A-Z BIR

CO

Key to Map Pages	2-3
Large Scale City Centres	4-5, 170
Map Pages	6-169

REFERENCE

Motorway	**M6**
A Road	A38
Under Construction	
Proposed	
B Road	B4284
Dual Carriageway	
One Way Street Traffic flow on A Roads is also indicated by a heavy line on the driver's left	➡ ➡
City Centre Ring Road & Junction Numbers	①
Restricted Access	
Pedestrianized Road	
Track / Footpath	- - - - -
Cycleway (Selected)	• • • • •
Railway	⧫
Station Heritage Level Tunnel Station Crossing	
Midland Metro The boarding of Metro trams at stops may be limited to a single direction, indicated by the arrow.	Stop
Built Up Area	NEWTON PL.
Local Authority Boundary	— · · — · · —
Posttown Boundary	——————
Postcode Boundary (within Posttown)	— — — —
Map Continuation **20** Large Scale City Centre **4**	

Car Park (Selected)	P
Church or Chapel	†
Fire Station	■
Hospital	H
House Numbers A and B Roads only	20 40
Information Centre	🛈
Junction Name (M6 Toll only)	BURNTWOOD JUNCTION
National Grid Reference	⁴12
Park & Ride	Monkspath P+🚌
Police Station	▲
Post Office	★

Toilet:
  without facilities for the Disabled
  with facilities for the Disabled
  for exclusive use by the Disabled
	▽
	▽
	▽

Viewpoint	☀ 🔆
Educational Establishment	▭
Hospital or Hospice	▭
Industrial Building	▭
Leisure or Recreational Facility	▭
Place of Interest	▭
Public Building	▭
Shopping Centre or Market	▭
Other Selected Buildings	▭

SCALE

Map Pages 6-169 1:18103 3½ inches to 1 mile	Map Pages 4-5, 170 1:9051 7 inches to 1 mile
0 ¼ ½ Mile	0 ⅛ ¼ Mile
0 250 500 750 Metres	0 100 200 300 Metres
5.52 cm to 1 km 8.89 cm to 1 mile	11.05 cm to 1 km 17.78 cm to 1 mile

Copyright of Geographers' A-Z Map Company Ltd.

Head Office:
Fairfield Road, Borough Green, Sevenoaks, Kent TN15 8PP
Telephone: 01732 781000 (Enquiries & Trade Sales)
          01732 783422 (Retail Sales)
www.a-zmaps.co.uk
Copyright © Geographers' A-Z Map Co. Ltd.

Ordnance Survey This product includes mapping data licensed from Ordnance Survey® with the permission of the Controller of Her Majesty's Stationery Office.

KEY TO MAP PAGES

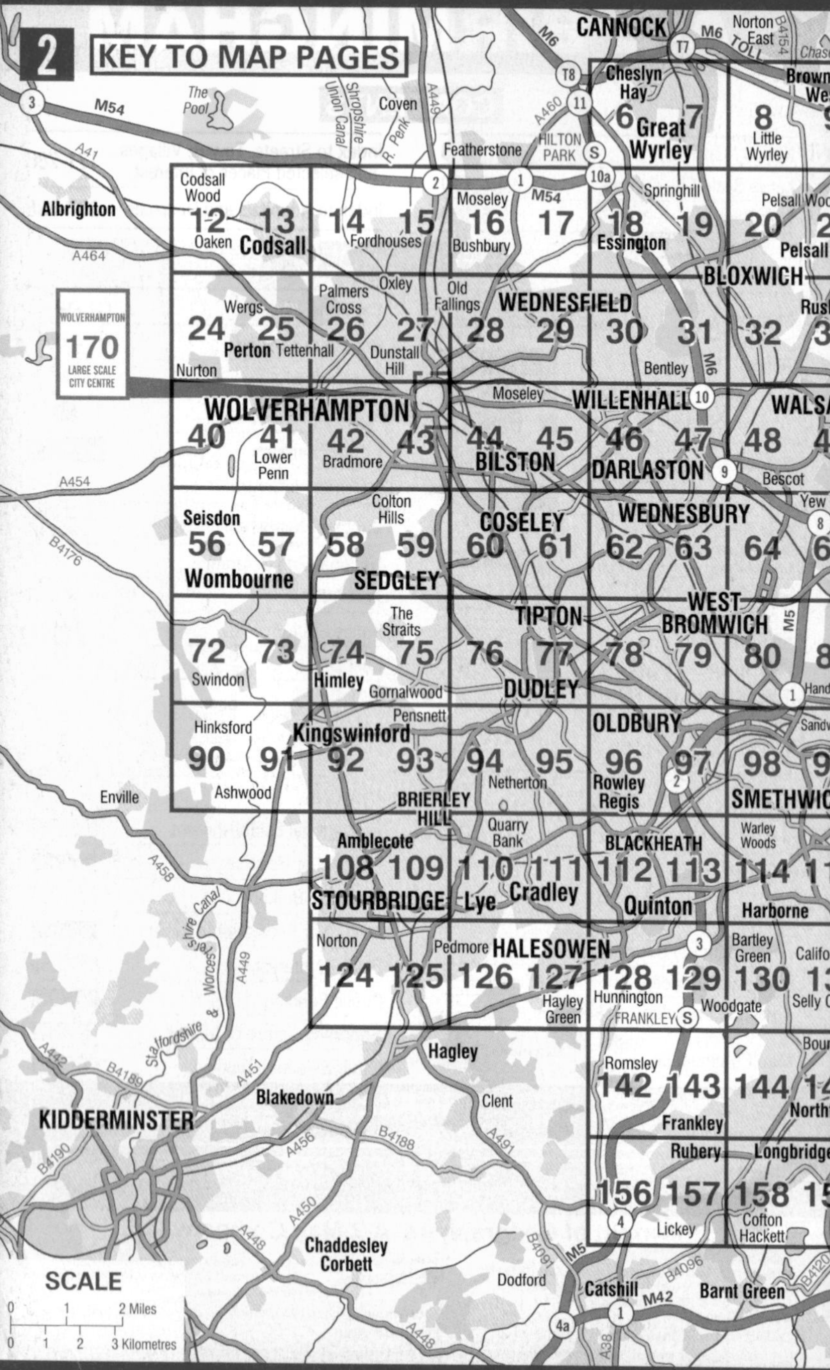
CANNOCK
WOLVERHAMPTON
170
LARGE SCALE CITY CENTRE
12 13 14 15 16 17 18 19 20
24 25 26 27 28 29 30 31 32
40 41 42 43 44 45 46 47 48
56 57 58 59 60 61 62 63 64
72 73 74 75 76 77 78 79 80
90 91 92 93 94 95 96 97 98
108 109 110 111 112 113 114
124 125 126 127 128 129 130
142 143 144
156 157 158
6 7 8
Cheslyn Hay
Great Wyrley
Little Wyrley
Codsall Wood
Codsall
Oaken
Albrighton
Fordhouses
Bushbury
Essington
Pelsall
BLOXWICH
Wergs
Perton
Tettenhall
Nurton
Palmers Cross
Oxley
Dunstall Hill
Old Fallings
WEDNESFIELD
Bentley
WILLENHALL
WALSALL
Moseley
WOLVERHAMPTON
Lower Penn
Bradmore
BILSTON
DARLASTON
Bescot
Seisdon
Wombourne
Colton Hills
SEDGLEY
COSELEY
WEDNESBURY
WEST BROMWICH
TIPTON
The Straits
Swindon
Himley
Gornalwood
DUDLEY
Hinksford
Ashwood
Kingswinford
Pensnett
Netherton
OLDBURY
Rowley Regis
SMETHWICK
BRIERLEY HILL
Quarry Bank
Amblecote
STOURBRIDGE
Lye
Cradley
BLACKHEATH
Quinton
Warley Woods
Harborne
Norton
Pedmore
HALESOWEN
Hayley Green
Hunnington
FRANKLEY
Woodgate
Bartley Green
Romsley
Frankley
Rubery
Longbridge
Lickey
Cofton Hackett
Enville
Hagley
Clent
Blakedown
KIDDERMINSTER
Chaddesley Corbett
Dodford
Catshill
Barnt Green
Coven
Featherstone
HILTON PARK
Springhill
Norton East
The Pool
Shropshire Union Canal
R. Penk
Staffordshire & Worcestershire Canal
M54
M6
M6 TOLL
M5
M42
A41
A464
A454
B4176
A458
A449
A442
B4189
A451
A456
B4188
A491
A450
A448
B4190
B4091
B4096
A38
A460
SCALE
0 1 2 Miles
0 1 2 3 Kilometres

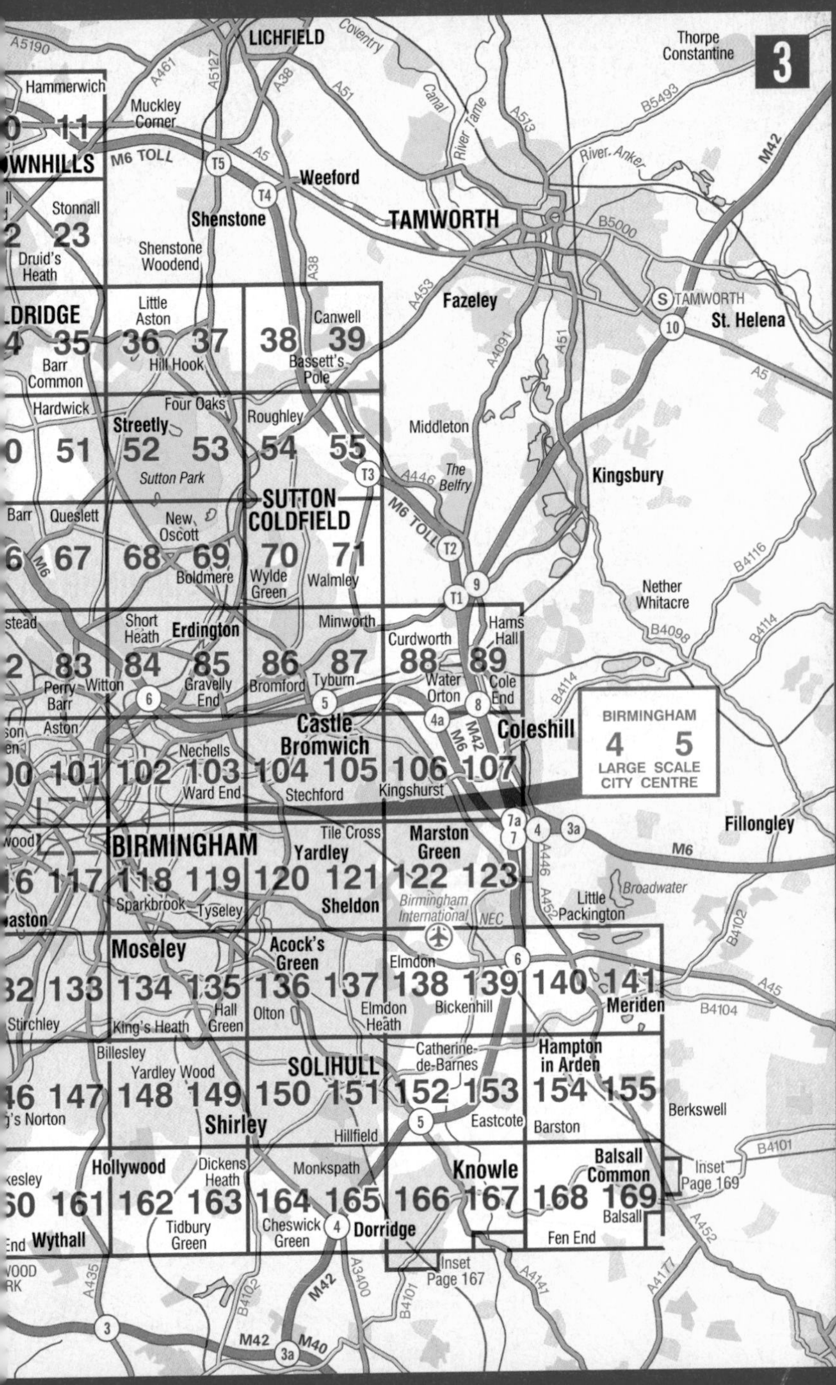
LICHFIELD
TAMWORTH
SUTTON COLDFIELD
BIRMINGHAM
SOLIHULL
Coleshill
Shenstone
Weeford
Fazeley
Kingsbury
St. Helena
Thorpe Constantine
Hammerwich
Muckley Corner
Stonnall
Druid's Heath
Shenstone Woodend
Little Aston
Canwell
Bassett's Pole
Barr Common
Hill Hook
Four Oaks
Hardwick
Streetly
Roughley
Middleton
The Belfry
Sutton Park
Queslett
New Oscott
Boldmere
Wylde Green
Walmley
Nether Whitacre
Short Heath
Erdington
Minworth
Curdworth
Hams Hall
Perry Barr
Witton
Gravelly End
Bromford
Tyburn
Water Orton
Cole End
Aston
Castle Bromwich
Nechells
Ward End
Stechford
Kingshurst
Tile Cross
Marston Green
Yardley
Sheldon
Sparkbrook
Tyseley
Birmingham International
NEC
Little Packington
Broadwater
Fillongley
Moseley
Acock's Green
Elmdon
Olton
Elmdon Heath
Bickenhill
Meriden
Stirchley
King's Heath
Hall Green
Billesley
Yardley Wood
Catherine-de-Barnes
Hampton in Arden
Shirley
Eastcote
Barston
Berkswell
Hillfield
Hollywood
Dickens Heath
Monkspath
Knowle
Balsall Common
Balsall
Fen End
Tidbury Green
Cheswick Green
Dorridge
Wythall
Inset Page 167
Inset Page 169
BIRMINGHAM 4 5 LARGE SCALE CITY CENTRE
M6 TOLL
M6
M42
M40
A5190
A461
A5127
A38
A51
A5
A513
A453
A4091
A446
A452
A45
A435
A3400
A4141
A4177
B5493
B5000
B4116
B4114
B4098
B4102
B4104
B4101
Coventry Canal
River Tame
River Anker
11
23
35
36
37
38
39
51
52
53
54
55
67
68
69
70
71
83
84
85
86
87
88
89
101
102
103
104
105
106
107
117
118
119
120
121
122
123
133
134
135
136
137
138
139
140
141
147
148
149
150
151
152
153
154
155
161
162
163
164
165
166
167
168
169

A
B
C
D
1
2
3
4
5
6
101
100
116
117
406
JEWELLERY QUARTER
BIRMINGHAM
B18
B19
B3
B2
B1
B15
Warstone La. Cemetery
Chamberlain Clock
WARSTONE LANE
THE CARPATHIAN
Jewellery & Silver Cen.
HOCKLEY CEN.
THE BIG PEG
VYSE ST.
AUGUSTA ST.
SPENCER ST.
HALL ST.
KENYON
CAROLINE
MARY
CONSTITUTION HILL
B4100
St. Pauls
MOTT ST.
HAMPTON
COLMORE FLATS
HOSPITAL
BOND ST.
HOWARD ST.
SUMMER LANE
CLIVE PL.
CITY HEIGHTS
WILLIAM BOOTH LA.
OLD SNOW HILL
ST. CHADS
QUEENSWAY
HENRIETTA
BISMILLAH BUILDING
LIVERY
SAPPHIRE CT.
KINGS CT.
MIDLAND CT.
QUEENS CT.
ST. PAUL'S
COX
UCE (Sch. of Jewellery)
ROSE PL.
VITTORIA
WARSTONE CT.
REGENT
HERITAGE CT.
REGENT PDE
ROW
FREDERICK STREET
REGENT ST.
REGENT PL.
Works
ST. PAULS TER.
NORTHWOOD
JAMES ST.
RBSA Gall.
BROOK ST.
Rec. Grd.
ST. HELEN'S PAS.
SOVEREIGN CT.
WEXLER LOFTS
TENBY
ALBION
LEGGE
GRAHAM
POINT 3
FARTHING CT.
Sikh Temple
NEWHALL PL.
NEWHALL CT.
NEWHALL HILL
NEWHALL STREET
CAMDEN DR.
CAMDEN STREET
SLOANE HO.
SLOANE ST.
ARTHUR PL.
Greek Cath.
SUMMER HILL T.
SAND PITS
GEORGE
HOLLAND ST.
CHARLOTTE
Offices
Office
THE OLD CHAPEL
LUDGATE HILL
WATER ST.
LUDGATE LOFT APARTMENTS
MARY ANN
Telecom Tower
MILLENNIUM APARTMENTS
Sub.
Locks
FLEET
LIONEL STREET
Chest Clinic
Coll.
A38
GREAT CHARLES ST. QUEENSWAY
NEW MKT. ST.
CHURCH STREET
PARADE
B4284
SUMMER ROW
ST. HELENA
JOHN SMYTH HO.
LESLIE BENTLEY HO.
RICHARD LIGHTON HO.
PROSPECT TRAD. EST.
QUBE
SCOTLAND ST.
CLEMENT
TOWNSEND WY.
TUDOR CT.
LOUISA ST.
EDWARD
BALMORAL CT.
BRINDLEY WK.
CAMBRIDGE TWR.
BRINDLEY DR.
JAMES CRESCENT TWR.
City Cen. Gds.
KINGSTON RW.
GALTON TWR.
CIVIC CL.
NORTON TWR.
CAMBRIDGE STREET
KING EDWARDS RD.
AUSTIN CT.
National Indoor Arena
Sea Life Centre
Birmingham Canal
BICC & Symphony Hall
Repertory Theatre
Hall of Memory
CENTENARY SQ.
BROAD STREET
328
PARADISE CIRCUS QUEENSWAY
Lib.
PARADISE PLACE
CONGREVE PAS.
CHAMBERLAIN SQUARE
Adrian Boult Hall
FLETCHERS WK.
Town Hall
STOCK EXCHANGE BUILDING
CORNWALL
MARGARET ST.
Uni.
Mus. & Art Gall.
EDMUND
BARTON PAS.
EDEN PL.
Council Ho.
COLMORE ROW
WATERLOO
WATERLOO PAS.
VICTORIA SQUARE
BENNETT'S HILL
WELLINGTON PAS.
TEMPLE ROW W.
TEMPLE PAS.
TEMPLE
BARWICK ST.
NEW ST.
PINFOLD
ETHEL ST.
PICCADILLY ARC.
LWR. TEMPLE ST.
STEPHENSON STREET
PARADISE ST.
HILL ST.
SWALLOW ST.
BRUNEL ST.
NAVIGATION
SUFFOLK ST. QUEENSWAY
JOHN BRIGHT ST.
Gala Casino
THE PALLASADES SHOP.
QUEENS DR.
STEPHENSON TWR.
LWR. SEVERN ST.
BEAK ST.
SUFFOLK PL.
Theatre
STATION STREET
ST. JUDES PAS.
SMALLBROOK
HOLLOWAY CIRCUS
A38
BRISTOL ST.
HORSE FAIR
BRINDLEYPLACE
CENTRAL SQ.
THE WATERS EDGE
Ikon Gallery
Gall.
OOZELLS ST.
OOZELLS SQ.
CUMBERLAND
BRUNSWICK
BRUNSWICK SQ.
SHEEPCOTE ST.
Syn.
GAS ST.
Gas St. Basin
WORCESTER BAR
THE WHARF
BRIDGE STREET
ALPHA TOWER
Registry Office
Footbri.
Carlton TV
BERKLEY STREET
SATURDAY BRI.
FRIDAY WHARF
BERKLEY CT.
BROADWALK
UPPER WILLIAM ST.
GRANVILLE STREET
TRIDENT HO.
GRANVILLE SQ.
STOKE WY.
SANDY WY.
RAKE WY.
TENNANT STREET
BISHOPSGATE ST.
WILLIAM STREET
HOLLIDAY
HOLLIDAY ST.
CENTENARY PLAZA
HOLLIDAY WHARF
QUEENS COURT
KINGS COURT
Birmingham Canal
Worcester &
Works
WASHINGTON WHARF
COMMERCIAL STREET
WASHINGTON CT.
WASHINGTON ST.
THE MALTINGS
RIDLEY ST.
Peace Gdn.
MAILBOX SQ.
THE MAILBOX
ROYAL ARCH APARTMENTS
WHARFSIDE STREET
SEVERN STREET PL.
SEVERN
Synagogue
BLUCHER
UPPER MARSHALL ST.
UPPER GOUGH ST.
GOUGH ST.
MARSHALL ST.
CHAPMANS PAS.
ELLIS
BROWNSEA DR.
CLEVELAND TWR.
HOLLOWAY HEAD
ERNEST ST.
FLORENCE ST.
EXETER ST.
CLYDESDALE TWR.
WINDMILL ST.
BOW ST.

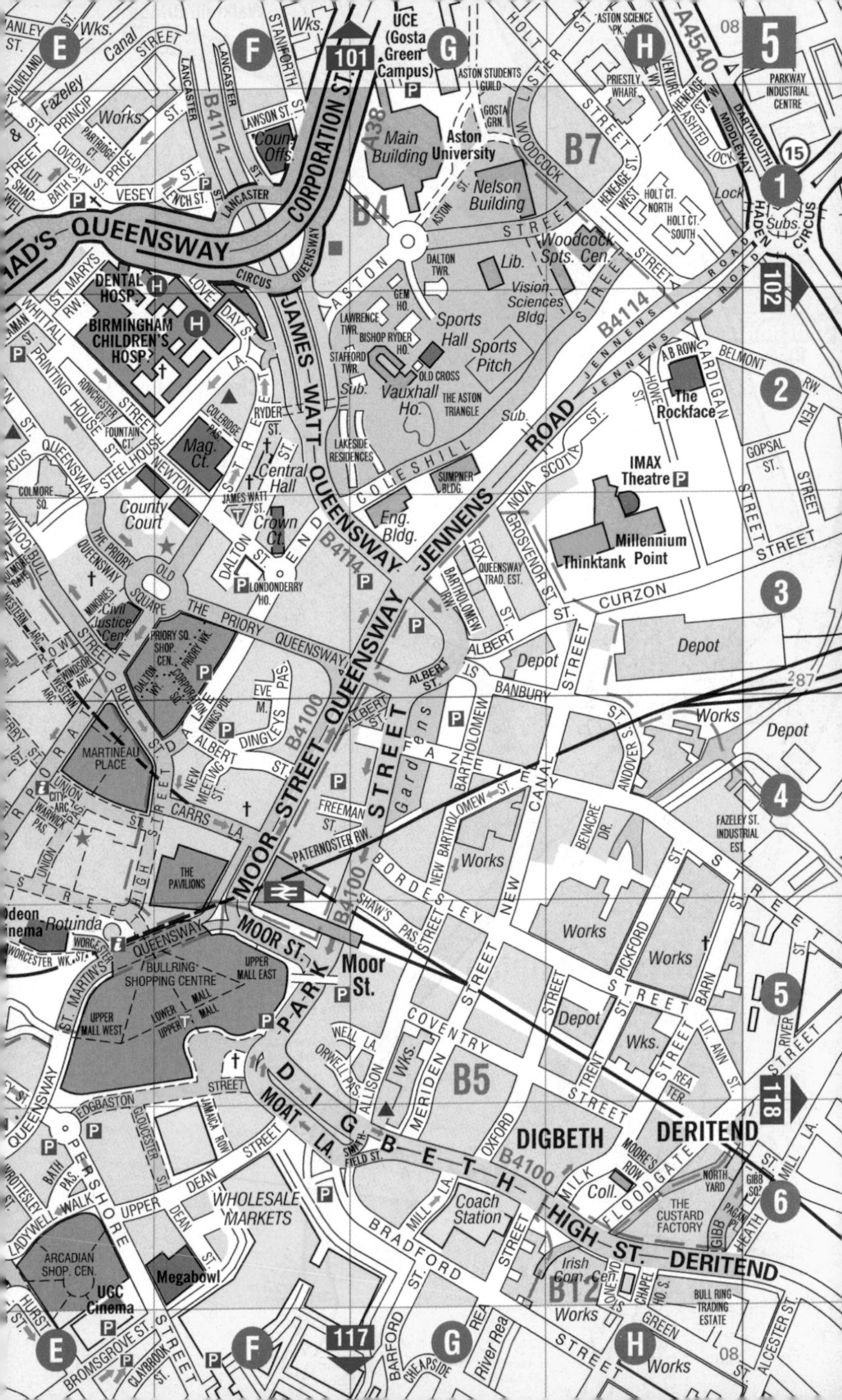

6
A
B
C
D
Walkmill Bridge
396
97
08
07
06
305
Lodge Farm
WS11
Middle Hill
Middle Hill Farm
Cannock
International Freight Terminal
SOUTH STAFFORDSHIRE BUSINESS PARK
Public Open Space
Littlew
Tile Works
Works
M6 TOLL MOTORWAY
M6 TOLL
MIDDLE HILL JUNCTION
Junction T8
1
2
3
4
5
6
A460
SAREDON ROAD
WOLVERHAMPTON ROAD
SAREDON RD.
WOLVER-HAMPTON RD.
HAWKINS
LODGE LA.
WALKMILL LA.
DRIVE
COPPICE
ROSEMARY ROAD
Playing Fields
Cheslyn Hay
Cheslyn Hay Prim. Sch.
Cheslyn Hay Leisure Cen.
Cheslyn Hay High Sch.
LODGE VW.
CLOVER RIDGE
LOW STREET
HIGH ST
WESLEY AV.
QUEEN ST.
ZION CL.
Lib.
HOSPITAL LANE
B4156
HILL ST.
HATHERTON ST.
DENEFIELD DR.
MITRE LANE
ROAD
CAMPIANS AV.
CEMETERY ST.
Cemetery
PINFORD
FALCON CL.
BESOM WY.
KESTREL WAY
EAGLE CL.
COLLIER CL.
FAIRVIEW CL.
RAVEN CL.
SWAN CL.
DUNDALK
MOONS LANE
LAPWING CL.
THE NOOK
ROSEWOOD
TUDOR WAY
SEYMOUR CL.
MEADOW
HARRISON CL.
GILPINS CFT.
POOL
HIGHFIELDS
THORN LEY CFT.
BRAMWELL DR.
WALLACE
GRANGE
CHILTERN
Campian's Wood
Laney Green
Hollies Farm
WARSTONE
WV10
Junc. 11
Holly Bush Farm
Garden Centre
The Hayes Farm
WOLVERHAMPTON
BUSH LA.
HOLLY
Blacklees Farm
The Bungalow
A462
Tile Works
Wolverhampton
HOLLY BUSH LA.
M6
The Beeches
Warren Farm
Upper Warstone Farm
Lower Warstone Farm
OLD WARSTONE LA.
Warstone
The Yells Farm
HILTON
M6 MOTORWAY
Sewage Works
Old Yells Farm
Wakeman's Wood
Warstone Belt
WV11
LANE
Hilton Park Service Area
Redhurst Wood
Holly Bank Gorse
LANDYWOOD
OLD
18
Haven Meadows
Farm

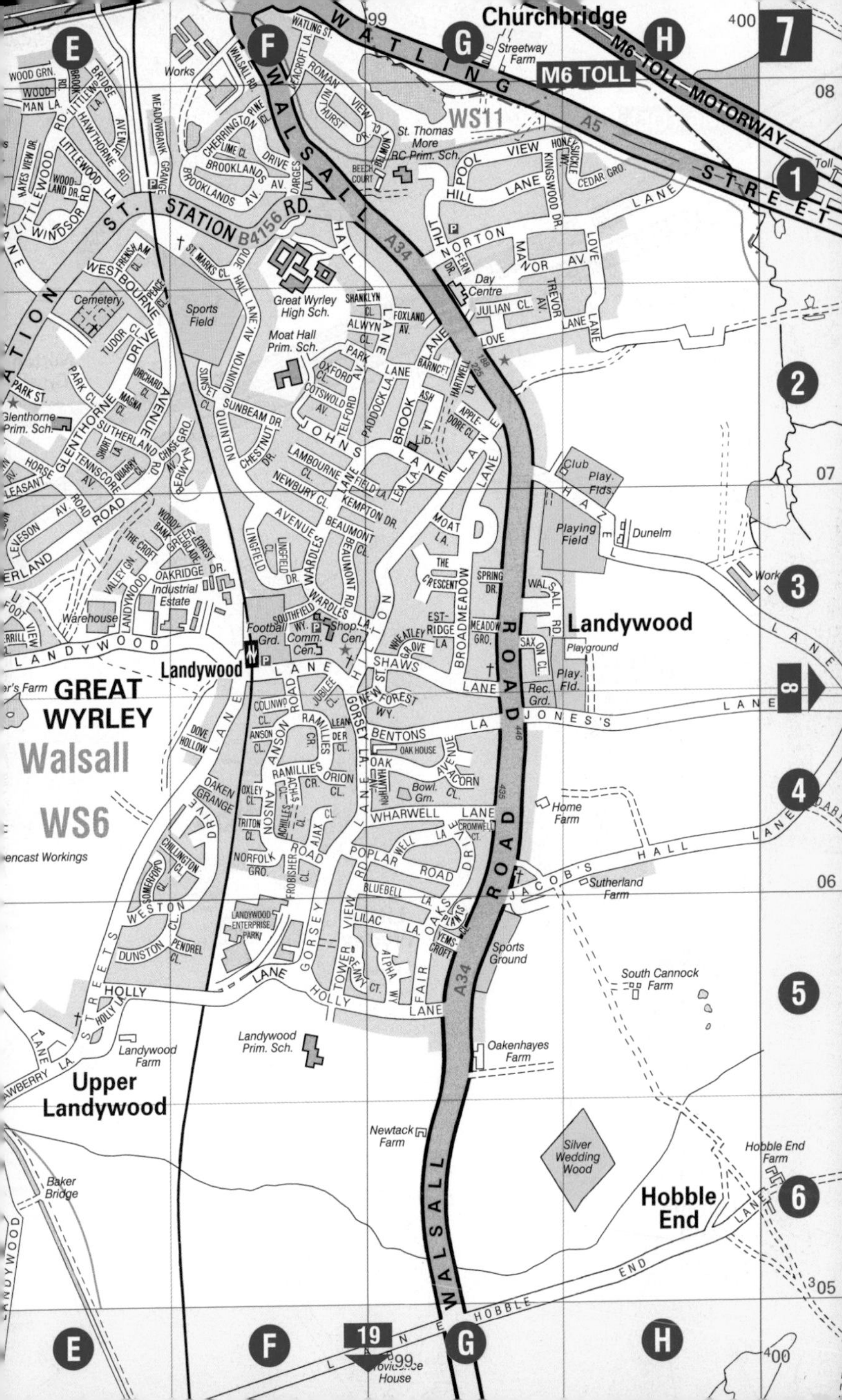

7
Churchbridge
M6 TOLL
M6 TOLL MOTORWAY
WATLING STREET
A5
WS11
WALSALL RD.
A34
STATION RD.
B4156
Great Wyrley High Sch.
Moat Hall Prim. Sch.
St. Thomas More RC Prim. Sch.
Streetway Farm
Day Centre
Cemetery
Sports Field
Glenthorne Prim. Sch.
Industrial Estate
Warehouse
Football Grd.
Comm. Cen.
Shop. Cen.
Landywood
GREAT WYRLEY
Walsall
WS6
Playing Field
Play. Flds.
Club
Dunelm
Playground
Play. Fld.
Rec. Grd.
JONES'S LANE
LANDYWOOD LANE
WALSALL ROAD
Home Farm
Sutherland Farm
HALL LANE
Sports Ground
South Cannock Farm
Landywood Prim. Sch.
Landywood Farm
Oakenhayes Farm
Upper Landywood
Newtack Farm
Silver Wedding Wood
Hobble End Farm
Hobble End
HOBBLE END LANE
Baker Bridge
LANDYWOOD ENTERPRISE PARK
19
8
E
F
G
H
1
2
3
4
5
6
99
400
08
07
06
05

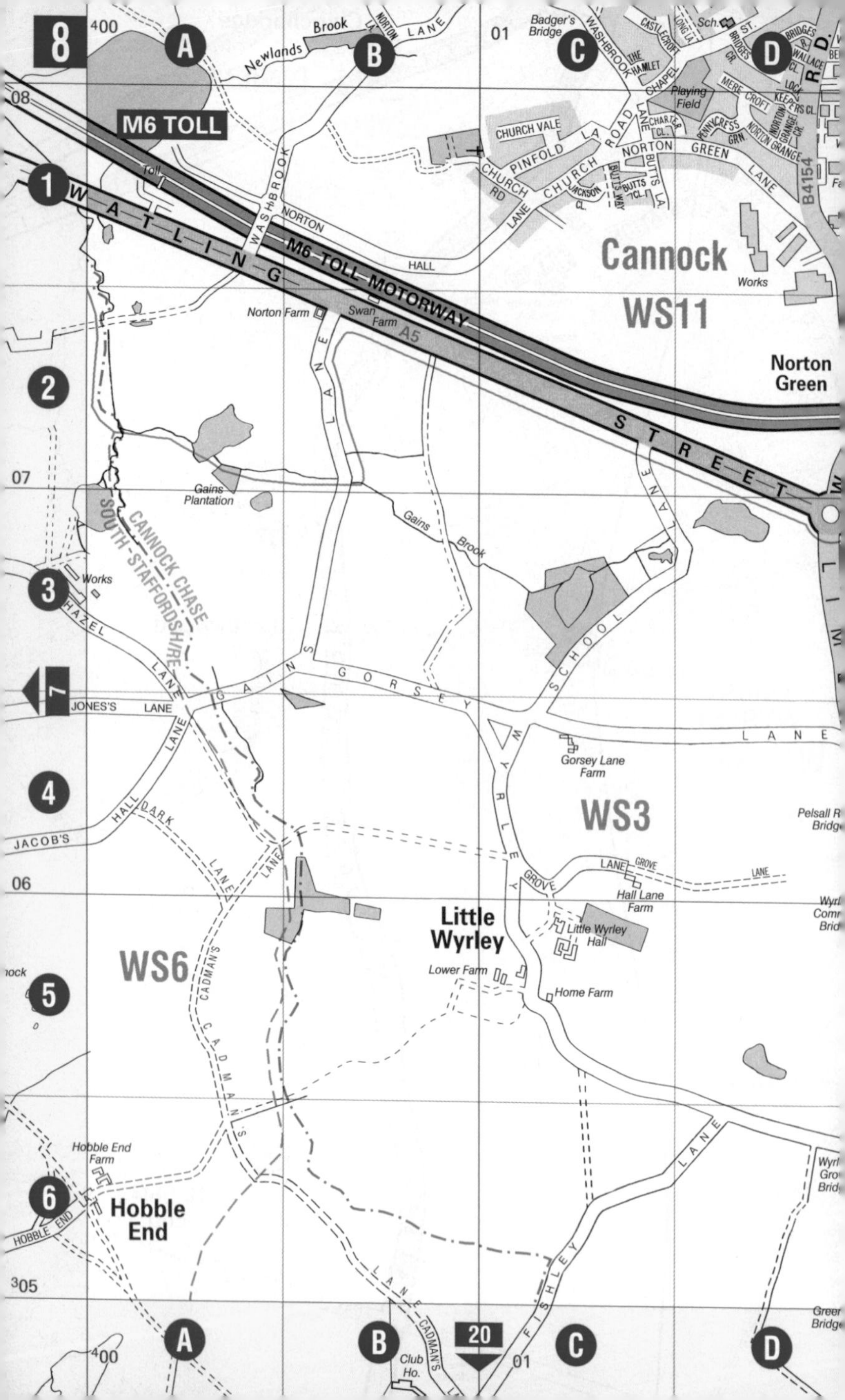

M6 TOLL
M6 TOLL MOTORWAY
WATLING STREET
A5
Cannock
WS11
Norton Green
WS3
WS6
Little Wyrley
Hobble End
Newlands Brook
NORTON LANE
Badger's Bridge
WASHBROOK
THE HAMLET
CASTLECROFT
LONG LA.
Sch.
BRIDGES CR.
WALLACE CL.
LOCK KEEPERS CL.
CHAPEL LANE
Playing Field
MERE CROFT
CHURCH VALE
PINFOLD LA.
CHURCH ROAD
CHARTER CL.
PENNYCRESS GRN.
NORTON GRANGE
NORTON GREEN LANE
CHURCH RD
CHURCH LANE
JACKSON CL.
BUTTS WAY
BUTTS CL.
BUTTS LA.
B4154
NORTON HALL
Works
Norton Farm
Swan Farm
Gains Plantation
Gains Brook
CANNOCK CHASE
SOUTH STAFFORDSHIRE
HAZEL LANE
GAINS LANE
GORSEY LANE
SCHOOL LANE
JONES'S LANE
JACOB'S HALL LANE
DARK LANE
WYRLEY
Gorsey Lane Farm
Pelsall Bridge
GROVE LANE
Hall Lane Farm
Little Wyrley Hall
Lower Farm
Home Farm
CADMAN'S LANE
Hobble End Farm
HOBBLE END
FISHLEY LANE
Club Ho.
Green Bridge
400
01
08
07
06
305
A
B
C
D
1
2
3
4
5
6
7
20

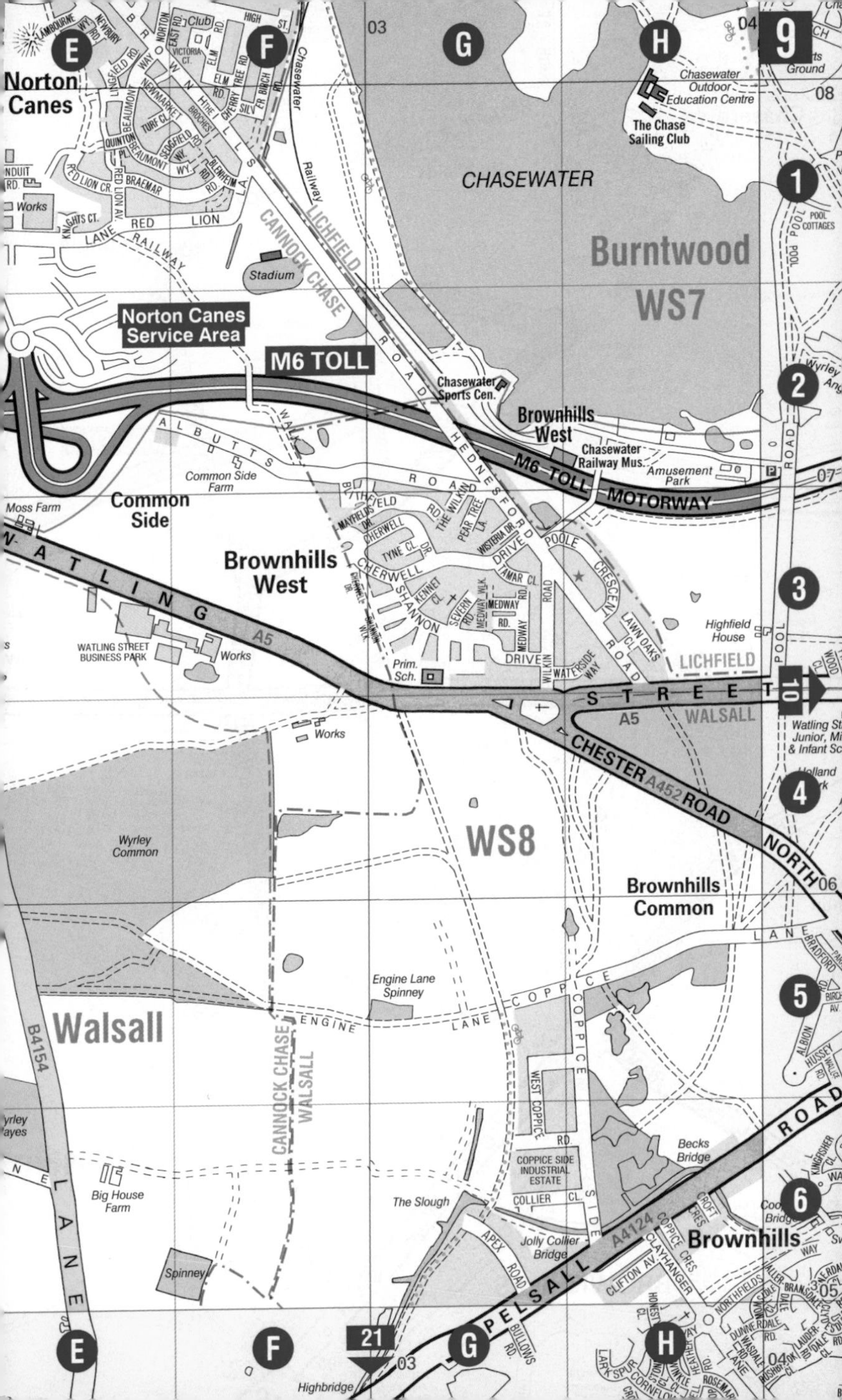
9
Norton Canes
Chasewater
CHASEWATER
Chasewater Outdoor Education Centre
The Chase Sailing Club
Burntwood
WS7
Stadium
Norton Canes Service Area
M6 TOLL
Chasewater Sports Cen.
Brownhills West
Chasewater Railway Mus.
Amusement Park
M6 TOLL MOTORWAY
Common Side Farm
Common Side
Moss Farm
Brownhills West
WATLING STREET BUSINESS PARK
Works
A5
Prim. Sch.
Highfield House
LICHFIELD
WALSALL
10
Watling St Junior, Mi & Infant Sc
CHESTER A452 ROAD NORTH
WS8
Wyrley Common
Brownhills Common
Engine Lane Spinney
Walsall
B4154
COPPICE SIDE INDUSTRIAL ESTATE
Becks Bridge
The Slough
Big House Farm
Jolly Collier Bridge
Spinney
PELSALL ROAD A4124
Brownhills
21
Highbridge
E
F
G
H
1
2
3
4
5
6

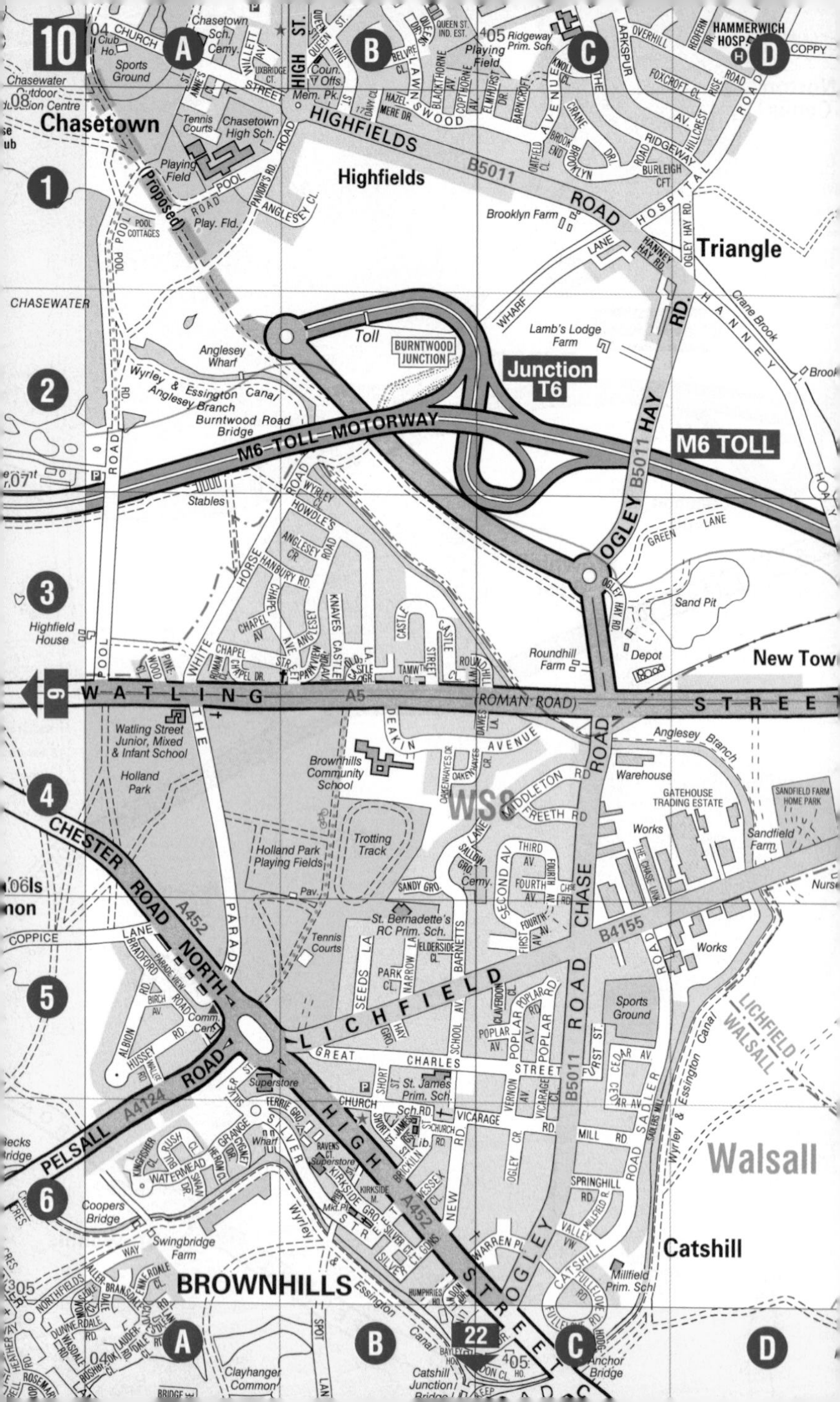
Chasetown
Chasewater Outdoor Education Centre
Chasetown Sch.
Cemy.
Sports Ground
Club Ho.
CHURCH ST.
HIGH ST.
Coun. Offs.
Mem. Pk.
Ridgeway Prim. Sch.
Playing Field
HAMMERWICH HOSP.
COPPY
Tennis Courts
Chasetown High Sch.
HIGHFIELDS ROAD
B5011
Highfields
LAWNSWOOD
RIDGEWAY
OVERHILL
LARKSPUR
FOXCROFT CL.
HILLCREST
BURLEIGH CFT.
BROOKLYN
CRANE DRI.
HOSPITAL ROAD
(Proposed)
POOL ROAD
Play. Fld.
POOL COTTAGES
ANGLESEY CL.
PAVIOR'S RD.
Brooklyn Farm
Triangle
HANNEY HAY RD.
OGLEY HAY RD.
CHASEWATER
Anglesey Wharf
Toll
BURNTWOOD JUNCTION
Lamb's Lodge Farm
Junction T6
Crane Brook
WHARF LANE
Wyrley & Essington Canal/ Anglesey Branch
Burntwood Road Bridge
M6 TOLL MOTORWAY
M6 TOLL
OGLEY HAY RD.
Stables
WYRLEY CL.
HOWDLE'S
ANGLESEY CR.
ANGLESEY ROAD
HANBURY RD.
WHITE HORSE ROAD
CHAPEL AV.
KNAVES CASTLE
CASTLE STREET
GREEN LANE
Sand Pit
Highfield House
Roundhill Farm
Depot
New Tow
9
WATLING STREET
A5
(ROMAN ROAD)
THE PARADE
Watling Street Junior, Mixed & Infant School
Holland Park
DEAKIN AVENUE
Brownhills Community School
WS8
MIDDLETON RD
FREETH RD
CHASE ROAD
Anglesey Branch
Warehouse
GATEHOUSE TRADING ESTATE
SANDFIELD FARM HOME PARK
Sandfield Farm
Works
Holland Park Playing Fields
Trotting Track
Cemy.
SECOND AV.
THIRD AV.
FOURTH AV.
FIRST AV.
CHESTER ROAD NORTH
A452
COPPICE LANE
BRADFORD
PARADE VIEW
SANDY GRO.
St. Bernadette's RC Prim. Sch.
Tennis Courts
SEEDS LA.
NARROW LA.
ELDERSIDE CL.
BARNETTS
B4155
LICHFIELD ROAD
Works
Sports Ground
LICHFIELD WALSALL
Comm. Cen.
HUSSEY RD.
ALBION RD.
BIRCH AV.
POPLAR AV.
SCHOOL AV.
GREAT CHARLES STREET
B5011
FIRST ST.
CEDAR AV.
SADLER ROAD
Wyrley & Essington Canal
Superstore
PELSALL ROAD
A4124
St. James Prim. Sch.
CHURCH RD.
VICARAGE RD.
VERNON AV.
MILL RD
Walsall
Wharf
SILVER ST.
HIGH STREET
A452
Superstore
GRANGE
KINGFISHER CL.
RUSH CL.
WATERMEAD
SWAN DR.
HERON CL.
CYGNET DR.
KIRKSIDE GRO.
NEW RD.
OGLEY CR.
SPRINGHILL RD.
VALLEY VW.
Coopers Bridge
Swingbridge Farm
Wyrley & Essington Canal
WARREN PL.
OGLEY
CATSHILL RD.
Catshill
Millfield Prim. Sch.
BROWNHILLS
NORTHFIELDS
BRANSDALE
ENNERDALE
DUNNERDALE RD.
WASDALE RD.
22
Clayhanger Common
Catshill Junction Bridge
Anchor Bridge
FULLELOVE RD.
A B C D
1 2 3 4 5 6

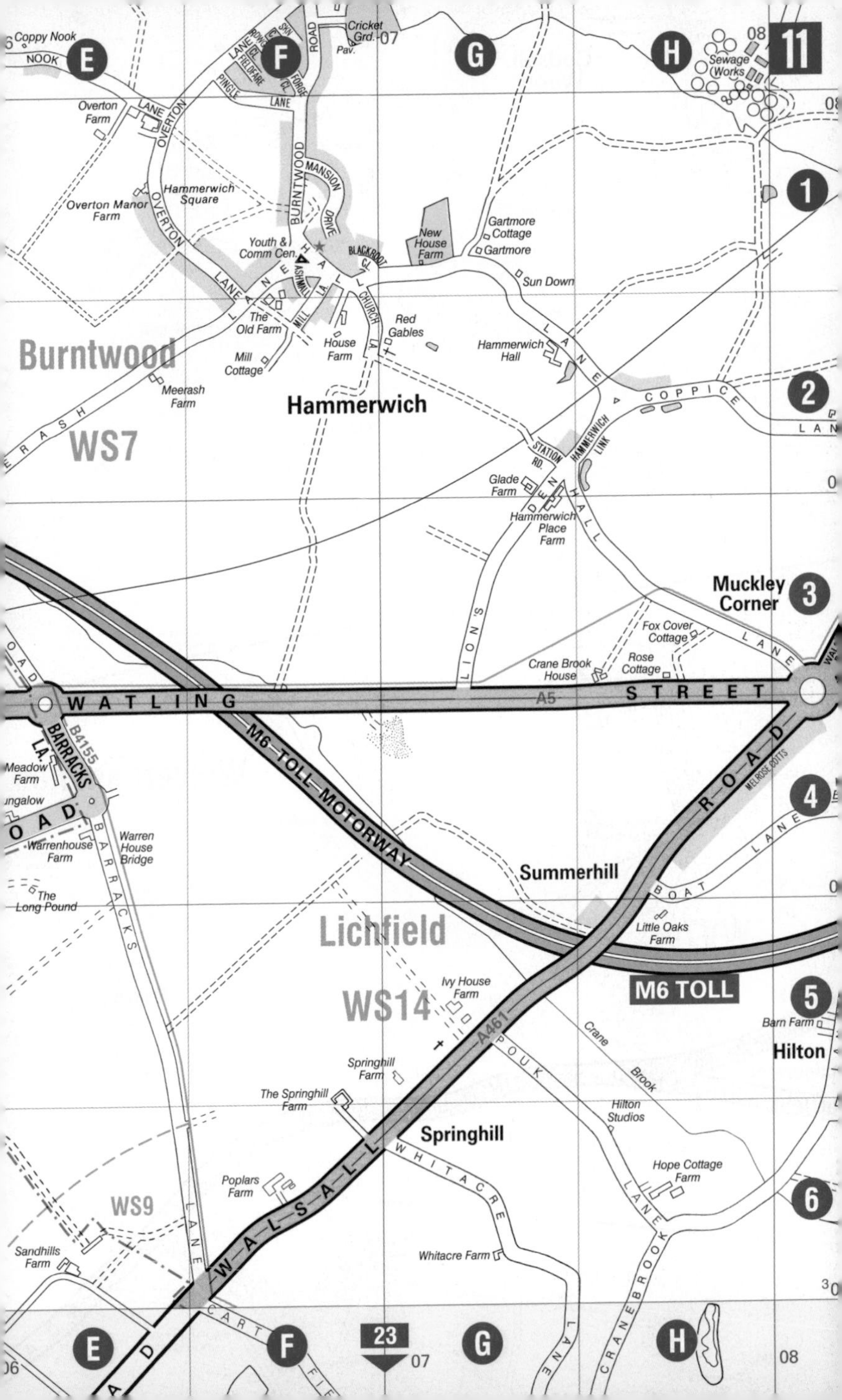
11
E
F
G
H
1
2
3
4
5
6
Coppy Nook
NOOK
Cricket Grd.
Pav.
07
08
Sewage Works
Overton Farm
OVERTON LANE
PINGLE LANE
FIELDFARE CL.
FORGE CL.
BURNTWOOD ROAD
MANSION DRIVE
Hammerwich Square
Overton Manor Farm
Youth & Comm Cen.
New House Farm
Gartmore Cottage
Gartmore
BLACKROOT CL.
ASHMILL
HALL LANE
MILL LA.
CHURCH LA.
Sun Down
The Old Farm
Red Gables
Burntwood
Mill Cottage
House Farm
Hammerwich Hall
Meerash Farm
Hammerwich
MEERASH LANE
WS7
COPPICE LANE
STATION RD.
HAMMERWICH LINK
Glade Farm
DEN HALL
Hammerwich Place Farm
LION'S DEN
Muckley Corner
Fox Cover Cottage
Crane Brook House
Rose Cottage
WATLING STREET
A5
B4155
BARRACKS LA.
Meadow Farm
M6 TOLL MOTORWAY
ROAD
MELROSE COTTS
Warrenhouse Farm
Warren House Bridge
BARRACKS LANE
Summerhill
BOAT LANE
The Long Pound
Lichfield
Little Oaks Farm
M6 TOLL
Ivy House Farm
WS14
Barn Farm
Crane Brook
Hilton
A461
POUK LANE
Springhill Farm
The Springhill Farm
Hilton Studios
Springhill
WHITACRE LANE
Hope Cottage Farm
Poplars Farm
WS9
WALSALL ROAD
CRANEBROOK LANE
Sandhills Farm
Whitacre Farm
CARTERS FIELD
23
06

Codsall Wood
A
B
C
D
1
2
3
4
5
6
84
385
05
Harriots Hayes Rd.
Wisley House
White House
Whitehouse Lane
Codsall Wood Road
Bridgnorth
South Staffordshire
The Cottage
Wood Hall Cottages
Pendrell Hall
Ledene Golf Centre (Pitch & Putt)
Wood Hall Farm
Leighton Pool
Wheatstone Park Farm
Leighton Cottage
Nursery Farm
Wheatstone Park
Little Harriot's Hayes Farm
Lane
The Wood
Lilac Cottage
Husphins Lane
Husphins Farm
The Stockings
Moatbrook Lane
Wheatstone Lodge Farm
Slate La.
Chillington Lane
Wood Road
Moat House Farm
Husphins Bridge
Moor Hall Bridge
Oaken Park Farm
Wolverhampton
Ivy Cottage
Oaken Lawn Riding School
Strawmoor Farm
Oaken Lawn Farm
Strawmoor Lane
Oaken
Springfield House
Manor House
Oaken Manor
WV7
Oaken
The Fold
Oaken Lane
Manor Fold
Nursery
The Meadows
The Shieling
Albrighton Rd.
A41
Kingswood
Shifnal Road
A464
Holyhead Road
Middle Lane
Shop Lane
Wayside Cottage
Stafford Road
A41
Keepers Cottage
Orchard House
Wrottesley Home Farm
Wrottesley Park Golf Course
Simmond's Wood

24

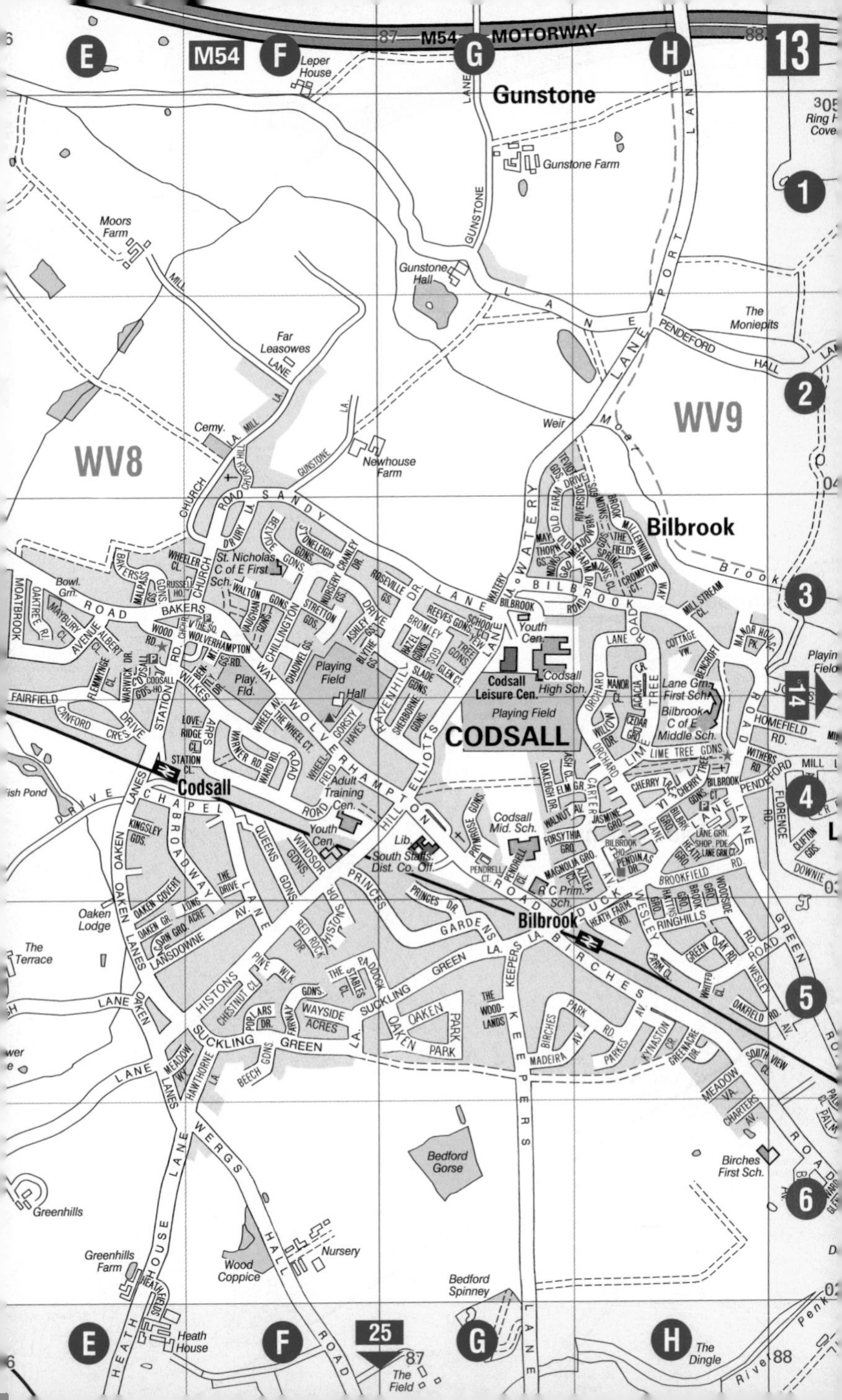
M54 MOTORWAY
Gunstone
Gunstone Farm
Leper House
Moors Farm
Gunstone Hall
Far Leasowes
The Moniepits
PENDEFORD HALL LANE
WV9
WV8
Cemy.
Newhouse Farm
Weir
Bilbrook
CODSALL
Codsall Leisure Cen.
Codsall High Sch.
Playing Field
St. Nicholas C of E First Sch.
Codsall
Codsall Mid. Sch.
Lane Grn. First Sch.
Bilbrook C of E Middle Sch.
Adult Training Cen.
Youth Cen.
Lib.
South Staffs. Dist. Co. Off.
R C Prim. Sch.
Bilbrook
Oaken Lodge
The Terrace
Fish Pond
Bedford Gorse
Greenhills
Greenhills Farm
Wood Coppice
Nursery
Bedford Spinney
Birches First Sch.
Heath House
The Dingle
The Field

14

25

M54 MOTORWAY
M54
The Middle Hattons
Ring Hill Covert
Lower Pendeford Farm
Ash Coppice
The Hattons
Shropshire Union Canal
River Penk
The Moniepits
PENDEFORD HALL LANE
Upper Hattons Bridge
The Long Wood
The Round Wood
Island Pool
Roman Road (Course Of)
COVEN LANE
Fish Pond
PENDEFORD HALL LA.
Fish Pond
MIDDLE LANE
PENDEFORD HALL MOBILE HOME PARK
Moat Brook
Bilbrook
Sewage Works
Shooting Pit
Playing Field
Pendeford Mill
ROAD
Pendeford Bridge
WOBASTON LANE
Wolverhampton
MILL LANE
JOEYS LA.
HOMEFIELD RD.
MILL GRO.
BALLIOL BUSINESS PARK
Aldersley House
OVERSTRAND
Upper Pendeford Farm
BARNHURST
Depot
Lane Green
Works
Pendeford
SOUTH STAFFORDSHIRE
WOLVERHAMPTON
WV8
Turnover Bridge
Filter Tank No. 3
Filter Tank
Weir
Public Open Space
Bilbrook Bridge
Sports Centre
Aldersley High School
Dovecotes Prim. Sch.
Birches First Sch.
LANE GRN. AV.
Penk
Dam Mill
River
CODSALL ROAD
RYEFIELD
The Dingle
SEWAGE WORKS
Brookside Farm
26

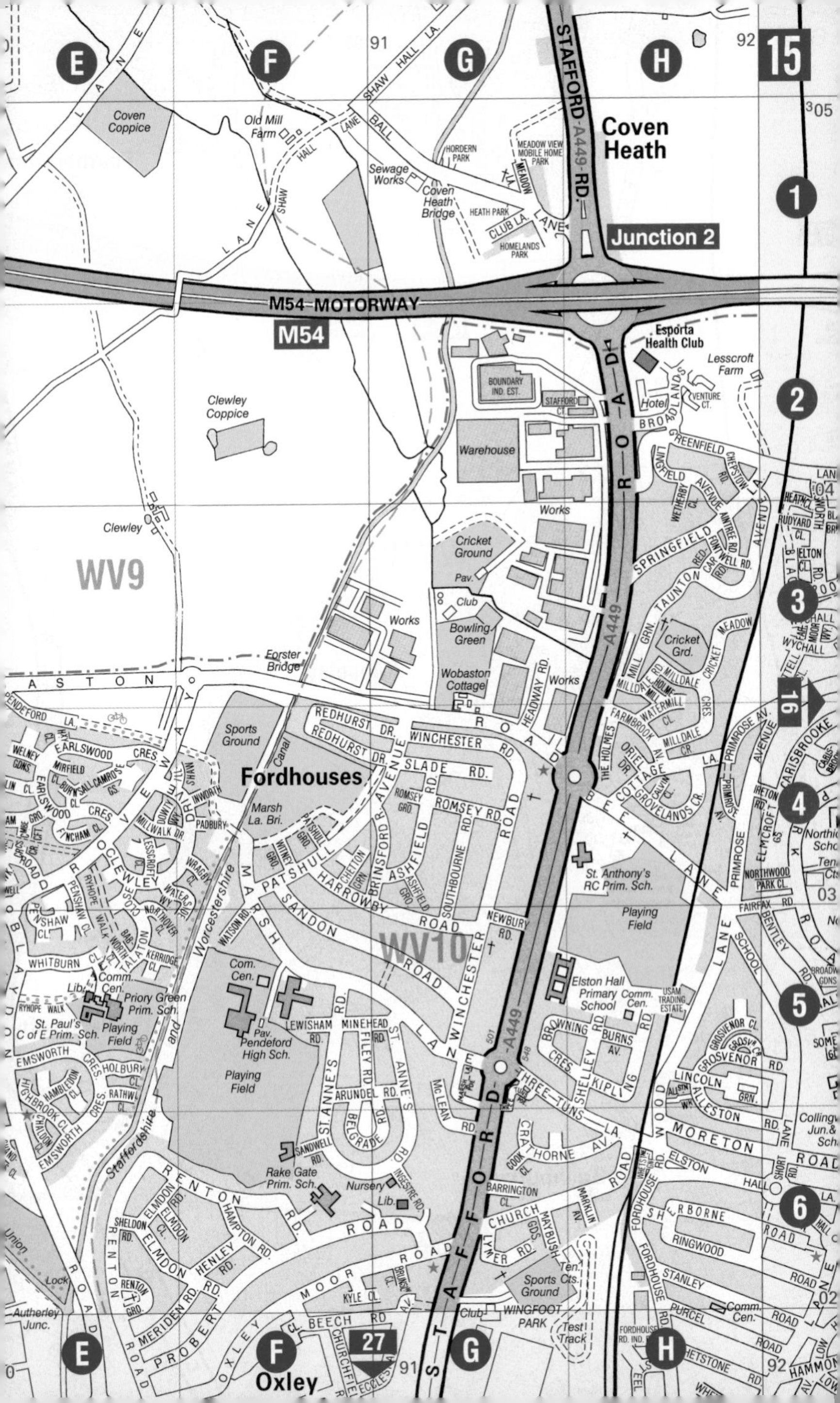

Coven Heath
Junction 2
M54 MOTORWAY
M54
Coven Coppice
Old Mill Farm
Sewage Works
Coven Heath Bridge
HORDERN PARK
MEADOW VIEW MOBILE HOME PARK
HEATH PARK
CLUB LA.
HOMELANDS PARK
STAFFORD RD. A449
Esporta Health Club
Lesscroft Farm
BOUNDARY IND. EST.
Hotel
VENTURE CT.
Clewley Coppice
Warehouse
Works
Clewley
WV9
Cricket Ground
Pav.
Club
Bowling Green
Wobaston Cottage
Forster Bridge
Cricket Grd.
ASTON
Fordhouses
Sports Ground
Canal
Marsh La. Bri.
St. Anthony's RC Prim. Sch.
Playing Field
WV10
Com. Cen.
Pendeford High Sch.
Elston Hall Primary School
Comm. Cen.
USAM TRADING ESTATE
Priory Green Prim. Sch.
St. Paul's C of E Prim. Sch.
Lib.
Staffordshire and Worcestershire
Rake Gate Prim. Sch.
Nursery
Collingwood Jun.& Sch.
Sports Ground
Ten. Cts.
Test Track
Club
WINGFOOT PARK
Union
Lock
Autherley Junc.
FORDHOUSE RD. IND. EST.
Oxley
27
16
E
F
G
H
1
2
3
4
5
6
91
92

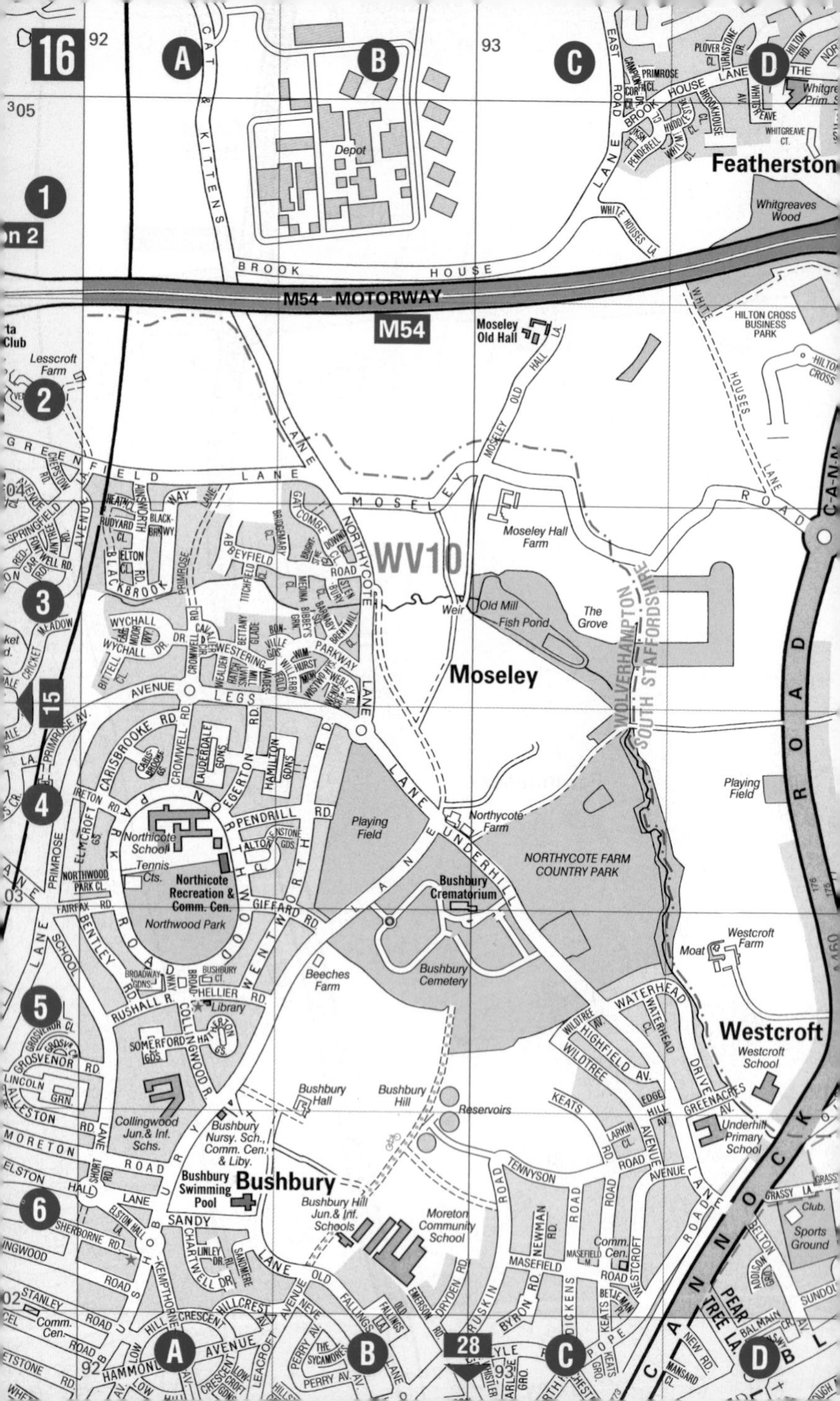

Depot
Featherston
Whitgreaves Wood
M54 MOTORWAY
M54
Moseley Old Hall
HILTON CROSS BUSINESS PARK
Lesscroft Farm
GREENFIELD LANE
MOSELEY ROAD
WV10
Moseley Hall Farm
Old Mill
Weir
Fish Pond
The Grove
Moseley
WOLVERHAMPTON
SOUTH STAFFORDSHIRE
Playing Field
Northycote Farm
NORTHYCOTE FARM COUNTRY PARK
Northicote School
Tennis Cts.
Northicote Recreation & Comm. Cen.
Northwood Park
Bushbury Crematorium
Bushbury Cemetery
Beeches Farm
Westcroft Farm
Moat
Westcroft
Westcroft School
Library
Collingwood Jun.& Inf. Schs.
Bushbury Nursy. Sch., Comm. Cen. & Liby.
Bushbury Hall
Bushbury Hill
Reservoirs
Underhill Primary School
Bushbury Swimming Pool
Bushbury
Bushbury Hill Jun.& Inf. Schools
Moreton Community School
Comm. Cen.
Club
Sports Ground
CANNOCK ROAD
A460
UNDERHILL LANE
NORTHYCOTE LANE
BUSHBURY LANE

15
28

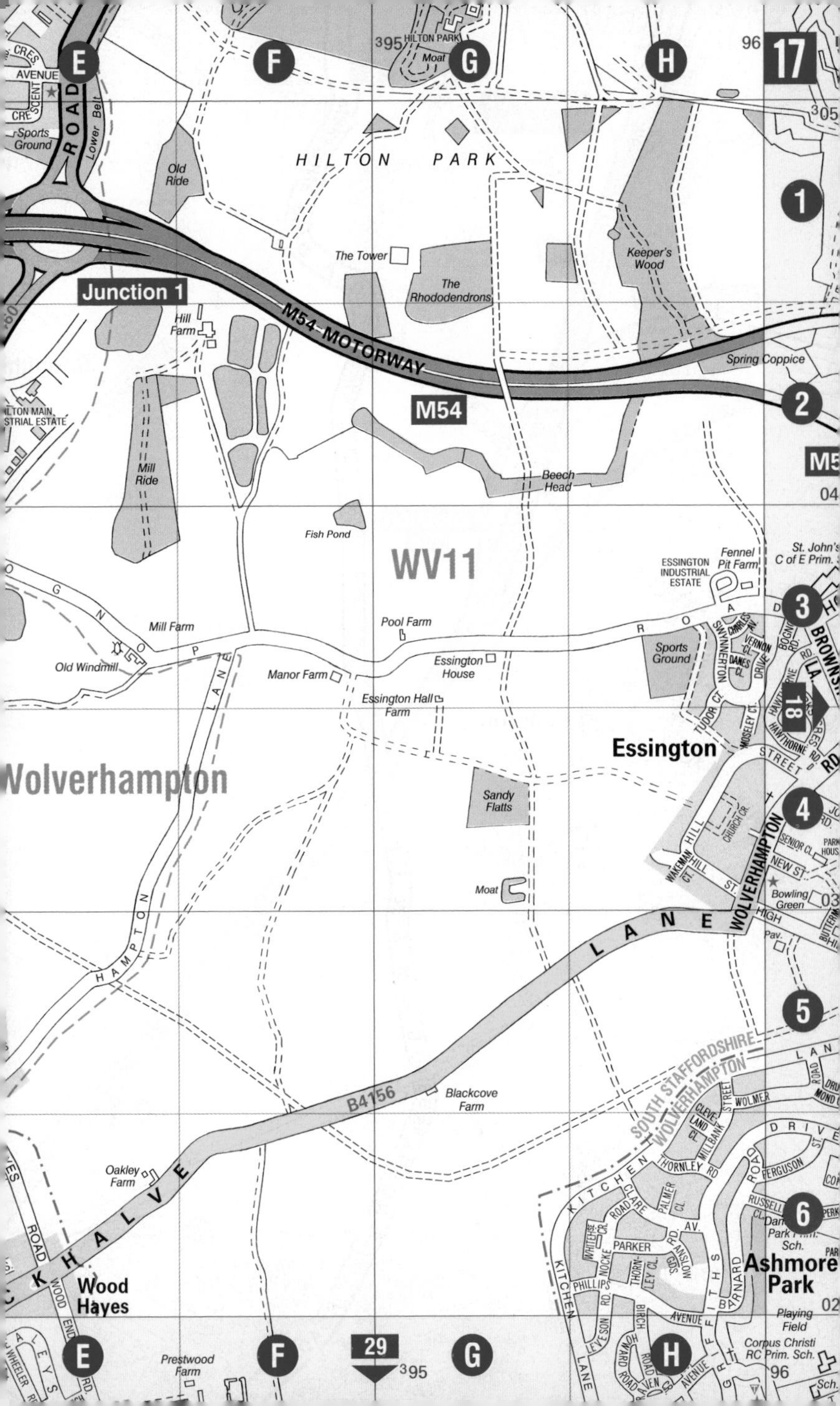

E **F** **G** **H**

395 HILTON PARK
Moat

305

HILTON PARK

Old Ride

The Tower

Keeper's Wood

The Rhododendrons

Junction 1

Hill Farm

1

M54-MOTORWAY

Spring Coppice

M54

Beech Head

2

M5

04

HILTON MAIN INDUSTRIAL ESTATE

Mill Ride

Fish Pond

WV11

ESSINGTON INDUSTRIAL ESTATE

Fennel Pit Farm

St. John's C of E Prim.

Mill Farm

Pool Farm

Sports Ground

3

BROWNS

Old Windmill

Essington House

Manor Farm

Essington Hall Farm

SWINNERTON

VERNON

DRIVE

18

HAWTHORNE

Wolverhampton

Essington

HAMPTON LANE

STREET

RD

Sandy Flatts

WAKHAM HILL

CHURCH

CR

SENIOR CL

NEW ST

PARK HOUS.

4

JO

03

Moat

WOLVERHAMPTON

HIGH

Bowling Green

Pav.

5

LANE

SOUTH STAFFORDSHIRE WOLVERHAMPTON

LAN

DRUMMOND

B4156

Blackcove Farm

WOLMER

DRIVE

KITCHEN

HORNLEY

CLEVE

Ferguson

RUSSELL

Dam Park Farm Sch.

6

Oakley Farm

LANE

WHITE

NOCKE

PALMER

CLOSE

AV.

BIRCH

GRIFFITHS

Ashmore Park

PARKER

THORNLEY

HALVE

Phillips

ROAD

KITCHEN LANE

MOSELEY

AVENUE

Playing Field

Wood Hayes

BIRCH HDW

HAWN

Corpus Christi RC Prim. Sch.

96

E **F** **29** **G** **H**

395

18
Wakeman's Wood
Hilton Park Service Area
Haven Meadows
Burn's Wood
M6
MOTORWAY
M54
Spring Coppice
The Hag
HOBNOCK ROAD
B4156
School Farm
Junction 10a
Upper Ryde Farm
Holly Bank Gorse
WARSTONE RD.
OLD LANDYWOOD LANE
Hollybank Farm
Horsefields Gorse
BROAD ROAD
B4210
Chapel Farm
Playing Field
Pav.
Springhi
Caravan Park
A462
Barn Farm
Fennel Pit Farm
St. John's C of E Prim. Sch.
Comm. Cen.
Wolverhampton
WV11
The Clu
Essington
Works
BROWNSHORE LA.
BROWNSHORE LANE
WOLVERHAMPTON RD.
Reservoir
Bowling Green
Hilton Colliery Farm
Sneyd Colliery
BURSNIPS ROAD
Depot
Sneyd Farm
HIGH HILL
STH. STAFFORDSHIRE
WOLVERHAMPTON
LANE
Coppice Farm
SNEYD RD.
ESSINGTON ROAD
KITCHEN LANE
SNAPE DRIVE
Danesmore Park Prim. Sch.
Ashmore Park
Playing Field
Corpus Christi RC Prim. Sch.
St. Alban's C of E Prim. Sch.
Allen's Rough Prim. Sch.
WV12
Beacon Prim. Sch.
6
17
30

E
F
G
H
7
31
20
1
2
3
4
5
6
WALSALL RD.
STAFFORD ROAD
A34
HOBBLE END LANE
Providence House
Long Lane Bridge
Day Nursery
Cannock Lodge Cottage
WS6
Newtown
Newtown Farm
Fishley Bridge No. 3
Fishley Bridge No. 2
Newtown Bridge
Lord Hays Branch (Disused)
Springhill Covert
Wyrley & Essington Canal
Yieldfields Hall
North Walsall Cemetery
Bowling Green
BLOXWICH GOLF COURSE
Club Ho.
Walsall
BROAD LANE
B4210
Bloxwich North
Baytree House
The Hills
King George V Memorial Playing Fields
Pav.
STH. STAFFORDSHIRE WALSALL
Abbey Primary School
Football Ground
The Sneyd School
Sneyd Reservoir
Play. Field
Youth Centre
BLOXWICH
Wallington Heath
A4124
BELL LANE
SNEYD LANE
LICHFIELD RD.
WS3
Bloxwich
HOSP.
Mossley Prim. Sch.
Home
St. Peter's RC Prim. Sch.
T.P. Riley Commun. Sch.
Arrowcraft Marina
Sneyd Junction Bridge
Busill Jones Prim. Sch.
Elmore Green Prim. Sch.
BLOXWICH HOSP.
HIGH ST.
ELMORE GREEN RD.
SANDBANK
Market Centre
Lib. & Thtre.
Dudley's

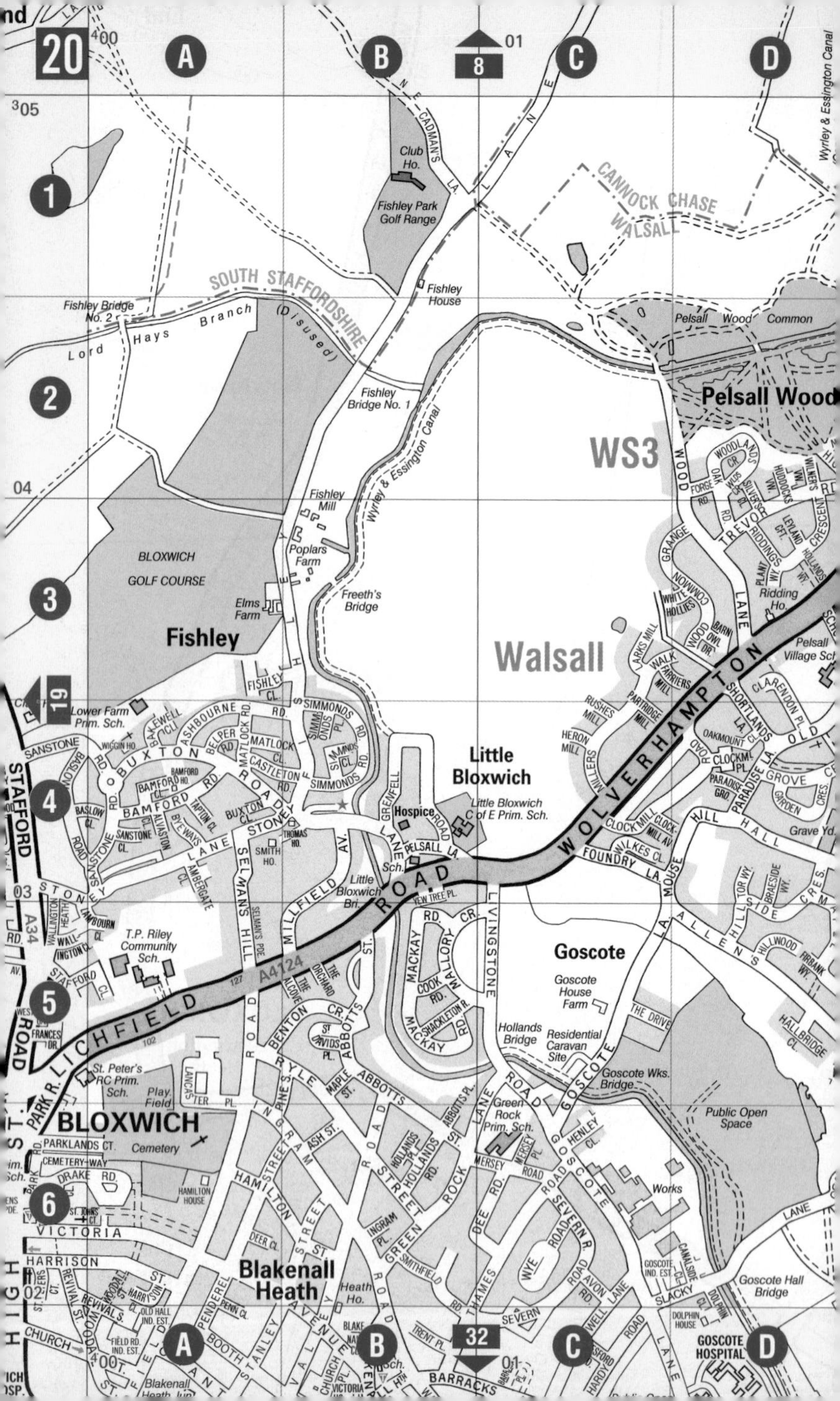
A
B
C
D
8
1
2
3
4
5
6
19
32
Fishley Park Golf Range
Club Ho.
CADMAN'S LA.
CANNOCK CHASE
WALSALL
SOUTH STAFFORDSHIRE
(Disused)
Lord Hays Branch
Fishley Bridge No. 2
Fishley House
Fishley Bridge No. 1
Wyrley & Essington Canal
Pelsall Wood Common
Pelsall Wood
WS3
Fishley Mill
Poplars Farm
Freeth's Bridge
BLOXWICH GOLF COURSE
Elms Farm
Fishley
Walsall
Little Bloxwich
Little Bloxwich C of E Prim. Sch.
Hospice
Lower Farm Prim. Sch.
WOLVERHAMPTON ROAD
LICHFIELD ROAD
A4124
A34
STAFFORD ROAD
T.P. Riley Community Sch.
Goscote
Goscote House Farm
Hollands Bridge
Residential Caravan Site
Goscote Wks. Bridge
Public Open Space
Works
Goscote Hall Bridge
GOSCOTE HOSPITAL
BLOXWICH
Cemetery
Blakenall Heath
St. Peter's RC Prim. Sch.
Play Field
Green Rock Prim. Sch.
Pelsall Village Sch.
Ridding Ho.
Grave Yd.
Little Bloxwich Bri.
HIGH ST.
Wyrley & Essington Canal

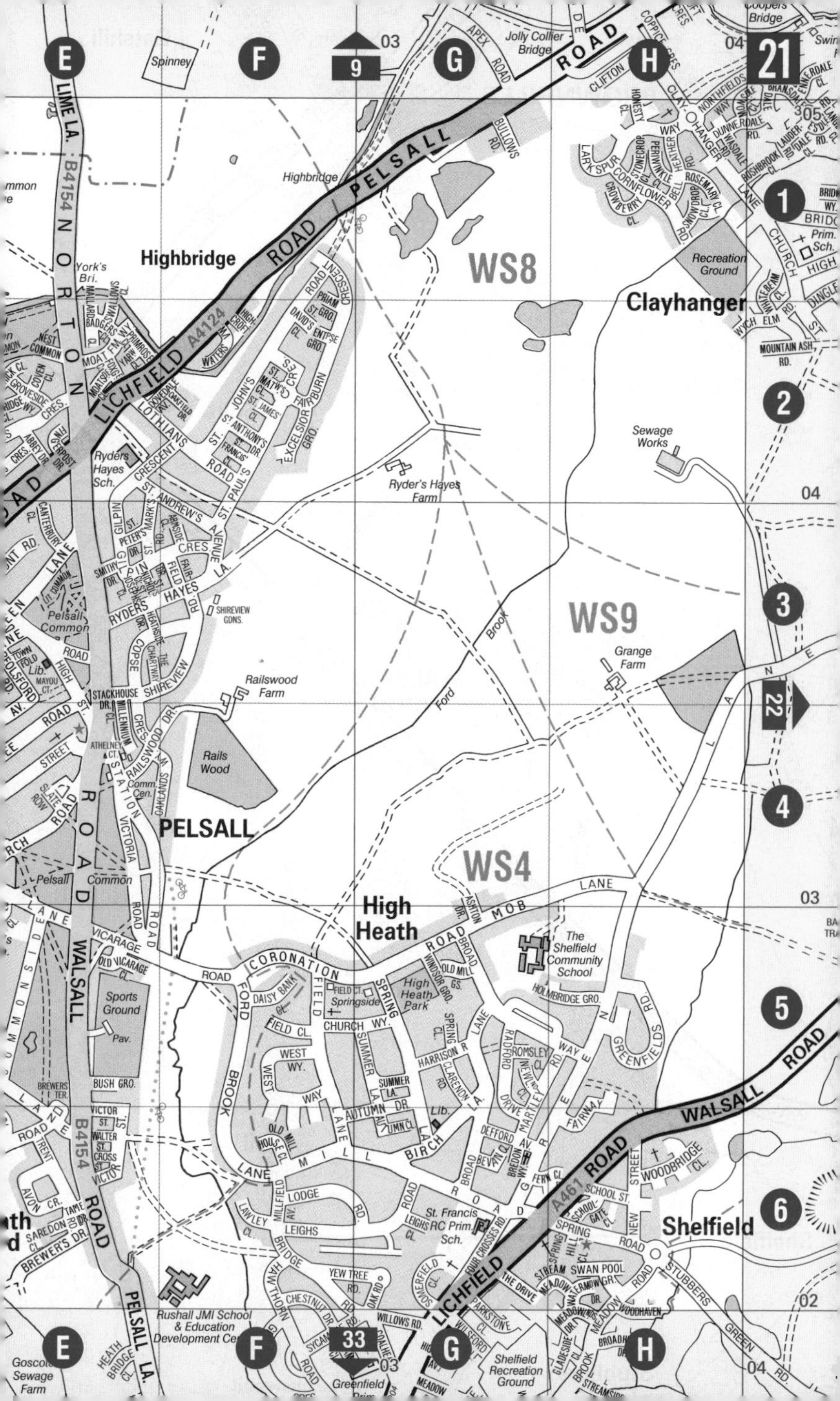

21
9
22
33
E
F
G
H
1
2
3
4
5
6
03
04
05
02
Spinney
Jolly Collier Bridge
Coopers Bridge
APEX ROAD
CLIFTON
PELSALL ROAD
Highbridge
LIME LA.
B4154
NORTON ROAD
York's Bri.
LICHFIELD ROAD
A4124
BULLOWS RD.
WS8
WS9
WS4
Clayhanger
Recreation Ground
CHURCH
Prim. Sch.
Sewage Works
Ryder's Hayes Farm
Ryders Hayes Sch.
LOTHIANS
CRESCENT
ST. PAUL'S
ST. ANDREW'S AVENUE
RYDERS HAYES LA.
SHIREVIEW GDNS.
Railswood Farm
Rails Wood
Ford Brook
Grange Farm
LANE
Pelsall Common
PELSALL
STATION
VICTORIA
Comm. Cen.
High Heath
MOB LANE
CORONATION ROAD
The Shelfield Community School
HOLMBRIDGE GRO.
GREENFIELDS RD.
VICARAGE ROAD
WALSALL ROAD
Sports Ground
Pav.
BUSH GRO.
BREWERS TER.
FORD BROOK LANE
DAISY BANK
FIELD CL.
WEST WAY
CHURCH WY.
SUMMER LA.
AUTUMN DR.
High Heath Park
Springside
SPRING LANE
HARRISON RD.
Lib.
BIRCH LA.
MILL LANE
LODGE RD.
LEIGHS RD.
LAWLEY CL.
MILLFIELD AV.
HAWTHORN
YEW TREE RD.
St. Francis RC Prim. Sch.
FOUR CROSSES RD.
BROAD LANE
GREEN LANE
FAIRWAY
DEFFORD AV.
A461
LICHFIELD ROAD
WALSALL ROAD
WOODBRIDGE CL.
NEW STREET
SCHOOL ST.
Shelfield
SPRING ROAD
SWAN POOL GR.
STUBBERS GREEN RD.
Shelfield Recreation Ground
Rushall JMI School & Education Development Ce
Goscote Sewage Farm
PELSALL LA.
HEATH BRIDGE
Greenfield

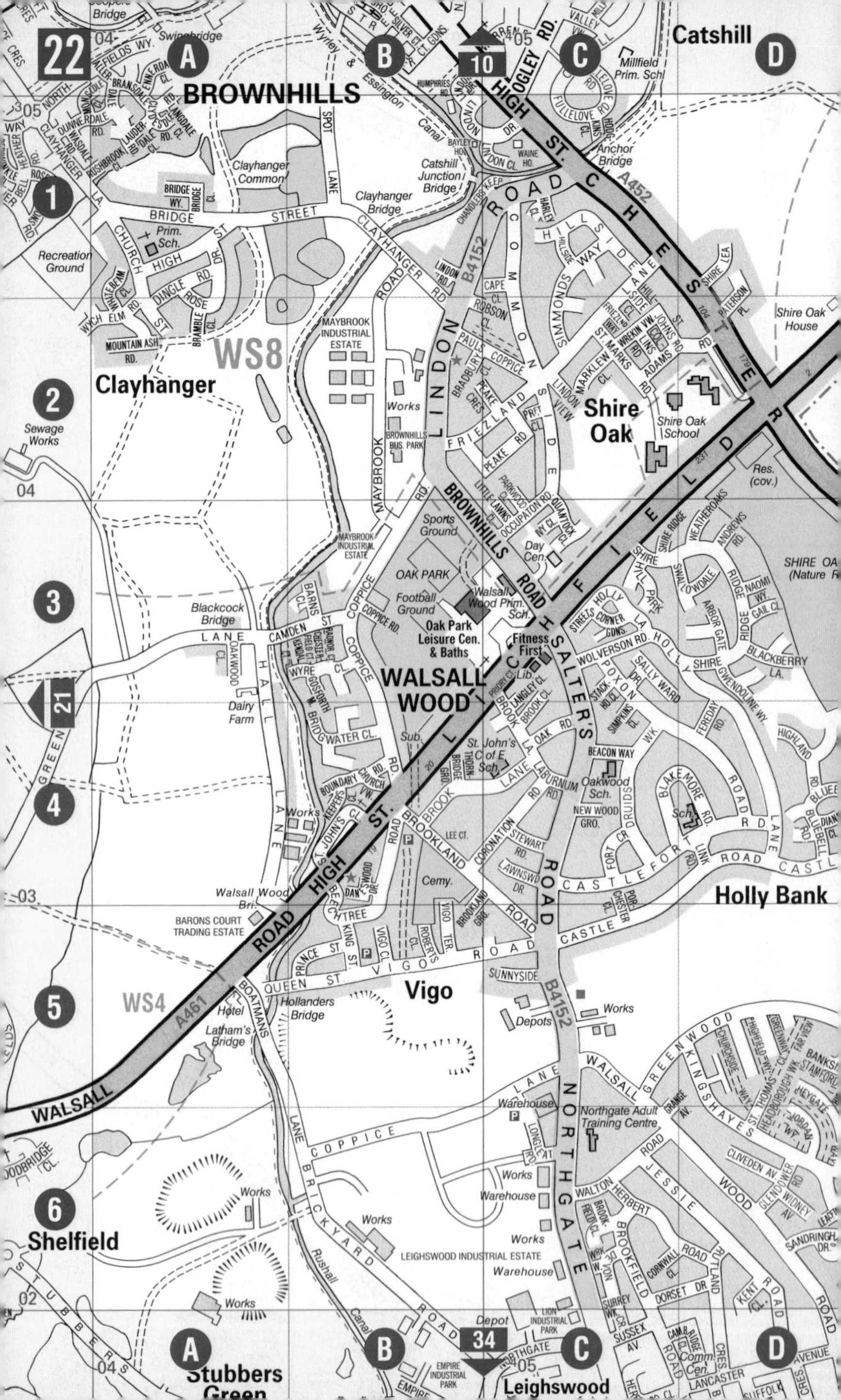
A
B
C
D
1
2
3
4
5
6
10
21
34
BROWNHILLS
Catshill
Clayhanger
WS8
Shire Oak
WALSALL WOOD
Holly Bank
Vigo
WS4
Shelfield
Stubbers Green
Leighswood
Clayhanger Common
Recreation Ground
Sewage Works
MAYBROOK INDUSTRIAL ESTATE
BROWNHILLS BUS. PARK
Sports Ground
OAK PARK
Football Ground
Oak Park Leisure Cen. & Baths
Walsall Wood Prim. Sch.
Shire Oak School
Shire Oak House
Blackcock Bridge
Dairy Farm
Walsall Wood Bri.
BARONS COURT TRADING ESTATE
Hollanders Bridge
Latham's Bridge
Northgate Adult Training Centre
LEIGHSWOOD INDUSTRIAL ESTATE
LION INDUSTRIAL PARK
EMPIRE INDUSTRIAL PARK
HIGH ST.
A452
CHESTER RD.
LINDON RD.
B4152
BROWNHILLS ROAD
SALTER'S ROAD
NORTHGATE
WALSALL ROAD
A461
HIGH ST.
LICHFIELD RD.
COPPICE LANE
BRICKYARD ROAD
HALL LANE
VIGO ROAD
CASTLE ROAD
BRIDGE STREET
CLAYHANGER RD.
MAYBROOK RD.
COMMON SIDE
Rushall Canal
Wyrley & Essington Canal

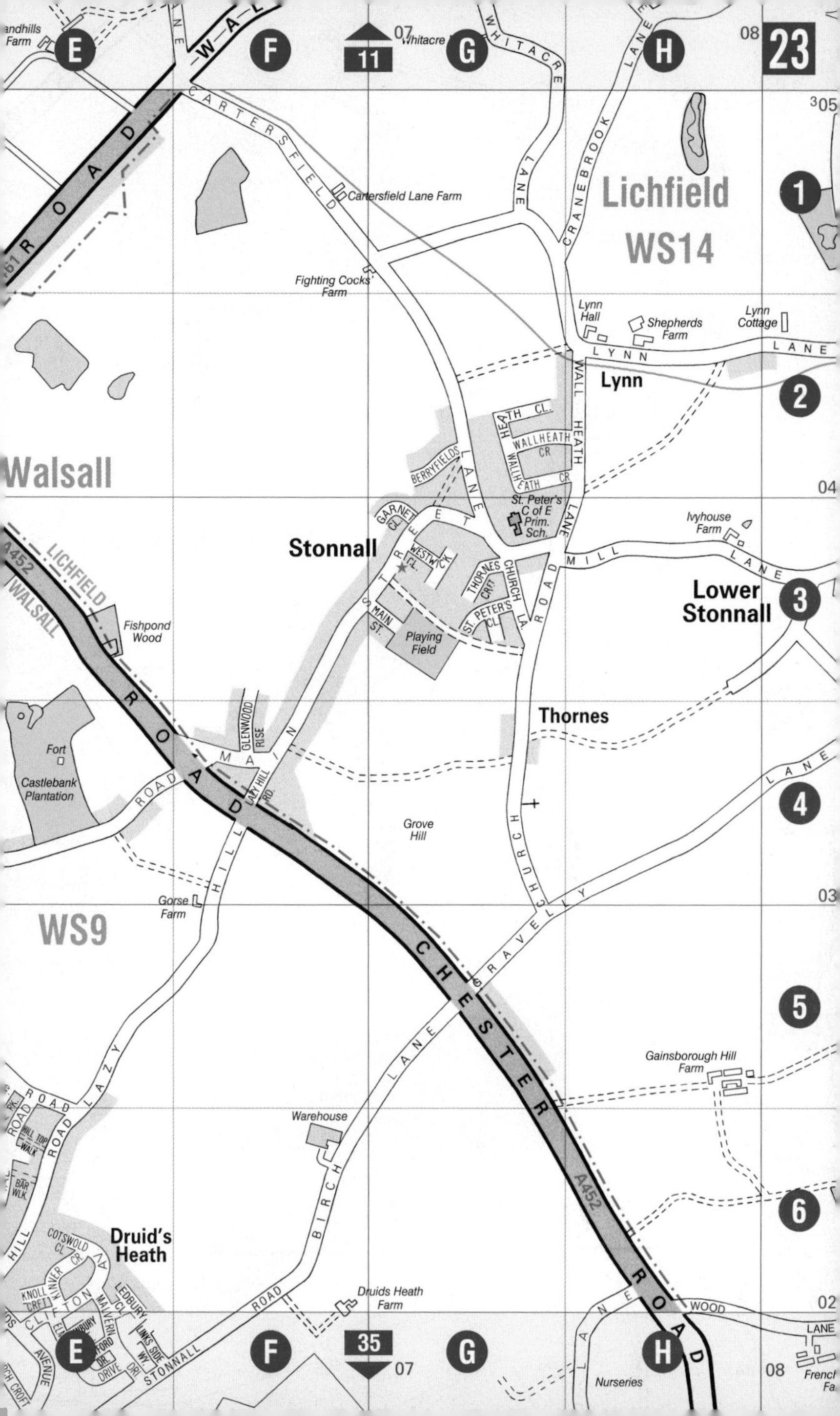
Lichfield
WS14
Walsall
WS9
Stonnall
Lower Stonnall
Lynn
Thornes
Druid's Heath
Cartersfield Lane Farm
Fighting Cocks' Farm
Lynn Hall
Shepherds Farm
Lynn Cottage
Ivyhouse Farm
St. Peter's C of E Prim. Sch.
Playing Field
Fishpond Wood
Fort
Castlebank Plantation
Grove Hill
Gorse Farm
Gainsborough Hill Farm
Warehouse
Druids Heath Farm
Nurseries
Whitacre
CARTERSFIELD LANE
WHITACRE LANE
CRANEBROOK LANE
LYNN LANE
WALL HEATH LANE
HEATH CL.
WALLHEATH CR
BERRYFIELDS
GARNET CL.
WESTWICK CL.
THORNES CRFT
CHURCH LA.
ST. PETER'S CL.
MAIN ST.
MAIN STREET
MILL LANE
CHURCH ROAD
GLENWOOD RISE
LAZY HILL RD.
LICHFIELD ROAD
CHESTER ROAD
A452
GRAVELLY LANE
BIRCH LANE
LAZY HILL
HILL TOP WALK
BAR WLK
COTSWOLD CL
KINVER CR.
KNOLL CRFT
CLIFTON AVENUE
MALVERN DRIVE
LEDBURY CL
LINKS SIDE WY.
STONNALL ROAD
WOOD LANE
E
F
G
H
1
2
3
4
5
6
11
35
07
08
305
04
03
02

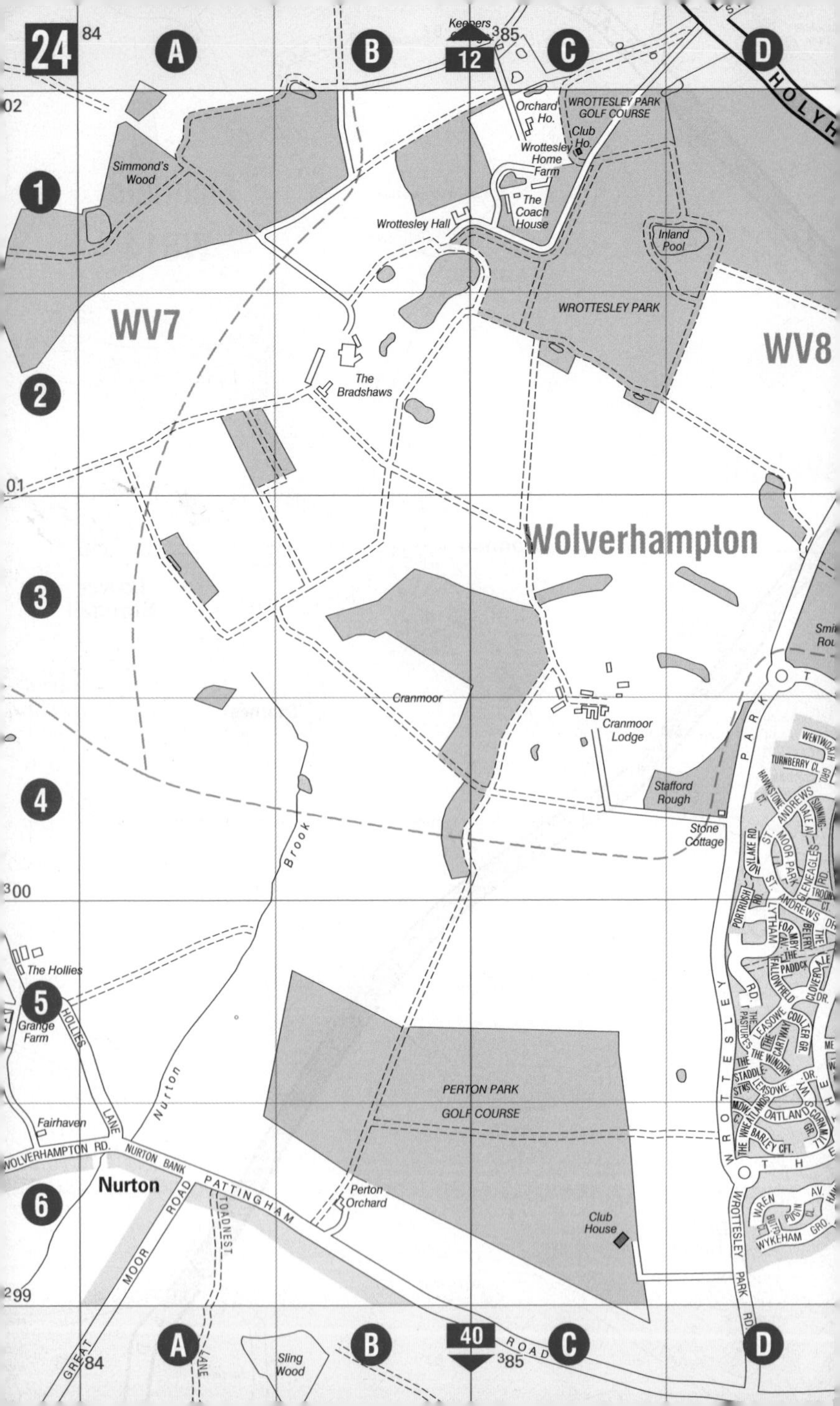

24 84

A   B   C   D

Keepers 385
12

Orchard Ho.

WROTTESLEY PARK
GOLF COURSE

Club Ho.

Wrottesley Home Farm

1 Simmond's Wood

The Coach House

Wrottesley Hall

Inland Pool

WV7

WROTTESLEY PARK

WV8

2 The Bradshaws

Wolverhampton

3

Cranmoor

Smi Rou

WENTWO

TURNBERRY C.

PARK

4 Cranmoor Lodge

Stafford Rough

Stone Cottage

ST ANDREWS CL
HAWKSTONE
ST ANDREWS DR
MOOR PARK
TROON CT
ST MARY
THE PADDOCK
LYTHAM
FALCONFIELD

300

5 The Hollies
Grange Farm

HOLLIES

THE LEASOW
THE PASTURES
THE WINDOW
THE STADDLE
STREET
MUIRFIELD DR
WENTLOE
OATLANDS
BARLEY CFT.

6 Fairhaven
WOLVERHAMPTON RD.
Nurton
NURTON BANK

PERTON PARK
GOLF COURSE

Perton Orchard

Club House

WREN
PIGEON
WYKEHAM GRO.
AV.

299

A   84   B   40 385   C   D

MOOR ROAD   PATTINGHAM   (ROAD)

Sling Wood

WROTTESLEY PARK ROAD

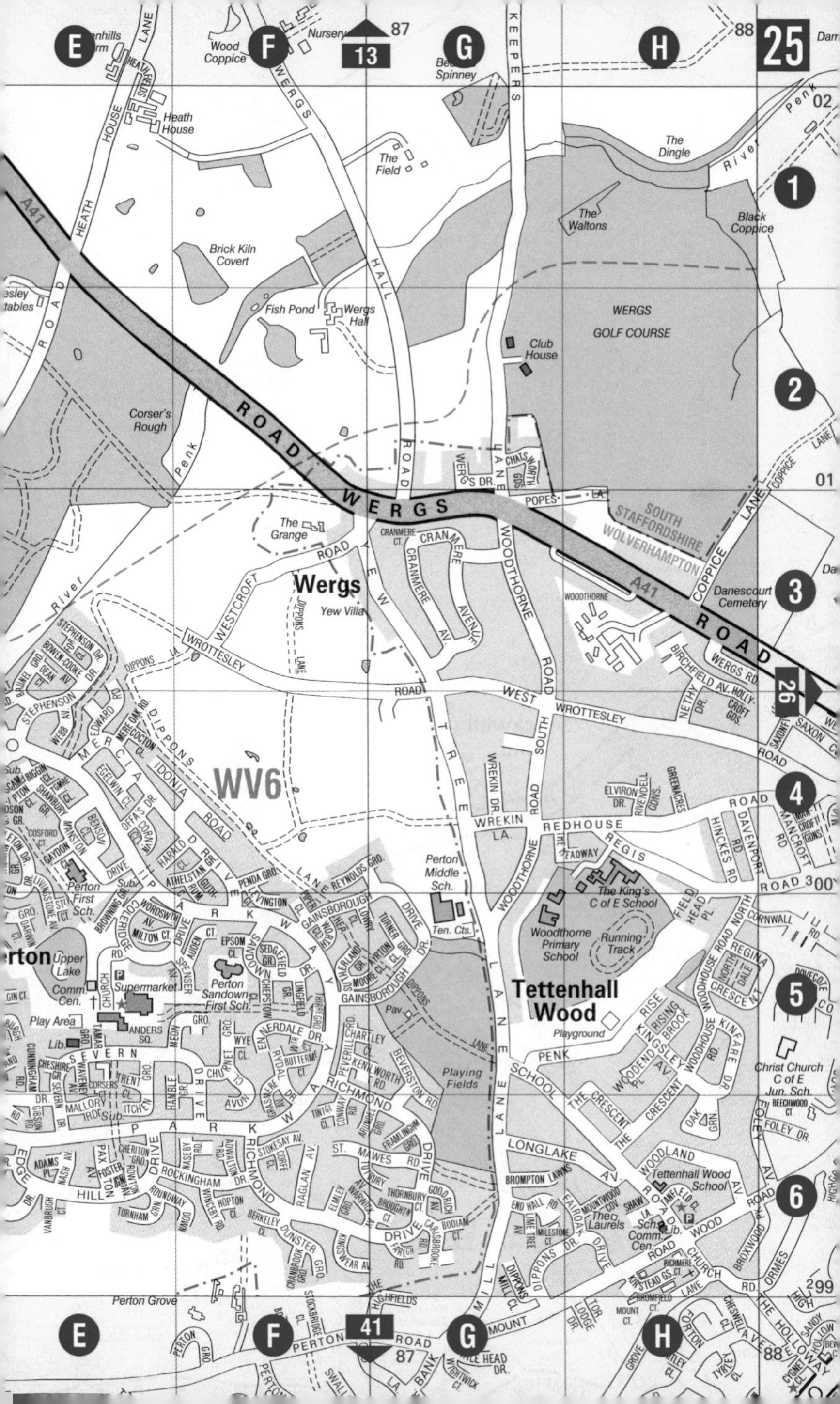

13
87
88
E
F
G
H
Wood Coppice
Nursery
Beech Spinney
Heath House
HEATH HOUSE LANE
WERGS HALL ROAD
KEEPERS LANE
The Field
The Dingle
River Penk
Black Coppice
The Waltons
Brick Kiln Covert
Fish Pond
Wergs Hall
WERGS GOLF COURSE
Club House
A41
WERGS ROAD
Corser's Rough
Penk
CHATSWORTH GDS.
WERGS DR.
POPES LA.
SOUTH STAFFORDSHIRE
WOLVERHAMPTON
COPPICE LANE
Danescourt Cemetery
The Grange
WESTCROFT ROAD
CRANMERE AVENUE
CRANMERE CT.
Wergs
Yew Villa
WOODTHORNE ROAD
DIPPONS LANE
WROTTESLEY ROAD
WEST WROTTESLEY
YEW TREE LANE
SOUTH ROAD
BIRCHFIELD AV.
HOLLYCROFT GDS.
NETHY DR.
WERGS RD.
26
SAXON
WV6
MERCIA
IDONIA ROAD
WREKIN DR.
WREKIN LA.
ELVIRON DR.
RIVENDELL GDNS.
GREENACRES
REDHOUSE ROAD
REGIS ROAD
HINCKES RD.
DAVENPORT RD.
MANCROFT RD.
Perton Middle Sch.
Ten. Cts.
The King's C of E School
Woodthorne Primary School
Running Track
Tettenhall Wood
Playground
PARK WAY
Perton First Sch.
Upper Lake
Supermarket
Perton Sandown First Sch.
Comm. Cen.
Play Area
Lib.
SEVERN DRIVE
GAINSBOROUGH DR.
Playing Fields
Pav.
RICHMOND
PARK DRIVE
PENK
SCHOOL
THE CRESCENT
KINGSLEY AV.
WOODHOUSE ROAD NORTH
REGINA CRESCENT
Christ Church C of E Jun. Sch.
FOLEY AV.
LONGLAKE AV.
WOODLAND AV.
Tettenhall Wood School
The Laurels
Sch. Comm. Cen.
CHURCH RD.
WOOD ROAD
MILL LANE
DIPPONS DR.
ROCKINGHAM DR.
HILL
EDGE
Perton Grove
PERTON ROAD
MOUNT
THE HOLLOWAY
41
87
300
299
01
02
1
2
3
4
5
6

Palmer's Cross
Wolverhampton
SOUTH STAFFORDSHIRE GOLF COURSE
Stockwell End
Tettenhall
Newbridge
Tettenhall Wood
WV8
WV6
WV3
Danescourt Cemetery
Wolverhampton Cricket Ground
Claregate Playing Field
Tettenhall College
THE WOLVERHAMPTON NUFFIELD HOSPITAL
St. Peter's Collegiate School
Wolverhampton Girls' High School
Smestow Valley Local Nature Reserve
Wildside Activity Centre
Wulfrun College
Newbridge Playing Fields
University of Wolverhampton (Compton Campus)

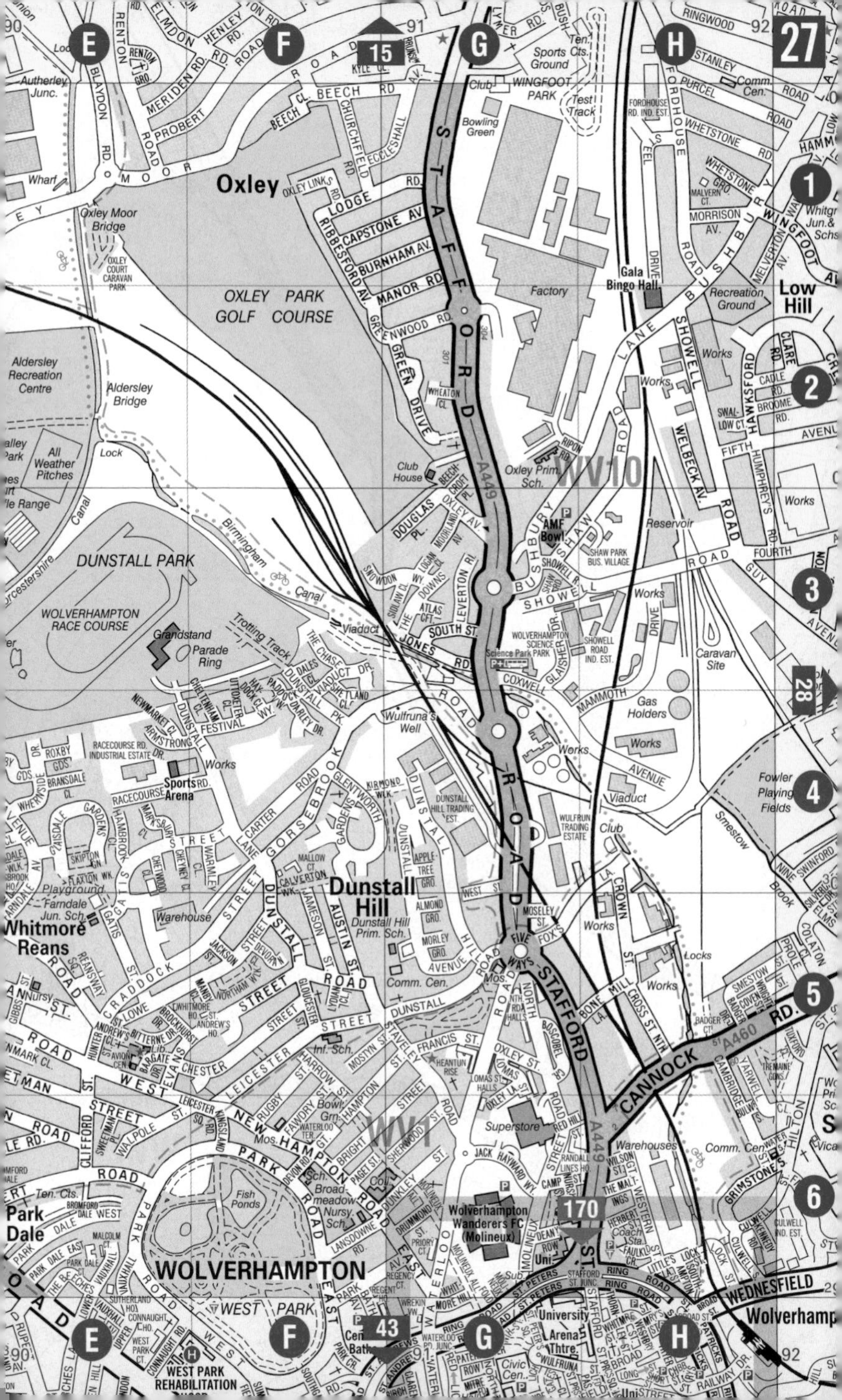
E
F
G
H
15
1
2
3
4
5
6
28
170
43
Oxley
OXLEY PARK
GOLF COURSE
Oxley Moor Bridge
OXLEY COURT CARAVAN PARK
Aldersley Recreation Centre
Aldersley Bridge
All Weather Pitches
DUNSTALL PARK
WOLVERHAMPTON RACE COURSE
Grandstand
Parade Ring
Trotting Track
Birmingham Canal
Viaduct
Wulfruna's Well
Dunstall Hill
Dunstall Hill Prim. Sch.
Comm. Cen.
Whitmore Reans
Farndale Jun. Sch.
Sports Arena
RACECOURSE RD. INDUSTRIAL ESTATE
DUNSTALL HILL TRADING EST.
STAFFORD ROAD
A449
Sports Cts. Ground
WINGFOOT PARK
Test Track
Bowling Green
Factory
Gala Bingo Hall
Recreation Ground
Low Hill
Oxley Prim. Sch.
WV10
AMF Bowl
SHAW PARK BUS. VILLAGE
Reservoir
WOLVERHAMPTON SCIENCE PARK
SHOWELL ROAD IND. EST.
Science Park
Caravan Site
Gas Holders
Works
Fowler Playing Fields
Smestow Brook
WULFRUN TRADING ESTATE
Locks
CANNOCK RD.
A460
Warehouses
Superstore
Wolverhampton Wanderers FC (Molineux)
WV1
Park Dale
WOLVERHAMPTON
WEST PARK
Fish Ponds
WEST PARK REHABILITATION
University
Arena Thtre.
Civic Cen.
Wolverhampton
WEDNESFIELD
RING ROAD
ST. PETERS
STAFFORD ST. JUNC.
WATERLOO RD. JUNC.
Coach Sta.
CULWELL IND. EST.
FORDHOUSE RD. IND. EST.
Autherley Junc.
Lock
Wharf
90
91
92

A
B
C
D
16
92
93
1
2
3
4
5
6
27
170
44
Old Fallings
Low Hill
Scotlands
Newbolds
Wolverhampton
WV10
Fallings Park
Park Village
New Cross
NEW CROSS HOSPITAL
Heath Town
WV1
Springfield
Heath Town Leisure Cen.
HEATH TOWN PARK
Cineworld Cinema
Bentley Bri. Leisure Pk.
Whitgreave Jun.& Inf. Schs.
Our Lady & St. Chad RC Sch.
Fallings Park Prim. Sch.
St. Christopher's Park
St. Mary's RC Prim. Sch.
D'Eyncourt Prim. Sch.
Heath Park High Sch.
Trinity C of E Prim. Sch.
St. Stephen's C of E Prim. Sch.
Woden Primary School
Wodensfield Prim. Sch.
Royal Mail Sorting Office
Fowler Playing Fields
Recreation Ground
Playing Field
Play. Fld.
Playground
Cold Stores
Bus Depot
Activity Cen.
Sikh Temple
Vicarage
Works
Comm. Cen.
PARK LANE TRAD. EST.
BLUEBIRD TRADING ESTATE
MERRYHILLS ENT. PK.
FALLINGS PK. IND. EST.
CULWELL TRAD. EST.
MANDERS INDUSTRIAL ESTATE
NEW CROSS IND. EST.
CROSSWAYS SHOP. CEN.
Wyrley & Essington Canal
Smestow Brook
A460
A4124
B4156
B4484
CANNOCK ROAD
WEDNESFIELD ROAD
WOLVERHAMPTON RD.
BLACKHALVE LA.
LONG KNOWLE LA.
BUSHBURY RD.
PRIMROSE LANE
SHOWELL CIRCUS
FOURTH AVENUE
FIRST AVENUE
SECOND AVENUE
THIRD AVENUE
FIFTH AVENUE
OLD FALLINGS CRESCENT
FALLINGS PARK
GUY AVENUE
PARK LANE
VICTORIA ROAD
KINGSWAY
WIMBORNE RD.
CORONATION RD.
CHURCH ROAD
POWELL STREET
LONGFORD RD.
DEANS ROAD
ASHBOURNE RD.
FRIESLAND DRIVE
LEWIS ROAD
STAFFORD ROAD

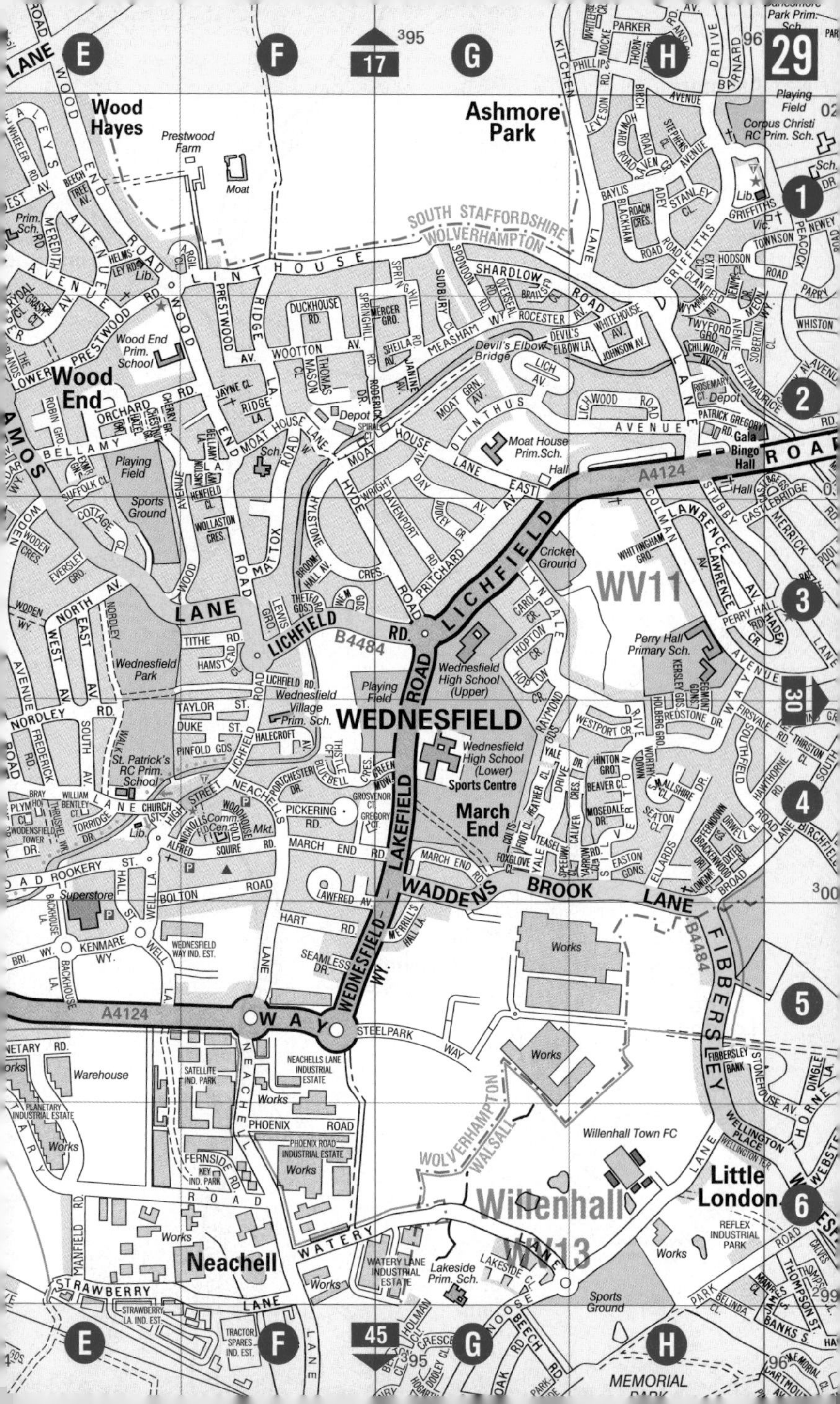
29
17
395
45
E
F
G
H
1
2
3
4
5
6
30
Wood Hayes
Prestwood Farm
Moat
Ashmore Park
Playing Field
Corpus Christi RC Prim. Sch.
SOUTH STAFFORDSHIRE
WOLVERHAMPTON
LINTHOUSE
Wood End Prim. School
Wood End
WOODEND
PRESTWOOD RD.
LOWER PRESTWOOD
ORCHARD
BELLAMY
Playing Field
Sports Ground
Devil's Elbow Bridge
Depot
Moat House Prim.Sch.
Gala Bingo Hall
A4124
LICHFIELD
ROAD
Cricket Ground
WV11
Perry Hall Primary Sch.
LANE
LICHFIELD RD.
B4484
Wednesfield Park
Wednesfield Village Prim. Sch.
Wednesfield High School (Upper)
WEDNESFIELD
Wednesfield High School (Lower)
Sports Centre
March End
St. Patrick's RC Prim. School
HIGH STREET
Lib.
Mkt.
Superstore
WADDENS BROOK LANE
LAKEFIELD ROAD
WEDNESFIELD WY.
WEDNESFIELD WAY IND. EST.
Works
KENMARE WY.
WAY
STEELPARK WAY
NEACHELLS LANE INDUSTRIAL ESTATE
Warehouse
SATELLITE IND. PARK
PLANETARY INDUSTRIAL ESTATE
PHOENIX ROAD
PHOENIX ROAD INDUSTRIAL ESTATE
KEY IND. PARK
WOLVERHAMPTON
WALSALL
Willenhall Town FC
FIBBERSLEY
Little London
Willenhall
WV13
REFLEX INDUSTRIAL PARK
Neachell
WATERY LANE
WATERY LANE INDUSTRIAL ESTATE
Lakeside Prim. Sch.
Sports Ground
STRAWBERRY LANE
STRAWBERRY LA. IND. EST.
TRACTOR SPARES IND. EST.
MEMORIAL

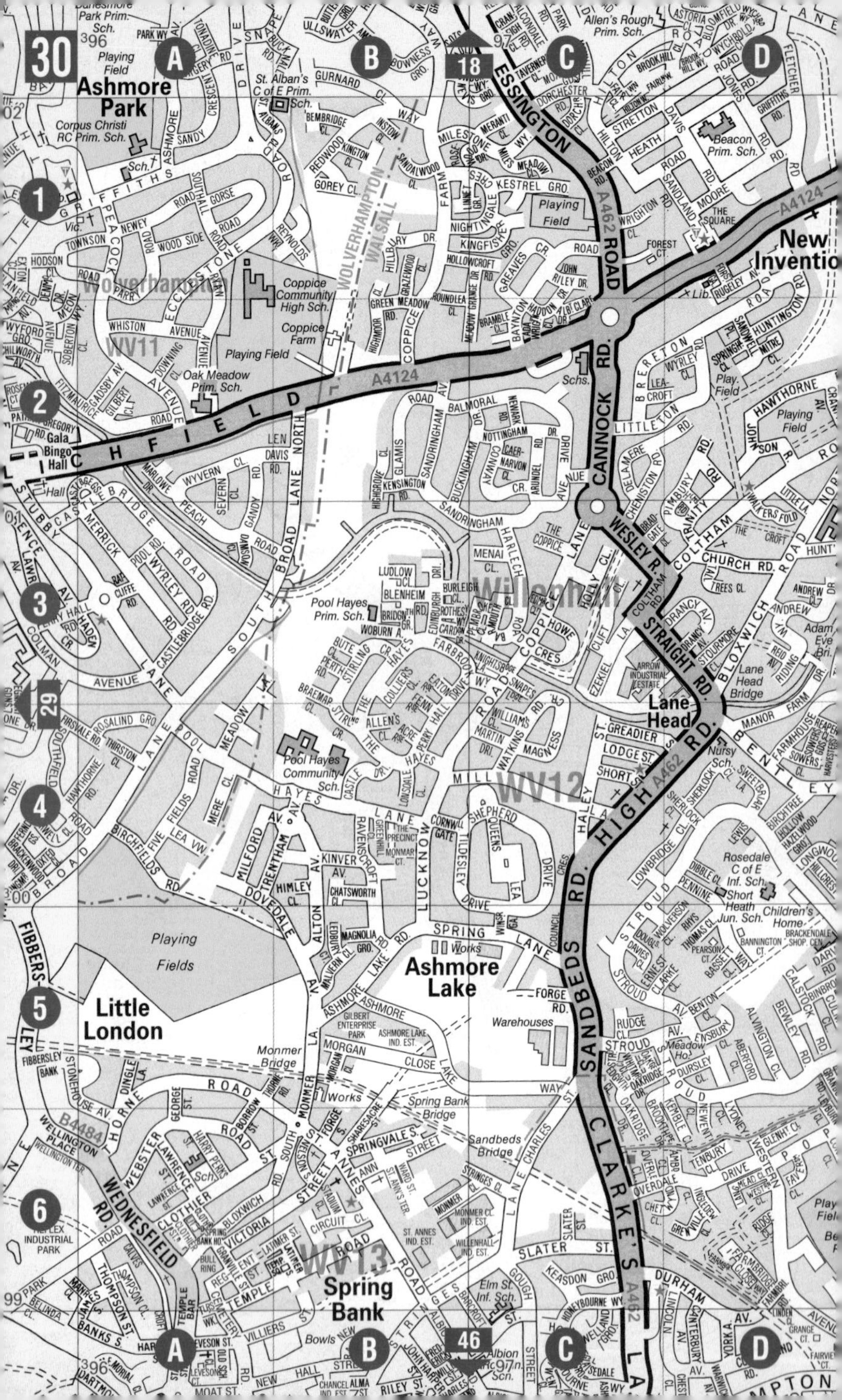
A
B
C
D
18
1
2
3
4
5
6
29
46
Ashmore Park
Playing Field
Corpus Christi RC Prim. Sch.
St. Alban's C of E Prim. Sch.
Allen's Rough Prim. Sch.
Beacon Prim. Sch.
New Invention
Coppice Community High Sch.
Coppice Farm
Playing Field
Oak Meadow Prim. Sch.
Gala Bingo Hall
WV11
Wolverhampton
Walsall
A4124
A462
ESSINGTON ROAD
CANNOCK RD.
LICHFIELD
Pool Hayes Prim. Sch.
Pool Hayes Community Sch.
Willenhall
WV12
Lane Head
Arrow Industrial Estate
Rosedale C of E Inf. Sch.
Short Heath Jun. Sch.
Children's Home
Playing Fields
Little London
Ashmore Lake
Works
Warehouses
Gilbert Enterprise Park
Ashmore Lake Ind. Est.
Monmer Bridge
Spring Bank Bridge
Sandbeds Bridge
WV13
Spring Bank
Elm St. Inf. Sch.
Bowls
Albion
Flexx Industrial Park
SANDBEDS RD.
HIGH RD.
CLARKE'S
STRAIGHT RD.
WESLEY R.
BLOXWICH ROAD
WEDNESFIELD RD.
B4484
SOUTH BROAD LANE NORTH
POOL LANE
HAYES LANE
SPRING LANE
STROUD AV.
SLATER ST.
DURHAM
BENTLEY
FIBBERSLEY

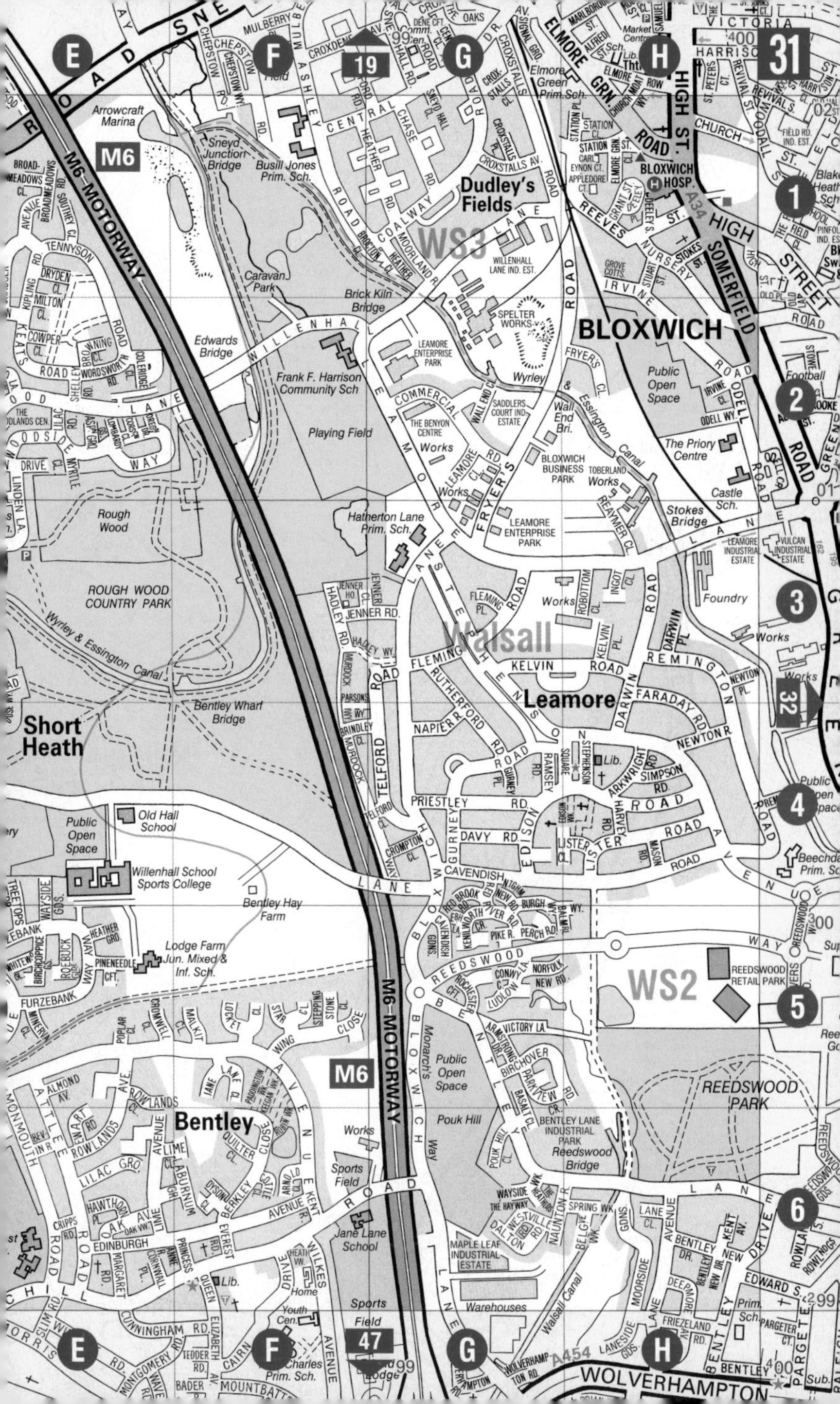

31
19
47
32
E
F
G
H
1
2
3
4
5
6
M6
M6 MOTORWAY
BLOXWICH
Dudley's Fields
WS3
WS2
Walsall
Leamore
Short Heath
Bentley
ROUGH WOOD COUNTRY PARK
Rough Wood
Arrowcraft Marina
Sneyd Junction Bridge
Busill Jones Prim. Sch.
Caravan Park
Brick Kiln Bridge
Edwards Bridge
Frank F. Harrison Community Sch
Playing Field
Hatherton Lane Prim. Sch.
WILLENHALL LANE IND. EST.
SPELTER WORKS
LEAMORE ENTERPRISE PARK
THE BENYON CENTRE
SADDLERS COURT IND. ESTATE
BLOXWICH BUSINESS PARK
Wyrley & Essington Canal
Wall End Bri.
Stokes Bridge
The Priory Centre
Castle Sch.
Public Open Space
LEAMORE INDUSTRIAL ESTATE
VULCAN INDUSTRIAL ESTATE
Foundry
Works
BLOXWICH HOSP.
Elmore Green Prim.Sch.
Bentley Wharf Bridge
Old Hall School
Willenhall School Sports College
Bentley Hay Farm
Lodge Farm Jun. Mixed & Inf. Sch.
REEDSWOOD RETAIL PARK
REEDSWOOD PARK
Beechdale Prim. Sch.
Monarch's Way
Pouk Hill
BENTLEY LANE INDUSTRIAL PARK
Reedswood Bridge
MAPLE LEAF INDUSTRIAL ESTATE
Warehouses
Walsall Canal
Jane Lane School
Sports Field
Youth Cen.
St. Charles Prim. Sch.
A34
A454
HIGH ST.
SOMERFIELD ROAD
WILLENHALL LANE
LEAMORE LANE
BLOXWICH ROAD
BENTLEY LANE
BENTLEY ROAD
WOLVERHAMPTON ROAD
REEDSWOOD WAY
CAVENDISH LANE
KELVIN ROAD
REMINGTON ROAD
STEPHENSON AVENUE

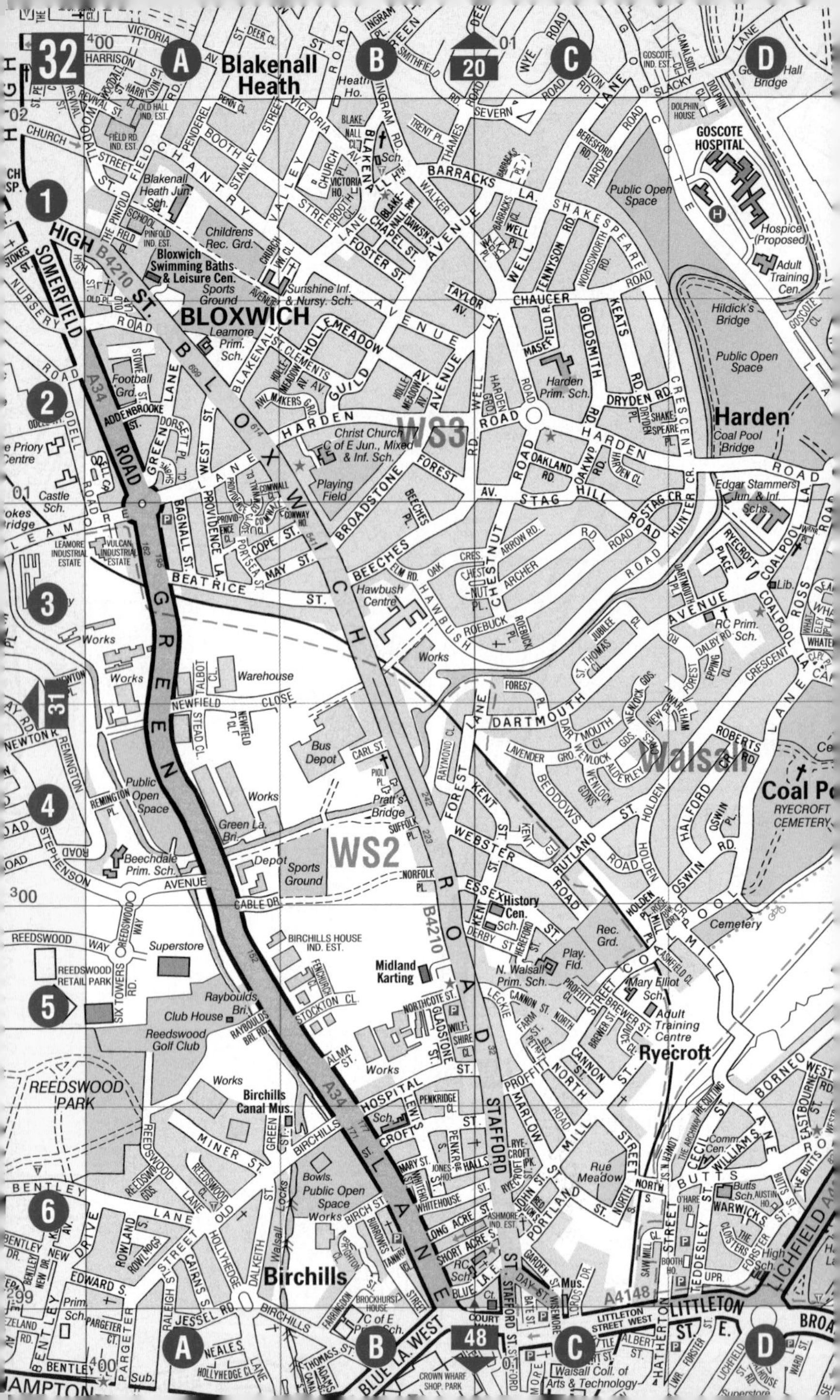
A
B
C
D
20
Blakenall Heath
BLOXWICH
Harden
Walsall
Coal Pool
Ryecroft
Birchills
WS3
WS2
GOSCOTE HOSPITAL
Public Open Space
Hildick's Bridge
Goscote Hall Bridge
Coal Pool Bridge
Harden Prim. Sch.
Christ Church C of E Jun., Mixed & Inf. Sch.
Playing Field
Hawbush Centre
Bus Depot
Works
Warehouse
Superstore
REEDSWOOD RETAIL PARK
Reedswood Golf Club
REEDSWOOD PARK
Birchills Canal Mus.
Midland Karting
Rec. Grd.
Cemetery
RYECROFT CEMETERY
Walsall Coll. of Arts & Technology
1
2
3
4
5
6
31
48

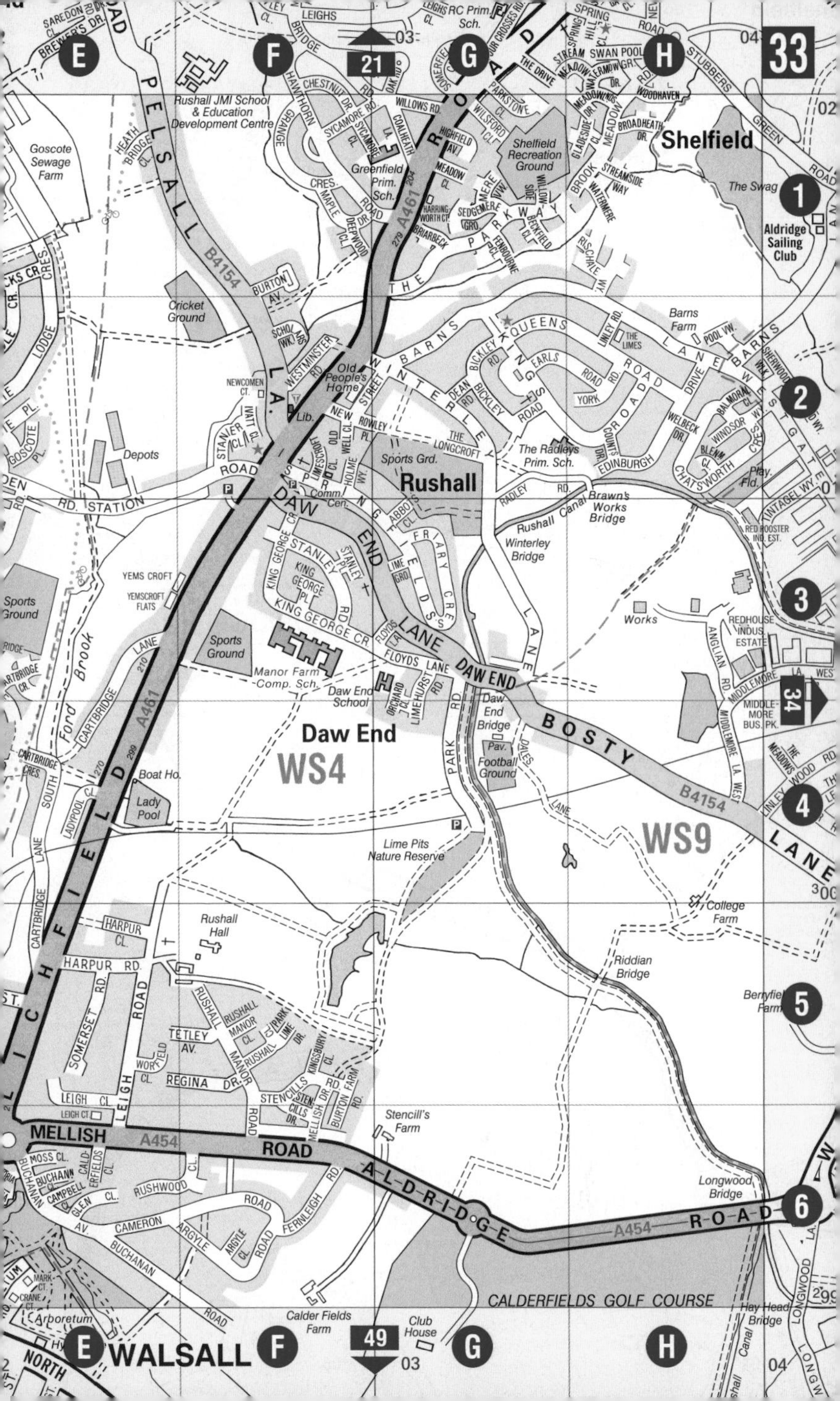

E
F
G
H
21
Rushall JMI School & Education Development Centre
Goscote Sewage Farm
Greenfield Prim. Sch.
Shelfield Recreation Ground
Shelfield
The Swag
Aldridge Sailing Club
Cricket Ground
Barns Farm
Old People's Home
Lib.
Depots
The Radleys Prim. Sch.
Sports Grd.
Rushall
Brawn's Works Bridge
Rushall Canal
Winterley Bridge
Works
Redhouse Indus. Estate
Sports Ground
Manor Farm Comp. Sch.
Daw End School
Daw End Bridge
Daw End
WS4
Pav.
Football Ground
Boat Ho.
Lady Pool
WS9
Lime Pits Nature Reserve
College Farm
Rushall Hall
Riddian Bridge
Stencill's Farm
Longwood Bridge
Calderfields Golf Course
Calder Fields Farm
Club House
Hay Head Bridge
Arboretum
WALSALL
49
34
1
2
3
4
5
6
PELSALL LA.
LICHFIELD ROAD
A461
B4154
DAW END LANE
BOSTY LANE
MELLISH ROAD
A454
ALDRIDGE ROAD
BARNS LANE
WINTERLEY LANE
STATION RD.

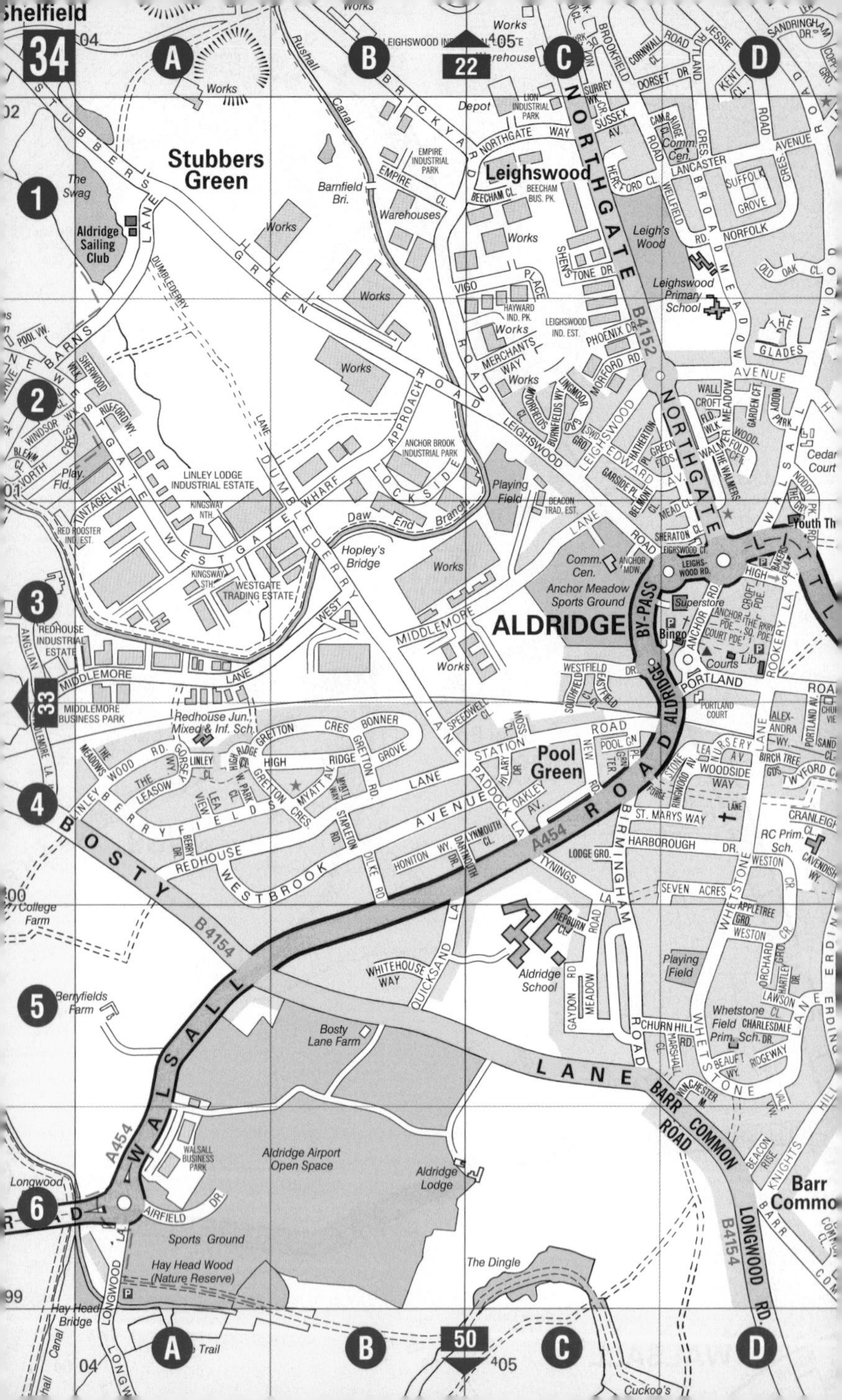
Shelfield
Stubbers Green
Leighswood
ALDRIDGE
Pool Green
Barr Common
Aldridge Sailing Club
The Swag
Works
Depot
Warehouse
Warehouses
Barnfield Bri.
Rushall Canal
LEIGHSWOOD INDUSTRIAL ESTATE
LION INDUSTRIAL PARK
EMPIRE INDUSTRIAL PARK
BEECHAM BUS. PK.
HAYWARD IND. PK.
LEIGHSWOOD IND. EST.
ANCHOR BROOK INDUSTRIAL PARK
LINLEY LODGE INDUSTRIAL ESTATE
RED ROOSTER IND. EST.
WESTGATE TRADING ESTATE
REDHOUSE INDUSTRIAL ESTATE
MIDDLEMORE BUSINESS PARK
BEACON TRAD. EST.
WALSALL BUSINESS PARK
Leigh's Wood
Leighswood Primary School
Playing Field
Play. Fld.
Hopley's Bridge
Daw End Branch
Comm. Cen.
Anchor Meadow Sports Ground
Superstore
Bingo
Courts
Lib.
Youth Th
Cedar Court
Redhouse Jun., Mixed & Inf. Sch.
RC Prim. Sch.
Whetstone Field Prim. Sch.
Aldridge School
College Farm
Berryfields Farm
Bosty Lane Farm
Aldridge Airport Open Space
Aldridge Lodge
Sports Ground
Hay Head Wood (Nature Reserve)
Hay Head Bridge
The Dingle
Longwood
Cuckoo's
Trail
STUBBERS GREEN
BRICKYARD ROAD
NORTHGATE
B4152
BY-PASS
ALDRIDGE ROAD
A454
WALSALL ROAD
BOSTY LANE
B4154
LONGWOOD RD.
LONGWOOD LA.
BARR COMMON ROAD
LEIGHSWOOD ROAD
MIDDLEMORE LANE
WESTGATE
DUMBLEDERRY LANE
APPROACH ROAD
WHARF
LOCKSIDE
STATION ROAD
HIGH ST
PORTLAND
ROOKERY LANE
BIRMINGHAM ROAD
WHETSTONE LANE
BERRYFIELDS
REDHOUSE AVENUE
WESTBROOK
HIGH RIDGE
GRETTON CRES
BONNER GROVE
LINLEY WOOD RD.
THE LEASOW
SPEEDWELL CL.
PADDOCK LA.
OAKLEY AV.
QUICKSAND LA.
WHITEHOUSE WAY
AIRFIELD DR.
VIGO PLACE
MERCHANTS WAY
PHOENIX DR.
MORFORD RD.
NORTHGATE WAY
SUSSEX AV.
LANCASTER
SUFFOLK GROVE
NORFOLK
BROADMEADOW
WALSALL WOOD
AVENUE
THE GLADES
CHURN HILL RD.
LODGE GRO.
HARBOROUGH DR.
ST. MARYS WAY
WOODSIDE WAY
NURSERY AV.
BEACON RISE
KNIGHTS
WESTON CR.
SEVEN ACRES
LAWSON CL.
CHARLESDALE DR.
RIDGEWAY
BEAUFORT WY.
WINCHESTER M.
MARSHALL CL.
HEPBURN CL.
GAYDON RD.
MEADOW
TYNINGS LA.
A B C D
1 2 3 4 5 6
04
405
02
01
00
99
22
33
50

Druid's Heath
E
F
23
07
G
H
08
Druids Heath Farm
CHESTER ROAD
A452
WOOD LANE
Nurseries
HOLLY LANE
BACK LANE
DRUIDS HEATH GOLF COURSE
Club House
Millgreen Farm
Mill Green Farm
MILL LANE
Sports Grd.
Mill Green
Nursery
FORGE LA
Nuttall's Farm
HOLE LANE
GOULD FIRM LANE
Cricket Grd.
Pav.
Cemy.
Sports Grd.
Cooper & Jordan C of E Prim. Sch.
Nursing Home
THE MALTINGS
Fairlawns
A454
ASTON RD.
ALDRIDGE RD.
36
Osier Bed
Brooklands Nursery
GREEN LA
POTHERLEY BROOK RD.
Walsall
WS9
BRANTON HILL LA.
BRANTON HILL LANE
St. Francis of Assisi RC Comp. Sch.
Branton Hill
Lowlands Wood
Bourne
LANE
LICHFIELD
WALSALL
COTTAGE MEWS
Corporation Wood
Shrubbery Farm
B74
Tower Covert
Waterworks Farm
Nursery
RAGLAN CL.
WINDERMERE DR.
LINDROSA ROAD
CONISTON ROAD
HINGLEY CL.
BRANOR CL.
LEACLIFFE WAY
Hingleys Covert
Hardwick Wood
LEAFY GLADE
BOURNE VALE
BOURNE VALE AVE
Bourne Vale
Playing Field
Pav.
VALE
51
LESTER GRO.
CHESTER WOOD
DERWENT CL.
KESWICK GRO.
HARDWICK ROAD
LITTLE HARDWICK ROAD
BARLEY
NURSERY VW.
1
2
3
4
5
6
02
01
300
299

Biddle's Field Wood
French Croft Farm
Forge Farm
Forge Wood
Sewage Works
Mill Green Farm
Walsall
WS9
Mill Green
The Belt
New Wood
Aston Wood
ASTON W
Nursery
FORGE LANE
Mill Farm
Osier Bed
Home Farm
Little Aston Primary School
Claypit Rough
The Rookery
Little Aston
Brooklands Nursery
ALDRIDGE
A454
ROAD
WALSALL
LITTLE ASTON
A4026
THE GROVE
POPLAR
ROSEMARY NOOK
LAKESIDE
Little Aston Hall
THE SPINNEY
ROMAN GRANGE
WOODSIDE DR.
Lowlands Wood
LITTLE ASTON BUPA HOSPITAL
Hornton Manor
BIRCH
ROSE BANK
LOXTON CL.
SQUIRREL WLK.
KEEPERS RD.
BEECH
GATE
HORNTON CL.
LITTLE ASTON GOLF COURSE
LONGACRES
LONGFIELD DR.
PARK DRIVE
Club House
B74
SELWYN WLK.
CHARTWELL
Barns Farm
ROMAN PK.
STONEHOUSE DR.
ENDWOOD DRIVE
JERVIS PK.
LICHFIELD
B4138
HILL
BIRMINGHAM
WOODSTOCK DRI.
TALL TREES CL.
Roundabout Wood
CLAVERDON DRI.
ROMAN LANE
BARNS CROFT
ALDERHITHE GRO.
ROSEMARY DR.
THE HEADLANDS
WAYSIDE DR.
JERVIS CRESCENT
VIEW
Hingleys Covert
VERCOURT
FALLOW FLD.
ROYSTON CHASE
NEWICK AVENUE
Ten. Cts.
LICHFIELD
WALSALL
ROSEMARY
HIGHBURY RD.
ST. MARGARET'S
PINEWAYS
STREETLY
Hardwick Wood
LEAFY GLADE
AVENUE
TALBOT
LITTLE ASTON PARK ROAD
PARK
B4151
BENNETT
CHESTNUT CL.
KIMBERLEY CL.
Hardwick Lodge
GRASMERE AV.
STREETLY
HARDWICK ROAD
52
35
08
09

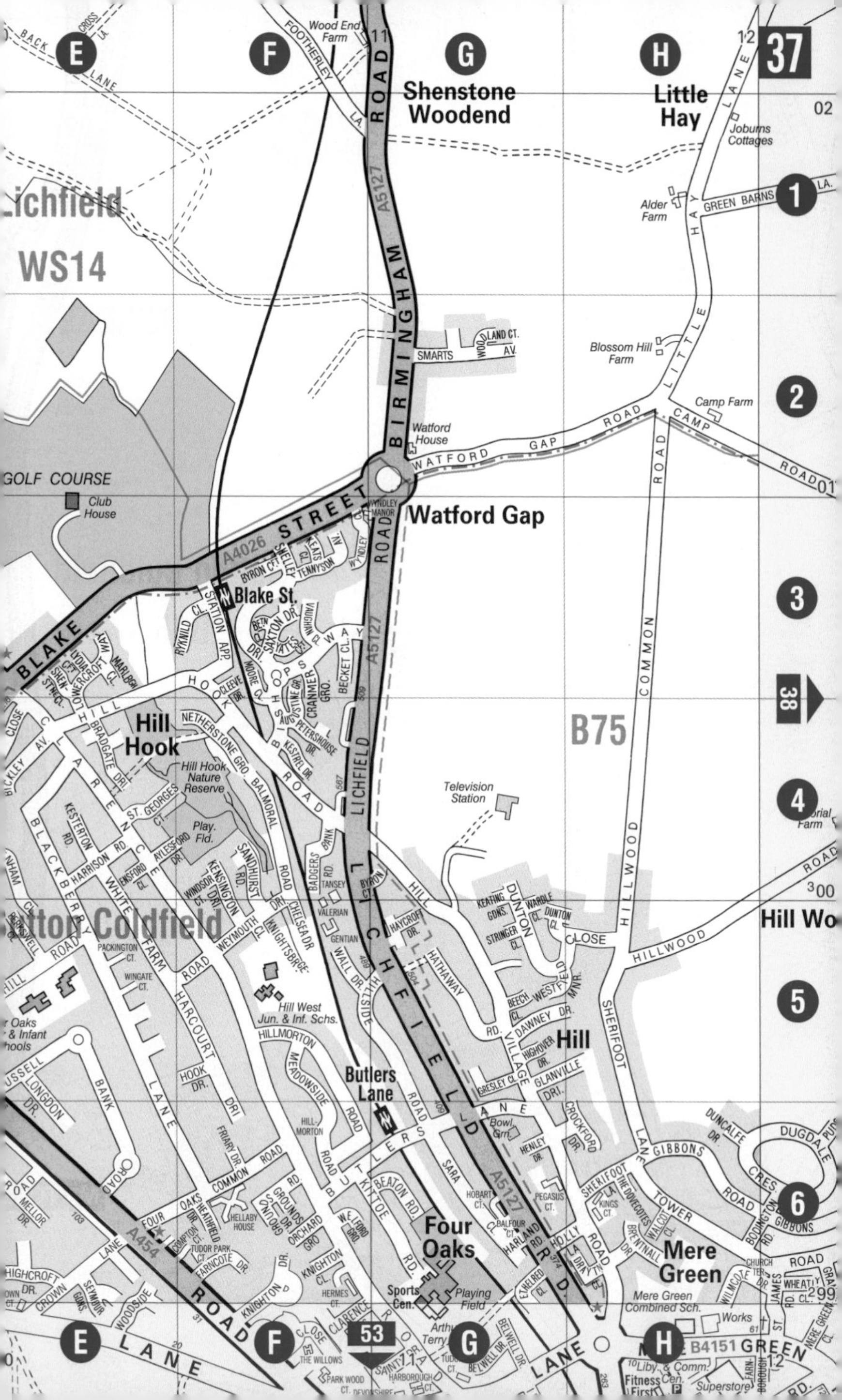
E
F
G
H
Shenstone Woodend
Little Hay
Lichfield
WS14
Wood End Farm
Footherley La.
Birmingham Road
A5127
Back Lane
Cross La.
Joburns Cottages
Alder Farm
Green Barns La.
Hay Lane
Little Hay Lane
Blossom Hill Farm
Camp Farm
Camp Road
Smarts Av.
Woodland Ct.
Watford House
Watford Gap Road
Road
Common Road
Golf Course
Club House
Watford Gap
Windley Manor
Blake Street
A4026
Blake St.
Byron Ct.
Shelley
Keats Cl.
Tennyson Av.
Windley
Station App.
Ryknild Cl.
Saxton Dr.
Vaughan
Yates
Bishops Way
Becket Cl.
Cranmer Gro.
Augustine Gro.
Petershouse Dr.
Kestrel Dr.
Lichfield Road
Hill Hook Road
Hill Hook
Hill Hook Nature Reserve
Netherstone Gro.
Balmoral
Cleeve Dr.
Moore Cl.
Lowercroft Way
Marlborough
Lydia Ct.
Clarence Road
Bickley Av.
Close
B75
Television Station
Memorial Farm
Hill Wood
Hillwood Road
Hillwood Common Road
Hillwood Close
Kesterton Rd.
St. Georges Ct.
Harrison Rd.
Aylesford Dr.
Play. Fld.
Ensford Cl.
Blackberry Lane
White Farm Road
Sandhurst
Kensington Dr.
Windsor Ct.
Badgers Bank Rd.
Tansey
Valerian
Gentian
Byron Ct.
Haycroft Dr.
Hathaway
Hill Village Rd.
Keating Gdns.
Stringer Cl.
Dunton Cl.
Wardle Cl.
Westfield Mnr.
Beech Cl.
Dawney Dr.
Highover Dr.
Hill
Gresley Cl.
Glanville Dri.
Sutton Coldfield
Packington Ct.
Wingate Ct.
Weymouth Cl.
Knightsbridge
Chelsea Dr.
Hill West Jun. & Inf. Schs.
Hillmorton
Meadowside Road
Wall Dr.
Hillside
Harcourt Road
Hook Dr.
Friary Dr.
Common Road
Four Oaks Common Road
Heathfield
Compton Dr.
Hellaby House
Tudor Park Ct.
Farncote Dr.
Grounds Rd.
Grounds Dr.
Orchard Gro.
Butlers Lane
Kittoe Road
Beaton Rd.
Wilford Gro.
Knighton Cl.
Knighton Dr.
Hermes Ct.
Clarence Road
Sara
Bowl. Grn.
Henley Dr.
Crockford Dr.
Sherifoot Lane
Sherifoot La.
Kings Ct.
The Dovecotes
Hobart Ct.
Balfour Ct.
Harland Rd.
Pegasus Ct.
Holly Road
La Drayton
Brentnall Dr.
Walcot Cl.
Tower Road
Gibbons Road
Duncalfe Dr.
Dugdale Cres.
Bodington Rd.
Mere Green
Church Ter.
Wilmcote Dr.
James Rd.
Wheatley Cl.
Grange
Mere Green Combined Sch.
Works
Four Oaks
Sports Cen.
Playing Field
Arthur Terry
Ethelred Cl.
Belwell Dr.
Belwell Lane
Tudor Ct.
Harborough Ct.
Saintbury
Four Oaks Road
A454
Lane
Crown Lane
Seymour Gdns.
Woodside
Highcroft Dr.
Mellor Dr.
Longdon Dr.
Russell Bank Road
Hill Road
Four Oaks & Infant Schools
The Willows
Park Wood Ct.
Devonshire
Mere Green Road
B4151
Liby. & Comm. Cen.
Fitness First
Superstore
Farnborough
Mere Green
1
2
3
4
5
6
38
53

38
A
B
C
D
1
2
3
4
5
6
37
54
Lichfield
WS14
Sutton Coldfield
B75
Hill Wood
Roughley
M6 TOLL
M6 TOLL MOTORWAY
LONDON
B4151
Manley Wood
Old Windmill
Works
Green Wood
Black Fir Wood
Joburns Cottages
Hovel Covert
Weeford Park Farm
Pine Tree Cottage
Springhill Farm
Manorial Farm Cottage
Springhill Plantation
Manorial Wood
Manorial Farm
Hilltop Farm
Dale Farm
Woodstile Cottage
Little Sutton Prim. Sch.
Marlpit Hall Fm.
The Keep
Fish Pond
Superstore
GREEN BARNS LANE
HAY LANE
LITTLE HAY LANE
MILL HOUSE LA.
CAMP ROAD
LICHFIELD
BIRMINGHAM
LICHFIELD ROAD
HILLWOOD ROAD
WORCESTER LANE
DUTTON'S LANE
WEEFORD ROAD
TURF PITTS LANE
SLADE ROAD
MAYALL DRIVE
LOXLEY
ST. JOHN CL.
HOMESTEAD DR.
DUNCALFE DR.
DUGDALE CRESCENT
PUDSEY DR.
RANDLE DR.
GRANGE ROAD
CARTWRIGHT RD.
CLARENDON RD.
EDWARDS RD.
HURST RD.
WILLMOTT RD.
MARLPIT LANE
GIBBONS RD.
BODINGTON RD.
TOWER ROAD
FIELDS WAY
SCARECROW
CANWELL GA.
ROUGHLEY DR.
LITTLE SUTTON
FOX HILL ROAD
SUTTON

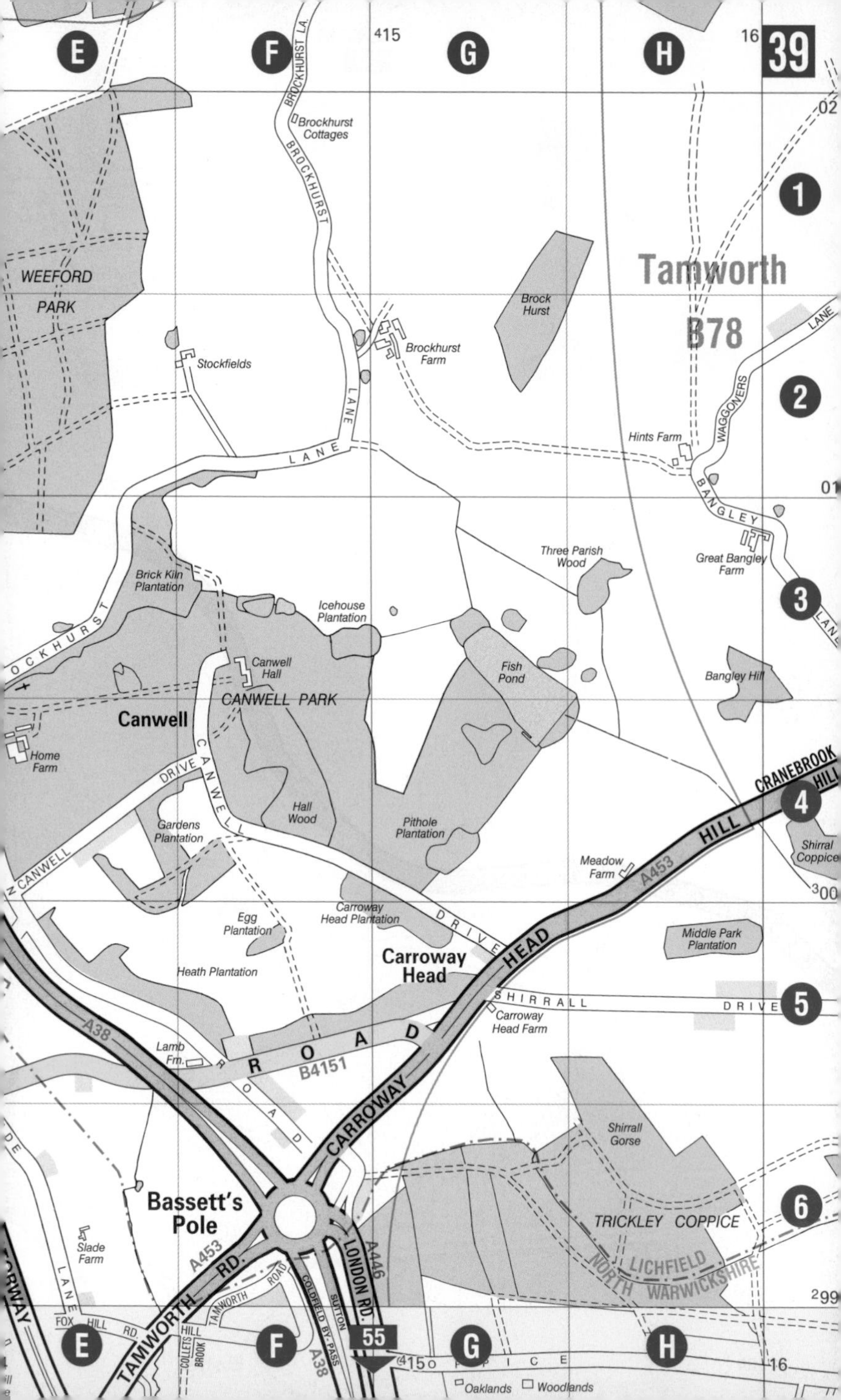
E
F
G
H
415
16
02
01
300
299
1
2
3
4
5
6
Tamworth
B78
BROCKHURST LA.
Brockhurst Cottages
BROCKHURST
LANE
Brockhurst Farm
Brock Hurst
WEEFORD PARK
Stockfields
LANE
WAGGONERS
LANE
Hints Farm
BANGLEY
Great Bangley Farm
LANE
Three Parish Wood
Brick Kiln Plantation
Icehouse Plantation
BROCKHURST
Canwell Hall
CANWELL PARK
Fish Pond
Bangley Hill
Canwell
Home Farm
CANWELL
DRIVE
CRANEBROOK HILL
Hall Wood
Pithole Plantation
Gardens Plantation
CANWELL
Shirral Coppice
Meadow Farm
A453
HILL
Carroway Head Plantation
DRIVE
Egg Plantation
Middle Park Plantation
Carroway Head
HEAD
Heath Plantation
SHIRRALL
DRIVE
Carroway Head Farm
A38
Lamb Fm.
ROAD
B4151
ROAD
CARROWAY
Shirrall Gorse
Bassett's Pole
TRICKLEY COPPICE
Slade Farm
A453
LONDON RD.
A446
LICHFIELD
NORTH WARWICKSHIRE
TAMWORTH RD.
ROAD
TAMWORTH
COLDFIELD BY-PASS
SUTTON
LANE
FOX HILL RD.
HILL
COLLETS BROOK
A38
TAMWORTH
55
COPPICE
Oaklands
Woodlands

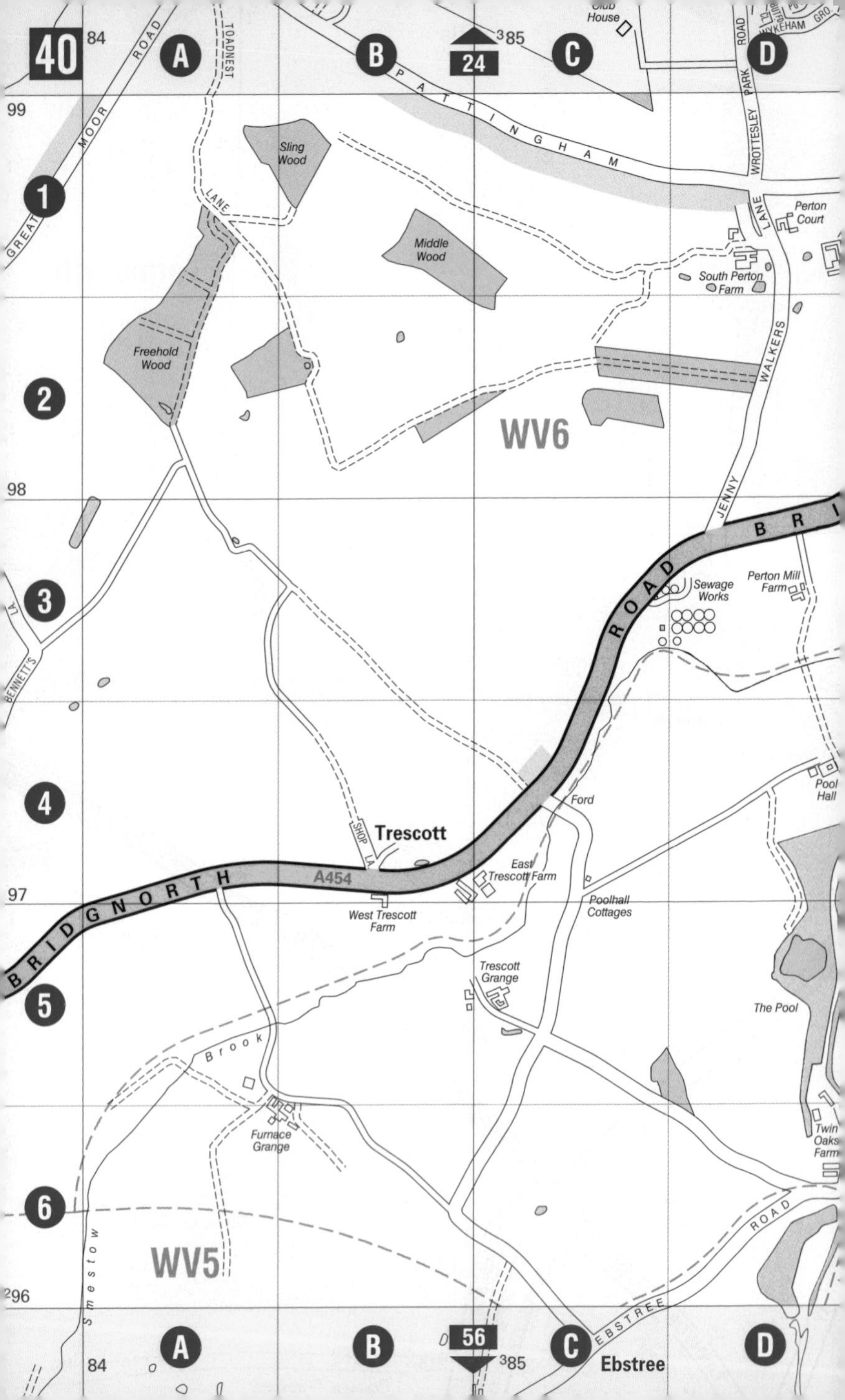

40 84

99

A

GREAT MOOR ROAD

TOADNEST LANE

Sling Wood

Middle Wood

1

B

PATTINGHAM

▲ 385
24

C

D

Club House

WROTTESLEY PARK ROAD

PICKHAM GRO

Perton Court

South Perton Farm

2

Freehold Wood

WV6

WALKERS LANE

JENNY

98

3

BENNETT'S PL

Sewage Works

Perton Mill Farm

ROAD

BRI

4

Ford

Pool Hall

Shop LA

Trescott

East Trescott Farm

97

5

BRIDGNORTH

A454

West Trescott Farm

Trescott Grange

Poolhall Cottages

The Pool

6

Brook

Furnace Grange

Smestow

WV5

Twin Oaks Farm

ROAD

296

84

A

B

▼ 56
385

EBSTREE

C

Ebstree

D

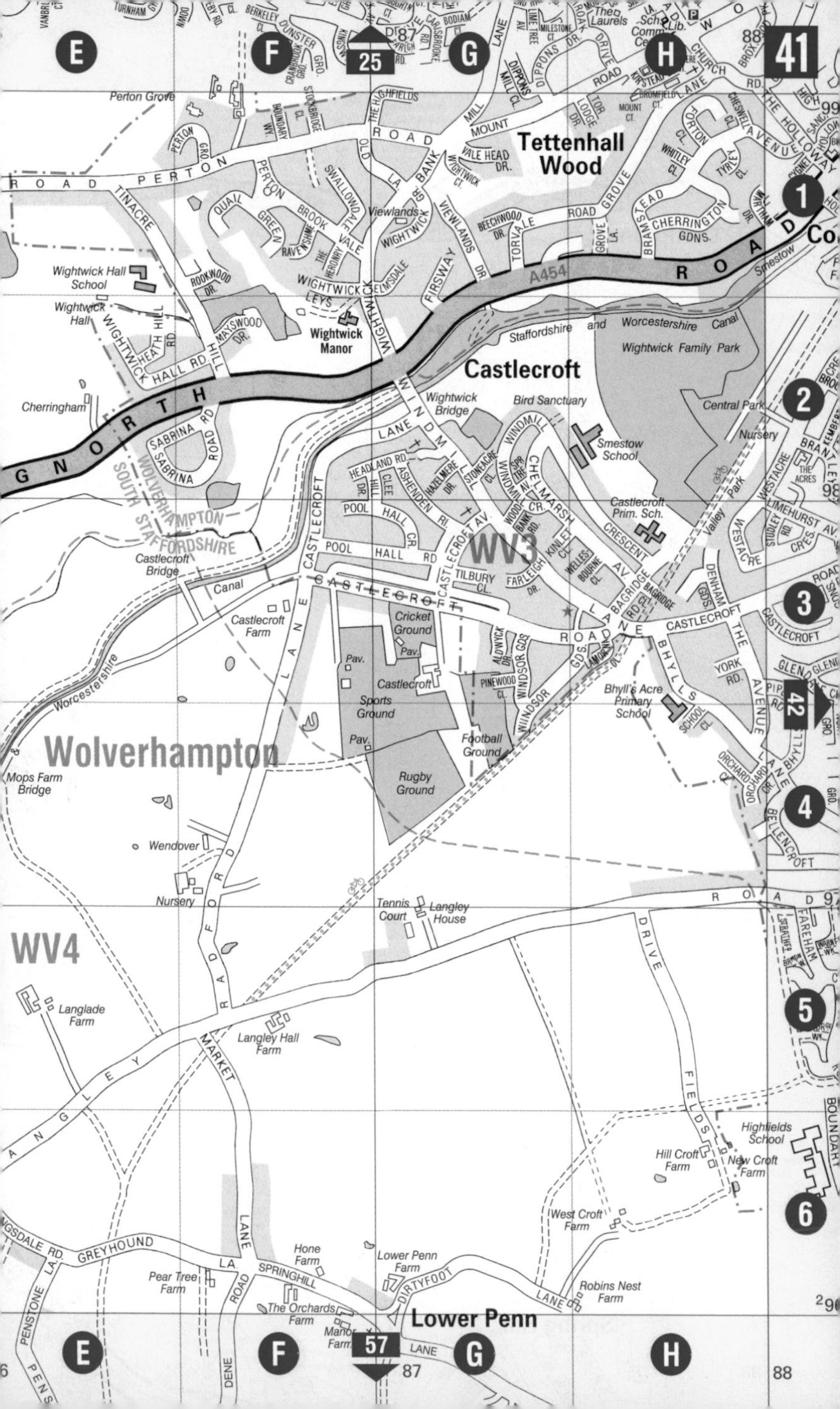

25
57
42
Tettenhall Wood
Castlecroft
WV3
WV4
Wolverhampton
Lower Penn
Wightwick Manor
Wightwick Hall School
Wightwick Hall
Cherringham
Staffordshire and Worcestershire Canal
Wightwick Family Park
Bird Sanctuary
Central Park
Smestow School
Castlecroft Prim. Sch.
Wightwick Bridge
Castlecroft Bridge
Castlecroft Farm
Cricket Ground
Castlecroft Sports Ground
Rugby Ground
Football Ground
Bhyll's Acre Primary School
Mops Farm Bridge
Wendover
Nursery
Tennis Court
Langley House
Langlade Farm
Langley Hall Farm
Highfields School
Hill Croft Farm
New Croft Farm
West Croft Farm
Robins Nest Farm
Hone Farm
Lower Penn Farm
Pear Tree Farm
The Orchards Farm
Manor Farm
Perton Grove
Viewlands
A454
NORTH ROAD
PERTON ROAD
CASTLECROFT ROAD
CASTLECROFT LANE
WINDMILL LANE
RADFORD ROAD
LANGLEY ROAD
MARKET LANE
FIELDS DRIVE
GREYHOUND LA.
SPRINGHILL
DIRTYFOOT LANE
WOLVERHAMPTON
SOUTH STAFFORDSHIRE
86
87
88

Compton
WV6
WV3
WV4
Merridale
Bradmore
BANTOCK PARK
Merry Hill
Penn
Spring Hill
University of Wolverhampton (Compton Park Campus)
City of Wolverhampton College (The Cedars, Horticultural Unit)
Wolverhampton Grammar School
Bantock Ho. Mus.
Uplands Jun. Sch.
Westacre Inf. Sch.
St. Michael's RC Prim. Sch.
Warstone Primary School
Windsor Avenue Playing Fields
Bradmore Rec. Grd.
Springdale Jun.& Inf. Schs.
Highfields School
Hospice
COMPTON ROAD
FINCHFIELD HILL
FINCHFIELD ROAD WEST
BROAD LANE
BIRCHES BARN
CASTLECROFT ROAD
LANGLEY ROAD
WARSTONES DRIVE
26
41
58

43
27
170
59
44
E
F
G
H
1
2
3
4
5
6
Wolverhampton Wanderers FC (Molineux)
WEST PARK
Bandstand
WV1
WV2
WEST PARK REHABILITATION HOSP.
Central Baths
University
Arena Thtre.
Civic Cen.
Wolverhampton
WOLVERHAMPTON
Wolverhampton
CHAPEL ASH
RING ROAD ST. PETERS
RING ROAD ST. ANDREWS
RING ROAD ST. MARKS
RING RD. ST. JOHNS
RING ROAD ST. GEORGES
RING ROAD ST. DAVIDS
RING ROAD ST. PATRICKS
St. Georges
Bus Sta.
Mander Cen.
Wulfrun Cen.
The Orchard Cen.
Merridale Prim. Sch.
Mosque
Sikh Temple
Hindu Temple
Bowl. Grn.
Graiseley Rec. Cen.
Blakenhall Rec. Grd.
Superstore
Music Sch.
AMF Bowling
Royal Wolverhampton Jun. Sch.
Blakenhall
IMEX BUSINESS PARK
St. Luke's C of E Prim. Sch.
The Royal Wolverhampton School
St. Mary & St. Johns RC Prim. Sch.
Learning Disability Services
Phoenix Nursery School
Phoenix Park
Playground
PENN ROAD
DUDLEY ROAD
BIRMINGHAM RD.
THOMPSON RD.
WOLVERHAMPTON RD. EAST
GOLDTHORN HILL
GOLDTHORN HILL ROAD
A4039
A449
A459
A4150
A4123
A4124
A41
A454
A4161
Penn Fields
Woodfield Social and Sports Club
Goldthorn Hill
Res. (cov.)
Goldthorn Park
Goldthorn Park Prim. Sch.
Colton Hills Community
Playing Fields
The Royal

WOLVERHAMPTON
Wolverhampton
WV10
WV1
WV2
WV4
WEDNESFIELD RD.
Royal Mail Sorting Office
Wyrley & Essington Canal
MANDERS INDUSTRIAL ESTATE
NEW CROSS IND. EST.
BRICKHEATH RD.
HELMING DRIVE
DEANS ROAD
LEWIS
RUDGE AV.
BURCOT
ST. GILES
STANTON RD.
OSIER ST.
HEATH RD.
DEANSFIELD RD.
BARNFIELD RD.
COVENTRY ST.
BROOKLANDS
ESSINGTON
HAWKLEY
SYDENHAM
PARADE
ABINGDON
HORSELEY FLDS.
LWR. HORSELEY FLD.
A454
WILLENHALL
MIDDLE CROSS
BILSTON ST. ISLAND
RING ROAD ST. DAVIDS
WALSALL STREET
LWR. WALSALL ST.
MOORE ST.
ST. MATTHEWS ST.
CHILLINGTON WORKS INDUSTRIAL ESTATE
CHANCEL IND. EST.
BI-TEC IND. PK.
PARKSIDE INDUSTRIAL ESTATE
EAST PARK TRADING ESTATE
Holy Rosary RC Prim. Sch.
Plascom
PLASCOM RD.
EAST PARK WAY
PARKLANDS
MAYFIELD
SELBOURNE CR.
HURSTBOURNE
WOODSTOCK RD.
HOLLINGTON RD.
THORNTON RD.
East Park Jun. & Inf. Schs.
EAST PARK
Tennis Cts.
Clock Tower
BILSTON ROAD
The Royal
CLEVELAND RD.
SUTHERLAND PL.
GORDON ST.
STEELHOUSE LA.
Warehouse
CHILLINGTON ST.
LANDPORT RD.
A41
Monmore Green
Works
ALL SAINTS' ROAD
All Saints' Prim. Sch.
CABLE STREET
COOPER STREET
SUTHERLAND AV.
Monmore Green Stadium
AVENUE
Wholesale Market
NEW ENTERPRISE CENTRE
MONMORE RD.
GULLWICK
Stow Heath
Training Centre
LILAC RD.
GIFFARD RD.
City of Wolverhampton Coll. (Wellington Rd. Campus)
WELLINGTON ROAD
CALEDONIA RD.
Grove Prim. Sch.
Youth Cen.
CENTRAL TRADING ESTATE
MONMORE BUSINESS PARK
MAJOR STREET
BRADLEY RD.
POND LA.
Recreation Ground
ETTINGSHALL RD.
D'URBERVILLE RD. IND. EST.
MONMORE PARK IND. EST.
HOLCROFT ST.
PEMBROKE
Priestfield
BRUNEL WY.
GEORGE STREET
JOHN STREET
FROST ST.
SIDWICK CR.
VICTOR CL.
HALL PARK ST.
Priestfield
Bilston C of E Prim. Sch.
THOMPSON AV.
A4123
KENT ROAD
COTSWOLD
ROUGH HILLS RD.
WEBNOR INDUSTRIAL ESTATE
A4126
Recreation Ground
Depot
Gas Works
CHESTON ROAD IND. EST.
PARKFIELD ROAD
A4039
Playground
Football Ground
WATERSIDE IND. EST.
MILLFIELDS
A4039
Windsor Nursery School
TAYLOR RD.
DIMMOCK
Parkfield
St. Teresa's RC Prim. Sch.
Parkfield High Sch.
BIRMINGHAM NEW ROAD
WOLVERHAMPTON RD. EAST
A459
MANOR RD.
SPRING RD.
Ettingshall
Foundry
HILTON TRADING ESTATE
SPRING ROAD INDUSTRIAL ESTATE
Depot
Basin
TARMAC RD.
Lanesfield
Spring Vale
LAWNSWOOD AV.
KENILWORTH
28
60
43
170
A B C D
1 2 3 4 5 6
92 93 96 97 98 99

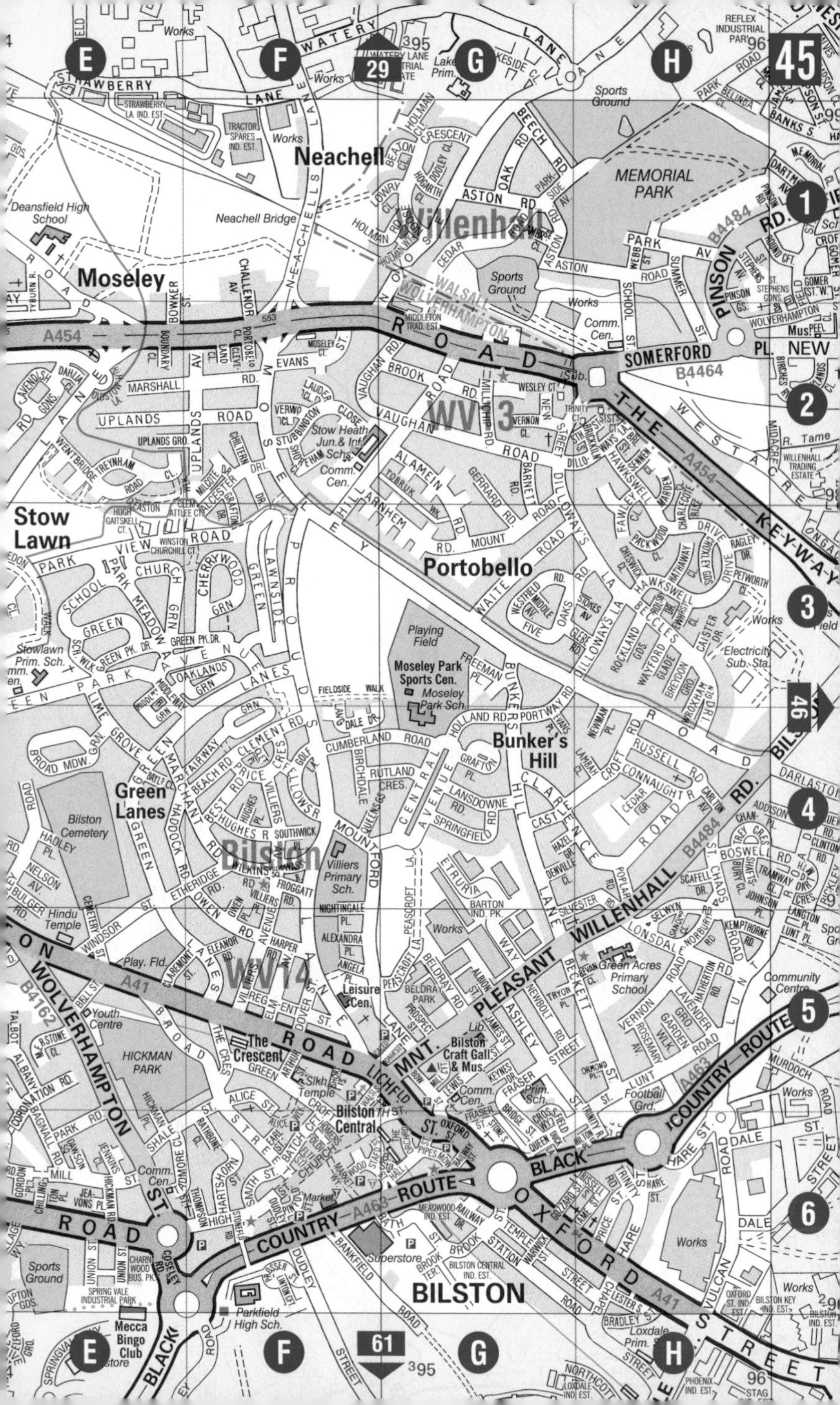
E
F
G
H
29
61
46
1
2
3
4
5
6
395
96
Neachell
Moseley
Willenhall
Stow Lawn
Portobello
Bunker's Hill
Green Lanes
Bilston
BILSTON
WV13
WV14
MEMORIAL PARK
Sports Ground
Deansfield High School
Neachell Bridge
Strawberry La. Ind. Est.
Tractor Spares Ind. Est.
Watery Lane Industrial Estate
Reflex Industrial Park
Middleton Trad. Est.
Stow Heath Jun. & Inf. Schs.
Comm. Cen.
Stowlawn Prim. Sch.
Playing Field
Moseley Park Sports Cen.
Moseley Park Sch.
Electricity Sub. Sta.
Willenhall Trading Estate
Bilston Cemetery
Hindu Temple
Villiers Primary Sch.
Barton Ind. Pk.
Green Acres Primary School
Community Centre
Leisure Cen.
Hickman Park
Youth Centre
The Crescent
Sikh Temple
Bilston Central
Bilston Craft Gall. & Mus.
Football Grd.
Market
Superstore
Meadwood Ind. Est.
Bilston Central Ind. Est.
Spring Vale Industrial Park
Mecca Bingo Club
Parkfield High Sch.
Loxdale Prim. Sch.
Oxford St. Ind. Est.
Bilston Key Ind. Est.
Phoenix Ind. Est.
Loxdale Ind. Est.
Play. Fld.
Works
A454
A41
A463
B4484
B4464
B4162
WOLVERHAMPTON ROAD
THE KEYWAY
WILLENHALL ROAD
PLEASANT MNT.
LICHFIELD ST.
OXFORD ST.
BLACK COUNTRY ROUTE
WALSALL WOLVERHAMPTON
SOMERFORD PL.
PINSON RD.
NEACHELLS LANE
WATERY LANE
STRAWBERRY LANE
MOSELEY ROAD
PROUDS LANE
CENTRAL AVENUE
MOUNTFORD LA.
GREEN LANES
BROAD LANES
UPLANDS ROAD
PARK VIEW ROAD
CHURCH GRN
GREEN PARK AVENUE
HOLLAND RD
CUMBERLAND ROAD
DILLOWAY'S LA
WESTACRE CRES
BECKETT ST.
LUNT ROAD
HARE ST.
DALE ST.
VULCAN ROAD
OXFORD STREET
BRADLEY ST.
NORTHCOTT

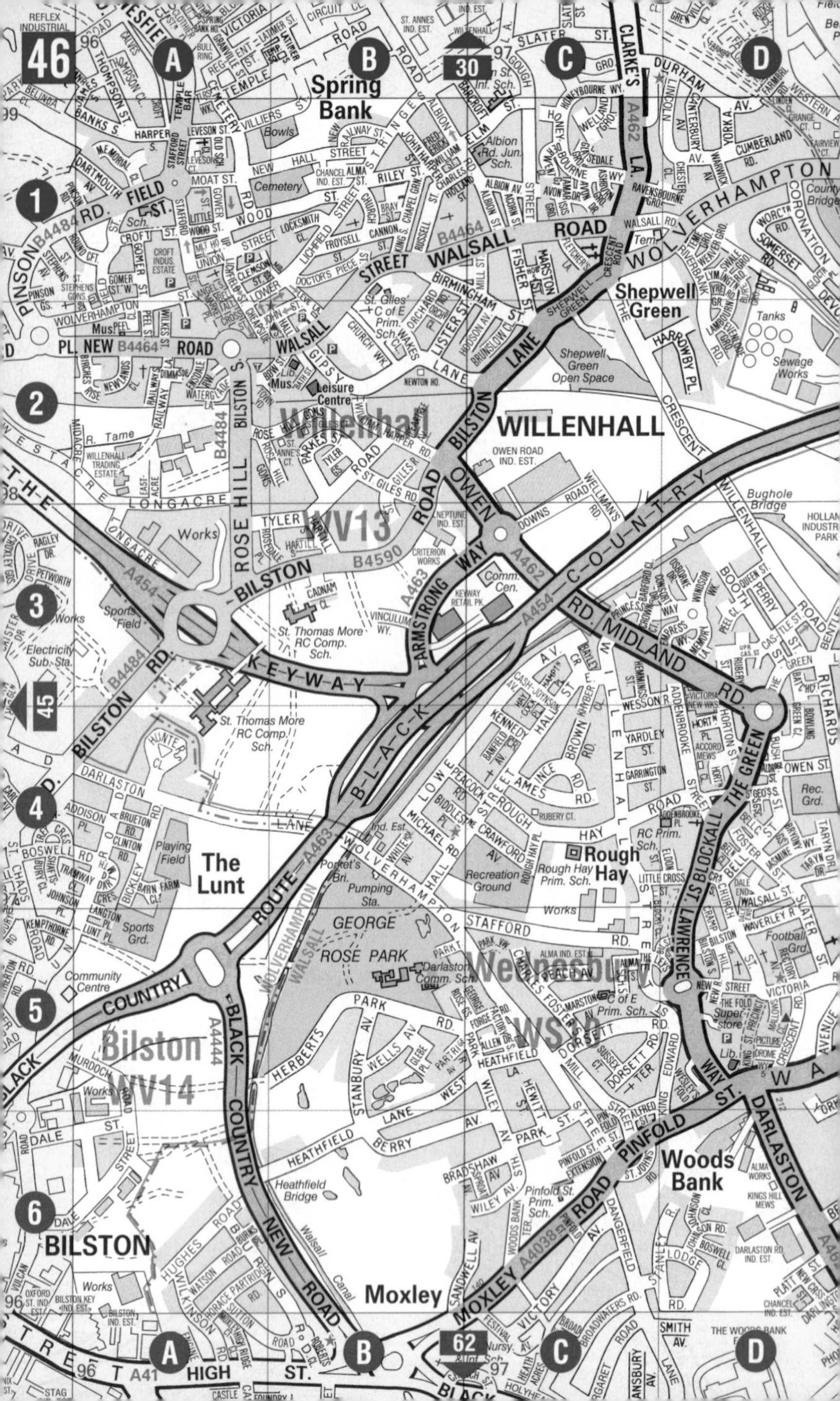

46
A
B
C
D
30
Spring Bank
1
2
3
4
5
6
45
62
WILLENHALL
Willenhall
WV13
Shepwell Green
Shepwell Green Open Space
Sewage Works
Tanks
Cemetery
Bowls
Leisure Centre
OWEN ROAD IND. EST.
Bughole Bridge
Works
Sports Field
Electricity Sub. Sta.
St. Thomas More RC Comp. Sch.
KEYWAY RETAIL PK
Comm. Cen.
The Lunt
Playing Field
Sports Grd.
Community Centre
Rough Hay
Rough Hay Prim. Sch.
Recreation Ground
Pumping Sta.
GEORGE ROSE PARK
Darlaston Comm. Sch.
Wednesbury WS10
Bilston WV14
BILSTON
Moxley
Woods Bank
Heathfield Bridge
Walsall Canal
Rec. Grd.
Football Grd.
WALSALL ROAD
WOLVERHAMPTON
BLACK COUNTRY ROUTE
KEYWAY
BILSTON ROAD
ROSE HILL
BILSTON LANE
ARMSTRONG WAY
MIDLAND RD.
WILLENHALL
ST. LAWRENCE WAY
THE GREEN
BLACK COUNTRY NEW ROAD
MOXLEY ROAD
PINFOLD ST.
DARLASTON
HIGH ST.
CLARKE'S LA.
A462
A454
A463
A4444
A4038
A41
B4464
B4484
B4590

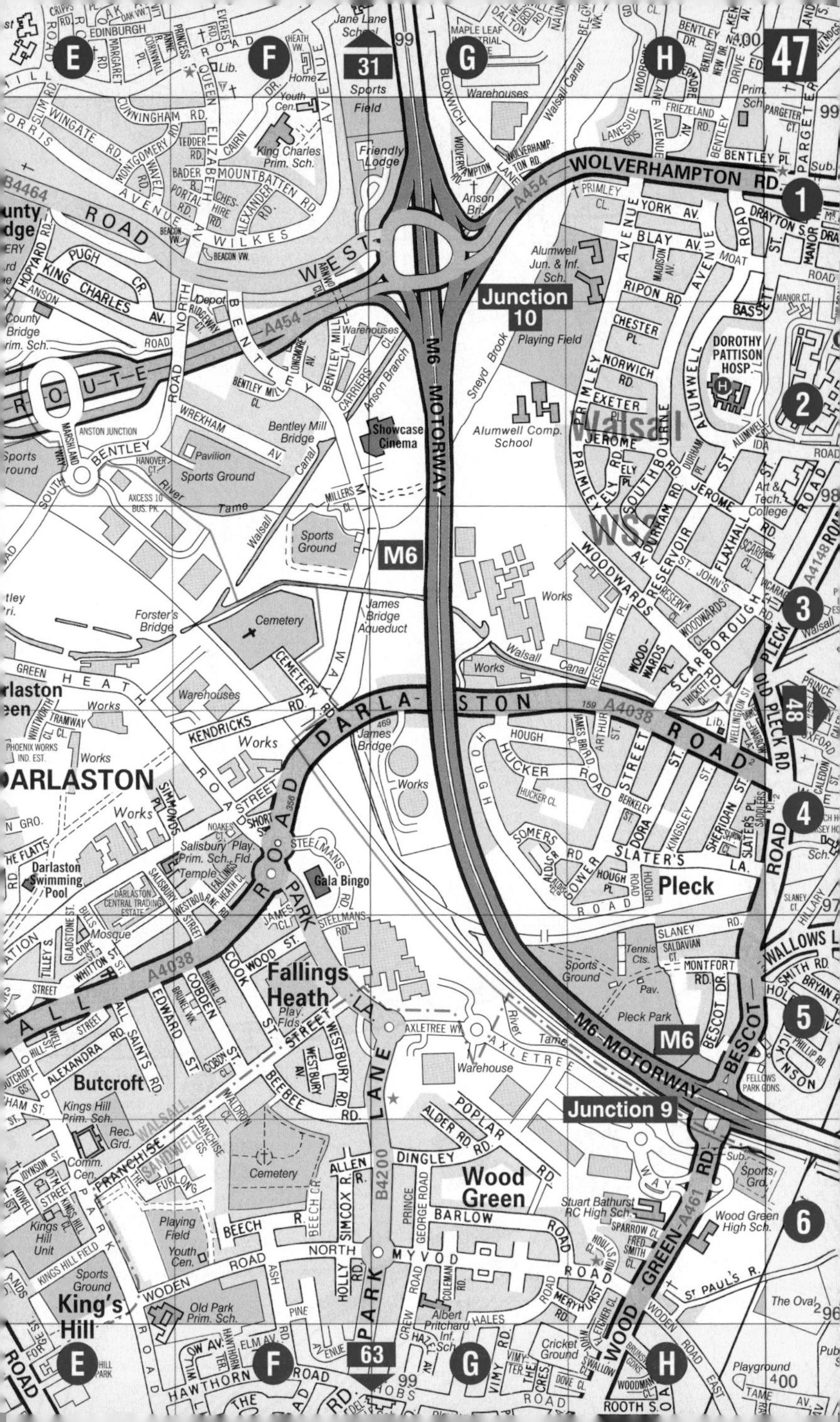
47
E
F
G
H
31
63
48
1
2
3
4
5
6
Walsall
DARLASTON
Pleck
Fallings Heath
Butcroft
Wood Green
King's Hill
Junction 10
Junction 9
M6 MOTORWAY
M6
WOLVERHAMPTON RD.
DARLASTON ROAD
WEST ROAD
BLACK COUNTRY ROUTE
PARK LANE
B4200
A454
A4038
A461
A4148
B4464
Alumwell Comp. School
Alumwell Jun. & Inf. Sch.
DOROTHY PATTISON HOSP.
King Charles Prim. Sch.
Showcase Cinema
Gala Bingo
Cemetery
Sports Ground
Playing Field
Walsall Canal
River Tame
Pleck Park
James Bridge Aqueduct
Bentley Mill Bridge
Forster's Bridge
Darlaston Swimming Pool
Kings Hill Prim. Sch.
Old Park Prim. Sch.
Stuart Bathurst RC High Sch.
Wood Green High Sch.
Albert Pritchard Inf. Sch.
Cricket Ground
The Oval
Art & Tech. College
Friendly Lodge
Warehouses
Works

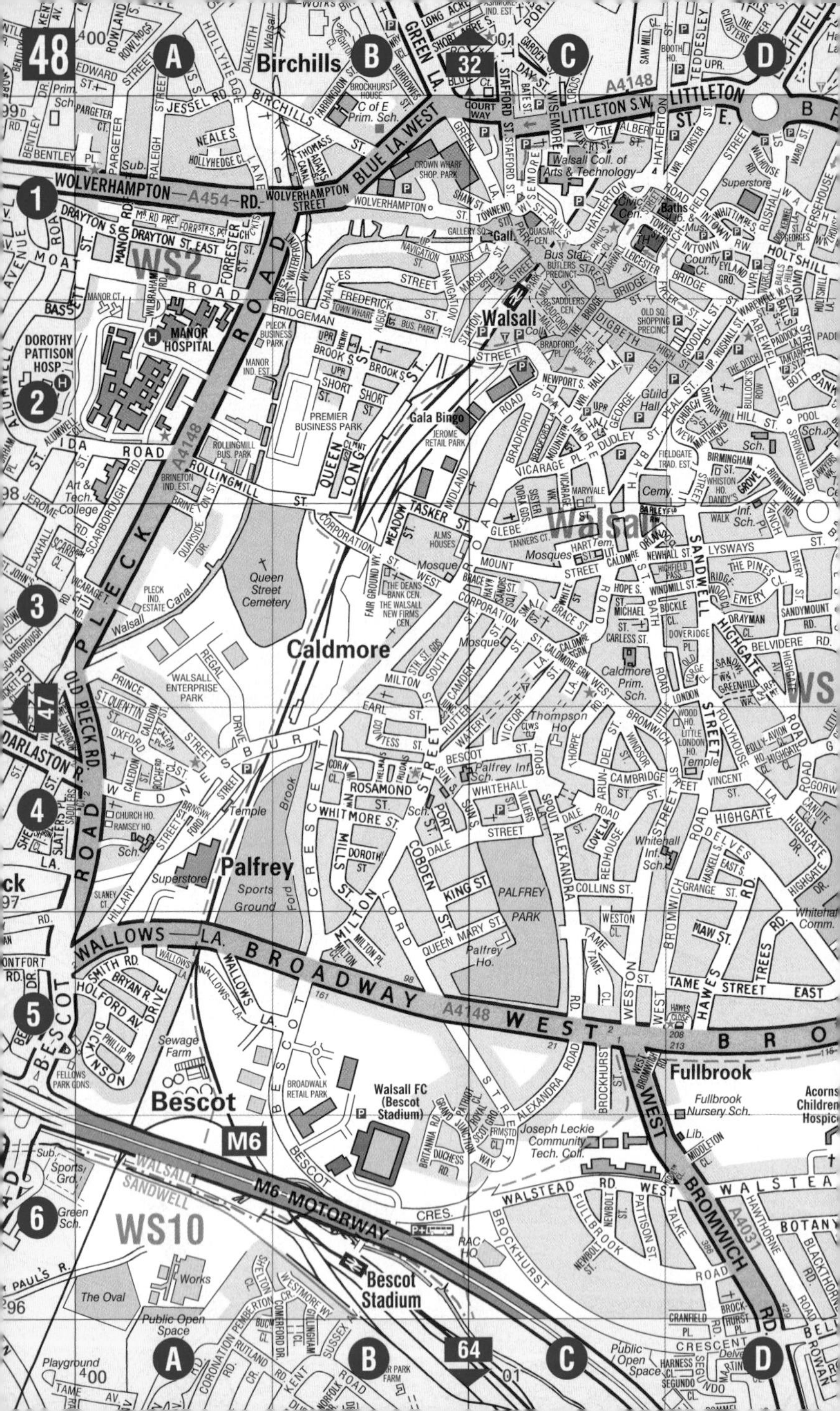

Birchills
Walsall
Caldmore
Palfrey
Bescot
Fullbrook
WS2
WS10
Manor Hospital
Dorothy Pattison Hosp.
Walsall Coll. of Arts & Technology
Crown Wharf Shop. Park
Queen Street Cemetery
Walsall Enterprise Park
Premier Business Park
Jerome Retail Park
Gala Bingo
Palfrey Park
Sports Ground
Broadwalk Retail Park
Walsall FC (Bescot Stadium)
Bescot Stadium
Joseph Leckie Community Tech. Coll.
Fullbrook Nursery Sch.
Sewage Farm
The Oval
M6 Motorway
A4148
A454
A4031
32
47
64

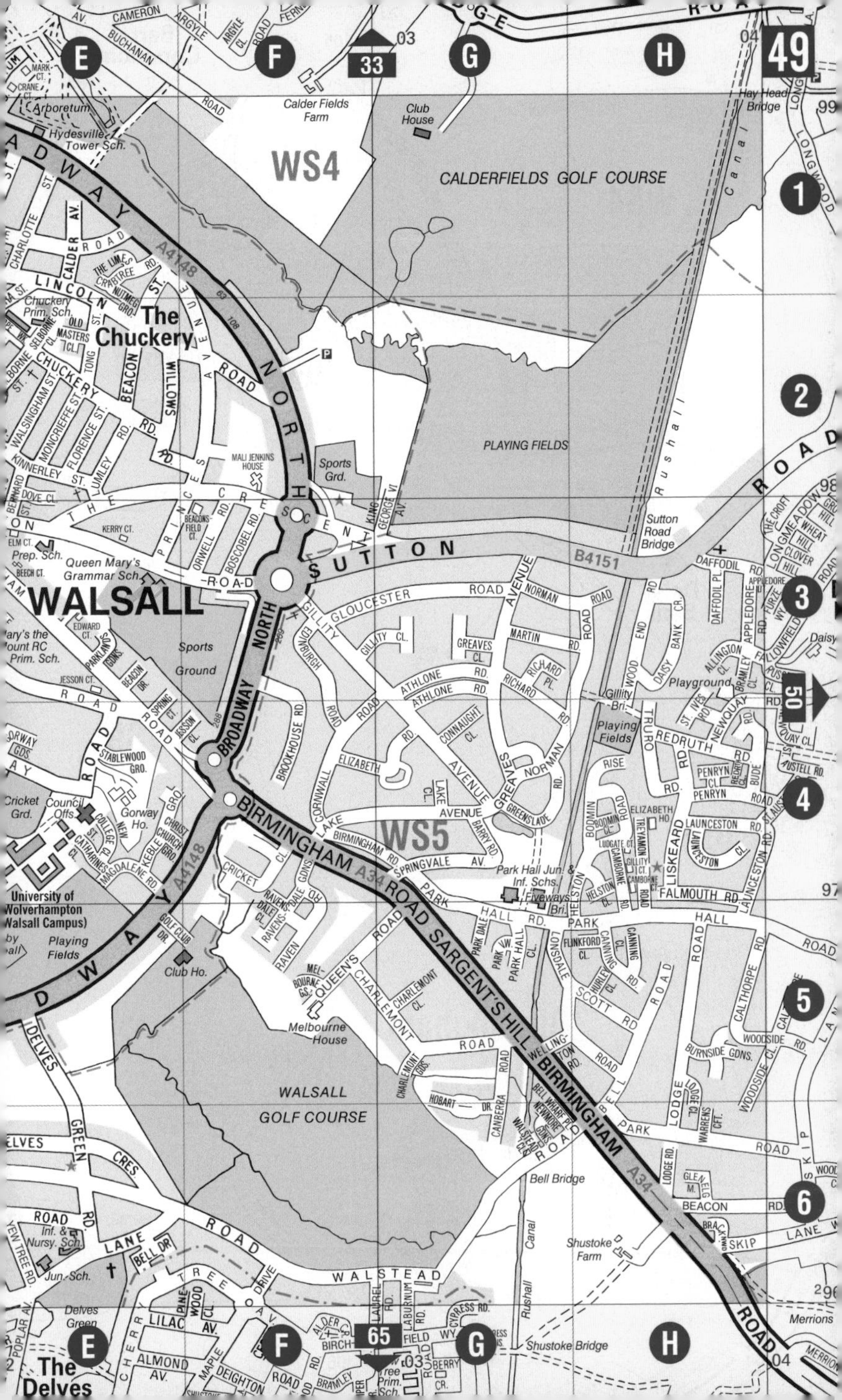

33
65
50
WS4
WS5
WALSALL
The Chuckery
The Delves
CALDERFIELDS GOLF COURSE
WALSALL GOLF COURSE
PLAYING FIELDS
Calder Fields Farm
Club House
Arboretum
Hydesville Tower Sch.
Chuckery Prim. Sch.
Queen Mary's Grammar Sch.
Prep. Sch.
Sports Ground
Sports Grd.
Council Offs.
Cricket Grd.
University of Wolverhampton Walsall Campus)
Playing Fields
Club Ho.
Melbourne House
Park Hall Jun. & Inf. Schs.
Fiveways Bri.
Gillity Bri.
Sutton Road Bridge
Hay Head Bridge
Bell Bridge
Shustoke Farm
Shustoke Bridge
Rushall Canal
Playground
Inf. & Nursy. Sch.
Jun. Sch.
Delves Green
Merrions
SUTTON ROAD
B4151
BROADWAY NORTH
A4148
BIRMINGHAM ROAD
A34
SARGENT'S HILL
PARK HALL RD.
WALSTEAD ROAD
GLOUCESTER ROAD
NORMAN AVENUE
LAKE AVENUE
SPRINGVALE AV.
CHARLEMONT ROAD
QUEEN'S ROAD
LODGE ROAD
BEACON RD.
SKIP LANE
LONGWOOD

Sports Ground
Hay Head Bridge
Nature Trail
WS4
Hay Head Farm
34
The Dingle
Barr Common
Cuckoo's Nook
LONGWOOD
Birch Wood
Potters Wood
Walsall
SUTTON ROAD
B4151
Three Crowns School
Moat
Beacon Hill Farm
Pine Hurst
Daisy Bank
Wren's Nest
Pool House Farm
WS9
49
BODENS LANE
Crook Cottage Farm
BARR LAKES LANE
WS5
SKIP LANE
CROOK LANE
Beacon Farm
PINFOLD LANE
HALL ROAD
Birmingham
B43
BEACON HEIGHTS
Crook House
Crook House Farm
GREAT BARR GOLF COURSE
PARK ROAD
WOODFIELD CL.
WOODLANDS AV.
Birch Grove
BEACON RD.
The Old Hall
OLD HALL LANE
Barr Beacon School
BIRMINGHAM RD.
A34
Merrions Wood
Club
Chapel Farm
The Duckery
66
CHAPEL
MERRIONS CLO
CORONATION

Hardwick
Streetly
Sutton Coldfield
B74
Pheasey
B43
Barr Beacon Reservoirs
BARR BEACON
Streetly Crematorium
Cemetery
Blackwood Park
Blackwood Sch.
Foley Wood
Community Centre
Industrial Estate
Common Farm
Blue House Farm
Beacon Park Farm
Beacon Dairy Farm
Pheasey Playing Fields
Doe Bank Wood
Meadow View Jun. Mixed & Inf. Sch.
Doe Bank Farm
Streetly School Playing Fields
Lindens Prim. Sch.
King George's Playing Field
Sports Ground
FOLEY ROAD WEST
FOLEY RD. EAST
BEACON HILL
CHESTER ROAD
QUESLETT ROAD
BRIDLE LANE
ALDRIDGE ROAD
HUNDRED ACRE ROAD
35
52
67

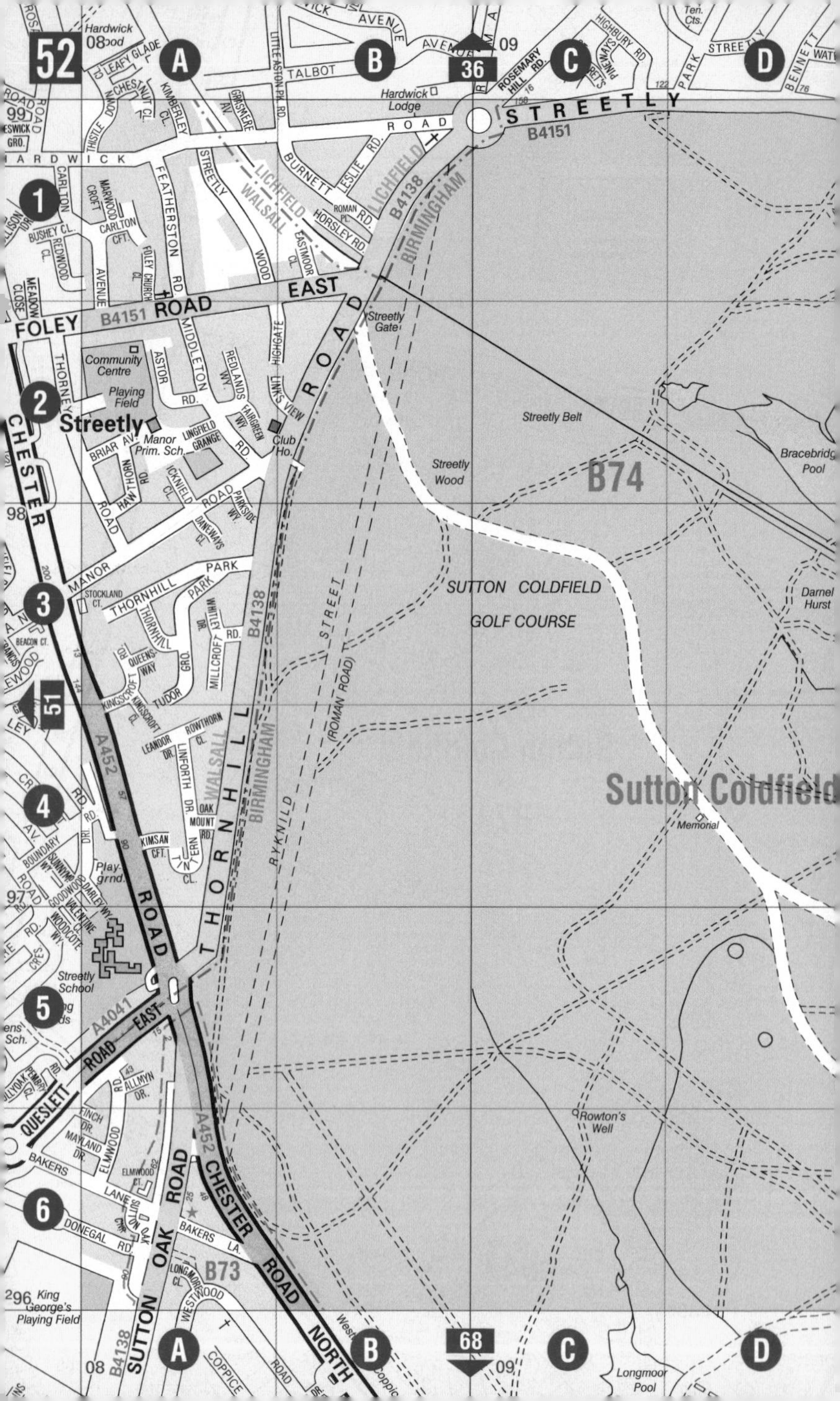

Hardwick Wood
Leafy Glade
Talbot
Hardwick Lodge
Streetly Road
B4151
Lichfield Road
B4138
Birmingham Road
Foley Road East
Community Centre
Playing Field
Streetly
Manor Prim. Sch.
Club Ho.
Streetly Gate
Streetly Belt
Streetly Wood
B74
Bracebridge Pool
Sutton Coldfield Golf Course
Darnel Hurst
Sutton Coldfield
Memorial
Rykneld Street (Roman Road)
Thornhill Road
Chester Road
A452
Manor Road
Thornhill Park
Streetly School
A4041
Queslett Road East
Rowton's Well
Bakers Lane
Donegal Rd.
Sutton Oak Road
Chester Road North
B73
King George's Playing Field
Longmoor Pool
Westwood
Coppice Road
36
51
68

E
F
G
H
37
69
54
1
2
3
4
5
6
WALSALL ROAD
A454
B4151
LANE
BELWELL LANE
FOUR OAKS ROAD
MERE GREEN RD.
LICHFIELD RD.
A5127
Mere Green
Four Oaks
Ley Hill
Four Oaks Park
Doe Bank
B75
BRACEBRIDGE RD.
BLACKROOT ROAD
BARKER ROAD
WYVERN ROAD
MIDLAND ROAD
MULROY RD.
TUDOR HILL
Tudor Hill
SUTTON COLDFIELD
B73
Sutton Coldfield
SUTTON PARK
Pool Hollies
Gravel Pit
Earthworks
Ford
Upper Nut Hurst
Lower Nut Hurst
Blackroot Pool
Boat Houses
Hartop Gate
Keeper's Pool
Hill Hurst
Holly Hurst
Plants Brook
Park House
Youth Centre
All Weather Pitch
Sutton Park Visitors Centre
Wyndley Leisure Centre
Running Track
Wyndley Swimming Baths
Mere Green Combined Sch.
Sports Cen.
Playing Field
Arthur Terry Sch.
Superstore
Coppice Prim. Sch.
Tennis Cts.
Depot
Town Hall
GRACECHURCH SHOP. CEN.
HIGH ST.
MANOR ROAD
BRASSINGTON RD.

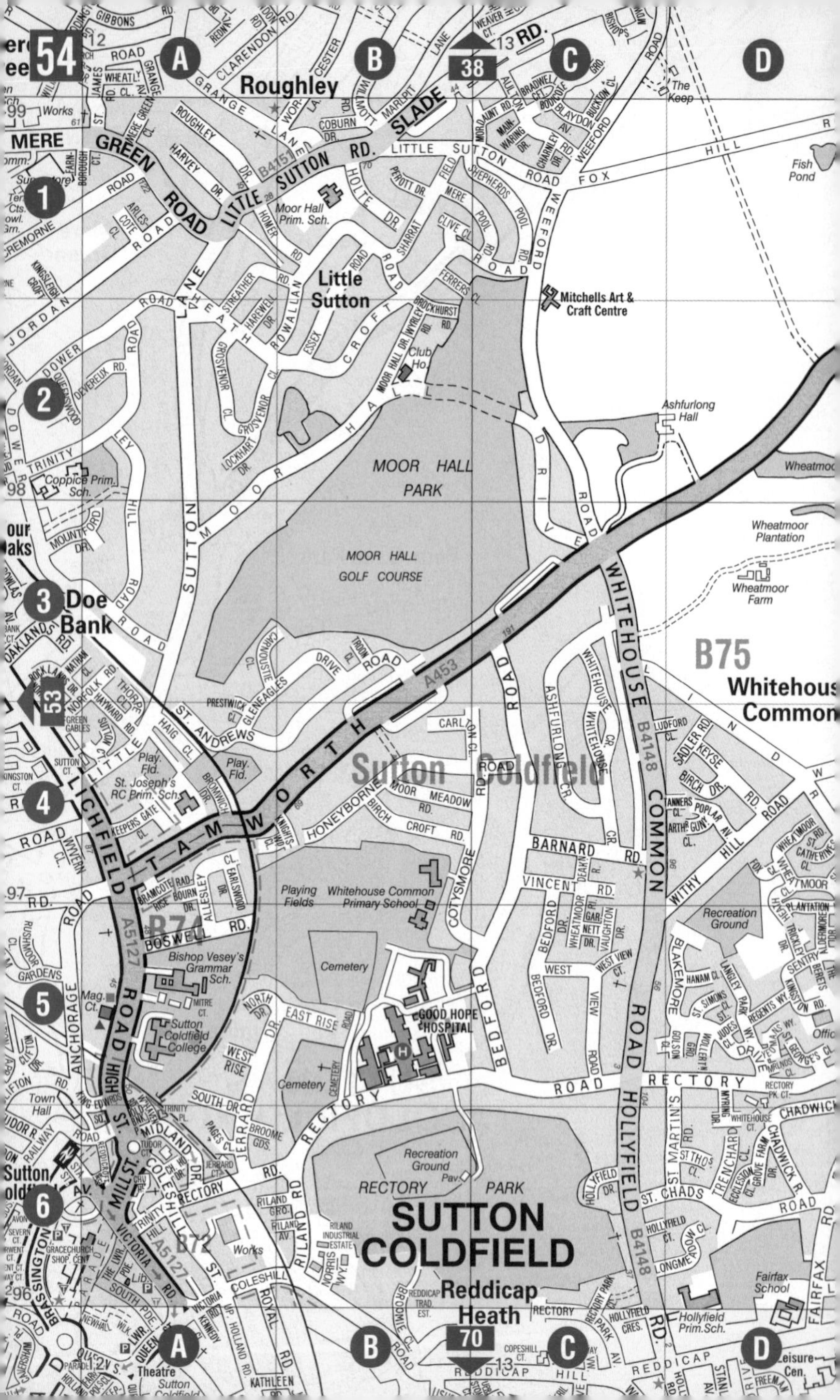

Roughley
Little Sutton
MOOR HALL PARK
MOOR HALL GOLF COURSE
Mitchells Art & Craft Centre
Ashfurlong Hall
Wheatmoor Plantation
Wheatmoor Farm
B75
Whitehouse Common
Sutton Coldfield
Doe Bank
Four Oaks
Moor Hall Prim. Sch.
Coppice Prim. Sch.
St. Joseph's RC Prim. Sch.
Whitehouse Common Primary School
Playing Fields
Cemetery
GOOD HOPE HOSPITAL
Bishop Vesey's Grammar Sch.
Sutton Coldfield College
Recreation Ground
RECTORY PARK
SUTTON COLDFIELD
Reddicap Heath
Fairfax School
Hollyfield Prim.Sch.
Fish Pond
The Keep
TAMWORTH ROAD A453
LITTLE SUTTON RD.
WEEFORD ROAD
WHITEHOUSE COMMON ROAD B4148
HOLLYFIELD RD.
RECTORY ROAD
LICHFIELD ROAD A5127
HIGH ST.
MILL ST.
B72
B74
38
53
70

TRICKLEY COPPICE
COPPICE LANE
FOX HILL RD.
HILL LANE
TAMWORTH RD.
COLLETS BROOK
Bassett's Pole
Sewage Works
Sutton Coldfield Crematorium
A453
ROAD
LONDON ROAD
SUTTON COLDFIELD BY PASS
A38
Sports Ground
Oaklands
Woodlands
Parkwood House Farm
Woodside Farm
Tamworth
B78
Collets Brook
M6 TOLL
M6 TOLL MOTORWAY
LANGLEY MILL JUNCTION
Junction T3
Woodlands Farm
NEW PARK WOOD
New Park Farm
A446
Littleworth End
Fish Pond
Highfields
Cottage Farm
High Heath
Bercot
HILL
Withy Hill Farm
Langley Brook Farm
Langley Mill Farm
Franfield
Osier Bed
Sutton New Hall Cemetery
Lindridge Pool
Langley Pool
Fish Pond
BIRMINGHAM
NTH. WARWICKSHIRE
Toll
Works
The Kennels
Galanthus
YEOMANRY CL.
CASERN PL.
INFANTRY VW.
BARRACK CL.
DRIVE
ROAD
Langley Sch.
LANGLEY RD.
WYATT
REPINGTON WAY
LODGE
CARHAMPTON
BIGWOOD DR.
DUNCUMB RD
CUMBER LAND WK.
GOODEVE WALK
LANGLEY HALL DR.
New Hall Jun. & Inf. Sch.
COLMORE DR.
BRACK DR.
WILSON DR.
WILSN DR.
LEIGH R.
LEIGH
LANGLEY HALL RD.
THE FALCONS
REGAN CT.
SPRINGFIELD CT.
FALSTAFF CT.
KNIGHT CT.
WOODINGTON RD.
ARDEN DR.
ARDEN CRES.
WYATT RD.
KEEP
DELANCY
Comm. Cen.
CHURCHILL PDE
JESSON RD.
NEWDIGATE R.
STONE AV.
FOWLER RD.
CATTELL DR.
HOLBECHE R.
Rec. Grd.
NUTHURST CL.
SPRINGFIELD ROAD
Falcon Lodge
B76
HOLLY LANE
E F G H
1 2 3 4 5 6
415
16
99
98
97
96
39
71

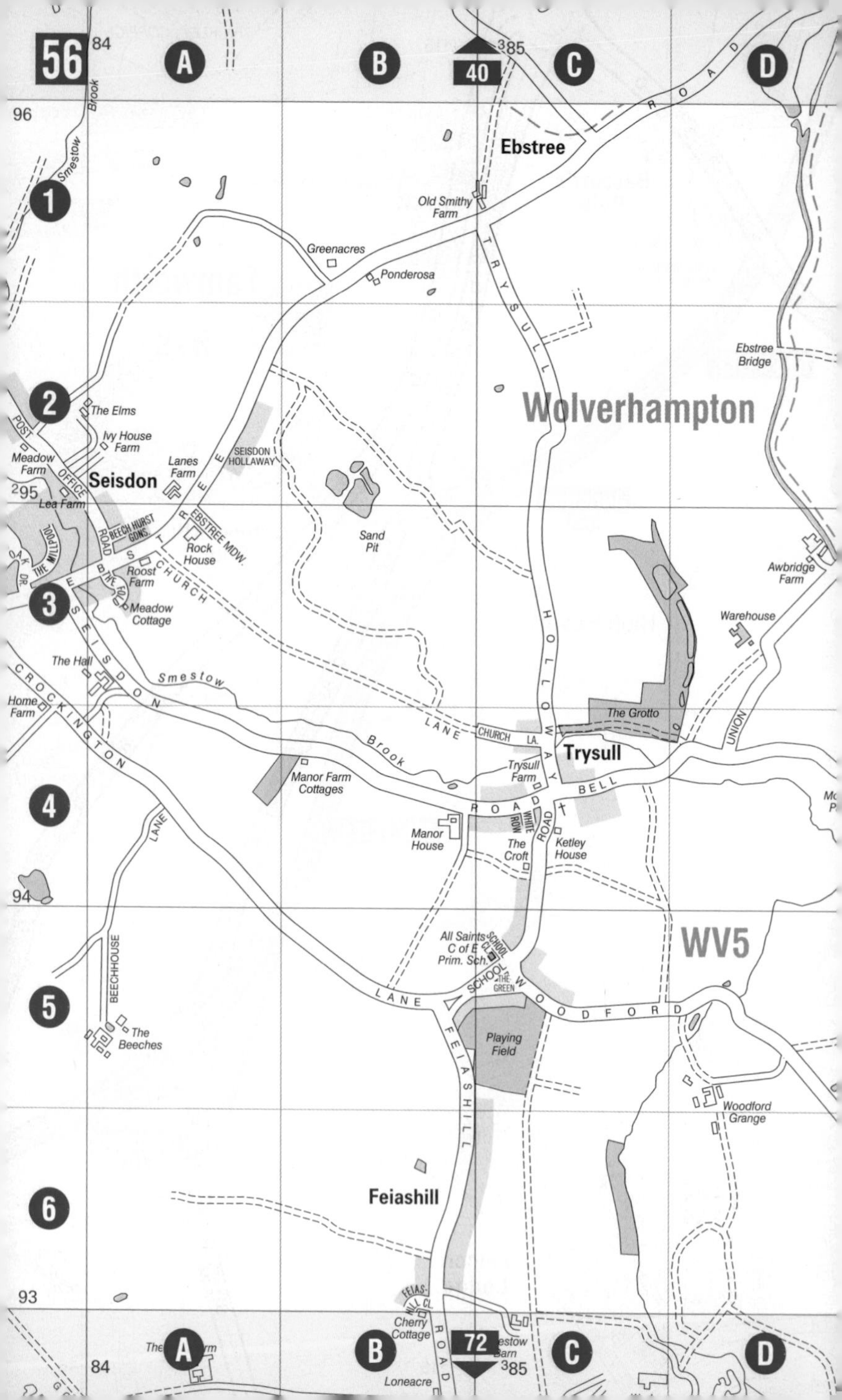

40
72
Ebstree
Old Smithy Farm
Greenacres
Ponderosa
Wolverhampton
Ebstree Bridge
The Elms
Ivy House Farm
Meadow Farm
Seisdon
Lanes Farm
SEISDON HOLLAWAY
Lea Farm
BEECH HURST GDNS.
EBSTREE MDW.
Rock House
Roost Farm
Meadow Cottage
Sand Pit
Awbridge Farm
Warehouse
The Hall
Home Farm
Smestow
Brook
The Grotto
Trysull
Trysull Farm
Manor Farm Cottages
CHURCH LA.
Manor House
The Croft
Ketley House
All Saints C of E Prim. Sch.
WV5
The Beeches
Playing Field
Woodford Grange
Feiashill
Cherry Cottage
Loneacre

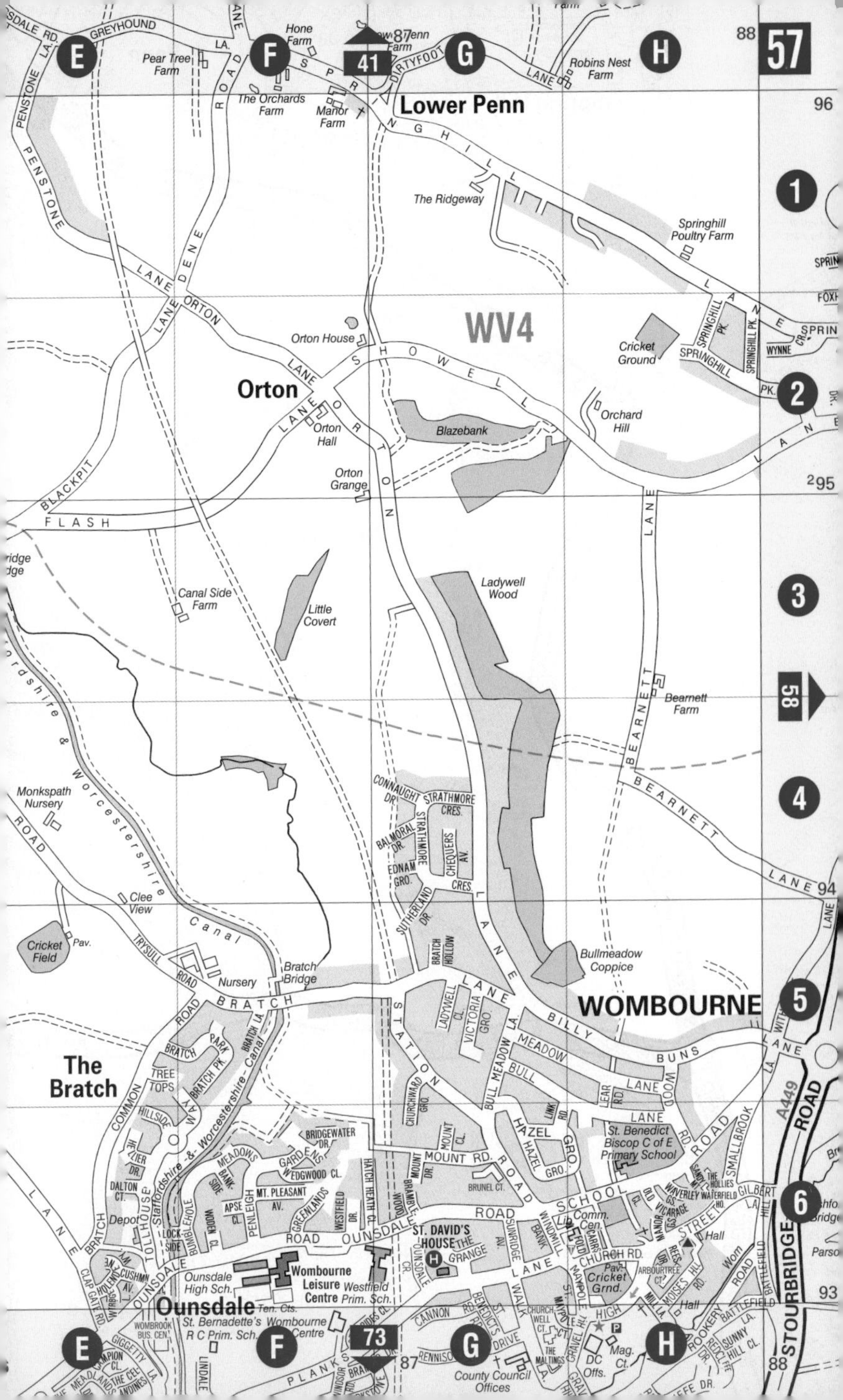

Lower Penn
Orton
WV4
WOMBOURNE
The Bratch
Ounsdale
Hone Farm
Pear Tree Farm
The Orchards Farm
Manor Farm
Robins Nest Farm
The Ridgeway
Springhill Poultry Farm
Orton House
Cricket Ground
Orton Hall
Orton Grange
Blazebank
Orchard Hill
Canal Side Farm
Little Covert
Ladywell Wood
Bearnett Farm
Monkspath Nursery
Clee View
Cricket Field
Pav.
Nursery
Bratch Bridge
Bullmeadow Coppice
St. Benedict Biscop C of E Primary School
ST. DAVID'S HOUSE
Ounsdale High Sch.
Wombourne Leisure Centre
Westfield Prim. Sch.
St. Bernadette's R C Prim. Sch.
Wombourne Centre
County Council Offices
DC Offs.
Mag. Ct.
Pav. Cricket Grnd.
Comm. Cen.
Depot
GREYHOUND LA.
PENSTONE LA.
DIRTYFOOT LANE
SPRINGHILL LANE
ORTON LANE
DENE ROAD
SHOWELL LANE
BLACKPIT LANE
FLASH LANE
ORTON LANE
BEARNETT LANE
Staffordshire & Worcestershire Canal
TRYSULL ROAD
BRATCH LANE
STATION ROAD
BILLY BUNS LANE
MEADOW LANE
BULL LANE
HAZEL GRO.
SCHOOL ROAD
OUNSDALE ROAD
MOUNT RD.
COMMON ROAD
CHURCH RD.
HIGH ST.
STOURBRIDGE ROAD
A449
SMALLBROOK ROAD
WOOD RD.
ROOKERY LA.
PLANKS LANE
41
73
58
E F G H
1 2 3 4 5 6
87 88 93 94 95 96

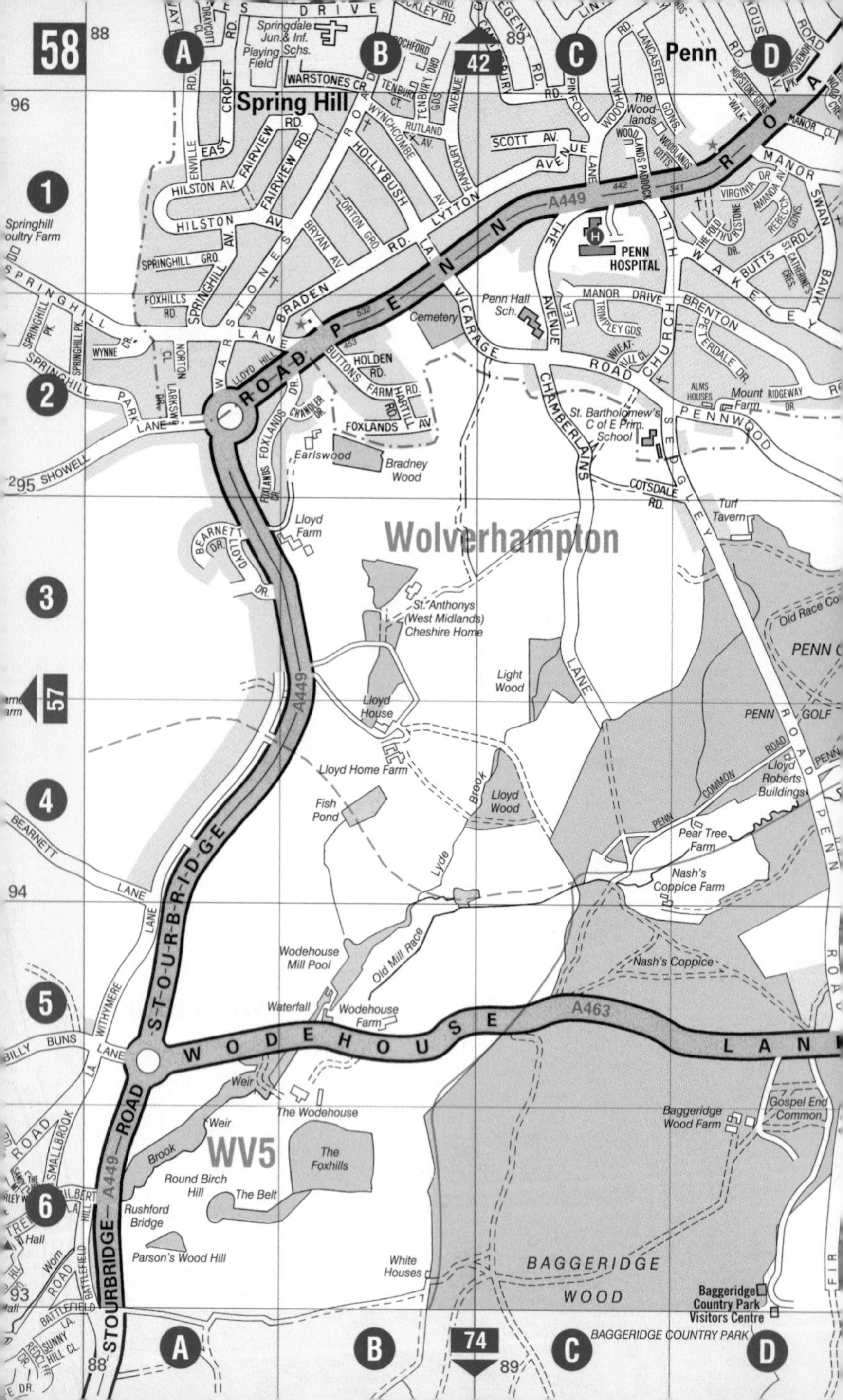

Spring Hill
Penn
Springdale Jun.& Inf. Schs.
Playing Field
Springhill Poultry Farm
PENN HOSPITAL
Penn Hall Sch.
Cemetery
St. Bartholomew's C of E Prim. School
Earlswood
Bradney Wood
Lloyd Farm
Wolverhampton
St. Anthonys (West Midlands) Cheshire Home
Light Wood
Lloyd House
Lloyd Home Farm
Fish Pond
Lloyd Wood
Pear Tree Farm
Nash's Coppice Farm
Nash's Coppice
Turf Tavern
Old Race Co
PENN GOLF
Lloyd Roberts Buildings
Wodehouse Mill Pool
Old Mill Race
Waterfall
Wodehouse Farm
Weir
The Wodehouse
WV5
The Foxhills
Round Birch Hill
The Belt
Rushford Bridge
Parson's Wood Hill
White Houses
BAGGERIDGE WOOD
Baggeridge Wood Farm
Gospel End Common
Baggeridge Country Park Visitors Centre
BAGGERIDGE COUNTRY PARK
PENN ROAD
A449
STOURBRIDGE ROAD
WODEHOUSE LANE
A463
WARSTONES LANE
VICARAGE ROAD
CHAMBERLAINS LANE
SEDGLEY ROAD
PENNWOOD LANE
WAKELEY HILL

42
57
74

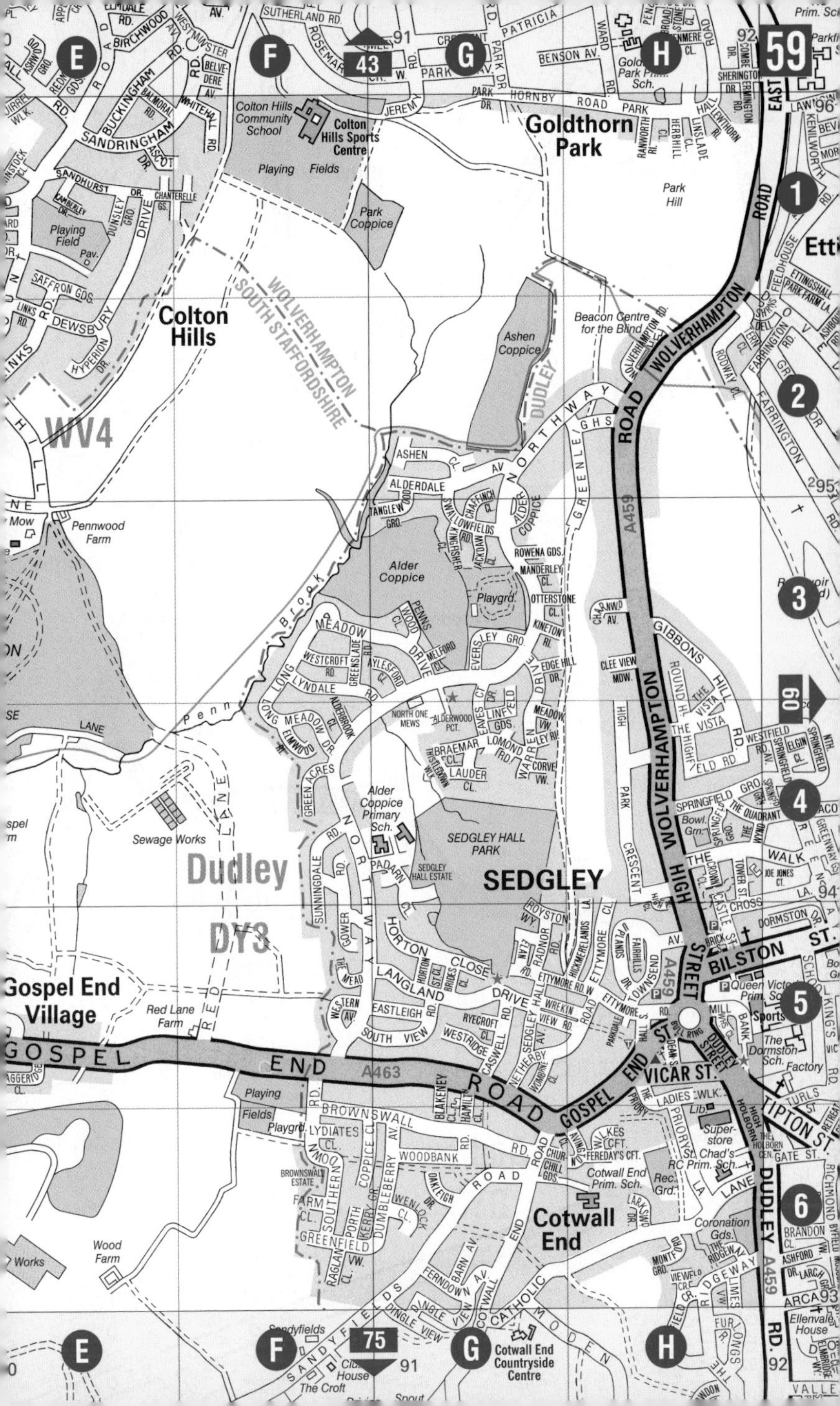

43
75
60
Goldthorn Park
Colton Hills
Colton Hills Community School
Colton Hills Sports Centre
Playing Fields
Park Coppice
Park Hill
Ashen Coppice
Beacon Centre for the Blind
WOLVERHAMPTON
SOUTH STAFFORDSHIRE
DUDLEY
WV4
Pennwood Farm
Alder Coppice
Alder Coppice Primary Sch.
SEDGLEY HALL PARK
SEDGLEY
Dudley
DY3
Sewage Works
Gospel End Village
Red Lane Farm
GOSPEL END ROAD
A463
A459
WOLVERHAMPTON ROAD
HIGH STREET
BILSTON ST.
VICAR ST.
TIPTON ST.
DUDLEY RD.
Cotwall End
Cotwall End Prim. Sch.
Cotwall End Countryside Centre
Wood Farm
Sandyfields
The Croft
The Dormston Sch.
St. Chad's RC Prim. Sch.
Coronation Gds.
Ellenvale House
Playing Fields
Playgrd.
E
F
G
H
1
2
3
4
5
6
91
92
93
94
95
96

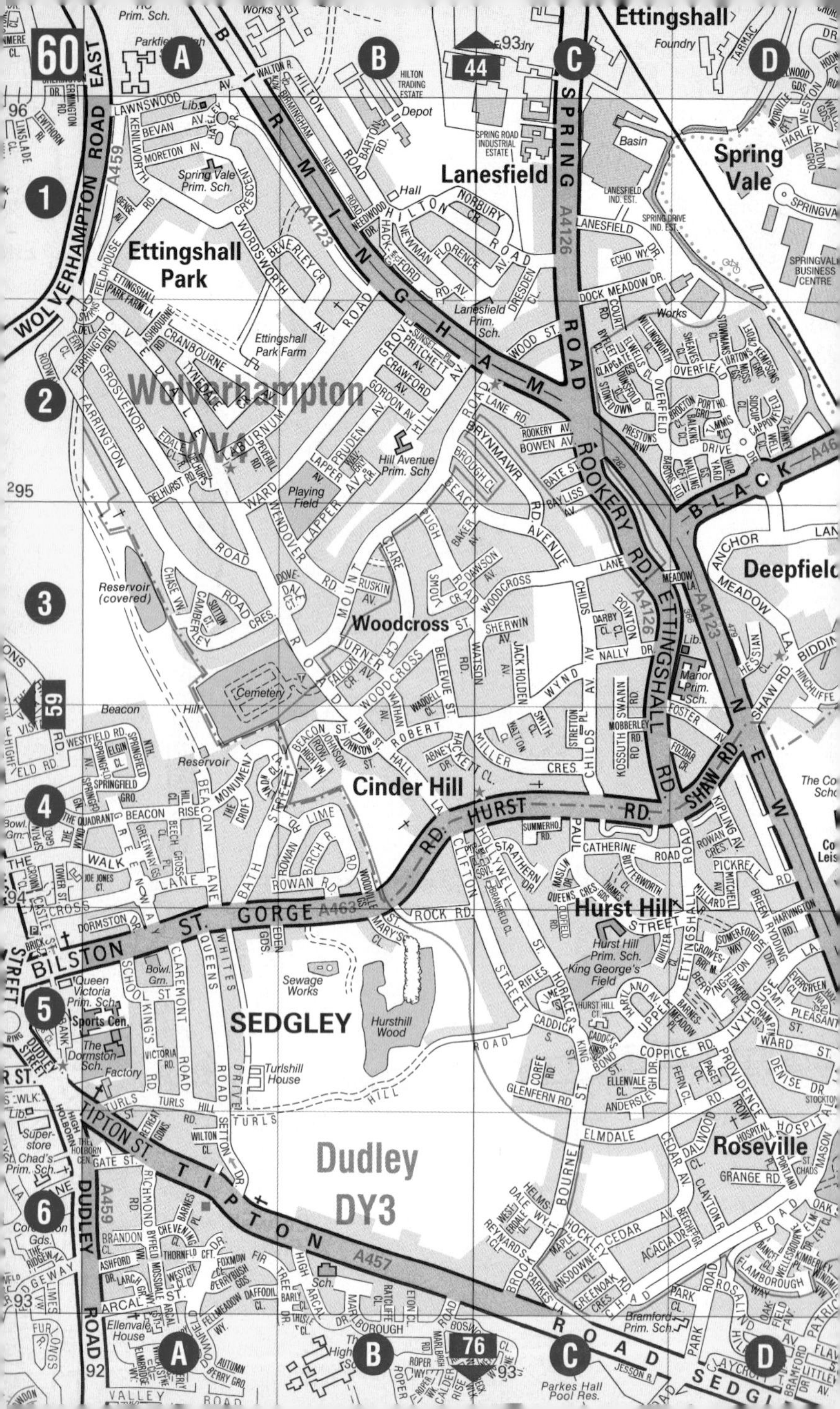

44
76
59
Ettingshall
Lanesfield
Spring Vale
Ettingshall Park
Wolverhampton WV4
Deepfield
Woodcross
Cinder Hill
Hurst Hill
SEDGLEY
Dudley DY3
Roseville
BIRMINGHAM NEW ROAD
SPRING ROAD
ROOKERY RD.
ETTINGSHALL RD.
WOLVERHAMPTON ROAD EAST
BILSTON ST.
GORGE RD.
HURST RD.
TIPTON ST.
TIPTON ROAD
DUDLEY ROAD
BLACK COUNTRY NEW ROAD
Hilton Trading Estate
Spring Road Industrial Estate
Lanesfield Ind. Est.
Spring Drive Ind. Est.
Springvale Business Centre
Spring Vale Prim. Sch.
Lanesfield Prim. Sch.
Hill Avenue Prim. Sch.
Manor Prim. Sch.
Hurst Hill Prim. Sch.
Queen Victoria Prim. Sch.
The Dormston Sch.
Bramford Prim. Sch.
Ettingshall Park Farm
Reservoir (covered)
Cemetery
Beacon Hill
Sewage Works
Hursthill Wood
Turlshill House
King George's Field
Playing Field
Sports Cen.
Parkes Hall Pool Res.

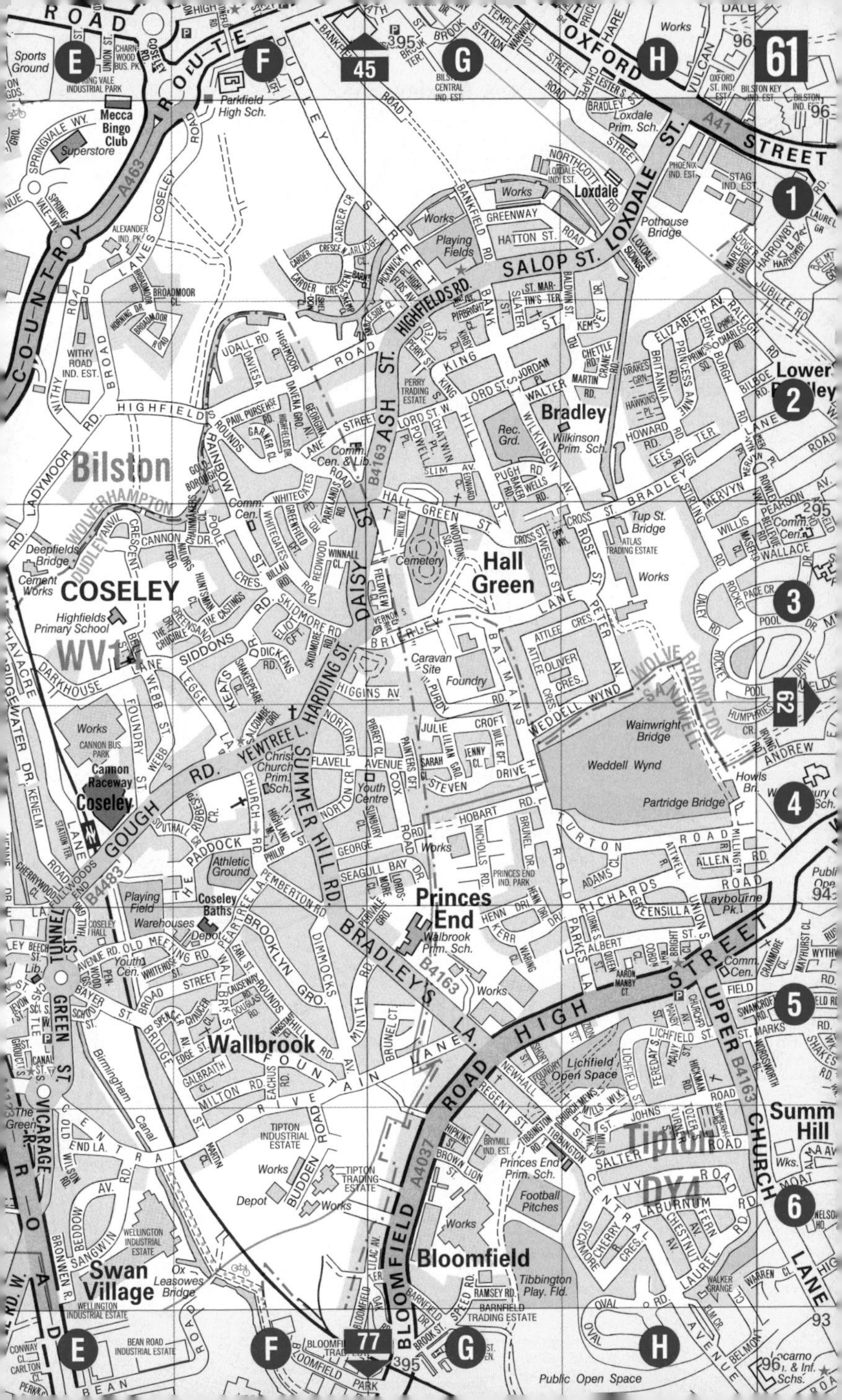

45
77
62
E
F
G
H
1
2
3
4
5
6
Bilston
COSELEY
WV14
Hall Green
Bradley
Loxdale
Princes End
Wallbrook
Bloomfield
Swan Village
Tipton
DY4
Lower Bradley
Summer Hill
Sports Ground
Mecca Bingo Club
Superstore
Springvale Industrial Park
Parkfield High Sch.
Bilston Central Ind. Est.
Oxford St. Ind. Est.
Bilston Key Ind. Est.
Bilston Ind. Est.
Loxdale Prim. Sch.
Phoenix Ind. Est.
Stag Ind. Est.
Loxdale Ind. Est.
Pothouse Bridge
Works
Playing Fields
Alexander Ind. Pk.
Withy Road Ind. Est.
Perry Trading Estate
Comm. Cen. & Lib.
Rec. Grd.
Wilkinson Prim. Sch.
Comm. Cen.
Tup St. Bridge
Atlas Trading Estate
Deepfields Bridge
Cement Works
Highfields Primary School
Cemetery
Caravan Site
Foundry
Wainwright Bridge
Weddell Wynd
Partridge Bridge
Howls Br.
Cannon Bus. Park
Cannon Raceway
Coseley
Christ Church Prim. Sch.
Youth Centre
Athletic Ground
Playing Field
Coseley Baths
Warehouses
Depot
Princes End Ind. Park
Walbrook Prim. Sch.
Laybourne Pk.
Lichfield Open Space
Birmingham Canal
Tipton Industrial Estate
Tipton Trading Estate
Brymill Ind. Est.
Princes End Prim. Sch.
Football Pitches
Wellington Industrial Estate
Ox Leasowes Bridge
Tibbington Play. Fld.
Barnfield Trading Estate
Bean Road Industrial Estate
Walker Grange
Public Open Space
Locarno Inf. & Jun. Schs.
COUNTRY ROUTE
A463
A41
B4163
B4483
A4037
OXFORD STREET
SALOP ST.
LOXDALE ST.
HIGHFIELDS RD.
ASH ST.
DAISY ST.
HARDING ST.
YEWTREE L.
GOUGH RD.
SUMMER HILL RD.
BRADLEY'S LA.
HIGH ROAD
UPPER CHURCH LANE
HIGH STREET
BLOOMFIELD ROAD
FOUNTAIN LANE
CENTRAL DRIVE
VICARAGE RD.
TUNNEL ST.
GREEN ST.
LADYMOOR RD.
WOLVERHAMPTON
DUDLEY
SANDWELL
BRIERLEY LANE
BATMANS HILL RD.
TURTON ROAD
RICHARDS ROAD
DUDLEY STREET
HIGHFIELDS RD.
BRADLEY LANE
PEARSON ST.
HALL GREEN ST.
KING ST.
WILKINSON AV.
BROAD LANES
COSELEY RD.
OLD MEETING RD.
BROAD STREET
395
96
93
94

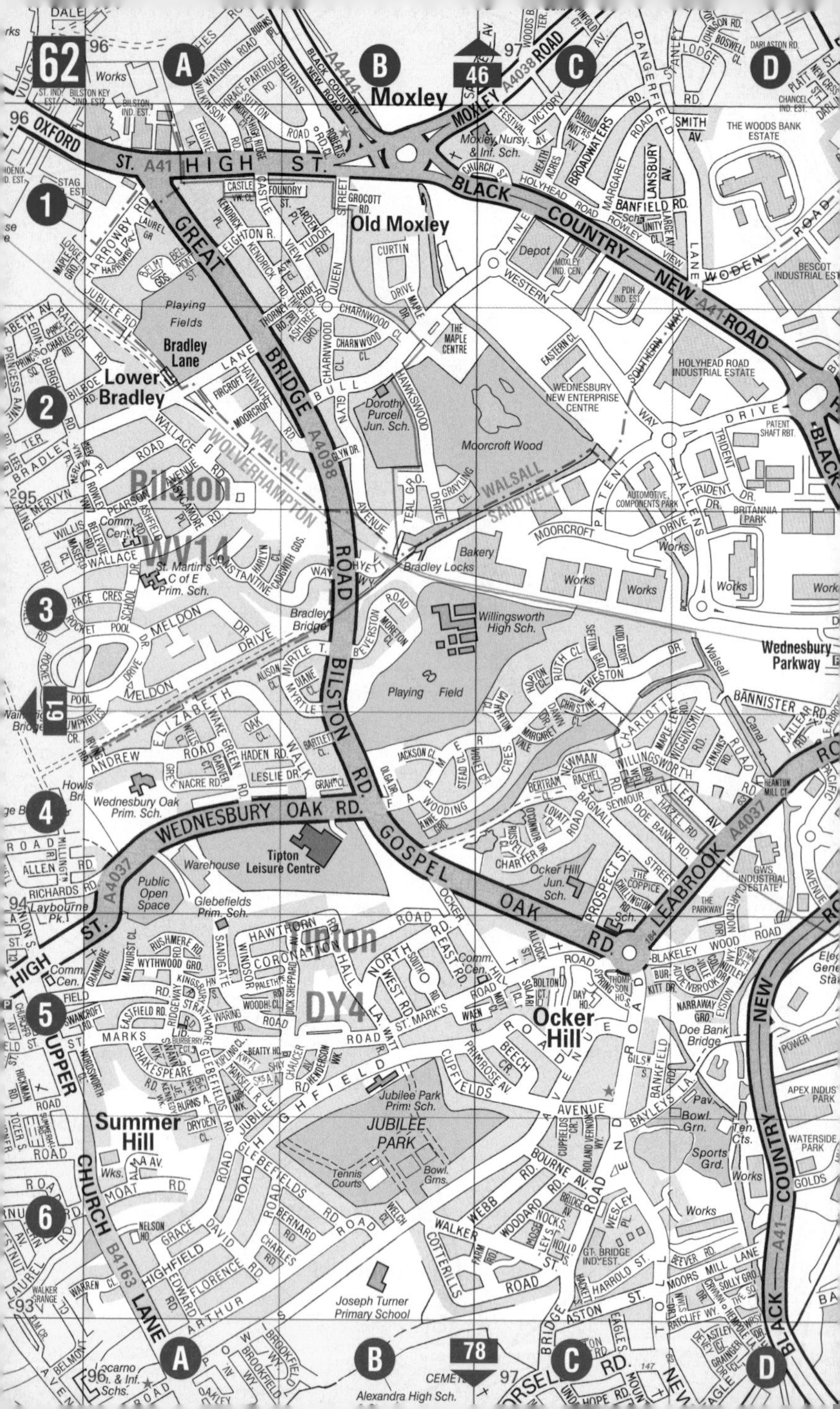
Moxley
Old Moxley
Lower Bradley
Bilston
WV14
Bradley Lane
Playing Fields
Moorcroft Wood
Bradley Locks
Bradley Bridge
Willingsworth High Sch.
Playing Field
Wednesbury Parkway
Tipton Leisure Centre
Tipton
DY4
Ocker Hill
Summer Hill
JUBILEE PARK
Joseph Turner Primary School
Alexandra High Sch.
Wednesbury Oak Prim. Sch.
St. Martin's C of E Prim. Sch.
Dorothy Purcell Jun. Sch.
Glebefields Prim. Sch.
Jubilee Park Prim. Sch.
Ocker Hill Jun. Sch.
Moxley Nursy. & Inf. Sch.
THE WOODS BANK ESTATE
BESCOT INDUSTRIAL EST.
HOLYHEAD ROAD INDUSTRIAL ESTATE
WEDNESBURY NEW ENTERPRISE CENTRE
AUTOMOTIVE COMPONENTS PARK
BRITANNIA PARK
GWS INDUSTRIAL ESTATE
APEX INDUS. PARK
WATERSIDE PARK
THE MAPLE CENTRE
BLACK COUNTRY NEW ROAD
GREAT BRIDGE ROAD
BILSTON RD.
GOSPEL OAK RD.
WEDNESBURY OAK RD.
HIGH ST.
OXFORD ST.
LEABROOK
CHURCH LANE
A41
A4098
A4037
A4038
A4444
B4163
46
78
61
A
B
C
D
1
2
3
4
5
6
96
97
95
94
93

King's Hill
Church Hill
Wednesbury
WS10
WEDNESBURY
Mesty Croft
Balls Hill
Hill Top
Harvills Hawthorn
B70
B71
Wednesbury Great Western Street
Brunswick Park
Cemetery
Sandwell College (Wednesbury Campus)
Tame Valley Canal
Wodensborough Comm. Technology College
Hateley Heath Prim. Sch.
Kent Close Prim. Sch.
Moorlands Prim. Sch.
Harvills Hawthorn Prim. Sch.
St. John's C of E Prim. Sch.
Tameside Prim. Sch.
Old Park Prim. Sch.
Albert Pritchard Inf. Sch.
Wednesbury Leis. Cen.
Mecca Bingo Club
Holloway Bank Trading Estate
Hill Top Industrial Estate
Siddons Factory Estate
Howard St. Ind. Estate
Robins Business Park
The Parkway Industrial Centre
Wednesbury Trading Estate
Kings Hill Bus. Park
Old Pk. Trad. Est.
Brookside Ind. Est.
Bridge St. Ind. Est.
Spartan Ind. Cen.
Ridgacre Enterprise
A462
A461
A4196
B4200
47
79
64
E
F
G
H
1
2
3
4
5
6

A
B
C
D
1
2
3
4
5
6
48
63
80
M6
M6 MOTORWAY
Junction 8
Wednesbury
WS10
Friar Park
The Woods
Mesty Croft
Hall Green
Hateley Heath
Charlemont
West Bromwich
B71
Hall End
The Oval
Public Open Space
Park Hill Prim. Sch.
Manor High Sch.
Friar Park Millennium Cen.
Playing Field
Works
Factory
Tame Bridge Parkway
Tameside Prim. Sch.
Play. Field
The Priory Prim. Sch.
Playground
Wodensborough Comm. Technology College
Tame Valley Canal
Crankhall Lane Bridge
Hall Green Prim. Sch.
The Westminster School
Running Track
Menzies High Sch.
Ten. Cts.
West Bromwich Cemetery
HEATH LANE HOSPITAL
Hollyhedge Sch.
Charlemont Sch.
Kent Close Prim. Sch.
John Bosco Prim. Sch.
WALSALL ROAD
A4031
A4041
NEWTON ROAD
FRIAR PARK ROAD
HALL GREEN ROAD
HOLLYHEDGE ROAD
WESTMINSTER ROAD
CHARLEMONT
CRANKHALL LANE
WALSALL
SANDWELL
RIDGACRE ENTERPRISE

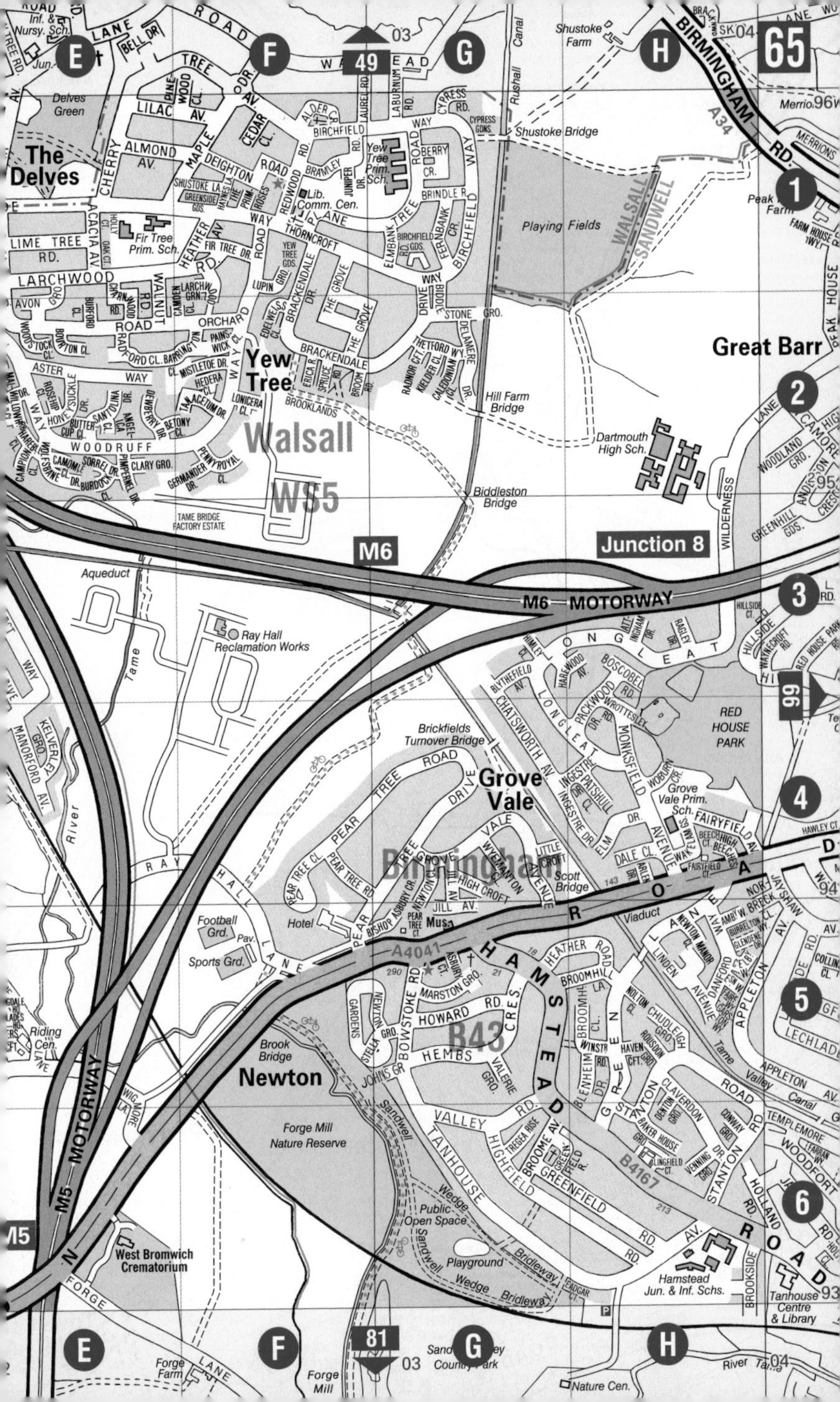

The Delves
Delves Green
Yew Tree
Walsall
WS5
Great Barr
Grove Vale
Birmingham
B43
Newton
Forge Mill Nature Reserve
Playing Fields
Shustoke Farm
Shustoke Bridge
Hill Farm Bridge
Biddleston Bridge
Dartmouth High Sch.
Junction 8
M6 MOTORWAY
M5 MOTORWAY
TAME BRIDGE FACTORY ESTATE
Aqueduct
Ray Hall Reclamation Works
Brickfields Turnover Bridge
RED HOUSE PARK
Grove Vale Prim. Sch.
Scott Bridge
Viaduct
Hotel
Mus.
Football Grd.
Sports Grd.
Riding Cen.
Brook Bridge
Public Open Space
Playground
West Bromwich Crematorium
Hamstead Jun. & Inf. Schs.
Tanhouse Centre & Library
Forge Farm
Forge Mill
Sandwell Valley Country Park
Nature Cen.
Fir Tree Prim. Sch.
Yew Tree Prim. Sch.
Lib. Comm. Cen.
Peak Farm
BIRMINGHAM RD.
HAMSTEAD ROAD
A4041
A34
B4167
49
81
96

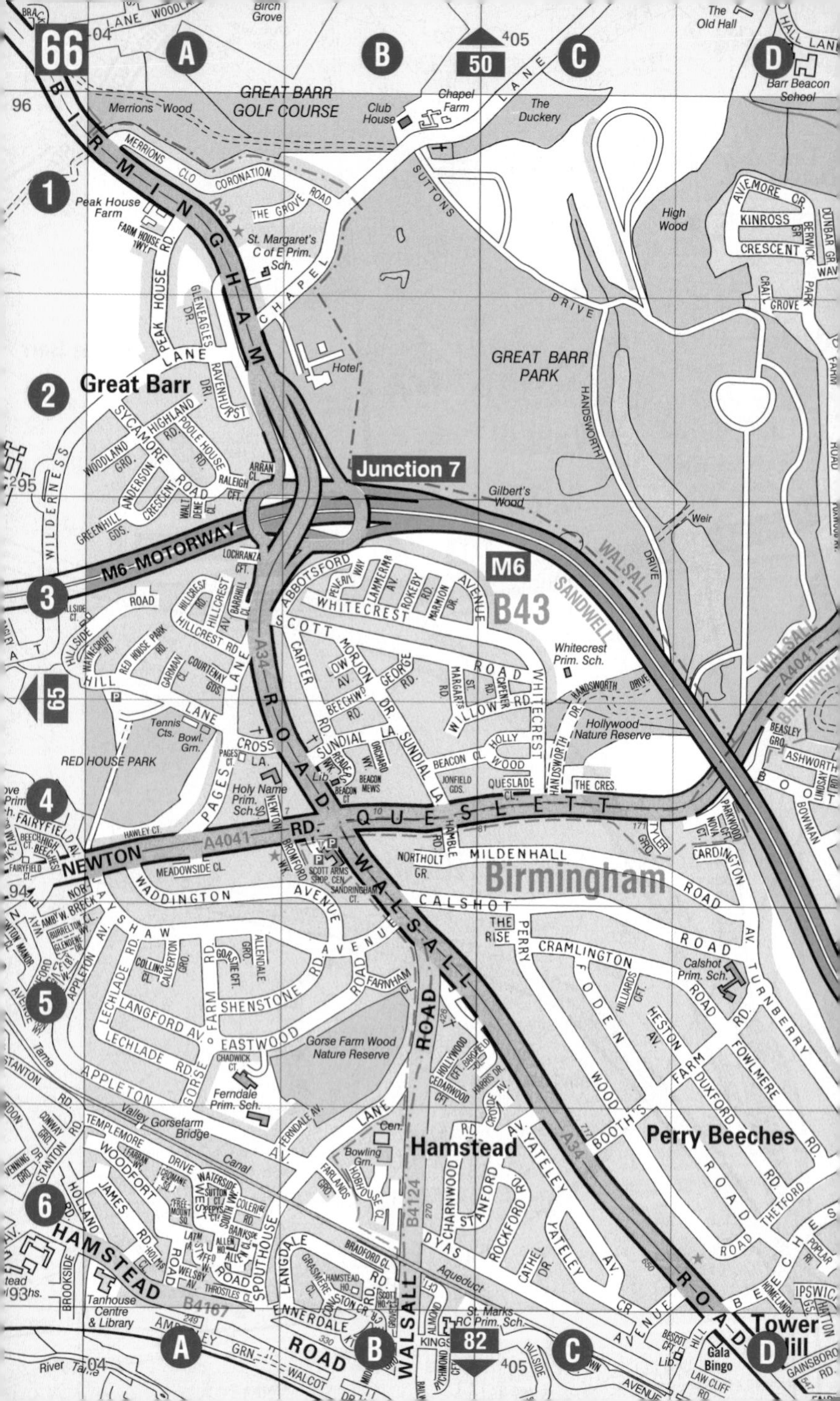

A
B
C
D
1
2
3
4
5
6
50
65
82
GREAT BARR GOLF COURSE
Merrions Wood
Birch Grove
Club House
Chapel Farm
The Duckery
The Old Hall
Barr Beacon School
Peak House Farm
St. Margaret's C of E Prim. Sch.
Hotel
Great Barr
GREAT BARR PARK
High Wood
Junction 7
Gilbert's Wood
M6 MOTORWAY
M6
B43
WALSALL
SANDWELL
Whitecrest Prim. Sch.
Hollywood Nature Reserve
Weir
RED HOUSE PARK
Tennis Cts.
Bowl. Grn.
Holy Name Prim. Sch.
NEWTON RD.
QUESLETT
A4041
A34
Scott Arms Shop. Cen.
Lib.
Birmingham
Calshot Prim. Sch.
Gorse Farm Wood Nature Reserve
Ferndale Prim. Sch.
Valley Gorsefarm Bridge
Canal
Hamstead
Perry Beeches
Bowling Grn.
B4124
B4167
Tanhouse Centre & Library
Aqueduct
St. Marks RC Prim. Sch.
Tower Hill
Gala Bingo
River Tame
BIRMINGHAM ROAD
WALSALL ROAD
HAMSTEAD ROAD
ENNERDALE ROAD

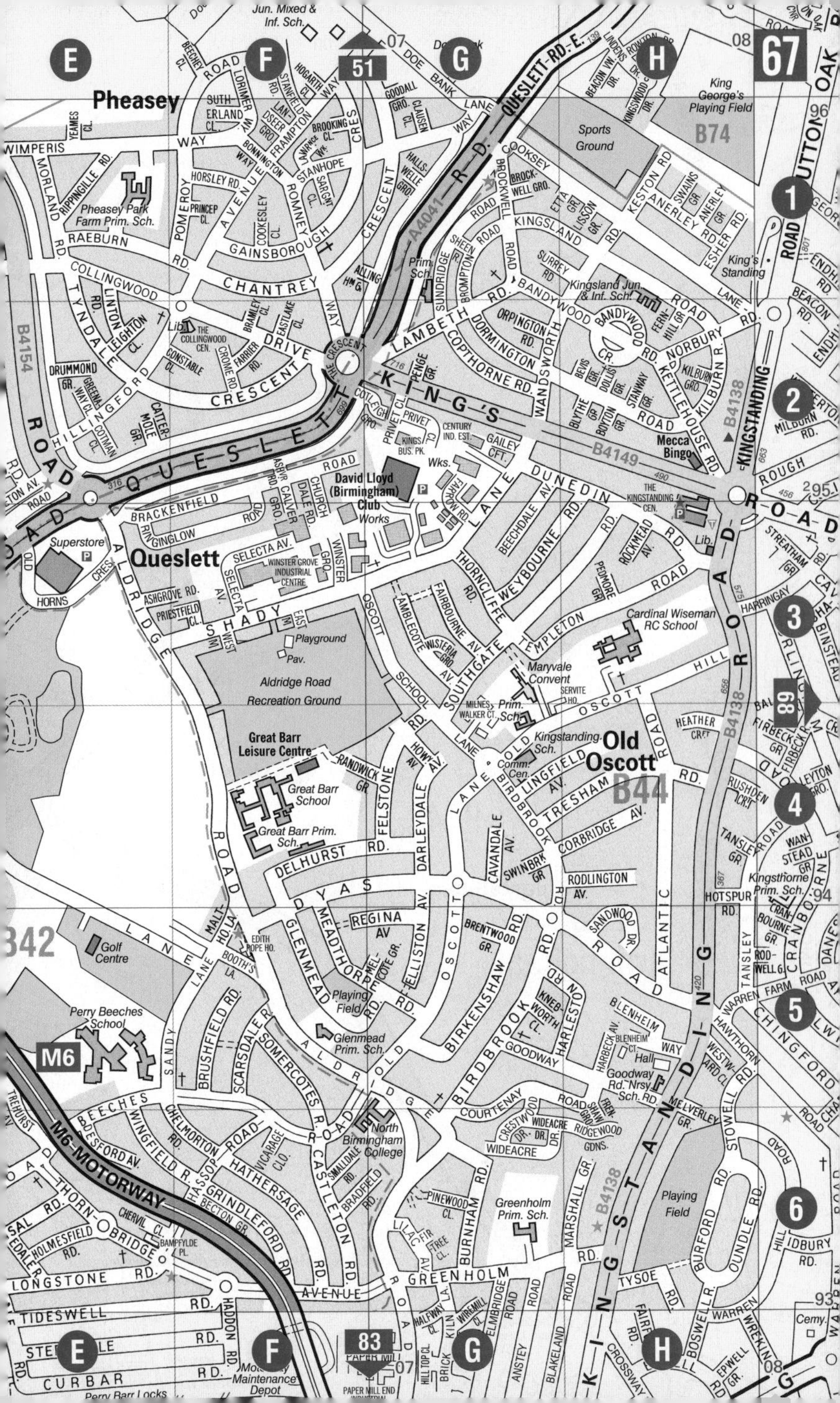

E
F
G
H
51
83
89
1
2
3
4
5
6
Pheasey
Queslett
Old Oscott
B74
B44
B4154
B4138
B4149
A4041
M6
M6-MOTORWAY
QUESLETT ROAD
KING'S ROAD
KINGSTANDING ROAD
QUESLETT RD. E.
Pheasey Park Farm Prim. Sch.
King George's Playing Field
Sports Ground
King's Standing
Kingsland Jun. & Inf. Sch.
Mecca Bingo
THE KINGSTANDING CEN.
David Lloyd (Birmingham) Club
Works
Superstore
WINSTER GROVE INDUSTRIAL CENTRE
CENTURY IND. EST.
KINGS BUS. PK.
Playground
Pav.
Aldridge Road Recreation Ground
Great Barr Leisure Centre
Great Barr School
Great Barr Prim. Sch.
Cardinal Wiseman RC School
Maryvale Convent
SERVITE HO.
MILNES WALKER CT.
Prim. Sch.
Kingstanding Sch.
Comm. Cen.
Kingsthorne Prim. Sch.
Golf Centre
Perry Beeches School
EDITH POPE HO.
Playing Field
Glenmead Prim. Sch.
North Birmingham College
Greenholm Prim. Sch.
Goodway Rd. Nrsy Sch.
Hall
Playing Field
Motorway Maintenance Depot
Perry Barr Locks
PAPER MILL END INDUSTRIAL
Cemy.
Jun. Mixed & Inf. Sch.
THE COLLINGWOOD CEN.
Lib.

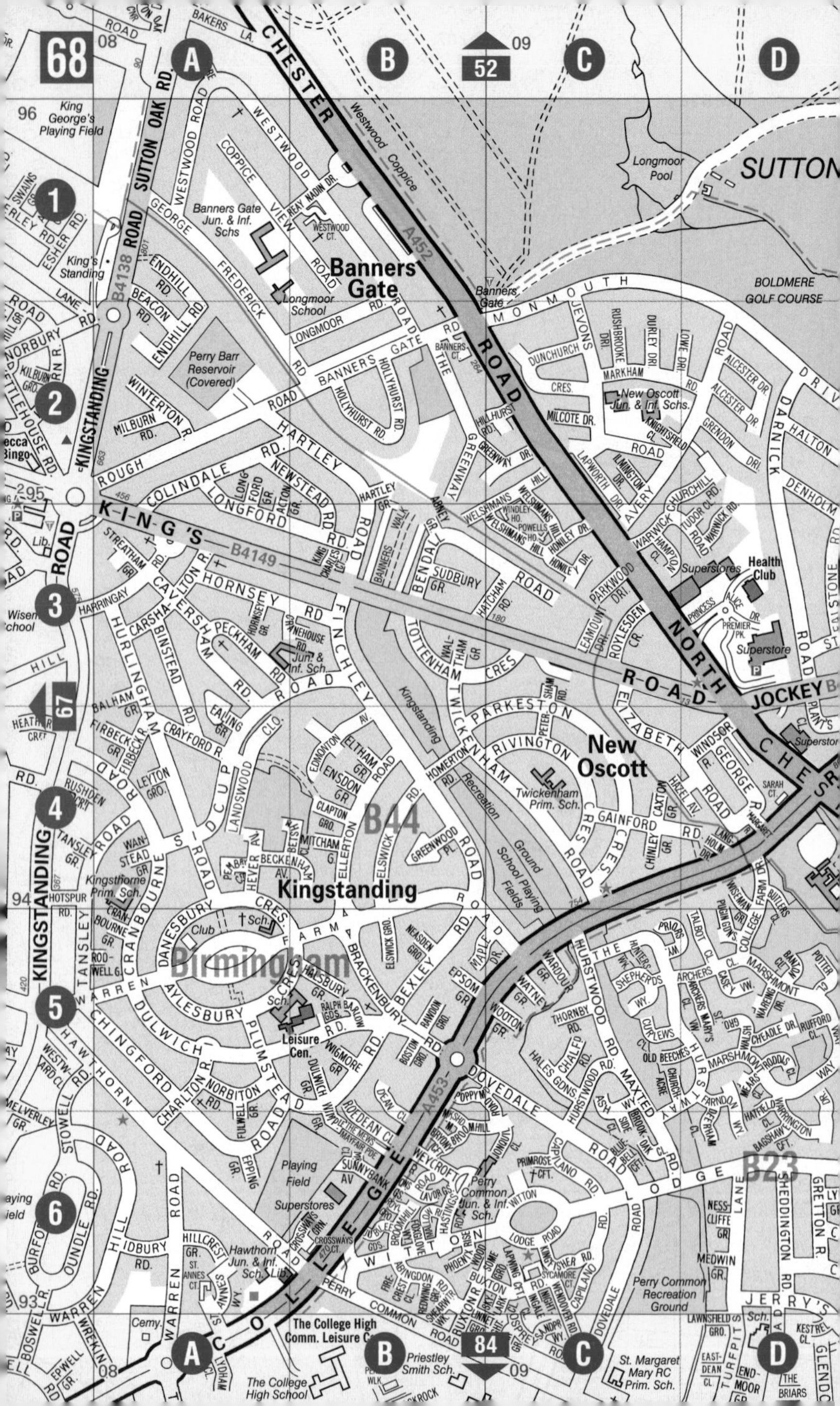
A
B
C
D
52
09
08
96
93
94
1
2
3
4
5
6
67
84
SUTTON
Longmoor Pool
BOLDMERE GOLF COURSE
King George's Playing Field
King's Standing
Banners Gate
Banners Gate Jun. & Inf. Schs
Longmoor School
Perry Barr Reservoir (Covered)
Westwood Coppice
CHESTER ROAD
A452
SUTTON OAK RD.
KINGSTANDING ROAD
B4138
KING'S ROAD
B4149
NORTH ROAD
JOCKEY
MONMOUTH
New Oscott Jun. & Inf. Schs.
Health Club
Superstores
Superstore
New Oscott
Twickenham Prim. Sch.
Kingstanding Recreation Ground
School Playing Fields
Cranehouse Rd. Jun. & Inf. Sch.
B44
Kingstanding
Kingsthorne Prim. Sch.
Birmingham
Leisure Cen.
Playing Field
Superstores
Perry Common Jun. & Inf. Sch.
Perry Common Recreation Ground
Hawthorn Jun. & Inf. Sch.
The College High Comm. Leisure Cen.
The College High School
Priestley Smith Sch.
St. Margaret Mary RC Prim. Sch.
A453
B23
LODGE ROAD
COLLEGE ROAD
DOVEDALE ROAD
WITTON LODGE ROAD
PERRY COMMON ROAD
JERRY'S LANE
Cemy.

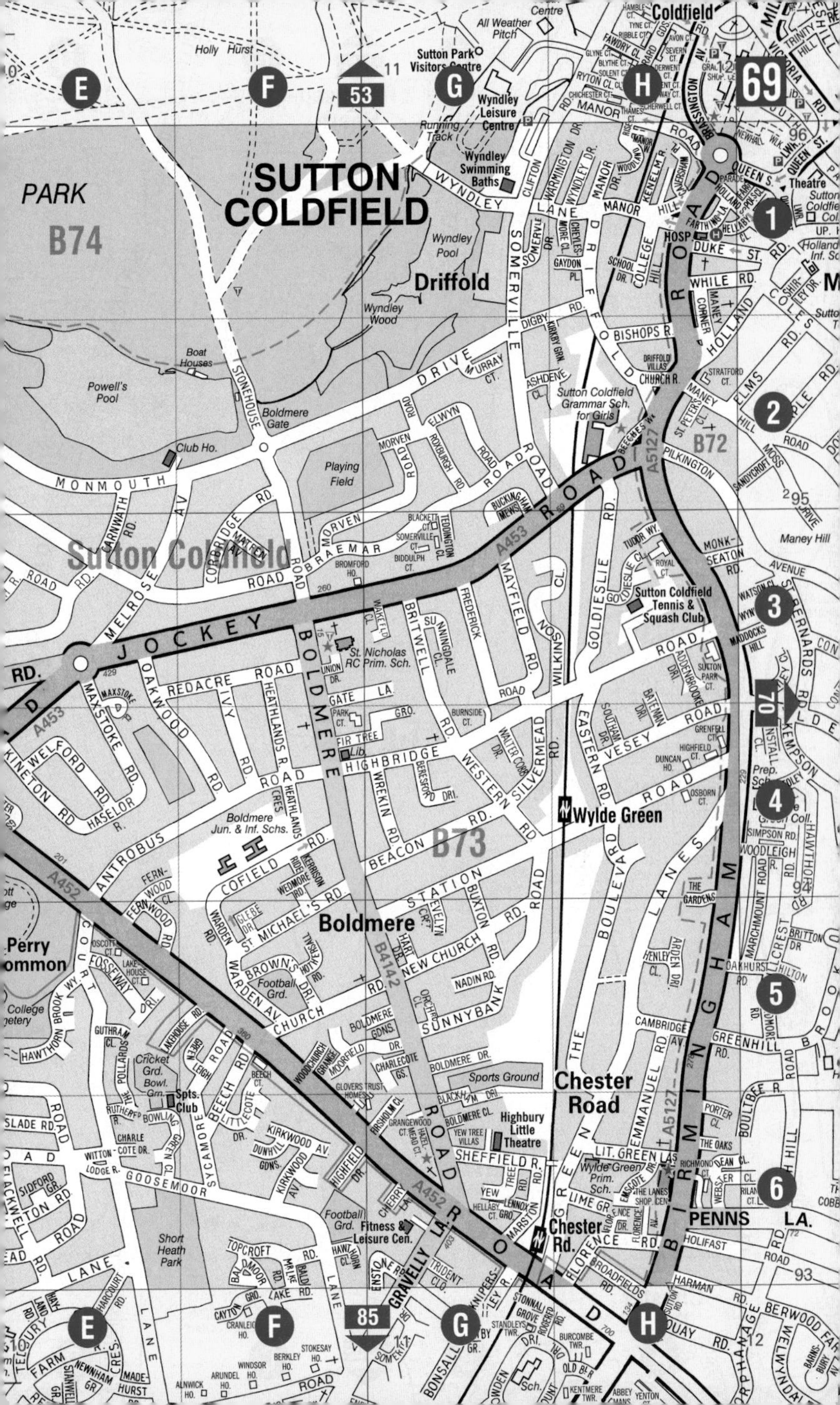
69
53
85
70
E
F
G
H
1
2
3
4
5
6
SUTTON
COLDFIELD
PARK
B74
B72
B73
Sutton Coldfield
Driffold
Boldmere
Chester
Road
Maney Hill
Perry
Holly Hurst
Sutton Park
Visitors Centre
All Weather
Pitch
Centre
Coldfield
Wyndley
Leisure
Centre
Running
Track
Wyndley
Swimming
Baths
Wyndley
Pool
Wyndley
Wood
Boat
Houses
Powell's
Pool
Boldmere
Gate
Club Ho.
Playing
Field
Sutton Coldfield
Grammar Sch.
for Girls
Sutton Coldfield
Tennis &
Squash Club
St. Nicholas
RC Prim. Sch.
Boldmere
Jun. & Inf. Schs.
Wylde Green
Football
Grd.
Sports Ground
Highbury
Little
Theatre
Wylde Green
Prim.
Sch.
Cricket
Grd.
Spts.
Club
Short
Heath
Park
Fitness &
Leisure Cen.
Chester
Rd.
Theatre
HOSP.
WYNDLEY LANE
MONMOUTH
DRIVE
JOCKEY RD.
ROAD
A453
A452
A5127
B4142
BIRMINGHAM ROAD
BOLDMERE ROAD
SOMERVILLE
DRIFFOLD
MANOR HILL
MANOR ROAD
COLLEGE HILL
SCHOOL DR.
DIGBY RD.
BISHOPS R.
CHURCH R.
DUKE ST.
WHILE RD.
HOLLAND
MANEY CORNER
ELMS RD.
PILKINGTON
MONK-SEATON RD.
AVENUE
ST BERNARDS RD.
MADDOCKS HILL
KEMPSON
STONEHOUSE
MELROSE AV
CARNWATH RD.
CORBRIDGE RD.
MATFEN AV
MORVEN ROAD
BRAEMAR ROAD
ELWYN ROAD
ROXBURGH RD.
BUCKINGHAM MEWS
MAYFIELD RD.
FREDERICK ROAD
BRITWELL RD.
SUNNINGDALE CL.
WILKINS CL.
GOLDIESLIE RD.
TUDOR WY.
REDACRE ROAD
OAKWOOD RD.
IVY RD.
HEATHLANDS R.
MAXSTOKE RD.
WELFORD RD.
KINETON RD
HASELOR R.
HIGHBRIDGE ROAD
GATE LA.
FIR TREE
WREKIN RD.
WESTERN RD
SILVERMEAD RD.
EASTERN RD
VESEY ROAD
ANTROBUS RD.
BEACON RD.
COFIELD RD.
STATION ROAD
BUXTON RD.
ST. MICHAEL'S RD.
BROWN'S DR.
NEW CHURCH RD.
CHURCH RD.
WARDEN AV
SUNNYBANK
BOULEVARD
LANES
THE GREEN
EMMANUEL RD.
CAMBRIDGE AV.
GREENHILL RD.
LIT. GREEN LA
LIME GR
FLORENCE RD.
BROADFIELDS RD.
PENNS LA.
HOLIFAST
HARMAN RD.
QUAY RD.
BERWOOD
GOOSEMOOR LANE
SYCAMORE
BEECH RD
GRAVELLY LA.
SHEFFIELD R.
MARSTON
KIRKWOOD AV.
TOPCROFT RD.
COURT
FOSSEWAY DRI.
SLADE RD.
WITTON LODGE R.
HAWTHORN BROOK WY.

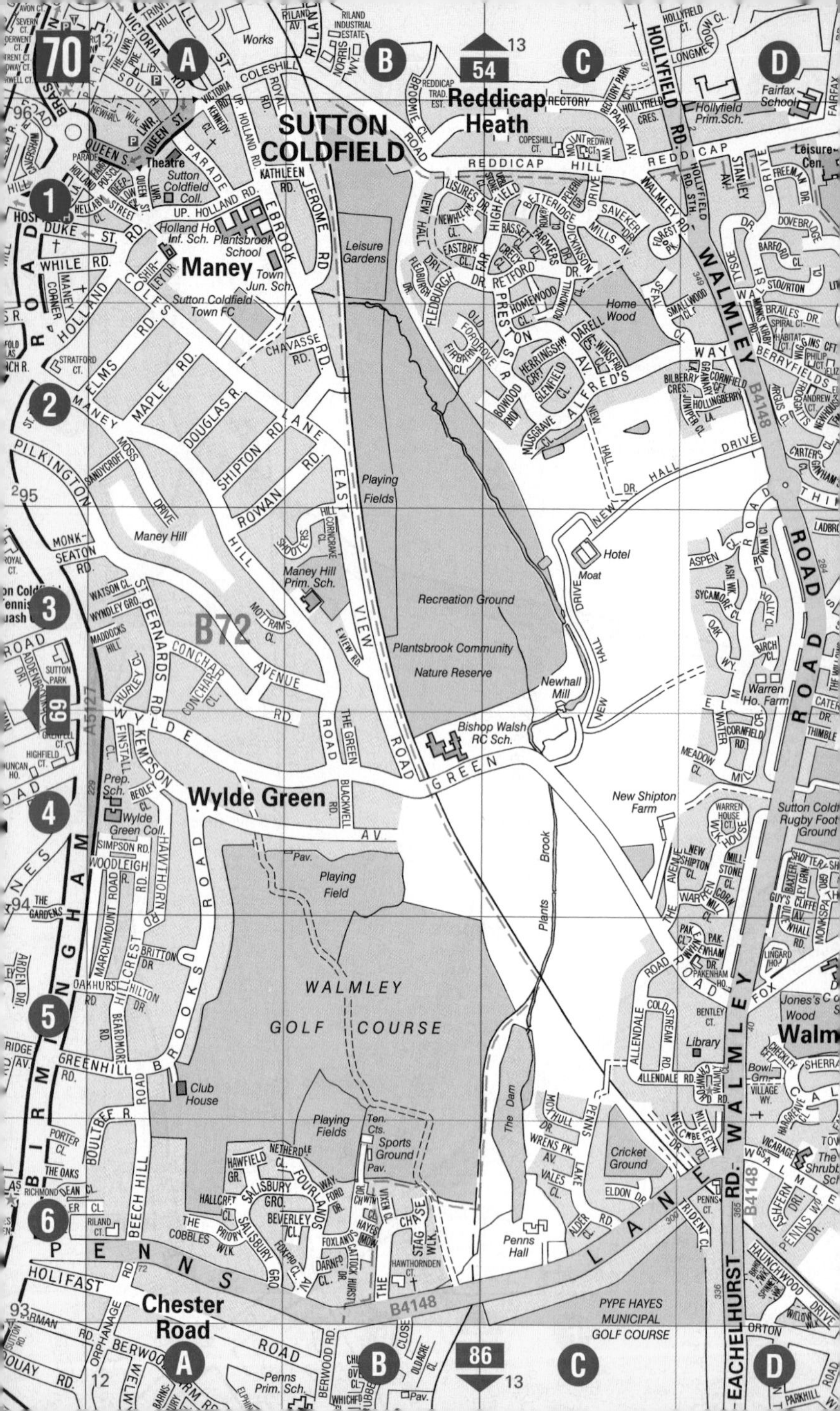

A
B
C
D
54
13
Reddicap Heath
SUTTON COLDFIELD
Works
RILAND INDUSTRIAL ESTATE
REDDICAP TRAD. EST.
Fairfax School
Hollyfield Prim.Sch.
Leisure Cen.
Theatre
Sutton Coldfield Coll.
Lib.
Holland Ho. Inf. Sch.
Plantsbrook School
Maney
Town Jun. Sch.
Sutton Coldfield Town FC
Leisure Gardens
Home Wood
1
2
3
4
5
6
95
94
93
96
B72
Maney Hill
Maney Hill Prim. Sch.
Playing Fields
Recreation Ground
Plantsbrook Community Nature Reserve
Hotel
Moat
Newhall Mill
Bishop Walsh RC Sch.
Wylde Green
Prep. Sch.
Wylde Green Coll.
New Shipton Farm
Warren Ho. Farm
Sutton Coldfield Rugby Football Ground
Playing Field
WALMLEY GOLF COURSE
Club House
Playing Fields
Ten. Cts.
Sports Ground
Pav.
The Dam
Plants Brook
Cricket Ground
Penns Hall
Library
Jones's Wood
Walm
PYPE HAYES MUNICIPAL GOLF COURSE
Chester Road
Penns Prim. Sch.
86
12
13
69
A5127
B4148
SUTTON COLDFIELD
PARADE
QUEEN ST.
COLESHILL ST.
REDDICAP HILL
HOLLYFIELD RD.
WALMLEY ROAD
PENNS LANE
CHESTER ROAD
BIRMINGHAM ROAD
WYLDE GREEN ROAD
EAST VIEW ROAD
MANEY HILL ROAD
BROOKS ROAD
HOLLAND ROAD
NEW HALL DRIVE
EACHELHURST RD.
WALMLEY RD.

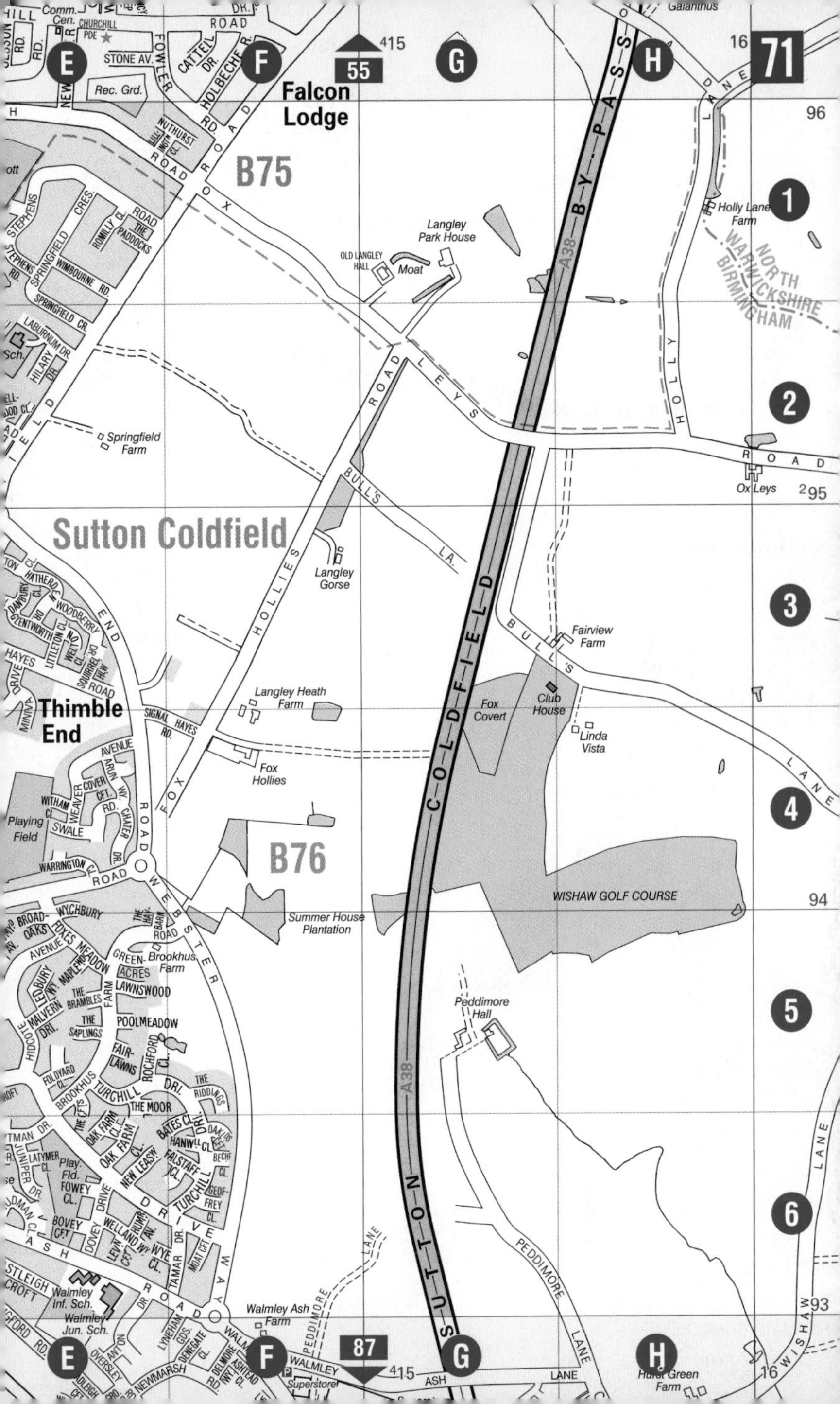

E F G H 16

Comm. Cen. CHURCHILL PDE.
CHURCHILL
STONE AV.
FOWLER RD.
CATTELL DR.
HOLBECHE RD.
ROAD

55

415

96

Falcon Lodge

Rec. Grd.

B75

1

Holly Lane Farm

Langley Park House

OLD LANGLEY HALL
Moat

NORTH WARWICKSHIRE BIRMINGHAM

Springfield Farm

2

LEYS

A38 BY-PASS

ROAD
Ox Leys
95

Sutton Coldfield

HOLLIES

BULL'S LA.

Langley Gorse

3

Fairview Farm

BULL'S

Thimble End

SIGNAL
HAYES RD.

Langley Heath Farm

Fox Hollies

Fox Covert

Club House

Linda Vista

COLDFIELD

4

Playing Field

WEBSTER

B76

WARRINGTON ROAD

Summer House Plantation

WISHAW GOLF COURSE

94

GREEN
Brookhus Farm

LAWNSWOOD

POOLMEADOW

FAIR-LAWNS

BROOKHUS

TURCHILL

THE MOOR

RIDDINGS

Peddimore Hall

5

Walmley Inf. Sch.
Walmley Jun. Sch.

Walmley Ash Farm

87

415
ASH

WALMLEY

Superstore

PEDDIMORE LANE

WISHAW LANE

Hurst Green Farm

6

93

E F G H 16

84
A
B
56
385
C
D
93
The Park Farm
Cherry Cottage
Smestow Barn
Loneacre
GORSE LANE
FEIASHILL ROAD
Works
Wolverhampton
WV5
Hartford House
B4176
SMESTOW GATE
BRIDGNORTH
POOL
WOODFORD
North Lodge
WOMBOURNE ENTERPRISE PARK
Works
Smestow Grange Farm
Smestow Gate Farm
SMESTOW LA.
92
SWINDON GOLF COURSE
CHAPEL LA.
Blackhill Plantation
Smestow
Smestow Mill
Smestow Wildlife Cen.
Club House
NEW ROAD
MILL LA.
New Road Farm
Church Cottage Farm
Depot
New Lodge
CHURCH
Pine View
91
Whitehouse Plantation
Kidderminster
FOREST COVERT
DY7
Whitehouse Farm
LANE
South Lodge
Old Plantation
THE
ROAD
WHITEHOUSE
290
HIGHGATE COMMON COUNTRY PARK
90
CHASEPOOL
Chasepool

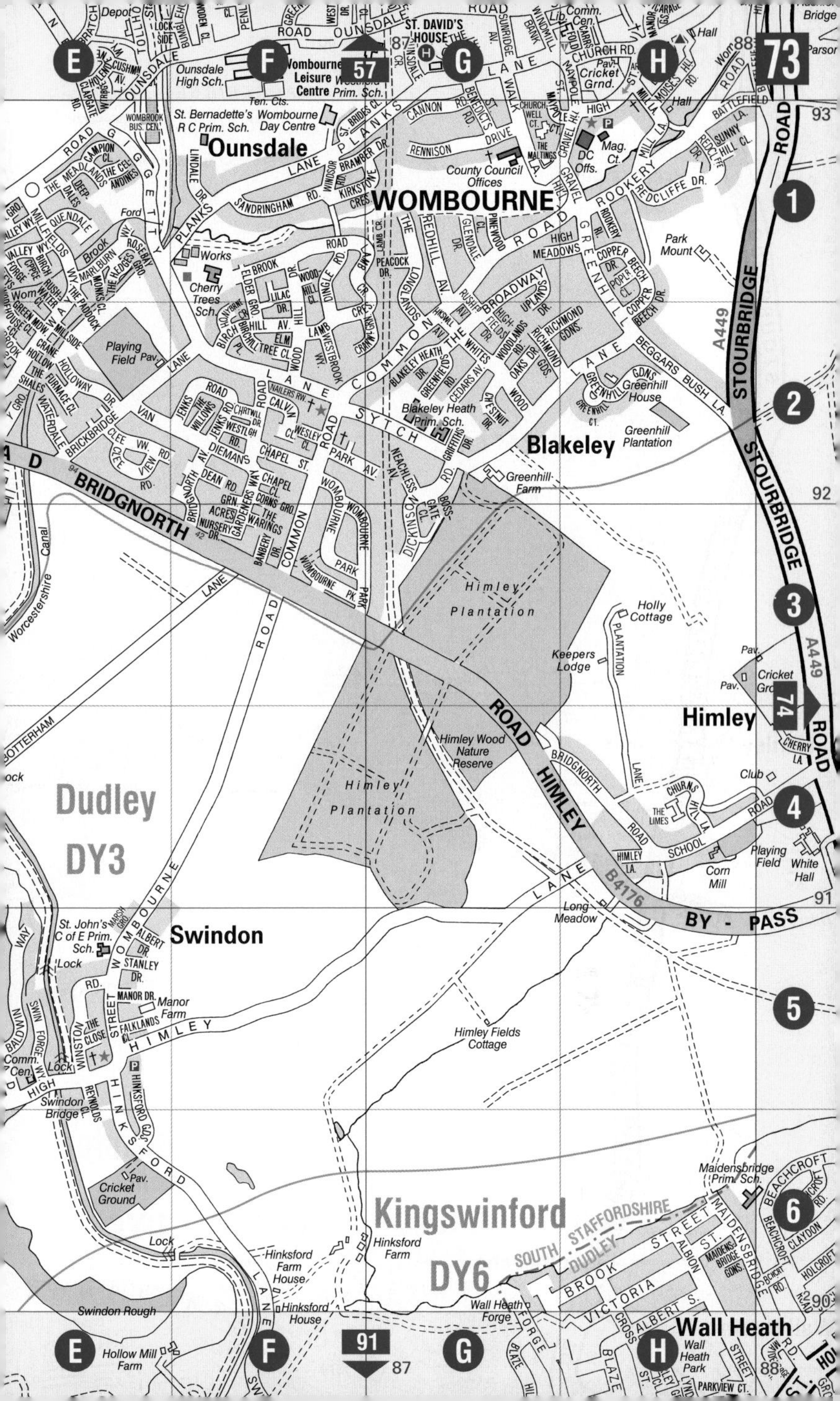

WOMBOURNE
Ounsdale
Blakeley
Himley
Swindon
Wall Heath
Dudley
DY3
Kingswinford
DY6
Wombourne Leisure Centre
Ounsdale High Sch.
St. Bernadette's R C Prim. Sch.
Wombourne Day Centre
County Council Offices
DC Offs.
Mag. Ct.
Cherry Trees Sch.
Playing Field
Blakeley Heath Prim. Sch.
Greenhill House
Greenhill Plantation
Greenhill Farm
Himley Plantation
Himley Wood Nature Reserve
Holly Cottage
Keepers Lodge
Park Mount
Cricket Grnd.
The Limes
Corn Mill
White Hall
Long Meadow
Himley Fields Cottage
St. John's C of E Prim. Sch.
Manor Farm
Swindon Bridge
Cricket Ground
Hinksford Farm
Hinksford Farm House
Hinksford House
Swindon Rough
Hollow Mill Farm
Wall Heath Forge
Wall Heath Park
Maidensbridge Prim. Sch.
Worcestershire Canal
BRIDGNORTH ROAD
STOURBRIDGE ROAD
A449
B4176
HIMLEY ROAD
BY - PASS
SOUTH STAFFORDSHIRE
DUDLEY
57
91
74

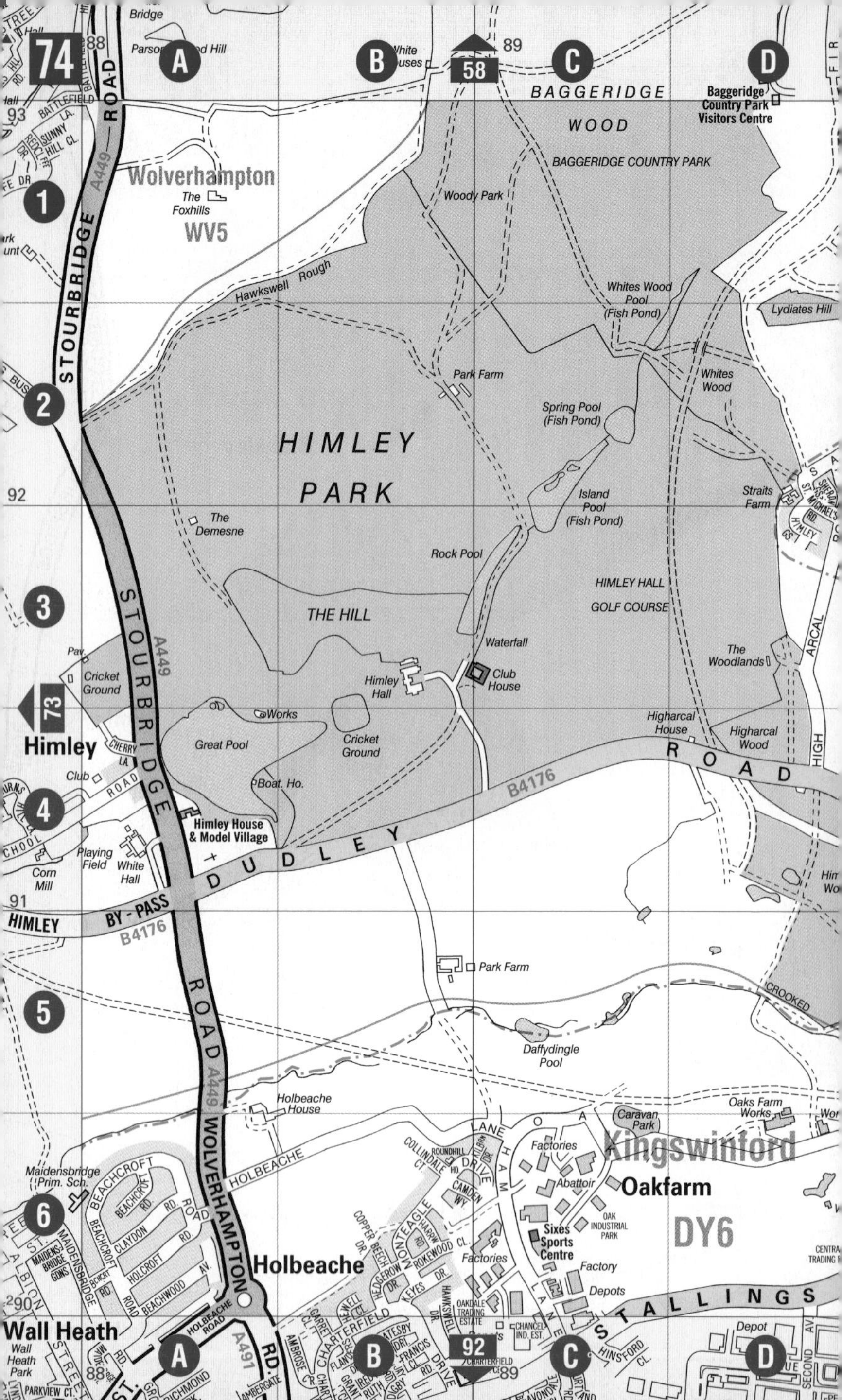
A
B
C
D
1
2
3
4
5
6
58
73
92
88
89
93
92
91
90
Bridge
White Houses
BAGGERIDGE
WOOD
Baggeridge Country Park Visitors Centre
BAGGERIDGE COUNTRY PARK
Wolverhampton
The Foxhills
WV5
Woody Park
Hawkswell Rough
Whites Wood Pool (Fish Pond)
Lydiates Hill
Park Farm
Whites Wood
Spring Pool (Fish Pond)
HIMLEY PARK
Island Pool (Fish Pond)
Straits Farm
The Demesne
Rock Pool
HIMLEY HALL GOLF COURSE
THE HILL
Waterfall
Club House
Himley Hall
The Woodlands
Cricket Ground
Works
Great Pool
Higharcal House
Higharcal Wood
Boat. Ho.
Himley House & Model Village
Pav.
Himley
Club
Playing Field
White Hall
Corn Mill
STOURBRIDGE ROAD
A449
DUDLEY ROAD
B4176
HIMLEY BY-PASS
WOLVERHAMPTON ROAD
ARCAL
HIGH
CHERRY LA.
Park Farm
CROOKED
Daffydingle Pool
Holbeache House
Caravan Park
Oaks Farm Works
Kingswinford
Oakfarm
DY6
Factories
Abattoir
OAK INDUSTRIAL PARK
Sixes Sports Centre
Factory
Depots
Maidensbridge Prim. Sch.
HOLBEACHE
BEACHCROFT
CLAYDON RD.
HOLCROFT RD.
BEACHWOOD AV.
MAIDENSBRIDGE
Holbeache
Wall Heath
Wall Heath Park
PARKVIEW CT.
RICHMOND
A491
CHARTERFIELD
STALLINGS
Depot
HINSFORD CL.
OAKDALE TRADING ESTATE
CHANCEL IND. EST.
COLLINDALE CT.
ROUNDHILL
CAMDEN WY.
COPPER BEECH DR.
MONTEAGLE
ROKEWOOD CL.
HEDGEROW DR.
KEYES DR.
HAWKSWELL DR.
AMBROSE CR.
SUNNY HILL CL.
BATTLEFIELD LA.

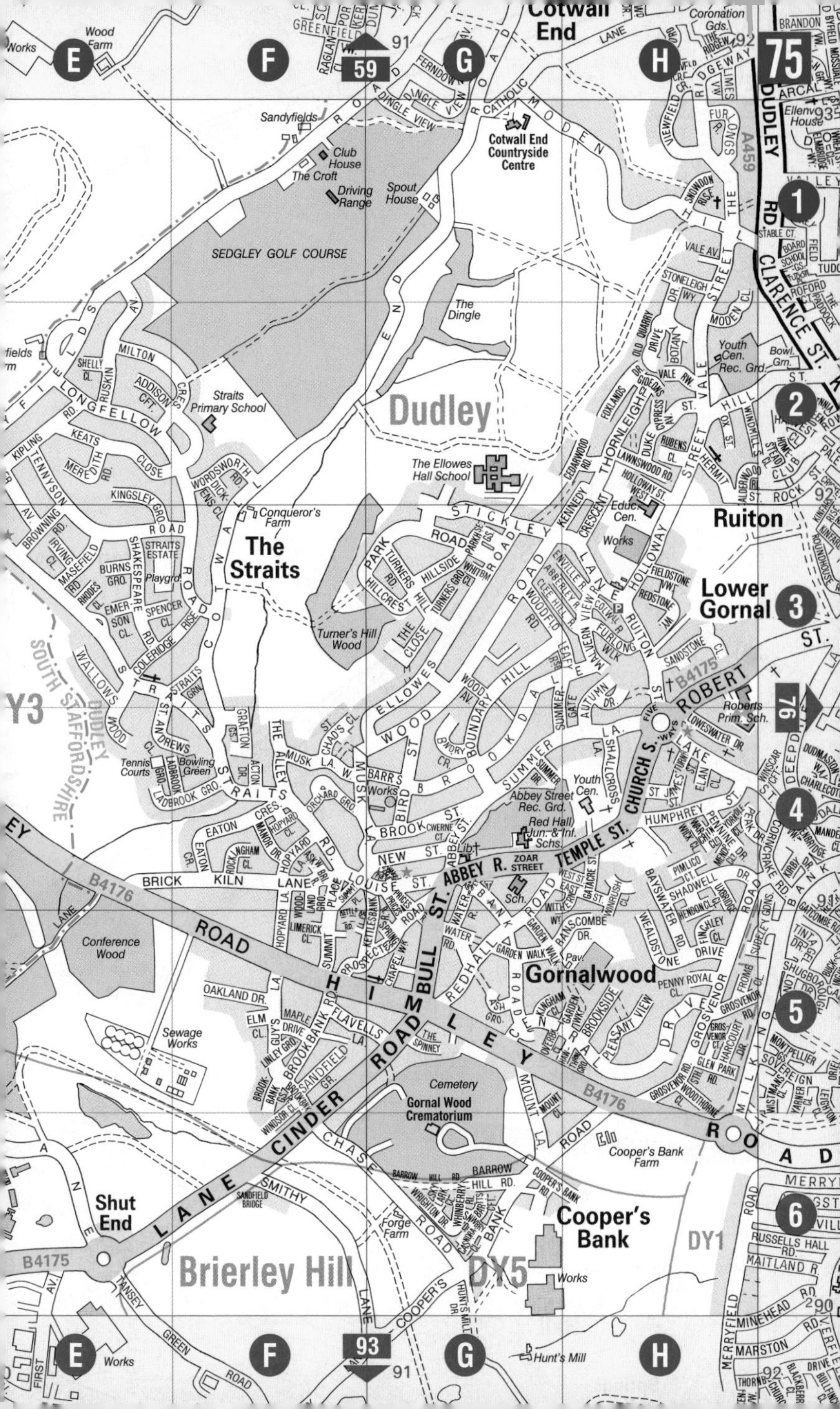
E
F
G
H
59
91
93
76
1
2
3
4
5
6
Cotwall End
Coronation Gds.
Wood Farm
Works
Sandyfields
Club House
The Croft
Driving Range
Spout House
SEDGLEY GOLF COURSE
Cotwall End Countryside Centre
The Dingle
Straits Primary School
Dudley
The Ellowes Hall School
Conqueror's Farm
The Straits
STRAITS ESTATE
Playgrd.
Turner's Hill Wood
Educ. Cen.
Works
Ruiton
Lower Gornal
Youth Cen.
Rec. Grd.
Bowl. Grn.
Ellenvale House
Roberts Prim. Sch.
Tennis Courts
Bowling Green
Barrs Works
Youth Cen.
Abbey Street Rec. Grd.
Red Hall Jun. & Inf. Schs.
Zoar Street Sch.
Conference Wood
Sewage Works
Gornalwood
Cemetery
Gornal Wood Crematorium
Cooper's Bank Farm
Shut End
Forge Farm
Cooper's Bank
Works
Brierley Hill
DY5
DY1
Y3
Hunt's Mill
SOUTH STAFFORDSHIRE
DUDLEY
SEDGLEY ROAD
CATHOLIC LANE
MODEN
COTWALL END ROAD
RIDGEWAY
LONGFELLOW RD.
MILTON CRES.
STICKLEY LANE
THORNLEIGH
HOLLOWAY
RUITON
ROBERT ST.
CHURCH ST.
TEMPLE ST.
ABBEY R.
BULL ST.
HIMLEY ROAD
BRICK KILN LANE
STRAITS RD.
BROOKDALE
WOOD ST.
ELLOWES
CINDER ROAD
LANE
CHASE
SMITHY
BARROW HILL RD.
COOPER'S BANK
MOUNT LA.
PENNY ROYAL CL.
GROSVENOR
MILKING BANK
CLARENCE ST.
DUDLEY RD.
A459
B4175
B4176
MERRYFIELD
RUSSELLS HALL RD.
MAITLAND R.
MINEHEAD RD.
MARSTON RD.
TANSEY GREEN ROAD

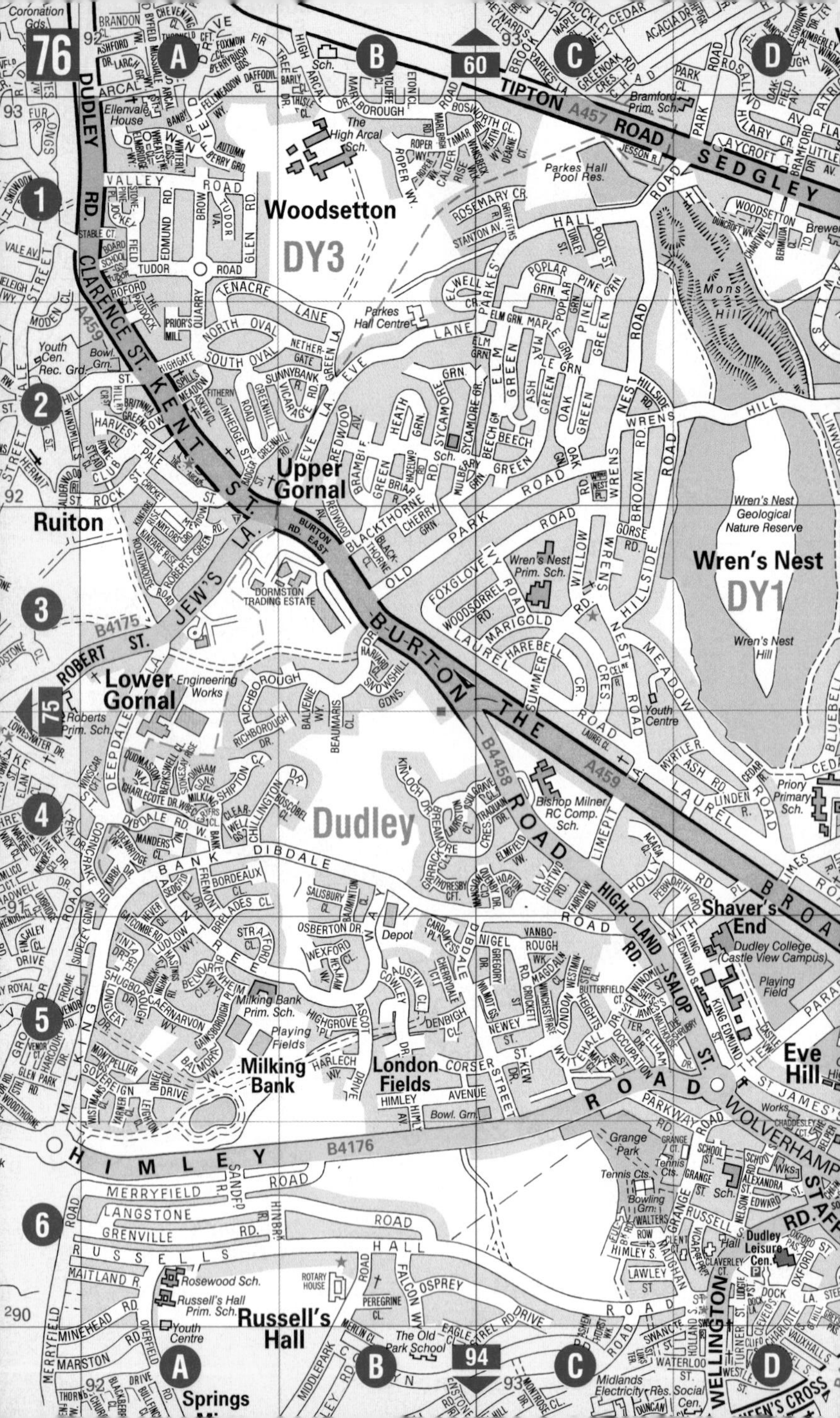
76
A
B
C
D
60
1
2
3
4
5
6
75
94
Woodsetton
DY3
Upper Gornal
Ruiton
Lower Gornal
Dudley
Wren's Nest
DY1
Wren's Nest Geological Nature Reserve
Wren's Nest Hill
Mons Hill
Shaver's End
Eve Hill
Milking Bank
London Fields
Russell's Hall
Springs
Grange Park
TIPTON ROAD
SEDGLEY ROAD
A457
A459
B4175
B4458
B4176
DUDLEY RD.
CLARENCE ST.
KENT ST.
BURTON ROAD
THE BROADWAY
HIMLEY ROAD
JEW'S LA.
ROBERT ST.
HIGHLAND RD.
SALOP ST.
WOLVERHAMPTON ST.
STAFFORD ST.
WELLINGTON RD.
The High Arcal Sch.
Ellenvale House
Parkes Hall Pool Res.
Parkes Hall Centre
Bramford Prim. Sch.
Wren's Nest Prim. Sch.
Dormston Trading Estate
Engineering Works
Roberts Prim. Sch.
Bishop Milner RC Comp. Sch.
Priory Primary Sch.
Dudley College (Castle View Campus)
Playing Field
Youth Centre
Milking Bank Prim. Sch.
Playing Fields
Depot
Bowl. Grn.
Tennis Cts.
Bowling Grn.
Dudley Leisure Cen.
Rosewood Sch.
Russell's Hall Prim. Sch.
Rotary House
The Old Park School
Midlands Electricity Res.
Social Cen.
Youth Cen. Rec. Grd.

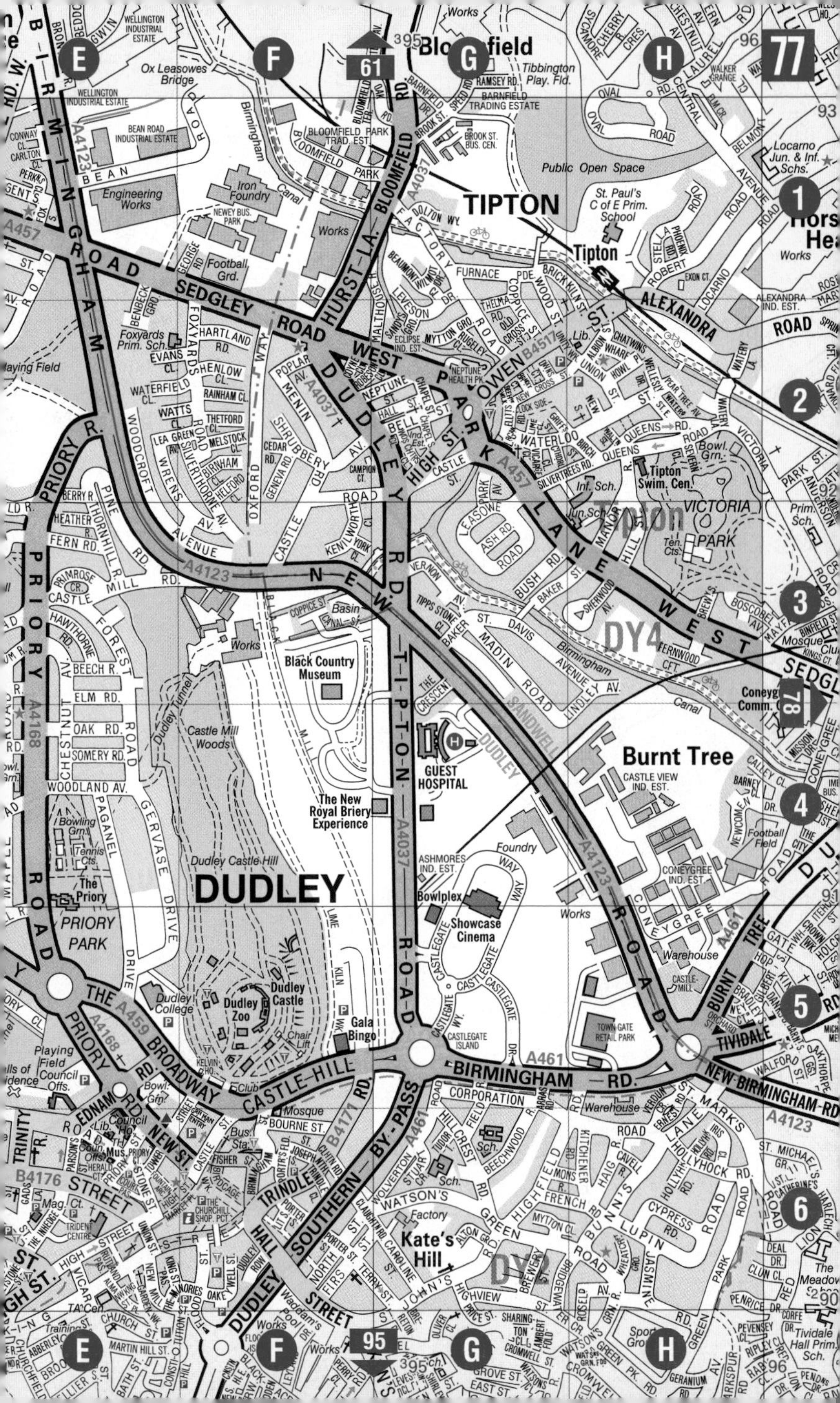

Bloomfield
Tibbington Play. Fld.
Wellington Industrial Estate
Ox Leasowes Bridge
Bean Road Industrial Estate
Engineering Works
Iron Foundry
Bloomfield Park Trad. Est.
Barnfield Trading Estate
Brook St. Bus. Cen.
Public Open Space
TIPTON
St. Paul's C of E Prim. School
Locarno Jun. & Inf. Schs.
Tipton
Works
Football Grd.
Foxyards Prim. Sch.
Playing Field
Alexandra Ind. Est.
Sedgley Road West
Dudley Road
Park Lane West
Owen St.
Neptune Health Pk.
Tipton Swim. Cen.
Victoria Park
Inf. Sch.
Jun. Sch.
Ten. Cts.
Prim. Sch.
New Road
Priory Road
Castle Mill Rd.
Black Country Museum
Basin
DY4
Birmingham Canal
Coneygree Comm.
Burnt Tree
Castle View Ind. Est.
Dudley Tunnel
Castle Mill Woods
Guest Hospital
The New Royal Briery Experience
Tipton Road
Football Field
Dudley Castle Hill
DUDLEY
Foundry
Ashmores Ind. Est.
Bowlplex
Showcase Cinema
Coneygree Ind. Est.
Works
Warehouse
The Priory
Priory Park
Dudley College
Dudley Zoo
Dudley Castle
Chair Lift
Gala Bingo
Castlegate Island
Town Gate Retail Park
Tividale
Birmingham Rd.
New Birmingham Rd.
The Broadway
Castle Hill
Southern By-Pass
Playing Field
Council Offs.
Mosque
Bus. Sta.
Lib.
Council Ho.
Mus.
Trident Centre
The Churchill Shop. Pct.
Factory
Kate's Hill
DY2
Training Cen.
Wadam's Pool
Sports Grd.
The Meadows
Tividale Hall Prim. Sch.
61
78
95

A
B
C
D
1
2
3
4
5
6
62
77
96
Horseley Heath
TIPTON
Tipton
DY4
Dudley Port
Tividale
Oldbury
B69
Tree
UPPER CHURCH LANE
LOWER CHURCH LA.
ALEXANDRA RD.
HORSELEY RD.
HORSELEY HEATH
HORSELEY
NEW ROAD
GREAT WESTERN
TAME RD.
SHEEPWASH LA.
PORT
SEDGLEY ROAD EAST
TIPTON ROAD
DUDLEY PORT
DUDLEY ROAD WEST
DUDLEY ROAD
NEW BIRMINGHAM ROAD
BURNT TREE
TEMPLE WAY
CITY ROAD
A461
A457
A4033
A4123
B4517
B4163
B4166
CEMETERY
Alexandra High Sch. & Sixth Form Centre
Tipton College
Joseph Turner Primary School
Locarno Jun. & Inf. Schs.
Works
ALEXANDRA IND. EST.
HALE TRADING EST.
GREAT BRIDGE WEST IND. CEN.
Sheepwash Nature Reserve
River Tame
VICTORIA PARK
Bowl. Grn.
Prim. Sch.
The Mosque
Mosque
Club
Liby.
Coneygree Comm. Cen.
IMEX BUS. PK.
Football Field
VAUGHAN TRADING ESTATE
Netherton Tunnel Branch
Depot
Tividale Road Bri.
CLETON ST. BUS. PK.
Aqueduct
Bus Depot
Foundry
Warehouse
Tividale Park
Tividale Prim. Sch.
Burnt Tree Prim. Sch.
Football Ground
Tividale High School & Comm. Coll.
Tividale Comm. Rec. Cen.
Sports Ground
Cycle Race Track
Fishers Bridge
Locks
The Meadows School
Tividale Hall Prim. Sch.
Library
Brad Villa

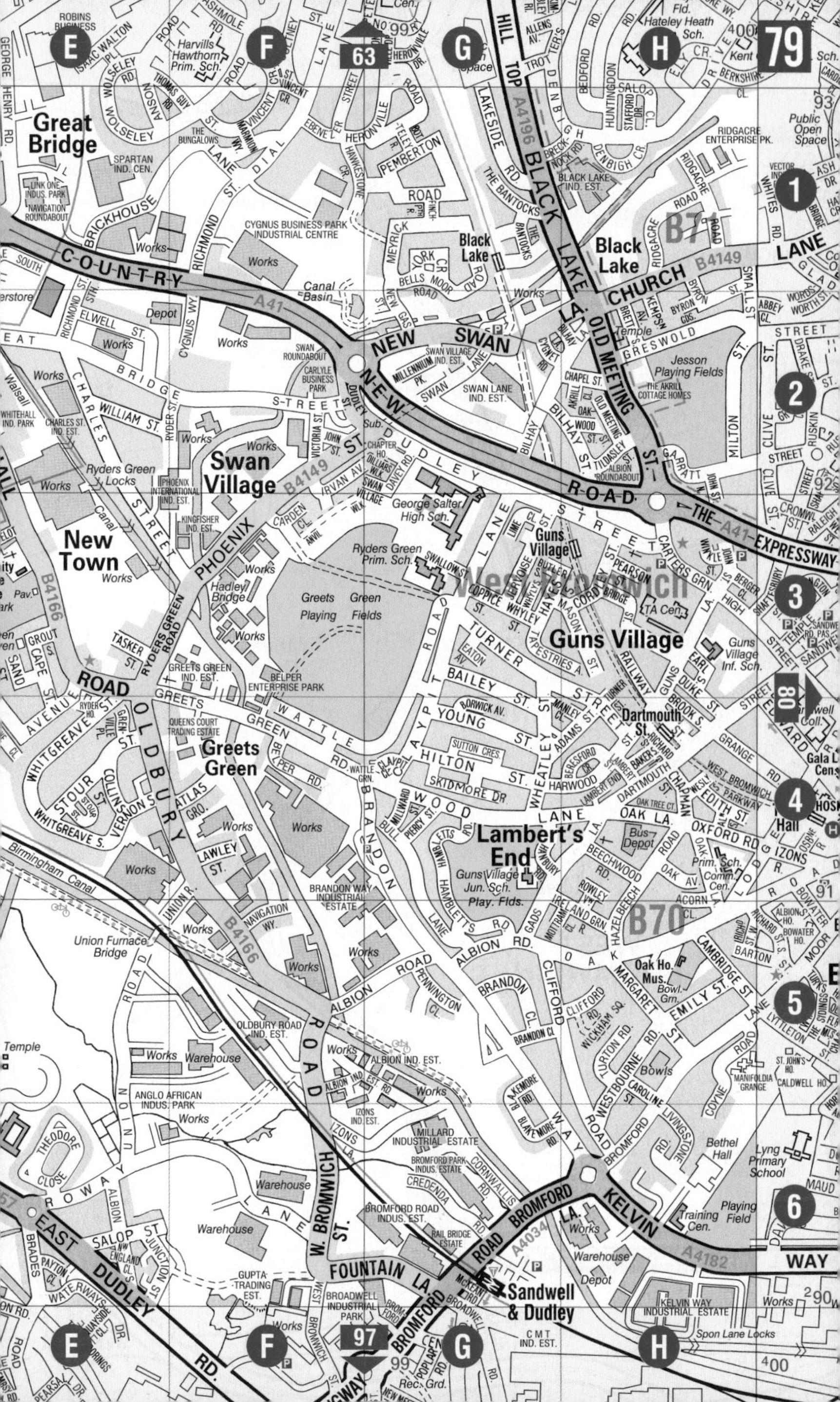

Great Bridge
Swan Village
New Town
Greets Green
Black Lake
Guns Village
West Bromwich
Lambert's End
Sandwell & Dudley
COUNTRY ROAD
NEW SWAN LANE
BLACK LAKE
HILL TOP
OLD MEETING ST.
CHURCH LANE
PHOENIX STREET
OLDBURY ROAD
WATTLE GREEN RD.
BRANDON WAY
W. BROMWICH ST.
KELVIN WAY
BROMFORD RD.
EAST DUDLEY RD.
THE EXPRESSWAY
A41
A4196
A4182
A4034
B4149
B4166
B71
B70
Cygnus Business Park Industrial Centre
George Salter High Sch.
Ryders Green Prim. Sch.
Greets Green Playing Fields
Jesson Playing Fields
Guns Village Jun. Sch. Play. Flds.
Guns Village Inf. Sch.
Oak Ho. Mus.
Lyng Primary School
Bethel Hall
Harvills Hawthorn Prim. Sch.
Hateley Heath Sch.
Birmingham Canal
Ryders Green Locks
Spon Lane Locks
Union Furnace Bridge
Kelvin Way Industrial Estate
Brandon Way Industrial Estate
Millard Industrial Estate
Anglo African Indus. Park
Bus Depot
Works
Warehouse
Depot
63
97
80
E
F
G
H
1
2
3
4
5
6

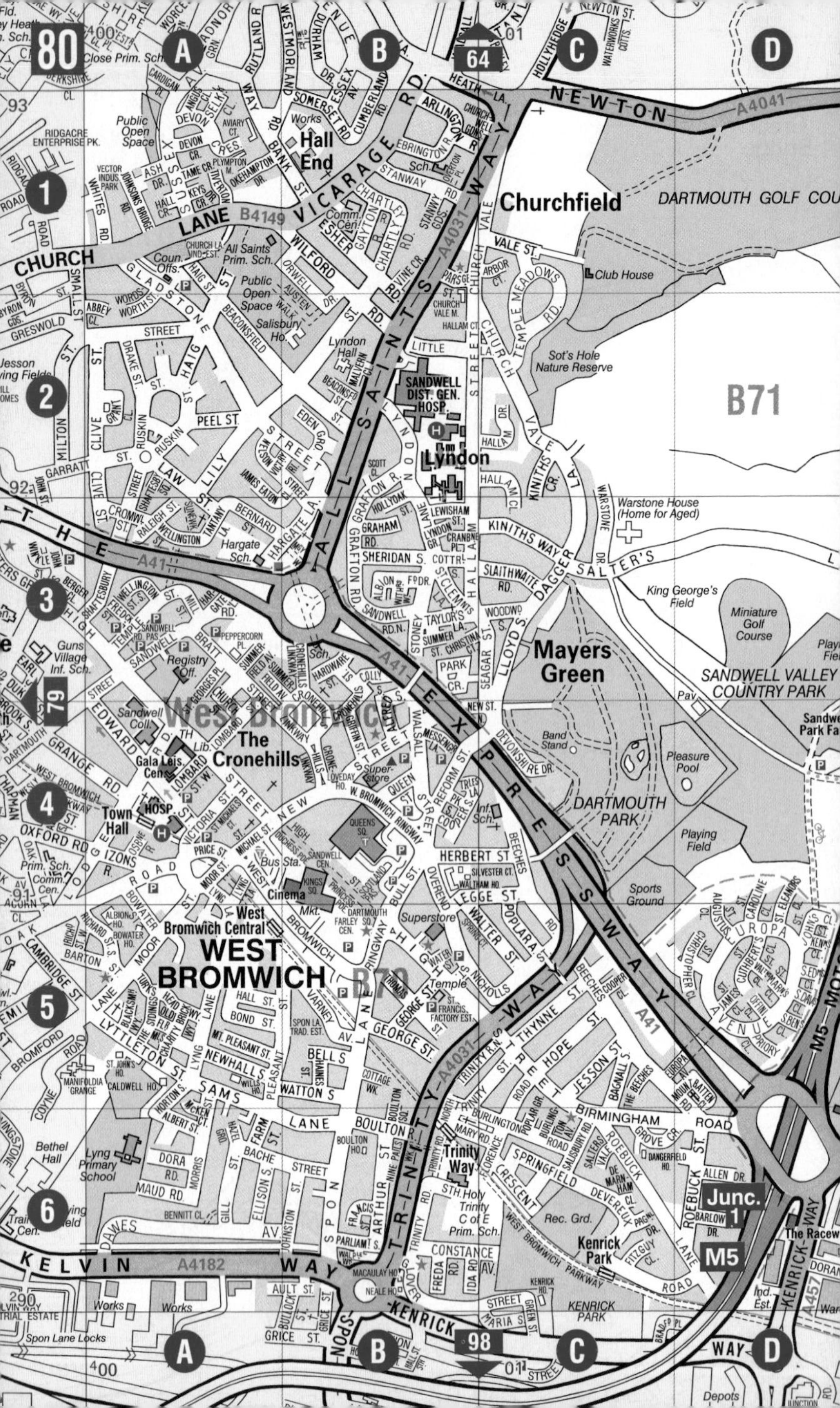
64
A
B
C
D
1
2
3
4
5
6
Hall End
Churchfield
DARTMOUTH GOLF COU
Sot's Hole Nature Reserve
B71
Lyndon
SANDWELL DIST. GEN. HOSP.
Warstone House (Home for Aged)
King George's Field
Miniature Golf Course
Mayers Green
SANDWELL VALLEY COUNTRY PARK
West Bromwich
The Cronehills
DARTMOUTH PARK
Pleasure Pool
Playing Field
Sports Ground
WEST BROMWICH
B70
79
VICARAGE RD.
CHURCH LANE B4149
ALL SAINTS WAY A4031
NEWTON A4041
THE EXPRESSWAY A41
TRINITY WAY A4031
KELVIN WAY A4182
BIRMINGHAM ROAD
Trinity Way
Kenrick Park
Junc. 1
M5
KENRICK WAY A457
Lyng Primary School
Bethel Hall
West Bromwich Central
Town Hall
Gala Leis. Cen.
Sandwell Coll.
Registry Off.
Hargate Sch.
Guns Village Inf. Sch.
Club House
Band Stand
Rec. Grd.
KENRICK PARK
Spon Lane Locks
98

West Bromwich Crematorium
E
F
G
H
65
M5
M5 MOTORWAY
FORGE LANE
Forge Farm
Forge Mill Farm
River Tame
Sandwell Valley Country Park
B43
Nature Cen.
RSPB Sandwell Valley Nature Reserve
Forge Mill Lake
Hamstead Hall School
Comm. Cen.
Tanhouse Centre & Library
Jun. & Inf. Schs.
BROOKSIDE
Bridleway
EADGAR CT.
ACFOLD
CHALCOT
CRAYTHORNE
PARK LANE
Sailing Cen.
Swan Pool
Priory Woods Nature Reserve
B20
HANDSWORTH GOLF COURSE
Fish Pond
Club House
Park Farm
HILLTOP GOLF COURSE
Birmingham
82
BIRMINGHAM
SANDWELL
SILVERCROFT
Sports Ground
Benedictine Priory (site of)
Holy Well
AVENUE
THE LEVERRETTS
CRADLEY CROFT
WILKS GRN.
POSEY CL.
St. John Wall RC School
OXHILL
SANDWELL PARK GOLF COURSE
HANDSWORTH CEMETERY
Bowl. Grn.
LARCH AV.
FRIARY GDS.
OXHILL RD.
LANE
ROAD
B21
COPTHALL RD.
LINCHMERE RD.
CRANBROOK RD.
LANDGATE R.
FELL GRO.
BUSH GR.
A4040
Prim. Sch.
GREENHILL RD.
AVENUE RD.
FARNHAM RD.
UPLANDS
NEWCOMBE ROAD
ROAD
FARCROFT RD.
FARCROFT GR.
AYLESFORD R.
MERVYN RD.
ASTLEY RD.
AYLESFORD RD.
HOLLYCROFT
CLENT R.
ALBION RD.
GRAFTON RD.
Handsworth
SANDWELL RD.
CAMP LANE
RALEIGH
RALEIGH IND. EST.
Wks. Train. Cen.
Sandwell Rec. Grd.
Bakery
PARK LANE IND. EST.
Pav.
Rec. Grd.
MINGHAM
A41
ROAD
HOLYHEAD
ISLAND RD.
Government Offices
BOUNDARY PL.
MILTON DR.
CL.
Depot
Depot
Sandwell Academy
Albion Jun. Sch.
COLLIERY RD.
LANE
West Bromwich Albion FC (The Hawthorns)
HAWTHORNS INDUSTRIAL ESTATE
Training Centre
MIDDLEMORE RD.
PADDINGTON R.
MALVERN RD.
SAMPSON CL.
AUSTIN RD.
LAWNSWOOD GR.
ONIBURY
NIJON CL.
WESTBOURNE
RD.
CARLTON AV.
SINGH CL.
St. James' C of E Prim. Sch.
REGENT ROAD
NEW INNS CL.
MILTON RD.
BERD DR.
Hamilton School
Oaklands Sports & Social Cen.
Sports Ground
Bowling Green
HALFORD'S LA.
ALBION RD.
LONES RD.
STEPHENS RD.
ST. STEPHENS RD.
The Hawthorns
99
MIDDLEMORE INDUSTRIAL ESTATE
WINCHESTER GR.
BELMONT
GREEN
CLEEA
ROAD
HOLYHEAD WAY
1
2
3
4
5
6
03
04
93
92
02

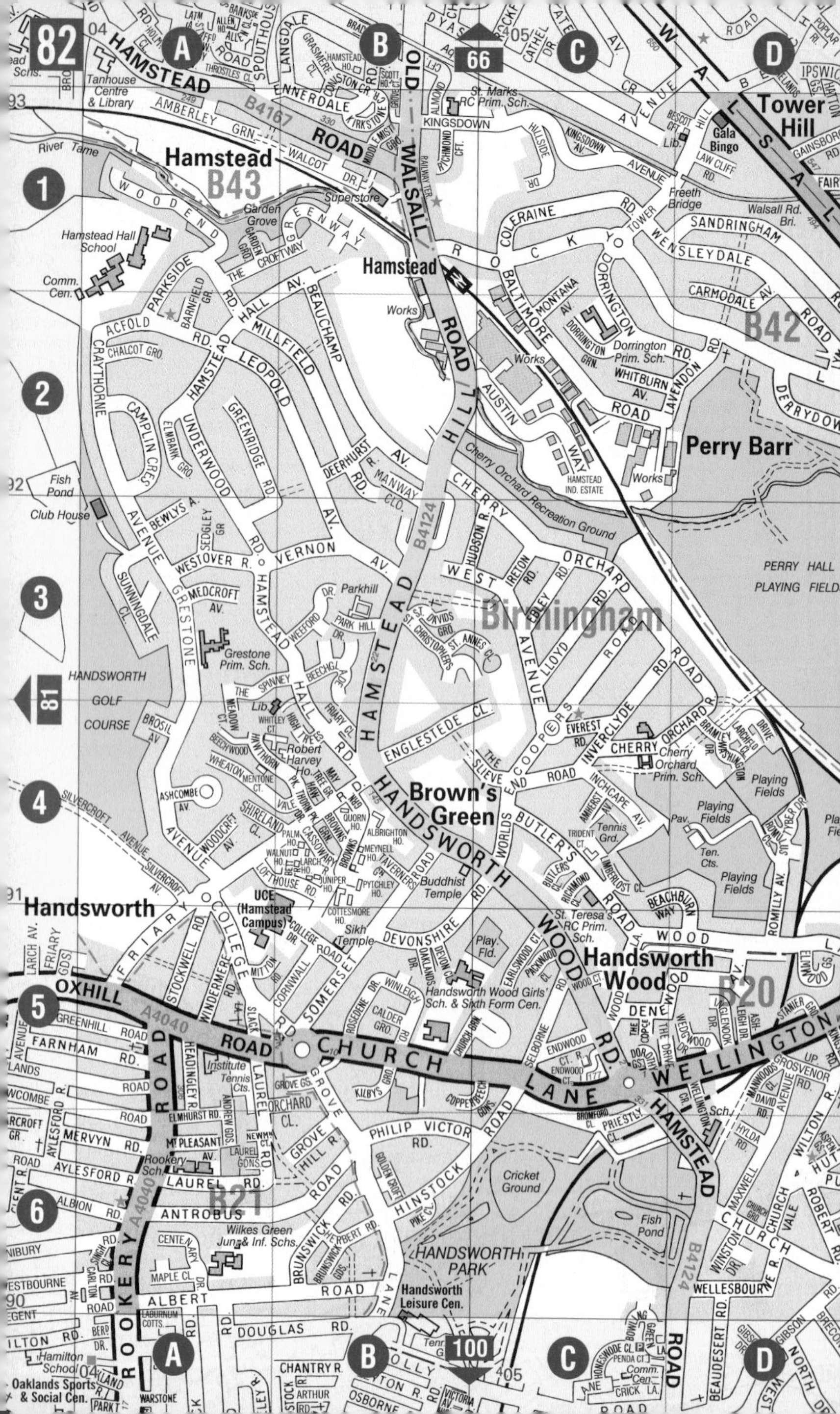

HAMSTEAD ROAD
Tanhouse Centre & Library
AMBERLEY GRN.
Hamstead
B43
River Tame
WOODEND
Hamstead Hall School
Comm. Cen.
PARKSIDE
BARNFIELD GR.
ACFOLD RD.
CHALCOT GRO.
CRAYTHORNE
HAMSTEAD HALL AV.
MILLFIELD
BEAUCHAMP
LEOPOLD
UNDERWOOD
GREENRIDGE RD.
CAMPLIN CRES.
ELMBANK GRO.
Fish Pond
Club House
BEWLYS A.
SEDGLEY GR.
WESTOVER R.
VERNON AV.
MEDCROFT AV.
GRESTONE
SUNNINGDALE CL.
Grestone Prim. Sch.
HANDSWORTH GOLF COURSE
81
BROSIL AV.
ASHCOMBE AV.
SILVERCROFT AVENUE
WOODCROFT AV.
SHIRELAND CL.
UCE (Hamstead Campus)
Handsworth
FRIARY RD.
COLLEGE
STOCKWELL RD.
OXHILL ROAD
A4040
CHURCH ROAD
B4167
ENNERDALE
WALCOT DR.
Superstore
Garden Grove
GREENWAY
THE CROFTWAY
OLD WALSALL ROAD
Hamstead
Works
HAMSTEAD HILL ROAD
B4124
St. Marks RC Prim. Sch.
KINGSDOWN
KINGSDOWN AV.
AVENUE
ROCKY LANE
COLERAINE RD.
BALTIMORE
MONTANA AV.
DORRINGTON RD.
Dorrington Prim. Sch.
WHITBURN AV.
AUSTIN WAY
HAMSTEAD IND. ESTATE
Perry Barr
Cherry Orchard Recreation Ground
CHERRY ORCHARD
WEST AV.
PERRY HALL PLAYING FIELDS
Birmingham
Parkhill
ST. DAVIDS GRO.
ST. CHRISTOPHERS
ST. ANNES CL.
ENGLESTEDE CL.
HANDSWORTH WOOD ROAD
Brown's Green
Buddhist Temple
Sikh Temple
DEVONSHIRE RD.
Play. Fld.
Handsworth Wood Girls' Sch. & Sixth Form Cen.
St. Teresa's RC Prim. Sch.
Handsworth Wood
B20
WELLINGTON ROAD
Cherry Orchard Prim. Sch.
Playing Fields
Tennis Grd.
Cricket Ground
Fish Pond
HANDSWORTH PARK
Handsworth Leisure Cen.
100
66
Tower Hill
Gala Bingo
Freeth Bridge
Walsall Rd. Bri.
SANDRINGHAM
WENSLEYDALE
CARMODALE AV.
B42
B21
ROOKERY ROAD
A4040
Rookery Sch.
Wilkes Green Jun. & Inf. Schs.
ANTROBUS
ALBERT ROAD
DOUGLAS RD.
Hamilton School
Oaklands Sports & Social Cen.
PHILIP VICTOR RD.
HINSTOCK ROAD
GROVE
LAUREL
HAMSTEAD RD.
CHURCH VALE
WELLESBOURNE R.
BEAUDESERT RD.
A
B
C
D
1
2
3
4
5
6

Perry
Birmingham Alexander Sports Stadium
Perry Reservoir (Boating)
Leisure Gardens
Bowling Green
M6
PERRY PARK
Playground
Playing Field
Hall of Remembrance
Birmingham Crematorium
Warehouses
Perry Barr Locks
Motorway Maintenance Depot
PAPER MILL END
PAPER MILL END INDUSTRIAL ESTATE
Superstore
Moor Lane Sports Ground
Birmingham Canal
CONTAINERBASE
Works
Depot
THE POPLARS INDUSTRIAL ESTATE
M6 MOTORWAY
COLLEGE
ROAD
KINGSTANDING
B44
B4138
A453
A34
Sports Ground
Perry Bridge
River Tame
TAMEBRIDGE INDUSTRIAL ESTATE
Refuse Disposal Works
MOOR LANE IND. EST.
B6
BROOKVALE TRADING ESTATE
HOLFORD IND. PK.
Perry Barr Stadium (Greyhound)
ALDRIDGE
HOLFORD
THE COPPICE
Corporation Bus Depot
Playing Field
OSCOTT GARDENS
ONE STOP SHOPPING CEN.
UCE (Perry Barr Campus)
Perry Barr
A4040
ASTON
Witton
Works
ATLAS ESTATE
IMI HQ
Holy Trinity C of E Prim. Sch.
Birchfield
Leisure Cen.
Broadway Sch.
Lib.
Westminster Prim. Sch.
Birchfield Prim. Sch.
Sacred Heart RC Prim. Sch.
Cricket & Football Ground
Aston Villa FC (Villa Park)
Mus.
Yew Tree Comm. Sch.
B4140
B4137
Buddhist Temple
ASTON
Aston Hall
ASTON PARK
Hindu Temple
WITTON
LANE

67
84
101

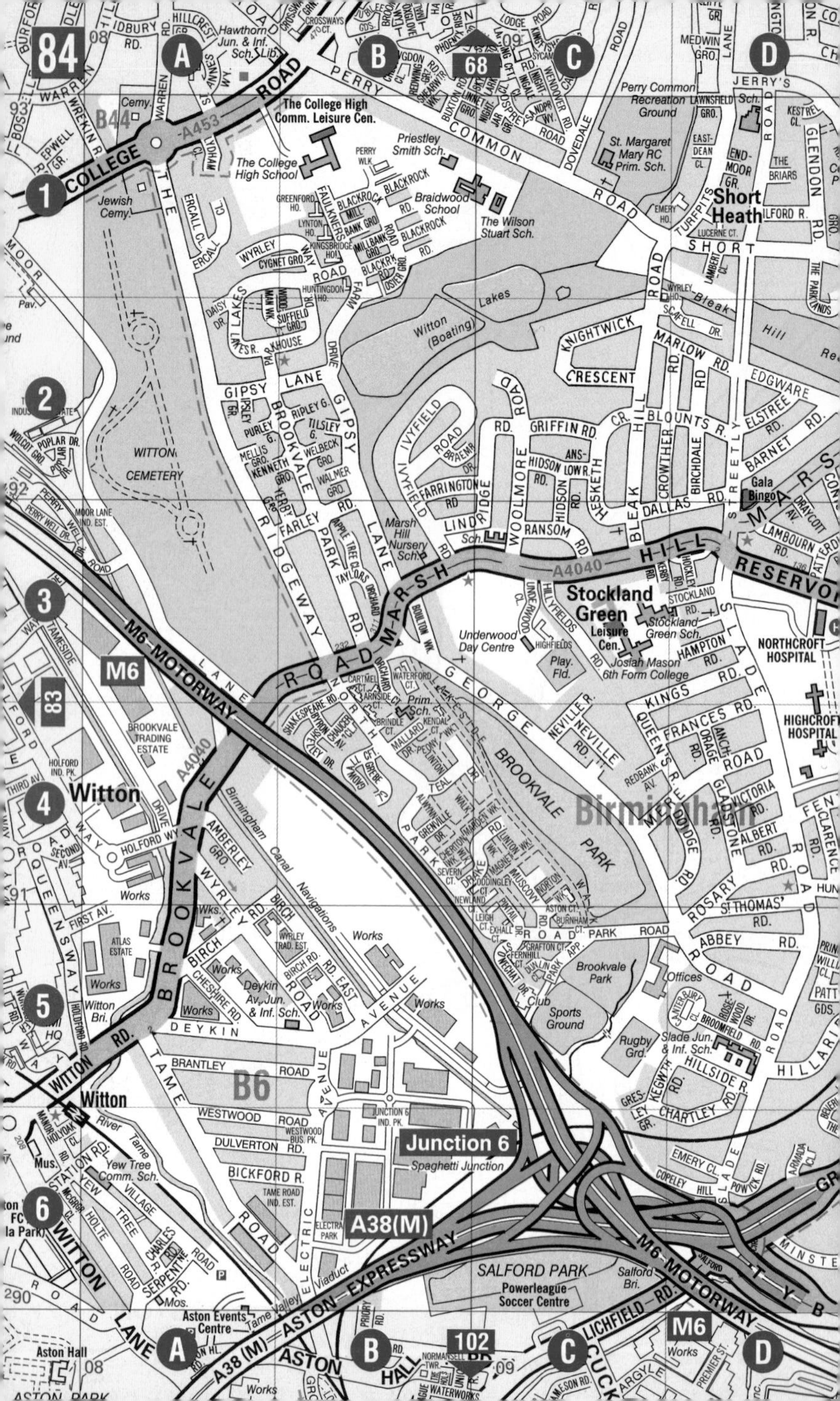
68
83
102
A
B
C
D
1
2
3
4
5
6
COLLEGE ROAD
PERRY COMMON ROAD
The College High Comm. Leisure Cen.
The College High School
Priestley Smith Sch.
Braidwood School
The Wilson Stuart Sch.
Hawthorn Jun. & Inf. Sch.
Jewish Cemy.
Perry Common Recreation Ground
St. Margaret Mary RC Prim. Sch.
Short Heath
Witton (Boating) Lakes
WITTON CEMETERY
GIPSY LANE
BROOKVALE ROAD
RIDGEWAY
MARSH HILL
A4040
A453
B44
B6
M6 MOTORWAY
M6
Stockland Green
Stockland Green Sch.
Stockland Green Leisure Cen.
Josiah Mason 6th Form College
Underwood Day Centre
NORTHCROFT HOSPITAL
HIGHCROFT HOSPITAL
Gala Bingo
BROOKVALE PARK
Birmingham
Witton
BROOKVALE TRADING ESTATE
Birmingham Canal Navigations
Deykin Av. Jun. & Inf. Sch.
Brookvale Park
Sports Ground
Rugby Grd.
Slade Jun. & Inf. Sch.
Junction 6
Spaghetti Junction
A38(M)
ASTON EXPRESSWAY
SALFORD PARK
Powerleague Soccer Centre
Salford Bri.
Aston Events Centre
Aston Hall
ASTON PARK
Yew Tree Comm. Sch.
WITTON LANE
LICHFIELD RD.
ASTON HALL RD.
Tame Valley Viaduct

E
F
G
H
1
2
3
4
5
6
69
103
86
Erdington
ERDINGTON
Gravelly Hill
Birches Green
Chester Rd.
B23
B24
Short Heath Park
Erdington Reservoir
Rookery Park
Abbey RC Jun. & Inf. Sch.
St. Edmund Campion RC School
Highclere Sch.
St. Barnabas C of E Prim. Sch.
The Queensbury School
Kingsbury School
Kingsbury Leisure Cen.
Birches Green Jun. & Inf. Schs.
St. Mary & St. John RC Prim. Sch.
Yenton Jun. & Inf. Schs.
School Playing Fields
Playing Field
Playing Fields
HASTINGWOOD IND. PARK
BROMFORD MILLS INDUSTRIAL ESTATE
THE FORT SHOPPING PARK
Bus Depot
Works
Warehouse
Tanks
BROMFORD GATE
GRAVELLY HILL NORTH
SUTTON NEW ROAD
HIGH ST. SUTTON
SUMMER RD.
STATION ROAD
ORPHANAGE ROAD
SIX WAYS
WOOD END RD.
BROMFORD LANE
KINGSBURY ROAD
TYBURN ROAD
FORT PARKWAY
A38
A4040
A452
A5127
A47
B4142
B4531

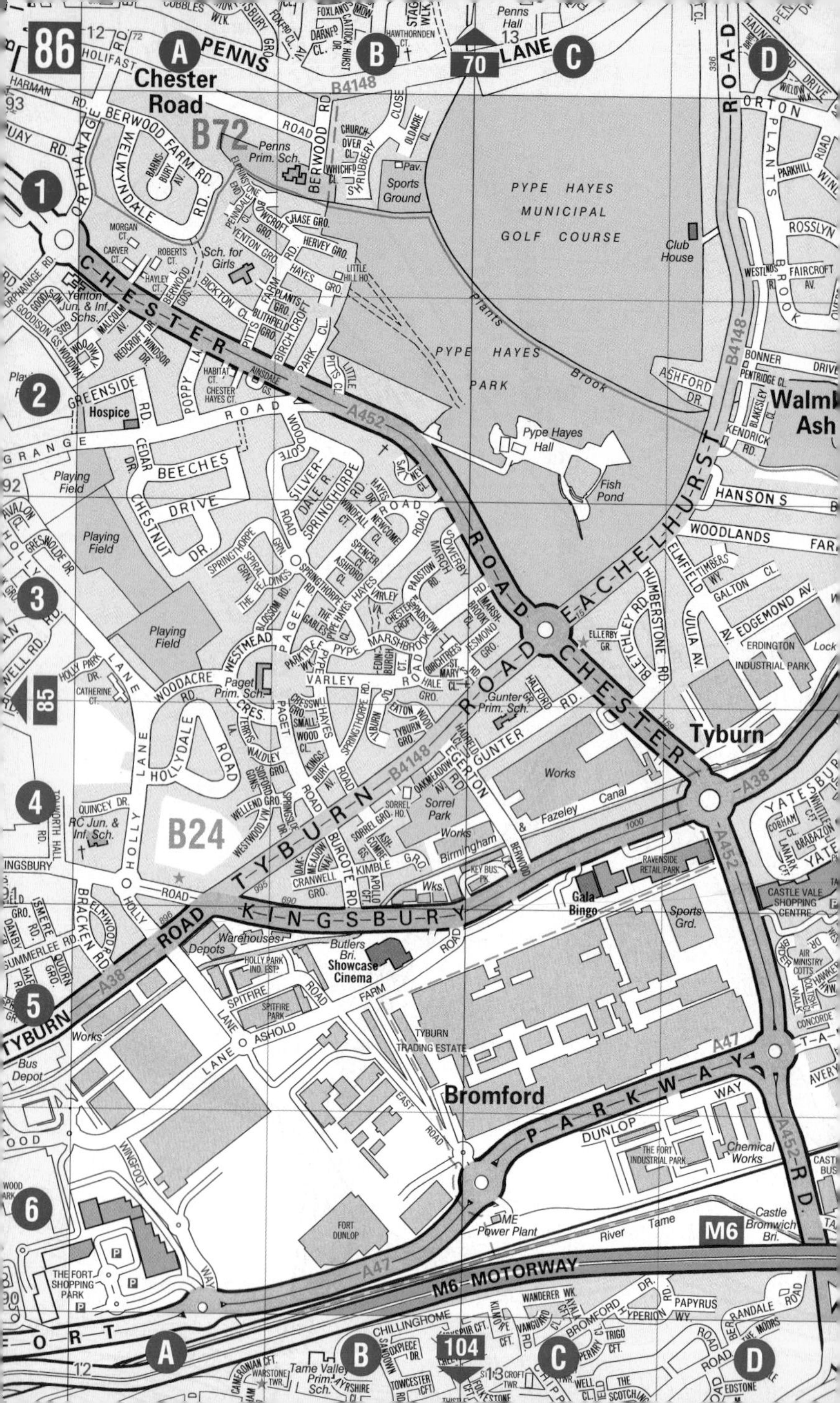

PENNS LANE
Chester Road
B72
Penns Prim. Sch.
Sports Ground
PYPE HAYES MUNICIPAL GOLF COURSE
Club House
Sch. for Girls
Yenton Jun. & Inf. Schs.
CHESTER ROAD
PYPE HAYES PARK
Plants Brook
Pype Hayes Hall
Fish Pond
Hospice
GRANGE ROAD
Playing Field
BEECHES DRIVE
CHESTNUT DR.
Paget Prim. Sch.
Gunter Prim. Sch.
EACHELHURST ST
Walmley Ash
WOODLANDS
ERDINGTON INDUSTRIAL PARK
Tyburn
Works
Birmingham & Fazeley Canal
Sorrel Park
B24
RC Jun. & Inf. Sch.
TYBURN ROAD
KINGSBURY ROAD
RAVENSIDE RETAIL PARK
Gala Bingo
Sports Grd.
CASTLE VALE SHOPPING CENTRE
Warehouses
Depots
Butlers Bri.
Showcase Cinema
HOLLY PARK IND. EST.
SPITFIRE PARK
TYBURN TRADING ESTATE
Bromford
PARKWAY
DUNLOP WAY
THE FORT INDUSTRIAL PARK
Chemical Works
Bus Depot
FORT DUNLOP
Power Plant
River Tame
Castle Bromwich Bri.
M6
M6 MOTORWAY
A47
THE FORT SHOPPING PARK
FORT PARKWAY
Tame Valley Prim. Sch.
A452
A38
B4148

70
85
104

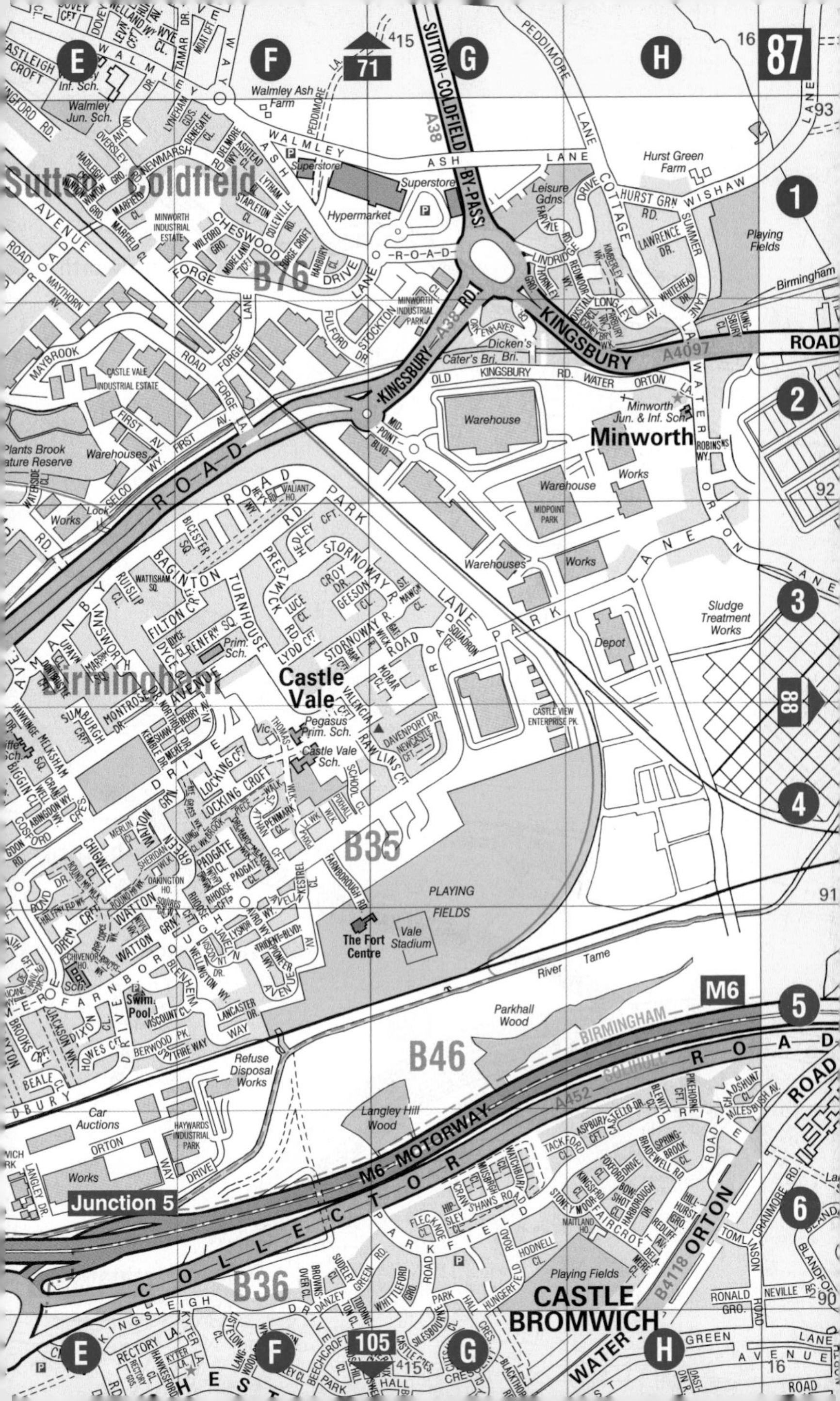
87
71
105
88
E
F
G
H
1
2
3
4
5
6
16
93
92
91
90
415
Sutton Coldfield
Birmingham
Castle Vale
Minworth
CASTLE BROMWICH
B76
B35
B46
B36
A38
A4097
A452
B4118
M6
Junction 5
M6 MOTORWAY
SUTTON COLDFIELD BY-PASS
KINGSBURY RD.
KINGSBURY ROAD
WALMLEY ASH LANE
WALMLEY ROAD
PEDDIMORE LANE
COTTAGE LANE
WISHAW LANE
HURST GRN. RD.
LAWRENCE DR.
SUMMER LANE
WATER ORTON LANE
OLD KINGSBURY RD.
PARK LANE
FORGE LANE
CHESWOOD DRIVE
TURNHOUSE ROAD
FARNBOROUGH ROAD
COLLECTOR ROAD
BIRMINGHAM ROAD
SOLIHULL ROAD
CHESTER ROAD
ORTON WAY
WATER ORTON
PARKFIELD ROAD
HESTER
KINGSLEIGH DRIVE
Walmley Ash Farm
Walmley Inf. Sch.
Walmley Jun. Sch.
Superstore
Hypermarket
Leisure Gdns.
Hurst Green Farm
Playing Fields
MINWORTH INDUSTRIAL ESTATE
MINWORTH INDUSTRIAL PARK
CASTLE VALE INDUSTRIAL ESTATE
Dicken's Bri.
Cater's Bri.
Warehouse
Warehouses
Works
Lock
Plants Brook Nature Reserve
Minworth Jun. & Inf. Sch.
MIDPOINT PARK
Sludge Treatment Works
Depot
CASTLE VIEW ENTERPRISE PK.
Prim. Sch.
Pegasus Prim. Sch.
Castle Vale Sch.
PLAYING FIELDS
The Fort Centre
Vale Stadium
River Tame
Parkhall Wood
Swim. Pool
Refuse Disposal Works
Car Auctions
HAYWARDS INDUSTRIAL PARK
Langley Hill Wood
Playing Fields

Wiggins Hill Farm
Curdworth Bridge
Curdworth Church Bridge
Wigginshill Road Bridge
Broad Balk Bridge
Playing Fields
Playing Field
Birmingham & Fazeley Canal
KINGSBURY BUSINESS PARK
KINGSBURY ROAD
A4097
Curdworth
Filter Beds
SEWAGE WORKS
Sutton Coldfield
B76
ORTON LANE
Conduit
River Tame
Sludge Treatment Works
Works
Depot
Water Orton
MINWORTH RD.
MARSH
Parkhall Wood
BIRMINGHAM ROAD B4118
PLANK LANE
Water Orton
The Green
Water Orton Prim. Sch.
M6
M6 MOTORWAY
COLLECTOR ROAD
A452
Lanchester Park
Park Hall School
Forest Oak School
Lanchester School
B36
Bosworth Wood Prim. Sch.
Attleboro' Farm
Junction 4a
87
106
A
B
C
D
1
2
3
4
5
6
16
17
93
92
91
90

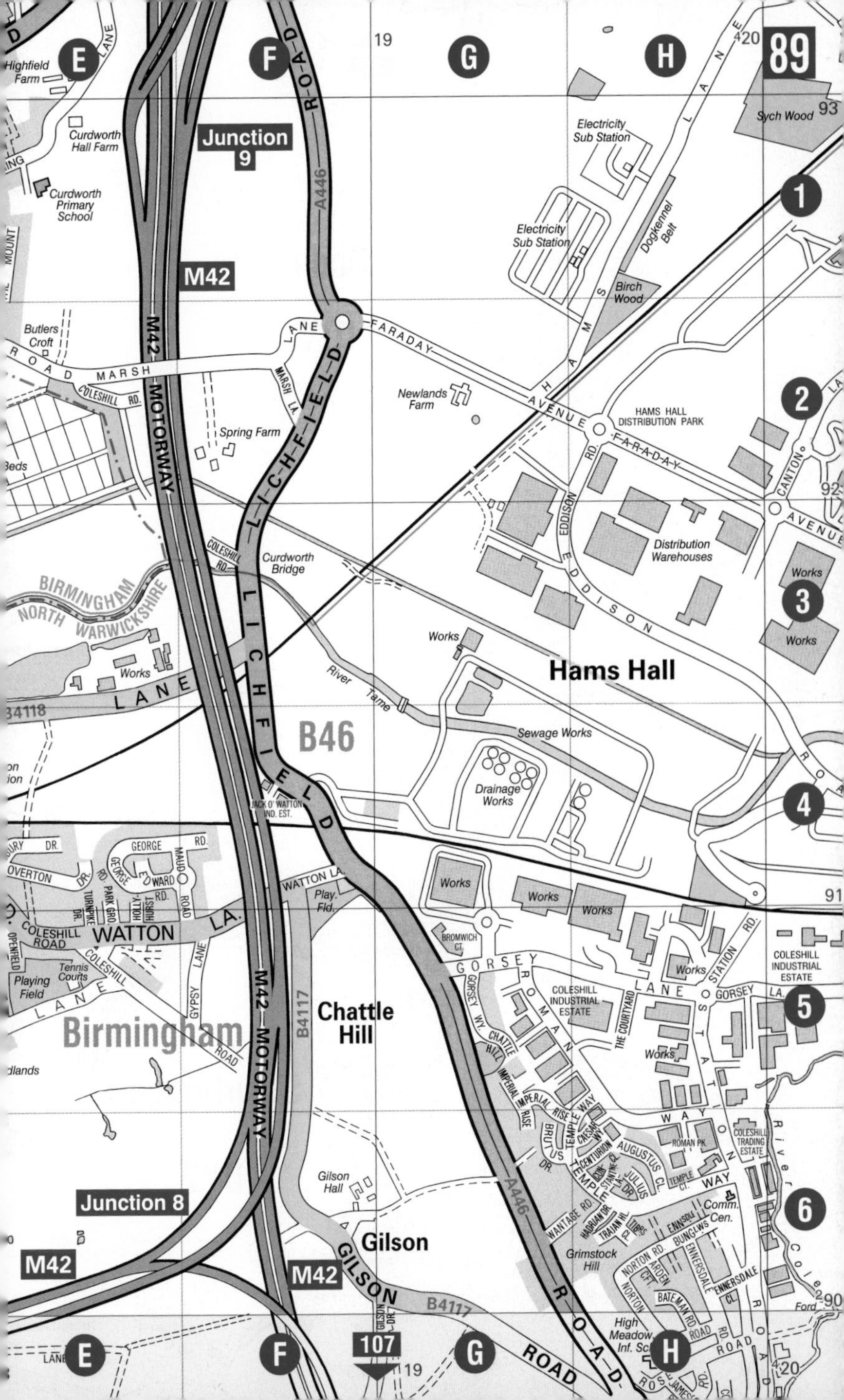
E
F
G
H
19
420
93
Sych Wood
Highfield Farm
Curdworth Hall Farm
Curdworth Primary School
Junction 9
M42
A446
LICHFIELD ROAD
Electricity Sub Station
Electricity Sub Station
Dogkennel Belt
Birch Wood
HAMS LANE
1
Butlers Croft
MARSH LANE
FARADAY AVENUE
MARSH LA.
COLESHILL RD.
Newlands Farm
Spring Farm
M42 MOTORWAY
HAMS HALL DISTRIBUTION PARK
2
CANTON
EDDISON RD.
92
Distribution Warehouses
Works
3
Works
Curdworth Bridge
BIRMINGHAM
NORTH WARWICKSHIRE
Works
Works
River Tame
Hams Hall
B4118
B46
Sewage Works
Drainage Works
4
JACK O' WATTON IND. EST.
GEORGE RD.
OVERTON DR.
WARD RD.
MAUD ROAD
TURNPIKE DR.
PARK GRO.
HOLLYOAK
HURST RD.
WATTON LA.
Play. Fld.
Works
Works
Works
91
COLESHILL ROAD
WATTON LA.
BROMWICH CT.
GORSEY LANE
Works
STATION RD.
COLESHILL INDUSTRIAL ESTATE
OPENFIELD
Tennis Courts
Playing Field
GYPSY LANE
B4117
Chattle Hill
ROMAN WAY
COLESHILL INDUSTRIAL ESTATE
THE COURTYARD
GORSEY LA.
5
Birmingham
GORSEY WY.
CHATTLE HILL
Works
IMPERIAL RISE
BRUTUS DR.
TEMPLE WAY
CAESAR WY.
CENTURION
AUGUSTUS CL.
JULIUS DR.
ROMAN PK
TEMPLE CT.
COLESHILL TRADING ESTATE
River Cole
Gilson Hall
Junction 8
WANTAGE RD.
HADRIAN DR.
TRAJAN HL.
TIBBS CL.
ENNSDALE
BUNGLWS
Comm. Cen.
6
Gilson
M42
M42
GILSON ROAD
B4117
Grimstock Hill
NORTON RD.
ARDEN CFT.
BATEMAN RD.
ENNERSDALE CL.
ENNERSDALE ROAD
Ford
90
High Meadow Inf. Sch.
107
GILSON DR.
ROSE
JAMES
420
LANE

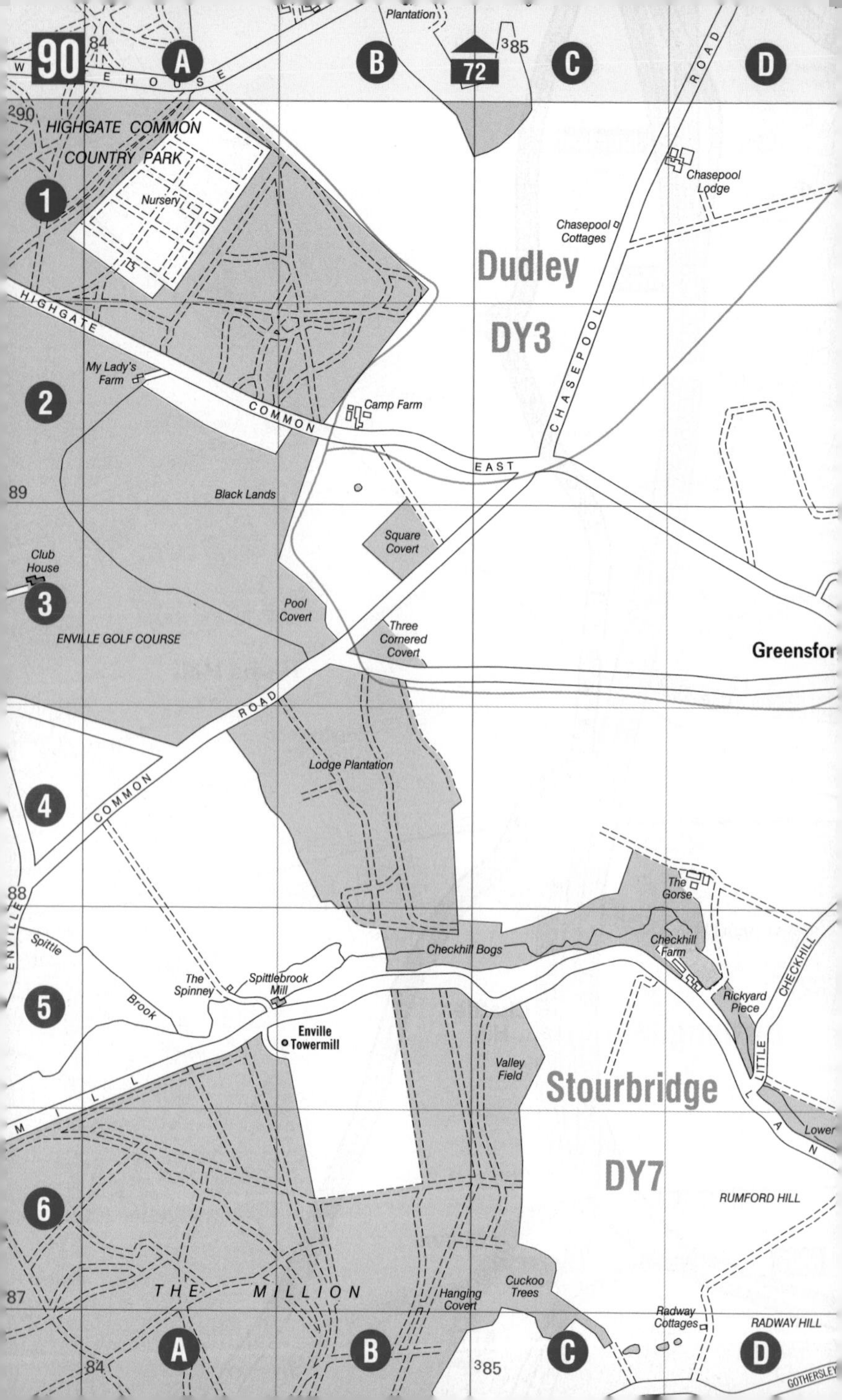

W

84

A

B

72

C

ROAD

D

290

HIGHGATE COMMON

COUNTRY PARK

Nursery

1

HIGHGATE

Chasepool Lodge

Chasepool Cottages

Dudley

DY3

My Lady's Farm

2

COMMON

Camp Farm

EAST

CHASEPOOL

89

Black Lands

Square Covert

Club House

3

Pool Covert

Three Cornered Covert

Greensfor

ENVILLE GOLF COURSE

ROAD

Lodge Plantation

COMMON

4

The Gorse

88

Spittle

Checkhill Bogs

Checkhill Farm

CHECKHILL

Brook

The Spinney

Spittlebrook Mill

5

Enville Towermill

Valley Field

Stourbridge

Rickyard Piece

LITTLE

A

N

Lower

MILL

DY7

RUMFORD HILL

6

Cuckoo Trees

THE   MILLION

Hanging Covert

Radway Cottages

RADWAY HILL

87

84

A

B

385

C

D

GOTHERSLEY

E
F
G
H
73
Lock
Hinksford
Swindon Rough
Hinksford House
Wall Heath Forge
Hollow Mill Farm
Hinksford Bridge
HINKSFORD PARK RESIDENTIAL MOBILE HOMES
Hinksford
Staffordshire & Worcestershire Canal
Wall Heath
Wall Heath Park
BROOK STREET
VICTORIA
ALBERT S.
CROSS ST.
BLAZE PK.
BLAZE HILL
FORGE
LANE
ROAD
PARKVIEW CT.
THE GABLES
Comm. Cen.
Recreation Ground
ENVILLE
SWINDON
ROAD
GROVE
HEATHBROOK AV.
HIGH
ST.
A449
FOUNDRY
Prim. Sch.
NEW
FLATT
MILE
LANE
Pav.
Pavilion
Sports Ground
Dudley Kingswinford Rugby Football Club
OSTLER CL.
Dawley Brook
SWINDON
B4178
ROAD
SOUTH STAFFORDSHIRE
DUDLEY
Kingswinford
DY6
The Paddocks
Lock
LODGE
LANE
A4101
The Summerhill School
92
Herons Reach
ASHWOOD
Ashwood Lodge
Ashwood Bridge
Ashwood Marina
DOCTORS
Ashwood
LANE
Ashwoodfield House
KINGSLEY RD.
KINGSLEY COURT
RIDGE
KINGSLEY RD.
MOUNT
Ridgehill Wood
Gorse Corner
Nursery
Flatheridge Bridge
Waterworks Cottages
Pumping Station
Rocky Lock Bed
KIDDERMINSTER
A449
LAWNSWOOD
LOWER
ROMAN
ROAD
Lock
Staffordshire & Worcestershire Canal
Lawneswood
Fish Ponds
Holloway House
Lock
Gothersley Bridge
Gothersley
Gothersley Cottage
Lawns Wood
Lawneswood Farm
HUNTERS RIDE
LAWNSWOOD DR.
Dudley Lodge
Foley Fane
Gothersley Rough
PLEASANT
ASHLEY CL.
HILLWOOD CL.
ARDEN CL.
HORSHAM AV.
SPINNEY CL.
BALMORAL
ELMWOOD
HATHAWAY M.
CHATSWORTH M.
AVON M.
BLUE BELL
88
89
90
87
1
2
3
4
5
6

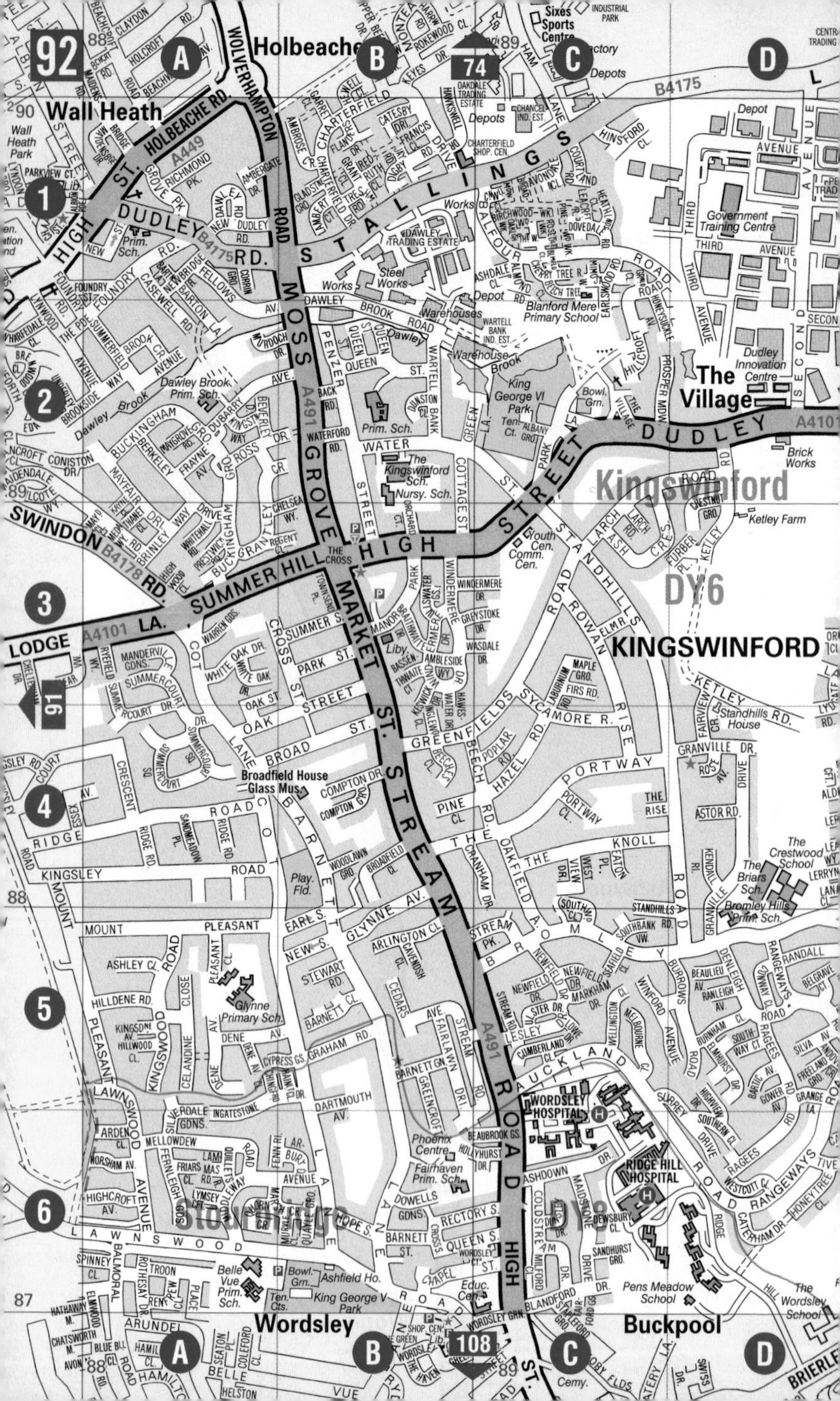

Wall Heath
Holbeache
Sixes Sports Centre
74
Kingswinford
DY6
KINGSWINFORD
The Village
Government Training Centre
Dudley Innovation Centre
King George VI Park
The Kingswinford Sch.
Broadfield House Glass Mus.
Glynne Primary Sch.
Wordsley Hospital
Ridge Hill Hospital
Stourbridge
DY8
Wordsley
Buckpool
Pens Meadow School
The Wordsley School
The Crestwood School
Bromley Hills Prim. Sch.
Blanford Mere Primary School
Dawley Brook Prim. Sch.
Belle Vue Prim. Sch.
King George V Park
Fairhaven Prim. Sch.
Phoenix Centre
91
108
A449
A491
A4101
B4175
B4178

75
Bank
Works
Hunt's Mill
Tansey Green
Tile Works
Works
Warehouses
Enterprise Workshops
Tansey Green House
Barrowhill Copse
DY1
RUSSELL'S HALL HOSPITAL
BUSHEY FIELDS HOSPITAL
St. Marks C of E Prim. Sch.
HIGH STREET
A4101
GIBBONS INDUSTRIAL ESTATE
Pensnett
Community Centre
Brierley Hill
Middle Pool
Fens Pool
Mullet Park
Bromley Prim. Sch.
Playing Field
The Pensnett Sch. of Technology
Bromley
Grove Pool
Wide Waters
DY5
94
PADDYS WIDE WATER IND. EST.
THE WALLOWS INDUSTRIAL ESTATE
COMMONSIDE
B4179
Crestwood Park Prim. Sch.
The Dell Stadium
Recreation Ground
Brockmoor
Dudley Fields
Next Generation Health Club
PENSNETT ROAD
B4180
Round Oak
A461
Comm. Cen.
Dingle Primary School
The Leys Depot
Cressett La. Bridge
The Leys
PREMIER PARTNERSHIP IND. EST.
COCKLEY WHARF IND. EST.
WATERFRONT BUSINESS PARK
Playing Field
Pav. Cricket Grd.
Brockmoor Prim. Sch. Play. Flds.
BRIERLEY HILL
Farmer's Bridge
Stourbridge Canal
LEYS RD.
BROOKMOOR IND. EST.
MOOR STREET
MOOR ST. IND. EST.
THE BRIERLEY TRAD. EST.
THE MOOR CENTRE
FIVE WAYS
Megabowl
The Brier School
Brierley Hill Baths
109
E
F
G
H
1
2
3
4
5
6

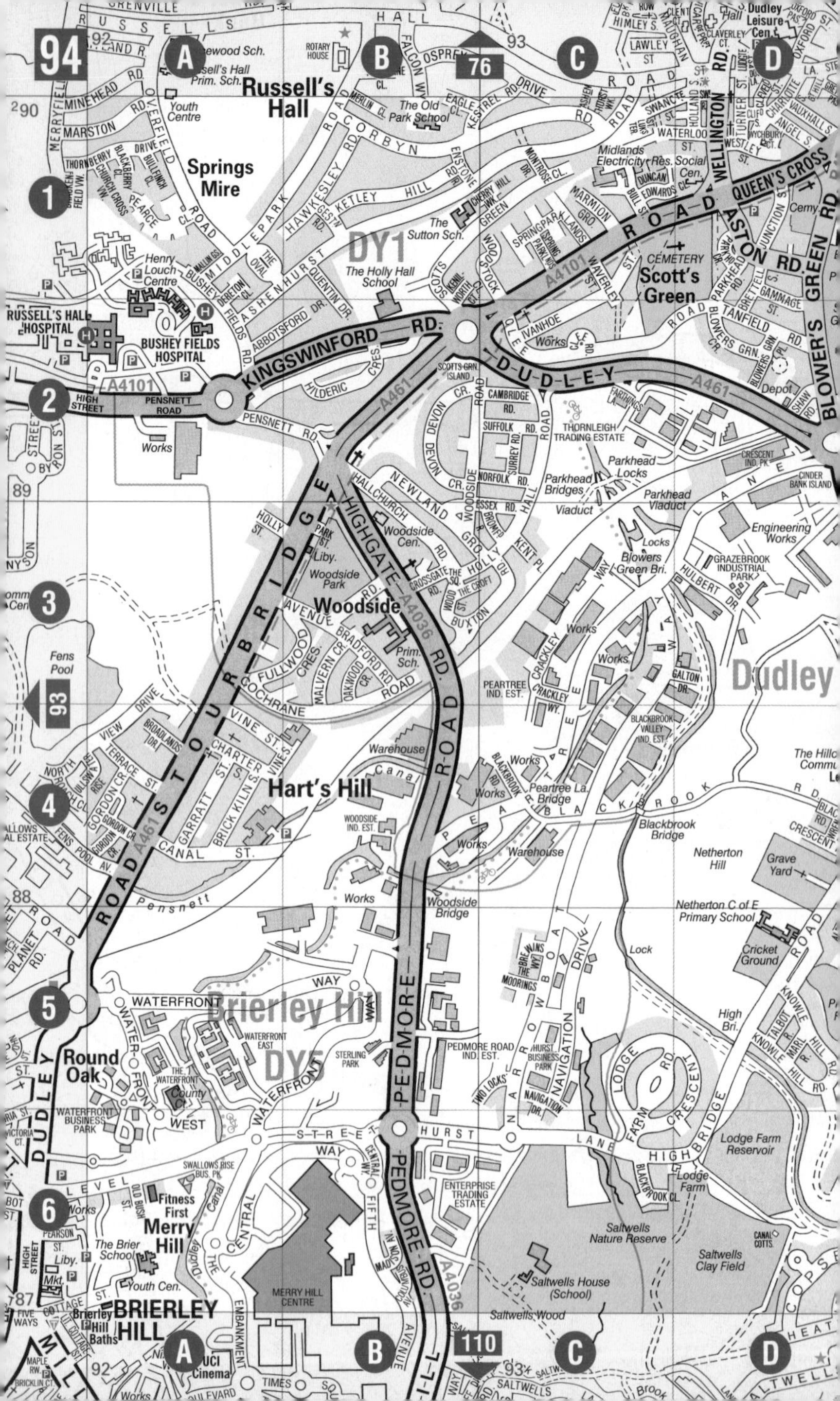
Russell's Hall
Springs Mire
DY1
The Holly Hall School
The Sutton Sch.
Scott's Green
CEMETERY
Midlands Electricity Res. Social Cen.
Dudley Leisure Cen.
RUSSELL'S HALL HOSPITAL
BUSHEY FIELDS HOSPITAL
Henry Louch Centre
Youth Centre
Russell's Hall Prim. Sch.
The Old Park School
ROTARY HOUSE
KINGSWINFORD RD.
DUDLEY ROAD
QUEEN'S CROSS
A4101
A461
A4036
SCOTTS GRN. ISLAND
THORNLEIGH TRADING ESTATE
Parkhead Locks
Parkhead Bridges
Parkhead Viaduct
Viaduct
CRESCENT IND. PK.
CINDER BANK ISLAND
Engineering Works
GRAZEBROOK INDUSTRIAL PARK
Blowers Green Bri.
Woodside
Woodside Cen.
Woodside Park
Liby.
Prim. Sch.
Fens Pool
Dudley
STOURBRIDGE ROAD
HIGHGATE RD.
PEDMORE ROAD
PEARTREE IND. EST.
BLACKBROOK VALLEY IND. EST.
Warehouse
Hart's Hill
Works
Peartree La. Bridge
Blackbrook Bridge
Netherton Hill
Grave Yard
Netherton C of E Primary School
Cricket Ground
WOODSIDE IND. EST.
Woodside Bridge
Canal
Pensnett
Brierley Hill
DY5
Round Oak
WATERFRONT EAST
THE WATERFRONT
County Ct.
WATERFRONT BUSINESS PARK
STERLING PARK
PEDMORE ROAD IND. EST.
HURST BUSINESS PARK
NARROW BOAT WAY
NAVIGATION DRIVE
THE MOORINGS
TWO LOCKS
Lock
High Bri.
LODGE FARM CRESCENT
Lodge Farm Reservoir
Lodge Farm
HURST LANE
HIGH BRIDGE
ENTERPRISE TRADING ESTATE
Saltwells Nature Reserve
Saltwells Clay Field
Saltwells House (School)
Saltwells Wood
CANAL COTTS.
SWALLOWS RISE BUS. PK.
Fitness First
Merry Hill
MERRY HILL CENTRE
The Brier School
Youth Cen.
Liby.
Mkt.
BRIERLEY HILL
Brierley Hill Baths
UCI Cinema
FIVE WAYS
LEVEL ST.
DUDLEY RD.
76
93
110
A
B
C
D
1
2
3
4
5
6

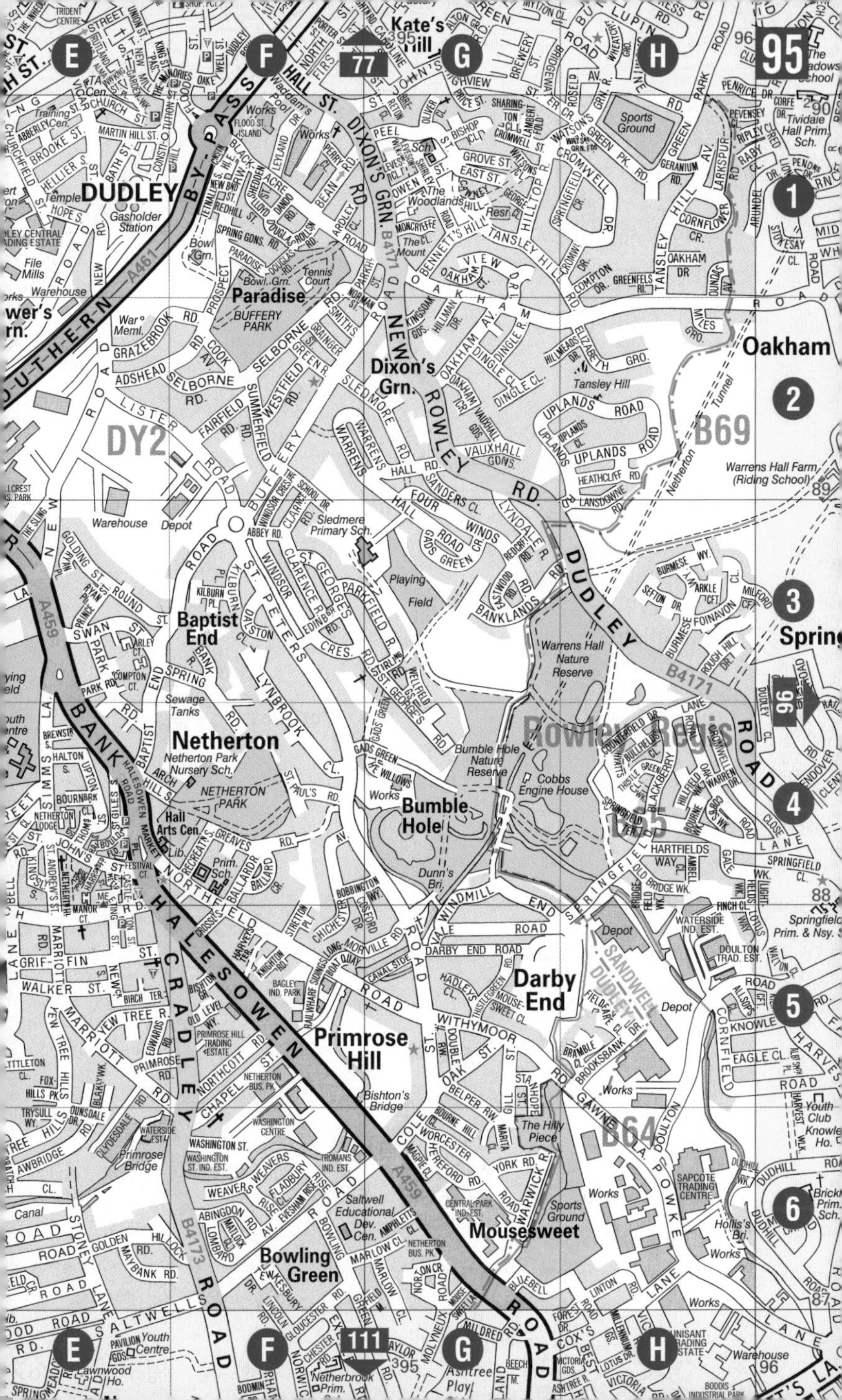
95
77
111
E
F
G
H
1
2
3
4
5
6
DUDLEY
Kate's Hill
Paradise
BUFFERY PARK
Dixon's Grn.
Oakham
DY2
B69
B65
B64
Warrens Hall Farm (Riding School)
Tansley Hill
Netherton Tunnel
Baptist End
Sledmere Primary Sch.
Playing Field
Warrens Hall Nature Reserve
Rowley Regis
Spring
Netherton
Netherton Park Nursery Sch.
NETHERTON PARK
Bumble Hole Nature Reserve
Cobbs Engine House
Bumble Hole
Dunn's Bri.
Hall Arts Cen.
Lib.
Prim. Sch.
Sewage Tanks
Darby End
Primrose Hill
Bishton's Bridge
The Hilly Piece
Mousesweet
Sports Ground
Bowling Green
Saltwell Educational Dev. Cen.
Primrose Bridge
Canal
Pavilion Youth Centre
Lawnwood Ho.
Netherbrook Prim.
Ashtree Play
SAPCOTE TRADING CENTRE
Hollis's Bri.
Works
Warehouse
Depot
WATERSIDE IND. EST.
DOULTON TRAD. EST.
Springfield Prim. & Nsy. S
Youth Club
Knowle Ho.
BAGLEY IND. PARK
PRIMROSE HILL TRADING ESTATE
NETHERTON BUS. PK.
WASHINGTON CENTRE
TROMANS IND. EST.
CENTRAL PARK IND. EST.
UNISANT TRADING ESTATE
BODDIS INDUSTRIAL PARK
Gasholder Station
DUDLEY CENTRAL TRADING ESTATE
File Mills
War Meml.
Temple
Training Cen.
Wadham's Pool
Tennis Court
Bowl. Grn.
The Woodlands
The Mount
Resr.
Sports Ground
Tividale Hall Prim. Sch.
The Meadows School
SOUTHERN BY-PASS
A461
A459
B4171
B4173
NEW ROWLEY RD.
DUDLEY ROAD
HALESOWEN ROAD
CRADLEY ROAD
OAKHAM ROAD
BUFFERY ROAD
SALTWELLS ROAD
WINDMILL END
SPRINGFIELD LANE
POWKE LANE
GAWNE LA.
WITHYMOOR RD.
DARBY END ROAD
NORTHFIELD RD.
COX'S RD.
89
88
87
90
96
395

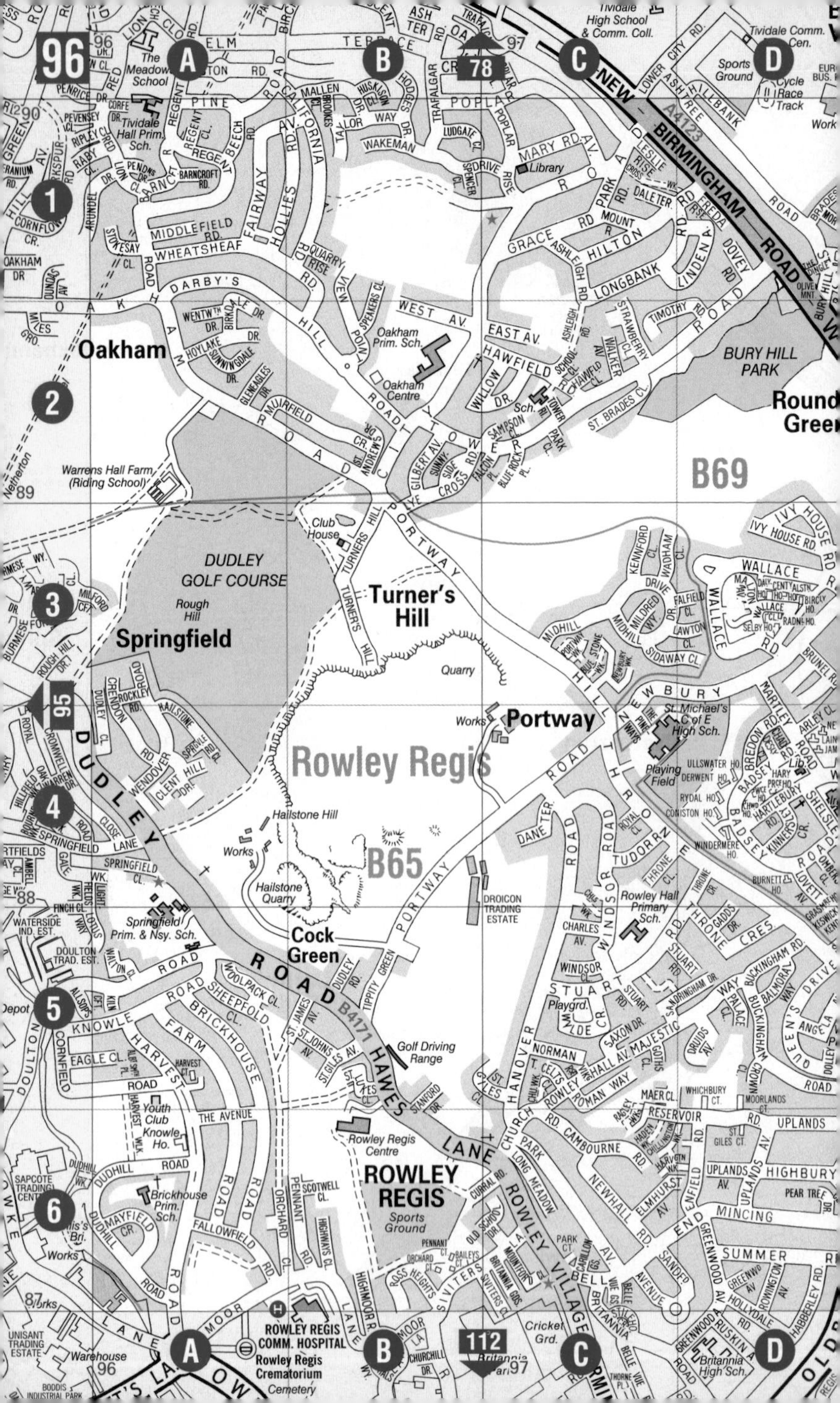

96
78
97
95
112
A
B
C
D
1
2
3
4
5
6
90
89
88
87
96
97
Oakham
Springfield
Turner's Hill
Portway
Rowley Regis
ROWLEY REGIS
Cock Green
Round Green
B69
B65
Tividale High School & Comm. Coll.
Tividale Comm. Cen.
Sports Ground
Cycle Race Track
The Meadows School
Tividale Hall Prim. Sch.
Library
Oakham Prim. Sch.
Oakham Centre
BURY HILL PARK
Warrens Hall Farm (Riding School)
DUDLEY GOLF COURSE
Rough Hill
Club House
Quarry
Works
Hailstone Hill
Hailstone Quarry
DROICON TRADING ESTATE
St. Michael's C of E High Sch.
Playing Field
Rowley Hall Primary Sch.
Springfield Prim. & Nsy. Sch.
WATERSIDE IND. EST.
DOULTON TRAD. EST.
Depot
Golf Driving Range
Rowley Regis Centre
Youth Club
Knowle Ho.
Brickhouse Prim. Sch.
SAPCOTE TRADING CENTRE
Rowley Regis Sports Ground
ROWLEY REGIS COMM. HOSPITAL
Rowley Regis Crematorium
Cemetery
UNISANT TRADING ESTATE
Warehouse
BODDIS INDUSTRIAL PARK
Cricket Grd.
Britannia High Sch.
NEW BIRMINGHAM ROAD
A4123
OAKHAM ROAD
DUDLEY ROAD
B4171
HAWES LANE
ROWLEY VILLAGE
PORTWAY HILL
PORTWAY ROAD
CITY ROAD
TOWER ROAD
NEWBURY LANE
HALL AV.
HANOVER RD.
WINDSOR RD.
STUART RD.
THRONE CRES.
CAMBOURNE RD.
RESERVOIR RD.
UPLANDS AV.
HIGHBURY RD.
MINCING LANE
SUMMER LANE
KNOWLE RD.
HARVEST RD.
FARM RD.
BRICKHOUSE RD.
DUDHILL RD.
MOOR LANE
SPRINGFIELD LANE
DARBY'S HILL RD.
WHEATSHEAF RD.
MIDDLEFIELD RD.
POPLAR RD.
MARY RD.
GRACE RD.
HILTON RD.
LONGBANK RD.
WALLACE RD.
IVY HOUSE RD.
QUEEN'S DRIVE
BUCKINGHAM RD.
ROWLEY HALL AV.
ROMAN WAY
NEWHALL RD.
GREENWOOD AV.
HABBERLEY RD.

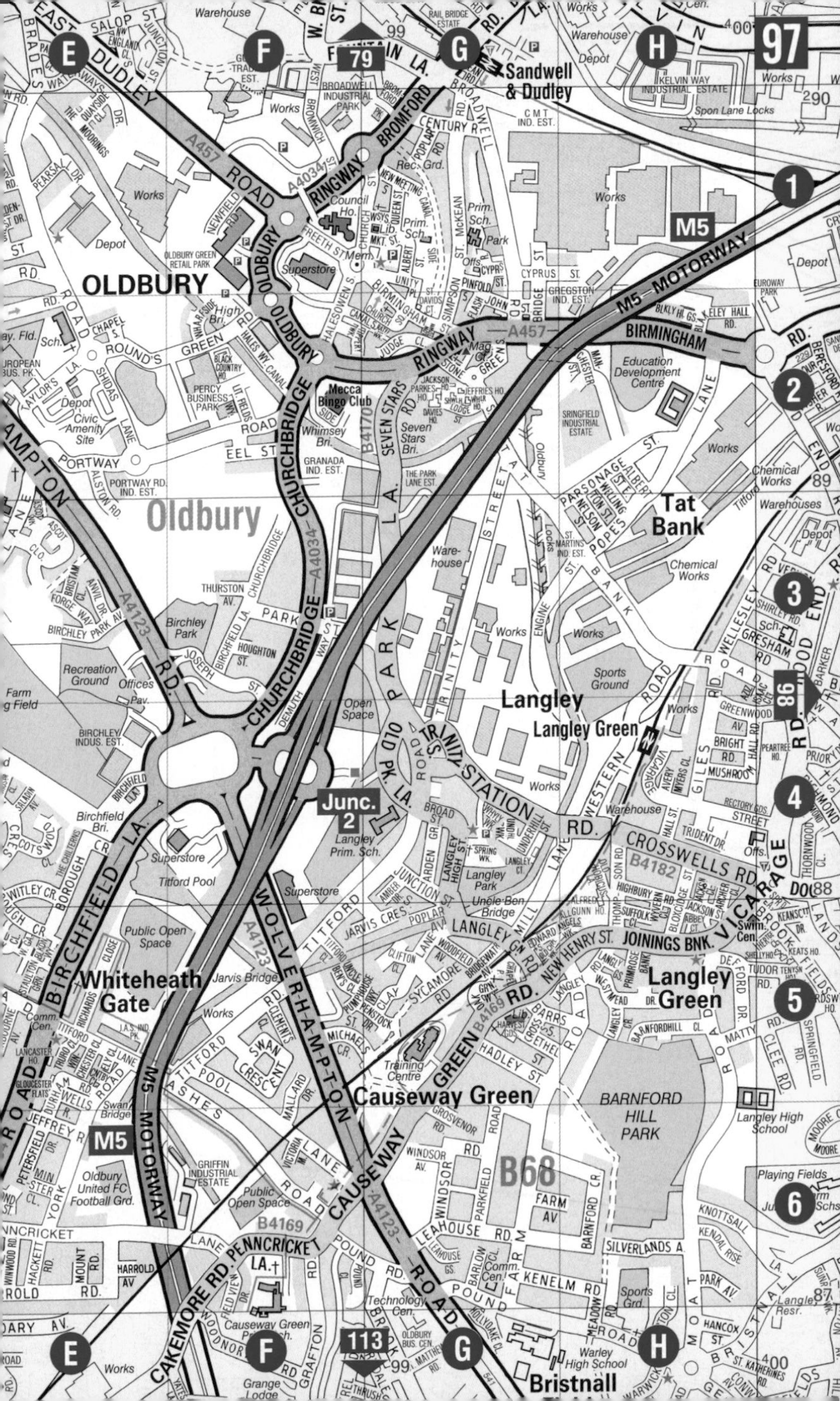
OLDBURY
Oldbury
Sandwell & Dudley
Tat Bank
Langley
Langley Green
Whiteheath Gate
Causeway Green
Bristnall
BARNFORD HILL PARK
B68
M5 MOTORWAY
Junc. 2
BIRMINGHAM
RINGWAY
A457
A4034
A4123
B4169
B4182
B4170
CHURCHBRIDGE
WOLVERHAMPTON ROAD
CAUSEWAY GREEN
TITFORD ROAD
CROSSWELLS RD.
VICARAGE
EAST DUDLEY ROAD
BIRCHFIELD LA.
PARK LA.
STATION RD.
Mecca Bingo Club
Education Development Centre
Langley High School
Warley High School
Oldbury United FC Football Grd.
KELVIN WAY INDUSTRIAL ESTATE
Spon Lane Locks
79
86
113

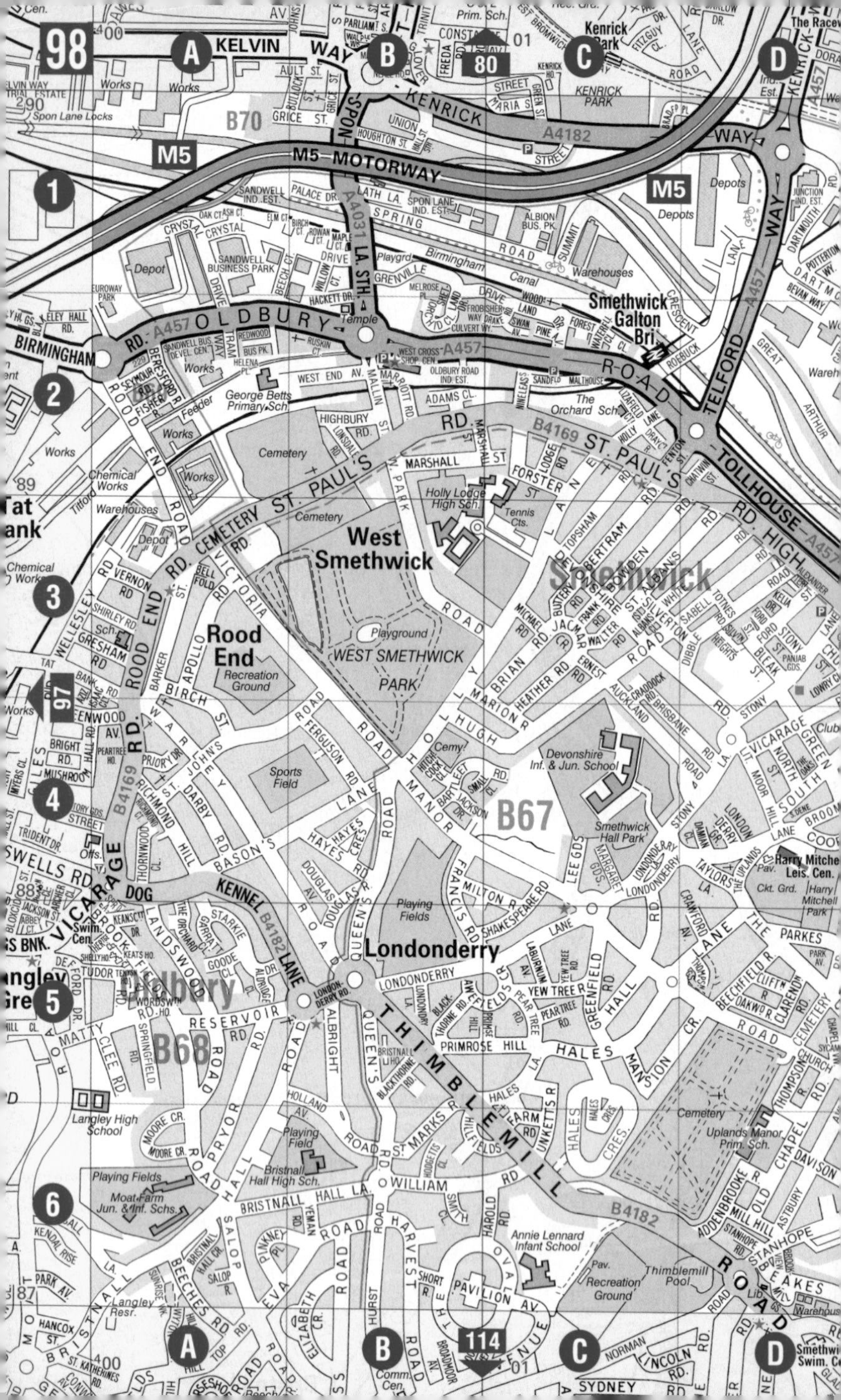

98
A
B
C
D
1
2
3
4
5
6
80
97
114
KELVIN WAY
Kenrick Park
KENRICK PARK
KENRICK WAY
A4182
B70
M5
M5 MOTORWAY
Spon Lane Locks
SPON LANE
A4031
SPON LANE IND. EST.
SANDWELL IND. EST.
SANDWELL BUSINESS PARK
CRYSTAL DRIVE
Depot
Depots
Warehouses
ALBION BUS. PK.
SPRING ROAD
Birmingham Canal
GRENVILLE DRIVE
Smethwick Galton Bri.
JUNCTION IND. EST.
TELFORD WAY
A457
OLDBURY ROAD
BIRMINGHAM RD.
Temple
WEST CROSS SHOP. CEN.
OLDBURY ROAD IND. EST.
George Betts Primary Sch.
The Orchard Sch.
TOLLHOUSE RD.
HIGH
B4169
ST. PAUL'S RD.
CEMETERY RD.
Cemetery
Holly Lodge High Sch.
Tennis Cts.
West Smethwick
WEST SMETHWICK PARK
Playground
Smethwick
Works
Chemical Works
Warehouses
Tat Bank
Rood End
Recreation Ground
ROOD END RD.
VICTORIA RD.
Sports Field
HOLLY LANE
MANOR ROAD
Cemy.
B67
Devonshire Inf. & Jun. School
Smethwick Hall Park
LONDONDERRY LANE
Harry Mitchell Leis. Cen.
Ckt. Grd.
Harry Mitchell Park
VICARAGE RD.
DOG KENNEL LANE
B4182
Swim. Cen.
Oldbury
Langley Green
Londonderry
Playing Fields
THIMBLEMILL ROAD
RESERVOIR RD.
B68
PRIMROSE HILL
HALES LANE
Cemetery
Uplands Manor Prim. Sch.
Langley High School
Playing Field
Bristnall Hall High Sch.
BRISTNALL HALL LA.
Playing Fields
Moat Farm Jun. & Inf. Schs.
Annie Lennard Infant School
Pav.
Recreation Ground
Thimblemill Pool
Langley Resr.
PAVILION AV.
Smethwick Swim. Cen.
SYDNEY RD.

99
Handsworth
Soho
SMETHWICK
The Hawthorns
Smethwick Rolfe St.
Handsworth Booth St.
Black Patch Rec. Grd.
VICTORIA PARK
Victoria Park Prim. Sch.
Council House
Sandwell Coll. (Smethwick Campus)
Hadley Stadium
B66
B16
B18
B71
81
100
115
E
F
G
H
1
2
3
4
5
6
HOLYHEAD ROAD
ROLFE STREET
SOHO WAY
CRANFORD ST.
HEATH ST.
DUDLEY ROAD
CAPE HILL
WATERLOO ROAD
BEARWOOD ROAD
CITY ROAD

A
B
C
D
82
Handsworth
Handsworth Leisure Cen.
B20
B21
B18
B16
B1
1
2
3
4
5
6
Wilkes Green Jun. & Inf. Schs.
Oaklands Sports & Social Cen.
Hamilton School
SOHO ROAD
A41
ROOKERY RD.
BOULTON RD.
A4040
DOUGLAS RD.
HOLLY
LEYTON R.
OSBORNE R.
MOSTYN R.
MONTAGUE R.
GOLDS HILL
HAMSTEAD RD.
B4124
GIBSON ROAD
WELFORD RD.
Welford Prim. Sch.
VILLA RD.
SOHO HILL
Sikh Temple
King Edward VI Handsworth Sch.
St. Michael's C of E Jun. & Inf. Sch.
Gib Heath
Winson Green/ Outer Circle
Winson Green
HMP Birmingham
Mary Seacole Ho.
Soho Benson Rd.
Benson Prim. Sch.
St. Stephen's Cen.
HANDSWORTH NEW RD.
WINSON GREEN RD.
DUDLEY ROAD
SPRING HILL
A457
ICKNIELD ST.
A4540
MIDDLEWAY
LADYWOOD
CITY HOSPITAL
Eye Centre
Maternity Centre
Birmingham Canal
HEATH ST.
B4135
Summerfield Cen.
SUMMERFIELD PARK
A4040
Midland Sailing Club
PORT ROAD
B4126
Ladywood Arts & Leisure Cen.
116
99
EDGBASTON RESERVOIR
Buddhist Tower Temple
All Saints
Hockley
Birmingham
Jewellery Quarter
HOCKLEY CIRCUS
HOCKLEY FLYOVER
Bus Depot
Lozells
Nelson Prim.
National Indoor Arena
Ladywood
Key Cemetery
Warstone Cemetery
Works

101
83
102
117
E
F
G
H
1
2
3
4
5
6
ASTON
Aston Hall
ASTON PARK
A38(M)
King Edward VI Aston Sch.
Cricket & Football Ground
(Villa Park)
Buddhist Temple
Westminster Prim. Sch.
Sacred Heart Prim. Sch.
TRINITY
FREER ROAD
ARDEN ROAD
BIRCHFIELD ROAD
WITTON ROAD
B4140
A34
PRESTBURY RD.
ETTINGTON RD.
Broadway Sch.
FREDERICK
ALBERT
B6
VICTORIA ROAD
Mosque
BEVINGTON ROAD
LOZELLS
B4144
WELLS RD.
HATFIELD RD.
WILSON RD.
LEONARD
ROLAND
FINCH RD.
CARLYLE RD.
JOHNSTONE ST.
BENNETT ST.
Lozells Centre
Holte Sch.
Leis. Cen.
Lozells Jun. & Inf. Sch.
B4515
GERRARD ST
CLIFFORD ST.
HIGH ST.
PARK LANE
B4144
BROMFIELD CL.
HANOVER CL.
NUGENT CL.
CAMBORNE CL.
BROOKLYN AV.
ESTONE WK.
ASTON EXPRESSWAY
Police Depot
Aston Manor Sch.
Royal Mail Depot
Swim. Pool
Comm. Cen.
NEWTOWN SHOP. CEN.
PHILLIPS ST.
BURLINGTON ST.
ALMA ST.
B4498
SUMMER LA.
NEW TOWN ROW
New Town Row
A34
Burbury Park
Mayfield Sch.
B19
BIRMINGHAM
Newtown
St. George's Church Cen.
GREAT KING STREET NORTH
10
11
12
13
14
15
LUCAS CIRCUS
MIDDLEWAY
NEW JOHN A4540 ST. WEST
NEWTOWN MIDDLEWAY
DARTMOUTH MIDDLEWAY
A4540
ASTON ROAD
A38
CORPORATION ST.
UCE (Gosta Green Campus)
Aston Univ.
Aston University
Sports Pitch
Liby.
Uni.
Sports Cen.
GT. HAMPTON ST.
B4100
CONSTITUTION HILL
St. Pauls
St. George's Park
6th Form Centre
Jewellery & Silver Cen.
Elec. Sta.
St.Chads RC Cath.
ST. CHADS QUEENSWAY
HOSP.
CHILDREN'S HOSP.
Snow Hill
St.Philips Cath.
Chest Clinic
Telecom Twr.
B3
B4
B5
JAMES WATT QUEENSWAY
JENNENS ROAD
B4114
Imax Thtre.
Millennium Point
Thinktank
The Rockface
CURZON
Depot
MOOR ST. QUEENSWAY
PRIORY QUEENSWAY
PARADE
FAZELEY ST.
Aston Cross Business Park
Ringway Business Park
LICHFIELD
ROCKY
Factory
Works

ASTON
ASTON PARK
Aston Hall
A38(M)
ASTON EXPRESSWAY
Aston Events Centre
Powerleague Soccer Centre
Junc. 6
84
Star City
ASTON HALL RD.
LICHFIELD ROAD
CUCKOO ROAD
Aston
B6
B7
ROCKY LANE
HEARTLANDS
NECHELLS PARKWAY
SALTLEY RD.
Vauxhall
Duddeston
Gas Works
Rail Traffic Control Cen.
ADDERLEY PARK
Saltley
BIRMINGHAM
Freightliner Terminal
LANDOR STREET
GARRISON
Birmingham Wheels Adventure Park
101
118
B4

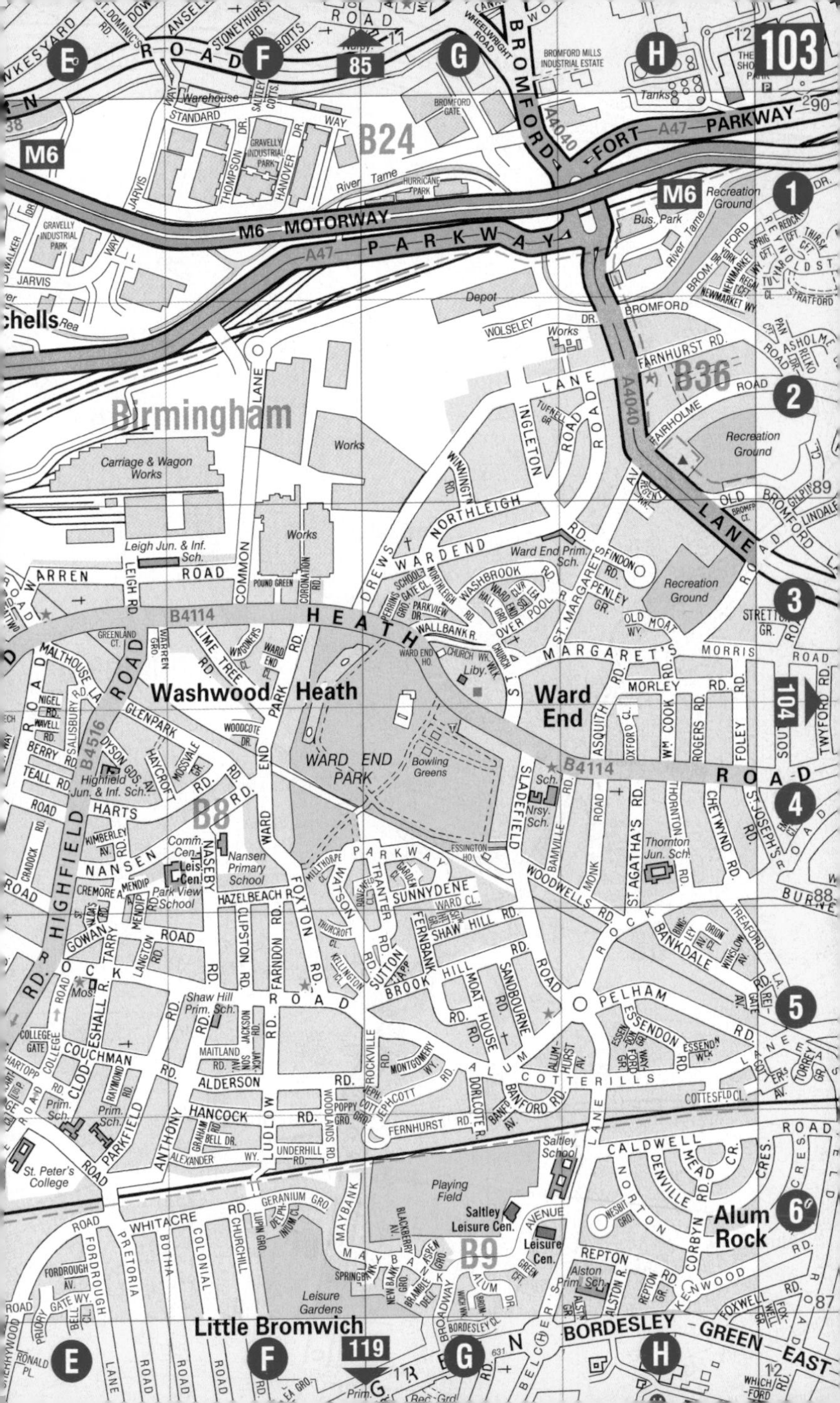

103
85
104
119
B24
B36
B8
B9
M6
M6 MOTORWAY
A47 PARKWAY
FORT PARKWAY
BROMFORD LANE
A4040
B4114
B4516
Bromford Mills Industrial Estate
Gravelly Industrial Park
Hurricane Park
River Tame
Recreation Ground
Bus. Park
Depot
Works
Birmingham
Carriage & Wagon Works
Leigh Jun. & Inf. Sch.
WARREN ROAD
HEATH ROAD
Washwood Heath
Ward End
WARD END PARK
Bowling Greens
Ward End Prim. Sch.
HIGHFIELD ROAD
Highfield Jun. & Inf. Sch.
Nansen Primary School
Park View School
Shaw Hill Prim. Sch.
ROCK ROAD
PARKWAY
SUNNYDENE
Thornton Jun. Sch.
PELHAM
COTTERILLS
ALUM ROCK
Alum Rock
Saltley School
Playing Field
Saltley Leisure Cen.
Leisure Cen.
Alston Prim. Sch.
St. Peter's College
Leisure Gardens
Little Bromwich
BORDESLEY GREEN EAST

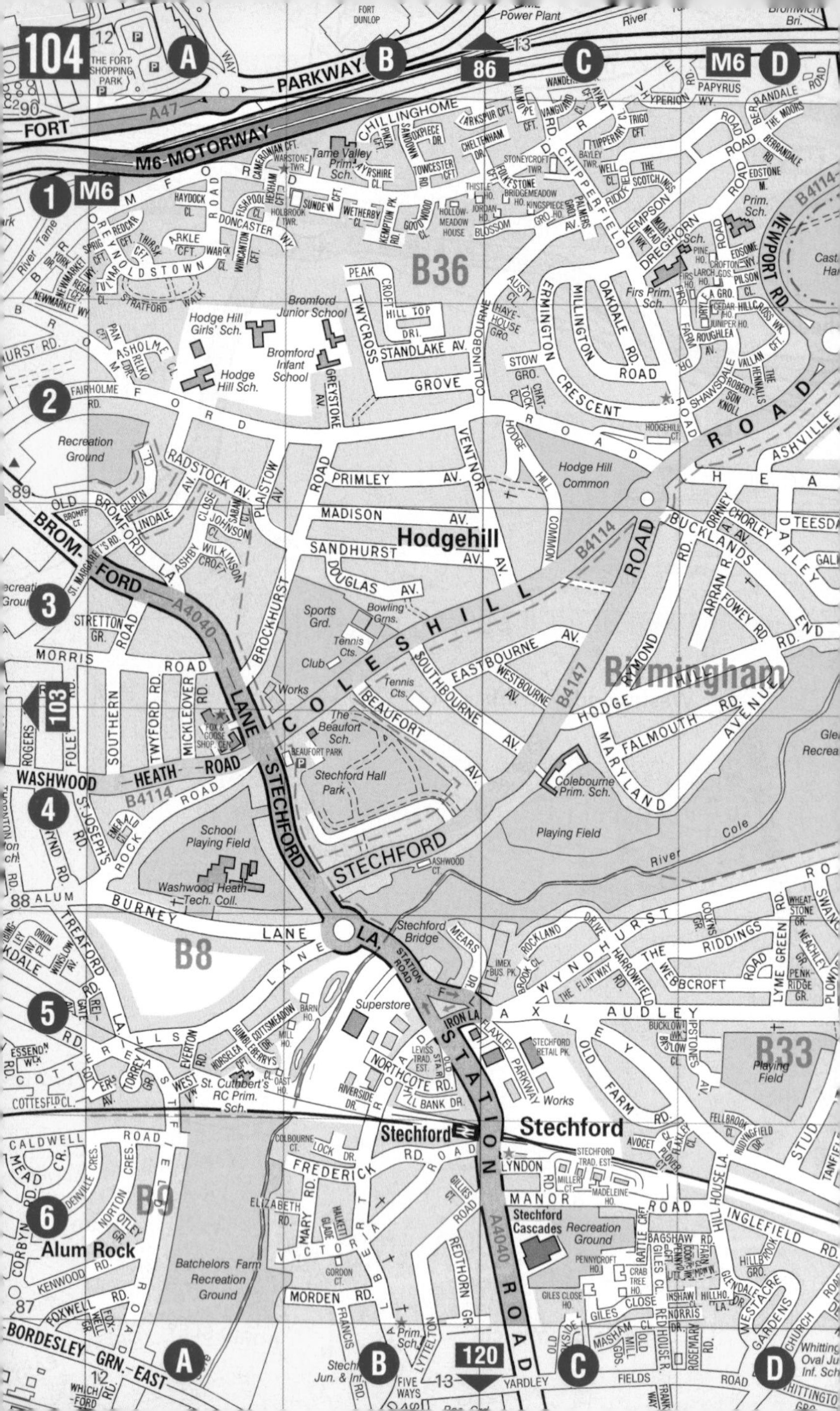

A
B
C
D
1
2
3
4
5
6
86
103
120
M6
M6-MOTORWAY
FORT PARKWAY
A47
THE FORT SHOPPING PARK
FORT DUNLOP
Power Plant
River
Bromwich Bri.
Tame Valley Prim. Sch.
B36
Hodge Hill Girls' Sch.
Bromford Junior School
Bromford Infant School
Hodge Hill Sch.
Recreation Ground
Hodge Hill Common
Hodgehill
Sports Grd.
Bowling Grns.
Tennis Cts.
Club
Works
The Beaufort Sch.
Stechford Hall Park
Colebourne Prim. Sch.
Playing Field
River Cole
Birmingham
School Playing Field
Washwood Heath Tech. Coll.
B8
Stechford Bridge
Superstore
IMEX BUS. PK.
STECHFORD RETAIL PK.
St. Cuthbert's RC Prim. Sch.
Stechford
Stechford Cascades
Recreation Ground
B33
B9
Alum Rock
Batchelors Farm Recreation Ground
Firs Prim. Sch.
Edstone Prim. Sch.
BROMFORD LANE
COLESHILL ROAD
STECHFORD LANE
STATION ROAD
WASHWOOD HEATH ROAD
HODGE HILL ROAD
BURNEY LANE
B4114
B4147
A4040
BORDESLEY GRN. EAST
YARDLEY FIELDS ROAD
MANOR ROAD
AUDLEY ROAD
WYNDHURST ROAD
HODGE HILL AVENUE
MARYLAND AVENUE
FALMOUTH RD.
BUCKLANDS END
NEWPORT RD.
CHIPPERFIELD RD.
ERMINGTON CRESCENT
MILLINGTON ROAD
OAKDALE RD.
PRIMLEY AV.
MADISON AV.
SANDHURST AV.
DOUGLAS AV.
BROCKHURST RD.
EASTBOURNE AV.
SOUTHBOURNE AV.
BEAUFORT AV.
STANDLAKE AV.
GROVE
TWYCROSS
COLLINGBOURNE AV.
VENTNOR AV.
MORRIS ROAD
SOUTHERN RD.
TWYFORD RD.
MICKLEOVER RD.
STRETTON GR.
FREDERICK RD.
VICTORIA RD.
MORDEN RD.
REDTHORN GR.
INGLEFIELD RD.
HILL HOUSE LA.
CALDWELL ROAD
KENWOOD RD.
FOXWELL RD.
CORBYN RD.
NORTHCOTE RD.
IRON LA.
FLAXLEY PARKWAY
OLD FARM RD.

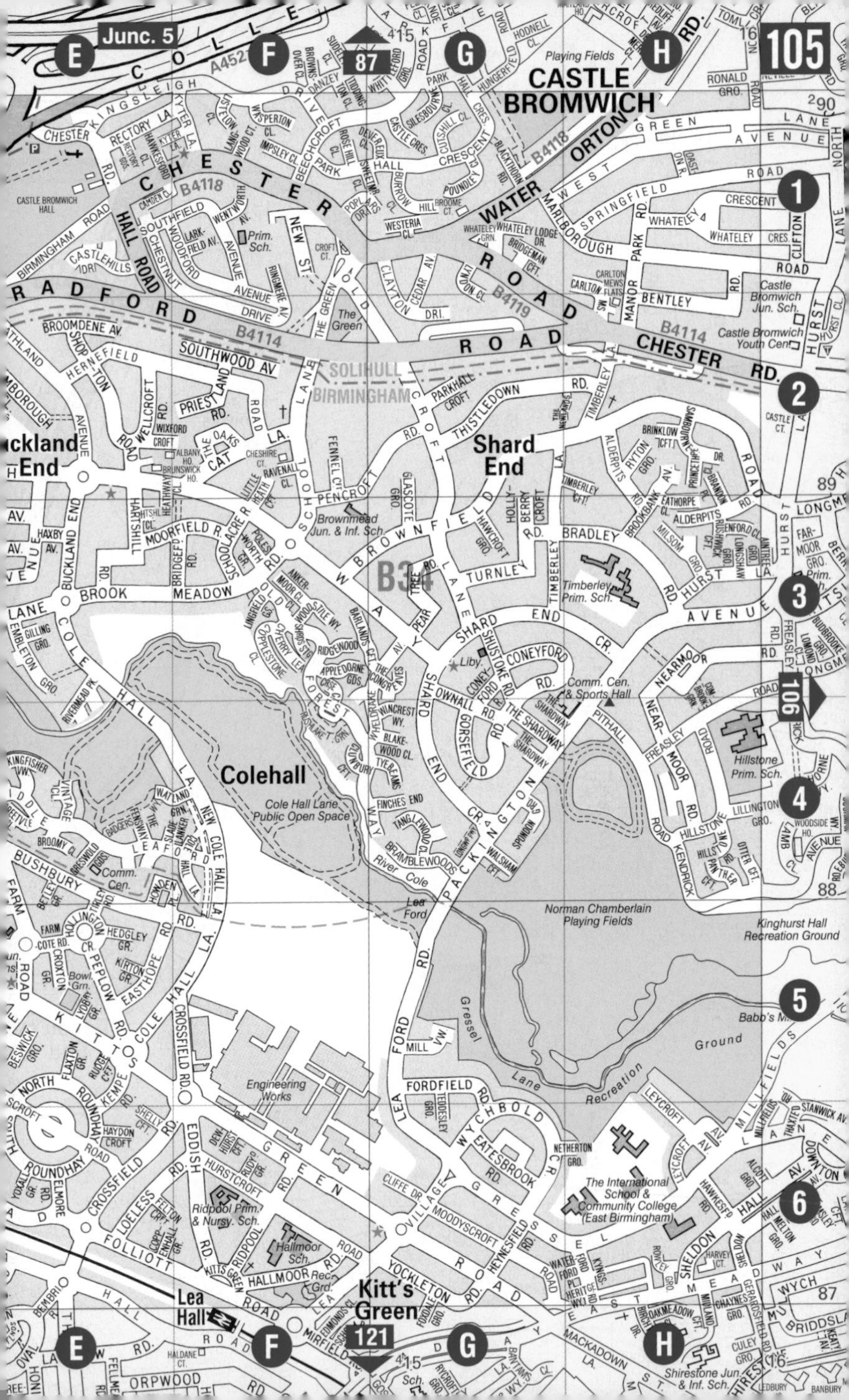
105
Junc. 5
87
121
106
CASTLE BROMWICH
Shard End
Colehall
Kitt's Green
Buckland End
Lea Hall
B34
SOLIHULL
BIRMINGHAM
CHESTER ROAD
BRADFORD ROAD
WATER ORTON
CASTLE BROMWICH HALL
Playing Fields
Castle Bromwich Jun. Sch.
Castle Bromwich Youth Cen.
Brownmead Jun. & Inf. Sch.
Timberley Prim. Sch.
Hillstone Prim. Sch.
Comm. Cen. & Sports Hall
Cole Hall Lane Public Open Space
River Cole
Lea Ford
Norman Chamberlain Playing Fields
Kinghurst Hall Recreation Ground
Gressel Lane Recreation Ground
Babb's Mill
Engineering Works
Ridpool Prim. & Nursy. Sch.
Hallmoor Sch.
The International School & Community College (East Birmingham)
Shirestone Jun. & Inf. Sch.
The Green
Liby.
Comm. Cen.
Bowl. Grn.
Rec. Grd.
Prim. Sch.
B4118
B4119
B4114
A452

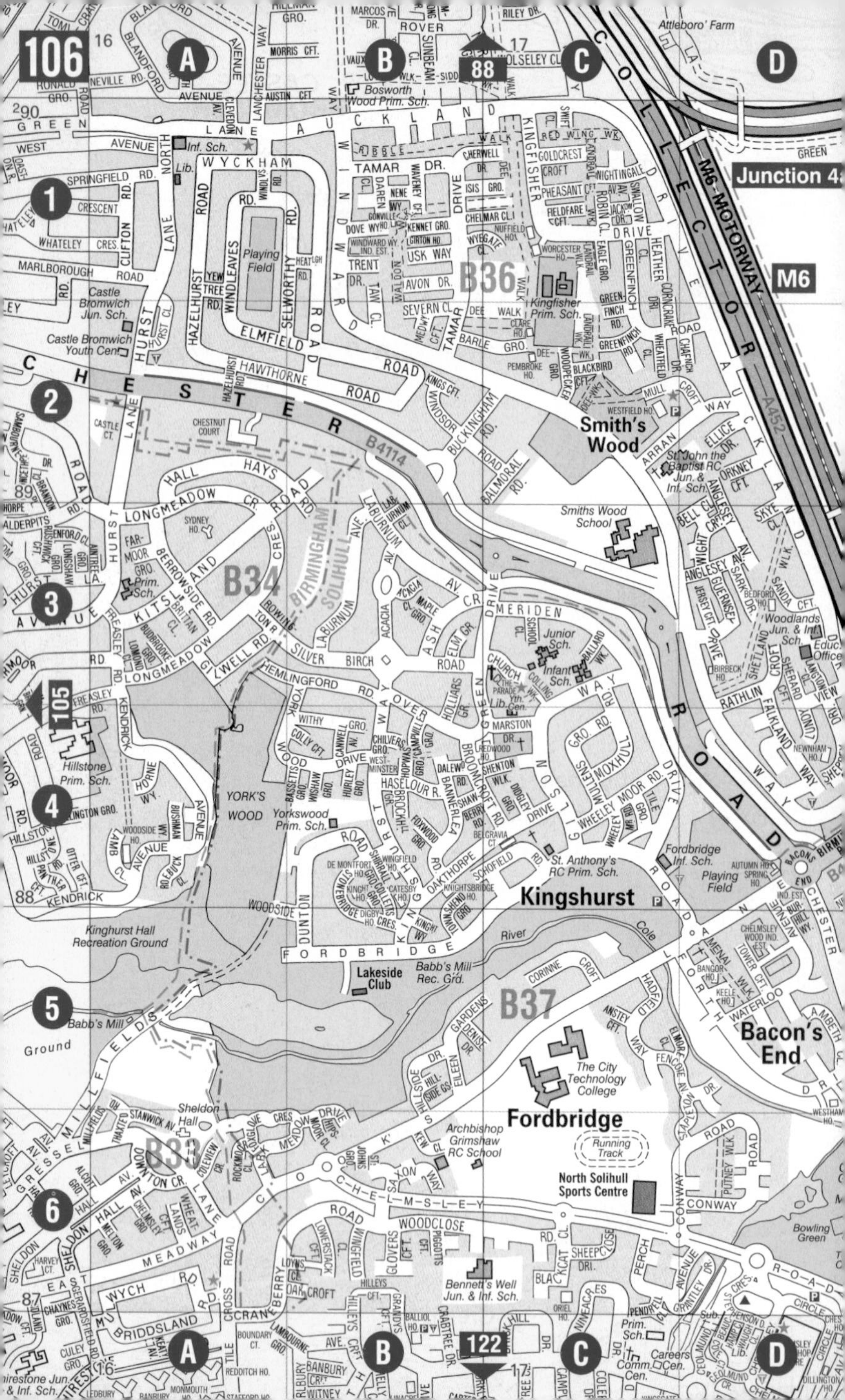
A
B
C
D
1
2
3
4
5
6
88
105
122
Junction 4
M6
M6 MOTORWAY
COLLECTOR ROAD
CHESTER ROAD
B4114
A452
AUCKLAND DRIVE
WINDWARD WAY
KINGFISHER DRIVE
WYCKHAM RD.
ELMFIELD ROAD
HAWTHORNE ROAD
HAZELHURST ROAD
NORTH LANE
LONGMEADOW CR.
KITSLAND ROAD
HALL HAYS ROAD
SILVER BIRCH ROAD
HEMLINGFORD RD.
KINGSHURST WAY
FORDBRIDGE ROAD
MILLFIELDS
CHELMSLEY ROAD
MEADWAY
CONWAY AVENUE
WHEELEY MOOR RD.
GILSON WAY
MERIDEN DRIVE
Smith's Wood
Smiths Wood School
Kingfisher Prim. Sch.
B36
B34
B37
B33
BIRMINGHAM
SOLIHULL
Castle Bromwich Jun. Sch.
Castle Bromwich Youth Cen.
Playing Field
Inf. Sch.
Lib.
Bosworth Wood Prim. Sch.
St. John the Baptist RC Jun. & Inf. Sch.
Woodlands Jun. & Inf. Sch.
Educ. Office
Junior Sch.
Infant Sch.
Lib. Cen.
Hillstone Prim. Sch.
YORK'S WOOD
Yorkswood Prim. Sch.
St. Anthony's RC Prim. Sch.
Kingshurst
Fordbridge Inf. Sch.
Playing Field
Kinghurst Hall Recreation Ground
River Cole
Lakeside Club
Babb's Mill Rec. Grd.
Babb's Mill
Ground
The City Technology College
Fordbridge
Running Track
North Solihull Sports Centre
Archbishop Grimshaw RC School
Sheldon Hall
Bacon's End
Bennett's Well Jun. & Inf. Sch.
Bowling Green
Prim. Sch.
Careers Cen.
Comm. Cen.
Attleboro' Farm

Gilson
89
Junction 8
GILSON ROAD
B4117
LICHFIELD RD.
Grimstock Hill
High Meadow Inf. Sch.
Coleshill Bridge
Cole End
Cole End Park
STATION ROAD
HIGH STREET
The Belt
GREEN LANE
M42 MOTORWAY
M42
COLESHILL
The Catmore
irmingham
STONEBRIDGE ROAD
A446
B4114
BIRMINGHAM RD.
SOUTH DRIVE
River Cole
Leisure Cen.
Phoenix House
Rec. Grd.
Coleshill Hall Farm
HALL WALK
Woodlands Cemetery
The Decoy
Woodlands Crematorium
BIRMINGHAM ROAD
M6 TOLL MOTORWAY
B46
NORTH WARWICKSHIRE
SOLIHULL
Solihull College (Chelmsley Campus)
M6
M6 MOTORWAY
A452
CHESTER ROAD
Bishop Wilson C of E Prim. School
Junc. 4 (M6)
Junction 7a (M42)
COVENTRY ROAD
Blythe Sch.
The Coleshill School
Play. Flds.
Pool Farm
COLESHILL HEATH ROAD
123

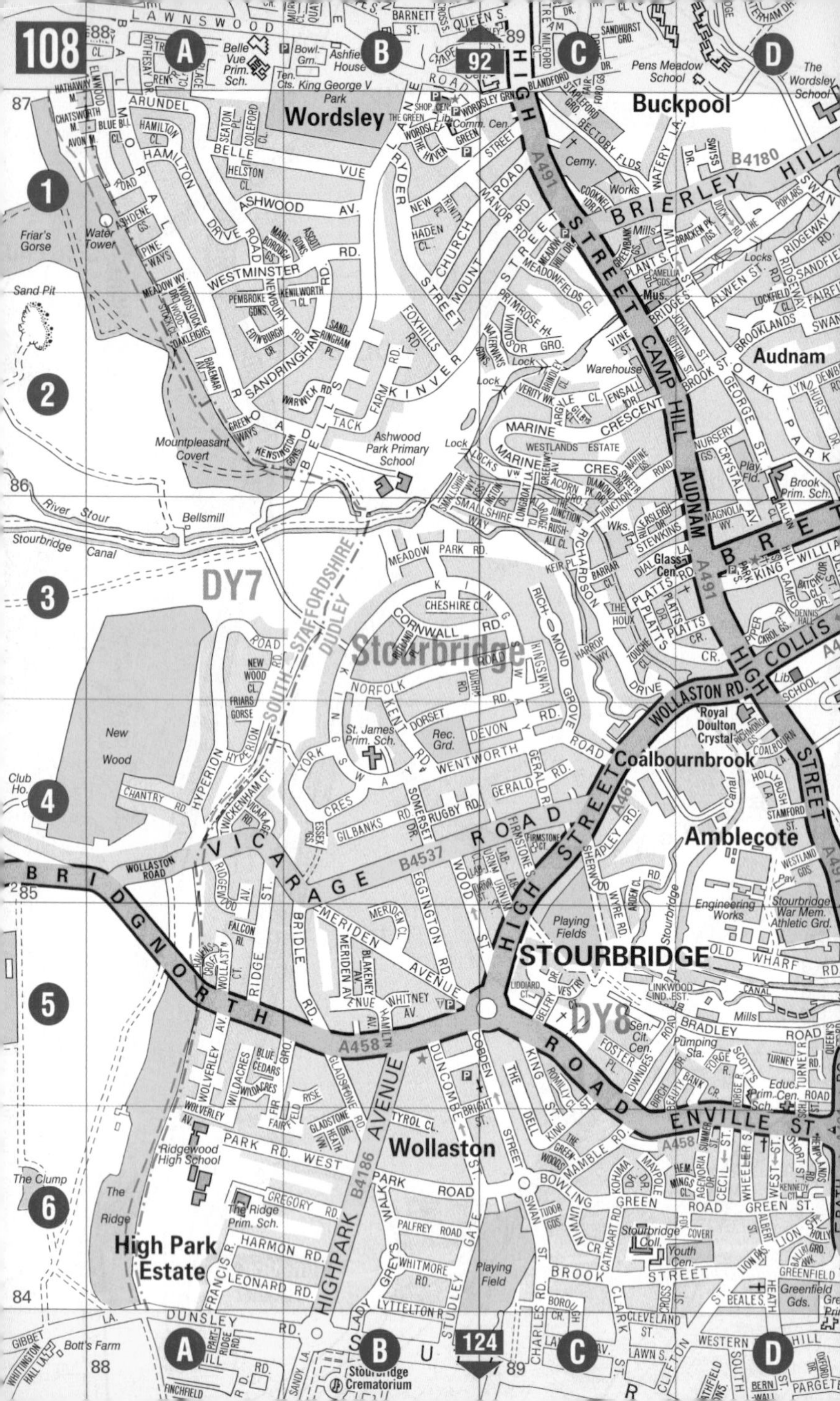

108
A
B
C
D
1
2
3
4
5
6
87
86
85
84
88
89
92
124
Wordsley
Buckpool
Audnam
Stourbridge
STOURBRIDGE
Amblecote
Coalbournbrook
Wollaston
High Park Estate
DY7
DY8
LAWNSWOOD
QUEEN ST.
BARNETT ST.
Belle Vue Prim. Sch.
Bowl. Grn.
Ashfield House
Ten. Cts.
King George V Park
Pens Meadow School
The Wordsley School
ARUNDEL
HAMILTON
BELLE VUE
HELSTON CL.
ASHWOOD AV.
WESTMINSTER RD.
SANDRINGHAM RD.
KINVER STREET
CHURCH STREET
MOUNT STREET
MANOR RD.
RYDER
BELLS LA.
TACK FARM
FOXHILLS RD.
Friar's Gorse
Sand Pit
Water Tower
Mountpleasant Covert
Ashwood Park Primary School
River Stour
Bellsmill
Stourbridge Canal
HIGH STREET
A491
BRIERLEY HILL
B4180
Cemy.
RECTORY FLDS.
WATERY LA.
Works
Mills
Mus.
CAMP HILL
AUDNAM
BROOK ST.
GEORGE ST.
OAK PARK
MARINE CRESCENT
WESTLANDS ESTATE
MARINE CRES.
Warehouse
Lock
SMALLSHIRE WAY
Brook Prim. Sch.
Glass Cen.
MEADOW PARK RD.
KINGSWAY
CHESHIRE CL.
CORNWALL RD.
NORFOLK RD.
DORSET RD.
DEVON RD.
WENTWORTH RD.
Rec. Grd.
St. James Prim. Sch.
RICHMOND GROVE
KINGSWAY
GROVE ROAD
RICHARDSON
HARROP WY.
PLATTS RD.
PLATTS CR.
COLLIS
WOLLASTON RD.
Royal Doulton Crystal
Lib.
SCHOOL
SOUTH STAFFORDSHIRE DUDLEY
New Wood
Club Ho.
CHANTRY RD.
HYPERION
VICARAGE ROAD
B4537
GILBANKS RD.
RUGBY RD.
GERALD RD.
BRIDGNORTH ROAD
A458
WOLLASTON ROAD
MERIDEN AVENUE
EGGINGTON RD.
WOOD ST.
HIGH STREET
A461
Playing Fields
Stourbridge
Engineering Works
Stourbridge War Mem. Athletic Grd.
OLD WHARF
LINKWOOD IND. EST.
CANAL
Mills
BRADLEY ROAD
Pumping Sta.
Sen. Cit. Cen.
FOSTER PL.
ROAD
ENVILLE ST.
HIGHPARK AVENUE
B4186
DUNCOMBE ST.
COBDEN STREET
THE DELL
KING ST.
MAMBLE RD.
PARK RD. WEST
PARK ROAD
PALFREY ROAD
WHITMORE RD.
HARMON RD.
LEONARD RD.
GREGORY RD.
The Ridge Prim. Sch.
Ridgewood High School
The Clump
The Ridge
BOWLING GREEN ROAD
GREEN ST.
Stourbridge Coll.
Youth Cen.
BROOK STREET
Playing Field
STUDLEY GATE
LADY GREYS WALK
LYTTELTON R.
DUNSLEY RD.
Bott's Farm
GIBBET LA.
Stourbridge Crematorium
CLEVELAND ST.
WESTERN HILL
Greenfield Gds.
BEALES ST.
Educ. Cen.

BRIERLEY HILL
Hawbush
High Ercal
Silver End
Withymoor Village
Brierley Hill
DY5
Holloway End
Bouchall
Clatterbatch
LYE
Hay Green
Stourbridge Town
DY9
Grange Estate
CORBETT HOSPITAL
Sewage Works
Freehold Farm
Mousehall Farm
Thorns Community College
River Stour
93
125
110

BRIERLEY HILL
MERRY HILL CENTRE
Saltwells Nature Reserve
Saltwells Wood
Saltwells Clay Field
Mushroom Green
Quarry Bank
Brierley Hill
DY5
STEVENS PARK
Dunn's Bank
Thorns Community College
Leisure Centre
Thorns Primary School
Mousehall Farm
Sewage Works
Cridden Works
LYE
Lye
Hay Green
Netherend
The Hayes
Cradley
Homer Hill
Cradley Heath
Wollescote
Halesowen Harriers Football Club
West Midlands Resettlement Unit
Mousesweet Brook Nature Reserve
Bob's Coppice
SALTBROOK TRADING ESTATE
GK DAVIES TRADING ESTATE
TIPPER TRADING ESTATE
OLD FORGE TRADING ESTATE
Beech Farm
94
109
126
A
B
C
D
1
2
3
4
5
6

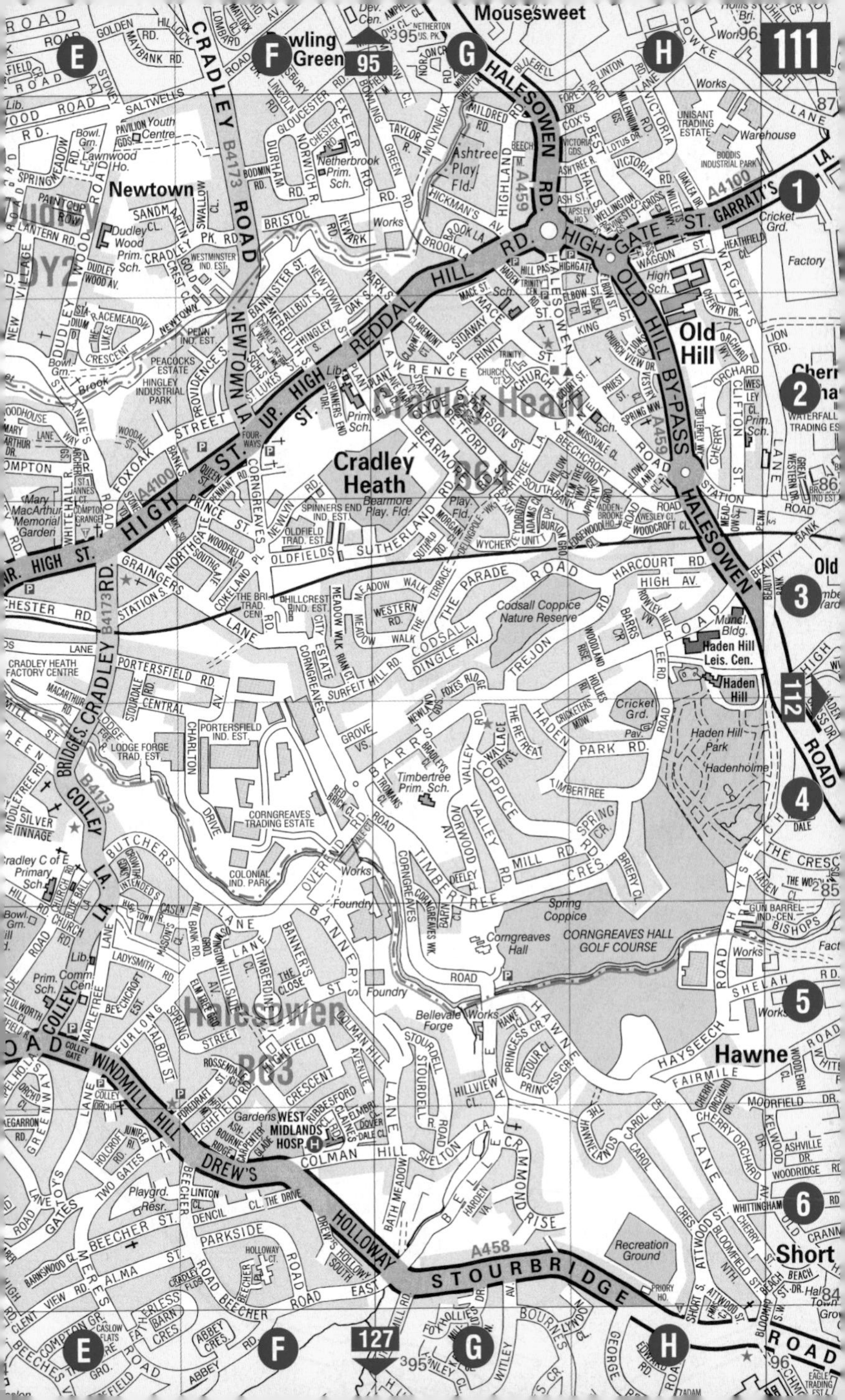

96
111
128

A
B
C
D
1
2
3
4
5
6
96
97
87
86
85
84
ROWLEY REGIS COMM. HOSPITAL
Rowley Regis Crematorium
Cemetery
POWKE LA
A4100
GARRATT'S LA.
Powke Lane Open Space
Totnal Bridge
POWKE LA INDUSTRIAL ESTATE
Factory
Cricket Grd.
Warehouse
Works
Cricket Grd.
Britannia Park
Britannia High Sch.
BIRMINGHAM RD.
B4171
Rowley Regis
HIGH ST.
HENDERSON WY.
OLDBURY RD.
STATION RD.
A4034
Superstore
Cherry Orchard
WATERFALL LANE TRADING ESTATE
Old Hill
Timber Yard
Cradley Heath
B64
B65
Haden Hill Leis. Cen.
Haden Hill Park
Hadenholme
HALESOWEN RD.
A459
HADEN HILL RD.
Blackheath Tunnel
Waterfall Lane Bridge
Depot
GORSTY HILL
COOMBS ROAD
A4099
College
COOMBESWOOD BUS. PK.
HIGHLAND HOUSE
Coombeswood
Halesowen
Olive Hill Primary School
Furnace Coppice
Factory
Works
Hawne
B63
Newfield Park Primary School
Halesowen College
HALESOWEN INDUSTRIAL PARK
Warehouse
Works Training Centre
Hawne Basin
MUCKLOW HILL TRADING ESTATE
MUCKLOW HILL
A458
Midlands Electricity
Heywood Bridge
Breaches Pool
DUDLEY RD.
HALESOWEN
Short Cross
Halesowen Town FC
STOURBRIDGE RD.
LEASOWES

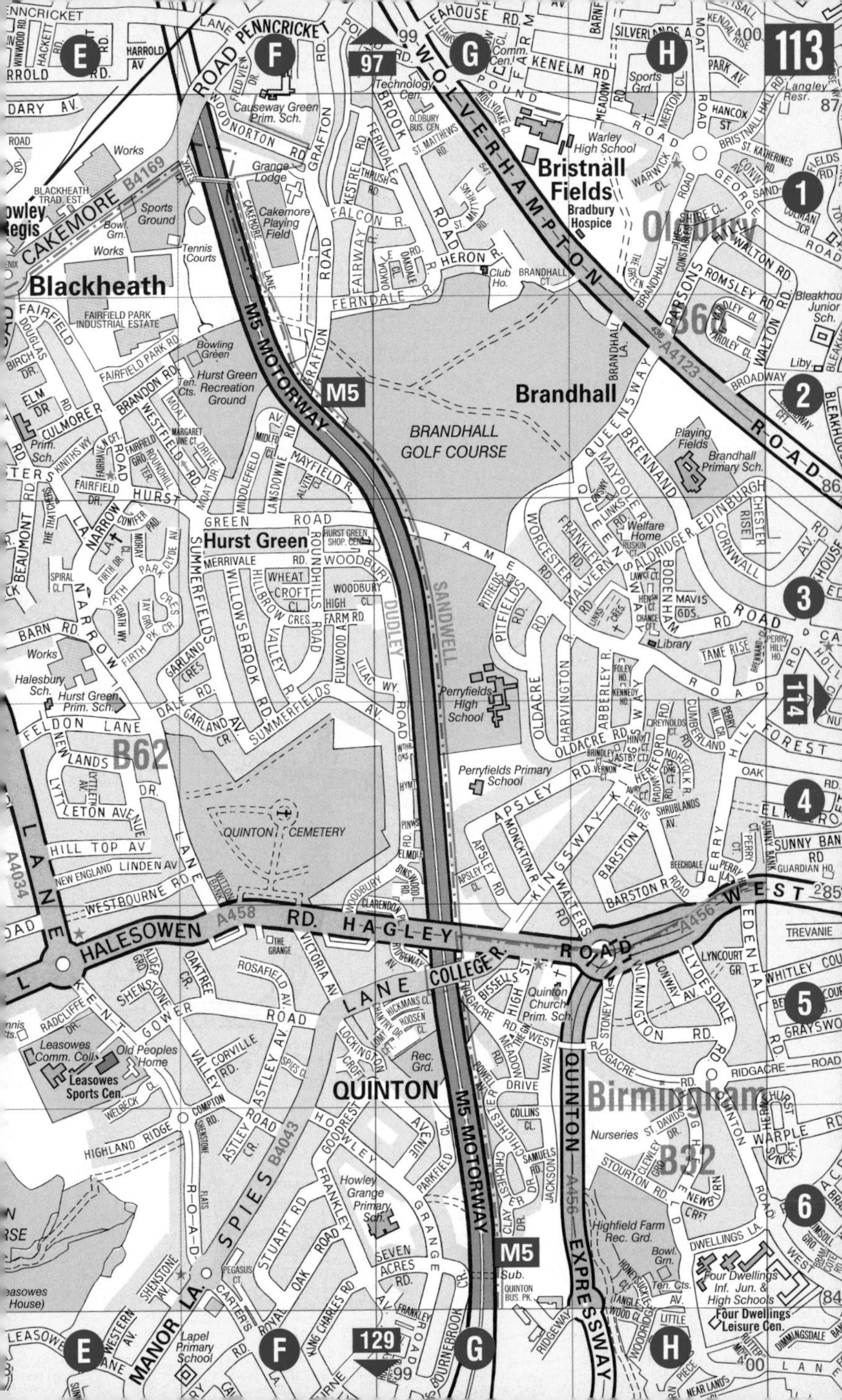
Blackheath
Bristnall Fields
Oldbury
Brandhall
BRANDHALL GOLF COURSE
Hurst Green
QUINTON
Birmingham
B62
B68
B32
M5 MOTORWAY
WOLVERHAMPTON ROAD
HAGLEY ROAD WEST
HALESOWEN RD.
QUINTON EXPRESSWAY
QUINTON CEMETERY
Perryfields High School
Warley High School
Bradbury Hospice
Brandhall Primary Sch.
Four Dwellings Inf. Jun. & High Schools
Four Dwellings Leisure Cen.
Leasowes Sports Cen.
Howley Grange Primary Sch.
Quinton Church Prim. Sch.
Lapel Primary School
Perryfields Primary School
Hurst Green Prim. Sch.
Causeway Green Prim. Sch.
97
114
129

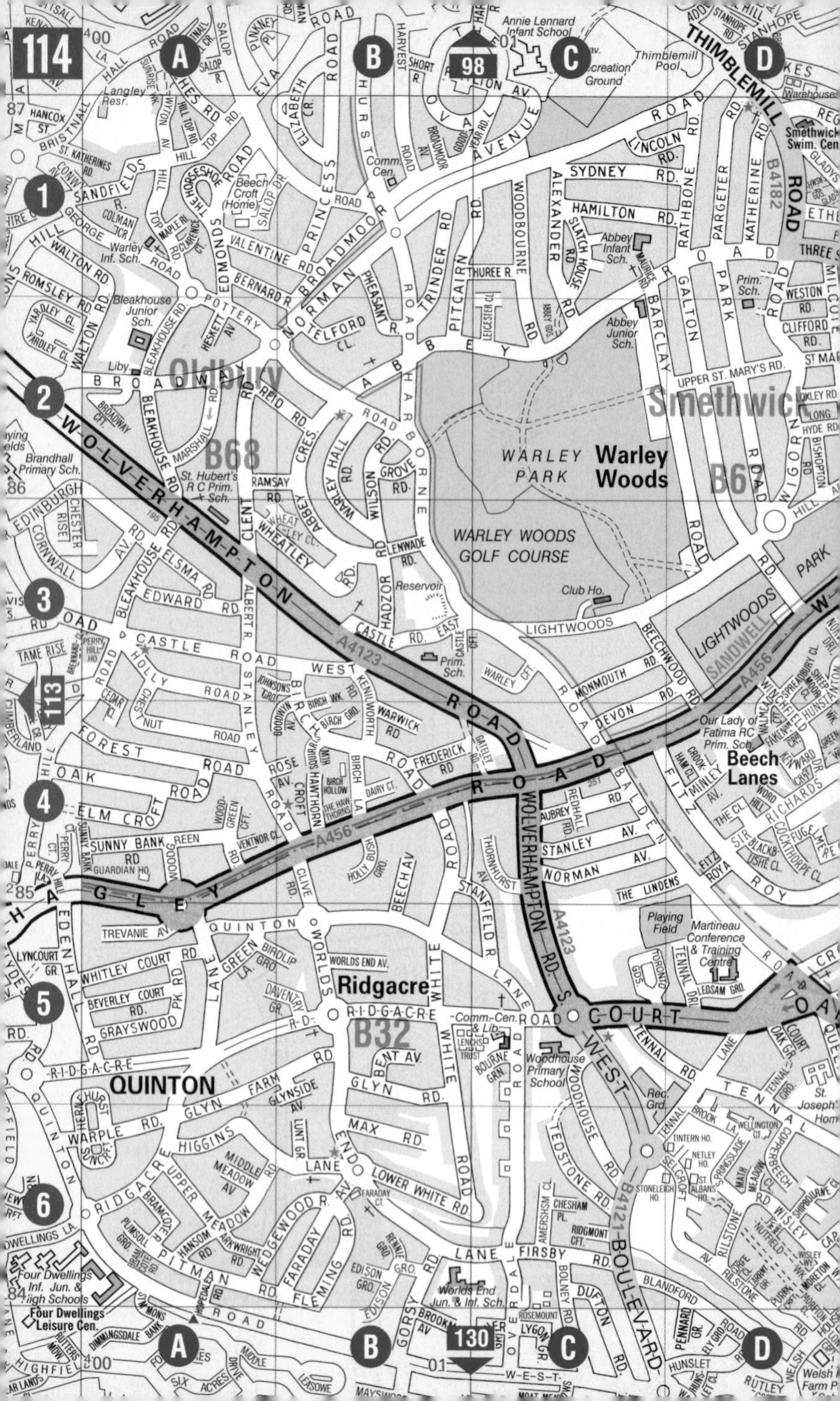

A
B
C
D
98
Annie Lennard Infant School
Thimblemill Pool
THIMBLEMILL ROAD
Langley Resr.
Smethwick Swim. Cen.
B4182
SANDFIELDS
SYDNEY RD.
HAMILTON RD.
LINCOLN RD.
Beech Croft (Home)
Comm. Cen.
Warley Inf. Sch.
Abbey Infant Sch.
Bleakhouse Junior Sch.
Abbey Junior Sch.
Prim. Sch.
Liby.
Oldbury
BROADWAY
Smethwick
WOLVERHAMPTON
B68
Brandhall Primary Sch.
St. Hubert's R C Prim. Sch.
WARLEY PARK
Warley Woods
WARLEY WOODS GOLF COURSE
Reservoir
Club Ho.
LIGHTWOODS
B67
CASTLE ROAD
A4123
ROAD
113
A456
Our Lady of Fatima RC Prim. Sch.
Beech Lanes
HAGLEY
QUINTON
Ridgacre
B32
Playing Field
Martineau Conference & Training Centre
Comm. Cen. & Lib.
Woodhouse Primary School
COURT ROAD
WEST BOULEVARD
B4121
Rec. Grd.
St. Joseph's Hom
Four Dwellings Inf. Jun. & High Schools
Four Dwellings Leisure Cen.
Worlds End Jun. & Inf. Sch.
130
Welsh Farm Pr

E
F
G
H
99
131
116
1
2
3
4
5
6
Bearwood
Birmingham
Chad Valley
HARBORNE
Harts Green
B16
B15
B17
B66
Hadley Stadium
Cardinal Newman RC Sch.
Sports Ground
Playing Field
The Portland Centre
Bowling Greens
Cricket Grd.
Club Ho.
The George Dixon Schools
Hindu Temple
Birmingham Squash Rackets Cen.
St. Paul's Convent
St. Paul's Girls' Sch.
School Play
Lordswood Boys' Sch. & Sixth Form Centre
Playing Fields
Oakhill House Children's Home
Leisure Gardens
Lordswood Girls Sch. & The Sixth Form Centre
Reservoir (covered)
WOODBOURNE PRIORY HOSP.
Norfolk Ho. Sch.
Fish Pond
Chad Vale Primary School
Sports Grd.
Fitness First
Queen Alexandra College
Baskerville School
Swim. Pool
Gala Bingo
Eccleston School
Harborne Prim. Sch.
St. Mary's RC Prim. Sch.
St. Peter's C of E Jun. Sch.
Cricket Grd.
Comm. Cen.
Lib.
School Playing Field
Pavilions
BIRMINGHAM WOMEN'S HOSPITAL
PORTLAND ROAD
CITY ROAD
HAGLEY ROAD
SANDON ROAD
BEARWOOD ROAD
LORDSWOOD ROAD
ROTTON PARK ROAD
NORFOLK RD.
NURSERY RD.
METCHLEY LANE
HIGH STREET
HARBORNE PARK RD.
WOODBOURNE ROAD
KNIGHTLOW ROAD
PEREIRA RD.
WESTFIELD RD.
AUGUSTUS ROAD
VERNON ROAD
YORK RD.
YATELEY ROAD
HARBORNE RD.
BARLOW'S RD.
WAR LANE
VICTORIA RD.
VICARAGE RD.
GREENFIELD RD.
MOOR POOL AV.
PARK HILL RD.
STATION RD.
GILLHURST RD.
OAKHAM RD.
RAVENHURST RD.
A4030
A4040
A456
B4182
B4125
B4129
B4124
B4123

EDGBASTON RESERVOIR
Midland Sailing Club
Ladywood Arts & Leisure Cen.
Ladywood
National Indoor Arena
Nelson Prim. Sch.
Birmingham Squash Rackets Cen.
St. Paul's RC Girls' Sch.
St. Paul's Convent
Perrott's Folly
Chamberlain Gdns.
The Oratory
Sixth Form Coll.
HAGLEY ROAD
MIDDLEWAY
BROAD
ISLINGTON ROW
FIVE WAYS
Five Ways
PORTLAND ROAD
VERNON ROAD
ICKNIELD PORT ROAD
MONUMENT RD.
HIGHFIELD RD.
CALTHORPE RD.
University of Central England (Westbourne Campus)
Edgbaston C of E College
The Princess Royal Centre
Worcs. & Birmingham Canal
Chad Valley
EDGBASTON
Birmingham Botanical Gardens
Edgbaston High Sch. for Girls
Edgbaston Archery & Lawn Tennis Society
Hallfield Sch.
Birmingham
CHURCH ROAD
HARBORNE ROAD
The Vale Halls of Residence
Harborne Hill School
The Blue Coat School
Queens Coll. (Theological)
THE BIRMINGHAM NUFFIELD HOSPITAL
University of Birmingham
EDGBASTON GOLF COURSE
Edgbaston Pool (Fish Pond)
QUEEN ELIZABETH HOSPITAL
BIRMINGHAM WOMEN'S HOSPITAL
Winterbourne Research Garden
PRIORY RD.
Priory Sch.
100
115
132
A B C D
1 2 3 4 5 6

E
F
G
H
101
1
2
3
4
5
6
4
5
118
133
BIRMINGHAM
Digbeth
Highgate
Lee Bank
Balsall Heath
B12
B15
B5
New St.
Moor St.
CALTHORPE PARK
Warwickshire County Cricket Club (Edgbaston)
Police Training College
Midlands Arts Centre
BICC & Symphony Hall
Theatre
Registry Office
Casino
Bowling Alley
Wholesale Markets
BRISTOL STREET
MIDDLEWAY
BELGRAVE
EDGBASTON ROAD
PERSHORE ROAD
BRISTOL ROAD
MOSELEY RD.
HADEN WAY
DIGBETH
HIGH ST. DERITEND
BRADFORD ST.
B4284
A38
A441
A4540
B4217
A435
A4167
B4100

Millennium Point
Freightliner Terminal
A
B
C
D
102
1
2
3
4
5
6
117
134
B4
B5
B8
B9
B11
B12
Birmingham Wheels Adventure Park
St. Andrews Industrial Estate
IMEX Business Park
Bordesley Green Girls Sch.
Whitworth Industrial Park
Garrison Circus
Garrison La. Pk.
Watery Lane Middleway
Bordesley
Kingston Hill Local Pk.
Birmingham City FC (St. Andrews)
Deritend
Digbeth
Coventry Rd.
Cattell Rd.
Bordesley Circus
Bordesley Middleway
Camp Hill
Camp Hill Circus
Highgate Middleway
Calthorpe Sch.
Stratford Road
Small Heath Highway
Sparkbrook
Farm Park
Grand Union Canal
Montgomery St.
Small Heath
Poets Corner
Highgate Road
Balsall Heath
Pickwick Park
Nelson Mandela Sch.
Golden Hillock Sch.
Golden Hillock Rd.
Warwick Road
Walford Road
Sports Grd.
Small Heath Trading Estate
Armoury Trading Estate
Victoria St.
Muntz St.
Leisure Cen.
Mosque
Balsall Heath Park
Sara Pk.
Superstores
Camp Hill Ind. Est.

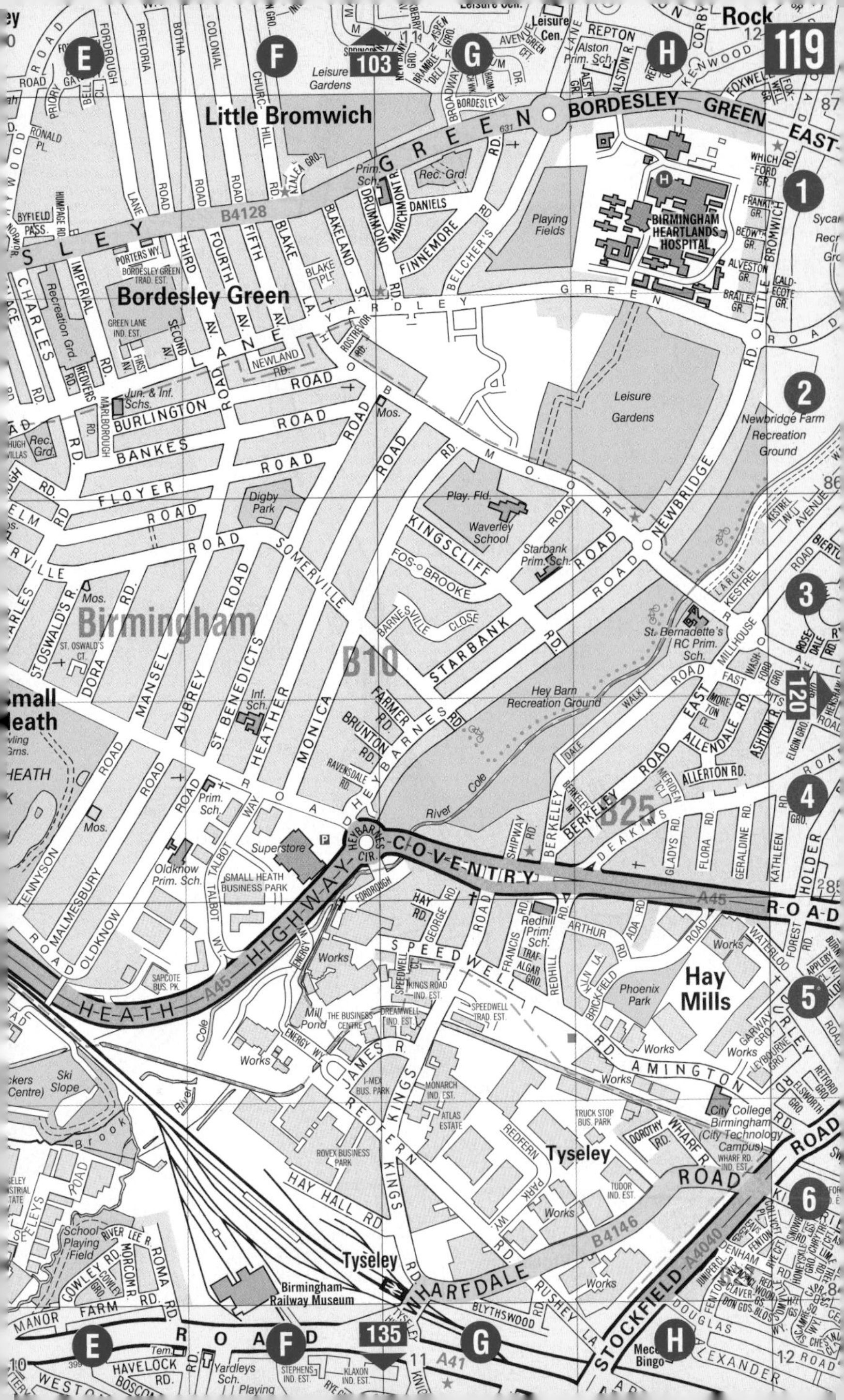
Little Bromwich
Bordesley Green
Birmingham
Small Heath
B10
B25
Hay Mills
Tyseley
Birmingham Heartlands Hospital
Leisure Gardens
Playing Fields
Newbridge Farm Recreation Ground
Hey Barn Recreation Ground
Waverley School
Starbank Prim. Sch.
St. Bernadette's RC Prim. Sch.
Digby Park
Oldknow Prim. Sch.
Small Heath Business Park
Superstore
Phoenix Park
City College Birmingham (City Technology Campus)
Birmingham Railway Museum
Ski Slope
Bordesley Green
Coventry Road
Heybarnes Cir.
Highway
Heath
Wharfdale
Stockfield
Yardley Green
Speedwell
Amington
Redfern
Hay Hall Rd.
Kings Rd.
A45
A4040
B4146
B4128
A41
103
120
135

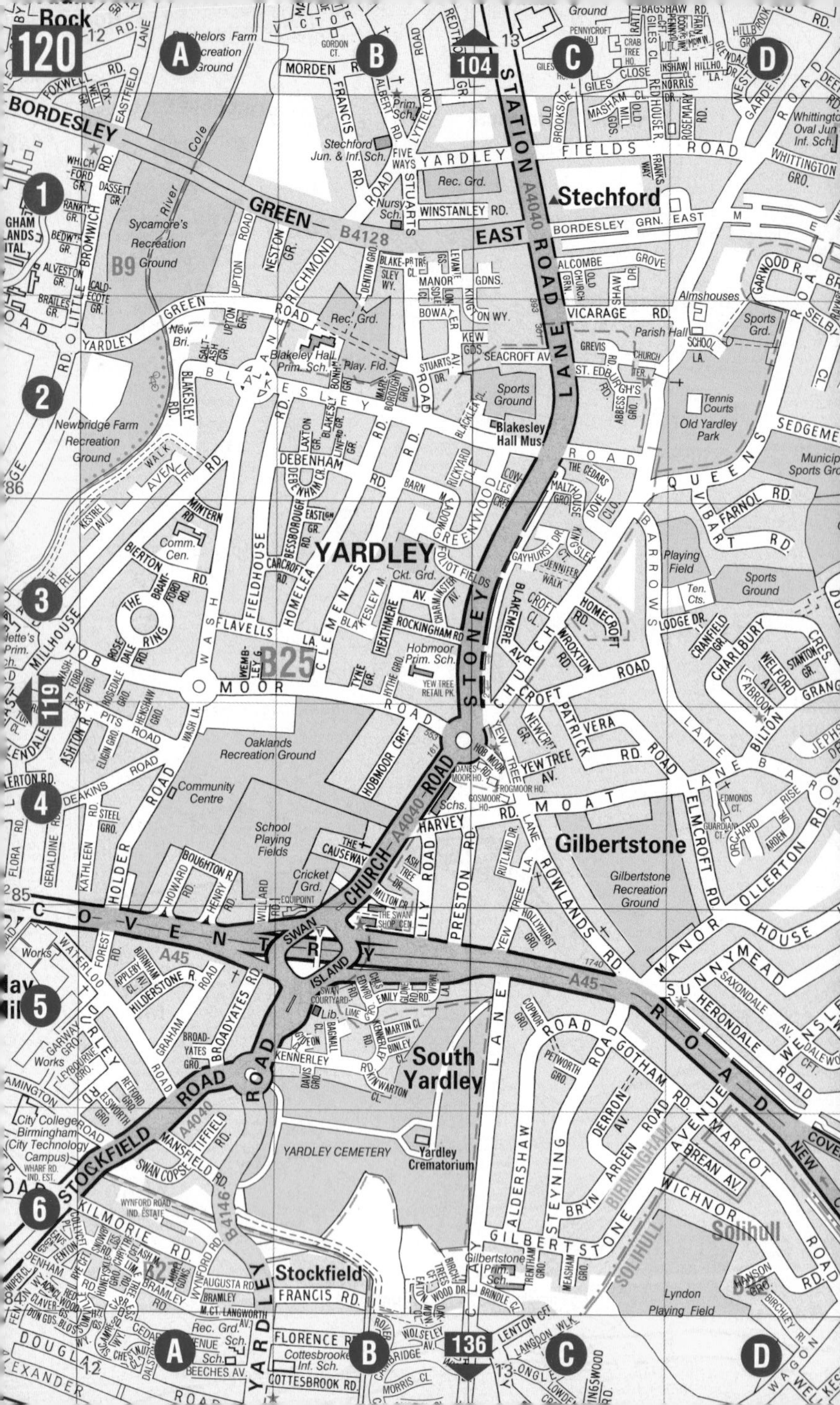

Stechford
YARDLEY
Gilbertstone
South Yardley
Stockfield
STATION ROAD
STONEY LANE
COVENTRY ROAD
BORDESLEY GREEN EAST
YARDLEY CEMETERY
Yardley Crematorium
Old Yardley Park
Oaklands Recreation Ground
Gilbertstone Recreation Ground
Sycamore's Recreation Ground
Newbridge Farm Recreation Ground
Lyndon Playing Field
City College Birmingham (City Technology Campus)
Blakesley Hall Mus.
Hobmoor Prim. Sch.
B25
B9
A45
A4040
B4128
B4146
Solihull
104
119
136

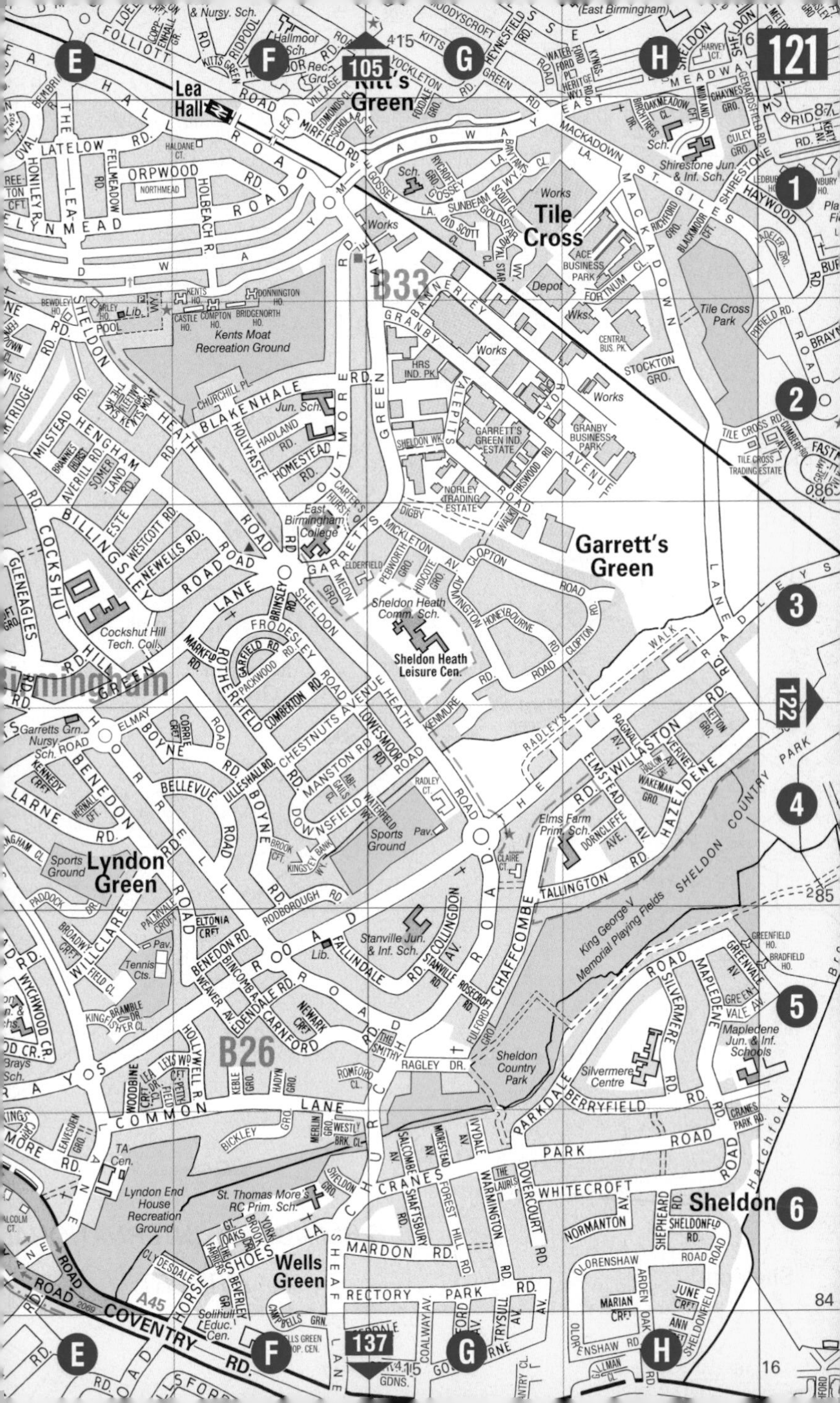
E
F
G
H
105
Kitt's Green
Lea Hall
Tile Cross
B33
Garrett's Green
Kents Moat Recreation Ground
Sheldon Heath Comm. Sch.
Sheldon Heath Leisure Cen.
East Birmingham College
Cockshut Hill Tech. Coll.
Lyndon Green
B26
Sheldon Country Park
King George V Memorial Playing Fields
Tile Cross Park
Lyndon End House Recreation Ground
St. Thomas More's RC Prim. Sch.
Wells Green
Sheldon
Stanville Jun. & Inf. Sch.
Elms Farm Prim. Sch.
Mapledene Jun. & Inf. Schools
Silvermere Centre
Shirestone Jun. & Inf. Sch.
Solihull Educ. Cen.
COVENTRY RD.
A45
122
137
1
2
3
4
5
6
E
F
G
H

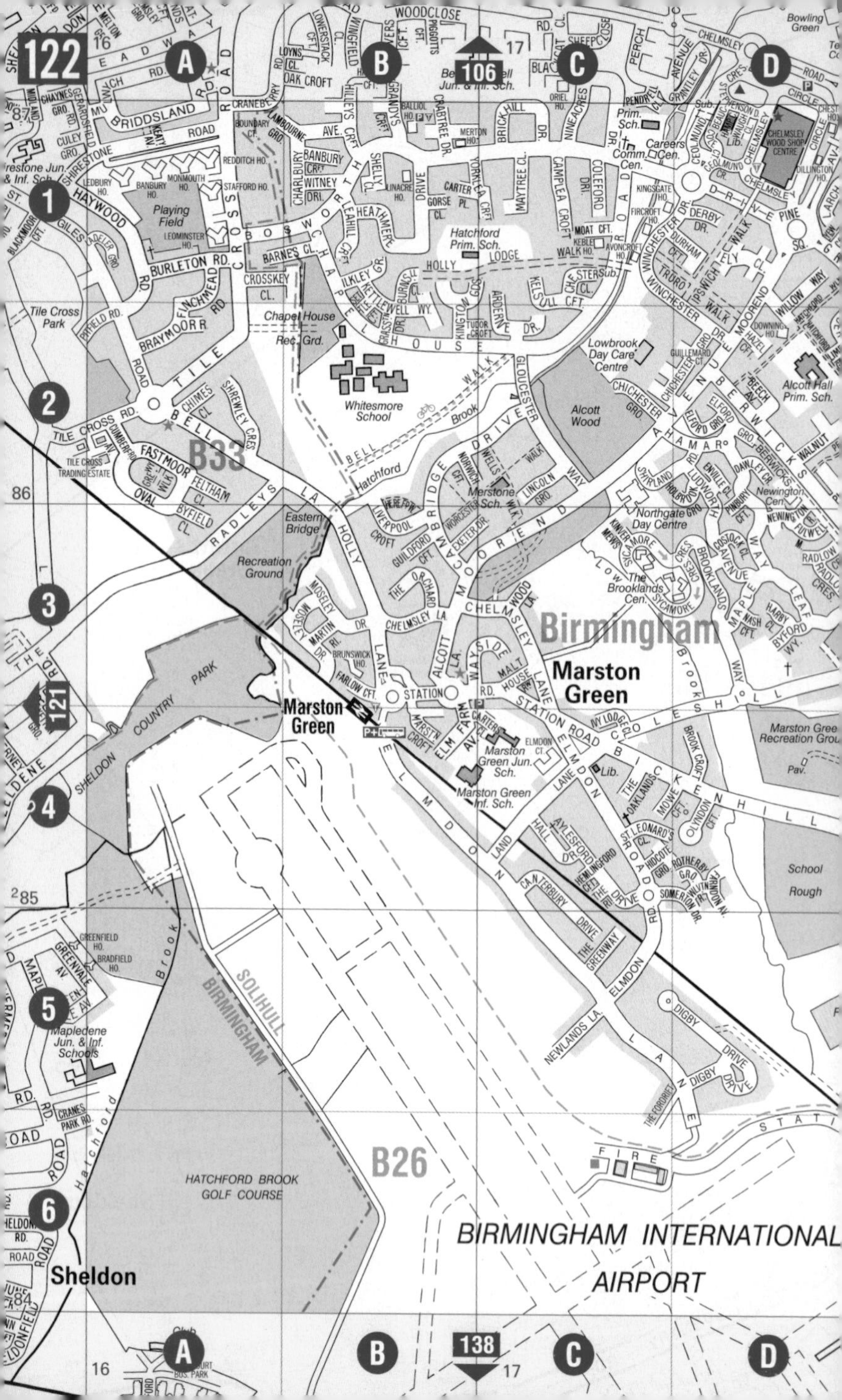
A
B
C
D
106
16
17
1
2
3
4
5
6
86
85
84
121
138
WOODCLOSE
PIGGOTTS
WINGFIELD
LOWERSTACK CFT.
LOYNS CL.
OAK CROFT
BRIDDSLAND
SHIRESTONE ROAD
CRANEBERRY ROAD
LAMBOURNE GRO.
AVE.
BANBURY CFT.
WITNEY DRI.
CHARLBURY
SHELLY CL.
LINACRE HO.
DRIVE
GORSE CL.
CARTER PL.
YORKLEA CFT.
MAYTREE CL.
CAMPLEA CROFT
COLEFORD DRI.
NINEACRES
BRICK HILL DR.
CRABTREE DR.
MERTON HO.
BALLIOL HO.
GRANDYS CFT.
HILLEYS CFT.
Prim. Sch.
Careers Cen.
Comm. Cen.
CHELMSLEY WOOD SHOP CENTRE
Lib.
CHELMSLEY CIRCLE
DILLINGTON HO.
CHELMSLEY DRIVE
PINE SQ.
KINGSGATE HO.
FIRCROFT HO.
MOAT CFT.
KEBLE HO.
WALK
AVONCROFT HO.
Hatchford Prim. Sch.
HOLLY
LODGE
HEATHMERE
LEAHILL CFT.
ILKLEY GR.
KETTLEWELL WY.
BURNS CL.
KINGTON GDS.
ARDERNE DR.
TUDOR CROFT
KELSULL CFT.
CHESTER CL.
WINCHESTER DR.
DERBY DR.
DURHAM CFT.
TRURO
ELY CL.
IPSWICH WALK
WINCHESTER WALK
MOOREND
WILLOW WAY
DOWNING HO.
HAZEL CFT.
Alcott Hall Prim. Sch.
Lowbrook Day Care Centre
GUILLEMARD CT.
CHICHESTER GRO.
BEECH AV.
ELFORD GRO.
HAMAR
BERWICKS
WALNUT
Playing Field
LEOMINSTER HO.
BANBURY HO.
MONMOUTH HO.
REDDITCH HO.
STAFFORD HO.
BOUNDARY CFT.
LEDBURY HO.
Firestone Jun. & Inf. Sch.
HAYWOOD
GILES
BLACKMOOR CFT.
BURLETON RD.
CROSS
BOSWORTH
BARNES CL.
CHAPEL HOUSE
CROSSKEY CL.
Chapel House Rec. Grd.
FINCHMEAD RD.
BRAYMOOR RD.
Tile Cross Park
PYFIELD RD.
ROAD
TILE
TILE CROSS RD.
CHIMES CL.
SHREWLEY CRES.
BELL
Whitesmore School
GLOUCESTER
Alcott Wood
FASTMOOR OVAL
FELTHAM CL.
BYFIELD CL.
TILE CROSS TRADING ESTATE
B33
RADLEYS
BELL WALK
Brook
Hatchford
DRIVE
CAMBRIDGE
LIVERPOOL CROFT
WELLS
Merstone Sch.
LINCOLN GRO.
WAY
MOOREND
Northgate Day Centre
SYCAMORE CRES.
KINVER MEWS
The Brooklands Cen.
BROOKLANDS
AVENUE
MAPLE
LEAF
WAY
NEWINGTON
Newington Cen.
RADLOW CRES.
HARBY CL.
BYFORD WY.
NASH CFT.
Eastern Bridge
HOLLY
LA.
Recreation Ground
GUILDFORD CFT.
THE ORCHARD
MOSELEY DR.
MARTIN DR.
BRUNSWICK HO.
CHELMSLEY LA.
ALCOTT LA.
CHELMSLEY
WAYSIDE
MALT HOUSE
LANE
Birmingham
Marston Green
SHELDON COUNTRY PARK
Marston Green
STATION
FARLOW CFT.
MARSTON CROFT
ELM FARM AV.
Marston Green Jun. Sch.
Marston Green Inf. Sch.
STATION ROAD
IVY LODGE CL.
COLESHILL
BICKENHILL
Lib.
THE OAKLANDS
MOWE CFT.
OLYNDON CFT.
BROOK CROFT
Marston Green Recreation Ground
Pav.
School Rough
ELMDON
LANE
HALL
AYLESFORD DR.
HEMLINGFORD CFT.
THE DRIVE
ST. LEONARD'S CL.
HIDCOTE GRO.
ROTHERBY GRO.
SOMERTON DR.
CANTERBURY DRIVE
THE GREENWAY
ELMDON LANE
NEWLANDS LA.
DIGBY DRIVE
THE FORDRIFT
FIRE STATION
SOLIHULL
BIRMINGHAM
GREENFIELD HO.
BRADFIELD HO.
GREENVALE AV.
Mapledene Jun. & Inf. Schools
CRANES PARK RD.
ROAD
Hatchford
Brook
HATCHFORD BROOK GOLF COURSE
B26
BIRMINGHAM INTERNATIONAL AIRPORT
Sheldon
SHELDON RD.
Club
BUS. PARK

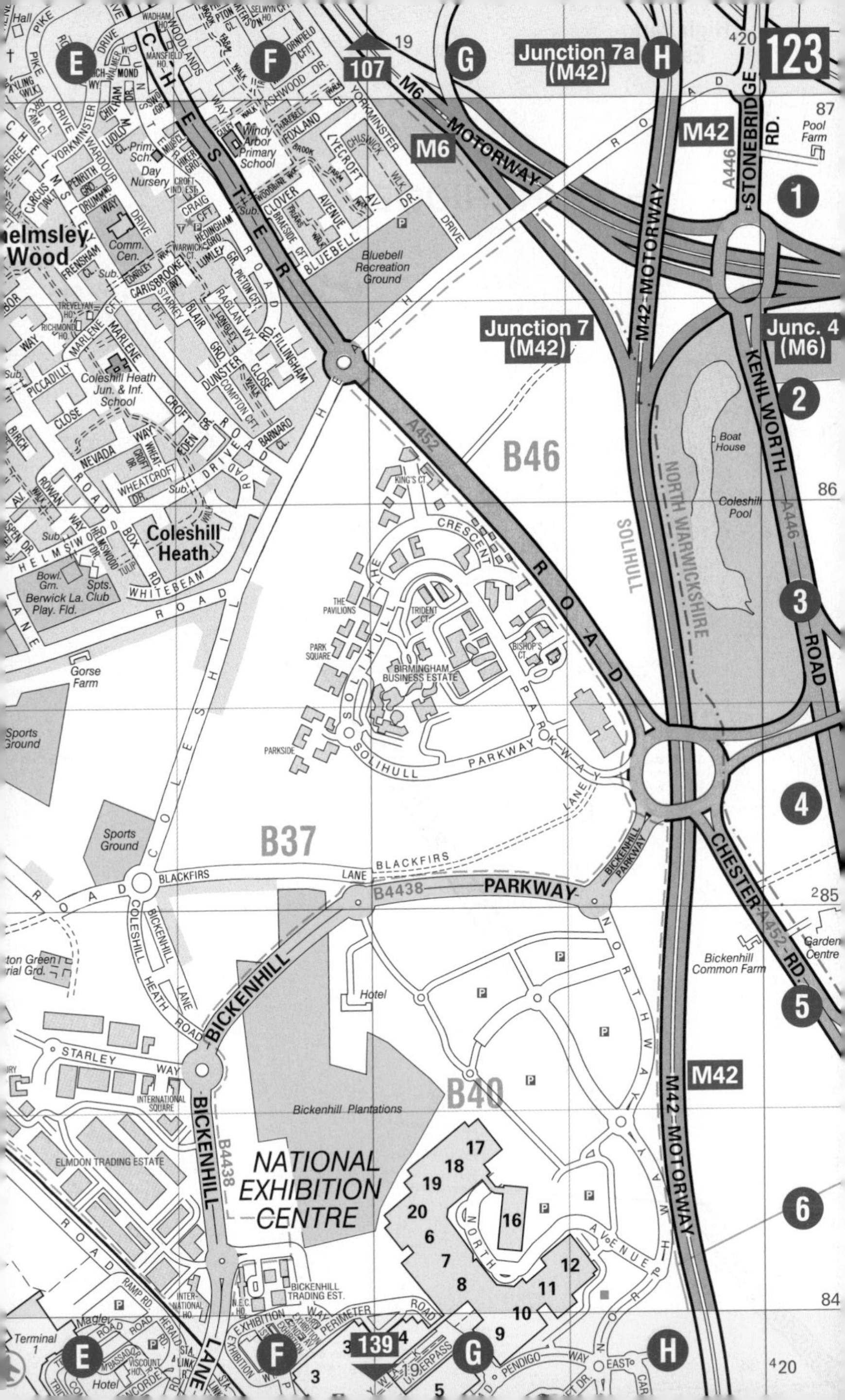
Junction 7a (M42)
M6 MOTORWAY
M42
Junction 7 (M42)
Junc. 4 (M6)
STONEBRIDGE RD.
KENILWORTH ROAD
CHESTER ROAD
M42 MOTORWAY
Pool Farm
Boat House
Coleshill Pool
NORTH WARWICKSHIRE
SOLIHULL
B46
B37
B40
Chelmsley Wood
Coleshill Heath
Windy Arbor Primary School
Day Nursery
Comm. Cen.
Coleshill Heath Jun. & Inf. School
Bluebell Recreation Ground
BIRMINGHAM BUSINESS ESTATE
SOLIHULL PARKWAY
BLACKFIRS LANE
PARKWAY
BICKENHILL LANE
COLESHILL HEATH ROAD
Gorse Farm
Sports Ground
Berwick La. Play. Fld.
Bickenhill Common Farm
Garden Centre
Hotel
Bickenhill Plantations
NATIONAL EXHIBITION CENTRE
ELMDON TRADING ESTATE
BICKENHILL TRADING EST.
STARLEY WAY
INTERNATIONAL SQUARE
PERIMETER ROAD
NORTH WAY
NORTH AVENUE
PENDIGO WAY
Terminal 1
107
139

High Park Est
STOURBRIDGE
Stourbridge Crematorium
Cemetery
Heath
Norton
Stourbridge
Gig Mill Prim. Sch.
Adult Educ. Cen.
Comm. Cen.
Council Offices
Heath Pool
Mary Stevens Park
Swinford Common
Pedmore Common
STOURBRIDGE
Racecourse Farm
Norton Covert
Little Iverley Covert
Frog Hall Cotts.
High Lodge
High Lodge Farm
DY7
Stourbridge Lawn Tennis & Squash Club
Tennis Courts
Sugar Loaf Kennels
Beechlands
Beehive Bungalow
Iverley Park Farm
Sugarloaf Farm
Iverley
Rickstones
DY10
Iverley Hay Farm
Upper Brake Farm
The Birches
DY8
Bury's Hill
Bott's Farm
NORTON ROAD
A451
B4186
SOUTH ROAD
KIDDERMINSTER ROAD
SUGAR LOAF LANE
SOUTH STAFFORDSHIRE
DUDLEY
RACECOURSE LANE
COUNTY LANE
Roman Road
CROWN LANE
ROMAN ROAD
CLENT VIEW ROAD
108
A B C D
1 2 3 4 5 6
84 83 82 81
88 89

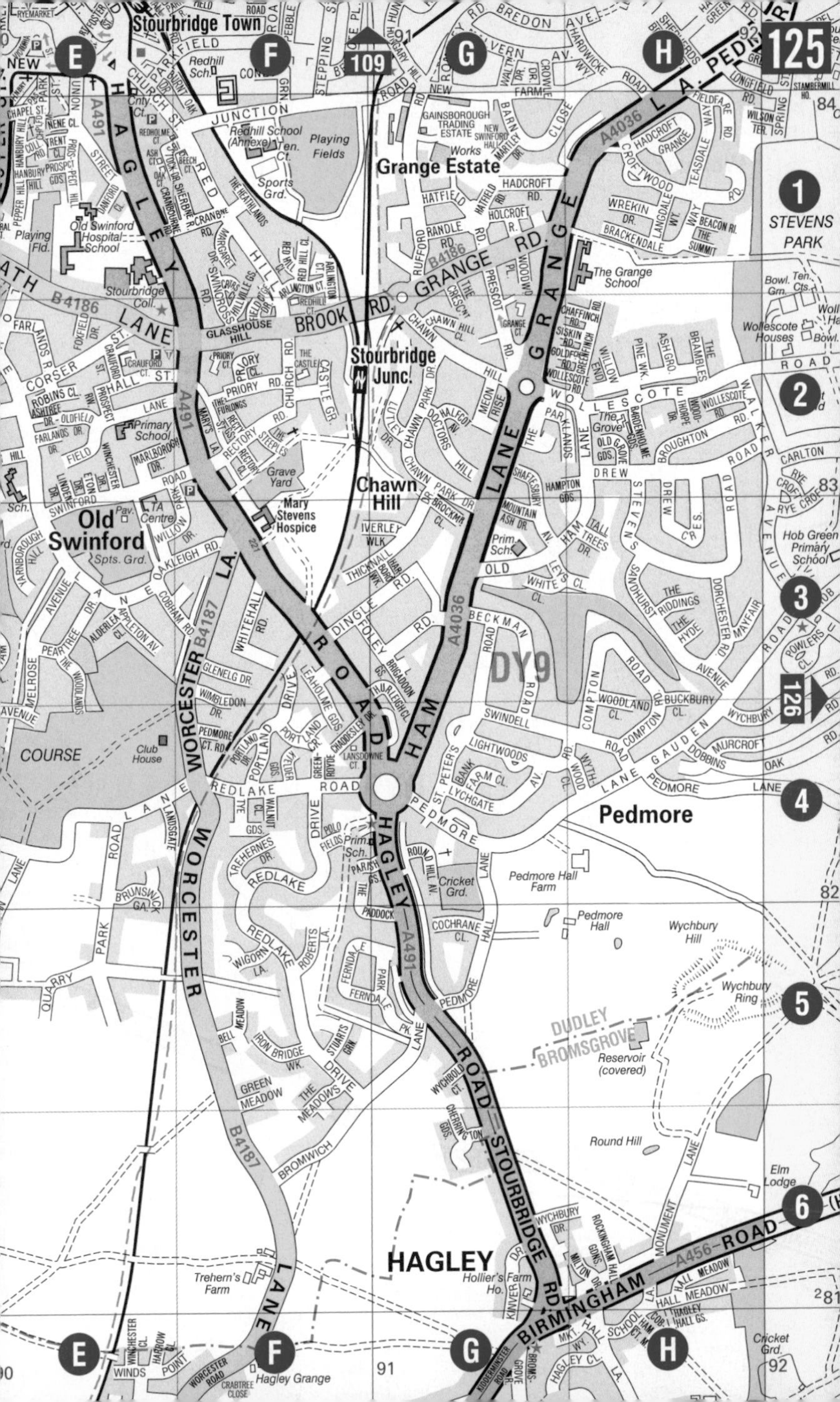
125
109
126
Stourbridge Town
Grange Estate
Stourbridge Junc.
Chawn Hill
Old Swinford
Pedmore
HAGLEY
DY9
STEVENS PARK
Playing Fields
Redhill Sch.
Redhill School (Annexe)
Sports Grd.
Old Swinford Hospital School
Stourbridge Coll.
The Grange School
Wollescote Houses
Hob Green Primary School
Primary School
Mary Stevens Hospice
Grave Yard
COURSE
Club House
Pedmore Hall Farm
Pedmore Hall
Wychbury Hill
Wychbury Ring
DUDLEY
BROMSGROVE
Reservoir (covered)
Round Hill
Elm Lodge
Cricket Grd.
Trehern's Farm
Hollier's Farm Ho.
Hagley Grange
HAGLEY ROAD
WORCESTER LANE
WORCESTER LA.
GRANGE LANE
GRANGE RD.
BROOK RD.
HAMLANE
STOURBRIDGE ROAD
BIRMINGHAM RD.
A456 ROAD
A491
A4036
B4186
B4187
REDLAKE ROAD
PEDMORE LANE
GAUDEN ROAD
WOLLESCOTE ROAD
DREW ROAD

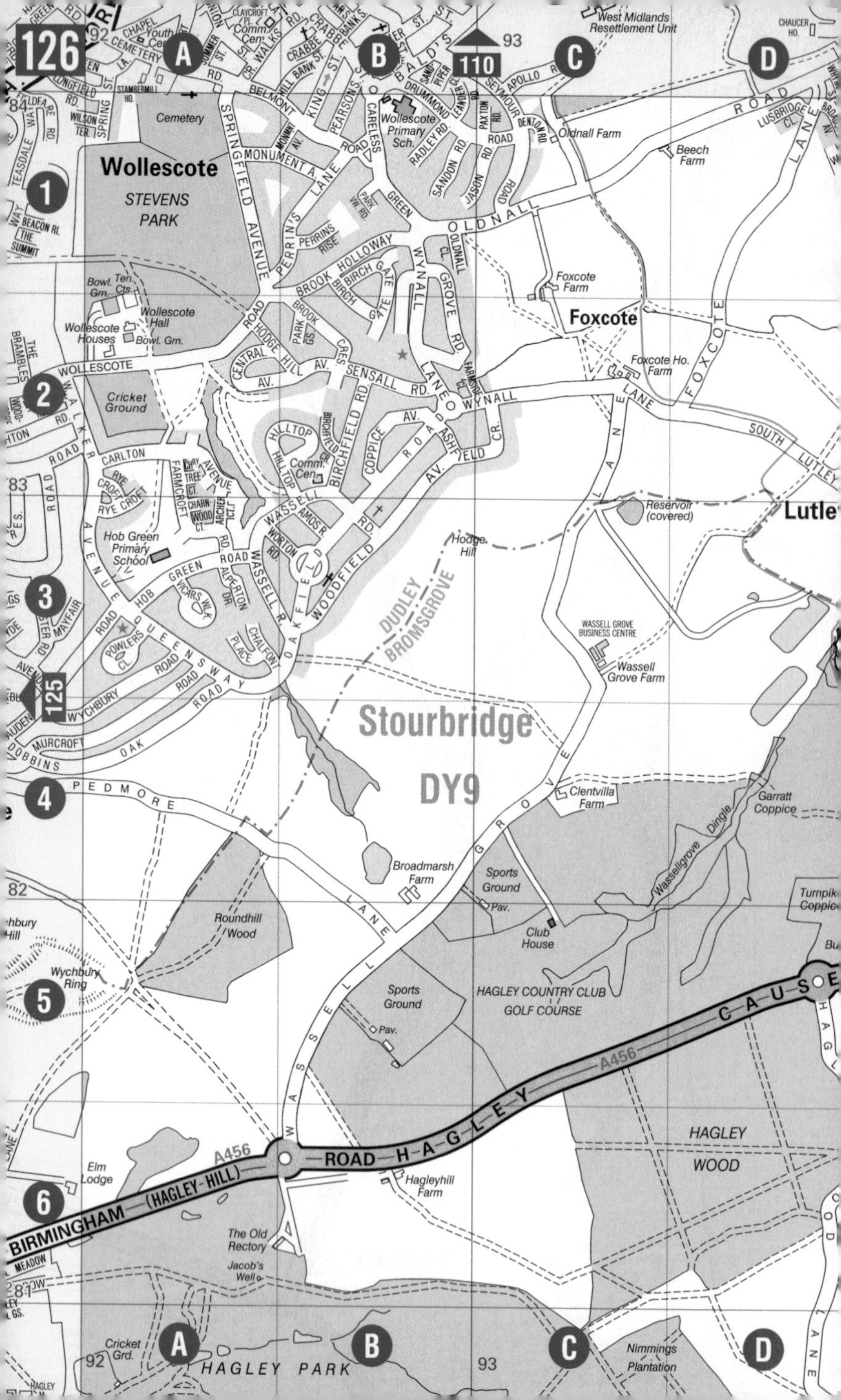
Wollescote
STEVENS PARK
Cemetery
Foxcote
Stourbridge
DY9
HAGLEY COUNTRY CLUB GOLF COURSE
HAGLEY WOOD
HAGLEY PARK
Roundhill Wood
Wychbury Ring
Broadmarsh Farm
Foxcote Farm
Foxcote Ho. Farm
Oldnall Farm
Beech Farm
Wassell Grove Farm
WASSELL GROVE BUSINESS CENTRE
Clentvilla Farm
Garratt Coppice
Wassellgrove Dingle
Reservoir (covered)
Hodge Hill
DUDLEY
BROMSGROVE
Sports Ground
Club House
Hagleyhill Farm
The Old Rectory
Jacob's Well
Elm Lodge
Nimmings Plantation
Cricket Ground
Hob Green Primary School
Wollescote Hall
Wollescote Houses
Wollescote Primary Sch.
West Midlands Resettlement Unit
HAGLEY ROAD
BIRMINGHAM (HAGLEY HILL)
A456
WASSELL GROVE LANE
PEDMORE LANE
OLDNALL ROAD
SOUTH ROAD
FOXCOTE LANE
QUEENSWAY
WYNALL LANE
SPRINGFIELD AVENUE
PERRIN'S LANE
WOODFIELD AV.
110
125

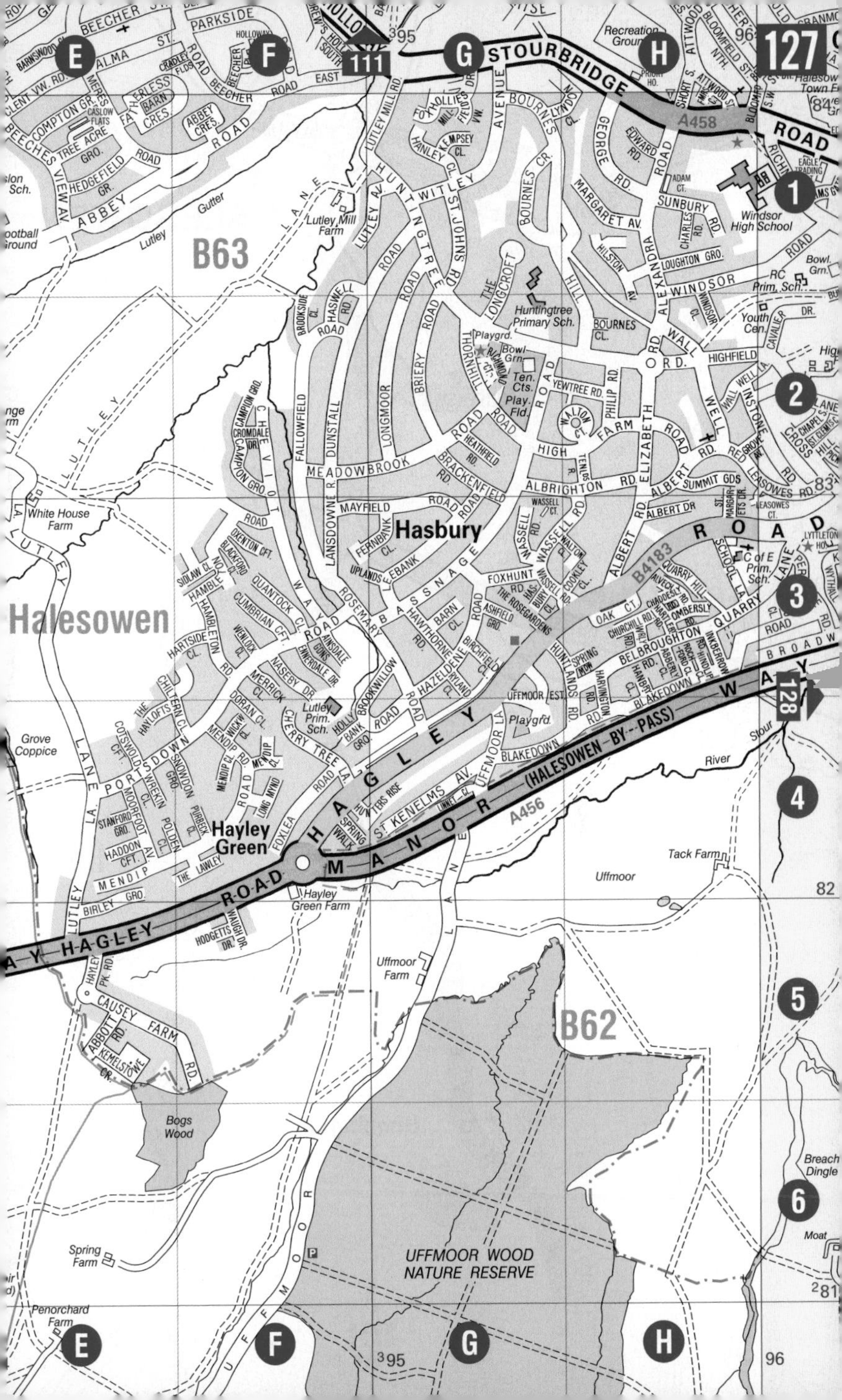
STOURBRIDGE ROAD
A458
Halesowen
Hasbury
Hayley Green
HAGLEY ROAD
MANOR WAY (HALESOWEN BY-PASS)
A456
B4183
B63
B62
Windsor High School
Huntingtree Primary Sch.
Lutley Prim. Sch.
Lutley Mill Farm
White House Farm
Grove Coppice
Hayley Green Farm
Uffmoor Farm
Tack Farm
Uffmoor
Bogs Wood
Spring Farm
Penorchard Farm
UFFMOOR WOOD NATURE RESERVE
Breach Dingle
River Stour
111
128

A
B
C
D
1
2
3
4
5
6
112
127
142
96
97
84
83
82
81
HALESOWEN
Halesowen
STOURBRIDGE ROAD
A458
MUCKLOW HILL
QUEENSWAY
HIGH ST.
HAGLEY ROAD
B4183
MANOR WAY (HALESOWEN BY-PASS)
A456
BROMSGROVE RD.
A459
GRANGE HILL
GRANGE ROAD
BROMSGROVE ROAD
B4551
ILLEY
B63
B62
DUDLEY
BROMSGROVE
River Stour
Halesowen Town FC
Windsor High School
The Earls High School
Shenstone Trad. Est.
Belfont Trad. Est.
Breaches Pool
Heywood Bridge
Manor Way Primary Sch.
Seth Somers Pk. Cricket Grd.
Seth Somers Track
Halesowen Abbey
Manor Abbey Farm
The Grange
Sports Ground
Grange Hill House
Oatenfields Farm
Illey Mill
Illeybrook Farm
Doverhousefields Farm
Goodrest Farm
Hunnington
Blue Bird Park
Rec. Grd.
Breach Dingle
Moat
Breach Farm
Illey House Farm
Paddock Wood
GOLF

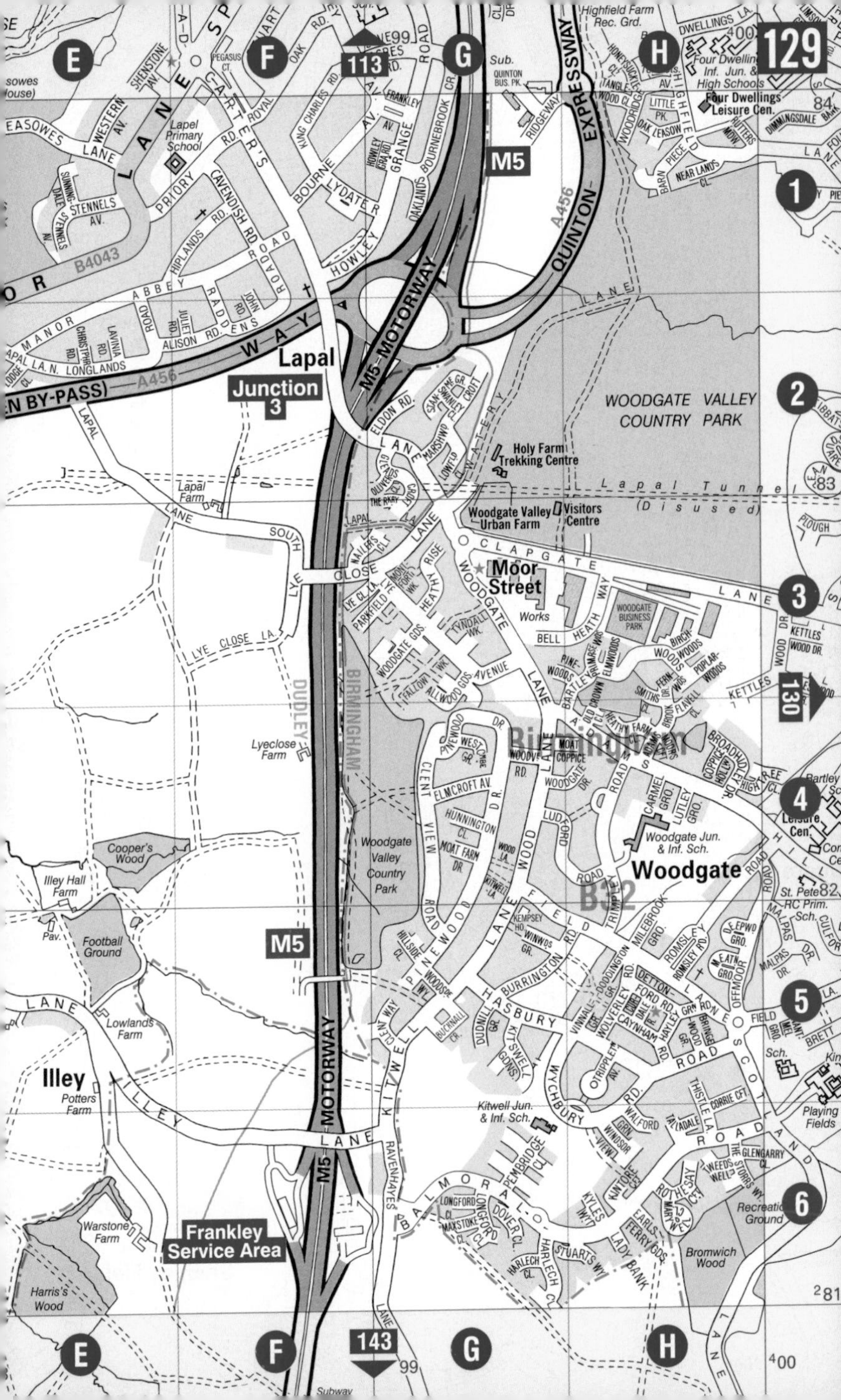

E
F
G
H
113
129
1
2
3
4
5
6
130
143
M5
Lapal
Junction 3
Lapal Primary School
WOODGATE VALLEY COUNTRY PARK
Holy Farm Trekking Centre
Woodgate Valley Urban Farm
Visitors Centre
Moor Street
Lapal Tunnel (Disused)
Woodgate Valley Country Park
Woodgate Jun. & Inf. Sch.
Woodgate
B32
Kitwell Jun. & Inf. Sch.
Illey
Potters Farm
Lyeclose Farm
Lapal Farm
Cooper's Wood
Illey Hall Farm
Football Ground
Lowlands Farm
Warstone Farm
Harris's Wood
Frankley Service Area
M5 MOTORWAY
QUINTON EXPRESSWAY
A456
B4043
Four Dwellings Inf. Jun. & High Schools
Four Dwellings Leisure Cen.
Highfield Farm Rec. Grd.
Bromwich Wood
Recreation Ground
Playing Fields
St. Peter's RC Prim. Sch.
WOODGATE BUSINESS PARK
Works

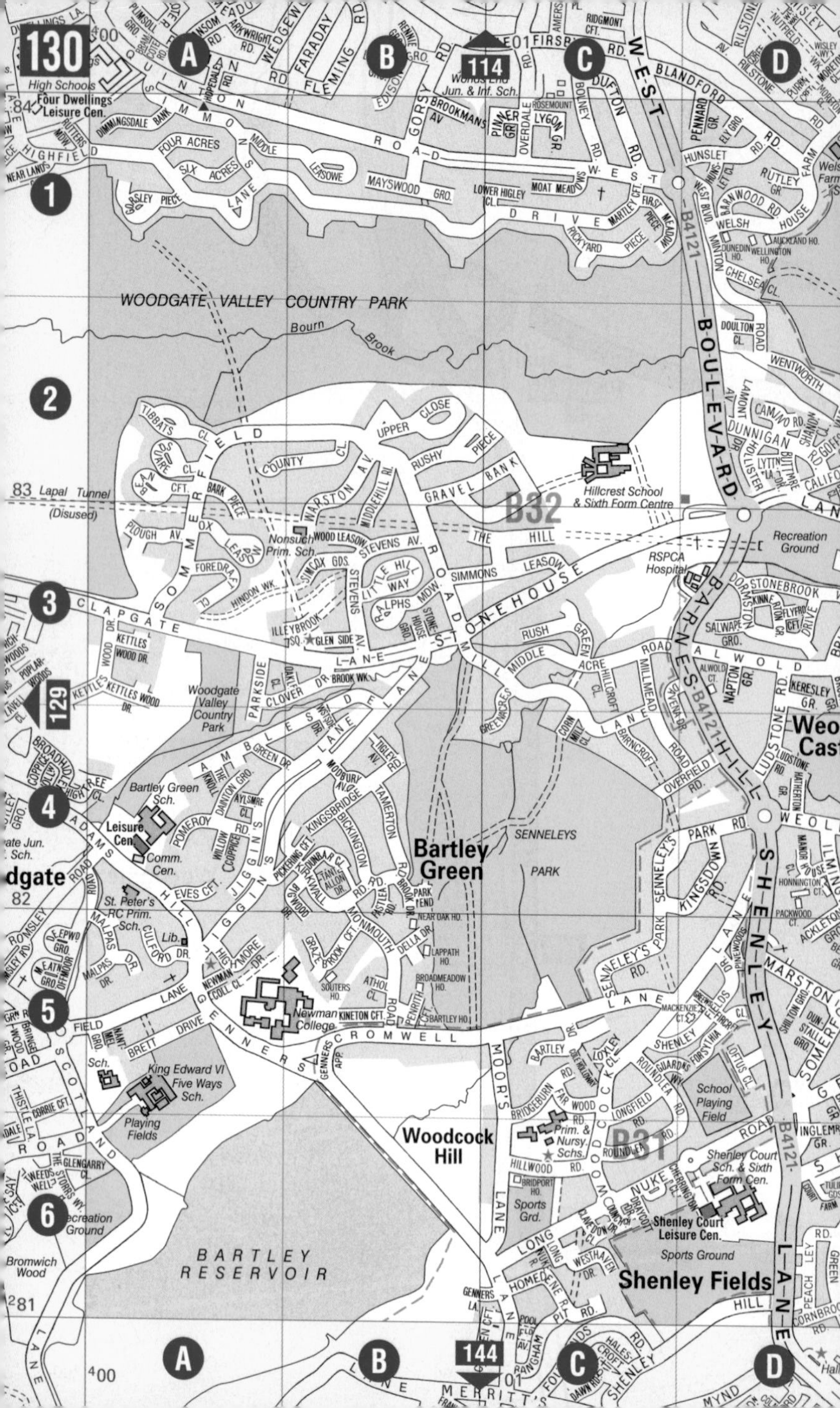

A
B
C
D
1
2
3
4
5
6
114
144
129
High Schools
Four Dwellings Leisure Cen.
WOODGATE VALLEY COUNTRY PARK
Bourn Brook
Lapal Tunnel (Disused)
Hillcrest School & Sixth Form Centre
B32
Nonsuch Prim. Sch.
Recreation Ground
RSPCA Hospital
Woodgate Valley Country Park
Bartley Green Sch.
Leisure Cen.
Comm. Cen.
St. Peter's RC Prim. Sch.
Lib.
Bartley Green
SENNELEYS PARK
Newman College
King Edward VI Five Ways Sch.
Playing Fields
Woodcock Hill
Prim. & Nursy. Schs.
B31
Sports Grd.
School Playing Field
Shenley Court Sch. & Sixth Form Cen.
Shenley Court Leisure Cen.
Sports Ground
Shenley Fields
BARTLEY RESERVOIR
Bromwich Wood
Recreation Ground
Weoley Castle
SIMMONS ROAD
WEST BOULEVARD
B4121
STONEHOUSE
CLAPGATE LANE
SOMMERFIELD
BARNES HILL
SHENLEY LANE
CROMWELL LANE
GENNERS
MOOR'S LANE
SCOTLAND LANE
ADAMS HILL
JIGGINS LANE
MILL ROAD

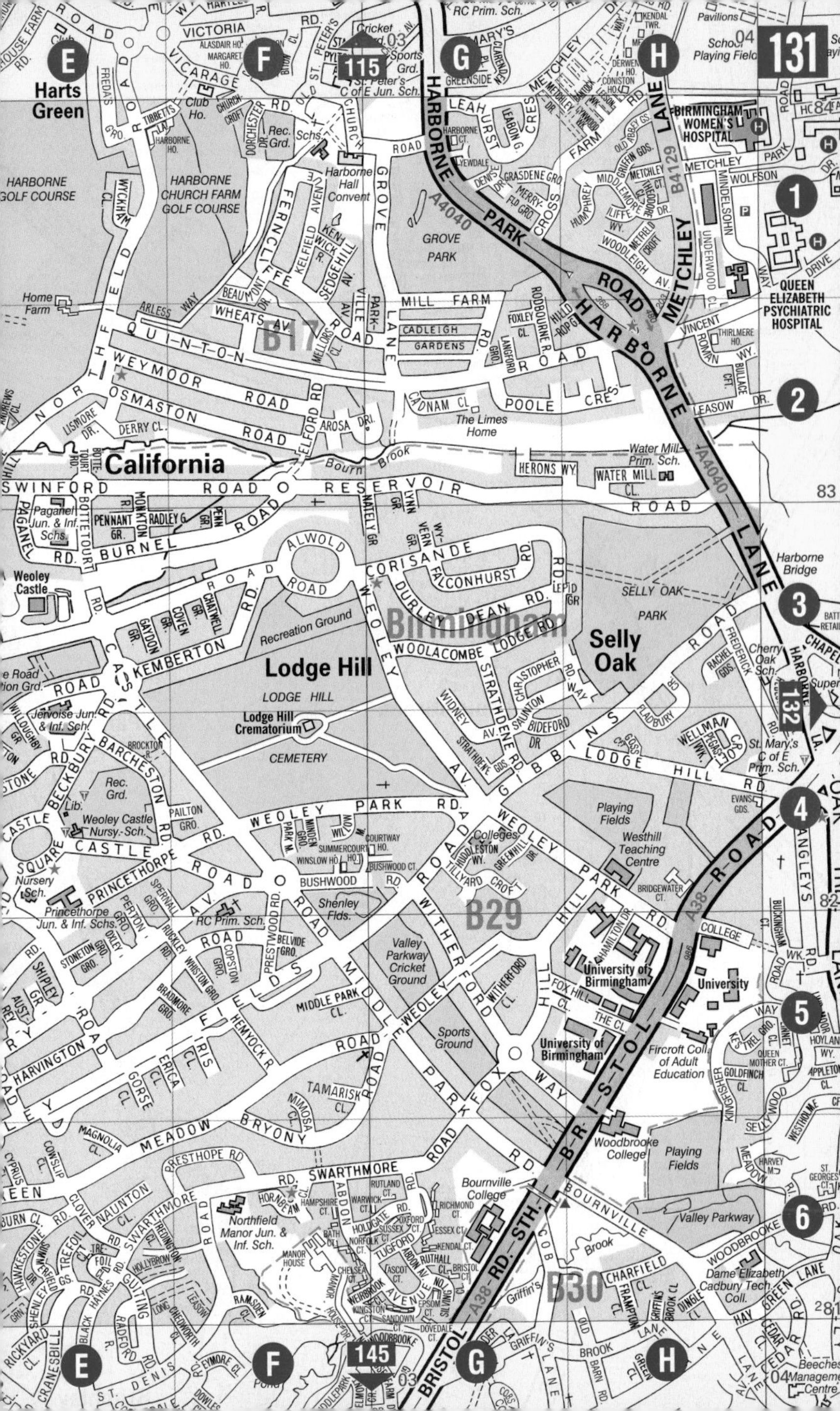

Harts Green
HARBORNE GOLF COURSE
HARBORNE CHURCH FARM GOLF COURSE
California
Weoley Castle
Lodge Hill
Lodge Hill Crematorium
CEMETERY
Birmingham
Selly Oak
SELLY OAK PARK
GROVE PARK
BIRMINGHAM WOMEN'S HOSPITAL
QUEEN ELIZABETH PSYCHIATRIC HOSPITAL
University of Birmingham
Woodbrooke College
Bournville College
Valley Parkway
Northfield Manor Jun. & Inf. Sch.
Dame Elizabeth Cadbury Tech. Coll.
Fircroft Coll. of Adult Education
Westhill Teaching Centre
Valley Parkway Cricket Ground
Sports Ground
Recreation Ground
The Limes Home
Water Mill Prim. Sch.
Harborne Hall Convent
Harborne Bridge
B17
B29
B30
115
132
145

University of Birmingham
116
Queen Elizabeth Hospital
Birmingham Women's Hospital
Queen Elizabeth Psychiatric Hospital
University
Edgbaston Pool (Fish Pond)
Edgbaston Golf Course
Winterbourne Research Garden
King Edward VI High School for Girls
King Edward's School
University House
Moseley RUFC
B15
B29
B30
Selly Oak
Bournbrook
Selly Park
Selly Oak Hospital
Ten Acres
Cadbury World
Bournville Works
Bournville
Stirchley
Stirchley Indoor Bowling Cen.
131
146

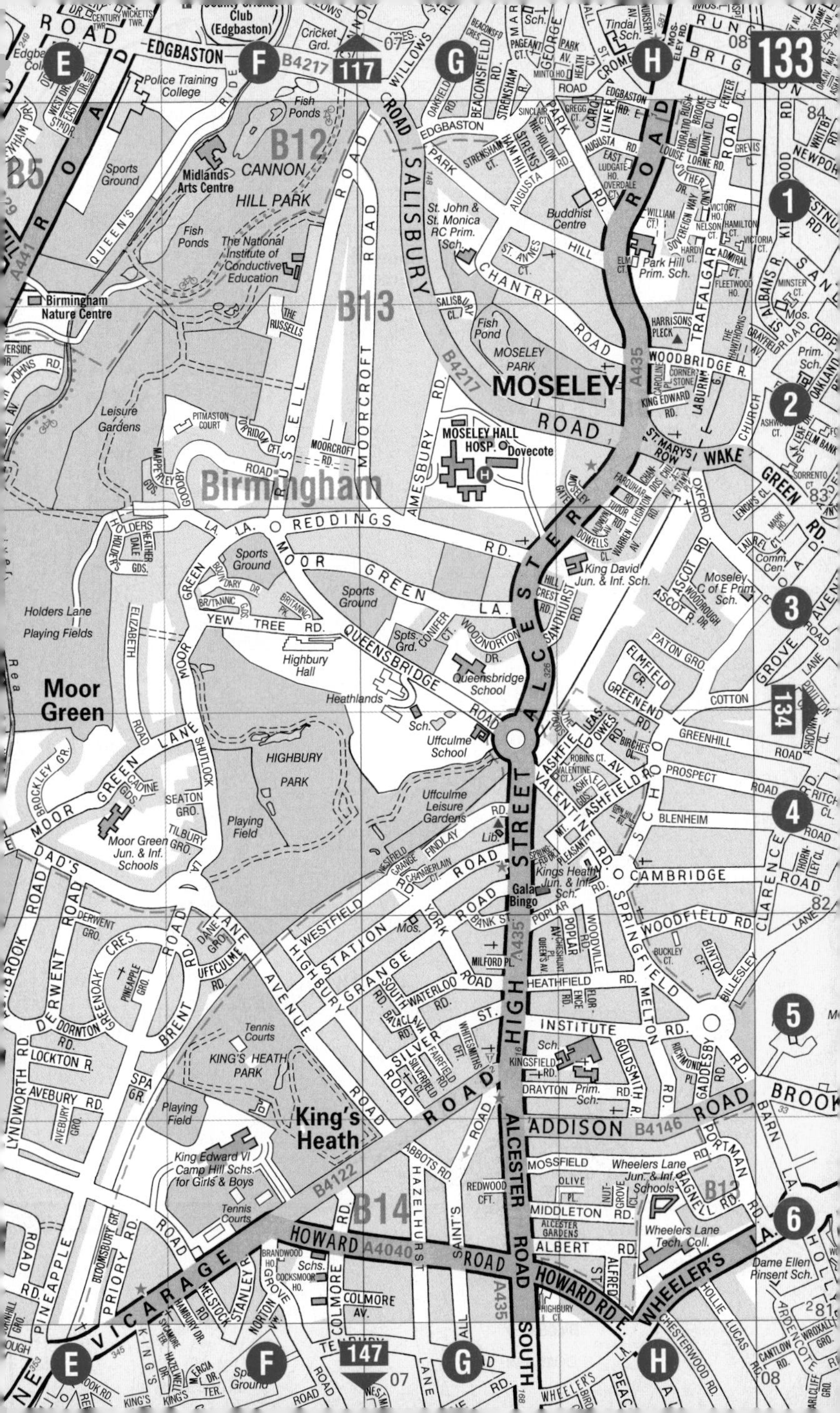133
117
134
147
E
F
G
H
1
2
3
4
5
6
B12
B13
B14
B5
Birmingham
MOSELEY
Moor Green
King's Heath
EDGBASTON
Police Training College
Fish Ponds
Midlands Arts Centre
CANNON HILL PARK
Sports Ground
The National Institute of Conductive Education
Birmingham Nature Centre
Leisure Gardens
Holders Lane Playing Fields
SALISBURY ROAD
MOORCROFT ROAD
RUSSELL ROAD
St. John & St. Monica RC Prim. Sch.
Buddhist Centre
Park Hill Prim. Sch.
MOSELEY PARK
Fish Pond
MOSELEY ROAD
MOSELEY HALL HOSP.
Dovecote
REDDINGS LA.
MOOR GREEN LA.
YEW TREE RD.
Highbury Hall
QUEENSBRIDGE ROAD
Queensbridge School
Uffculme School
Uffculme Leisure Gardens
HIGHBURY PARK
Playing Field
King David Jun. & Inf. Sch.
Moseley C of E Prim. Sch.
ALCESTER ROAD
HIGH STREET
Kings Heath Jun. & Inf. Sch.
Gala Bingo
CAMBRIDGE ROAD
WOODFIELD RD.
HEATHFIELD RD.
INSTITUTE RD.
ADDISON ROAD
Wheelers Lane Jun. & Inf. Schools
Wheelers Lane Tech. Coll.
Dame Ellen Pinsent Sch.
WHEELER'S LA.
HOWARD ROAD
VICARAGE ROAD
KING'S HEATH PARK
Tennis Courts
King Edward VI Camp Hill Schs. for Girls & Boys
Moor Green Jun. & Inf. Schools
DAD'S LANE
A435
A4040
B4217
B4122
B4146
A441

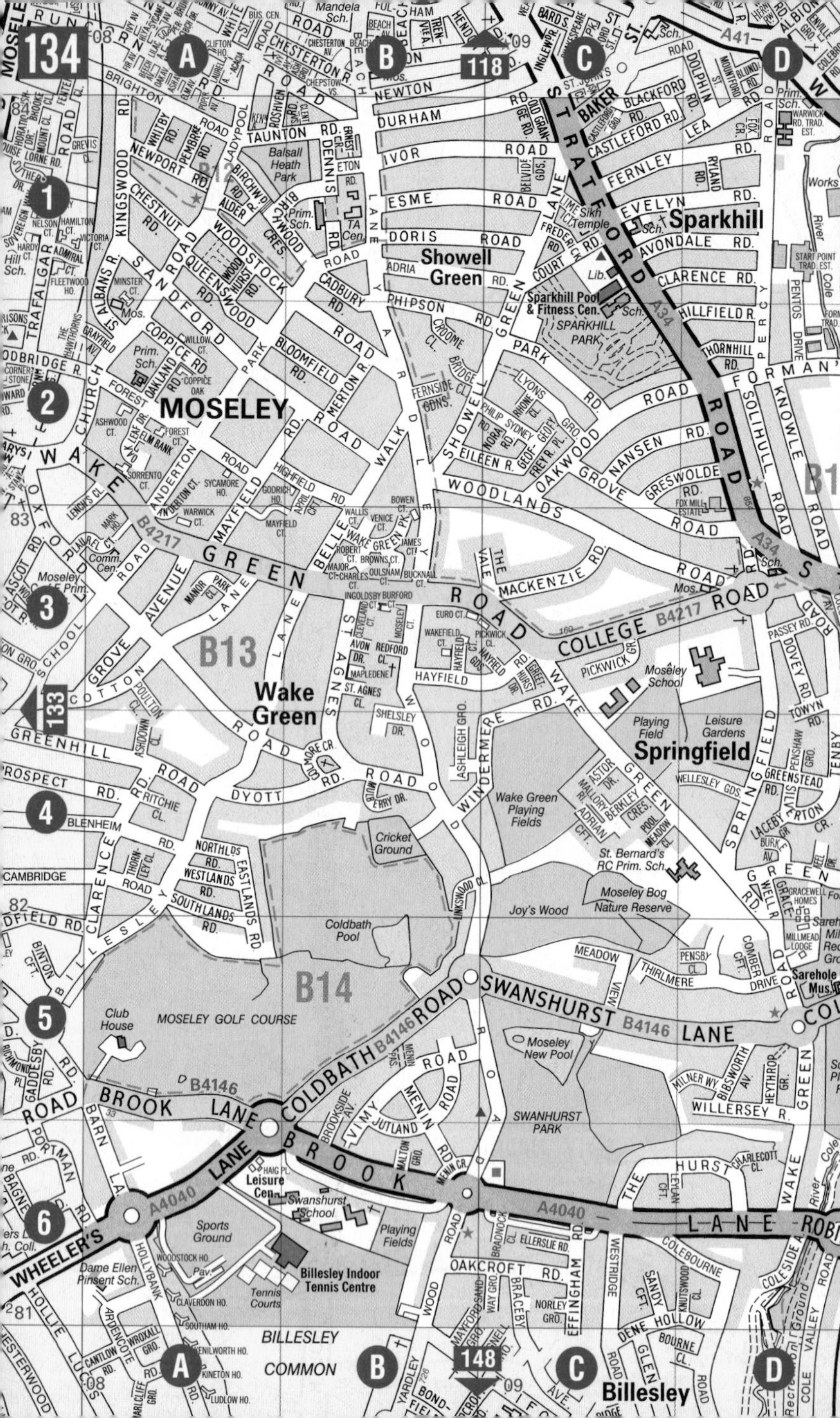

118
133
148
MOSELEY
Sparkhill
Showell Green
Wake Green
Springfield
Billesley
B12
B13
B14
STRATFORD ROAD
A34
WAKE GREEN ROAD
B4217
COLLEGE ROAD
SWANSHURST LANE
B4146
COLDBATH ROAD
BROOK LANE
A4040
WHEELER'S LANE
YARDLEY WOOD ROAD
SANDFORD ROAD
WOODSTOCK ROAD
SPRINGFIELD ROAD
WOODLANDS ROAD
OAKWOOD ROAD
SHOWELL GREEN LANE
Balsall Heath Park
Sparkhill Pool & Fitness Cen.
SPARKHILL PARK
Moseley School
Playing Field
Leisure Gardens
Wake Green Playing Fields
Cricket Ground
Coldbath Pool
Joy's Wood
Moseley Bog Nature Reserve
St. Bernard's RC Prim. Sch.
MOSELEY GOLF COURSE
Club House
Moseley New Pool
SWANHURST PARK
Leisure Cen.
Swanshurst School
Playing Fields
Sports Ground
Billesley Indoor Tennis Centre
Tennis Courts
Dame Ellen Pinsent Sch.
BILLESLEY COMMON
Sikh Temple
Lib.
Works
START POINT TRAD. EST.
WARWICK RD. TRAD. EST.
FOX MILL ESTATE

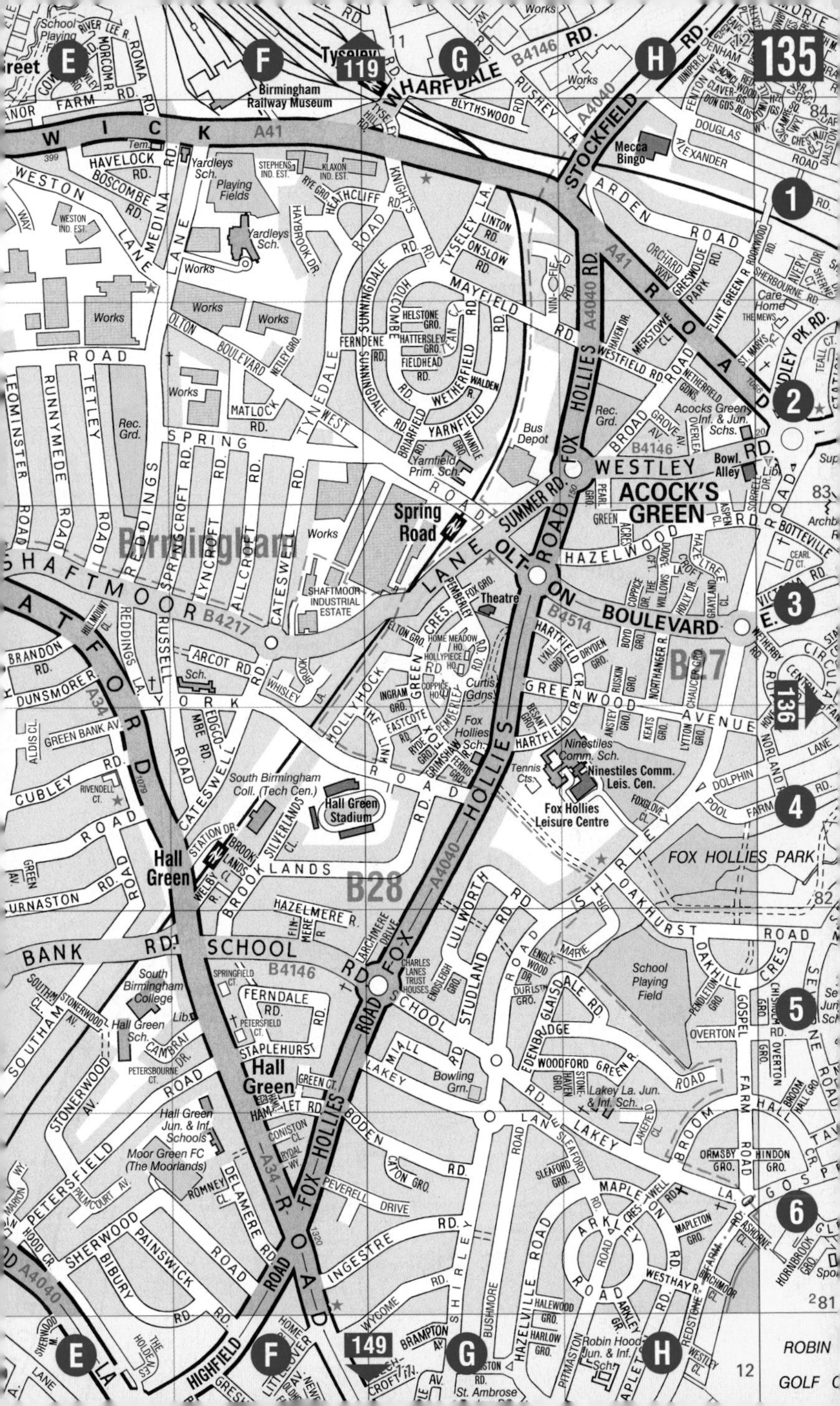
E
F
G
H
119
149
136
1
2
3
4
5
6
Tyseley
Birmingham Railway Museum
WHARFDALE
WICK A41
STOCKFIELD RD.
Mecca Bingo
ALEXANDER
DOUGLAS
ARDEN ROAD
HAVELOCK RD.
BOSCOMBE RD.
WESTON LANE
Weston Ind. Est.
Yardleys Sch.
Playing Fields
MEDINA RD.
Works
OLTON BOULEVARD
SUNNINGDALE RD.
HOLCOMBE RD.
TYSELEY LA.
LINTON RD.
ONSLOW RD.
MAYFIELD RD.
HELSTONE GRO.
HATTERSLEY GRO.
FIELDHEAD RD.
WETHERFIELD
YARNFIELD
Yarnfield Prim. Sch.
TYNEDALE
Rec. Grd.
SPRING ROAD
Spring Road
Bus Depot
FOX HOLLIES RD.
A4040
WESTLEY RD.
ACOCK'S GREEN
Bowl. Alley
Acocks Green Inf. & Jun. Schs.
BROAD RD.
WESTFIELD RD.
Birmingham
SHAFTMOOR LANE B4217
STRATFORD RD. A34
REDDINGS
RUSSELL
SPRINGCROFT RD.
LYNCROFT
ALLCROFT RD.
CATESWELL RD.
SHAFTMOOR INDUSTRIAL ESTATE
SUMMER RD.
OLTON BOULEVARD B4514
HAZELWOOD
Theatre
Curtis Gdns.
Fox Hollies Sch.
GREENWOOD AVENUE
B27
Ninestiles Comm. Sch.
Ninestiles Comm. Leis. Cen.
Fox Hollies Leisure Centre
FOX HOLLIES PARK
South Birmingham Coll. (Tech Cen.)
Hall Green Stadium
Hall Green
BROOKLANDS
B28
SHIRLEY RD.
OAKHURST ROAD
School Playing Field
SCHOOL RD. B4146
South Birmingham College
Hall Green Sch.
FERNDALE RD.
STAPLEHURST
Bowling Grn.
LAKEY LANE
Lakey La. Jun. & Inf. Sch.
Hall Green Jun. & Inf. Schools
Moor Green FC (The Moorlands)
PETERSFIELD
SHERWOOD
PAINSWICK ROAD
INGESTRE RD.
WYCOME RD.
MAPLETON RD.
ARKLEY RD.
HAZELVILLE ROAD
Robin Hood Jun. & Inf. Sch.
HIGHFIELD RD.
St. Ambrose
ROBIN
GOLF

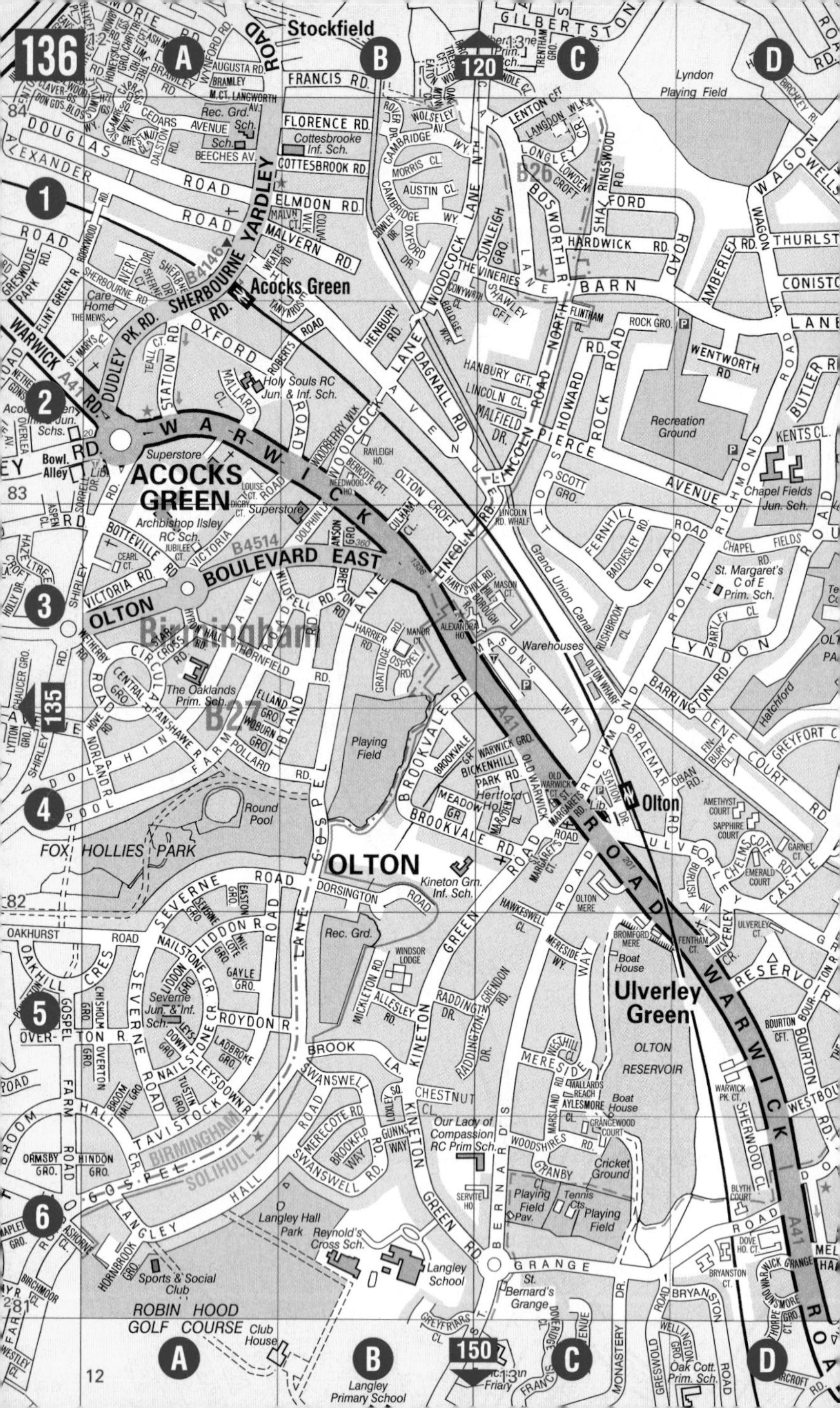

Stockfield
120
135
150
ACOCKS GREEN
Acocks Green
OLTON
Olton
Birmingham
Ulverley Green
OLTON RESERVOIR
FOX HOLLIES PARK
ROBIN HOOD GOLF COURSE
Lyndon Playing Field
Recreation Ground
Playing Field
Round Pool
Grand Union Canal
WARWICK ROAD
BOULEVARD EAST
SHERBOURNE RD.
YARDLEY ROAD
DOUGLAS ROAD
ALEXANDER ROAD
LINCOLN ROAD NORTH
RICHMOND ROAD
LYNDON ROAD
GOSPEL LANE
GOSPEL FARM ROAD
LANGLEY HALL RD.
KINETON GREEN RD.
SEVERNE ROAD
DOLPHIN LANE
FARM RD.
BARN LANE
PIERCE AVENUE
ULVERLEY CRES.
GRANGE RD.
Holy Souls RC Jun. & Inf. Sch.
Archbishop Ilsley RC Sch.
The Oaklands Prim. Sch.
Severne Jun. & Inf. Sch.
Kineton Grn. Inf. Sch.
Our Lady of Compassion RC Prim Sch.
Langley School
Reynold's Cross Sch.
Langley Hall Park
Sports & Social Club
Chapel Fields Jun. Sch.
St. Margaret's C of E Prim. Sch.
Cottesbrooke Inf. Sch.
Oak Cott. Prim. Sch.
Langley Primary School
St. Bernard's Grange
Cricket Ground
Boat House
Warehouses
Superstore
A41
B4146
B4514
B26
B27
A
B
C
D
1
2
3
4
5
6

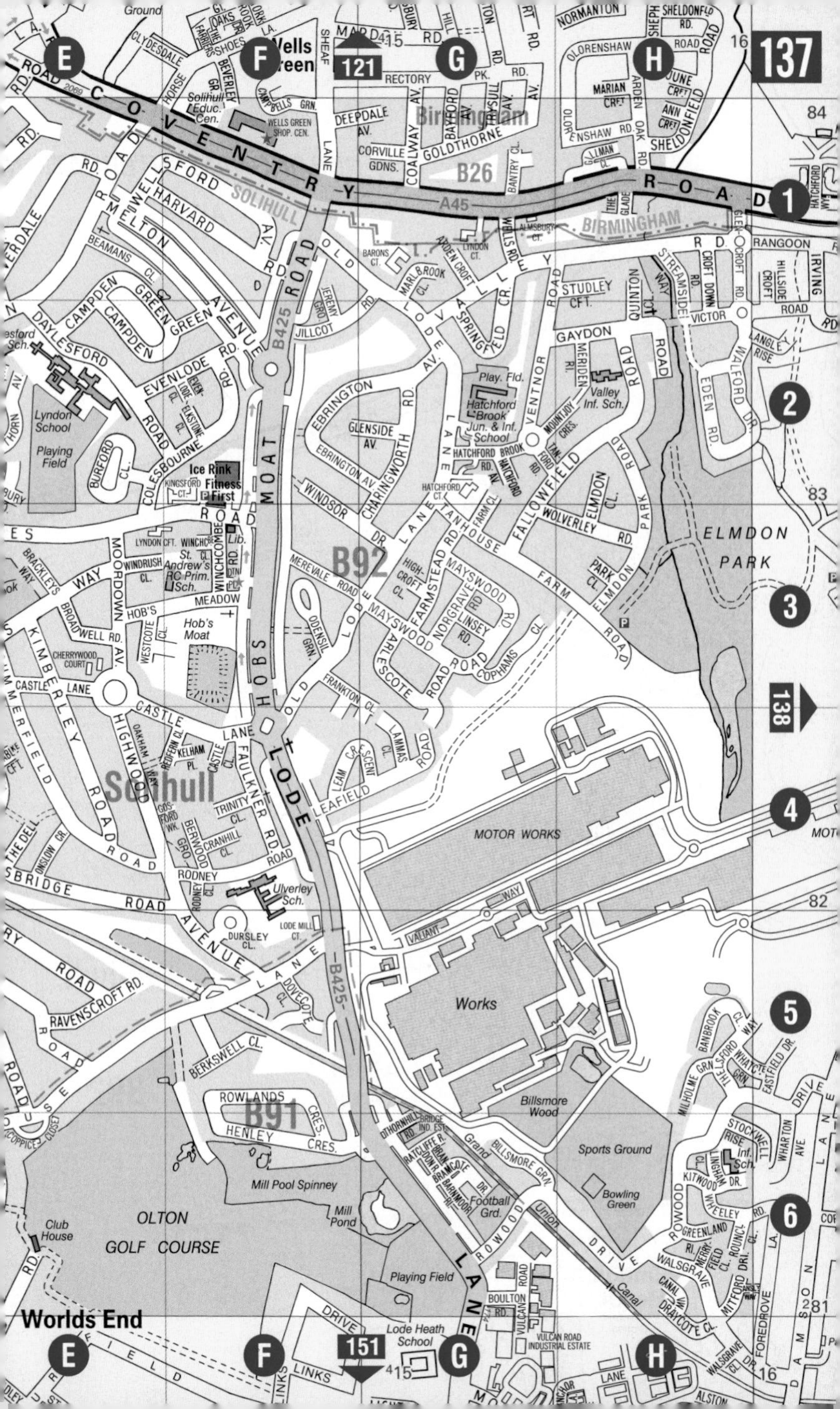
Wells Green
121
Birmingham
B26
COVENTRY ROAD
SOLIHULL
BIRMINGHAM
A45
B425
B92
Hatchford Brook Jun. & Inf. School
Valley Inf. Sch.
Lyndon School
Playing Field
Ice Rink
Fitness First
St. Andrew's RC Prim. Sch.
Hob's Moat
ELMDON PARK
138
Solihull
MOTOR WORKS
Works
Ulverley Sch.
Billsmore Wood
Sports Ground
Bowling Green
B91
Mill Pool Spinney
Mill Pond
Football Grd.
OLTON GOLF COURSE
Club House
Playing Field
Lode Heath School
Worlds End
151
VULCAN ROAD INDUSTRIAL ESTATE
Grand Union Canal

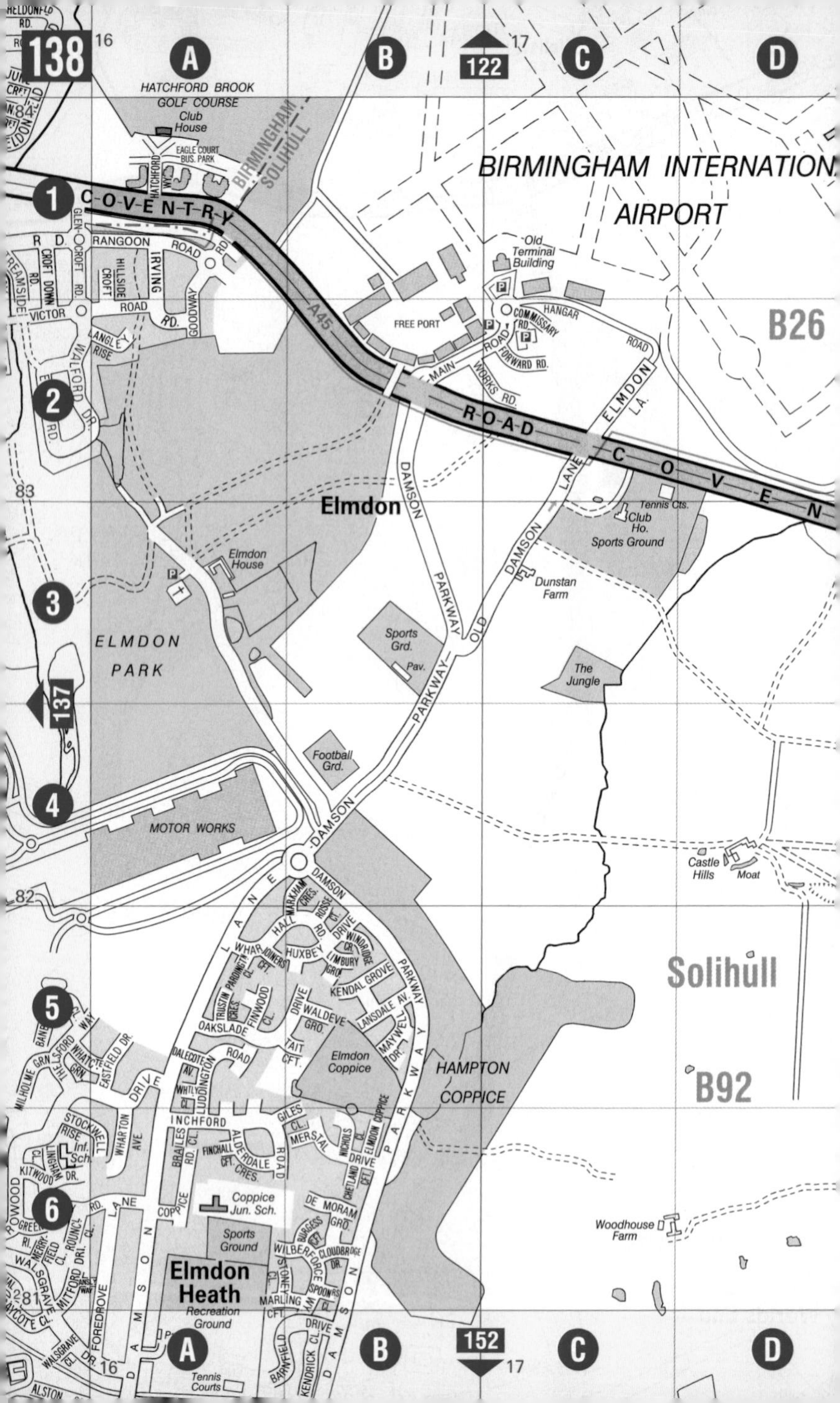

A **B** 122 17 **C** **D**

HATCHFORD BROOK
GOLF COURSE
Club
House
EAGLE COURT
BUS. PARK

BIRMINGHAM INTERNATIONAL

AIRPORT

1 COVENTRY

BIRMINGHAM SOLIHULL

Old
Terminal
Building

HANGAR

RANGOON
CROFT
HILLSIDE
ROAD
IRVING
GOODWAY
ROAD

COMMISSARY
RD.

FREE PORT

FORWARD RD.

B26

GLEN RD.
CROFT DOWN RD.
REAMSIDE RD.
VICTOR RD.
WALFORD DR.
LANGLE RISE

A45
MAIN
WORKS
RD.

2 ROAD

83

Elmdon

DAMSON

Tennis Cts.
Club
Ho.
Sports Ground

OLD
DAMSON
LANE

ELMDON
LA.

COVEN

3

ELMDON
PARK

Elmdon House

PARKWAY

Dunstan
Farm

137

Sports
Grd.
Pav.

The
Jungle

4

82

MOTOR WORKS

Football
Grd.

DAMSON

PARKWAY

Castle
Hills
Moat

HALAM
CRES.
HUXBEY

THE WINDING

TIMBURY

WHAR.
JONES
FENWOOD
KENDAL GROVE

LANSDALE AV.

HAMPTON
COPPICE

5

MILLHOLME GRN.
THE GATE
SHIFORD WHATCLIFFE
EASTFIELD RD.

WHARF
TRIGON PARDINGTON CRES.
FENWOOD CL.
OAKSLADE
DALECOTE
WALDEVE GRO.
TAIT CFT.

Elmdon
Coppice

MAYWELL

PARKWAY

B92

Solihull

MILHOLME GRN.
GOODWAY
GREEN
KITWOOD DR.
WHARTON AVE.
STOCKWELL RISE
Inf. Sch.
INGRAM
COPPICE
LUDINGTON
INCHFORD
BRAILES CL.
FINDHALL CFT.
ALDESDALE CRES.
GILES CL.
MERSIAL
ELMDON COPPICE
WORDS
DR.

Woodhouse
Farm

6

GOODWAY RD.
281
FOREDROVE
MITFORD DR.
ROUNDS RD.
CL.
WALSGRAVE
WINSMORE CL.

Coppice
Jun. Sch.
Sports
Ground

DE MORAM
BURGESS
WILBER
CLOUDBRIDGE DR.
SPOONWAYS
MARLING
DRIVE

**Elmdon
Heath**

Recreation
Ground

ALSTON

A 16 **B** 152 17 **C** **D**

Tennis
Courts

KENDRICK CL.
BAYFIELD

DAMSON

NATIONAL EXHIBITION CENTRE
Birmingham International
Birmingham
Bickenhill
M42
MOTORWAY
Junction 6
A45
B4438
B40
B37
Pendigo Lake
Crescent Wood Island
Hotel
ARENA
FORUM
PAVILION
Offices
Longacre Farm
Wyckhams Close
National Motorcycle Museum
Play. Field
HAVEN CARAVAN PK.
Club House
Playing Field
Church Farm
Yew Tree Farm
Vicarage
Grange Farm
Pavilion
Sports Ground
Heathend Farm
Heath Farm
Home Farm
Hampton Manor
Hampton Hall Farm
Terminal 1
Terminal 2
CATHERINE DE BARNES LANE
BICKENHILL LANE
SHADOWBROOK LANE
Shadow Brook
PERIMETER ROAD
PENDIGO WAY
NORTHWAY
EASTWAY
CAR PARK ROAD
SOUTH CAR PARK ROAD
CHURCH LANE
PITT LANE
CLOCK LANE
ST. PETERS LANE
OLD STATION ROAD
AIRPORT WAY
BICKENHILL TRADING EST.
123
153
140

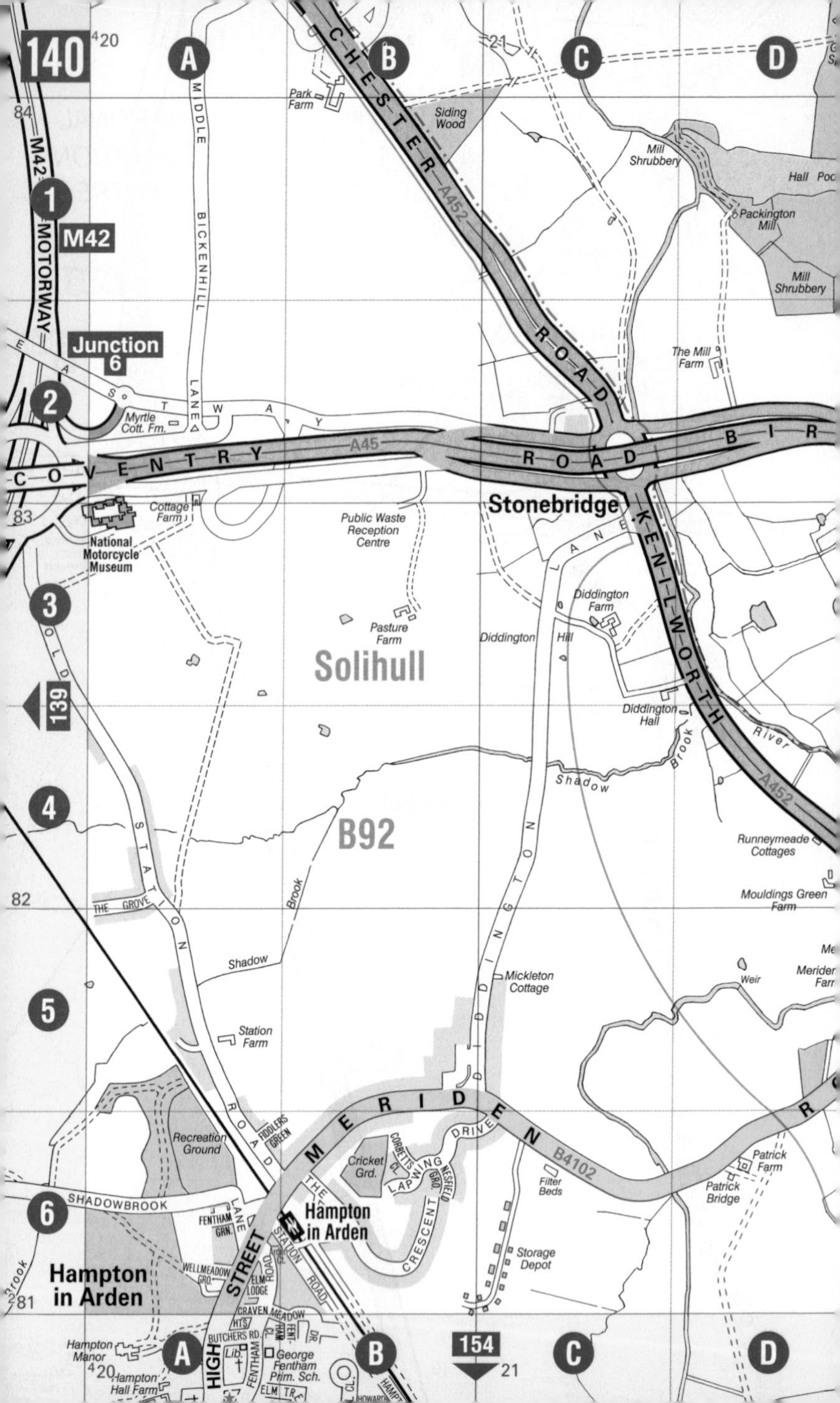

420
A
B
C
D
84
83
82
81
1
2
3
4
5
6
M42 MOTORWAY
M42
Junction 6
MIDDLE BICKENHILL LANE
CHESTER ROAD
A452
Park Farm
Siding Wood
21
Mill Shrubbery
Hall Poo
Packington Mill
Mill Shrubbery
The Mill Farm
EASTWAY
Myrtle Cott. Fm.
COVENTRY ROAD
A45
ROAD
BIR
Stonebridge
KENILWORTH
A452
Cottage Farm
National Motorcycle Museum
Public Waste Reception Centre
Pasture Farm
LANE
Diddington Farm
Diddington Hill
Diddington Hall
Solihull
River
Shadow Brook
OLD STATION ROAD
THE GROVE
B92
Brook
Shadow
Runneymeade Cottages
Mouldings Green Farm
DIDDINGTON LANE
Mickleton Cottage
Weir
Meriden Farm
Station Farm
MERIDEN ROAD
B4102
Recreation Ground
FIDDLERS GREEN
Cricket Grd.
CORBETTS CL.
LAPWING GRO.
NESFIELD GRO.
DRIVE
Filter Beds
Patrick Farm
Patrick Bridge
SHADOWBROOK LANE
FENTHAM GRN.
THE CRESCENT
Hampton in Arden
STATION ROAD
Storage Depot
WELLMEADOW GRO.
ELM LODGE
HIGH STREET
Hampton in Arden
CRAVEN MEADOW
HTS
BUTCHERS RD.
FENTHAM CL.
FENTHAM RD.
Lib.
George Fentham Prim. Sch.
ELM TREE
HOWARD
HAMPTON
Hampton Manor
Hampton Hall Farm
DR.
Brook

139
154

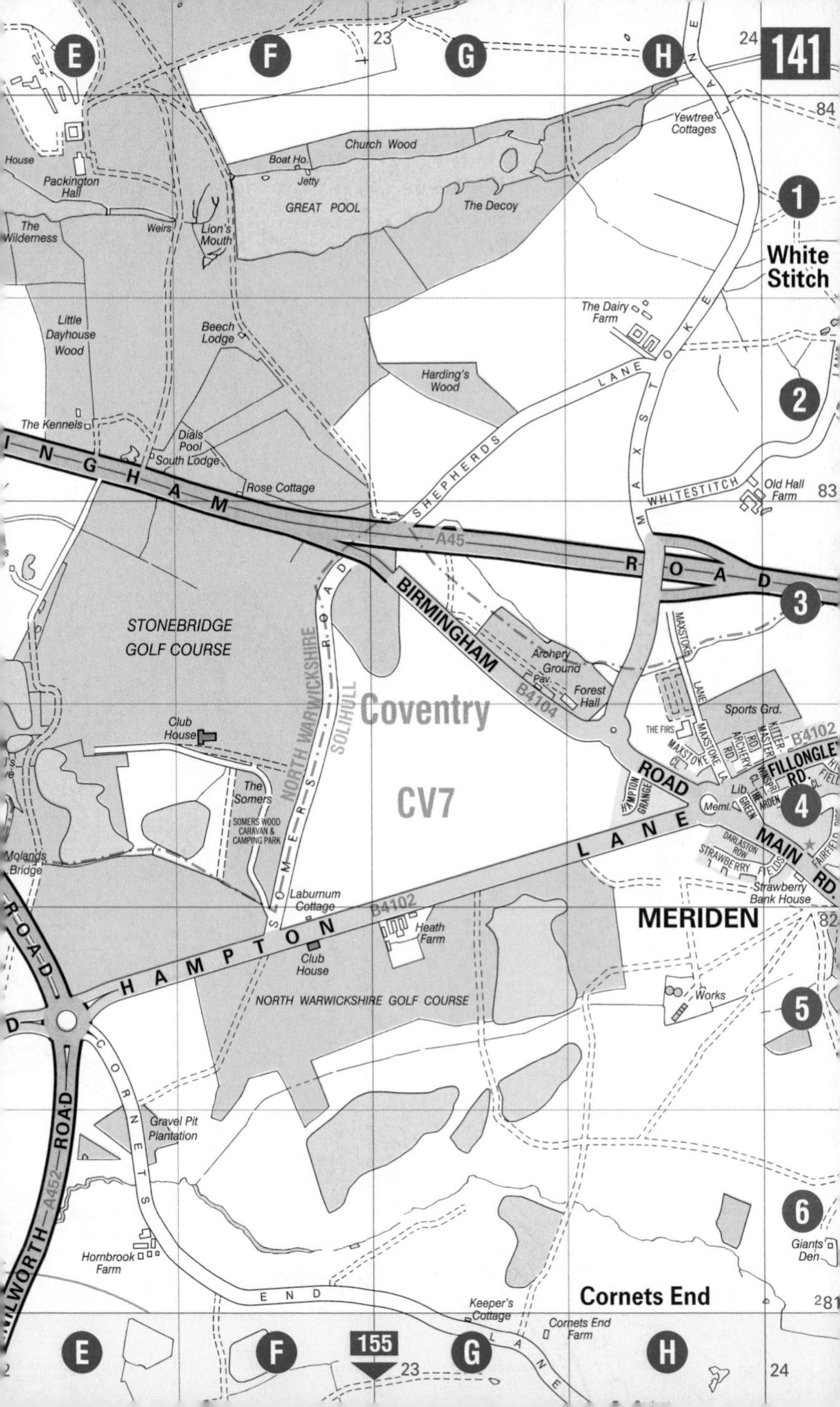

84

1

White Stitch

2

House
Packington Hall
The Wilderness
Church Wood
Boat Ho.
Jetty
GREAT POOL
The Decoy
Weirs
Lion's Mouth
Yewtree Cottages
The Dairy Farm
Little Dayhouse Wood
Beech Lodge
Harding's Wood
The Kennels
Dials Pool
South Lodge
Rose Cottage
SHEPHERDS LANE
MAXSTOKE LANE
WHITESTITCH
Old Hall Farm
83

INGHAM

A45

ROAD

3

STONEBRIDGE GOLF COURSE

BIRMINGHAM
ROAD
B4104

NORTH WARWICKSHIRE
SOLIHULL

Coventry

CV7

Archery Ground Pav.
Forest Hall
THE FIRS
Sports Grd.
MAXSTOKE LANE
ARCHERY
MAXSTOKE RD.
B4102

FILLONGLEY RD.

4

Club House
The Somers
SOMERS WOOD CARAVAN & CAMPING PARK
Molands Bridge
Laburnum Cottage
B4102
Heath Farm
MEERSON ROAD
Lib.
Meml.
GRANGE
HAMPTON
GREEN
CHURCH
DARLASTON ROW
STRAWBERRY
MAIN RD.

MERIDEN

Strawberry Bank House
82

HAMPTON
LANE
Club House

NORTH WARWICKSHIRE GOLF COURSE

Works

5

ROAD
A452
KENILWORTH ROAD

CORNETS
Gravel Pit Plantation
Hornbrook Farm

END

Giants Den

6

Keeper's Cottage
Cornets End Farm
Cornets End
LANE

281

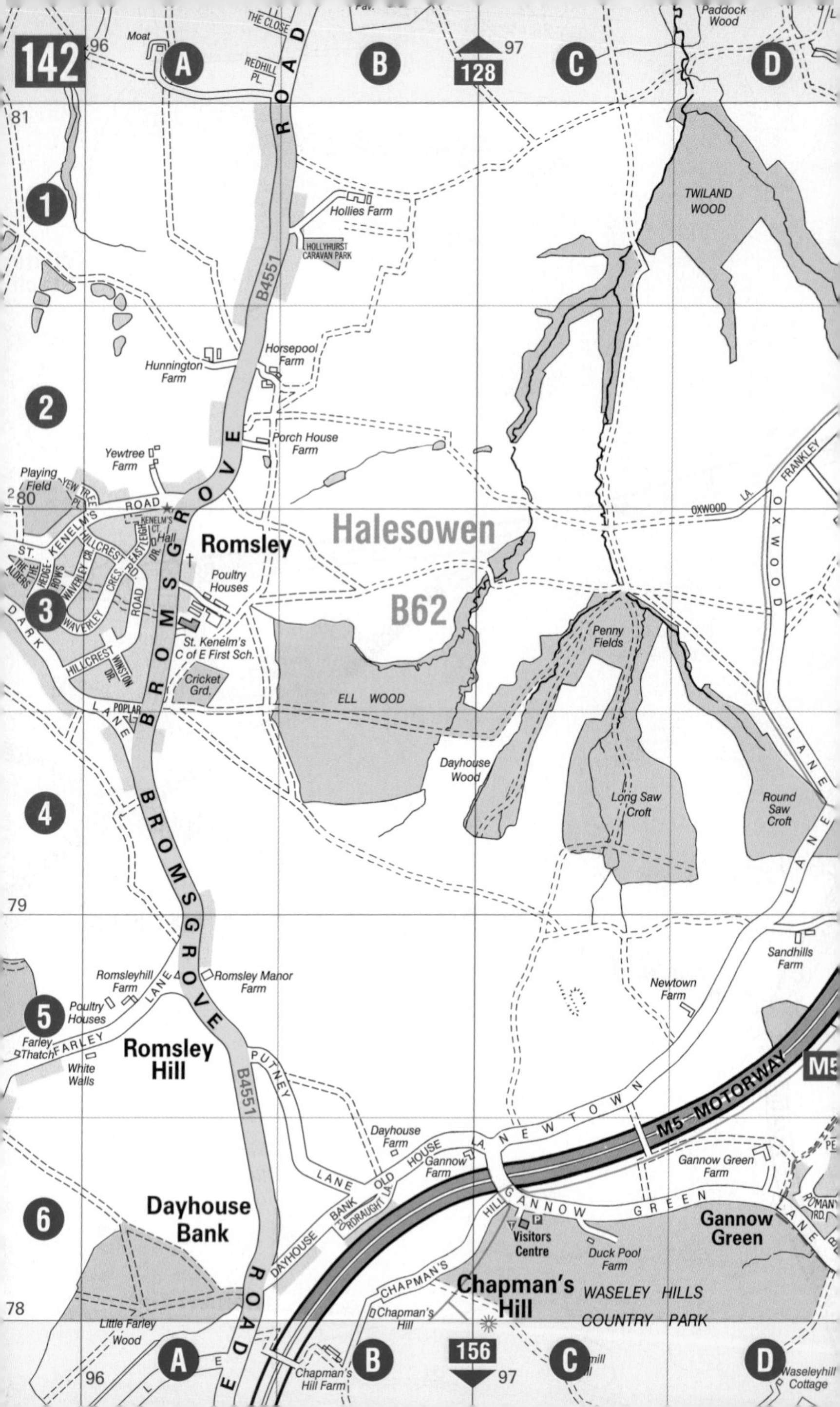

Moat
THE CLOSE
REDHILL PL.
BROMSGROVE ROAD
B4551
128
96
97
81
80
79
78
A
B
C
D
1
2
3
4
5
6
Paddock Wood
Hollies Farm
HOLLYHURST CARAVAN PARK
TWILAND WOOD
Horsepool Farm
Hunnington Farm
Porch House Farm
Yewtree Farm
Playing Field
YEW TREE PL.
ROAD
KENELM'S CT.
Hall
ST. KENELM'S
HILLCREST RD.
EASTLEIGH DR.
Romsley
Halesowen
B62
FRANKLEY
OXWOOD LA.
OXWOOD LANE
THE ALDERS
THE HEDGE ROWS
WAVERLEY CR.
CRES.
ROAD
WAVERLEY
DARK
Poultry Houses
St. Kenelm's C of E First Sch.
HILLCREST
WINSTON DR.
Cricket Grd.
ELL WOOD
Penny Fields
POPLAR LANE
Dayhouse Wood
Long Saw Croft
Round Saw Croft
LANE
Sandhills Farm
Romsleyhill Farm
Romsley Manor Farm
Newtown Farm
Poultry Houses
Farley Thatch
FARLEY
Romsley Hill
White Walls
PUTNEY
M5
M5 MOTORWAY
NEWTOWN
Dayhouse Farm
OLD HOUSE LA.
Gannow Farm
Gannow Green Farm
LANE
DAYHOUSE BANK
RDRAUGHT LA.
HILL
GANNOW GREEN LANE
ROMANY RD.
Dayhouse Bank
Visitors Centre
Duck Pool Farm
Gannow Green
CHAPMAN'S
Chapman's Hill
WASELEY HILLS COUNTRY PARK
Chapman's Hill
Little Farley Wood
Chapman's Hill Farm
156
Waseleyhill Cottage

Frankley Service Area
129
M5
M5 MOTORWAY
Harris's Wood
Kettles Wood
Raven Hays Wood
Frankley Green
Frankley
BARTLEY RESERVOIR
Westminster Farm
Moat
Park Farm
Long Kettles Wood
Greenwood Cott.
Brookhouse Farm
B32
B31
B45
Birmingham
Frankley Beeches
Yew Tree Cottages
Yew Tree Farm
Frankley Hill
Lower Hill Cottages
Frankley Hill Farm
Upper Hill Farm
Egg Hill
Egghill Farm
Egghill Dingle
Lower Hill Farm
Public Open Space
BROMSGROVE
BIRMINGHAM
Playing Field
Frogmill Comm. Jun. Sch.
The Beeches Inf. Sch.
Holly Hill Methodist C of E Inf. & Nursy. Sch.
Leisure Cen.
Frankley Comm. High Sch.
Lib.
HOLLY HILL SHOP. CEN.
GANNOW SHOP. CEN.
FRANKLEY INDUSTRIAL PARK
Balaam's Wood
Reaside Jun. Sch.
Great Park
Laundry
REASIDE CLINIC
UGC Cinema
Gala Bingo
Fitness Club
Sports Pitch
Reservoir
144
157
Subway
E F G H
1 2 3 4 5 6
99
81
80
79
78
400
Ground
Bromwich Wood

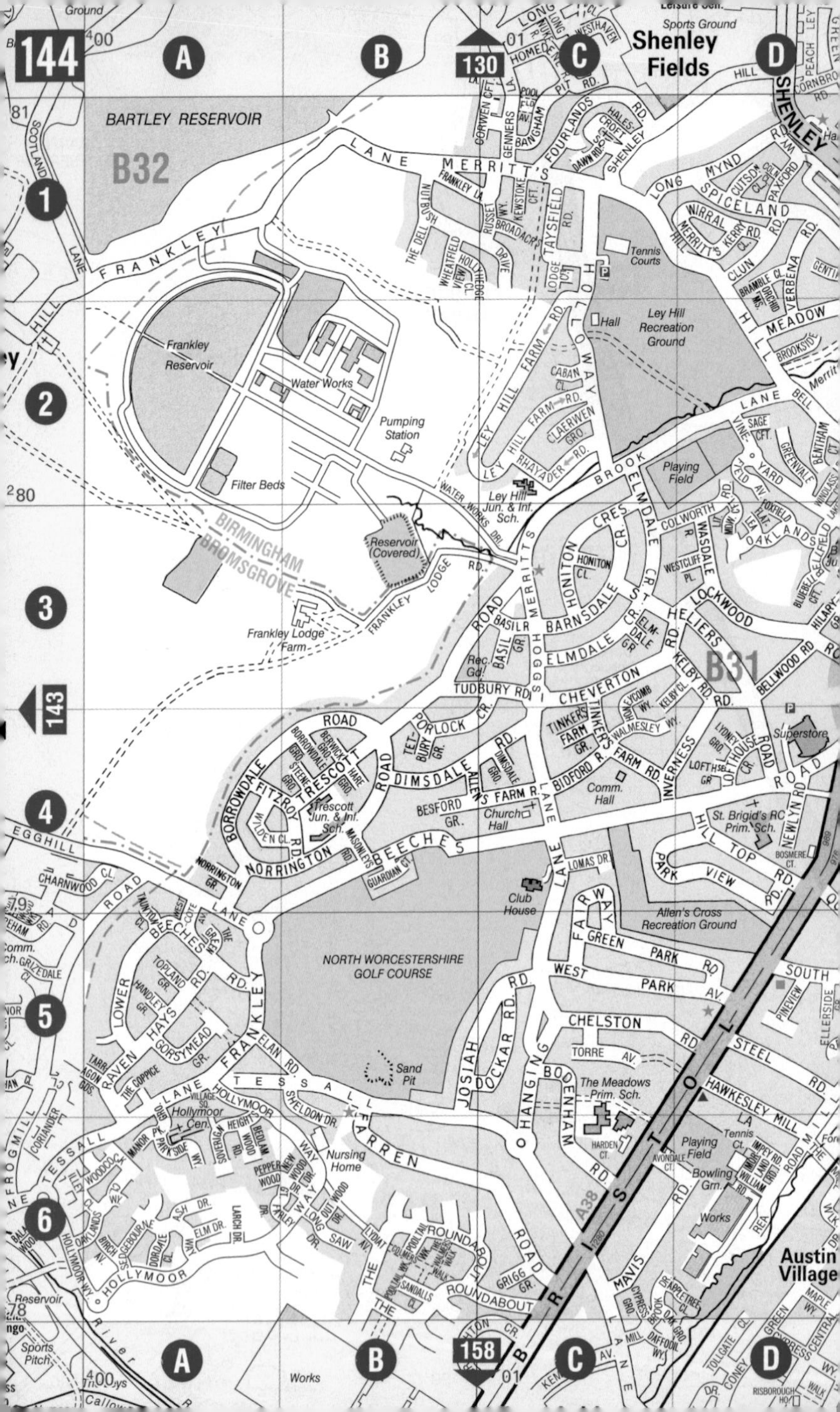
A
B
C
D
1
2
3
4
5
6
130
143
158
Shenley Fields
Sports Ground
BARTLEY RESERVOIR
B32
B31
FRANKLEY LANE
SCOTLAND LANE
HILL
MERRITT'S
Frankley Reservoir
Water Works
Pumping Station
Filter Beds
Reservoir (Covered)
Frankley Lodge Farm
FRANKLEY LODGE RD.
BIRMINGHAM
BROMSGROVE
WATER WORKS DRI.
Tennis Courts
Hall
Ley Hill Recreation Ground
LEY HILL FARM RD.
HOLLOWAY
Ley Hill Jun. & Inf. Sch.
MERRITTS BROOK LANE
Playing Field
SHENLEY HILL
LONG MYND
SPICELAND RD.
WIRRAL
CLUN
VERBENA
MEADOW
BROOKSIDE
BELL
BENTHAM
OAKLANDS
COLWORTH
WASDALE
WESTCLIFF PL.
LOCKWOOD
HELIERS
HONITON CRES
ELMDALE
BARNSDALE
BASIL RD.
Rec. Gd.
TUDBURY RD.
CHEVERTON
KELBY RD.
BELLWOOD RD
TINKERS FARM GR.
WALMESLEY WY.
HONEYCOMB WY.
INVERNESS
LOFTHOUSE CR.
Superstore
PORLOCK CR.
TETBURY GR.
DIMSDALE RD.
ALLENS FARM R.
BIDFORD R.
FARM RD.
Comm. Hall
BORROWDALE ROAD
TRESCOTT ROAD
FITZROY
Trescott Jun. & Inf. Sch.
NORRINGTON RD.
BESFORD GR.
Church Hall
HOGGS LANE
BEECHES ROAD
HILL TOP RD.
St. Brigid's RC Prim. Sch.
NEWLYN RD.
PARK VIEW RD.
EGGHILL
CHARNWOOD CL.
GUARDIAN CT.
LOMAS DR.
Club House
FAIRWAY
Allen's Cross Recreation Ground
NORTH WORCESTERSHIRE GOLF COURSE
GREEN PARK RD.
WEST PARK AV.
SOUTH
PINEVIEW
ELLERSIDE
BEECHES RD.
TOPLAND GR.
LOWER
HAYS RD.
GORSYMEAD GR.
RAVEN
FRANKLEY LANE
ELAN RD.
Sand Pit
JOSIAH RD.
DOCKAR RD.
HANGING LANE
BODENHAM RD.
CHELSTON RD
TORRE AV.
STEEL RD.
The Meadows Prim. Sch.
HAWKESLEY MILL LA
TESSALL LANE
FARREN
THE COPPICE
HOLLYMOOR
Hollymoor Cen.
SHELDON DR.
Nursing Home
Playing Field
Tennis Ct.
Bowling Grn.
Works
Austin Village
FROGMILL
CORIANDER
WOODCOCK
OAKLANDS
ASH DR.
ELM DR.
LARCH DR.
HOLLYMOOR WY.
SEDGEBOURNE
DORDALE CL.
ROUNDABOUT
GRIGG GR.
MAVIS RD.
BRISTOL RD
A38
Reservoir
River
Sports Pitch
Works
CONEY GREEN
TOLLGATE CL.
MAPLE WY.
CENTRAL
400
401
280
278

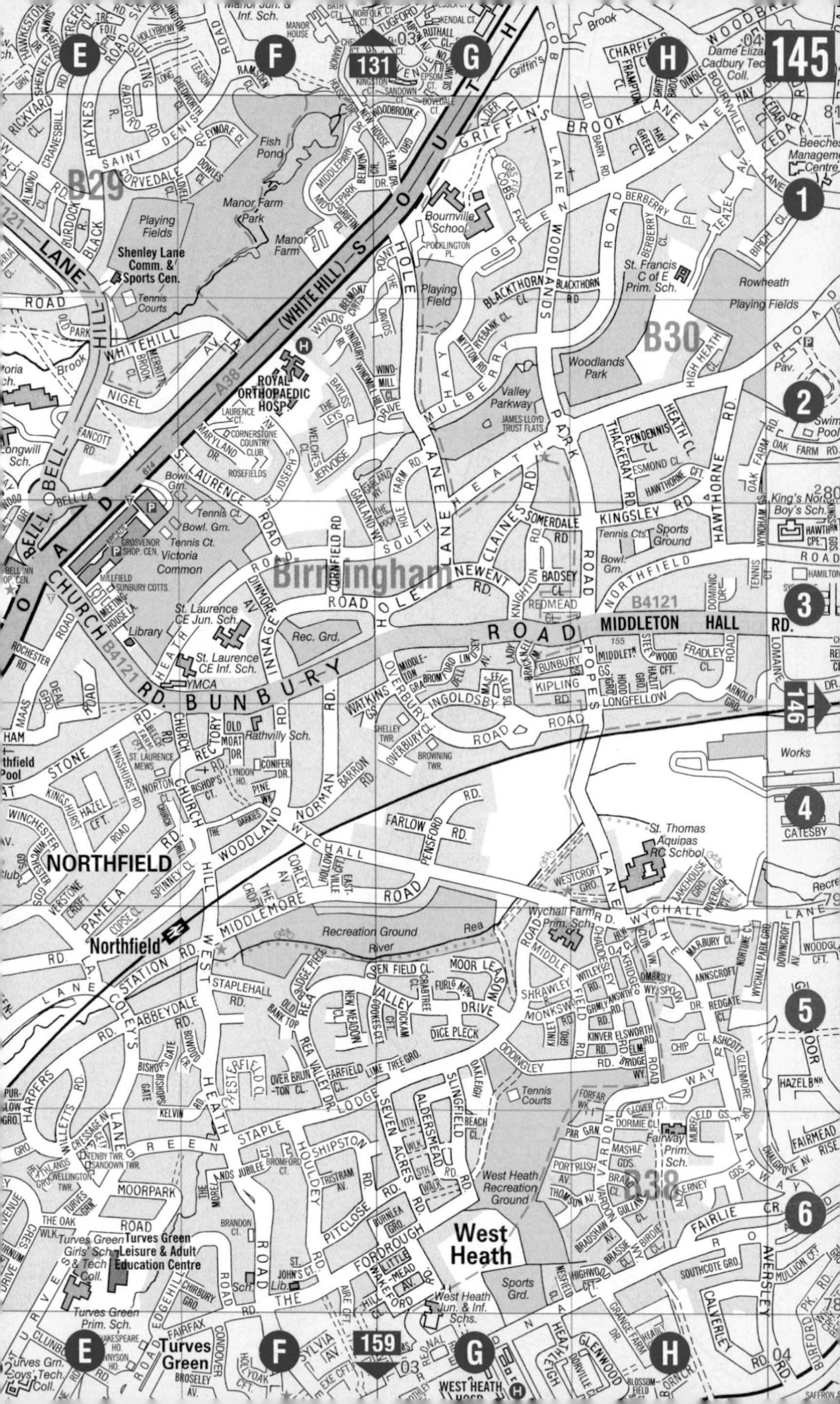

145
131
159
146
E
F
G
H
1
2
3
4
5
6
B29
B30
B38
Birmingham
NORTHFIELD
Northfield
West Heath
Turves Green
Manor Farm Park
Fish Pond
Playing Fields
Shenley Lane Comm. & Sports Cen.
ROYAL ORTHOPAEDIC HOSP.
Bournville School
St. Francis C of E Prim. Sch.
Rowheath Playing Fields
Woodlands Park
Valley Parkway
Victoria Common
Rec. Grd.
St. Laurence CE Jun. Sch.
St. Laurence CE Inf. Sch.
Rathvilly Sch.
St. Thomas Aquinas RC School
Wychall Farm Prim. Sch.
Recreation Ground
River Rea
West Heath Recreation Ground
Fairway Prim. Sch.
Turves Green Leisure & Adult Education Centre
Turves Green Girls' Sch. & Tech Coll.
Turves Green Prim. Sch.
West Heath Jun. & Inf. Schs.
Sports Grd.
Works
MIDDLETON HALL RD.
BUNBURY ROAD
BRISTOL ROAD SOUTH (WHITE HILL)
A38
B4121
NORTHFIELD ROAD
WYCHALL ROAD
HOLE LANE
WOODLANDS PARK ROAD
GRIFFIN'S BROOK LANE
BOURNVILLE LANE
HAWTHORNE RD.
POPES LANE
CHURCH RD.
STONE RD.
MIDDLEMORE RD.
STATION RD.
WEST HEATH RD.
LONGFELLOW ROAD
STAPLEHALL RD.
LODGE RD.
FAIRWAY
FAIRLIE CR.
AVERSLEY RD.

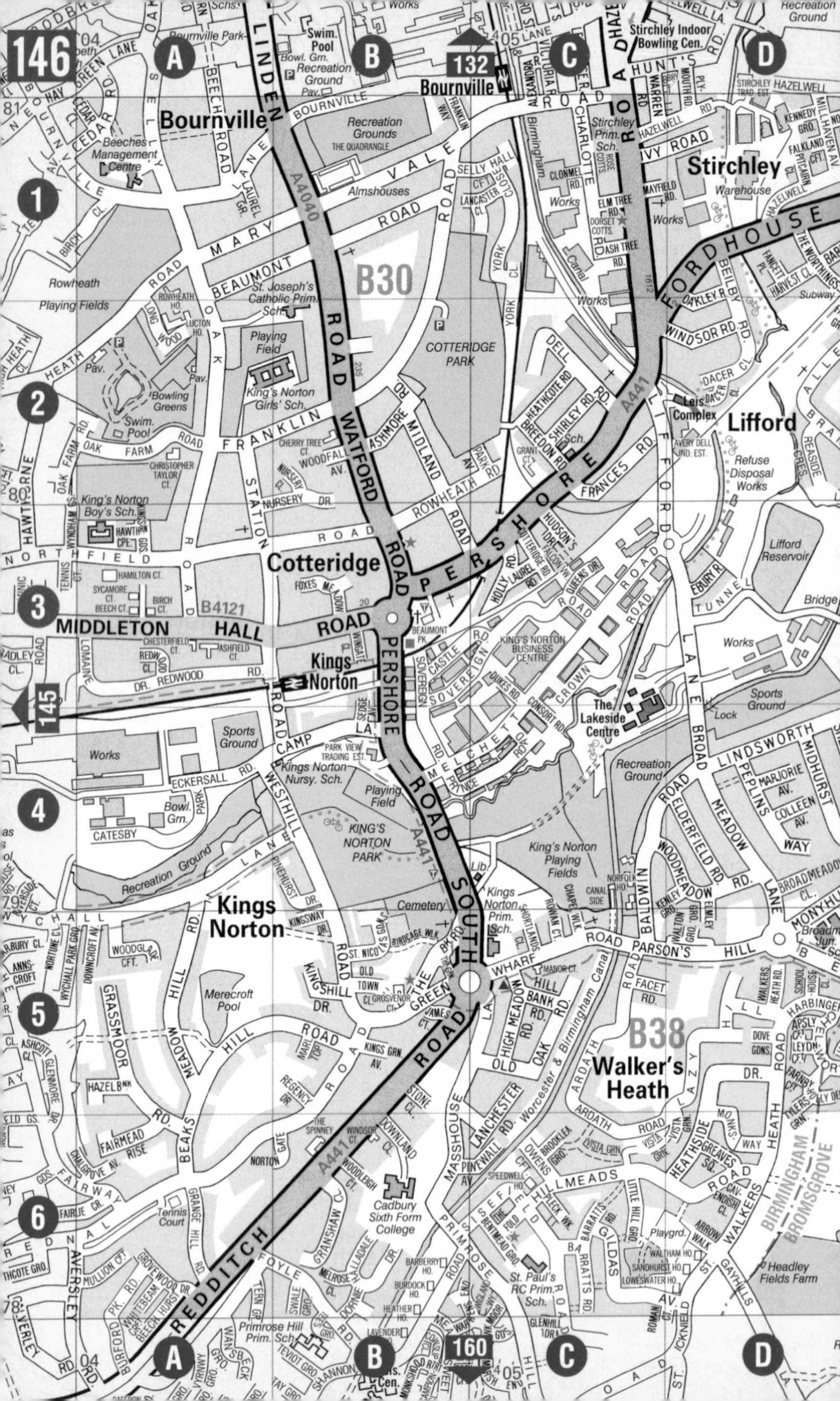
A
B
C
D
1
2
3
4
5
6
132
145
160
Bournville
Stirchley
Lifford
Cotteridge
Kings Norton
Walker's Heath
B30
B38
MIDDLETON HALL ROAD
PERSHORE ROAD
WATFORD ROAD
REDDITCH ROAD
FORDHOUSE
LINDEN ROAD
BOURNVILLE LANE
MARY VALE ROAD
Rowheath Playing Fields
Cotteridge Park
King's Norton Park
Lifford Reservoir
The Lakeside Centre
King's Norton Business Centre
Cadbury Sixth Form College
Mercroft Pool
Stirchley Indoor Bowling Cen.
BIRMINGHAM
BROMSGROVE

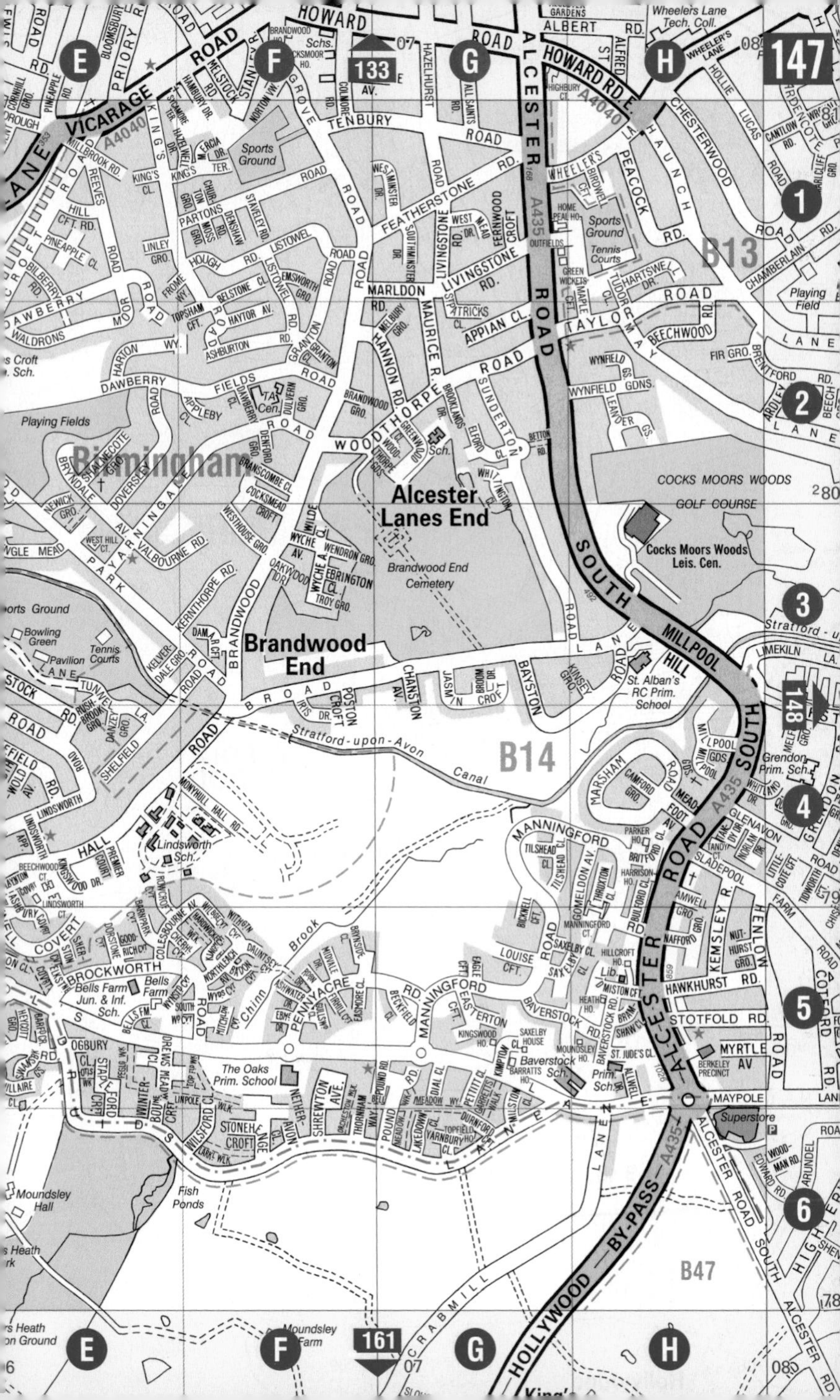

Alcester Lanes End
Brandwood End
Birmingham
B13
B14
B47
Brandwood End Cemetery
Cocks Moors Woods Golf Course
Cocks Moors Woods Leis. Cen.
St. Alban's RC Prim. School
Grendon Prim. Sch.
Lindsworth Sch.
Bells Farm Jun. & Inf. Sch.
The Oaks Prim. School
Baverstock Sch.
Moundsley Hall
Fish Ponds
Stratford-upon-Avon Canal
Playing Fields
Sports Ground
Playing Field
Superstore
ALCESTER ROAD SOUTH
HOLLYWOOD BY-PASS
VICARAGE ROAD
HOWARD RD. E.
WHEELER'S LANE
BRANDWOOD ROAD
BROAD LANE
DAWBERRY FIELDS ROAD
WOODTHORPE ROAD
MILLPOOL HILL
MAYPOLE LANE
TAYLOR ROAD
CHAMBERLAIN ROAD
PEACOCK RD.
HAUNCH LA.
MANNINGFORD RD.
BROCKWORTH
A435
A4040
E
F
G
H
1
2
3
4
5
6
133
148
161

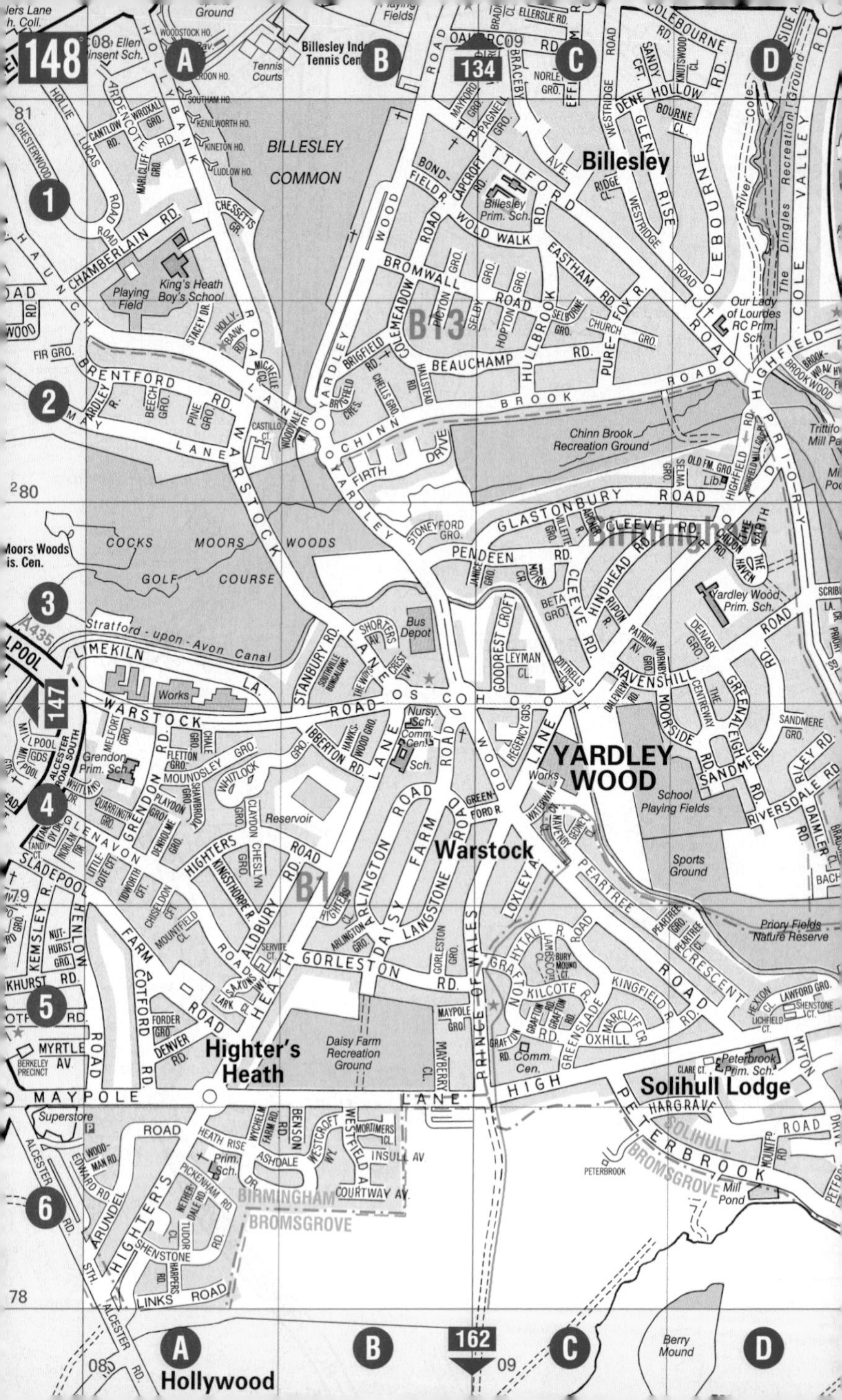

A
B
C
D
1
2
3
4
5
6
134
147
162
BILLESLEY COMMON
Billesley
B13
Chinn Brook Recreation Ground
COCKS MOORS WOODS GOLF COURSE
Stratford - upon - Avon Canal
YARDLEY WOOD
Warstock
B14
Highter's Heath
Solihull Lodge
Daisy Farm Recreation Ground
Hollywood
Berry Mound
King's Heath Boy's School
Billesley Prim. Sch.
Yardley Wood Prim. Sch.
Grendon Prim. Sch.
Peterbrook Prim. Sch.
Our Lady of Lourdes RC Prim. Sch.
Bus Depot
Reservoir
School Playing Fields
Sports Ground
Priory Fields Nature Reserve
BIRMINGHAM
BROMSGROVE
SOLIHULL

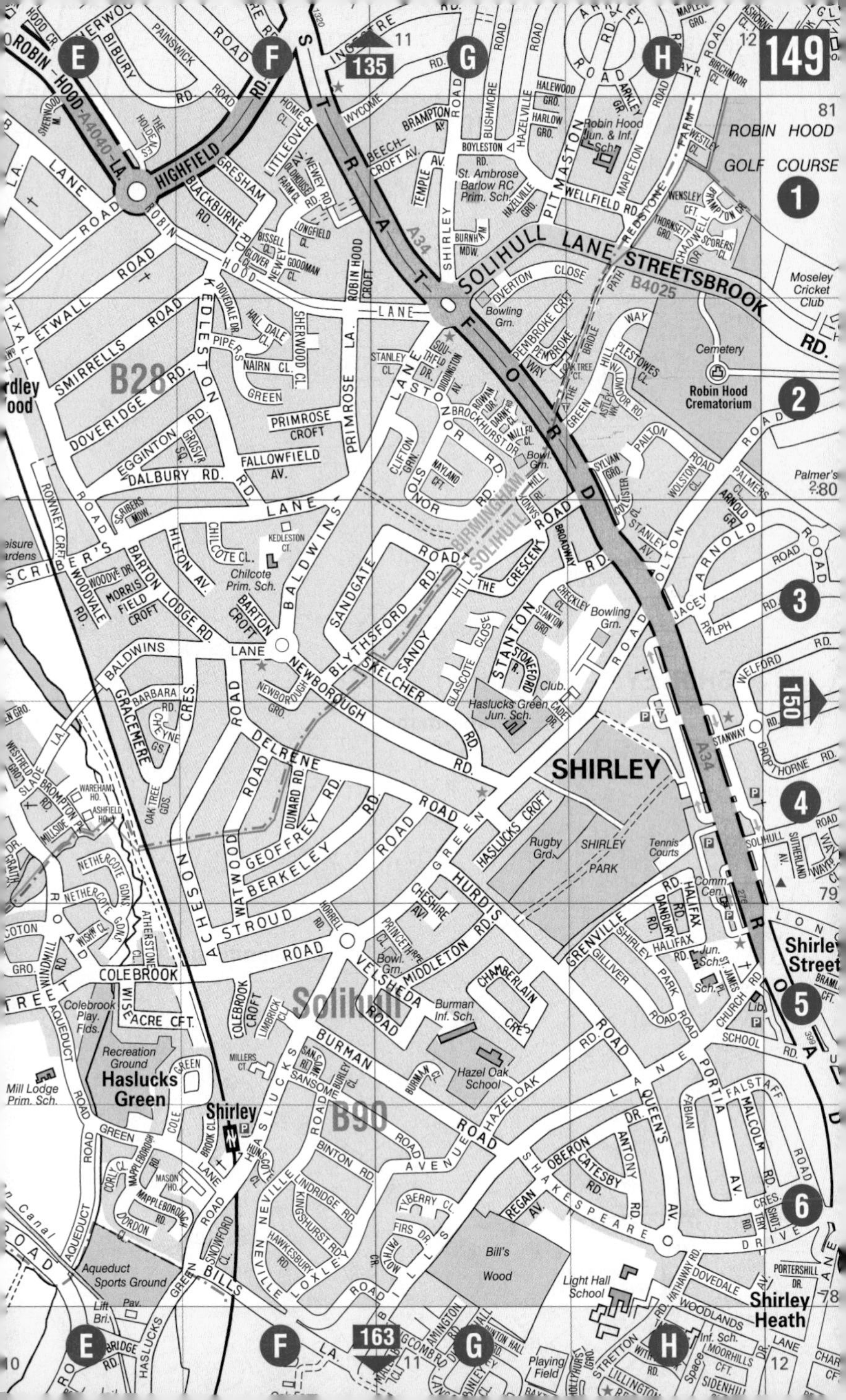
149
135
163
150
E
F
G
H
1
2
3
4
5
6
11
12
81
80
79
78
ROBIN HOOD GOLF COURSE
Moseley Cricket Club
Cemetery
Robin Hood Crematorium
Robin Hood Jun. & Inf. Sch.
St. Ambrose Barlow RC Prim. Sch.
Bowling Grn.
Bowl. Grn.
Chilcote Prim. Sch.
Haslucks Green Jun. Sch.
Club
SHIRLEY
Rugby Grd.
SHIRLEY PARK
Tennis Courts
Comm. Cen.
Jun. Sch.
Lib.
Burman Inf. Sch.
Hazel Oak School
Bill's Wood
Light Hall School
Playing Field
Inf. Sch.
Shirley Heath
Shirley Street
Solihull
B28
B90
Colebrook Play. Flds.
Recreation Ground
Haslucks Green
Mill Lodge Prim. Sch.
Aqueduct Sports Ground
Shirley
STRATFORD ROAD
A34
A4040
B4025
HIGHFIELD RD.
ROBIN HOOD LA.
SOLIHULL LANE
STREETSBROOK RD.
ETWALL ROAD
SMIRRELLS ROAD
DOVERIDGE RD.
EGGINTON RD.
DALBURY RD.
KEDLESTON RD.
SCRIBERS LANE
BALDWINS LANE
PRIMROSE LA.
PRIMROSE CROFT
FALLOWFIELD AV.
BLYTHSFORD RD.
SANDGATE ROAD
SANDY HILL RD.
NEWBOROUGH RD.
DELRENE ROAD
GEOFFREY RD.
BERKELEY ROAD
STROUD ROAD
HASLUCKS GREEN ROAD
HURDIS RD.
MIDDLETON RD.
VELSHEDA ROAD
BURMAN ROAD
HAZELOAK ROAD
ACHESON ROAD
WATWOOD ROAD
COLEBROOK
WISE ACRE CFT.
BILLS LANE
NEVILLE RD.
LOXLEY AVENUE
SHAKESPEARE DRIVE
QUEEN'S AV.
PORTIA AV.
GRENVILLE RD.
HALIFAX RD.
SCHOOL RD.
CHURCH RD.
WOODLANDS
AQUEDUCT ROAD
WINDMILL RD.
BIRMINGHAM
SOLIHULL

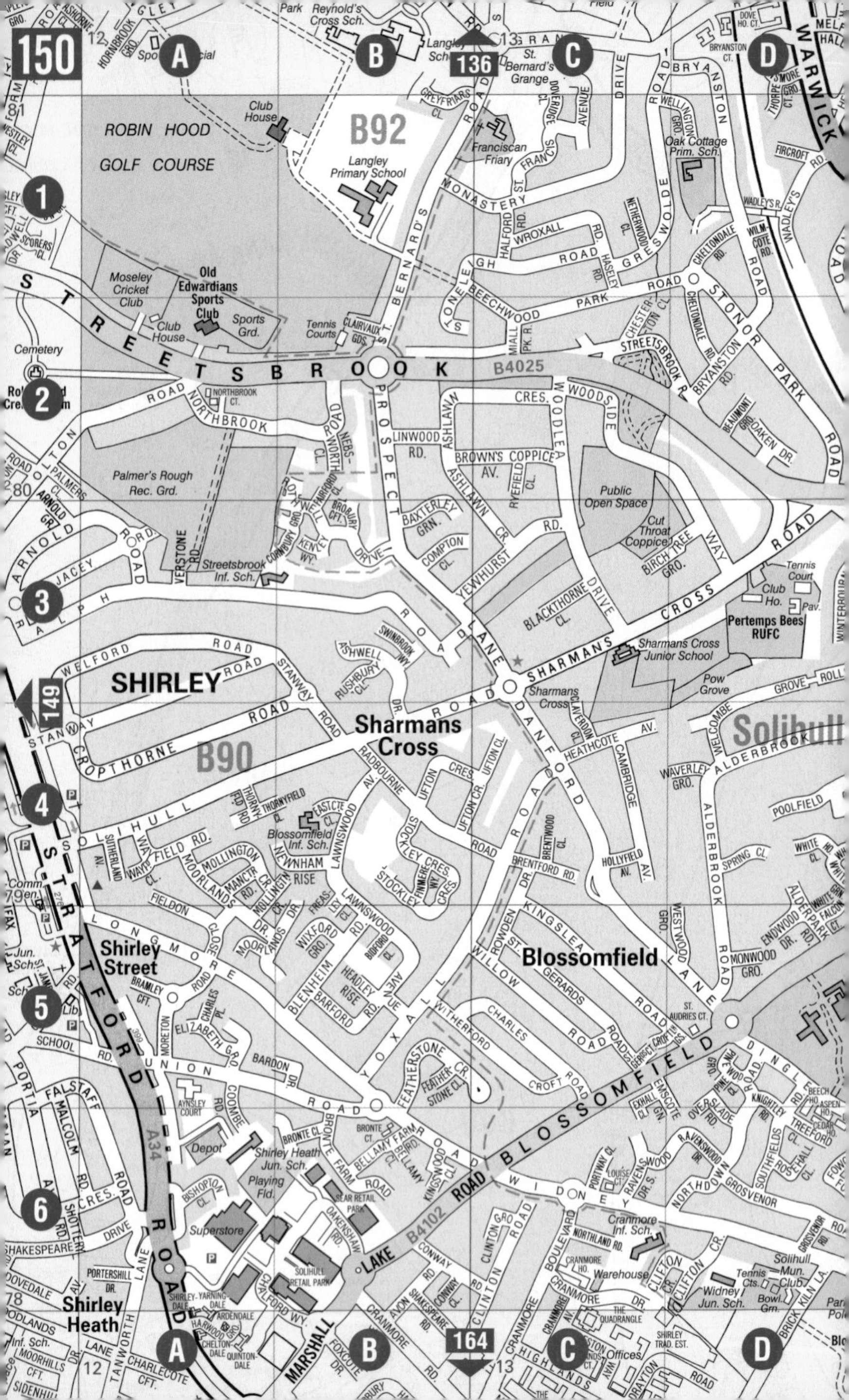

ROBIN HOOD GOLF COURSE
Club House
B92
Langley Primary School
Franciscan Friary
Oak Cottage Prim. Sch.
Moseley Cricket Club
Old Edwardians Sports Club
Sports Grd.
Cemetery
STREETSBROOK
B4025
Palmer's Rough Rec. Grd.
Public Open Space
Cut Throat Coppice
Streetsbrook Inf. Sch.
Pertemps Bees RUFC
Sharmans Cross Junior School
SHIRLEY
Sharmans Cross
B90
Solihull
Blossomfield Inf. Sch.
Shirley Street
Blossomfield
Shirley Heath Jun. Sch.
Playing Fld.
Superstore
Depot
SOLIHULL RETAIL PARK
Cranmore Inf. Sch.
Warehouse
Widney Jun. Sch.
Solihull Mun. Club
Shirley Heath
BLOSSOMFIELD
B4102
A34
STRATFORD ROAD
136
149
164

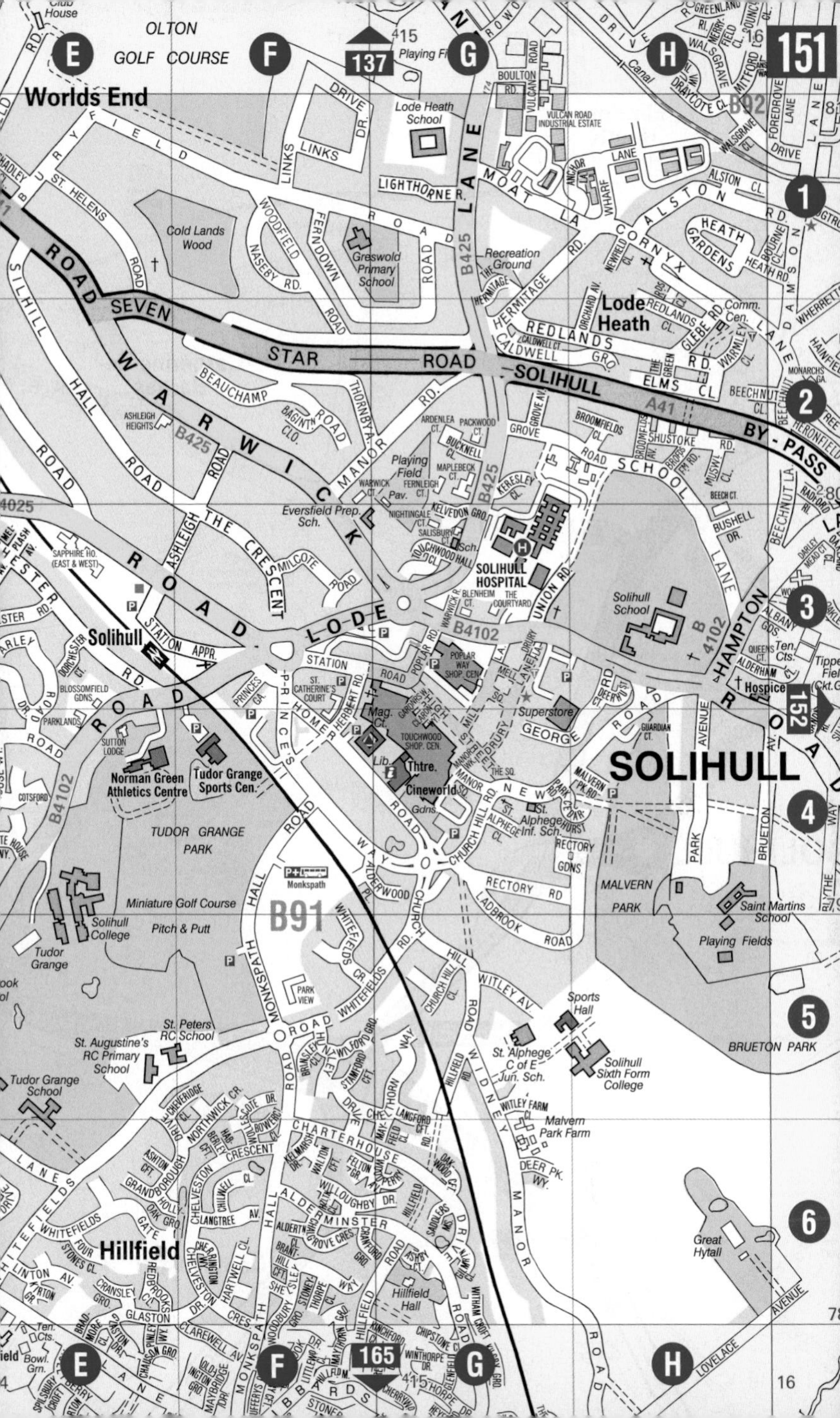

OLTON GOLF COURSE
Worlds End
137
Lode Heath School
Cold Lands Wood
Greswold Primary School
Recreation Ground
Lode Heath
SEVEN STAR ROAD
SOLIHULL BY-PASS
WARWICK ROAD
Playing Field
Eversfield Prep. Sch.
SOLIHULL HOSPITAL
Solihull School
Solihull
LODE LANE
STATION ROAD
Norman Green Athletics Centre
Tudor Grange Sports Cen.
TUDOR GRANGE PARK
Miniature Golf Course
Pitch & Putt
Solihull College
Tudor Grange
SOLIHULL
Superstore
TOUCHWOOD SHOP. CEN.
Thtre.
Cineworld
MALVERN PARK
Saint Martins School
Playing Fields
BRUETON PARK
Sports Hall
St. Alphege C of E Jun. Sch.
Solihull Sixth Form College
Malvern Park Farm
St. Peters RC School
St. Augustine's RC Primary School
Tudor Grange School
Hillfield
Hillfield Hall
Great Hytall
B91
152
165

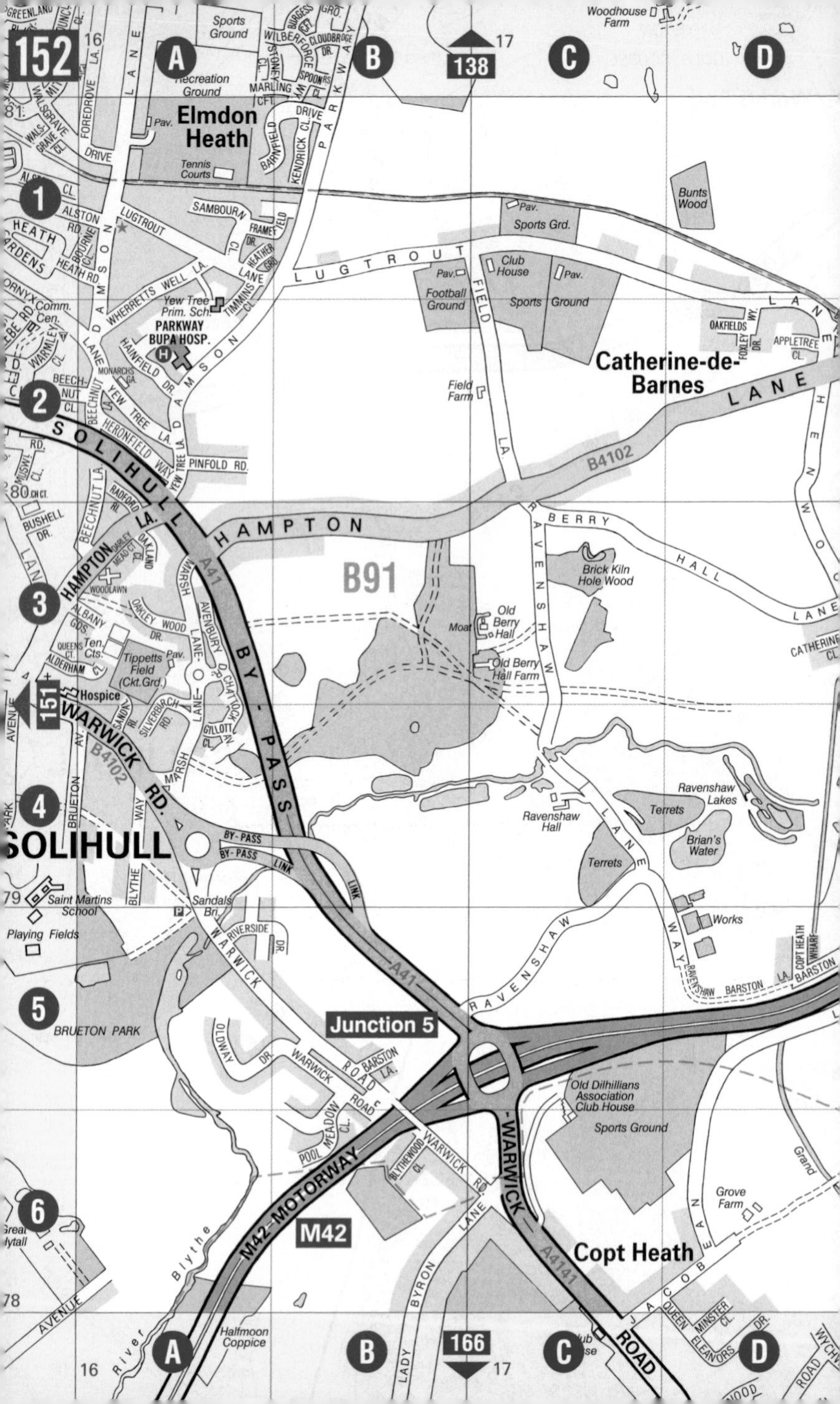
Elmdon Heath
Sports Ground
Recreation Ground
Tennis Courts
Pav.
Catherine-de-Barnes
Bunts Wood
Sports Grd.
Club House
Football Ground
Sports Ground
Field Farm
Yew Tree Prim. Sch.
PARKWAY BUPA HOSP.
Comm. Cen.
LUGTROUT LANE
DAMSON PARKWAY
CATHERINE-DE-BARNES LANE
B4102
HAMPTON LANE
SOLIHULL BY-PASS
A41
B91
Brick Kiln Hole Wood
Old Berry Hall
Moat
Old Berry Hall Farm
BERRY HALL LANE
RAVENSHAW LANE
Ravenshaw Hall
Ravenshaw Lakes
Terrets
Brian's Water
Works
Tippetts Field (Ckt.Grd.)
Hospice
WARWICK RD.
SOLIHULL
Saint Martins School
Playing Fields
BRUETON PARK
Sandals Bri.
Junction 5
M42 MOTORWAY
M42
WARWICK ROAD
A4141
Old Dilhillians Association Club House
Sports Ground
Grove Farm
Copt Heath
JACOBEAN LANE
Halfmoon Coppice
River Blythe
Woodhouse Farm
138
151
166
A
B
C
D
1
2
3
4
5
6
16
17
78
79
80
81

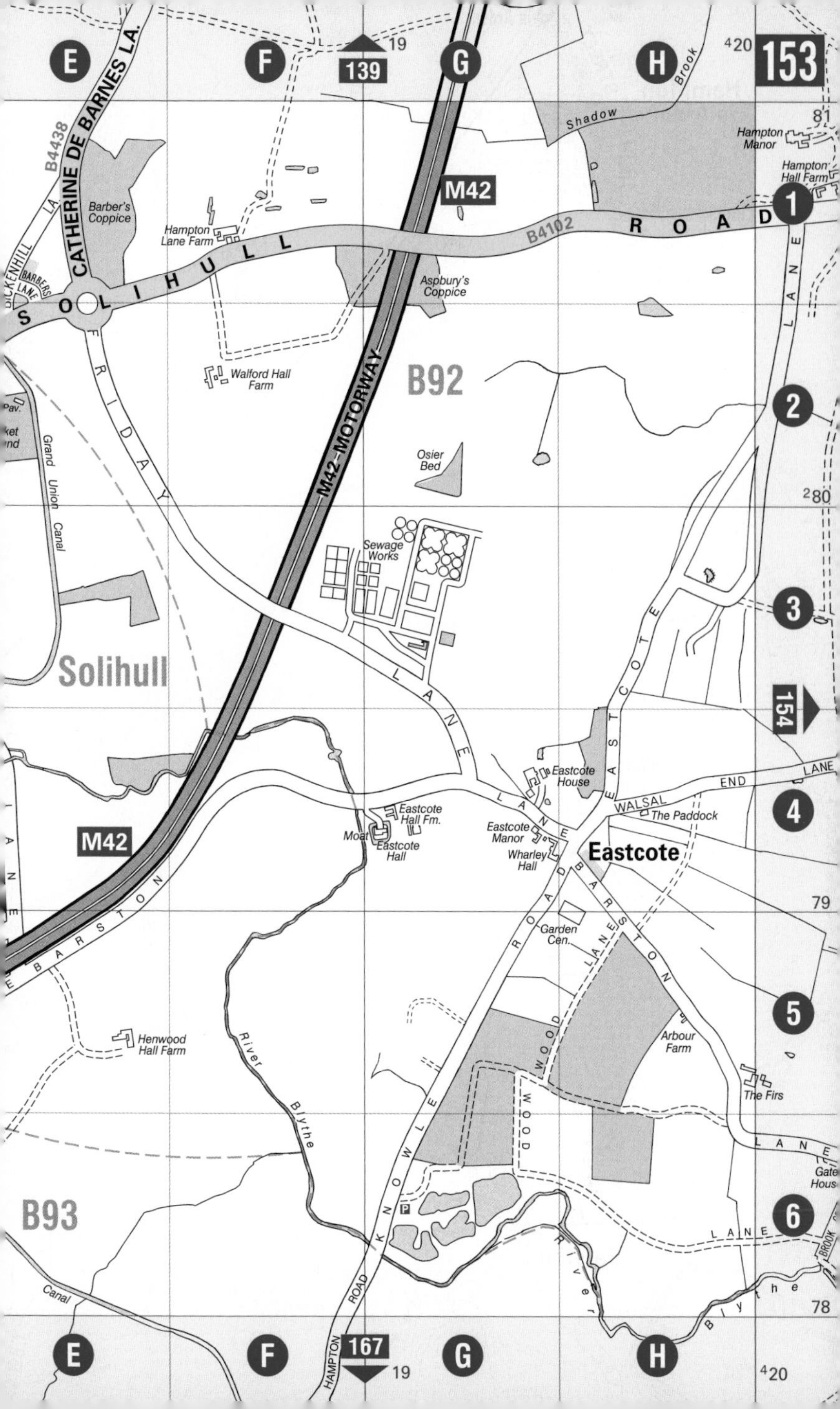

E
F
G
H
139
19
420
Brook
Shadow
81
Hampton Manor
Hampton Hall Farm
CATHERINE DE BARNES LA.
B4438
Barber's Coppice
M42
Hampton Lane Farm
B4102
ROAD
SOLIHULL
BICKENHILL LA.
BARBERS LANE
Aspbury's Coppice
LANE
FRIDAY
Walford Hall Farm
B92
M42-MOTORWAY
Grand Union Canal
Osier Bed
280
Sewage Works
EASTCOTE
Solihull
LANE
154
Eastcote House
WALSAL END LANE
The Paddock
Eastcote Hall Fm.
Moat
Eastcote Hall
Eastcote Manor
Wharley Hall
Eastcote
M42
BARSTON
ROAD
BARSTON LANE
Garden Cen.
79
Henwood Hall Farm
River Blythe
WOOD LANE
Arbour Farm
The Firs
WOOD
LANE
Gate House
B93
KNOWLE
LANE
BROOK
Canal
River Blythe
78
HAMPTON ROAD
167
19
420
1
2
3
4
5
6

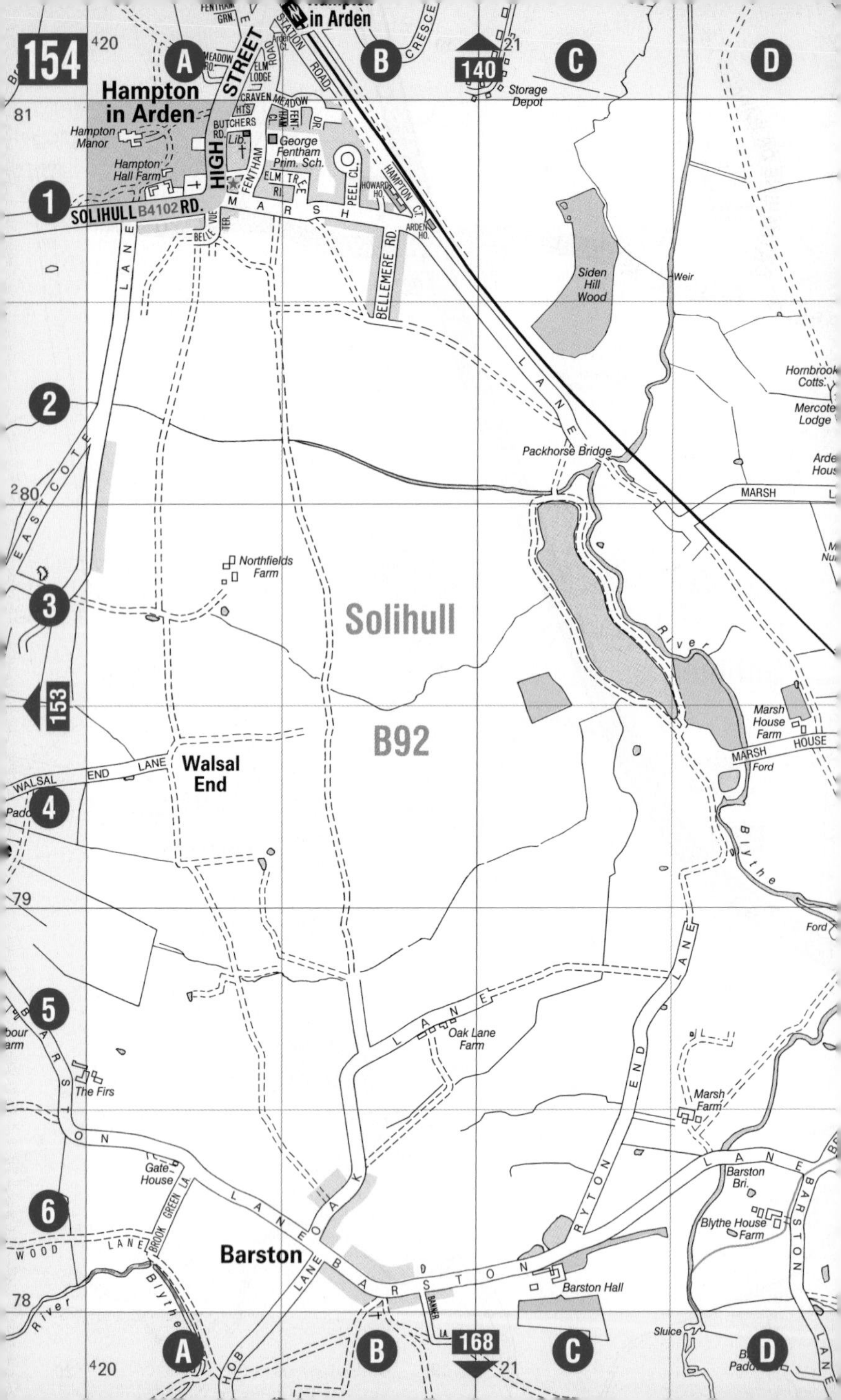

Hampton in Arden
Hampton Manor
Hampton Hall Farm
HIGH STREET
MEADOW RD.
ELM LODGE
CRAVEN HTS.
MEADOW
BUTCHERS RD.
Lib.
George Fentham Prim. Sch.
FENTHAM
ELM TREE RI.
PEEL CL.
HOWARDS HO.
HAMPTON CT.
ARDEN HO.
STATION ROAD
SOLIHULL B4102 RD.
MARSH
BELLE VUE TER.
BELLEMERE RD.
LANE
Storage Depot
Siden Hill Wood
Weir
Hornbrook Cotts.
Mercote Lodge
Packhorse Bridge
MARSH
EASTCOTE
Northfields Farm
Solihull
B92
River
Marsh House Farm
MARSH HOUSE
Ford
Blythe
WALSAL END LANE
Walsal End
Oak Lane Farm
LANE
RYTON END LANE
Marsh Farm
The Firs
BARSTON LANE
Gate House
BROOK GREEN LA.
WOOD LANE
Barston
OAK
BARSTON LANE
Barston Bri.
Blythe House Farm
Barston Hall
BANNER LA.
River Blythe
HOB LANE
Sluice

140
153
168

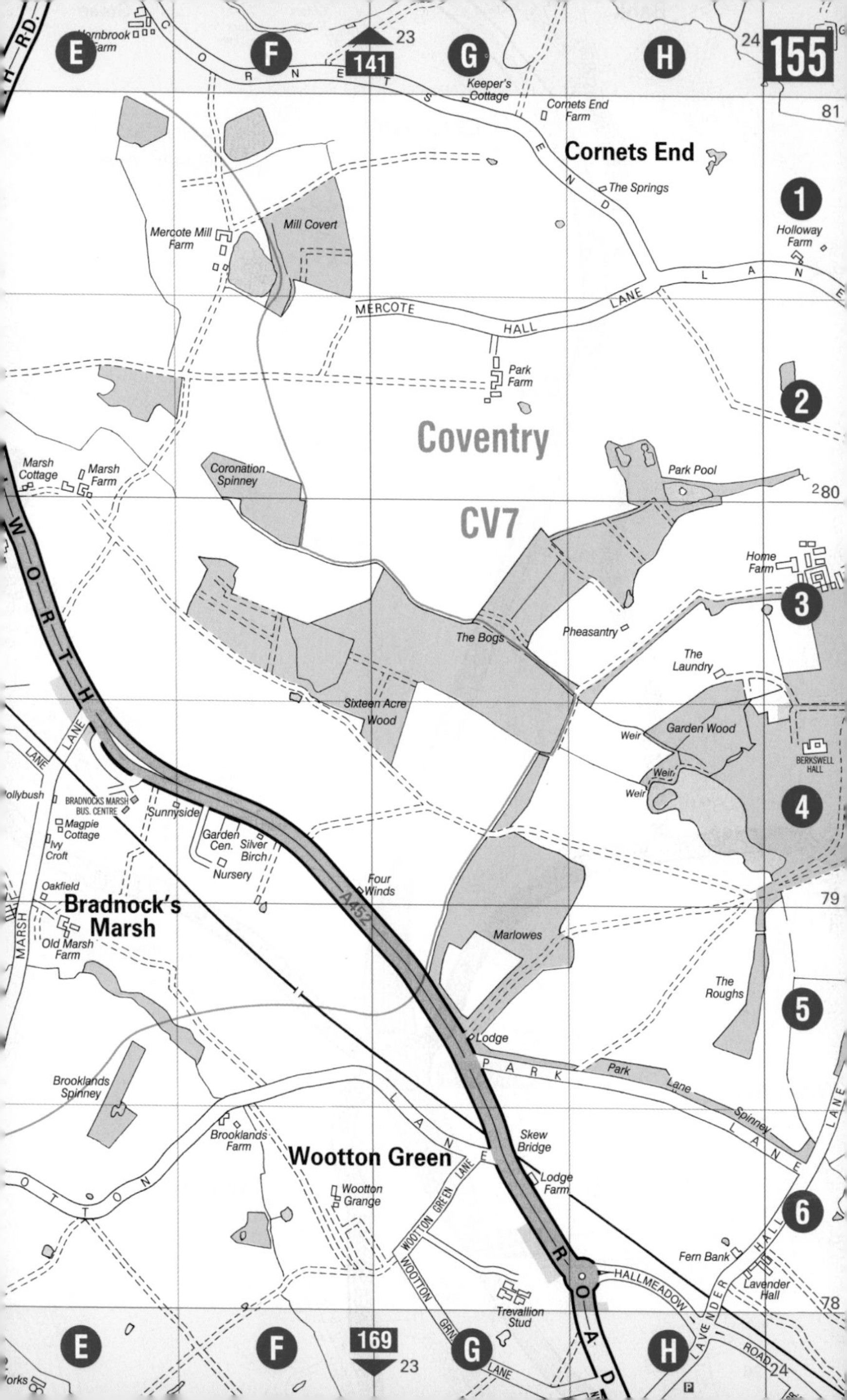

E   F   141   23   G   H   24   155

81

Hornbrook Farm

Keeper's Cottage

Cornets End Farm

Cornets End

The Springs

1

Holloway Farm

Mercote Mill Farm

Mill Covert

MERCOTE HALL LANE   LANE

2

80

Park Farm

Coventry

Marsh Cottage

Marsh Farm

Coronation Spinney

CV7

Park Pool

Home Farm

3

BERKSWELL HALL

The Bogs

Pheasantry

The Laundry

Garden Wood

Weir

Weir

Weir

4

Sixteen Acre Wood

W O R T H   L A N E   L A N E

Hollybush

BRADNOCKS MARSH BUS. CENTRE

Sunnyside

Magpie Cottage

Ivy Croft

Garden Cen.

Silver Birch

Nursery

Oakfield

Four Winds

A452

Bradnock's Marsh

Old Marsh Farm

Marlowes

79

The Roughs

5

M A R S H   L A N E

Brooklands Spinney

Brooklands Farm

Wootton Green

Lodge

P A R K   Park   Lane

Spinney

L A N E

Skew Bridge

Wootton Grange

Lodge Farm

6

W O O T T O N   WOOTTON GREEN LANE

R O A D

Fern Bank

Lavender Hall

H A L L   L A N E

78

Trevallion Stud

HALLMEADOW

P

E   F   169   23   G   H   24

L A V E N D E R   ROAD

orks

Bank
Green
Visitors Centre
Duck Pool Farm
142
Chapman's Hill
Chapman's Hill Farm
B62
Little Farley Wood
Bromsgrove Rd.
Dayhouse
Chapman's
Windmill Hill
WASELEY HILLS COUNTRY PARK
Waseleyhill Cottage
Quantry
DY9
Poultry Houses
Bell Heath Country Study Centre
Segbourne Coppice
WASELEY HILL
Waseleyhill Farm
Gunner
Chadwich Manor Estate
Chadwich Lane
Thatchers Cottage
M5
M5 Motorway
Holywell Primary School
Waseley Hills High Sch. & Sixth Form Cen.
Bromsgrove
Chadwich Grange
Rabbit Hill Plantation
B4551
Subway
B61
Holywell Farm
Holywell Lane
Three Acres
Youth Cen
Holy Well (Chalybeate)
RED HILL
Money Lane
Money Lane Farm
Yewtree Farm
Redhill Farm
Broadmoor Wood
Malthouse Lane
Subway
Reservoir (covered)
Redhill
Chadwich Manor Farm
Malt House La.
Malt House
Manor
Territory Bank
Harbours Hl.
Sandy Lane
A491
Chadwich Heights
Subway
Spring Pools
Chadwich Manor
Cherry Trees
Road
Wildmoor Farm
Top Road
Keys Hill Farm
Brookhouse Farm
Birmingham Road
A38
BEACON
Middle Road
Third
Chadwich House
The Winsel
Lane Road
Yard
Chadwich Farm
Junction 4
Wildmoor
Sand Pit
Lydiate Ash Rd.
Halesowen Road
A38
Meadow View
Lydiate Ash
Lydiate Ash Rd.
The Limes
B60
Alvechurch
Mill
Lane
Mount Pleasant
Woodrow Farm
Woodrow La.
Beacon
Marlbrook La.
Nursery
Wildmoor
78
77
96
97
75

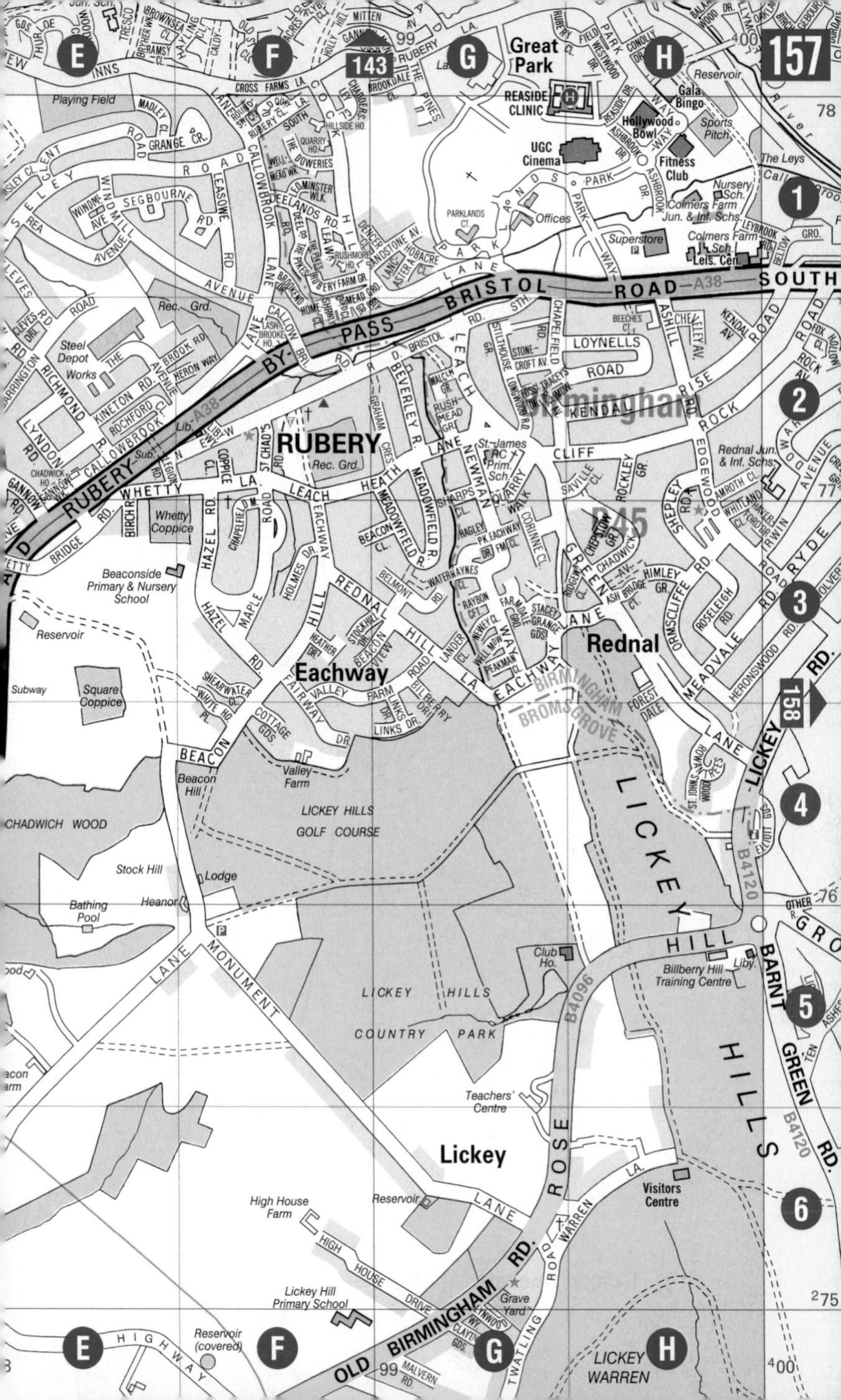

Great Park
Reaside Clinic
UGC Cinema
Hollywood Bowl
Gala Bingo
Fitness Club
Sports Pitch
Reservoir
River
The Leys
Colmers Farm Jun. & Inf. Schs.
Colmers Farm Sch.
Leis. Cen.
Superstore
Offices
Parklands Ct.
Playing Field
Rec. Grd.
Steel Depot Works
BRISTOL ROAD SOUTH
A38
RUBERY BY-PASS
RUBERY
Birmingham
B45
St. James RC Prim. Sch.
Rednal Jun. & Inf. Schs.
Whetty Coppice
Beaconside Primary & Nursery School
Reservoir
Subway
Square Coppice
Eachway
Rednal
BIRMINGHAM
BROMSGROVE
Valley Farm
Beacon Hill
LICKEY HILLS GOLF COURSE
CHADWICH WOOD
Stock Hill
Lodge
Bathing Pool
Heanor
Club Ho.
Billberry Hill Training Centre
Liby.
LICKEY HILLS COUNTRY PARK
LICKEY HILLS
Teachers' Centre
Lickey
Visitors Centre
High House Farm
Reservoir
Lickey Hill Primary School
Grave Yard
Reservoir (covered)
LICKEY WARREN
B4096
B4120
ROSE
OLD BIRMINGHAM RD.
BARNT GREEN RD.
LICKEY RD.
MONUMENT LANE
HIGHWAY
143
158
E
F
G
H
1
2
3
4
5
6
78
77
76
275
99
400

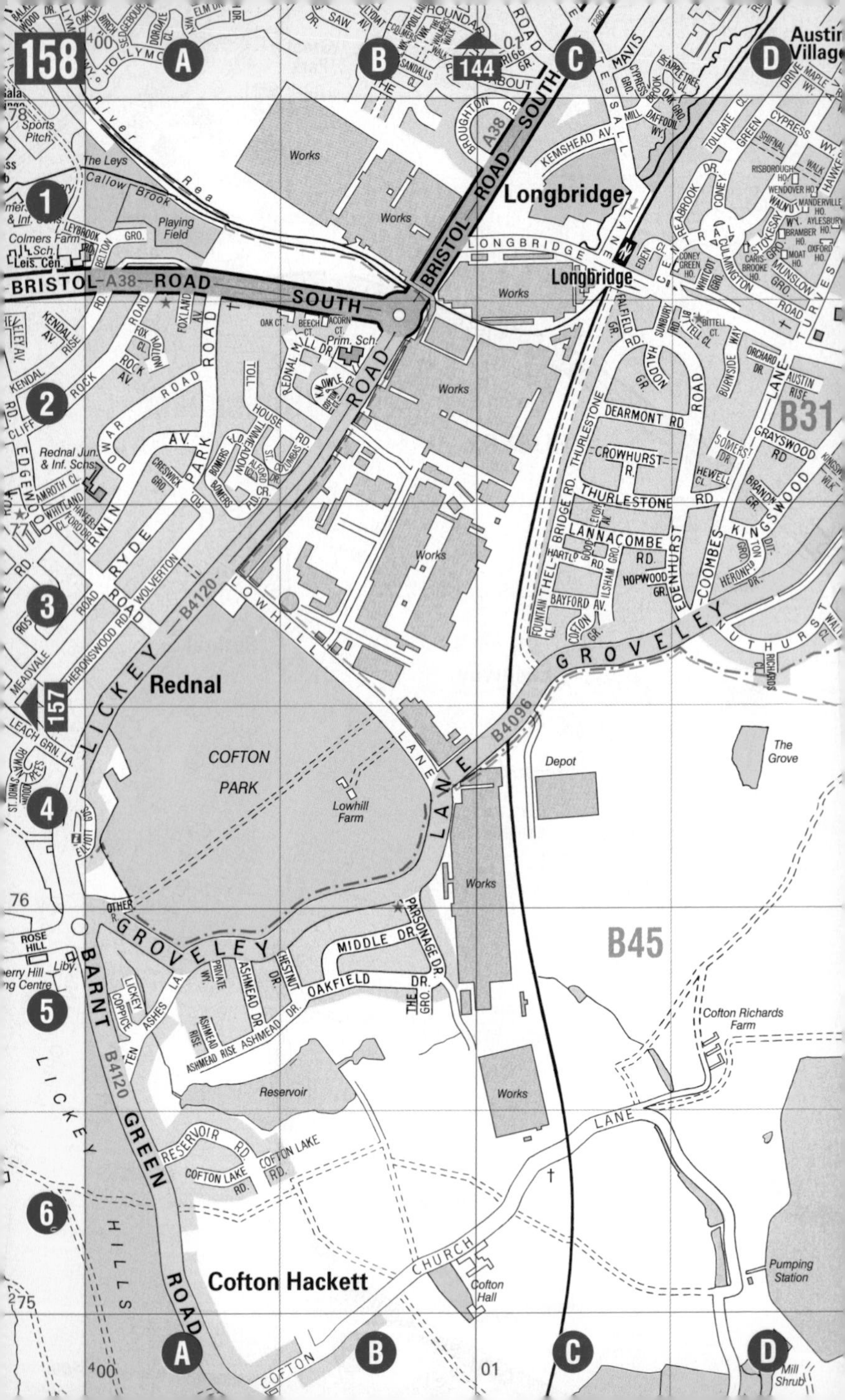

144
157
A
B
C
D
1
2
3
4
5
6
Longbridge
Rednal
Cofton Hackett
Austin Village
COFTON PARK
Lowhill Farm
Works
Depot
The Grove
Cofton Richards Farm
Reservoir
Pumping Station
Cofton Hall
Mill Shrub
Playing Field
Sports Pitch
The Leys
Callow Brook
River Rea
Colmers Farm Sch.
Leis. Cen.
Rednal Jun. & Inf. Schs.
Prim. Sch.
BRISTOL ROAD SOUTH
A38
B4120
B4096
LICKEY ROAD
BARNT GREEN ROAD
LICKEY HILLS
GROVELEY LANE
LOWHILL LANE
LONGBRIDGE LANE
CHURCH LANE
COFTON LANE
B31
B45
76
75
400
01

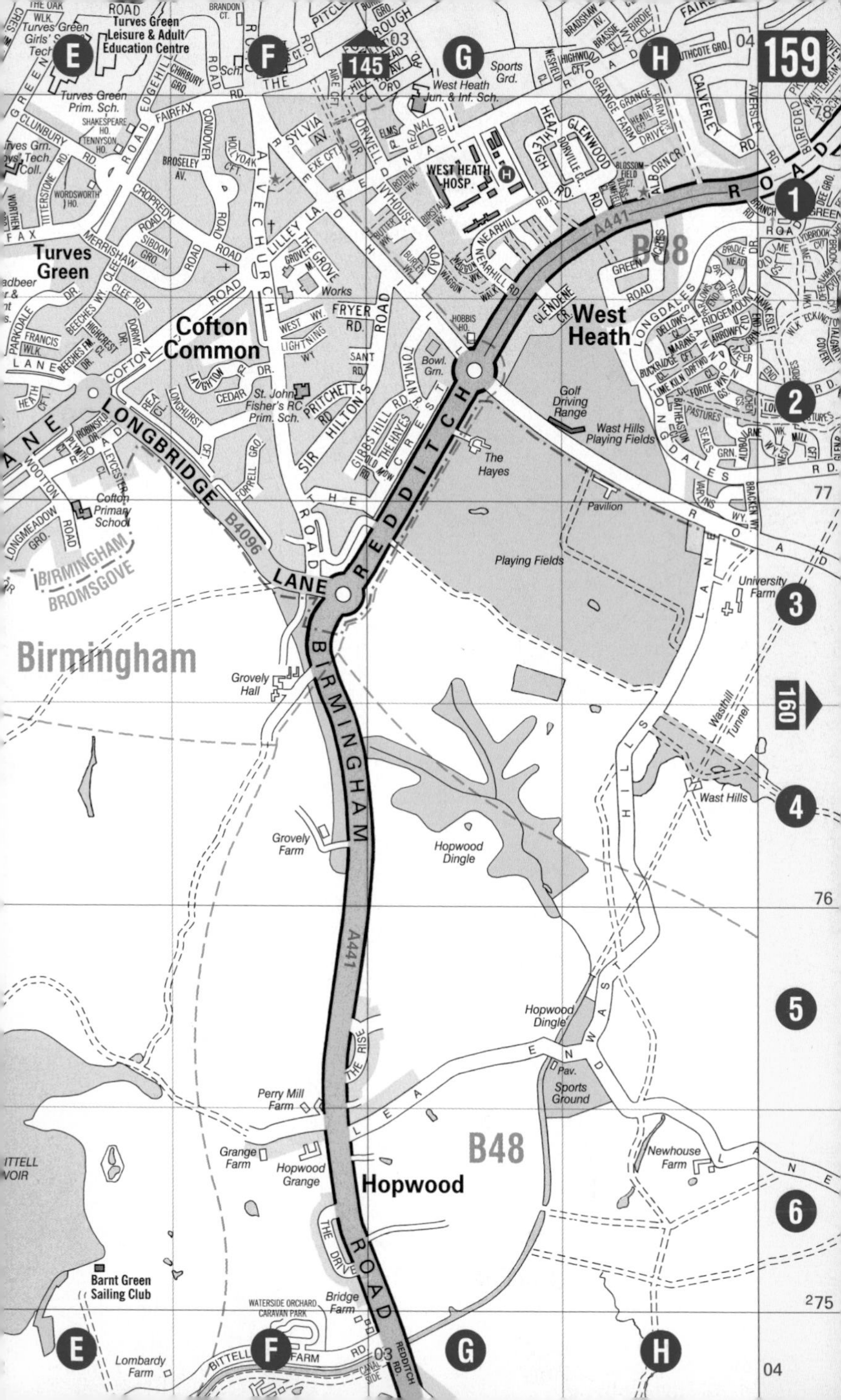
Turves Green
Leisure & Adult
Education Centre
Turves Green Girls' Sch.
Turves Green Prim. Sch.
Turves Green
Cofton Common
West Heath
WEST HEATH HOSP.
West Heath Jun. & Inf. Sch.
Sports Grd.
St. John Fisher's RC Prim. Sch.
Cofton Primary School
Works
Bowl. Grn.
Golf Driving Range
Wast Hills Playing Fields
The Hayes
Pavilion
Playing Fields
University Farm
Birmingham
BIRMINGHAM
BROMSGOVE
Grovely Hall
Wasthill Tunnel
Wast Hills
Grovely Farm
Hopwood Dingle
Perry Mill Farm
Sports Ground
Grange Farm
Hopwood Grange
Hopwood
B48
B38
Newhouse Farm
Barnt Green Sailing Club
WATERSIDE ORCHARD CARAVAN PARK
Bridge Farm
Lombardy Farm
LONGBRIDGE LANE
REDDITCH ROAD
BIRMINGHAM ROAD
A441
B4096
ALVECHURCH ROAD
COFTON ROAD
LEA END LANE
WAST HILLS LANE
LONGDALES RD.
145
160

Hawkesley
Gay Hill
B38
Bell Green
Birmingham
Forhill
Lea End
B48
REDDITCH ROAD
A441
Primrose Hill Prim. Sch.
Kings Norton High Sch.
Leis. Cen.
Comm. Cen.
Prim. Sch.
St. Pauls RC Prim. Sch.
College
BIRMINGHAM
BROMSGROVE
Goodrest Farm
Red Hill
University Farm
Wasthill
Tunnel
Seal's Green Farm
Colebrook Farm
Forhill Farm
Forhill House
Sports Grd.
Forhill Picnic Site
Brockhill Dingle
Swanshill Wood
Swan's Hill
Ryknild Street (Roman Road)
GRIMPITS LANE
GOODREST LANE
LILLYCROFT LA.
ICKNIELD STREET
HEADLEY HEATH
BELL GREEN
CLEWSHAW LANE
BROCKHILL
LEA END
WATERY LANE
REDHILL ROAD
LONGDALE ROAD
PRIMROSE HILL
SHANNON ROAD
GAY HILL
146
159
A
B
C
D
1
2
3
4
5
6
04
405
78
77
76
75

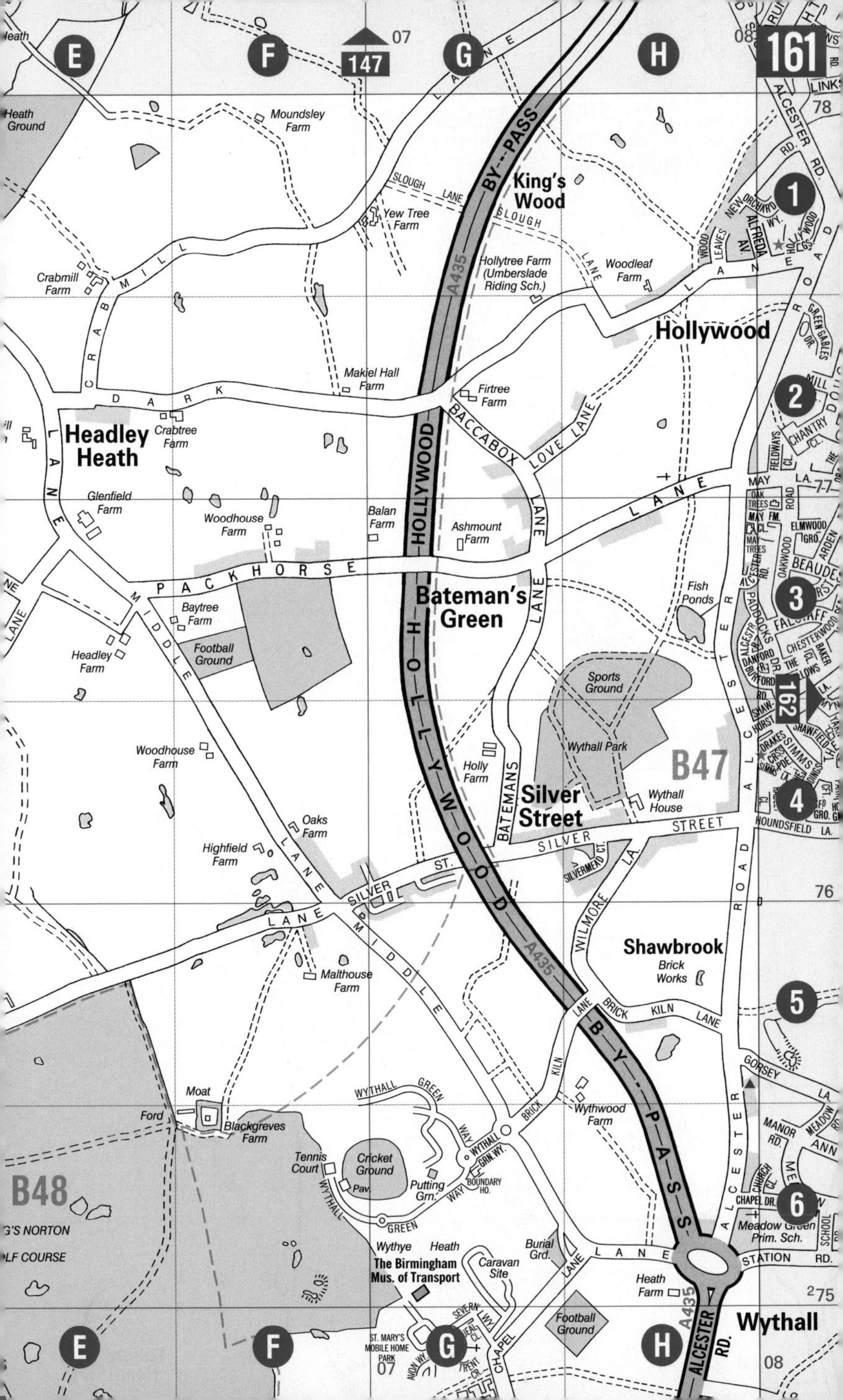

E **F** 07 147 **G** **H** 08 LINK 78

King's Wood

SLOUGH LANE

Moundsley Farm

SLOUGH

Yew Tree Farm

Hollytree Farm (Umberslade Riding Sch.)

Woodleaf Farm

1 ALFRIDA HOLLYWOOD

Crabmill Farm

Hollywood

GREY GABLES DR.

DARK

Makiel Hall Farm

Firtree Farm

MILL

CHANTRY THE

2 REDWALS

Headley Heath

Crabtree Farm

BACCABOX LANE

LOVE LANE

HOLLYWOOD

MAY LA.

OAK TREES

ELMWOOD 'GRO.

BEAUDE

Glenfield Farm

Woodhouse Farm

Balan Farm

Ashmount Farm

LANE

OAKWOOD

3 PATROCKS DR

ALCESTER

DANFORD

CHESTERMAN

THE BURFORD

PACKHORSE

Bateman's Green

Fish Ponds

FALCRAFT

Baytree Farm

Football Ground

Sports Ground

Wythall Park

162

SHAW HORST

DRAKES SIMMS

STRO POF

SHAWFIELD

Headley Farm

MIDDLE

Woodhouse Farm

HOLLYWOOD

Holly Farm

BATEMANS

Silver Street

Wythall House

B47

4 HOUNDSFIELD LA.

Oaks Farm

Highfield Farm

SILVER ST.

SILVER STREET

SILVERMERE CT.

WILMORE LA.

ROAD

76

LANE

Malthouse Farm

MIDDLE

Shawbrook

Brick Works

5 GORSEY

B48

Moat

Ford

Blackgreves Farm

WYTHALL GREEN WAY

BRICK KILN LANE

BRICK KILN LANE

Wythwood Farm

ALCESTER

MANOR RD.

MEADOW ANN

G'S NORTON

LF COURSE

Tennis Court

Cricket Ground

Pav.

Putting Grn.

WYTHALL GRN. WAY

BOUNDARY HO.

BY—PASS

CHAPEL DR.

CHURCH

6 Meadow Green Prim. Sch.

WYTHALL

GREEN

Wythye Heath

The Birmingham Mus. of Transport

Caravan Site

Burial Grd.

LANE

Heath Farm

STATION RD.

2 75

ST. MARY'S MOBILE HOME PARK 07

Football Ground

Wythall

ALCESTER RD.

E **F** **G** **H** 08

Hollywood
GAY HILL GOLF COURSE
Berry Mound
Brookhouse Farm
Major's Green
Trueman's Heath Farm
Trueman's Heath
Little Trueman's Heath Farm
Pond
Sewage Works
Ford
River Cole
The Coppice Prim. Sch.
The Woodrush High School
Playing Field
Woodrush Youth Cen.
Houndsfield Farm
Birmingham
B47
Barn Hill
Leagreen Farm
Wythall
Lowbrook Farm
Gravel Pit
Shawbrook
Bleakhouse Farm
Manor Farm
Meadow Green Prim. Sch.
Grove Farm
FULFORD HEATH GOLF COURSE
Fulford Hall Farm
Fulford Hall
Fulford Heath
Club House
BROMSGROVE
SOLIHULL
HOLLYWOOD LANE
ALCESTER ROAD
MAY LANE
HOUNDSFIELD LANE
TRUEMANS HEATH LANE
NORTON LANE
GORSEY LANE
STATION ROAD
LINKS ROAD
161
148

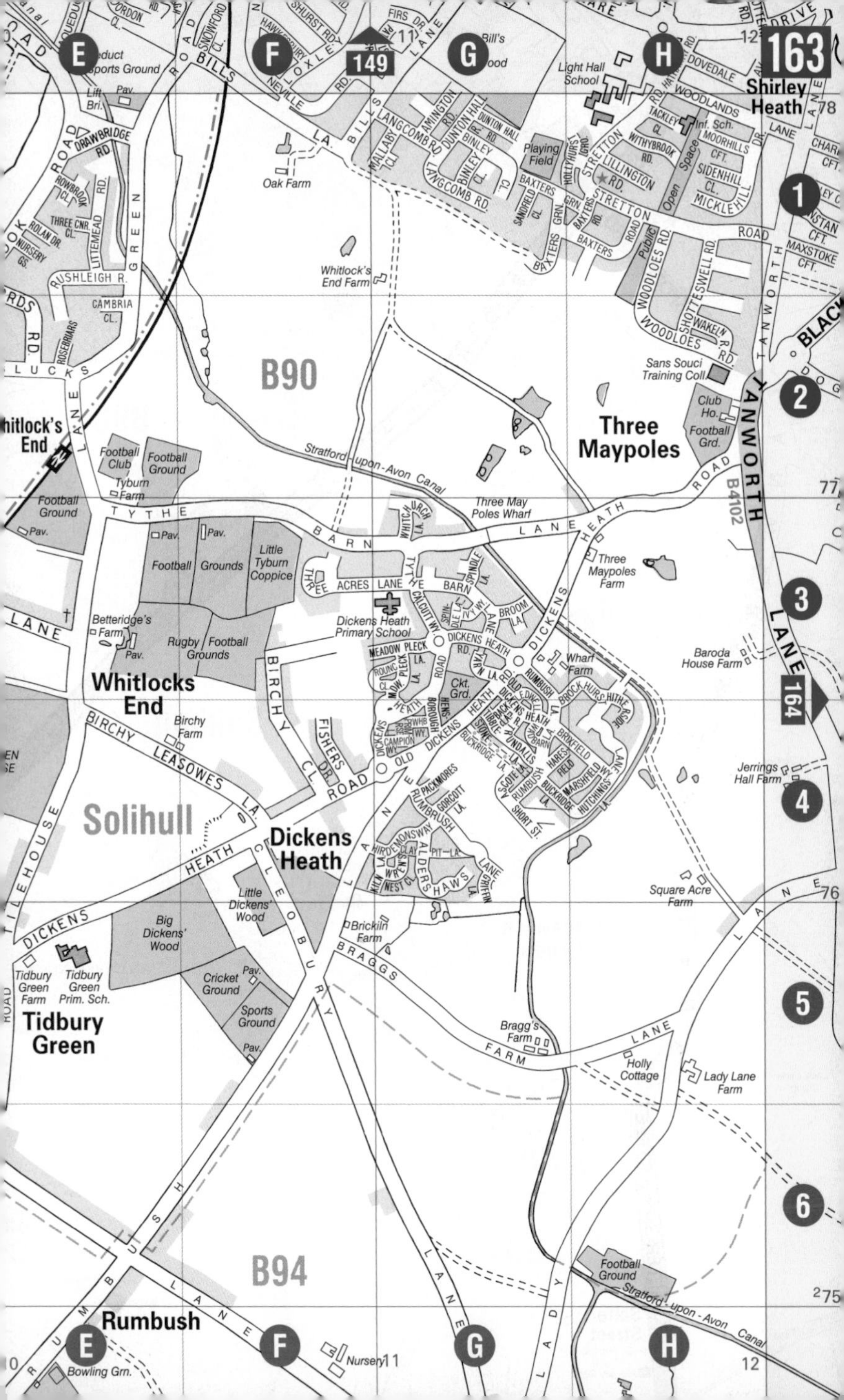

E
F
G
H
149
Shirley Heath
Light Hall School
Bill's Wood
Aqueduct Sports Ground
DRAWBRIDGE RD.
ROWBROOK CL.
THREE CNR. CL.
ROLAN DR.
NURSERY GS.
LITTLEMEAD RD.
RUSHLEIGH R.
CAMBRIA CL.
ROSEBRIARS
BILLS LA.
NEVILLE RD.
LOXLEY
LANGCOMB RD.
MALLABY CL.
AMINGTON RD.
DUNTON HALL RD.
BINLEY CL.
Oak Farm
Playing Field
HOLLYHURST GRO.
STRETTON RD.
LILLINGTON RD.
WITHYBROOK RD.
TACKLEY CL.
Inf. Sch.
MOORHILLS CFT.
SIDENHILL CL.
MICKLEHILL
WOODLANDS LANE
DOVEDALE
Open Space
BAXTERS GRN.
BAXTERS RD.
SANDFIELD CL.
Public
WOODLOES RD.
SHOTTESWELL RD.
WAKEFIN R.
WOODLOES RD.
MAXSTOKE CFT.
Whitlock's End Farm
B90
Sans Souci Training Coll.
Club Ho.
Football Grd.
Three Maypoles
TANWORTH LANE
B4102
ROAD
Whitlock's End
LUCKS LANE
GREEN
Football Club
Football Ground
Tyburn Farm
Football Ground
Pav.
Stratford-upon-Avon Canal
Three May Poles Wharf
TYTHE BARN LANE
HEATH
Football Grounds
Little Tyburn Coppice
THREE ACRES LANE
TYTHE BARN LA.
SPINDLE LA.
BROOM LA.
Three Maypoles Farm
Dickens Heath Primary School
Betteridge's Farm
Rugby Football Grounds
MEADOW PLECK
DICKENS HEATH RD.
Wharf Farm
Baroda House Farm
164
Whitlocks End
Birchy Farm
BIRCHY LEASOWES LA.
BIRCHY CL.
FISHERS DR.
OLD ROAD
Ckt. Grd.
RUMBUSH
BROCK HURST
HITHE RISE
BRIMFIELD
HARESFIELD
MARSHFIELD WY.
HUTCHINGS LA.
SHORT ST.
BUCKRIDGE LA.
ASCOTE LA.
PACKMORES
GORCOTT LA.
RUMBRUSH
Jerrings Hall Farm
Solihull
Dickens Heath
TILEHOUSE
DICKENS HEATH
CLEOBURY
Little Dickens' Wood
HIRDEMONSWAY
ALDERS
HAWS
WRENS
NEST CL.
PIT LA.
Square Acre Farm
Brickiln Farm
BRAGGS FARM LANE
Big Dickens' Wood
Tidbury Green Farm
Tidbury Green Prim. Sch.
Tidbury Green
Cricket Ground
Sports Ground
Bragg's Farm
Holly Cottage
Lady Lane Farm
B94
RUMBUSH LANE
LANE
LADY
Football Ground
Stratford-upon-Avon Canal
Rumbush
Bowling Grn.
Nursery
1
2
3
4
5
6
78
77
76
75
11
12

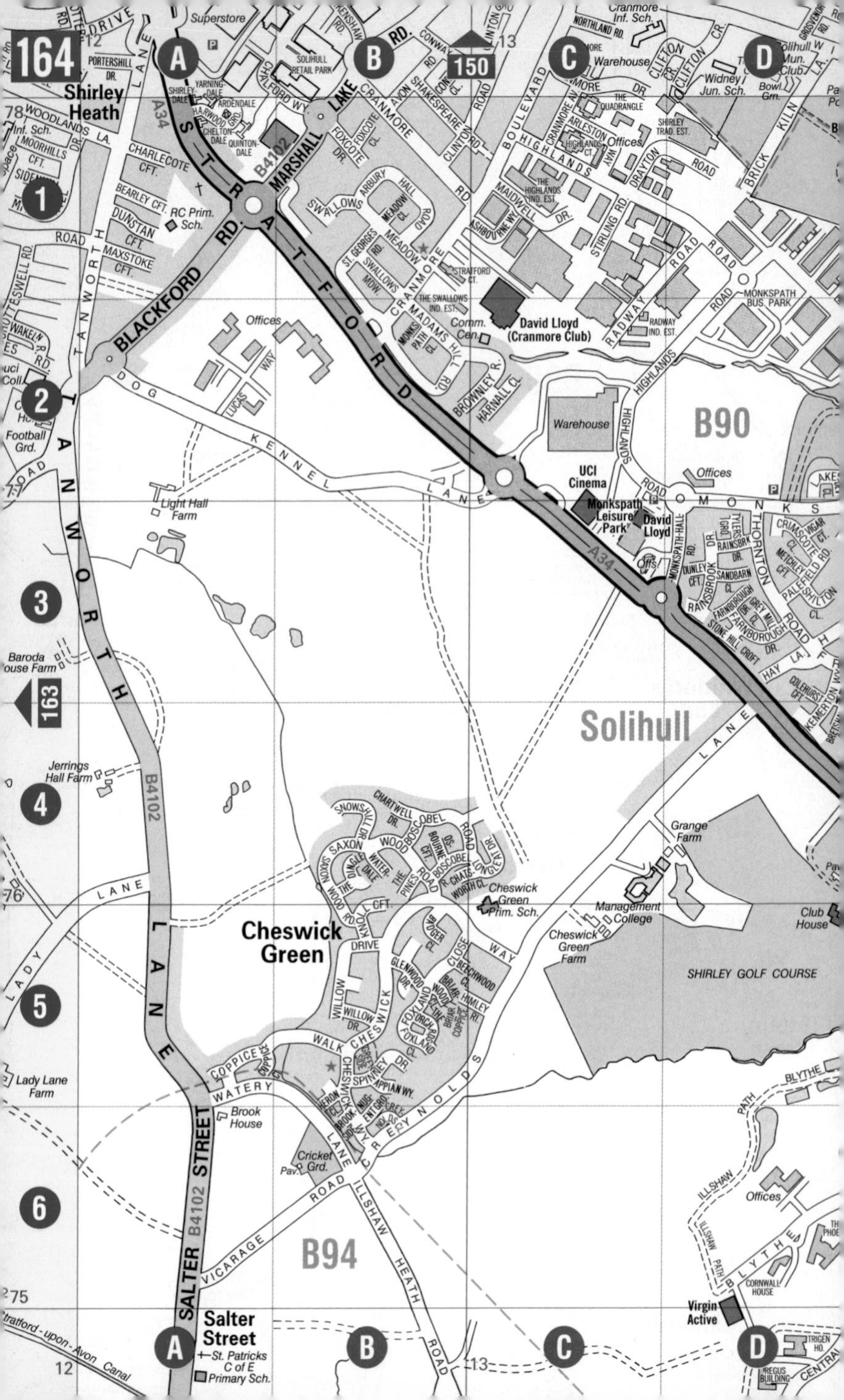
Shirley Heath
Solihull
Cheswick Green
Salter Street
B90
B94
A34
B4102
STRATFORD RD.
BLACKFORD RD.
MARSHALL LAKE
TANWORTH LANE
SALTER STREET
DOG KENNEL LANE
CRANMORE BOULEVARD
MONKSPATH
HIGHLANDS
Superstore
Solihull Retail Park
RC Prim. Sch.
Offices
Comm. Cen.
David Lloyd (Cranmore Club)
Warehouse
UCI Cinema
Monkspath Leisure Park
Light Hall Farm
Baroda House Farm
Jerrings Hall Farm
Lady Lane Farm
Brook House
Cricket Grd.
Grange Farm
Management College
Cheswick Green Farm
Cheswick Green Prim. Sch.
SHIRLEY GOLF COURSE
Club House
Virgin Active
Cornwall House
Regus Building
Monkspath Bus. Park
The Highlands Ind. Est.
Shirley Trad. Est.
Radway Ind. Est.
The Swallows Ind. Est.
St. Patricks C of E Primary Sch.
Stratford-upon-Avon Canal
Football Grd.
Widney Jun. Sch.
Cranmore Inf. Sch.
150
163

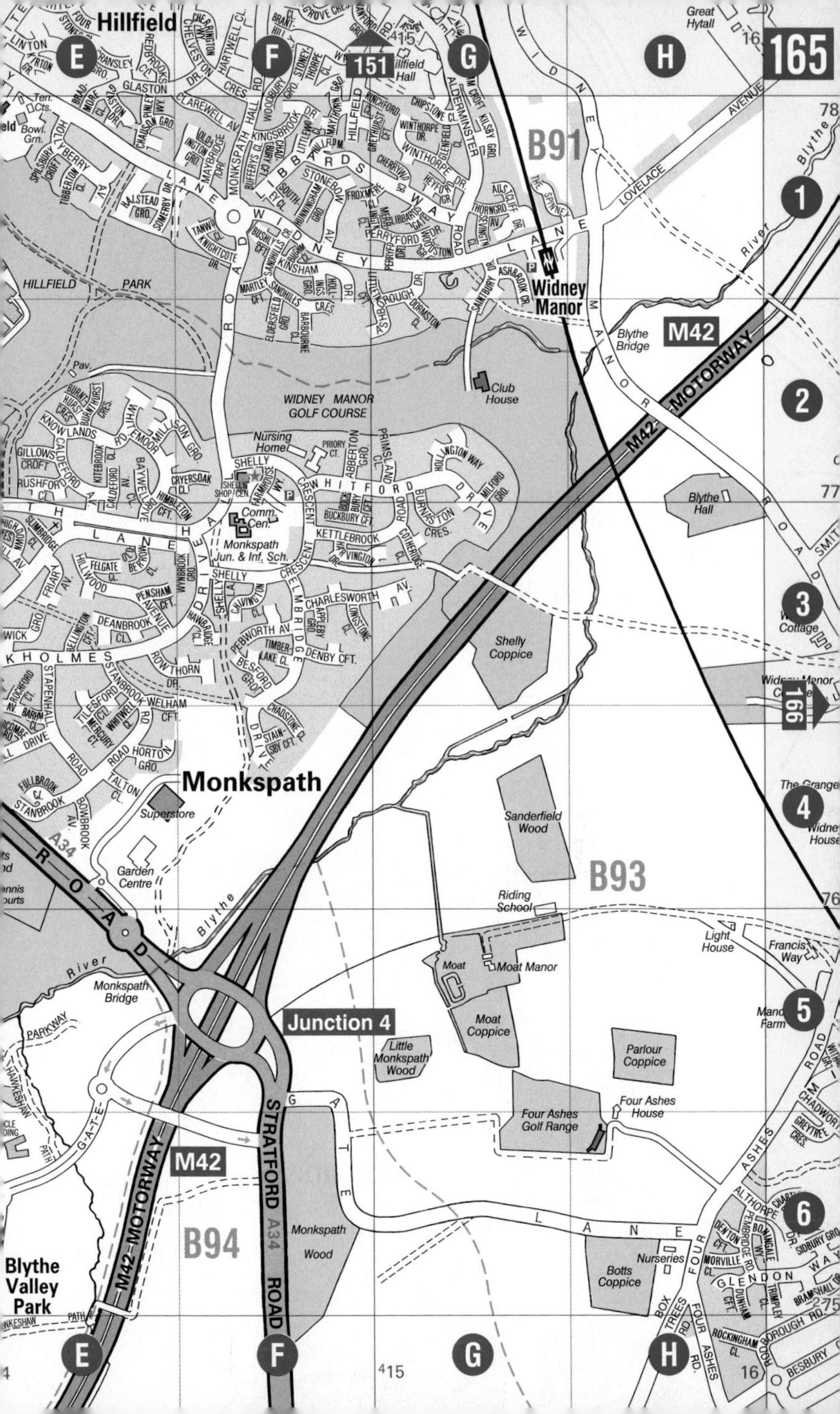
Hillfield
151
Hillfield Hall
Great Hytall
E
F
G
H
B91
Widney Manor
Blythe Bridge
M42
M42 MOTORWAY
HILLFIELD PARK
WIDNEY MANOR GOLF COURSE
Club House
Nursing Home
Monkspath Jun. & Inf. Sch.
Comm. Cen.
Blythe Hall
Shelly Coppice
Sanderfield Wood
B93
Riding School
Moat Manor
Moat Coppice
Little Monkspath Wood
Parlour Coppice
Four Ashes Golf Range
Four Ashes House
Botts Coppice
Nurseries
Monkspath
Superstore
Garden Centre
Monkspath Bridge
Junction 4
STRATFORD ROAD A34
Monkspath Wood
B94
Blythe Valley Park
Light House
Francis Way
166
1
2
3
4
5
6
415

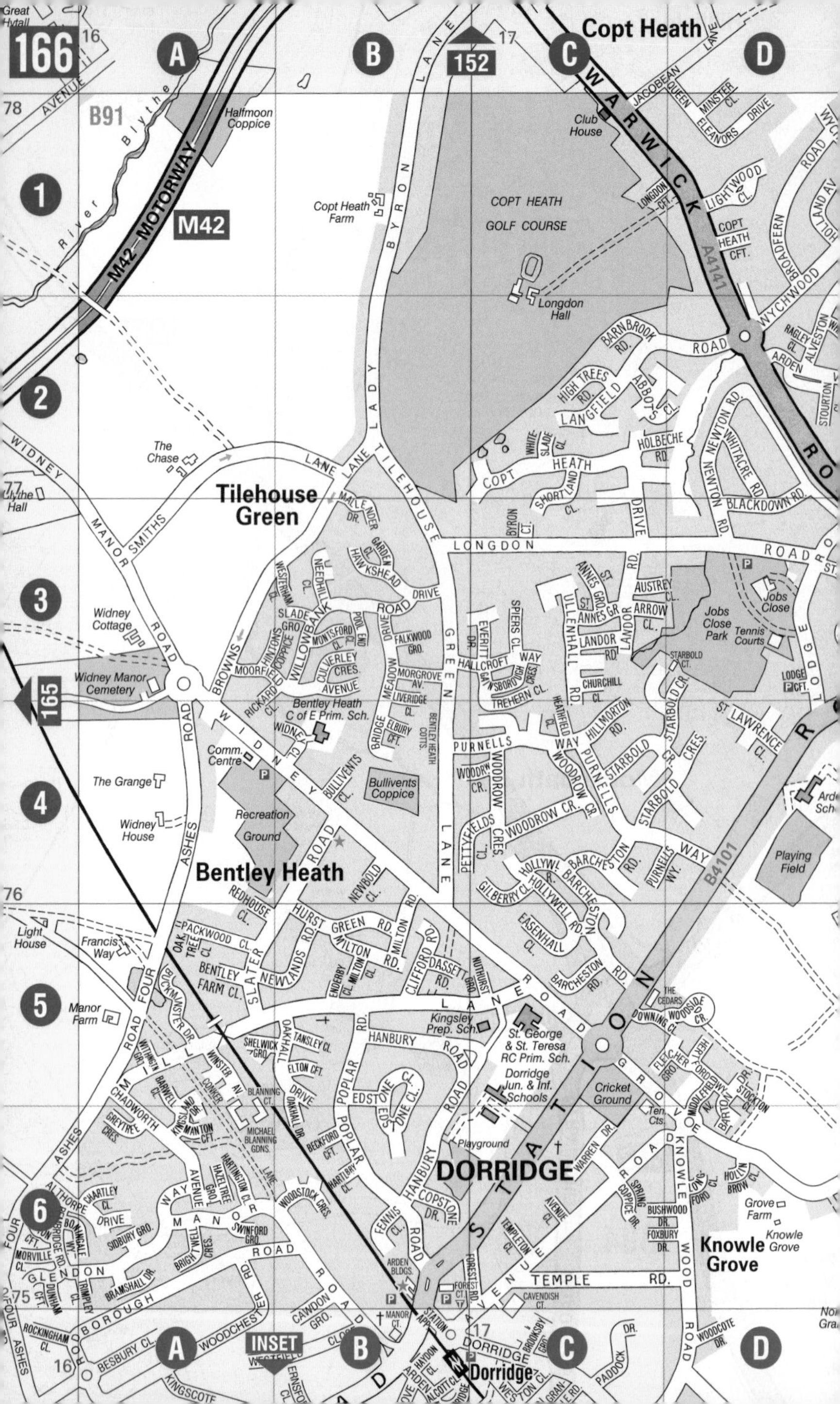

Copt Heath
152
A
B
C
D
1
2
3
4
5
6
165
INSET
Halfmoon Coppice
M42 MOTORWAY
M42
B91
River Blythe
Copt Heath Farm
COPT HEATH GOLF COURSE
Club House
Longdon Hall
WARWICK
A4141
B4101
The Chase
Tilehouse Green
Widney Cottage
Widney Manor Cemetery
Bentley Heath C of E Prim. Sch.
Comm. Centre
The Grange
Widney House
Recreation Ground
Bullivents Coppice
Bentley Heath
Jobs Close Park
Jobs Close
Tennis Courts
Playing Field
Light House
Francis Way
Manor Farm
Kingsley Prep. Sch.
St. George & St. Teresa RC Prim. Sch.
Dorridge Jun. & Inf. Schools
Cricket Ground
Playground
DORRIDGE
Grove Farm
Knowle Grove
Knowle Grove
Dorridge

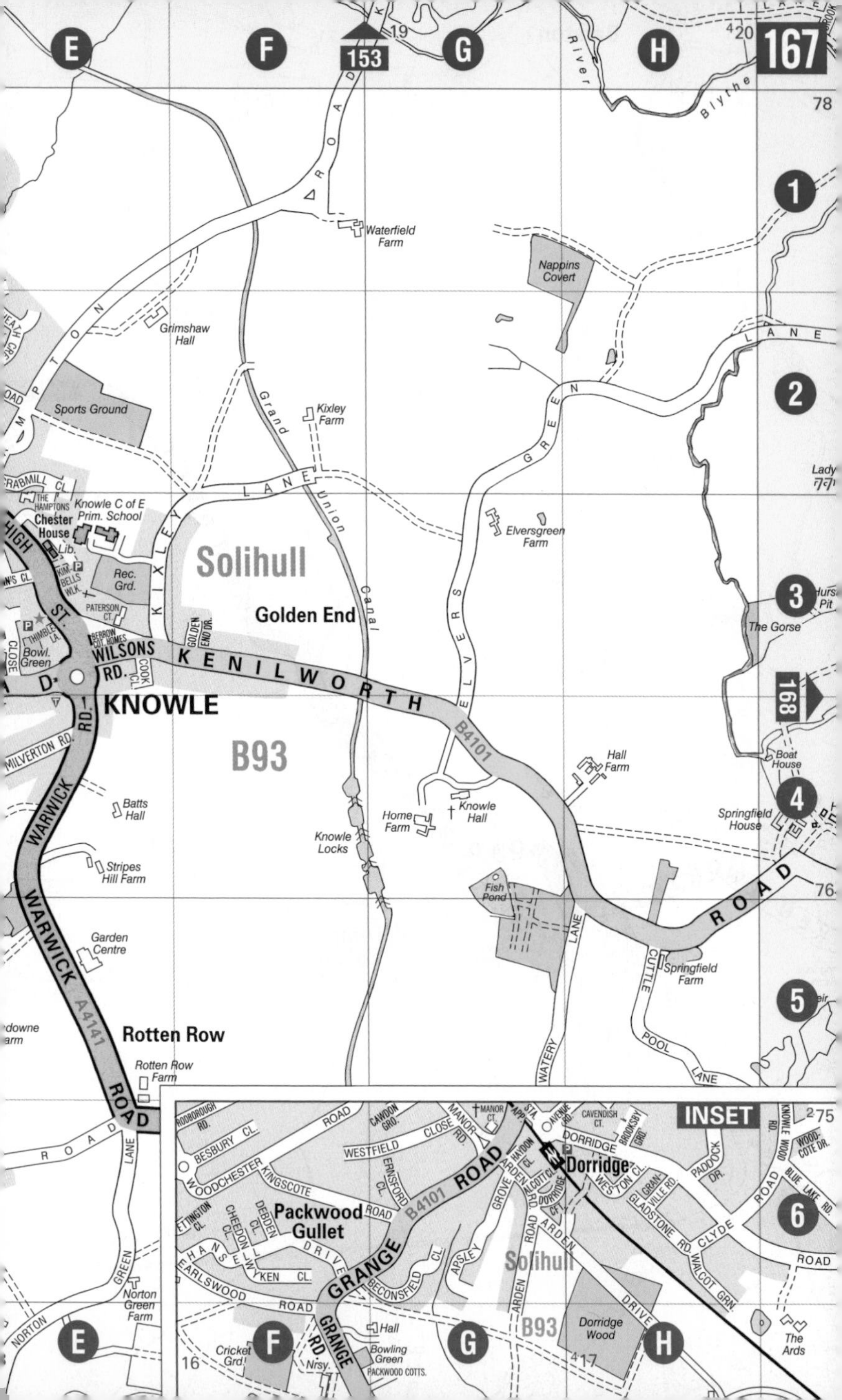

E F 153 G H 167

78

River Blythe

19 420

1

Waterfield Farm

Nappins Covert

Grimshaw Hall

GREEN LANE

2

Sports Ground

Kixley Farm

Lady

CRABMILL CL.
THE HAMPTONS
Knowle C of E Prim. School

KIXLEY LANE

Grand Union Canal

Elversgreen Farm

3

Chester House
Lib.

Rec. Grd.

Solihull

The Gorse

Hurst Pit

PATERSON
CHERBON CT. HOMES

Bowl. Green

WILSONS RD.
COOK CL.
GOLDEN END DR.

Golden End

ELVERS

168

KNOWLE

KENILWORTH

B4101

Hall Farm

Boat House

4

Springfield House

WARWICK RD.
MILVERTON ROAD

B93

Batts Hall

Home Farm
Knowle Hall

Knowle Locks

ROAD

76

Springfield Farm

Stripes Hill Farm

Garden Centre

Fish Pond

CUTTLE

5

WARWICK ROAD A4141

Rotten Row

...downe Farm

Rotten Row Farm

WATERY LANE

POOL LANE

INSET

275

6

DORRIDGE

Dorridge

CAVENDISH CT.

KNOWLE WOOD RD.
WOODCOTE DR.

RODBOROUGH RD.
BESBURY CL.
ROAD
WESTFIELD

MANOR CT.
CARDON GRO.
CLOSE RD.

MAJOR RD.

PADDOCK DR.
BLUE LANE RD.

Packwood Gullet

KINGSCOTE
WOODCHESTER
ETTINGTON CL.
CHEDDON CL.
DEBDEN CL.
'KEN CL.

ERNSFORD CL.

ARDEN

DRIVE

WESTON CL.
OLCOTT CL.
GLADSTONE RD.
SMALL CL.
CLYDE
WALCOT GRN.
GRENVILLE RD.

ROAD

EARLSWOOD ROAD
BEANS

GRANGE RD.

BECONSFIELD CL.

GROVE RD.
ARSLEY

B4101

GRANGE

Solihull

ARDEN DRIVE

Dorridge Wood

ROAD

The Ards

E 16 F GRANGE RD. G B93 H 417

Norton Green Farm

NORTON

GREEN LANE

Hall

Cricket Grd.

Nrsy.

Bowling Green
PACKWOOD COTTS.

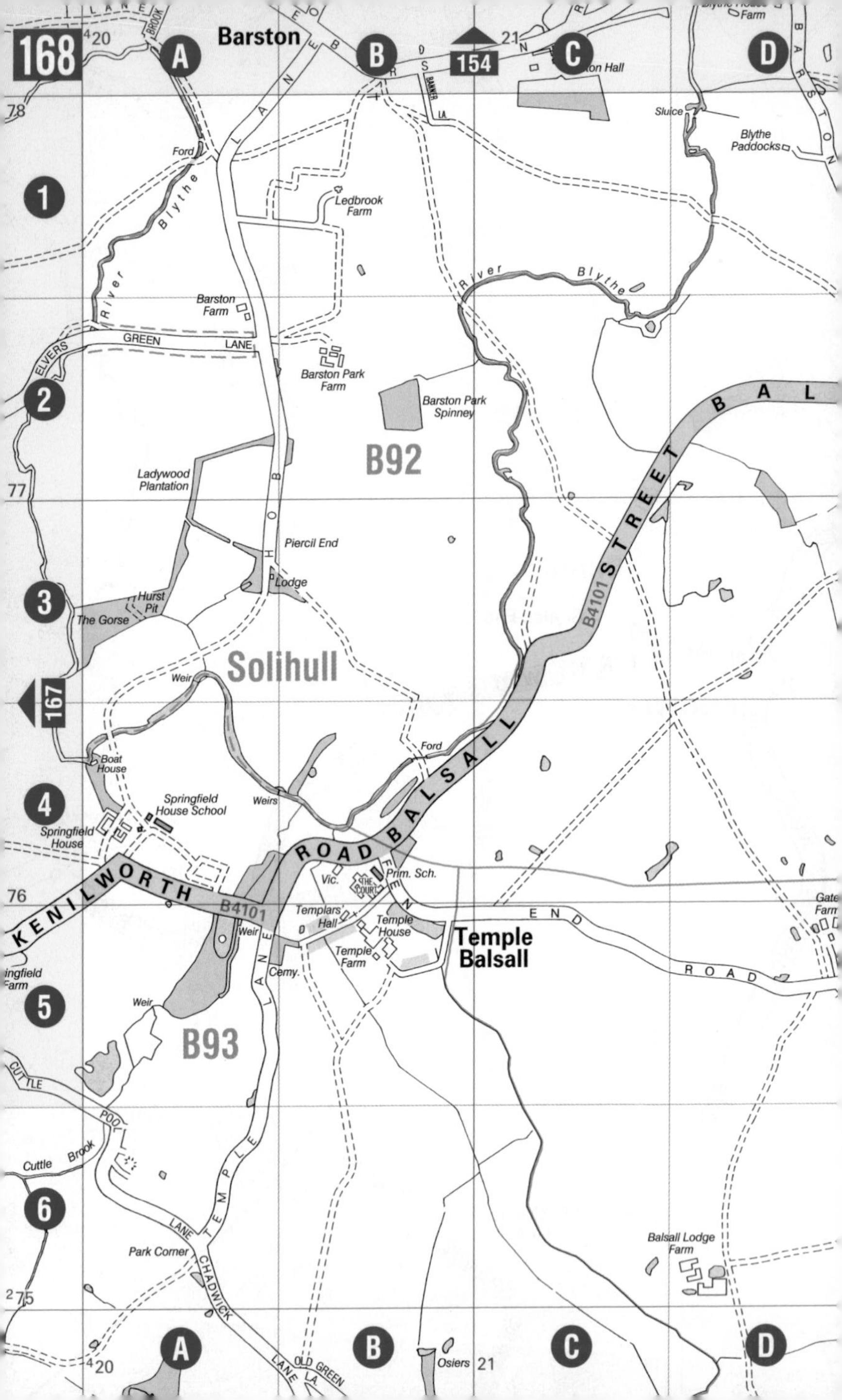

Barston
A
B
C
D
154
167
1
2
3
4
5
6
Brook
Lane
Barston Lane
Banner La
Ford
River Blythe
Ledbrook Farm
Sluice
Blythe Paddocks
Blythe House Farm
Barston Farm
Elvers Green Lane
Barston Park Farm
Barston Park Spinney
B92
Ladywood Plantation
Hob Lane
Piercil End
Lodge
Hurst Pit
The Gorse
Solihull
Weir
Boat House
Springfield House School
Springfield House
Weirs
Ford
Balsall Street
B4101
Kenilworth Road
Vic.
The Court
Prim. Sch.
Templars' Hall
Temple House
Temple Farm
Fen End Road
Temple Balsall
Gate Farm
ingfield Farm
Cemy.
Weir
B93
Temple Lane
Cuttle Pool Lane
Cuttle Brook
Park Corner
Chadwick Lane
Old Green La.
Balsall Lodge Farm
Osiers
420
21
78
77
76
275

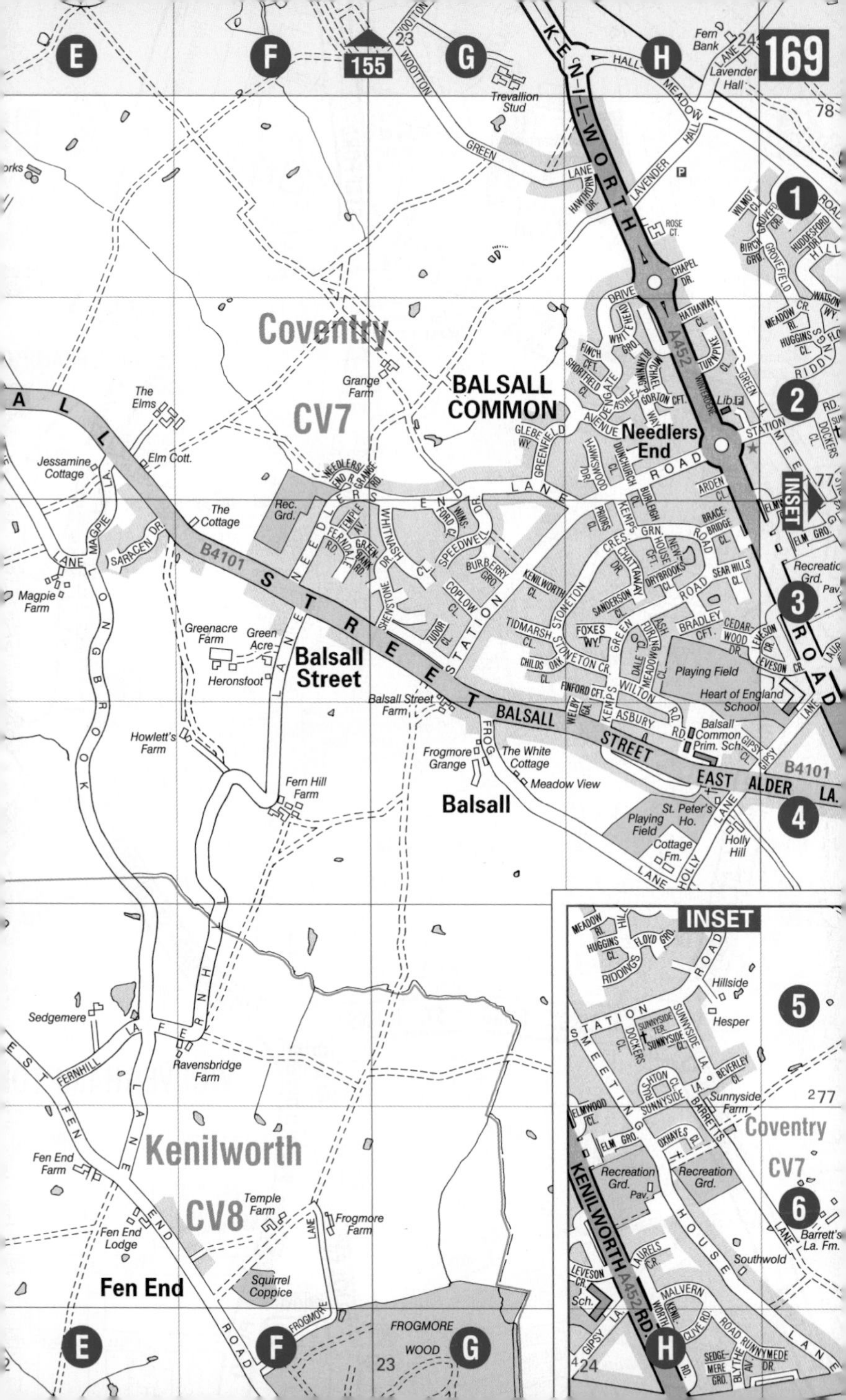
155
Coventry
CV7
BALSALL COMMON
Needlers End
Balsall Street
Balsall
Kenilworth
CV8
Fen End
INSET
KENILWORTH ROAD
A452
B4101
BALSALL STREET
EAST ALDER LA.
STATION ROAD
Trevallion Stud
Fern Bank
Lavender Hall
Grange Farm
The Elms
Jessamine Cottage
Elm Cott.
The Cottage
Rec. Grd.
Magpie Farm
Greenacre Farm
Green Acre
Heronsfoot
Howlett's Farm
Fern Hill Farm
Balsall Street Farm
Frogmore Grange
The White Cottage
Meadow View
Playing Field
Heart of England School
Balsall Common Prim. Sch.
St. Peter's Ho.
Cottage Fm.
Holly Hill
Sedgemere
Ravensbridge Farm
Fen End Farm
Fen End Lodge
Temple Farm
Frogmore Farm
Squirrel Coppice
FROGMORE WOOD
Recreation Grd.
Pav.
Hillside
Hesper
Sunnyside Farm
Southwold
Barrett's La. Fm.
Sch.

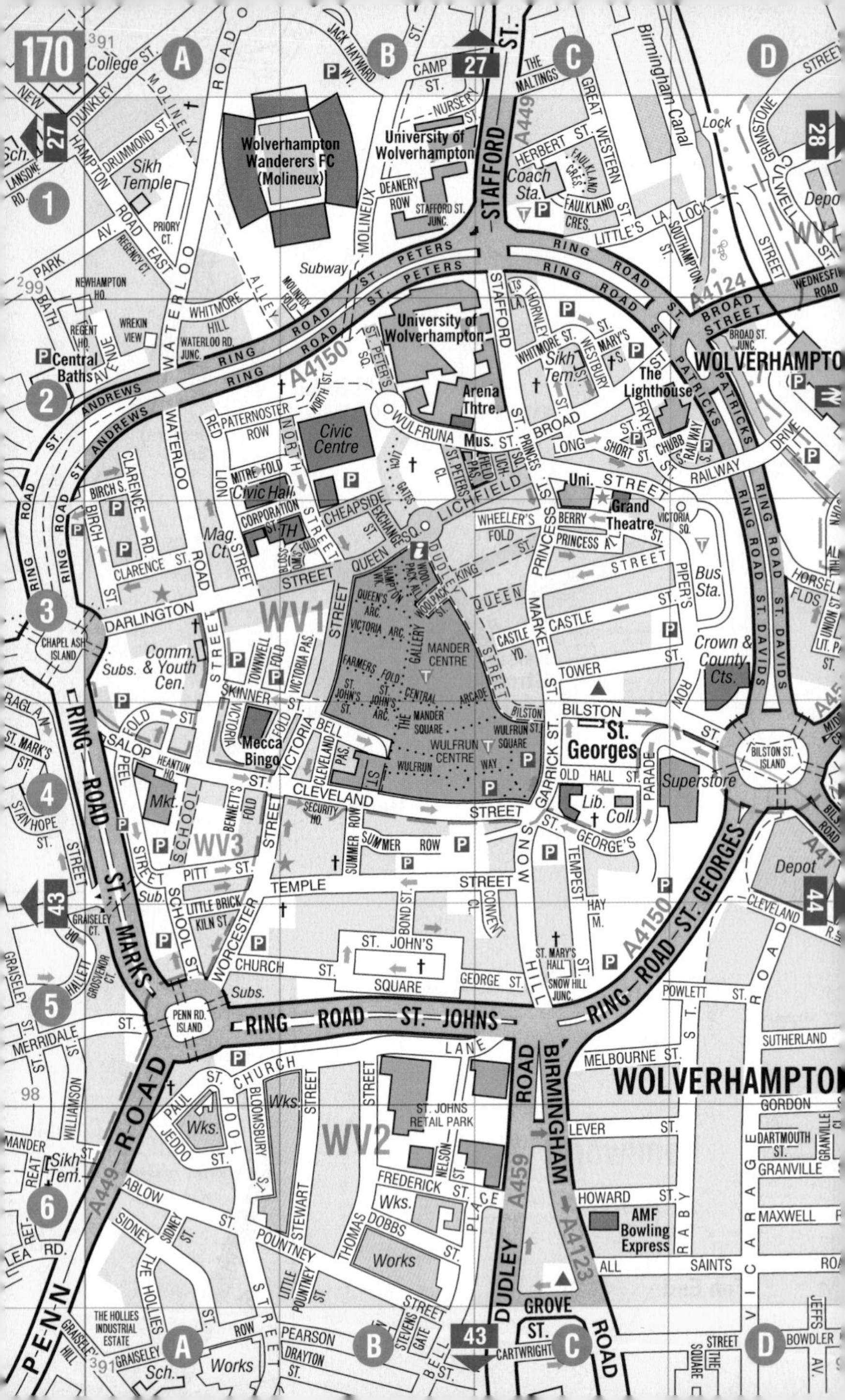

Wolverhampton Wanderers FC (Molineux)
University of Wolverhampton
STAFFORD ST.
RING ROAD ST. PETERS
RING ROAD ST. ANDREWS
Central Baths
Sikh Temple
Coach Sta.
Birmingham Canal
BROAD STREET
WOLVERHAMPTON
The Lighthouse
Arena Thtre.
Civic Centre
Civic Hall
Grand Theatre
Bus Sta.
WV1
MANDER CENTRE
WULFRUN CENTRE
Mecca Bingo
Comm. & Youth Cen.
CHAPEL ASH ISLAND
Crown & County Cts.
BILSTON ST. ISLAND
St. Georges
Superstore
WV3
Mkt.
RING ROAD ST. MARKS
RING ROAD ST. GEORGES
PENN RD. ISLAND
RING ROAD ST. JOHNS
ST. JOHN'S SQUARE
WV2
ST. JOHNS RETAIL PARK
WOLVERHAMPTON
AMF Bowling Express
Depot
THE HOLLIES INDUSTRIAL ESTATE
Works
PENN ROAD
DUDLEY ROAD
BIRMINGHAM ROAD
27
28
43
44

INDEX

Including Streets, Places & Areas, Hospitals & Hospices, Industrial Estates,
Selected Flats & Walkways, Stations, Junctions and Selected Places of Interest.

HOW TO USE THIS INDEX

1. Each street name is followed by its Postcode District and then by its Locality abbreviation(s) and then by its map reference;
   e.g. **Abberley Rd.** B68: O'bry . . . .4H **113** is in the B68 Postcode District and the Oldbury Locality and is to be found in square 4H on page **113**. The page number is shown in bold type.

2. A strict alphabetical order is followed in which Av., Rd., St., etc. (though abbreviated) are read in full and as part of the street name;
   e.g. **Abbeydale Rd.** appears after **Abbey Cres.** but before **Abbey Dr.**

3. Streets and a selection of flats and walkways too small to be shown on the maps, appear in the index with the thoroughfare to which it is
   connected shown in brackets; e.g. **Abberton Ct.** B23: Erd . . . .5C **84** (off Dunlin Cl.)

4. Addresses that are in more than one part are referred to as not continuous.

5. Places and areas are shown in the index in **BLUE TYPE** and the map reference is to the actual map square in which the town centre or area is
   located and not to the place name shown on the map; e.g. **ALDRIDGE** 3D **34**

6. An example of a selected place of interest is Aston Manor Transport Mus. 6H **83**

7. An example of a station is Adderley Park Station (Rail) . . . .6D **102** Included are Rail (**Rail**) Stations and Midland Metro (**MM**) Stations.

8. Junction names are shown in the index in BOLD TYPE; e.g. **BURNTWOOD JUNC.** 2B **10**

9. Map references shown in brackets; e.g **Ablow St.** WV2: Wolv . . . .3G **43** (6A **170**) refer to entries that also appear on the large scale
   pages **4-5** & **170**.

GENERAL ABBREVIATIONS

All. : Alley	**Ent.** : Enterprise	**Nth.** : North
App. : Approach	**Est.** : Estate	**Pde.** : Parade
Arc. : Arcade	**Fld.** : Field	**Pk.** : Park
Av. : Avenue	**Flds.** : Fields	**Pas.** : Passage
Blvd. : Boulevard	**Gdns.** : Gardens	**Pl.** : Place
Bri. : Bridge	**Ga.** : Gate	**Pct.** : Precinct
Bldg. : Building	**Gt.** : Great	**Res.** : Residential
Bldgs. : Buildings	**Grn.** : Green	**Ri.** : Rise
Bungs. : Bungalows	**Gro.** : Grove	**Rd.** : Road
Bus. : Business	**Hgts.** : Heights	**Rdbt.** : Roundabout
Cvn. : Caravan	**Ho.** : House	**Shop.** : Shopping
C'way. : Causeway	**Ho's.** : Houses	**Sth.** : South
Cen. : Centre	**Ind.** : Industrial	**Sq.** : Square
Chu. : Church	**Info.** : Information	**Sta.** : Station
Circ. : Circle	**Intl.** : International	**St.** : Street
Cir. : Circus	**Junc.** : Junction	**Ter.** : Terrace
Cl. : Close	**La.** : Lane	**Twr.** : Tower
Coll. : College	**Lit.** : Little	**Trad.** : Trading
Comn. : Common	**Lwr.** : Lower	**Up.** : Upper
Cnr. : Corner	**Mnr.** : Manor	**Va.** : Vale
Cott. : Cottage	**Mans.** : Mansions	**Vw.** : View
Cotts. : Cottages	**Mkt.** : Market	**Vs.** : Villas
Ct. : Court	**Mdw.** : Meadow	**Vis.** : Visitors
Cres. : Crescent	**Mdws.** : Meadows	**Wlk.** : Walk
Cft. : Croft	**M.** : Mews	**W.** : West
Dr. : Drive	**Mt.** : Mount	**Yd.** : Yard
E. : East	**Mus.** : Museum	

LOCALITY ABBREVIATIONS

A Grn : **Acock's Green**	Bly P : **Blythe Valley Park**	Clent : **Clent**
Alb : **Albrighton**	Bold : **Boldmere**	Cod : **Codsall**
A'rdge : **Aldridge**	Bord G : **Bordesley Green**	Cod W : **Codsall Wood**
A'chu : **Alvechurch**	B'vlle : **Bournville**	Coft H : **Cofton Hackett**
Amb : **Amblecote**	Brie H : **Brierley Hill**	Col : **Coleshill**
Aston : **Aston**	B'frd : **Brinsford**	Cose : **Coseley**
Bal C : **Balsall Common**	Bwnhls : **Brownhills**	Coven : **Coven**
Bal H : **Balsall Heath**	Burn : **Burntwood**	Cov H : **Coven Heath**
B Grn : **Barnt Green**	Bush : **Bushbury**	Crad : **Cradley**
Bars : **Barston**	Cann : **Cannock**	Crad H : **Cradley Heath**
Bart G : **Bartley Green**	Can : **Canwell**	Curd : **Curdworth**
Bass P : **Bassetts Pole**	Cas B : **Castle Bromwich**	Darl : **Darlaston**
Belb : **Belbroughton**	Cas V : **Castle Vale**	Dic H : **Dickens Heath**
Ben H : **Berkley Heath**	Cath B : **Catherine-de-Barnes**	Dorr : **Dorridge**
Berk : **Berkswell**	Cats : **Catshill**	Dray B : **Drayton Bassett**
Bick : **Bickenhill**	C'wich : **Chadwich**	Dud : **Dudley**
Bilb : **Bilbrook**	Chad E : **Chadwick End**	Earls : **Earlswood**
Bils : **Bilston**	Chase : **Chasetown**	Edg : **Edgbaston**
Birm : **Birmingham**	Chel W : **Chelmsley Wood**	Env : **Enville**
Birm A : **Birmingham Int. Airport**	C Hay : **Cheslyn Hay**	Erd : **Erdington**
B'brook : **Bilbrook**	Ches G : **Cheswick Green**	Ess : **Essington**
Blox : **Bloxwich**	Clay : **Clayhanger**	E'shll : **Ettingshall**

LOCALITY ABBREVIATIONS

F'stne : **Featherstone**
Fen E : **Fen End**
Foot : **Footherley**
F'bri : **Fordbridge**
F'hses : **Fordhouses**
Forh : **Forhill**
Four C : **Four Crosses**
Four O : **Four Oaks**
Fran : **Frankley**
Gorn : **Gornalwood**
Gt Barr : **Great Barr**
Gt Wyr : **Great Wyrley**
Hag : **Hagley**
Hale : **Halesowen**
Hall G : **Hall Green**
Hamm : **Hammerwich**
H Ard : **Hampton in Arden**
Hand : **Handsworth**
Harb : **Harborne**
Head H : **Headley Heath**
Hilt : **Hilton**
Himl : **Himley**
Hints : **Hints**
Hock : **Hockley**
H'ley H : **Hockley Heath**
Hodg H : **Hodge Hill**
H'wd : **Hollywood**
Hopw : **Hopwood**
Hunn : **Hunnington**
I'ley : **Iverley**
K Hth : **King's Heath**
K'hrst : **Kingshurst**
K Nor : **King's Norton**
K'sdng : **Kingstanding**
K'wfrd : **Kingswinford**
Kinv : **Kinver**
Kitts G : **Kitt's Green**
Know : **Knowle**
Lapw : **Lapworth**
Lea M : **Lea Marston**
Lich : **Lichfield**
Lick : **Lickey**
Lit A : **Little Aston**
Lit H : **Little Hay**
Lit P : **Little Packington**
Lit W : **Little Wyrley**
Longb : **Longbridge**
Lwr G : **Lower Gornal**
Lwr P : **Lower Penn**
Loz : **Lozells**
Lutley : **Lutley**

L Ash : **Lydiate Ash**
Lye : **Lye**
Lynn : **Lynn**
Maj G : **Major's Green**
Marl : **Marlbrook**
Mars G : **Marston Green**
Mer : **Meriden**
Midd : **Middleton**
Min : **Minworth**
M'path : **Monkspath**
Mose : **Moseley**
Mox : **Moxley**
Muck C : **Muckley Corner**
Nat E C : **National Exhibition Centre**
Nech : **Nechells**
Neth : **Netherton**
New O : **New Oscott**
N'fld : **Northfield**
Nort C : **Norton Canes**
Nur : **Nurton**
Oaken : **Oaken**
O'bry : **Oldbury**
Old H : **Old Hill**
Olton : **Olton**
Oxl : **Oxley**
Patt : **Pattingham**
Pedm : **Pedmore**
Pels : **Pelsall**
Pend : **Pendeford**
Penn : **Penn**
P'ntt : **Pensnett**
P Barr : **Perry Barr**
Pert : **Perton**
Quar B : **Quarry Bank**
Quin : **Quinton**
Redn : **Rednal**
Roms : **Romsley**
R'ley : **Roughley**
Row R : **Rowley Regis**
Rubery : **Rubery**
Rus : **Rushall**
Salt : **Saltley**
Sed : **Sedgley**
Seis : **Seisdon**
S Oak : **Selly Oak**
S End : **Shard End**
Share : **Shareshill**
Sheld : **Sheldon**
S'fld : **Shelfield**
Shens : **Shenstone**
Shen W : **Shenstone Woodend**

Shir : **Shirley**
Small H : **Small Heath**
Smeth : **Smethwick**
Sol : **Solihull**
S'brk : **Sparkbrook**
S'hll : **Sparkhill**
Stech : **Stechford**
Stir : **Stirchley**
Ston : **Stonnall**
Stourb : **Stourbridge**
Stourt : **Stourton**
S'tly : **Streetly**
S Cold : **Sutton Coldfield**
Swind : **Swindon**
Tett : **Tettenhall**
Tid G : **Tidbury Green**
Tip : **Tipton**
Tiv : **Tividale**
Tres : **Trescott**
Try : **Trysull**
Tys : **Tyseley**
Up Gor : **Upper Gornal**
Wall : **Wall**
W Hth : **Wall Heath**
Walm : **Walmley**
Wals : **Walsall**
Wals W : **Walsall Wood**
W End : **Ward End**
Wat O : **Water Orton**
W'bry : **Wednesbury**
Wed : **Wednesfield**
W'frd : **Weeford**
W Cas : **Weoley Castle**
W Brom : **West Bromwich**
Wild : **Wildmoor**
W'hall : **Willenhall**
Win G : **Winson Green**
Wis : **Wishaw**
Witt : **Witton**
Woll : **Wollaston**
W'cte : **Wollescote**
Wolv : **Wolverhampton**
Wom : **Wombourne**
Word : **Wordsley**
W Grn : **Wylde Green**
Wyt : **Wythall**
Yard : **Yardley**
Yard W : **Yardley Wood**

3B Business Village B21: Hand 2H **99**

A

A1 Trad. Est. B66: Smeth 2F **99**
Aaron Manby Ct. DY4: Tip 5H **61**
Abberley Cl. B63: Hale. 3H **127**
Abberley Ind. Cen.
  B66: Smeth 4H **99**
Abberley Rd. B68: O'bry 4H **113**
  DY3: Lwr G 3G **75**
Abberley St. B66: Smeth 4H **99**
  DY2: Dud 1E **95**
Abberton Cl. B63: Hale. 2C **128**
Abberton Ct. B23: Erd 5C **84**
                               (off Dunlin Cl.)
Abberton Gro. B90: M'path 2F **165**
Abbess Gro. B25: Yard 2C **120**
Abbey Cl. B71: W Brom 2A **80**
Abbey Ct. B68: O'bry 5H **97**
Abbey Cres. B63: Crad 1F **127**
  B68: O'bry 3B **114**
Abbeydale Rd. B31: N'fld 5E **145**
Abbey Dr. WS3: Pels 2E **21**
Abbeyfield Rd. B23: Erd 6D **68**
  WV10: Bush. 3A **16**
Abbey Gdns. B67: Smeth 2C **114**
Abbey Mans. B24: Erd 1H **85**

Abbey Rd. B17: Harb 6H **115**
  B23: Erd 5D **84**
  B63: Crad 1E **127**
  B67: Smeth 2B **114**
  DY2: Dud 3F **95**
  DY3: Gorn 4G **75**
Abbey Sq. WS3: Blox 5E **19**
Abbey St. B18: Hock 4C **100**
  DY3: Gorn 4G **75**
Abbey St. Nth. B18: Hock 4C **100**
Abbots Cl. WS3: Know 2C **166**
  WS4: Rus. 3G **33**
Abbotsford Av. B43: Gt Barr 3B **66**
Abbotsford Dr. DY1: Dud 2A **94**
Abbotsford Rd. B11: S'brk 5B **118**
Abbots Rd. B14: K Hth 6G **133**
Abbots Way B18: Hock. 3D **100**
  WV3: Wolv 2C **42**
Abbott Rd. B63: Hale 5E **127**
Abbotts M. DY5: Brie H 2H **109**
Abbotts Pl. WS3: Blox 6B **20**
Abbotts Rd. B24: Erd 6F **85**
Abbotts St. WS3: Blox 5B **20**
Abdon Av. B29: W Cas 6F **131**
Aberdeen St. B18: Win G 5A **100**
Aberford Cl. WV12: W'hall 5D **30**
Abigails Cl. B26: Sheld. 4F **121**
Abingdon Cl. WV1: Wolv 1D **44**
Abingdon Rd. B23: Erd. 6B **68**
  DY2: Neth 6F **95**
  WS3: Blox. 5F **19**
  WV1: Wolv 1D **44**

Abingdon Way B35: Cas V 4E **87**
  WS3: Blox. 5F **19**
Ablewell St. WS1: Wals 2D **48**
Ablow St. WV2: Wolv 3G **43** (6A **170**)
Abney Dr. WV14: Cose 4B **60**
Abney Gro. B44: K'sdng 3B **68**
Aboyne Cl. B5: Edg 5F **117**
Ab Row B4: Birm 6H **101** (2H **5**)
Acacia Av. B37: K'hrst 3B **106**
  WS5: Wals 1E **65**
Acacia Cl. B37: K'hrst 3B **106**
  B69: Tiv 5B **78**
  DY1: Dud 4C **76**
Acacia Cres. WV8: Bilb 3H **13**
Acacia Dr. WV14: Cose 6C **60**
Acacia Rd. B30: B'vlle 5A **132**
Acacia Ter. B12: Bal H 6A **118**
Accord M. WS10: Darl 4D **46**
Ace Bus. Pk. B33: Kitts G 1H **121**
Acfold Rd. B20: Hand. 2A **82**
Acheson Rd.
  B90: Hall G, Shir. 5F **149**
Acheston Rd. B28: Hall G 5F **149**
Achilles Cl. WS6: Gt Wyr 4F **7**
                          (not continuous)
Ackers, The (Activity Cen.). 5D **118**
Ackleton Gdns.
  WV3: Wolv 4D **42**
Ackleton Gro. B29: W Cas 5D **130**
ACOCKS GREEN 2A **136**
Acocks Green Bowl 2H **135**
Acocks Green Station (Rail) 1A **136**

Acorn Cl. B27: A Grn . . . 6H **119**
B30: B'vlle . . . 5A **132**
B70: W Brom . . . 4H **79**
WS6: Gt Wyr . . . 4G **7**
Acorn Ct. B45: Redn . . . 2B **158**
Acorn Gdns. B30: Stir . . . 5C **132**
Acorn Gro. B1: Birm . . . 6D **100**
DY8: Word . . . 2C **108**
WV8: Cod . . . 5E **13**
Acorn Rd. B62: B'hth . . . 3C **112**
WV11: Wed . . . 6A **18**
Acorn St. WV13: W'hall . . . 1C **46**
Acre Ri. WV12: W'hall . . . 4B **30**
Acres, The WV3: Wolv . . . 2A **42**
Acres Rd. DY5: Quar B . . . 3H **109**
Acton Dr. DY3: Lwr G . . . 4F **75**
Acton Gro. B44: K'sdng . . . 2A **68**
WV14: Bils . . . 1D **60**
Adam Ct. B63: Hale . . . 1H **127**
Adams Brook Dr. B32: Bart G . . . 4H **129**
Adams Cl. B66: Smeth . . . 2B **98**
DY4: Tip . . . 4H **61**
Adams Hill B32: Bart G . . . 4H **129**
Adams Rd. WS8: Bwnhls . . . 2C **22**
WV3: Wolv . . . 4A **42**
Adams St. B7: Birm . . . 4H **101**
B70: W Brom . . . 4H **79**
WS2: Wals . . . 1B **48**
Ada Rd. B9: Birm . . . 1B **118**
B25: Yard . . . 5H **119**
B66: Smeth . . . 6F **99**
Ada Wrighton Cl. WV12: W'hall . . . 2C **30**
Addenbrooke Ct. B64: Old H . . . 3H **111**
Addenbrooke Dr. B73: W Grn . . . 3H **69**
Addenbrooke Pl. WS10: Darl . . . 4D **46**
Addenbrooke Rd. B67: Smeth . . . 6D **98**
Addenbrooke St. WS3: Blox . . . 2A **32**
WS10: Darl . . . 3D **46**
Addenbrook Way DY4: Tip . . . 5D **62**
Adderley Gdns. B8: Salt . . . 4D **102**
(not continuous)
Adderley Pk. Cl. B8: Salt . . . 5E **103**
Adderley Park Station (Rail) . . . 6D **102**
Adderley Rd. B8: Salt . . . 6C **102**
Adderley Rd. Sth. B8: Salt . . . 6C **102**
Adderley St. B9: Birm . . . 2A **118**
Adderley Trad. Est. B8: Salt . . . 5C **102**
Addington Way B69: Tiv . . . 5D **78**
Addison Cl. WS10: W'bry . . . 3C **64**
Addison Cft. DY3: Lwr G . . . 2E **75**
Addison Gro. WV11: Wed . . . 6D **16**
Addison Pl. B46: Wat O . . . 4D **88**
WV14: Bils . . . 4A **46**
Addison Rd. B7: Nech . . . 1C **102**
B14: K Hth . . . 6G **133**
DY5: Brie H . . . 1F **109**
WS10: W'bry . . . 3C **64**
WV3: Wolv . . . 3D **42**
Addison St. WS10: W'bry . . . 3F **63**
Addison Ter. WS10: W'bry . . . 3F **63**
Adelaide Av. B70: W Brom . . . 6G **63**
Adelaide St. DY5: Brie H . . . 6H **93**
Adelaide Twr. *B34: S End* . . . *4G* ***105***
(off Packington Av.)
Adelaide Wlk. WV2: Wolv . . . 3A **44**
Adelphi Ct. *DY5: Brie H* . . . *1H* ***109***
(off Promenade, The)
Adey Rd. WV11: Wed . . . 1H **29**
Adkins La. B67: Smeth . . . 2D **114**
Admington Rd. B33: Sheld . . . 3G **121**
Admiral Pl. B13: Mose . . . 1H **133**
Admirals Way B65: Row R . . . 1B **112**
Adrian Boult Hall . . . 1F **117** (4C **4**)
Adrian Ct. B24: Erd . . . 1H **85**
Adrian Cft. B13: Mose . . . 4C **134**
Adria Rd. B11: S'hll . . . 1B **134**
Adshead Rd. DY2: Dud . . . 2E **95**
Adstone Gro. B31: N'fld . . . 6D **144**
Advent Gdns. *B70: W Brom* . . . *4H* ***79***
(off Brook St.)
Adwalton Rd. WV6: Pert . . . 6F **25**
Agenoria Dr. DY8: Stourb . . . 6D **108**
Ainsdale Cl. DY8: Stourb . . . 3D **124**
Ainsdale Gdns. B24: Erd . . . 2A **86**
B63: Hale . . . 3F **127**
Ainsworth Rd. B31: N'fld . . . 5H **145**
WV10: Bush . . . 2A **16**
Aintree Gro. B34: S End . . . 3A **106**
Aintree Rd. WV10: F'hses . . . 3H **15**
Aintree Way DY1: Dud . . . 4A **76**
Aire Cft. B31: N'fld . . . 6F **145**
Airfield Dr. WS9: A'rdge . . . 6A **34**
Air Ministry Cotts. B35: Cas V . . . 5D **86**
Airport Way B26: Birm A . . . 1E **139**
Ajax Cl. WS6: Gt Wyr . . . 4F **7**
Akrill Cl. B70: W Brom . . . 2H **79**
Akrill Cott. Homes, The
B70: W Brom . . . 2H **79**
Alamein Rd. WV13: W'hall . . . 2G **45**
Alasdair Ho. B17: Harb . . . 6F **115**
Albany Ct. *B62: Quin* . . . *4G* ***113***
(off Binswood Rd.)
Albany Cres. WV14: Bils . . . 5E **45**
Albany Gdns. B91: Sol . . . 3A **152**
Albany Gro. DY6: K'wfrd . . . 2C **92**
WV11: Ess . . . 6C **18**
Albany Ho. B34: S End . . . 2F **105**
Albany Rd. B17: Harb . . . 5G **115**
WV1: Wolv . . . 1F **43**
Albemarle Rd. DY8: Stourb . . . 3D **124**
Albermarle Rd. DY6: K'wfrd . . . 4E **93**
Albert Av. B12: Bal H . . . 5A **118**
Albert Clarke Dr. WV12: W'hall . . . 2C **30**
Albert Cl. WV8: Cod . . . 3E **13**
Albert Dr. B63: Hale . . . 3H **127**
DY3: Swind . . . 5E **73**
Albert Ho. *WS10: Darl* . . . *5C* ***46***
(off Factory St.)
Albert Rd. B6: Aston . . . 1F **101**
B14: K Hth . . . 6G **133**
B17: Harb . . . 6F **115**
B21: Hand . . . 6A **82**
B23: Erd . . . 4D **84**
B33: Stech . . . 1B **120**
B63: Hale . . . 3H **127**
B68: O'bry . . . 3A **114**
WV6: Wolv . . . 6D **26**
Albert Smith Pl. B65: Row R . . . 5A **96**
Albert St. B4: Birm . . . 1G **117** (4F **5**)
B5: Birm . . . 6H **101**
B69: O'bry . . . 1G **97**
B70: W Brom . . . 6A **80**
DY4: Tip . . . 5H **61**
DY5: P'ntt . . . 2H **93**
DY6: W Hth . . . 1H **91**
DY8: Stourb . . . 6D **108**
DY9: Lye . . . 6A **110**
WS2: Wals . . . 1C **48**
WS10: W'bry . . . 3F **63**
Albert St. E. B69: O'bry . . . 2H **97**
Albert Wlk. B17: Harb . . . 6G **115**
Albion Av. WV13: W'hall . . . 1C **46**
Albion Bus. Pk. B66: Smeth . . . 1C **98**
Albion Fld. Dr. B71: W Brom . . . 3B **80**
Albion Ho. B70: W Brom . . . 5A **80**
Albion Ind. Est. B70: W Brom . . . 5G **79**
Albion Ind. Est. Rd. B70: W Brom . . . 5F **79**
Albion Pde. DY6: W Hth . . . 1H **91**
Albion Rd. B11: S'brk . . . 6D **118**
B21: Hand . . . 6H **81**
B70: W Brom . . . 5F **79**
(not continuous)
B71: W Brom . . . 1F **99**
WS8: Bwnhls . . . 5A **10**
WV13: W'hall . . . 1B **46**
Albion Rdbt. B70: W Brom . . . 3H **79**
Albion St. B1: Birm . . . 6D **100** (2A **4**)
B69: O'bry . . . 6E **79**
DY4: Tip . . . 2H **77**
DY5: Brie H . . . 6H **93**
DY6: W Hth . . . 6H **73**
WV1: Wolv . . . 1H **43** (3D **170**)
WV13: W'hall . . . 1C **46**
WV14: Bils . . . 5G **45**
Albion Ter. *B46: Wat O* . . . *4D* ***88***
(off St Pauls Ct.)
Alborn Cres. B38: K Nor . . . 1H **159**
Albright Ho. *B69: O'bry* . . . *5E* ***97***
(off Kempsey Cl.)
Albrighton Ho. B20: Hand . . . 4B **82**
Albrighton Rd. B63: Hale . . . 2G **127**
WV7: Alb . . . 5A **12**
Albright Rd. B68: O'bry . . . 5B **98**
Albury Wlk. B11: S'brk . . . 4A **118**
Albutts Rd. WS8: Nort C . . . 2F **9**
Alcester Dr. B73: New O . . . 2D **68**
(not continuous)
WV13: W'hall . . . 2F **45**
Alcester Gdns. B14: K Hth . . . 6G **133**
ALCESTER LANES END . . . 2G **147**
Alcester Rd. B13: Mose . . . 3G **133**
B47: H'wd . . . 6A **148**
B47: Wyt . . . 6H **161**
Alcester Rd. Sth. B14: K Hth . . . 6G **133**
(not continuous)
Alcester St. B12: Birm . . . 3H **117** (6H **5**)
Alcombe Gro. B33: Stech . . . 1C **120**
Alcott Cl. B93: Dorr . . . 6G **167**
Alcott Gro. B33: Kitts G . . . 6H **105**
Alcott La. B37: Mars G . . . 3B **122**
Alcove, The WS3: Blox . . . 5B **20**
Aldbourne Way B38: K Nor . . . 2H **159**
Aldbury Rd. B14: K Hth . . . 5A **148**
Aldeburgh Cl. WS3: Blox . . . 4G **19**
Aldeford Dr. DY5: Brie H . . . 3H **109**
Alderbrook Cl. DY3: Sed . . . 4F **59**
Alderbrook Rd. B91: Sol . . . 4D **150**
Alder Cl. B47: H'wd . . . 3B **162**
B76: Walm . . . 6C **70**
Alder Coppice DY3: Sed . . . 3G **59**
Alder Cres. WS5: Wals . . . 1F **65**
Alder Dale WV3: Wolv . . . 2C **42**
Alderdale Av. DY3: Sed . . . 2G **59**
Alderdale Cres. B92: Sol . . . 6A **138**
Alder Dr. B37: Chel W . . . 2D **122**
Alderflat Pl. B7: Birm . . . 4C **102**
Alderford Cl. WV8: Pend . . . 1D **26**
Alder Gro. B62: Quin . . . 5E **113**
Alderham Cl. B91: Sol . . . 3H **151**
Alderhithe Gro. B74: Lit A . . . 6B **36**
Alder La. B30: B'vlle . . . 1G **145**
CV7: Bal C . . . 4H **169**
Alderlea Cl. DY8: Stourb . . . 3E **125**
Alderley Cres. WS3: Wals . . . 4C **32**
Alderman Bowen Leisure Cen. . . . 6G **103**
Alderminster Rd. B91: Sol . . . 6F **151**
Aldermore Dr. B75: S Cold . . . 5D **54**
Alderney Gdns. B38: K Nor . . . 6H **145**
Alderpark Rd. B91: Sol . . . 4D **150**
Alderpits Rd. B34: S End . . . 2H **105**
(not continuous)
Alder Rd. B12: Bal H . . . 1A **134**
DY6: K'wfrd . . . 4D **92**
WS10: W'bry . . . 5G **47**
Alders, The B62: Roms . . . 3A **142**
Aldersea Dr. B6: Aston . . . 2H **101**
Aldershaw Rd. B26: Yard . . . 6C **120**
Aldershaws B90: Dic H . . . 4G **163**
Aldersley Av. WV6: Tett . . . 2C **26**
Aldersley Cl. WV6: Tett . . . 2D **26**
Aldersley High School Sports Cen. . . . 6B **14**
Aldersley Leisure Village . . . 3D **26**
Aldersley Rd. WV6: Tett . . . 4C **26**
Aldersley Stadium . . . 3D **26**
Aldersmead Rd. B31: N'fld . . . 5G **145**
Alderson Rd. B8: Salt . . . 5F **103**
Alderton Cl. B91: Sol . . . 6F **151**
Alderton Dr. WV3: Wolv . . . 3C **42**
Alder Way B74: S'tly . . . 3G **51**
Alderwood Pl. B91: Sol . . . 4F **151**
Alderwood Pct. DY3: Sed . . . 4G **59**
Alderwood Ri. DY3: Up Gor . . . 2H **75**
Aldgate Dr. DY5: Brie H . . . 4G **109**
Aldgate Gro. B19: Birm . . . 4F **101**
Aldis Cl. B28: Hall G . . . 4E **135**
WS2: Wals . . . 4G **47**
Aldis Rd. WS2: Wals . . . 4G **47**
ALDRIDGE . . . 3D **34**
Aldridge By-Pass WS9: A'rdge . . . 4D **34**
Aldridge Cl. B68: O'bry . . . 5A **98**
DY8: Word . . . 3C **108**
Aldridge Rd. B44: Gt Barr . . . 3E **67**
B68: O'bry . . . 3H **113**
B74: Lit A . . . 4H **35**
B74: S'tly . . . 2F **51**
WS4: Wals . . . 6G **33**
WS9: A'rdge . . . 4H **35**
Aldridge Sailing Club . . . 1A **34**
Aldridge St. WS10: Darl . . . 4D **46**
Aldridge Youth Theatre . . . 3D **34**
Aldwych Cl. WS9: A'rdge . . . 1D **34**

Aldwyck Dr.—Andover Cres.

Aldwyck Dr. WV3: Wolv 3G **41**
Aldwyn Av. B13: Mose 3H **133**
Alexander Gdns. B42: P Barr 4F **83**
Alexander Hill DY5: Quar B 3B **110**
Alexander Ind. Pk. WV14: Bils 1E **61**
Alexander Rd. B27: A Grn 1H **135**
B67: Smeth 1C **114**
WS2: Wals 1F **47**
WV8: Bilb 4A **14**
Alexander Ter. B67: Smeth 3D **98**
Alexander Way B8: Salt 6F **103**
Alexandra Av. B21: Hand 2H **99**
Alexandra Ct. *DY3: Gorn* *4G 75*
(off Redhall Rd.)
Alexandra Cres. B71: W Brom 5C **64**
Alexandra Ho. B27: A Grn 3B **136**
Alexandra Ind. Est. DY4: Tip 1A **78**
Alexandra Pl. DY1: Dud 3D **76**
WV14: Bils 5F **45**
Alexandra Rd. B5: Bal H 5G **117**
B21: Hand 2H **99**
B30: Stir 1C **146**
B63: Hale 2H **127**
DY4: Tip 2H **77**
WS1: Wals 4C **48**
WS10: Darl 5E **47**
WV4: Penn 6E **43**
Alexandra St. DY1: Dud 6D **76**
WV3: Wolv 2F **43**
Alexandra Theatre 1F 117 (5D 4)
Alexandra Way B69: Tiv 5A **78**
WS9: A'rdge 4D **34**
Alford Cl. B45: Redn 2A **158**
Alfreda Av. B47: H'wd 1H **161**
Alfred Gunn Ho. B68: O'bry 5H **97**
Alfred Rd. B11: S'hll 6B **118**
B21: Hand 1A **100**
Alfred Squire Rd. WV11: Wed 4E **29**
Alfred St. B6: Aston 1B **102**
B12: Bal H 6B **118**
B14: K Hth 6H **133**
B66: Smeth 2G **99**
B70: W Brom 4B **80**
WS3: Blox 6H **19**
WS10: Darl 6C **46**
Alfryth Ct. *B15: Edg* *3E 117*
(off Lee Cres.)
Algernon Rd. B16: Edg 5H **99**
Alice St. WV14: Bils 5F **45**
Alice Wlk. WV14: Bils 6F **45**
Alison Cl. DY4: Tip 3A **62**
Alison Dr. DY8: Stourb 3D **124**
Alison Rd. B62: Hale 2F **129**
Allan Cl. B66: Smeth 4F **99**
DY8: Word 3D **108**
All Angels Wlk. B68: O'bry 5H **97**
Allbut St. B64: Crad H 2F **111**
Allcock St. B9: Birm 2A **118**
DY4: Tip 5C **62**
Allcroft Rd. B11: Tys 3F **135**
Allenby Cl. DY6: K'wfrd 4E **93**
Allen Cl. B43: Gt Barr 6A **66**
Allendale Gro. B43: Gt Barr 5A **66**
Allendale Rd. B25: Yard 4H **119**
B76: Walm 5C **70**
Allen Dr. B70: W Brom 6D **80**
WS10: Darl 5C **46**
Allen Ho. B43: Gt Barr 6A **66**
Allen Rd. DY4: Tip 4H **61**
WS10: W'bry 6F **47**
WV6: Wolv 6D **26**
Allens Av. B18: Hock 3B **100**
B71: W Brom 6G **63**
Allen's Cl. WV12: W'hall 4B **30**
Allens Cft. Rd. B14: K Hth 2D **146**
Allens Farm Rd. B31: N'fld 4B **144**
Allen's La. WS3: Pels 5D **20**
Allen's Rd. B18: Hock 3B **100**
Allen St. B70: W Brom 4H **79**
Allerdale Rd. WS8: Clay 6A **10**
Allerton Ct. B71: W Brom 4A **64**
Allerton La. B71: W Brom 5A **64**
Allerton Rd. B25: Yard 4H **119**
Allesley Cl. B74: S Cold 5A **54**
Allesley Rd. B92: Olton 5B **136**
Allesley St. B6: Aston 4G **101**
Alleston Rd. WV10: Bush 5H **15**
Alleston Wlk. WV10: Bush 5H **15**
Alley, The DY3: Lwr G 4F **75**
Alleyne Gro. B24: Erd 5G **85**
Alleyne Rd. B24: Erd 6G **85**
Allingham Gro. B43: Gt Barr 1G **67**
Allington Cl. WS5: Wals 3H **49**
Allison St. B5: Birm 1H **117** (5G **5**)
Allman Rd. B24: Erd 3H **85**
Allmyn Dr. B74: S'tly 5A **52**
ALL SAINTS **4C 100**
All Saints Dr. B74: Four O 1F **53**
All Saints Ind. Est. B18: Hock 4C **100**
All Saints Rd. B14: K Hth 1G **147**
B18: Hock 4D **100**
WS10: Darl 5E **47**
WV2: Wolv 3H **43** (6C **170**)
All Saints St. B18: Hock 4C **100**
All Saints Way B71: W Brom 3B **80**
Allsops Cl. B65: Row R 5H **95**
Allwell Dr. B14: K Hth 5H **147**
Allwood Gdns. B32: Bart G 3G **129**
Alma Av. DY4: Tip 6A **62**
Alma Cres. B7: Birm 5B **102**
Alma Ind. Est. WS10: Darl 5C **46**
Alma Pas. B17: Harb 5H **115**
Alma Pl. B12: Bal H 6B **118**
DY2: Dud 6E **77**
Almar Ct. WV8: Pend 6D **14**
Alma St. B19: Hock 3G **101**
B63: Crad 6E **111**
B66: Smeth 3G **99**
WS2: Wals 5B **32**
WS10: Darl 5C **46**
WS10: W'bry 2H **63**
WV10: Wolv 6B **28**
WV13: W'hall 1B **46**
Alma Way B19: Loz 2F **101**
Alma Works WS10: Darl 6D **46**
Almond Av. WS2: Wals 5E **31**
WS5: Wals 1E **65**
Almond Cl. B29: W Cas 1E **145**
WS3: Pels 5D **20**
Almond Cft. B42: Gt Barr 1B **82**
Almond Gro. WV6: Wolv 5G **27**
Almond Rd. DY6: K'wfrd 1C **92**
Almsbury Ct. B26: Sheld 1G **137**
Alms Ho's. WS1: Wals 3B **48**
WV4: Penn 2D **58**
Alnwick Ho. B23: Erd 1F **85**
Alnwick Rd. WS3: Blox 3H **19**
Alperton Dr. DY9: W'cte 3A **126**
Alpha Cl. B12: Bal H 5G **117**
Alpha Twr. B1: Birm 1E **117** (5B **4**)
Alpha Way WS6: Gt Wyr 5G **7**
Alpine Dr. DY2: Neth 5D **94**
Alpine Way WV3: Wolv 1A **42**
Alport Cft. B9: Birm 1B **118**
Alston Cl. B74: Four O 1G **53**
B91: Sol 1H **151**
Alston Gro. B9: Bord G 6H **103**
Alston Ho. B69: O'bry 3D **96**
Alston Rd. B9: Bord G 6H **103**
B69: O'bry 2E **97**
B91: Sol 1H **151**
Alston St. B16: Birm 1C **116**
Althorpe Dr. B93: Dorr 6H **165**
Alton Av. WV12: W'hall 5B **30**
Alton Cl. WV10: Bush 4A **16**
Alton Gro. B71: W Brom 6C **64**
DY2: Dud 6G **77**
Alton Rd. B29: S Oak 2B **132**
Alum Dr. B9: Bord G 6G **103**
Alumhurst Av. B8: W End 5G **103**
ALUM ROCK 6H 103
Alum Rock Rd. B8: Salt 4D **102**
Alumwell Cl. WS2: Wals 2H **47**
Alumwell Rd. WS2: Wals 2H **47**
Alvaston Cl. WS3: Blox 4A **20**
Alvechurch Highway B60: L Ash 6C **156**
Alvechurch Rd. B31: Longb 1F **159**
B63: Hale 3H **127**
Alverley Cl. DY6: W Hth 1H **91**
Alverstoke Cl. WV9: Pend 5E **15**
Alveston Gro. B9: Bord G 1H **119**
B93: Know 2D **166**
Alveston Rd. B47: H'wd 2A **162**
Alvin Cl. B62: B'hth 2F **113**
Alvington Cl. WV12: W'hall 5D **30**
Alvis Wlk. B36: Cas B 6B **88**
Alwen St. DY8: Word 1D **108**
Alwin Rd. B65: Row R 1B **112**
Alwold Ct. B29: W Cas 3D **130**
Alwold Rd. B29: W Cas, S Oak 3D **130**
Alwyn Cl. WS6: Gt Wyr 2F **7**
Alwynn Wlk. B23: Erd 4B **84**
Amal Way B6: Witt 5H **83**
(not continuous)
Amanda Av. WV4: Penn 1D **58**
Amanda Dr. B26: Yard 2E **121**
Amazon Lofts *B1: Birm* *5D 100*
(off Tenby St.)
Ambassador Rd. B26: Birm A 1E **139**
Ambell Cl. B65: Row R 4H **95**
Amber Dr. B69: O'bry 4G **97**
Ambergate Cl. WS3: Blox 4A **20**
Ambergate Dr. DY6: W Hth 1A **92**
Amberley Ct. B29: S Oak 5A **132**
Amberley Grn. B43: Gt Barr 1A **82**
Amberley Gro. B6: Witt 4A **84**
Amberley Rd. B92: Olton 1D **136**
Amberley Way B74: S'tly 2G **51**
Amber Way B62: Hale 5B **112**
Amberwood Cl. WS2: Wals 6D **30**
AMBLECOTE **4C 108**
Amblecote Av. B44: Gt Barr 3G **67**
Amblecote Rd. DY5: Brie H 4G **109**
Ambleside B32: Bart G 4A **130**
Ambleside Cl. WV14: Bils 2G **61**
Ambleside Dr. DY5: Brie H 3G **109**
Ambleside Gro. WV12: W'hall 6B **18**
Ambleside Way DY6: K'wfrd 3B **92**
Ambrose Cl. WV13: W'hall 1G **45**
Ambrose Cres. DY6: K'wfrd 1B **92**
Ambury Way B43: Gt Barr 5H **65**
AMC Cinema 2C **116**
Amelas Cl. DY5: Brie H 2E **109**
Amersham Cl. B32: Quin 6C **114**
Amesbury Rd. B13: Mose 2G **133**
Ames Rd. WS10: Darl 4C **46**
Amethyst Ct. B92: Olton 4D **136**
AMF Bowling
Wolverhampton 3H 43 (6C 170)
Oxley 3G 27
Amherst Av. B20: Hand 4C **82**
Amington Cl. B75: R'ley 5B **38**
Amington Rd. B25: Yard 5H **119**
B90: Shir 1G **163**
Amiss Gdns. B10: Small H 3C **118**
Amity Cl. B66: Smeth 4F **99**
Amos Av. WV11: Wed 2D **28**
Amos La. WV11: Wed 2E **29**
Amos Rd. DY9: W'cte 3B **126**
Amphlett Cft. DY4: Tip 3B **78**
Amphletts Cl. DY2: Neth 6G **95**
Ampton Rd. B15: Edg 4D **116**
Amroth Cl. B45: Redn 2H **157**
Amwell Gro. B14: K Hth 4H **147**
Anchorage Rd. B23: Erd 4D **84**
B74: S Cold 5H **53**
Anchor Brook Ind. Pk. WS9: A'rdge 2B **34**
Anchor Cl. B16: Edg 2A **116**
Anchor Cres. B18: Win G 4B **100**
Anchor Hill DY5: Brie H 2G **109**
Anchor La. B91: Sol 1H **151**
WV14: Cose 3D **60**
(not continuous)
Anchor Mdw. WS9: A'rdge 3C **34**
Anchor Pde. WS9: A'rdge 3D **34**
Anchor Rd. WS9: A'rdge 3D **34**
WV14: Cose 3E **61**
Andersleigh Dr. WV14: Cose 5C **60**
Anderson Cres. B43: Gt Barr 2A **66**
Anderson Gdns. DY4: Tip 3A **78**
Anderson Rd. B23: Erd 1E **85**
B66: Smeth 2E **115**
B67: Smeth 2E **115**
DY4: Tip 2A **78**
Anders Sq. WV6: Pert 5E **25**
Anderton Cl. B74: S Cold 4G **53**
Anderton Ct. B13: Mose 3A **134**
Anderton Pk. Rd. B13: Mose 2A **134**
Anderton Rd. B11: S'brk 5B **118**
Anderton St. B1: Birm 6D **100**
Andover Cres. DY6: K'wfrd 5D **92**

Andover St. B5: Birm 1H 117 (4H 5)
Andrew Cl. WV12: W'hall 3D 30
Andrew Ct. B76: Walm 2D 70
Andrew Dr. WV12: W'hall 3D 30
Andrew Gdns. B21: Hand 5A 82
Andrew Rd. B63: Hale 2A 128
B71: W Brom 3D 64
DY4: Tip 4A 62
Andrews Cl. DY5: Quar B 3A 110
Andrews Rd. WS9: Wals W 3D 22
Anerley Gro. B44: Gt Barr 1H 67
Anerley Rd. B44: Gt Barr 1H 67
Angela Av. B65: Row R 5D 96
Angela Pl. WV14: Bils 5F 45
Angelica Cl. WS5: Wals 2E 65
Angelina St. B12: Birm 3H 117
Angel Pas. DY8: Stourb 6E 109
Angel St. DY1: Dud 1D 94
WV13: W'hall 1A 46
Anglesey Av. B36: Cas B 2D 106
Anglesey Cl. WS7: Chase 1A 10
Anglesey Cres. WS8: Bwnhls 3B 10
Anglesey Rd. WS8: Bwnhls 3B 10
Anglesey St. B19: Loz 2E 101
Anglian Rd. WS9: A'rdge 3H 33
Anglo African Ind. Pk. B69: O'bry 5E 79
Angus Cl. B71: W Brom 1A 80
Anita Av. DY4: Tip 5A 78
Anita Cft. B23: Erd 5D 84
Ankadine Rd. DY8: Amb 5F 109
Ankerdine Ct. B63: Hale 2A 128
Ankermoor Cl. B34: S End 3F 105
Annan Av. WV10: Bush 2A 28
Ann Cft. B26: Sheld 1H 137
Anne Cl. B70: W Brom 4E 79
Anne Ct. B76: Walm 2E 71
Anne Gro. DY4: Tip 4B 62
Anne Rd. B66: Smeth 2G 99
DY5: Quar B 2C 110
WV4: Penn 5F 43
Ann Rd. B47: Wyt 6A 162
Annscroft B38: K Nor 5H 145
Ann St. WV13: W'hall 6B 30
Ansbro Cl. B18: Win G 4B 100
Ansculf Rd. DY5: Brie H 2F 109
Ansell Rd. B11: S'brk 5C 118
B24: Erd 6F 85
Ansley Way B92: Sol 6H 137
Anslow Gdns. WV11: Wed 6H 17
Anslow Rd. B23: Erd 2C 84
Anson Cl. WS6: Gt Wyr 4F 7
WV6: Pert 4E 25
Anson Ct. B70: W Brom 6F 63
Anson Gro. B27: A Grn 3B 136
Anson Rd. B70: W Brom 1E 79
WS2: Wals 1E 47
WS6: Gt Wyr 4F 7
Anstey Cft. B37: F'bri 5C 106
Anstey Gro. B27: A Grn 4H 135
Anstey Rd. B44: K'sdng 1G 83
Anston Junc. WS2: Wals 2E 47
Anston Way WV11: Wed 2F 29
Anstree Cl. WS6: C Hay 4D 6
Anstruther Rd. B15: Edg 4H 115
Anthony Rd. B8: Salt 6E 103
Anton Dr. B76: Walm 1E 87
Antony Rd. B90: Shir 6H 149
Antringham Gdns. B15: Edg 3H 115
Antrobus Rd. B21: Hand 6A 82
B73: Bold 4E 69
Anvil Cres. WV14: Cose 3E 61
Anvil Dr. B69: O'bry 3E 97
Anvil Wlk. B70: W Brom 3F 79
Apex Bus. Pk. WS11: Nort C 1D 8
Apex Ind. Pk. DY4: Tip 5D 62
Apex Rd. WS8: Bwnhls 6G 9
Apley Rd. DY8: Woll 4C 108
Apollo Cft. B24: Erd 4B 86
Apollo Rd. B68: O'bry 3A 98
DY9: W'cte 6C 110
Apollo Way B20: Hand 6F 83
B66: Smeth 4G 99
Apperley Way B63: Crad 4D 110
Appian Cl. B14: K Hth 2G 147
Appian Way B90: Ches G 5B 164
Appleby Cl. B14: K Hth 2F 147
Appleby Gdns. WV11: Ess 5C 18
Appleby Gro. B90: M'path 3F 165
Applecross B74: Four O 2F 53
Appledore Cl. WS6: Gt Wyr 2G 7
Appledore Ct. WS3: Blox 1H 31
Appledore Rd. WS5: Wals 3H 49
Appledore Ter. WS5: Wals 3H 49
Appledorne Gdns. B34: S End 3F 105
Applesham Cl. B11: S'brk 5D 118
Appleton Av. B43: Gt Barr 5H 65
DY8: Stourb 3E 125
Appleton Cl. B30: B'vlle 5A 132
Appleton Cres. WV4: Penn 6E 43
Apple Tree Cl. B23: Erd 3B 84
Appletree Cl. B31: Longb 6D 144
B91: Cath B 2D 152
Appletree Gro. WS9: A'rdge 5D 34
WV6: Wolv 4G 27
Applewood Gro. B64: Old H 3H 111
April Cft. B13: Mose 2B 134
Apse Cl. WV5: Wom 6F 57
Apsley Cl. B68: O'bry 4G 113
Apsley Cft. B38: K Nor 5D 146
Apsley Gro. B24: Erd 5G 85
B93: Dorr 6G 167
Apsley Ho. B64: Old H 1H 111
Apsley Rd. B68: O'bry 4G 113
Aqueduct Rd. B90: Shir 5E 149
Aragon Dr. B73: S Cold 5G 53
Arbor Ct. B71: W Brom 1C 80
Arboretum Rd. WS1: Wals 1D 48
Arbor Way B37: Chel W 2E 123
Arbour Ga. WS9: Wals W 3D 22
Arbourtree Ct. WV5: Wom 6H 57
Arbury Dr. DY8: Word 6B 92
Arbury Hall Rd. B90: Shir 1B 164
Arbury Wlk. B76: Min 2H 87
Arcade B31: N'fld 3E 145
Arcade, The DY3: Up Gor 2A 76
WS1: Wals 2C 48
Arcadia *B70: W Brom* *4A 80*
(off W. Bromwich Ringway)
Arcadian Cinema 2G 117
Arcadian Shop. Cen.
B5: Birm 2G 117 (6E 5)
Arcal St. DY3: Sed 6A 60
Arch, The B9: Birm 1A 118
Archer Cl. B68: O'bry 4H 97
WS10: W'bry 2E 63
Archer Ct. DY9: W'cte 3A 126
Archer Gdns. B64: Crad H 2E 111
Archer Rd. B14: Yard W 3C 148
WS3: Blox 3C 32
Archers Cl. B23: Erd 5D 68
(not continuous)
Archery Rd. CV7: Mer 4H 141
Arches, The B10: Small H 3B 118
Arch Hill St. DY2: Neth 4E 95
Archibald Rd. B19: Loz 1E 101
Archway, The WS4: Wals 6D 32
Arcot Rd. B28: Hall G 3F 135
Ardath Rd. B38: K Nor 5C 146
Ardav Rd. B70: W Brom 5F 63
Ardedale B90: Shir 1A 164
Arden Bldgs. B93: Dorr 6B 166
Arden Cl. CV7: Bal C 2H 169
CV7: Mer 4H 141
DY8: Woll 4C 108
DY8: Word 6A 92
Ardencote Rd. B13: Mose 6A 134
Arden Ct. B24: Erd 4H 85
B42: P Barr 3F 83
B92: H Ard 6A 140
DY3: Lwr G *4H 75*
(off Chiltern Cl.)
Arden Cft. B46: Col 6H 89
B92: Sol 1G 137
Arden Dr. B26: Yard 4D 120
B73: W Grn 5H 69
B75: S Cold 6F 55
(not continuous)
B93: Dorr 6G 167
Arden Gro. B19: Loz 1E 101
B69: O'bry 4G 97
Arden Ho. B92: H Ard 1B 154
Ardenlea Ct. B91: Sol 2G 151
Arden Oak Rd. B26: Sheld 6H 121
Arden Pl. WV14: Bils 1B 62
Arden Rd. B6: Aston 1F 101
B8: Salt 6C 102
B27: A Grn 1H 135
B45: Fran 6G 143
B47: H'wd 3A 162
B67: Smeth 5E 99
B93: Dorr 6G 167
Arden Va. Rd. B93: Know 2D 166
Arderne Dr. B37: F'bri 2C 122
Ardingley Wlk. DY5: Brie H 4F 109
Ardley Cl. DY2: Dud 1F 95
Ardley Rd. B14: K Hth 2A 148
Arena B40: Nat E C 2G 139
Arena Theatre 1G 43 (2B 170)
Arena Wlk. B1: Birm 5A 4
Aretha Cl. DY6: K'wfrd 3E 93
Argil Cl. WV11: Wed 1F 29
Argus Cl. B76: Walm 2D 70
Argyle Cl. DY8: Word 2C 108
WS4: Wals 6F 33
Argyle Rd. WS4: Wals 6F 33
WV2: Wolv 5F 43
Argyle St. B7: Nech 1C 102
Argyll Ho. WV1: Wolv 5G 27
Arkle Cft. B36: Hodg H 1A 104
B65: Row R 3H 95
Arkley Gro. B28: Hall G 6H 135
Arkley Rd. B28: Hall G 6H 135
Arkwright Rd. B32: Quin 6A 114
WS2: Wals 4H 31
Arlen Dr. B43: Gt Barr 4H 65
Arlescote Cl. B75: Four O 1A 54
Arlescote Rd. B92: Sol 3G 137
Arless Way B17: Harb 2E 131
Arleston Way B90: Shir 1C 164
Arley Cl. B69: O'bry 4D 96
Arley Ct. DY2: Neth 3E 95
Arley Dr. DY8: Stourb 2C 124
Arley Gro. WV4: Penn 6B 42
Arley Ho. B26: Yard 2E 121
Arley Rd. B8: Salt 4D 102
B29: S Oak 2B 132
B91: Sol 3E 151
Arley Vs. *B18: Win G* *5H 99*
(off Cape St.)
Arlidge Cl. WV14: Bils 1F 61
Arlington Cl. DY6: K'wfrd 5B 92
Arlington Ct. DY8: Stourb 1F 125
Arlington Gro. B14: K Hth 5B 148
Arlington Rd. B14: K Hth 5B 148
B71: W Brom 1B 80
Armada Cl. B23: Erd 6D 84
Armoury Rd. B11: Small H 5D 118
Armoury Trad. Est. B11: Small H 5D 118
Armside Cl. WS3: Pels 3F 21
Armstead Rd. WV9: Pend 4D 14
Armstrong Cl. DY8: Amb 4F 109
Armstrong Dr. B36: Cas B 6B 88
WS2: Wals 5G 31
WV6: Wolv 4E 27
Armstrong Way WV13: W'hall 3B 46
Arnhem Cl. WV11: Wed 1D 28
Arnhem Rd. WV13: W'hall 3G 45
Arnhem Way DY4: Tip 2C 78
Arnold Cl. WS2: Wals 6F 31
Arnold Gro. B30: K Nor 3H 145
B90: Shir 3H 149
Arnold Rd. B90: Shir 3H 149
Arnside Ct. B23: Erd 3B 84
Arnwood Cl. WS2: Wals 1F 47
Arosa Dr. B17: Harb 2F 131
Arps Rd. WV8: Cod 4F 13
Arran Cl. B43: Gt Barr 2A 66
Arran Rd. B34: Hodg H 3D 104
Arran Way B36: Cas B 2C 106
Arras Rd. DY2: Dud 5G 77
Arrow Cl. B93: Know 3C 166
Arrowfield Grn. B38: K Nor 2H 159
Arrow Ind. Est.
WV12: W'hall 3C 30
Arrow Rd. WS3: Blox 3C 32
Arrow Wlk. B38: K Nor 6D 146
Arsenal St. B9: Bord G 2C 118
Arter St. B12: Bal H 5H 117
Arthur Gunby Cl. B75: S Cold 4D 54
Arthur Harris Cl. B66: Smeth 6G 99
Arthur Pl. B1: Birm 6D 100 (3A 4)

Arthur Rd.—Aston Station (Rail)

Arthur Rd. B15: Edg 5D **116**
B21: Hand 1B **100**
B24: Erd 3H **85**
B25: Yard 5H **119**
DY4: Tip 1A **78**
Arthur St. B10: Small H 2B **118**
B70: W Brom 6B **80**
WS2: Wals 4H **47**
WV2: Wolv 5H **43**
WV14: Bils 5F **45**
Arthur Terry Sports Cen., The 6G **37**
Artillery St. B9: Birm 1B **118**
Arton Cft. B24: Erd 5F **85**
Arundel Av. WS10: W'bry 2F **63**
Arundel Ct. *B29: W Cas* *6G* ***131***
(off Abdon Av.)
Arundel Cres. B92: Olton 4E **137**
Arundel Dr. B69: Tiv 1A **96**
Arundel Gro. WV6: Pert 6F **25**
Arundel Ho. B23: Erd 1F **85**
Arundel Pl. B11: S'brk 5A **118**
Arundel Rd. B14: K Hth 6A **148**
DY8: Word 1A **108**
WV10: Oxl 5F **15**
WV12: W'hall 2C **30**
Arundel St. WS1: Wals 4C **48**
(not continuous)
Arun Way B76: Walm 4E **71**
Asbury Ct. B43: Gt Barr 5G **65**
Asbury Rd. CV7: Bal C 4H **169**
WS10: W'bry 3C **64**
Ascot Cl. B16: Birm 1B **116**
B69: O'bry 3E **97**
Ascot Dr. DY1: Dud 5B **76**
WV4: Penn 1E **59**
Ascote La. B90: Dic H 4G **163**
Ascot Gdns. DY8: Word 1B **108**
Ascot Rd. B13: Mose 3H **133**
Ascot Wlk. B69: O'bry 3E **97**
Ash Av. B12: Bal H 6A **118**
Ashborough Dr. B91: Sol 2G **165**
Ashbourne Gro. B6: Aston 1G **101**
Ashbourne Ridge B63: Crad 6F **111**
Ashbourne Rd. B16: Edg 6H **99**
WS3: Blox 4A **20**
WV1: Wolv 6C **28**
WV4: E'shll 2A **60**
Ashbourne Way B90: Shir 1C **164**
Ash Bridge Ct. B45: Redn 3H **157**
Ashbrook Cres. B91: Sol 1G **165**
Ashbrook Dr. B45: Redn 1H **157**
Ashbrook Gro. B30: Stir 5D **132**
Ashbrook Rd. B30: Stir 5E **133**
Ashburn Gro. WV13: W'hall 1C **46**
Ashburton Rd. B14: K Hth 2F **147**
Ashbury Covert B30: K Nor 4E **147**
Ashby Cl. B8: W End 3A **104**
Ashby Ct. B91: Sol 6G **151**
Ash Cl. WV8: Bilb 4G **13**
Ashcombe Av. B20: Hand 4A **82**
Ashcombe Gdns. B24: Erd 4B **86**
Ashcott Cl. B38: K Nor 5H **145**
Ash Ct. B66: Smeth 1A **98**
DY8: Stourb 1E **125**
Ash Cres. B37: K'hrst 3B **106**
DY6: K'wfrd 3C **92**
Ashcroft B15: Edg 6A **116**
B66: Smeth 4G **99**
Ashcroft Gro. B20: Hand 5F **83**
Ashdale Cl. DY6: K'wfrd 1C **92**
Ashdale Dr. B14: K Hth 6B **148**
Ashdale Gro. B26: Yard 3E **121**
Ashdene Cl. B73: S Cold 2G **69**
Ashdene Gdns. DY8: Word 1A **108**
Ashdown Cl. B13: Mose 4A **134**
B45: Fran 5G **143**
Ashdown Dr. DY8: Word 6C **92**
Ash Dr. B31: Longb 6A **144**
B71: W Brom 1A **80**
Ashen Cl. DY3: Sed 2G **59**
Ashenden Ri. WV3: Wolv 2G **41**
Ashenhurst Rd. DY1: Dud 2A **94**
Ashenhurst Wlk. DY1: Dud 1C **94**
Ashes Rd. B69: O'bry 5F **97**
Ashfern Dr. B76: Walm 6D **70**
Ashfield Av. B14: K Hth 4G **133**
Ashfield Cl. WS3: Wals 5D **32**
Ashfield Ct. B30: K Nor 3A **146**
Ashfield Cres. DY2: Neth 6E **95**
DY9: W'cte 2B **126**
Ashfield Gdns. B14: K Hth 4H **133**
Ashfield Gro. B63: Hale 3G **127**
WV10: F'hses 4G **15**
Ashfield Ho. B28: Hall G. 4E **149**
Ashfield Rd. B14: K Hth 4H **133**
WV3: Wolv 1B **42**
WV10: F'hses 4G **15**
WV14: Bils 3A **62**
Ashford Cl. B24: Erd 3B **86**
Ashford Dr. B76: Walm 2D **86**
DY3: Sed 6A **60**
Ashford Twr. B12: Birm 3A **118**
Ash Furlong Cl. CV7: Bal C 3H **169**
Ashfurlong Cres. B75: S Cold 4C **54**
Ash Grn. DY1: Dud 2C **76**
Ash Gro. B12: Bal H 6B **118**
B31: N'fld 3D **144**
DY3: Gorn 5G **75**
DY9: W'cte 2H **125**
Ashgrove Ho. *B45: Rubery* *2E* ***157***
(off Callowbrook La.)
Ashgrove Rd. B44: Gt Barr 3E **67**
Ash Hill WV3: Wolv 2B **42**
Ashill Rd. B45: Redn 2H **157**
Ash La. WS6: Gt Wyr 2G **7**
Ashlawn Cres. B91: Sol 2B **150**
Ashleigh Dr. B20: Hand 5D **82**
Ashleigh Gro. B13: Mose 4B **134**
Ashleigh Hgts. B91: Sol 2E **151**
Ashleigh Rd. B69: Tiv 1C **96**
B91: Sol 3F **151**
Ashley Cl. B15: Edg 4E **117**
DY6: K'wfrd 5A **92**
DY8: Stourb 3B **124**
Ashley Gdns. B8: Salt 5D **102**
WV8: Cod 3F **13**
Ashley Mt. WV6: Tett 4B **26**
Ashley Rd. B23: Erd 4E **85**
B66: Smeth 5G **99**
WS3: Blox 6F **19**
WV4: Penn 6C **42**
Ashley St. WV14: Bils 5G **45**
Ashley Ter. B29: S Oak 4A **132**
Ashley Way CV7: Bal C 2H **169**
Ashmall WS7: Hamm 1F **11**
Ashmead Dr. B45: Coft H 5A **158**
Ashmead Gro. B24: Erd 5G **85**
Ashmead Ri. B45: Coft H 5A **158**
Ash M. B27: A Grn 6A **120**
Ashmole Rd. B70: W Brom 6F **63**
ASHMOOR LAKE 4B **30**
Ashmore Av. WV11: Wed 1A **30**
Ashmore Ind. Est. WS2: Wals 6C **32**
Ashmore Lake Ind. Est. WV12: W'hall 5B **30**
Ashmore Lake Rd. WV12: W'hall 5B **30**
Ashmore Lake Way WV12: W'hall 5B **30**
ASHMORE PARK **6A 18**
Ashmore Rd. B30: K Nor 2B **146**
Ashmores Ind. Est. DY1: Dud 4G **77**
Ashold Farm Rd. B24: Erd 5B **86**
Asholme Cl. B36: Hodg H 2A **104**
Ashorne Cl. B28: Hall G 6H **135**
Ashover Gro. *B18: Win G* *5A* ***100***
(off Heath Grn. Rd.)
Ashover Rd. B44: Gt Barr 2F **67**
Ash Rd. B8: Salt 5D **102**
DY1: Dud 4D **76**
DY4: Tip 3G **77**
WS10: W'bry 6F **47**
Ash St. B64: Old H 1H **111**
WS3: Blox 6B **20**
WV3: Wolv 2E **43**
WV14: Bils 2G **61**
Ashtead Cl. B76: Walm 1F **87**
Ashted Lock B7: Birm 5H **101** (1H **5**)
Ashted Wlk. B7: Birm 5B **102**
Ash Ter. B69: Tiv 6B **78**
Ashton Cft. B91: Sol 6E **151**
Ashtoncroft B16: Birm 1C **116**
Ashton Dr. WS4: S'fld 4G **21**
Ashton Pk. Dr. DY5: Brie H 2G **109**
Ashton Rd. B25: Yard 4H **119**
Ashtree Cl. DY5: Brie H 3E **109**
Ash Tree Dr. B26: Yard 4B **120**
Ashtree Dr. DY8: Stourb 2E **125**
Ashtree Gro. WV14: Bils 2B **62**
Ash Tree Rd. B30: Stir 1C **146**
Ashtree Rd. B64: Old H 1H **111**
B69: Tiv 6C **78**
WS3: Pels 4E **21**
Ashurst Rd. B76: Walm 1D **86**
Ashville Av. B34: Hodg H 2D **104**
Ashville Dr. B63: Hale 6A **112**
Ash Wlk. B76: Walm 3D **70**
Ashwater Dr. B14: K Hth 5F **147**
Ash Way B23: Erd 5C **68**
Ashway B11: S'hll 6B **118**
Ashwell Dr. B90: Shir 3B **150**
Ashwells Gro. WV9: Pend 5E **15**
Ashwin Rd. B21: Hand 2B **100**
ASHWOOD **4E 91**
Ashwood Av. DY8: Word 1A **108**
Ashwood Cl. B74: S'tly 3G **51**
Ashwood Ct. B13: Mose 2A **134**
B34: Hodg H 4B **104**
Ashwood Dr. B37: Chel W 6F **107**
Ashwood Gro. WV4: Penn 6E **43**
Ashwood Lwr. La. DY6: K'wfrd 4E **91**
DY7: Stourt 4E **91**
Ashworth Rd. B42: Gt Barr 4D **66**
Askew Bri. Rd. DY3: Gorn 4F **75**
Askew Cl. DY3: Up Gor 2A **76**
Aspbury Cft. B36: Cas B 6H **87**
Aspen Cl. B27: A Grn 3H **135**
B76: Walm 3D **70**
Aspen Dr. B37: Chel W 3E **123**
Aspen Gdns. B20: Hand 6D **82**
Aspen Gro. B9: Bord G 6G **103**
B47: Wyt 4B **162**
WV12: W'hall 2E **31**
Aspen Ho. B91: Sol 5D **150**
Aspen Way WV3: Wolv 2E **43**
Asquith Dr. B69: Tiv 5C **78**
Asquith Rd. B8: W End 4H **103**
Asra Cl. B66: Smeth 1E **99**
Asra Ho. *B66: Smeth* *1E* ***99***
(off Oxford Rd.)
Astbury Av. B67: Smeth 6D **98**
Astbury Cl. WS3: Blox 3G **19**
WV1: Wolv 2C **44**
Astbury Ct. B68: O'bry 4H **113**
Aster Wlk. WV9: Pend 4E **15**
Aster Way WS5: Wals 2E **65**
Astley Av. B62: Quin 5F **113**
Astley Cl. DY4: Tip 1D **78**
Astley Cres. B62: Quin 6F **113**
Astley Pl. WV2: Wolv 5H **43**
Astley Rd. B21: Hand 6H **81**
Astley Wlk. B90: Shir 2H **149**
ASTON **6H 83**
Aston Bri. B6: Aston 4H **101**
Aston Brook Grn. B6: Aston 4H **101**
Aston Brook St. B6: Aston 3H **101**
(not continuous)
Aston Brook St. E. B6: Aston 4H **101**
Aston Bury B15: Edg 4H **115**
Aston Chu. Rd. B7: Nech 2C **102**
B8: Salt 2C **102**
Aston Chu. Trad. Est. B7: Nech 3D **102**
Aston Cl. WV14: Bils 1B **62**
Aston Ct. B23: Erd 5C **84**
Aston Cross Bus. Pk. B6: Aston 3A **102**
Aston Events Cen. 1A **102**
Aston Expressway B6: Aston 4H **101**
Aston Hall 1H **101**
Aston Hall Rd. B6: Aston 1A **102**
Aston La. B20: Hand 5F **83**
Aston Mnr. Cl. B20: Hand 5G **83**
Aston Manor Transport Mus. 6H **83**
Aston Newton Pool & Fitness Cen. 3G **101**
Aston Rd. B6: Birm 4H **101**
(not continuous)
B69: Tiv 6A **78**
DY2: Dud 1D **94**
WV13: W'hall 1G **45**
Aston Rd. Nth. B6: Aston 3H **101**
Aston Science Pk. B7: Birm 5H **101** (1H **5**)
Aston's Cl. DY5: Brie H 4H **109**
Aston Seedbed Cen. B7: Nech 3A **102**
Aston's Fold DY5: Brie H 4H **109**
Aston Station (Rail) 1B **102**

Aston St.—Bakers La.

Aston St. B4: Birm. 5H **101** (2F **5**)
(not continuous)
DY4: Tip 6C **62**
WV3: Wolv 3E **43**
Aston Students Guild 1G **5**
Aston Triangle, The B4: Birm . . . 6H **101** (2G **5**)
Aston University 5H 101 (1G 5)
Aston Villa FC 6H **83**
Astor Dr. B13: Mose 4C **134**
Astoria Cl. WV12: W'hall 6D **18**
Astoria Gdns. WV12: W'hall. 6D **18**
Astor Rd. B74: S'tly 2A **52**
DY6: K'wfrd 4D **92**
Athelney Ct. WS3: Pels 4E **21**
Athelstan Gro. WV6: Pert 4F **25**
Atherstone Cl. B90: Shir. 5E **149**
Atherstone Rd. WV1: Wolv 1D **44**
Athlone Rd. WS5: Wals 3G **49**
Athol Cl. B32: Bart G 5B **130**
Athole St. B12: Birm 4A **118**
Atlantic Ct. *WV13: W'hall. 2A 46*
(off Cheapside)
Atlantic Rd. B44: Gt Barr 5H **67**
Atlantic Way WS10: W'bry 4E **63**
Atlas Cft. WV10: Oxl 3G **27**
Atlas Est. B6: Witt 5A **84**
B11: Tys. 6G **119**
Atlas Gro. B70: W Brom 4F **79**
Atlas Trad. Est. WV14: Bils 3H **61**
Atlas Way B1: Birm 5A **4**
Attenborough Cl. B19: Hock 4F **101**
Attingham Dr. B43: Gt Barr 3H **65**
Attleboro La. B46: Wat O 5C **88**
Attlee Cl. B69: Tiv 5D **78**
Attlee Cres. WV14: Bils 3G **61**
Attlee Rd. WS2: Wals. 5E **31**
Attwell Pk. WV3: Wolv 4B **42**
Attwell Rd. DY4: Tip 4H **61**
Attwood Cl. B8: Salt. 3E **103**
Attwood Gdns. WV4: E'shll. 6A **44**
Attwood St. B63: Hale 6H **111**
DY9: Lye. 6B **110**
Aubrey Rd. B10: Small H 3F **119**
B32: Harb. 4C **114**
Auchinleck Ho. *B16: Birm 2D 116*
(off Broad St.)
Auchinleck Sq. *B15: Birm 2D 116*
(off Islington Row Middleway)
Auckland Dr. B36: Cas B 1B **106**
Auckland Ho. B32: Quin. 1D **130**
Auckland Rd. B11: S'brk 4A **118**
B67: Smeth 3C **98**
DY6: K'wfrd 5C **92**
Auden Ct. WV6: Pert. 5F **25**
Audleigh Ho. B15: Birm 3E **117**
Audlem Wlk. WV10: Wolv 4C **28**
Audley Rd. B33: Stech 5C **104**
AUDNAM 2D **108**
Audnam DY8: Word 2D **108**
Augusta Rd. B13: Mose 1G **133**
B27: A Grn 6A **120**
Augusta Rd. E. B13: Mose. 1H **133**
Augusta St. B18: Birm. 5E **101** (1A **4**)
Augustine Gro. B18: Hock 3B **100**
B74: Four O 4F **37**
Augustus Cl. B46: Col 6H **89**
Augustus Ct. B15: Edg 3B **116**
Augustus Rd. B15: Edg 3H **115**
Augustus St. WS2: Wals 2B **48**
Aulton Rd. B75: R'ley. 6C **38**
Ault St. B70: W Brom. 6B **80**
Austcliff Dr. B91: Sol 1G **165**
Austen Pl. B15: Edg. 3D **116**
Austen Wlk. B71: W Brom 2B **80**
Austin Cl. B27: A Grn. 1B **136**
DY1: Dud 5B **76**
Austin Ct. B1: Birm 1D **116** (4A **4**)
Austin Cft. B36: Cas B 6A **88**
Austin Ho. WS4: Wals 6D **32**
Austin Ri. B31: Longb 2D **158**
Austin Rd. B21: Hand. 6G **81**
Austin St. WV6: Wolv. 5F **27**
AUSTIN VILLAGE 6D **144**
Austin Way B42: P Barr 2C **82**
Austrey Cl. B93: Know 3C **166**
Austrey Gro. B29: W Cas 5E **131**
Austrey Rd. DY6: K'wfrd. 4E **93**
Austy Cl. B36: Hodg H 1C **104**
Automotive Components Pk.
WS10: W'bry 2C **62**
Autumn Berry Gro. DY3: Sed 1A **76**
Autumn Cl. WS4: S'fld 6G **21**
Autumn Dr. DY3: Lwr G 3H **75**
WS4: S'fld 6G **21**
Autumn Gro. B19: Hock 3E **101**
Autumn Ho. B37: K'hrst 4D **106**
Avalon Cl. B24: Erd 3H **85**
Avebury Gro. B30: Stir 6E **133**
Avebury Rd. B30: Stir. 5E **133**
Ave Maria Cl. B64: Old H. 2G **111**
Avenbury Dr. B91: Sol 3A **152**
Avenue, The B27: A Grn. 1B **136**
B45: Rubery 2E **157**
B65: Row R 6A **96**
B76: Walm 4C **70**
WV3: Wolv. 3H **41**
WV4: Penn. 1C **58**
WV10: F'stne 1D **16**
WV10: Wolv 4B **28**
Avenue Cl. B7: Nech 3A **102**
B93: Dorr 6C **166**
Avenue Rd. B6: Aston 3H **101**
B7: Nech 3H **101**
B14: K Hth 5F **133**
B21: Hand 5H **81**
B23: Erd 3F **85**
B65: B'hth, Row R 2D **112**
B93: Dorr 6C **166**
DY2: Dud 3B **94**
WS10: Darl 5D **46**
WV3: Wolv. 1C **42**
WV14: Cose 5E **61**
Averill Rd. B26: Yard 2E **121**
Avern Cl. DY4: Tip 1B **78**
Aversley Rd. B38: K Nor 6H **145**
Avery Ct. B68: O'bry 4H **113**
Avery Cft. B35: Cas V. 5D **86**
Avery Dell Ind. Est. B30: K Nor. 2D **146**
Avery Dr. B27: A Grn 1A **136**
Avery Ho. B16: Edg 2C **116**
Avery Myers Cl. B68: O'bry 4H **97**
Avery Rd. B66: Smeth 3H **99**
B73: New O 3C **68**
Aviary Ct. B71: W Brom. 1A **80**
Aviemore Cres. B43: Gt Barr 1D **66**
Avington Cl. DY3: Sed 6H **59**
Avion Cen. WV6: Wolv 5E **27**
Avion Cl. WS1: Wals 4D **48**
Avocet Cl. B33: Stech. 6C **104**
Avon Cl. B14: K Hth 6F **147**
DY5: P'ntt. 3F **93**
WV6: Pert. 6F **25**
Avon Ct. B73: S Cold 6H **53**
Avon Cres. WS3: Pels. 6E **21**
Avoncroft Ho. B37: Chel W. 1C **122**
Avondale Cl. DY6: K'wfrd. 1C **92**
Avondale Ct. B31: N'fld 6C **144**
Avondale Rd. B11: S'hll. 1C **134**
WV6: Wolv. 6D **26**
Avon Dr. B13: Mose 3B **134**
B36: Cas B 1B **106**
WV13: W'hall. 1C **46**
Avon Gro. WS5: Wals 2E **65**
Avon Ho. B15: Birm 3F **117**
Avon M. DY8: Word 6H **91**
Avon Rd. B63: Crad 6D **110**
B90: Shir 6B **150**
DY8: Stourb 2D **124**
WS3: Blox 6C **20**
Avon St. B11: S'hll 6C **118**
Avon Way B47: Wyt 6G **161**
Avro Way B35: Cas V 5F **87**
Awbridge Rd. DY2: Neth 6E **95**
Awefields Cres. B67: Smeth 5B **98**
Awlmakers Gro. WS3: Blox 2A **32**
Axcess 10 Bus. Pk. WS10: W'bry 2E **47**
Axletree Way WS10: W'bry 5G **47**
Ayala Cft. B36: Hodg H 6C **86**
Aylesbury Cres. B44: K'sdng 5A **68**
Aylesbury Ho. B31: Longb. 1D **158**
Aylesford Cl. DY3: Sed 3G **59**
Aylesford Dr. B37: Mars G 4C **122**
B74: Four O 4E **37**
Aylesford Rd. B21: Hand 6H **81**
Aylesmore Cl. B32: Bart G. 4A **130**
B92: Olton 5C **136**
Aynsley Ct. B90: Shir. 5A **150**
Ayre Rd. B24: Erd 3H **85**
Ayrshire Cl. B36: Hodg H. 1B **104**
Ayrton Cl. WV6: Pert 5G **25**
Azalea Cl. WV8: Bilb 4H **13**
Azalea Gro. B9: Bord G 1F **119**
Aziz Isaac Cl. B68: O'bry 3H **97**

B

Babington Rd. B21: Hand. 2A **100**
Bablake Cft. B92: Olton 4E **137**
Babors Fld. WV14: Cose 2C **60**
Babworth Cl. WV9: Pend 5E **15**
Baccabox La. B47: H'wd 2G **161**
Bacchus Rd. B18: Hock 3B **100**
Bache St. B70: W Brom. 6A **80**
Bach Mill Dr. B28: Hall G. 4D **148**
Backhouse La.
WV11: Wed 5E **29**
Back La. B64: Crad H. 2D **110**
B90: Dic H 4G **163**
WS9: A'rdge. 2H **35**
WS14: Foot 1E **37**
Back Rd. B38: K Nor 5B **146**
DY6: K'wfrd 2B **92**
BACONS END 5D **106**
Bacons End B37: K'hrst 4D **106**
Baddesley Rd. B92: Olton 3C **136**
Bader Rd. WS2: Wals. 1F **47**
WV6: Pert. 6E **25**
Bader Wlk. B35: Cas V. 5D **86**
Badger Cl. B90: Ches G 5B **164**
Badgers Bank Rd.
B74: Four O 4F **37**
Badgers Cl. WS3: Pels. 2E **21**
Badgers Cft. B62: Hale. 4B **112**
Badger St. DY3: Up Gor. 2A **76**
DY9: Lye. 5A **110**
Badgers Way B34: Stech 4E **105**
Badminton Cl. DY1: Dud 4B **76**
Badon Covert B14: K Hth 5F **147**
Badsey Cl. B31: N'fld. 3G **145**
Badsey Rd. B69: O'bry. 4D **96**
Baggeridge Cl. DY3: Sed 5E **59**
Baggeridge Country Pk. 1C **74**
Baggeridge Country Pk. Vis. Cen.
. . . . . 6D **58**
Baggott St. WV2: Wolv 4G **43**
Baginton Cl. B91: Sol. 2F **151**
Baginton Rd. B35: Cas V 3E **87**
Bagley Ind. Pk. DY2: Neth 5F **95**
Bagley's Rd. DY5: Brie H. 5G **109**
Bagley St. DY9: Lye. 6G **109**
Bagnall Cl. B25: Yard. 5B **120**
Bagnall Rd. WV14: Bils 6E **45**
Bagnall St. B70: W Brom. 5C **80**
(Beeches Rd.)
B70: W Brom. 6D **62**
(Shaw St.)
DY4: Tip. 6D **62**
(Chimney Rd.)
DY4: Tip. 4C **62**
(Newman Rd.)
WS3: Blox 3A **32**
Bagnall Wlk. DY5: Brie H. 2H **109**
Bagnell Rd. B13: Mose 6H **133**
Bagot St. B4: Birm. 5G **101**
Bagridge Cl. WV3: Wolv 3H **41**
Bagridge Rd. WV3: Wolv. 3H **41**
Bagshawe Cft. B23: Erd. 6D **68**
Bagshaw Rd. B33: Stech 6C **104**
Bailey Rd. WV14: Bils 4D **44**
Baileys Ct. B65: Row R 6B **96**
Bailey St. B70: W Brom. 3G **79**
WV1: Wolv. 1A **44**
Bakeman Ho. *B25: Yard. 5B 120*
(off Tivoli, The)
Baker Av. WV14: Cose 3B **60**
Baker Ho. Gro. B43: Gt Barr 6H **65**
Baker Rd. WV14: Bils. 2G **61**
Bakers Gdns. WV8: Cod. 3E **13**
Bakers La. B74: S'tly 6H **51**
WS9: A'rdge. 3D **34**

Baker St.—Barnswood Cl.

Baker St. B10: Small H 2D 118
B11: S'hll 1C 134
B21: Hand 1B 100
B70: W Brom 4H 79
DY4: Tip 3G 77
(not continuous)
Bakers Way WV8: Cod 3E 13
Bakewell Cl. WS3: Blox 4A 20
Balaams Wood Dr. B31: Longb 6H 143
Balaclava Rd. B14: K Hth 5G 133
Balcaskie Cl. B15: Edg 4A 116
Balden Rd. B32: Harb 4C 114
Baldmoor Lake Rd. B23: Erd 6F 69
Bald's La. DY9: Lye 6B 110
Baldwin Cl. B69: Tiv 5D 78
Baldwin Rd. B30: K Nor 5C 146
Baldwins Ho. *DY5: Quar B* *3B* 110
(off Maughan St.)
Baldwins La. B28: Hall G 3E 149
Baldwin St. B66: Smeth 3F 99
WV14: Bils 1H 61
Baldwin Way DY3: Swind 5E 73
Balfour Ct. B74: Four O 6G 37
WV6: Wolv *5D* 26
(off Balfour Cres.)
Balfour Cres. WV6: Wolv 5D 26
Balfour Dr. B69: Tiv 5C 78
Balfour Ho. B16: Edg 2B 116
Balfour Rd. DY6: K'wfrd 1C 92
Balfour St. B12: Bal H 5G 117
Balham Gro. B44: K'sdng 3A 68
Balholm B62: Hale 6D 112
Balking Cl. WV14: Cose 2D 60
Ballarat Wlk. DY8: Stourb 6D 108
Ballard Cres. DY2: Neth 4F 95
Ballard Rd. DY2: Neth 4F 95
Ballard Wlk. B37: K'hrst 3C 106
Ballfields DY4: Tip 2D 78
Ball Ho. *WS3: Blox* *1H* 31
(off Somerfield Rd.)
Balliol Bus. Pk. WV9: Pend 4B 14
Balliol Ho. B37: F'bri 1B 122
Ball La. WV10: Cov H 1G 15
Ballot St. B66: Smeth 4F 99
BALLS HILL 5G 63
Balls Hill WS1: Wals 1D 48
Balls St. WS1: Wals 2D 48
Balmain Cres. WV11: Wed 1D 28
Balmoral Cl. B62: Hale 4B 112
WS4: Rus 2H 33
Balmoral Ct. B1: Birm 3A 4
Balmoral Dr. WV5: Wom 4G 57
WV12: W'hall 2B 30
Balmoral Rd. B23: Erd 2F 85
B32: Bart G 6G 129
B36: Cas B 2C 106
B74: Four O 4F 37
DY8: Word 6A 92
WV4: Penn 6E 43
Balmoral Vw. DY1: Dud 5A 76
Balmoral Way B65: Row R 5D 96
WS2: Wals 5G 31
BALSALL 4H 169
BALSALL COMMON 3H 169
BALSALL HEATH 6H 117
Balsall Heath Rd. B5: Bal H 4F 117
B12: Bal H 5G 117
BALSALL STREET 3G 169
Balsall St. CV7: Bal C 4B 168
Balsall St. E. CV7: Bal C 4G 169
Baltimore Rd. B42: P Barr 1C 82
Balvenie Way DY1: Dud 4B 76
Bamber Cl. WV3: Wolv 3C 42
Bamford Cl. WS3: Blox 4A 20
Bamford Ho. WS3: Blox 4A 20
Bamford Rd. WS3: Blox 4A 20
WV3: Wolv 3E 43
Bampfylde Pl. B42: Gt Barr 6E 67
Bamville Rd. B8: W End 4G 103
Banbery Dr. WV5: Wom 3F 73
Banbrook Cl. B92: Sol 5H 137
Banbury Cl. DY3: Sed 1A 76
Banbury Cft. B37: F'bri 1B 122
Banbury Ho. B33: Kitts G 1A 122
Banbury St. B5: Birm 6H 101 (3G 5)
Bancroft Cl. WV14: Cose 6D 60
Bandywood Cres. B44: Gt Barr 2H 67
Bandywood Rd. B44: Gt Barr 1G 67
Banfield Av. WS10: Darl 4C 46
Banfield Rd. WS10: Darl 1C 62
Banford Av. B8: W End 5G 103
Banford Rd. B8: W End 5G 103
Bangham Pit Rd. B31: N'fld 1C 144
Bangley La. B78: Hints 3H 39
Bangor Ho. B37: F'bri 5D 106
Bangor Rd. B9: Bord G 1D 118
Bankdale Rd. B8: W End 5H 103
Bankes Rd. B10: Small H 2E 119
Bank Farm Cl. DY9: Pedm 4G 125
Bankfield Rd. DY4: Tip 5C 62
WV14: Bils 6F 45
(not continuous)
Banklands Rd. DY2: Dud 3G 95
Bank Rd. DY2: Neth 3F 95
DY3: Gorn 4G 75
(not continuous)
Bankside B13: Mose 3D 134
B43: Gt Barr 6A 66
WV5: Wom 6F 57
Bankside Cres. B74: S'tly 4H 51
Bankside Way WS9: A'rdge 5D 22
Banks St. WV13: W'hall 1A 46
Bank St. B14: K Hth 5G 133
B64: Crad H 2E 111
B71: W Brom 1A 80
DY5: Brie H 6H 93
DY9: Lye 6B 110
WS1: Wals 2D 48
WV10: Wolv 4A 28
WV14: Bils 2G 61
WV14: Cose 5D 60
Bankwell St. DY5: Brie H 5G 93
Banner La. B92: Bars 6B 154
Bannerlea Rd. B37: K'hrst 4B 106
Bannerley Rd. B33: Sheld 2G 121
Banners Ct. B73: S'tly 2B 68
BANNERS GATE 1B 68
Banners Ga. Rd. B73: S'tly 2B 68
Banners Gro. B23: Erd 1G 85
Banner's La. B63: Crad 5F 111
Banner's St. B63: Crad 5F 111
Banners Wlk. B44: K'sdng 3B 68
Bannington Ct. WV12: W'hall 5D 30
Bannister Rd. WS10: W'bry 3D 62
Bannister St. B64: Crad H 2F 111
Banstead Cl. WV2: Wolv 4A 44
Bantams Cl. B33: Kitts G 1G 121
Bantock Av. WV3: Wolv 3D 42
Bantock Ct. WV3: Wolv 3C 42
Bantock Gdns. WV3: Wolv 2C 42
Bantock House Mus. 2D 42
Bantocks, The B70: W Brom 1G 79
Bantock Way B17: Harb 6H 115
Banton Cl. B23: Erd 5D 68
Bantry Cl. B26: Sheld 1G 137
BAPTIST END 3E 95
Baptist End Rd. DY2: Dud, Neth 4E 95
Barbara Rd. B28: Hall G 3E 149
Barbel Dr. WV10: Wolv 5C 28
Barberry Ho. B38: K Nor 6B 146
Barbers La. B92: Cath B 1E 153
Barbourne Cl. B91: Sol 2F 165
Barbrook Dr. DY5: Brie H 4F 109
Barcheston Rd. B29: W Cas 4E 131
B93: Know 4C 166
Barclay Ct. WV3: Wolv 1E 43
Barclay Rd. B67: Smeth 2C 114
Barcroft WV13: W'hall 6B 30
Bardenholme Gdns. DY9: W'cte 2H 125
Bardfield Cl. B42: Gt Barr 5B 66
Bardon Dr. B90: Shir 5A 150
Bard St. B11: S'hll 6C 118
Bardwell Cl. WV8: Pend 1D 26
Barford Cl. B76: Walm 1D 70
WS10: Darl 3C 46
Barford Cres. B38: K Nor 5E 147
Barford Ho. B5: Birm 4G 117
Barford Rd. B16: Birm 5A 100
B90: Shir 5B 150
Barford St. B5: Birm 3G 117
Bargate Dr. WV6: Wolv 5E 27
Bargehouse Wlk. B38: K Nor 2A 160
Bargery Rd. WV11: Wed 6A 18
Barham Cl. B90: M'path 4E 165
Barker Rd. B74: S Cold 4H 53
Barker St. B19: Loz 2D 100
B68: O'bry 3A 98
Bark Piece B32: Bart G 2A 130
Barlands Cft. B34: S End 3F 105
Barle Gro. B36: Cas B 2B 106
Barley Cl. DY3: Sed 6B 60
WS9: A'rdge 1G 51
WV8: Pend 6C 14
Barley Cft. WV6: Pert 6D 24
Barleyfield Ho. *WS1: Wals* *3C* 48
(off Bath St.)
Barleyfield Ri. DY6: W Hth 1G 91
Barleyfield Row WS1: Wals 3C 48
Barlow Cl. B45: Fran 5E 143
B68: O'bry 6G 97
Barlow Dr. B70: W Brom 6D 80
Barlow Rd. WS10: W'bry 6G 47
Barlow's Rd. B15: Edg 6H 115
Barmouth Cl. WV12: W'hall 3C 30
Barnabas Rd. B23: Erd 3F 85
Barnaby Sq. WV10: Bush 3B 16
Barnard Cl. B37: Chel W 2F 123
Barnardo's Cen. B7: Birm 4A 102
Barnard Pl. WV2: Wolv 5A 44
Barnard Rd. B75: S Cold 4C 54
WV11: Wed 6H 17
Barn Av. DY3: Sed 6G 59
Barnbrook Rd. B93: Know 2C 166
Barn Cl. B30: Stir 1D 146
B63: Hale 3G 127
B64: Crad H 5G 111
DY9: Lye 1G 125
Barncroft B32: Bart G 4C 130
WS6: Gt Wyr 2G 7
WS7: Chase 1C 10
Barncroft Rd. B69: Tiv 1A 96
Barncroft St. B70: W Brom 5G 63
Barnes Cl. B37: F'bri 1A 122
Barnes Hill B29: W Cas 3D 130
Barnesmeadow Pl. WV14: Cose 5D 60
Barnesville Cl. B10: Small H 3G 119
Barnet Rd. B23: Erd 2D 84
Barnett Cl. DY6: K'wfrd 5B 92
WV14: Bils 1F 61
Barnett Grn. DY6: K'wfrd 5B 92
Barnett La. DY6: K'wfrd 4B 92
DY8: Word 4B 92
Barnett Rd. WV13: W'hall 2G 45
Barnetts La. WS8: Bwnhls 5B 10
Barnett St. B69: Tiv 5A 78
DY4: Tip 3A 78
DY8: Word 6B 92
Barney Cl. DY4: Tip 4H 77
Barn Farm Cl. WV14: Bils 4A 46
Barnfield Dr. B92: Sol 1A 152
Barnfield Gro. B20: Hand 2A 82
Barnfield Rd. B62: B'hth 4D 112
DY4: Tip 6G 61
WV1: Wolv 1C 44
Barnfield Trad. Est. DY4: Tip 6G 61
Barnford Cl. B10: Small H 2C 118
Barnford Cres. B68: O'bry 6H 97
Barnfordhill Cl. B68: O'bry 5H 97
Barn Grn. WV3: Wolv 4D 42
BARN HILL 4C 162
Barn Ho. B8: W End 5B 104
Barnhurst La. WV8: Bilb, Pend 4B 14
Barn La. B13: Mose 6A 134
B21: Hand 2A 100
B92: Olton 1C 136
Barn Mdw. B25: Yard 2B 120
Barnmoor Ri. B91: Sol 6G 137
Barn Owl Dr. WS3: Pels 3D 20
Barn Owl Wlk. DY5: Brie H 5G 109
Barnpark Covert B14: K Hth 5E 147
Barn Piece B32: Quin 1H 129
Barnsbury Av. B72: W Grn 1A 86
Barns Cl. WS9: Wals W 3B 22
Barns Cft. B74: Lit A 5B 36
Barnsdale Cres. B31: N'fld 3C 144
Barns La. WS4: Rus 2G 33
WS9: A'rdge 2H 33
Barnsley Rd. B17: Edg 2E 115
Barnstaple Rd. B66: Smeth 4F 99
Barn St. B5: Birm 1H 117 (5H 5)
Barnswood Cl. B63: Crad 6E 111

Barnt Grn. Rd.—Beaton Cl.

Barnt Grn. Rd. B45: Coft H 5A **158**
Barnt Green Sailing Club 6E **159**
Barnwood Rd. B32: Quin 1D **130**
WV8: Pend 6C **14**
Barons Cl. B17: Harb 5E **115**
Barons Ct. B92: Sol 1G **137**
Barons Ct. Trad. Est. WS9: Wals W 5A **22**
Barrack Cl. B75: S Cold 5E **55**
Barrack La. B63: Crad 5D **110**
Barracks Cl. WS3: Blox 1C **32**
Barracks La. WS3: Blox 1B **32**
WS8: Bwnhls 4E **11**
Barracks Pl. WS3: Blox 1C **32**
Barrack St. B7: Birm 5A **102**
B70: W Brom 5G **63**
Barra Cft. B35: Cas V 3F **87**
Barrar Cl. DY8: Amb 3C **108**
Barratts Cft. DY5: P'ntt 6G **75**
Barratts Ho. B14: K Hth 5G **147**
Barratts Rd. B38: K Nor 6C **146**
BARR COMMON 6D **34**
Barr Comn. Cl. WS9: A'rdge 6D **34**
Barr Comn. Rd. WS9: A'rdge 6D **34**
Barretts La. CV7: Bal C 6H **169**
Barrhill Cl. B43: Gt Barr 3A **66**
Barrington Cl. WS5: Wals 2E **65**
WV10: Oxl 6G **15**
Barrington Rd. B45: Rubery 2E **157**
B92: Olton 3C **136**
Barr Lakes La. WS9: A'rdge 4A **50**
Barron Rd. B31: N'fld 4F **145**
Barrow Hill Rd. DY5: P'ntt 6G **75**
Barrow Ho. *B16: Edg* *2B 116*
(off Meyrick Wlk.)
Barrows La. B26: Yard 3C **120**
(not continuous)
Barrows Rd. B11: S'brk 5C **118**
Barrow Wlk. B5: Birm 4G **117**
(not continuous)
Barrs Cres. B64: Crad H 3H **111**
Barrs Rd. B64: Crad H 4G **111**
Barrs St. B68: O'bry 5G **97**
Barr St. B19: Hock 4E **101**
(not continuous)
DY3: Lwr G 4G **75**
Barry Jackson Twr. B6: Aston 2H **101**
Barry Rd. WS5: Wals 4G **49**
Barsham Cl. B5: Edg 5E **117**
Barsham Dr. DY5: Brie H 3G **109**
BARSTON 6A **154**
Barston La. B91: Sol 5D **152**
(Ravenshaw, not continuous)
B91: Sol 5B **152**
(Warwick Rd.)
B92: Bars, H Ard 4H **153**
CV7: Bal C 6D **154**
Barston Rd. B68: O'bry 4H **113**
Bartholomew Row B5: Birm 6H **101** (3G **5**)
Bartholomew St. B5: Birm 1H **117** (4G **5**)
Bartic Av. DY6: K'wfrd 5D **92**
Bartleet Rd. B67: Smeth 4B **98**
Bartlett Cl. DY4: Tip 4B **62**
Bartley Cl. B92: Olton 3D **136**
Bartley Dr. B31: N'fld 5C **130**
BARTLEY GREEN 4B **130**
Bartley Green Leisure Cen. 4A **130**
Bartley Ho. B32: Bart G 5B **130**
Bartley Woods B32: Bart G 3H **129**
Barton Cft. B28: Hall G 3F **149**
Barton Dr. B93: Know 6D **166**
Barton Ind. Pk. WV14: Bils 4G **45**
Barton La. DY6: W Hth 1A **92**
Barton Lodge Rd. B28: Hall G 3E **149**
Barton Pas. B3: Birm 4C **4**
Barton Rd. WV4: E'shll 1B **60**
Bartons Bank B6: Aston 2G **101**
Barton St. B70: W Brom 5H **79**
Bar Wlk. WS9: A'rdge 6E **23**
Barwell Cl. B93: Dorr 5A **166**
Barwell Ct. B9: Birm 1B **118**
Barwell Rd. B9: Birm 1B **118**
Barwick St. B3: Birm 6F **101** (3D **4**)
Basalt Cl. WS2: Wals 5G **31**
Basil Gro. B31: N'fld 3C **144**
Basil Rd. B31: N'fld 3C **144**
Baslow Cl. B33: Stech 5C **104**
WS3: Blox 4H **19**
Baslow Rd. WS3: Blox 4H **19**
Bason's La. B68: O'bry 4A **98**
Bassano Rd. B65: B'hth 2C **112**
Bassenthwaite Ct. DY6: K'wfrd 3B **92**
Bassett Cl. B76: Walm 1C **70**
WV4: Penn 5A **42**
WV12: W'hall 5D **30**
Bassett Cft. B10: Small H 3B **118**
Bassett Rd. B63: Crad 5C **110**
WS10: W'bry 2A **64**
(not continuous)
Bassetts Gro. B37: K'hrst 4B **106**
BASSETT'S POLE 1F **55**
Bassett St. WS2: Wals 2H **47**
Bassnage Rd. B63: Hale 3G **127**
Batch Cft. WV14: Bils 6F **45**
Batchcroft WS10: Darl 3D **46**
Batchelor Cl. DY8: Amb 3D **108**
Bateman Dr. B73: W Grn 3H **69**
Bateman Rd. B46: Col 6H **89**
BATEMAN'S GREEN 3G **161**
Batemans La. B47: H'wd, Wyt 4G **161**
Bates Cl. B76: Walm 6F **71**
Bates Gro. WV10: Wolv 4C **28**
Bate St. WS2: Wals 6C **32**
WV4: E'shll 2C **60**
Bath Av. WV1: Wolv 1F **43** (2A **170**)
Bath Ct. B15: Birm 2E **117**
B29: W Cas 6F **131**
Batheaston Cl. B38: K Nor 2H **159**
Bath Mdw. B63: Crad 6G **111**
Bath Pas. B5: Birm 2G **117** (6E **5**)
Bath Rd. DY4: Tip 2A **78**
DY5: Quar B 1C **110**
DY8: Stourb 6D **108**
WS1: Wals 3C **48**
WV1: Wolv 1F **43**
Bath Row B15: Birm 2E **117**
B69: O'bry 1D **96**
Bath St. B4: Birm 5G **101** (1E **5**)
DY2: Dud 1E **95**
DY3: Sed 4A **60**
WS1: Wals 2C **48**
WV1: Wolv 2A **44**
WV13: W'hall 2B **46**
WV14: Bils 6G **45**
Bath Wlk. B12: Bal H 6G **117**
Batmans Hill Rd. DY4: Tip 3G **61**
WV14: Bils 3G **61**
Batson Ri. DY5: Brie H 3E **109**
Battenhall Rd. B17: Harb 6E **115**
Battery Retail Pk. B29: S Oak 3A **132**
Battery Way B11: Tys 1E **135**
Battlefield Hill WV5: Wom 6A **58**
Battlefield La. WV5: Wom 1H **73**
Bavaro Gdns. DY5: Quar B 1C **110**
Baverstock Rd. B14: K Hth 5G **147**
Baxterley Grn. B76: Walm 4D **70**
B91: Sol 3B **150**
Baxter Rd. DY5: Brie H 1G **109**
Baxters Grn. B90: Shir 1G **163**
Baxters Rd. B90: Shir 1H **163**
Bayer St. WV14: Cose 5E **61**
Bayford Av. B26: Sheld 1G **137**
B31: Longb 3C **158**
Bayley Cres. WS10: Darl 3C **46**
Bayley Ho. WS8: Bwnhls 1B **22**
Bayleys La. DY4: Tip 5C **62**
Bayley Twr. B36: Hodg H 1C **104**
Baylie Ct. *DY8: Stourb* *6D 108*
(off Green St.)
Baylie St. DY8: Stourb 1D **124**
Baylis Av. WV11: Wed 1H **29**
Bayliss Av. WV4: E'shll 2C **60**
Bayliss Cl. B31: N'fld 2F **145**
WV14: Bils 4E **45**
Baynton Rd. WV12: W'hall 2C **30**
Bayston Av. WV3: Wolv 3C **42**
Bayston Rd. B14: K Hth 3G **147**
Bayswater Rd. B20: Hand 6F **83**
DY3: Lwr G 4H **75**
Bay Tree Cl. B38: K Nor 1H **159**
Baytree Cl. WS3: Blox 5G **19**
Baytree Rd. WS3: Blox 5G **19**
Baywell Cl. B90: M'path 2E **165**
Beach Av. B12: Bal H 6B **118**
WV14: Cose 2B **60**
Beach Brook Cl. B11: S'hll 6B **118**
Beachburn Way B20: Hand 4C **82**
Beach Cl. B31: N'fld 6G **145**
Beachcroft Rd. DY6: W Hth 6A **74**
Beach Dr. B63: Hale 6A **112**
Beach Rd. B11: S'hll 6B **118**
WV14: Bils 4F **45**
Beach St. B63: Hale 6A **112**
Beach Trade Cen. B12: Bal H 6B **118**
Beachwood Av. DY6: W Hth 6A **74**
Beacon Cl. B43: Gt Barr 4B **66**
B45: Rubery 3G **157**
B66: Smeth 2E **99**
Beacon Ct. B43: Gt Barr 4B **66**
B74: S'tly 3H **51**
Beacon Dr. WS1: Wals 3E **49**
Beacon Hgts. WS9: A'rdge 5D **50**
Beacon Hill B6: Aston 1G **101**
B45: Rubery 4F **157**
WS9: A'rdge 2E **51**
Beacon Ho. *B45: Rubery* *2E 157*
(off Callowbrook La.)
Beacon La. B45: Lick 6D **156**
B60: L Ash 6D **156**
DY3: Sed 4A **60**
Beacon M. B43: Gt Barr 4B **66**
Beacon Pas. *DY3: Sed* *5H 59*
(off High St.)
Beacon Ri. DY3: Sed 4A **60**
DY9: W'cte 1H **125**
WS9: A'rdge 6D **34**
Beacon Rd. B43: Gt Barr 3D **50**
B44: K'sdng 1A **68**
B73: Bold 4G **69**
WS5: Wals 6H **49**
WS9: A'rdge 3D **50**
WV12: W'hall 1C **30**
Beaconsfield Av. WV4: E'shll 5H **43**
Beaconsfield Ct. WS1: Wals 3F **49**
Beaconsfield Cres. B12: Bal H 6G **117**
Beaconsfield Dr. WV4: E'shll 5H **43**
Beaconsfield Rd. B12: Bal H 1G **133**
B74: S Cold 4H **53**
Beaconsfield St. B71: W Brom 2A **80**
Beacon St. WS1: Wals 2E **49**
WV14: Cose 4B **60**
Beacon Trad. Est. WS9: A'rdge 3C **34**
Beacon Vw. B45: Rubery 3F **157**
WS2: Wals 1F **47**
(not continuous)
Beacon Vw. Dr. B74: S'tly 6H **51**
Beaconview Ho. B71: W Brom 4D **64**
Beacon Vw. Rd. B71: W Brom 3C **64**
Beacon Way WS9: Wals W 4C **22**
Beakes Rd. B67: Smeth 6D **98**
Beaks Farm Gdns. B16: Edg 1H **115**
Beaks Hill Rd. B38: K Nor 6A **146**
Beak St. B1: Birm 1F **117** (5D **4**)
Beale Cl. B35: Cas V 5E **87**
Beale Ho. B16: Edg 2B **116**
Beales St. B6: Aston 1B **102**
Beale St. DY8: Stourb 6D **108**
Bealeys Av. WV11: Wed 1E **29**
Bealeys Cl. WS3: Blox 4G **19**
Bealeys Fold *WV11: Wed* *4F 29*
(off Nicholls Fold)
Bealeys La. WS3: Blox 4G **19**
Beamans Cl. B92: Olton 1E **137**
Beaminster Rd. B91: Sol 3E **151**
Beamish La. WV8: Cod W 2A **12**
Beamont Cl. DY4: Tip 1G **77**
Bean Cft. B32: Bart G 2A **130**
Bean Rd. DY2: Dud 1F **95**
DY4: Tip 1E **77**
Bean Rd. Ind. Est. DY4: Tip 1E **77**
Beardmore Rd. B72: W Grn 5A **70**
Bearley Cft. B90: Shir 1A **164**
Bearmore Rd. B64: Old H 2G **111**
Bearnett Dr. WV4: Penn 3A **58**
Bearnett La. WV4: Lwr P 4H **57**
WV5: Wom 4H **57**
BEAR WOOD 2E **115**
Bearwood Ho. B66: Smeth 5E **99**
Bearwood Rd. B66: Smeth 2E **115**
Bearwood Shop. Cen. B66: Smeth 2E **115**
Beasley Gro. B43: Gt Barr 4D **66**
Beaton Cl. WV13: W'hall 1G **45**

Beaton Rd.—Bellis St.

Beaton Rd. B74: Four O . . . 6G **37**
Beatrice St. WS3: Blox. . . . 3A **32**
Beatrice Wlk. B69: Tiv . . . 5A **78**
Beatty Ho. DY4: Tip . . . 5A **62**
Beaubrook Gdns. DY8: Word . . . 6C **92**
Beauchamp Av. B20: Hand. . . . 2B **82**
Beauchamp Cl. B37: Chel W . . . 1D **122**
B76: Walm . . . 6F **71**
Beauchamp Rd. B13: Mose . . . 2B **148**
B91: Sol . . . 2F **151**
Beaudesert Cl. B47: H'wd . . . 3A **162**
Beaudesert Rd. B20: Hand . . . 1D **100**
B47: H'wd . . . 3A **162**
Beaufort Av. B34: Hodg H . . . 3B **104**
Beaufort Pk. B8: W End . . . 4B **104**
Beaufort Rd. B16: Edg . . . 2B **116**
B23: Erd . . . 5E **85**
Beaufort Way WS9: A'rdge. . . . 5D **34**
Beaulieu Av. DY6: K'wfrd. . . . 5D **92**
Beaumaris Cl. DY1: Dud . . . 4B **76**
Beaumont Cl. WS6: Gt Wyr . . . 3F **7**
Beaumont Dr. B17: Harb. . . . 1F **131**
DY5: Brie H. . . . 4F **109**
Beaumont Gdns. B18: Hock. . . . 3B **100**
Beaumont Gro. B91: Sol . . . 2D **150**
Beaumont Pk. B30: K Nor . . . 3B **146**
Beaumont Rd. B30: B'vlle . . . 1A **146**
B62: B'hth . . . 3E **113**
WS6: Gt Wyr . . . 3F **7**
WS10: W'bry . . . 1F **63**
Beaumont Way WS11: Nort C . . . 1E **9**
Beausale Dr. B93: Know . . . 2D **166**
Beauty Bank B64: Crad H. . . . 3A **112**
Beauty Bank Cres. DY8: Stourb. . . . 5C **108**
Beaver Cl. WV11: Wed . . . 4H **29**
Bebington Cl. WV8: Pend . . . 1D **26**
Beccles Dr. WV13: W'hall . . . 3H **45**
Beckbury Av. WV4: Penn . . . 6A **42**
Beckbury Rd. B29: W Cas . . . 4E **131**
Beck Cl. B66: Smeth. . . . 5E **99**
Beckenham Av. B44: K'sdng . . . 4A **68**
Beckensall Cl. DY1: Dud . . . 6D **76**
Becket Cl. B74: Four O . . . 3F **37**
Beckett St. WV14: Bils. . . . 5G **45**
Beckfield Cl. B14: K Hth . . . 5G **147**
WS4: S'fld . . . 1G **33**
Beckford Cft. B93: Dorr . . . 6B **166**
Beckman Rd. DY9: Pedm. . . . 3G **125**
Beckminster Rd. WV3: Wolv . . . 4D **42**
Beconsfield Cl. B93: Dorr . . . 6G **167**
Becton Gro. B42: Gt Barr . . . 6F **67**
Bedcote Pl. DY8: Stourb. . . . 6F **109**
Beddoe Cl. DY4: Tip. . . . 2D **78**
Beddow Av. WV14: Cose . . . 6E **61**
Beddows Rd. WS3: Wals . . . 4C **32**
Bedford Dr. B75: S Cold . . . 5C **54**
Bedford Ho. B36: Cas B . . . 3D **106**
WV1: Wolv. . . . 5G **27**
Bedford Rd. B11: S'brk . . . 2A **118**
B71: W Brom . . . 6H **63**
B75: S Cold . . . 5C **54**
Bedford St. DY4: Tip . . . 2B **78**
WV1: Wolv. . . . 4D **44**
Bedford Ter. B19: Loz. . . . 1F **101**
Bedlam Wood Rd. B31: Longb . . . 6A **144**
Bedworth Cft. DY4: Tip. . . . 3B **78**
Bedworth Gro. B9: Bord G. . . . 1H **119**
Beebee Rd. WS10: W'bry. . . . 5F **47**
Beecham Bus. Pk. WS9: A'rdge. . . . 1C **34**
Beecham Cl. WS9: A'rdge . . . 1C **34**
Beech Av. B12: Bal H . . . 6A **118**
B32: Quin. . . . 4B **114**
B37: Chel W. . . . 2D **122**
B62: B'hth . . . 3C **112**
Beech Cl. B75: Four O . . . 5G **37**
DY3: Sed . . . 4A **60**
WV10: Oxl . . . 1F **27**
Beech Ct. B8: Salt. . . . 4E **103**
B30: K Nor . . . 3A **146**
B43: Gt Barr. . . . 4H **65**
B45: Redn . . . 2B **158**
B66: Smeth . . . 1A **98**
B73: Bold . . . 5F **69**
B91: Sol. . . . 2H **151**
DY8: Stourb . . . 1F **125**
WS1: Wals . . . 3E **49**
WS6: Gt Wyr . . . 1G **7**
Beech Cres. DY4: Tip. . . . 5C **62**
WS10: W'bry . . . 6F **47**
Beechcroft B15: Edg. . . . 4C **116**
Beechcroft Av. B28: Hall G. . . . 1G **149**
Beechcroft Ct. B74: Four O . . . 2G **53**
Beechcroft Cres. B74: S'tly. . . . 2F **51**
Beechcroft Est. B63: Crad . . . 5E **111**
Beechcroft Pl. WV10: Oxl . . . 2G **27**
Beechcroft Rd. B36: Cas B . . . 1F **105**
B64: Old H . . . 2G **111**
Beechdale B68: O'bry . . . 4H **113**
Beechdale Av. B44: Gt Barr. . . . 3G **67**
Beech Dene Gro. B23: Erd . . . 2E **85**
Beecher Pl. B63: Crad . . . 6F **111**
Beecher Rd. B63: Crad. . . . 6F **111**
Beecher Rd. E. B63: Crad. . . . 6F **111**
Beecher St. B63: Crad . . . 6E **111**
Beeches, The B15: Edg . . . 3E **117**
B70: W Brom . . . 5C **80**
B74: Four O . . . 5D **36**
WV1: Wolv . . . 6E **27**
Beeches Av. B27: A Grn. . . . 1A **136**
Beeches Cl. B45: Rubery. . . . 2D **156**
DY6: K'wfrd . . . 4B **92**
Beeches Ct. B45: Redn . . . 2H **157**
Beeches Dr. B24: Erd . . . 2A **86**
Beeches Farm Dr. B31: Longb . . . 2E **159**
Beeches Pl. WS3: Blox . . . 2B **32**
Beeches Rd. B42: Gt Barr . . . 6D **66**
B65: B'hth . . . 2B **112**
B68: O'bry . . . 6A **98**
B70: W Brom . . . 4C **80**
(not continuous)
WS3: Blox . . . 3B **32**
Beeches Vw. Av. B63: Crad . . . 1E **127**
Beeches Wlk. B73: W Grn. . . . 2H **69**
Beeches Way B31: Longb . . . 2E **159**
Beechey Cl. B43: Gt Barr . . . 6F **51**
Beech Farm Cft. B31: N'fld. . . . 4E **145**
Beechfield Av. B11: S'brk . . . 5B **118**
Beechfield Cl. B62: B'hth. . . . 3C **112**
Beechfield Gro. WV14: Cose . . . 6D **60**
Beechfield Rd. B11: S'brk . . . 5B **118**
B67: Smeth . . . 5D **98**
Beech Gdns. WV8: Cod . . . 5F **13**
Beech Ga. B74: Lit A . . . 4B **36**
Beechglade B20: Hand. . . . 3B **82**
Beech Grn. DY1: Dud. . . . 2C **76**
Beech Gro. B14: K Hth. . . . 2A **148**
Beech Hill Rd. B72: W Grn . . . 6A **70**
Beech Ho. *B31: N'fld . . . 4F 145*
(off Church Rd.)
B91: Sol. . . . 5D **150**
Beechhouse La. WV5: Seis . . . 5A **56**
Beech Hurst B38: K Nor . . . 1A **160**
Beech Hurst Gdns. WV5: Seis . . . 3A **56**
BEECH LANES . . . 4D **114**
Beech M. B64: Old H . . . 1G **111**
Beechmore Rd. B26: Sheld . . . 6D **120**
Beechmount Dr. B23: Erd . . . 1G **85**
Beechnut Cl. B91: Sol . . . 2H **151**
Beechnut La. B91: Sol . . . 3A **152**
(not continuous)
Beech Rd. B23: Erd . . . 6F **69**
B30: B'vlle . . . 6A **132**
B47: H'wd . . . 3B **162**
B69: Tiv . . . 1A **96**
DY1: Dud . . . 3E **77**
DY6: K'wfrd . . . 4C **92**
DY8: Stourb . . . 2C **124**
WS10: W'bry . . . 6F **47**
WV10: Oxl . . . 1F **27**
WV13: W'hall . . . 1G **45**
Beech St. WV14: Cose . . . 5E **61**
Beech Tree Av. WV11: Wed . . . 1E **29**
Beech Tree Cl. DY6: K'wfrd . . . 1C **92**
Beechtree Rd. WS9: Wals W . . . 4B **22**
Beech Wlk. B38: K Nor . . . 1B **160**
Beech Way B66: Smeth . . . 4F **99**
Beechwood B20: Hand. . . . 4A **82**
Beechwood Av. WV11: Wed. . . . 1D **28**
Beechwood Cl. B90: Ches G . . . 5C **164**
WS3: Blox . . . 4H **19**
Beechwood Ct. B30: K Nor. . . . 4E **147**
WV6: Tett . . . 6A **26**
Beechwood Cft. B74: Lit A. . . . 4D **36**
Beechwood Dr. WV6: Tett . . . 1G **41**
Beechwood Pk. Rd. B91: Sol. . . . 1C **150**
Beechwood Rd. B14: K Hth . . . 2H **147**
B43: Gt Barr . . . 4B **66**
B67: Smeth . . . 3C **114**
B70: W Brom . . . 4H **79**
DY2: Dud . . . 6G **77**
Beehive La. B76: Curd . . . 1E **89**
Beehive Wlk. DY4: Tip. . . . 2G **77**
Bee La. WV10: F'hses . . . 4H **15**
Beeston Cl. B6: Aston . . . 2A **102**
DY5: Brie H . . . 3H **109**
Beeton Rd. B18: Win G . . . 3A **100**
Beet St. B65: B'hth. . . . 2C **112**
Beever Rd. DY4: Tip . . . 6D **62**
Beggars Bush La. WV5: Wom . . . 2H **73**
Beighton Cl. B74: Four O . . . 3F **37**
Beilby Rd. B30: Stir . . . 1D **146**
Belbroughton Rd. B63: Hale . . . 3H **127**
DY8: Stourb . . . 2C **124**
Belcher's La. B9: Bord G . . . 1G **119**
Beldray Pk. WV14: Bils . . . 5G **45**
Beldray Rd. WV14: Bils . . . 5G **45**
Belfont Trad. Est. B62: Hale. . . . 1C **128**
Belfry, The WV6: Pert . . . 5D **24**
Belfry Cl. WS3: Blox . . . 4G **19**
Belfry Dr. DY8: Woll . . . 5C **108**
Belgrade Rd. WV10: Oxl. . . . 6F **15**
Belgrave Ct. DY6: K'wfrd . . . 5D **92**
Belgrave Interchange B5: Birm . . . 4F **117**
Belgrave Middleway B5: Birm. . . . 4G **117**
B12: Birm. . . . 4G **117**
Belgrave Rd. B62: B'hth . . . 3D **112**
Belgrave Ter. B21: Hand . . . 2C **100**
Belgrave Wlk. WS2: Wals . . . 6H **31**
Belgravia Cl. B5: Bal H . . . 4G **117**
Belgravia Cl. Walkway
B5: Bal H . . . 4G **117**
Belgravia Ct. B37: K'hrst . . . 4C **106**
Belgrove Cl. B15: Edg . . . 5A **116**
Belinda Cl. WV13: W'hall. . . . 6H **29**
Bellamy Cl. B90: Shir. . . . 6B **150**
Bellamy Farm Rd. B90: Shir . . . 6B **150**
Bellamy La. WV11: Wed . . . 2E **29**
Bell Av. WV13: W'hall . . . 1A **46**
Bell Barn Rd. B15: Birm. . . . 3E **117**
Bell Barn Shop. Cen. B15: Birm . . . 2E **117**
Bell Cl. B9: Bord G. . . . 1E **119**
B36: Cas B. . . . 3D **106**
WS10: Darl . . . 4D **46**
Bellcroft B16: Birm. . . . 1D **116**
Bell Dr. B8: Salt . . . 6F **103**
WS5: Wals . . . 6E **49**
Bellefield Av. B18: Win G . . . 5A **100**
Bellefield Rd. B18: Win G . . . 5A **100**
Belle Isle DY5: Brie H . . . 6G **93**
Bellemere Rd. B92: H Ard . . . 2B **154**
Bellencroft Gdns. WV3: Wolv . . . 4A **42**
Bell End B65: Row R . . . 6C **96**
Bellevale B63: Hale . . . 6G **111**
Belle Vue DY8: Word. . . . 1A **108**
Bellevue B5: Bal H . . . 4F **117**
Bellevue Av. B16: Edg . . . 5H **99**
Belle Vue Dr. B62: Hale . . . 5D **112**
Belle Vue Gdns. B65: Row R. . . . 6C **96**
Belle Vue Rd. B65: Row R. . . . 1C **112**
DY5: Quar B. . . . 2C **110**
Bellevue Rd. B26: Sheld. . . . 4F **121**
WV14: Bils . . . 3A **62**
Bellevue St. WV14: Cose . . . 3B **60**
Belle Vue Ter. B92: H Ard . . . 1A **154**
Belle Wlk. B13: Mose . . . 3B **134**
Bellfield B31: N'fld. . . . 3D **144**
Bellfield Ho. *B14: K Hth. . . . 6F 147*
(off Thornham Way)
Bell Flwer Dr. WS5: Wals . . . 2D **64**
Bell Fold B68: O'bry . . . 3A **98**
BELL GREEN
Birmingham . . . 3D **160**
Bell Grn. La. B38: Head H . . . 4D **160**
Bell Heather Rd. WS8: Clay. . . . 1H **21**
Bell Heath Way B32: Bart G. . . . 3G **129**
Bell Hill B31: N'fld . . . 2E **145**
Bell Holloway B31: N'fld . . . 2D **144**
Bellington Cft. B90: M'path . . . 3E **165**
Bell Inn Shop. Cen., The
B31: N'fld . . . 3E **145**
Bellis St. B16: Edg . . . 2B **116**

180 A-Z Birmingham

Bell La. B31: N'fld 3E **145**
   B33: Kitts G 2A **122**
   WS3: Blox 5G **19**
   WS5: Wals 1D **64**
Bellman Cl. WS10: Darl 4D **46**
Bell Mdw. DY9: Pedm 5F **125**
Bell Mdw. Way B14: K Hth 5G **147**
   (not continuous)
Bell Pl. WV2: Wolv 3G **43** (6B **170**)
Bell Rd. DY2: Neth 4E **95**
   WS5: Wals 5H **49**
   WV5: Try 4C **56**
Bells Farm Cl. B14: K Hth 5E **147**
Bellsize Cl. WS11: Nort C 1D **8**
Bells La. B14: K Hth 5D **146**
   DY8: Word 2B **108**
Bells Moor Rd. B70: W Brom 1G **79**
Bell St. B70: W Brom 5B **80**
   DY4: Tip 2G **77**
   DY5: Brie H 1H **109**
   DY5: P'ntt 3H **93**
     (Belmont Rd.)
   DY5: P'ntt 2H **93**
     (Hartland St.)
   DY8: Stourb 6D **108**
   WS10: Darl 5G **47**
   WV1: Wolv 2G **43** (4B **170**)
   WV14: Bils 5E **45**
   WV14: Cose 3E **61**
Bell St. Sth. DY5: Brie H 1H **109**
Bell Wlk. B37: F'bri 2B **122**
Bell Wharf Pl. WS5: Wals 5G **49**
Bellwood Rd. B31: N'fld 3D **144**
Belmont Cl. DY4: Tip 1H **77**
   WS9: A'rdge 3C **34**
   WS11: Cann 1G **7**
Belmont Covert B31: N'fld 2F **145**
Belmont Cres. B31: N'fld 1F **145**
Belmont Gdns. WV14: Bils 1A **62**
Belmont Pas. B9: Birm. 1A **118**
Belmont Rd. B21: Hand 1G **99**
   B45: Rubery 3G **157**
   B66: Smeth 1E **115**
   DY5: P'ntt 3H **93**
   DY9: W'cte 6A **110**
   WV4: Penn 6E **43**
Belmont Rd. E. B21: Hand. 1G **99**
Belmont Row B4: Birm 6A **102** (2H **5**)
Belmont St. WV14: Bils 1A **62**
Belper, The DY1: Dud 6D **76**
Belper Ent. Pk. B70: W Brom. 3F **79**
Belper Rd. B70: W Brom 4F **79**
   WS3: Blox 4A **20**
Belper Row DY2: Neth 5G **95**
Belstone Cl. B14: K Hth 1F **147**
Belton Av. WV11: Wed 6D **16**
Belton Gro. B45: Redn 1A **158**
Belvedere Av. WV4: Penn. 6F **43**
Belvedere Cl. DY6: K'wfrd 5D **92**
   WS7: Chase 1B **10**
Belvedere Gdns. WV6: Tett 2C **26**
Belvedere Rd. B24: Erd 5G **85**
Belvide Gdns. WV8: Cod 3F **13**
Belvide Gro. B29: W Cas 5F **131**
Belvidere Gdns. B11: S'hll 1C **134**
Belvidere Rd. WS1: Wals 3D **48**
Belvoir Cl. DY1: Dud 5A **76**
Belwell Dr. B74: Four O 1G **53**
Belwell La. B74: Four O 1G **53**
Bembridge Cl. WV12: W'hall 1B **30**
Bembridge Rd. B33: Yard 6E **105**
Benacre Dr. B5: Birm 1H **117** (4H **5**)
Benbeck Gro. DY4: Tip 2E **77**
Bencroft WV8: Bilb 3H **13**
Bendall Rd. B44: K'sdng 3B **68**
Benedon Rd. B26: Sheld 4E **121**
Benmore Av. B5: Bal H 5F **117**
Bennett Av. DY1: Dud 1D **76**
Bennett Rd. B74: Four O 6D **36**
Bennett's Fold WV3: Wolv . . . 2G **43** (4A **170**)
Bennett's Hill B2: Birm . . . 1F **117** (4D **4**)
   DY2: Dud 1G **95**
Bennett's La. WV6: Tres. 3A **40**
Bennett's Rd. B8: Salt 3D **102**
Bennett St. B19: Loz 1F **101**
Ben Nevis Way DY8: Amb 5E **109**
Bennitt Cl. B70: W Brom 6A **80**

Benson Av. WV4: Penn 6G **43**
Benson Cl. WV6: Pert. 4E **25**
Benson Ind. Est. B18: Hock 3B **100**
Benson Rd. B14: K Hth 6B **148**
   B18: Hock 3B **100**
Bent Av. B32: Quin 5B **114**
Bentham Ct. B31: N'fld 2D **144**
BENTLEY 6F **31**
Bentley Bridge Leisure Pk. 5D **28**
Bentley Bri. Way WV11: Wed 5D **28**
Bentley Ct. B76: Walm. 5D **70**
Bentley Dr. WS2: Wals 1H **47**
   WV8: Cod 3F **13**
Bentley Farm Cl. B93: Ben H 5A **166**
Bentley Gro. B29: W Cas 5D **130**
BENTLEY HEATH 4B **166**
Bentley Heath Cotts. B93: Know . . . 4B **166**
Bentley La. WS2: Wals 5G **31**
   WV12: W'hall 4D **30**
Bentley La. Ind. Pk. WS2: Wals 6G **31**
Bentley Mill Cl. WS2: Wals 2F **47**
Bentley Mill La. WS2: Wals 2F **47**
Bentley Mill Way WS2: Wals 2F **47**
Bentley New Dr. WS2: Wals 6H **31**
Bentley Pl. WS2: Wals 1H **47**
Bentley Rd. B36: Cas B 2H **105**
   WV10: Bush 5A **16**
Bentley Rd. Nth. WS2: Wals 2E **47**
Bentley Rd. Sth. WS10: Darl 3D **46**
Bentmead Gro. B38: K Nor 6C **146**
Benton Av. B11: S'hll 5C **118**
Benton Cl. WV12: W'hall 5D **30**
Benton Cres. WS3: Blox. 5B **20**
Benton Rd. B11: S'brk 5C **118**
Bentons La. WS6: Gt Wyr 4G **7**
Bentons Mill Cft. B7: Nech. 1C **102**
Bent St. DY5: Brie H. 5H **93**
Ben Willetts Wlk. B65: B'hth 2C **112**
Benyon Cen., The WS2: Wals 2G **31**
Beoley Cl. B72: W Grn 4A **70**
Beoley Gro. B45: Rubery 2F **157**
Berberry Cl. B30: B'vlle 1H **145**
Beresford Cres. B70: W Brom 4H **79**
Beresford Dr. B73: Bold. 4G **69**
Beresford Rd. B69: O'bry 2A **98**
   WS3: Blox 1C **32**
Berets, The B75: S Cold 5D **54**
Bericote Cft. B27: A Grn 2B **136**
Berkeley Cl. WV6: Pert. 6F **25**
Berkeley Dr. DY6: K'wfrd 2A **92**
Berkeley M. B25: Yard. 4G **119**
Berkeley Pct. B14: K Hth 5H **147**
Berkeley Rd. B25: Yard 4G **119**
   B90: Shir 4F **149**
Berkeley Rd. E. B25: Yard 4H **119**
Berkeley St. WS2: Wals 4H **47**
Berkley Cl. WS2: Wals 6F **31**
Berkley Ct. B1: Birm 2E **117** (6A **4**)
Berkley Cres. B13: Mose 4C **134**
Berkley Ho. B23: Erd 1F **85**
Berkley St. B1: Birm 1E **117** (5A **4**)
Berkshire, The WS3: Blox 4G **19**
Berkshire Cl. B71: W Brom 6H **63**
Berkshire Cres. WS10: W'bry 1A **64**
Berkswell Cl. B74: Four O 5E **37**
   B91: Sol 5F **137**
   DY1: Dud 4A **76**
Berkswell Hall CV7: Berk. 4H **155**
Berkswell Rd. B24: Erd 3H **85**
Bermuda Cl. DY1: Dud. 1D **76**
Bernard Pl. B18: Hock 4B **100**
Bernard Rd. B17: Edg. 1F **115**
   B68: O'bry 1A **114**
   DY4: Tip 6B **62**
Bernard St. B71: W Brom 3A **80**
   WS1: Wals 3E **49**
Berners St. B19: Loz. 2F **101**
Bernhard Dr. B21: Hand 1A **100**
Bernwall Cl. DY8: Stourb. 1D **124**
Berrandale Rd. B36: Hodg H 1D **104**
Berrington Dr. WV14: Cose 5D **60**
Berrington Wlk. B5: Birm 4G **117**
Berrow Cott. Homes B93: Know. . . . 3E **167**
Berrow Dr. B15: Edg. 4A **116**
Berrowside Rd. B34: S End 3A **106**
Berry Av. WS10: Darl 6B **46**
Berrybush Gdns. DY3: Sed 6A **60**

Berry Cl. B19: Hock 3F **101**
Berry Cres. WS5: Wals 1G **65**
Berry Dr. B66: Smeth 3E **99**
   WS9: A'rdge 4A **34**
Berryfield Rd. B26: Sheld 5H **121**
Berryfields WS9: A'rdge 4A **34**
   WS9: Ston 2G **23**
Berryfields Rd. B76: Walm 2D **70**
Berry Hall La. B91: Cath B, Sol . . . 3C **152**
Berrymound Vw. B47: H'wd 2C **162**
Berry Rd. B8: Salt. 4E **103**
   DY1: Dud 2E **77**
Berry St. B18: Hock 3B **100**
   WV1: Wolv 1H **43** (3C **170**)
Bertha Rd. B11: S'brk 6D **118**
Bertram Cl. DY4: Tip 4C **62**
Bertram Rd. B9: Small H 2D **118**
   B67: Smeth 3C **98**
Berwick Gro. B31: N'fld 4B **144**
   B43: Gt Barr. 1D **66**
Berwicks La. B37: Chel W 2D **122**
   (not continuous)
Berwood Farm Rd. B72: W Grn. 1A **86**
Berwood Gdns. B24: Erd 2A **86**
Berwood Gro. B92: Olton 4F **137**
Berwood La. B24: Erd 4C **86**
Berwood Pk. B35: Cas V 5E **87**
Berwood Rd. B72: W Grn. 1B **86**
Berwyn Gro. WS6: C Hay 2F **7**
Besant Gro. B27: A Grn 4G **135**
Besbury Cl. B93: Dorr 6F **167**
BESCOT 5A **48**
Bescot Cres. WS1: Wals 5B **48**
Bescot Cft. B42: Gt Barr. 1D **82**
Bescot Dr. WS2: Wals 5H **47**
Bescot Ind. Est. WS10: W'bry 1D **62**
Bescot Rd. WS2: Wals 5H **47**
Bescot Stadium 5B **48**
Bescot Stadium Station (Rail) 6B **48**
Bescot St. WS1: Wals 4B **48**
Besford Gro. B31: N'fld 4B **144**
   B90: M'path 3F **165**
Besom Way WS6: C Hay 3C **6**
Bessborough Rd. B25: Yard. 3B **120**
Best Rd. WV14: Bils 4F **45**
Best St. B64: Old H 1H **111**
Beswick Gro. B33: Kitts G 5E **105**
Beta Gro. B14: Yard W 3C **148**
Betjeman Pl. WV10: Bush 6C **16**
Betley Gro. B33: Stech 4E **105**
Betony Cl. WS5: Wals 2E **65**
Betsham Cl. B44: K'sdng 4B **68**
Bettany Glade WV10: Bush 3A **16**
Betteridge Dr. B76: Walm 1C **70**
Betton Rd. B14: K Hth 2G **147**
Bett Rd. B20: Hand. 4B **82**
Betty's La. WS11: Nort C 1D **8**
Beulah Ct. B63: Hale 1A **128**
Bevan Av. WV4: E'shll 1A **60**
Bevan Cl. WS4: S'fld 6G **21**
   WV14: Bils 5H **45**
Bevan Ind. Est. DY5: Brie H 1E **109**
Bevan Rd. DY4: Tip 3B **78**
   DY5: Brie H 1E **109**
Bevan Way B66: Smeth 1D **98**
Beverley Cl. B72: W Grn 6A **70**
   CV7: Bal C 5H **169**
Beverley Ct. Rd. B32: Quin 5A **114**
Beverley Cres. WV4: E'shll 1B **60**
Beverley Cft. B23: Erd 6D **84**
Beverley Dr. DY6: K'wfrd 2A **92**
Beverley Gro. B26: Sheld 6F **121**
Beverley Rd. B45: Rubery 2G **157**
   B71: W Brom 4B **64**
Beverston Rd. DY4: Tip 3B **62**
   WV6: Pert 5G **25**
Bevington Rd. B6: Aston 6H **83**
Bevin Rd. WS2: Wals 6E **31**
Bevis Gro. B44: Gt Barr 2H **67**
Bewdley Av. B12: Bal H 5A **118**
Bewdley Dr. WV1: Wolv. 1D **44**
Bewdley Ho. B26: Yard. 1E **121**
Bewdley Rd. B30: Stir 5D **132**
Bewdley Vs. B18: Win G 5H **99**
   (off Cape St.)
Bewlay Cl. DY5: Brie H 4F **109**
Bewley Rd. WV12: W'hall 5D **30**

Bewlys Av.—Birmingham Rd.

Bewlys Av. B20: Hand . . . 3A **82**
Bexley Gro. B71: W Brom . . . 6C **64**
Bexley Rd. B44: K'sdng . . . 5B **68**
Bhylls Cres. WV3: Wolv . . . 4A **42**
Bhylls La. WV3: Wolv . . . 3H **41**
Bibbey's Grn. WV10: Bush . . . 3B **16**
Bibsworth Av. B13: Mose . . . 5D **134**
Bibury Rd. B28: Hall G . . . 6E **135**
BICC & Symphony Hall . . . 1E **117** (4A 4)
Bicester Sq. B35: Cas V . . . 3F **87**
BICKENHILL . . . 4F **139**
Bickenhill Grn. Ct. B92: Bick . . . 4F **139**
Bickenhill La. B37: Mars G . . . 5E **123**
(not continuous)
B92: Cath B . . . 1E **153**
Bickenhill Pk. Rd. B92: Olton . . . 4B **136**
Bickenhill Parkway B40: Nat E C . . . 5F **123**
Bickenhill Rd. B37: Mars G . . . 4C **122**
Bickenhill Trad. Est. B40: Mars G . . . 6F **123**
Bickford Rd. B6: Witt . . . 6A **84**
WV10: Wolv . . . 4B **28**
Bickington Rd. B32: Bart G . . . 4B **130**
Bickley Av. B11: S'brk . . . 5C **118**
B74: Four O . . . 4E **37**
Bickley Gro. B26: Sheld . . . 6F **121**
Bickley Rd. WS4: Rus . . . 2G **33**
WV14: Bils . . . 4A **46**
Bicknell Cft. B14: K Hth . . . 5G **147**
Bickton Cl. B24: Erd . . . 1A **86**
Biddings La. WV14: Cose . . . 3D **60**
Biddlestone Gro. WS5: Wals . . . 1G **65**
Biddlestone Pl. WS10: Darl . . . 4B **46**
Biddulph Ct. B73: S Cold . . . 3G **69**
Bideford Dr. B29: S Oak . . . 4G **131**
Bideford Rd. B66: Smeth . . . 4F **99**
Bidford Cl. B90: Shir . . . 5B **150**
Bidford Rd. B31: N'fld . . . 4C **144**
Bierton Rd. B25: Yard . . . 3A **120**
Biggin Cl. B35: Cas V . . . 4E **87**
WV6: Pert . . . 4E **25**
Big Peg, The B18: Birm . . . 5E **101** (1A 4)
Bigwood Dr. B32: Bart G . . . 4B **130**
B75: S Cold . . . 5E **55**
Bilberry Cres. B76: Walm . . . 2C **70**
Bilberry Dr. B45: Rubery . . . 3G **157**
Bilberry Rd. B14: K Hth . . . 1E **147**
Bilboe Rd. WV14: Bils . . . 2H **61**
BILBROOK . . . 3H **13**
Bilbrook Ct. WV8: Bilb . . . 4H **13**
Bilbrook Gro. B29: W Cas . . . 3D **130**
WV8: Bilb . . . 4H **13**
Bilbrook Ho. WV8: Bilb . . . 4H **13**
Bilbrook Rd. WV8: Bilb, Cod . . . 3G **13**
(not continuous)
Bilbrook Station (Rail) . . . 5H **13**
Bilhay La. B70: W Brom . . . 2G **79**
Bilhay St. B70: W Brom . . . 2G **79**
Billau Rd. WV14: Cose . . . 3F **61**
BILLESLEY . . . 1C **148**
Billesley Indoor Tennis Cen. . . . 6B **134**
Billesley La. B13: Mose . . . 5H **133**
Billingham Cl. B91: Sol . . . 1F **165**
Billingsley Rd. B26: Yard . . . 3E **121**
Bills La. B90: Shir . . . 6F **149**
Billsmore Grn. B92: Sol . . . 6G **137**
Bills St. WS10: Darl . . . 4E **47**
Billy Buns La. WV5: Wom . . . 5G **57**
Billy Wright Cl. WV4: Penn . . . 5C **42**
Bilport La. WS10: W'bry . . . 5F **63**
BILSTON . . . 6H **45**
Bilston Central Ind. Est. WV14: Bils . . . 6G **45**
Bilston Central (MM) . . . 6F **45**
Bilston Craft Gallery & Mus. . . . 5G **45**
Bilston Ind. Est. WV14: Bils . . . 6A **46**
Bilston Key Ind. Est. WV14: Bils . . . 6H **45**
Bilston Leisure Cen. . . . 5F **45**
Bilston Rd. DY4: Tip . . . 3B **62**
WS10: W'bry . . . 2D **62**
WV2: Wolv . . . 2A **44** (4D 170)
WV13: W'hall . . . 4A **46**
Bilston St. DY3: Sed . . . 5H **59**
WS10: Darl . . . 5D **46**
(not continuous)
WV1: Wolv . . . 2H **43** (4C 170)
WV13: W'hall . . . 2A **46**
Bilston St. Island
WV1: Wolv . . . 2H **43** (4D 170)
Bilton Grange Rd. B26: Yard . . . 4D **120**
Bilton Ind. Est. B38: K Nor . . . 1A **160**
Binbrook Rd. WV12: W'hall . . . 5D **30**
Bincomb Av. B26: Sheld . . . 5F **121**
Binfield St. DY4: Tip . . . 3A **78**
Bingley Av. B8: W End . . . 5H **103**
Bingley Ent. Cen. *WV3: Wolv . . . 3E 43*
(off Norfolk Rd.)
Bingley St. WV3: Wolv . . . 3E **43**
Binley Cl. B25: Yard . . . 5B **120**
B90: Shir . . . 1G **163**
Binstead Rd. B44: K'sdng . . . 3A **68**
Binswood Rd. B62: Quin . . . 4G **113**
Binton Cft. B13: Mose . . . 5H **133**
Binton Rd. B90: Shir . . . 6F **149**
Birbeck Ho. B36: Cas B . . . 3D **106**
Birbeck Pl. DY5: P'ntt . . . 3F **93**
Birchall St. B12: Birm . . . 2H **117**
Birch Av. B31: Longb . . . 6A **144**
DY5: Quar B . . . 1C **110**
WS8: Bwnhls . . . 5A **10**
Birch Cl. B17: Harb . . . 6H **115**
B30: B'vlle . . . 1H **145**
B76: Walm . . . 3D **70**
Birch Coppice DY5: Quar B . . . 2C **110**
(not continuous)
WV5: Wom . . . 1E **73**
Birchcoppice Gdns. WV12: W'hall . . . 5E **31**
Birch Ct. B30: K Nor . . . 3A **146**
B66: Smeth . . . 1B **98**
WS4: Wals . . . 5E 33
(off Lichfield Rd.)
WV1: Wolv . . . 5G **27**
Birch Cres. B69: Tiv . . . 6A **78**
Birch Cft. B24: Erd . . . 2B **86**
B37: Chel W . . . 2E **123**
WS9: A'rdge . . . 1E **35**
Birchcroft B66: Smeth . . . 4G **99**
Birch Cft. Rd. B75: S Cold . . . 4B **54**
Birchdale WV14: Bils . . . 4F **45**
Birchdale Av. B23: Erd . . . 3E **85**
Birchdale Rd. B23: Erd . . . 2D **84**
Birch Dr. B62: B'hth . . . 2E **113**
B74: Lit A . . . 4D **36**
B75: S Cold . . . 4D **54**
DY8: Stourb . . . 5C **108**
Birches Av. WV8: Bilb . . . 6A **14**
Birches Barn Av. WV3: Wolv . . . 4D **42**
Birches Barn Rd. WV3: Wolv . . . 3D **42**
Birches Cl. B13: Mose . . . 4H **133**
BIRCHES GREEN . . . 5G **85**
Birches Grn. Rd. B24: Erd . . . 5H **85**
Birches Pk. Rd. WV8: Cod . . . 5G **13**
Birches Ri. WV13: W'hall . . . 2A **46**
Birches Rd. WV8: Bilb . . . 5G **13**
BIRCHFIELD . . . 5E **83**
Birchfield Av. WV6: Tett . . . 3H **25**
Birchfield Cl. B63: Hale . . . 3G **127**
Birchfield Cres. DY9: W'cte . . . 2B **126**
Birchfield Gdns. B6: Aston . . . 1F **101**
WS5: Wals . . . 1G **65**
Birchfield La. B69: O'bry . . . 5E **97**
(not continuous)
Birchfield Rd. B19: Loz . . . 1F **101**
B20: Hand . . . 6F **83**
DY9: W'cte . . . 2B **126**
Birchfields Rd. WV12: W'hall . . . 4A **30**
Birchfield Twr. B20: Hand . . . 6F **83**
Birchfield Way WS5: Wals . . . 1F **65**
Birch Ga. DY9: W'cte . . . 1B **126**
Birchglade WV3: Wolv . . . 2B **42**
Birch Gro. B68: O'bry . . . 4B **114**
CV7: Bal C . . . 1H **169**
Birch Hill Av. WV5: Wom . . . 2F **73**
Birch Hollow B15: Edg . . . 5B **116**
B68: O'bry . . . 4B **114**
Birchill Pl. WV5: Wom . . . 2F **73**
Birchills Canal Mus. . . . 5A **32**
Birchills Ho. Ind. Est. WS2: Wals . . . 5B **32**
Birchills St. WS2: Wals . . . 6A **32**
Birch La. B68: O'bry . . . 4B **114**
WS4: S'fld . . . 6G **21**
WS9: A'rdge . . . 6F **23**
Birchley Ho. B69: O'bry . . . 3D **96**
Birchley Ind. Est. B69: O'bry . . . 4E **97**
Birchley Pk. Av. B69: O'bry . . . 3E **97**
Birchley Ri. B92: Olton . . . 6D **120**
Birchmoor Cl. B28: Hall G . . . 6H **135**
Birchover Rd. WS2: Wals . . . 5G **31**
Birch Rd. B6: Witt . . . 5A **84**
B45: Rubery . . . 3E **157**
B68: O'bry . . . 3B **114**
DY3: Sed . . . 4B **60**
WV11: Wed . . . 6H **17**
Birch Rd. E. B6: Witt . . . 5B **84**
Birch St. B68: O'bry . . . 3A **98**
DY4: Tip . . . 2H **77**
WS2: Wals . . . 6B **32**
WV1: Wolv . . . 1G **43** (2A 170)
Birch Ter. DY2: Neth . . . 5E **95**
Birch Tree Gdns. WS9: A'rdge . . . 4D **34**
Birchtree Gdns. DY5: Quar B . . . 2C **110**
Birch Tree Gro. B91: Sol . . . 3C **150**
Birchtree Hollow WV12: W'hall . . . 4D **30**
Birchtrees B24: Erd . . . 3B **86**
Birchtrees Cft. B26: Yard . . . 6B **120**
Birchtrees Dr. B33: Kitts G . . . 1H **121**
Birch Wlk. B68: O'bry . . . 4B **114**
Birchwood Cl. WV11: Ess . . . 4A **18**
Birchwood Cres. B12: Bal H . . . 1B **134**
Birchwood Rd. B12: Bal H . . . 1A **134**
WV4: Penn . . . 6E **43**
Birchwoods B32: Bart G . . . 3H **129**
Birchwood Wlk. DY6: K'wfrd . . . 1C **92**
Birchy Cl. B90: Dic H . . . 3F **163**
Birchy Leasowes La. B90: Dic H . . . 4E **163**
Birdbrook Rd. B44: Gt Barr . . . 4G **67**
Birdcage Wlk. B38: K Nor . . . 5B **146**
DY2: Dud . . . 6F **77**
Bird End B71: W Brom . . . 5D **64**
Birdie Cl. B38: K Nor . . . 6H **145**
Birdlip Gro. B32: Quin . . . 5A **114**
Birds Mdw. DY5: P'ntt . . . 2F **93**
Bird St. DY3: Lwr G . . . 4G **75**
Birdwell Cft. B13: Mose . . . 1H **147**
Birkdale Av. B29: S Oak . . . 4B **132**
Birkdale Cl. DY8: Stourb . . . 4D **124**
WV1: Wolv . . . 1C **44**
Birkdale Dr. B69: Tiv . . . 2A **96**
Birkdale Gro. B29: S Oak . . . 5C **132**
Birkdale Rd. WS3: Blox . . . 4G **19**
Birkenshaw Rd. B44: Gt Barr . . . 5G **67**
Birley Gro. B63: Hale . . . 5E **127**
BIRMINGHAM . . . 1F **117** (5D 4)
Birmingham Alexander Sports Stadium
. . . 1E **83**
Birmingham Botanical Gdns. . . . 4B **116**
Birmingham Bus. Est. B37: Mars G . . . 3G **123**
Birmingham City FC . . . 2C **118**
Birmingham Crematorium B42: P Barr . . . 2E **83**
Birmingham Hippodrome Theatre
. . . 2G **117** (6D 4)
BIRMINGHAM INTERNATIONAL AIRPORT
. . . 1C **138**
Birmingham International Station (Rail)
. . . 1F **139**
Birmingham Mus. & Art Gallery
. . . 1F **117** (3C 4)
Birmingham Mus. of Transport, The
. . . 6G **161**
Birmingham Nature Cen. . . . 1E **133**
Birmingham New Rd. DY1: Dud . . . 2E **77**
DY4: Tip . . . 2E **77**
WV4: E'shll . . . 6A **44**
WV14: Cose . . . 6A **44**
Birmingham One Bus. Pk. B1: Birm . . . 6D **100**
Birmingham Railway Mus. . . . 6F **119**
Birmingham Repertory Theatre
. . . 1E **117** (4B 4)
Birmingham Rd. B31: Hopw . . . 3F **159**
B36: Cas B . . . 1E **105**
B37: K'hrst . . . 4D **106**
B43: Gt Barr . . . 1A **66**
B45: Rubery . . . 5C **156**
B46: Col . . . 4E **107**
B46: Wat O . . . 5B **88**
B48: Hopw . . . 3F **159**
B61: L Ash, Rubery . . . 5C **156**
B63: Hale . . . 2B **128**
B65: Row R . . . 1C **112**
B69: O'bry . . . 2H **97**
B70: W Brom . . . 6C **80**
B71: W Brom . . . 6E **81**
B72: W Grn . . . 6H **69**

182 A-Z Birmingham

Birmingham Rd. CV7: Mer. 2D **140**
  DY1: Dud 5G **77**
  DY9: Hag 6G **125**
  WS1: Wals 2D **48**
  WS5: Wals 4F **49**
    (not continuous)
  WS9: A'rdge 4C **34**
  WS14: Shens, Shen W. . . . . (5C **170**)
  WV2: Wolv 2H **43** (5C **170**)
Birmingham Sports Cen. 5H **117**
Birmingham Squash Rackets Cen. . . 1H **115**
Birmingham B63: Hale 2B **128**
  B69: O'bry 2G **97**
  DY2: Dud 6F **77**
  DY8: Stourb 6E **109**
  DY9: Stourb 6E **109**
  WS1: Wals 2D **48**
  WS10: Darl. 5E **47**
  WV13: W'hall 1H **45**
Birmingham Wheels Adventure Pk. . . 1C **118**
Birnham Cl. DY4: Tip 2F **77**
Birstall Way B38: K Nor. 1G **159**
Bisell Way DY5: Brie H 4H **109**
Bishbury Cl. B15: Edg 3A **116**
Bishop Asbury Cottage Mus. 5G **65**
Bishop Asbury Cres. B43: Gt Barr . . . 5G **65**
Bishop Cl. B45: Fran. 6E **143**
  DY2: Dud 1G **95**
Bishop Rd. WS10: W'bry 3A **64**
Bishop Ryder Ho. B4: Birm 2G **5**
Bishops Cl. B66: Smeth. 5G **99**
Bishop's Ct. B31: N'fld 4F **145**
  B37: Mars G 3G **123**
Bishops Ga. B31: N'fld 5A **145**
Bishopsgate St. B15: Birm . . . 2D **116** (6A **4**)
Bishops Mdw. B75: R'ley 6C **38**
Bishops Rd. B73: S Cold 2H **69**
Bishop St. B5: Birm 3G **117**
Bishops Wlk. B64: Crad H 5A **112**
Bishops Way B74: Four O. 4F **37**
Bishopton Cl. B90: Shir 6A **150**
Bishopton Rd. B67: Smeth. 2D **114**
Bishton Gro. DY2: Neth 5F **95**
Bisley Gro. B24: Erd 5G **85**
Bismillah Bldg. B19: Birm. 5F **101** (1C **4**)
Bissell Cl. B28: Hall G 1F **149**
Bissell Dr. WS10: W'bry 2H **63**
Bissell St. B5: Birm 3G **117**
  B32: Quin 5G **113**
  WV14: Bils 6H **45**
Bi-Tec Ind. Pk. WV1: Wolv. 2C **44**
Biton Cl. B17: Harb. 6F **115**
Bittell Cl. B31: Longb 2D **158**
  WV10: Bush. 3A **16**
Bittell Ct. B31: Longb 2D **158**
Bittell Farm Rd. B48: Hopw 6F **159**
Bitterne Dr. WV6: Wolv 5E **27**
Bittern Wlk. DY5: Brie H 5G **109**
Blackacre Rd. DY2: Dud 1F **95**
Blackberry Av. B9: Bord G 6G **103**
Blackberry Cl. DY1: Dud 1A **94**
Blackberry La. B63: Hale 3A **128**
  B65: Row R 4H **95**
  B74: Four O 4E **37**
  WS9: Wals W 3D **22**
Blackbird Cft. B36: Cas B 2C **106**
Blackbrook Cl. DY2: Dud, Neth 4C **94**
Blackbrook Valley Ind. Est. DY2: Dud. . . 4C **94**
Blackbrook Way WV10: Bush. 3A **16**
Blackburn Av. WV6: Tett. 2C **26**
Blackburne Rd. B28: Hall G 1F **149**
Blackbushe Cl. B17: Harb 4D **114**
Blackcat Cl. B37: F'bri 6C **106**
Black Country Ho. B69: O'bry. 3F **77**
Black Country Mus. 3F **77**
Black Country New Rd. B70: W Brom . . 1D **78**
  DY4: Tip 1D **78**
  WS10: Darl, W'bry 1B **62**
  WS10: Tip, W'bry. 2D **62**
  WV14: Bils 5A **46**
Black Country Route WS2: Wals 4B **46**
  WV13: W'hall 4B **46**
  WV14: Cose, Bils 2D **60**
Blackdown Cl. B45: Fran 5G **143**
Blackdown Rd. B93: Know. 3D **166**
Blackett Ct. B73: S Cold 3G **69**

Blackfirs La. B37: Mars G 4E **123**
Blackford Cl. B63: Hale. 3F **127**
Blackford Rd. B11: S'hll 1C **134**
  B90: Shir 2A **164**
Blackford St. B18: Win G 4A **100**
Blackhalve La. WV11: Wed, Ess 1D **28**
Blackham Dr. B73: Bold. 6G **69**
Blackham Rd. WV11: Wed. 1H **29**
Black Haynes Rd. B29: W Cas 1E **145**
BLACKHEATH 2C **112**
Blackheath Mkt. B65: B'hth 2D **112**
Blackheath Trad. Est. B65: Row R . . . 1E **113**
Blackhorse La. DY5: Brie H 2A **110**
BLACK LAKE 1H **79**
Black Lake B70: W Brom 1G **79**
Black Lake Ind. Est. B70: W Brom . . . 1H **79**
Black Lake Stop (MM) 1G **79**
Blacklea Cl. B25: Yard 2B **120**
Black Mill DY1: Dud 3F **77**
Blackmoor Cft. B33: Kitts G 1H **121**
Blackpit La. WV4: Lwr P 2E **57**
Blackrock Rd. B23: Erd 1B **84**
Blackroot Cl. WS7: Hamm 1F **11**
Blackroot Ho. B73: New O 3C **68**
    (off Welshmans Hill)
Blackroot Rd. B74: S Cold 4G **53**
Blacksmith Dr. B75: R'ley 6C **38**
Blacksmith Way B70: W Brom 5A **80**
Blackthorn Cl. B30: B'vlle 1G **145**
Blackthorne Av. WS7: Chase 1B **10**
Blackthorne Cl. B91: Sol 3C **150**
  DY1: Dud 3B **76**
Blackthorne Rd. B67: Smeth 5B **98**
  DY1: Dud 3B **76**
  WS5: Wals 6D **48**
Blackthorn Rd. B30: B'vlle 1G **145**
  B36: Cas B 1G **105**
  DY8: Word 2D **108**
Blackwater Cl. DY5: P'ntt. 3E **93**
Blackwell Rd. B72: W Grn 4B **70**
Blackwood Av. WV11: Wed 1D **28**
Blackwood Dr. B74: S'tly 3G **51**
Blackwood Rd. B74: S'tly. 2G **51**
Blades Ho. B71: W Brom 5E **65**
Blades Rd. B70: W Brom 3D **78**
Blaenwern Dr. B63: Crad 4D **110**
Blagdon Rd. B63: Hale. 5A **112**
Blair Gro. B37: Chel W 2F **123**
Blakedon Rd. WS10: W'bry 2E **63**
Blakedown Rd. B63: Hale 4G **127**
Blakedown Way B69: O'bry 5E **97**
Blake Hall Cl. DY5: Brie H 4G **109**
Blake Ho. WS2: Wals 3A **48**
    (off St Johns Rd.)
Blakeland Rd. B44: K'sdng 1G **83**
Blakeland St. B9: Bord G 1F **119**
Blake La. B9: Bord G 1F **119**
BLAKELEY 2G **73**
Blakeley Av. WV6: Tett. 2D **26**
Blakeley Hall Gdns. B69: O'bry. 2H **97**
Blakeley Hall Rd. B69: O'bry. 2H **97**
Blakeley Heath Dr. WV5: Wom 2G **73**
Blakeley Ri. WV6: Tett. 2D **26**
Blakeley Wlk. DY2: Neth 5E **95**
Blakeley Wood Rd. DY4: Tip 5C **62**
Blakemere Av. B25: Yard 3C **120**
Blakemere Ho. B16: Birm 1C **116**
    (off Graston Cl.)
Blakemore Cl. B32: Bart G. 2D **130**
Blakemore Dr. B75: S Cold 5D **54**
Blakemore Rd. B70: W Brom 5G **79**
  WS9: Wals W 4C **22**
Blakenall Cl. WS3: Blox. 1B **32**
BLAKENALL HEATH 1B **32**
Blakenall Heath WS3: Blox 1B **32**
Blakenall La. WS3: Blox 2A **32**
Blakenall Row WS3: Blox 1B **32**
Blakeney Av. B17: Harb 4E **115**
  B8: Woll. 5B **108**
Blakeney Cl. DY3: Sed. 5G **59**
Blakenhale Rd. B33: Sheld. 2F **121**
BLAKENHALL 4G **43**
Blakenhall Gdns. WV2: Wolv. 4G **43**
Blakenhall Ind. Est. WV2: Wolv. 4F **43**
Blake Pl. B9: Bord G. 1F **119**
Blakesley Cl. B76: Walm 2D **86**
Blakesley Gro. B25: Yard 2B **120**

Blakesley Hall Mus. 2C **120**
Blakesley M. B25: Yard 3B **120**
Blakesley Rd. B25: Yard 2A **120**
Blakesley Way B33: Stech 1B **120**
Blake St. B74: Four O. 3E **37**
Blake Street Station (Rail). 3F **37**
Blakewood Cl. B34: S End. 4G **105**
Blandford Av. B36: Cas B 6A **88**
Blandford Dr. DY8: Word 6C **92**
Blandford Rd. B32: Quin 6C **114**
Blanefield WV8: Pend 5C **14**
Blanning Ct. B93: Dorr. 5A **166**
Blay Av. WS2: Wals 1H **47**
Blaydon Av. B75: R'ley 1C **54**
Blaydon Ct. B17: Harb 1H **131**
    (off Metchley La.)
Blaydon Rd. WV9: Pend. 5E **15**
Blaythorn Av. B92: Olton 2E **137**
Blaze Hill Rd. DY6: W Hth. 1G **91**
Blaze Pk. DY6: W Hth 1H **91**
Bleak Hill Rd. B23: Erd 3C **84**
Bleakhouse Rd. B68: O'bry 2A **114**
Bleak St. B67: Smeth. 3D **98**
Blenheim Cl. WS4: Rus. 2H **33**
Blenheim Ct. B44: Gt Barr 5H **67**
  B91: Sol 3G **151**
Blenheim Dr. B43: Gt Barr 5H **65**
Blenheim Rd. B13: Mose. 4H **133**
  B90: Shir 5B **150**
  DY6: K'wfrd 3D **92**
  WS11: Nort C 1F **9**
  WV12: W'hall 3B **30**
Blenheim Way B35: Cas V 5F **87**
  B44: Gt Barr 5H **67**
  DY1: Dud 5A **76**
Bletchley Rd. B24: Erd. 3C **86**
Blewitt Cl. B36: Cas B 5H **87**
Blewitt St. DY5: P'ntt. 3G **93**
Blews St. B6: Birm. 4G **101**
Blithe Cl. DY8: Amb 3E **109**
Blithfield Dr. DY5: Brie H 4F **109**
Blithfield Gro. B24: Erd 2A **86**
Blithfield Rd. WS8: Bwnhls 3F **9**
Blockall WS10: Darl. 4D **46**
Blockall Cl. WS10: Darl 5C **46**
BLOOMFIELD 6G **61**
Bloomfield Cl. WV5: Wom. 1D **72**
Bloomfield Dr. WV12: W'hall. 6D **18**
Bloomfield Pk. DY4: Tip 1F **77**
Bloomfield Pk. Trad. Est. DY4: Tip . . . 1F **77**
Bloomfield Rd. B13: Mose. 2B **134**
  DY4: Tip. 1G **77**
Bloomfield Sth. Nth. B63: Hale 6H **111**
Bloomfield St. W. B63: Hale 1H **127**
Bloomfield Ter. DY4: Tip 1F **77**
Bloomsbury Gro. B14: K Hth 6E **133**
Bloomsbury St. WV2: Wolv . . . 3G **43** (5A **170**)
Bloomsbury Wlk. B7: Nech 4B **102**
    (not continuous)
Blossom Av. B29: S Oak. 3B **132**
BLOSSOMFIELD 5D **150**
Blossomfield Cl. B38: K Nor 1H **159**
  DY6: K'wfrd 1C **92**
Blossomfield Club 1E **165**
Blossomfield Ct. B38: K Nor 1H **159**
Blossomfield Gdns. B91: Sol 3E **151**
Blossomfield Rd. B91: Sol. 6C **150**
Blossom Gro. B36: Hodg H 1C **104**
  B64: Old H 2H **111**
    (off Cherry Dr.)
Blossom Hill B24: Erd 3G **85**
Blossom Rd. B24: Erd 3A **86**
Blossom's Fold WV1: Wolv. . . . 1G **43** (3B **170**)
Blossomville Way B27: A Grn 1H **135**
Blounts Rd. B23: Erd 2C **84**
BLOWER'S GREEN 2D **94**
Blowers Grn. Cres. DY2: Dud 2D **94**
Blowers Grn. Pl. DY2: Dud 2D **94**
Blowers Grn. Rd. DY2: Dud 2D **94**
Bloxcidge St. B68: O'bry 5H **97**
BLOXWICH 6H **19**
Bloxwich Bus. Pk. WS2: Wals 2G **31**
Bloxwich La. WS2: Wals 5G **31**
Bloxwich Library Theatre. 6H **19**
Bloxwich North Station (Rail). 4F **19**
Bloxwich Rd. WS2: Wals 2A **32**
  WS3: Blox 2A **32**

Bloxwich Rd. Nth. WV12: W'hall 3D **30**
Bloxwich Rd. Sth. WV13: W'hall 6A **30**
Bloxwich Station (Rail) 6G **19**
Bloxwich Swimming Baths & Leisure Cen.
. . . . 1A **32**
Blucher St. B1: Birm 2F **117** (6C **4**)
Blue Ball La. B92: Crad 5E **111**
Blue Bell Cl. DY8: Word 1A **108**
Bluebell Cres. WV11: Wed 4F **29**
Bluebell Cft. B23: Erd 6C **68**
  B31: N'fld 3D **144**
Bluebell La. WS6: Gt Wyr 4G **7**
Bluebell Rd. B64: Old H. 6G **95**
  DY1: Dud 4D **76**
  WS9: Wals W 4D **22**
Bluebellwood Cl. B76: Walm 2E **71**
Blue Bird Pk. B62: Hunn 5A **128**
Bluebird Trad. Est. WV10: Wolv 4A **28**
Blue Cedars DY8: Woll 5A **108**
Blue Lake Rd. B93: Dorr 6H **167**
Blue La. E. WS2: Wals 6B **32**
Blue La. W. WS2: Wals 1B **48**
Blue Rock Pl. B69: Tiv 2C **96**
Blue Stone Wlk. B65: Row R 3C **96**
Blundell Rd. B11: S'hll. 6D **118**
Blyth Cl. B92: Olton 6D **136**
Blythe Av. CV7: Bal C 6H **169**
Blythe Ct. B46: Col 2H **107**
  B73: S Cold 6H **53**
Blythefield Av. B43: Gt Barr 3G **65**
Blythe Gdns. WV8: Cod 3F **13**
Blythe Gro. B44: Gt Barr 2H **67**
Blythe Rd. B46: Col 2H **107**
BLYTHE VALLEY PARK 6D **164**
Blythe Valley Parkway B90: Bly P 5D **164**
Blythe Way B91: Sol. 4A **152**
Blythewood Cl. B91: Sol 6B **152**
Blythsford Rd. B28: Hall G 3F **149**
Blythswood Rd. B11: Tys 1G **135**
Blyton Cl. B16: Birm 6B **100**
Board School Gdns. DY3: Up Gor 1A **76**
Boar Hound Cl. B18: Hock 5C **100**
Boat La. WS14: Muck C 4H **11**
Boatmans La. WS9: Wals W 5A **22**
Bobbington Way DY2: Neth 4F **95**
Bob's Coppice Wlk. DY5: Quar B 4B **110**
Boddis Ind. Pk. B64: Old H 1H **111**
Bodenham Rd. B31: N'fld. 5C **144**
  B68: O'bry 3H **113**
Boden Rd. B28: Hall G 6F **135**
Bodens La. WS9: A'rdge 4C **50**
Bodiam Cl. WV6: Pert 6G **25**
Bodicote Gro. B75: R'ley 1C **54**
Bodington Rd. B75: Four O 6H **37**
Bodmin Cl. WS5: Wals. 4H **49**
Bodmin Ct. DY5: Brie H 1H **109**
Bodmin Gro. B7: Birm 4B **102**
Bodmin Ri. WS5: Wals 4H **49**
Bodmin Rd. DY2: Neth 1F **111**
Bognop Rd. WV11: Ess 3E **17**
BOLDMERE 5F **69**
Boldmere Cl. B73: Bold 6G **69**
Boldmere Ct. B43: Gt Barr 6A **66**
  (off South Vw.)
Boldmere Dr. B73: Bold. 5G **69**
Boldmere Gdns. B73: Bold. 5F **69**
Boldmere Rd. B73: Bold. 3F **69**
Boldmere Ter. B29: S Oak 4A **132**
Boleyn Cl. WS6: C Hay 3D **6**
Boleyn Rd. B45: Fran 6D **142**
Bolney Rd. B32: Quin 6C **114**
Bolton Ct. DY4: Tip. 5C **62**
Bolton Ind. Cen. B19: Hock 3D **100**
Bolton Rd. B10: Small H 3B **118**
  WV11: Wed 4E **29**
Bolton St. B9: Birm 1B **118**
Bolton Way WS3: Blox 4F **19**
Bomers Fld. B45: Redn 2A **158**
Bond, The B5: Birm 1A **118**
Bond Dr. B35: Cas V 4E **87**
Bondfield Rd. B13: Mose. 1B **148**
Bond Sq. B18: Hock 5C **100**
Bond St. B19: Birm 5F **101** (1C **4**)
  B30: Stir. 6C **132**
  B65: Row R 6E **97**
  B70: W Brom 5A **80**
  WV2: Wolv 2G **43** (5B **170**)

Bond St. WV14: Cose. 5C **60**
Bonham Gro. B25: Yard 2B **120**
Boningale Way B93: Dorr 6H **165**
Bonner Dr. B76: Walm 2D **86**
Bonner Gro. WS9: A'rdge. 4B **34**
Bonnington Way B43: Gt Barr 1F **67**
Bonny Stile La. WV11: Wed 3D **28**
Bonsall Rd. B23: Erd 1G **85**
Bonville Gdns. WV10: Bush. 3A **16**
Booth Cl. DY6: K'wfrd. 3E **93**
  WS3: Blox 1B **32**
Booth Ct. DY5: Brie H 1H **109**
Booth Ho. WS4: Wals 6D **32**
Booth Rd. WS10: W'bry 3A **64**
Booth's Farm Rd. B42: Gt Barr 6C **66**
Booth's La. B42: Gt Barr 4D **66**
  (not continuous)
Booth St. B21: Hand. 2G **99**
  B66: Hand, Smeth 2G **99**
  WS3: Blox 1A **32**
  WS10: Darl 3D **46**
Bordeaux Cl. DY1: Dud 4A **76**
Borden Cl. WV8: Pend 1D **26**
BORDESLEY
  Birmingham 1B **118**
Bordesley Cir. B10: Small H. 2B **118**
Bordesley Cl. B9: Bord G. 1G **119**
BORDESLEY GREEN. 1E **119**
Bordesley Grn. B9: Bord G 1D **118**
Bordesley Grn. E. B9: Bord G 1H **119**
  B33: Stech 1A **120**
Bordesley Grn. Rd. B8: Salt. 1D **118**
  B9: Bord G 1D **118**
Bordesley Grn. Trad. Est.
  B9: Bord G 1E **119**
Bordesley Middleway B11: S'brk. 3A **118**
Bordesley Station (Rail) 2A **118**
Bordesley St. B5: Birm 1H **117** (4G **5**)
Bordesley Trad. Est. B8: Salt. 6D **102**
Borneo Cl. WS4: Wals 5D **32**
Borough Cres. B69: O'bry 4E **97**
  DY8: Stourb 6C **108**
Borrowdale Cl. DY5: Brie H 4F **109**
Borrowdale Gro. B31: N'fld 4B **144**
Borrowdale Rd. B31: N'fld 4A **144**
Borrow St. WV13: W'hall 6A **30**
Borwick Av. B70: W Brom 4G **79**
Bosbury Ter. B30: Stir 6D **132**
Boscobel Av. DY4: Tip 3H **77**
Boscobel Cl. DY1: Dud. 4B **76**
Boscobel Cres. WV1: Wolv 5G **27**
Boscobel Rd. B43: Gt Barr. 3H **65**
  B90: Ches G 4B **164**
  WS1: Wals 3F **49**
Boscombe Av. B11: S'brk. 5C **118**
Boscombe Rd. B11: Tys 1E **135**
Bosmere Ct. B31: N'fld 4D **144**
Bossgate Cl. WV5: Wom 3G **73**
Boston Gro. B44: K'sdng 5B **68**
Bosty La. WS9: A'rdge 4G **33**
Boswell Cl. WS10: Darl 6D **46**
  WS10: W'bry 4C **62**
Boswell Rd. B44: K'sdng 1H **83**
  B74: S Cold 5A **54**
  WV14: Bils 4H **45**
Bosworth Cl. DY3: Sed 1B **76**
Bosworth Ct. B26: Sheld. 6E **121**
Bosworth Dr. B37: Chel W, F'bri. 1B **122**
  B37: F'bri 1B **122**
Bosworth Rd. B26: Yard. 1C **136**
Botany Dr. DY3: Up Gor 2H **75**
Botany Rd. WS5: Wals 6D **48**
Botany Wlk. B16: Birm 1C **116**
Botha Rd. B9: Bord G. 6E **103**
Botteley Rd. B70: W Brom. 1G **79**
Botterham La. DY3: Swind. 4E **73**
Bottetourt Rd. B29: W Cas 2E **131**
  (not continuous)
Botteville Rd. B27: A Grn. 3A **136**
Bott La. DY9: Lye. 5H **109**
  WS1: Wals 2D **48**
BOUCHALL 5F **109**
Boughton Rd. B25: Yard. 4A **120**
Boulevard, The B73: W Grn. 5H **69**
  DY5: Brie H 1A **110**
Boultbee Rd. B72: W Grn. 6A **70**
Boulton Ho. B70: W Brom 6B **80**

Boulton Ind. Cen. B18: Hock 4D **100**
Boulton Middleway B18: Birm. 4D **100**
Boulton Retreat B21: Hand 2A **100**
Boulton Rd. B21: Hand. 2A **100**
  B66: Smeth 3H **99**
  B70: W Brom 6B **80**
  B91: Sol 6G **137**
Boulton Sq. B70: W Brom 6B **80**
Boulton Wlk. B23: Erd 3B **84**
Boundary Av. B65: Row R 1E **113**
Boundary Cl. WV13: W'hall 2E **45**
Boundary Ct. B37: F'bri 1A **122**
Boundary Cres. DY3: Lwr G. 4G **75**
Boundary Dr. B13: Mose. 3F **133**
Boundary Hill DY3: Lwr G 4G **75**
Boundary Ho. B5: Edg 6E **117**
  B47: Wyt 6G **161**
Boundary Ind. Est. WV10: F'hses 2G **15**
Boundary Pl. B21: Hand 6G **81**
Boundary Rd. B74: S'tly. 4H **51**
  WS9: Wals W 4B **22**
Boundary Way WV4: Penn. 6A **42**
  WV6: Tett 1F **41**
Bourlay Cl. B45: Fran. 5E **143**
BOURNBROOK 3B **132**
Bournbrook Ct. B5: S Oak 2C **132**
Bournbrook Rd. B29: S Oak 2C **132**
Bourne Av. B62: Quin 1F **129**
  DY4: Tip 6C **62**
Bournebrook Cl. DY2: Neth 4E **95**
Bournebrook Cres. B62: Quin 1G **129**
Bourne Cl. B13: Mose 1D **148**
  B91: Sol 1A **152**
Bourne Grn. B32: Quin 5C **114**
Bourne Hill Cl. DY2: Neth 6G **95**
Bourne Rd. B6: Aston. 2B **102**
Bournes Cl. B63: Hale 2H **127**
Bournes Cres. B63: Hale 1G **127**
Bournes Hill B63: Hale. 1G **127**
Bourne St. DY2: Dud 6F **77**
  DY3: Sed 6C **60**
  WV14: Cose 6C **60**
Bourne Va. WS9: A'rdge 6F **35**
Bourne Wlk. B65: Row R 4H **95**
Bourne Way Gdns. B29: S Oak 5C **132**
Bourn Mill Dr. B6: Aston 3G **101**
BOURNVILLE 6A **132**
Bournville La. B30: B'vlle 6H **131**
Bournville Station (Rail) 6C **132**
Bourton Cl. WS5: Wals 2E **65**
Bourton Cft. B92: Olton 5D **136**
Bourton Rd. B92: Olton 5D **136**
Bovey Cft. B76: Walm. 6E **71**
Bovingdon Rd. B35: Cas V 4E **87**
Bowater Av. B33: Stech 2B **120**
Bowater Ho. B19: Birm. 4F **101**
  (off Aldgate Gro.)
  B70: W Brom 5A **80**
Bowater St. B70: W Brom 4A **80**
Bowbrook Av. B90: M'path 4E **165**
Bowcroft Gro. B24: Erd 1A **86**
Bowden Rd. B67: Smeth 3C **98**
Bowdler Rd. WV2: Wolv. 3H **43** (6D **170**)
Bowen Av. WV4: E'shll 2C **60**
Bowen-Cooke Av. WV6: Pert 3E **25**
Bowen Ct. B13: Mose. 2B **134**
Bowen St. WV4: E'shll 6A **44**
Bowercourt Cl. B91: Sol 6F **151**
Bower La. DY5: Quar B 3B **110**
Bowes Rd. B45: Rubery 2E **157**
Bowker St. WV13: W'hall 2E **45**
Bowlas Av. B74: Four O 3H **53**
BOWLING GREEN 6F **95**
Bowling Grn. Cl. B23: Erd 6E **69**
  WS10: Darl 4D **46**
Bowling Grn. La. B20: Hand 1C **100**
Bowling Grn. Rd. DY2: Neth. 6F **95**
  DY8: Stourb 6C **108**
Bowlplex
  Birmingham 2C **116**
  Dudley. 4G **77**
Bowman Rd. B42: Gt Barr 4D **66**
Bowmans Ri. WV1: Wolv 6C **28**
Bowness Gro. WV12: W'hall 6B **18**
Bowood Cres. B31: N'fld. 5F **145**
Bowood Dr. WV6: Tett 3B **26**
Bowood End B76: Walm 2C **70**

Bowshot Cl. B36: Cas B 6H 87
Bowstoke Rd. B43: Gt Barr 5G 65
Bow St. B1: Birm 2F 117 (6D 4)
  WV13: W'hall 2B 46
  WV14: Bils 5G 45
Bowyer Rd. B8: Salt 5E 103
Bowyer St. B10: Small H 2A 118
Boxhill Cl. B6: Aston 3H 101
Box Rd. B37: Chel W 3E 123
Box St. WS1: Wals 2D 48
Box Trees Rd. B93: Dorr 6H 165
Boyd Gro. B27: A Grn 3H 135
Boydon Cl. WV2: E'shll 5C 44
Boyleston Rd. B28: Hall G 1G 149
Boyne Rd. B26: Sheld 4E 121
Boyton Gro. B44: Gt Barr 2H 67
Brabazon Gro. B35: Cas V 4D 86
Bracadale Av. B24: Erd 3G 85
Bracebridge Cl. B17: Harb 6H 115
Bracebridge Rd. B24: Erd 6F 85
  B74: Four O 3F 53
Bracebridge St. B6: Aston 3G 101
Braceby Av. B13: Mose 6C 134
Brace St. WS1: Wals 3C 48
  (not continuous)
Brackenbury Rd. B44: K'sdng 5B 68
Bracken Cl. WV8: Pend 6C 14
Bracken Cft. B37: Chel W 6E 107
Brackendale Dr. WS5: Wals 2F 65
Brackendale Shop. Cen.
  WV12: W'hall 5D 30
Brackendale Way DY9: W'cte 1H 125
Bracken Dr. B75: S Cold 6E 55
Brackenfield Rd. B44: Gt Barr 3E 67
  B63: Hale 2G 127
Brackenfield Vw. DY1: Dud 1H 93
Bracken Pk. Gdns. DY8: Word 1D 108
Bracken Rd. B24: Erd 5A 86
Brackenwood B38: K Nor 2H 159
  B74: S'tly 3H 51
Brackenwood WS5: Wals 6H 49
Brackley Av. B20: Hand 6E 83
Brackleys Way B92: Olton 3D 136
Bradbeer Ho. B16: Edg 2C 116
Bradburne Way B7: Birm 4A 102
Bradburn Rd. WV11: Wed 1D 28
Bradbury Cl. WS8: Bwnhls 2B 22
Bradbury Rd. B92: Olton 4D 136
Braden Rd. WV4: Penn 2B 58
Brades Cl. B63: Crad 4D 110
Brades Ri. B69: O'bry 1D 96
Brades Rd. B69: O'bry 6E 79
BRADES VILLAGE 1D 96
Bradewell Rd. B36: Cas B 6H 87
Bradfield Ho. B26: Sheld 5A 122
Bradfield Rd. B42: Gt Barr 6F 67
Bradford Cl. B43: Gt Barr 6B 66
Bradford Ct. B12: Birm 3A 118
Bradford La. WS1: Wals 2C 48
Bradford Mall WS1: Wals 2C 48
Bradford Pl. B11: S'brk 5A 118
  B70: W Brom 1C 98
  WS1: Wals 2C 48
Bradford Rd. B36: Cas B 1E 105
  DY2: Dud 3B 94
  WS8: Bwnhls 5A 10
Bradford St. B5: Birm 2H 117 (6G 5)
  WS1: Wals 2C 48
Bradgate Cl. WV12: W'hall 3C 30
Bradgate Dr. B74: Four O 4E 37
Bradgate Pl. B12: Bal H 6A 118
BRADLEY 2G 61
Bradley Cft. CV7: Bal C 3H 169
Bradley La. WV14: Bils 2H 61
Bradleymore Rd. DY5: Brie H 6H 93
Bradley Rd. B34: S End 3H 105
  DY8: Stourb 5D 108
Bradleys Cl. B64: Crad H 4G 111
Bradley's La. DY4: Tip 5F 61
  WV14: Cose 5F 61
Bradley St. DY4: Tip 5H 77
  DY5: P'ntt 2F 93
  WV14: Bils 1H 61
BRADMORE 3C 42

Bradmore Cl. B91: Sol 1E 165
Bradmore Gro. B29: W Cas 5E 131
Bradmore Rd. WV3: Wolv 3D 42
Bradnock Cl. B13: Mose 6C 134
BRADNOCK'S MARSH 4E 155
Bradnocks Marsh Bus. Cen.
  B92: H Ard 4F 155
Bradnocks Marsh La. B92: H Ard . . . 6D 154
Bradshaw Av. B38: K Nor 6H 145
  WS10: Darl 6B 46
Bradshaw Cl. DY4: Tip 4A 78
Bradshawe Cl. B28: Hall G 4D 148
Bradshaw St. WV1: Wolv 1A 44
Bradstock Rd. B30: K Nor 3E 147
Bradwell Cft. B75: R'ley 6C 38
Braemar Av. DY8: Word 2A 108
Braemar Cl. DY3: Sed 4G 59
  WV12: W'hall 3B 30
Braemar Dr. B23: Erd 2B 84
Braemar Rd. B73: S Cold 3F 69
  B92: Olton 4C 136
  WS1: Nort C 1E 9
Braeside Cft. B37: Chel W 1F 123
Braeside Av. WS3: Pels 4D 20
Bragg Rd. B20: Hand 5F 83
Braggs Farm La. B90: Dic H, Shir . . . 5F 163
Braid Cl. B38: K Nor 6H 145
Brailes Cl. B92: Sol 6A 138
Brailes Dr. B76: Walm 2D 70
Brailes Gro. B9: Bord G 2H 119
Brailsford Cl. WV11: Wed 1G 29
Brailsford Dr. B66: Smeth 4E 99
Bramah Way DY4: Tip 1C 78
Bramber Dr. WV5: Wom 1F 73
Bramber Ho. B31: Longb 1D 158
Bramber Way DY8: Stourb 3D 124
Bramble Cl. B6: Aston 2G 101
  B31: N'fld 1D 144
  B46: Col 2H 107
  B64: Old H 5H 95
  WS8: Clay 2A 22
  WV12: W'hall 2C 30
Bramble Dell B9: Bord G 6G 103
Bramble Dr. B26: Sheld 5E 121
Bramble Grn. DY1: Dud 2B 76
Brambles, The B76: Walm 5E 71
Brambleside DY8: Word 2D 108
Bramblewood WV5: Wom 6G 57
Bramblewood Dr. WV3: Wolv 3C 42
Bramblewoods B34: S End 4G 105
Brambling Wlk. B15: Edg 4E 117
  DY5: Brie H 5G 109
Brampton Av. B91: Sol 6G 137
Bramcote Cl. B75: S Cold 4A 54
Bramcote Ri. B75: S Cold 4A 54
Bramcote Rd. B32: Quin 6A 114
  (not continuous)
Bramdean Wlk. WV4: Penn 5A 42
Bramerton Cl. WV11: Wed. 3C 28
Bramford Dr. DY1: Dud 1D 76
Bramley Cl. B43: Gt Barr 2F 67
  WS5: Wals 3H 49
Bramley Dr. B90: Shir 3A 150
Bramley Dr. B20: Hand 6A 120
  B47: H'wd 3B 162
Bramley M. Ct. B27: A Grn 6A 120
Bramley Rd. B27: A Grn. 6A 120
  WS5: Wals 1F 65
Brampton Av. B28: Hall G 1G 149
Brampton Cres. B90: Shir 1H 149
Bramshall Dr. B93: Dorr 6A 166
Bramshaw Cl. B14: K Hth 5H 147
Bramshill Cl. B15: Edg 3D 116
Bramstead Av. WV6: Tett 1H 41
Bramwell Dr. WS6: C Hay 4D 6
Branchal Rd. WS9: A'rdge 6E 23
Branch Rd. B38: K Nor 1A 160
BRANDHALL 3H 113
Brandhall Ct. B68: O'bry 1G 113
Brandhall La. B68: O'bry 2H 113
Brandhall Rd. B68: O'bry 1H 113
Brandon Cl. B70: W Brom 5G 79
  DY3: Sed 6A 60
  WS9: A'rdge 6H 35
Brandon Ct. B31: N'fld 6F 145

Brandon Gro. B31: Longb 2D 158
Brandon Pk. WV3: Wolv. 4C 42
Brandon Pas. B16: Birm. 6A 100
Brandon Pl. B34: S End 2H 105
Brandon Rd. B28: Hall G 3E 135
  B62: B'hth 2E 113
  B91: Sol 6G 137
Brandon Thomas Ct. B6: Aston 1B 102
Brandon Way B70: W Brom 4G 79
  DY5: Quar B 3A 110
Brandon Way Ind. Est. B70: W Brom . . . 4F 79
BRANDWOOD END 3F 147
Brandwood Gro. B14: K Hth 2F 147
Brandwood Ho. B14: K Hth 6F 133
Brandwood Pk. Rd. B14: K Hth 2D 146
Brandwood Rd. B14: K Hth 3F 147
Branfield Cl. WV14: Cose 4C 60
Branksome Av. B21: Hand 1B 100
Branscombe Cl. B14: K Hth 2F 147
Bransdale Av. WV6: Wolv 4E 27
Bransdale Rd. WS8: Clay 6A 10
Bransford Ri. B91: Cath B 2D 152
Bransford Twr. B12: Birm. 3H 117
Branston Cl. B18: Birm. 4E 101
Branston St. B18: Birm. 4E 101
Brantford Rd. B25: Yard 3A 120
Branthill Cft. B91: Sol 6F 151
Brantley Av. WV3: Wolv 2A 42
Brantley Rd. B6: Witt 5A 84
Branton Hill La. WS9: A'rdge 4E 35
Brasshouse La. B66: Smeth 3D 98
Brassie Cl. B38: K Nor 6H 145
Brassington Av. B73: S Cold 1H 69
BRATCH, THE 6E 57
Bratch Cl. DY2: Neth 6E 95
Bratch Comn. Rd. WV5: Wom 6E 57
Bratch Hollow WV5: Wom 5G 57
Bratch La. WV5: Wom 5F 57
Bratch Pk. WV5: Wom 5F 57
Bratt St. B70: W Brom 3A 80
Braunston Cl. B76: Walm 3E 71
Brawnes Hurst B26: Yard 2E 121
Brayford Av. DY5: Brie H 4F 109
Bray Ho. WV11: Wed 4E 29
Braymoor Rd. B33: Kitts G 2A 122
Brays Rd. B26: Sheld 5E 121
Bray St. WV13: W'hall 1B 46
Bream Cl. B37: Chel W 1E 123
  WV10: Wolv 5D 28
Breamore Cres. DY1: Dud 4B 76
Brean Av. B26: Yard 6D 120
Brearley Cl. B19: Birm 4G 101
Brearley St. B19: Birm 4F 101
  B21: Hand 1H 99
Breaside Wlk. B37: Chel W 6E 107
Brecknock Rd.
  B71: W Brom 1G 79
Brecon Dr. DY8: Amb 5F 109
Brecon Rd. B20: Hand 1D 100
Bredon Av. DY9: Lye 6G 109
Bredon Ct. B63: Hale 2A 128
Bredon Cft. B18: Birm 4C 100
Bredon Rd. B69: O'bry 4D 96
  DY8: Amb 5E 109
Breech Cl. B74: S'tly 4G 51
Breeden Dr. B76: Curd 1D 88
Breedon Rd. B30: K Nor 2C 146
Breedon Ter. B18: Hock 4C 100
  (off Brookfield Rd.)
Breedon Way WS4: S'fld 6G 21
Breener Ind. Est. DY5: Brie H 2F 109
Brelades Cl. DY1: Dud 5A 76
Brennand Cl. B68: O'bry 3H 113
Brennand Rd. B68: O'bry 2H 113
Brentford Rd. B14: K Hth 2A 148
  B91: Sol 4C 150
Brentmill Cl. WV10: Bush 3B 16
Brentnall Dr. B75: Four O 6H 37
Brenton Rd. WV4: Penn 2D 58
Brent Rd. B30: Stir 5F 133
Brentwood Cl. B91: Sol 4C 150
Brentwood Gro. B44: Gt Barr 5G 67
Brenwood Cl. DY6: K'wfrd 2H 91
Brereton Cl. DY2: Dud 1G 95
Brereton Rd. WV12: W'hall 2C 30

Bretby Gro. B23: Erd	1G **85**
Bretshall Cl. B90: M'path.	4D **164**
Brett Dr. B32: Bart G	5A **130**
Brettell La. DY5: Brie H	3D **108**
DY8: Amb	3D **108**
Brettell St. DY2: Dud	1D **94**
Bretton Gdns. WV10: Wolv	3B **28**
Bretton Rd. B27: A Grn	3B **136**
Brett St. B71: W Brom	2H **79**
Brevitt Rd. WV2: Wolv	5H **43**
Brewer's Dr. WS3: Pels	6E **21**
Brewers Ter. WS3: Pels	5E **21**
Brewer St. WS2: Wals	5C **32**
Brewery St. B6: Birm	4G **101**
B21: Hand	1H **99**
B67: Smeth	3D **98**
DY2: Dud	6G **77**
DY4: Tip	3H **77**
Brewins Way DY5: Brie H.	5C **94**
Brewster St. DY2: Neth	4E **95**
Breydon Gro. WV13: W'hall	3H **45**
Brian Rd. B67: Smeth	3C **98**
Briar Av. B74: S'tly	2A **52**
Briarbeck WV4: S'fld	1G **33**
Briar Cl. B24: Erd	3G **85**
Briar Coppice B90: Ches G	5B **164**
Briar Ct. DY5: Brie H	1H **109**
(off Hill St.)	
Briarfield Rd. B11: Tys	2G **135**
Briarley B71: W Brom	4D **64**
Briar Rd. DY1: Dud	2B **76**
Briars, The B23: Erd	1D **84**
Briars Cl. DY5: Brie H	5G **93**
Briarwood Cl. B90: Ches G	5B **164**
WV2: E'shll	4C **44**
Brickbridge La. WV5: Wom	2E **73**
Brickfield Rd. B25: Yard	5H **119**
Brickheath Rd. WV1: Wolv.	6C **28**
Brickhill Dr. B37: F'bri	1C **122**
Brickhouse La. B70: W Brom	1E **79**
Brickhouse La. Sth.	
DY4: Tip	1D **78**
Brickhouse Rd.	
B65: Row R	5A **96**
Brickiln St. WS8: Bwnhls	6B **10**
Brick Kiln La. B44: Gt Barr	1G **83**
B47: Wyt	6G **161**
B91: Sol	1D **164**
DY3: Gorn	4E **75**
Brick Kiln St. DY4: Tip	1G **77**
DY5: Brie H	4A **94**
DY5: Quar B	3C **110**
Brickkiln St. WV13: W'hall	2H **45**
Bricklin Ct. DY5: Brie H	1H **109**
Brick St. DY3: Sed	5H **59**
Brickyard Rd. WS9: A'rdge	6B **22**
Briddsland Rd. B33: Kitts G	1A **122**
Brides Wlk. B38: K Nor	2A **160**
Bridge, The WS1: Wals	2C **48**
Bridge Av. DY4: Tip	6C **62**
WS6: C Hay	1E **7**
Bridgeburn Rd. B31: N'fld	5C **130**
Bridge Cl. B11: S'hll	2B **134**
WS8: Clay	1A **22**
Bridge Ct. B64: Old H	3H **111**
(off Edgewood Cl.)	
Bridge Cft. B12: Bal H	5G **117**
Bridgefield Wlk. B65: Row R	4H **95**
Bridgefoot Wlk. WV8: Pend	6D **14**
Bridgeford Rd. B34: S End	3F **105**
Bridgehead Wlk. B76: Walm	6D **70**
Bridge Ind. Est. B91: Sol	6G **137**
Bridgelands Way B20: Hand.	6F **83**
Bridgeman Cft. B36: Cas B	1G **105**
Bridgeman St. WS2: Wals	2B **48**
Bridgemary Cl. WV10: Bush	3B **16**
Bridge Mdw. Dr. B93: Know.	4B **166**
Bridgemeadow Ho.	
B36: Hodg H	1C **104**
Bridgend Cft. DY5: P'ntt	3F **93**
Bridgenorth Ho. B33: Yard	2F **121**
Bridge Piece B31: N'fld	5F **145**
Bridge Rd. B8: Salt.	5E **103**
DY4: Tip	1C **78**
WS4: S'fld	6F **21**
Bridges Cres. WS11: Nort C	1D **8**
Bridges Rd. WS11: Nort C	1D **8**

Bridge St. B1: Birm	1E **117** (5B **4**)
B63: Crad	4E **111**
B69: O'bry	2G **97**
B70: W Brom	3H **79**
DY8: Word	2C **108**
WS1: Wals	1C **48**
WS8: Clay	1A **22**
WS10: W'bry	4F **63**
WV10: Wolv	4A **28**
WV13: W'hall	2H **45**
WV14: Bils	6G **45**
WV14: Cose	5E **61**
Bridge St. Ind. Est. WS10: W'bry	4F **63**
Bridge St. Nth. B66: Smeth	3F **99**
Bridge St. Sth. B66: Smeth	3F **99**
Bridge St. W. B19: Hock.	4F **101**
Bridge Trad. Cen., The B64: Crad H	3F **111**
Bridge Trad. Est., The B66: Smeth	3F **99**
Bridge Wlk. B27: A Grn	2B **136**
Bridgewater Av. B69: O'bry	5G **97**
Bridgewater Ct. B29: S Oak	4H **131**
Bridgewater Cres. DY2: Dud	6G **77**
Bridgewater Dr. WV5: Wom	6F **57**
WV14: Cose	3E **61**
Bridge Way WS8: Clay	1A **22**
Bridgnorth Av. WV5: Wom	3F **73**
Bridgnorth Gro. WV12: W'hall	3B **30**
Bridgnorth Rd. DY3: Himl	4H **73**
DY3: Swind	2A **72**
DY7: Stourt	3A **108**
(not continuous)	
DY8: Woll	4A **108**
WV5: Wom	2E **73**
WV6: Pert, Tett, Tres	5A **40**
Bridgwater Cl. WS9: Wals W	4B **22**
Bridle Gro. B71: W Brom	5D **64**
Bridle La. B74: S'tly	4G **51**
WS9: A'rdge	5E **51**
Bridle Mead B38: K Nor	1H **159**
Bridle Path, The B90: Shir.	2H **149**
Bridle Rd. DY8: Woll	5B **108**
Bridlewood B74: S'tly	3H **51**
Bridport Ho. B31: N'fld	1C **144**
BRIERLEY HILL	1H **109**
Brierley Hill Baths	1H **109**
BRIERLEY HILL. DY5: Brie H.	1E **109**
DY8: Word	1C **108**
Brierley La. WV14: Bils, Cose	3G **61**
Brierley Trad. Est., The DY5: Brie H	6G **93**
Brier Mill Rd. B63: Hale.	2C **128**
Briery Cl. B64: Crad H	4H **111**
Briery Rd. B63: Hale	2G **127**
Briffen Ho. B16: Birm.	1D **116**
Brigadoon Gdns. DY9: Pedm	3G **125**
Brigfield Cres. B13: Mose	2B **148**
Brigfield Rd. B13: Mose.	2B **148**
Brighton Cl. WS2: Wals	6B **32**
Brighton Pl. WV3: Wolv	1E **43**
Brighton Rd. B12: Bal H.	6H **117**
Bright Rd. B68: O'bry.	4H **97**
Brightside Cl. WV10: Bush	3B **16**
Brightstone Rd. B45: Fran	5H **143**
Bright St. DY8: Woll	6B **108**
WS10: Darl	6D **46**
WV1: Wolv	6F **27**
Brightwell Cres. B93: Dorr.	6A **166**
Brimfield Pl. WV6: Wolv	5D **26**
(off Newbridge St.)	
Brindle Cl. B26: Yard	6C **120**
Brindle Ct. B23: Erd	4B **84**
Brindlefields Way DY4: Tip	5A **78**
Brindle Rd. WS5: Wals	1G **65**
Brindley Av. WV11: Wed	6A **18**
Brindley Cl. DY8: Word	2C **108**
WS2: Wals	4F **31**
WV5: Wom.	1D **72**
Brindley Ct. B68: O'bry	4H **113**
DY4: Tip	2G **77**
Brindley Pl. B1: Birm	1E **117** (4A **4**)
Brindley Point B16: Birm	1D **116**
Brindley Rd. B71: W Brom	5G **63**
Brindley Way B66: Smeth	4G **99**
Brineton Gro. B29: W Cas	4E **131**
Brineton Ind. Est. WS2: Wals	2A **48**
Brineton St. WS2: Wals	2A **48**
Bringewood Gro. B32: Bart G	5H **129**

Brinklow Cft. B34: S End	2H **105**
Brinklow Rd. B29: W Cas.	3D **130**
Brinklow Twr. B12: Birm	4H **117**
Brinley Way DY6: K'wfrd	3A **92**
Brinsford Rd. WV10: F'hses.	4G **15**
Brinsley Cl. B91: Sol	5F **151**
Brinsley Rd. B26: Sheld	3F **121**
Brisbane Rd. B67: Smeth.	4C **98**
Briseley Cl. DY5: Brie H.	3G **109**
Bristam Cl. B69: O'bry	3E **97**
BRISTNALL FIELDS	1H **113**
Bristnall Hall Cres. B68: O'bry	6A **98**
Bristnall Hall La. B68: O'bry	6A **98**
Bristnall Hall Rd. B68: O'bry	1H **113**
Bristnall Ho. B67: Smeth	5B **98**
Bristol Ct. B29: W Cas	6G **131**
Bristol Rd. B5: S Oak	2B **132**
B23: Erd	4E **85**
B29: S Oak.	6H **131**
DY2: Neth	1F **111**
Bristol Rd. Sth. B31: Longb.	1B **158**
B45: Redn	1G **157**
Bristol St. B5: Birm	3F **117** (6D **4**)
Briston Cl. DY5: Brie H	3G **109**
Britannia Gdns. B65: Row R	6C **96**
Britannia Grn. DY3: Up Gor	2A **76**
Britannia Pk. WS10: W'bry	2D **62**
Britannia Rd. B65: Row R	1C **112**
WS1: Wals	6B **48**
WV14: Bils.	2H **61**
Britannia St. B69: Tiv.	5C **78**
Britannic Gdns. B13: Mose.	3F **133**
Britannic Pk. B13: Mose.	3F **133**
Britford Cl. B14: K Hth	4H **147**
Brittan Cl. B34: S End	3A **106**
Britton Dr. B72: W Grn	5A **70**
Britwell Rd. B73: W Grn	3G **69**
Brixfield Way B90: Dic H	4G **163**
Brixham Rd. B16: Edg	5H **99**
Broadacres B31: N'fld	1C **144**
Broadcott Ind. Est. B64: Old H	2A **112**
Broad Cft. DY4: Tip	1C **78**
Broadfern Rd. B93: Know	1D **166**
Broadfield Cl. B71: W Brom	4D **64**
DY6: K'wfrd	4B **92**
Broadfield House Glass Mus.	4A **92**
Broadfields Rd. B23: Erd	6H **69**
Broadfield Wlk. B16: Birm.	2D **116**
Broadheath Dr. WS4: S'fld	1H **33**
Broadhidley Dr. B32: Bart G	4H **129**
Broadlands WV10: F'hses	2H **15**
Broadlands Dr. DY5: Brie H	4A **94**
Broad La. B14: K Hth	3F **147**
WS3: Blox.	4F **19**
WS4: S'fld	6G **21**
WV3: Wolv	3C **42**
WV11: Ess	1C **18**
Broad La. Gdns. WS3: Blox.	5G **19**
Broad La. Nth. WV12: W'hall	3B **30**
Broad Lanes WV14: Bils.	2E **61**
Broad La. Sth. WV11: Wed	4H **29**
Broadmeadow DY6: K'wfrd	1C **92**
WS9: A'rdge.	1D **34**
Broadmeadow Cl. B30: K Nor	4D **146**
Broad Mdw. Grn. WV14: Bils	4E **45**
Broadmeadow Ho. B32: Bart G	5B **130**
Broad Mdw. La. B30: K Nor.	4D **146**
Broadmeadow La. WS6: Gt Wyr	3G **7**
Broadmeadows Cl. WV12: W'hall	1E **31**
Broadmeadows Rd. WV12: W'hall .	1E **31**
Broadmoor Av. B67: Smeth	1B **114**
B68: O'bry	1B **114**
Broadmoor Cl. WV14: Bils	1E **61**
Broadmoor Rd. WV14: Bils	1E **61**
Broadoaks B76: Walm	5E **71**
Broad Oaks Rd. B91: Sol	1D **150**
Broad Rd. B27: A Grn	2H **135**
Broadstone Av. B63: Crad	1D **126**
WS3: Blox	3B **32**
Broadstone Cl. WV4: Penn	6H **43**
Broadstone Rd. B26: Yard	1D **120**
Broad St. B1: Birm	2D **116**
B15: Birm	2D **116** (6A **4**)
B69: O'bry	4G **97**
DY5: P'ntt	3G **93**
DY6: K'wfrd	4B **92**
WV1: Wolv	1H **43** (2C **170**)

Broad St.—Broomfields Farm Rd.

Broad St. WV14: Bils 5E 45
WV14: Cose 5E 61
Broad St. Junc. WV1: Wolv 1H 43 (2D 170)
Broadwalk B1: Birm 2E 117 (6A 4)
Broadwalk Retail Pk. WS1: Wals 5B 48
Broadwaters Av. WS10: Darl 1C 62
Broadwaters Rd. WS10: Darl 1C 62
Broad Way WS4: S'fld 5G 21
Broadway B68: O'bry 2A 114
B90: Shir 3G 149
WS1: Wals 5D 48
WV3: Wolv 2A 42
WV8: Cod 4E 13
WV10: Bush 5A 16
Broadway, The B20: Hand 5F 83
B71: W Brom 6G 63
DY1: Dud 4C 76
DY8: Stourb 2B 124
WV5: Wom 2G 73
Broadway Av. B9: Bord G 1G 119
B63: Hale 3A 128
Broadway Community Leisure Cen. 5G 83
Broadway Cft. B26: Sheld 5E 121
B68: O'bry 2A 114
Broadway Gdns. WV10: Bush 5A 16
Broadway Nth. WS1: Wals 1D 48
Broadway Plaza 2C 116
Broadway W. WS1: Wals 5A 48
Broadwell Ind. Pk. B69: O'bry 6F 79
Broadwell Rd. B69: O'bry 1G 97
B92: Olton 3E 137
Broadwyn Trad. Est. B64: Old H 2A 112
Broadyates Gro. B25: Yard 5A 120
Broadyates Rd. B25: Yard 5A 120
Brobury Cft. B91: Shir 3B 150
Broches, The WS11: Nort C 1F 9
Brockeridge Cl. WV12: W'hall 6C 18
Brockfield Ho. WV10: Wolv 5B 28
Brockhall Gro. B37: K'hrst 4B 106
Brockhill La. B48: A'chu 6D 160
Brockhurst Cres. WS5: Wals 6C 48
Brockhurst Dr. B28: Hall G 2G 149
WV6: Wolv 5E 27
Brockhurst Ho. WS2: Wals 6B 32
Brockhurst La. B75: Can 3E 39
Brockhurst Pl. WS5: Wals 6D 48
Brockhurst Rd. B36: Hodg H 3A 104
B75: R'ley 2B 54
Brockhurst St. WS1: Wals 5C 48
Brockley Cl. DY5: Brie H 6H 93
Brockley Gro. B13: Mose 4E 133
Brockley Pl. B7: Nech 2C 102
BROCKMOOR 5G 93
Brockmoor Cl. DY9: Pedm 3G 125
Brock Rd. DY4: Tip 3C 78
Brockton Rd. B29: W Cas 4E 131
Brockwell Gro. B44: Gt Barr 1G 67
Brockwell Rd. B44: Gt Barr 1G 67
Brockworth Rd. B14: K Hth 5E 147
Brocton Cl. WS3: Blox 1G 31
WV14: Cose 2D 60
Brogden Cl. B71: W Brom 5D 64
Bromfield Cl. B6: Aston 2G 101
Bromfield Ct. WV6: Tett 1H 41
Bromfield Cres. WS10: W'bry 1A 64
Bromfield Rd. WS10: W'bry 2A 64
BROMFORD 5B 86
Bromford Cl. B20: Hand 6C 82
B23: Erd 2E 85
Bromford Ct. B31: N'fld 6F 145
Bromford Cres. B24: Erd 5G 85
Bromford Dale WV1: Wolv 6E 27
WV6: Wolv 6E 27
Bromford Dell B31: N'fld 3G 145
Bromford Dr. B36: Hodg H 1H 103
Bromford Gdns. B15: Edg 3G 115
Bromford Ga. B24: Erd 1G 103
Bromford Hill B20: Hand 4E 83
Bromford Ho. B73: Bold 3F 69
Bromford La. B8: W End 3H 103
B24: Erd 5G 85
B70: W Brom 6G 79
Bromford Mere B92: Olton 5C 136
Bromford Mills Ind. Est. B24: Erd 6G 85
Bromford Pk. B69: O'bry 1G 97
Bromford Pk. Ho. *B13: Mose* 3B 134
(off Wake Grn. Pk.)
Bromford Pk. Ind. Est. B70: W Brom 6G 79
Bromford Ri. WV3: Wolv 3F 43
Bromford Rd. B36: Hodg H 2H 103
B69: O'bry 1G 97
B70: W Brom 6G 79
DY2: Dud 3C 94
Bromford Rd. Ind. Est. B69: O'bry 6G 79
Bromford Wlk. B43: Gt Barr 4B 66
BROMLEY 4F 93
Bromley DY5: P'ntt 4F 93
Bromley Gdns. WV8: Cod 3G 13
Bromley La. DY6: K'wfrd 5C 92
Bromley Pl. WV4: Penn 6E 43
Bromley St. B9: Birm 2A 118
DY9: Lye 5B 110
WV2: Wolv 4G 43
Brompton Dr. DY5: Brie H 4F 109
Brompton Lawns WV6: Tett 6G 25
Brompton Pool Rd. B28: Hall G 4E 149
Brompton Rd. B44: Gt Barr 1G 67
Bromsgrove Rd. B62: Hunn, Roms 3A 142
B63: Hale 2C 128
DY9: Clent, Hag 6G 125
Bromsgrove St. B5: Birm 2G 117 (6E 5)
B63: Hale 1C 128
Bromwall Rd. B13: Mose 1B 148
Bromwich Ct. B46: Col 5G 89
Bromwich Dr. B75: S Cold 4A 54
Bromwich La. DY9: Pedm 6F 125
Bromwich Wlk. B9: Bord G 6G 103
Bromwynd Cl. WV2: Wolv 5F 43
Bromyard Av. B76: Walm 5E 71
Bromyard Rd. B11: S'hll 2E 135
Bronte Cl. B90: Shir 6B 150
Bronte Ct. B90: Shir 6B 150
Bronte Farm Rd. B90: Shir 6B 150
Bronte Rd. WV2: E'shll 5B 44
Bronwen Rd. WV14: Cose 6E 61
Brookbank Av. B34: S End 3H 105
Brookbank Gdns. DY3: Gorn 5F 75
Brookbank Rd. DY3: Gorn 5F 75
Brook Cl. B33: Stech 5C 104
B90: Shir 6F 149
WS9: Wals W 4C 22
Brook Cres. DY6: W Hth 2A 92
DY9: W'cte 2B 126
Brook Cft. B26: Sheld 4F 121
B37: Mars G 4D 122
Brookdale DY3: Lwr G 4G 75
Brookdale Cl. B45: Redn 6G 143
Brookdale Dr. WV4: Penn 5C 42
Brook Dr. B32: Bart G 4B 130
Brook End WS7: Chase 1C 10
Brookend Dr. B45: Rubery 1F 157
Brookes Cl. B69: Tiv 1B 96
Brookes Ho. *WS1: Wals* 2D 48
(off Paddock La.)
Brooke St. DY2: Dud 1E 95
Brook Farm Wlk. B37: Chel W 6F 107
Brookfield Cl. WS9: A'rdge 6C 22
Brookfield Rd. B18: Hock 4C 100
WS9: A'rdge 6C 22
WV8: Bilb 4H 13
BROOKFIELDS 5D 100
Brookfields Rd. B68: O'bry 5A 98
Brookfield Ter. B18: Hock 4C 100
Brookfield Way B92: Olton 6B 136
DY4: Tip 1A 78
Brook Grn. La. B92: Bars 6A 154
Brook Gro. WV8: Bilb 4H 13
Brookhill Cl. WV12: W'hall 6C 18
Brook Hill Rd. B8: W End 5G 103
Brookhill Way WV12: W'hall 6D 18
Brook Holloway DY9: W'cte 1B 126
Brookhouse Cl. WV10: F'stne 1D 16
Brook Ho. La. WV10: F'stne 1A 16
Brookhouse Rd. WS5: Wals 4F 49
Brookhurst La. B90: Dic H 3H 163
Brookhus Farm Rd. B76: Walm 5E 71
Brooking Cl. B43: Gt Barr 1F 67
Brookland Gro. WS9: Wals W 5B 22
Brookland Rd. WS9: Wals W 4B 22
Brooklands DY3: Swind 6E 73
DY8: Word 2D 108
WS5: Wals 2F 65
Brooklands Av. WS6: Gt Wyr 1F 7
Brooklands Cl. B28: Hall G 4F 135
Brooklands Dr. B14: K Hth 2G 147
Brooklands Pde. WV1: Wolv 2C 44
Brooklands Rd. B28: Hall G 4F 135
Brooklands Way B37: Mars G 3D 122
Brook La. B13: Mose 5A 134
B32: Harb 6D 114
B64: Old H 1G 111
B92: Olton 5B 136
WS6: Gt Wyr 2G 7
WS9: Wals W 4B 22
Brooklea Gro. B38: K Nor 6C 146
Brooklyn Av. B6: Aston 2H 101
Brooklyn Gro. DY6: W Hth 1H 91
WV14: Cose 5F 61
Brooklyn Rd. WS7: Chase 1C 10
Brookmans Av. B32: Quin 1B 130
Brook Mdw. Ct. B28: Hall G 1D 148
Brook Mdw. Rd. B34: S End 3E 105
WS4: S'fld 1H 33
Brook Mdws. WV8: Bilb 3H 13
Brookmoor Ind. Est. DY5: Brie H 6E 93
Brookpiece Ho. *B14: K Hth* 5G 147
(off Milston Cl.)
Brook Piece Wlk. B35: Cas V 4F 87
Brook Rd. B15: Edg 4A 116
B45: Rubery 2E 157
B68: O'bry 1G 113
DY8: Stourb 2F 125
WS6: C Hay 1E 7
WV5: Wom 1F 73
WV13: W'hall 2G 45
Brooksbank Dr. B64: Old H 5H 95
Brooksby Gro. B93: Dorr 6H 167
Brooks Cft. B35: Cas V 5E 87
Brookside B31: N'fld 2D 144
B43: Gt Barr 6H 65
B90: Ches G 6B 164
DY3: Gorn 5H 75
WS10: W'bry 2H 63
Brookside Av. B13: Mose 6B 134
Brookside Cl. B23: Erd 6C 68
B63: Hale 2F 127
WV5: Wom 1E 73
Brookside Ind. Est. WS10: W'bry 2H 63
Brookside Way DY6: W Hth 2H 91
Brooks Rd. B72: W Grn 5A 70
Brook St. B3: Birm 6E 101 (2B 4)
B66: Smeth 3F 99
B70: W Brom 4H 79
DY3: Gorn 4G 75
DY3: Sed 6C 60
DY4: Tip 1G 77
DY5: Quar B 3C 110
DY6: W Hth 6H 73
DY8: Stourb 6C 108
DY8: Word 2D 108
DY9: Lye 6B 110
WS2: Wals 2B 48
WV14: Bils 6G 45
Brook St. Bus. Cen. DY4: Tip 1G 77
Brook Ter. WV14: Bils 6G 45
Brookthorpe Dr. WV12: W'hall 6C 30
Brookvale Gro. B92: Olton 4B 136
Brookvale M. B29: S Oak 3D 132
Brookvale Pk. Rd. B23: Erd 2B 84
Brookvale Rd. B6: Witt 5A 84
B92: Olton 4B 136
Brookvale Trad. Est. B6: Witt 4H 83
Brookview B67: Smeth 6D 98
Brook Vw. Cl. B19: Hock 3E 101
Brook Wlk. B32: Bart G 3B 130
Brookwillow Rd. B63: Hale 4F 127
Brookwood Av. B28: Hall G 2D 148
Broomcroft Rd. B37: K'hrst 4B 106
Broomdene Av. B34: S End 2E 105
Broom Dr. B14: K Hth 3G 147
Broome Av. B43: Gt Barr 6G 65
Broome Cl. B63: Hale 2A 128
Broome Ct. B36: Cas B 1G 105
Broome Gdns. B75: S Cold 6A 54
Broomehill Cl. DY5: Brie H 4G 109
Broome Rd. WV10: Bush 2A 28
Broomfield B67: Smeth 4D 98
Broomfield Rd. B23: Erd 5D 84
Broomfields Av. B91: Sol 2H 151
Broomfields Cl. B91: Sol 2H 151
Broomfields Farm Rd. B91: Sol 2H 151

Broomhall Av. WV11: Wed 3F **29**
Broom Hall Cres. B27: A Grn. 6H **135**
Broom Hall Gro. B27: A Grn 5A **136**
Broomhill Cl. B43: Gt Barr. 5H **65**
Broomhill La. B43: Gt Barr 5H **65**
Broomhill Rd. B23: Erd 6B **68**
(not continuous)
Broom Ho. B71: W Brom 4D **64**
Broomhurst B15: Edg 3A **116**
Broomie Cl. B75: S Cold 6B **54**
Broom La. B90: Dic H 3G **163**
Broomlea Cl. B74: S'tly 3G **51**
Broom Rd. DY1: Dud 2C **76**
WS5: Wals 2F **65**
Broom St. B12: Birm 3A **118**
Broomy Cl. B34: Stech 4E **105**
Broseley Av. B31: Longb 1F **159**
Broseley Brook Cl.
B9: Bord G 2C **118**
Brosil Av. B20: Hand 4A **82**
Brougham St. B19: Loz 2D **100**
(not continuous)
Brough Cl. B7: Nech. 3B **102**
WV4: E'shll. 2B **60**
Broughton Ct. WV6: Pert 6G **25**
Broughton Cres. B31: Longb 1B **158**
Broughton Rd. B20: Hand 1C **100**
DY9: W'cte. 2H **125**
WV3: Wolv 2A **42**
Brownfield Rd. B34: S End 3G **105**
BROWNHILLS. 6B **10**
Brownhills Bus. Pk. WS8: Bwnhls. 2B **22**
BROWNHILLS COMMON 5A **10**
Brownhills Rd. WS8: Wals W 2B **22**
WS11: Nort C 1E **9**
BROWNHILLS WEST 3G **9**
Brownhills West Station
Chasewater Railway 2G **9**
Browning Cl. WV12: W'hall 2E **31**
Browning Cres. WV10: F'hses 5G **15**
Browning Gro. WV6: Pert. 5E **25**
Browning Rd. DY3: Lwr G 3E **75**
Browning St. B16: Birm. 1D **116**
Browning Twr. B31: N'fld 4G **145**
Brownley Rd. B90: Shir 2B **164**
Brown Lion St. DY4: Tip 6G **61**
Brown Rd. WS10: Darl 4C **46**
Brown's Coppice Av. B91: Sol 2B **150**
Browns Ct. B13: Mose 3B **134**
Brown's Dr. B73: Bold. 5F **69**
Brownsea Cl. B45: Fran 6E **143**
Brownsea Dr. B1: Birm 2F **117** (6C **4**)
BROWN'S GREEN
Birmingham 4B **82**
Browns Grn. B20: Hand 4B **82**
Brownshore La. WV11: Ess 3A **18**
Browns La. B93: Know. 3A **166**
Brownsover Cl. B36: Cas B. 6F **87**
Brown St. WV2: Wolv. 4H **43**
Brownswall Est. DY3: Sed 6F **59**
Brownswall Rd. DY3: Sed 6F **59**
Broxwood Pk. WV6: Tett 6H **25**
Brueton Av. B91: Sol 4H **151**
Brueton Dr. B24: Erd 4G **85**
Brueton Rd. WV14: Bils 4A **46**
Bruford Rd. WV3: Wolv 3E **43**
Brunel Cl. B12: Bal H 6A **118**
Brunel Ct. WS10: Darl 5F **47**
WV5: Wom. 6G **57**
WV14: Cose. 5G **61**
Brunel Dr. DY4: Tip 4G **61**
Brunel Gro. WV6: Pert 3E **25**
Brunel Rd. B69: O'bry 3D **96**
Brunel St. B2: Birm 1F **117** (5C **4**)
Brunel Wlk. WS10: Darl 5F **47**
Brunel Way WV2: E'shll 4C **44**
Brunslow Cl. WV10: Oxl. 6G **15**
WV13: W'hall 2C **46**
Brunswick Arc. *B1: Birm 1D **116***
(off Brunswick St.)
Brunswick Ct. WS10: W'bry. 2A **64**
Brunswick Gdns. B21: Hand. 6B **82**
WS10: W'bry 1H **63**
Brunswick Ga. DY8: Stourb 4E **125**
Brunswick Ho. B34: S End 2E **105**
B37: Mars G. 3B **122**
Brunswick Pk. Rd. WS10: W'bry 2G **63**
Brunswick Rd. B12: Bal H 6A **118**
B21: Hand 6B **82**
Brunswick Sq. B1: Birm 1D **116** (5A **4**)
Brunswick St. B1: Birm. 1D **116** (5A **4**)
WS2: Wals 4A **48**
Brunswick Ter. WS10: W'bry 2F **63**
Brunton Rd. B10: Small H. 4F **119**
Brushfield Rd. B42: Gt Barr 5F **67**
Brutus Dr. B46: Col 6G **89**
Bryan Av. WV4: Penn 1B **58**
Bryan Rd. WS2: Wals. 5A **48**
Bryanston Ct. B91: Sol. 6D **136**
Bryanston Rd. B91: Sol 6D **136**
Bryant St. B18: Win G 4A **100**
Bryce Rd. DY5: P'ntt 4E **93**
(not continuous)
Bryher Wlk. B45: Fran 6E **143**
Brylan Cft. B44: K'sdng 1H **83**
Brymill Ind. Est. DY4: Tip 6G **61**
Bryn Arden Rd. B26: Yard 6C **120**
Bryndale Av. B14: K Hth. 2E **147**
Brynmawr Rd. WV14: Cose 2C **60**
Brynside Cl. B14: K Hth 5F **147**
Bryony Cft. B23: Erd. 6B **68**
Bryony Gdns. WS10: Darl 4D **46**
Bryony Rd. B29: W Cas 6F **131**
BSA Bus. Pk. B11: Small H 5D **118**
Buchanan Av. WS4: Wals. 6E **33**
Buchanan Cl. WS4: Wals 6E **33**
Buchanan Rd. WS4: Wals 6E **33**
Buckbury Cl. DY9: Pedm 4H **125**
Buckbury Cft. B90: M'path 3F **165**
Buckingham Cl. WS10: W'bry 1A **64**
Buckingham Ct. B29: S Oak. 4A **132**
Buckingham Dr. WV12: W'hall 2B **30**
Buckingham Gro. DY6: K'wfrd 2A **92**
Buckingham Ho. B31: Longb. 1D **158**
Buckingham M. B73: W Grn 2G **69**
Buckingham Ri. DY1: Dud 5A **76**
Buckingham Rd. B36: Cas B 2B **106**
B65: Row R 5D **96**
WV4: Penn 1E **59**
Buckingham St. B19: Birm. 5F **101**
BUCKLAND END 2D **104**
Buckland End B34: S End. 3E **105**
Buckland Ho. *B15: Edg. 4E **117***
(off Summer Rd.)
Bucklands End La. B34: Hodg H 3D **104**
Buckle Cl. WS1: Wals 3D **48**
Buckley Ct. B13: K Hth. 5H **133**
Buckley Rd. WV4: Penn 6B **42**
Bucklow Wlk. B33: Stech 5C **104**
Buckminster Dr. B93: Dorr. 5A **166**
Bucknall Ct. B13: Mose 3B **134**
Bucknall Cres. B32: Bart G 5G **129**
Bucknall Rd. WV11: Wed. 6B **18**
Bucknell Cl. B91: Sol. 2G **151**
BUCKPOOL 1D **108**
Buckridge Cl. B38: K Nor. 2H **159**
Buckridge La. B90: Dic H. 4G **163**
(not continuous)
Buckton Cl. B75: R'ley 1C **54**
Budbrooke Gro. B34: S End 3A **106**
Budden Rd. WV14: Cose 6F **61**
Bude Rd. WS5: Wals 4H **49**
Buffery Rd. DY2: Dud. 2F **95**
Bufferys Cl. B91: Sol 1F **165**
Buildwas Cl. WS3: Blox 5F **19**
Bulford Cl. B14: K Hth 5H **147**
Bulger Rd. WV14: Bils 4E **45**
Bullace Cft. B15: Edg. 2H **131**
Buller St. WV4: E'shll. 6A **44**
Bullfields Cl. B65: Row R 4H **95**
Bullfinch Cl. DY1: Dud. 1A **94**
Bullivents Cl. B93: Ben H. 4B **166**
Bull La. B70: W Brom 4G **79**
WS10: Mox 2B **62**
WV5: Wom. 5G **57**
WV14: Bils 2B **62**
Bull Mdw. La. WV5: Wom 5G **57**
Bullock's Row WS1: Wals 2D **48**
Bullock St. B7: Birm. 4A **102**
B70: W Brom 1B **98**
Bullows Rd. WS8: Bwnhls 1G **21**
Bull Ring B63: Hale 2B **128**
DY3: Sed 5H **59**
WV13: W'hall 6A **30**
Bullring Shop. Cen. B5: Birm . . . 1G **117** (5F **5**)
Bull Ring Trad. Est.
B12: Birm 2H **117** (6H **5**)
Bull's La. B76: Walm 2F **71**
(not continuous)
Bull St. B4: Birm. 6G **101** (3E **5**)
B17: Harb. 5H **115**
B70: W Brom 4B **80**
DY1: Dud 1C **94**
DY3: Gorn 5G **75**
DY5: Brie H. 2F **109**
(Goldencross Way)
DY5: Brie H 1E **109**
(Hawbush Rd.)
WS10: Darl. 5E **47**
Bull St. Trad. Est. DY5: Brie H 1F **109**
Bulrush Cl. WS8: Bwnhls. 6A **10**
Bulwell Cl. B6: Aston. 2A **102**
Bulwer St. WV10: Wolv 6H **27**
BUMBLE HOLE 4G **95**
Bumblehole Mdws. WV5: Wom 6F **57**
Bumble Hole Nature Reserve 4G **95**
Bunbury Gdns. B30: K Nor. 3G **145**
Bunbury Rd. B31: N'fld. 3F **145**
Bundle Hill B63: Hale. 2A **128**
Bungalows, The B70: W Brom 1F **79**
BUNKER'S HILL 4G **45**
Bunkers Hill La. WV14: Bils 3G **45**
Bunn's La. DY2: Dud 6H **77**
Burbage Cl. WV10: Wolv 3B **28**
Burberry Ct. DY4: Tip. 5A **62**
Burberry Gro. CV7: Bal C. 3G **169**
Burbidge Rd. B9: Bord G. 6D **102**
Burbury St. B19: Loz 2E **101**
Burbury St. Sth. B19: Hock 3E **101**
Burcombe Twr. B23: Erd 1H **85**
Burcot Av. WV1: Wolv 1C **44**
Burcot Ct. B74: Four O 1F **53**
Burcote Rd. B24: Erd 4B **86**
Burcot Wlk. WV1: Wolv 1C **44**
Burdock Cl. WS5: Wals 2E **65**
Burdock Ho. B38: K Nor. 6B **146**
Burdock Rd. B29: W Cas 1E **145**
Burdons Cl. B34: Stech 4E **105**
Bure Gro. WV13: W'hall. 1D **46**
Burfield Rd. B63: Crad 5E **111**
Burford Cl. B92: Olton 2E **137**
WS5: Wals 2E **65**
Burford Ct. B13: Mose 3B **134**
Burford Pk. Rd. B38: K Nor 1A **160**
Burford Rd. B44: K'sdng 6H **67**
B47: H'wd 3H **161**
Burgess Cft. B92: Sol. 6B **138**
Burghley Dr. B71: W Brom 3D **64**
Burghley Wlk. DY5: Brie H. 3F **109**
Burgh Way WS2: Wals. 4G **31**
Burhill Way B37: F'bri 4D **106**
Burke Av. B13: Mose 4D **134**
Burkitt Dr. DY4: Tip 5C **62**
Burland Av. WV6: Tett 2C **26**
Burleigh Cl. CV7: Bal C 2H **169**
WV12: W'hall 3B **30**
Burleigh Cft. WS7: Chase. 1C **10**
Burleigh Rd. WV3: Wolv 4E **43**
Burleigh St. WS1: Wals 2E **49**
Burleton Rd. B33: Kitts G. 1A **122**
Burley Cl. B90: Shir 5F **149**
Burley Way B38: K Nor 1G **159**
Burlington Arc. B2: Birm 4D **4**
Burlington Av. B70: W Brom 6C **80**
Burlington Pas. B2: Birm. 4D **4**
Burlington Rd. B10: Small H 2E **119**
B70: W Brom 6C **80**
Burlington St. B6: Aston 3G **101**
Burlish Av. B92: Olton 4D **136**
Burman Cl. B90: Shir. 5G **149**
Burman Dr. B46: Col 4H **107**
Burman Rd. B90: Shir. 5F **149**
Burmarsh Wlk. WV8: Pend 1D **26**
Burmese Way B65: Row R. 3H **95**
Burnaston Cres. B90: M'path. 3G **165**
Burnaston Rd. B28: Hall G 4E **135**
Burnbank Gro. B24: Erd. 3H **85**
Burn Cl. B66: Smeth. 5E **99**
Burncross Way WV10: Wolv 3B **28**
Burnell Gdns. WV3: Wolv 3C **42**
Burnel Rd. B29: W Cas. 3E **131**

Burnett Ho. B69: O'bry 4D **96**
Burnett Rd. B74: Lit A 1B **52**
Burney La. B8: W End 4A **104**
Burnfields Way WS9: A'rdge 2C **34**
Burnham Av. B25: Yard 5A **120**
WV10: Oxl 1F **27**
Burnham Cl. DY6: K'wfrd. 5D **92**
Burnham Ct. B23: Erd 5C **84**
DY5: Brie H 1H 109
(off Hill St.)
Burnham Mdw. B28: Hall G 1G **149**
Burnham Rd. B44: Gt Barr. 6G **67**
Burnhill Gro. B29: W Cas. 5E **131**
Burnlea Gro. B31: N'fld 6G **145**
Burnsall Cl. B37: F'bri 1B **122**
WV9: Pend 4E **15**
Burns Av. DY4: Tip 5A **62**
WV10: F'hses. 5H **15**
Burns Cl. DY8: Amb 3E **109**
Burns Gro. DY3: Lwr G. 3E **75**
Burnside Ct. B73: W Grn 4G **69**
Burnside Gdns. WS5: Wals 5H **49**
Burnside Way B31: Longb 2D **158**
Burns Pl. WS10: Mox. 6A **46**
Burns Rd. WS10: Mox 6A **46**
Burnthurst Cres. B90: M'path 2E **165**
Burnt Oak Dr. DY8: Stourb 6F **109**
BURNT TREE 5H 77
Burnt Tree DY4: Tip 5H **77**
BURNTWOOD JUNC. **2B 10**
Burntwood Rd. WS7: Hamm. 1F **11**
Burrelton Way B43: Gt Barr 5H **65**
Burrington Rd. B32: Bart G 5G **129**
Burrowes St. WS2: Wals 6B **32**
Burrow Hill Cl. B36: Cas B. 1G **105**
Burrows Ho. *WS2: Wals. 6B 32*
(off Burrowes St.)
Burrows Rd. DY6: K'wfrd. 5D **92**
Bursledon Wlk. WV1: Wolv 3E **45**
Burslem Cl. WS3: Blox 3G **19**
Bursnips Rd. WV11: Ess 5B **18**
Burton Av. WS4: Rus 1F **33**
Burton Cres. WV10: Wolv 6A **28**
Burton Farm Rd. WS4: Wals 6F **33**
Burton Gro. B64: Old H 3G **111**
Burton Rd. DY1: Dud 3B **76**
WV10: Wolv. 6A **28**
Burton Rd. E. DY1: Dud 3B **76**
Burton Wood Dr. B20: Hand 5F **83**
Buryfield Rd. B91: Sol 1E **151**
Bury Hill Rd. B69: O'bry 2D **96**
Bury Mound Ct. B90: Shir 5C **148**
Bush Av. B66: Smeth 4G **99**
BUSHBURY 6A 16
Bushbury Ct. WV10: Bush 5A **16**
Bushbury Crematorium WV10: Bush 4B **16**
Bushbury Cft. B37: Chel W. 6E **107**
Bushbury La. WV10: Oxl, Bush 3G **27**
Bushbury Rd. B33: Stech 4E **105**
WV10: Wolv 3C **28**
Bushbury Swimming Pool 6A 16
Bushell Dr. B91: Sol. 3H **151**
Bushey Cl. B74: S'tly 1H **51**
Bushey Flds. Rd. DY1: Dud 1A **94**
Bush Gro. B21: Hand 6G **81**
WS3: Pels. 5E **21**
Bushley Cft. B91: Sol 1F **165**
Bushman Way B34: S End 4A **106**
Bushmore Rd. B28: Hall G 1G **149**
Bush Rd. DY2: Neth 1E **111**
DY4: Tip. 3G **77**
Bush St. WS10: Darl 4D **46**
Bushway Cl. DY5: Brie H 1E **109**
Bushwood Ct. B15: Edg 3E **117**
B29: S Oak. 4G **131**
Bushwood Dr. B93: Dorr 6C **166**
Bushwood Rd. B29: S Oak 4F **131**
(not continuous)
Business Cen., The B11: Tys 5F **119**
Bustleholme Av. B71: W Brom 4D **64**
Bustleholme Cres. B71: W Brom. 4C **64**
Bustleholme La. B71: W Brom 4C **64**
(not continuous)
Butchers La. B63: Crad 4E **111**
Butchers Rd. B92: H Ard 1A **154**
BUTCROFT. 5E 47
Butcroft Gdns. WS10: Darl 5E **47**
Bute Cl. B45: Fran 6E **143**
WV12: W'hall 3B **30**
Butler Lane Station (Rail) 6G 37
Butler Rd. B92: Olton. 2D **136**
Butlers Cl. B20: Hand. 4C **82**
B23: Erd. 4D **68**
Butlers La. B74: Four O 6F **37**
Butlers Pct. WS1: Wals 1C **48**
Butler's Rd. B20: Hand. 4C **82**
Butler St. B70: W Brom 3G **79**
Butlin St. B7: Nech. 2C **102**
Buttercup Cl. WS5: Wals 2E **65**
Butterfield Cl. WV6: Pert 6D **24**
Butterfield Ct. DY1: Dud 5C **76**
Butterfield Rd. DY5: P'ntt. 2F **93**
Butterfly Way B64: Old H. 2H **111**
Buttermere Cl. DY5: Brie H 4F **109**
WV6: Tett 1B **26**
Buttermere Ct. WV6: Pert. 5F **25**
Buttermere Dr. B32: Bart G 2D **130**
WV11: Ess 5A **18**
Buttermere Gro. WV12: W'hall. 6B **18**
Butter Wlk. B38: K Nor 1G **159**
Butterworth Cl. WV14: Cose 4C **60**
Buttery Rd. B67: Smeth 3C **98**
Buttons Farm Rd. WV4: Penn 2B **58**
Buttress Way B66: Smeth. 3E **99**
Butts, The WS4: Wals 6D **32**
Butts Cl. WS11: Nort C. 1C **8**
Butts La. WS11: Nort C 1C **8**
Butts Rd. WS4: Wals 6D **32**
WV4: Penn. 1D **58**
Butts St. WS4: Wals. 6D **32**
Butts Way WS11: Nort C 1C **8**
Buxton Cl. WS3: Blox. 4A **20**
Buxton Rd. B23: Erd. 1B **84**
B73: W Grn 4G **69**
DY2: Dud 3B **94**
WS3: Blox 4A **20**
Byeways WS3: Blox. 4A **20**
Byfield Cl. B33: Kitts G 3A **122**
Byfield Pas. B9: Bord G 1E **119**
Byfield Vw. DY3: Sed 6A **60**
Byfleet Cl. WV14: Cose 2C **60**
Byford Way B37: Mars G 3D **122**
Byland Way WS3: Blox. 5F **19**
By-Pass Link B91: Sol 4A **152**
Byrchen Moor Gdns. DY5: P'ntt 2F **93**
Byrne Rd. WV2: Wolv 4H **43**
Byron Av. B23: Erd. 4B **84**
Byron Cl. B10: Small H 4D **118**
Byron Ct. B74: Four O 4G **37**
B93: Know 3C **166**
Byron Cres. DY1: Dud 2D **76**
Byron Cft. B74: Four O 3F **37**
DY3: Lwr G. 2E **75**
Byron Gdns. B71: W Brom. 2H **79**
Byron Ho. B63: Crad 6D **110**
Byron Rd. B10: Small H. 4D **118**
WV10: Bush. 1C **28**
WV12: W'hall 2E **31**
Byron St. B71: W Brom 1H **79**
DY5: P'ntt 2H **93**
Bywater Ho. *WS1: Wals. 2D 48*
(off Paddock La.)

C

Caban Cl. B31: N'fld. 2C **144**
Cable Dr. WS2: Wals 4A **32**
Cabot Gro. WV6: Pert. 5E **25**
Cadbury Dr. B35: Cas V 6E **87**
Cadbury Ho. *B19: Birm. 4F 101*
(off Gt. Hampton Row)
Cadbury Rd. B13: Mose 1B **134**
Cadbury Way B17: Harb 6F **115**
Cadbury World 6B 132
Caddick Cres. B71: W Brom 6B **64**
Caddick Rd. B42: Gt Barr. 4D **66**
Caddick St. WV14: Cose 5C **60**
(not continuous)
Cadet Dr. B90: Shir 4G **149**
Cadgwith Gdns. WV14: Bils 3A **62**
Cadine Gdns. B13: Mose 4E **133**
Cadleigh Gdns. B17: Harb 2G **131**
Cadle Rd. WV10: Bush. 2A **28**
Cadman Cres. WV10: Wolv 3C **28**
Cadman's La. WS3: Blox 1B **20**
WS6: Gt Wyr 5A **8**
(not continuous)
Cadnam Cl. B17: Harb 2G **131**
WV13: W'hall 3B **46**
Caernarvon Cl.
WV12: W'hall 2C **30**
Caernarvon Way DY1: Dud 5A **76**
Caesar Way B46: Col 6H **89**
Cahill Av. WV10: Wolv 5C **28**
Cairn Dr. WS2: Wals. 1F **47**
Cairns St. WS2: Wals. 6A **32**
Caister Dr. WV13: W'hall 3H **45**
Cakemore La. B68: O'bry 1F **113**
Cakemore Rd. B65: Row R 1E **113**
Cala Dr. B15: Edg. 4D **116**
Calcot Dr. WV6: Tett. 2C **26**
Calcutt Way B90: Dic H 3G **163**
(not continuous)
Caldecote Gro. B9: Bord G. 1A **120**
Caldeford Av. B90: M'path 2E **165**
Calder Av. WS1: Wals 1E **49**
Calder Dr. B76: Walm 5D **70**
Calderfields Cl. WS4: Wals 6E **33**
Calder Gro. B20: Hand. 5B **82**
Calder Ri. DY3: Sed. 1B **76**
Calder Twr. B20: Hand 6F **83**
CALDMORE 3C 48
Caldmore Grn. WS1: Wals. 3C **48**
Caldmore Rd. WS1: Wals 2C **48**
Caldwell Ct. B91: Sol. 2G **151**
Caldwell Gro. B91: Sol 2G **151**
Caldwell Ho. B70: W Brom 5A **80**
Caldwell Rd. B9: Bord G 6H **103**
Caldwell St. B71: W Brom. 5B **64**
Caldy Wlk. B45: Fran 6F **143**
Caledonia DY5: Quar B 4H **109**
Caledonian Cl. WS5: Wals. 2G **65**
Caledonia Rd. WV2: Wolv 3H **43**
(not continuous)
Caledonia St. WV14: Bils. 5G **45**
Caledon Pl. WS2: Wals 4A **48**
Caledon St. WS2: Wals 4A **48**
(not continuous)
Calewood Rd. DY5: Quar B 4H **109**
CALIFORNIA. 2D 130
California Ho. *B32: Bart G 3C 130*
(off Millmead Rd.)
California Rd. B69: Tiv. 1B **96**
California Way B32: Bart G 2D **130**
Callcott Dr. DY5: Quar B 4H **109**
Callear Rd. WS10: W'bry 4D **62**
Calley Cl. DY4: Tip. 4H **77**
Callow Bri. Rd. B45: Rubery 2F **157**
Callowbrook La. B45: Rubery 1F **157**
Calshot Rd. B42: Gt Barr 4B **66**
Calstock Rd. WV12: W'hall 5D **30**
Calthorpe Cl. WS5: Wals 5A **50**
Calthorpe Mans. B15: Edg. 2D **116**
Calthorpe Rd. B15: Edg 3C **116**
B20: Hand 5E **83**
WS5: Wals 5H **49**
Calver Cres. WV11: Wed 4H **29**
Calver Gro. B44: Gt Barr. 2F **67**
Calverley Rd. B38: K Nor. 6H **145**
Calverton Gro. B43: Gt Barr. 5A **66**
Calverton Wlk. WV6: Wolv. 4F **27**
Calves Cft. WV13: W'hall. 6A **30**
Calvin Cl. WV5: Wom. 2F **73**
WV10: F'hses. 4H **15**
Camberley B71: W Brom. 4D **64**
Camberley Cres. WV4: E'shll 3A **60**
Camberley Dr. WV4: Penn 1E **59**
Camberley Gro. B23: Erd. 1E **85**
Camberley Rd. DY6: K'wfrd. 6D **92**
Camborne Cl. B6: Aston 2G **101**
Camborne Ct. WS5: Wals 4H **49**
Camborne Rd. WS5: Wals. 4H **49**
Cambourne Rd. B65: Row R 6C **96**
Cambrai Dr. B28: Hall G. 5E **135**
Cambria Cl. B90: Maj G 2E **163**
Cambridge Av. B73: W Grn 5H **69**
B91: Sol 4C **150**
Cambridge Cl. WS9: A'rdge 1C **34**
Cambridge Cres. B15: Edg. 4E **117**
Cambridge Dr. B37: Mars G. 3B **122**

Cambridge Rd. B13: Mose. 4H 133
B66: Smeth 2E 99
DY2: Dud 2C 94
Cambridge St. B1: Birm 1E 117 (4A 4)
B70: W Brom 5H 79
WS1: Wals 4C 48
WV10: Wolv 5H 27
Cambridge Twr. B1: Birm 6E 101 (4A 4)
Cambridge Way B27: A Grn 1B 136
Camden Cl. B36: Cas B 1E 105
WS5: Wals 2F 65
Camden Dr. B1: Birm 6D 100 (2A 4)
Camden St. B1: Birm 5C 100 (2A 4)
B18: Hock 5C 100
WS1: Wals 3B 48
WS9: Wals W 3A 22
Camden Way DY6: K'wfrd 6B 74
Camellia Gdns. DY8: Word 1C 108
WV9: Pend 4D 14
Camelot Way B10: Small H 3C 118
Cameo Dr. DY8: Amb 3D 108
Cameronian Cft. B36: Hodg H 1A 104
Cameron Rd. WS4: Wals 6E 33
Camford Gro. B14: K Hth 4H 147
Cam Gdns. DY5: P'ntt 3F 93
Camino Rd. B32: Bart G 2D 130
Camomile Cl. WS5: Wals 2E 65
Campbell Cl. WS4: Wals 6E 33
Campbells Grn. B26: Sheld 1F 137
Campbell St. DY5: Brie H 5G 93
Campden Grn. B92: Olton 2E 137
Camp Hill B12: Birm 3A 118
DY8: Word 2C 108
Camp Hill Cir. B11: S'brk 3A 118
Camp Hill Ind. Est. B12: Birm 4A 118
Camphill La. WS10: W'bry 3F 63
Camphill Pct. WS10: W'bry 3F 63
Campians Av. WS6: C Hay 3D 6
Campion Cl. B38: K Nor 1B 160
WS5: Wals 2E 65
WV5: Wom 1E 73
Campion Ct. DY4: Tip 2F 77
Campion Dr. WV10: F'stne 1C 16
Campion Gro. B63: Hale 2F 127
Campion Ho. B38: K Nor 1A 160
WV10: Wolv 5B 28
Campion Way B90: Dic H 4G 163
Camp La. B21: Hand 6F 81
B38: K Nor 4B 146
Camplea Cft. B37: F'bri 1C 122
Camplin Cres. B20: Hand 2A 82
Camp Rd. B75: R'ley 2A 38
WS14: Lit H 2H 37
Camp St. B9: Bord G 2C 118
WS10: W'bry 3F 63
WV1: Wolv 6G 27 (1B 170)
Campville Cres. B71: W Brom 4C 64
Campville Gro. B37: K'hrst 4B 106
Campwood Cl. B30: B'vlle 5A 132
Camrose Cft. B12: Bal H 6H 117
B34: S End 3F 105
Camrose Gdns. WV9: Pend 4E 15
Canal Cotts. DY2: Neth 6D 94
Canal La. B24: Erd 6G 85
Canal Side B30: K Nor 4C 146
B48: Hopw 6G 159
B69: O'bry 2F 97
DY2: Neth 5G 95
Canalside Cl. WS3: Blox 6D 20
WS10: W'bry 3C 64
Canalside Ind. Est. DY5: Brie H 2G 109
Canal St. B69: O'bry 2F 97
DY4: Tip 3F 77
DY5: Brie H 4A 94
DY8: Amb 5D 108
WS2: Wals 1B 48
WV14: Cose 5E 61
Canal Vw. Ind. Est.
DY5: Brie H 2F 109
Canary Gro. B19: Loz 1E 101
Canberra Rd. WS5: Wals 6G 49
Canberra Way B12: Birm 3A 118
Canford Cl. B12: Birm 4H 117
Canford Cres. WV8: Cod 4E 13
Canning Cl. WS5: Wals 5H 49
Canning Gdns. B18: Win G 5A 100
Canning Rd. WS5: Wals 5H 49
Cannock Rd.
WV10: Bush, F'stne, Share 2D 16
WV10: Wolv 5H 27
WV12: W'hall 2C 30
Cannon Bus. Pk. WV14: Cose 4E 61
Cannon Dr. WV14: Cose 3E 61
Cannon Hill Gro. B12: Bal H 6G 117
Cannon Hill Pl. B12: Bal H 6G 117
Cannon Hill Rd. B12: Bal H 6F 117
Cannon Raceway 4E 61
Cannon Rd. WV5: Wom 1G 73
Cannon St. B2: Birm 1G 117 (4D 4)
WS2: Wals 5C 32
WV13: W'hall 1B 46
Cannon St. Nth. WS2: Wals 5C 32
Canterbury Av. WV13: W'hall 1D 46
Canterbury Cl. B23: Erd 5D 84
B65: Row R 5E 97
B71: W Brom 5C 64
WS3: Pels 3E 21
Canterbury Dr. B37: Mars G 4C 122
WV6: Pert 5D 24
Canterbury Rd. B20: Hand 6F 83
B71: W Brom 5B 64
WV4: Penn 6C 42
Canterbury Twr. *B1: Birm* *6D 100*
(off St Marks St.)
Cantlow Ho. B12: Birm 4H 117
Cantlow Rd. B13: Mose 1A 148
Canton La. B46: Col 2H 89
Canute Cl. WS1: Wals 4D 48
Canvey Cl. B45: Fran 6E 143
CANWELL 4E 39
Canwell Av. B37: K'hrst 4B 106
Canwell Dr. B75: Can 4E 39
Canwell Gdns. WV14: Bils 1E 61
Canwell Ga. B75: R'ley 5C 38
Capcroft Rd. B13: Mose 1B 148
Cape Cl. WS8: Bwnhls 1C 22
Cape Hill B66: Smeth 5F 99
Cape Hill Retail Cen. B66: Smeth 5F 99
Capener Rd. B43: Gt Barr 3C 66
Capern Gro. B32: Harb 6D 114
Cape St. B18: Win G 5H 99
B70: W Brom 3E 79
Capethorn Rd. B66: Smeth 6E 99
Capilano Rd. B23: Erd 6C 68
Capponfield Cl. WV14: Cose 2D 60
Capstone Av. B18: Hock 5C 100
WV10: Oxl 1F 27
Captain's Cl. WV3: Wolv 1B 42
Carcroft Rd. B25: Yard 3B 120
Cardale St. B65: B'hth 1D 112
Carden Cl. B70: W Brom 3F 79
Carder Cres. WV14: Bils 1F 61
Carder Dr. DY5: Brie H 1G 109
Cardigan Cl. B71: W Brom 6A 64
Cardigan Dr. WV12: W'hall 3B 30
Cardigan St. B4: Birm 6H 101 (2H 5)
Cardington Av. B42: Gt Barr 4D 66
Cardoness Pl. DY1: Dud 5B 76
Careless Grn. DY9: Lye, W'cte 1B 126
Careynon Ct. WS3: Blox 1H 31
Carhampton Rd. B75: S Cold 5E 55
Carillon Gdns. B65: Row R 6C 96
Carisbrooke Av. B37: Chel W 1E 123
Carisbrooke Cl. WS10: W'bry 3C 64
Carisbrooke Cres. WS10: W'bry 2C 64
Carisbrooke Dr. B62: Hale 1D 128
Carisbrooke Gdns. WV10: Bush 4A 16
Carisbrooke Ho. B31: Longb 1D 158
Carisbrooke Rd. B17: Edg 2F 115
WS10: W'bry 3B 64
WV6: Pert 6G 25
WV10: Bush 4A 16
Carless Av. B17: Harb 4F 115
Carless St. WS1: Wals 3C 48
Carlisle St. B18: Win G 4A 100
Carlson Pk. B17: Harb 6F 115
Carl St. WS2: Wals 4B 32
Carlton Av. B21: Hand 6A 82
B74: S'tly 1H 51
DY9: W'cte 2A 126
WV11: Wed 2C 28
WV14: Bils 4H 45
Carlton Cl. B75: S Cold 4B 54
DY1: Dud 1E 77
Carlton Cft. B74: S'tly 1A 52
Carlton M. B36: Cas B 1H 105
Carlton M. Flats B36: Cas B 1H 105
Carlton Rd. B9: Small H 2D 118
B66: Smeth 1E 99
WV3: Wolv 4E 43
Carlyle Bus. Pk. B70: W Brom 2F 79
Carlyle Gro. WV10: Bush 1C 28
Carlyle Rd. B16: Edg 2A 116
B19: Loz 1E 101
B65: Row R 1C 112
WV10: Bush 1C 28
Carmel Gro. B32: Bart G 4H 129
Carmodale Av. B42: P Barr 1D 82
Carnegie Av. DY4: Tip 3A 78
Carnegie Dr. WS10: W'bry 2G 63
Carnegie Rd. B65: Row R 1B 112
Carnford Rd. B26: Sheld 5F 121
Carnforth Cl. DY6: K'wfrd 2H 91
Carnoustie Cl. B75: S Cold 3A 54
WS3: Blox 4G 19
Carnwath Rd. B73: New O 3E 69
Carol Cres. B63: Hale 6H 111
WV11: Wed 3G 29
Carol Gdns. DY8: Amb 3D 108
Caroline Pl. B13: Mose 2H 133
Caroline Rd. B13: Mose 1H 133
Caroline St. B3: Birm 5E 101 (1B 4)
B70: W Brom 5H 79
DY2: Dud 6G 77
Carpathian, The B18: Birm 1A 4
Carpathian Ct. B18: Birm 5E 101
Carpenter Glade B63: Crad 6F 111
Carpenter Pl. B12: Bal H 5A 118
Carpenter Rd. B15: Edg 4C 116
Carpenters Ct. *B12: Birm* *3H 117*
(off Vaughton St.)
Carpenter's Rd. B19: Loz 2E 101
Carrick Cl. WS3: Pels 2E 21
Carriers Cl. WS2: Wals 2F 47
Carriers Fold WV5: Wom 6H 57
Carrington Rd. WS10: W'bry 3B 64
CARROWAY HEAD 5G 39
Carroway Head Hill B75: Bass P, Can 6F 39
Carrs La. B4: Birm 1G 117 (4F 5)
Carshalton Gro. WV2: Wolv 4A 44
Carshalton Rd. B44: K'sdng 3A 68
Cartbridge Cres. WS3: Wals 3D 32
(not continuous)
Cartbridge La. WS4: Wals 4E 33
Cartbridge La. Sth. WS4: Wals 5E 33
Cartbridge Wlk. WS3: Wals 3E 33
Carter Av. WV8: Bilb 4H 13
Carter Rd. B43: Gt Barr 3B 66
WV6: Wolv 4F 27
Carters Cl. B37: Mars G 4C 122
B76: Walm 2D 70
Cartersfield La. WS9: Ston 1F 23
Carters Grn. B70: W Brom 3H 79
Carter's Hurst B33: Sheld 2F 121
Carter's La. B62: Quin 6F 113
Cartland Rd. B11: S'brk 4C 118
B14: K Hth 5D 132
B30: Stir 5D 132
Cartmel Ct. B23: Erd 3B 84
Cartway, The WV6: Pert 5D 24
Cartwright Gdns. B69: Tiv 5C 78
Cartwright Ho. WS3: Blox 6H 19
Cartwright Rd. B75: R'ley 6A 38
Cartwright St. WV2: Wolv 3H 43 (6C 170)
Carver Ct. B24: Erd 1A 86
DY4: Tip 4A 62
Carver Gdns. DY8: Stourb 3C 124
Carver St. B1: Birm 5D 100
Casern Vw. B75: S Cold 5E 55
Casewell Rd. DY6: W Hth 1A 92
Casey Av. B23: Erd 5D 68
Cash-Joynson Av. WS10: Darl 3C 46
Caslon Cres. DY8: Stourb 1B 124
Caslon Rd. B63: Crad 5E 111
Caslow Flats B63: Crad 1E 127
Cassandra Cl. DY5: P'ntt 6G 75
Cassowary Rd. B20: Hand 4B 82
Castello Dr. B36: Cas B 6H 87
Castillo Ct. B14: K Hth 2A 148
Castings, The WV14: Cose 3F 61
Castle, The DY8: Stourb 2F 125

Castlebridge Gdns. WV11: Wed 2H 29
Castlebridge Rd. WV11: Wed 3H 29
CASTLE BROMWICH 1F 105
Castle Bromwich Bus. Pk.
B35: Cas V 6D 86
Castle Bromwich Hall B36: Cas B 1E 105
Castle Cl. B64: Old H 2B 112
B92: Olton 4F 137
WS8: Bwnhls 3B 10
Castle Ct. B34: S End 2A 106
Castle Cres. B36: Cas B 1G 105
CASTLECROFT 2G 41
Castle Cft. B68: O'bry 3B 114
Castlecroft WS11: Nort C 1C 8
Castlecroft Av. WV3: Wolv 3G 41
Castlecroft Gdns. WV3: Wolv 3A 42
Castlecroft La. WV3: Wolv 3F 41
Castle Cft. Rd. WV14: Bils 4G 45
Castlecroft Rd. WV3: Wolv 3F 41
Castle Dr. B46: Col 4H 107
WV12: W'hall 4B 30
Castleford Gro. B11: S'hll 1C 134
Castleford Rd. B11: S'hll 1C 134
Castlefort Rd. WS9: Wals W 4C 22
Castlegate Dr. DY1: Dud 5G 77
Castlegate Island DY1: Dud 5G 77
Castlegate Way DY1: Dud 5G 77
Castle Gro. DY8: Stourb 2F 125
Castle Hgts. B64: Old H 3B 112
(off Granville Rd.)
Castle Hill DY1: Dud 5F 77
Castlehill Rd. WS9: Wals W 4D 22
Castlehills Dr. B36: Cas B 1E 105
Castle Ho. B33: Yard 2F 121
Castle La. B92: Olton 4D 136
Castlemill DY4: Tip 5H 77
Castle Mill Rd. DY1: Dud 3E 77
Castle Rd. B29: W Cas 3E 131
B30: K Nor 3B 146
DY4: Tip 3F 77
WS9: Wals W 5C 22
Castle Rd. E. B68: O'bry 3B 114
Castle Rd. W. B68: O'bry 3A 114
Castle Sq. B29: W Cas 4E 131
Castle St. B70: W Brom 5G 63
DY1: Dud 6F 77
DY3: Sed 5H 59
DY4: Tip 2G 77
WS8: Bwnhls 3B 10
WS10: Darl 3D 46
(not continuous)
WV1: Wolv 1H 43 (3C 170)
WV14: Cose 5E 61
Castleton Rd. B42: Gt Barr 6F 67
WS3: Blox 4A 20
Castleton St. DY2: Neth 4E 95
CASTLE VALE 3F 87
Castle Vale Baths 5E 87
Castle Va. Ind. Est. B76: Min 2E 87
Castle Va. Shop. Cen. B35: Cas V 4D 86
Castle Vw. DY1: Dud 5D 76
Castle Vw. Cl. WS10: Mox 1A 62
Castle Vw. Enterprise Pk. B35: Cas V 4G 87
Castle Vw. Ind. Est. DY4: Tip 4H 77
Castle Vw. Rd. WV14: Bils 1A 62
Castle Vw. Ter. WV14: Cose 5D 60
Castle Yd. WV1: Wolv 1H 43 (3C 170)
Caswell Rd. DY3: Sed 5G 59
Cat & Kittens La. WV10: F'stne 1A 16
Cater Dr. B76: Walm 3D 70
Caterham Dr. DY6: K'wfrd 6D 92
Catesby Dr. DY6: K'wfrd 1B 92
Catesby Ho. B37: K'hrst 4B 106
Catesby Pk. B38: K Nor 4A 146
Catesby Rd. B90: Shir 6H 149
Cateswell Rd. B11: Tys 3F 135
B28: Hall G 4F 135
Cathcart Rd. DY8: Stourb 6C 108
Cathedral Cl. DY4: Tip 2G 77
Cathel Dr. B42: Gt Barr 6C 66
Catherine Ct. B24: Erd 3A 86
CATHERINE-DE-BARNES 2D 152
Catherine de Barnes La.
B92: Bick, Cath B 1E 153
Catherine Dr. B73: S Cold 5G 53
Catherine Rd. WV14: Cose 4C 60
Catherines Cl. B91: Cath B 3D 152
Catherine St. B6: Aston 2A 102
Catherton Cl. DY4: Tip 3C 62
Catholic La. DY3: Sed 1G 75
Catisfield Cres. WV8: Pend 6D 14
Cat La. B34: S End 2F 105
Caton Gro. B28: Hall G 6G 135
Cato St. B7: Birm 5B 102
Cato St. Nth. B7: Nech 4C 102
CATSHILL
Walsall 6C 10
Catshill Rd. WS8: Bwnhls 6C 10
Cattell Dr. B75: S Cold 6F 55
Cattell Rd. B9: Bord G 2C 118
Cattells Gro. B7: Nech 3C 102
Cattermole Gro. B43: Gt Barr 2E 67
Cattock Hurst Dr.
B72: W Grn 6B 70
Causeway B65: Row R 1C 112
Causeway, The B25: Yard 4B 120
CAUSEWAY GREEN 6F 97
Causeway Grn. Rd. B68: O'bry 6F 97
Causeway Rd. WV14: Cose 5F 61
Causey Farm Rd. B63: Hale 5E 127
Cavalier Cir. WV10: Bush 3A 16
Cavalier Dr. B63: Hale 2A 128
Cavandale Av. B44: Gt Barr 4G 67
Cavell Cl. WS2: Wals 1B 48
Cavell Rd. DY2: Dud 6H 77
Cavendish Cl. B38: K Nor 6D 146
DY6: K'wfrd 5B 92
Cavendish Ct. B17: Harb 3F 115
B93: Dorr 6C 166
Cavendish Gdns. WS2: Wals 5G 31
WV1: Wolv 2E 45
Cavendish Rd. B16: Edg 6H 99
B62: Hale 1F 129
WS2: Wals 4G 31
WV1: Wolv 2D 44
Cavendish Way WS9: A'rdge 4D 34
Caversham Pl. B73: S Cold 1H 69
Caversham Rd. B44: K'sdng 3A 68
Cawdon Gro. B93: Dorr 6G 167
Cawdor Cres. B16: Edg 2B 116
Cawney Hill DY2: Dud 1G 95
Caxton Ga. B2: Birm 4E 5
Caxton Gate Shop. Cen.
B2: Birm 1G 117
Caxton Gro. B44: K'sdng 4C 68
Caynham Rd. B32: Bart G 5H 129
Cayton Gro. B23: Erd 1F 85
Cearl Ct. B27: A Grn 3A 136
Cecil Dr. B69: Tiv 5D 78
Cecil Rd. B24: Erd 4F 85
B29: S Oak 4E 133
Cecil St. B19: Birm 5G 101
DY8: Stourb 6D 108
WS4: Wals 6D 32
Cedar Av. B36: Cas B 1G 105
WS8: Bwnhls 5C 10
WV14: Cose 6D 60
Cedar Bri. Cft. B74: Four O 3H 53
Cedar Cl. B30: B'vlle 1A 146
B68: O'bry 3A 114
DY8: Stourb 3B 124
WS5: Wals 1F 65
Cedar Dr. B24: Erd 2A 86
B31: Longb 2F 159
B74: S'tly 2G 51
Cedar Gro. WS6: Gt Wyr 1H 7
WV3: Wolv 4D 42
WV8: Bilb 4H 13
WV14: Bils 4H 45
Cedar Ho. B36: Hodg H 1D 104
B91: Sol 6D 150
Cedarhurst B32: Harb 6E 115
B91: Sol 4G 151
Cedar Pk. Rd. WV12: W'hall 6C 18
Cedar Rd. B30: B'vlle 1A 146
DY1: Dud 4D 76
(not continuous)
DY4: Tip 2F 77
WS10: W'bry 3G 63
WV13: W'hall 1G 45
Cedars, The B25: Yard 2C 120
B93: Know 5C 166
WV6: Tett 4B 26
WV6: Wolv 6D 26
Cedars Av. B27: A Grn 1A 136
DY6: K'wfrd 5B 92
WV5: Wom 2G 73
Cedar Tree B23: Erd 5E 85
Cedar Wlk. B37: Chel W 1D 122
(off Chelmsley Wood Shop. Cen.)
Cedar Way B31: Longb 6D 144
WV11: Wed 2E 29
Cedarwood B74: Four O 3H 53
Cedarwood Cft. B42: Gt Barr 5B 66
Cedarwood Dr. CV7: Bal C 3H 169
Cedarwood Rd. DY3: Up Gor 2H 75
Celandine Cl. DY6: K'wfrd 5A 92
Celandine Rd. DY1: Dud 3C 76
Celandines, The WV5: Wom 1E 73
Celbury Way B43: Gt Barr 5H 65
Celts Cl. B65: Row R 5C 96
Cemetery La. B18: Birm 4D 100
Cemetery Rd. B66: Smeth 3A 98
B67: Smeth 5D 98
B68: O'bry 3A 98
B75: S Cold 5B 54
DY9: Lye 6H 109
WS10: Darl 3F 47
WV13: W'hall 6A 30
Cemetery St. WS6: C Hay 3C 6
WV14: Bils 5E 45
Cemetery Way WS3: Blox 6H 19
Centenary Cl. B31: N'fld 6E 145
Centenary Dr. B21: Hand 6A 82
Centenary Plaza B1: Birm 1E 117 (5B 4)
Centenary Sq. B1: Birm 1E 117 (4B 4)
Centenary Way B1: Birm 2F 117
(off Blucher St.)
B1: Birm 4B 4
(off Queensway)
Central Arc. WV1: Wolv 1G 43 (3B 170)
Central Av. B31: Longb 1C 158
B64: Crad H 4E 111
B65: Row R 1C 112
DY4: Tip 6H 61
DY9: W'cte 2A 126
WV14: Bils 4G 45
Central Baths 1F 43 (2A 170)
Central Blvd. B90: Bly P 6D 164
Central Bus. Pk. B33: Kitts G 2H 121
Central Cl. WS3: Blox 6G 19
Central Dr. DY3: Gorn 5G 75
WS3: Blox 1F 31
WV14: Cose 6E 61
Central Gro. B27: A Grn 3A 136
Central Links Ind. Est. B7: Nech 3B 102
Central Pk. Dr. B18: Win G 4B 100
Central Pk. Ind. Est. DY2: Neth 6G 95
Central Sq. B1: Birm 1D 116 (5A 4)
B23: Erd 3G 85
Central Trad. Est. DY6: K'wfrd 6D 74
Central Way DY5: Brie H 6A 94
Centre City B5: Birm 6D 4
Centre La. B63: Hale 2B 128
Centreway, The B14: Yard W 3D 148
Centurion Cl. B46: Col 6H 89
Century Ho. B69: O'bry 3D 96
Century Ind. Est. B44: Gt Barr 2G 67
Century Pk. B9: Bord G 1C 118
B37: Mars G 5E 123
Century Rd. B69: O'bry 1G 97
Century Twr. B5: Edg 6E 117
Ceolmund Cres. B37: Chel W 1D 122
Chaceley Gro. B23: Erd 6D 68
Chadbrook Crest B15: Edg 4A 116
Chadbury Cft. B91: Sol 1F 165
Chadbury Rd. B63: Hale 2C 128
Chaddersley Cl. B45: Rubery 6F 143
Chaddesley Cl. B69: O'bry 4D 96
Chaddesley Ct. DY1: Dud 6D 76
Chaddesley Dr. DY9: Pedm 4F 125
Chaddesley Rd. B31: N'fld 5H 145
B63: Hale 3H 127
Chadley Cl. B91: Sol 1E 151
Chad Rd. B15: Edg 3B 116
WV14: Cose 6C 60
Chadshunt Cl. B36: Cas B 5H 87
Chad Sq. B15: Edg 4A 116
Chadstone Cl. B90: M'path 4F 165
CHAD VALLEY 4A 116
Chad Valley Cl. B17: Harb 5H 115

Chadwell Dr. B90: Shir 1H **149**
Chadwell Gdns. WV8: Cod 3F **13**
Chadwich La. B61: C'wich 2A **156**
Chadwick Av. B45: Redn 3H **157**
Chadwick Cl. WV4: Penn 5A **42**
Chadwick Ct. B43: Gt Barr 5A **66**
Chadwick Ho. B45: Rubery 2E **157**
Chadwick La. B93: Chad E, Know 6A **168**
Chadwick Rd. B75: S Cold 6D **54**
Chadworth Av. B93: Dorr 5A **166**
Chaffcombe Rd. B26: Sheld 5G **121**
Chaffinch Cl. DY3: Sed 3G **59**
Chaffinch Dr. B36: Cas B 2D **106**
Chaffinch Rd. DY9: W'cte 2H **125**
Chainmakers Cl. WV14: Cose 3F **61**
Chain Wlk. B19: Loz 1F **101**
Chalcot Gro. B20: Hand 2A **82**
Chaldon Cl. WV9: Pend 6E **15**
Chale Gro. B14: K Hth 4A **148**
Chalfont Pl. DY9: W'cte 3A **126**
Chalfont Rd. B20: Hand 5D **82**
Chalford Rd. B23: Erd 5C **68**
Chalford Way B90: Shir 6A **150**
Chalgrove Av. B38: K Nor 6H **145**
Chalgrove Cres. B91: Sol 6F **151**
Challenge Way WV10: Wolv 4A **28**
Challenor Av. WV13: W'hall 1F **45**
Chalybeate Cl. B45: Fran 6F **143**
Chamberlain Clock 5D **100** (1A **4**)
Chamberlain Cl. B69: Tiv 5D **78**
Chamberlain Ct. B14: K Hth 4G **133**
B18: Birm 5E **101**
Chamberlain Cres. B90: Shir 5G **149**
Chamberlain Hall B15: Edg 5C **116**
Chamberlain Ho. *B16: Edg 2C* ***116***
(off Skipton Rd.)
Chamberlain Rd. B13: Mose 1H **147**
Chamberlains La. WV4: Penn 2C **58**
Chamberlain Sq. B3: Birm 1F **117** (4C **4**)
(not continuous)
Chamberlain Wlk. B66: Smeth 4F **99**
Chance Cft. B68: O'bry 3H **113**
Chancel Ind. Est. DY6: K'wfrd 1C **92**
WS10: Darl 6D **46**
WV1: Wolv 2C **44**
WV13: W'hall 1B **46**
Chancellors Cl. B15: Edg 3A **116**
Chancel Way B6: Witt 2H **83**
B62: Hale 5C **112**
Chancery Way DY5: Quar B 1B **110**
Chandler Dr. WV4: Penn 2B **58**
Chandler Ho. B69: O'bry 5D **96**
Chandlers Cl. B18: Win G 4B **100**
WV9: Pend 6E **15**
Chandlers Keep WS8: Bwnhls 1B **22**
Chandos Av. B13: Mose 2H **133**
Chandos Rd. B12: Birm 3A **118**
Channon Dr. DY5: Brie H 3H **109**
Chanston Av. B14: K Hth 3G **147**
Chanterelle Gdns. WV4: Penn 1E **59**
Chantrey Cres. B43: Gt Barr 1F **67**
WV14: Bils 4H **45**
Chantry Av. WS3: Blox 1A **32**
Chantry Cl. B47: H'wd 2A **162**
Chantry Dr. B62: Quin 5G **113**
Chantry Heath Cres. B93: Know 1E **167**
Chantry Rd. B13: Mose 1G **133**
B21: Hand 1B **100**
DY7: Stourt 4A **108**
Chapel Ash WV3: Wolv 1F **43**
Chapel Ash Island
WV1: Wolv 1F **43** (3A **170**)
Chapel Av. WS8: Bwnhls 3A **10**
Chapel Cl. B64: Old H 3B **112**
WV5: Wom 2F **73**
Chapel Ct. *DY5: Brie H 1H* ***109***
(off Promenade, The)
DY5: P'ntt 2G ***93***
(off Chapel St.)
Chapel Dr. B47: Wyt 6H **161**
CV7: Bal C 1H **169**
WS8: Bwnhls 3A **10**
Chapelfield M. B45: Rubery 3F **157**
DY8: Stourb 1E **125**
Chapelfield Rd. B45: Redn 2G **157**
Chapel Flds. Rd. B92: Olton 3D **136**
Chapel Grn. WV13: W'hall 1B **46**
Chapel Ho. La. B63: Crad 5E **111**
Chapelhouse Rd. B37: F'bri 1B **122**
Chapel Ho. St. B12: Birm 2H **117** (6H **5**)
Chapel La. B29: S Oak 3A **132**
B43: Gt Barr 2A **66**
B47: Wyt 6G **161**
DY3: Swind 3C **72**
WV8: Cod 4E **13**
Chapel Pas. B69: O'bry 5G **97**
Chapel Sq. WS6: C Hay 2D **6**
Chapel St. B21: Hand 2H **99**
B63: Hale 2A **128**
B69: O'bry 2E **97**
B70: W Brom 2H **79**
DY2: Neth 5F **95**
DY4: Tip 2G **77**
(not continuous)
DY5: P'ntt 2G **93**
DY5: Quar B 3B **110**
DY6: W Hth 1H **91**
DY8: Stourb 1E **125**
DY8: Word 6B **92**
DY9: Lye 6A **110**
WS3: Blox 1B **32**
WS3: Pels 4D **20**
WS8: Bwnhls 3A **10**
WS11: Nort C 1C **8**
WV2: Wolv 4H **43**
WV5: Wom 2F **73**
(not continuous)
WV14: Bils 6H **45**
Chapel Vw. B67: Smeth 5D **98**
Chapel Wlk. B30: K Nor 4C **146**
DY3: Gorn 5G **75**
Chapelwood Gro. B42: P Barr 2F **83**
Chapman Rd. B10: Small H 3C **118**
CHAPMAN'S HILL 6B **142**
Chapman's Hill B62: Roms 6B **142**
Chapmans Pas. B1: Birm 2F **117** (6C **4**)
Chapman St. B70: W Brom 4H **79**
Chapter Ho. B70: W Brom 2G **79**
Charfield Cl. B30: B'vlle 6H **131**
Charingworth Rd. B92: Sol 3G **137**
Charity Brick Way B70: W Brom 5A **80**
Charlbury Av. B37: F'bri 1B **122**
Charlbury Cres. B26: Yard 3D **120**
Charlbury Twr. *B5: Birm 3G* ***117***
(off Southacre Av.)
Charlecote Cft. B90: Shir 1A **164**
Charlecote Dr. B23: Erd 6E **69**
DY1: Dud 4A **76**
Charlecote Gdns. B73: Bold 5G **69**
Charlecote Ri. WV13: W'hall 3H **45**
Charlecott Cl. B13: Mose 6D **134**
CHARLEMONT 5C **64**
Charlemont Av. B71: W Brom 5C **64**
Charlemont Cl. WS5: Wals 5G **49**
Charlemont Cres. B71: W Brom 5C **64**
Charlemont Gdns. WS5: Wals 5G **49**
Charlemont Rd. B71: W Brom 5C **64**
WS5: Wals 5F **49**
Charles Av. B65: Row R 5C **96**
WV4: Penn 6F **43**
WV11: Ess 3H **17**
Charles Cl. B8: Salt 5D **102**
WS6: C Hay 4D **6**
Charles Ct. B13: Mose 3B **134**
B76: Walm 2D ***70***
(off Berryfields Rd.)
Charles Cres. WS3: Pels 2E **21**
Charlesdale Dr. WS9: A'rdge 5D **34**
Charles Edward Rd. B26: Yard 5B **120**
Charles Foster St. WS10: Darl 5C **46**
Charles Henry St. B12: Birm 3H **117**
Charles Holland St. WV13: W'hall 1B **46**
Charles Lanes Trust Ho's.
B28: Hall G 5G **135**
Charles Pearson Ct. *B66: Smeth 4F* ***99***
(off Mill Dr.)
Charles Rd. B6: Aston 6A **84**
B9: Small H 1E **119**
B20: Hand 6E **83**
B63: Hale 1H **127**
B91: Sol 5C **150**
DY4: Tip 6A **62**
DY5: Quar B 2C **110**
DY8: Stourb 1C **124**
Charles St. B66: Smeth 2G **99**
B70: W Brom 2E **79**
WS2: Wals 1B **48**
WV13: W'hall 6C **30**
Charles St. Ind. Est. B70: W Brom 2E **79**
Charles Wlk. B65: Row R 4C **96**
Charles Wesley Ct. *WV3: Wolv 4E* ***43***
(off Claremont Rd.)
Charlesworth Av. B90: M'path 3F **165**
Charleville Rd. B19: Hock 2D **100**
Charlotte Cl. B69: Tiv 5A **78**
Charlotte Gdns. B66: Smeth 4F **99**
Charlotte Rd. B15: Edg 4E **117**
B30: Stir 1C **146**
WS10: W'bry 4C **62**
Charlotte St. B3: Birm 6E **101** (3B **4**)
DY1: Dud 1D **94**
WS1: Wals 1E **49**
Charlton Dr. B64: Crad H 4F **111**
Charlton Pl. B8: Salt 4D **102**
Charlton Rd. B44: K'sdng 6A **68**
Charlton St. DY1: Dud 6D **76**
DY5: Brie H 6E **93**
Charminster Av. B25: Yard 3B **120**
Charnley Dr. B75: R'ley 1C **54**
Charnwood Av. DY3: Sed 3H **59**
Charnwood Bus. Pk. WV14: Bils 6E **45**
Charnwood Cl. B45: Fran 4H **143**
DY5: Brie H 4F **109**
WV14: Bils 2B **62**
Charnwood Ct. DY9: W'cte 3A **126**
Charnwood Rd. B42: Gt Barr 6B **66**
WS5: Wals 1E **65**
Charter Cl. WS11: Nort C 1C **8**
Charter Cres. B64: Old H 3B **112**
Charterfield Dr. DY6: K'wfrd 1B **92**
Charterfield Shop. Cen. DY6: K'wfrd 1C **92**
Charterhouse Dr. B91: Sol 6F **151**
Charter Rd. DY4: Tip 4C **62**
Charters Av. WV8: Bilb 6H **13**
Charters Cl DY4: Tip 2G **77**
Charter St. DY5: Brie H 4A **94**
Chartist Rd. B8: Salt 3D **102**
Chartley Cl. B93: Dorr 6A **166**
WV6: Pert 5F **25**
Chartley Rd. B23: Erd 6D **84**
B71: W Brom 1B **80**
Chartway, The WS3: Pels 3E **21**
Chartwell Cl. DY1: Dud 1D **76**
Chartwell Dr. B74: Four O 5D **36**
B90: Ches G 4B **164**
WV5: Wom 2F **73**
WV10: Bush 6A **16**
Chase, The B76: Walm 6B **70**
WV6: Wolv 3F **27**
Chase Av. WS6: C Hay 2F **7**
Chase Gro. B24: Erd 1B **86**
Chase Link, The WS8: Bwnhls 4C **10**
Chasepool Rd. DY3: Swind 2C **90**
Chase Rd. DY3: Gorn 6F **75**
DY5: P'ntt 6G **75**
WS3: Blox 1G **31**
WS8: Bwnhls 4C **10**
Chase Sailing Club, The 1H **9**
Chase Vw. WV4: E'shll 3A **60**
Chasewater Railway Mus. 2H **9**
Chasewater Sports Cen. 2G **9**
Chassieur Wlk. B46: Col 1H **107**
Chater Dr. B76: Walm 4E **71**
Chatham Rd. B31: N'fld 4E **145**
Chatsworth Av. B43: Gt Barr 4G **65**
Chatsworth Cl. B72: W Grn 6B **70**
B90: Ches G 4B **164**
WV12: W'hall 4B **30**
Chatsworth Cres. WS4: Rus 2H **33**
Chatsworth Gdns. WV6: Tett 2G **25**
Chatsworth M. DY8: Word 6H **91**
Chatsworth Rd. B62: Hale 4A **112**
Chattaway Dr. CV7: Bal C 3H **169**
Chattaway St. B7: Nech 2C **102**
CHATTLE HILL 5G **89**
Chattle Hill B46: Col 5G **89**
Chattock Av. B91: Sol 3A **152**
Chattock Cl. B36: Hodg H 2C **104**
Chatwell Gro. B29: S Oak 3F **131**
Chatwin Pl. WV14: Bils 2G **61**
Chatwin St. B66: Smeth 2D **98**

Chatwins Wharf DY4: Tip 2H **77**
Chaucer Av. DY3: Lwr G 2E **75**
DY4: Tip 5B **62**
WV12: W'hall 1E **31**
Chaucer Cl. B23: Erd 4B **84**
DY8: Amb 3E **109**
WV14: Cose 5F **61**
Chaucer Gro. B27: A Grn 3H **135**
Chaucer Ho. B63: Crad 6D **110**
Chaucer Rd. WS3: Blox 1C **32**
Chauson Gro. B91: Sol 1E **165**
Chavasse Rd. B72: S Cold 2A **70**
CHAWN HILL **2G 125**
Chawn Hill DY9: Pedm 2G **125**
Chawn Hill Cl. DY9: Pedm 2G **125**
Chawn Pk. Dr. DY9: Pedm 2G **125**
Chaynes Gro. B33: Kitts G 6H **105**
Cheadle Dr. B23: Erd 5D **68**
Cheam Gdns. WV6: Tett 1C **26**
Cheapside B5: Birm 2H **117** (6G **5**)
B12: Birm 2H **117**
WV1: Wolv 1G **43** (3B **170**)
WV13: W'hall 2A **46**
Cheapside Ind. Est. B12: Birm 2H **117**
Cheatham St. B7: Nech 3C **102**
Checketts St. WS2: Wals 1A **48**
Checkley Cl. B90: Shir 3G **149**
Checkley Cft. B76: Walm 5D **70**
Cheddar Rd. B12: Bal H 5G **117**
Chedworth Cl. B29: W Cas 6F **131**
Chedworth Ct. B29: S Oak 5A **132**
Cheedon Cl. B93: Dorr 6F **167**
Chelford Cres. DY6: K'wfrd 6E **93**
Chells Gro. B13: Mose 2B **148**
Chelmar Cl. B36: Cas B 1B **106**
Chelmar Dr. DY5: P'ntt 3E **93**
Chelmarsh Av. WV3: Wolv 2G **41**
Chelmorton Rd. B42: Gt Barr 6F **67**
Chelmscote Rd. B92: Olton 4D **136**
Chelmsley Av. B46: Col 3H **107**
Chelmsley Circ. B37: Chel W 1D **122**
Chelmsley Gro. B33: Kitts G 6A **106**
Chelmsley La. B37: Mars G 3B **122**
(not continuous)
Chelmsley Rd. B37: Chel W, F'bri 6B **106**
CHELMSLEY WOOD **1D 122**
Chelmsley Wood Ind. Est. B37: F'bri . . . 5D **106**
Chelmsley Wood Shop. Cen.
B37: Chel W 1D **122**
Chelsea *B37: K'hrst* *4B* ***106***
(off Chilvers Gro.)
Chelsea Cl. B32: Quin 1D **130**
Chelsea Ct. B29: W Cas 6F **131**
Chelsea Dr. B74: Four O 5F **37**
Chelsea Way DY6: K'wfrd 3B **92**
Chelston Dr. WV6: Wolv 5C **26**
Chelston Rd. B31: N'fld 5C **144**
Cheltenham Cl. WV6: Wolv 3F **27**
Cheltenham Dr. B36: Hodg H 1B **104**
DY6: K'wfrd 3H **91**
Chelthorn Way B91: Sol 5G **151**
Cheltondale Rd. B91: Sol 1D **150**
Chelveston Cres. B91: Sol 6F **151**
Chelwood Gdns. WV14: Bils 6D **44**
Chelworth Rd. B38: K Nor 5D **146**
Chem Rd. WV14: Bils 6E **45**
Cheniston Rd. WV12: W'hall 3C **30**
Chepstow Cl. WV6: Pert 5F **25**
Chepstow Gro. B45: Redn 3H **157**
Chepstow Rd. WS3: Blox 6F **19**
WV10: F'hses 2H **15**
Chepstow Vs. B12: Bal H 6B **118**
Chepstow Way WS3: Blox 6F **19**
Chequerfield Dr. WV3: Wolv 5E **43**
Chequers Av. WV5: Wom 4G **57**
Chequer St. WV3: Wolv 5E **43**
Cherhill Covert B14: K Hth 5E **147**
Cherington Rd. B29: S Oak 5C **132**
Cherish Ho. B12: Birm 3A **118**
Cheriton Gro. WV6: Pert 6E **25**
Cheriton Wlk. B23: Erd 4B **84**
Cherrington Cl. B31: N'fld 6C **130**
Cherrington Dr. WS6: Gt Wyr 1F **7**
Cherrington Gdns. DY9: Pedm 6G **125**
WV6: Tett 1H **41**
Cherrington Way B91: Sol 6F **151**
Cherry Cres. B24: Erd 4F **85**
Cherrydale Ct. DY1: Dud 5B **76**
Cherry Dr. B9: Birm 2B **118**
B64: Old H 2H **111**
Cherry Gdns. *B73: W Grn* *6H* ***69***
(off Emscote Dr.)
Cherry Grn. DY1: Dud 3B **76**
Cherry Gro. *B66: Smeth* *4G* ***99***
(off Rosedale Av.)
DY8: Stourb 1C **124**
WV11: Wed 2E **29**
Cherry Hill Wlk. DY1: Dud 1C **94**
Cherry La. B73: Bold 6G **69**
DY3: Himl 4A **74**
WS10: W'bry 3G **63**
Cherry Lea B34: S End 3F **105**
CHERRY ORCHARD **2H 111**
Cherry Orchard B64: Old H 2H **111**
Cherry Orchard Av. B63: Hale 6H **111**
Cherry Orchard Cres.
B63: Hale 5H **111**
Cherry Orchard Rd. B20: Hand 2B **82**
Cherry Rd. DY4: Tip 6H **61**
Cherry St. B2: Birm 1G **117** (4E **5**)
B63: Hale 6H **111**
DY8: Stourb 1C **124**
Cherry Tree Av. WS5: Wals 1E **65**
Cherry Tree Ct. B30: K Nor 2B **146**
Cherrytree Ct. DY9: W'cte 2A **126**
Cherry Tree Cft. B27: A Grn 6A **120**
Cherry Tree Gdns. WV8: Bilb 4H **13**
Cherry Tree La. B63: Hale 4F **127**
WV8: Bilb 4H **13**
Cherry Tree Rd. DY6: K'wfrd 1C **92**
WS11: Nort C 1F **9**
Cherry Wlk. B47: H'wd 4B **162**
Cherrywood Cl. WV14: Cose 4E **61**
Cherrywood Ct. B92: Olton 3E **137**
Cherrywood Cres. B91: Sol 1G **165**
Cherrywood Grn. WV14: Bils 3F **45**
Cherrywood Ind. Est. B9: Bord G 6D **102**
Cherrywood Rd. B9: Bord G 1D **118**
B74: S'tly 2F **51**
Cherrywood Way B74: Lit A 4D **36**
Chervil Cl. B42: Gt Barr 6E **67**
Chervil Ri. WV10: Wolv 6B **28**
Cherwell Ct. B73: S Cold 6H **53**
Cherwell Dr. B36: Cas B 1B **106**
WS8: Bwnhls 3G **9**
(not continuous)
Cherwell Gdns. B6: Aston 1F **101**
Cheshire Av. B90: Shir 4G **149**
Cheshire Cl. DY8: Woll 3B **108**
Cheshire Ct. B34: S End 2F **105**
Cheshire Gro. WV6: Pert 5E **25**
Cheshire Rd. B6: Witt 5A **84**
B67: Smeth 5E **99**
WS2: Wals 1F **47**
Cheslyn Dr. WS6: C Hay 2D **6**
Cheslyn Gro. B14: K Hth 4A **148**
CHESLYN HAY **3D 6**
Cheslyn Hay Leisure Cen. **2C 6**
Chessetts Gro. B13: Mose 1A **148**
Chester Av. WV6: Tett 2D **26**
Chester Cl. B37: F'bri 1C **122**
WV13: W'hall 1D **46**
Chester Ct. *B29: W Cas* *6F* ***131***
(off Abdon Av.)
B37: Chel W *1F* ***123***
(off Hedingham Gro.)
Chesterfield Cl. B31: N'fld 5F **145**
Chesterfield Ct. B30: K Nor 3A **146**
WS9: Wals W 3B **22**
Chester Gdns. B73: New O 4E **69**
Chestergate Cft. B24: Erd 3B **86**
Chester Hayes Ct. B24: Erd 2A **86**
Chester House **3E 167**
Chester Pl. WS2: Wals 2H **47**
Chester Ri. B68: O'bry 3H **113**
CHESTER ROAD **6A 70**
Chester Rd. B24: Erd 2A **86**
B35: Cas V 3C **86**
B36: Cas B 1E **105**
B37: Chel W, F'bri 4D **106**
B46: Col 4H **123**
B64: Crad H 3E **111**
B71: W Brom 4H **63**
B73: New O 4D **68**
Chester Rd. B74: S'tly 1H **51**
CV7: Lit P 1B **140**
DY2: Neth 1F **111**
WS8: Bwnhls, Wals W 2D **22**
WS9: A'rdge, Wals W 4G **35**
Chester Rd. Nth. B73: S'tly, New O 6A **52**
WS8: Bwnhls 4H **9**
Chester Road Station (Rail) **6G 69**
Chester St. B6: Aston 4H **101**
Chester St. Wharf B6: Aston 4H **101**
Chesterton Av. B12: Bal H 6B **118**
Chesterton Cl. B91: Sol 2C **150**
Chesterton Rd. B12: Bal H 6A **118**
WV10: Bush 1C **28**
Chesterwood B47: H'wd 3A **162**
WS9: A'rdge 1H **51**
Chesterwood Gdns. B20: Hand 5F **83**
Chesterwood Rd. B13: Mose 1H **147**
Chestnut Av. DY1: Dud 4E **77**
DY4: Tip 6H **61**
Chestnut Cl. B27: A Grn 1A **136**
B74: S'tly 6A **36**
B92: Olton 5B **136**
DY8: Stourb 3B **124**
WV8: Cod 5F **13**
Chestnut Ct. B36: Cas B 2A **106**
Chestnut Dr. B24: Erd 3A **86**
B36: Cas B 1E **105**
B45: Coft H 5B **158**
WS4: S'fld 6F **21**
WS6: C Hay 2D **6**
WS6: Gt Wyr 2F **7**
WV5: Wom 2G **73**
Chestnut Gro. B17: Harb 6H **115**
B46: Col 2H **107**
DY6: K'wfrd 2D **92**
WV11: Wed 2E **29**
Chestnut Ho. B37: Chel W 1D **122**
Chestnut Pl. B14: K Hth 5H **133**
WS3: Blox 3B **32**
Chestnut Rd. B13: Mose 1A **134**
B68: O'bry 4A **114**
WS3: Blox 3C **32**
WS10: W'bry 4G **63**
Chestnuts Av. B26: Sheld 4F **121**
Chestnut Wlk. *B37: Chel W* *1D* ***122***
(off Chelmsley Wood Shop. Cen.)
Chestnut Way WV3: Wolv 3B **42**
Chestom Rd. WV14: Bils 5D **44**
Chestom Rd. Ind. Est. WV14: Bils 5D **44**
Cheston Ind. Est. B7: Nech 3A **102**
Cheston Rd. B7: Nech 3A **102**
Cheswell Cl. WV6: Tett 1H **41**
Cheswick Cl. WV13: W'hall 3H **45**
CHESWICK GREEN **5B 164**
Cheswick Way B90: Ches G 5B **164**
Cheswood Dr. B76: Walm 1F **87**
Chetland Cft. B92: Sol 6B **138**
Chettle Rd. WV14: Bils 2H **61**
Chetton Grn. WV10: F'hses 4F **15**
Chetwood Cl. WV6: Wolv 4E **27**
Chetwynd Cl. WS2: Wals 6C **30**
Chetwynd Rd. B8: W End 4H **103**
WV2: Wolv 5F **43**
Cheveley Av. B45: Redn 2H **157**
Chevening Cl. DY3: Sed 6A **60**
Cheveridge Cl. B91: Sol 5F **151**
Cheverton Rd. B31: N'fld 3C **144**
Cheviot Rd. DY8: Amb 5E **109**
WV2: E'shll 4B **44**
Cheviot Way B63: Hale 2F **127**
Cheylesmore Cl. B73: S Cold 1H **69**
Cheyne Ct. *B17: Harb* *6H* ***115***
(off Greenfield Rd.)
Cheyne Gdns. B28: Hall G 4E **149**
Cheyne Pl. B17: Harb 6H **115**
Cheyne Wlk. DY5: Brie H 4G **109**
Cheyne Way B17: Harb 6H **115**
Cheyney Cl. WV6: Wolv 4E **27**
Chichester Av. DY2: Neth 5F **95**
Chichester Ct. B73: S Cold 6H **53**
Chichester Dr. B32: Quin 6G **113**
Chichester Gro. B37: Chel W 2C **122**
(not continuous)
Chigwell Cl. B35: Cas V 4E **87**
Chilcote Cl. B28: Hall G 3F **149**
Childs Av. WV14: Cose 3C **60**

Childs Oak Cl. CV7: Bal C 3G **169**
Chilgrove Gdns. WV6: Tett 4A **26**
Chilham Dr. B37: Chel W 1E **123**
Chillenden Ct. *WV13: W'hall 1C* ***46***
(off Mill St.)
Chillinghome Rd.
B36: Hodg H 1B **104**
Chillington Cl. WS6: Gt Wyr 4F **7**
Chillington Dr. DY1: Dud 4A **76**
WV8: Cod 3F **13**
Chillington Flds. WV1: Wolv 2C **44**
Chillington La. WV8: Cod 2D **12**
Chillington Pl. WV14: Bils 6E **45**
Chillington Rd. DY4: Tip 4C **62**
Chillington Wlk. B65: Row R 6C **96**
Chillington Works Ind. Est.
WV1: Wolv 2B **44**
Chiltern Cl. B63: Hale 3E **127**
DY3: Lwr G 4H **75**
WS6: C Hay 4D **6**
Chiltern Dr. WV13: W'hall 2F **45**
Chiltern Rd. DY8: Amb 5F **109**
Chilterns, The B69: O'bry 4E **97**
Chilton Ct. *B23: Erd 5C* ***84***
(off Park App.)
Chilton Rd. B14: Yard W 3D **148**
Chilvers Gro. B37: K'hrst 4B **106**
Chilwell Cl. B91: Sol 6F **151**
Chilwell Cft. B19: Hock 4G **101**
Chilworth Av. WV11: Wed 2H **29**
Chilworth Cl. B6: Aston 3H **101**
Chimes Cl. B33: Kitts G 2A **122**
Chimney Rd. DY4: Tip 6D **62**
Chingford Cl. DY8: Word 5A **92**
Chingford Rd. B44: K'sdng 5A **68**
Chinley Gro. B44: K'sdng 4C **68**
Chinn Brook Rd. B13: Mose 2B **148**
Chip Cl. B38: K Nor 5H **145**
Chipperfield Rd. B36: Hodg H 1C **104**
Chipstead Rd. B23: Erd 6D **68**
Chipstone Cl. B91: Sol 1G **165**
Chirbury Gro. B31: Longb 6F **145**
Chirton Gro. B14: K Hth 1F **147**
Chiseldon Cft. B14: K Hth 4A **148**
Chisholm Gro. B27: A Grn 5A **136**
Chiswell Rd. B18: Win G 5A **100**
Chiswick Ct. B23: Erd 5E **85**
Chiswick Ho. *B15: Birm 3E* ***117***
(off Bell Barn Rd.)
Chiswick Wlk. B37: Chel W 1F **123**
Chivenor Ho. B35: Cas V 5E **87**
Chivington Cl. B90: M'path 3F **165**
Chorley Av. B34: Hodg H 3D **104**
Chorley Gdns. WV14: Bils 6D **44**
Christchurch Cl. B15: Edg 3A **116**
Christ Chu. Gro. WS1: Wals 4E **49**
Christina Ct. B71: W Brom 3B **80**
Christine Cl. DY4: Tip 3C **62**
Christopher Ct. *B23: Erd 5D* ***68***
(off Marshmount Way)
Christopher Rd. B29: S Oak 3G **131**
B62: Hale 2E **129**
WV2: Wolv 3A **44**
Christopher Taylor Ct. B30: B'vlle 2A **146**
Chubb St. WV1: Wolv 1H **43** (2D **170**)
CHUCKERY, THE 2E **49**
Chuckery Rd. WS1: Wals 2E **49**
Chudleigh Gro. B43: Gt Barr 5H **65**
Chudleigh Rd. B23: Erd 3E **85**
Churchacre B23: Erd 5C **68**
Church Av. B13: Mose 2H **133**
B20: Hand 1E **101**
B46: Wat O 4D **88**
DY8: Amb 4E **109**
CHURCHBRIDGE **1G 7**
Churchbridge B69: O'bry 4F **97**
(not continuous)
Churchbridge Ind. Est. *B69: O'bry 4F* ***97***
(off Churchbridge)
Church Cl. B37: K'hrst 3C **106**
B47: Wyt 6A **162**
Church Ct. B64: Old H 2G **111**
Church Cres. WV11: Ess 4H **17**
Church Cft. B63: Hale 1A **128**
Churchcroft B17: Harb 1F **131**
Chu. Cross Vw. DY1: Dud 1A **94**
Chu. Dale Rd. B44: Gt Barr 2F **67**
Churchdown Ct. *B23: Erd 5C* ***84***
(off Dunlin Ct.)
Church Dr. B30: Stir 6D **132**
CHURCHFIELD **1B 80**
Churchfield Av. DY4: Tip 5H **61**
Churchfield Cl. B7: Nech 3C **102**
Churchfield Rd. WV10: Oxl 1F **27**
Churchfields Rd. WS10: W'bry 1F **63**
Churchfield St. DY2: Dud 1E **95**
Church Gdns. B67: Smeth 5E **99**
Church Grn. B20: Hand 5B **82**
WV14: Bils 3E **45**
Church Gro. B13: Mose 2C **148**
B20: Hand 6D **82**
CHURCH HILL
Wednesbury **2F 63**
Church Hill B31: N'fld 4F **145**
(not continuous)
B32: Fran 2G **143**
B46: Col 2H **107**
B72: S Cold 6A **54**
DY5: Brie H 1H **109**
WS1: Wals 2D **48**
WS10: W'bry 2F **63**
(Ethelfleda Ter.)
WS10: W'bry 2F **63**
(Walsall St.)
WV4: Penn 2C **58**
WV8: Cod 2F **13**
Chu. Hill Cl. B91: Sol 5G **151**
Chu. Hill Ct. WS10: W'bry 2F **63**
Chu. Hill Dr. WV6: Tett 4C **26**
Chu. Hill Rd. B20: Hand 6D **82**
B91: Sol 4G **151**
WV6: Tett 3B **26**
Chu. Hill St. B67: Smeth 3D **98**
Church Ho. WS2: Wals 4A **48**
Church Ho. Dr. B72: S Cold 6A **54**
Churchill Cl. B69: Tiv 5C **78**
Churchill Dr. B65: Row R 1B **112**
DY8: Amb 4E **109**
Churchill Gdns. DY3: Sed 6G **59**
Churchill Pde. B75: S Cold 6E **55**
Churchill Pl. B33: Sheld 2F **121**
Churchill Rd. B9: Bord G 6F **103**
B63: Hale 3H **127**
B73: New O 2D **68**
B75: S Cold 6E **55**
WS2: Wals 1D **46**
Churchill Shop. Pct., The DY2: Dud 6F **77**
Churchill Wlk. DY4: Tip 5A **62**
Church La. B6: Aston 1A **102**
B20: Hand 5B **82**
B33: Stech 6D **104**
B63: Hale 1B **128**
B71: W Brom 1H **79**
B76: Curd 1D **88**
B92: Bick 4F **139**
WS7: Hamm 2F **11**
WS9: Ston 3G **23**
WV2: Wolv 2G **43** (5A **170**)
WV5: Seis, Try 3A **56**
(not continuous)
WV8: Cod 3F **13**
Church La. Ind. Est. B71: W Brom 1A **80**
Church M. DY4: Tip 6H **61**
Chu. Moat Way WS3: Blox 1H **31**
Churchover Cl. B76: Walm 1B **86**
Church Pl. WS3: Blox 1B **32**
Church Rd. B6: Aston 2B **102**
B13: Mose 2A **134**
B15: Edg 4C **116**
B24: Erd 3F **85**
B25: Yard 4B **120**
B26: Sheld 6F **121**
B31: N'fld 3E **145**
B33: Yard 2C **120**
B42: P Barr 2F **83**
B63: Crad 4E **111**
B65: Row R 6C **96**
B67: Smeth 5D **98**
B73: Bold 5F **69**
B73: S Cold 2H **69**
B90: Shir 5H **149**
DY2: Neth 4D **94**
DY3: Swind 4D **72**
DY8: Stourb 2F **125**
Church Rd. DY8: Word 1B **108**
DY9: Lye 6A **110**
WS3: Pels 4E **21**
WS8: Bwnhls 6B **10**
(not continuous)
WS9: Ston 4G **23**
WS11: Nort C 1C **8**
WV3: Wolv 4C **42**
WV5: Wom 6H **57**
WV6: Pert 5E **25**
WV6: Tett 4C **26**
(Rock, The)
WV6: Tett 6H **25**
(School Rd.)
WV8: Cod 3F **13**
(not continuous)
WV10: Oxl 6G **15**
WV12: W'hall 3D **30**
WV14: Cose 4F **61**
Churchside Way WS9: A'rdge 5D **22**
Church Sq. B69: O'bry 2G **97**
Church St. B3: Birm 6F **101** (3D **4**)
B19: Loz 2E **101**
B62: B'hth 2D **112**
B64: Old H 2G **111**
B69: O'bry 1G **97**
B70: W Brom 3A **80**
DY2: Dud 1E **95**
DY3: Lwr G 4H **75**
DY4: Tip 5A **78**
DY5: Brie H 2G **109**
DY5: P'ntt 2H **93**
DY5: Quar B 2B **110**
DY8: Stourb 6E **109**
WS1: Wals 2D **48**
WS3: Blox 1H **31**
WS7: Chase 1A **10**
WS8: Clay 1A **22**
WS10: Darl 4D **46**
(Bell St.)
WS10: Darl 1B **62**
(Black Country New Rd.)
WV2: Wolv 2G **43** (5A **170**)
WV10: Wolv 5C **28**
WV11: Wed 4E **29**
WV13: W'hall 1B **46**
(not continuous)
WV14: Bils 6F **45**
Church Ter. B33: Yard 2C **120**
B75: Four O 6H **37**
Church Va. B20: Hand 6D **82**
B71: W Brom 1B **80**
WS11: Nort C 1C **8**
Church Va. M. B71: W Brom 2B **80**
Church Vw. B11: S'brk 5D **118**
WS9: A'rdge 4D **34**
WS9: Wals W 4B **22**
Church Vw. Cl. WS3: Blox 1A **32**
Church Vw. Dr. B64: Old H 2H **111**
Church Wlk. B8: W End 3G **103**
B46: Col 3H **107**
B65: Row R 5C **96**
WV3: Wolv 4D **42**
WV6: Tett 4C **26**
WV13: W'hall 2B **46**
Churchward Cl. DY8: Amb 5F **109**
Churchward Gro. WV5: Wom 6G **57**
Church Way WS4: S'fld 5F **21**
Churchwell Ct. B63: Hale 2B **128**
Churchwell Gdns.
B71: W Brom 1B **80**
Churchyard Rd. DY4: Tip 2B **78**
Churnet Gro. WV6: Pert 5F **25**
Churn Hill Rd. WS9: A'rdge 5C **34**
Churns Hill La. DY3: Himl 4H **73**
Churston Cl. WS3: Blox 4G **19**
Churton House (Crystal Glass Cen., The)
3C **108**
Churwell Ct. WV5: Wom 1G **73**
Cider Av. DY5: Quar B 3A **110**
(not continuous)
Cinder Bank DY2: Neth 2D **94**
Cinder Bank Island
DY2: Dud 2D **94**
CINDER HILL **4B 60**
Cinder Rd. DY3: Gorn 6F **75**
Cinder Way WS10: W'bry 2E **63**

Cineworld
Solihull 4G **151**
Wednesfield 5D **28**
Cinquefoil Leasow DY4: Tip. 1C **78**
Circle, The B17: Harb 4G **115**
Circuit Cl. WV13: W'hall. 6B **30**
Circular Rd. B27: A Grn 3A **136**
Circus Av. B37: Chel W. 1E **123**
City, The DY4: Tip 4A **78**
City Arc. *B2: Birm. 4E **5***
(off Corporation St.)
City Est. B64: Crad H 3F **111**
City Hgts. B4: Birm 1D **4**
City Plaza B2: Birm. 4E **5**
City Rd. B16: Edg 2F **115**
B17: Edg. 2F **115**
B69: Tiv 2B **96**
City Trad. Est. B16: Birm 6C **100**
City Vw. B8: Salt 5D **102**
City Wlk. B5: Birm. 2G **117** (6E **5**)
Civic Cl. B1: Birm 1E **117** (4A **4**)
Claerwen Gro. B31: N'fld 2C **144**
Claines Rd. B31: N'fld 3G **145**
B63: Crad 6F **111**
Claire Ct. B26: Sheld 4G **121**
Clairvaux Gdns. B92: Olton 2B **150**
Clandon Cl. B14: K Hth 5E **147**
Clanfield Av. WV11: Wed. 1H **29**
Clapgate Gdns. WV14: Cose 2C **60**
Clap Ga. Gro. WV5: Wom 1E **73**
Clapgate La. B32: Bart G. 3G **129**
Clapgate Rd. WV5: Wom 6E **57**
Clapton Gro. B44: K'sdng. 4B **68**
Clare Av. WV11: Wed. 6H **17**
Clare Ct. B90: Shir. 5D **148**
Clare Cres. WV14: Cose. 3B **60**
Clare Dr. B15: Edg 3B **116**
Clare Ho. B36: Cas B 2C **106**
Clarel Av. B8: Salt 6C **102**
Claremont Ct. B64: Old H 2G **111**
Claremont M. WV3: Wolv. 4E **43**
Claremont Pl. B18: Win G 4B **100**
Claremont Rd. B11: S'brk 4B **118**
B18: Hock 3D **100**
B66: Smeth. 5F **99**
DY3: Sed 5A **60**
WV3: Wolv 4E **43**
Claremont St. B64: Old H 2G **111**
WV14: Bils 5E **45**
Claremont Way B63: Hale 2B **128**
Clarence Av. B21: Hand. 1G **99**
Clarence Ct. B68: O'bry 1A **114**
Clarence Gdns.
B74: Four O 1F **53**
Clarence M. B17: Harb 5H **115**
Clarence Rd. B11: S'hll 1C **134**
B13: K Hth 4A **134**
B17: Harb. 5H **115**
B21: Hand 1G **99**
B23: Erd. 4D **84**
B74: Four O 4E **37**
DY2: Dud 3F **95**
WV1: Wolv 1G **43** (2A **170**)
WV14: Bils. 4G **45**
Clarence St. DY3: Up Gor 1A **76**
WV1: Wolv 1G **43** (3A **170**)
Clarenden Pl. B17: Harb 6G **115**
Clarendon Dr. DY4: Tip 4D **62**
Clarendon Pl. B62: Quin. 4F **113**
WS3: Pels 3D **20**
Clarendon Rd. B16: Edg. 2A **116**
B67: Smeth 5D **98**
B75: R'ley. 6A **38**
WS4: S'fld 5G **21**
Clarendon St. WS3: Blox 6H **19**
WV3: Wolv 1E **43**
Clarendon Way B91: Sol 4G **151**
Clare Rd. WS3: Wals 3E **33**
WV10: Bush. 2A **28**
Clarewell Av. B91: Sol 1F **165**
Clarke Ho. WS3: Blox 6H **19**
Clarkes Gro. DY4: Tip 1C **78**
Clarke's La. B71: W Brom 6A **64**
WV13: W'hall 6C **30**
Clark Rd. WV3: Wolv 1D **42**
Clarkson Pl. DY5: Quar B. 5A **110**
Clarkson Rd. WS10: W'bry 1G **63**
Clark St. B16: Birm 1B **116**
DY8: Stourb 6C **108**
Clarry Dr. B74: Four O 3F **53**
Clary Gro. WS5: Wals. 2E **65**
CLATTERBATCH. 6F **109**
Claughton Rd. DY2: Dud 6F **77**
Claughton Rd. Nth. DY2: Dud 6F **77**
Clausen Cl. B43: Gt Barr 1G **67**
Clavedon Cl. B31: N'fld 6C **130**
Claverdon Cl. B91: Sol. 4C **150**
WS8: Bwnhls 5C **10**
Claverdon Dr. B43: Gt Barr 5H **65**
B74: Lit A. 5B **36**
Claverdon Gdns. B27: A Grn 6H **119**
Claverdon Ho. B13: Mose 6A **134**
Claverley Ct. DY1: Dud 6D **76**
Claverley Dr. WV4: Penn 6B **42**
Claybrook St. B5: Birm 2G **117** (6E **5**)
Claycroft Pl. DY9: Lye 6A **110**
Claycroft Ter. DY1: Dud 1D **76**
Claydon Gro. B14: K Hth 4A **148**
Claydon Rd. DY6: W Hth 6A **74**
Clay Dr. B32: Quin 6G **113**
CLAYHANGER. 1A **22**
Clayhanger La. WS8: Bwnhls, Clay 6H **9**
Clayhanger Rd. WS8: Bwnhls 1B **22**
Clay La. B26: Yard 6C **120**
B69: O'bry 5G **97**
Claypit Cl. B70: W Brom 4G **79**
Clay Pit La. B90: Dic H 4G **163**
(not continuous)
Claypit La. B70: W Brom 4G **79**
Clayton Cl. WV2: Wolv. 4G **43**
Clayton Dr. B36: Cas B. 1G **105**
Clayton Gdns. B45: Lick. 6G **157**
Clayton Ho. B16: Edg 2B **116**
Clayton Rd. B8: Salt. 4D **102**
WV14: Cose 6D **60**
Clayton Wlk. B35: Cas V 5E **87**
Clear Vw. DY6: K'wfrd 3H **91**
Clearwell Gdns. DY1: Dud. 4A **76**
Clee Hill Dr. WV3: Wolv 2G **41**
Clee Hill Rd. DY3: Lwr G. 3G **75**
Clee Rd. B31: Longb 1E **159**
B68: O'bry 5A **98**
DY2: Dud 2C **94**
DY8: Amb. 5E **109**
Cleeve Dr. B74: Four O. 3F **37**
Cleeve Ho. B24: Erd. 5G **85**
Cleeve Rd. B14: Yard W. 3C **148**
WS3: Blox. 4F **19**
Cleeve Way WS3: Blox 5F **19**
Clee Vw. Mdw. DY3: Sed 3H **59**
Clee Vw. Rd. WV5: Wom 2E **73**
Clematis Dr. WV9: Pend 4D **14**
Clem Attlee Ct. WV14: Wolv 3E **45**
Clement Pl. WV14: Bils 4F **45**
Clement Rd. B62: B'hth 2D **112**
WV14: Bils 4F **45**
Clements Cl. B69: O'bry. 5F **97**
Clements Rd. B25: Yard. 3B **120**
Clement St. B1: Birm 6D **100** (3A **4**)
WS2: Wals 2B **48**
Clemson St. WV13: W'hall 1A **46**
Clent Ct. DY1: Dud. 6D **76**
Clent Hill Dr. B65: Row R 4A **96**
Clent Ho. B63: Hale 3A **128**
Clent Rd. B21: Hand 6H **81**
B45: Rubery 1E **157**
B68: O'bry 3A **114**
DY8: Amb. 5E **109**
Clent Vw. B66: Smeth. 6F **99**
Clent Vw. Rd. B32: Bart G 4G **129**
B63: Crad 1E **127**
DY8: Stourb 2A **124**
(not continuous)
Clent Vs. B12: Bal H. 1B **134**
Clent Way B32: Bart G 5G **129**
Cleobury La. B90: Tid G 4F **163**
B94: Earls. 4F **163**
Cleton St. DY4: Tip. 4B **78**
Cleton St. Bus. Pk. DY4: Tip 4B **78**
Clevedon Av. B36: Cas B 1A **106**
Clevedon Rd. B12: Bal H 5G **117**
Cleveland Cl. WV11: Wed 6H **17**
WV13: W'hall 2F **45**
Cleveland Ct. B13: Mose 3B **134**
Cleveland Pas. WV1: Wolv. . . . 2G **43** (4B **170**)
Cleveland Rd. WV2: Wolv 2H **43** (5D **170**)
Cleveland St. DY1: Dud. 6D **76**
DY8: Stourb 1C **124**
WV1: Wolv 2G **43** (4B **170**)
Cleveland Twr. B1: Birm 6D **4**
Cleves Cres. WS6: C Hay. 4D **6**
Cleves Dr. B45: Rubery 2E **157**
Cleves Rd. B45: Rubery. 1E **157**
Clewley Dr. WV9: Pend 4E **15**
Clewley Gro. B32: Quin 6H **113**
Clews Cl. WS1: Wals 4C **48**
Clewshaw La. B38: Head H 5D **160**
Cley Cl. B5: Edg 5F **117**
Cliff, The DY8: Stourb 5E **109**
Cliffe Dr. B33: Kitts G. 6G **105**
Clifford Rd. B67: Smeth. 2D **114**
B70: W Brom. 5G **79**
B93: Ben H. 5B **166**
Clifford St. B19: Loz 2F **101**
DY1: Dud 1D **94**
WV6: Wolv 6E **27**
Clifford Wlk. B19: Loz 2F **101**
(not continuous)
Cliff Rock Rd. B45: Redn. 2H **157**
Clift Cl. WV12: W'hall. 3C **30**
Clifton Av. WS8: Bwnhls 6H **9**
WS9: A'rdge 1E **35**
Clifton Cl. B6: Aston 2H **101**
B69: O'bry 5G **97**
Clifton Cres. B91: Sol. 6C **150**
Clifton Dr. B73: S Cold. 5H **53**
Clifton Gdns. WV8: Bilb 4A **14**
Clifton Grn. B28: Hall G 2G **149**
Clifton Ho. B12: Bal H 6A **118**
Clifton La. B71: W Brom 5C **64**
Clifton Rd. B6: Aston. 2H **101**
B12: Bal H 6H **117**
B36: Cas B 1A **106**
B62: B'hth 3D **112**
B67: Smeth 5D **98**
B73: S Cold 1G **69**
WV6: Tett 4B **26**
Clifton Rd. Ind. Est. *B12: Bal H. 6H **117***
(off Clifton Rd.)
Clifton St. B64: Old H. 2H **111**
DY8: Stourb 1C **124**
WV14: Cose 4B **60**
Clifton Ter. B23: Erd 3F **85**
Clinic Dr. DY9: Lye. 6A **110**
Clinton Gro. B90: Shir 6C **150**
Clinton Rd. B46: Col 3H **107**
B90: Shir 1B **164**
WV14: Bils 4A **46**
Clinton St. B18: Win G. 4A **100**
Clipper Vw. B16: Edg. 2A **116**
Clipston Rd. B8: Salt 5F **103**
Clissold Cl. B12: Birm 4G **117**
Clissold Pas. B18: Hock. 5C **100**
Clissold St. B18: Hock 5C **100**
Clive Cl. B75: R'ley 1B **54**
Cliveden Av. B42: P Barr 3E **83**
WS9: A'rdge. 6D **22**
Cliveden Coppice B74: Four O 2F **53**
Clivedon Way B62: Hale. 4A **112**
Cliveland St. B19: Birm 5G **101** (1E **5**)
Clive Pl. B19: Birm 5F **101** (1D **4**)
Clive Rd. B32: Quin 4B **114**
CV7: Bal C 6H **169**
Clive St. B71: W Brom. 2A **80**
Clockfields Dr. DY5: Brie H 2E **109**
Clock La. B92: Bick. 3F **139**
Clockmill Av. WS3: Pels. 4C **20**
Clockmill Pl. WS3: Pels. 4D **20**
Clockmill Rd. WS3: Pels 4C **20**
Clodeshall Rd. B8: Salt 5E **103**
Cloister Dr. B62: Hale 2D **128**
Cloisters, The WS4: Wals 6D **32**
Clonmel Rd. B30: Stir 1C **146**
Clopton Cres. B37: F'bri. 5D **106**
Clopton Rd. B33: Sheld 3G **121**
Close, The B17: Harb. 4D **114**
B29: S Oak. 5H **131**
B47: H'wd 4A **162**
B62: Hunn 6A **128**
B63: Crad 5F **111**
B92: Olton 5D **136**

Close, The—Colton Hills

Close, The DY3: Lwr G 3G 75
DY3: Swind 5E 73
WS10: W'bry 2E 63
Clothier Gdns. WV13: W'hall 6A 30
Clothier St. WV13: W'hall 6A 30
Cloudbridge Dr. B92: Sol 6B 138
Cloudsley Gro. B92: Olton 2D 136
Clover Av. B37: Chel W 1F 123
Clover Ct. B38: K Nor 5H 145
Cloverdale WV6: Pert 5D 24
Clover Dr. B32: Bart G 3A 130
Clover Hill WS5: Wals 3A 50
Clover La. DY6: W Hth 2G 91
Clover Lea Sq. B8: W End 3G 103
Clover Ley WV10: Wolv 6B 28
Clover Piece DY4: Tip 1C 78
Clover Ridge WS6: C Hay 2C 6
Clover Rd. B29: W Cas 6E 131
Club La. WV10: Cov H 1G 15
Club Row DY3: Up Gor 2A 76
Club Vw. B38: K Nor 5H 145
Clunbury Cft. B34: S End 4F 105
Clunbury Rd. B31: Longb 1E 159
Clun Cl. B69: Tiv 6H 77
Clun Rd. B31: N'fld 1D 144
Clyde Av. B62: B'hth 3E 113
Clyde Ct. B73: S Cold 6H 53
Clyde M. DY5: P'ntt 3F 93
Clyde Rd. B93: Dorr 6H 167
Clydesdale B26: Sheld 6E 121
Clydesdale Rd. B32: Quin 5H 113
DY2: Neth 6E 95
WS8: Clay 1A 22
Clydesdale Twr. B1: Birm 6D 4
Clyde St. B12: Birm 2A 118
B64: Old H 2G 111
Clyde Twr. B19: Loz 1F 101
C M T Ind. Est. B69: O'bry 1G 97
COALBOURNBROOK 3D 108
Coalbourn La. DY8: Amb 4D 108
Coalbourn Way DY5: Brie H 6E 93
Coalheath La. WS4: S'fld 1G 33
Coalmeadow Cl. WS3: Blox 4F 19
COAL POOL 3D 32
Coalpool La. WS3: Wals 3D 32
Coalpool Pl. WS3: Wals 3D 32
Coalport Rd. WV1: Wolv 2C 44
Coalway Av. B26: Sheld 1G 137
WV3: Penn 5E 43
Coalway Gdns. WV3: Wolv 5B 42
Coalway Rd. WS3: Blox 1G 31
WV3: Penn 5B 42
Coatsgate Wlk. WV8: Pend 6D 14
Cobbles, The B72: W Grn 6A 70
Cobble Wlk. B18: Hock 4C 100
Cobbs Wlk. B65: Row R 4H 95
Cobden Cl. DY4: Tip 5H 61
WS10: Darl 5F 47
Cobden Gdns. B12: Bal H 5G 117
Cobden St. DY8: Woll 5B 108
WS1: Wals 4B 48
WS10: Darl 5F 47
Cobham Bus. Cen. B9: Bord G 1D 118
Cobham Cl. B35: Cas V 4D 86
Cobham Ct. M. DY9: Hag 6H 125
Cobham Rd. B9: Bord G 1D 118
B63: Hale 1B 128
DY8: Stourb 3E 125
WS10: W'bry 3C 64
Cob La. B30: B'vlle 6G 131
Cobs Fld. B30: B'vlle 1G 145
Coburg Cft. DY4: Tip 1C 78
Coburn Dr. B75: R'ley 1B 54
Cochrane Cl. DY4: Tip 1C 78
DY9: Pedm 5G 125
Cochrane Rd. DY2: Dud 3A 94
COCK GREEN 5B 96
Cock Hill La. B45: Rubery 6F 143
Cockley Wharf Ind. Est. DY5: Brie H 5F 93
Cockshed La. B62: B'hth 3C 112
Cockshut Hill B26: Yard 3E 121
Cockshutt La. WV2: Wolv 4H 43
Cocksmead Cft. B14: K Hth 2F 147
Cocksmoor Ho. B14: K Hth 6F 133
Cocks Moor Woods Leisure Cen.
B14: K Hth 3H 147
Cockthorpe Cl. B17: Harb 4D 114
Cocton Cl. WV6: Pert 4E 25
CODSALL 3F 13
Codsall Coppice Nature Reserve 3G 111
Codsall Gdns. WV8: Cod 3E 13
Codsall Ho. WV8: Cod 3E 13
Codsall Leisure Cen. 3G 13
Codsall Rd. B64: Crad H 3G 111
WV6: Tett 2C 26
WV8: Tett 6A 14
Codsall Station (Rail) 4E 13
CODSALL WOOD 1B 12
Codsall Wood Rd. WV8: Cod, Cod W 1B 12
Cofield Rd. B73: Bold 4F 69
Cofton Chu. La. B45: Coft H 6A 158
COFTON COMMON 2F 159
Cofton Ct. B45: Redn 2B 158
Cofton Gro. B31: Longb 3C 158
COFTON HACKETT 6A 158
Cofton Lake Rd. B45: Coft H 6A 158
Cofton Rd. B31: Longb 2E 159
Cokeland Pl. B64: Crad H 3F 111
Colaton Cl. WV10: Wolv 5A 28
Colbourne Ct. B33: Stech 6B 104
Colbourne Rd. DY4: Tip 3A 78
Coldbath Rd. B13: Mose 5B 134
Coldridge Cl. WV8: Pend 6D 14
Coldstream Dr. DY8: Word 6C 92
Coldstream Rd. B76: Walm 5C 70
Coldstream Way B6: Witt 5G 83
(not continuous)
Cole Bank Rd. B13: Mose 5D 134
B28: Hall G 5D 134
Colebourne Rd. B13: Mose 6C 134
Colebridge Cres. B46: Col 1H 107
Colebrook Cft. B90: Shir 5F 149
Colebrook Rd. B11: S'hll 6D 118
B90: Shir 5E 149
Cole Ct. B37: Chel W 1D 122
COLE END 1H 107
Coleford Cl. DY8: Word 1A 108
Coleford Dr. B37: F'bri 1C 122
Cole Grn. B90: Shir 6E 149
COLEHALL 4G 105
Cole Hall La. B34: S End 3E 105
(not continuous)
Cole Holloway B31: N'fld 5C 130
Colehurst Cft. B90: M'path 3D 164
Coleman Rd. WS10: W'bry 6G 47
Coleman St. WV6: Wolv 5D 26
Colemeadow Rd. B13: Mose 2B 148
B46: Col 2H 107
Colenso Rd. B16: Edg 5H 99
Coleraine Rd. B42: Gt Barr 1C 82
Coleridge Cl. WS3: Pels 2E 21
WV12: W'hall 2E 31
Coleridge Dr. WV6: Pert 5E 25
Coleridge Pas. B4: Birm 6G 101 (2F 5)
Coleridge Ri. DY3: Lwr G 3E 75
Coleridge Rd. B43: Gt Barr 6A 66
Colesbourne Av. B14: K Hth 5E 147
Colesbourne Rd. B92: Olton 2E 137
Coles Cres. B71: W Brom 6H 63
Colesden Wlk. WV4: Penn 5A 42
Coleshaven B46: Col 3H 107
COLESHILL 2H 107
COLESHILL HEATH 3E 123
Coleshill Heath Rd. B37: Mars G 4E 123
B46: Col 1G 123
Coleshill Ind. Est. B46: Col 5H 89
(Gorsey La.)
B46: Col 5G 89
(Roman Way)
Coleshill Leisure Cen. 3H 107
Coleshill Rd. B36: Hodg H 3B 104
B37: Mars G 4C 122
B46: Wat O 4D 88
B75: S Cold 6A 54
B76: Curd 1D 88
(not continuous)
Coleshill St. B4: Birm 6H 101 (2G 5)
B72: S Cold 6A 54
Coleshill Trad. Est. B46: Col 6H 89
Coleside Av. B13: Mose 6D 134
Coles La. B71: W Brom 6G 63
B72: S Cold 1A 70
Cole St. DY2: Neth 6G 95
Cole Valley Rd. B28: Hall G 1D 148
Coleview Cres. B33: Kitts G 6A 106
Coleville Rd. B76: Walm 1F 87
Coley's La. B31: N'fld 5E 145
Colgreave Av. B11: Mose 3D 134
Colindale Rd. B44: K'sdng 2A 68
Colinwood Cl. WS6: Gt Wyr 4F 7
Collector Rd. B36: Cas B 6F 87
B37: F'bri 4E 107
Colleen Av. B30: K Nor 4D 146
College Cl. WS10: W'bry 3G 63
College Ct. WV6: Tett 5B 26
College Dr. B20: Hand 5B 82
Coll. Farm Dr. B23: Erd 5D 68
College Ga. B8: Salt 5E 103
College Gro. B20: Hand 2D 100
College High Community Leisure Cen., The 1B 84
College Hill B73: S Cold 1H 69
College Rd. B8: Salt 6E 103
B13: Mose 3C 134
B20: Hand 5A 82
B32: Quin 5G 113
B44: P Barr, K'sdng 2G 83
B73: New O 1A 84
DY8: Stourb 1E 125
WV6: Tett 5B 26
College St. B18: Hock 5C 100
College Vw. WV6: Tett 6B 26
College Wlk. B29: S Oak 5H 131
Collets Brook B75: Bass P 1F 55
Collett Cl. DY8: Amb 5E 109
Collett Rd. WV6: Pert 4E 25
Colletts Gro. B37: K'hrst 4B 106
Colley Av. WV10: Bush 1B 28
Colley Ga. B63: Crad 5E 111
Colley La. B63: Crad 4E 111
Colley Orchard B63: Crad 5E 111
Colley St. B70: W Brom 3B 80
Collier Cl. WS6: C Hay 3D 6
WS8: Bwnhls 6G 9
Collier's Cl. WV12: W'hall 3B 30
Colliers Fold DY5: P'ntt 4F 93
Colliery Dr. WS3: Blox 4F 19
Colliery Rd. B71: W Brom 6E 81
WV1: Wolv 1B 44
Collindale Ct. DY6: K'wfrd 6B 74
Collingbourne Av. B36: Hodg H 2B 104
Collingdon Av. B26: Sheld 5G 121
Collings Ho. B16: Edg 2C 116
Colling Wlk. B37: K'hrst 3C 106
Collingwood Cen., The B43: Gt Barr 2F 67
Collingwood Dr. B43: Gt Barr 1E 67
Collingwood Rd. WV10: Bush 5A 16
Collins Cl. B32: Quin 6G 113
Collins Rd. WS8: Bwnhls 2C 22
WS10: W'bry 2A 64
Collins St. B70: W Brom 4E 79
WS1: Wals 4C 48
Collis St. DY8: Amb 3D 108
Collister Cl. B90: Shir 3H 149
Colly Cft. B37: K'hrst 4B 106
Collycroft Pl. B27: A Grn 6H 119
Colman Av. WV11: Wed 3H 29
Colman Cres. B68: O'bry 1A 114
Colman Hill B63: Crad 6F 111
Colman Hill Av. B63: Crad 5F 111
Colmers Farm Leisure Cen. 1H 157
Colmers Wlk. B31: Longb 6B 144
Colmore Av. B14: K Hth 6F 133
Colmore Cir. Queensway
B4: Birm 6G 101 (3E 5)
Colmore Cres. B13: Mose 4B 134
Colmore Dr. B75: S Cold 6E 55
Colmore Flats B19: Birm 5F 101 (1D 4)
Colmore Ga. B3: Birm 3E 5
Colmore Rd. B14: K Hth 6F 133
Colmore Row B3: Birm 1F 117 (4C 4)
Colmore Sq. B4: Birm 6G 101 (2E 5)
Coln Cl. B31: N'fld 1D 144
Colonial Ind. Pk. B64: Crad H 4F 111
Colonial Rd. B9: Bord G 6F 103
Colshaw Rd. DY8: Stourb 1C 124
Colston Rd. B24: Erd 5H 85
Colt Cl. B74: S'tly 4G 51
Coltham Rd. WV12: W'hall 3C 30
Coltishall Cl. B35: Cas V 5D 86
COLTON HILLS 1E 59

Colton Hills Sports Cen. 1F 59
Coltsfoot Cl. WV11: Wed 4G 29
Coltsfoot Vw. WS6: C Hay 3E 7
Columbia Cl. B5: Bal H 5F 117
Columbine Cl. WS5: Wals 2E 65
Columbus Av. DY5: Brie H 6B 94
Colville Cl. DY4: Tip 5D 62
Colville Rd. B12: Bal H 6B 118
Colville Wlk. B12: Bal H. 6B 118
Colwall Rd. DY3: Lwr G. 3H 75
Colwall Wlk. B27: A Grn 1B 136
Colworth Rd. B31: N'fld 3C 144
Colyns Gro. B33: Stech 4D 104
Comber Cft. B13: Mose 5D 134
Comber Dr. DY5: P'ntt 3F 93
Comberford Dr. WS10: W'bry 3G 63
Comberford Rd. WS10: W'bry 6B 48
Comberton Rd. B26: Sheld 4F 121
Combine Cl. B75: R'ley 5B 38
Combrook Grn. B34: S End 3H 105
Comet Rd. B26: Birm A 1E 139
Commercial Rd. WS2: Wals 2G 31
WV1: Wolv 2A 44
Commercial St. B1: Birm 2E 117 (6B 4)
Commissary Rd. B26: Birm A 2C 138
Commonfield Cft. B8: Salt 4D 102
Common La. B8: Salt 3F 103
B26: Sheld 6E 121
Common Rd. WV5: Wom 3F 73
COMMON SIDE 3E 9
Commonside DY5: P'ntt 3G 93
WS3: Pels. 5E 21
WS8: Bwnhls 1C 22
Communication Row B15: Birm 2E 117
COMPTON 1A 42
Compton Cl. B91: Sol. 3B 150
Compton Ct. B74: Four O 6F 37
DY2: Neth 3E 95
WV3: Wolv 1D 42
Compton Cft. B37: Chel W 2F 123
Compton Dr. B74: S'tly 4G 51
DY2: Dud 1H 95
DY6: K'wrfd 4B 92
Compton Grange B64: Crad H 3E 111
Compton Gro. B63: Crad 1E 127
DY6: K'wrfd 4B 92
Compton Hill Dr. WV3: Wolv 1B 42
Compton Ho. B33: Yard 2F 121
Compton Pk. WV3: Wolv 1C 42
Compton Pk. Recreation Cen. 6C 26
Compton Rd. B24: Erd 6E 85
B62: Quin 6F 113
B64: Crad H 2E 111
DY9: Pedm. 4H 125
WV3: Wolv 1C 42
Compton Rd. W. WV3: Wolv 1A 42
Comsey Rd. B43: Gt Barr 2D 66
Comwall Cl. WS3: Blox 3A 32
(not continuous)
Conchar Cl. B72: W Grn 3A 70
Conchar Rd. B72: W Grn 3A 70
Concorde Dr. B35: Cas V 5D 86
Concorde Rd. B26: Birm A 1E 139
Condover Cl. WS2: Wals 6D 30
Condover Rd. B31: Longb 1F 159
Conduit Rd. WS11: Nort C 1E 9
Coneybury Wlk. B76: Min 2H 87
Coneyford Rd. B34: S End 3G 105
(not continuous)
Coneygree Ind. Est.
DY4: Tip 4H 77
Coney Grn. DY8: Stourb 6F 109
Coney Grn. Dr. B31: Longb 1D 158
Coney Grn. Ho. B31: Longb 1D 158
Coneygree Rd. DY4: Tip 5H 77
Congreve Pas. B3: Birm 1F 117 (4C 4)
Conifer Cl. DY5: Brie H 3G 109
Conifer Ct. B13: Mose 3G 133
Conifer Dr. B21: Hand 2A 100
B31: N'fld 4F 145
Conifer Paddock B62: B'hth 3E 113
Conifer Rd. B74: S'tly 3G 51
Conington Gro. B17: Harb 6E 115
Coniston Av. B92: Olton 1D 136
Coniston Cl. B28: Hall G 6F 135
Coniston Cres. B43: Gt Barr 6B 66
Coniston Dr. DY6: K'wrfd 2H 91

Coniston Ho. B17: Harb 6H 115
B69: O'bry 4D 96
Coniston Rd. B23: Erd 2D 84
B74: S'tly 6H 35
WV6: Tett 1B 26
Conker La. B93: Dorr 5A 166
Connaught Av. WS10: W'bry 2A 64
Connaught Cl. WS5: Wals 4G 49
Connaught Dr. WV5: Wom 4G 57
Connaught Gdns. B5: Bal H 5G 117
Connaught Ho. WV1: Wolv 1E 43
Connaught Rd. WV1: Wolv. 1E 43
WV14: Bils 4H 45
Connops Way DY9: Lye 6A 110
Connor Rd. B71: W Brom 5C 64
Conolly Dr. B45: Redn 6H 143
Conrad Cl. B11: S'brk 4A 118
Consort Cres. DY5: P'ntt 3G 93
Consort Dr. WS10: Darl 3D 46
Consort Rd. B30: K Nor 4C 146
Constable Cl. B43: Gt Barr 2F 67
Constables, The B68: O'bry. 1H 113
Constance Av. B70: W Brom 6B 80
Constance Rd. B5: Edg. 6F 117
Constantine La. B46: Col 6H 89
Constantine Way WV14: Bils 3A 62
Constitution Hill B19: Birm . . . 5F 101 (1C 4)
DY2: Dud 1E 95
Constitution Hill E. DY2: Dud. 1F 95
Containerbase B44: P Barr 2G 83
Convent Cl. WV2: Wolv. 2H 43 (5C 170)
Conway Av. B32: Quin 5H 113
B68: O'bry 1H 113
B71: W Brom 4H 63
Conway Cl. B90: Shir 6B 150
DY1: Dud 1E 77
DY6: K'wrfd 5D 92
Conway Cres. WV12: W'hall. 2C 30
Conway Gro. B43: Gt Barr 6H 65
Conway Rd. B11: S'brk 5C 118
B37: F'bri 6D 106
B90: Shir 6B 150
WV6: Pert 6F 25
Conwy Cl. WS2: Wals 5G 31
Conybere St. B12: Birm 4G 117
Conyworth Cl. B27: A Grn 1B 136
Cook Av. DY2: Dud 2F 95
Cook Cl. B93: Know 3E 167
WV6: Pert 5E 25
WV10: Oxl 6G 15
Cookes Cl. B31: N'fld 5F 145
Cookesley Cl. B43: Gt Barr 1F 67
Cookley Cl. B63: Hale 3H 127
Cookley Way B69: O'bry. 4E 97
Cooknell Dr. DY8: Word 1C 108
Cook Rd. WS3: Blox 5B 20
Cooksey La. B44: Gt Barr. 1G 67
B44: Gt Barr. 1G 67
Cooksey Rd. B10: Small H 3B 118
(not continuous)
Cook's La. B37: K'hrst 6B 106
Cookspiece Wlk. B33: Stech 6D 104
Cook St. B7: Nech 2C 102
WS10: Darl 5F 47
WV2: Wolv. 4G 43
Coombe Cft. WV9: Pend. 4E 15
Coombe Hill B64: Old H 3B 112
Coombe Pk. B74: Four O 4F 53
Coombe Rd. B20: Hand 6G 83
B90: Shir 5A 150
Coombes La. B31: Longb 3D 158
COOMBESWOOD 3D 112
Coombeswood Bus. Pk. B62: B'hth . . 3B 112
Coombs Rd. B62: Hale 5B 112
Coombswood Way B62: B'hth 4B 112
Cooper Av. DY5: Brie H 1E 109
Cooper Cl. B70: W Brom 5C 80
COOPER'S BANK 6G 75
Cooper's Bank Rd. DY3: Gorn 6G 75
DY5: P'ntt 6G 75
Cooper's La. B67: Smeth 4D 98
Coopers Rd. B20: Hand 4C 82
Cooper St. B70: W Brom 4B 80
WV2: Wolv. 3B 44
Copeley Hill B23: Erd. 6C 84
Copes Cres. WV10: Wolv. 3C 28

Copeshill Ct. B75: S Cold. 1C 70
Cope St. B18: Hock 6C 100
WS3: Blox 3A 32
WS10: Darl 5E 47
Cophall St. DY4: Tip 2D 78
Cophams Cl. B92: Sol 3G 137
Coplow Cl. CV7: Bal C 3G 169
Coplow Cotts. B16: Birm 6B 100
Coplow Ho. B16: Birm 6B 100
Coplow St. B16: Birm 6B 100
Coplow Ter. B16: Birm 6B 100
(off Coplow St.)
Copnor Gro. B26: Yard 5C 120
Coppenhall Gro. B33: Kitts G. 6E 105
Copperbeech Cl. B32: Harb 6D 114
Copper Beech Dr. DY6: K'wrfd 6B 74
WV5: Wom. 1H 73
Copperbeech Dr. B12: Bal H 6A 118
Copperbeech Gdns. B20: Hand 5B 82
Coppice, The B20: Hand 5C 82
B31: Longb 5A 144
B42: P Barr 4G 83
DY4: Tip 4C 62
WV12: W'hall 3C 30
Coppice Ash Cft. B19: Loz 1F 101
Coppice Av. DY9: W'cte 2B 126
Coppice Cl. B24: Erd 4F 85
B45: Rubery 2F 157
B90: Ches G 5A 164
B91: Sol 6E 137
DY3: Sed 6F 59
DY5: Quar B 2B 110
WS6: C Hay 1D 6
WV11: Wed 6A 18
Coppice Cres. WS8: Bwnhls 6H 9
Coppice Dr. B27: A Grn 3H 135
Coppice Farm Way WV12: W'hall . . . 6B 18
Coppice Hollow B32: Bart G 4H 129
Coppice Ho. B27: A Grn. 3G 135
Coppice La. B78: Midd 1G 55
DY5: Quar B 2B 110
WS6: C Hay 1D 6
WS7: Hamm 2H 11
WS8: Bwnhls 5G 9
WS9: A'rdge 6B 22
WV6: Tett 3H 25
WV12: W'hall 3C 30
Coppice Oak B13: Mose 2A 134
Coppice Ri. DY5: Quar B 1C 110
Coppice Rd. B13: Mose 2A 134
B64: Crad H 4G 111
B92: Sol 6A 138
WS9: Wals W 3B 22
WV3: Wolv 3B 42
WV14: Cose 5C 60
Coppice Side WS8: Bwnhls 5H 9
Coppice Side Ind. Est. WS8: Bwnhls. . . . 6G 9
Coppice St. B70: W Brom 3G 79
DY4: Tip 3F 77
(Canal St.)
DY4: Tip 3F 77
(Furnace Pde.)
Coppice Vw. Rd. B73: S'tly 1A 68
Coppice Wlk. B90: Ches G 5A 164
Coppice Way B37: Chel W 1D 122
(off Chelmsley Wood Shop. Cen.)
Copplestone Cl. B34: S End 3F 105
Coppy Hall Gro. WS9: A'rdge 6D 22
Coppy Nook La. WS7: Hamm 1D 10
Copse, The B74: Four O 2F 53
Copse Cl. B31: N'fld 5E 145
Copse Cres. WS3: Pels. 3E 21
Copse Rd. DY2: Neth 6D 94
Copstone Dr. B93: Dorr 6B 166
Copston Gro. B29: W Cas 5F 131
Copthall Rd. B21: Hand. 5G 81
COPT HEATH 6C 152
Copt Heath Cft. B93: Know 1D 166
Copt Heath Dr. B93: Know 2C 166
Copt Heath Golf Course 1C 166
Copt Heath Wharf B91: Sol 5D 152
Copthorne Av. WS7: Chase 1B 10
Copthorne Rd. B44: Gt Barr 2G 67
WV3: Wolv 4E 43
Coralin Cl. B37: Chel W 1D 122
Corbett Cres. DY8: Amb 4E 109
Corbett Rd. B47: H'wd 2A 162
DY5: Brie H 2H 109

Corbetts Cl. B92: H Ard 6B **140**
Corbett St. B66: Smeth. 5F **99**
Corbridge Av. B44: Gt Barr 4H **67**
Corbridge Rd. B73: S Cold 3F **69**
Corbyn Rd. B9: Bord G. 6H **103**
DY1: Dud 1B **94**
Corbyn's Cl. DY5: P'ntt. 2F **93**
Corbyn's Hall La. DY5: P'ntt. 2F **93**
Corbyn's Hall Rd. DY5: P'ntt 3F **93**
Cordley St. B70: W Brom. 3H **79**
Corfe Cl. B32: Harb 6D **114**
WV6: Pert 6F **25**
Corfe Dr. B69: Tiv. 1A **96**
Corfe Rd. WV14: Cose 5C **60**
Corfton Dr. WV6: Tett 5A **26**
Coriander Cl. B45: Fran 6H **143**
Corinne Cl. B45: Redn 3G **157**
Corinne Cft. B37: K'hrst 5C **106**
Corisande Rd. B29: S Oak 3G **131**
Corley Av. B31: N'fld. 4F **145**
Corley Cl. B90: Shir 6E **149**
Cornbow Cen. B63: Hale 2B **128**
Cornbrook Rd. B29: W Cas 6D **130**
Cornbury Gro. B91: Shir. 3B **150**
Corncrake Cl. B72: S Cold 3B **70**
Corncrake Dr. B36: Cas B. 1C **106**
Corncrake Rd. DY3: Lwr G. 4A **76**
Cornel Cl. B37: Chel W. 3E **123**
Cornerstone B13: Mose 2H **133**
Cornerstone Country Club B31: N'fld . . . 2F **145**
Cornerway B38: K Nor 2B **160**
CORNETS END 1H **155**
Cornets End La. CV7: Mer 5E **141**
Cornfield WV8: Pend 6C **14**
Cornfield Cl. DY6: W Hth. 1G **91**
Cornfield Cft. B37: Chel W 6F **107**
B76: Walm 2D **70**
Cornfield Pl. *B65: Row R. 5H 95*
(off Allsops Cl.)
Cornfield Rd. B31: N'fld 3F **145**
B65: Row R 5H **95**
B76: Walm 4D **70**
Cornflower Cl. WV10: F'stne 1C **16**
Cornflower Cres. DY2: Dud 1H **95**
Cornflower Rd. WS8: Clay 1H **21**
Corngreaves, The B34: S End 3G **105**
Corngreaves Rd. B64: Crad H 2F **111**
Corngreaves Trad. Est. B64: Crad H . . . 4F **111**
Corngreaves Wlk. B64: Crad H 4G **111**
Corn Hill WS5: Wals. 3A **50**
WV10: Wolv 1H **43** (3D **170**)
Cornhill Gro. B30: Stir 1E **147**
Corn Mill Cl. B32: Bart G 4C **130**
B76: Walm 4D **70**
WS1: Wals 4B **48**
Cornmill Gro. WV6: Pert 6D **24**
Cornovian Cl. WV6: Pert 4E **25**
Corns Gro. WV5: Wom 2F **73**
Corns Ho. *WS10: Darl 5E 47*
(off Birmingham St.)
Corns St. WS10: Darl 6E **47**
Cornwall Av. B68: O'bry. 3H **113**
Cornwall Cl. DY6: K'wfrd 1C **92**
WS9: A'rdge. 6C **22**
WS10: W'bry 2B **64**
Cornwall Ga. WV12: W'hall 4B **30**
Cornwall Ho. B90: Bly P 6D **164**
Cornwallis Rd. B70: W Brom. 6G **79**
Cornwall Pl. WS2: Wals. 6E **31**
Cornwall Rd. B20: Hand. 5B **82**
B45: Fran 6E **143**
B66: Smeth. 2F **99**
DY8: Woll. 3B **108**
WS5: Wals 4F **49**
WV6: Tett 5A **26**
Cornwall Rd. Ind. Est. B66: Smeth 2F **99**
Cornwall St. B3: Birm 6F **101** (3C **4**)
Cornwall Twr. B18: Hock 4D **100**
Cornwell Cl. DY4: Tip. 2A **78**
Cornyx La. B91: Sol. 1H **151**
Coronation Av. WV13: W'hall. 1D **46**
Coronation Rd. B8: Salt 3F **103**
B29: S Oak. 3B **132**
B43: Gt Barr. 1A **66**
DY4: Tip. 5A **62**
WS4: S'fld 5F **21**
WS9: Wals W. 4C **22**
Coronation Rd. WS10: W'bry. 2A **64**
WV10: Wolv. 4C **28**
WV14: Bils 6E **45**
Corporation Rd. DY2: Dud. 5G **77**
Corporation Sq. B4: Birm 6G **101** (3F **5**)
Corporation St. B2: Birm. 1G **117** (4E **5**)
(not continuous)
B4: Birm 5G **101** (1F **5**)
WS1: Wals 3C **48**
WS10: W'bry. 3G **63**
WV1: Wolv 1G **43** (3A **170**)
Corporation St. W. WS1: Wals. 3B **48**
Corrie Cft. B26: Sheld. 4F **121**
B32: Bart G 5H **129**
Corrin Gro. DY6: W Hth 1A **92**
Corron Hill *B63: Hale. 1B 128*
(off Cobham Rd.)
Corsers Ct. WV6: Pert 5E **25**
Corser St. DY1: Dud. 5B **76**
DY8: Stourb 2E **125**
WV1: Wolv. 2B **44**
Corsican Cl. WV12: W'hall 2E **31**
Corvedale Rd. B29: W Cas. 1E **145**
Corve Gdns. WV6: Tett. 4C **26**
Corve Vw. DY3: Sed. 4G **59**
Corville Gdns. B26: Sheld 1G **137**
Corville Rd. B62: Quin 5F **113**
Corwen Cft. B31: N'fld 1C **144**
Cory Cft. DY4: Tip. 2A **78**
COSELEY 5E **61**
Coseley Baths 4F **61**
Coseley Hall WV14: Cose. 5E **61**
Coseley Leisure Cen. 4D **60**
Coseley Rd. WV14: Bils 6E **45**
Coseley Station (Rail) 4E **61**
Cosford Ct. WV6: Pert 4E **25**
Cosford Cres. B35: Cas V. 4E **87**
Cosford Dr. DY2: Neth 5G **95**
Cosgrove Wlk. WV8: Pend. 6D **14**
Cossington Rd. B23: Erd 6D **68**
Costock Cl. B37: Mars G 3D **122**
Cotford Rd. B14: K Hth. 5A **148**
Cotheridge Cl. B90: M'path 3G **165**
Cot La. DY6: K'wfrd 3A **92**
DY8: Word 4A **92**
Cotleigh Gro. B43: Gt Barr. 2G **67**
Cotman Cl. B43: Gt Barr. 2E **67**
Coton Gro. B90: Shir 5E **149**
Coton La. B23: Erd 3F **85**
Coton Rd. WV4: Penn. 6F **43**
Cotsdale Rd. WV4: Penn 2C **58**
Cotsford B91: Sol 4E **151**
Cotswold Av. WS6: Gt Wyr. 2F **7**
Cotswold Cl. B45: Fran 5H **143**
B69: O'bry 4E **97**
WS9: A'rdge 6E **23**
Cotswold Cft. B63: Hale 4E **127**
Cotswold Gro. WV12: W'hall 6B **18**
Cotswold Rd. DY8: Amb. 5F **109**
WV2: E'shll. 4B **44**
Cotsworld Ct. *WV2: Wolv. 5F 43*
(off Goldthorn Hill)
Cottage Cl. WV11: Wed 3E **29**
(not continuous)
Cottage Gdns. B45: Rubery 4F **157**
Cottage La. B76: Min. 1H **87**
WV10: F'hses. 4H **15**
Cottage M. WS9: A'rdge. 5G **35**
Cottage St. DY5: Brie H 6H **93**
DY6: K'wfrd 2B **92**
Cottage Vw. WV8: Bilb. 3H **13**
Cottage Wlk. B70: W Brom 5B **80**
COTTERIDGE 3A **146**
Cotteridge Rd. B30: K Nor. 3C **146**
Cotterills Av. B8: W End. 5A **104**
Cotterills La. B8: W End 5G **103**
Cotterills Rd. DY4: Tip 6B **62**
Cottesbrook Rd. B27: A Grn. 1B **136**
Cottesfield Cl. B8: W End 5H **103**
Cottesmore Cl. B71: W Brom 5D **64**
Cottesmore Ho. B20: Hand 5B **82**
Cottle Cl. WS2: Wals 6F **31**
Cotton La. B13: Mose 3H **133**
Cottrells Cl. B14: Yard W. 3C **148**
Cottrells M. B46: Wat O. 5D **88**
Cottrell St. B71: W Brom 3B **80**
Cottsmeadow Dr. B8: W End 5A **104**
COTWALL END 6G **59**
Cotwall End Countryside Cen. 1G **75**
Cotwall End Rd. DY3: Lwr G, Sed 3F **75**
Cotysmore Rd. B75: S Cold 5B **54**
Couchman Rd. B8: Salt 5E **103**
Coulter Gro. WV6: Pert 5D **24**
Council Cres. WV12: W'hall. 5C **30**
Counterfield Dr. B65: Row R 4H **95**
Countess Dr. WS4: Rus 2H **33**
Countess St. WS1: Wals 4B **48**
COUNTY BRIDGE 1D **46**
County Cl. B30: Stir 1D **146**
B32: Bart G 2A **130**
County La. DY8: I'ley 5B **124**
WV7: Alb 2A **12**
WV8: Cod W 2A **12**
County Pk. Av. B62: Hale 2C **128**
Court, The B93: Know 4B **168**
Court Cres. DY6: K'wfrd. 4H **91**
Courtenay Gdns. B43: Gt Barr 3A **66**
Courtenay Rd. B44: Gt Barr. 6G **67**
Court Farm Rd. B23: Erd 1E **85**
Court Farm Way B29: W Cas 6D **130**
Courtland Rd. DY6: K'wfrd. 1C **92**
Courtlands, The WV6: Wolv. 5C **26**
Courtlands Cl. B5: Edg. 5E **117**
Court La. B23: Erd 5E **69**
Court Oak Gro. B32: Harb 5D **114**
Court Oak Rd. B32: Harb 5C **114**
Court Pde. WS9: A'rdge. 3D **34**
Court Pas. DY1: Dud 6E **77**
Court Rd. B11: S'hll 1C **134**
B12: Bal H 5G **117**
WV4: E'shll. 2C **60**
WV6: Wolv. 5D **26**
Court St. B64: Old H. 2H **111**
DY8: Stourb 6E **109**
Court Way WS2: Wals 1C **48**
Courtway Av. B14: K Hth 6B **148**
Courtway Ho. B29: S Oak. 4G **131**
Court Yd., The *B70: W Brom. 4G 79*
(off Hambletts Rd.)
Courtyard, The B46: Col. 5H **89**
B91: Sol 3G **151**
Coveley Gro. B18: Hock 4C **100**
Coven Cl. WS3: Pels. 2E **21**
Coven Gro. B29: S Oak. 3F **131**
COVEN HEATH 1H **15**
Coven La. WV9: Coven 2D **14**
Coventry Rd. B10: Small H 2A **118**
B25: Yard. 4G **119**
B26: Yard, Sheld 5C **120**
B46: Col 6H **107**
B92: Bick 2C **138**
Coventry St. B5: Birm. 1H **117** (5G **5**)
DY8: Stourb 6E **109**
WV1: Wolv 1C **44**
Cover Cft. B76: Walm. 4E **71**
Coverdale Rd. B92: Olton. 1E **137**
Covert, The WV8: Pend 6C **14**
Covert La. DY8: Stourb 4B **124**
Cowles Cft. B25: Yard 2C **120**
Cowley Cl. B36: Cas B 6B **88**
Cowley Dr. B27: A Grn 1B **136**
DY1: Dud 5B **76**
Cowley Gro. B11: Tys. 6E **119**
Cowley Rd. B11: Tys 6E **119**
Cowper Cl. WV12: W'hall 2E **31**
Cowslip Cl. B29: W Cas 6E **131**
B38: K Nor. 1B **160**
Cowslip Wlk. DY5: Brie H 5G **109**
Coxcroft Av. DY5: Quar B 3B **110**
Coxmoor Cl. WS3: Blox 4F **19**
Cox Rd. WV14: Cose 4G **61**
Cox's La. B64: Old H 1H **111**
Cox St. B3: Birm 5F **101** (1C **4**)
Coxwell Av. WV10: Wolv 3G **27**
Coxwell Gdns. B16: Birm. 1B **116**
Coyne Cl. DY4: Tip 2F **77**
Coyne Rd. B70: W Brom 5H **79**
Crabbe St. DY9: Lye. 6B **110**
Crab La. DY6: K'wfrd 5E **93**
WV12: W'hall. 6D **18**
Crabmill Cl. B38: K Nor. 2A **160**
B93: Know 2E **167**
Crabmill La. B38: Head H 2E **161**
Crabourne Rd. DY2: Neth 1D **110**

Crabtree Cl.—Cross La.

Crabtree Cl. B31: N'fld . . . 5G **145**
B71: W Brom . . . 5D **64**
DY9: Hag . . . 6F **125**
Crabtree Dr. B37: F'bri . . . 1B **122**
Crab Tree Ho. B33: Stech . . . 6C **104**
Crabtree Rd. B18: Hock . . . 4C **100**
WS1: Wals . . . 1E **49**
Crackley Way DY2: Dud . . . 3C **94**
Craddock Rd. B67: Smeth . . . 3C **98**
Craddock St. WV6: Wolv . . . 5E **27**
CRADLEY . . . 4E **111**
Cradley Cft. B21: Hand . . . 4G **81**
Cradley Flds. B63: Crad . . . 6E **111**
Cradley Forge DY5: Quar B . . . 3C **110**
CRADLEY HEATH . . . 2G **111**
Cradley Heath Factory Cen.
B64: Crad H . . . 3E **111**
Cradley Heath Station (Rail) . . . 3D **110**
Cradley Leisure Cen. . . . 4D **110**
Cradley Mill DY5: Quar B . . . 4B **110**
Cradley Pk. Rd. DY2: Neth . . . 1E **111**
Cradley Rd. B64: Crad H . . . 3E **111**
DY2: Neth . . . 5F **95**
Cradock Rd. B8: Salt . . . 4E **103**
Craig Cft. B37: Chel W . . . 1F **123**
Crail Gro. B43: Gt Barr . . . 1D **66**
Cramlington Rd. B42: Gt Barr . . . 5C **66**
Cramp Hill WS10: Darl . . . 5D **46**
Cranbourne Av. WV4: E'shll . . . 2A **60**
Cranbourne Cl. B45: Fran . . . 5G **143**
Cranbourne Gro. B44: K'sdng . . . 5A **68**
Cranbourne Pl. B71: W Brom . . . 3B **80**
Cranbourne Rd. B44: K'sdng . . . 5A **68**
DY8: Stourb . . . 1E **125**
Cranbrook Ct. *WV13: W'hall* . . . *1C* ***46***
(off Mill St.)
Cranbrook Gro. WV6: Pert . . . 6F **25**
Cranbrook Rd. B21: Hand . . . 6G **81**
Cranby St. B8: Salt . . . 4C **102**
Craneberry Rd. B37: F'bri . . . 1A **122**
Cranebrook Hill B78: Hints . . . 4H **39**
Cranebrook La. WS14: Hilt, Lynn . . . 1H **23**
Crane Ct. WS1: Wals . . . 6E **33**
Crane Dr. WS7: Chase . . . 1C **10**
Crane Hollow WV5: Wom . . . 2E **73**
Cranehouse Rd. B44: K'sdng . . . 3B **68**
Cranemoor Cl. B7: Nech . . . 3C **102**
Crane Rd. WV14: Bils . . . 2H **61**
Cranesbill Rd. B29: W Cas . . . 1E **145**
Cranes Pk. Rd. B26: Sheld . . . 6G **121**
Crane Ter. WV6: Tett . . . 4C **26**
Cranfield Gro. B26: Yard . . . 3D **120**
Cranfield Pl. WS5: Wals . . . 1D **64**
Cranford Gro. B91: Sol . . . 6F **151**
Cranford Rd. WV3: Wolv . . . 3A **42**
Cranford St. B66: Smeth . . . 4G **99**
Cranford Way B66: Smeth . . . 4G **99**
Cranham Dr. DY6: K'wfrd . . . 4C **92**
Cranhill Cl. B92: Olton . . . 4F **137**
Crankhall La. B71: W Brom . . . 2H **63**
WS10: W'bry . . . 2H **63**
Cranleigh Cl. WS9: A'rdge . . . 4D **34**
WV12: W'hall . . . 6C **18**
Cranleigh Ho. B23: Erd . . . 1F **85**
Cranleigh Pl. B44: P Barr . . . 2G **83**
Cranley Dr. WV8: Cod . . . 3F **13**
Cranmer Av. WV12: W'hall . . . 2D **30**
Cranmer Cl. WS6: C Hay . . . 4D **6**
Cranmere Av. WV6: Tett . . . 3G **25**
Cranmere Ct. WV6: Tett . . . 3G **25**
Cranmer Gro. B74: Four O . . . 3F **37**
Cranmoor Cres. B63: Hale . . . 6A **112**
Cranmore Av. B21: Hand . . . 2H **99**
B90: Shir . . . 1C **164**
Cranmore Blvd. B90: Shir . . . 1B **164**
Cranmore Cl. DY4: Tip . . . 5A **62**
Cranmore Dr. B90: Shir . . . 6C **150**
Cranmore Rd. B36: Cas B . . . 6H **87**
B90: Shir . . . 1B **164**
WV3: Wolv . . . 6D **26**
Cransley Gro. B91: Sol . . . 6E **151**
Crantock Cl. WV11: Ess . . . 6C **18**
Crantock Rd. B42: P Barr . . . 3E **83**
Cranwell Grn. WV5: Wom . . . 2F **73**
Cranwell Gro. B24: Erd . . . 4B **86**
Cranwell Way B35: Cas V . . . 4E **87**
Crathorne Av. WV10: Oxl . . . 6G **15**
Crauford Ct. DY8: Stourb . . . 2E **125**
Crauford St. DY8: Stourb . . . 2E **125**
Craven Hgts. B92: H Ard . . . 6A **140**
Craven St. WV2: E'shll . . . 5B **44**
Crawford Av. B67: Smeth . . . 4D **98**
WS10: Darl . . . 4C **46**
WV4: E'shll . . . 2B **60**
Crawford Rd. B76: Walm . . . 5D **70**
WV3: Wolv . . . 1E **43**
Crawford St. B8: Salt . . . 5C **102**
Crawley Wlk. B64: Crad H . . . 2F **111**
Crawshaws Rd. B36: Cas B . . . 6G **87**
Crayford Rd. B44: K'sdng . . . 4A **68**
Craythorne Av. B20: Hand . . . 2A **82**
Crecy Cl. B76: Walm . . . 1C **70**
Credenda Rd. B70: W Brom . . . 6G **79**
Credon Gro. B15: Edg . . . 1B **132**
Cregoe St. B15: Birm . . . 2E **117**
Cremore Av. B8: Salt . . . 4E **103**
Cremorne Rd. B75: Four O . . . 1H **53**
Cremorne Wlk. B75: Four O . . . 1H **53**
Crendon Rd. B65: Row R . . . 3A **96**
Crescent, The B18: Hock . . . 3D **100**
B37: Mars G . . . 3G **123**
B43: Gt Barr . . . 4C **66**
(Handsworth Dr.)
B43: Gt Barr . . . 2F **67**
(King's Rd.)
B46: Wat O . . . 4D **88**
B64: Crad H . . . 4A **112**
B65: Row R . . . 1B **112**
B90: Shir . . . 3G **149**
B91: Sol . . . 3F **151**
B92: H Ard . . . 6B **140**
DY1: Dud . . . 3G **77**
DY9: Lye . . . 1G **125**
WS1: Wals . . . 3E **49**
WS6: Gt Wyr . . . 3G **7**
WS10: W'bry . . . 1G **63**
WV6: Tett . . . 6H **25**
WV13: W'hall . . . 2C **46**
WV14: Bils . . . 5F **45**
Crescent Arc. *B91: Sol* . . . *4G* ***151***
(off Touchwood Shop. Cen.)
Crescent Av. DY5: Brie H . . . 1G **109**
Crescent Ind. Pk. DY2: Dud . . . 2D **94**
Crescent, The (MM) . . . 5F **45**
Crescent Rd. DY2: Neth . . . 4D **94**
WS10: Darl . . . 5D **46**
WV13: W'hall . . . 1C **46**
Crescent Studios B18: Hock . . . 3C **100**
Crescent Theatre . . . 1D **116**
Crescent Twr. B1: Birm . . . 4A **4**
Cressage Av. B31: N'fld . . . 6E **145**
Cressett Av. DY5: Brie H . . . 5F **93**
Cressett La. DY5: Brie H . . . 5G **93**
Cressington Dr. B74: Four O . . . 2G **53**
Cresswell Ct. WV9: Pend . . . 4E **15**
Cresswell Cres. WS3: Blox . . . 5F **19**
Cresswell Gro. B24: Erd . . . 3B **86**
Crest, The B31: Longb . . . 2F **159**
Crest Vw. B14: K Hth . . . 3B **148**
B74: S'tly . . . 3H **51**
Crestwood Dr. B44: Gt Barr . . . 6G **67**
Crestwood Glen WV6: Tett . . . 2C **26**
Creswell Rd. B28: Hall G . . . 6H **135**
Creswick Gro. B45: Redn . . . 2A **158**
Crew Rd. WS10: W'bry . . . 1G **63**
Creynolds Cl. B90: Ches G . . . 6B **164**
Creynolds La. B90: Ches G . . . 6B **164**
Cricket Cl. WS5: Wals . . . 4F **49**
Cricketers Mdw. B64: Crad H . . . 4G **111**
Cricket Mdw. DY3: Up Gor . . . 2A **76**
WV10: F'hses . . . 3H **15**
Cricket St. B70: W Brom . . . 6F **63**
Crick La. B20: Hand . . . 1C **100**
Cricklewood Dr. B62: Hale . . . 2D **128**
Crimmond Ri. B63: Hale . . . 6G **111**
Crimscote Cl. B90: M'path . . . 3D **164**
Cripps Rd. WS2: Wals . . . 6E **31**
Criterion Works WV13: W'hall . . . 3B **46**
Crocketts Av. B21: Hand . . . 2H **99**
Crockett's La. B66: Smeth . . . 4E **99**
Crocketts Rd. B21: Hand . . . 2G **99**
Crockett St. DY1: Dud . . . 5C **76**
Crockford Dr. B75: Four O . . . 6H **37**
Crockford Rd. B71: W Brom . . . 4A **64**
Crockington La. WV5: Seis, Try . . . 3A **56**
Crocus Cres. WV9: Pend . . . 4E **15**
Croft, The B31: N'fld . . . 4F **145**
DY2: Dud . . . 3B **94**
DY3: Sed . . . 4A **60**
WS5: Wals . . . 3A **50**
WS6: C Hay . . . 3E **7**
WV5: Wom . . . 2D **72**
WV12: W'hall . . . 3D **30**
Croft Apartments *WV13: W'hall* . . . *1A* ***46***
(off Croft St.)
Croft Cl. B25: Yard . . . 3C **120**
Croft Ct. B36: Cas B . . . 1F **105**
Croft Cres. WS8: Bwnhls . . . 6H **9**
Cft. Down Rd. B92: Sol . . . 1H **137**
Croftdown Rd. B17: Harb . . . 5D **114**
Crofters Cl. DY8: Stourb . . . 1F **125**
Crofters Ct. B15: Edg . . . 5A **116**
Crofters La. B75: R'ley . . . 6C **38**
Crofters Wlk. WV8: Pend . . . 6C **14**
Croft Ho. *WS1: Wals* . . . *2D* ***48***
(off Paddock La.)
Croft Ind. Est. B37: Chel W . . . 1F **123**
WV13: W'hall . . . 1A **46**
Croft La. WV10: Bush . . . 2C **28**
Croftleigh Gdns. B91: Sol . . . 5C **150**
Croft Pde. WS9: A'rdge . . . 3D **34**
Croft Rd. B26: Yard . . . 3C **120**
Crofts, The B76: Walm . . . 6E **71**
Croft St. WS2: Wals . . . 6B **32**
WV13: W'hall . . . 1A **46**
(not continuous)
Croftway, The B20: Hand . . . 1A **82**
Croftwood Rd. DY9: W'cte . . . 1H **125**
Cromane Sq. B43: Gt Barr . . . 6A **66**
Cromdale Dr. B63: Hale . . . 2F **127**
Cromer Gdns. WV6: Wolv . . . 4D **26**
Crome Rd. B43: Gt Barr . . . 2F **67**
Cromer Rd. B12: Bal H . . . 6H **117**
Crompton Av. B20: Hand . . . 6E **83**
Crompton Cl. WS2: Wals . . . 4G **31**
Crompton Ct. WV8: Bilb . . . 3H **13**
Crompton Rd. B7: Nech . . . 1C **102**
B20: Hand . . . 6E **83**
B45: Fran . . . 6D **142**
DY4: Tip . . . 3A **78**
Cromwell Cl. B65: Row R . . . 4H **95**
WS2: Wals . . . 5E **31**
Cromwell Ct. WS6: Gt Wyr . . . 4G **7**
Cromwell Dr. DY2: Dud . . . 1H **95**
Cromwell La. B31: N'fld . . . 5B **130**
Cromwell Rd. WV10: Bush . . . 4A **16**
Cromwell St. B7: Nech . . . 4B **102**
B71: W Brom . . . 3A **80**
DY2: Dud . . . 1G **95**
Crondal Pl. B15: Edg . . . 4D **116**
CRONEHILLS, THE . . . 4A **80**
Cronehills Linkway B70: W Brom . . . 3B **80**
Cronehills St. B70: W Brom . . . 4B **80**
Crooked Ho. La. DY3: Gorn, Himl . . . 5D **74**
Crookham Cl. B17: Harb . . . 4D **114**
Crookhay La. B71: W Brom . . . 5G **63**
Crook La. WS9: A'rdge . . . 4C **50**
Croome Cl. B11: S'hll . . . 2B **134**
Cropredy Rd. B31: Longb . . . 1E **159**
Cropthorne Dr. B47: H'wd . . . 2B **162**
Cropthorne Rd. B90: Shir . . . 4A **150**
Crosbie Rd. B17: Harb . . . 5F **115**
Crosby Cl. B1: Birm . . . 6D **100**
WV6: Wolv . . . 4D **26**
Cross, The DY6: K'wfrd . . . 3B **92**
Cross Cl. B64: Old H . . . 1H **111**
Cross Farm Mnr. *B17: Harb* . . . *1H* ***131***
(off Cross Farm Rd.)
Cross Farm Rd. B17: Harb . . . 1G **131**
Cross Farms La. B45: Rubery . . . 6F **143**
Crossfield Rd. B33: Kitts G . . . 5F **105**
Crossgate Rd. DY2: Dud . . . 3B **94**
Cross Ho. *WV2: Wolv* . . . *4G* ***43***
(off Blakenhall Gdns.)
Crossings Ind. Est., The *WS3: Blox* . . . *1H* ***31***
(off Fryer's Rd.)
Crosskey Cl. B33: Kitts G . . . 1A **122**
Crossland Cres. WV6: Tett . . . 3D **26**
Cross La. B43: Gt Barr . . . 4A **66**
DY3: Sed . . . 5H **59**
WS14: Foot . . . 1E **37**

Crossley St. DY2: Neth 5F 95
Cross Pl. DY3: Sed 4A 60
Cross Quays Ind. Est. B69: Tiv 5B 78
     (off Hallbridge Way)
Cross St. B21: Hand 1G 99
  B63: Hale 2A 128
  B65: B'hth 2C 112
  B66: Smeth 3E 99
  B68: O'bry 5G 97
  DY1: Dud 6D 76
  DY6: K'wfrd 3B 92
  DY6: W Hth 1H 91
  DY8: Stourb 6C 108
  DY8: Word 6B 92
  WS3: Pels 6E 21
  WS6: C Hay 3D 6
  WS10: Darl 4D 46
  WS10: W'bry 2E 63
  WV1: Wolv 2B 44
  WV13: W'hall 2A 46
  WV14: Bils 3G 61
     (not continuous)
Cross St. Nth. WV1: Wolv 5H 27
Cross St. Sth. WV2: Wolv 4G 43
Cross Wlk. B69: Tiv 1C 96
Cross Walks Rd. DY9: Lye 6A 110
Crossway La. B44: K'sdng 1H 83
Crossways Ct. B44: K'sdng 6B 68
Crossways Grn. B44: K'sdng 6B 68
Crossways Shop. Cen. WV10: Wolv 6C 28
Crosswells Rd. B68: O'bry 4H 97
Crosswell Way WV14: Bils 6G 45
Crowberry Cl. WS8: Clay 1H 21
Crowesbridge M. WV14: Cose 5D 60
Crowhurst Rd. B31: Longb 2C 158
Crowland Av. WV6: Pert 5E 25
Crowle Dr. DY9: Lye 6G 109
Crown Av. B20: Hand 5F 83
Crown Cen., The DY8: Stourb 6E 109
Crown Cl. B65: Row R 5D 96
  DY3: Sed 4H 59
Crown Ct. B74: Four O 6E 37
  WS10: Darl 3C 46
Crown La. B74: Four O 6E 37
  DY8: I'ley 6A 124
  DY8: Stourb 6D 108
Crownmeadow Dr. DY4: Tip 6D 62
Crown Rd. B9: Bord G 1D 118
  B30: K Nor 3C 146
Crown St. WV1: Wolv 5H 27
Crown Wharf Shop. Pk. WS2: Wals 1B 48
Crows Nest Cl. B76: Walm 2D 70
Crowther Gdns. B63: Crad 4E 111
Crowther Gro. WV6: Wolv 5D 26
Crowther Rd. B23: Erd 2C 84
  WV6: Wolv 5C 26
Crowther St. WV10: Wolv 5A 28
Croxall Way B66: Smeth 4F 99
Croxdene Av. WS3: Blox 6F 19
     (not continuous)
Croxley Gdns. WV13: W'hall 3H 45
Croxstalls Av. WS3: Blox 1G 31
Croxstalls Cl. WS3: Blox 6G 19
Croxstalls Pl. WS3: Blox 1G 31
Croxstalls Rd. WS3: Blox 6G 19
Croxton Gro. B33: Stech 5E 105
Croyde Av. B42: Gt Barr 6C 66
Croydon Cl. B29: W Cas 6G 131
     (off Abdon Av.)
Croydon Rd. B24: Erd 6F 85
  B29: S Oak 2B 132
Croy Dr. B35: Cas V 3F 87
Crucible, The WV14: Cose 3E 61
Crusader Cl. B69: O'bry 4E 97
Crychan Cl. B45: Fran 5H 143
Cryersoak Cl. B90: M'path 2F 165
Crystal Av. DY8: Word 2D 108
Crystal Dr. B66: Smeth 1A 98
Crystal Ho. B66: Smeth 3F 99
Crystal Leisure Cen. 6D 108
Cubley Rd. B28: Hall G 4E 135
Cuckoo Rd. B7: Aston, Nech 1C 102
Cuin Rd. B66: Smeth 3F 99
Cuin Wlk. B66: Smeth 4G 99
     (off Cuin Rd.)
Culey Gro. B33: Kitts G 1H 121

Culey Wlk. B37: Chel W 1F 123
Culford Dr. B32: Bart G 5A 130
Culham Cl. B27: A Grn 3B 136
Cullwick St. WV1: Wolv 4C 44
Culmington Rd. B31: Longb 1D 158
Culmore Cl. WV12: W'hall 5D 30
Culmore Rd. B62: B'hth 2E 113
Culverhouse Dr. DY5: Brie H 2E 109
Culverley Cres. B93: Know 3B 166
Culvert Way B66: Smeth 2B 98
Culwell Ind. Est. WV10: Wolv 6A 28
Culwell St. WV10: Wolv 6H 27 (1D 170)
Culwell Trad. Est. WV10: Wolv 5B 28
Cumberford Av. B33: Kitts G 2A 122
Cumberland Av. B5: Birm 4G 117
Cumberland Cl. DY6: K'wfrd 5C 92
Cumberland Ho. WV1: Wolv 5G 27
Cumberland Rd. B68: O'bry 4H 113
  B71: W Brom 1B 80
  WV13: W'hall 1D 46
  WV14: Bils 4F 45
Cumberland St. B1: Birm 1E 117 (5A 4)
Cumberland Wlk. B75: S Cold 6F 55
Cumbrian Cl. B63: Hale 3F 127
Cumbria Way B8: Salt 3D 102
Cunningham Rd. WS2: Wals 1E 47
  WV6: Pert 5E 25
Cupfields Av. DY4: Tip 5B 62
Cupfields Cres. DY4: Tip 6C 62
Curbar Rd. B42: Gt Barr 1E 83
Curdale Rd. B32: Bart G 5H 129
CURDWORTH 1D 88
Curlews Cl. B23: Erd 5C 68
Curral Rd. B65: Row R 6B 96
Curtin Dr. WS10: Mox 1B 62
Curtis Cl. B66: Smeth 5G 99
Curzon Circ. B4: Birm 6A 102
Curzon St. B4: Birm 6H 101 (3H 5)
  WV2: Wolv 4H 43
Cushman Av. WV5: Wom 6E 57
Custard Factory, The
  B9: Birm 2H 117 (6H 5)
Cuthbert Rd. B18: Win G 5A 100
Cutlers Rough Cl. B31: N'fld 2D 144
Cutler St. B66: Smeth 3F 99
Cutsdean Cl. B31: N'fld 1D 144
Cutshill Cl. B36: Cas B 1G 105
Cutting, The WS4: Wals 6D 32
Cuttle Pool La. B93: Know 5H 167
Cutworth Cl. B76: Walm 2E 71
Cwerne Ct. DY3: Gorn 4G 75
Cygnet Cl. WV6: Tett 1A 42
Cygnet Dr. WS8: Bwnhls 6A 10
Cygnet Gro. B23: Erd 1A 84
Cygnet La. DY5: P'ntt 2G 93
Cygnet Rd. B70: W Brom 2G 79
Cygnus Bus. Pk. Ind. Cen.
  B70: W Brom 1F 79
Cygnus Way B70: W Brom 2F 79
Cypress Av. DY3: Up Gor 2H 75
Cypress Gdns. B74: S Cold 4G 53
  DY6: K'wfrd 5A 92
  WS5: Wals 1G 65
Cypress Gro. B31: N'fld 6C 144
Cypress Rd. DY2: Dud 6H 77
  WS5: Wals 1G 65
Cypress Sq. B27: A Grn 6A 120
Cypress Way B31: Longb 1D 158
Cyprus Cl. B29: W Cas 6E 131
Cyprus St. B69: O'bry 1G 97
     (not continuous)
  WV2: Wolv 5G 43
Cyril Rd. B10: Small H 3C 118

D

Dacer Cl. B30: Stir 2D 146
Dace Rd. WV10: Wolv 5D 28
Dadford Vw. DY5: Brie H 1F 109
Dad's La. B13: Mose 4E 133
Daffodil Cl. DY3: Sed 6A 60
Daffodil Pl. WS5: Wals 3H 49
Daffodil Rd. WS5: Wals 3H 49
Daffodil Way B31: Longb 1C 158
Dagger La. B71: W Brom 3C 80
Dagnall Rd. B27: A Grn 2B 136

Dahlia Ct. WV1: Wolv 2E 45
Daimer Cl. B36: Cas B 6B 88
Daimler Rd. B14: Yard W 4D 148
Dainton Gro. B32: Bart G 4A 130
Dairy Cl. DY4: Tip 2B 78
Dairy Ct. B68: O'bry 4B 114
DAISY BANK 3H 49
Daisy Bank Cl. WS3: S'fld 5F 21
Daisy Bank Cres. WS5: Wals 3H 49
Daisy Dr. B23: Erd 2A 84
Daisy Farm Rd. B14: K Hth 5B 148
Daisy Mdw. DY4: Tip 1C 78
Daisy Rd. B16: Edg 1B 116
Daisy St. WV14: Cose 3F 61
Daisy Wlk. WV9: Pend 4E 15
Dakota Apartments B16: Birm 1D 116
     (off Grosvenor St. W.)
Dalbeg Cl. WV8: Pend 1C 26
Dalbury Rd. B28: Hall G 2E 149
Dalby Rd. WS3: Wals 3D 32
Dale Cl. B43: Gt Barr 4H 65
  B66: Smeth 6E 99
  DY4: Tip 2D 78
Dalecote Av. B92: Sol 5A 138
Dale End B4: Birm 1G 117 (4F 5)
  WS10: Darl 5D 46
     (not continuous)
Dale Mdw. Cl. CV7: Bal C 3H 169
Dale Rd. B29: S Oak 2A 132
  B62: B'hth 4E 113
  DY8: Stourb 3D 124
Dales Cl. WV6: Wolv 3F 27
Dales La. WS9: A'rdge 4G 33
Dalesman Cl. DY6: K'wfrd 2H 91
Dale St. B66: Smeth 6E 99
  WS1: Wals 4B 48
     (not continuous)
  WS10: W'bry 2E 63
  WV3: Wolv 2F 43
  WV14: Bils 6H 45
Dale Ter. B69: Tiv 1C 96
Daleview Rd. B14: Yard W 3C 148
Dale Wlk. B25: Yard 4H 119
Dalewood Cft. B26: Sheld 5D 120
Dalewood Rd. B37: K'hrst 4B 106
Daley Cl. B1: Birm 6D 100
Daley Rd. WV14: Bils 3H 61
Dalkeith Rd. B73: New O 3D 68
Dalkeith St. WS2: Wals 6A 32
Dallas Rd. B23: Erd 3C 84
Dallimore Cl. B92: Olton 2D 136
Dalloway Cl. B5: Edg 5F 117
Dalston Cl. DY2: Dud 3F 95
Dalston Rd. B27: A Grn 1A 136
Dalton Ct. B23: Erd 4B 84
  WV5: Wom 6E 57
Dalton Pl. B92: Olton 3F 137
Dalton Rd. WS2: Wals 6G 31
Dalton St. B4: Birm 6G 101 (3F 5)
Dalton Twr. B4: Birm 1G 5
Dalton Way B4: Birm 6G 101 (3E 5)
Dalvine Rd. DY2: Neth 1D 110
Dalwood Cl. WV14: Cose 6D 60
Damar Cft. B14: K Hth 3F 147
Damian Cl. B67: Smeth 4D 98
Damson Cl. WV12: W'hall 3A 30
Damson La. B91: Sol 2A 152
  B92: Sol 2A 152
Damson Parkway B91: Sol 2A 152
  B92: Sol 2B 138
Damson Wharf DY4: Tip 4A 78
Danbury Cl. B76: Walm 3E 71
Danbury Rd. B90: Shir 5H 149
Danby Gro. B24: Erd 5H 85
Dando Rd. DY2: Dud 1F 95
Dandy Bank Rd. DY6: P'ntt 1E 93
Dandy's Wlk. WS1: Wals 2D 48
Dane Gro. B13: Mose 5F 133
Danehill Wlk. WV8: Pend 1D 26
Danesbury Cres. B44: K'sdng 5A 68
Danes Cl. WV11: Ess 3H 17
Danescourt Rd. WV6: Tett 3A 26
Danesmoor Ho. B25: Yard 4B 120
Daneswood Dr. WS9: Wals W 4B 22
Dane Ter. B65: Row R 4C 96
Daneways Cl. B74: S'tly 3A 52
Danford Cl. DY8: Stourb 1E 125

Danford Gdns.—Dene Av.

Danford Gdns. B10: Small H 3C **118**
Danford La. B91: Sol 4C **150**
Danford Rd. B47: H'wd 3H **161**
Danford Way B43: Gt Barr 5H **65**
Dangerfield Ho. B70: W Brom 6C **80**
Dangerfield La. WS10: Darl 6C **46**
Daniels La. WS9: A'rdge 5E **35**
Daniels Rd. B9: Bord G 1G **119**
Danks St. DY4: Tip 5A **78**
Danzey Grn. Rd. B36: Cas B 6F **87**
Danzey Gro. B14: K Hth 4E **147**
Darby Cl. WV14: Cose 3C **60**
DARBY END **5G 95**
Darby End Rd. DY2: Neth 5G **95**
Darby Ho. *WS2: Wals* *4A 48*
(off Caledon St.)
Darby Rd. B68: O'bry 4A **98**
WS10: W'bry 2H **63**
Darby's Hill Rd. B69: Tiv 1A **96**
Darby St. B65: B'hth 2C **112**
Darbys Way DY4: Tip 2B **78**
Darell Cft. B76: Walm 2C **70**
Daren Cl. B36: Cas B 1B **106**
Dare Rd. B23: Erd 3E **85**
Darfield Wlk. B12: Birm 3H **117**
Darges La. WS6: Gt Wyr 1F **7**
Darkhouse La. WV14: Cose 3E **61**
Darkies, The B31: N'fld 4F **145**
(not continuous)
Dark La. B38: Head H 2E **161**
B47: H'wd 2E **161**
B62: Roms 3A **142**
WS6: Gt Wyr 4A **8**
DARLASTON **4D 46**
Darlaston Central Trad. Est.
WS10: Darl 4E **47**
DARLASTON GREEN **3D 46**
Darlaston La. WV14: Bils 4A **46**
Darlaston Rd. WS2: Wals 4F **47**
WS10: Darl, W'bry 6D **46**
Darlaston Rd. Ind. Est. WS10: Darl 6D **46**
Darlaston Row CV7: Mer 4H **141**
Darlaston Swimming Pool 4E **47**
Darley Av. B34: Hodg H 3D **104**
Darleydale Av. B44: Gt Barr 4G **67**
Darley Dr. WV6: Wolv 4F **27**
Darley Ho. B69: O'bry 3D **96**
Darley Mead Ct. B91: Sol 3A **152**
Darley Way B74: S'tly 4A **52**
Darlington St. WS10: Darl 1D **62**
WV1: Wolv 1F **43** (3A **170**)
WV3: Wolv 1F **43**
Darnel Cft. B10: Small H 2B **118**
Darnel Hurst Rd. B75: R'ley 6A **38**
Darnford Cl. B28: Hall G 2G **149**
B72: W Grn 6B **70**
Darnick Rd. B73: New O 2D **68**
Darnley Rd. B16: Birm 1C **116**
Darris Rd. B29: S Oak 5C **132**
Dartford Rd. WS3: Blox 6F **19**
Dartmoor Cl. B45: Fran 5G **143**
Dartmouth Av. DY8: Word 5B **92**
WS3: Wals 4C **32**
WV13: W'hall 1A **46**
Dartmouth Cir. B6: Birm 4H **101**
Dartmouth Cl. WS3: Wals 4C **32**
Dartmouth Cres. WV14: Bils 4A **46**
Dartmouth Dr. WS9: A'rdge 4B **34**
Dartmouth Ho. *WS3: Wals* *3D 32*
(off Ryecroft Pl.)
Dartmouth Middleway B6: Birm 4H **101**
B7: Birm 4H **101** (1H **5**)
Dartmouth Pl. WS3: Wals 3D **32**
Dartmouth Rd. B29: S Oak 3B **132**
B66: Smeth 1D **98**
Dartmouth Sq. B70: W Brom 5B **80**
Dartmouth Steet Stop (MM) 4H **79**
Dartmouth St. B70: W Brom 4H **79**
WV2: Wolv 3H **43** (6D **170**)
(not continuous)
Darvel Rd. WV12: W'hall 5D **30**
Darwall St. WS1: Wals 1C **48**
Darwin Ct. WV6: Pert 5E **25**
Darwin Ho. B37: Chel W 2E **123**
Darwin Pl. WS2: Wals 3H **31**
Darwin Rd. WS2: Wals 4H **31**
Dassett Gro. B9: Bord G 1A **120**
Dassett Rd. B93: Ben H 5B **166**
Dauntsey Covert B14: K Hth 5F **147**
Davena Dr. B29: W Cas 3C **130**
Davena Gro. WV14: Cose 2F **61**
Davenport Dr. B35: Cas V 4G **87**
Davenport Rd. WV6: Tett 4H **25**
WV11: Wed 3G **29**
Daventry Gro. B32: Quin 5A **114**
Davey Rd. B20: Hand 6G **83**
B70: W Brom 2G **79**
David Harman Dr. B71: W Brom 6D **64**
David Lloyd Leisure
Birmingham Club 2F **67**
Cranmore Club 2C **164**
Solihull 3C **164**
David Peacock Cl. DY4: Tip 2A **78**
David Rd. B20: Hand 5D **82**
DY4: Tip 6A **62**
Davids, The B31: N'fld 1G **145**
Davies Av. WV14: Cose 2F **61**
Davies Ho. B69: O'bry 2G **97**
WS3: Blox 5H **19**
Davis Av. DY4: Tip 3G **77**
Davis Gro. B25: Yard 5B **120**
Davison Rd. B67: Smeth 6D **98**
Davis Rd. WV12: W'hall 1D **30**
Davy Cl. WS7: Chase 1B **10**
Davy Rd. WS2: Wals 4G **31**
Dawberry Cl. B14: K Hth 2F **147**
Dawberry Flds. Rd. B14: K Hth 2E **147**
Dawberry Rd. B14: K Hth 2E **147**
DAW END **3G 33**
Daw End WS4: Rus 3G **33**
Daw End La. WS4: Rus 2F **33**
Dawes Av. B70: W Brom 6A **80**
Dawes La. WS8: Bwnhls 4C **10**
Dawley Brook Rd. DY6: K'wfrd 2B **92**
Dawley Cl. WS2: Wals 4H **47**
Dawley Cres. B37: Mars G 2D **122**
Dawley Rd. DY6: W Hth 1A **92**
Dawley Trad. Est. DY6: K'wfrd 1B **92**
Dawlish Rd. B29: S Oak 2B **132**
B66: Smeth 4F **99**
DY1: Dud 1D **76**
Dawn Dr. DY4: Tip 3C **62**
Dawney Dr. B75: Four O 5G **37**
Dawn Rd. B31: N'fld 1C **144**
Dawson Av. WV14: Cose 3C **60**
Dawson Ct. B24: Erd 4F **85**
Dawson Rd. B21: Hand 1A **100**
Dawson Sq. WV14: Bils 6E **45**
Dawson St. B66: Smeth 6E **99**
WS3: Blox 1B **32**
Day Av. WV11: Wed 2G **29**
Day Ho. DY4: Tip 5C **62**
DAYHOUSE BANK **6B 142**
Dayhouse Bank B62: Roms 6B **142**
Daylesford Rd. B92: Olton 2E **137**
Day St. WS2: Wals 6C **32**
Deakin Av. WS8: Bwnhls 4B **10**
Deakin Rd. B24: Erd 4F **85**
B75: S Cold 4C **54**
Deakins Rd. B25: Yard 4H **119**
Deal Dr. B69: Tiv 6A **78**
Deal Gro. B31: N'fld 3E **145**
Deanbrook Cl. B90: M'path 3E **165**
Dean Cl. B44: K'sdng 5B **68**
B72: W Grn 6H **69**
DY8: Amb 5F **109**
Dean Ct. *DY5: Brie H* *1H 109*
(off Promenade, The)
WV6: Pert 3E **25**
Deanery Row WV1: Wolv 6G **27** (1B **170**)
Dean Rd. B23: Erd 2F **85**
WS4: Rus 2G **33**
WV5: Wom 2F **73**
Deans Bank Cen., The WS1: Wals 3B **48**
Deansfield Rd. WV1: Wolv 1C **44**
Deans Pl. WS3: Wals 3D **32**
Dean's Rd. WV1: Wolv 6C **28**
Dean St. B5: Birm 2G **117** (6F **5**)
DY3: Sed 5H **59**
Dearman Rd. B11: S'brk 4B **118**
Dearmont Rd. B31: Longb 2C **158**
Dearne Ct. DY3: Sed 1C **76**
Debden Cl. B93: Dorr 6F **167**
Debenham Cres. B25: Yard 2B **120**
Debenham Rd. B25: Yard 2B **120**
Deblen Dr. B16: Edg 2H **115**
Deborah Cl. WV2: Penn 5G **43**
Dee Gro. B38: K Nor 1A **160**
Deelands Rd. B45: Rubery 1F **157**
Deeley Cl. B15: Edg 4E **117**
B64: Crad H 4G **111**
Deeley Dr. DY4: Tip 1C **78**
Deeley Pl. WS3: Blox 1H **31**
Deeley St. DY5: Quar B 2A **110**
WS3: Blox 1H **31**
Deepdale Av. B26: Sheld 1F **137**
Deepdale La. DY3: Lwr G 4A **76**
Deepdales WV5: Wom 1E **73**
DEEPFIELDS **3D 60**
Deeplow Cl. B72: S Cold 1A **70**
Deepmoor Rd. B33: Yard 6D **104**
Deepmore Av. WS2: Wals 6H **31**
Deepwood Cl. WS4: S'fld 1F **33**
Deepwood Gro. B32: Bart G 5H **129**
Deer Cl. WS3: Blox 6A **20**
Deerham Cl. B23: Erd 6D **68**
Deerhurst Ct. B91: Sol 3H **151**
Deerhurst Rd. B20: Hand 2B **82**
Dee Rd. WS3: Blox 6C **20**
Deer Pk. Way B91: Sol 6G **151**
Deer Wlk. WV8: Pend 5D **14**
Dee Wlk. B36: Cas B 1C **106**
(not continuous)
Defford Av. WS4: S'fld 6G **21**
Defford Dr. B68: O'bry 5H **97**
De Havilland Dr. B35: Cas V 5E **87**
Deighton Rd. WS5: Wals 1F **65**
Delamere Cl. B36: Cas B 6H **87**
Delamere Dr. WS5: Wals 2G **65**
Delamere Rd. B28: Hall G 6F **135**
WV12: W'hall 2C **30**
Delancey Keep B75: S Cold 6E **55**
Delhurst Rd. B44: Gt Barr 4F **67**
WV4: E'shll 2A **60**
Delingpole Wlk. B64: Old H 3G **111**
Delius Ho. B16: Birm 1D **116**
Dell, The B31: N'fld 1B **144**
B36: Cas B 6B **88**
B74: Four O 3G **53**
B92: Olton 4E **137**
DY8: Woll 5C **108**
Della Dr. B32: Bart G 5B **130**
Dell Farm Cl. B93: Know 3D **166**
Dellows Cl. B38: K Nor 2H **159**
Dell Rd. B30: K Nor 2C **146**
DY5: P'ntt 4F **93**
Dell Stadium, The 4F **93**
Delmore Way B76: Walm 1F **87**
Delph Dr. DY5: Quar B 4A **110**
Delphinium Cl. B9: Bord G 6F **103**
Delph La. DY5: Brie H 3H **109**
Delph Rd. DY5: Brie H 2G **109**
Delph Rd. Ind. Est. DY5: Brie H 2G **109**
Delrene Rd. B28: Hall G 4F **149**
B90: Shir 4F **149**
DELVES, THE **6D 48**
Delves Cres. WS5: Wals 6E **49**
Delves Grn. Rd. WS5: Wals 5E **49**
Delves Rd. WS1: Wals 4D **48**
Delville Cl. WS10: W'bry 1F **63**
Delville Rd. WS10: W'bry 1F **63**
Delville Ter. WS10: W'bry 1F **63**
De Marnham Cl. B70: W Brom 6C **80**
De Montfort Ho. B37: K'hrst 4B **106**
De Montfort M. B46: Col 3H **107**
De Moram Gro. B92: Sol 6B **138**
Demuth Way B69: O'bry 4F **97**
Denaby Gro. B14: Yard W 3D **148**
Denbigh Cl. DY1: Dud 5B **76**
Denbigh Ct. *B29: W Cas* *6G 131*
(off Tugford Rd.)
Denbigh Cres. B71: W Brom 1H **79**
Denbigh Dr. B71: W Brom 6G **63**
WS10: W'bry 1B **64**
Denbigh Rd. DY4: Tip 2C **78**
Denbigh St. B9: Bord G 1D **118**
Denby Cl. B7: Birm 4B **102**
Denby Cft. B90: M'path 3F **165**
Dencer Cl. B45: Rubery 1F **157**
Dencil Cl. B63: Crad 6F **111**
Dene Av. DY6: K'wfrd 5A **92**

A-Z Birmingham 201

Dene Ct. Rd. B92: Olton 4D **136**
Dene Cft. WS3: Blox 6G **19**
Denegate Cl. B76: Walm 1F **87**
Dene Hollow B13: Mose. 1C **148**
Dene Rd. DY8: Stourb 2D **124**
WV4: Lwr P 1F **57**
Denewood Av. B20: Hand. 5C **82**
Denford Gro. B14: K Hth. 2F **147**
Dengate Dr. CV7: Bal C 2H **169**
Denham Ct. *B23: Erd 5C 84*
(off Park App.)
Denham Gdns. WV3: Wolv 3H **41**
Denham Rd. B27: A Grn 6H **119**
Denholme Gro. B14: K Hth 4A **148**
Denholm Rd. B73: New O 2D **68**
Denise Dr. B17: Harb 1G **131**
B37: K'hrst. 5B **106**
WV14: Cose 5D **60**
Denleigh Rd. DY6: K'wfrd 5D **92**
Denmark Cl. WV6: Wolv. 5E **27**
Denmead Dr. WV11: Wed 1H **29**
Denmore Gdns. WV1: Wolv. 1D **44**
Dennfield Dr. WS6: C Hay 2C **6**
Dennis Hall DY8: Amb. 3D **108**
Dennis Hall Rd. DY8: Amb. 3E **109**
Dennis Rd. B12: Bal H 1B **134**
Dennis St. DY8: Amb. 3D **108**
Denshaw Rd. B14: K Hth 1F **147**
Denstone Gdns. WV10: Bush. 4A **16**
Denton Cft. B93: Dorr 6H **165**
Denton Gro. B33: Stech 1B **120**
B43: Gt Barr. 6H **65**
Denton Rd. DY9: W'cte 1C **126**
Denver Rd. B14: K Hth. 5A **148**
Denville Cl. WV14: Bils 4G **45**
Denville Cres. B9: Bord G 6H **103**
Derby Av. WV6: Tett 2C **26**
Derby Dr. B37: Chel W 1D **122**
Derby St. B9: Birm 1A **118**
WS2: Wals 5B **32**
Dereham Cl. B8: Salt. 5D **102**
Dereham Wlk. WV14: Bils 3G **61**
Dereton Cl. DY1: Dud. 1A **94**
DERITEND . . . . . **2A 118 (6H 5)**
Derron Av. B26: Yard 6C **120**
Derry Cl. B17: Harb 2E **131**
Derrydown Cl. B23: Erd 4E **85**
Derrydown Rd. B42: P Barr 2D **82**
Derry St. DY5: Brie H. 1H **109**
WV2: Wolv. 3H **43**
Derwent Cl. B74: S'tly 1H **51**
DY5: P'ntt. 3E **93**
WV13: W'hall 1C **46**
Derwent Ct. B73: S Cold 6H **53**
Derwent Gro. B30: Stir. 5E **133**
Derwent Ho. B17: Harb 6H **115**
B69: O'bry 4D **96**
Derwent Rd. B30: Stir 5E **133**
WV6: Tett 1B **26**
Desford Av. B42: Gt Barr 6E **67**
Dettonford Rd. B32: Bart G 5H **129**
Devereux Cl. B36: Cas B 1G **105**
Devereux Rd. B70: W Brom. 6C **80**
B75: Four O 2A **54**
Devey Dr. DY4: Tip. 1D **78**
Devil's Elbow La. WV11: Wed. 2G **29**
Devine Cft. DY4: Tip. 2A **78**
Devitts Cl. B90: M'path 2D **164**
Devon Cl. B20: Hand 5B **82**
Devon Ct. *B29: W Cas 6F 131*
(off Holdgate Rd.)
Devon Cres. B71: W Brom. 1A **80**
DY2: Dud 2B **94**
WS9: A'rdge. 6C **22**
Devon Rd. B45: Fran 5E **143**
B67: Smeth 4C **114**
DY8: Woll. 4C **108**
WS10: W'bry 1A **64**
WV1: Wolv 6F **27**
WV13: W'hall. 1D **46**
Devonshire Av. B18: Hock 3B **100**
Devonshire Ct. B74: Four O 1F **53**
Devonshire Dr. B71: W Brom. 4C **80**
Devonshire Rd. B20: Hand. 5B **82**
B67: Smeth 3C **98**
Devonshire St. B18: Hock 3B **100**
Devon St. B7: Birm. 5C **102**
Devoran Cl. WV6: Wolv 5F **27**
Dewberry Dr. WS5: Wals 2E **65**
Dewberry Rd. DY8: Word 2D **108**
Dewhurst Cft. B33: Kitts G 6F **105**
Dewsbury Cl. DY8: Word. 6C **92**
Dewsbury Dr. WV4: Penn. 2E **59**
Dewsbury Gro. B42: P Barr 2E **83**
Deykin Av. B6: Witt 5A **84**
Deyncourt Rd. WV10: Wolv 2C **28**
Dial Cl. B14: K Hth. 5G **147**
Dial La. B70: W Brom 1F **79**
DY8: Amb. 3C **108**
Diamond Pk. Dr. DY8: Word 2C **108**
Diana Cl. WS9: Wals W. 4D **22**
Diane Cl. DY4: Tip 3B **62**
Dibble Cl. WV12: W'hall 4D **30**
Dibble Rd. B67: Smeth 3D **98**
Dibdale Ct. *DY3: Lwr G 4H 75*
(off Yorkdale Cl.)
Dibdale Rd. DY1: Dud 4A **76**
Dibdale Rd. W. DY1: Dud 4A **76**
Dibdale St. DY1: Dud. 5B **76**
Dice Pleck B31: N'fld. 5G **145**
Dickens Cl. DY3: Lwr G 2F **75**
DICKENS HEATH **4F 163**
Dickens Heath Rd.
B90: Dic H, Tid G 5E **163**
Dickens Rd. WV10: Bush. 1C **28**
WV14: Cose 3F **61**
Dickinson Av. WV10: Bush. 1A **28**
Dickinson Dr. B76: Walm 1C **70**
WS2: Wals 5A **48**
Dickinson Rd. WV5: Wom 3G **73**
Dick Sheppard Av. DY4: Tip. 5B **62**
Diddington Av. B28: Hall G 2G **149**
Diddington La. B92: Bick, H Ard 5C **140**
Didgley Gro. B37: K'hrst 4C **106**
DIGBETH . . . . . **2H 117 (6H 5)**
Digbeth B5: Birm. 1G **117** (5F **5**)
WS1: Wals 2C **48**
Digby Ct. B27: A Grn 2A **136**
Digby Cres. B46: Wat O. 4D **88**
Digby Dr. B37: Mars G. 5D **122**
Digby Ho. B37: K'hrst. 5B **106**
Digby Rd. B46: Col. 3H **107**
B73: S Cold 2G **69**
DY6: K'wfrd 1B **92**
Digby Wlk. B33: Sheld. 3G **121**
Dilke Rd. WS9: A'rdge 4B **34**
Dilliars Wlk. B70: W Brom 2G **79**
Dillington Ho. B37: Chel W 1D **122**
Dilloway's La. WV13: W'hall 2G **45**
Dimmingsdale Bank B32: Quin 1A **130**
Dimmingsdale Rd. WV4: Lwr P. 6E **41**
Dimminsdale WV13: W'hall. 2A **46**
Dimmocks Av. WV14: Cose 5F **61**
Dimmock St. WV4: E'shll 6A **44**
Dimsdale Gro. B31: N'fld. 4C **144**
Dimsdale Rd. B31: N'fld 4B **144**
Dingle, The B29: S Oak 3A **132**
B69: O'bry 1D **96**
B90: Ches G. 4B **164**
WV3: Wolv. 2B **42**
Dingle Av. B64: Crad H 3G **111**
Dingle Cl. B30: B'vlle. 6H **131**
DY2: Dud 2G **95**
Dingle Ct. *B69: O'bry. 1E 97*
(off Dingle St.)
B91: Sol. 6D **150**
Dingle Hollow B69: O'bry 1D **96**
Dingle La. B91: Sol 5D **150**
WV13: W'hall. 5A **30**
Dingle Mead B14: K Hth. 3E **147**
Dingle Mdw. Ct. B69: O'bry. 1E **97**
Dingle Rd. DY2: Dud 2G **95**
DY6: K'wfrd 5E **93**
DY9: Pedm. 3F **125**
WS8: Clay 1A **22**
WV5: Wom 1F **73**
Dingle St. B69: O'bry. 1D **96**
Dingle Vw. DY3: Sed 1G **75**
Dingley Rd. WS10: W'bry 6G **47**
Dingleys Pas. B4: Birm. 1G **117** (4F **5**)
Dinham Gdns. DY1: Dud 4A **76**
Dinmore Av. B31: N'fld. 3F **145**
Dinsdale Wlk. WV6: Wolv 4E **27**
Dippons Dr. WV6: Tett 6G **25**
Dippons La. WV6: Pert. 3E **25**
WV6: Tett 3F **25**
Dippons Mill Cl. WV6: Tett 6G **25**
DIRCHILLS. **1A 48**
Dirtyfoot La. WV4: Lwr P. 6G **41**
Discovery Cl. DY4: Tip. 2C **78**
Ditch, The WS1: Wals 2D **48**
Ditton Gro. B31: Longb 3D **158**
Dixon Cl. B35: Cas V 5E **87**
DY4: Tip. 1C **78**
Dixon Ct. B10: Small H. 3B **118**
Dixon Ho. B16: Edg 2C **116**
Dixon Rd. B10: Small H 3B **118**
DIXON'S GREEN **1G 95**
Dixon's Grn. Ct. *DY2: Dud. 1G 95*
(off Dixon's Grn. Rd.)
Dixon's Grn. Rd. DY2: Dud. 1F **95**
Dixon St. WV2: E'shll 5A **44**
Dobbins Oak Rd. DY9: W'cte. 4H **125**
Dobbs Mill Cl. B29: S Oak. 3D **132**
Dobbs St. WV2: Wolv 3G **43** (6B **170**)
Dock, The DY9: Lye 6B **110**
Dockar Rd. B31: N'fld. 5C **144**
Dockers Cl. CV7: Bal C. 5H **169**
Dock La. DY1: Dud. 6D **76**
Dock La. Ind. Est. *DY1: Dud 6D 76*
(off Dock La.)
Dock Mdw. Dr. WV4: E'shll. 1C **60**
Dock Rd. DY8: Word 1D **108**
Doctors Hill DY9: Pedm. 2G **125**
Doctors La. DY6: K'wfrd. 4F **91**
Doctor's Piece WV13: W'hall. 1B **46**
Doddington Gro. B32: Bart G. 5H **129**
Dodford Cl. B45: Rubery 2F **157**
DOE BANK **3H 53**
Doe Bank Ct. B74: Four O 3H **53**
Doe Bank La. B43: Gt Barr. 5E **51**
WS9: A'rdge. 5E **51**
Doe Bank Rd. DY4: Tip 4C **62**
Dogge La. Cft. B27: A Grn. 3H **135**
Dog Kennel La. B68: O'bry 4A **98**
B90: Shir 2A **164**
WS1: Wals 1D **48**
Dogkennel La. B63: Hale. 2B **128**
Dogpool La. B30: Stir 4D **132**
Doidge Rd. B23: Erd 4D **84**
Dollery Dr. B5: Edg. 6E **117**
Dollis Gro. B44: Gt Barr. 2H **67**
Dolman Rd. B6: Aston. 1G **101**
Dolobran Rd. B11: S'brk 4B **118**
Dolphin Cl. WS3: Blox. 6D **20**
Dolphin Ct. *WV12: W'hall 2D 30*
(off Huntington Rd.)
Dolphin Ho. WS3: Blox 1D **32**
Dolphin La. B27: A Grn 4H **135**
(not continuous)
Dolphin Rd. B11: S'hll 6D **118**
Dolton Way DY4: Tip 1G **77**
Dominic Dr. B30: K Nor. 3H **145**
Doncaster Way B36: Hodg H 1A **104**
Don Cl. B15: Edg 3H **115**
Donegal Rd. B74: S'tly. 6H **51**
Donibristle Cft. B35: Cas V 3E **87**
Donnington Ho. B33: Yard 1F **121**
Donovan Dr. B73: S Cold. 5G **53**
Dooley Cl. WV13: W'hall 1G **45**
Dora Herbert Ct. B12: Bal H. 6G **117**
Doran Cl. B63: Hale 4F **127**
Doranda Way B71: W Brom. 6D **80**
Doranda Way Ind. Pk.
B71: W Brom. 6D **80**
Dora Rd. B10: Small H. 3E **119**
B21: Hand 2A **100**
B70: W Brom 6A **80**
Dora St. WS2: Wals. 4H **47**
Dorchester Cl. WV12: W'hall 1C **30**
Dorchester Ct. B91: Sol 3E **151**
Dorchester Dr. B17: Harb 1F **131**
Dorchester Rd. B91: Sol. 3E **151**
DY9: W'cte. 3H **125**
WV12: W'hall. 1C **30**
Dordale Cl. B31: Longb 6A **144**
Dordon Cl. B90: Shir 6E **149**
Doreen Gro. B24: Erd. 5G **85**
Doris Rd. B9: Bord G 1D **118**
B11: S'hll 1B **134**
B46: Col. 1H **107**

Dorking Ct. B29: W Cas 6G **131**
    (off Abdon Av.)
Dorlcote Rd. B8: Salt 5G **103**
Dormie Cl. B38: K Nor 6H **145**
Dormington Rd. B44: Gt Barr 2G **67**
Dormston Cl. B31: Sol 2G **165**
Dormston Dr. B29: W Cas 3D **130**
  DY3: Sed 5A **60**
Dormston Sports & Art Cen. 5A **60**
Dormston Trad. Est. DY1: Dud. 3A **76**
Dormy Dr. B31: Longb 2E **159**
Dorncliffe Av. B33: Sheld. 4H **121**
Dornie Dr. B38: K Nor 6B **146**
Dornton Rd. B30: Stir 5E **133**
Dorothy Adams Cl. B64: Old H 3G **111**
Dorothy Gdns. B20: Hand. 5C **82**
Dorothy Rd. B11: Tys. 6H **119**
  B67: Smeth 6E **99**
Dorothy St. WS1: Wals. 4B **48**
DORRIDGE 6B **166**
Dorridge Cft. B93: Dorr 6G **167**
Dorridge Rd. B93: Dorr 6H **167**
Dorridge Station (Rail) 6G **167**
Dorrington Grn. B42: P Barr 2C **82**
Dorrington Rd. B42: P Barr 1C **82**
Dorset Cl. B45: Fran 5F **143**
Dorset Cotts. B30: Stir 1C **146**
Dorset Ct. B29: W Cas 6F **131**
    (off Abdon Av.)
Dorset Dr. WS9: A'rdge 6C **22**
Dorset Rd. B17: Edg. 6F **99**
  DY8: Woll. 4B **108**
Dorset Pl. WS3: Blox 2A **32**
Dorsett Rd. WS10: Darl 5C **46**
  WS10: W'bry 3B **64**
Dorsett Rd. Ter. WS10: Darl 5C **46**
Dorsheath Gdns. B23: Erd 3F **85**
Dorsington Rd. B27: A Grn 4B **136**
Dorstone Covert B14: K Hth 5E **147**
Dorville Cl. B38: K Nor 1H **159**
Douay Rd. B24: Erd 1H **85**
Double Row DY2: Neth 5G **95**
Doughty St. DY4: Tip 2C **78**
Douglas Av. B36: Hodg H. 3B **104**
  B68: O'bry 4B **98**
Douglas Davies Cl. WV12: W'hall 5C **30**
Douglas Pl. WV10: Oxl 3G **27**
Douglas Rd. B21: Hand 1A **100**
  B27: A Grn 1H **135**
  B47: H'wd 2A **162**
  B62: B'hth 2E **113**
  B68: O'bry 5B **98**
  B72: S Cold 2A **70**
  DY2: Dud 1F **95**
  WV14: Cose 5F **61**
Doulton Cl. B32: Quin 2D **130**
Doulton Dr. B66: Smeth 3E **99**
Doulton Rd. B64: Old H 6H **95**
  B65: Row R 6H **95**
Doulton Trad. Est. B65: Row R 5H **95**
Dovebridge Cl. B76: Walm 1D **70**
Dove Cl. B25: Yard 3C **120**
  WS1: Wals 2E **49**
  WS10: W'bry 1G **63**
Dovecote 2G **133**
Dovecote Cl. B91: Sol. 5F **137**
  DY4: Tip 2C **78**
  WV6: Tett 5A **26**
Dovecotes, The B75: Four O 6H **37**
Dovedale Av. B90: Shir 6H **149**
  WS3: Pels. 2E **21**
  WV12: W'hall 4A **30**
Dovedale Cl. B29: W Cas. 6G **131**
  B46: Wat O. 4C **88**
  WV4: E'shll 3B **60**
Dovedale Dr. B28: Hall G 1F **149**
Dovedale Rd. B23: Erd. 5C **68**
  DY6: K'wfrd 1C **92**
  WV4: E'shll 2A **60**
Dove Dr. DY8: Amb 3E **109**
Dove Gdns. B38: K Nor 5D **146**
Dove Hollow WS6: Gt Wyr 4F **7**
Dove Ho. Ct. B91: Sol 6D **136**
Dovehouse La. B91: Sol 6D **136**
Dovehouse Pool Rd. B6: Aston 1G **101**
Dover Cl. B32: Bart G. 6G **129**

Dover Ct. B29: W Cas 6G **131**
    (off Abdon Av.)
Dovercourt Rd. B26: Sheld 6G **121**
Doverdale Cl. B63: Crad. 6F **111**
Dover Ho. WS3: Blox 2A **32**
    (off Providence Cl.)
Dove Ridge DY8: Amb 4E **109**
Doveridge Cl. B91: Sol. 6C **136**
Doveridge Pl. WS1: Wals 3D **48**
Doveridge Rd. B28: Hall G 2E **149**
Doversley Rd. B14: K Hth 2E **147**
Dover St. B18: Hock. 3C **100**
  WV14: Bils 5F **45**
Dove Way B36: Cas B. 1B **106**
Dovey Dr. B76: Walm 6E **71**
Dovey Rd. B13: Mose 3D **134**
  B69: Tiv 1D **96**
Dovey Twr. B7: Birm. 5A **102**
Dowar Rd. B45: Redn. 2A **158**
Dowells Cl. B13: Mose 3H **133**
Dowells Gdns. DY8: Word 6B **92**
Doweries, The B45: Rubery 1F **157**
Dower Rd. B75: Four O 2H **53**
Dowles Cl. B29: W Cas. 1F **145**
Downcroft Av. B38: K Nor 5A **146**
Downend Cl. WV10: Bush 3B **16**
Downes Ct. DY4: Tip 2G **77**
Downey Cl. B11: S'brk 4B **118**
Downfield Cl. WS3: Blox 3G **19**
Downfield Dr. DY3: Sed 1A **76**
Downham Cl. WS5: Wals 2A **50**
Downham Pl. WV3: Wolv. 3D **42**
Downham Wood WS5: Wals 3A **50**
Downie Rd. WV8: Bilb 4A **14**
Downing Cl. B65: B'hth 2C **112**
  B93: Know 5C **166**
  WV11: Wed 2A **30**
Downing Ct. B68: O'bry 4H **113**
Downing Ho. B37: Chel W 2D **122**
Downing St. B63: Hale 6A **112**
  B66: Smeth. 2F **99**
Downing St. Ind. Est. B66: Smeth. 2G **99**
Downland Cl. B38: K Nor 6B **146**
Downs, The WS9: A'rdge 1G **51**
  WV10: Oxl 3G **27**
Downsfield Rd. B26: Sheld. 4F **121**
Downside Rd. B24: Erd 6E **85**
Downs Rd. WV13: W'hall 3C **46**
Downton Cres. B33: Kitts G 6A **106**
Dowry Ho. B45: Rubery 1F **157**
    (off Rubery La. Sth.)
Dowty Way WV9: Pend. 4E **15**
Drainage Board Cotts. B24: Erd. 6F **85**
    (off Saltley Cotts.)
Drake Cl. WS3: Blox 6H **19**
Drake Rd. B23: Erd 4B **84**
  B66: Smeth 2C **98**
  WS3: Blox 6H **19**
Drakes Cross Pde. B47: H'wd 4A **162**
Drakes Grn. WV14: Bils 2H **61**
Drakes Hill Cl. DY8: Stourb 1A **124**
Drake St. B71: W Brom 2A **80**
Drancy Av. WV12: W'hall 3D **30**
    (not continuous)
Drawbridge Rd. B90: Maj G 1E **163**
Draycote Cl. B92: Sol. 6H **137**
Draycott Av. B23: Erd 3D **84**
Draycott Cl. WV4: Penn 6A **42**
Draycott Dr. B31: N'fld 6C **130**
Draycott Rd. B66: Smeth 2C **98**
Drayman Cl. WS1: Wals 3D **48**
Drayton Cl. B75: Four O 6H **37**
Drayton Rd. B14: K Hth 5G **133**
  B66: Smeth 2E **115**
  B90: Shir 1C **164**
Drayton St. WS2: Wals 1H **47**
  WV2: Wolv 3G **43** (6B **170**)
Drayton St. E. WS2: Wals 1A **48**
Dreadnought Rd. DY5: P'ntt. 2F **93**
Dreamwell Ind. Est. B11: Tys 5G **119**
Dreel, The B15: Edg. 4A **116**
Dreghorn Rd. B36: Hodg H 1C **104**
Drem Cft. B35: Cas V 5E **87**
Dresden Cl. WV4: E'shll 1C **60**
Drew Cres. DY9: W'cte 3H **125**
Drew Rd. DY9: W'cte 2H **125**
Drew's Holloway B63: Crad 6F **111**

Drew's Holloway Sth. B63: Crad 6F **111**
Drews Ho. B14: K Hth. 6F **147**
    (off Netheravon Cl.)
Drews La. B8: W End. 3G **103**
Drews Mdw. Cl. B14: K Hth 5E **147**
DRIFFOLD 1G **69**
Driffold B73: S Cold 1H **69**
Driffold Vs. B73: S Cold 2H **69**
Driftwood Cl. B38: K Nor 2H **159**
Drive, The B20: Hand. 5C **82**
  B23: Erd 5E **85**
  B48: Hopw 6F **159**
  B63: Crad 6F **111**
  B63: Hale 2A **128**
  DY5: Brie H 4G **93**
  WS3: Blox 5C **20**
  WV6: Tett 4A **26**
  WV8: Cod 4F **13**
Drive Flds. WV4: Lwr P 5H **41**
Droicon Trad. Est. B65: Row R 4C **96**
Droveway, The WV8: Pend. 5C **14**
  WV9: Pend 5C **14**
Droxford Wlk. WV8: Pend 6C **14**
Druid Pk. Rd. WV12: W'hall. 6C **18**
Druids Av. B65: Row R 5D **96**
  WS9: A'rdge 6E **23**
DRUID'S HEATH 6D **22**
Druids La. B14: K Hth 5E **147**
Druids Wlk. WS9: Wals W 4C **22**
Drummond Cl. WV11: Wed 5A **18**
Drummond Gro. B43: Gt Barr 2E **67**
Drummond Rd. B9: Bord G. 1F **119**
  DY9: W'cte 6B **110**
Drummond St. WV1: Wolv . . . 6G **27** (1A **170**)
Drummond Way B37: Chel W. 1E **123**
Drury La. B91: Sol 4G **151**
    (not continuous)
  DY8: Stourb 6E **109**
  WV8: Cod 3F **13**
Drybrook Cl. B38: K Nor 1A **160**
Drybrooks Cl. CV7: Bal C 3H **169**
Dryden Cl. DY4: Tip 6A **62**
  WV12: W'hall 1E **31**
Dryden Gro. B27: A Grn 3H **135**
Dryden Pl. WS3: Blox 2C **32**
Dryden Rd. WS3: Blox 2C **32**
  WV10: Bush 6B **16**
Drylea Gro. B36: Hodg H 2D **104**
Dubarry Av. DY6: K'wfrd 2A **92**
Duchess Pde. B70: W Brom 4B **80**
Duchess Pl. B16: Edg. 2C **116**
Duchess Rd. B16: Edg 2C **116**
  WS1: Wals 6B **48**
Duckhouse Rd. WV11: Wed 2F **29**
Duck La. WV8: Bilb 5H **13**
  WV14: Bils 6G **45**
Duddeston Dr. B8: Salt. 5D **102**
Duddeston Mnr. Rd. B7: Birm 5A **102**
Duddeston Mill Rd. B7: Birm. 5B **102**
  B8: Birm, Salt. 5C **102**
Duddeston Mill Trad. Est. B8: Salt 5C **102**
Duddeston Station (Rail) 5B **102**
Dudding Rd. WV4: Penn 6H **43**
Dudhill Rd. B65: Row R. 6A **96**
Dudhill Wlk. B65: Row R 6H **95**
DUDLEY. 6E **77**
Dudley Castle 5F **77**
Dudley Central Trad. Est. DY2: Dud 1E **95**
Dudley Cl. B65: Row R 3A **96**
Dudley Cres. WV11: Wed 3G **29**
DUDLEY FIELDS 5G **93**
Dudley Gro. B18: Win G 5A **100**
Dudley Leisure Cen. 6D **76**
Dudley Mus. & Art Gallery 6E **77**
Dudley Pk. Rd. B27: A Grn 2A **136**
DUDLEY PORT 3B **78**
Dudley Port DY4: Tip 4A **78**
Dudley Port Station (Rail) 3B **78**
Dudley Rd. B18: Win G 5H **99**
  B63: Hale 5B **112**
  B65: Row R 3H **95**
  B69: O'bry 6E **79**
  DY3: Himl. 4A **74**
  DY3: Sed 6A **60**
  DY4: Tip 2F **77**
  DY5: Brie H 6H **93**

Dudley Rd. DY6: K'wfrd . . . 2D **92**
DY6: W Hth . . . 1A **92**
DY9: Lye . . . 5A **110**
WV2: Wolv . . . 3H **43** (6C **170**)
Dudley Rd. E. B69: O'bry, Tiv . . . 5C **78**
Dudley Rd. W. B69: Tiv . . . 5A **78**
DY4: Tip . . . 5A **78**
Dudley Row DY2: Dud . . . 6F **77**
DUDLEY'S FIELDS . . . 1G **31**
Dudley Southern By-Pass DY2: Dud . . . 2C **94**
Dudley St. B5: Birm . . . 1G **117** (5E **5**)
B70: W Brom . . . 2F **79**
DY3: Sed . . . 5H **59**
WS1: Wals . . . 2C **48**
WS10: W'bry . . . 3E **63**
WV1: Wolv . . . 1G **43** (3B **170**)
WV14: Bils . . . 6F **45**
Dudley Wlk. WV4: Penn . . . 6G **43**
Dudley Wood Av. DY2: Neth . . . 1E **111**
Dudley Wood Rd. DY2: Neth . . . 2E **111**
Dudley Zoo . . . 5F **77**
Dudmaston Way DY1: Dud . . . 4A **76**
Dudnill Gro. B32: Bart G . . . 5G **129**
Duffield Cl. WV8: Pend . . . 6D **14**
Dufton Rd. B32: Quin . . . 6C **114**
Dugdale Cres. B75: Four O . . . 6A **38**
Dugdale Ho. B71: W Brom . . . 5E **65**
Dugdale St. B18: Win G . . . 5H **99**
Dukes Rd. B30: K Nor . . . 3C **146**
Duke St. B65: Row R . . . 1B **112**
B70: W Brom . . . 3H **79**
B72: S Cold . . . 1H **69**
DY3: Up Gor . . . 2H **75**
DY8: Stourb . . . 5E **109**
WV1: Wolv . . . 2A **44**
WV3: Wolv . . . 4E **43**
WV11: Wed . . . 4F **29**
Dulvern Gro. B14: K Hth . . . 2F **147**
Dulverton Rd. B6: Witt . . . 6A **84**
Dulwich Gro. B44: K'sdng . . . 5B **68**
Dulwich Rd. B44: K'sdng . . . 5A **68**
Dumbleberry Av. DY3: Sed . . . 6G **59**
Dumblederry La. WS9: A'rdge . . . 1A **34**
(not continuous)
Dunard Rd. B90: Shir . . . 4F **149**
Dunbar Cl. B32: Bart G . . . 4B **130**
Dunbar Gro. B43: Gt Barr . . . 1D **66**
Duncalfe Dr. B75: Four O . . . 6H **37**
Duncan Edwards Cl. DY1: Dud . . . 1C **94**
Duncan Ho. B73: W Grn . . . 4H **69**
Dunchurch Cl. CV7: Bal C . . . 2H **169**
Dunchurch Cres. B73: New O . . . 2C **68**
Dunchurch Dr. B31: N'fld . . . 6C **130**
Dunchurch Ho. B5: Birm . . . 3G **117**
Duncombe Grn. B46: Col . . . 2H **107**
Duncombe Gro. B17: Harb . . . 4D **114**
Duncombe St. DY8: Woll . . . 5B **108**
Duncroft Rd. B26: Yard . . . 3D **120**
Duncroft Wlk. DY1: Dud . . . 1D **76**
Duncumb Rd. B75: S Cold . . . 6E **55**
Dundalk La. WS6: C Hay . . . 3D **6**
Dundas Av. DY2: Dud . . . 1H **95**
Dunedin Ho. B32: Quin . . . 1D **130**
Dunedin Rd. B44: Gt Barr . . . 2G **67**
Dunham Cft. B93: Dorr . . . 6H **165**
Dunkirk Av. B70: W Brom . . . 3D **78**
Dunkley St. WV1: Wolv . . . 6G **27** (1A **170**)
Dunley Ct. *B23: Erd . . . 5C 84*
(off Dunlin Cl.)
Dunley Cft. B90: M'path . . . 3D **164**
Dunlin Cl. B23: Erd . . . 5C **84**
DY6: K'wfrd . . . 3E **93**
Dunlop Way B35: Cas V . . . 6C **86**
Dunnerdale Rd. WS8: Clay . . . 1H **21**
Dunnigan Rd. B32: Bart G . . . 2D **130**
DUNN'S BANK . . . 4B **110**
Dunn's Bank DY5: Quar B . . . 4B **110**
(Lynval Rd.)
DY5: Quar B . . . 4C **110**
(Saltbrook Rd.)
Dunsfold Cl. WV14: Cose . . . 2C **60**
Dunsfold Cft. B6: Aston . . . 3H **101**
Dunsford Cl. DY5: Brie H . . . 4F **109**
Dunsford Rd. B66: Smeth . . . 1E **115**
Dunsink Rd. B6: Aston . . . 6H **83**
Dunslade Cres. DY5: Quar B . . . 3B **110**
Dunslade Rd. B23: Erd . . . 6D **68**
Dunsley Dr. DY8: Word . . . 6C **92**
Dunsley Gro. WV4: Penn . . . 1E **59**
Dunsley Rd. DY8: Woll . . . 1A **124**
Dunsmore Dr. DY5: Quar B . . . 3B **110**
Dunsmore Gro. B91: Sol . . . 6D **136**
Dunsmore Rd. B28: Hall G . . . 3E **135**
Dunstall Av. WV6: Wolv . . . 4G **27**
Dunstall Gro. B29: W Cas . . . 5D **130**
DUNSTALL HILL . . . 4F **27**
Dunstall Hill WV6: Wolv . . . 4G **27**
Dunstall Hill Trad. Est. WV6: Wolv . . . 4G **27**
Dunstall La. WV6: Wolv . . . 4E **27**
Dunstall Pk. . . . 3E **27**
Dunstall Pk. WV6: Wolv . . . 3F **27**
Dunstall Rd. B63: Hale . . . 2F **127**
WV6: Wolv . . . 5F **27**
Dunstan Cft. B90: Shir . . . 1A **164**
Dunster Cl. B30: K Nor . . . 3D **146**
Dunster Gro. WV6: Pert . . . 6F **25**
Dunster Rd. B37: Chel W . . . 6E **107**
Dunston Cl. DY6: K'wfrd . . . 2B **92**
WS6: Gt Wyr . . . 5E **7**
Dunton Cl. B75: Four O . . . 5G **37**
Dunton Hall Rd. B90: Shir . . . 1G **163**
Dunton Rd. B37: K'hrst . . . 5B **106**
Dunton Trad. Est. B7: Nech . . . 2D **102**
Dunvegan Rd. B24: Erd . . . 3G **85**
Durant Cl. B45: Fran . . . 5D **142**
Durban Rd. B66: Smeth . . . 5G **99**
D'Urberville Cl. *WV2: E'shll . . . 5B 44*
(off D'urberville Rd.)
D'Urberville Rd. WV2: E'shll . . . 4B **44**
(not continuous)
Durberville Rd. Ind. Est. WV2: E'shll . . . 4B **44**
Durham Av. WV13: W'hall . . . 6C **30**
Durham Ct. *B29: W Cas . . . 6G 131*
(off Abdon Av.)
Durham Cft. B37: Chel W . . . 1D **122**
Durham Dr. B71: W Brom . . . 6B **64**
Durham Ho. WV1: Wolv . . . 5G **27**
Durham Pl. WS2: Wals . . . 2H **47**
Durham Rd. B11: S'hll . . . 1B **134**
B65: Row R . . . 5E **97**
DY2: Neth . . . 1F **111**
DY8: Woll . . . 3B **108**
WS2: Wals . . . 3H **47**
WS10: W'bry . . . 1B **64**
Durham Twr. B1: Birm . . . 6D **100**
Durley Dean Rd. B29: S Oak . . . 3G **131**
Durley Dr. B73: New O . . . 2C **68**
Durley Rd. B25: Yard . . . 5A **120**
Durlston Gro. B28: Hall G . . . 5G **135**
Durnford Cft. B14: K Hth . . . 6G **147**
Dursley Cl. B92: Olton . . . 5F **137**
WV12: W'hall . . . 5D **30**
Dutton's La. B75: R'ley . . . 5C **38**
Duxford Rd. B42: Gt Barr . . . 5D **66**
Dwellings La. B32: Quin . . . 6H **113**
Dyas Av. B42: Gt Barr . . . 6B **66**
Dyas Rd. B44: Gt Barr . . . 4F **67**
B47: H'wd . . . 2A **162**
Dyce Cl. B35: Cas V . . . 3E **87**
Dymoke St. B12: Birm . . . 3H **117**
Dynes Wlk. B67: Smeth . . . 4E **99**
Dyott Rd. B13: Mose . . . 4A **134**
Dyson Cl. WS2: Wals . . . 6F **31**
Dyson Gdns. B8: Salt . . . 4E **103**

E

Eachelhurst Rd. B24: Erd . . . 3C **86**
B76: Walm . . . 2D **86**
Eachus Rd. WV14: Cose . . . 5F **61**
EACHWAY . . . 3F **157**
Eachway B45: Rubery . . . 3F **157**
Eachway Farm Cl. B45: Redn . . . 3G **157**
Eachway La. B45: Redn . . . 3G **157**
Eadgar Ct. B43: Gt Barr . . . 6H **65**
Eagle Cl. B65: Row R . . . 5H **95**
DY1: Dud . . . 1B **94**
WS6: C Hay . . . 3D **6**
Eagle Ct. WV3: Wolv . . . 5E **43**
Eagle Ct. Bus. Pk. B26: Sheld . . . 1A **138**
Eagle Cft. B14: K Hth . . . 5G **147**
Eagle Gdns. B24: Erd . . . 5G **85**
Eagle Gro. B36: Cas B . . . 1C **106**
Eagle Ind. Est. DY4: Tip . . . 6E **63**
Eagle La. DY4: Tip . . . 1D **78**
Eagle St. DY4: Tip . . . 1C **78**
WV2: Wolv . . . 3A **44**
WV3: Wolv . . . 4E **43**
Eagle Trad. Est. B63: Hale . . . 1A **128**
Ealing Gro. B44: K'sdng . . . 4A **68**
Eanwulf Ct. B15: Edg . . . 3E **117**
Earlsbury Gdns. B20: Hand . . . 6F **83**
Earls Ct. Rd. B17: Harb . . . 5E **115**
Earls Ferry Gdns. B32: Bart G . . . 6H **129**
Earlsmead Rd. B21: Hand . . . 1G **99**
Earls Rd. WS4: Rus . . . 2G **33**
Earlston Way B43: Gt Barr . . . 5H **65**
Earl St. B70: W Brom . . . 3H **79**
DY6: K'wfrd . . . 5B **92**
WS1: Wals . . . 4B **48**
WV14: Bils . . . 6F **45**
WV14: Cose . . . 5F **61**
Earls Way B63: Hale . . . 1B **128**
Earlswood Ct. B20: Hand . . . 5C **82**
Earlswood Cres. WV9: Pend . . . 4E **15**
Earlswood Dr. B74: S Cold . . . 4A **54**
Earlswood Ho. *B5: Birm . . . 4G 117*
(off Barrow Wlk.)
Earlswood Rd. B93: Dorr . . . 6F **167**
DY6: K'wfrd . . . 2C **92**
Easby Way B8: Salt . . . 4E **103**
WS3: Blox . . . 5F **19**
Easenhall Cl. B93: Know . . . 5C **166**
Easmore Cl. B14: K Hth . . . 5F **147**
Eastacre WV13: W'hall . . . 2A **46**
East Av. B69: Tiv . . . 2C **96**
WV11: Wed . . . 3E **29**
Eastbourne Av. B34: Hodg H . . . 3B **104**
Eastbourne St. WS4: Wals . . . 6D **32**
Eastbrook Cl. B76: Walm . . . 1B **70**
Eastbury Dri B92: Olton . . . 2E **137**
Eastbury Dr. B92: Olton . . . 2E **137**
E. Car Pk. Rd. B40: Nat E C . . . 1H **139**
EASTCOTE . . . 4H **153**
Eastcote Cl. B90: Shir . . . 4B **150**
Eastcote La. B92: H Ard . . . 4H **153**
Eastcote Rd. B27: A Grn . . . 4G **135**
WV10: Wolv . . . 4B **28**
East Cft. Rd. WV4: Penn . . . 1A **58**
Eastdean Cl. B23: Erd . . . 1D **84**
East Dr. B5: Edg . . . 1E **133**
Eastern Av. DY5: Brie H . . . 1F **109**
Eastern Cl. WS10: Mox . . . 2C **62**
Eastern Rd. B29: S Oak . . . 2D **132**
B73: W Grn . . . 4H **69**
Easterton Cft. B14: K Hth . . . 5G **147**
E. Farm Cft. B10: Small H . . . 3D **118**
Eastfield Cl. WS9: A'rdge . . . 3C **34**
Eastfield Dr. B92: Sol . . . 5A **138**
Eastfield Gro. WV1: Wolv . . . 1B **44**
Eastfield Retreat WV1: Wolv . . . 1B **44**
Eastfield Rd. B8: W End . . . 5A **104**
B9: Bord G . . . 5A **104**
DY4: Tip . . . 5A **62**
WV1: Wolv . . . 1B **44**
East Ga. B16: Edg . . . 6A **100**
East Grn. WV4: Penn . . . 5B **42**
Eastham Rd. B13: Mose . . . 1C **148**
East Holme B9: Bord G . . . 1C **118**
Easthope Rd. B33: Stech . . . 5E **105**
Eastlake Cl. B43: Gt Barr . . . 2F **67**
Eastlands Rd. B13: Mose . . . 4A **134**
Eastleigh DY3: Sed . . . 5G **59**
Eastleigh Cft. B76: Walm . . . 6E **71**
Eastleigh Dr. B62: Roms . . . 3A **142**
Eastleigh Gro. B25: Yard . . . 3B **120**
E. Meadway B33: Kitts G . . . 1H **121**
East M. B44: Gt Barr . . . 3F **67**
E. Moor Cl. B74: S'tly . . . 1B **52**
Eastney Cres. WV8: Pend . . . 1C **26**
Easton Gdns. WV11: Wed . . . 4H **29**
Easton Gro. B27: A Grn . . . 4A **136**
B47: H'wd . . . 2B **162**
East Pk. Trad. Est. WV1: Wolv . . . 3B **44**
East Pk. Way WV1: Wolv . . . 2D **44**
East Pathway B17: Harb . . . 5G **115**
East Ri. B75: S Cold . . . 5B **54**
East Rd. B24: Erd . . . 5B **86**
DY4: Tip . . . 5B **62**
WV10: B'frd, F'stne . . . 1C **16**

East St. DY2: Dud . . . 1G 95
— DY3: Gorn . . . 4H 75
— DY5: Quar B . . . 3C 110
— WS1: Wals . . . 4D 48
— WV1: Wolv . . . 2A 44
East Vw. Rd. B72: S Cold. . . 2B 70
Eastville B31: N'fld. . . 4F 145
Eastward Glen WV8: Bilb. . . 6A 14
East Way B17: Harb . . . 5G 115
Eastway B40: Nat E C . . . 2H 139
— B92: Bick . . . 2H 139
Eastwood Rd. B12: Bal H . . . 6F 117
— B43: Gt Barr. . . 5A 66
— DY2: Dud . . . 3G 95
Eatesbrook Rd. B33: Kitts G . . . 6G 105
Eathorpe Cl. B34: S End . . . 3H 105
Eaton Av. B70: W Brom . . . 3G 79
Eaton Ct. B74: S Cold. . . 4H 53
Eaton Cres. DY3: Gorn . . . 4F 75
Eaton Pl. DY6: K'wfrd. . . 4C 92
Eaton Ri. WV12: W'hall . . . 3B 30
Eaton Wood B24: Erd . . . 4B 86
Eaton Wood Dr. B26: Yard . . . 6B 120
Eaves Ct. Dr. DY3: Sed . . . 4G 59
Eaves Grn. Gdns. B27: A Grn . . . 6H 119
Ebenezer St. B70: W Brom. . . 1F 79
— WV14: Cose. . . 5D 60
Ebley Rd. B20: Hand . . . 3C 82
Ebmore Dr. B14: K Hth . . . 5F 147
Ebrington Av. B92: Sol . . . 2F 137
Ebrington Cl. B14: K Hth . . . 3F 147
Ebrington Rd. B71: W Brom . . . 1B 80
Ebrook Rd. B72: S Cold . . . 1A 70
EBSTREE . . . 1C 56
Ebstree Mdw. WV5: Seis . . . 3A 56
Ebstree Rd. WV5: Seis, Try . . . 3A 56
Ebury Rd. B30: K Nor. . . 3D 146
Eccleshall Av. WV10: Oxl . . . 1F 27
Eccleston Cl. B75: S Cold . . . 6D 54
Ecclestone Rd. WV11: Wed . . . 1A 30
Echo Way WV4: E'shll. . . 1C 60
Eckersall Rd. B38: K Nor . . . 4A 146
Eckington Wk. B38: K Nor. . . 2A 160
Eclipse Ind. Est. DY4: Tip . . . 2G 77
Edale Cl. DY6: K'wfrd . . . 2H 91
— WV4: E'shll. . . 2A 60
Edale Rd. B42: Gt Barr. . . 6E 67
Eddish Rd. B33: Kitts G . . . 6F 105
Eddison Rd. B46: Col. . . 3G 89
Edelweiss Cl. WS5: Wals . . . 2F 65
Edenbridge Rd. B28: Hall G . . . 5G 135
Edenbridge Vw. DY1: Dud . . . 4A 76
Eden Cl. B31: Longb . . . 1C 158
— B69: Tiv . . . 5D 78
Edencroft B15: Edg . . . 3E 117
Edendale Rd. B26: Sheld . . . 5F 121
Eden Gdns. DY3: Sed . . . 5A 60
Eden Gro. B37: Chel W . . . 2F 123
— B71: W Brom . . . 2B 80
Edenhall Rd. B32: Quin . . . 5H 113
Eden Ho. DY8: Stourb . . . 6E 109
Edenhurst Rd. B31: Longb . . . 3D 158
Eden Pl. B3: Birm . . . 1F 117 (4C 4)
Eden Rd. B92: Sol . . . 2H 137
Edensor Cl. WV10: Wolv . . . 5A 28
EDGBASTON. . . 6C 116
Edgbaston . . . 6F 117
Edgbaston Archery & Lawn Tennis Society
. . . 4B 116
Edgbaston Pk. Rd. B15: Edg . . . 6C 116
Edgbaston Priory Club . . . 5E 117
Edgbaston Rd. B5: Edg . . . 6F 117
— B12: Bal H . . . 6F 117
— B66: Smeth . . . 5E 99
Edgbaston Rd. E. B12: Bal H . . . 6H 117
Edgbaston Shop. Cen.
— B16: Edg . . . 3C 116
Edgbaston St. B5: Birm. . . 2G 117 (6E 5)
Edgcombe Rd. B28: Hall G . . . 4F 135
Edgbaston Rd. DY8: Woll . . . 4B 108
Edge Hill Av. WV10: Bush . . . 5C 16
Edge Hill Dr. DY3: Sed . . . 3G 59
— WV6: Pert. . . 6E 25
Edge Hill Rd. B74: Four O . . . 5D 36
Edgehill Rd. B31: Longb . . . 1E 159
Edgemond Av. B24: Erd . . . 3D 86
Edge St. WV14: Cose . . . 5F 61
Edgewood Cl. B64: Old H. . . 3H 111

Edgewood Rd. B38: K Nor . . . 2A 160
— B45: Redn . . . 2H 157
Edgeworth Cl. WV12: W'hall . . . 5C 30
Edgware Rd. B23: Erd . . . 2D 84
Edinburgh Av. WS2: Wals. . . 6E 31
Edinburgh Ct. B24: Erd. . . 3B 86
Edinburgh Cres. DY8: Word. . . 2A 108
Edinburgh Dr. WS4: Rus . . . 2H 33
— WV12: W'hall. . . 3B 30
Edinburgh La. WS2: Wals . . . 5G 31
Edinburgh Rd. B68: O'bry . . . 3H 113
— DY2: Dud . . . 3F 95
— WS5: Wals . . . 3F 49
— WV14: Bils . . . 2H 61
Edison Ct. WV12: W'hall . . . 2D 30
(off Huntington Rd.)
Edison Gro. B32: Quin . . . 6B 114
Edison Rd. WS2: Wals . . . 4G 31
Edison Wlk. WS2: Wals . . . 4H 31
Edith Pope Ho. B42: Gt Barr. . . 5F 67
Edith Rd. B66: Smeth. . . 6F 99
Edith St. B70: W Brom. . . 4H 79
Edmonds Cl. B33: Kitts G . . . 1F 121
Edmonds Ct. B10: Small H. . . 4D 118
— B26: Yard . . . 4D 120
Edmonds Rd. B68: O'bry . . . 1A 114
Edmonton Av. B44: K'sdng . . . 4B 68
Edmonton Ho. B5: Bal H . . . 4F 117
Edmoor Cl. WV12: W'hall. . . 3C 30
Edmund Rd. B8: Salt . . . 5D 102
— DY3: Up Gor. . . 1A 76
Edmund St. B3: Birm . . . 6F 101 (3C 4)
Ednam Cl. B71: W Brom . . . 5D 64
Ednam Gro. WV5: Wom . . . 4G 57
Ednam Rd. DY1: Dud . . . 6E 77
— WV4: Penn. . . 5G 43
Edsome Way B36: Hodg H . . . 1D 104
Edstone Cl. B93: Dorr . . . 5B 166
Edstone M. B36: Hodg H . . . 1D 104
Edward Cl. WV14: Bils . . . 2G 61
Edward Ct. B16: Edg . . . 2G 115
— B76: Walm . . . 2D 70
— WS1: Wals . . . 3E 49
Edward Fisher Dr. DY4: Tip . . . 2A 78
Edward Rd. B5: Edg . . . 5F 117
— B12: Bal H . . . 5F 117
— B14: K Hth . . . 6H 147
— B46: Wat O . . . 4E 89
— B63: Hale . . . 1H 127
— B67: Smeth . . . 5D 98
— B68: O'bry . . . 3A 114
— DY4: Tip . . . 6A 62
— WV6: Penn . . . 4E 25
Edwards Rd. B24: Erd . . . 2G 85
— B75: R'ley . . . 6B 38
— DY2: Neth. . . 5E 95
Edward St. B1: Birm . . . 1D 116 (4A 4)
— B68: O'bry . . . 5G 97
— B70: W Brom . . . 4A 80
— DY1: Dud . . . 6D 76
— WS2: Wals . . . 6H 31
— WS10: Darl. . . 5E 47
— WV4: E'shll . . . 5B 44
Edwin Phillips Dr. B71: W Brom . . . 5H 63
Edwin Rd. B30: Stir . . . 6D 132
Eel St. B69: O'bry. . . 2F 97
Effingham Rd. B13: Mose . . . 1C 148
Egbert St. B6: Aston. . . 1B 102
Egelwin Cl. WV6: Pert . . . 4E 25
Egerton Rd. B24: Erd . . . 4B 86
— B74: S'tly . . . 2H 51
— WV10: Bush . . . 4A 16
EGG HILL. . . 4H 143
Egghill La. B31: N'fld. . . 4A 144
— B32: Fran . . . 3G 143
— B45: Fran . . . 3G 143
Eggington Rd. DY8: Woll . . . 4B 108
Egginton Rd. B28: Hall G . . . 2E 149
Egmont Gdns. WV11: Wed. . . 3H 29
Eileen Gdns. B37: K'hrst . . . 5B 106
Eileen Rd. B11: S'hll . . . 2B 134
Elan Cl. DY3: Lwr G. . . 4H 75
Elan Rd. B31: Longb . . . 5A 144
— DY3: Sed . . . 5G 59
Elbow St. B64: Old H . . . 1H 111
Elbury Cft. B93: Know . . . 4B 166

Elcock Dr. B42: P Barr . . . 2F 83
Eldalade Way WS10: W'bry. . . 3B 64
Elderberry Cl. DY8: Stourb . . . 2A 124
— WS5: Wals . . . 2D 64
Elderfield B33: Sheld . . . 3F 121
Elderfield Rd. B30: K Nor . . . 4D 146
Elder Gro. WV5: Wom . . . 1F 73
Eldersfield Gro.
— B91: Sol . . . 2F 165
Elderside Cl. WS8: Bwnhls . . . 5B 10
Elder Way B23: Erd . . . 5E 85
Eldon Ct. WS1: Wals . . . 2D 48
(off Eldon St.)
Eldon Dr. B76: Walm . . . 6C 70
Eldon Rd. B16: Edg . . . 2B 116
— B62: Quin. . . 2G 129
Eldon St. WS1: Wals . . . 2D 48
— WS10: Darl . . . 4D 46
Eldridge Cl. WV9: Pend. . . 5D 14
Eleanor Rd. WV14: Bils . . . 5F 45
Electra Pk. B6: Witt . . . 6B 84
Electric Av. B6: Witt . . . 6B 84
Elford Cl. B14: K Hth . . . 2G 147
Elford Gro. B37: Mars G. . . 2D 122
— WV14: Bils . . . 1E 61
Elford Rd. B17: Harb. . . 2F 131
— B71: W Brom . . . 4C 64
Elgar Cl. B15: Edg . . . 4C 116
Elgar Cres. DY5: P'ntt . . . 2H 93
Elgar Ho. B16: Birm . . . 1D 116
Elgin Cl. DY3: Sed . . . 4A 60
— DY8: Amb. . . 4E 109
Elgin Ct. WV6: Pert. . . 5E 25
Elgin Rd. WS3: Blox. . . 3G 19
Eligin Gro. B25: Yard . . . 4A 120
Eliot Cl. WV14: Cose . . . 3F 61
Eliot St. B7: Nech. . . 1C 102
Elizabeth Av. WS10: W'bry . . . 2A 64
— WV4: Penn . . . 6F 43
— WV14: Bils . . . 2H 61
Elizabeth Ct. B17: Harb . . . 1H 131
(off Metchley La.)
Elizabeth Cres. B68: O'bry. . . 1B 114
Elizabeth Gro. B90: Shir. . . 5A 150
— DY2: Dud . . . 2H 95
Elizabeth Ho. B76: Walm . . . 2D 70
— DY9: Lye . . . 6H 109
— WS5: Wals. . . 4H 49
Elizabeth M. B69: Tiv . . . 5A 78
Elizabeth Prout Gdns.
— B65: B'hth . . . 2B 112
Elizabeth Rd. B13: Mose . . . 3E 133
— B33: Stech . . . 6A 104
— B63: Hale . . . 2H 127
— B70: W Brom . . . 3D 78
— B73: New O . . . 3C 68
— WS5: Wals . . . 4F 49
Elizabeth Wlk. DY4: Tip . . . 4A 62
Elkington Cft. B90: M'path . . . 4E 165
Elkington St. B6: Aston . . . 4G 101
Elkstone Cl. B92: Olton. . . 2F 137
Elkstone Covert B14: K Hth . . . 5E 147
Elland Gro. B27: A Grn . . . 3A 136
Ellards Dr. WV11: Wed . . . 4H 29
Ellen St. B18: Hock . . . 5C 100
(not continuous)
Ellenvale Cl. WV14: Cose . . . 5C 60
Ellerby Gro. B24: Erd . . . 3C 86
Ellerside Gro. B31: N'fld . . . 5D 144
Ellerslie Cl. DY5: Quar B . . . 3H 109
Ellerslie Rd. B13: Mose . . . 6C 134
Ellerton Rd. B44: K'sdng . . . 4B 68
Ellerton Wlk. WV10: Wolv . . . 4B 28
Ellesborough Rd. B17: Harb. . . 3F 115
Ellesmere Rd. B8: Salt. . . 5D 102
Ellice Dr. B36: Cas B . . . 2D 106
Elliott Cl. B45: Redn . . . 4A 158
Elliott Rd. B29: S Oak . . . 4A 132
Elliotts La. WV8: Cod. . . 4G 13
Elliotts Rd. DY4: Tip . . . 2G 77
Elliott Way B6: Witt . . . 3G 83
Elliot Way B6: Witt. . . 4H 83
Ellis Av. DY5: Brie H. . . 1E 109
Ellison St. B70: W Brom . . . 6A 80
Ellis St. B1: Birm. . . 2F 117 (6C 4)
Elliston Av. B44: Gt Barr . . . 5G 67
Ellowes Rd. DY3: Lwr G . . . 3G 75

Elm Av. B12: Bal H . . . 6A **118**
WS10: W'bry . . . 1F **63**
WV11: Wed . . . 1D **28**
WV14: Bils . . . 5F **45**
Elmay Rd. B26: Sheld . . . 4E **121**
Elm Bank B13: Mose . . . 2A **134**
Elmbank Gro. B20: Hand . . . 2A **82**
Elmbank Rd. WS5: Wals . . . 1G **65**
Elmbridge Cl. B63: Crad . . . 6F **111**
Elmbridge Dr. B90: M'path . . . 3F **165**
Elmbridge Rd. B44: K'sdng . . . 1G **83**
Elmbridge Way B31: N'fld . . . 5H **145**
DY3: Sed . . . 1A **76**
Elm Cl. DY3: Gorn . . . 5F **75**
DY8: Stourb . . . 3B **124**
Elm Ct. B13: Mose . . . 1H **133**
B66: Smeth . . . 1A **98**
WS1: Wals . . . 3E **49**
Elm Cres. DY4: Tip . . . 1H **77**
Elm Cft. B68: O'bry . . . 4A **114**
Elmcroft B66: Smeth . . . 4G **99**
Elmcroft Av. B32: Bart G . . . 4G **129**
Elmcroft Gdns. WV10: Bush . . . 4A **16**
Elmcroft Rd. B26: Yard . . . 4D **120**
Elmdale B62: Quin . . . 4G **113**
Elmdale Cres. B31: N'fld . . . 2C **144**
Elmdale Dr. WS9: A'rdge . . . 1E **35**
Elmdale Gro. B31: N'fld . . . 3C **144**
Elmdale Rd. WV4: Penn . . . 6E **43**
WV14: Cose . . . 6C **60**
ELMDON . . . 3B **138**
Elmdon Cl. B92: Sol . . . 3H **137**
WV10: Oxl . . . 6E **15**
Elmdon Coppice B92: Sol . . . 6B **138**
Elmdon Ct. *B29: W Cas* . . . *6G 131*
(off Abdon Av.)
B37: Mars G . . . 4C **122**
ELMDON HEATH . . . 1A **152**
Elmdon La. B26: Birm A . . . 2C **138**
B37: Mars G . . . 4B **122**
Elmdon Pk. . . . 3A 138
Elmdon Pk. Rd. B92: Sol . . . 3H **137**
Elmdon Rd. B27: A Grn . . . 1B **136**
B29: S Oak . . . 3C **132**
B37: Mars G . . . 4C **122**
WV10: Oxl . . . 6E **15**
Elmdon Trad. Est. B37: Mars G . . . 6E **123**
Elm Dr. B31: Longb . . . 6A **144**
B43: Gt Barr . . . 4H **65**
B62: B'hth . . . 2E **113**
Elm Farm Av. B37: Mars G . . . 4B **122**
Elm Farm Rd. WV2: Wolv . . . 4H **43**
Elmfield Av. B24: Erd . . . 3D **86**
Elmfield Cres. B13: Mose . . . 3H **133**
Elmfield Rd. B36: Cas B . . . 2A **106**
Elmfield Vw. DY1: Dud . . . 4C **76**
Elm Grn. DY1: Dud . . . 2C **76**
Elm Gro. B37: K'hrst . . . 3B **106**
CV7: Bal C . . . 6H **169**
WV8: Bilb . . . 4G **13**
Elmhurst Av. B65: Row R . . . 6C **96**
Elmhurst Dr. DY6: K'wfrd . . . 5D **92**
WS7: Chase . . . 1C **10**
Elmhurst Rd. B21: Hand . . . 6A **82**
Elmley Cl. WV14: Cose . . . 6D **60**
Elmley Gro. B30: K Nor . . . 5D **146**
WV6: Pert . . . 6F **25**
Elm Lodge B92: H Ard . . . 6A **140**
Elmore Cl. B37: F'bri . . . 5C **106**
Elmore Grn. Cl. WS3: Blox . . . 1H **31**
Elmore Grn. Rd. WS3: Blox . . . 6G **19**
Elmore Rd. B33: Kitts G . . . 6E **105**
Elmore Row WS3: Blox . . . 6H **19**
Elm Rd. B30: B'vlle . . . 5B **132**
B76: Walm . . . 3D **70**
DY1: Dud . . . 3E **77**
DY6: K'wfrd . . . 3C **92**
WS3: Blox . . . 3B **32**
WS11: Nort C . . . 1F **9**
Elms, The B16: Birm . . . 6B **100**
Elms Cl. B38: K Nor . . . 1G **159**
B91: Sol . . . 2H **151**
Elmsdale WV6: Tett . . . 1G **41**
Elmsdale Ct. WS1: Wals . . . 3D **48**
Elms Rd. B15: Edg . . . 1B **132**
B72: S Cold . . . 2A **70**
Elmstead Av. B33: Sheld . . . 4H **121**
Elmstead Cl. WS5: Wals . . . 2A **50**
Elmstead Twr. *B5: Birm* . . . *4G 117*
(off Berrington Wlk.)
Elmstead Wood WS5: Wals . . . 2A **50**
Elm St. WV3: Wolv . . . 2E **43**
WV13: W'hall . . . 1C **46**
Elm Ter. B69: Tiv . . . 6A **78**
Elm Tree Cl. WV5: Wom . . . 2F **73**
Elm Tree Gro. B63: Crad . . . 5F **111**
Elm Tree Ri. B92: H Ard . . . 1A **154**
Elm Tree Rd. B17: Harb . . . 5E **115**
B30: Stir . . . 1C **146**
Elmtree Rd. B74: S'tly . . . 2F **51**
Elm Tree Way B64: Old H . . . 2H **111**
Elmwood Av. WV11: Ess . . . 4A **18**
Elmwood Cl. B5: Edg . . . 5F **117**
CV7: Bal C . . . 6H **169**
Elmwood Ct. B73: S'tly . . . 6A **52**
Elmwood Gdns. B20: Hand . . . 5D **82**
Elmwood Gro. B47: H'wd . . . 3A **162**
Elmwood Ri. DY3: Sed . . . 4F **59**
Elmwood Rd. B24: Erd . . . 5A **86**
B74: S'tly . . . 6A **52**
DY8: Word . . . 6A **92**
Elmwoods B32: Bart G . . . 3H **129**
Elphinstone End B24: Erd . . . 1A **86**
Elsma Rd. B68: O'bry . . . 3A **114**
Elston Hall La. WV10: Bush . . . 6H **15**
Elstree Rd. B23: Erd . . . 2D **84**
Elswick Gro. B44: K'sdng . . . 5B **68**
Elswick Rd. B44: K'sdng . . . 4B **68**
Elsworth Gro. B25: Yard . . . 5A **120**
Elsworth Rd. B31: N'fld . . . 5H **145**
Eltham Gro. B44: K'sdng . . . 4B **68**
Elton Cl. WV10: Bush . . . 3A **16**
Elton Cft. B93: Dorr . . . 5B **166**
Elton Gro. B27: A Grn . . . 3G **135**
Eltonia Cft. B26: Sheld . . . 5F **121**
Elva Cft. B36: Cas B . . . 6B **88**
Elvers Grn. La. B93: Know . . . 3G **167**
Elvetham Rd. Nth. B15: Birm . . . 3E **117**
Elviron Dr. WV6: Tett . . . 4H **25**
Elwell Cres. DY1: Dud . . . 1B **76**
Elwells Cl. WV14: Cose . . . 2C **60**
Elwell St. B70: W Brom . . . 2E **79**
WS10: W'bry . . . 2H **63**
Elwyn Rd. B73: S Cold . . . 2G **69**
Ely Cl. B37: Chel W . . . 1D **122**
B65: Row R . . . 5E **97**
Ely Cres. B71: W Brom . . . 6H **63**
Ely Gro. B32: Quin . . . 1D **130**
Ely Pl. WS2: Wals . . . 2H **47**
Ely Rd. WS2: Wals . . . 2H **47**
Emay Cl. B70: W Brom . . . 5F **63**
Embankment, The DY5: Brie H . . . 6A **94**
Embassy Dr. B15: Edg . . . 3C **116**
B69: O'bry . . . 1E **97**
Embassy Rd. B69: O'bry . . . 1E **97**
Embleton Gro. B34: Hodg H . . . 3E **105**
Emerald Ct. B8: W End . . . 4A **104**
B92: Olton . . . 4D **136**
Emerson Cl. DY3: Lwr G . . . 3E **75**
Emerson Gro. WV10: Bush . . . 1B **28**
Emerson Rd. B17: Harb . . . 5G **115**
WV10: Bush . . . 6B **16**
Emery Cl. B23: Erd . . . 6D **84**
WS1: Wals . . . 3D **48**
Emery Ho. B23: Erd . . . 1C **84**
Emery St. WS1: Wals . . . 3D **48**
Emily Gdns. B16: Birm . . . 6B **100**
Emily Rd. B26: Yard . . . 5B **120**
Emily St. B12: Birm . . . 3H **117**
B70: W Brom . . . 5H **79**
Emmanuel Rd. B73: W Grn . . . 6H **69**
Emmeline St. B9: Birm . . . 2B **118**
Empire Cl. WS9: A'rdge . . . 1B **34**
Empire Ind. Pk. WS9: A'rdge . . . 1B **34**
Empress Way WS10: Darl . . . 3D **46**
Emscote Dr. B73: W Grn . . . 6H **69**
Emscote Grn. B91: Sol . . . 5C **150**
Emscote Rd. B6: Aston . . . 6H **83**
Emsworth Cres. WV9: Pend . . . 5E **15**
Emsworth Gro. B14: K Hth . . . 1F **147**
Enderby Cl. B93: Ben H . . . 5B **166**
Enderby Dr. WV4: Penn . . . 1D **58**
Enderley Cl. WS3: Blox . . . 4H **19**
Enderley Dr. WS3: Blox . . . 4H **19**
End Hall Rd. WV6: Tett . . . 6G **25**
Endhill Rd. B44: K'sdng . . . 1A **68**
Endicott Rd. B6: Aston . . . 6H **83**
Endmoor Gro. B23: Erd . . . 1D **84**
Endsleigh Gro. B28: Hall G . . . 5G **135**
Endwood Ct. B20: Hand . . . 5C **82**
Endwood Ct. Rd. B20: Hand . . . 5C **82**
Endwood Dr. B74: Lit A . . . 5C **36**
B91: Sol . . . 5D **150**
Energy Way B10: Small H . . . 5F **119**
(not continuous)
Enfield Cl. B23: Erd . . . 1F **85**
Enfield Ct. *B29: W Cas* . . . *6G 131*
(off Abdon Av.)
Enfield Rd. B15: Edg . . . 3D **116**
B65: Row R . . . 6D **96**
Enford Cl. B34: S End . . . 3H **105**
Engine La. DY9: Lye . . . 5H **109**
WS8: Bwnhls . . . 5F **9**
WS10: Mox . . . 1A **62**
Engine St. B66: Smeth . . . 3F **99**
B69: O'bry . . . 3G **97**
Englestede Cl. B20: Hand . . . 4B **82**
Englewood Dr. B28: Hall G . . . 5G **135**
Ennerdale Cl. WS8: Clay . . . 6A **10**
Ennerdale Dr. B63: Hale . . . 3F **127**
WV6: Pert . . . 5F **25**
Ennerdale Rd. B43: Gt Barr . . . 1B **82**
WV6: Tett . . . 1B **26**
Ennersdale Bungs. B46: Col . . . 6H **89**
Ennersdale Cl. B46: Col . . . 6H **89**
Ennersdale Rd. B46: Col . . . 6H **89**
Ensall Dr. DY8: Word . . . 2C **108**
Ensbury Cl. WV12: W'hall . . . 5D **30**
Ensdale Row WV13: W'hall . . . 2A **46**
Ensdon Gro. B44: K'sdng . . . 4B **68**
Ensford Cl. B74: Four O . . . 4E **37**
Enstone Rd. B23: Erd . . . 6G **69**
DY1: Dud . . . 1B **94**
Enterprise Dr. B74: S'tly . . . 4G **51**
DY9: Lye . . . 5C **110**
Enterprise Gro. WS3: Pels . . . 2F **21**
Enterprise Trad. Est. DY5: Brie H . . . 6B **94**
Enterprise Way B7: Birm . . . 5H **101**
Enville Cl. B37: Mars G . . . 2D **122**
WS3: Blox . . . 4G **19**
Enville Comn. Rd. DY7: Env . . . 5A **90**
Enville Gro. B11: S'brk . . . 6D **118**
Enville Pl. *DY8: Stourb* . . . *6D 108*
(off Short St.)
Enville Rd. DY3: Lwr G . . . 3H **75**
DY6: W Hth . . . 1G **91**
WV4: Penn . . . 1A **58**
Enville St. DY8: Stourb . . . 6D **108**
Enville Twr. Mill DY7: Env . . . 5B **90**
Epping Cl. B45: Fran . . . 5H **143**
WS3: Wals . . . 3D **32**
Epping Gro. B44: K'sdng . . . 6A **68**
Epsom Cl. WV6: Pert . . . 5F **25**
Epsom Ct. B29: W Cas . . . 6G **131**
Epsom Gro. B44: K'sdng . . . 5B **68**
Epwell Gro. B44: K'sdng . . . 1H **83**
Epwell Rd. B44: K'sdng . . . 1H **83**
Epworth Ct. DY5: P'ntt . . . 4F **93**
Equipoint B25: Yard . . . 4B **120**
Erasmus Rd. B11: S'brk . . . 4A **118**
Ercall Cl. B23: Erd . . . 1A **84**
ERDINGTON . . . 3F **85**
Erdington Hall Rd. B24: Erd . . . 5E **85**
Erdington Ind. Pk. B24: Erd . . . 3D **86**
Erdington Rd. WS9: A'rdge . . . 5D **34**
Erdington Sports Club . . . 5F 69
Erdington Station (Rail) . . . 2F **85**
Erdington Swimming Pool & Turkish Suite . . . 3G 85
Erica Cl. B29: W Cas . . . 5E **131**
Erica Rd. WS5: Wals . . . 2F **65**
Ermington Cres. B36: Hodg H . . . 1C **104**
Ermington Rd. WV4: Penn . . . 6H **43**
Ernest Clarke Cl.
WV12: W'hall . . . 5C **30**
Ernest Rd. B12: Bal H . . . 1B **134**
B67: Smeth . . . 3C **98**
DY2: Dud . . . 6H **77**
Ernest St. B1: Birm . . . 2F **117** (6C **4**)
Ernsford Cl. B93: Dorr . . . 6G **167**
Erskine St. B7: Birm . . . 5B **102**

Esher Rd. B44: Gt Barr . . . 1H 67
B71: W Brom . . . 1B 80
Eskdale Cl. WV1: Wolv . . . 1C 44
Eskdale Wlk. DY5: Brie H . . . 3F 109
Esme Rd. B11: S'hll . . . 1B 134
Esmond Cl. B30: B'vlle . . . 2H 145
Esporta Health & Fitness
Birmingham . . . 2C 116
Broadlands . . . 2H 15
Essendon Gro. B8: W End . . . 5H 103
Essendon Rd. B8: W End . . . 5H 103
Essendon Wlk. B8: W End . . . 5H 103
Essex Av. B71: W Brom . . . 6A 64
DY6: K'wfrd . . . 4H 91
WS10: W'bry . . . 1A 64
Essex Ct. B29: W Cas . . . 6G 131
Essex Gdns. DY8: Woll . . . 4B 108
Essex Ho. WV1: Wolv . . . 5G 27
Essex Rd. B75: R'ley . . . 2B 54
DY2: Dud . . . 3C 94
Essex St. B5: Birm . . . 2F 117 (6D 4)
WS2: Wals . . . 4C 32
ESSINGTON . . . 4A 18
Essington Cl. DY8: Word . . . 2C 108
Essington Ho. B8: W End . . . 4G 103
Essington Ind. Est. WV11: Ess . . . 3H 17
Essington Rd. WV12: W'hall . . . 5B 18
Essington St. B16: Birm . . . 2D 116
Essington Way WV1: Wolv . . . 2D 44
Este Rd. B26: Yard . . . 3E 121
Estone Wlk. B6: Aston . . . 2H 101
Estria Rd. B15: Edg . . . 4D 116
Estridge La. WS6: Gt Wyr . . . 3G 7
Ethelfleda Ter. WS10: W'bry . . . 2F 63
Ethelred Cl. B74: Four O . . . 6G 37
Ethel Rd. B17: Harb . . . 6H 115
Ethel St. B2: Birm . . . 1F 117 (4D 4)
B67: Smeth . . . 1D 114
B68: O'bry . . . 5G 97
Etheridge Rd. WV14: Bils . . . 4E 45
Eton Cl. DY3: Sed . . . 6B 60
Eton Ct. *B74: Four O* . . . *1F 53*
(off Vesey Cl.)
Eton Dr. DY8: Stourb . . . 2E 125
Eton Rd. B12: Bal H . . . 1B 134
Etruria Way WV14: Bils . . . 4G 45
Etta Gro. B44: Gt Barr . . . 1H 67
ETTINGSHALL . . . 6C 44
ETTINGSHALL PARK . . . 1A 60
Ettingshall Pk. Farm La. WV4: E'shll . . . 1A 60
Ettingshall Rd. WV2: E'shll . . . 4C 44
WV14: Cose . . . 3C 60
Ettington Cl. B93: Dorr . . . 6F 167
Ettington Rd. B6: Aston . . . 1G 101
Ettymore Cl. DY3: Sed . . . 5H 59
Ettymore Rd. DY3: Sed . . . 5H 59
Ettymore Rd. W. DY3: Sed . . . 5G 59
Etwall Rd. B28: Hall G . . . 2E 149
Euan Cl. B17: Harb . . . 3G 115
Euro Bus. Pk. B69: O'bry . . . 6D 78
Euro Ct. B13: Mose . . . 3B 134
Europa Av. B70: W Brom . . . 5D 80
(not continuous)
European Bus. Pk. B69: O'bry . . . 2E 97
Euroway Pk. B69: O'bry . . . 1A 98
Evans Cl. DY4: Tip . . . 2E 77
Evans Gdns. B29: S Oak . . . 4H 131
Evans Pl. WV14: Bils . . . 4G 45
Evans St. WV6: Wolv . . . 5E 27
WV13: W'hall . . . 2F 45
WV14: Cose . . . 4B 60
Eva Rd. B18: Win G . . . 3H 99
B68: O'bry . . . 6A 98
Evason Ct. B6: Aston . . . 6G 83
EVE HILL . . . 5D 76
Eve La. DY1: Dud . . . 2B 76
Evelyn Cft. B73: Bold . . . 5G 69
Evelyn Rd. B11: S'hll . . . 1C 134
Evenlode Cl. B92: Olton . . . 2F 137
Evenlode Gro. WV13: W'hall . . . 2D 46
Evenlode Rd. B92: Olton . . . 2E 137
Evered Bardon Ho. *B69: O'bry* . . . *2E 97*
(off Round's Grn. Rd.)
Everest Rd. B20: Hand . . . 4C 82
WS2: Wals . . . 6F 31
Evergreen Cl. WV14: Cose . . . 5D 60
Everitt Dr. B93: Know . . . 3C 166
Eversley Dale B24: Erd . . . 5G 85
Eversley Gro. DY3: Sed . . . 3G 59
WV11: Wed . . . 3E 29
Eversley Rd. B9: Small H . . . 2D 118
(not continuous)
Evers St. DY5: Quar B . . . 3C 110
Everton Rd. B8: W End . . . 5A 104
Eves Cft. B32: Bart G . . . 4A 130
Evesham Cres. WS3: Blox . . . 4F 19
Evesham Ri. DY2: Neth . . . 6F 95
Eveson Rd. DY8: Stourb . . . 3B 124
Ewart Rd. WS2: Wals . . . 6E 31
Ewell Rd. B24: Erd . . . 3H 85
Ewhurst Av. B29: S Oak . . . 4B 132
(Heeley Rd.)
B29: S Oak . . . 5C 132
(Umberslade Rd.)
Ewhurst Cl. WV13: W'hall . . . 3H 45
Exbury Cl. WV9: Pend . . . 5D 14
Excel Cl. B11: S'brk . . . 4B 118
Excelsior Gro. WS3: Pels . . . 2F 21
Exchange, The WS3: Blox . . . 6H 19
Exchange St. DY5: Brie H . . . 5H 93
WV1: Wolv . . . 1G 43 (3B 170)
Exe Cft. B31: Longb . . . 1F 159
Exeter Dr. B37: Mars G . . . 3B 122
Exeter Pas. B1: Birm . . . 2F 117
Exeter Pl. WS2: Wals . . . 2H 47
Exeter Rd. B29: S Oak . . . 3B 132
B66: Smeth . . . 4F 99
DY2: Neth . . . 1F 111
Exeter St. B1: Birm . . . 2F 117 (6D 4)
Exford Cl. DY5: Brie H . . . 4F 109
Exhall Cl. B91: Sol . . . 5C 150
Exhall Ct. B23: Erd . . . 5C 84
Exhibition Way B40: Nat E C . . . 1F 139
Exmoor Grn. WV11: Wed . . . 2E 29
Exon Ct. DY4: Tip . . . 1H 77
Expressway, The B70: W Brom . . . 3H 79
Exton Cl. WV11: Wed . . . 1H 29
Exton Gdns. *B66: Smeth* . . . *3H 99*
(off Foundry La.)
Exton Way B8: Salt . . . 4D 102
Eyland Gro. WS1: Wals . . . 1D 48
Eymore Cl. B29: W Cas . . . 1F 145
Eyre St. B18: Hock . . . 6C 100
Eyston Av. DY4: Tip . . . 5D 62
Eyton Cft. B12: Birm . . . 4H 117
Ezekiel La. WV12: W'hall . . . 3C 30

F

Fabian Cl. B45: Fran . . . 5F 143
Fabian Cres. B90: Shir . . . 6H 149
Facet Rd. B38: K Nor . . . 5C 146
Factory Est. B44: P Barr . . . 1G 83
Factory Rd. B18: Hock . . . 3B 100
DY4: Tip . . . 1G 77
Factory St. WS10: Darl . . . 5C 46
Fairbourne Av. B44: Gt Barr . . . 3G 67
B65: Row R . . . 5E 97
Fairbourn Twr. B23: Erd . . . 1G 85
Fairburn Cres. WS3: Pels . . . 2F 21
Faircroft Av. B76: Walm . . . 1D 86
Faircroft Rd. B36: Cas B . . . 6H 87
Fairdene Way B43: Gt Barr . . . 5H 65
Fairfax Rd. B31: Longb . . . 1E 159
B75: S Cold . . . 6D 54
WV10: Bush . . . 5H 15
Fairfield Dr. B62: B'hth . . . 2E 113
WS3: Pels . . . 3F 21
WV8: Cod . . . 3E 13
Fairfield Gro. B62: B'hth . . . 2E 113
Fairfield Mt. WS1: Wals . . . 3D 48
Fairfield Pk. Ind. Est. B62: B'hth . . . 2E 113
Fairfield Pk. Rd. B62: B'hth . . . 2E 113
Fairfield Ri. CV7: Mer . . . 4H 141
DY8: Woll . . . 6A 108
Fairfield Rd. B14: K Hth . . . 5G 133
B62: B'hth . . . 2E 113
B63: Hale . . . 3A 128
DY2: Dud . . . 2F 95
DY8: Word . . . 1D 108
Fairford Cl. B91: Shir . . . 2B 150
Fairford Gdns. DY8: Word . . . 6C 92
Fairford Rd. B44: K'sdng . . . 1H 83
Fairgreen Gdns. DY5: P'ntt . . . 4F 93
Fairgreen Way B29: S Oak . . . 4B 132
B74: S'tly . . . 2A 52
Fair Ground Way WS1: Wals . . . 3B 48
Fairhaven Cft. B62: B'hth . . . 2E 113
Fairhills DY3: Sed . . . 5H 59
Fairhill Way B11: S'brk . . . 4B 118
Fairholme Rd. B36: Hodg H . . . 2H 103
Fairlawn B15: Edg . . . 4C 116
Fairlawn Cl. WV12: W'hall . . . 6C 18
Fairlawn Dr. DY6: K'wfrd . . . 5B 92
Fairlawns B26: Yard . . . 2E 121
B76: Walm . . . 5E 71
Fairlawn Way WV12: W'hall . . . 6C 18
Fairlie Cres. B38: K Nor . . . 6H 145
Fairmead Ri. B38: K Nor . . . 6A 146
Fairmile Rd. B63: Hale . . . 5H 111
Fairoak Dr. WV6: Tett . . . 6H 25
Fair Oaks Dr. WS6: Gt Wyr . . . 5G 7
Fairview Av. B42: Gt Barr . . . 1D 82
Fairview Cl. WS6: C Hay . . . 3D 6
WV11: Wed . . . 3D 28
Fairview Ct. WS2: Wals . . . 1D 46
Fairview Cres. DY6: K'wfrd . . . 4D 92
WV11: Wed . . . 2D 28
Fairview Gro. WV11: Wed . . . 2D 28
Fairview Ind. Est. B76: Curd . . . 1D 88
Fairview Rd. DY1: Dud . . . 4C 76
WV4: Penn . . . 1A 58
WV11: Wed . . . 2D 28
Fairway B31: N'fld . . . 5C 144
WS4: S'fld . . . 6H 21
Fairway, The B38: K Nor . . . 5H 145
Fairway Av. B69: Tiv . . . 1A 96
Fairway Dr. B45: Rubery . . . 3F 157
Fairway Grn. WV14: Bils . . . 4F 45
Fairway Rd. B68: O'bry . . . 1F 113
Fairways Av. DY8: Stourb . . . 3C 124
Fairways Cl. DY8: Stourb . . . 3C 124
Fairyfield Av. B43: Gt Barr . . . 4H 65
Fairyfield Ct. B43: Gt Barr . . . 4H 65
Fakenham Cft. B17: Harb . . . 4D 114
Falcon Cl. WS6: C Hay . . . 3C 6
Falcon Cres. WV14: Cose . . . 3B 60
Falcondale Rd. WV12: W'hall . . . 6C 18
Falconhurst Rd. B29: S Oak . . . 3G 131
FALCON LODGE . . . 6F 55
Falcon Lodge Cres. B75: S Cold . . . 6D 54
Falcon Pl. B69: Tiv . . . 2C 96
Falcon Ri. DY8: Woll . . . 5A 108
Falcon Rd. B68: O'bry . . . 1F 113
Falcons, The B75: S Cold . . . 6F 55
Falcon Vw. B30: K Nor . . . 3C 146
Falcon Way DY1: Dud . . . 6B 76
Falfield Cl. B65: Row R . . . 3D 96
Falfield Gro. B31: Longb . . . 2C 158
Falkland Cft. B30: Stir . . . 1D 146
Falklands Cl. DY3: Swind . . . 5E 73
Falkland Way B36: Cas B . . . 4D 106
Falkwood Gro. B93: Know . . . 3B 166
Fallindale Rd. B26: Sheld . . . 5F 121
FALLINGS HEATH . . . 5F 47
Fallings Heath Cl. WS10: Darl . . . 4F 47
FALLINGS PARK . . . 4B 28
Fallings Pk. Ind. Est. WV10: Wolv . . . 4B 28
Fallow Fld. B74: Lit A . . . 6B 36
Fallowfield B15: Edg . . . 3A 116
WV6: Pert . . . 5D 24
WV8: Pend . . . 5C 14
Fallowfield Av. B28: Hall G . . . 2F 149
Fallowfield Rd. B63: Hale . . . 2F 127
B65: Row R . . . 6A 96
B92: Sol . . . 3G 137
WS5: Wals . . . 3A 50
Fallows Ho. B19: Hock . . . 4G 101
Fallows Rd. B11: S'brk . . . 5C 118
Fallow Wlk. B32: Bart G . . . 3G 129
Falmouth Rd. B34: Hodg H . . . 4C 104
WS5: Wals . . . 4H 49
Falstaff Av. B47: H'wd . . . 3A 162
Falstaff Cl. B76: Walm . . . 6F 71
Falstaff Ct. B75: S Cold . . . 6G 55
Falstaff Rd. B90: Shir . . . 5H 149
Falstone Rd. B73: New O . . . 3D 68
Fancott Rd. B31: N'fld . . . 2E 145
Fancourt Av. WV4: Penn . . . 1B 58
Fane Rd. WV11: Wed . . . 6A 18

Fanshawe Rd. B27: A Grn 4A 136
Fanum Ho. B63: Hale 2B 128
Faraday Av. B32: Quin 6B 114
B46: Col 2H 89
B76: Curd 2G 89
Faraday Ct. B32: Quin 6B 114
Faraday Ho. B15: Birm 3E 117
Faraday Rd. WS2: Wals 3H 31
Faraday Wharf B7: Birm 5H 101
Farbrook Way WV12: W'hall 3B 30
Farclose Ho. B15: Edg 4E 117
Farcroft Av. B21: Hand 1H 99
Farcroft Gro. B21: Hand 6H 81
Farcroft Rd. B21: Hand 6H 81
Fareham Cres. WV4: Penn 5A 42
Farfield Cl. B31: N'fld 5F 145
Far High Dr. DY4: Tip 2B 78
Far Highfield B76: Walm 1B 70
Farhill Cl. B71: W Brom 5D 64
Farlands Dr. DY8: Stourb 2E 125
Farlands Gro. B43: Gt Barr 6B 66
Farlands Rd. DY8: Stourb 2E 125
Farleigh Dr. WV3: Wolv 3G 41
Farleigh Rd. WV6: Pert 6G 25
Farley Cen. B70: W Brom 5B 80
Farley La. B62: Roms 5A 142
Farley Rd. B23: Erd 3B 84
Farley St. DY4: Tip 2D 78
Farlow Cft. B37: Mars G 3B 122
Farlow Rd. B31: N'fld 4G 145
Farlows End B38: K Nor 2H 159
Farmacre B9: Birm 1B 118
Farm Av. B68: O'bry 6G 97
Farmbridge Cl. WS2: Wals 6D 30
Farmbridge Rd. WS2: Wals 6D 30
Farmbridge Way WS2: Wals 6D 30
Farmbrook Av. WV10: F'hses 4H 15
Farm Cl. B92: Sol 3G 137
DY3: Sed 6F 59
WV8: Bilb 5H 13
Farmcote Rd. B33: Stech 5E 105
Farm Cft. B19: Hock 3E 101
Farmcroft Rd. DY9: W'cte 2A 126
Farmdale Gro. B45: Redn 3G 157
Farmer Rd. B10: Small H 4G 119
Farmers Cl. B76: Walm 1C 70
Farmers Ct. B63: Hale 1H 127
Farmers Fold WV1: Wolv 1G 43 (3B 170)
Farmers Wlk. B21: Hand 2H 99
Farmer Way DY4: Tip 4B 62
Farm Ho. La. B75: R'ley 6C 38
Farmhouse Rd. WV12: W'hall 4D 30
Farm Ho. Way B43: Gt Barr 1A 66
Farmhouse Way B90: M'path 2F 165
WV12: W'hall 4E 31
Farmoor Gro. B34: S End 3A 106
Farmoor Way WV10: Bush 3A 16
Farm Rd. B11: S'brk 4B 118
B65: Row R 5A 96
B67: Smeth 6C 98
B68: O'bry 6G 97
DY2: Neth 6C 94
DY4: Tip 6C 62
DY5: Quar B 2A 110
WV3: Wolv 3A 42
Farmside Cl. DY9: W'cte 2B 126
Farmside Grn. WV9: Pend 5D 14
Farmstead Cl. B75: R'ley 6B 38
WS1: Wals 6C 48
Farmstead Rd. B92: Sol 3G 137
Farm St. B19: Hock 3D 100
B70: W Brom 6A 80
WS2: Wals 5C 32
Farnborough Ct. B75: Four O 1H 53
Farnborough Dr. B90: M'path 3D 164
Farnborough Rd. B35: Cas V 5E 87
Farnbury Cft. B38: K Nor 5D 146
Farn Cl. B33: Stech 6D 104
Farncote Dr. B74: Four O 6F 37
Farndale Av. WV6: Wolv 4D 26
Farndale Cl. DY5: Brie H 5F 109
Farndon Av. B37: Mars G 4D 122
Farndon Rd. B8: Salt 5F 103
Farndon Way B23: Erd 5D 68
Farnham Cl. B43: Gt Barr 5B 66
Farnham Rd. B21: Hand 5H 81
Farnhurst Rd. B36: Hodg H 2H 103
Farnol Rd. B26: Yard 3D 120
Farnworth Gro. B36: Cas B 6A 88
Farquhar Rd. B13: Mose 2H 133
B15: Edg 5B 116
Farquhar Rd. E. B15: Edg 5B 116
Farran Way B43: Gt Barr 6A 66
Farren Rd. B31: Longb 6B 144
Farrier Cl. B76: Walm 5D 70
Farrier Rd. B43: Gt Barr 2F 67
Farriers, The B26: Sheld 6F 121
Farriers Mill WS3: Pels 3C 20
Farrier Way DY6: W Hth 2G 91
Farringdon Ho. *WS2: Wals* *6B 32*
(off Green La.)
Farringdon St. WS2: Wals 1B 48
Farrington Rd. B23: Erd 2B 84
WV4: E'shll 2H 59
Farrow Rd. B44: Gt Barr 2G 67
Farthing Ct. B1: Birm 6E 101 (2A 4)
Farthing La. B72: S Cold 1H 69
B76: Curd 1E 89
Farthing Pools Cl. B72: S Cold 1A 70
Farthings, The B17: Harb 5H 115
Farthings La. DY2: Dud 2C 94
Farvale Rd. B76: Min 1G 87
Far Vw. WS9: A'rdge 5D 22
Farway Gdns. WV8: Cod 5F 13
Far Wood Rd. B31: N'fld 5C 130
Fashoda Rd. B29: S Oak 4D 132
Fastlea Rd. B32: Bart G 4B 130
Fastmoor Oval B33: Kitts G 2A 122
Fast Pits Rd. B25: Yard 3H 119
Fatherless Barn Cres. B63: Crad 1E 127
Faulkland Cres. WV1: Wolv 6H 27 (1C 170)
Faulkner Cl. DY8: Stourb 1D 124
Faulkner Rd. B92: Olton 4F 137
Faulkners Farm Dr. B23: Erd 1B 84
Faulknor Dr. DY5: P'ntt 2F 93
Faversham Cl. WS2: Wals 6D 30
WV8: Pend 1C 26
Fawdry Cl. B73: S Cold 6H 53
Fawdry St. B9: Birm 1A 118
B66: Smeth 4G 99
WV1: Wolv 6F 27
Fawley Cl. WV13: W'hall 3H 45
Fawley Gro. B14: K Hth 2D 146
Fazeley St. B5: Birm 1H 117 (4G 5)
Fazeley St. Ind. Est.
B5: Birm 1A 118 (4H 5)
Fearon Pl. B66: Smeth 4E 99
FEATHERSTONE 1D 16
Featherstone Cl. B90: Shir 5B 150
Featherstone Cres. B90: Shir 5B 150
Featherstone Rd. B14: K Hth 1G 147
Featherston Rd. B74: S'tly 1A 52
FEIASHILL 6B 56
Feiashill Cl. WV5: Try 6B 56
Feiashill Rd. WV5: Try 5B 56
Felbrigg Cl. DY5: Brie H 3G 109
Feldings, The B24: Erd 3A 86
Feldon La. B62: B'hth 4E 113
Felgate Cl. B90: M'path 3E 165
Fellbrook Cl. B33: Stech 5D 104
Fell Gro. B21: Hand 5G 81
Fellmeadow Rd. B33: Yard 1E 121
Fellmeadow Way DY3: Sed 1A 76
Fellows Av. DY6: W Hth 1A 92
Fellows La. B17: Harb 5E 115
Fellows Pk. Gdns. WS2: Wals 5H 47
Fellows Rd. WV14: Bils 4F 45
Fellows St. WV2: Wolv 3G 43
Felsted Way B7: Birm 5A 102
Felstone Rd. B44: Gt Barr 4G 67
Feltham Cl. B33: Kitts G 2A 122
Felton Cft. B33: Kitts G 6E 105
Felton Gro. B91: Sol 6F 151
Fenbourne Cl. WS4: S'fld 1G 33
Fenchurch Cl. WS2: Wals 5B 32
Fencote Av. B37: F'bri 5C 106
FEN END 6F 169
Fen End Rd. CV8: Fen E 6E 169
Fen End Rd. W. B93: Know 4B 168
CV8: Fen E 4B 168
Fenmere Cl. WV4: Penn 6H 43
Fennel Cl. WS6: C Hay 2D 6
Fennel Cft. B34: S End 2F 105
Fennel Rd. DY5: Brie H 4G 109
Fennis Cl. B93: Dorr 6B 166
Fenn Ri. DY8: Word 6B 92
WV12: W'hall 3B 30
Fens Cres. DY5: Brie H 4G 93
Fens Pool Av. DY5: Brie H 4H 93
Fensway, The B34: Stech 4E 105
Fenter Cl. B13: Mose 6H 117
Fentham Cl. B92: H Ard 1B 154
Fentham Ct. B92: Olton 5D 136
Fentham Grn. B92: H Ard 6A 140
Fentham Rd. B6: Aston 1F 101
B23: Erd 4D 84
B92: H Ard 1A 154
Fenton Rd. B27: A Grn 6H 119
B47: H'wd 2A 162
Fenton St. B66: Smeth 2C 98
DY5: Brie H 6H 93
Fenton Way B27: A Grn 1H 135
Fereday Rd. WS9: Wals W 4D 22
Fereday's Cft. DY3: Sed 6H 59
Fereday St. DY4: Tip 5H 61
Ferguson Dr. DY4: Tip 1B 78
Ferguson Rd. B68: O'bry 4B 98
Ferguson St. WV11: Wed 6A 18
Fern Av. DY4: Tip 6H 61
Fern Bank Cl. B63: Hale 3F 127
Fernbank Cres. WS5: Wals 1G 65
Fernbank Rd. B8: W End 5G 103
Ferncliffe Rd. B17: Harb 1F 131
Fern Cl. WS4: S'fld 6G 21
WV14: Cose 5D 60
Ferndale Av. B43: Gt Barr 6B 66
Ferndale Ct. *B17: Harb* *1H 131*
(off Metchley La.)
B46: Col 4H 107
Ferndale Cres. B12: Birm 3A 118
Ferndale M. B46: Col 4H 107
Ferndale Pk. DY9: Pedm 5F 125
Ferndale Rd. B28: Hall G 5F 135
B46: Col 4H 107
B68: O'bry 2F 113
B74: S'tly 3H 51
CV7: Bal C 3F 169
WV11: Ess 4B 18
Ferndene Rd. B11: Tys 2F 135
Ferndown Av. DY3: Sed 6G 59
Ferndown Cl. B26: Yard 2E 121
WS3: Blox 3H 19
Ferndown Gdns. WV11: Wed 4H 29
Ferndown Rd. B91: Sol 1F 151
Fern Dr. WS6: Gt Wyr 1G 7
Fernfail Ct. B23: Erd 2E 85
Fernhill Ct. B23: Erd 5C 84
Fernhill Gro. B44: Gt Barr 2H 67
Fernhill La. CV7: Bal C 5F 169
CV8: Fen E 5E 169
Fernhill Rd. B92: Olton 3C 136
Fernhurst Dr. DY5: P'ntt 2F 93
Fernhurst Rd. B8: Salt 6G 103
Fernleigh Ct. B91: Sol 2G 151
Fernleigh Gdns. DY8: Word 6A 92
Fernleigh Rd. WS4: Wals 6F 33
Fernley Av. B29: S Oak 3D 132
Fernley Rd. B11: S'hll 1C 134
Fern Leys WV3: Wolv 2B 42
Fern Rd. B24: Erd 3G 85
DY1: Dud 3E 77
WV3: Wolv 3F 43
Fernside Gdns. B13: Mose 2B 134
Fernside Rd. WV13: W'hall 6F 29
Fernwood Cl. B73: Bold 4E 69
Fernwood Cft. B14: K Hth 1G 147
DY4: Tip 3H 77
Fernwood Rd. B73: Bold 5E 69
Fernwoods B32: Bart G 3H 129
Ferrers Cl. B75: R'ley 1B 54
Ferrie Gro. WS8: Bwnhls 6A 10
Ferris Gro. B27: A Grn 4G 135
Festival Av. WS10: Darl 1C 62
Festival Ct. DY2: Neth 4E 95
Festival Way WV6: Wolv 4F 27
Fibbersley WV11: Wed 5H 29
WV13: W'hall 5H 29
Fibbersley Bank
WV13: W'hall 5H 29
Fiddlers Grn. B92: H Ard 6A 140
Field Av. B31: N'fld 2D 144

Field Cl. B26: Sheld 5E **121**
  DY8: Word 1E **109**
  WS3: Blox 1A **32**
  WS4: S'fld 5F **21**
Field Cott. Dr. DY8: Stourb 2F **125**
Field Ct. WS4: S'fld 5F **21**
Fieldfare WS7: Hamm 1F **11**
Fieldfare Cl. B64: Old H. 5H **95**
Fieldfare Cft. B36: Cas B 1C **106**
Fieldfare Rd. DY9: W'cte 1H **125**
Fieldgate Trad. Est. WS1: Wals. 2D **48**
Fld. Head Pl. WV6: Tett 5H **25**
Fieldhead Rd. B11: Tys 2G **135**
Fieldhouse Rd. B25: Yard 3A **120**
  WV4: E'shll 1A **60**
Field La. B32: Bart G 5G **129**
  B91: Sol 1C **152**
  DY8: Stourb 2E **125**
  WS4: S'fld 5F **21**
  WS6: Gt Wyr 2F **7**
Field M. DY2: Neth 6G **95**
Fieldon Cl. B90: Shir 4A **150**
Field Rd. DY2: Dud 6G **77**
  DY4: Tip 5H **61**
  WS3: Blox 1A **32**
Field Rd. Ind. Est. WS3: Blox 1A **32**
Fields, The WV8: Bilb 3H **13**
Fieldside Wlk. WV14: Bils 3F **45**
Fieldstone Vw. DY3: Lwr G 3H **75**
Field St. WV10: Wolv 6A **28**
  WV13: W'hall 1A **46**
  WV14: Bils 2G **61**
Fieldview Cl. WV14: Cose 3G **61**
Field Vw. Dr. B65: Row R. 6F **97**
Field Wlk. WS9: A'rdge 2D **34**
Fieldways Cl. B47: H'wd 2A **162**
Fifield Gro. B33: Yard 6D **104**
Fifth Av. B9: Bord G 1F **119**
  DY5: Brie H 6B **94**
  WV10: Bush 2H **27**
Filey Rd. WV10: Oxl 5F **15**
Fillingham Cl. B37: Chel W 2F **123**
Fillongley Rd. CV7: Mer 4H **141**
Filton Cft. B35: Cas V 3E **87**
Fimbrell Cl. DY5: Brie H. 3E **109**
Finbury Cl. B92: Olton 4D **136**
Finchall Cft. B92: Sol 6A **138**
Fincham Cl. WV9: Pend 4E **15**
Finch Cl. B65: Row R. 5H **95**
Finch Cft. CV7: Bal C 2H **169**
Finchdene Gro. WV3: Wolv 2B **42**
Finch Dr. B74: S'tly 6A **52**
Finches End B34: S End. 4G **105**
Finchfield Cl. DY8: Stourb. 1A **124**
Finchfield Gdns. WV3: Wolv 2C **42**
Finchfield Hill WV3: Wolv 1A **42**
          (not continuous)
Finchfield La. WV3: Wolv 3A **42**
Finchfield Rd. WV3: Wolv 2C **42**
Finchfield Rd. W. WV3: Wolv 2B **42**
Finchley Av. B19: Loz 1E **101**
Finchley Cl. DY3: Lwr G 5H **75**
Finchley Rd. B44: K'sdng 3B **68**
Finchmead Rd. B33: Kitts G 2A **122**
Finchpath Rd. B70: W Brom 1G **79**
Finch Rd. B19: Loz 1E **101**
Findlay Rd. B14: K Hth 4G **133**
Findon Rd. B8: W End 3H **103**
Finford Cft. CV7: Bal C 3H **169**
Fingerpost Dr. WS3: Pels 2E **21**
Finlarigg Dr. B15: Edg 5B **116**
Finmere Rd. B28: Hall G. 5F **135**
Finmere Way B90: Shir 4B **150**
Finnemore Rd. B9: Bord G 1G **119**
Finneywell Cl. WV14: Cose 2D **60**
Finsbury Dr. DY5: Brie H 4G **109**
Finsbury Gro. B23: Erd 1D **84**
Finstall Cl. B7: Birm. 5A **102**
  B72: W Grn 4A **70**
Finwood Cl. B92: Sol 5A **138**
Fir Av. B12: Bal H 6A **118**
Firbank Cl. B30: B'ville 6A **132**
Firbank Way WS3: Pels 5D **20**
Firbarn Cl. B76: Walm 2B **70**
Firbeck Gro. B44: K'sdng 4A **68**
Firbeck Rd. B44: K'sdng 4A **68**
Fir Cft. DY5: Brie H 3G **109**

Fircroft B31: N'fld 5D **130**
  B91: Sol 1D **150**
  WV14: Bils 2A **62**
Fircroft Ho. B37: Chel W 1C **122**
Firecrest Cl. B23: Erd. 6B **68**
Fire Sta. Rd.
  B26: Birm A 6C **122**
Fir Gro. B14: K Hth 2H **147**
  DY8: Woll 5A **108**
  WV3: Wolv 2E **43**
Firhill Cft. B14: K Hth 5F **147**
Firmstone Ct. DY8: Woll 4C **108**
Firmstone St. DY8: Woll 4C **108**
Firs, The B11: S'brk 5C **118**
  CV7: Mer 4H **141**
Firsbrook Cl. WV6: Wolv 4D **26**
Firsbrook Ho. WV6: Wolv 4E **27**
Firsby Rd. B32: Quin 6C **114**
Firs Cl. B67: Smeth 4E **99**
Firs Dr. B90: Shir 6G **149**
Firs Farm Dr.
  B36: Hodg H 1D **104**
Firsholm Cl. B73: Bold. 6G **69**
Firs Ho. B36: Hodg H. 1D **104**
Firs La. B67: Smeth 4E **99**
Firs Rd. DY6: K'wfrd 3C **92**
Firs St. DY2: Dud 6F **77**
First Av. B6: Witt 5H **83**
  B9: Bord G 2E **119**
  B29: S Oak 2D **132**
  B76: Min. 2E **87**
  DY6: P'ntt 6E **75**
  WS8: Bwnhls 5C **10**
  WV10: Bush 3A **28**
First Exhibition Av.
  B40: Nat E C 1F **139**
First Mdw. Piece B32: Quin 1C **130**
Fir St. DY3: Sed 6D **58**
Firsvale Rd. WV11: Wed 4H **29**
Firsway WV6: Tett 1G **41**
Firswood Rd. B33: Sheld 2G **121**
Firth Dr. B14: Yard W. 2B **148**
  B62: B'hth 3E **113**
Firth Pk. Cres. B62: B'hth 3E **113**
Firtree Cl. B44: Gt Barr 6G **67**
Fir Tree Dr. DY3: Sed 6A **60**
  WS5: Wals 1F **65**
Fir Tree Gro. B73: Bold. 4F **69**
Fir Tree Rd. WV3: Wolv 3B **42**
Firtree Rd. B24: Erd. 4H **85**
Fisher Cl. B45: Fran 5E **143**
Fisher Rd. B69: O'bry 2A **98**
  WS3: Blox. 5F **19**
Fishers Dr. B90: Dic H 4F **163**
Fisher St. DY2: Dud 6F **77**
  DY4: Tip 2D **78**
              (Dudley Port)
  DY4: Tip 2D **78**
             (Great Bridge)
  DY5: Brie H. 1F **109**
  WV13: W'hall 1C **46**
FISHLEY 4A **20**
Fishley Cl. WS3: Blox 3A **20**
Fishley La. WS3: Blox, Lit W 4B **20**
Fishpool Cl. B36: Hodg H 1A **104**
Fistral Gdns. WV3: Wolv 4D **42**
Fithern Cl. DY3: Up Gor 2A **76**
Fitness First Health Club
  Brierley Hill 6A **94**
  Mere Green 1H **53**
  Solihull 2F **137**
  Stirchley 5D **132**
  Walsall Wood 3C **22**
  Wednesbury. 3D **62**
  Wolverhampton *6C* **170**
        (in AMF Bowling Express)
Fitters Mill Cl. B5: Bal H 5G **117**
Fitton Av. DY6: K'wfrd 4E **93**
Fitzgerald Pl. DY5: Brie H 5F **109**
Fitzguy Cl. B70: W Brom 6C **80**
Fitzmaurice Rd. WV11: Wed 2H **29**
Fitz Roy Av. B17: Harb 4D **114**
Fitzroy Rd. B31: N'fld 4A **144**
Five Flds. Rd. WV12: W'hall 4A **30**
Five Oaks Rd. WV13: W'hall 3G **45**
FIVE WAYS
  Birmingham 3E **117**

Five Ways B15: Birm 2D **116**
  B33: Stech 1B **120**
  DY3: Lwr G 4H **75**
  DY5: Brie H 1H **109**
  WV1: Wolv. 5G **27**
  WV3: Penn. 4A **42**
Five Ways Shop. Cen. B15: Birm 2D **116**
Five Ways Station (Rail) 3D **116**
Flackwell Rd. B23: Erd. 6E **69**
Fladbury Cl. DY2: Neth. 6F **95**
Fladbury Cres. B29: S Oak 4H **131**
Fladbury Gdns. B19: Hand 1E **101**
Fladbury Pl. B19: Loz. 2E **101**
Flamborough Cl. B34: Hodg H. 2E **105**
Flamborough Way WV14: Cose 6D **60**
Flanders Dr. DY6: K'wfrd 1B **92**
Flash La. WV4: Lwr P 3E **57**
Flash Rd. B69: O'bry 2G **97**
Flatlea B31: N'fld 3D **144**
Flatts, The WS10: Darl. 4E **47**
Flavell Av. WV14: Cose 4F **61**
Flavell Cl. B32: Bart G. 4H **129**
Flavells La. B25: Yard 3A **120**
  DY3: Gorn. 5F **75**
Flavell St. DY1: Dud 1D **76**
Flax Cl. B47: H'wd 4A **162**
Flax Gdns. B38: K Nor 1B **160**
Flaxhall St. WS2: Wals 3H **47**
Flaxley Cl. B33: Stech 6D **104**
Flaxley Parkway B33: Stech. 5C **104**
Flaxley Rd. B33: Stech, Kitts G 5B **104**
Flaxton Gro. B33: Kitts G 5E **105**
Flaxton Wlk. WV6: Wolv 4E **27**
Flecknoe Cl. B36: Cas B 6G **87**
Fledburgh Dr. B76: Walm. 1B **70**
Fleet St. B3: Birm 6E **101** (3B **4**)
  WV14: Bils 6F **45**
Fleetwood Gro. B26: Yard 2E **121**
Fleetwood Ho. B13: Mose 1H **133**
Fleming Pl. WS2: Wals 3G **31**
Fleming Rd. B32: Quin. 6B **114**
  WS2: Wals 3G **31**
           (not continuous)
Flemmynge Cl. WV8: Cod 3E **13**
Fletcher Gro. B93: Know 5C **166**
Fletcher Rd. WV12: W'hall. 6D **18**
Fletcher's La. WV13: W'hall. 1C **46**
Fletcher St. DY9: Lye 6B **110**
Fletchers Wlk. B3: Birm 1E **117** (4B **4**)
Fletton Gro. B14: K Hth 4A **148**
Flinkford Cl. WS5: Wals. 5H **49**
Flint Grn. Rd. B27: A Grn 2H **135**
Flintham Cl. B27: A Grn. 2C **136**
Flint Ho. WV1: Wolv 5G **27**
Flintway, The B33: Stech 5C **104**
Floodgate St. B5: Birm. 2H **117** (6H **5**)
Flood St. DY2: Dud 1F **95**
Flood St. Island DY2: Dud 1F **95**
Flora Rd. B25: Yard 4H **119**
Florence Av. B11: S'hll. 5C **118**
  B73: W Grn 6H **69**
  WV4: E'shll 1B **60**
Florence Bldgs. B29: S Oak 3B **132**
Florence Dr. B73: W Grn 6H **69**
Florence Gro. B18: Win G 5A **100**
  B71: W Brom 4C **64**
Florence Rd. B14: K Hth 5H **133**
  B21: Hand 1H **99**
  B27: A Grn 1B **136**
  B66: Smeth. 5F **99**
  B69: O'bry 2D **96**
  B70: W Brom 6C **80**
  B73: W Grn 6H **69**
  DY4: Tip 6A **62**
  WV8: Bilb 4H **13**
Florence St. B1: Birm 2F **117** (6C **4**)
  WS1: Wals 2E **49**
Florian Gro. WS10: Darl. 4E **47**
Florida Way DY6: K'wfrd 3E **93**
Flowerdale Cl.
  WV14: Cose 5D **60**
Floyd Gro. CV7: Bal C 5H **169**
Floyds La. WS4: Rus 3G **33**
Floyer Rd. B10: Small H. 2E **119**
Flyford Cft. B29: W Cas 3D **130**
Foden Rd. B42: Gt Barr 5C **66**
Foinavon Cl. B65: Row R. 3H **95**

Fold, The B38: K Nor 6C **146**
  WS10: Darl 5D **46**
  WV4: Penn 1D **58**
  WV5: Seis 3A **56**
  WV8: Oaken 5D **12**
Fold St. WV1: Wolv. 2G **43** (4A **170**)
Foldyard Cl. B76: Walm 5E **71**
Foley Av. WV6: Tett 6A **26**
Foley Chu. Cl. B74: S'tly 1A **52**
Foley Ct. B74: S'tly 2H **51**
Foley Dr. WV6: Tett 6A **26**
Foley Gro. WV5: Wom 2E **73**
Foley Ho. B68: O'bry 3H **113**
Foley Rd. B8: W End 4H **103**
  DY9: Pedm 3F **125**
Foley Rd. E. B74: S'tly 2H **51**
Foley Rd. W. B74: S'tly 2F **51**
Foley St. WS10: W'bry 2G **63**
Foley Wood Cl. B74: S'tly 2G **51**
Foliot Flds. B25: Yard 3B **120**
Folkes Rd. DY9: Lye 5C **110**
Folkestone Cft. B36: Hodg H 1C **104**
Folliott Rd. B33: Kitts G 6E **105**
Follyhouse Cl. WS1: Wals 4D **48**
Follyhouse La. WS1: Wals 4D **48**
Fontley Cl. B26: Yard 2D **120**
Fontwell Rd. WV10: F'hses 3H **15**
Footherley La.
  WS14: Foot, Shen W 1F **37**
FORDBRIDGE 6C **106**
Fordbridge Rd. B37: K'hrst 5B **106**
Ford Brook La. WS3: S'fld 5F **21**
Fordbrough, The
  B74: Four O 2G **53**
Forder Gro. B14: K Hth 5A **148**
Forde Way Gdns. B38: K Nor 2H **159**
Fordfield Rd. B33: Kitts G 5G **105**
Fordham Gro. WV9: Pend 4E **15**
Fordhouse La. B30: Stir. 1D **146**
Fordhouse Rd. WV10: Bush. 6H **15**
Fordhouse Rd. Ind. Est.
  WV10: Bush. 1H **27**
FORDHOUSES 4F **15**
Fordraught La. B62: Roms 6B **142**
Fordrift, The B37: Mars G 6C **122**
Fordrough B25: Yard 4F **119**
Fordrough, The B31: N'fld 6F **145**
  B90: Maj G 1B **162**
Fordrough Av. B9: Bord G 6E **103**
Fordrough La. B9: Bord G 6E **103**
Fords Rd. B90: Maj G 2E **163**
Ford St. B18: Hock. 4D **100**
  B67: Smeth 3D **98**
  WS2: Wals 4A **48**
Fordwater Rd. B74: S'tly 5H **51**
Foredraft Cl. B32: Bart G 3A **130**
Foredraft St. B63: Crad. 6F **111**
Foredrove La. B92: Sol 1A **152**
Forest Av. WS3: Blox 2B **32**
Forest Cl. B66: Smeth 2C **98**
  B74: S'tly 4G **51**
Forest Ct. B13: Mose 2A **134**
  B93: Dorr 6B **166**
  WV12: W'hall 1C **30**
Forest Dale B45: Redn 3H **157**
Forest Dr. B17: Harb 5H **115**
  B64: Old H 1H **111**
Foresters Way B75: R'ley 6C **38**
Forest Ga. WV12: W'hall 1D **30**
Forest Glade WS6: C Hay 3F **7**
Forest Hill Rd. B26: Sheld 6G **121**
Forest La. WS2: Wals 4B **32**
Forest Pk. B76: Walm 1C **70**
Forest Pl. WS3: Wals 3C **32**
Fore St. B2: Birm 1G **117** (4E **5**)
Forest Rd. B13: Mose 2A **134**
  B25: Yard 5A **120**
  B68: O'bry 4A **114**
  B93: Dorr 6C **166**
  DY1: Dud 3E **77**
Forest Way B47: H'wd 3B **162**
  WS6: Gt Wyr 4G **7**
Forfar Wlk. B38: K Nor 5H **145**
Forge, The B63: Crad. 3D **110**
Forge Cl. WS7: Hamm 1F **11**
  WV8: Pend 6C **14**
Forge Cft. B76: Walm 1F **87**

Forge La. B62: Hale 6C **112**
  B64: Crad H 3D **110**
  B71: W Brom 6E **65**
  B74: Lit A 3C **36**
  B76: Min. 1F **87**
                  (not continuous)
  B76: Walm 1F **87**
          (off Walmley Ash La.)
  DY6: W Hth 1G **91**
  WS9: A'rdge 4C **34**
              (Birmingham)
  WS9: A'rdge 2H **35**
               (Mill La.)
  WS14: Foot 1B **36**
Forge Leys WV5: Wom 1E **73**
Forge Mill Nature Reserve 6F **65**
Forge Rd. DY8: Stourb. 5D **108**
                  (not continuous)
  WS3: Pels 2D **20**
  WS10: Darl 5C **46**
  WV12: W'hall 5C **30**
Forge St. WS10: Darl 1E **63**
  WV13: W'hall 6B **30**
Forge Trad. Est. B62: Hale 6C **112**
Forge Valley Way WV5: Wom 1E **73**
Forge Way B69: O'bry 3E **97**
FORHILL 5C **160**
Forman's Rd. B11: S'hll 2D **134**
Forman Trad. Est. B11: S'hll 2D **134**
Formby Av. WV6: Pert 5D **24**
Formby Way WS3: Blox 4G **19**
Forrell Gro. B31: Longb 2F **159**
Forrest Av. WV11: Ess 3A **18**
Forrester St. WS2: Wals 1A **48**
Forrester St. Pct. WS2: Wals. 1A **48**
Forster St. B7: Birm 6A **102**
  B67: Smeth 2C **98**
Forsythia Cl. B31: N'fld 5D **130**
Forsythia Gro. WV8: Bilb 4G **13**
Fort Cen., The 5F **87**
Fort Cres. WS9: Wals W 4C **22**
Fort Dunlop 6B **86**
Forth Dr. B37: F'bri. 5D **106**
Forth Gro. B38: K Nor 1A **160**
Forth Way B62: B'hth 3E **113**
Fort Ind. Est., The B35: Cas V 6C **86**
Fortnum Cl. B33: Kitts G 1H **121**
Forton Cl. WV6: Tett. 1H **41**
Fort Parkway B24: Erd 1H **103**
  B35: Cas V 6C **86**
Fort Shop. Pk., The B24: Erd. 6H **85**
Forum B40: Nat E C 2G **139**
Forward Rd. B26: Birm A. 2C **138**
Fosbrooke Rd. B10: Small H 3G **119**
Fosseway Dr. B23: Erd 5E **69**
Fossil Dr. B45: Redn 2G **157**
Foster Av. WV14: Cose 4D **60**
Foster Gdns. B18: Hock 3B **100**
Foster Grn. WV6: Pert 6E **25**
Foster Pl. DY8: Woll. 5C **108**
Foster Rd. WV10: Bush 3A **28**
Foster St. DY8: Stourb 6E **109**
  WS3: Blox 1B **32**
  WS10: Darl 4D **46**
Foster St. E. DY8: Stourb. 6E **109**
Foster Way B5: Edg 6E **117**
                  (not continuous)
Fotherley Brook Rd. WS9: A'rdge 4H **35**
Foundry La. B66: Smeth 2G **99**
  WS3: Pels 4C **20**
Foundry Rd. B18: Win G 4H **99**
  DY6: W Hth 1H **91**
Foundry St. DY4: Tip 5G **61**
  DY6: W Hth 1A **92**
  WV14: Bils 1A **62**
  WV14: Cose 4E **61**
Fountain Arc. DY1: Dud 6E **77**
Fountain Cl. B31: Longb 3C **158**
Fountain Ct. B4: Birm. 2E **5**
Fountain Ho. B63: Hale 2B **128**
Fountain La. B69: O'bry 6F **79**
  DY4: Tip 5F **61**
  WV14: Cose 5F **61**
Fountain Rd. B17: Edg 2F **115**
Fountains Rd. WS3: Blox 5E **19**
Fountains Way WS3: Blox 5E **19**
Four Acres B32: Quin 1A **130**

Four Ashes Rd. B93: Ben H, Dorr 6H **165**
Four Crosses Rd. WS4: S'fld 6G **21**
Four Dwellings Leisure Cen. 1H **129**
Fourlands Av. B72: W Grn 6B **70**
Fourlands Rd. B31: N'fld 1C **144**
FOUR OAKS
  Sutton Coldfield 6G **37**
Four Oaks Comn. Rd. B74: Four O 6E **37**
Four Oaks Ct. B74: Four O 2H **53**
FOUR OAKS PARK 3F **53**
Four Oaks Rd. B74: Four O 1G **53**
Four Oaks Station (Rail) 3H **53**
Four Stones Cl. B91: Sol 6E **151**
Four Stones Gro. B5: Bal H 5G **117**
Fourth Av. B9: Bord G. 1F **119**
  B29: S Oak 2E **133**
  WS8: Bwnhls 4C **10**
                  (not continuous)
  WV10: Bush. 3H **27**
Fourways B64: Crad H 2F **111**
Four Winds Rd. DY2: Dud 3G **95**
Fowey Cl. B76: Walm 6E **71**
Fowey Rd. B34: Hodg H 3D **104**
Fowgay Dr. B91: Sol 6D **150**
Fowler Cl. B66: Smeth 1E **99**
  WV6: Pert. 3E **25**
Fowler Rd. B75: S Cold 6E **55**
Fowler St. B7: Nech 4B **102**
  WV2: Wolv. 5G **43**
Fowlmere Rd. B42: Gt Barr 5D **66**
Fox & Goose Shop. Cen. B8: W End . . . 4A **104**
Foxbury Dr. B93: Dorr 6C **166**
Fox Cl. B75: S Cold 4D **54**
FOXCOTE 2C **126**
Foxcote Av. B21: Hand 2A **100**
Foxcote Cl. B90: Shir. 1B **164**
Foxcote Dr. B90: Shir. 1B **164**
Foxcote La. B63: Crad 2D **126**
Fox Covert DY8: Stourb 6D **108**
Fox Cres. B11: S'hll 1D **134**
Foxcroft Cl. WS7: Burn 1C **10**
Foxdale Dr. DY5: Brie H 6F **93**
Foxdale Gro. B33: Kitts G 1G **121**
Foxes Mdw. B30: K Nor 3B **146**
  B76: Walm 5E **71**
Foxes Ridge B64: Crad H 3G **111**
Foxes Way CV7: Bal C 3H **169**
Foxfield B31: N'fld 3D **144**
Foxfield Dr. DY8: Stourb 2E **125**
Fox Foot Dr. DY5: Brie H 5G **93**
Foxford Cl. B36: Cas B. 6H **87**
  B72: W Grn 6B **70**
Foxglove Cl. B27: A Grn 4H **135**
  WS3: Pels. 2E **21**
  WV11: Wed 4G **29**
Foxglove Cres. B37: K'hrst 6A **106**
Foxglove Rd. DY1: Dud 3B **76**
Foxglove Way B21: Hand 2H **99**
  B23: Erd 6B **68**
Fox Grn. Cres. B27: A Grn 4G **135**
Fox Gro. B27: A Grn 3G **135**
Fox Hill B29: S Oak 5G **131**
Fox Hill Cl. B29: S Oak 5G **131**
Fox Hill Rd. B75: R'ley 1C **54**
                  (not continuous)
Foxhills Pk. DY2: Neth 5E **95**
Foxhills Rd. DY8: Word 2B **108**
  WV4: Penn 2A **58**
Foxhollies Dr. B63: Hale 1G **127**
Fox Hollies Leisure Cen. 4G **135**
Fox Hollies Rd. B28: Hall G 6F **135**
  B76: Walm 5D **70**
                  (not continuous)
Fox Hollow WV6: Tett. 1A **42**
Fox Hollow Cl. B45: Redn 2A **158**
Foxhope Cl. B38: K Nor 5E **147**
Foxhunt Rd. B63: Hale 3G **127**
Foxland Av. B45: Redn 2A **158**
  WS6: Gt Wyr 2G **7**
Foxland Cl. B37: Chel W 1F **123**
  B90: Ches G 5B **164**
Foxlands Av. WV4: Penn 2B **58**
Foxlands Cres. WV4: Penn 2A **58**
Foxlands Dr. B72: W Grn 6B **70**
  DY3: Up Gor 2H **75**
  WV4: Penn 2A **58**
Foxlea Rd. B63: Hale 4F **127**

Foxley Dr. B91: Cath B 2D **152**
Foxmeadow Cl. DY3: Sed 6A **60**
Fox Mill Est. B11: S'hll 2D **134**
Foxoak Ent. Cen. B64: Crad H 2F **111**
    (off Foxoak St.)
Foxoak St. B64: Crad H 2E **111**
Fox's La. WV1: Wolv 5G **27**
Fox St. B5: Birm 6H **101** (3G **5**)
    DY1: Dud 1E **77**
Foxton Rd. B8: Salt. 4F **103**
Fox Wlk. WS9: Wals W 4D **22**
Foxwell Gro. B9: Bord G 6A **104**
Foxwell Rd. B9: Bord G 6H **103**
Foxwood Av. B43: Gt Barr 3D **66**
Foxwood Gro. B37: K'hrst 4B **106**
Foxyards Rd. DY4: Tip 2F **77**
Foyle Rd. B38: K Nor 6A **146**
Fozdar Cres. WV14: Cose 4D **60**
Fradley Cl. B30: K Nor 3H **145**
Framefield Dr. B91: Sol 1A **152**
Framlingham Gro. WV6: Pert 6G **25**
Frampton Cl. B30: B'ville 6H **131**
    B37: Chel W 6F **107**
Frampton Way B43: Gt Barr 1F **67**
Frances Dr. WS3: Blox 5H **19**
Frances Rd. B19: Loz 1E **101**
    B23: Erd 4D **84**
    B30: K Nor 2C **146**
Franchise Gdns. WS10: W'bry 6F **47**
Franchise St. B42: P Barr 5G **83**
    WS10: W'bry 6E **47**
Francis Cl. B74: S'tly 3H **51**
    DY6: K'wfrd 1B **92**
Francis Rd. B16: Edg 2C **116**
    B25: Yard 5G **119**
    B27: A Grn 6B **120**
    B33: Stech 1B **120**
    B67: Smeth 4B **98**
    B78: Woll 6A **108**
Francis Sharp Ho. WS3: Blox 5G **19**
Francis St. B7: Birm 6A **102**
    B70: W Brom 6B **80**
    WV1: Wolv 5G **27**
Francis Wlk. B31: Longb 2E **159**
Francis Ward Cl.
    B71: W Brom 5G **63**
Frankburn Rd. B74: S'tly 3G **51**
Frankfort St. B19: Hock 3F **101**
Frankholmes Dr. B90: M'path 3D **164**
FRANKLEY 2H **143**
Frankley Av. B62: Quin 6F **113**
FRANKLEY BEECHES 3G **143**
Frankley Beeches Rd.
    B31: Longb, N'fld 5A **144**
Frankley Community Leisure Cen. . . . 6F **143**
FRANKLEY GREEN 2G **143**
Frankley Grn. B32: Fran 2D **142**
Frankley Grn. La. B32: Fran 2E **143**
FRANKLEY HILL 4F **143**
Frankley Hill La. B32: Fran 4F **143**
Frankley Hill Rd. B45: Fran 4F **143**
Frankley Ind. Pk. B45: Fran 5H **143**
Frankley La. B31: N'fld 1B **144**
    B32: Bart G, N'fld 1A **144**
Frankley Lodge Rd.
    B31: Fran 3B **144**
Frankley Rd. B68: O'bry 3H **113**
Frankley Ter. B17: Harb 6F **115**
Franklin Rd. B30: B'ville 2A **146**
Franklin St. B18: Win G 4A **100**
Franklin Way B30: B'ville 1B **146**
Franklyn Cl. WV6: Pert 4E **25**
Frank Rd. B67: Smeth 3C **98**
Frank St. B12: Birm 4H **117**
Franks Way B33: Stech 1C **120**
Frank Tommey Cl. B65: B'hth 2C **112**
Frankton Cl. B92: Sol 3F **137**
Frankton Gro. B9: Bord G 1H **119**
Fraser Rd. B11: S'brk 6D **118**
Fraser St. WV14: Bils. 6G **45**
    (not continuous)
Frayne Av. DY6: K'wfrd 2A **92**
Freasley Cl. B90: Shir 5B **150**
Freasley Rd. B34: S End 4H **105**
Freda Ri. B69: Tiv 1D **96**
Freda Rd. B70: W Brom 6B **80**
Freda's Gro. B17: Harb 6E **115**

Frederick Rd. B6: Aston 1G **101**
    B11: S'hll 1C **134**
    B15: Edg 3D **116**
    B23: Erd 5D **84**
    B29: S Oak 3H **131**
    B33: Stech 6B **104**
    B68: O'bry 4B **114**
    B73: W Grn 3G **69**
    WV11: Wed 4E **29**
Fredericks Cl. DY8: Stourb 1C **124**
Frederick St. B1: Birm 5E **101** (1A **4**)
    B70: W Brom 3A **80**
    WS2: Wals 1B **48**
    WV2: Wolv 3G **43** (6B **170**)
Frederick William St. WV13: W'hall . . 1B **46**
Fred Smith Cl. WS10: W'bry 6H **47**
Freeland Gro. DY6: K'wfrd. 5D **92**
Freeman Dr. B76: Walm 1D **70**
Freeman Pl. WV14: Bils. 3G **45**
Freeman Rd. B7: Nech 3B **102**
    WS10: W'bry 2A **64**
Freeman St. B5: Birm 1G **117** (4F **5**)
    WV10: Wolv 1B **44**
Freemount Sq. B43: Gt Barr 6A **66**
Free Port B26: Birm A 2B **138**
Freer Rd. B6: Aston 1F **101**
Freer St. WS1: Wals 1C **48**
Freeth Rd. WS8: Bwnhls 4C **10**
Freeth St. B16: Birm 1B **116**
    B69: O'bry 1F **97**
Freezeland St. WV14: Bils. 5D **44**
Fremont Dr. DY1: Dud 4A **76**
French Rd. DY2: Dud 6G **77**
French Walls B66: Smeth 4G **99**
Frensham Cl. B37: Chel W 1E **123**
    WS6: C Hay 1E **7**
Frensham Way B17: Harb 5G **115**
Frenshaw Gro. B44: Gt Barr 5H **67**
Freshwater Dr. DY5: Brie H 3F **109**
Friardale Cl. WS10: W'bry 2B **64**
FRIAR PARK 3A **64**
Friar Pk. Farm WS10: W'bry 1B **64**
Friar Pk. Rd. WS10: W'bry 2A **64**
Friars Cl. DY8: Word 6A **92**
Friars Gorse DY7: Stourt 4A **108**
Friar St. WS10: W'bry 2H **63**
Friars Wlk. B37: Chel W 1F **123**
Friary Av. B90: M'path 3E **165**
Friary Cl. B20: Hand 4B **82**
Friary Cres. WS4: Rus 3G **33**
Friary Dr. B74: Four O 6F **37**
Friary Gdns. B21: Hand 5H **81**
Friary Rd. B20: Hand 5A **82**
Friday La. B92: Cath B, H Ard 2E **153**
Friday Wharf B1: Birm 6A **4**
Friesland Dr. WV1: Wolv 6D **28**
Friezeland Rd. WS2: Wals 1H **47**
Friezland La. WS8: Bwnhls 2B **22**
Friezland Way WS8: Bwnhls 2C **22**
Frinton Gro. B21: Hand 2G **99**
Friston Av. B16: Birm. 2D **116**
Frobisher Cl. WS6: Gt Wyr. 4F **7**
Frobisher Rd. B66: Smeth 2B **98**
Frodesley Rd. B26: Sheld. 3F **121**
Froggatt Rd. WV14: Bils. 4F **45**
Froggatts Ride B76: Walm. 2D **70**
Frog Hall Cotts. DY7: I'ley 2A **124**
Frog La. CV7: Bal C 4G **169**
Frogmill Rd. B45: Fran 6H **143**
Frogmoor Ho. B25: Yard 4C **120**
Frogmore La. CV8: Fen E 6F **169**
Frome Cl. DY3: Lwr G 5H **75**
Frome Dr. WV11: Wed 4E **29**
Frome Way B14: K Hth 1E **147**
Frost St. WV2: E'shll. 5C **44**
Froxmere Cl. B91: Sol 1F **165**
Froyle Cl. WV6: Tett. 4A **26**
Froysell St. WV13: W'hall 1B **46**
Fryer Rd. B31: Longb 2F **159**
Fryer's Cl. WS3: Blox 2H **31**
Fryer's Rd. WS2: Wals 3G **31**
    WS3: Blox 3G **31**
Fryer St. WV1: Wolv 1H **43** (2C **170**)
Fuchsia Cl. WV9: Pend 4D **14**
Fugelmere Cl. B17: Harb. 4D **114**
Fulbrook Gro. B29: W Cas 5D **130**
Fulbrook Rd. DY1: Dud 6C **76**

Fulford Dr. B76: Min. 2F **87**
Fulford Gro. B26: Sheld 5G **121**
Fulford Hall La. B90: Tid G 6D **162**
Fulford Hall Rd. B94: Earls 6D **162**
FULFORD HEATH 6D **162**
Fulham Rd. B11: S'hll 6B **118**
FULLBROOK 5D **48**
Fullelove Rd. WS8: Bwnhls 6C **10**
Fullbrook Rd. WS5: Wals. 6C **48**
Fuller M. B24: Erd 4F **85**
Fullerton Cl. WV8: Pend 6C **14**
Fullwood Cres. DY2: Dud. 3A **94**
Fullwoods End WV14: Cose 4E **61**
Fulwell Gro. B44: K'sdng. 6A **68**
Fulwell M. B37: Mars G. 3D **122**
Fulwood Av. B62: B'hth 3F **113**
Furber Pl. DY6: K'wfrd 3D **92**
Furlong, The WS10: W'bry 6E **47**
Furlong La. B63: Crad 5E **111**
Furlong Mdw. B31: N'fld 5G **145**
Furlongs, The DY8: Stourb. 2F **125**
    WV11: Wed 4D **28**
Furlongs Rd. DY3: Sed 1H **75**
Furlong Wlk. DY3: Lwr G. 3H **75**
Furnace Cl. WV5: Wom 2E **73**
Furnace Hill B63: Hale 5B **112**
Furnace La. B63: Hale 6B **112**
Furnace Pde. DY4: Tip 1G **77**
Furnace Rd. DY2: Dud 1E **95**
Furness Cl. WS3: Blox 4F **19**
Furst St. WS8: Bwnhls 5C **10**
Furzebank Way WV12: W'hall 5E **31**
Furze Way WS5: Wals 3A **50**

G

Gables, The B24: Erd 3B **86**
    DY6: W Hth 1H **91**
Gaddesby Rd. B14: K Hth 5H **133**
Gadds Dr. B65: Row R 5D **96**
Gadsby Av. WV11: Wed 2A **30**
Gads Grn. DY2: Neth 4G **95**
Gads Grn. Cres. DY2: Dud. 3G **95**
Gads La. B70: W Brom 5G **79**
    DY1: Dud 6E **77**
Gadwall Cft. B23: Erd. 4B **84**
Gail Cl. WS9: Wals W 3D **22**
Gailey Cft. B44: Gt Barr 2G **67**
Gail Pk. WV3: Wolv 4B **42**
Gainford Cl. WV8: Pend. 6D **14**
Gainford Rd. B44: K'sdng. 4C **68**
Gainsborough Cres. B43: Gt Barr. 1F **67**
    B93: Know 3C **166**
Gainsborough Dr. WV6: Pert 5F **25**
Gainsborough Hill DY8: Stourb 2D **124**
Gainsborough Pl. DY1: Dud. 5A **76**
Gainsborough Rd. B42: Gt Barr 1D **82**
Gainsborough Trad. Est. DY9: Lye. . . . 1G **125**
Gainsford Dr. B62: Hale 5B **112**
Gains La. WS3: Lit W. 3A **8**
    WS11: Lit W 3A **8**
Gairloch Rd. WV12: W'hall 6B **18**
Gaitskell Ter. B69: Tiv 5D **78**
Gaitskell Way B66: Smeth 2D **98**
Gala Bingo
    Aldridge 3D **34**
    Bushbury 1H **27**
    Darlaston 4F **47**
    Dudley 6E **77**
    Gala Casino 1F **117** (5D **4**)
    Great Park 6H **143**
    Harborne 6G **115**
    Kings Heath 4G **133**
    Stockland Green 2D **84**
    Tower Hill 1D **82**
    Tyburn 4C **86**
    Walsall 2B **48**
    Wednesfield 2H **29**
    Yardley 5B **120**
    (off Swan Shop. Cen., The)
Galahad Way WS10: W'bry 3G **63**
Gala Leisure Cen. 4A **80**
Galbraith Cl. WV14: Cose. 5F **61**
Galena Way B6: Aston 3G **101**
Gale Wlk. B65: Row R 4H **95**

Gallagher Ct. _B13:_ Mose . . . . _3B_ **134**
(off Wake Grn. Pk.)
Gallery, The WV1: Wolv 2G **43** (4B **170**)
Gallery Sq. WS2: Wals 1B **48**
Galloway Av. B43: Hodg H. 3D **104**
Galton Cl. B24: Erd 3D **86**
DY4: Tip 1C **78**
Galton Dr. DY2: Dud 3D **94**
Galton Rd. B67: Smeth 1D **114**
Galton Twr. B1: Birm 1E **117** (4A **4**)
Gamesfield Grn. WV3: Wolv 2D **42**
Gammage St. DY2: Dud. 1D **94**
Gandy Rd. WV12: W'hall 3A **30**
Gannah's Farm Cl. B76: Walm 2D **70**
GANNOW GREEN 6C **142**
Gannow Grn. La. B45: Roms 6C **142**
Gannow Mnr. Cres. B45: Fran 5E **143**
Gannow Mnr. Gdns. B45: Fran 6F **143**
Gannow Rd. B45: Rubery 2E **157**
Gannow Shop. Cen. B45: Fran 6E **143**
Gannow Wlk. B45: Rubery 2E **157**
Ganton Rd. WS3: Blox 3G **19**
Ganton Wlk. WV8: Pend 1D **26**
Garden Cl. B8: W End 4G **103**
B45: Fran 5G **143**
B93: Know .3B **166**
Garden Cres. WS3: Pels 4D **20**
Garden Cft. WS9: A'rdge 2D **34**
Gardeners Wlk. B91: Sol 4G **151**
Gardeners Way WV5: Wom 3F **73**
Garden Gro. B20: Hand 1A **82**
Gardens, The B23: Erd 4E **85**
B72: W Grn 5H **69**
Garden St. WS2: Wals 6C **32**
Garden Wlk. DY2: Dud 6E **77**
DY3: Gorn 5G **75**
(not continuous)
WV14: Bils .5H **45**
Garfield Rd. B26: Sheld 3F **121**
Garland Cres. B62: B'hth 3E **113**
Garlands, The WV11: Wed 2E **29**
Garland St. B9: Birm 6C **102**
Garland Way B31: N'fld 2F **145**
(not continuous)
Garman Cl. B43: Gt Barr 3A **66**
Garner Cl. WV14: Cose. 2F **61**
Garnet Av. B43: Gt Barr 1D **66**
Garnet Cl. WS9: Ston. 3G **23**
Garnet Ct. B92: Olton. 4D **136**
Garnett Dr. B75: S Cold 5C **54**
Garrard Gdns. B73: S Cold 6H **53**
Garratt Cl. B68: O'bry 5A **98**
Garratt's La. B64: Old H. 1H **111**
Garratt St. B71: W Brom 2H **79**
DY5: Brie H 4A **94**
Garret Cl. DY6: K'wfrd 1B **92**
GARRETT'S GREEN 3G **121**
Garrett's Grn. Ind. Est. B33: Sheld . . . 2G **121**
Garretts Grn. La. B26: Sheld 4D **120**
Garretts Wlk. B14: K Hth 5G **147**
Garrick Cl. DY1: Dud 4B **76**
Garrick St. WV1: Wolv 2H **43** (4C **170**)
Garrington St. WS10: Darl 4C **46**
Garrison Cir. B9: Birm 1A **118**
Garrison Ct. B9: Birm . . . . _1B_ **118**
(off Barwell Rd.)
Garrison La. B9: Birm 1B **118**
Garrison St. B9: Birm 1B **118**
Garston Way B43: Gt Barr 5H **65**
Garth, The B14: Yard W 3D **148**
Garway Gro. B25: Yard 5H **119**
Garwood Rd. B26: Yard 1D **120**
Gas St. B1: Birm 1E **117** (5A **4**)
Gatacre St. DY3: Gorn 4H **75**
Gatcombe Cl. WV10: Bush. 3B **16**
Gatcombe Rd. DY1: Dud 5A **76**
Gatehouse Fold _DY2:_ Dud . . . . _6F_ **77**
(off Birmingham St.)
Gatehouse Trad. Est. WS8: Bwnhls. 4D **10**
Gate La. B73: Bold 3F **69**
B93: Dorr 5F **165**
B94: H'ley H 5F **165**
Gateley Rd. B68: O'bry 4C **114**
Gate St. B8: Salt. 4D **102**
DY3: Sed 6A **60**
DY4: Tip 5A **78**
Gatis St. WV6: Wolv. 5E **27**

Gatwick Rd. B35: Cas V. 3G **87**
Gauden Rd. DY9: W'cte. 4H **125**
Gavin Way B6: Witt 3H **83**
Gaydon Cl. WV6: Pert. 4E **25**
Gaydon Gro. B29: S Oak. 3E **131**
Gaydon Pl. B73: S Cold 1H **69**
Gaydon Rd. B92: Sol 2H **137**
WS9: A'rdge 5C **34**
Gayfield Av. DY5: Brie H 2H **109**
GAY HILL 2D **160**
Gayhill La. B38: Head H 6D **146**
Gayhurst Dr. B25: Yard. 3C **120**
Gayle Gro. B27: A Grn 5A **136**
Gayton Rd. B71: W Brom. 1B **80**
Geach Twr. _B19:_ Birm. 4F **101**
(off Uxbridge St.)
Gedney Cl. B90: Shir. 4C **148**
Geeson Cl. B35: Cas V 3F **87**
Gee St. B19: Hock. 3F **101**
Gem Ho. B4: Birm. 2G **5**
Geneva Rd. DY4: Tip 2F **77**
Genge Av. WV4: E'shll 1A **60**
Genners App. B31: N'fld 5B **130**
Genners La. B31: N'fld. 6B **130**
B32: Bart G 5A **130**
Genthorn Cl. WV4: E'shll 1B **60**
Gentian B74: Four O. 5F **37**
Gentian Cl. B31: N'fld. 1D **144**
Geoffrey Cl. B76: Walm 6F **71**
Geoffrey Pl. B11: S'hll 2C **134**
Geoffrey Rd. B11: S'hll 2C **134**
B90: Shir 4F **149**
George Arthur Rd. B8: Salt 5D **102**
George Av. B65: Row R 1D **112**
George Bird Cl. B66: Smeth. 3E **99**
George Cl. DY2: Dud 1G **95**
George Frederick Rd. B73: S'tly 1A **68**
George Henry Rd. DY4: Tip 6E **63**
George Rd. B15: Edg 3D **116**
B23: Erd 3B **84**
B25: Yard .5G **119**
B29: S Oak 2A **132**
B43: Gt Barr 3B **66**
B46: Wat O .4E **89**
B63: Hale .1H **127**
B68: O'bry 1H **113**
B73: New O 4D **68**
B91: Sol 4G **151**
DY4: Tip 1F **77**
WV14: Cose 4F **61**
George Rose Gdns. WS10: Darl. 5C **46**
George St. B3: Birm 6E **101** (3A **4**)
B12: Bal H .6G **117**
B19: Loz. 2D **100**
B21: Hand .1G **99**
B70: W Brom 5B **80**
DY1: Dud 1D **76**
DY8: Word 2D **108**
WS1: Wals .2C **48**
WV2: E'shll. 4C **44**
WV2: Wolv 2H **43** (5C **170**)
WV13: W'hall 5A **30**
George St. W. B18: Hock. 5C **100**
Georgian Gdns. WS10: W'bry 2F **63**
Georgina Av. WV14: Cose 2F **61**
Geraldine Rd. B25: Yard 4H **119**
Gerald Rd. DY8: Woll. 4C **108**
Geranium Gro. B9: Bord G 6F **103**
Geranium Rd. DY2: Dud 1H **95**
Gerardsfield Rd. B33: Kitts G 6H **105**
Germander Dr. WS5: Wals 2F **65**
Gerrard Cl. B19: Loz. 2E **101**
Gerrard Rd. WV13: W'hall 2G **45**
Gerrard St. B19: Loz. 2E **101**
Gertrude Pl. B18: Hock 4C **100**
Gervase Dr. DY1: Dud 4E **77**
Geston Rd. DY1: Dud. 1B **94**
Gibbet La. DY7: Kinv 1A **124**
(not continuous)
Gibbins Rd. B29: S Oak 4G **131**
Gibbons Gro. WV6: Wolv. 5D **26**
Gibbons Hill Rd. DY3: Sed 3H **59**
Gibbons Ind. Est. DY6: K'wfrd 2E **93**
Gibbon's La. DY5: P'ntt 2E **93**
Gibbons Rd. B75: Four O 6H **37**
WV6: Wolv. 5D **26**
Gibbs Hill Rd. B31: Longb. 2F **159**

Gibb Sq. B9: Birm. 2A **118** (6H **5**)
Gibbs Rd. DY9: Lye 6C **110**
Gibbs St. WV6: Wolv 5E **27**
Gibb St. B9: Birm 2H **117** (6H **5**)
GIB HEATH 3B **100**
Gibson Dr. B20: Hand 1D **100**
B66: Smeth 3E **99**
Gibson Rd. B20: Hand 1D **100**
WV6: Pert. .6E **25**
Gideon Cl. B25: Yard 5B **120**
Gideons Cl. DY3: Up Gor. 2H **75**
Giffard Rd. WV1: Wolv. 4D **44**
WV10: Bush. 4A **16**
Gifford Ct. _DY5:_ Brie H. 1H **109**
(off Hill St.)
Giggetty La. WV5: Wom. 1E **73**
Gigmill Way DY8: Stourb. 1C **124**
Gilbanks Rd. DY8: Woll 4B **108**
Gilberry Cl. B93: Know 4C **166**
Gilbert Av. B69: Tiv 2B **96**
Gilbert Cl. WV11: Wed. 2A **30**
Gilbert Ct. _WS4:_ Wals . . . . _5E_ **33**
(off Lichfield Rd.)
Gilbert Ent. Pk.
WV12: W'hall 5B **30**
Gilbert La. WV5: Wom. 6H **57**
Gilbert Rd. B66: Smeth 5F **99**
GILBERTSTONE. 4C **120**
Gilbertstone Av. B26: Yard. 6C **120**
Gilbert St. DY4: Tip 5H **77**
Gilbeys Cl. DY8: Word 2C **108**
Gilby Rd. B16: Birm 1C **116**
Gilchrist Dr. B15: Edg 3A **116**
Gildas Av. B38: K Nor 6C **146**
Giles Cl. B33: Stech. 6C **104**
B92: Sol 6B **138**
Giles Cl. Ho. B33: Stech 6C **104**
Giles Hill DY8: Stourb 5E **109**
Giles Rd. B68: O'bry 4H **97**
Gilldown Pl. B15: Edg 4D **116**
Gillespie Cft. B6: Aston 2H **101**
Gillhurst Rd. B17: Harb 4F **115**
Gillies Ct. B33: Stech. 6B **104**
Gilling Gro. B34: Hodg H 3E **105**
Gillingham Cl. WS10: W'bry 6B **48**
Gillity Av. WS5: Wals. 3F **49**
Gillity Cl. WS5: Wals 3F **49**
Gillity Ct. WS5: Wals 4H **49**
Gilliver Rd. B90: Shir. 5H **149**
Gillman Cl. B26: Sheld 1H **137**
Gillott Cl. B91: Sol 4A **152**
Gillott Rd. B16: Edg. 2G **115**
Gillows Cft. B90: M'path 2E **165**
Gillscroft Rd. B33: Kitts G 5E **105**
Gill St. B70: W Brom 6A **80**
DY2: Neth 5G **95**
Gilmorton Cl. B17: Harb 4F **115**
B91: Sol 6G **151**
Gilpin Cl. B8: W End 2A **104**
Gilpin Cres. WS3: Pels. 3E **21**
Gilpins Cft. WS6: C Hay. 4D **6**
GILSON 6F **89**
Gilson Dr. B46: Col 2F **107**
Gilson Rd. B46: Col 6F **89**
Gilson St. DY4: Tip. 5C **62**
Gilson Way B37: K'hrst 4C **106**
Gilwell Rd. B34: S End 3A **106**
Gimble Wlk. B17: Harb 3E **115**
(not continuous)
Gin Cridden DY9: Lye. 5A **110**
Gipsy Cl. CV7: Bal C. 4H **169**
Gipsy La. B23: Erd 2A **84**
CV7: Bal C 4H **169**
WV13: W'hall 2B **46**
Girton Ho. B36: Cas B 1B **106**
Gisborn Cl. B10: Small H 3B **118**
GK Davies Trad. Est.
B63: Crad. 5C **110**
Glade, The B26: Sheld 1H **137**
B74: S'tly. .2G **51**
DY9: Lye. .6A **110**
WV8: Pend .6C **14**
Glades, The WS9: A'rdge 2D **34**
Gladeside Cl. WS4: S'fld 1H **33**
Gladstone Dr. B69: Tiv 5C **78**
DY8: Woll. .6B **108**
Gladstone Gro. DY6: K'wfrd 1B **92**

Gladstone Rd.—Gosmoor Ho.

Gladstone Rd. B11: S'brk. 5B 118
B23: Erd 4D 84
B26: Yard 5B 120
B93: Dorr 6H 167
DY8: Woll 5B 108
Gladstone St. B6: Aston 1A 102
B71: W Brom 1A 80
WS2: Wals 5B 32
WS10: Darl 5E 47
Gladys Rd. B25: Yard 4H 119
B67: Smeth 1D 114
Gladys Ter. B67: Smeth 1D 114
Glaisdale Gdns. WV6: Wolv 4E 27
Glaisdale Rd. B28: Hall G 5G 135
Glaisedale Gro. WV13: W'hall 1C 46
Glaisher Dr. WV10: Wolv 3G 27
Glamis Rd. WV12: W'hall 2B 30
Glanville Dr. B75: Four O 5G 37
Glasbury Cft. B38: K Nor 2A 160
Glascote Cl. B90: Shir 3G 149
Glascote Gro. B34: S End 2G 105
Glassford Dr. WV6: Tett 3C 26
Glasshouse Hill DY8: Stourb 2F 125
Glastonbury Cres. WS3: Blox 5E 19
Glastonbury Rd. B14: Yard W 3C 148
B71: W Brom 4B 64
Glastonbury Way WS3: Blox 6E 19
Glaston Dr. B91: Sol 6E 151
Gleads Cft. B62: Quin 2G 129
Gleaston Wlk. WV1: Wolv 3E 45
Gleave Rd. B29: S Oak 4A 132
Glebe Dr. B73: Bold 5F 69
Glebe Farm Rd. B33: Stech 4E 105
Glebe Flds. B76: Curd 1D 88
Glebefields Rd. DY4: Tip 5A 62
Glebeland Cl. B16: Birm 2D 116
Glebe La. DY8: Stourb 1C 124
Glebe Pl. WS10: Darl 5B 46
Glebe Rd. B91: Sol 2H 151
WV13: W'hall 3H 45
Glebe St. WS1: Wals 3C 48
Glebe Way CV7: Bal C 2G 169
Glenavon Rd. B14: K Hth 4H 147
Glen Cl. WS4: Wals 6E 33
Glencoe Rd. B16: Edg 5G 99
Glen Ct. WV3: Wolv 1C 42
WV8: Cod 3G 13
Glencroft Rd. B92: Sol 1H 137
Glendale Cl. B63: Hale 1B 128
WV3: Wolv 3A 42
Glendale Dr. B33: Stech 6D 104
WV5: Wom 1G 73
Glendale Twr. B23: Erd 1H 85
Glendene Cres. B38: K Nor 2G 159
Glendene Dr. B43: Gt Barr 5H 65
Glendevon Cl. B45: Fran 5G 143
Glendon Rd. B23: Erd 1D 84
Glendon Way B93: Dorr 6H 165
Glendower Rd. B42: P Barr 3E 83
WS9: A'rdge 6D 22
Gleneagles Dr. B43: Gt Barr 2A 66
B69: Tiv 2A 96
B75: S Cold 4A 54
Gleneagles Rd. B26: Yard 3E 121
WS3: Blox 4F 19
WV6: Pert 4D 24
Glenelg Dr. DY8: Stourb 3F 125
Glenelg M. WS5: Wals 6H 49
Glenfern Rd. WV14: Cose 5C 60
Glenfield WV8: Pend 5C 14
Glenfield Cl. B76: Walm 2C 70
B91: Sol 1G 165
Glenfield Gro. B29: S Oak 4C 132
Glengarry Cl. B32: Bart G 6H 129
Glengarry Gdns. WV3: Wolv 2D 42
Glenhill Dr. B38: K Nor 1C 160
Glenhurst Cl. WS2: Wals 6D 30
Glenmead Rd. B44: Gt Barr 5F 67
Glenmore Cl. WV3: Wolv 4C 42
Glenmore Dr. B38: K Nor 5H 145
Glen Pk. Rd. DY3: Gorn 5H 75
Glenpark Rd. B8: Salt 4E 103
Glen Ri. B13: Mose 1C 148
Glen Rd. DY3: Up Gor 1A 76
DY8: Stourb 2D 124
Glenroyde B38: K Nor 2A 160
Glen Side B32: Bart G 3B 130
Glenside Av. B92: Sol 2G 137
Glenthorne Dr. WS6: C Hay 2E 7
Glenthorne Rd. B24: Erd 5G 85
Glenthorne Way B24: Erd 5G 85
Glentworth B76: Walm 3E 71
Glentworth Gdns. WV6: Wolv 4F 27
Glenville Dr. B23: Erd 2E 85
Glenwood Cl. DY5: Quar B 3H 109
Glenwood Dr. B90: Ches G 5B 164
Glenwood Ri. WS9: Ston 4F 23
Glenwood Rd. B38: K Nor 1H 159
Globe St. WS10: W'bry 4F 63
Gloucester Flats B65: Row R 5E 97
Gloucester Ho. WV1: Wolv 5G 27
Gloucester Pl. WV13: W'hall 1D 46
Gloucester Rd. DY2: Neth 1F 111
WS5: Wals 3F 49
WS10: W'bry 2A 64
Gloucester St. B5: Birm 2G 117 (6E 5)
WV6: Wolv 5F 27
Gloucester Way B37: Mars G 2C 122
Glover Cl. B28: Hall G 1F 149
Glover Rd. B75: S Cold 6D 54
Glovers Cft. B37: F'bri 6B 106
Glovers Fld. Dr. B7: Nech 2C 102
Glover's Rd. B10: Small H 3C 118
Glover St. B9: Birm 1A 118
B70: W Brom 6B 80
Glovers Trust Homes B73: Bold 5F 69
Glyme Dr. WV6: Tett 4C 26
Glyn Av. WV14: Bils 2B 62
Glyn Dr. WV14: Bils 2B 62
Glyne Ct. B73: S Cold 6H 53
Glyn Farm Rd. B32: Quin 6A 114
Glynn Cres. B63: Crad 4D 110
Glynne Av. DY6: K'wfrd 5B 92
Glyn Rd. B32: Quin 5B 114
Glynside Av. B32: Quin 5B 114
Godrich Ho. B13: Mose 2A 134
Goffs Cl. B32: Bart G 2D 130
Goldborough Cl. WV14: Cose 2F 61
Gold Crest Cl. DY2: Neth 1F 111
Goldcrest Cft. B36: Cas B 1C 106
Goldencrest Dr. B69: O'bry 1E 97
Golden Cft. B20: Hand 6B 82
Goldencross Way DY5: Brie H 2F 109
GOLDEN END 3F 167
Golden End Dr. B93: Know 3F 167
Golden Hillock Rd. B10: Small H 4D 118
B11: S'brk 6D 118
DY2: Neth 6E 95
Goldfinch Cl. B30: B'vlle 5H 131
Goldfinch Rd. DY9: W'cte 2G 125
Goldicroft Rd. WS10: W'bry 1G 63
Goldieslie Cl. B73: W Grn 3H 69
Goldieslie Rd. B73: W Grn 3H 69
Golding St. DY2: Neth 3E 95
GOLDS GREEN 6E 63
Golds Hill Gdns. B21: Hand 2B 100
Golds Hill Rd. B21: Hand 1B 100
Golds Hill Way DY4: Tip 6D 62
Goldsmith Rd. B14: K Hth 5H 133
WS3: Blox 2C 32
Goldstar Way B33: Kitts G 1G 121
Goldthorn Av. WV4: Penn 5F 43
Goldthorn Cres. WV4: Penn 5E 43
Goldthorne Av. B26: Sheld 1G 137
GOLDTHORN HILL 6F 43
Goldthorn Hill WV2: Penn 5E 43
Goldthorn Hill Rd. WV2: Penn 5F 43
GOLDTHORN PARK 1G 59
Goldthorn Rd. WV2: Wolv 5F 43
Goldthorn Ter. WV2: Wolv 4F 43
Goldthorn Wlk. DY5: Brie H 3H 109
Golf Club Dr. WS1: Wals 5E 49
Golf La. WV14: Bils 4F 45
Golson Cl. B75: S Cold 5D 54
Gomeldon Av. B14: K Hth 4H 147
Gomer St. WV13: W'hall 1A 46
Gomer St. W. WV13: W'hall 1A 46
Gonville Ho. B36: Cas B 1B 106
Gooch Cl. DY8: Amb 5E 109
Gooch St. B5: Birm 3G 117
Gooch St. Nth. B5: Birm 2G 117
Goodall Gro. B43: Gt Barr 6G 51
Goodall St. WS1: Wals 2D 48
Goodby Rd. B13: Mose 2F 133
Goode Av. B18: Hock 4C 100
Goode Cl. B68: O'bry 5A 98
Goodeve Wlk. B75: S Cold 6F 55
Goodison Gdns. B24: Erd 2H 85
Goodleigh Av. B31: Longb 3C 158
Goodman Cl. B28: Hall G 1F 149
Goodman St. B1: Birm 6D 100
Goodrest Av. B62: Quin 6F 113
Goodrest Cft. B14: Yard W 3C 148
Goodrest La. B38: Head H 3B 160
(not continuous)
Goodrich Av. WV6: Pert 6G 25
Goodrich Covert B14: K Hth 5E 147
Goodrick Way B7: Nech 3B 102
Goodway Ho. *B4: Birm 1E 5*
(off Shadwell St.)
Goodway Rd. B44: Gt Barr 5G 67
B92: Sol 2A 138
Goodwood Cl. B36: Hodg H 1B 104
Goodwood Dr. B74: S'tly 4H 51
Goodwyn Av. B68: O'bry 4B 114
Goodyear Av. WV10: Bush 1A 28
Goodyear Rd. B67: Smeth 1B 114
Goosemoor La. B23: Erd 6E 69
Gopsal St. B4: Birm 6A 102 (2H 5)
Gorcott La. B90: Dic H 4G 163
Gordon Av. B19: Loz 2F 101
B71: W Brom 5A 64
WV4: E'shll 2B 60
Gordon Cl. B69: Tiv 5D 78
Gordon Ct. B33: Stech 6B 104
Gordon Cres. DY5: Brie H 4A 94
Gordon Dr. DY4: Tip 1C 78
Gordon Pl. WV14: Bils 6E 45
Gordon Rd. B17: Harb 5H 115
B19: Loz 1E 101
Gordon St. *B9: Birm 1B 118*
(off Garrison La.)
WS10: Darl 5D 46
WV2: Wolv 3H 43 (6D 170)
Gorey Cl. WV12: W'hall 1B 30
Gorge Rd. DY3: Sed 5A 60
WV14: Cose 5A 60
Gorleston Gro. B14: K Hth 5B 148
Gorleston Rd. B14: K Hth 5B 148
GORNALWOOD 4G 75
Gornal Wood Crematorium
DY3: Gorn 5G 75
Gorsebrook Rd. WV6: Wolv 4F 27
WV10: Wolv 4G 27
Gorse Cl. B29: W Cas 5E 131
B37: F'bri 1B 122
Gorse Farm Rd. B43: Gt Barr 5A 66
Gorse Farm Wood Nature Reserve 5B 66
Gorsefield Rd. B34: S End 4G 105
Gorse La. WV5: Try 1A 72
Gorsemoor Way WV11: Ess 4B 18
Gorse Rd. DY1: Dud 3C 76
WV11: Wed 1A 30
Gorsey La. B46: Col 5G 89
B47: Wyt 5A 162
WS3: Lit W 3B 8
WS6: Gt Wyr 4F 7
Gorsey Way B46: Col 5G 89
WS9: A'rdge 4A 34
Gorsly Piece B32: Quin 1A 130
Gorstie Cft. B43: Gt Barr 5A 66
Gorsty Av. DY5: Brie H 6G 93
Gorsty Cl. B71: W Brom 5D 64
Gorsty Hayes WV8: Cod 4F 13
Gorsty Hill Rd. B65: B'hth 3B 112
Gorsymead Gro. B31: Longb 5A 144
Gorsy Rd. B32: Quin 1B 130
Gorton Cft. CV7: Bal C 2H 169
Gorway Cl. WS1: Wals 4D 48
Gorway Gdns. WS1: Wals 4E 49
Gorway Rd. WS1: Wals 4D 48
GOSCOTE 5C 20
Goscote Cl. WS3: Wals 2D 32
Goscote Ind. Est. WS3: Blox 6C 20
Goscote La. WS3: Blox, Wals 6C 20
Goscote Lodge Cres. WS3: Wals 2E 33
Goscote Pl. WS3: Wals 2E 33
Goscote Rd. WS3: Pels 6D 20
Gosford St. B12: Bal H 5H 117
Gosford Wlk. B92: Olton 4F 137
Gosmoor Ho. B26: Yard 4C 120

Gospel End Rd.—Green, The

Gospel End Rd. DY3: Sed. 5E **59**
Gospel End St. DY3: Sed 6H **59**
GOSPEL END VILLAGE. 5E 59
Gospel Farm Rd. B27: A Grn. 5H **135**
Gospel La. B27: A Grn. 6A **136**
Gospel Oak Rd. DY4: Tip 4B **62**
Gosport Cl. WV1: Wolv 4D **44**
Goss, The DY5: Brie H 2H **109**
Goss Cft. B29: S Oak 4H **131**
Gossey La. B33: Kitts G. 1G **121**
Gosta Grn. B4: Birm 5H **101** (1G **5**)
Gotham Rd. B26: Yard 5C **120**
GOTHERSLEY 6E 91
Gothersley La. DY7: Stourt 6D **90**
Goths Cl. B65: Row R 5C **96**
Gough Av. WV11: Wed 1D **28**
Gough Rd. B11: S'brk 6D **118**
B15: Edg. 4E **117**
WV14: Cose 4E **61**
Gough St. B1: Birm 2F **117** (6C **4**)
WV1: Wolv 1A **44**
WV13: W'hall 6C **30**
Gould Firm La. WS9: A'rdge 3G **35**
Gowan Rd. B8: Salt 5E **103**
Gower Av. DY6: K'wfrd. 5D **92**
Gower Ho. *B62: Quin* *5F* ***113***
(off Lockington Cft.)
Gower Rd. B62: Quin 5E **113**
DY3: Sed 5F **59**
Gower St. B19: Loz. 2F **101**
WS2: Wals 4H **47**
WV2: Wolv 3A **44**
(not continuous)
WV13: W'hall 1A **46**
Gozzard St. WV14: Bils 6G **45**
Gracechurch Cen. B72: S Cold 6H **53**
Gracemere Cres. B28: Hall G. 4E **149**
Grace Rd. B11: S'brk 4C **118**
B69: Tiv 1C **96**
DY4: Tip 6A **62**
Gracewell Homes B13: Mose 4D **134**
Gracewell Rd. B13: Mose 4D **134**
Grafton Ct. WV6: Wolv. 5D **26**
Grafton Dr. WV13: W'hall 3F **45**
Grafton Gdns. DY3: Lwr G 4F **75**
Grafton Gro. B19: Loz. 2E **101**
Grafton Pl. WV14: Bils. 4G **45**
Grafton Rd. B11: S'brk. 4B **118**
B21: Hand 6H **81**
B68: O'bry 2F **113**
B71: W Brom 3B **80**
B90: Shir 5C **148**
Graham Cl. DY4: Tip 4B **62**
Graham Cres. B45: Rubery 2G **157**
Graham Rd. B8: Salt. 6F **103**
B25: Yard 5A **120**
B62: B'hth 3C **112**
B71: W Brom 3B **80**
DY8: Word 5B **92**
Graham St. B1: Birm. 6E **101** (2A **4**)
B19: Loz 2E **101**
Grainger Cl. DY4: Tip. 1D **78**
Graingers La. B64: Crad H. 3E **111**
Grainger St. DY2: Dud 2F **95**
Graiseley Ct. WV3: Wolv 2G **43** (5A **170**)
Graiseley Hill WV2: Wolv. 3G **43** (6A **170**)
Graiseley La. WV11: Wed 4D **28**
Graiseley Recreation Cen. 3G 43
Graiseley Row WV2: Wolv 3G **43** (6A **170**)
Graiseley St. WV3: Wolv. 2F **43** (5A **170**)
Graith Cl. B28: Hall G. 4E **149**
Grammar School La. B63: Hale. 1A **128**
Grampian Rd. DY8: Amb 5E **109**
Granada Ind. Est. B69: O'bry 2F **97**
Granary, The WS9: A'rdge 2D **34**
Granary Cl. DY6: W Hth. 1G **91**
Granary La. B76: Walm 2D **70**
Granary Rd. WV8: Pend. 6C **14**
Granbourne Rd. WS2: Wals. 5D **30**
Granby Av. B33: Sheld. 2G **121**
Granby Bus. Pk. B33: Sheld. 2H **121**
Granby Cl. B92: Olton 6C **136**
Grandborough Dr. B91: Sol 6E **151**
Grand Cl. B66: Smeth. 6F **99**
Grand Junc. Way WS1: Wals 5B **48**
Grand Theatre. 1H 43 (3C 170)
Grandys Cft. B37: F'bri. 6B **106**
Grange, The B62: Quin. 5F **113**
WV5: Wom. 6G **57**
Grange Av. B75: Four O 6A **38**
WS9: A'rdge 5C **22**
Grange Ct. DY1: Dud 6C **76**
DY9: Lye 2G **125**
WS2: Wals. 1D **46**
WV3: Wolv 2F **43**
Grange Cres. B45: Rubery 1E **157**
B63: Hale 2B **128**
WS4: S'fld 1F **33**
GRANGE ESTATE. 1G 125
Grange Farm Dr. B38: K Nor 6H **145**
Grangefield Cl. WV8: Pend 6D **14**
Grange Hill B62: Hale. 3C **128**
Grange Hill Rd. B38: K Nor 6A **146**
Grange La. B75: R'ley 6A **38**
DY6: K'wfrd 5D **92**
DY9: Lye 2G **125**
Grange Ri. B38: K Nor. 2B **160**
Grange Rd. B6: Aston 1G **101**
B10: Small H 2D **118**
B14: K Hth 5F **133**
B24: Erd. 2H **85**
B29: S Oak. 2B **132**
B63: Hale 2B **128**
B64: Old H 2A **112**
B66: Smeth 6E **99**
B70: W Brom 4H **79**
B91: Sol 6C **136**
B93: Dorr 6F **167**
CV7: Bal C 2F **169**
DY1: Dud 6D **76**
DY9: Lye 1G **125**
WV2: Wolv 5F **43**
WV6: Tett 4A **26**
WV14: Cose. 6D **60**
Grange St. DY1: Dud 6D **76**
WS1: Wals 4D **48**
Grangewood B73: Bold 6G **69**
Grangewood Ct. B92: Olton 6C **136**
Granmore Ho. B90: Shir. 6C **150**
Granshaw Cl. B38: K Nor. 6B **146**
Grant Cl. B71: W Brom 2A **80**
DY6: K'wfrd 1B **92**
Grant Ct. B30: K Nor 2C **146**
Grantham Rd. B11: S'brk. 4B **118**
B66: Smeth. 6F **99**
Grantley Cres.
DY6: K'wfrd 3A **92**
Grantley Dr. B37: F'bri 6D **106**
Granton Cl. B14: K Hth. 2F **147**
Granton Rd. B14: K Hth 2F **147**
Grantown Gro. WS3: Blox 3G **19**
Grant St. B15: Birm 3F **117**
WS3: Blox 1H **31**
Granville Cl. WV2: Wolv. 3H **43** (6D **170**)
Granville Dr. DY6: K'wfrd 4D **92**
Granville Rd. B64: Old H 3B **112**
B93: Dorr. 6H **167**
Granville Sq. B15: Birm 2E **117** (6A **4**)
Granville St. B1: Birm. 2E **117** (6A **4**)
WV2: Wolv 3H **43** (6D **170**)
WV13: W'hall 6A **30**
Grasdene Gro. B17: Harb. 1G **131**
Grasmere Av. B74: Lit A. 1A **52**
WV6: Pert 6F **25**
Grasmere Cl. B43: Gt Barr. 6B **66**
DY6: K'wfrd 2H **91**
WV6: Tett 1C **26**
WV11: Wed 2E **29**
Grasmere Ho. B69: O'bry 5D **96**
Grasmere Rd. B21: Hand. 2B **100**
Grassington Dr. B37: F'bri 2B **122**
Grassmere Ct. WS6: C Hay 2D **6**
Grassmere Dr. DY8: Stourb. 1D **124**
Grassmoor Rd. B38: K Nor 5A **146**
Grassy La. WV11: Wed 6D **16**
Graston Cl. B16: Birm 1C **116**
Gratham Cl. DY5: Brie H. 4F **109**
Grattidge Rd. B27: A Grn. 3B **136**
Gravel Bank B32: Bart G 2B **130**
Gravel Hill WV5: Wom. 1H **73**
GRAVELLY HILL 5E 85
Gravelly Hill B23: Erd 6D **84**
Gravelly Hill Nth. B23: Erd. 5E **85**
Gravelly Hill Station (Rail) 5E **85**
Gravelly Ind. Pk. B24: Erd 1E **103**
(Jarvis Way)
B24: Erd 1F **103**
(Thompson Dr.)
Gravelly La. B23: Erd 2F **85**
WS9: Ston 5G **23**
Graydon Ct. B74: S Cold 4H **53**
Grayfield Av. B13: Mose 2A **134**
Grayland Cl. B27: A Grn 3H **135**
Grayling Cl. WS10: Mox 2B **62**
Grayling Rd. DY9: Lye. 5G **109**
Grayling Wlk. B37: Chel W. 6E **107**
WV10: Wolv. 5D **28**
Grayshott Cl. B23: Erd 2E **85**
Grays Rd. B17: Harb 5H **115**
Gray St. B9: Birm. 1B **118**
Grayswood Pk. Rd. B32: Quin 5A **114**
Grayswood Rd. B31: Longb. 2D **158**
Grazebrook Cft. B32: Bart G. 5B **130**
Grazebrook Ind. Pk. DY2: Dud. 3D **94**
Grazebrook Rd. DY2: Dud 2E **95**
Grazewood Cl. WV12: W'hall 1B **30**
Greadier St. WV12: W'hall. 4C **30**
Gt. Arthur St. B66: Smeth 2D **98**
GREAT BARR 1A 66
Great Barr Leisure Cen. 4F 67
Gt. Barr St. B9: Birm 1A **118**
Gt. Brickkiln St. WV3: Wolv. 2E **43**
GREAT BRIDGE. 1E 79
Great Bri. DY4: Tip. 2D **78**
Gt. Bridge Ind. Est. DY4: Tip 6C **62**
Gt. Bridge Rd. WV14: Bils 1A **62**
Gt. Bridge St. B70: W Brom. 2E **79**
Gt. Bridge W. Ind. Cen. DY4: Tip 1D **78**
Gt. Brook St. B7: Birm 5A **102** (1H **5**)
Gt. Charles St. WS8: Bwnhls. 5B **10**
Gt. Charles St. Queensway
B3: Birm 6F **101** (3C **4**)
Gt. Colmore St. B15: Birm 3F **117**
Gt. Cornbow B63: Hale. 2B **128**
Great Cft. Ho. *WS10: Darl* *5D* ***46***
(off Lawrence Way)
Gt. Farley Dr. B31: Longb 6A **144**
Gt. Francis St. B7: Birm. 5B **102**
Gt. Hampton Row B19: Birm 5E **101**
Gt. Hampton St. B18: Birm 4E **101**
WV1: Wolv 6F **27**
(not continuous)
Great Hill DY1: Dud 6D **76**
Gt. King St. B19: Birm 4E **101**
(not continuous)
Gt. King St. Nth. B19: Hock 3E **101**
Gt. Lister St. B7: Birm 5H **101**
Great Mdw. DY4: Tip 2B **78**
Gt. Moor Rd. WV6: Patt. 1A **40**
Great Oaks B26: Sheld 6F **121**
Greatorex Ct. B71: W Brom 5H **63**
GREAT PARK 6H 143
Gt. Stone Rd. B31: N'fld. 4E **145**
Gt. Tindal St. B16: Birm. 1C **116**
Gt. Western Arc. B2: Birm 6G **101** (3E **5**)
Gt. Western Cl. B18: Win G. 3A **100**
Gt. Western Dr. B64: Old H 2A **112**
Gt. Western Ind. Est. B18: Win G 3A **100**
Gt. Western St. WS10: W'bry 3E **63**
WV1: Wolv 6H **27** (1C **170**)
Gt. Western Way DY4: Tip. 1D **78**
Gt. Wood Rd. B10: Small H 2C **118**
GREAT WYRLEY 2E 7
Greaves, The B76: Min 1B **88**
Greaves Av. WS5: Wals 4G **49**
Greaves Cl. WS5: Wals 3G **49**
Greaves Cres. WV12: W'hall 1C **30**
Greaves Rd. DY2: Neth. 4F **95**
Greaves Sq. B38: K Nor. 6D **146**
Grebe Cl. B23: Erd 4B **84**
Greek Cathedral 3A 4
Green, The B23: Erd 2G **85**
B31: Longb 5A **144**
B32: Quin. 5G **113**
B36: Cas B 2F **105**
B38: K Nor 5B **146**
B68: O'bry 1H **113**
B72: W Grn 4B **70**
B91: Sol. 2H **151**
CV7: Mer 4H **141**
DY8: Word 1B **108**

Green, The—Griffin Rd.

Green, The WS3: Blox 6H **19**
(not continuous)
WS9: A'rdge 3D **34**
(not continuous)
WS10: Darl 4D **46**
WV5: Try 5C **56**
Greenacre Dr. WV8: Bilb 5H **13**
Greenacre Rd. DY4: Tip 4A **62**
Green Acres B27: A Grn 3H **135**
DY3: Sed 4F **59**
WV5: Wom 2F **73**
Greenacres B32: Bart G 4C **130**
B76: Walm 5E **71**
WV6: Tett 4H **25**
Greenacres Av. WV10: Bush 5D **16**
Greenacres Cl. WS9: A'rdge 1G **51**
Grn. Acres Rd. B38: K Nor 1H **159**
Greenaleigh Rd. B14: Yard W 3D **148**
Green Av. B28: Hall G 4E **135**
Greenaway Cl. B43: Gt Barr 2E **67**
Greenaway Ct. *WV10: F'stne* *1E 17*
(off Avenue, The)
Grn. Bank Av. B28: Hall G 4E **135**
Greenbank Gdns. DY8: Word 1C **108**
Greenbank Rd. CV7: Bal C 3F **169**
Grn. Barns La. WS14: Lit H 1H **37**
Greenbush Dr. B63: Hale 6A **112**
Green Cl. B47: Wyt 6A **162**
Green Ct. B24: Erd 5E **85**
B28: Hall G 5F **135**
Green Cft. B9: Bord G 6G **103**
WV14: Bils 5F **45**
Greencroft DY6: K'wfrd 5B **92**
Green Dr. B32: Bart G 4A **130**
WV10: Oxl 2G **27**
Greenend Rd. B13: Mose 3H **133**
Greenfels Ri. DY2: Dud 1H **95**
Greenfield Av. B64: Crad H 2D **110**
CV7: Bal C 2G **169**
DY8: Stourb 6D **108**
Greenfield Cft. WV14: Cose 3F **61**
Greenfield Ho. B26: Sheld 5H **121**
Greenfield La. WV10: F'hses 2H **15**
Greenfield Rd. B17: Harb 6G **115**
B43: Gt Barr 6G **65**
B67: Smeth 5C **98**
Green Flds. WS9: A'rdge 2C **34**
Greenfields Rd. DY6: K'wfrd 4B **92**
WS4: S'fld 5H **21**
WV5: Wom 2G **73**
Greenfield Vw. DY3: Sed 6F **59**
Greenfinch Rd. B36: Cas B 1C **106**
DY9: W'cte 2H **125**
Greenford Ho. B23: Erd 1B **84**
B70: W Brom *1C 98*
(off Maria St.)
Greenford Rd. B14: K Hth 4B **148**
Green Gables B74: S Cold 4H **53**
Grn. Gables Dr. B47: H'wd 2A **162**
Greenhill WV5: Wom 1H **73**
Grn. Hill Av. B14: K Hth 4H **133**
Greenhill Cl. WV12: W'hall 4B **30**
Greenhill Ct. WV5: Wom 2H **73**
Greenhill Dr. B29: S Oak 4G **131**
Greenhill Gdns. B43: Gt Barr 3A **66**
B62: Hale 5D **112**
WV5: Wom 2H **73**
Greenhill Rd. B13: Mose 4H **133**
B21: Hand 5H **81**
B62: B'hth 4D **112**
B72: W Grn 5H **69**
DY3: Up Gor 2A **76**
Greenhill Wlk. WS1: Wals 3D **48**
Grn. Hill Way B90: Shir 2H **149**
Greenhill Way WS9: A'rdge 6D **22**
Greenholm Rd. B44: Gt Barr 6G **67**
Greening Dr. B15: Edg 4C **116**
Greenland Cl. DY6: K'wfrd 1C **92**
Greenland Ct. B8: Salt 3E **103**
Greenland Ri. B92: Sol 6H **137**
Greenland Rd. B29: S Oak 4D **132**
Greenlands WV5: Wom 6F **57**
Greenlands Rd. B37: Chel W 1D **122**
Green La. B9: Small H 2C **118**
B21: Hand 1G **99**
B32: Quin 5A **114**
B36: Cas B 1H **105**
Green La. B38: K Nor 1A **160**
B43: Gt Barr 5H **65**
B46: Col 4H **107**
(Castle Dr., not continuous)
B46: Col 1D **106**
(Collector Rd., not continuous)
B46: Col 5F **107**
(Ryeclose Cft.)
B62: B'hth 2D **112**
B90: Shir 6E **149**
CV7: Bal C 2H **169**
DY3: Up Gor 2B **76**
DY6: K'wfrd 2B **92**
DY9: Lye 6H **109**
WS2: Wals 3A **32**
WS3: Blox 2A **32**
WS3: Pels 3E **21**
WS4: S'fld 6G **21**
WS7: Hamm 3C **10**
WS9: A'rdge 4G **35**
WS9: Wals W 6G **21**
WV6: Tett 2C **26**
Green La. Ind. Est. B9: Bord G 2E **119**
GREEN LANES 4E **45**
Green Lanes B73: W Grn 6H **69**
WV14: Bils 4E **45**
Green La. Wlk. B38: K Nor 1B **160**
Greenleas Gdns. B63: Hale 2C **128**
Green Leigh B23: Erd 5F **69**
Greenleighs DY3: Sed 2H **59**
Greenly Rd. WV4: Penn, E'shll 6H **43**
Grn. Man Entry DY1: Dud 6F **77**
Green Mdw. DY9: Pedm 5F **125**
WV11: Wed 4G **29**
Green Mdw. Cl. WV5: Wom 2E **73**
Green Mdw. Rd. B29: W Cas 6D **130**
WV12: W'hall 2B **30**
Greenoak Cres. B30: Stir 5E **133**
WV14: Cose 6C **60**
Grn. Oak Rd. WV8: Bilb 5H **13**
Green Pk. Av. WV14: Bils 3E **45**
Green Pk. Dr. WV14: Bils 3E **45**
Green Pk. Rd. B31: N'fld 5C **144**
DY2: Dud 1H **95**
Greenridge Rd. B20: Hand 2A **82**
Green Rd. B13: Mose 4D **134**
DY2: Dud 2F **95**
Grn. Rock La. WS3: Blox 6B **20**
Greenroyde DY9: Pedm 4F **125**
Greens, The *WV6: Pert* *6E 25*
(off Edge Hill Dr.)
Greensand WV14: Cose 3F **61**
GREENSFORGE 3D **90**
Greensforge La. DY7: Stourt 6E **91**
Greens Health & Fitness Club 1H **157**
Greenside B17: Harb 6G **115**
B90: Ches G 5B **164**
Greenside Gdns. WS5: Wals 1F **65**
Greenside Rd. B24: Erd 2A **86**
Greenside Way WS5: Wals 1D **64**
Greensill Av. DY4: Tip 5H **61**
Greenslade Cft. B31: N'fld 5E **145**
Greenslade Rd. B90: Shir 5C **148**
DY3: Sed 3F **59**
WS5: Wals 4G **49**
Greensleeves B74: Four O 2F **53**
Greenstead Rd. B13: Mose 4D **134**
Green St. B12: Birm 2H **117** (6H **5**)
B67: Smeth 4D **98**
B69: O'bry 2G **97**
B70: W Brom 6C **80**
DY8: Stourb 6D **108**
WS2: Wals 6A **32**
WV14: Cose 5E **61**
Greensway WV11: Wed 1D **28**
Greenvale B31: N'fld 2D **144**
Greenvale Av. B26: Sheld 5H **121**
Green Wlk. B17: Harb 4D **114**
Greenway B20: Hand 1B **82**
DY3: Sed 4A **60**
WS9: A'rdge 5D **22**
Greenway, The B37: Mars G 5C **122**
B73: S'tly 2B **68**
Greenway Av. DY8: Word 2C **108**
Greenway Dr. B73: S'tly 2B **68**
Greenway Gdns. B38: K Nor 2A **160**
DY3: Sed 4A **60**
Greenway Rd. WV14: Bils 1G **61**
Greenways B31: N'fld 5D **130**
B63: Crad 6E **111**
DY8: Word 2A **108**
Greenway St. B9: Bord G 2C **118**
Greenway Wlk. B33: Kitts G 2A **122**
Green Wickets B14: K Hth 1H **147**
Greenwood B25: Yard 3B **120**
Greenwood Av. B27: A Grn 3G **135**
B65: Row R 6D **96**
B68: O'bry 4H **97**
Greenwood Cl. B14: K Hth 2G **147**
Greenwood Cotts. *DY1: Dud* *2C 76*
(off Maple Grn.)
Greenwood Pk. WS9: A'rdge 5E **23**
Greenwood Pl. B44: K'sdng 4B **68**
Greenwood Rd. B71: W Brom 5H **63**
WS9: A'rdge 5C **22**
WV10: Oxl 2F **27**
Greenwoods, The DY8: Stourb 6C **108**
Greenwood Sq. *B37: Chel W* *1D 122*
(off Chelmsley Wood Shop. Cen.)
Greenwood Way *B37: Chel W* *1D 122*
(off Chelmsley Wood Shop. Cen.)
GREET 6D **118**
Greethurst Dr. B13: Mose 3C **134**
GREETS GREEN 4F **79**
Greets Grn. Ind. Est. B70: W Brom 3F **79**
Greets Grn. Rd. B70: W Brom 4F **79**
Greetville Cl. B34: Stech 4E **105**
Gregg Ct. B12: Bal H 1H **133**
Gregory Av. B29: W Cas 5D **130**
Gregory Cl. WS10: W'bry 3F **63**
Gregory Ct. WV11: Wed 4F **29**
Gregory Dr. DY1: Dud 5C **76**
Gregory Rd. DY8: Woll 6A **108**
Gregston Ind. Est. B69: O'bry 2H **97**
Grendon Dr. B73: New O 2D **68**
Grendon Gdns. WV3: Penn 5B **42**
Grendon Rd. B14: K Hth 4A **148**
B92: Olton 5C **136**
Grenfell Ct. B72: W Grn 4H **69**
Grenfell Dr. B15: Edg 3B **116**
Grenfell Rd. WS3: Blox 4B **20**
Grenville Cl. WS2: Wals 6D **30**
Grenville Dr. B23: Erd 4B **84**
B66: Smeth 1B **98**
Grenville Pl. B70: W Brom 4E **79**
Grenville Rd. B90: Shir 5H **149**
DY1: Dud 6A **76**
Gresham Rd. B28: Hall G 1F **149**
B68: O'bry 3A **98**
Gresham Twr. B12: Birm 3H **117**
Gresley Cl. B75: Four O 5G **37**
Gresley Gro. B23: Erd 5C **84**
Gressel La. B33: Kitts G 6G **105**
Grestone Av. B20: Hand 3A **82**
Greswolde Dr. B24: Erd 3H **85**
Greswolde Pk. Rd. B27: A Grn 1H **135**
Greswolde Rd. B11: S'hll 2C **134**
B91: Sol 1C **150**
Greswold Gdns. B34: Stech 4E **105**
Greswold St. B71: W Brom 2H **79**
Gretton Cres. WS9: A'rdge 4A **34**
Gretton Rd. B23: Erd 6D **68**
WS9: A'rdge 4B **34**
Greville Dr. B15: Edg 5E **117**
Grevis Cl. B13: Mose 1H **133**
Grevis Rd. B25: Yard 2C **120**
Greyfort Cres. B92: Olton 4D **136**
Greyfriars Cl. B92: Olton 1B **150**
DY1: Dud 4A **76**
Greyhound La. DY8: Stourb 3B **124**
WV4: Lwr P 6E **41**
Greyhurst Cft. B91: Sol 1G **165**
Grey Mill Cl. B90: M'path 3D **164**
Greystoke Av. B36: Hodg H 2B **104**
Greystoke Dr. DY6: K'wfrd 3B **92**
Greystone Pas. DY1: Dud 6D **76**
Greystone St. DY1: Dud 6E **77**
Greytree Cres. B93: Dorr 6A **166**
Grice St. B70: W Brom 1A **98**
Griffin Cl. B31: N'fld 1F **145**
Griffin Gdns. B17: Harb 1H **131**
Griffin Ind. Est. B65: Row R 6F **97**
Griffin La. B90: Dic H 4G **163**
Griffin Rd. B23: Erd 2C **84**

Griffin's Brook Cl. B30: B'vlle 6H **131**
Griffin's Brook La. B30: B'vlle 1G **145**
Griffin St. B70: W Brom. 4B **80**
DY2: Neth. 5E **95**
WV1: Wolv 2B **44**
Griffiths Dr. WV5: Wom 2G **73**
WV11: Wed 1H **29**
Griffiths Rd. B71: W Brom. 4A **64**
DY1: Dud 1C **76**
WV12: W'hall 1D **30**
Griffiths St. DY4: Tip 2G **77**
Grigg Gro. B31: Longb. 6C **144**
Grimley Rd. B31: N'fld. 5H **145**
Grimpits La. B38: Head H 2C **160**
Grimshaw Rd. B27: A Grn 4G **135**
Grimstone St. WV10: Wolv. . . . 6H **27** (1D **170**)
Grindleford Rd. B42: Gt Barr 6F **67**
Gristhorpe Rd. B29: S Oak. 4C **132**
Grizedale Cl. B45: Fran 5H **143**
Grocott Rd. WS10: Mox. 1B **62**
Grosmont Av. B12: Bal H 5A **118**
Grosvenor Av. B20: Hand. 5E **83**
B74: S'tly 2H **51**
Grosvenor Cl. B75: R'ley 2A **54**
WV10: Bush. 5H **15**
Grosvenor Ct. B20: Hand 5E **83**
B38: K Nor 5B **146**
DY3: Lwr G 5H **75**
DY9: Pedm 4F 125
(off Redlake Rd.)
WV3: Wolv 2G **43** (5A **170**)
WV11: Wed. 4F **29**
Grosvenor Cres. WV10: Bush 5H **15**
Grosvenor Ho. B23: Erd. 2G **85**
Grosvenor Pk. WV4: Penn 6D **42**
Grosvenor Rd. B6: Aston 1B **102**
B17: Harb. 5E **115**
B20: Hand 5E **83**
B68: O'bry 6G **97**
B91: Sol. 6D **150**
DY3: Lwr G 5H **75**
WV4: E'shll. 2A **60**
WV10: Bush. 5H **15**
Grosvenor Rd. Sth. DY3: Gorn 5H **75**
Grosvenor Shop. Cen. B31: N'fld. 3E **145**
Grosvenor Sq. B28: Hall G 2F **149**
Grosvenor St. B5: Birm. 6H **101** (3G **5**)
Grosvenor St. W. B16: Birm 2D **116**
Grosvenor Ter. B15: Birm 2D **116**
Grosvenor Way DY5: Quar B 4A **110**
Grotto La. WV6: Tett. 4C **26**
Groucutt St. WV14: Cose 5E **61**
Grounds Dr. B74: Four O 6F **37**
Grounds Rd. B74: Four O 6F **37**
Grout St. B70: W Brom. 3E **79**
Grove, The B8: Salt 5C **102**
B31: Longb. 1F **159**
B43: Gt Barr. 1A **66**
B45: Coft H 5B **158**
B46: Col. 5H **107**
B65: Row R 1C **112**
B74: Lit A. 4D **36**
B92: H Ard 4A **140**
DY5: Brie H 3G **109**
WS5: Wals 2F **65**
WV4: E'shll. 6A **44**
WV11: Wed 3D **28**
Grove Av. B13: Mose 3A **134**
B21: Hand 1B **100**
B27: A Grn. 2H **135**
B29: S Oak. 4A **132**
B63: Hale. 2H **127**
B91: Sol. 2G **151**
Grove Cott. Rd. B9: Small H 1D **118**
Grove Cotts. WS3: Blox 1H **31**
Grove Ct. B42: Gt Barr 1B **82**
Grove Cres. B70: W Brom 6C **80**
DY5: Brie H 4G **93**
WS3: Pels 4D **20**
GROVE END 2H **71**
Grove Farm Dr. B75: S Cold 6D **54**
Grovefield Cres. CV7: Bal C. 1H **169**
Grove Gdns. B20: Hand 5B **82**
Grove Hill WS5: Wals. 3A **50**
Grove Hill Rd. B21: Hand. 6B **82**
Groveland Rd. DY4: Tip 4A **78**
Grovelands Cres. WV10: F'hses 4H **15**
Grove La. B17: Harb 1G **131**
B20: Hand 5B **82**
B21: Hand 1B **100**
B66: Smeth 4G **99**
(not continuous)
WS3: Lit W. 4C **8**
WV6: Tett. 1H **41**
Groveley La. B31: Longb. 3C **158**
B45: Coft H 5A **158**
Grove M. B31: Longb. 1F **159**
Grove Pk. DY6: W Hth 1A **92**
Grove Rd. B11: S'hll. 2C **134**
B14: K Hth 6F **133**
B68: O'bry 2B **114**
B91: Sol. 2G **151**
B93: Know 5C **166**
DY9: W'cte. 1B **126**
Groveside Way WS3: Pels 2E **21**
Grove St. B66: Smeth 5H **99**
DY2: Dud 1G **95**
WV2: Wolv 3H **43** (6C **170**)
WV10: Wolv. 6B **28**
Grove Ter. WS1: Wals 2D **48**
GROVE VALE 4H **65**
Grove Va. Av. B43: Gt Barr 4G **65**
Grove Vs. B64: Crad H 4F **111**
Grove Way B74: S'tly 4H **51**
Grovewood Dr. B38: K Nor. 6A **146**
Guardian Ct. B26: Yard 4D **120**
B31: N'fld. 4B **144**
B91: Sol. 4H **151**
Guardian Ho. B68: O'bry 4A **114**
Guardians Way B31: N'fld 5C **130**
Guernsey Dr. B36: Cas B 3D **106**
Guest Av. WV11: Wed 1E **29**
Guest Gro. B19: Hock. 3E **101**
Guild Av. WS3: Blox. 2B **32**
Guild Cl. B16: Birm 1C **116**
Guildford Ct. *B29: W Cas. 6G 131*
(off Abdon Av.)
Guildford Cft. B37: Mars G. 3B **122**
Guildford Rd. B19: Hock. 3F **101**
Guildford St. B19: Loz 2F **101**
Guildhall M., The *WS1: Wals 2D 48*
(off Goodall St.)
Guillemard Ct. B37: Chel W. 2D **122**
Guiting Rd. B29: W Cas 6E **131**
Gullane Cl. B38: K Nor 6H **145**
Gullswood Cl. B14: K Hth. 5F **147**
Gumbleberrys Cl. B8: W End. 5A **104**
Gun Barrel Ind. Est. B64: Crad H. 5H **111**
Gunmakers Wlk. B19: Loz 2F **101**
Gunner Gro. B75: S Cold 5E **55**
Gunner La. B45: Rubery 2D **156**
Gunns Way B92: Olton 6B **136**
Guns La. B70: W Brom 3H **79**
Gunstock Cl. B74: S'tly 4G **51**
GUNSTONE 1G **13**
Gunstone La. WV8: Cod, Cod W 2F **13**
(not continuous)
GUNS VILLAGE. 3H **79**
Guns Village Stop (MM) 3H **79**
Gunter Rd. B24: Erd. 4C **86**
Gupta Trad. Est. B69: O'bry 6F **79**
Gurnard Cl. WV12: W'hall 6B **18**
Gurney Pl. WS2: Wals 4G **31**
Gurney Rd. WS2: Wals 4G **31**
Guthram Cl. B23: Erd 5E **69**
Guthrie Cl. B19: Hock. 3F **101**
Guthrum Cl. WV6: Pert. 4F **25**
Guy Av. WV10: Bush 3H **27**
Guys Cliffe Av. B76: Walm. 4D **70**
Guy's La. DY3: Gorn. 5F **75**
Guys Motors Ind. Pk. WV10: Wolv 4B **28**
Gwalia Gro. B23: Erd 3F **85**
Gwendoline Way WS9: Wals W. 3D **22**
GWS Ind. Est. WS10: W'bry 4D **62**
Gypsy La. B46: Wat O. 5F **89**

H

Habberley Cft. B91: Sol 6F **151**
Habberley Rd. B65: Row R 1D **112**
Habitat Ct. B24: Erd 2A **86**
B76: Walm 2D **70**
Hackett Cl. WV14: Cose 4B **60**
Hackett Ct. *B69: O'bry 2G 97*
(off Canal St.)
Hackett Dr. B66: Smeth 2B **98**
Hackett Rd. B65: Row R. 6E **97**
Hackett St. DY4: Tip. 6C **62**
Hackford Rd. WV4: E'shll 1B **60**
Hack St. B9: Birm. 2A **118**
Hackwood Ho. B69: O'bry 4D **96**
Hackwood Rd. WS10: W'bry 3H **63**
Hadcroft Grange DY9: W'cte 1H **125**
Hadcroft Rd. DY9: Lye 1G **125**
Haddock Rd. WV14: Bils 4E **45**
Haddon Cres. WV12: W'hall. 2C **30**
Haddon Cft. B63: Hale 4E **127**
Haddon Rd. B42: Gt Barr 6F **67**
Haddon Twr. B5: Birm. 3F **117**
Haden Cir. B7: Birm 5A **102** (1H **5**)
Haden Cl. B64: Crad H. 4H **111**
DY8: Word 1B **108**
Haden Ct. *B12: Birm 4H 117*
(off Belgrave Middleway)
Haden Cres. WV11: Wed 3A **30**
Haden Cross Dr. B64: Crad H. 4A **112**
Hadendale B64: Crad H 4A **112**
Haden Hill 3H **111**
Haden Hill WV3: Wolv 1E **43**
Haden Hill Leisure Cen. 3H **111**
Haden Hill Rd. B63: Hale. 5A **112**
Haden Pk. Rd. B64: Crad H 4G **111**
Haden Rd. B64: Old H 1G **111**
DY4: Tip. 4A **62**
Haden St. B12: Bal H. 5H **117**
Haden Wlk. B65: Row R 6C **96**
Haden Way B12: Bal H. 5H **117**
Hadfield Cl. B24: Erd 4B **86**
Hadfield Cft. B19: Birm 4E **101**
Hadfield Way B37: F'bri 5C **106**
Hadland Rd. B33: Sheld 2F **121**
Hadleigh Cft. B76: Walm 1E **87**
Hadley Cl. B47: Wyt. 4A **162**
Hadley Ct. B16: Edg. 2H **115**
Hadley Cft. B66: Smeth 2E **99**
Hadley Pl. WV14: Bils 4E **45**
Hadley Rd. WS2: Wals 3F **31**
WV14: Bils 4E **45**
Hadleys Cl. DY2: Neth 5G **95**
Hadley Stadium 6E **99**
Hadley St. B68: O'bry 5G **97**
Hadley Way WS2: Wals 3F **31**
Hadlow Cft. B33: Sheld 4H **121**
Hadrian Dr. B46: Col 6H **89**
Hadyn Gro. B26: Sheld 5F **121**
Hadzor Rd. B68: O'bry 3B **114**
Hafren Cl. B45: Fran 5H **143**
Hafton Gro. B9: Small H. 2D **118**
Haggar St. WV2: Wolv 5G **43**
HAGLEY. 6G **125**
Hagley C'way. DY9: Hag 6B **126**
Hagley Cl. DY9: Hag 6G **125**
Hagley Hall Gdns. DY9: Hag 6H **125**
Hagley Hill DY9: Hag. 6A **126**
Hagley Mall B63: Hale 2B **128**
Hagley Pk. Dr. B45: Redn 3G **157**
Hagley Rd. B16: Edg 2E **115**
B63: Hale 5E **127**
DY8: Pedm, Stourb 1E **125**
DY9: Pedm. 4G **125**
Hagley Rd. W. B17: Harb. 4A **114**
B32: Quin. 5G **113**
B62: Quin. 5G **113**
B68: O'bry 5G **113**
Hagley St. B63: Hale 2B **128**
Hagley Vw. Rd. DY2: Dud 1E **95**
Hagley Vs. *B12: Bal H 1B 134*
(off Taunton Rd.)
B12: S'hll 6B 118
(off Taunton Rd.)
Hagley Wood La. DY9: Hag 5D **126**
Haig Cl. B75: S Cold 4A **54**
Haig Pl. B13: Mose 6A **134**
Haig Rd. DY2: Dud. 6H **77**
Haig St. B71: W Brom 2A **80**
Hailes Pk. Cl. WV4: Wolv 5A **44**
Hailsham Rd. B23: Erd. 2F **85**
Hailstone Cl. B65: Row R 4A **96**
Haines Cl. DY4: Tip 3B **78**
Haines St. B70: W Brom 5B **80**

Hainfield Dr.—Hannah Rd.

Hainfield Dr. B91: Sol . . . 2A **152**
Hainge Rd. B69: Tiv . . . 5C **78**
Hainult Cl. DY8: Word . . . 5B **92**
Halas Ind. Est. B62: Hale . . . 6B **112**
Halberton St. B66: Smeth . . . 5H **99**
Haldane Ct. B33: Yard . . . 1F **121**
Haldon Gro. B31: Longb . . . 2C **158**
Halecroft Av. WV11: Wed . . . 4F **29**
Hale Gro. B24: Erd . . . 3B **86**
Halesbury Ct. *B63: Hale* . . . *3H 127*
(off Ombersley Rd.)
Hales Cres. B67: Smeth . . . 6C **98**
Halescroft Sq. B31: N'fld . . . 1C **144**
Hales Gdns. B23: Erd . . . 5C **68**
Hales La. B67: Smeth . . . 5C **98**
Halesmere Way B63: Hale . . . 2C **128**
HALESOWEN . . . **2B 128**
Halesowen By-Pass B62: Hale . . . 2D **128**
B62: Roms, Hale . . . 4H **127**
Halesowen Ind. Pk. B62: Hale . . . 5B **112**
(Coombs Rd.)
B62: Hale . . . 5C **112**
(Hereward Ri.)
Halesowen Leisure Cen. . . . 2B **128**
Halesowen Rd. B61: L Ash . . . 6C **156**
B62: Quin . . . 5E **113**
B64: Crad H . . . 3H **111**
B64: Old H . . . 1G **111**
B65: B'hth . . . 3C **112**
DY2: Neth . . . 4E **95**
(Baptist End Rd.)
DY2: Neth . . . 5F **95**
(Cradley Rd.)
Halesowen St. B69: O'bry . . . 2F **97**
Hales Rd. B63: Hale . . . 2A **128**
(Highfield La.)
B63: Hale . . . 1A **128**
(Islington)
WS10: W'bry . . . 1G **63**
Hales Way B69: O'bry . . . 2F **97**
Halesworth Rd. WV9: Pend . . . 6D **14**
Hale Trad. Est. DY4: Tip . . . 1B **78**
Halewood Gro. B28: Hall G . . . 6G **135**
Haley St. WV12: W'hall . . . 4C **30**
Halfcot Av. DY9: Pedm . . . 2G **125**
Halford Cres. WS3: Wals . . . 4D **32**
Halford Gro. B24: Erd . . . 3C **86**
Halford Rd. B91: Sol . . . 1C **150**
Halford's La. B66: Smeth . . . 2E **99**
B71: W Brom . . . 1E **99**
Halford's La. Ind. Est. B66: Smeth . . . 1E **99**
Halfords Pk. B66: Smeth . . . 1E **99**
Halfpenny Fld. Wlk. B35: Cas V . . . 5E **87**
Halfway Cl. B44: Gt Barr . . . 1G **83**
Halifax Ho. B5: Bal H . . . 4F **117**
Halifax Rd. B90: Shir . . . 4H **149**
Haliscombe Gro. B6: Aston . . . 1G **101**
Halkett Glade B33: Stech . . . 6B **104**
Halladale B38: K Nor . . . 6B **146**
Hallam Cl. B71: W Brom . . . 2C **80**
Hallam Ct. B71: W Brom . . . 2B **80**
Hallam Cres. WV10: Wolv . . . 3A **28**
Hallam Dr. B71: W Brom . . . 2C **80**
Hallam St. B12: Bal H . . . 6G **117**
B71: W Brom . . . 3B **80**
Hallbridge Cl. WS3: Pels . . . 5D **20**
Hallbridge Way B69: Tiv . . . 5B **78**
Hallchurch Rd. DY2: Dud . . . 2B **94**
Hall Cres. B71: W Brom . . . 1A **80**
Hallcroft Cl. B72: W Grn . . . 6A **70**
Hallcroft Way B93: Know . . . 3C **166**
WS9: A'rdge . . . 4E **35**
Hall Dale Cl. B28: Hall G . . . 2F **149**
Hall Dr. B37: Mars G . . . 4C **122**
HALL END
West Bromwich . . . **1B 80**
Hall End WS10: W'bry . . . 2F **63**
Hallens Dr. WS10: W'bry . . . 2D **62**
Hallett Dr. WV3: Wolv . . . 2F **43** (5A **170**)
Hallewell Rd. B16: Edg . . . 6H **99**
HALL GREEN
Bilston . . . **3G 61**
Birmingham . . . **5F 135**
West Bromwich . . . **4A 64**
Hall Green Little Theatre . . . 3G **135**
Hall Grn. Rd. B71: W Brom . . . 4A **64**
Hall Green Stadium . . . 4F **135**
Hall Green Station (Rail) . . . **4F 135**
Hall Grn. St. WV14: Bils . . . 2G **61**
Hall Gro. WV14: Cose . . . 5E **61**
Hall Hays Rd. B34: S End . . . 2A **106**
Hall La. DY2: Neth . . . 3E **95**
DY4: Tip . . . 5B **62**
DY9: Hag . . . 6H **125**
WS3: Pels . . . 4D **20**
WS6: Gt Wyr . . . 1F **7**
WS7: Hamm . . . 1F **11**
WS9: Wals W . . . 3A **22**
WS14: Muck C . . . 3H **11**
WV14: Cose . . . 4B **60**
Hall Mdw. DY9: Hag . . . 6H **125**
Hallmeadow Rd. CV7: Bal C . . . 6H **155**
Hallmoor Rd. B33: Kitts G . . . 6F **105**
Hall of Memory, The . . . 1E **117** (4B **4**)
Hallot Cl. B23: Erd . . . 5D **68**
Halloughton Rd. B74: S Cold . . . 4G **53**
Hall Pk. St. WV2: E'shll . . . 5D **44**
Hall Rd. B8: Salt . . . 5D **102**
B20: Hand . . . 1C **100**
B36: Cas B . . . 1E **105**
B67: Smeth . . . 5C **98**
Hall Rd. Av. B20: Hand . . . 1C **100**
Hallstead Rd. B13: Mose . . . 2B **148**
Hall St. B18: Birm . . . 5E **101** (1B **4**)
B64: Old H . . . 1H **111**
B68: O'bry . . . 4H **97**
B70: W Brom . . . 5A **80**
DY2: Dud . . . 6F **77**
DY3: Sed . . . 5H **59**
DY4: Tip . . . 2G **77**
DY8: Stourb . . . 2E **125**
WS2: Wals . . . 6B **32**
WS10: Darl . . . 4B **46**
WV11: Wed . . . 4E **29**
WV13: W'hall . . . 2B **46**
WV14: Bils . . . 6G **45**
Hall St. E. WS10: Darl . . . 4C **46**
Hall St. Sth. B70: W Brom . . . 1B **98**
Hallswelle Gro. B43: Gt Barr . . . 1G **67**
Hall Wlk. B46: Col . . . 4G **107**
(not continuous)
Halow Cl. B31: N'fld . . . 5H **145**
Halsbury Gro. B44: K'sdng . . . 5B **68**
Halstead Gro. B91: Sol . . . 1E **165**
Halton Rd. B73: New O . . . 2D **68**
Halton St. DY2: Neth . . . 4E **95**
Hamar Way B37: Mars G . . . 2D **122**
Hamberley Ct. B18: Win G . . . 5H **99**
Hamble Cl. DY5: P'ntt . . . 3E **93**
Hamble Ct. B73: S Cold . . . 6H **53**
Hambledon Cl. WV9: Pend . . . 5E **15**
Hamble Gro. WV6: Pert . . . 6E **25**
Hamble Rd. B42: Gt Barr . . . 4B **66**
WV4: Penn . . . 5A **42**
Hambleton Rd. B63: Hale . . . 3F **127**
Hambletts Rd. B70: W Brom . . . 4G **79**
Hambrook Cl. WV6: Wolv . . . 4E **27**
Hambury Dr. B14: K Hth . . . 6F **133**
Hamilton Av. B17: Harb . . . 3E **115**
B62: Hale . . . 2C **128**
DY8: Woll . . . 5B **108**
Hamilton Cl. DY3: Sed . . . 6G **59**
DY8: Word . . . 1A **108**
Hamilton Ct. B13: Mose . . . 1H **133**
B30: K Nor . . . 3A **146**
Hamilton Dr. B29: S Oak . . . 5H **131**
B69: Tiv . . . 5C **78**
DY8: Word . . . 1A **108**
Hamilton Gdns. WV10: Bush . . . 4A **16**
Hamilton Ho. B66: Smeth . . . 4G **99**
WS3: Blox . . . 6A **20**
Hamilton Rd. B21: Hand . . . 1H **99**
B67: Smeth . . . 1C **114**
DY4: Tip . . . 1C **78**
Hamilton St. WS3: Blox . . . 6A **20**
Ham La. DY6: K'wfrd . . . 6C **74**
DY9: Pedm . . . 4G **125**
Hamlet, The WS11: Nort C . . . 1C **8**
Hamlet Gdns. B28: Hall G . . . 5F **135**
Hamlet Rd. B28: Hall G . . . 5F **135**
Hammer Bank DY5: Quar B . . . 3C **110**
Hammersley Cl. B63: Crad . . . 4D **110**
HAMMERWICH . . . **1F 11**
Hammerwich Link WS7: Hamm . . . 2H **11**
Hammond Av. WV10: Bush . . . 1A **28**
Hammond Dr. B23: Erd . . . 2F **85**
Hammond Way DY8: Amb . . . 4E **109**
Hampden Cl. DY5: Quar B . . . 3C **110**
Hampden Retreat B12: Bal H . . . 5G **117**
Hampshire Ct. B29: W Cas . . . 6F **131**
Hampshire Dr. B15: Edg . . . 3A **116**
Hampshire Rd. B71: W Brom . . . 5G **63**
Hampson Cl. B11: S'brk . . . 5B **118**
Hampstead Glade B63: Hale . . . 3C **128**
Hampton Cl. B73: New O . . . 3C **68**
Hampton Ct. *B15: Edg* . . . *3D 116*
(off George Rd.)
B71: W Brom . . . 4A **64**
B92: H Ard . . . 1B **154**
WV10: Bush . . . 5D **16**
Hampton Ct. Rd. B17: Harb . . . 5D **114**
Hampton Dr. B74: Four O . . . 3H **53**
Hampton Gdns. DY9: Pedm . . . 2G **125**
Hampton Grange CV7: Mer . . . 4H **141**
Hampton Gro. WS3: Pels . . . 3D **20**
HAMPTON IN ARDEN . . . **1A 154**
Hampton in Arden Station (Rail) . . . **6B 140**
Hampton La. B91: Cath B, Sol . . . 3H **151**
(not continuous)
CV7: Mer . . . 5E **141**
Hampton Pl. WS10: Darl . . . 3C **46**
Hampton Rd. B6: Aston . . . 6F **83**
B23: Erd . . . 3D **84**
B93: Know . . . 2E **167**
WV10: Oxl . . . 6F **15**
Hamptons, The B93: Know . . . 3E **167**
Hampton St. B19: Birm . . . 5F **101** (1C **4**)
DY2: Neth . . . 4E **95**
WV14: Cose . . . 5D **60**
Hampton Vw. WV10: Wolv . . . 5B **28**
Hampton Wlk. WV1: Wolv . . . 1G **43** (3B **170**)
HAMS HALL . . . **3H 89**
Hams Hall Distribution Pk. B46: Col . . . 2H **89**
Hams La. B76: Lea M . . . 2G **89**
Hams Rd. B8: Salt . . . 5D **102**
HAMSTEAD . . . **6B 66**
Hamstead Cl. WV11: Wed . . . 3F **29**
Hamstead Hall Av. B20: Hand . . . 2A **82**
Hamstead Hall Rd. B20: Hand . . . 3A **82**
Hamstead Hill B20: Hand . . . 4B **82**
Hamstead Ho. B43: Gt Barr . . . 6B **66**
Hamstead Ind. Est. B42: P Barr . . . 2C **82**
Hamstead Rd. B20: Hand . . . 6D **82**
B43: Gt Barr . . . 5G **65**
Hamstead Station (Rail) . . . **1B 82**
Hamstead Ter. WS10: W'bry . . . 3G **63**
Hanam Cl. B75: S Cold . . . 5D **54**
Hanbury Cl. B63: Hale . . . 3H **127**
Hanbury Ct. *DY8: Stourb* . . . *1E 125*
(off College Rd.)
Hanbury Cres. WV4: Penn . . . 5C **42**
Hanbury Cft. B27: A Grn . . . 2C **136**
Hanbury Dr. B69: O'bry . . . 5E **97**
Hanbury Hill DY8: Stourb . . . 1E **125**
Hanbury Pas. DY8: Stourb . . . 6E **109**
Hanbury Rd. B70: W Brom . . . 4G **79**
B93: Dorr . . . 5B **166**
WS8: Bwnhls . . . 3A **10**
Hanch Pl. WS1: Wals . . . 3D **48**
Hancock Rd. B8: Salt . . . 5F **103**
Hancox St. B68: O'bry . . . 1H **113**
Handley Gro. B31: Longb . . . 5A **144**
Handley St. WS10: W'bry . . . 1G **63**
HANDSWORTH . . . **6A 82**
Handsworth Booth Street Stop (MM)
. . . 2G **99**
Handsworth Cl. B21: Hand . . . 2H **99**
Handsworth Dr. B43: Gt Barr . . . 2C **66**
Handsworth Horticultural Institute . . . *5A 82*
(off Oxhill Rd.)
Handsworth Leisure Cen. B20: Hand . . . 6B **82**
Handsworth New Rd. B18: Win G . . . 3A **100**
HANDSWORTH WOOD . . . **5C 82**
Handsworth Wood Rd. B20: Hand . . . 4B **82**
Hangar Rd. B26: Birm A . . . 2C **138**
Hanging La. B31: N'fld . . . 5C **144**
Hangleton Dr. B11: S'brk . . . 5D **118**
Hanley Cl. B63: Hale . . . 1G **127**
Hanley St. B19: Birm . . . 5F **101** (1E **5**)
Hannafore Rd. B16: Edg . . . 6H **99**
Hannah Rd. WV14: Bils . . . 2A **62**

A-Z Birmingham 217

Hanney Hay Rd.—Hathaway Cl.

Hanney Hay Rd. WS7: Chase, Hamm 1C **10**
Hannon Rd. B14: K Hth 2G **147**
Hanover Cl. B6: Aston 2G **101**
Hanover Ct. WS2: Wals 2E **47**
WV6: Tett 5A **26**
Hanover Dr. B24: Erd 1F **103**
Hanover Rd. B65: Row R 5C **96**
Hansell Dr. B93: Dorr 6F **167**
Hansom Rd. B32: Quin 6A **114**
Hanson Gro. B92: Olton 6D **120**
Hansons Bri. Rd. B24: Erd 2D **86**
Hanwell Cl. B76: Walm 6F **71**
Hanwood Cl. B12: Birm 3H **117**
Harald Cl. WV6: Pert 4E **25**
Harbeck Av. B44: Gt Barr 5H **67**
Harbet Dr. B40: Nat E C 1G **139**
Harbinger Rd. B38: K Nor 5D **146**
HARBORNE 5F **115**
Harborne Ct. B17: Harb 1G **131**
Harborne Ho. B17: Harb 1E **131**
Harborne La. B17: Harb, S Oak 2H **131**
B29: S Oak 3A **132**
Harborne Pk. Rd. B17: Harb 6G **115**
Harborne Pool & Fitness Cen. 6F **115**
Harborne Rd. B15: Edg 5A **116**
B68: O'bry 2B **114**
Harborough Ct. B74: Four O 1G **53**
Harborough Dr. B36: Cas B 6H **87**
WS9: A'rdge 4C **34**
Harborough Wlk. DY9: Pedm 3G **125**
Harbours Hill B61: Wild 4A **156**
Harbour Ter. WV3: Wolv 2E **43**
Harbury Cl. B76: Walm 1F **87**
Harbury Rd. B12: Bal H 6F **117**
Harby Cl. B37: Mars G 3D **122**
Harcourt Dr. B74: Four O 5F **37**
DY3: Gorn 5H **75**
Harcourt Rd. B23: Erd 1E **85**
B64: Crad H 3H **111**
WS10: W'bry 1F **63**
HARDEN 2C **32**
Harden Cl. WS3: Blox 2C **32**
Harden Ct. B31: N'fld 6C **144**
Harden Gro. WS3: Blox 2C **32**
Harden Keep B66: Smeth 5E **99**
Harden Mnr. Ct. B63: Hale 2C **128**
Harden Rd. WS3: Blox, Wals 2B **32**
Harden Va. B63: Hale 6G **111**
Harding St. WV14: Cose 3F **61**
Hardon Rd. WV4: E'shll 6B **44**
Hardware St. B70: W Brom 3B **80**
HARDWICK 2G **51**
Hardwick Ct. B74: S'tly 1H **51**
Hardwick Dr. B62: Hale 4A **112**
Hardwicke Wlk. B14: K Hth 5F **147**
Hardwicke Way DY9: Lye 6H **109**
Hardwick Rd. B26: Yard 1C **136**
B74: S'tly 1H **51**
B92: Olton 1C **136**
Hardy Ct. B13: Mose 1H **133**
Hardy Rd. WS3: Blox 1C **32**
WS10: W'bry 2G **63**
Hardy Sq. WV2: E'shll 5B **44**
Harebell Cl. WS5: Wals 2E **65**
Harebell Cres. DY1: Dud 3C **76**
Harebell Gdns. B38: K Nor 1B **160**
Harebell Wlk. B37: Chel W 1F **123**
Hare Gro. B31: N'fld 4B **144**
Haresfield B90: Dic H 4G **163**
Hare St. WV14: Bils 6H **45**
(not continuous)
Harewell Dr. B75: R'ley 2A **54**
Harewood Av. B43: Gt Barr 3G **65**
WS10: W'bry 2A **64**
Harewood Cl. B28: Hall G 2E **149**
Harford St. B19: Birm 5E **101**
Hargate La. B70: W Brom 3A **80**
B71: W Brom 3A **80**
Hargrave Cl. B46: Wat O 4D **88**
Hargrave Rd. B90: Shir 5C **148**
Hargreave Cl. B76: Walm 6D **70**
Hargreaves St. WV1: Wolv 4C **44**
Harland Rd. B74: Four O 6G **37**
Harlech Cl. B32: Bart G 6G **129**
B69: Tiv 6A **78**
Harlech Ho. *WS3: Blox 3A 32*
(off Providence Cl.)
Harlech Rd. WV12: W'hall 3C **30**
Harlech Twr. B23: Erd 1G **85**
Harlech Way DY1: Dud 5B **76**
Harleston Rd. B44: Gt Barr 5H **67**
Harley Cl. WS8: Bwnhls 1C **22**
Harley Dr. WV14: Bils 1D **60**
Harlow Gro. B28: Hall G 1G **149**
Harlstones Cl. DY8: Amb 3E **109**
Harlyn Cl. WV14: Bils 3A **62**
Harman Rd. B72: W Grn 6H **69**
Harmon Rd. DY8: Woll 6A **108**
Harmony Ho. B10: Small H 2C **118**
Harnall Cl. B90: Shir 2C **164**
Harness Cl. WS5: Wals 1D **64**
Harold Rd. B16: Edg 2B **116**
B67: Smeth 6C **98**
Harper Av. WV11: Wed 2E **29**
Harper Rd. WV14: Bils 5F **45**
Harpers Rd. B14: K Hth 6A **148**
B31: N'fld 6E **145**
Harper St. WV13: W'hall 1A **46**
Harpur Cl. WS4: Wals 5E **33**
Harpur Rd. WS4: Wals 5E **33**
Harrier Rd. B27: A Grn 3B **136**
Harrier Way B42: P Barr 4F **83**
Harriet Cl. DY5: P'ntt 4F **93**
Harringay Dr. DY8: Stourb 2C **124**
Harringay Rd. B44: K'sdng 3H **67**
Harrington Cft. B71: W Brom 6D **64**
Harringworth Ct. WS4: S'fld 1G **33**
Harriots Hayes Rd. WV8: Cod W 1A **12**
Harris Ct. B18: Hock 3C **100**
Harris Dr. B42: Gt Barr 5C **66**
B66: Smeth 6F **99**
Harrison Cl. WS3: Blox 6A **20**
WS6: C Hay 4D **6**
Harrison Ct. DY8: Amb 2E **109**
Harrison Ho. B14: K Hth 4H **147**
Harrison Rd. B24: Erd 3F **85**
B74: Four O 4E **37**
DY8: Word 2E **109**
WS4: S'fld 5G **21**
Harrison's Fold DY2: Neth 4E **95**
Harrisons Grn. B15: Edg 5A **116**
Harrisons Pleck B13: Mose 2H **133**
Harrison's Rd. B15: Edg 5A **116**
Harrison St. WS3: Blox 6H **19**
Harrold Av. B65: Row R 6E **97**
Harrold Rd. B65: Row R 6E **97**
Harrold St. DY4: Tip 6C **62**
Harrop Way DY8: Amb 3C **108**
Harrowby Dr. DY4: Tip 3A **78**
Harrowby Pl. WV13: W'hall 2D **46**
WV14: Bils 1A **62**
Harrowby Rd. WV10: F'hses 4F **15**
WV14: Bils 1A **62**
Harrow Cl. DY9: Hag 6E **125**
Harrowfield Rd. B33: Stech 5C **104**
Harrow Rd. B29: S Oak 2B **132**
DY6: K'wfrd 6B **74**
Harrow St. WV1: Wolv 5F **27**
Harry Mitchell Leisure Cen. 4D **98**
Harry Perks St. WV13: W'hall 6A **30**
Harry Price Ho. B69: O'bry 4D **96**
Hart Dr. B73: Bold 5G **69**
Hartfield Cres. B27: A Grn 3G **135**
Hartfields Way B65: Row R 4H **95**
Hartford Cl. B17: Harb 4E **115**
Hartill Rd. WV4: Penn 2B **58**
Hartill St. WV13: W'hall 3B **46**
Hartington Cl. B93: Dorr 6A **166**
Hartington Rd. B19: Loz 1F **101**
Hartland Av. WV14: Cose 5C **60**
Hartland Rd. B31: Longb 3C **158**
B71: W Brom 5D **64**
DY4: Tip 2F **77**
Hartland St. DY5: P'ntt 2H **93**
Hartlebury Cl. B93: Dorr 6B **166**
Hartlebury Rd. B63: Hale 3H **127**
B69: O'bry 4D **96**
Hartledon Rd. B17: Harb 6F **115**
Hartley Dr. WS9: A'rdge 5D **34**
Hartley Gro. B44: K'sdng 2B **68**
Hartley Pl. B15: Edg 3B **116**
Hartley Rd. B44: K'sdng 2B **68**
Hartley St. WV3: Wolv 1E **43**
Harton Way B14: K Hth 2E **147**
Hartopp Rd. B8: Salt 5E **103**
B74: Four O 2F **53**
Hart Rd. B24: Erd 2G **85**
WV11: Wed 5F **29**
Hartsbourne Dr. B62: Hale 1D **128**
Harts Cl. B17: Harb 5H **115**
HARTS GREEN 6E **115**
Harts Grn. Rd. B17: Harb 6E **115**
HART'S HILL 4A **94**
Hartshill Cl. B34: S End 3E **105**
Hartshill Rd. B27: A Grn 3B **136**
B34: S End 3E **105**
Hartshorn St. WV14: Bils 6F **45**
Hartside Cl. B63: Hale 3F **127**
Harts Rd. B8: Salt 4E **103**
Hart St. WS1: Wals 3C **48**
Hartswell Dr. B13: Mose 1H **147**
Hartwell Cl. B91: Sol 6F **151**
Hartwell La. WS6: Gt Wyr 2G **7**
Hartwell Rd. B24: Erd 5H **85**
Hartwood Cres. WV4: Penn 6D **42**
Harvard Cl. DY1: Dud 3B **76**
Harvard Rd. B92: Olton 1F **137**
Harvest Cl. B30: Stir 1D **146**
DY3: Up Gor 2A **76**
Harvest Ct. B65: Row R 5A **96**
Harvesters Cl. WS9: A'rdge 1G **51**
Harvesters Rd. WV12: W'hall 4D **30**
Harvesters Wlk. WV8: Pend 6C **14**
Harvesters Way WV12: W'hall 4D **30**
Harvester Way DY6: W Hth 1G **91**
Harvest Flds. Way B75: R'ley 5B **38**
Harvest Gdns. B68: O'bry 5G **97**
Harvest Rd. B65: Row R 5A **96**
B67: Smeth 6B **98**
Harvest Wlk. B65: Row R 5A **96**
Harvey Ct. B33: Kitts G 6H **105**
Harvey Dr. B75: R'ley 1A **54**
Harvey M. B30: B'vlle 6A **132**
Harvey Rd. B26: Yard 4B **120**
WS2: Wals 4H **31**
Harvey's Ter. DY2: Neth 5F **95**
HARVILLS HAWTHORN 6F **63**
Harvills Hawthorn B70: W Brom 6F **63**
Harvine Wlk. DY8: Stourb 2C **124**
Harvington Dr. B90: M'path 3F **165**
Harvington Rd. B29: W Cas 5E **131**
B63: Hale 3H **127**
B68: O'bry 4G **113**
WV14: Cose 5D **60**
Harvington Wlk. B65: Row R 6C **96**
Harvington Way B76: Walm 5E **71**
Harwin Cl. WV6: Tett 2D **26**
Harwood Gro. B90: Shir 1A **164**
Harwood St. B70: W Brom 4H **79**
HASBURY 3G **127**
Hasbury Cl. B63: Hale 3G **127**
Hasbury Rd. B32: Bart G 5G **129**
Haseley Rd. B21: Hand 2A **100**
B91: Sol 1C **150**
Haselor Rd. B73: New O 4E **69**
Haselour Rd. B37: K'hrst 4B **106**
Haskell St. WS1: Wals 4D **48**
Haslucks Cft. B90: Shir 4G **149**
HASLUCKS GREEN 6E **149**
Haslucks Grn. Rd. B90: Maj G 2E **163**
Hassop Rd. B42: Gt Barr 6F **67**
Hastings Ct. DY1: Dud 5A **76**
Hastings Rd. B23: Erd 6B **68**
(not continuous)
Hastingwood Ind. Pk. B24: Erd 6H **85**
Haswell Rd. B63: Hale 2F **127**
Hatcham Rd. B44: K'sdng 3C **68**
Hatchett St. B19: Birm 4G **101**
Hatchford Av. B92: Sol 2G **137**
Hatchford Brook Rd. B92: Sol 2G **137**
Hatchford Ct. B92: Sol 2G **137**
Hatchford Wlk. B37: Chel W 2D **122**
Hatchford Way B26: Sheld 1A **138**
Hatch Heath Cl. WV5: Wom 6F **57**
Hateley Dr. WV4: E'shll 1A **60**
HATELEY HEATH 6A **64**
Hatfield Cl. B23: Erd 6D **68**
Hatfield Rd. B19: Loz 1F **101**
DY9: Lye 1G **125**
Hathaway Cl. CV7: Bal C 2H **169**
WV13: W'hall 3H **45**

Hathaway M. DY8: Word 6H **91**
Hathaway Rd. B75: Four O 5G **37**
B90: Shir 6H **149**
Hatherden Dr. B76: Walm 3E **71**
Hathersage Rd. B42: Gt Barr 6F **67**
Hatherton Gdns. WV10: Bush 5A **16**
Hatherton Gro. B29: W Cas 4D **130**
Hatherton Pl. WS9: A'rdge 2C **34**
Hatherton Rd. WS1: Wals 1C **48**
WV14: Bils 5H **45**
Hatherton St. WS1: Wals 1C **48**
WS6: C Hay 3C **6**
Hattersley Gro. B11: Tys 2G **135**
Hatton Cres. WV10: Wolv 2C **28**
Hatton Gdns. B42: Gt Barr 6D **66**
Hatton Rd. WV6: Wolv 6D **26**
Hattons Gro. WV8: Bilb 5H **13**
Hatton St. WV14: Bils 1G **61**
Haughton Rd. B20: Hand 6E **83**
Haunch La. B13: Mose 1H **147**
Haunchwood Dr. B76: Walm 6D **70**
Havacre La. WV14: Cose 3E **61**
Havelock Cl. WV3: Wolv 3C **42**
Havelock Rd. B8: Salt 4D **102**
B11: Tys 1E **135**
B20: Hand 6E **83**
Haven, The B14: Yard W 3D **148**
DY8: Word 1B **108**
WV2: Wolv 3G **43**
Haven Cvn. Pk. B92: Bick 3E **139**
Haven Cft. B43: Gt Barr 5H **65**
Haven Dr. B27: A Grn 2H **135**
Haverford Dr. B45: Redn 3H **157**
Havergal Wlk. B63: Crad 1D **126**
Haverhill Cl. WS3: Blox 4G **19**
Hawbridge Cl. B90: M'path 3F **165**
HAWBUSH 1E **109**
Hawbush Gdns. DY5: Brie H 2E **109**
Hawbush Rd. DY5: Brie H 1E **109**
WS3: Blox 3B **32**
Hawbush Urban Farm Vis. Cen. 1F **109**
Hawcroft Gro. B34: S End 3G **105**
Hawes Cl. WS1: Wals 5D **48**
Hawes La. B65: Row R 5B **96**
Hawes Rd. WS1: Wals 5D **48**
Haweswater Dr. DY6: K'wfrd 3B **92**
Hawfield Cl. B69: Tiv 2C **96**
Hawfield Gro. B72: W Grn 6A **70**
Hawfield Rd. B69: Tiv 2C **96**
Hawker Dr. B35: Cas V 5D **86**
Hawkesbury Rd. B90: Shir 6F **149**
Hawkes Cl. B30: Stir 5C **132**
Hawkesford Cl. B36: Cas B 1E **105**
B74: Four O 2H **53**
Hawkesford Rd. B33: Kitts G 6H **105**
Hawkeshaw Path B90: Bly P 5E **165**
(not continuous)
Hawkes La. B70: W Brom 6G **63**
HAWKESLEY 2A **160**
Hawkesley Cres. B31: Longb 6D **144**
Hawkesley Dr. B31: Longb 1D **158**
Hawkesley End B38: K Nor 2A **160**
Hawkesley Mill La. B31: N'fld 5D **144**
Hawkesley Rd. DY1: Dud 1B **94**
Hawkesley Sq. B38: K Nor 2A **160**
Hawkes St. B10: Small H 3D **118**
Hawkestone Cres. B70: W Brom 1F **79**
Hawkestone Rd. B29: W Cas 6E **131**
Hawkeswell Cl. B92: Olton 4C **136**
Hawkesyard Rd. B24: Erd 6E **85**
Hawkhurst Rd. B14: K Hth 5H **147**
Hawkinge Dr. B35: Cas V 4E **87**
Hawkins Cl. B5: Bal H 5G **117**
Hawkins Cft. DY4: Tip 4A **78**
Hawkins Dr. WS11: Cann 1C **6**
Hawkins Pl. WV14: Bils 2H **61**
Hawkins St. B70: W Brom 5G **63**
Hawkley Cl. WV1: Wolv 1D **44**
Hawkley Rd. WV1: Wolv 1D **44**
Hawkmoor Gdns. B38: K Nor 1C **160**
Hawks Cl. WS6: C Hay 3D **6**
Hawksford Cres. WV10: Bush 2H **27**
Hawkshead Dr. B93: Know 3B **166**
Hawksmill Ind. Est. B9: Small H 2C **118**
Hawksmoor Dr. WV6: Pert 6D **24**
Hawkstone Ct. WV6: Pert 4D **24**
Hawkswell Av. WV5: Wom 2G **73**
Hawkswell Dr. DY6: K'wfrd 1B **92**
WV13: W'hall 2H **45**
Hawkswood Dr. CV7: Bal C 2H **169**
WS10: Mox 2B **62**
Hawkswood Gro. B14: K Hth 4B **148**
Hawley Cl. WS4: Wals 5D **32**
Hawley Ct. B43: Gt Barr 4A **66**
Hawnby Gro. B76: Walm 3E **71**
HAWNE 5G **111**
Hawne Cl. B63: Hale 5G **111**
Hawnelands, The B63: Hale 6H **111**
Hawne La. B63: Hale 5G **111**
Hawthorn Av. WS6: Gt Wyr 4G **7**
Hawthorn Brook Way B23: Erd 5E **69**
Hawthorn Cl. B23: Erd 6F **69**
Hawthorn Coppice B30: K Nor 3A **146**
Hawthorn Cft. B68: O'bry 4B **114**
Hawthornden Ct. B76: Walm 6B **70**
Hawthorn Dr. B47: H'wd 3B **162**
CV7: Bal C 1H **169**
Hawthorne Cft. B30: K Nor 2H **145**
Hawthorne Gro. DY3: Gorn 5H **75**
Hawthorne Ho. WV10: Wolv 6B **28**
Hawthorne La. WV8: Cod 5F **13**
Hawthorne Rd. B15: Edg 4A **116**
B30: K Nor 3H **145**
B36: Cas B 2A **106**
B63: Hale 3G **127**
DY1: Dud 3E **77**
WS5: Wals 6D **48**
WS6: C Hay 1E **7**
WV2: Wolv 5H **43**
WV11: Ess 3A **18**
WV11: Wed 4H **29**
WV12: W'hall 2D **30**
Hawthorn Gro. B19: Loz 1E **101**
Hawthorn Pk. B20: Hand 4A **82**
Hawthorn Pk. Dr. B20: Hand 4B **82**
Hawthorn Pl. WS2: Wals 6E **31**
Hawthorn Rd. B44: K'sdng 5H **67**
B72: W Grn 4A **70**
B74: S'tly 2A **52**
DY4: Tip 5A **62**
DY5: Quar B 3A **110**
WS4: S'fld 6F **21**
WS10: W'bry 1F **63**
WV1: Wolv 3D **44**
Hawthorns, The 6F **81**
Hawthorns, The B13: Mose 2H **133**
B68: O'bry 4B **114**
Hawthorns Bus. Cen. B66: Smeth 1E **99**
Hawthorns Ind. Est. B21: Hand 6F **81**
Hawthorns Station, The (Rail & MM) 1F **99**
Hawthorn Ter. WS10: W'bry 1F **63**
Haxby Av. B34: Hodg H 3E **105**
Haybarn, The B76: Walm 5E **71**
Haybrook Dr. B11: Tys 1F **135**
Haycock Pl. WS10: Darl 4C **46**
Haycroft Av. B8: Salt 4E **103**
Haycroft Dr. B74: Four O 5G **37**
Haydn Sanders Sq. WS1: Wals 3C **48**
Haydock Cl. B36: Hodg H 1A **104**
WV6: Wolv 3F **27**
Haydon Cl. B93: Dorr 6G **167**
Haydon Cft. B33: Kitts G 6E **105**
Hayehouse Gro. B36: Hodg H 2C **104**
HAYES, THE 5C **110**
Hayes, The B31: Longb 2G **159**
DY9: Lye 6B **110**
WV12: W'hall 3B **30**
Hayes Bus. Pk. DY9: Lye 5B **110**
Hayes Cres. B68: O'bry 4B **98**
Hayes Cft. B38: K Nor 2A **160**
Hayes Dr. B24: Erd 2B **86**
Hayes Gro. B24: Erd 1B **86**
Hayes La. DY9: Lye 5C **110**
Hayes Mdw. B72: W Grn 6B **70**
Hayes Rd. B68: O'bry 4B **98**
Hayes St. B70: W Brom 3G **79**
Hayes Trad. Est., The DY9: Lye 5C **110**
Hayes Vw. Dr. WS6: C Hay 1E **7**
Hayfield Ct. B13: Mose 3B **134**
Hayfield Gdns. B13: Mose 3C **134**
Hayfield Rd. B13: Mose 3B **134**
HAY GREEN 6H **109**
Hay Grn. DY9: Lye 6H **109**
Hay Grn. Cl. B30: B'vlle 1H **145**
Hay Grn. La. B30: B'vlle 2G **145**
Hay Gro. WS8: Bwnhls 5B **10**
Hay Hall Rd. B11: Tys 6F **119**
Hay Head Wood (Nature Reserve) 6A **34**
Hay Hill WS5: Wals 3A **50**
Hayland Rd. B23: Erd 1E **85**
Hay La. B90: M'path 3D **164**
Hayle Cl. B38: K Nor 5D **146**
Hayley Ct. B24: Erd 1A **86**
HAYLEY GREEN 4F **127**
Hayley Grn. Rd. B32: Bart G 5H **129**
Hayley Pk. Rd. B63: Hale 5E **127**
Hayling Cl. B45: Fran 6F **143**
Hayling Gro. WV2: Wolv 5F **43**
Haylofts, The B63: Hale 4E **127**
Haymarket, The WV8: Pend 6C **14**
HAY MILLS 5H **119**
Haynes La. WS5: Wals 1F **65**
Hay Pk. B5: Bal H 5F **117**
Haypits Cl. B71: W Brom 6C **64**
Hayrick Dr. DY6: W Hth 2G **91**
Hay Rd. B25: Yard 4G **119**
Hayseech B64: Crad H 4H **111**
Hayseech Rd. B63: Hale 5H **111**
Hays Kent Moat, The B26: Yard 2E **121**
Haytor Av. B14: K Hth 2F **147**
Haywain Cl. WV9: Pend 5E **15**
Hayward Ind. Pk. WS9: A'rdge 2C **34**
Hayward Rd. B75: S Cold 3A **54**
Haywards Cl. B23: Erd 2E **85**
WS3: Pels 4D **20**
Haywards Ind. Est. B35: Cas V 6F **87**
Hayward St. WV14: Cose 5D **60**
Hayway, The WS2: Wals 6G **31**
Haywharf Rd. DY5: P'ntt 4F **93**
Haywood Dr. B62: B'hth 3C **112**
WV6: Tett 5A **26**
Haywood Rd. B33: Kitts G 1A **122**
Haywood's Farm B71: W Brom 3D **64**
Hazel Av. B73: New O 4C **68**
WS10: W'bry 1G **63**
Hazelbank B38: K Nor 5A **146**
Hazelbeach Rd. B8: Salt 4F **103**
Hazelbeech Rd. B70: W Brom 5H **79**
Hazel Cft. B31: N'fld 4E **145**
B37: Chel W 2D **122**
Hazeldene Gro. B6: Aston 1G **101**
Hazeldene Rd. B33: Sheld 4H **121**
B63: Hale 3G **127**
Hazel Dr. B47: H'wd 4B **162**
Hazeley Cl. B17: Harb 4D **114**
Hazel Gdns. B27: A Grn 1A **136**
WV8: Cod 3G **13**
Hazelglen Gro. *B18: Win G* *5A **100***
(off Heath Grn. Rd.)
Hazel Gro. B70: W Brom 6A **80**
DY8: Stourb 2A **124**
WV5: Wom 6G **57**
WV11: Wed 2E **29**
WV14: Bils 4G **45**
Hazelhurst Rd. B14: K Hth 1G **147**
B36: Cas B 2A **106**
Hazel La. WS6: Gt Wyr 3H **7**
Hazelmead Ct. B73: Bold 6G **69**
Hazelmere Dr. WS7: Chase 1B **10**
WV3: Wolv 2G **41**
Hazelmere Rd. B28: Hall G 4F **135**
Hazeloak Rd. B90: Shir 6G **149**
Hazel Rd. B45: Rubery 3F **157**
DY1: Dud 5E **77**
DY4: Tip 4C **62**
DY6: K'wfrd 4C **92**
WV3: Wolv 4C **42**
Hazelton Cl. B91: Sol 6F **151**
Hazeltree Cft. B27: A Grn 3H **135**
Hazeltree Gro. B93: Dorr 6A **166**
Hazelville Gro. B28: Hall G 1G **149**
Hazelville Rd. B28: Hall G 1G **149**
Hazelwell Cres. B30: Stir 1D **146**
Hazelwell Dr. B14: K Hth 1F **147**
Hazelwell Fordrough B30: Stir 6D **132**
Hazelwell La. B30: Stir 6C **132**
Hazelwell Rd. B30: Stir 1C **146**
Hazelwell St. B30: Stir 6C **132**
Hazelwood Cl. WS6: C Hay 3D **6**
Hazelwood Dr. WV11: Wed 4C **28**

Hazelwood Gro. WV12: W'hall 4D **30**
Hazelwood Rd. B27: A Grn 3H **135**
B74: S'tly 2F **51**
DY1: Dud 2B **76**
Hazlemere Dr. B74: Four O 3G **53**
Hazlitt Gro. B30: K Nor 3H **145**
Headborough Wlk. WS9: A'rdge 6D **22**
Headingley Rd. B21: Hand 5A **82**
Headland Dr. B8: Salt 4D **102**
Headland Rd. WV3: Wolv 2F **41**
Headlands, The B74: Lit A 6C **36**
Headley Cft. B38: K Nor 1H **159**
HEADLEY HEATH 3E **161**
Headley Heath La. B38: Head H 2D **160**
Headley Ri. B90: Shir 5B **150**
Headway Rd. WV10: F'hses 4G **15**
Heale Cl. B63: Crad 4C **110**
Heanor Cft. B6: Aston 1B **102**
Heantum Cft. WV10: Wolv 4C **28**
Heantun Ho. WV3: Wolv 2G **43** (4A **170**)
Heantun Mill Ct. WS10: W'bry 4D **62**
Heantun Ri. WV1: Wolv 5G **27**
Heartland M. B65: Row R 1B **112**
Heartlands High Community Leisure Cen. 5A **102**
Heartlands Parkway B7: Nech 4C **102**
Heartlands Pl. B8: Salt 5E **103**
HEATH
Stourbridge 1D **124**
Heath Acres WS10: Darl 1C **62**
Heath Bri. Cl. WS4: Rus 1E **33**
Heathbrook Av. DY6: W Hth 2H **91**
Heathcliff Rd. B11: Tys 1F **135**
DY2: Dud 2H **95**
Heath Cl. B30: B'vlle 2H **145**
B75: S Cold 5D **54**
DY4: Tip 2B **78**
WS9: Ston 2G **23**
Heathcote Av. B91: Sol 4C **150**
Heathcote Ho. *B17: Harb* *6G* ***115***
(off Vivian Cl.)
Heathcote Rd. B30: K Nor 2C **146**
Heath Cft. B31: Longb 2E **159**
Heath Cft. Rd. B75: R'ley 2A **54**
HEATH END
Walsall 5E **21**
Heather Av. WS5: Wals 1F **65**
Heather Cl. B36: Cas B 1C **106**
WS3: Blox 1G **31**
WV11: Wed 4G **29**
Heather Ct. Gdns. B74: Four O 3H **53**
Heather Cft. B44: Gt Barr 4H **67**
Heather Dale B13: Mose 3E **133**
Heather Dr. B45: Rubery 3F **157**
Heather Gro. B91: Sol 1A **152**
WV12: W'hall 5E **31**
Heather Ho. B38: K Nor 6B **146**
Heatherleigh Rd. B36: Cas B 1B **106**
Heather Rd. B10: Small H 4F **119**
B43: Gt Barr 5G **65**
B67: Smeth 3C **98**
DY1: Dud 3E **77**
WS3: Blox 1G **31**
Heath Farm Rd. DY8: Stourb 3B **124**
WV8: Bilb 5H **13**
Heathfield Av. B20: Hand 1D **100**
Heathfield Cl. B64: Old H 1H **111**
B93: Know 4C **166**
Heathfield Ct. B19: Loz 2D **100**
Heathfield Dr. B74: Four O 6F **37**
WS3: Blox 5H **19**
Heathfield Gdns. DY8: Stourb 1D **124**
Heathfield La. WS10: Darl 5C **46**
Heathfield La. W. WS10: Darl 6B **46**
Heathfield Rd. B14: K Hth 5G **133**
B19: Hand 1D **100**
B63: Hale 2G **127**
Heathfields WV8: Cod 6E **13**
Heath Gdns. B91: Sol 1H **151**
Heath Grn. DY1: Dud 2B **76**
Heathgreen Cl. B37: Chel W 6F **107**
Heath Grn. Gro. *B18: Win G* *5A* ***100***
(off Heath Grn. Rd.)
Heath Grn. Rd. B18: Win G 5A **100**
Heath Gro. WV8: Bilb 4H **13**
Heath Hill Rd. WV6: Tett 2E **41**
Heath Ho. B14: K Hth 5H **147**
Heath Ho. Dr. WV5: Wom 2D **72**
Heath Ho. La. WV8: Cod 1E **25**
Heathland Av. B34: S End 2E **105**
Heathlands, The B65: B'hth 2C **112**
DY8: Stourb 1F **125**
WS2: Wals 6G **31**
WV5: Wom 2D **72**
Heathlands Cl. DY6: K'wfrd 1C **92**
Heathlands Cres. B73: Bold 4F **69**
Heathlands Gro. B31: N'fld 6E **145**
Heathlands Rd. B73: Bold 3F **69**
Heath La. B71: W Brom 6B **64**
DY8: Stourb 1E **125**
Heathleigh Rd. B38: K Nor 1G **159**
Heathmere Av. B25: Yard 3B **120**
Heathmere Dr. B37: F'bri 1B **122**
Heath Mill Cl. WV5: Wom 3D **72**
Heath Mill La. B9: Birm 2A **118** (6H **5**)
Heath Mill Rd. WV5: Wom 3D **72**
Heath Pk. WV10: Cov H 1G **15**
Heath Ri. B14: K Hth 6A **148**
Heath Rd. B30: B'vlle 2G **145**
B47: H'wd 2A **162**
B91: Sol 1H **151**
DY2: Neth 1D **110**
WS10: Darl 3E **47**
WV12: W'hall 1C **30**
Heath Rd. Sth. B31: N'fld 3E **145**
Heathside Dr. B38: K Nor 6D **146**
WS3: Pels 3E **21**
Heath St. B18: Win G 4H **99**
B65: B'hth 2C **112**
B66: Smeth 4H **99**
DY8: Stourb 6D **108**
Heath St. Ind. Est. B66: Smeth 4H **99**
Heath St. Sth. B18: Win G 5B **100**
HEATH TOWN 5D **28**
Heath Town Leisure Cen. 5C **28**
Heath Trad. Pk. B66: Smeth 4H **99**
Heath Vw. WS2: Wals 6F **31**
Heath Way B34: Hodg H, S End 2D **104**
Heathway Cl. B34: S End 3E **105**
Heathy Farm Cl. B32: Bart G 4H **129**
Heathy Ri. B32: Bart G 3G **129**
Heaton Cl. WV10: Bush 2A **16**
Heaton Dr. B15: Edg 3A **116**
B74: Four O 3F **53**
Heaton Rd. B91: Sol 1D **150**
Heaton St. B18: Hock 4D **100**
Hebden Gro. B28: Hall G 4E **149**
WV12: W'hall 6B **18**
Heddon Pl. B7: Birm 6A **102**
Hedera Cl. WS5: Wals 2F **65**
Hedgefield Gro. B63: Crad 1E **127**
Hedgerow Dr. DY6: K'wfrd 6B **74**
Hedgerows, The B62: Roms 3A **142**
Hedgerow Wlk. WV8: Pend 6C **14**
Hedges, The WV5: Wom 1E **73**
Hedgetree Cft. B37: Chel W 1E **123**
Hedgings, The *B34: S End* *3F* ***105***
(off Meadow Rd.)
Hedgley Gro. B33: Stech 5E **105**
Hedingham Gro. B37: Chel W 1F **123**
Hedley Cft. B35: Cas V 3F **87**
Hednesford Rd. WS8: Bwnhls 2G **9**
Heeley Rd. B29: S Oak 3A **132**
Hefford Dr. B66: Smeth 3E **99**
Helena Pl. B66: Smeth 2A **98**
Helena St. B1: Birm 6E **101** (3A **4**)
Helenny Cl. WV11: Wed 4C **28**
Helford Cl. DY4: Tip 2F **77**
Hellaby Cl. B72: S Cold 1H **69**
Hellaby Ct. B73: Bold 6G **69**
Hellaby Ho. B74: Four O 6F **37**
Hellier Av. DY4: Tip 3B **78**
Hellier Dr. WV5: Wom 6E **57**
Hellier Rd. WV10: Bush 5A **16**
Hellier St. DY2: Dud 1E **95**
Helming Dr. WV1: Wolv 6D **28**
Helmsdale Way DY3: Sed 6C **60**
Helmsley Cl. DY5: Brie H 3G **109**
Helmsley Rd. WV11: Wed 1E **29**
Helmswood Dr. B37: Chel W 3E **123**
Helston Cl. DY8: Word 1A **108**
WS5: Wals 4H **49**
Helstone Gro. B11: Tys 2G **135**
Helston Rd. WS5: Wals 4H **49**
Hembs Cres. B43: Gt Barr 5G **65**
Hemlingford Cft. B37: Mars G 4C **122**
Hemlingford Rd. B37: K'hrst 3A **106**
B76: Walm 6E **71**
Hemmings Cl. DY8: Stourb 6D **108**
Hemmings St. WS10: Darl 3C **46**
Hemplands Rd. DY8: Stourb 6D **108**
Hempole La. DY4: Tip 6D **62**
Hemyock Rd. B29: W Cas 5F **131**
Henbury Rd. B27: A Grn 2B **136**
Henderson Ct. B68: O'bry 3H **113**
Henderson Wlk. DY4: Tip 5B **62**
Henderson Way B65: B'hth 2C **112**
Hendon Cl. DY3: Lwr G 5H **75**
WV10: Bush 1A **28**
Hendon Rd. B11: S'hll 6B **118**
Heneage Pl. B7: Birm 5A **102**
Heneage St. B7: Birm 5A **102**
Heneage St. W. B7: Birm 5H **101** (1H **5**)
(not continuous)
Henfield Cl. WV11: Wed 2F **29**
Hengham Rd. B26: Yard 2E **121**
Henley Cl. B73: W Grn 5H **69**
DY4: Tip 2D **78**
WS3: Blox 6C **20**
Henley Cres. B91: Sol 6F **137**
Henley Dr. B75: Four O 6G **37**
Henley Rd. WV10: Oxl 6F **15**
Henley St. B11: S'brk 4A **118**
Henley Vs. *B12: Bal H* *6B* ***118***
(off Chesterton Rd.)
Henlow Cl. DY4: Tip 2F **77**
Henlow Rd. B14: K Hth 5H **147**
Hennalls, The B36: Hodg H 2D **104**
Henn Dr. DY4: Tip 5G **61**
Henne Dr. WV14: Cose 4E **61**
Henn St. DY4: Tip 5A **62**
Henrietta St. B19: Birm 5F **101** (1C **4**)
Henry Rd. B25: Yard 4A **120**
Henry St. WS2: Wals 2B **48**
Hensborough B90: Dic H 4G **163**
Hensel Dr. WV3: Wolv 3A **42**
Henshaw Gro. B25: Yard 4A **120**
Henshaw Rd. B10: Small H 3D **118**
Henstead St. B5: Birm 3F **117**
Henwood Cl. WV6: Tett 6A **26**
Henwood La. B91: Cath B 2D **152**
Henwood Rd. WV6: Tett 1A **42**
Hepburn Cl. WS9: A'rdge 5C **34**
Hepburn Edge B24: Erd 3H **85**
Hepworth Cl. WV6: Pert 5F **25**
Herald Ct. DY1: Dud 6E **77**
Herald Rd. B26: Birm A 1E **139**
Herbert Rd. B10: Small H 2C **118**
B21: Hand 6B **82**
B67: Smeth 2E **115**
B91: Sol 4F **151**
WS9: A'rdge 6C **22**
Herberts Pk. Rd. WS10: Darl 5B **46**
Herbert St. B70: W Brom 4B **80**
WV1: Wolv 6H **27** (1C **170**)
WV14: Bils 5D **44**
Herbhill Cl. WV4: Penn 1H **59**
Hereford Av. B12: Bal H 5A **118**
Hereford Cl. B45: Fran 5G **143**
WS9: A'rdge 1C **34**
Hereford Ho. WV1: Wolv 6G **27**
Hereford Pl. B71: W Brom 6H **63**
Hereford Rd. B68: O'bry 4H **113**
DY2: Neth 6G **95**
Hereford St. WS2: Wals 5C **32**
Hereford Wlk. B37: Mars G 2B **122**
Hereward Ri. B62: Hale 6B **112**
Heritage, The *WS1: Wals* *3C* ***48***
(off Sister Dora Gdns.)
Heritage Cl. B68: O'bry 5A **98**
Heritage Ct. B18: Birm 1A **4**
Heritage Way B33: Kitts G 6H **105**
DY4: Tip 2B **78**
Hermes Ct. B74: Four O 6F **37**
Hermes Rd. B26: Birm A 1E **139**
Hermitage, The B91: Sol 1G **151**
Hermitage Dr. B76: Walm 2D **70**
Hermitage Rd. B15: Edg 2G **115**
B23: Erd 4D **84**
B91: Sol 2G **151**
Hermit St. DY3: Up Gor 2H **75**

Hermon Row B11: S'brk 6D 118
Hernall Cft. B26: Sheld 4E 121
Hernefield Rd. B34: S End 2E 105
Hernehurst B32: Quin 6H 113
Hern Rd. DY5: Brie H 5G 109
Heron Cl. B90: Ches G 5B 164
WS8: Bwnhls 6A 10
Heron Ct. B73: W Grn 6H 69
(off Florence Av.)
Herondale Cres. DY8: Stourb 1A 124
Herondale Rd. B26: Sheld 5D 120
Heronfield Dr. B31: Longb 3D 158
Heronfield Way B91: Sol 2A 152
Heron Mill WS3: Pels 4C 20
Heron Rd. B68: O'bry 1G 113
Heronry, The WV6: Tett 1F 41
Heronsdale Rd. DY8: Stourb 2A 124
Herons Way B29: S Oak 2G 131
Heronswood Dr. DY5: Brie H 2H 109
Heronswood Rd. B45: Redn 3H 157
Heronville Dr. B70: W Brom 6G 63
Heronville Ho. DY4: Tip 4B 78
Heronville Rd. B70: W Brom 1F 79
Heron Way B45: Rubery 2F 157
Herrick Rd. B8: Salt 4E 103
Herrick St. WV3: Wolv 2F 43
Herringshaw Cft. B76: Walm 2C 70
Hertford St. B12: Bal H 6A 118
Hertford Way B93: Know 5D 166
Hervey Gro. B24: Erd 1B 86
Hesketh Cres. B23: Erd 2C 84
Heskett Av. B68: O'bry 2A 114
Hessian Cl. WV14: Cose 3D 60
Hestia Dr. B29: S Oak 5A 132
Heston Av. B42: Gt Barr 5C 66
Hever Av. B44: K'sdng 4A 68
Hever Cl. DY1: Dud 4A 76
Hewell Cl. B31: Longb 2D 158
DY6: K'wfrd 6B 74
Hewitson Gdns. B67: Smeth 1D 114
Hewitt St. WS10: Darl 5C 46
Hexham Cft. B36: Hodg H 1A 104
Hexham Way DY1: Dud 5B 76
Hexton Cl. B90: Shir 5D 148
Heybarnes Cir. B10: Small H 4F 119
Heybarnes Rd. B10: Small H 4F 119
Heycott Gro. B38: K Nor 5E 147
Heydon Rd. DY5: P'ntt 4F 93
Heyford Gro. B91: Sol 1G 165
Heyford Way B35: Cas V 2F 87
Heygate Way WS9: A'rdge 5D 22
Heynesfield Rd. B33: Kitts G 6G 105
Heythrop Gro. B13: Mose 5D 134
Hickman Av. WV1: Wolv 2C 44
Hickman Gdns. B16: Edg 2B 116
Hickman Pl. WV14: Bils 5E 45
Hickman Rd. B11: S'brk 5B 118
DY4: Tip 5H 61
DY5: Brie H 5G 93
WV14: Bils 6E 45
Hickman's Av. B64: Old H 1G 111
Hickmans Cl. B62: Quin 5G 113
Hickman St. DY9: Lye 5G 109
Hickmerelands La. DY3: Sed 5H 59
Hickory Dr. B17: Edg 1E 115
Hidcote Av. B76: Walm 5E 71
Hidcote Gro. B33: Sheld 3G 121
B37: Mars G 4C 122
Hidson Rd. B23: Erd 2C 84
Higgins Av. WV14: Cose 3F 61
Higgins La. B32: Quin 6A 114
Higgins Wlk. B66: Smeth 3F 99
Higgs Fld. Cres. B64: Old H 2A 112
Higgs Rd. WV11: Wed 6A 18
Highams Cl. B65: Row R 6B 96
Higham Way WV10: Wolv 3A 28
High Arcal Dr. DY3: Sed 6B 60
High Arcal Rd. DY3: Lwr G 4D 74
High Av. B64: Crad H 3H 111
High Beeches B43: Gt Barr 4H 65
HIGHBRIDGE 2E 21
Highbridge Rd. B73: Bold 4F 69
DY2: Neth 6C 94
High Brink Rd. B46: Col 2H 107
Highbrook Cl. WV9: Pend 5E 15
High Brow B17: Harb 4F 115
High Bullen WS10: W'bry 2F 63
Highbury Av. B21: Hand 1B 100
B65: Row R 6D 96
Highbury Cl. B65: Row R 6D 96
Highbury Ct. B13: Mose 6G 133
Highbury Little Theatre 6G 69
Highbury Rd. B14: K Hth 5F 133
B66: Smeth 2B 98
B68: O'bry 4H 97
B74: Four O 6C 36
High Clere B64: Crad H 4A 112
Highcrest Cl. B31: Longb 2E 159
High Cft. B43: Gt Barr 4G 65
WS3: Pels 2F 21
Highcroft WS9: A'rdge 5D 22
Highcroft Av. DY8: Word 6A 92
Highcroft Cl. B92: Sol 3G 137
Highcroft Dr. B74: Four O 6E 37
Highcroft Rd. B23: Erd 4E 85
Highdown Cres. B90: M'path 3E 165
HIGH ERCAL 1G 109
High Ercal Av. DY5: Brie H 1G 109
High Farm Rd. B62: B'hth 3F 113
B63: Hale 2G 127
Highfield CV7: Mer 4H 141
Highfield Av. WS4: S'fld 1G 33
WV10: Bush 5C 16
Highfield Cl. B28: Hall G 2D 148
Highfield Ct. B73: W Grn 4H 69
Highfield Cres. B63: Crad 5F 111
B65: B'hth 3B 112
WV11: Wed 3D 28
Highfield Dr. B73: Bold 6F 69
Highfield La. B32: Quin 5H 113
B63: Hale 2H 127
Highfield M. B63: Crad 5F 111
Highfield Pas. WS1: Wals 3C 48
Highfield Pl. B14: Yard W 2D 148
Highfield Rd. B8: Salt 5E 103
B13: Mose 2B 134
B14: Yard W 2D 148
B15: Edg 3C 116
B28: Hall G 2D 148
B43: Gt Barr 6G 65
B63: Crad 6F 111
B65: B'hth 2B 112
B67: Smeth 4D 98
DY2: Dud 6G 77
DY3: Sed 4H 59
DY4: Tip 6A 62
DY8: Word 1E 109
WS3: Pels 3E 21
Highfield Rd. Nth. WS3: Pels 2D 20
HIGHFIELDS 1B 10
Highfields B23: Erd 3C 84
Highfields, The WV6: Tett 1G 41
Highfields Av. WV14: Bils 1G 61
Highfields Ct. WV4: Penn 5A 42
Highfields Dr. WV5: Wom 2G 73
WV14: Cose 2F 61
Highfields Grange
WS6: C Hay 4D 6
Highfields Pk. WS6: C Hay 4D 6
Highfields Rd. WS7: Chase 1B 10
WV14: Bils, Cose 2E 61
Highfield Ter. B18: Hock 4C 100
Highfield Way WS9: A'rdge 5D 22
HIGHGATE 3H 117
Highgate B74: S'tly 2A 52
DY3: Up Gor 2A 76
Highgate Av. WS1: Wals 3D 48
WV4: Penn 5B 42
Highgate Bus. Cen. B12: Bal H 5B 118
Highgate Cl. B12: Birm 4H 117
WS1: Wals 4D 48
Highgate Common Country Pk. 1A 90
Highgate Comn. E.
DY3: Swind 2A 90
DY7: Env 2A 90
Highgate Dr. WS1: Wals 4D 48
Highgate Ho. B5: Birm 3G 117
(off Southacre Av.)
Highgate Middleway B12: Birm 4H 117
Highgate Pl. B12: Birm 4A 118
Highgate Rd. B12: Bal H 5A 118
DY2: Dud 3B 94
WS1: Wals 3D 48
Highgate Sq. B12: Birm 4H 117
Highgate St. B12: Birm 4H 117
B64: Old H 1H 111
(not continuous)
Highgate Trad. Est. B12: Birm 4A 118
Highgrove WV6: Tett 6A 26
Highgrove Cl. WV12: W'hall 2B 30
Highgrove Pl. DY1: Dud 5B 76
High Haden Cres.
B64: Crad H, Old H 3A 112
High Haden Rd. B64: Crad H, Old H 3A 112
HIGH HEATH
Sutton Coldfield 3F 55
Walsall 5G 21
High Heath Cl. B30: B'vlle 2H 145
High Hill WV11: Ess 5A 18
High Holborn DY3: Sed 6H 59
High Ho. Dr. B45: Lick 6F 157
Highland Ho. B62: B'hth 3C 112
Highland M. WV14: Cose 4F 61
Highland Ridge B62: Quin 6E 113
Highland Rd. B23: Erd 2F 85
B43: Gt Barr 2A 66
B64: Old H 1G 111
DY1: Dud 4C 76
WS9: Wals W 4D 22
Highlands Ct. B90: Shir 1C 164
Highlands Ind. Est., The B90: Shir 1C 164
Highlands Rd. B90: Shir 1C 164
WV3: Wolv 3B 42
High Leasowes B63: Hale 1A 128
High Mdw. Rd. B38: K Nor 5C 146
High Mdws. WV5: Wom 1G 73
WV6: Tett 1A 42
Highmoor Cl. WV12: W'hall 2B 30
WV14: Cose 2F 61
Highmoor Rd. B65: Row R 6B 96
Highmore Dr. B32: Bart G 5A 130
High Oak DY5: P'ntt 2G 93
Highover Dr. B75: Four O 5G 37
Highpark Av. DY8: Woll 6B 108
High Pk. Cl. B66: Smeth 4F 99
DY3: Sed 4H 59
High Pk. Cres. DY3: Sed 4H 59
HIGH PARK ESTATE 6A 108
High Pk. Rd. B63: Crad 6E 111
High Pk. St. B7: Nech 3B 102
High Point B15: Edg 5A 116
High Ridge WS9: A'rdge 4B 34
High Ridge Cl. WS9: A'rdge 4A 34
WS10: Mox 1A 62
High Rd. WV12: W'hall 4C 30
High St. B4: Birm 1G 117 (4E 5)
B6: Aston 2G 101
B8: Salt 4C 102
B14: K Hth 5G 133
B17: Harb 6G 115
B23: Erd 3F 85
B32: Quin 5G 113
B46: Col 1H 107
B63: Hale 1B 128
B64: Crad H 3E 111
B65: B'hth 2B 112
B66: Smeth 3D 98
B70: W Brom 3H 79
(not continuous)
B72: S Cold 5A 54
B90: Shir 5C 148
B91: Sol 3G 151
B92: H Ard 1A 154
B93: Know 3E 167
DY1: Dud 1E 95
DY3: Sed 4H 59
DY3: Swind 5E 73
DY4: Tip 5G 61
(Princes End)
DY4: Tip 2G 77
(Tipton)
DY5: Brie H 1H 109
(Brierley Hill)
DY5: Brie H 5F 93
(Brockmoor)
DY5: P'ntt 2E 93
DY5: Quar B 2B 110
DY6: K'wfrd 3B 92
DY6: W Hth 1H 91
DY8: Stourb 6E 109
DY8: Woll 5C 108

High St. DY8: Word 6C **92**
DY9: Lye 6A **110**
WS1: Wals 2C **48**
WS3: Blox 1H **31**
WS3: Pels 3E **21**
WS6: C Hay 3D **6**
WS7: Chase 1B **10**
(not continuous)
WS8: Bwnhls 6B **10**
WS8: Clay 1A **22**
WS9: A'rdge 3D **34**
(not continuous)
WS9: Wals W 4B **22**
WS10: Mox 1A **62**
WV5: Wom 1H **73**
WV6: Tett 5B **26**
WV11: Wed 4E **29**
WV14: Bils 6F **45**
High St. Amblecote DY8: Amb 3D **108**
High St. Bordesley B12: Birm 2A **118**
High St. Deritend B12: Birm 2H **117** (6H **5**)
Highters Cl. B14: K Hth 5B **148**
HIGHTER'S HEATH 5A **148**
Highter's Heath La. B14: K Hth 6A **148**
Highters Rd. B14: K Hth 4A **148**
High Timbers B45: Fran 6F **143**
High Town B63: Crad 5E **111**
Hightree Cl. B32: Bart G 4H **129**
High Trees B20: Hand 4B **82**
High Trees Rd. B93: Know 2C **166**
High Vw. WV14: Cose 4B **60**
Highview *WS1: Wals 3D 48*
(off Highgate Rd.)
Highview Dr. DY6: K'wfrd 5D **92**
Highview St. DY2: Dud 6G **77**
Highwood Av. B92: Olton 4E **137**
High Wood Cl. DY6: K'wfrd 3A **92**
Highwood Cft. B38: K Nor 6H **145**
Hiker Gro. B37: Chel W 1F **123**
Hilary Cres. DY1: Dud 1D **76**
Hilary Dr. B76: Walm 2E **71**
WS9: A'rdge 4C **34**
WV3: Wolv 4B **42**
Hilary Gro. B31: N'fld 3D **144**
Hilden Rd. B7: Birm 5A **102**
Hilderic Cres. DY1: Dud 2B **94**
Hilderstone Rd. B25: Yard 5A **120**
Hildicks Cres. WS3: Wals 2D **32**
Hildicks Pl. WS3: Wals 2D **32**
HILL 5G **37**
Hill, The B32: Bart G 3C **130**
Hillaire Cl. B38: K Nor 5E **147**
Hillaries Rd. B23: Erd 5D **84**
Hillary Av. WS10: W'bry 2A **64**
Hillary Crest DY3: Up Gor 2A **76**
Hillary St. WS2: Wals 4A **48**
Hill Av. WV4: E'shll 2B **60**
Hill Bank DY9: Lye 6B **110**
Hillbank B69: Tiv 6D **78**
Hill Bank Dr. B33: Stech 5B **104**
Hill Bank Rd. B38: K Nor 5C **146**
B63: Crad 5F **111**
Hillborough Rd. B27: A Grn 3C **136**
Hillbrook Gro. B33: Stech 6D **104**
Hillbrow Cres. B62: B'hth 3F **113**
Hillbury Dr. WV12: W'hall 1B **30**
Hill Cl. B31: N'fld 6F **145**
DY3: Sed 4A **60**
Hillcrest DY3: Lwr G 3G **75**
Hillcrest Av. B43: Gt Barr 3A **66**
B63: Crad 4D **110**
DY5: Brie H 2G **109**
WV10: Bush 6A **16**
Hillcrest Bus. Pk. DY2: Neth 2E **95**
Hillcrest Cl. DY2: Neth 4E **95**
Hillcrest Community Leisure Cen. 4D **94**
Hillcrest Gdns. WV12: W'hall 4D **30**
Hillcrest Gro. B44: K'sdng 6A **68**
Hillcrest Ind. Est. B64: Crad H 3F **111**
Hillcrest Ri. WS7: Burn 1D **10**
Hill Crest Rd. B13: Mose 3G **133**
Hillcrest Rd. B43: Gt Barr 3A **66**
B62: Roms 3A **142**
B72: W Grn 5A **70**
DY2: Dud 6G **77**
Hillcroft Ho. B14: K Hth 5H **147**
Hill Cft. Rd. B14: K Hth 1E **147**
Hillcroft Rd. DY6: K'wfrd 2C **92**
Hillcross Wlk. B36: Hodg H 1D **104**
Hilldene Rd. DY6: K'wfrd 5A **92**
Hilldrop Gro. B17: Harb 2H **131**
Hilleys Cft. B37: F'bri 6B **106**
HILLFIELD 6F **151**
Hillfield M. B91: Sol 1F **165**
Hillfield Rd. B11: S'hll 2D **134**
B91: Sol 1F **165**
(not continuous)
Hillfields B67: Smeth 6B **98**
Hillfields Rd. DY5: Brie H 4F **109**
Hillfield Wlk. B65: Row R 4H **95**
Hill Gro. B20: Hand 5E **83**
HILL HOOK 4E **37**
Hill Hook Nature Reserve 4F **37**
Hill Hook Rd. B74: Four O 4E **37**
Hill Ho. La. B33: Stech 6D **104**
(not continuous)
Hillhurst Gro. B36: Cas B 6H **87**
Hillhurst Rd. B73: New O 2B **68**
Hilliards Cft. B42: Gt Barr 5C **66**
Hillingford Av. B43: Gt Barr 2E **67**
Hill La. B43: Gt Barr 3A **66**
B75: Bass P 1F **55**
Hillman Dr. DY2: Dud 2G **95**
Hillman Gro. B36: Cas B 6A **88**
Hillmeads Dr. DY2: Dud 2G **95**
Hillmeads Rd. B38: K Nor 6C **146**
Hillmorton B74: Four O 6F **37**
Hill Morton Rd.
B74: Four O 5F **37**
Hillmorton Rd. B93: Know 4C **166**
Hillmount Cl. B28: Hall G 3E **135**
Hill Pk. WS9: Wals W 3C **22**
Hill Pas. B64: Old H 1G **111**
Hill Pl. WV11: Wed 6A **18**
Hill Rd. B69: Tiv 5A **78**
WV13: W'hall 3F **45**
Hillside DY3: Lwr G 3G **75**
WS8: Bwnhls 1C **22**
WV5: Wom 6E **57**
Hillside Av. B63: Crad 5F **111**
B65: B'hth 3B **112**
DY5: Quar B 3C **110**
Hillside Cl. B32: Bart G 5G **129**
WS8: Bwnhls 1C **22**
Hillside Ct. B43: Gt Barr 3H **65**
Hillside Cres. WS3: Pels 5D **20**
Hillside Cft. B92: Sol 1A **138**
Hillside Dr. B37: K'hrst 5B **106**
B42: Gt Barr 1C **82**
B74: S'tly 4H **51**
Hillside Gdns. B37: K'hrst 5B **106**
WV1: Wolv 6C **28**
Hillside Ho. B45: Rubery 1F **157**
Hillside Rd. B23: Erd 5D **84**
B43: Gt Barr 3H **65**
B74: Four O 5G **37**
DY1: Dud 2C **76**
Hillside Wlk. WV1: Wolv 6C **28**
Hillstone Gdns. WV10: Bush 1B **28**
Hillstone Rd. B34: S End 4H **105**
Hill St. B2: Birm 1F **117** (4C **4**)
B5: Birm 1F **117** (4C **4**)
B63: Hale 2A **128**
B66: Smeth 3E **99**
DY2: Neth 4D **94**
DY3: Up Gor 2H **75**
DY4: Tip 3H **77**
DY5: Brie H 1H **109**
DY5: Quar B 3C **110**
DY8: Amb 3D **108**
DY8: Stourb 1D **124**
DY9: Lye 6B **110**
WS1: Wals 2D **48**
WS6: C Hay 3C **6**
WS10: Darl 5E **47**
WV11: Ess 4H **17**
WV14: Bils 2G **61**
HILL TOP
West Bromwich 6G **63**
Hill Top B70: W Brom 5G **63**
Hilltop DY9: W'cte 2A **126**
Hill Top Av. B62: B'hth 4E **113**
Hill Top Cl. B44: Gt Barr 1G **83**
Hill Top Dr. B36: Hodg H 2B **104**
Hill Top Ind. Est. B70: W Brom 5F **63**
(Bilport La.)
B70: W Brom 5E **63**
(Pikehelve St.)
Hill Top Rd. B31: N'fld 4D **144**
B68: O'bry 1A **114**
Hilltop Rd. DY2: Dud 1G **95**
Hill Top Wlk. WS9: A'rdge 6E **23**
Hillview WS9: A'rdge 5D **22**
Hillview Cl. B63: Hale 5G **111**
Hillview Rd. B45: Rubery 1E **157**
Hill Village Rd. B75: Four O 4G **37**
Hillville Gdns. DY8: Stourb 2F **125**
HILL WOOD 5A **38**
Hillwood WS3: Pels 5D **20**
Hillwood Av. B90: M'path 3E **165**
Hillwood Cl. DY6: K'wfrd 5A **92**
Hillwood Comn. Rd. B75: Four O 5H **37**
Hillwood Rd. B31: N'fld 6C **130**
B62: B'hth 4C **112**
B75: Four O, R'ley 5H **37**
Hillyfields Rd. B23: Erd 3C **84**
Hilly Rd. WV14: Bils 3G **61**
Hilsea Cl. WV8: Pend 6D **14**
Hilston Av. B63: Hale 1H **127**
WV4: Penn 1A **58**
HILTON 5H **11**
Hilton Av. B28: Hall G 3E **149**
Hilton Cl. WS3: Blox 5F **19**
Hilton Cross WV10: F'stne 2D **16**
Hilton Cross Bus. Pk. WV10: F'stne 2D **16**
Hilton Dr. B72: W Grn 5A **70**
Hilton La. WS6: Gt Wyr 3F **7**
WV11: Ess 6A **6**
Hilton Main Ind. Est. WV10: F'stne 2E **17**
Hilton Pk. WV11: Ess 1G **17**
Hilton Pl. WV14: Bils 6H **45**
Hilton Rd. B69: Tiv 1C **96**
WV4: E'shll 6B **44**
WV10: F'stne 1D **16**
WV12: W'hall 1C **30**
Hilton St. B70: W Brom 4G **79**
WV10: Wolv 6A **28**
Hilton Trad. Est. WV4: E'shll 6B **44**
Hilton Way WV12: W'hall 1C **30**
Himbleton Cft. B90: M'path 2E **165**
HIMLEY 4H **73**
Himley Av. DY1: Dud 5B **76**
Himley By-Pass DY3: Himl 4G **73**
Himley Cl. B43: Gt Barr 3G **65**
WV12: W'hall 4B **30**
Himley Ct. *DY3: Lwr G 4A 76*
(off Peak Dr.)
Himley Cres. WV4: Penn 6F **43**
Himley Gdns. DY3: Lwr G 3D **74**
Himley Gro. B45: Redn 3H **157**
Himley House & Model Village 4A **74**
Himley La. DY3: Himl, Swind 5E **73**
(not continuous)
Himley Ri. B90: Ches G 5C **164**
Himley Rd. DY1: Dud 5G **75**
DY3: Gorn 4D **74**
Himley St. DY1: Dud 6C **76**
Himley Wood Nature Reserve 4G **73**
Hinbrook Rd. DY1: Dud 6A **76**
Hinchliffe Av. WV14: Cose 3D **60**
Hinckes Rd. WV6: Tett 4H **25**
Hinckley Ct. B68: O'bry 4H **113**
Hinckley St. B5: Birm 2F **117** (6D **4**)
Hincks St. WV2: E'shll 4C **44**
Hindhead Rd. B14: Yard W 3C **148**
Hindlip Cl. B63: Hale 3H **127**
Hindlow Cl. B7: Birm 5B **102**
Hindon Gro. B27: A Grn 6A **136**
Hindon Sq. B15: Edg 3B **116**
Hindon Wlk. B32: Bart G 3A **130**
Hingeston St. B18: Hock 5D **100**
Hingley Cft. WS9: A'rdge 6H **35**
Hingley Ind. Pk. B64: Crad H 2E **111**
Hingley Rd. B63: Crad 5C **110**
Hingley St. B64: Crad H 2F **111**
HINKSFORD 1F **91**
Hinksford Gdns. DY3: Swind 5E **73**
Hinksford La. DY3: Swind 5E **73**
DY6: K'wfrd 5E **73**
Hinksford Pk. Res. Mobile Homes
DY6: K'wfrd 1E **91**

Hinsford Cl. DY6: K'wfrd 1C **92**
Hinstock Cl. WV4: Penn 1E **59**
Hinstock Rd. B20: Hand 6B **82**
Hintlesham Av. B15: Edg 6H **115**
Hinton Gro. WV11: Wed 4H **29**
Hintons Coppice B93: Know 3A **166**
Hipkins St. DY4: Tip 6G **61**
Hiplands Rd. B62: Hale 1F **129**
Hipsley Cl. B36: Cas B 6G **87**
Hipsmoor Cl. B37: K'hrst 6B **106**
Hirdemonsway B90: Dic H 4G **163**
Histons Dr. WV8: Cod 5F **13**
Histons Hill WV8: Cod 5F **13**
Hitchcock Cl. B67: Smeth 4B **98**
Hitches La. B15: Edg 4D **116**
Hitherside B90: Dic H 4H **163**
Hive Development Cen. B18: Hock 2C **100**
HMP Birmingham B18: Win G 4A **100**
Hobacre Cl. B45: Rubery 1G **157**
Hobart Ct. B74: Four O 6G **37**
Hobart Cft. B7: Birm 5A **102**
Hobart Dr. WS5: Wals 5G **49**
Hobart Rd. DY4: Tip 4G **61**
Hobbis Ho. B38: K Nor 2G **159**
HOBBLE END 6G **7**
Hobble End La. WS6: Gt Wyr 1G **19**
Hobgate Cl. WV10: Wolv 5B **28**
Hobgate Rd. WV10: Wolv 5B **28**
Hob Grn. Rd. DY9: W'cte 3A **126**
Hobhouse Cl. B42: Gt Barr 6B **66**
Hob La. B92: Bars 3A **168**
Hobley St. WV13: W'hall 1C **46**
Hobmoor Cft. B25: Yard 4B **120**
Hob Moor Rd. B10: Small H 2F **119**
B25: Yard 3A **120**
Hobnock Rd. WV11: Ess 3A **18**
Hobs Hole La. WS9: A'rdge 2D **34**
Hob's Mdw. B92: Olton 3E **137**
Hobs Moat Rd. B92: Olton, Sol 3F **137**
Hobson Cl. B18: Hock 4C **100**
Hobson Rd. B29: S Oak 4D **132**
Hobs Rd. WS10: W'bry 1G **63**
HOCKLEY
Birmingham 4D **100**
Hockley Brook Trad. Est. B18: Hock . . . 3C **100**
Hockley Cen. *B18: Birm* *1A 4*
(off Big Pen, The)
Hockley Cir. B19: Hock 3D **100**
Hockley Cl. B19: Hock 3F **101**
Hockley Flyover B19: Hock 3D **100**
Hockley Hill B18: Birm 4D **100**
Hockley Hill Ind. Est. B18: Hock 4D **100**
Hockley Ind. Est. B18: Hock 4D **100**
Hockley La. DY2: Neth 6D **94**
Hockley Pool Cl. B18: Hock 4D **100**
Hockley Rd. B23: Erd 3D **84**
WV14: Cose 6C **60**
Hockley St. B18: Birm 5E **101**
B19: Birm 5E **101**
Hodder Gro. B71: W Brom 6D **64**
HODGEHILL 3B **104**
Hodge Hill Av. DY9: W'cte 2A **126**
Hodge Hill Comn. B36: Hodg H 2C **104**
Hodgehill Ct. B36: Hodg H 2C **104**
Hodge Hill Rd. B34: Hodg H 3C **104**
Hodges Dr. B69: Tiv 6B **78**
Hodgetts Cl. B67: Smeth 6B **98**
Hodgetts Dr. B63: Hale 5F **127**
Hodgkins Cl. WS8: Bwnhls 1C **22**
Hodgson Twr. B19: Hock 3F **101**
Hodnell Cl. B36: Cas B 6G **87**
Hodnet Cl. WV14: Bils 6D **44**
Hodnet Dr. DY5: P'ntt 3G **93**
Hodson Av. WV13: W'hall 2C **46**
Hodson Cl. WV11: Wed 1H **29**
Hoff Beck Ct. B9: Birm 1B **118**
Hogarth Cl. B43: Gt Barr 6F **51**
WV13: W'hall 1G **45**
Hogarth Ho. B15: Birm 3E **117**
Hogg's La. B31: N'fld 3C **144**
HOLBEACHE 6A **74**
Holbeache La. DY6: K'wfrd 6A **74**
Holbeache Rd. DY6: W Hth 1A **92**
Holbeach Rd. B33: Yard 1F **121**
Holbeche Rd. B75: S Cold 6F **55**
B93: Know 2C **166**
Holberg Gro. WV11: Wed 4H **29**
Holborn Cen., The DY3: Sed 6H **59**
Holborn Hill B6: Aston 1B **102**
Holbrook Gro. B37: Mars G 2D **122**
Holbrook Twr. B36: Hodg H 1A **104**
Holbury Cl. WV9: Pend 5E **15**
Holcombe Rd. B11: Tys 1G **135**
Holcroft Rd. B63: Crad 6E **111**
DY6: W Hth 6A **74**
DY9: Lye 1G **125**
Holcroft St. DY4: Tip 5A **78**
WV2: E'shll 4C **44**
Holden Cl. B23: Erd 5E **85**
Holden Cres. WS3: Wals 4C **32**
Holden Cft. DY4: Tip 4A **78**
Holden Pl. WS3: Wals 5C **32**
Holden Rd. WS10: W'bry 3G **63**
WV4: Penn 2B **58**
Holdens, The B28: Hall G 1E **149**
Holden Way B75: Four O 1H **53**
Holder Rd. B11: S'brk 5C **118**
B25: Yard 4A **120**
Holders Gdns. B13: Mose 3E **133**
Holders La. B13: Mose 3E **133**
Holdford Rd. B6: Witt 5H **83**
Holdgate Rd. B29: W Cas 6F **131**
Hole Farm Rd. B31: N'fld 3G **145**
Hole Farm Way B38: K Nor 2B **160**
Hole La. B31: N'fld 1G **145**
Holendene Way WV5: Wom 6E **57**
Holford Av. WS2: Wals 5A **48**
Holford Dr. B6: Witt 3G **83**
B42: P Barr 3G **83**
Holford Ind. Pk. B6: Witt 4H **83**
Holford Way B6: Witt 3H **83**
Holifast Rd. B72: W Grn 6H **69**
Holland Av. B68: O'bry 5B **98**
B93: Know 1D **166**
Holland Ho. *B19: Birm* *4F 101*
(off Gt. Hampton Row)
Holland Ind. Pk. WS10: Darl 3D **46**
Holland Rd. B43: Gt Barr 6H **65**
B72: S Cold 2H **69**
WV14: Bils 4G **45**
Holland Rd. W. B6: Aston 3H **101**
Hollands Pl. WS3: Blox 6B **20**
Hollands Rd. WS3: Blox 6B **20**
Holland St. B3: Birm 6E **101** (3A **4**)
B72: S Cold 1H **69**
DY1: Dud 1D **94**
DY4: Tip 6C **62**
Hollands Way WS3: Pels 3D **20**
Hollemeadow Av. WS3: Blox 2B **32**
Holliars Gro. B37: K'hrst 4B **106**
Holliday Pas. B1: Birm 2E **117** (6B **4**)
Holliday Rd. B21: Hand 2B **100**
B24: Erd 3G **85**
Holliday St. B1: Birm 2E **117** (6A **4**)
Holliday Wharf B1: Birm 2E **117** (6B **4**)
Hollie Lucas Rd. B13: Mose 6H **133**
Hollies, The B6: Aston 1B **102**
B16: Birm 6B **100**
WV2: Wolv 3G **43** (6A **170**)
WV5: Wom 6H **57**
Hollies Cft. B5: Edg 6E **117**
Hollies Dr. B62: Hale 5D **112**
WS10: W'bry 2F **63**
Hollies Ind. Est., The
WV2: Wolv 3G **43** (6A **170**)
Hollies La. WV6: Nur 5A **24**
Hollies Ri. B64: Crad H 3H **111**
Hollies Rd. B69: Tiv 1A **96**
Hollies St. DY5: P'ntt 2H **93**
Hollin Brow Cl. B93: Know 6D **166**
Hollingberry La. B76: Walm 2D **70**
Hollings Gro. B91: Sol 1F **165**
Hollington Cres. B33: Stech 5E **105**
Hollington Rd. WV1: Wolv 3D **44**
Hollington Way B90: M'path 2G **165**
Hollinwell Cl. WS3: Blox 4G **19**
Hollister Dr. B32: Bart G 2D **130**
Hollow, The B13: Mose 1G **133**
Holloway B31: N'fld 1C **144**
Holloway, The DY3: Swind 6D **72**
DY8: Amb 4D **108**
WV6: Tett 1A **42**
Holloway Bank B70: W Brom 4F **63**
WS10: W'bry 4F **63**
Holloway Bank Trad. Est.
WS10: W'bry 4F **63**
Holloway Cir. Queensway
B1: Birm 2F **117** (6D **4**)
Holloway Ct. B63: Crad 6F **111**
Holloway Dr. WV5: Wom 2E **73**
HOLLOWAY END 5F **109**
Holloway Head B1: Birm 2F **117** (6C **4**)
Holloway St. DY3: Lwr G, Up Gor 3H **75**
WV1: Wolv 4C **44**
Holloway St. W. DY3: Lwr G 2H **75**
Hollow Cft. B31: N'fld 4F **145**
Hollowcroft Rd. WV12: W'hall 1B **30**
Hollowmeadow Ho. B36: Hodg H 1B **104**
Holly Av. B12: Bal H 6A **118**
B29: S Oak 4D **132**
HOLLY BANK 4C **22**
Hollybank Av. WV11: Ess 4A **18**
Hollybank Cl. WS3: Blox 5G **19**
Hollybank Gro. B63: Hale 4F **127**
Hollybank Rd. B13: Mose 6A **134**
Hollyberry Av. B91: Sol 1E **165**
Hollyberry Cl. B63: Hale 2A **128**
Hollyberry Cft. B34: S End 3G **105**
Hollybrow B29: W Cas 6E **131**
Holly Bush Gro. B32: Quin 4B **114**
Holly Bush La. WV10: Share 5A **6**
(not continuous)
Hollybush La. DY8: Amb 4D **108**
WV4: Penn 1B **58**
WV8: Oaken 5D **12**
Holly Bush Wlk. B64: Crad H 2F **111**
Holly Cl. B76: Walm 3D **70**
WV12: W'hall 3C **30**
Hollycot Gdns. B12: Bal H 5H **117**
Holly Ct. B23: Erd 2G **85**
WS5: Wals 1E **65**
Hollycroft Gdns. WV6: Tett 4H **25**
Hollycroft Rd. B21: Hand 6H **81**
Hollydale Rd. B24: Erd 4A **86**
B65: Row R 6D **96**
Holly Dell B38: K Nor 5D **146**
Holly Dr. B27: A Grn 3H **135**
B47: H'wd 2B **162**
Hollyfaste Rd. B33: Sheld 2F **121**
Hollyfield Av. B91: Sol 4C **150**
Hollyfield Ct. B75: S Cold 6C **54**
Hollyfield Cres. B75: S Cold 1C **70**
Hollyfield Dr. B75: S Cold 6C **54**
Hollyfield Rd. B75: S Cold 6C **54**
Hollyfield Rd. Sth. B76: Walm 1D **70**
Holly Gro. B19: Hand 1D **100**
B29: S Oak 3B **132**
(not continuous)
B30: B'vlle 5B **132**
DY8: Stourb 6D **108**
WV3: Wolv 4D **42**
Holly Hall Rd. DY2: Dud 3C **94**
Hollyhedge Cl. B31: N'fld 1B **144**
WS2: Wals 1A **48**
Hollyhedge La. WS2: Wals 6A **32**
Hollyhedge Rd. B71: W Brom 6C **64**
Holly Hill B45: Fran 6F **143**
WS6: Gt Wyr *5E 7*
(off Holly La.)
Holly Hill Rd. B45: Fran 5G **143**
Holly Hill Shop. Cen. B45: Fran 6G **143**
Hollyhock Rd. B27: A Grn 4F **135**
DY2: Dud 6H **77**
Hollyhurst B46: Wat O 4E **89**
Hollyhurst Cvn. Pk. B62: Hunn 1B **142**
Hollyhurst Dr. DY8: Word 6B **92**
Hollyhurst Gro. B26: Yard 5C **120**
B90: Shir 1H **163**
Hollyhurst Rd. B73: S'tly 2B **68**
Holly La. B24: Erd 2H **85**
B37: Mars G 3B **122**
B66: Smeth 2C **98**
B67: Smeth 4B **98**
B74: Four O 6G **37**
B75: Four O 6G **37**
B76: Wis 2H **71**
CV7: Bal C 4H **169**
WS6: Gt Wyr 5E **7**
WS9: A'rdge 1H **35**
WS9: Wals W 3C **22**
(not continuous)

Holly Lodge Wlk. B37: F'bri 1B **122**
Hollymoor Way B31: Longb 5A **144**
Holly Mt. B16: Edg 2H **115**
Hollymount B62: Quin 4G **113**
Hollyoak Cft. B31: Longb 1F **159**
Hollyoake Cl. B68: O'bry 1G **113**
Hollyoak Gro. B91: Sol 6E **151**
Hollyoak Rd. B74: S'tly 5H **51**
Hollyoak St. B71: W Brom 3B **80**
Holly Pk. Dr. B24: Erd 3H **85**
Holly Pk. Ind. Est. B24: Erd 5A **86**
Hollypiece Ho. B27: A Grn 3G **135**
Holly Pl. B6: Aston 1G **101**
B29: S Oak 3D **132**
Holly Rd. B16: Edg 2G **115**
B20: Hand 1B **100**
B30: K Nor 3C **146**
B65: B'hth 2B **112**
B68: O'bry 3A **114**
B71: W Brom 5C **64**
DY1: Dud 4C **76**
WS10: W'bry 6F **47**
Holly St. B67: Smeth 4D **98**
DY1: Dud 3A **94**
Holly Vw. WV11: Ess 4A **18**
Hollywell Rd. B26: Sheld 5F **121**
B93: Know 4C **166**
Hollywell St. WV14: Cose 4C **60**
HOLLYWOOD 1A **162**
Holly Wood B43: Gt Barr 4C **66**
Hollywood Bowl 1H **157**
Hollywood By-Pass B38: Head H 3G **161**
B47: H'wd 3G **161**
Hollywood Cft. B42: Gt Barr 5B **66**
Hollywood Dr. B47: H'wd 1A **162**
Hollywood Gdns. B47: H'wd 1A **162**
Hollywood La. B47: H'wd 1A **162**
Hollywood Nature Reserve 4C **66**
Holman Cl. WV13: W'hall 1G **45**
Holman Rd. WV13: W'hall 1F **45**
Holman Way WV13: W'hall 1G **45**
Holmbridge Gro. WS4: S'fld 5H **21**
Holme Mill WV10: F'hses 3H **15**
Holmes, The WV10: F'hses 4H **15**
Holmes Cl. B43: Gt Barr 6A **66**
Holmes Dr. B45: Rubery 3F **157**
Holmesfield Rd. B42: Gt Barr 6E **67**
Holmes Rd. WV12: W'hall 2D **30**
Holme Way WS4: Rus 2F **33**
Holmwood Rd. B10: Small H 2D **118**
Holt Ct. Nth. B7: Birm 5H **101** (1H **5**)
Holt Ct. Sth. B7: Birm 5H **101** (1H **5**)
Holte Community Leisure Cen. 2F **101**
Holte Dr. B75: R'ley 1B **54**
Holte Rd. B6: Aston 6A **84**
B11: S'brk 6D **118**
Holtes Wlk. B6: Aston 1B **102**
Holt Rd. B62: B'hth 2E **113**
Holtshill La. WS1: Wals 1D **48**
Holt St. B7: Birm 5H **101** (1G **5**)
Holy Farm Trekking Cen. 2G **129**
Holyhead Community Leisure Cen. 1H **99**
Holyhead Rd. B21: Hand 6F **81**
WS10: Darl 1C **62**
WS10: W'bry 2D **62**
WV8: Cod, Oaken 5B **12**
Holyhead Rd. Ind. Est. WS10: W'bry 2D **62**
Holyhead Way B21: Hand 1H **99**
Holyoak Cl. B6: Aston 6H **83**
Holyrood Gro. B6: Aston 1G **101**
Holy Well Cl. B16: Edg 1C **116**
Holywell La. B45: Rubery 3D **156**
Home Cl. B28: Hall G 1F **149**
Homecroft Rd. B25: Yard 3C **120**
Homedene Rd. B31: N'fld 6C **130**
Homefield Rd. WV8: Bilb 4H **13**
Homelands B42: Gt Barr 6D **66**
Homelands Pk. WV10: Cov H 1G **15**
Homelea Rd. B25: Yard 3B **120**
Homemead Gro. B45: Rubery 2F **157**
Home Mdw. Ho. B27: A Grn 3G **135**
Home Peal Ho. B14: K Hth 1G **147**
HOMER HILL 4D **110**
Homer Hill Rd. B63: Crad 4E **111**
Homer Rd. B75: R'ley 1A **54**
B91: Sol 4F **151**
Homers Fold WV14: Bils 6F **45**
Homer St. B12: Bal H 6H **117**
Homerton Rd. B44: K'sdng 4B **68**
Homestead Cl. DY3: Up Gor 2A **76**
Homestead Dr. B75: R'ley 6A **38**
Homestead Rd. B33: Sheld 2F **121**
Home Twr. B7: Birm 4B **102**
Homewood Cl. B76: Walm 2C **70**
Honesty Cl. WS8: Clay 1H **21**
Honeswode Cl. B20: Hand 1C **100**
Honeyborne Rd. B75: S Cold 4B **54**
Honeybourne Cl. B63: Hale 2A **128**
Honeybourne Cres. WV5: Wom 2F **73**
Honeybourne Rd. B33: Sheld 3G **121**
B63: Hale 2C **128**
Honeybourne Way WV13: W'hall 1C **46**
Honeycomb Way B31: N'fld 4C **144**
Honeysuckle Av. DY6: K'wfrd 2C **92**
Honeysuckle Cl. B32: Quin 6H **113**
Honeysuckle Dr. WS5: Wals 2E **65**
Honeysuckle Gro. B27: A Grn 6A **120**
Honeysuckle Way WS6: Gt Wyr 1H **7**
Honeytree Cl. DY6: K'wfrd 6D **92**
Honiley Dr. B73: New O 3C **68**
Honiley Rd. B33: Yard 1E **121**
Honister Cl. DY5: Quar B 2B **110**
Honiton Cl. B31: N'fld 3C **144**
Honiton Cres. B31: N'fld 3C **144**
Honiton Wlk. B66: Smeth 4F **99**
Honiton Way WS9: A'rdge 4B **34**
Honnington Ct. B29: W Cas 4D **130**
Honor Av. WV4: Penn 6G **43**
Hood Gro. B30: K Nor 3H **145**
Hook Dr. B74: Four O 5F **37**
Hooper St. B18: Win G 5B **100**
Hoosen Cl. B62: Quin 5G **113**
Hopedale Rd. B32: Quin 6A **114**
Hope Pl. B29: S Oak 3B **132**
Hope Rd. DY4: Tip 1C **78**
Hope St. B5: Birm 3F **117**
B62: B'hth 3D **112**
B70: W Brom 5C **80**
DY2: Dud 1E **95**
DY8: Word 6B **92**
WS1: Wals 3C **48**
Hope Ter. DY2: Neth 4E **95**
WS10: Darl 1D **62**
Hopkins Ct. WS10: W'bry 2G **63**
Hopkins Dr. B71: W Brom 6C **64**
Hopkins St. DY4: Tip 5A **78**
Hopstone Gdns. WV4: Penn 6D **42**
Hopstone Rd. B29: W Cas 4E **131**
Hopton Cl. DY4: Tip 3C **62**
WV6: Pert 6F **25**
Hopton Cres. WV11: Wed 3G **29**
Hopton Gdns. DY1: Dud 4C **76**
Hopton Gro. B13: Mose 2C **148**
Hopwas Gro. B37: K'hrst 4B **106**
HOPWOOD 6G **159**
Hopwood Cl. B63: Hale 3A **128**
Hopwood Gro. B31: Longb 3C **158**
Hopyard Cl. DY3: Gorn 4F **75**
Hopyard Gdns. WV14: Cose 2D **60**
Hopyard La. DY3: Gorn 5F **75**
Hopyard Rd. WS2: Wals 1E **47**
Horace Partridge Rd. WS10: Mox 6A **46**
Horace St. WV14: Cose 5C **60**
Horatio Dr. B13: Mose 1H **133**
Hordern Cl. WV6: Wolv 4D **26**
Hordern Cres. DY5: Quar B 3H **109**
Hordern Gro. WV6: Wolv 4D **26**
Hordern Pk. WV10: Cov H 1G **15**
Hordern Rd. WV6: Wolv 4D **26**
Hornbeam Cl. B29: W Cas 6F **131**
Hornbeam Wlk. WV3: Wolv 2E **43**
Hornbrook Gro. B92: Olton 6A **136**
Hornby Gro. B14: Yard W 3C **148**
Hornby Rd. WV4: Penn 1G **59**
Horner Way B65: B'hth 2C **112**
Horne Way B34: S End 4A **106**
Horning Dr. WV14: Bils 2E **61**
Hornsey Gro. B44: K'sdng 3A **68**
Hornsey Rd. B44: K'sdng 3A **68**
Hornton Cl. B74: Lit A 4D **36**
Horrell Rd. B26: Sheld 4E **121**
B90: Shir 5F **149**
Horsecroft Dr. *B71: W Brom 5E 65*
(off Tompstone Rd.)
Horse Fair B5: Birm 2F **117** (6D **4**)
Horsehills Dr. WV3: Wolv 1C **42**
Horselea Cft. B8: W End 5A **104**
Horseley Flds. WV1: Wolv 1H **43** (3D **170**)
HORSELEY HEATH 1C **78**
Horseley Heath DY4: Tip 3B **78**
Horseley Rd. DY4: Tip 1C **78**
Horseshoe, The B68: O'bry 1A **114**
Horseshoe Cl. *WS2: Wals 4H 47*
(off Wellington St.)
Horse Shoes La. B26: Sheld 6F **121**
Horseshoe Wlk. *DY4: Tip 2G 77*
(off New Cross St.)
Horsfall Rd. B75: S Cold 6E **55**
Horsham Av. DY8: Word 6A **92**
Horsley Rd. B43: Gt Barr 1F **67**
B74: Lit A 1B **52**
Horton Cl. DY3: Sed 5G **59**
WS10: Darl 4D **46**
Horton Gro. B90: M'path 4E **165**
Horton Pl. WS10: Darl 4D **46**
Horton Sq. B12: Birm 4G **117**
Horton St. B70: W Brom 5A **80**
DY4: Tip 2D **78**
WS10: Darl 4D **46**
Hospital Dr. B15: Edg 1A **132**
Hospital La. B69: Tiv 5B **78**
WS6: C Hay 2B **6**
WV14: Cose 6D **60**
Hospital Rd. WS7: Burn 1C **10**
Hospital St. B19: Birm, Hock 4F **101** (1D **4**)
(not continuous)
WS2: Wals 5B **32**
WV2: Wolv 2H **43** (5D **170**)
Hothersall Dr. B73: Bold 5F **69**
Hotspur Rd. B44: K'sdng 4H **67**
Hough Pl. WS2: Wals 4H **47**
Hough Rd. B14: K Hth 1F **147**
WS2: Wals 4G **47**
Houghton Ct. B28: Hall G 3D **148**
Houghton St. B69: O'bry 3F **97**
B70: W Brom 1B **98**
Houldey Rd. B31: N'fld 6F **145**
Houliston Cl. WS10: W'bry 6H **47**
Houndsfield Cl. B47: H'wd 3C **162**
Houndsfield Ct. B47: Wyt 4A **162**
Houndsfield Gro. B47: Wyt 4A **162**
(not continuous)
Houndsfield La. B47: H'wd 3C **162**
B47: Wyt 4A **162**
B90: Dic H 3C **162**
Houndsfield M. B47: Wyt 4B **162**
Houx, The DY8: Amb 3C **108**
Hove Rd. B27: A Grn 4A **136**
Howard Ho. B92: H Ard 1B **154**
Howard Rd. B14: K Hth 6F **133**
B20: Hand 5D **82**
B25: Yard 4A **120**
B43: Gt Barr 5G **65**
B92: Olton 2C **136**
WV11: Wed 1H **29**
WV14: Bils 2H **61**
Howard Rd. E. B13: Mose 6H **133**
Howard St. B19: Birm 5F **101** (1C **4**)
B70: W Brom 6F **63**
DY4: Tip 2B **78**
WV2: Wolv 3H **43** (6C **170**)
Howard St. Ind. Est. B70: W Brom 6F **63**
Howarth Way B6: Aston 2A **102**
Howden Pl. B33: Stech 4E **105**
Howdle's La. WS8: Bwnhls 3B **10**
Howe Cres. WV12: W'hall 3C **30**
Howell Rd. WV2: Wolv 4A **44**
Howes Cft. B35: Cas V 5E **87**
Howe St. B4: Birm 6H **101** (2H **5**)
Howford Gro. B7: Birm 5B **102**
Howland Cl. WV9: Pend 5D **14**
Howley Av. B44: Gt Barr 4G **67**
Howley Grange Rd. B62: Quin 6F **113**
Howl Pl. DY4: Tip 2H **77**
Hoylake Cl. WS3: Blox 4H **19**
Hoylake Dr. B69: Tiv 2A **96**
Hoylake Rd. WV6: Pert 4D **24**
Hoyland Way B30: B'vlle 5A **132**
HRS Ind. Pk. B33: Sheld 2G **121**
Hubert Cft. B29: S Oak 3B **132**
Hubert Rd. B29: S Oak 3B **132**

Hubert St.—Irving Rd.

Hubert St. B6: Aston 4H 101
Hucker Cl. WS2: Wals 4G 47
Hucker Rd. WS2: Wals 4G 47
Huddesford Dr. CV7: Bal C 1H 169
Huddlestone Cl. WV10: F'stne 1D 16
Huddleston Way B29: S Oak 4G 131
Huddocks Vw. WS3: Pels 2D 20
Hudson Av. B46: Col 3H 107
Hudson Gro. WV6: Pert 4E 25
Hudson Rd. B20: Hand 3B 82
DY4: Tip 3C 78
Hudson's Dr. B30: K Nor 3C 146
Hudswell Dr. DY5: Brie H 3H 109
Huggins Cl. CV7: Bal C 5H 169
Hughes Av. WV3: Wolv 3D 42
Hughes Pl. WV14: Bils 4F 45
Hughes Rd. WS10: Mox 6A 46
WV14: Bils 4F 45
Hugh Gaitskell Ct. WV14: Wolv 3E 45
Hugh Porter Way WV6: Tett 2D 26
Hugh Rd. B10: Small H 2E 119
B67: Smeth 4B 98
Hugh Vs. B10: Small H 2E 119
Hulbert Dr. DY2: Dud 3D 94
Hulland Pl. DY5: Brie H 6G 93
Hullbrook Rd. B13: Mose 2C 148
Humber Av. B76: Walm 6E 71
Humber Gdns. B63: Crad 6E 111
Humber Gro. B36: Cas B 6B 88
Humber Rd. WV3: Wolv 2E 43
Humberstone Rd. B24: Erd 3C 86
Humber Twr. B7: Birm 5A 102
Hume St. B66: Smeth 5F 99
(not continuous)
Humpage Rd. B9: Bord G 1E 119
Humphrey Middlemore Dr. B17: Harb 1H 131
Humphrey's Rd. WV10: Bush 2H 27
Humphrey St. DY3: Lwr G 4H 75
Humphries Cres. WV14: Bils 4H 61
Humphries Ho. WS8: Bwnhls 6B 10
Hundred Acre Rd. B74: S'tly 4H 51
Hungary Cl. DY9: Lye 6G 109
Hungary Hill DY9: Lye 6G 109
Hungerfield Rd. B36: Cas B 6G 87
Hungerford Rd. DY8: Stourb 3C 124
Hunningham Gro. B91: Sol 1F 165
HUNNINGTON 6B 128
Hunnington Cl. B32: Bart G 4G 129
Hunnington Cres. B63: Hale 3B 128
Hunscote Cl. B90: Shir 6F 149
Hunslet Cl. B32: Quin 1D 130
Hunslet Rd. B32: Quin 1D 130
Hunstanton Av. B17: Harb 4D 114
Hunstanton Cl. DY5: Brie H 4G 109
Hunter Ct. B5: Edg 6F 117
Hunter Cres. WS3: Blox 3D 32
Hunters Cl. WV14: Bils 4A 46
Hunters Ride DY7: Stourt 6H 91
Hunters Ri. B63: Hale 4F 127
Hunter's Rd. B19: Hock 2D 100
Hunter St. WV6: Wolv 5E 27
Hunters Wlk. B23: Erd 5C 68
Huntingdon Ho. B23: Erd 1B 84
Huntingdon Rd. B71: W Brom 1H 79
Huntington Rd. WV12: W'hall 2D 30
Huntingtree Rd. B63: Hale 1G 127
Huntlands Rd. B63: Hale 3G 127
Huntley Dr. B91: Sol 5F 151
Huntly Rd. B16: Edg 2C 116
Hunton Ct. *B23: Erd 5E 85*
(off Gravelly Hill N.)
Hunton Hill B23: Erd 4D 84
Hunton Rd. B23: Erd 4E 85
Hunt's La. WV12: W'hall 3D 30
Huntsman Cl. WV14: Cose 3F 61
Hunts Mill Dr. DY5: P'ntt 6G 75
Hunt's Rd. B30: Stir 6C 132
Hurdis Rd. B90: Shir 4G 149
Hurdlow Av. B18: Hock 4D 100
Hurley Cl. B72: W Grn 3A 70
WS5: Wals 5H 49
Hurley Gro. B37: K'hrst 4B 106
Hurley's Fold DY2: Neth 4D 94
Hurlingham Rd. B44: K'sdng 3A 68
Hurricane Pk. B24: Erd 1G 103
Hurricane Way B35: Cas V 5E 87
Hursey Dr. DY4: Tip 2A 78
Hurst, The B13: Mose 6C 134
B47: H'wd 3A 162
Hurstbourne Cres. WV1: Wolv 2D 44
Hurst Cl. B36: Cas B 2A 106
Hurstcroft Rd. B33: Kitts G 6F 105
Hurst Grn. Rd. B62: B'hth 2E 113
B76: Min 1H 87
B93: Ben H 5B 166
Hurst Grn. Shop. Cen. B62: B'hth 3F 113
HURST HILL 5C 60
Hurst Hill Ct. *WV14: Cose 5C 60*
(off Caddick St.)
WV14: Cose 5C 60
(Hartland Av.)
Hurst La. B34: S End 3H 105
DY4: Tip 2F 77
DY5: Brie H 6B 94
Hurst La. Nth. B36: Cas B 2A 106
Hurst Rd. B67: Smeth 6B 98
WV14: Cose 4C 60
Hurst St. B5: Birm 2G 117 (6E 5)
(not continuous)
Hurstway, The B23: Erd 5C 68
Hurstwood Rd. B23: Erd 5C 68
Huskison Cl. B69: Tiv 6B 78
Husphins La. WV8: Cod, Cod W 2A 12
Hussey Rd. WS8: Bwnhls 5A 10
Hutchings La. B90: Dic H 4H 163
Hut Hill La. WS6: Gt Wyr 1G 7
Hutton Av. B8: Salt 4D 102
Hutton Rd. B8: Salt 4D 102
B20: Hand 6D 82
Huxbey Dr. B92: Sol 5B 138
Huxley Cl. WV9: Pend 4E 15
Hyacinth Cl. WS5: Wals 2D 64
Hyatt Sq. DY5: Brie H 4G 109
Hyatts Wlk. B65: Row R 4H 95
Hyde, The DY9: W'cte 3H 125
Hyde Rd. WV11: Wed 3F 29
Hydes Rd. B71: W Brom 4A 64
WS10: W'bry 2G 63
Hyett Way WV14: Bils 3B 62
Hylda Rd. B20: Hand 6D 82
Hylstone Cres. WV11: Wed 3F 29
Hylton St. B18: Birm 4E 101
Hyperion Dr. WV4: Penn 2E 59
Hyperion Rd. B36: Hodg H 6C 86
DY7: Stourt 4A 108
Hyron Hall Rd. B27: A Grn 3A 136
Hyssop Cl. B7: Birm 4A 102
Hytall Rd. B90: Shir 5C 148
Hythe Gro. B25: Yard 3B 120

I

Ibberton Rd. B14: K Hth 4B 148
Ibis Gdns. DY6: K'wfrd 3E 93
Ibstock Dr. DY8: Stourb 1E 125
Icknield Cl. B74: S'tly 2A 52
Icknield Port Rd. B16: Birm 5A 100
Icknield Sq. B16: Birm 6C 100
Icknield St. B18: Birm 5D 100
(not continuous)
B38: Forh 6C 160
B38: Head H, K Nor 1C 160
Ida Rd. B70: W Brom 6B 80
WS2: Wals 2H 47
Idbury Rd. B44: K'sdng 6A 68
Ideal Works DY9: Lye 5C 110
Idmiston Cft. B14: K Hth 5H 147
Idonia Rd. WV6: Pert 4E 25
Ikon Gallery 1E 117 (5A 4)
Ilford Rd. B23: Erd 1D 84
Iliffe Way B17: Harb 1H 131
Ilkley Gro. B37: F'bri 1B 122
ILLEY 5E 129
Illeybrook Sq. B32: Bart G 3B 130
Illey Cl. B31: Longb 6H 143
Illey La. B32: Fran 5E 129
B62: Hunn 4C 128
Illshaw WV9: Pend 4F 15
Illshaw Heath Rd. B94: H'ley H 6B 164
Illshaw Path B90: Bly P 6D 164
Ilmington Dr. B73: New O 2C 68
Ilmington Rd. B29: W Cas 4D 130
Ilsham Gro. B31: Longb 3C 158
Ilsley Rd. B23: Erd 3E 85
Imax Theatre 6H 101 (2H 5)
Imex Bus. Pk. B9: Bord G 1D 118
B11: Tys 5F 119
B33: Stech 5C 104
DY4: Tip 4A 78
WV2: Wolv 4G 43
Imperial Ri. B46: Col 5G 89
Imperial Rd. B9: Bord G 1E 119
Impey Rd. B31: N'fld 6D 144
Impsley Cl. B36: Cas B 1F 105
Ince Rd. WS10: Darl 4C 46
Inchcape Av. B20: Hand 4C 82
Inchford Rd. B92: Sol 6A 138
Inchlaggan Rd. WV10: Wolv 3B 28
Infantry Pl. B75: S Cold 5E 55
Ingatestone Dr. DY8: Word 6A 92
Ingestre Cl. WS3: Blox 4F 19
Ingestre Dr. B43: Gt Barr 4H 65
Inge St. B5: Birm 2G 117 (6D 4)
Ingestre Rd. B28: Hall G 6F 135
WV10: Oxl 6G 15
Ingham Way B17: Harb 3E 115
Ingleby Gdns. WV6: Wolv 4D 26
Ingledew Cl. WS2: Wals 6D 30
Inglefield Rd. B33: Stech 6D 104
Inglemere Gro. B29: W Cas 6D 130
Inglenook Dr. B20: Hand 5D 82
Ingleside Vs. *B11: S'hll 6C 118*
(off Warwick Rd.)
Ingleton Rd. B8: W End 2G 103
Inglewood Av. WV3: Wolv 3D 42
Inglewood Cl. DY6: K'wfrd 4B 92
Inglewood Gro. B74: S'tly 1H 51
Inglewood Rd. B11: S'hll 6C 118
Ingoldsby Ct. B13: Mose 3B 134
Ingoldsby Rd. B31: N'fld 3G 145
Ingot Cl. WS2: Wals 3H 31
Ingram Gro. B27: A Grn 3G 135
Ingram Pl. WS3: Blox 6B 20
Ingram Rd. WS3: Blox 6A 20
Inhedge, The DY1: Dud 6E 77
Inhedge St. DY3: Up Gor 2A 76
Inkberrow Cl. B69: O'bry 5E 97
Inkberrow Rd. B63: Hale 3H 127
Inkerman Gro. WV10: Wolv 1B 44
Inkerman Ho. *B19: Hock 3G 101*
(off Newtown Shop. Cen.)
Inkerman St. WV10: Wolv 6B 28
Inland Rd. B24: Erd 5H 85
Innage, The B47: H'wd 4A 162
Innage Rd. B31: N'fld 3F 145
Innisfree Cl. B47: Wyt 5C 162
Innsworth Dr. B35: Cas V 3E 87
Inshaw Cl. B33: Stech 6C 104
Institute Rd. B14: K Hth 5H 133
Instone Rd. B63: Hale 2H 127
Instow Cl. WV12: W'hall 1B 30
Insull Av. B14: K Hth 6B 148
Intended St. B63: Crad 4E 111
International Ho. B37: Mars G 6F 123
International Sq. B37: Mars G 5E 123
Intown WS1: Wals 1D 48
Intown Row WS1: Wals 1D 48
Inverclyde Rd. B20: Hand 4C 82
Inverness Ho. WV1: Wolv 6G 27
Inverness Rd. B31: N'fld 4C 144
Inworth WV9: Pend 4F 15
Ipsley Gro. B23: Erd 2A 84
Ipstones Av. B33: Stech 5D 104
Ipswich Cres. B42: Gt Barr 6D 66
Ipswich Wlk. B37: Chel W 1D 122
Ireland Grn. Rd. B70: W Brom 5H 79
Ireton Rd. B20: Hand 3C 82
WV10: Bush 4A 16
Iris Cl. B29: W Cas 5F 131
DY2: Dud 6H 77
Iris Dr. B14: K Hth 3F 147
Irnham Rd. B74: Four O 1G 53
Iron Bri. Wlk. DY9: Pedm 5F 125
Iron La. B33: Stech 5B 104
Irvan Av. B70: W Brom 2F 79
Irvine Cl. WS3: Blox 2H 31
Irvine Rd. WS3: Blox 1H 31
Irving Cl. DY3: Lwr G 3E 75
Irving Rd. B92: Sol 1A 138
WV14: Bils 4A 62

Irving St. B1: Birm 2F 117
Irwin Av. B45: Redn 3A 158
Isaac Walton Pl. B70: W Brom 6E 63
Isbourne Way B9: Birm 1B 118
Isis Gro. B26: Cas B. 1B 106
  WV13: W'hall 1C 46
Island Rd. B21: Hand. 6G 81
Islington B63: Hale. 1A 128
Islington Row Middleway B15: Birm. . 2D 116
Ismere Rd. B: Erd 5H 85
Itchen Gro. WV6: Pert 6E 25
Ithon Gro. B38: K Nor. 1A 160
Ivanhoe Rd. B43: Gt Barr. 2D 66
  WV2: E'shll. 5C 44
Ivanhoe St. DY2: Dud. 2C 94
Ivatt Cl. WS4: Rus 2F 33
IVERLEY 5B 124
Iverley Rd. B63: Hale 1C 128
Iverley Wlk. DY9: Pedm. 3G 125
Ivor Rd. B11: S'hll 1B 134
Ivy Av. B12: Bal H. 6A 118
                  (Clifton Rd.)
  B12: Bal H 6A 118
              (Runcorn Rd.)
Ivybridge Gro. B42: P Barr. 4E 83
Ivy Cl. WS8: Wals W 3C 22
Ivy Cft. WV9: Pend. 4D 14
Ivydale Av. B26: Sheld. 6G 121
Ivyfield Rd. B23: Erd 2B 84
Ivy Gro. B18: Win G 5A 100
         (off Heath Grn. Rd.)
Ivyhouse La. WV14: Cose 5D 60
Ivy Ho. Rd. B69: O'bry. 3D 96
Ivyhouse Rd. B38: K Nor 1G 159
Ivy Lodge Cl. B37: Mars G. 4C 122
Ivy Pl. B29: S Oak 3B 132
Ivy Rd. B21: Hand 2C 100
  B30: Stir 1C 146
  B73: Bold 3F 69
  DY1: Dud 3C 76
  DY4: Tip. 6H 61
Ivy Way B90: Dic H 3G 163
Izons Ind. Est. B70: W Brom 6F 79
Izons La. B70: W Brom. 6F 79
Izons Rd. B70: W Brom 4A 80

J

Jacey Rd. B16: Edg 1H 115
  B90: Shir 3H 149
Jack David Ho. DY4: Tip 2D 78
Jackdaw Cl. DY3: Sed 3G 59
Jackdaw Dr. B36: Cas B 1C 106
Jack Hayward Way
  WV1: Wolv 6G 27 (1B 170)
Jack Holden Av. WV14: Cose. 3C 60
Jack Newell Cl. WV14: Cose 5E 61
             (off Castle St.)
Jack O'Watton Ind. Est. B46: Wat O. . . 4F 89
Jackson Av. B8: Salt 5F 103
Jackson Cl. B11: S'brk. 4B 118
  B68: O'bry 4H 97
  DY4: Tip. 4B 62
  WS11: Nort C. 1C 8
  WV10: F'stne 1C 16
Jackson Ct. DY5: Quar B 2B 110
Jackson Dr. B67: Smeth. 4B 98
Jackson Ho. B69: O'bry 2G 97
Jackson Rd. B8: Salt. 5F 103
Jackson St. B68: O'bry 5H 97
  DY9: Lye. 6A 110
  WV6: Wolv 5F 27
Jackson Wlk. B35: Cas V 5E 87
Jackson Way B32: Quin 6G 113
Jacmar Cres. B67: Smeth 3C 98
Jacobean La. B91: Sol. 6C 152
  B93: Know 6C 152
Jacob's Hall La. WS6: Gt Wyr 4G 7
Jacoby Pl. B5: Edg 6E 117
Jaffray Cres. B24: Erd 4F 85
Jaffray Rd. B24: Erd 4F 85
Jakeman Rd. B12: Bal H 6G 117
Jamaica Row B5: Birm 2G 117 (6F 5)
James Bri. Cl. WS2: Wals 4H 47
James Brindley Wlk. B1: Birm. . . 1E 117 (4A 4)
James Clift Ho. B69: O'bry 4D 96

James Cl. B67: Smeth 4E 99
  WS10: Darl 5F 47
James Ct. B13: Mose 3B 134
  B38: K Nor 5B 146
James Dee Cl. DY5: Quar B. 2C 110
James Eaton Cl. B71: W Brom 2A 80
James Ho. B17: Harb 6F 115
          (off Cadbury Way)
  B19: Hock. 3E 101
         (off Newtown Dr.)
James Lloyd Trust Flats B30: B'vlle. . . 2G 145
James Memorial Homes B7: Nech . . . 2C 102
           (off Stuart St.)
Jameson Rd. B6: Aston 1C 102
Jameson St. WV6: Wolv 5F 27
James Rd. B11: Tys 5F 119
  B43: Gt Barr 6A 66
  B46: Col 1H 107
James Row B69: O'bry 1D 96
James Samuel Pl. B12: Birm 4H 117
James Scott Rd. B63: Crad 5C 110
James St. B3: Birm 6E 101 (2B 4)
  WV13: W'hall 6A 30
  WV14: Bils. 5G 45
James Turner St. B18: Win G 3A 100
James Watt Dr. B19: Hand 1D 100
James Watt Ho. B66: Smeth 4F 99
James Watt Ind. Pk. B66: Smeth 3G 99
James Watt Queensway
  B4: Birm 6G 101 (2F 5)
James Watt St. B4: Birm 3F 5
            (off Dalton St.)
  B71: W Brom 5H 63
         (not continuous)
Jane La. Cl. WS2: Wals 5F 31
Janice Gro. B14: Yard W 3C 148
Janine Av. WV11: Wed 2G 29
Jaques Cl. B46: Wat O. 5D 88
Jardine Rd. B6: Aston 6H 83
Jarratt Hall B29: S Oak 2A 132
Jarvis Cres. B69: O'bry 5F 97
Jarvis Rd. B23: Erd 1F 85
Jarvis Way B24: Erd 1E 103
J A S Ind. Pk. B65: Row R 5E 97
Jasmin Cft. B14: K Hth 3G 147
Jasmine Cl. WV9: Pend 4D 14
Jasmine Gro. WV8: Bilb. 4H 13
Jasmine Rd. DY2: Dud 6H 77
Jasmine Way WS10: Darl 4D 46
Jason Rd. DY9: W'cte 1B 126
Javelin Av. B35: Cas V 4F 87
Jayne Ct. B71: W Brom 4C 64
  WV11: Wed. 2F 29
Jay Rd. DY6: K'wfrd 1B 92
Jay's Av. DY4: Tip 3B 78
Jayshaw Av. B43: Gt Barr. 4A 66
Jeal Cl. B47: Wyt. 6G 161
Jean Dr. DY4: Tip 1D 78
Jeavons Pl. WV14: Bils 6E 45
Jedburgh Av. WV6: Pert 5E 25
Jeddo St. WV2: Wolv 3G 43 (6A 170)
Jeffcock Rd. WV3: Wolv 3D 42
Jefferson Cl. B71: W Brom 5H 63
Jeffrey Av. WV4: E'shll 6B 44
Jeffrey Rd. B65: Row R 6E 97
Jeffries Ho. B69: O'bry 2G 97
Jeffs Av. WV2: Wolv 3H 43 (6D 170)
Jenkins Cl. WV14: Bils 6E 45
Jenkinson Rd. WS10: W'bry 4D 62
Jenkins St. B10: Small H 3C 118
Jenks Av. WV10: Bush 1A 28
Jenks Rd. WV5: Wom. 2F 73
Jennens Rd. B4: Birm. 6H 101 (3G 5)
  B7: Birm 6H 101 (2H 5)
Jenner Cl. WS2: Wals 3G 31
Jenner Ho. WS2: Wals 3F 31
Jenner Rd. WS2: Wals 3F 31
Jenner St. WV2: Wolv 2A 44
Jennifer Wlk. B25: Yard 3C 120
Jennings St. B64: Old H. 1H 111
Jenny Cl. WV14: Bils 4G 61
Jennyns Ct. WS10: W'bry. 2F 63
Jenny Walkers La. WV6: Pert 3D 40
Jephcott Gro. B8: Salt 5G 103
Jephcott Rd. B8: Salt 5G 103
Jephson Dr. B26: Yard 4D 120
Jeremy Dr. B92: Sol 1F 137

Jeremy Rd. WV4: Penn 6G 43
Jerome Ct. B74: S'tly. 2H 51
Jerome K Jerome Birthplace Mus. 2C 48
         (off Bradford St.)
Jerome Retail Pk. WS1: Wals 2B 48
Jerome Rd. B72: S Cold. 1B 70
  WS2: Wals 2H 47
Jerrard Ct. B75: S Cold 6A 54
Jerrard Dr. B75: S Cold 6A 54
Jerry's La. B23: Erd 6D 68
Jersey Cft. B36: Cas B 3D 106
Jersey Rd. B8: Salt 5D 102
Jervis Cl. DY5: P'ntt 2G 93
Jervis Ct. WS1: Wals 1D 48
         (off Dog Kennel La.)
Jervis Cres. B74: Four O 6D 36
Jervis Pk. B74: Lit A 5C 36
Jervis Ter. B21: Hand. 1H 99
Jervoise Dr. B31: N'fld 2F 145
Jervoise La. B71: W Brom. 4C 64
Jervoise Rd. B29: W Cas. 4D 130
Jervoise St. B70: W Brom 3G 79
Jesmond Gro. B24: Erd 3C 86
Jessel Rd. WS2: Wals 1A 48
Jessie Rd. WS9: A'rdge 6C 22
Jesson Cl. WS1: Wals 4E 49
Jesson Ct. WS1: Wals 3E 49
Jesson Rd. B75: S Cold 6E 55
  DY3: Sed 1C 76
  WS1: Wals. 3D 48
Jesson St. B70: W Brom 5C 80
Jevons Dr. DY4: Tip 2B 78
Jevons Rd. B73: New O 2C 68
Jevon St. WV14: Cose 5D 60
         (not continuous)
JEWELLERY QUARTER 5D 100 (1A 4)
Jewellery Quarter Station (Rail & MM)
  . . . . 5D 100
Jew's La. DY3: Up Gor. 3A 76
Jiggin's La. B32: Bart G 5A 130
Jill Av. B43: Gt Barr 5G 65
Jillcot Rd. B92: Sol 2F 137
Jinnah Cl. B12: Birm 3H 117
Joan St. WV2: E'shll 5A 44
Jockey Fld. DY3: Up Gor 1A 76
Jockey La. WS10: W'bry 1G 63
Jockey Rd. B73: New O 3D 68
Joe Jones Ct. DY3: Sed 4A 60
Joey's La. WV8: Bilb 3A 14
John Bright Cl. DY4: Tip 5H 61
John Bright St. B1: Birm 1F 117 (5D 4)
John F Kennedy Wlk. DY4: Tip 5A 62
John Fletcher Cl.
  WS10: W'bry 1H 63
John Harper St. WV13: W'hall 1B 46
John Howell Dr. DY4: Tip. 2A 78
John Kempe Way B12: Birm 4A 118
John Riley Dr. WV12: W'hall 1C 30
John Rd. B62: Hale. 2F 129
Johns Gro. B43: Gt Barr. 5G 65
Johns La. B69: Tiv 4C 78
  DY4: Tip 3B 78
  WS6: Gt Wyr 2F 7
John Smyth Ho. B1: Birm 6E 101 (3A 4)
Johnson Av. WV11: Wed 2H 29
Johnson Cl. B8: W End 3A 104
  B11: S'hll 6C 118
  WS10: Darl 6D 46
Johnson Dr. B35: Cas V 4D 86
Johnson Pl. WV14: Bils 4H 45
Johnson Rd. B23: Erd. 2F 85
  WS10: Darl 6D 46
  WS10: W'bry 3A 64
  WV12: W'hall. 2D 30
Johnson Row WV14: Cose 4B 60
Johnsons Bri. Rd. B71: W Brom 1A 80
Johnsons Gro. B68: O'bry 3A 114
Johnson St. B7: Nech. 3C 102
  WV2: Wolv. 4H 43
  WV14: Cose 4B 60
Johnstone St. B19: Loz. 1F 101
Johnston St. B70: W Brom. 6B 80
John St. B19: Loz. 2D 100
  B65: B'hth 2C 112
  B69: O'bry 2G 97
  B70: W Brom 3H 79
             (Guns La.)

John St. B70: W Brom 2F 79
  (Phoenix St.)
DY5: Brie H 5H 93
DY8: Word 2D 108
WS2: Wals 6C 32
WV2: E'shll 5C 44
WV13: W'hall 2B 46
John St. Nth. B71: W Brom 2H 79
John Wilmott Community Leisure Cen.
. . . . 1D 70
John Wooton Ho. WS10: Darl 5D 46
  (off Lawrence Way)
Joiners Cft. B92: Sol 5A 138
Joinings Bank B68: O'bry 5H 97
Jones Fld. Cres. WV1: Wolv 1C 44
Jones Ho. WS2: Wals 6B 32
Jones Rd. WV10: Oxl 3G 27
WV12: W'hall 6D 18
Jones's La. WS6: Gt Wyr 4G 7
Jones Wood Cl. B76: Walm 6D 70
Jonfield Gdns. B43: Gt Barr 4B 66
Jordan Cl. B66: Smeth 4F 99
B75: Four O 2H 53
Jordan Ho. B36: Hodg H 1B 104
Jordan Leys DY4: Tip 2B 78
Jordan Pl. WV14: Bils 2G 61
Jordan Rd. B75: Four O 2H 53
Jordan Way WS9: A'rdge 6D 22
Joseph St. B69: O'bry 3F 97
Josiah Rd. B31: N'fld 5B 144
Jowett's La. B71: W Brom 5H 63
Joyberry Dr. DY8: Stourb 2D 124
Joynson St. WS10: Darl 6E 47
Jubilee Av. B71: W Brom 6H 63
Jubilee Cl. WS3: Wals 3C 32
WS6: Gt Wyr 3F 7
Jubilee Ct. B27: A Grn 3A 136
B31: N'fld 6F 145
Jubilee Gdns. B23: Erd 6B 68
Jubilee Rd. B45: Fran. 5E 143
DY4: Tip 6A 62
WV14: Bils 1A 62
Jubilee St. B71: W Brom 6B 64
Jubilee Trad. Cen. B5: Birm 2G 117
Judge Cl. B69: O'bry 2G 97
Judge Rd. DY5: Quar B 4B 110
Julia Av. B24: Erd 3D 86
Julia Gdns. B71: W Brom 5D 64
Julian Cl. WS6: Gt Wyr 2G 7
WV1: Wolv 1D 44
Julian Rd. WV1: Wolv 1D 44
Julie Cft. WV14: Bils 4G 61
Juliet Rd. B62: Hale 2F 129
Julius Dr. B46: Col 6H 89
Junction, The DY8: Word 3C 108
Junction 6 Ind. Pk. B6: Witt. 6B 84
Junction Ind. Est.
B66: Smeth 1D 98
Junction Rd. B21: Hand 1G 99
DY8: Stourb 1F 125
DY8: Word 3C 108
DY9: Stourb 1G 125
WV2: E'shll 4D 44
Junction St. B69: O'bry 6E 79
DY2: Dud 1D 94
WS1: Wals 3B 48
Junction St. Sth. B69: O'bry 4G 97
Junc. Two Ind. Est. B69: O'bry. 4F 97
  (off Demuth Way)
June Cft. B26: Sheld 6H 121
Juniper Cl. B27: A Grn 6H 119
B76: Walm 2D 70
Juniper Dr. B76: Walm 6E 71
WS5: Wals 1F 65
Juniper Ho. B20: Hand 4B 82
B36: Hodg H 2D 104
Juniper Ri. B63: Crad 6E 111
Jupiter B16: Birm 1D 116
  (not continuous)
Jury Rd. DY5: Quar B 4B 110
Jutland Rd. B13: Mose 6B 134

K

Karen Way DY5: Brie H 3H 109
KATE'S HILL 6H 77

Katherine Ho. B17: Harb 6F 115
  (off Cadbury Way)
Katherine Rd. B67: Smeth 1D 114
Kathleen Rd. B25: Yard 4A 120
B72: S Cold 1A 70
Katie Rd. B29: S Oak 4A 132
Kayne Cl. DY6: K'wfrd 3A 92
Keanscott Dr. B68: O'bry 5A 98
Keasdon Gro. WV13: W'hall. 6C 30
Keating Gdns. B75: Four O 5G 37
Keatley Av. B33: Kitts G 1A 122
Keats Av. B10: Small H 4D 118
Keats Cl. B74: Four O 3F 37
DY3: Lwr G. 2E 75
DY8: Amb 3E 109
Keats Dr. WV14: Cose 3F 61
Keats Gro. B27: A Grn 4H 135
WV10: Bush. 1C 28
Keats Ho. B68: O'bry 5A 98
Keats Rd. WS3: Blox 2C 32
WV10: Bush. 5C 16
WV12: W'hall 2E 31
Keble Gro. B26: Sheld 5F 121
WS1: Wals 4E 49
Keble Ho. B37: F'bri 1C 122
Kedleston Cl. WS3: Blox 4G 19
Kedleston Ct. B28: Hall G 3F 149
Kedleston Rd. B28: Hall G 1F 149
Keegan Wlk. WS2: Wals 5F 31
Keel Dr. B13: Mose 4D 134
Keele Ho. B37: F'bri 5D 106
Keeley St. B9: Birm 1B 118
Keelinge St. DY4: Tip. 2B 78
Keen St. B66: Smeth 5H 99
Keepers Cl. B18: Win G 4B 100
B46: Col 5H 107
DY6: W Hth 1H 91
WS9: Wals W 4B 22
Keepers Ga. Cl. B74: S Cold 4A 54
Keepers Ho. B73: New O 3C 68
  (off Welshmans Hill)
Keepers La. WV6: Tett 5G 13
WV8: Cod. 5G 13
Keepers Rd. B74: Lit A 4C 36
Keer Ct. B9: Birm 1B 118
Kegworth Rd. B23: Erd. 5C 84
Keir Hardie Wlk. B69: Tiv 5D 78
Keir Pl. DY8: Amb 3C 108
Keir Rd. WS10: W'bry 3A 64
Kelby Cl. B31: N'fld 3C 144
Kelby Rd. B31: N'fld 3D 144
Keldy Cl. WV6: Wolv 4D 26
Kelfield Av. B17: Harb 1F 131
Kelham Pl. B92: Olton 4F 137
Kelia Dr. B67: Smeth 3D 98
Kellett Rd. B7: Birm 5A 102
Kelling Cl. DY5: Brie H 3G 109
Kellington Cl. B8: W End 5F 103
Kelmarsh Dr. B91: Sol 6F 151
Kelmscott Rd. B17: Harb 4F 115
Kelsall Cl. WV1: Wolv 1D 44
Kelsall Cft. B1: Birm 6D 100
Kelsey Cl. B7: Birm 5B 102
Kelso Gdns. WV6: Pert 5D 24
Kelsull Cft. B37: F'bri 1C 122
Kelton Ct. B15: Edg 4C 116
Kelvedon Gro. B91: Sol 3G 151
Kelverdale Gro. B14: K Hth 3E 147
Kelverley Gro. B71: W Brom 4E 65
Kelvin Ho. DY1: Dud. 5F 77
Kelvin Pl. WS2: Wals 3H 31
Kelvin Rd. B31: N'fld 6E 145
WS2: Wals 3G 31
Kelvin Way B70: W Brom 6H 79
Kelvin Way Ind. Est. B70: W Brom . . 6H 79
Kelway Av. B43: Gt Barr. 2D 66
Kelwood Dr. B63: Hale 6A 112
Kelynmead Rd. B33: Yard 1E 121
Kemberton Cl. WV3: Wolv 2A 42
Kemberton Rd. B29: S Oak 3E 131
WV3: Wolv 2A 42
Kemble Cl. WV12: W'hall 6D 30
Kemble Cft. B5: Bal H 4G 117
Kemble Dr. B35: Cas V 4E 87
Kemelstowe Cres. B63: Hale 5E 127
Kemerton Way B90: M'path 4D 164
Kempe Rd. B33: Kitts G 5E 105

Kempsey Cl. B63: Hale 1G 127
B69: O'bry 5E 97
B92: Olton 2E 137
Kempsey Covert B38: K Nor 2A 160
Kempsey Ho. B32: Bart G 5G 129
Kemps Grn. Rd. CV7: Bal C 3H 169
Kempson Av. B71: W Brom 2H 79
B72: W Grn 4A 70
Kempson Rd. B36: Hodg H 1C 104
Kempsons Gro. WV14: Cose 2D 60
Kempthorne Av. WV10: Bush 6A 16
Kempthorne Gdns. WS3: Blox 5G 19
Kempthorne Rd. WV14: Bils 5H 45
Kempton Dr. WS6: Gt Wyr 3F 7
Kempton Pk. Rd. B36: Hodg H 1B 104
Kempton Way DY8: Stourb 2C 124
Kemsey Dr. WV14: Bils 2H 61
Kemshead Av. B31: Longb 1C 158
Kemsley Rd. B14: K Hth 5H 147
Kendal Av. B45: Redn 2H 157
B46: Col 2H 107
Kendal Cl. WV6: Tett 3D 26
Kendal Ct. B23: Erd 4B 84
B29: W Cas 6G 131
WS9: Wals W 3B 22
Kendal Gro. B92: Sol 5B 138
Kendal Ho. B69: O'bry 5D 96
Kendall Ri. DY6: K'wfrd 4D 92
Kendal Ri. B68: O'bry 6H 97
WV6: Tett 3D 26
Kendal Ri. Rd. B45: Redn 2H 157
Kendal Rd. B11: S'brk 4B 118
Kendal Twr. B17: Harb 6H 115
Kendrick Av. B34: S End 4A 106
Kendrick Cl. B92: Sol 1B 152
Kendrick Pl. WV14: Bils 1A 62
Kendrick Rd. B76: Walm 2D 86
WV10: Bush. 3A 28
WV14: Bils 1A 62
Kendricks Rd. WS10: Darl 4F 47
Kendrick St. WS10: W'bry 2G 63
Keneggy M. B29: S Oak 3B 132
Kenelm Rd. B10: Small H 3E 119
B68: O'bry 6G 97
B73: S Cold 1H 69
WV14: Cose 4E 61
Kenelm's Ct. B62: Roms 3A 142
Kenilworth Cl. B74: Four O 3G 53
CV7: Bal C 3G 169
DY4: Tip 3F 77
DY8: Word 1B 108
Kenilworth Ct. B16: Edg 3B 116
B24: Erd 5E 85
DY1: Dud 1B 94
Kenilworth Cres. WS2: Wals 5G 31
WV4: E'shll 1A 60
Kenilworth Ho. B13: Mose. 1A 148
WS3: Blox 3A 32
  (off Providence La.)
Kenilworth Rd. B20: Hand 6G 83
B46: Col 2H 123
B68: O'bry 3B 114
B92: H Ard 1D 154
B93: Know 3F 167
CV7: Bal C 2E 155
CV7: Mer 3C 140
WV6: Pert. 5F 25
Kenley Gro. B30: K Nor 4D 146
Kenley Way B91: Shir 3B 150
Kenmare Way WV11: Wed 5E 29
Kenmure Rd. B33: Sheld 4G 121
Kennedy Cl. B72: S Cold 1A 70
Kennedy Ct. DY8: Stourb 6D 108
Kennedy Cres. DY3: Lwr G 3H 75
WS10: Darl. 4C 46
Kennedy Cft. B26: Sheld. 4E 121
Kennedy Gro. B30: Stir 1D 146
Kennedy Ho. B68: O'bry 3H 113
Kennedy Rd. WV10: Wolv 6H 27
Kennedy Twr. B4: Birm. 2E 5
Kennerley Rd. B25: Yard 5B 120
Kennet Cl. WS8: Bwnhls 3G 9
Kennet Gro. B36: Cas B 1B 106
Kenneth Gro. B23: Erd 2A 84
Kennford Cl. B65: Row R. 3C 96
Kennington Rd. WV10: Wolv 4B 28
Kenrick Cft. B35: Cas V 5E 87

Kenrick Ho. B70: W Brom 6C **80**
Kenrick Park Stop (MM) 6C **80**
Kenrick Way B70: W Brom. 1B **98**
B71: W Brom 6D **80**
Kensington Av. B12: Bal H 1A **134**
Kensington Dr. B74: Four O 4F **37**
Kensington Gdns. DY8: Word 2A **108**
Kensington Rd. B29: S Oak 3C **132**
WV12: W'hall 2B **30**
Kensington St. B19: Hock. 3F **101**
Kenswick Dr. B63: Hale 3A **128**
Kent Av. WS2: Wals 6H **31**
Kent Cl. B71: W Brom 6H **63**
WS2: Wals 4C **32**
WS9: A'rdge. 6D **22**
Kentish Rd. B21: Hand. 1G **99**
Kentmere Twr. B23: Erd. 1H **85**
Kenton Av. WV6: Wolv 5D **26**
Kenton Wlk. B29: S Oak. 3B **132**
Kent Pl. DY2: Dud 3C **94**
Kent Rd. B45: Fran 6F **143**
B62: Quin 5E **113**
DY8: Woll. 4B **108**
WS2: Wals 6F **31**
WS10: W'bry 1A **64**
WV2: Wolv 4A **44**
Kents Cl. B92: Olton. 2D **136**
Kents Ho. B33: Yard 1F **121**
Kent St. B5: Birm 3G **117**
DY3: Up Gor. 2A **76**
WS2: Wals 4C **32**
Kent St. Nth. B18: Hock 4B **100**
Kenward Cft. B17: Harb 4D **114**
Kenway B47: H'wd 2A **162**
Kenwick Rd. B17: Harb. 1F **131**
Kenwood Rd. B9: Bord G. 6H **103**
Kenyon Cl. DY8: Amb. 4E **109**
Kenyon St. B18: Birm 5E **101** (1B **4**)
Kerby Rd. B23: Erd. 3C **84**
Kererwin Cl. B64: Old H. 2A **112**
Keresley Cl. B91: Sol. 2G **151**
Keresley Gro. B29: W Cas 3D **130**
Kernthorpe Rd. B14: K Hth. 3F **147**
Kerr Dr. DY4: Tip 5G **61**
Kerria Ct. B15: Birm 3F **117**
Kerridge Cl. WV9: Pend 5E **15**
Kerrison Ride B73: Bold 4F **69**
Kerry Cl. B31: N'fld 1D **144**
DY5: Brie H 5G **93**
Kerry Ct. WS1: Wals. 3E **49**
Kersley Gdns. WV11: Wed. 3H **29**
Kerswell Dr. B90: M'path. 4D **164**
Kesterton Rd. B74: Four O 4E **37**
Kesteven Cl. B15: Edg 5D **116**
Kesteven Rd. B71: W Brom 6A **64**
Keston Rd. B44: Gt Barr. 1H **67**
Kestrel Av. B25: Yard 3H **119**
Kestrel Cl. B23: Erd 1D **84**
B35: Cas V 4F **87**
Kestrel Dr. B74: Four O 4F **37**
Kestrel Gro. B30: B'vlle 5H **131**
WV12: W'hall 1C **30**
Kestrel Ri. WV6: Tett 2D **26**
Kestrel Rd. B63: Crad 4D **110**
B68: O'bry 1F **113**
DY1: Dud 1B **94**
Kestrel Way WS6: C Hay 3C **6**
Keswick Dr. DY6: K'wfrd 3B **92**
Keswick Gro. B74: S'tly 1H **51**
Keswick Ho. B69: O'bry. 5D **96**
Keswick Rd. B92: Olton 1D **136**
Ketley Cft. B12: Birm 4H **117**
Ketley Flds. DY6: K'wfrd 4E **93**
Ketley Hill Rd. DY1: Dud 1B **94**
Ketley Rd. DY6: K'wfrd 3D **92**
(not continuous)
Kettlebrook Rd. B90: M'path 3F **165**
Kettlehouse Rd. B44: Gt Barr 2H **67**
Kettles Bank Rd. DY3: Gorn 5G **75**
(not continuous)
Kettles Wood Dr. B32: Bart G 3H **129**
Kettlewell Way B37: F'bri. 1B **122**
Ketton Gro. B33: Sheld 4H **121**
Kew Cl. B37: K'hrst 6B **106**
Kew Dr. DY1: Dud 5C **76**
Kew Gdns. B33: Stech 2B **120**
Kewstoke Cl. WV12: W'hall 6B **18**
Kewstoke Cft. B31: N'fld 1C **144**
Kewstoke Rd. WV12: W'hall. 6B **18**
Key Bus. Pk. B24: Erd 4C **86**
Keyes Dr. DY6: K'wfrd 6B **74**
Key Hill B18: Birm 4D **100**
Key Hill Cir. B18: Birm. 4D **100**
Key Hill Dr. B18: Birm 4D **100**
Key Ind. Pk. WV13: W'hall 6F **29**
Keynell Covert B30: K Nor 4E **147**
Keynes Dr. WV14: Bils. 5G **45**
Keys Cres. B71: W Brom 1A **80**
Keyse Rd. B75: S Cold. 4D **54**
Keyte Cl. DY4: Tip 2A **78**
Keyway, The WV13: W'hall 2H **45**
Keyway Retail Pk. WV13: W'hall 3B **46**
Keyworth Cl. DY4: Tip 2A **78**
Khalsa Ind. Est. B66: Smeth 5H **99**
Khyber Cl. WS10: Darl 4C **46**
Kidd Cft. DY4: Tip. 3C **62**
Kidderminster Rd.
DY6: K'wfrd, W Hth 6G **91**
DY7: I'ley 6A **124**
DY7: Stourt 6G **91**
DY9: Hag 6G **125**
DY10: I'ley 6A **124**
Kielder Cl. WS5: Wals 2G **65**
Kielder Gdns. DY9: Pedm. 4F **125**
Kier's Bri. Cl. DY4: Tip. 4A **78**
Kilburn Dr. DY6: K'wfrd 6C **74**
Kilburn Gro. B44: Gt Barr. 2H **67**
Kilburn Pl. DY2: Dud 3F **95**
Kilburn Rd. B44: Gt Barr 2H **67**
Kilby Av. B16: Birm 1C **116**
(not continuous)
Kilbys Gro. B20: Hand 5B **82**
Kilcote Rd. B90: Shir 5C **148**
Kilmet Wlk. B67: Smeth. 4E **99**
Kilmore Cft. B36: Hodg H 6C **86**
Kilmorie Rd. B27: A Grn 6A **120**
Kiln Cft. B65: Row R 5A **96**
Kiln La. B25: Yard 5H **119**
B90: Dic H 4G **163**
Kilsby Gro. B91: Sol. 1G **165**
Kilvert Rd. WS10: W'bry 3H **63**
Kimbells Wlk. B93: Know 3E **167**
Kimberley Av. B8: Salt 4E **103**
Kimberley Cl. B74: S'tly. 6A **36**
Kimberley Pl. WV14: Cose 6D **60**
Kimberley Rd. B66: Smeth. 2E **99**
B92: Olton 3E **137**
Kimberley St. WV3: Wolv. 2E **43**
Kimberley Wlk. B76: Min. 1H **87**
Kimble Gro. B24: Erd. 4B **86**
Kimbley Ri. B71: W Brom 6G **63**
Kimpton Cl. B14: K Hth 5G **147**
Kimsan Cft. B74: S'tly 4A **52**
Kinchford Cl. B91: Sol 1G **165**
Kineton Cft. B32: Bart G. 5B **130**
Kineton Grn. Rd. B92: Olton 5B **136**
Kineton Ho. B13: Mose 1A **148**
Kineton Ri. DY3: Sed. 3G **59**
Kineton Rd. B45: Rubery 2E **157**
B73: New O 4E **69**
Kinfare Dr. WV6: Tett. 5H **25**
Kinfare Ri. DY3: Up Gor. 3A **76**
King Charles Av. WS2: Wals 1E **47**
King Charles Ct. B44: K'sdng. 3B **68**
King Charles Rd. B62: Quin 1F **129**
King Edmund St. DY1: Dud 5D **76**
(not continuous)
King Edward VI Ho. *B4: Birm. 6H 101*
(off Aston St.)
King Edward Ct. B63: Hale. 1A **128**
King Edward Rd. B13: Mose 2H **133**
King Edwards Cl. B20: Hand 1D **100**
King Edwards Dr. B16: Birm 1D **116**
King Edwards Gdns. B20: Hand. 2D **100**
King Edwards Rd. B1: Birm 6C **100**
(Ladywood Middleway)
B1: Birm 1D **116** (4A **4**)
(Summer Hill St.)
King Edward's Row WV2: Wolv 3G **43**
King Edwards Sq. B73: S Cold. 5A **54**
King Edward St. WS10: Darl 5D **46**
King Edwards Wharf
B16: Birm. 1D **116**
Kingfield Rd. B90: Shir 5C **148**
Kingfisher Cl. B26: Sheld. 5E **121**
DY3: Sed 3G **59**
WS8: Bwnhls 6A **10**
Kingfisher Dr. B36: Cas B 1C **106**
DY8: Stourb 2A **124**
Kingfisher Gro. WV12: W'hall 1B **30**
Kingfisher Ind. Est. B70: W Brom 3F **79**
Kingfisher Rd. B23: Erd. 6C **68**
Kingfisher Vw. B34: Stech 4E **105**
Kingfisher Way B30: B'vlle. 5H **131**
King George VI Av. WS1: Wals 3G **49**
King George Cres. WS4: Rus. 3F **33**
King George Pl. WS4: Rus. 3F **33**
Kingham Cl. DY3: Gorn 5G **75**
Kingham Covert B14: K Hth 5F **147**
Kings Av. B69: Tiv 5B **78**
Kingsbridge Ho. B23: Erd 1B **84**
Kingsbridge Rd. B32: Bart G 4B **130**
Kingsbridge Wlk. B66: Smeth 4F **99**
Kingsbrook Dr. B91: Sol. 1F **165**
Kingsbury Av. B24: Erd 4B **86**
Kingsbury Bus. Pk. B76: Min. 1A **88**
Kingsbury Cl. B76: Min 2H **87**
WS4: Wals 5F **33**
Kingsbury Leisure Cen. 5F **85**
Kingsbury Pl. B24: Erd 3H **85**
Kingsbury Rd. B24: Erd 5E **85**
B35: Cas V 5B **86**
B76: Min, Curd. 2G **87**
DY4: Tip 5A **62**
Kings Bus. Pk. B44: Gt Barr. 2G **67**
Kings Cinema. 4B **80**
Kingsclere Wlk. WV4: Penn. 5A **42**
Kingscliff Rd. B10: Small H 3G **119**
King's Cl. B14: K Hth 1E **147**
Kingscote Rd. B15: Edg. 5H **115**
B93: Dorr 6F **167**
Kings Ct. B37: Mars G 2G **123**
B1: Birm 2E **117** (6B **4**)
B3: Birm 2E **117** (1C **4**)
B75: Four O 6H **37**
DY4: Tip 3A **78**
WS10: W'bry 2E **63**
Kings Cft. B26: Sheld 6E **121**
B36: Cas B 2B **106**
Kingscroft Cl. B74: S'tly. 4A **52**
Kingscroft Rd. B74: S'tly 3A **52**
Kingsdene Av. DY6: K'wfrd 5A **92**
Kingsdown Av. B42: Gt Barr. 1B **82**
Kingsdown Rd. B31: N'fld 4D **130**
Kingsfield Rd. B14: K Hth 5G **133**
Kingsford Cl. B36: Cas B 6H **87**
Kingsford Ct. B92: Olton. 2F **137**
Kingsford Nouveau DY6: K'wfrd. 4E **93**
Kings Gdns. B30: K Nor 3A **146**
Kingsgate Ho. B37: Chel W 1C **122**
Kings Grn. Av. B38: K Nor 5B **146**
Kingshayes Rd. WS9: A'rdge. 5D **22**
KING'S HEATH 5G **133**
KING'S HILL 6D **46**
Kings Hill Bus. Pk. WS10: W'bry. 1E **63**
Kings Hill Cl. WS10: Darl. 6E **47**
Kingshill Dr. B38: K Nor. 5B **146**
Kings Hill Fld. WS10: Darl 6E **47**
Kings Hill M. WS10: Darl. 6D **46**
KINGSHURST 4B **106**
Kingshurst Ho. B37: K'hrst. 4B **106**
Kingshurst Rd. B31: N'fld. 4E **145**
B90: Shir 6F **149**
Kingshurst Way B37: K'hrst 5B **106**
Kingsland Dr. B93: Dorr. 6A **166**
Kingsland Rd. B44: Gt Barr 1G **67**
Kingslea Rd. B91: Sol 5C **150**
Kingsleigh Cft. B75: Four O. 1H **53**
Kingsleigh Dr. B36: Cas B 1E **105**
Kingsleigh Rd. B20: Hand 5D **82**
Kingsley Av. WV6: Tett. 5H **25**
Kingsley Bank Way B26: Sheld 4F **121**
Kingsley Ct. B25: Yard. 3C **120**
Kingsley Gdns. WV8: Cod 4E **13**
Kingsley Gro. DY3: Lwr G 2E **75**
Kingsley Rd. B12: Bal H. 5A **118**
B30: K Nor 3H **145**
DY6: K'wfrd 4H **91**
Kingsley St. DY2: Neth. 4E **95**
WS2: Wals 4H **47**
Kingslow Av. WV4: Penn 5B **42**

Kingsmere Cl. B24: Erd 5E **85**
KINGS NORTON 5H **145**
King's Norton Bus. Cen. B30: K Nor . . 3C **146**
Kings Norton Community Leisure Cen.
. . . . 1B **160**
Kings Norton Station (Rail) 3B **146**
Kingsoak Gdns. DY2: Dud 2G **95**
Kings Pde. B4: Birm 4F **5**
Kingspiece Ho. B36: Hodg H 1C **104**
Kings Rd. B14: K Hth 1E **147**
    B44: Gt Barr, K'sdng 2G **67**
    B73: New O 3A **68**
    DY3: Sed 5A **60**
    B11: Tys 6G **119**
    B23: Erd 3C **84**
    WS4: Rus 2G **33**
Kings Rd. Ind. Est. B11: Tys 5G **119**
Kings Sq. B70: W Brom 4B **80**
    WV14: Cose 5C **60**
King's Standing Ancient Monument . . . 1H **67**
KINGSTANDING 4B **68**
Kingstanding Cen., The B44: Gt Barr . . 2H **67**
Kingstanding Leisure Cen. 5A **68**
Kingstanding Rd. B44: K'sdng 1H **83**
King's Ter. B14: K Hth 1F **147**
Kingsthorpe Rd. B14: K Hth 4A **148**
Kingston Ct. B29: W Cas 6F **131**
    B74: S Cold 4H **53**
Kingston Ind. Est. B9: Birm 2B **118**
    (off Glover St.)
Kingston Rd. B9: Birm 2B **118**
    B75: S Cold 5D **54**
Kingston Row B1: Birm 1E **117** (4A **4**)
Kingston Way DY6: K'wfrd 2A **92**
King St. B11: S'brk 4A **118**
    B63: Hale 1A **128**
    B64: Old H 2H **111**
    B66: Smeth 2F **99**
    DY2: Dud 1E **95**
    DY5: Quar B 3C **110**
    DY8: Woll 5C **108**
    DY9: Lye 1B **126**
    WS1: Wals 4B **48**
    WS7: Chase 1B **10**
    WS9: Wals W 5B **22**
    WS10: W'bry 2E **63**
    WV1: Wolv 1G **43** (3B **170**)
    WV13: W'hall 1B **46**
    WV14: Bils 2G **61**
    WV14: Cose 5C **60**
King St. Pas. DY2: Dud 6E **77**
    DY5: Quar B 3C **110**
King St. Pct. WS10: Darl 5D **46**
Kingsway B68: O'bry 4G **113**
    DY8: Woll 3B **108**
    WV10: Wolv 3C **28**
    WV11: Ess 3A **18**
Kingsway Av. DY4: Tip 5A **62**
Kingsway Dr. B38: K Nor 5B **146**
Kingsway Nth. WS9: A'rdge 3A **34**
Kingsway Rd. WV10: Wolv 3C **28**
Kingsway Sth. WS9: A'rdge 3A **34**
Kingswear Av. WV6: Pert 6F **25**
KINGSWINFORD 3B **92**
Kingswinford Rd. DY1: Dud 2A **94**
KING'S WOOD 1G **161**
KINGSWOOD
    Wolverhampton 5A **12**
Kingswood Cl. B90: Shir 6B **150**
Kingswood Cft. B7: Nech 2C **102**
Kingswood Dr. B30: K Nor 4E **147**
    B74: S'tly 1H **67**
    WS6: Gt Wyr 1G **7**
Kingswood Gdns. WV4: Penn 5D **42**
Kingswood Ho. B14: K Hth 5G **147**
Kingswood Rd. B13: Mose 1A **134**
    B31: Longb 3D **158**
    DY6: K'wfrd 5A **92**
Kingswood Wlk. B31: Longb 2D **158**
Kington Cl. WV12: W'hall 1B **30**
Kington Gdns. B37: F'bri 2B **122**
Kington Way B33: Stech 1B **120**
King William St. DY8: Amb 3D **108**
Kiniths Cres. B71: W Brom 2C **80**
Kiniths Way B62: B'hth 2E **113**
    B71: W Brom 3C **80**
Kinlet Cl. WV3: Wolv 3G **41**

Kinlet Gro. B31: N'fld 5G **145**
Kinloch Dr. DY1: Dud 4B **76**
Kinnerley St. WS1: Wals 2E **49**
Kinnersley Cres. B69: O'bry 4D **96**
Kinnerton Cres. B29: W Cas 3D **130**
Kinross Cres. B43: Gt Barr 1D **66**
Kinsey Gro. B14: K Hth 3H **147**
Kinsham Dr. B91: Sol 1F **165**
Kintore Ct. B32: Bart G 6H **129**
Kintyre Cl. B45: Fran 6E **143**
Kinver Av. WV12: W'hall 4B **30**
Kinver Cres. WS9: A'rdge 6E **23**
Kinver Cft. B12: Bal H 4G **117**
    B76: Walm 5E **71**
Kinver Dr. DY9: Hag 6G **125**
    WV4: Penn 6A **42**
Kinver M. B37: Mars G 3C **122**
Kinver Rd. B31: N'fld 5H **145**
Kinver St. DY8: Word 2B **108**
Kinwarton Cl. B15: Yard 5B **120**
Kipling Av. WV14: Cose 4D **60**
Kipling Cl. DY4: Tip 5A **62**
Kipling Rd. B30: K Nor 3G **145**
    DY3: Lwr G 2E **75**
    WV10: F'hses 5H **15**
    WV12: W'hall 2E **31**
Kirby Cl. WV14: Bils 2G **61**
Kirby Dr. DY1: Dud 4A **76**
Kirby Rd. B18: Win G 3A **100**
Kirkby Grn. B73: S Cold 2H **69**
Kirkham Gdns. DY5: P'ntt 3G **93**
Kirkham Gro. B33: Stech 5D **104**
Kirkham Way DY4: Tip 2A **78**
Kirkside Gro. WS8: Bwnhls 6B **10**
Kirkside M. WS8: Bwnhls 6B **10**
Kirkstall Cl. WS3: Blox 5F **19**
Kirkstall Cres. WS3: Blox 5F **19**
Kirkstone Ct. DY5: Brie H 4F **109**
Kirkstone Cres. B43: Gt Barr 1B **82**
    WV5: Wom 1F **73**
Kirkstone Way DY5: Brie H 4F **109**
Kirkwall Rd. B32: Bart G 4B **130**
Kirkwood Av. B23: Erd 6F **69**
Kirmond Wlk. WV6: Wolv 4F **27**
Kirstead Gdns. WV6: Tett 6H **25**
Kirton Gro. B33: Stech 5E **105**
    B91: Sol 6E **151**
    WV6: Tett 4A **26**
Kitchener Rd. B29: S Oak 4D **132**
    DY2: Dud 6H **77**
Kitchener St. B66: Smeth 3H **99**
Kitchen La. WV11: Wed 6G **17**
Kitebrook Cl. B90: M'path 2E **165**
Kitsland Rd. B34: S End 3A **106**
Kitswell Gdns. B32: Bart G 5G **129**
Kittermaster Rd. CV7: Mer 4H **141**
Kittiwake Dr. DY5: Brie H 4G **109**
Kittoe Rd. B74: Four O 6F **37**
KITT'S GREEN 6G **105**
Kitts Grn. B33: Kitts G 6D **105**
Kitts Grn. Rd. B33: Kitts G 5E **105**
Kitwell La. B32: Bart G 5G **129**
Kitwood Dr. B92: Sol 6H **137**
Kixley La. B93: Know 3E **167**
Klaxon Ind. Est. B11: Tys 1F **135**
Knarsdale Cl. DY5: Brie H 3G **109**
Knaves Castle Av. WS8: Bwnhls . . . 3B **10**
Knebworth Cl. B44: Gt Barr 5G **67**
Knightcote Dr. B91: Sol 1F **165**
Knight Cl. B75: S Cold 6G **55**
Knightley Rd. B91: Sol 5D **150**
Knightlow Rd. B17: Harb 3E **115**
Knighton Cl. B74: Four O 6F **37**
Knighton Dr. B74: Four O 1F **53**
Knighton Rd. B31: N'fld 3G **145**
    B74: Four O 4D **36**
    DY2: Neth 5F **95**
Knights Av. WV6: Tett 3B **26**
Knightsbridge Cl. B74: Four O 5F **37**
Knightsbridge Ho. B37: K'hrst 4B **106**
Knightsbridge La. WV12: W'hall . . . 3C **30**
Knightsbridge Rd. B92: Olton 4D **136**
Knights Cl. B23: Erd 5E **85**
Knights Ct. WS11: Nort C 1E **9**
Knights Cres. WV6: Tett 2C **26**
Knightsfield Cl. B73: New O 2C **68**
Knights Hill WS9: A'rdge 6D **34**

Knight's Rd. B11: Tys 1G **135**
Knightstowe Av. B18: Hock 5C **100**
Knightswood Cl. B75: S Cold 4B **54**
Knightwick Cres. B23: Erd 2C **84**
Knipersley Rd. B73: Bold 1G **85**
Knoll, The B32: Bart G 4A **130**
    DY6: K'wfrd 4C **92**
Knoll Cl. WS7: Chase 1C **10**
Knoll Cft. B90: Ches G 5B **164**
    WS9: A'rdge 6E **23**
Knollcroft B16: Birm 1C **116**
Knott Ct. DY5: Brie H 1H **109**
Knottsall La. B68: O'bry 6H **97**
Knotts Farm Rd. DY6: K'wfrd 5E **93**
Knowlands Rd. B90: M'path 2E **165**
KNOWLE 3E **167**
Knowle Cl. B45: Redn 2B **158**
KNOWLE GROVE 6C **166**
Knowle Hill Rd. DY2: Neth 5D **94**
Knowle Rd. B11: S'hll 2D **134**
    B65: Row R 5H **95**
    B92: H Ard 6G **153**
Knowles Dr. B74: Four O 4G **53**
Knowles Rd. WV1: Wolv 2B **44**
Knowles St. WS10: W'bry 2G **63**
Knowle Wood Rd. B93: Dorr 6D **166**
Knox Rd. WV2: Wolv 5H **43**
Knoyle Ct. DY8: Stourb 5D **108**
    (off Scott's Rd.)
Knutsford St. B12: Bal H 5H **117**
Knutswood Cl. B13: Mose 6D **134**
Kohima Dr. DY8: Stourb 6C **108**
Kossuth Rd. WV14: Cose 4C **60**
Kyle Cl. WV10: Oxl 6F **15**
Kyles Way B32: Bart G 6H **129**
Kynaston Cres. WV8: Cod 5H **13**
Kyngsford Rd. B33: Kitts G 6H **105**
Kyotts Lake Rd. B11: S'brk 4A **118**
Kyrwicks La. B11: S'brk 5A **118**
Kyter La. B36: Cas B 1F **105**

L

Laburnum Av. B37: K'hrst 3B **106**
    B67: Smeth 5C **98**
Laburnum Cl. B37: K'hrst 3B **106**
    B47: H'wd 4A **162**
    DY8: Woll 4C **108**
    WS3: Pels 5E **21**
Laburnum Cotts. B21: Hand 1A **100**
Laburnum Cft. B69: Tiv 5B **78**
Laburnum Dr. B76: Walm 2E **71**
Laburnum Gro. B13: Mose 2H **133**
    WS2: Wals 6F **31**
Laburnum Ho. B30: B'vlle 6B **132**
Laburnum Rd. B30: B'vlle 5B **132**
    DY1: Dud 3D **76**
    DY4: Tip 6H **61**
    DY6: K'wfrd 3C **92**
    WS5: Wals 1G **65**
    WS9: Wals W 4C **22**
    WS10: W'bry 1H **63**
    WV1: Wolv 3D **44**
    WV4: E'shll 2A **60**
Laburnum St. DY8: Woll 4C **108**
    WV3: Wolv 2E **43**
Laburnum Trees B47: H'wd 3A **162**
    (off May Farm Cl.)
Laburnum Vs. B11: S'hll 6C **118**
Laburnum Way B31: Longb 6E **145**
Laceby Gro. B13: Mose 4D **134**
Ladbroke Dr. B76: Walm 3D **70**
Ladbroke Gro. B27: A Grn 5A **136**
Ladbrook Gro. DY3: Lwr G 4E **75**
Ladbrook Rd. B91: Sol 4G **151**
Ladbury Gro. WS5: Wals 1D **64**
Ladbury Rd. WS5: Wals 1E **65**
Ladeler Gro. B33: Kitts G 1A **122**
Ladies Wlk. DY3: Sed 5H **59**
Lady Bank B32: Bart G 6H **129**
Lady Bracknell M. B31: N'fld 3G **145**
Lady Byron La. B93: Know 2B **166**
Ladycroft B16: Birm 1C **116**
Lady Grey's Wlk. DY8: Stourb 1B **124**
Lady La. B90: Shir 6G **163**
    B94: Earls 6G **163**

Ladymoor Rd. WV14: Bils . . . 2E **61**
Ladypool Av. B11: S'brk. . . . 5B **118**
Ladypool Cl. B62: Hale. . . . 1C **128**
WS4: Wals . . . 4E **33**
Ladypool Rd. B12: Bal H . . . 1A **134**
Ladysmith Rd. B63: Crad . . . 5E **111**
Ladywell Cl. WV5: Wom . . . 5G **57**
Ladywell Wlk. B5: Birm . . . 2G **117** (6E **5**)
LADYWOOD . . . 1D **116**
Ladywood Arts & Leisure Cen. . . . 1B **116**
Ladywood Cir. B16: Birm . . . 1C **116**
Ladywood Cl. DY5: Quar B. . . . 2B **110**
Ladywood Middleway B1: Birm . . . 6C **100**
B16: Birm. . . . 6C **100**
Ladywood Rd. B16: Edg. . . . 2B **116**
B74: Four O . . . 4G **53**
LA Fitness . . . 6G **69**
Laing Ho. B69: O'bry . . . 4D **96**
Lake Av. WS5: Wals . . . 4F **49**
Lake Cl. WS5: Wals . . . 4G **49**
Lakedown Cl. B14: K Hth. . . . 6G **147**
Lakefield B31: N'fld . . . 3D **144**
Lakefield Cl. B28: Hall G . . . 6H **135**
Lakefield Rd. WV11: Wed . . . 4G **29**
Lakehouse Ct. B23: Erd . . . 5E **69**
Lakehouse Gro. B38: K Nor. . . . 4H **145**
Lakehouse Rd. B73: Bold. . . . 5E **69**
Laker Cl. DY8: Amb . . . 4E **109**
Lakeside B74: Lit A . . . 4B **36**
Lakeside Cen., The . . . 4C **146**
Lakeside Cl. WV13: W'hall . . . 6G **29**
Lakeside Club . . . 5B **106**
Lakeside Ct. DY5: Brie H . . . 3F **109**
Lakeside Dr. B90: M'path . . . 2D **164**
Lakeside Residences
B4: Birm . . . 6H **101** (2F **5**)
Lakeside Rd. B70: W Brom . . . 1G **79**
Lakeside Wlk. B23: Erd . . . 3B **84**
Lakes Rd. B23: Erd . . . 2A **84**
Lake St. DY3: Lwr G . . . 4H **75**
Lakewood Dr. B45: Redn . . . 6H **143**
Lakey La. B28: Hall G . . . 5G **135**
Lambah Cl. WV14: Bils . . . 4H **45**
Lamb Cl. B34: S End . . . 4A **106**
Lamb Cres. WV5: Wom . . . 1F **73**
(not continuous)
Lambert Cl. B23: Erd. . . . 1D **84**
Lambert Ct. DY6: K'wfrd . . . 1B **92**
Lambert End B70: W Brom . . . 4H **79**
Lambert Fold DY2: Dud . . . 1G **95**
Lambert Rd. WV10: Wolv . . . 3B **28**
LAMBERT'S END . . . 4H **79**
Lambert St. B70: W Brom . . . 4H **79**
Lambeth Cl. B37: F'bri. . . . 5D **106**
Lambeth Rd. B44: Gt Barr . . . 2G **67**
WV14: Bils. . . . 4D **44**
Lambourn Cl. WS3: Blox . . . 5A **20**
Lambourne Cl. WS6: Gt Wyr . . . 2F **7**
Lambourne Way DY5: Brie H . . . 3F **109**
WS11: Nort C. . . . 1E **9**
Lambourn Rd. B23: Erd. . . . 3D **84**
WV13: W'hall. . . . 2D **46**
Lambscote Cl. B90: Shir . . . 5C **148**
Lamgley Rd. WV3: Penn . . . 6E **41**
Lammas Cl. B92: Sol. . . . 4G **137**
Lammas Rd. DY8: Word . . . 6A **92**
Lammermoor Av. B43: Gt Barr. . . . 3B **66**
Lamont Av. B32: Bart G . . . 2D **130**
Lamorna Cl. WV3: Wolv . . . 3H **41**
Lanark Cl. DY6: K'wfrd . . . 4D **92**
Lanark Cft. B35: Cas V. . . . 4D **86**
Lancaster Av. B45: Rubery . . . 1G **157**
WS9: A'rdge. . . . 1D **34**
WS10: W'bry . . . 2A **64**
Lancaster Cir. Queensway
B4: Birm . . . 5G **101** (1F **5**)
Lancaster Cl. B30: B'vlle . . . 1C **146**
Lancaster Dr. B35: Cas V . . . 5F **87**
Lancaster Gdns. WV4: Penn . . . 6C **42**
Lancaster Ho. B65: Row R. . . . 5E **97**
Lancaster Pl. WS3: Blox . . . 5A **20**
Lancaster Rd. DY5: Brie H. . . . 1G **109**
Lancaster St. B4: Birm . . . 5G **101** (1F **5**)
Lancelot Cl. B8: Salt. . . . 6E **103**
Lancelot Pl. DY4: Tip. . . . 3E **79**
Lanchester Rd. B38: K Nor . . . 6C **146**
Lanchester Way B36: Cas B. . . . 6A **88**
Lander Cl. B45: Rubery . . . 3G **157**
Landgate Rd. B21: Hand . . . 5G **81**
Land La. B37: Mars G . . . 4C **122**
Landor Rd. B93: Know. . . . 3C **166**
Landor St. B8: Birm, Salt . . . 6B **102**
Landport Rd. WV2: Wolv . . . 3B **44**
Landrail Wlk. B36: Cas B. . . . 1C **106**
(not continuous)
Landrake Rd. DY6: K'wfrd . . . 4D **92**
Landseer Gro. B43: Gt Barr . . . 1F **67**
Landsgate DY8: Stourb . . . 4E **125**
Landswood Cl. B44: K'sdng. . . . 4A **68**
Landswood Rd. B68: O'bry . . . 5A **98**
LANDYWOOD. . . . 3G **7**
Landywood Ent. Pk. WS6: Gt Wyr . . . 5F **7**
Landywood Grn. WS6: C Hay. . . . 3E **7**
Landywood La. WS6: C Hay, Gt Wyr . . . 3D **6**
Landywood Station (Rail) . . . 3F **7**
Lane Av. WS2: Wals. . . . 6H **31**
Lane Cl. WS2: Wals. . . . 6H **31**
Lane Ct. WV1: Wolv. . . . 5G **27**
Lane Cft. B76: Walm . . . 5E **71**
LANE GREEN . . . 4H **13**
Lane Grn. Av. WV8: Bilb . . . 6A **14**
Lane Grn. Ct. WV8: Bilb. . . . 4H **13**
Lane Grn. Rd. WV8: Bilb . . . 4H **13**
Lane Grn. Shop. Pde WV8: Bilb . . . 4H **13**
LANE HEAD . . . 3C **30**
Lane Rd. WV4: E'shll . . . 2C **60**
Lanes Cl. WV5: Wom. . . . 2E **73**
LANESFIELD . . . 1B **60**
Lanesfield Dr. WV4: E'shll . . . 1C **60**
Lanesfield Ind. Est. WV4: E'shll. . . . 1C **60**
Laneside Av. B74: S'tly . . . 4H **51**
Laneside Gdns. WS2: Wals . . . 1H **47**
Lanes Shop. Cen., The B72: W Grn . . . 6H **69**
Lane St. WV14: Bils, Cose . . . 2F **61**
LANEY GREEN . . . 3A **6**
Langcomb Rd. B90: Shir . . . 1G **163**
Langdale Cl. WS8: Clay . . . 1A **22**
Langdale Cft. B21: Hand . . . 2A **100**
Langdale Dr. WV14: Bils . . . 4F **45**
Langdale Rd. B43: Gt Barr. . . . 6B **66**
Langdale Way DY9: W'cte . . . 1H **125**
Langdon St. B9: Birm. . . . 1B **118**
Langdon Wlk. B26: Yard . . . 1C **136**
Langfield Rd. B93: Know. . . . 2C **166**
Langford Av. B43: Gt Barr . . . 5A **66**
Langford Cl. WS1: Wals . . . 2E **49**
Langford Cft. B91: Sol . . . 5G **151**
Langford Gro. B17: Harb . . . 2G **131**
Langham Cl. B26: Sheld. . . . 4E **121**
Langham Grn. B74: S'tly . . . 2H **51**
Langholme Dr. B44: K'sdng. . . . 4D **68**
Langland Dr. DY3: Sed . . . 5G **59**
LANGLEY. . . . 4G **97**
Langley Av. WV14: Cose . . . 5E **61**
Langley Cl. WS9: Wals W . . . 3C **22**
Langley Ct. B69: O'bry. . . . 4G **97**
WV4: Penn. . . . 5B **42**
Langley Cres. B68: O'bry. . . . 5H **97**
Langley Dr. B35: Cas V . . . 6E **87**
Langley Gdns. B68: O'bry . . . 5H **97**
WV3: Wolv. . . . 4B **42**
LANGLEY GREEN . . . 5H **97**
Langley Grn. Rd. B69: O'bry . . . 5G **97**
Langley Green Station (Rail) . . . 4H **97**
Langley Gro. B10: Small H . . . 3D **118**
Langley Hall Dr. B75: S Cold . . . 6F **55**
Langley Hall Rd. B75: S Cold. . . . 6F **55**
B92: Olton . . . 6A **136**
Langley Heath Dr. B76: Walm . . . 2D **70**
Langley High St. B69: O'bry . . . 4G **97**
Langley Mill Junc.
Littleworth End. . . . 2G **55**
Falcon Lodge. . . . 5H **55**
Langley Pk. Way B75: S Cold . . . 5D **54**
Langley Ri. B92: Sol . . . 2A **138**
Langley Rd. B10: Small H . . . 3D **118**
B68: O'bry . . . 5H **97**
WV4: Lwr P . . . 6E **41**
Langleys Rd. B29: S Oak . . . 4A **132**
Langley Swimming Cen. . . . 5H **97**
Langmead Cl. WS2: Wals . . . 6D **30**
Langstone Rd. B14: K Hth . . . 5B **148**
DY1: Dud . . . 6A **76**
Langton Cl. B36: Cas B . . . 3D **106**
Langton Pl. WV14: Bils . . . 5A **46**
Langton Rd. B8: Salt . . . 5E **103**
Langtree Av. B91: Sol. . . . 6F **151**
Langwood Ct. B36: Cas B. . . . 1F **105**
Langworth Av. B27: A Grn . . . 6A **120**
Lannacombe Rd. B31: Longb . . . 3C **158**
Lansbury Av. WS10: Darl. . . . 1C **62**
Lansbury Grn. B64: Old H . . . 3B **112**
Lansbury Rd. B64: Old H . . . 3B **112**
Lansbury Wlk. DY4: Tip. . . . 5A **62**
Lansdale Av. B92: Sol . . . 5B **138**
Lansdowne Av. WV8: Cod . . . 5E **13**
Lansdowne Cl. WV14: Cose. . . . 6C **60**
Lansdowne Ct. DY9: Pedm. . . . 4F **125**
Lansdowne Ho. B15: Birm . . . 3F **117**
Lansdowne Rd. B21: Hand. . . . 2C **100**
B24: Erd . . . 4F **85**
B62: B'hth. . . . 3F **113**
B63: Hale . . . 3F **127**
DY2: Dud . . . 3H **95**
WV1: Wolv. . . . 6F **27** (1A **170**)
WV14: Bils. . . . 4G **45**
Lansdowne St. B18: Win G . . . 5B **100**
(not continuous)
Lansdown Pl. B18: Win G . . . 4B **100**
Lantern Rd. DY2: Neth . . . 1E **111**
LAPAL . . . 2F **129**
Lapal La. B62: Bart G. . . . 3F **129**
Lapal La. Nth. B62: Hale . . . 2E **129**
Lapal La. Sth. B62: Hale . . . 2E **129**
Lapley Cl. WV1: Wolv . . . 1D **44**
Lappath Ho. B32: Bart G . . . 5B **130**
Lapper Av. WV4: E'shll. . . . 2B **60**
Lapwing Cl. WS6: C Hay . . . 4C **6**
Lapwing Cft. B23: Erd . . . 6C **68**
Lapwing Dr. B92: H Ard . . . 6B **140**
Lapwood Av. DY6: K'wfrd . . . 3D **92**
Lapworth Dr. B73: New O. . . . 2C **68**
Lapworth Gro. B12: Bal H . . . 5H **117**
Lapworth Ho. B5: Birm . . . 4G **117**
Lapworth Mus. . . . 2B **132**
Lara Cl. B17: Harb . . . 3F **115**
Lara Gro. DY4: Tip . . . 5A **78**
Larch Av. B21: Hand . . . 5H **81**
Larch Cft. B37: Chel W. . . . 1D **122**
B69: Tiv . . . 5B **78**
Larch Dr. B31: Longb. . . . 6A **144**
Larches La. WV3: Wolv . . . 1E **43**
Larches St. B11: S'brk. . . . 5A **118**
Larchfield Cl. B20: Hand . . . 4D **82**
Larch Gro. DY3: Sed . . . 6A **60**
Larch Ho. B20: Hand . . . 4B **82**
B36: Hodg H . . . 1D **104**
Larchmere Dr. B28: Hall G . . . 5F **135**
WV11: Ess . . . 4B **18**
Larch Rd. DY6: K'wfrd . . . 3C **92**
Larch Wlk. B25: Yard. . . . 3H **119**
Larchwood Cres. B74: S'tly . . . 3G **51**
Larchwood Grn. WS5: Wals . . . 1F **65**
Larchwood Rd. WS5: Wals. . . . 1E **65**
Larcombe Dr. WV4: Penn . . . 6H **43**
Large Av. WS10: Darl. . . . 1C **62**
Lark Cl. B14: K Hth . . . 5A **148**
Larkfield Av. B36: Cas B. . . . 1F **105**
Larkhill Rd. DY8: Stourb . . . 1A **124**
Larkhill Wlk. B14: K Hth. . . . 6F **147**
Larkin Cl. WV10: Bush. . . . 6C **16**
Lark Mdw. Dr. B37: K'hrst . . . 6A **106**
Larksfield *B66: Smeth* . . . *5F **99***
(off Windmill La.)
Larksfield M. DY5: Brie H . . . 4G **109**
Larks Mill WS3: Pels . . . 3C **20**
Larkspur Av. WS7: Burn. . . . 1C **10**
Larkspur Cft. B36: Hodg H. . . . 1B **104**
Larkspur Rd. DY2: Dud . . . 1H **95**
Larkspur Way WS8: Clay . . . 1H **21**
Larkswood Dr. DY3: Sed . . . 6H **59**
WV4: Penn. . . . 2A **58**
Larne Rd. B26: Sheld. . . . 4E **121**
Lashbrooke Ho. B45: Rubery . . . 2F **157**
Latches Cl. WS10: Darl . . . 5E **47**
Latelow Rd. B33: Yard. . . . 1E **121**
Latham Av. B43: Gt Barr . . . 6A **66**
Latham Cres. DY4: Tip. . . . 4A **78**
Lath La. B66: Smeth . . . 1B **98**
Lathom Gro. B33: Stech. . . . 4D **104**
Latimer Gdns. B15: Edg. . . . 4F **117**

Latimer Pl.—Lelant Gro.

Latimer Pl. B18: Win G 3A 100
Latimer St. WV13: W'hall 6B 30
Latymer Cl. B76: Walm 6E 71
Lauder Cl. DY3: Sed 4G 59
WV13: W'hall 2F 45
Lauderdale Cl. WS8: Clay 1A 22
Lauderdale Gdns. WV10: Bush 4A 16
Laughton Cl. B31: Longb 2F 159
Launceston Cl. WS5: Wals 4H 49
Launceston Rd. WS5: Wals 4H 49
Launde, The B28: Hall G 4E 149
Laundry Rd. B66: Smeth 6G 99
Laureates Wlk. B74: Four O 2G 53
Laurel Av. B12: Bal H 6A 118
Laurel Cl. DY1: Dud 4C 76
Laurel Ct. B13: Mose 3H 133
Laurel Dr. B66: Smeth 1E 99
B74: S'tly 3G 51
Laurel Gdns. B21: Hand 6A 82
B27: A Grn 6A 120
Laurel Gro. B30: B'vlle 1A 146
WV3: Wolv 5C 42
WV14: Bils 1A 62
Laurel La. B63: Hale 2B 128
Laurel Rd. B21: Hand 6A 82
B30: K Nor 3C 146
DY1: Dud 3B 76
DY4: Tip 6H 61
WS5: Wals 1F 65
Laurels, The *B16: Birm* *6B 100*
(off Marroway St.)
B26: Sheld 6G 121
Laurels Cres. CV7: Bal C 6H 169
Laurel Ter. B6: Aston 6H 83
Laurence Ct. B31: N'fld 2F 145
Laurence Gro. WV6: Tett 2C 26
Lauriston Cl. DY1: Dud 4B 76
Lavender Cl. WS5: Wals 2D 64
WV9: Pend 4D 14
Lavender Ct. *B71: W Brom* *6A 64*
(off Sussex Av.)
Lavender Gdns. B23: Erd 6B 68
Lavender Gro. WS3: Wals 4C 32
WV14: Bils 5H 45
Lavender Hall La. CV7: Bal C 1H 169
Lavender Ho. B38: K Nor 1B 160
Lavender La. DY8: Stourb 2B 124
Lavender Rd. DY1: Dud 4D 76
Lavendon Rd. B42: P Barr 2D 82
Lavinia Rd. B62: Hale 2E 129
Law Cliff Rd. B42: Gt Barr 1D 82
Law Cl. B69: Tiv 5D 78
Lawden Rd. B10: Small H 3B 118
Lawford Cl. B7: Birm 6A 102
Lawford Gro. B5: Birm 3G 117
B90: Shir 5D 148
Lawfred Av. WV11: Wed 4F 29
Lawley, The B63: Hale 4F 127
Lawley Cl. WS4: S'fld 6F 21
Lawley Middleway B4: Birm 5A 102
Lawley Rd. WV14: Bils 5D 44
Lawley St. B70: W Brom 4F 79
DY1: Dud 6C 76
Lawn Av. DY8: Stourb 1C 124
Lawn La. WV9: Coven 2D 14
Lawn Oaks Cl. WS8: Bwnhls 3H 9
Lawn Rd. WV2: E'shll 5B 44
Lawnsdale Cl. B46: Col 2H 107
Lawnsdown Rd. DY5: Quar B 4B 110
Lawnsfield Gro. B23: Erd 1D 84
Lawnside Grn. WV14: Bils 3F 45
Lawn St. DY8: Stourb 1C 124
LAWNS WOOD 6G 91
Lawnswood B76: Walm 5E 71
DY7: Stourt 5G 91
Lawnswood Av. B90: Shir 4B 150
DY8: Word 5A 92
WS7: Chase 1B 10
WV4: E'shll 1A 60
WV6: Tett 1C 26
Lawnswood Dr. DY7: Stourt 6G 91
WS9: Wals W 4C 22
Lawnswood Gro. B21: Hand 6G 81
Lawnswood Ri. WV6: Tett 1D 26
Lawnswood Rd. DY3: Up Gor 2H 75
DY8: Word 6A 92
Lawnwood Rd. DY2: Neth 1D 110
Lawrence Av. WV10: Wolv 5C 28
WV11: Wed 3H 29
Lawrence Ct. B68: O'bry 3H 113
Lawrence Dr. B76: Min 1H 87
Lawrence La. B64: Old H 2G 111
Lawrence St. DY9: Lye 5G 109
WV13: W'hall 6A 30
Lawrence Twr. B4: Birm 2G 5
Lawrence Wlk.
B43: Gt Barr 1F 67
Lawson Cl. WS9: A'rdge 5D 34
Lawson St. B4: Birm 5G 101 (1F 5)
Law St. B71: W Brom 2A 80
Lawton Av. B29: S Oak 3D 132
Lawton Cl. B65: Row R 3D 96
Lawyers Wlk. WS1: Wals 2D 48
Laxey Rd. B16: Edg 6H 99
Laxford Cl. B12: Bal H 5G 117
Laxton Cl. DY6: K'wfrd 4E 93
Laxton Gro. B25: Yard 2B 120
Lazy Hill B38: K Nor 5D 146
WS9: A'rdge 5E 23
Lazy Hill Rd. WS9: A'rdge 1D 34
WS9: Ston 4F 23
Lea, The B33: Yard 1E 121
Lea Av. WS10: W'bry 4D 62
Lea Bank WV3: Wolv 1A 42
Lea Bank Rd. DY2: Neth 6D 94
Leabon Gro. B17: Harb 1G 131
Leabrook B26: Yard 3D 120
Leabrook Rd. DY4: Tip 4C 62
WS10: W'bry 4D 62
Leabrook Rd. Nth. WS10: W'bry 4D 62
Leach Grn. La. B45: Redn 2G 157
Leach Heath La. B45: Rubery 2F 157
Leacliffe Way WS9: A'rdge 6H 35
Leacote Dr. WV6: Tett 5A 26
Leacroft WV12: W'hall 2C 30
Leacroft Av. WV10: Bush 1A 28
Leacroft Cl. WS9: A'rdge 6D 22
Leacroft Gro. B71: W Brom 5H 63
Leacroft La. WS11: Cann 1F 7
Leacroft Rd. DY6: K'wfrd 1C 92
Leadbeater Ho. *WS3: Blox* *1H 31*
(off Somerfield Rd.)
Lea Dr. B26: Sheld 5E 121
LEA END 6B 160
Lea End La. B38: Forh 6A 160
B48: Hopw 5G 159
Leafield Cres. B33: Stech 4E 105
Leafield Gdns. B62: B'hth 3D 112
Leafield Rd. B92: Sol 4F 137
Lea Ford Rd. B33: Kitts G 5G 105
Leaford Way DY6: K'wfrd 4D 92
Leafy Glade B74: S'tly 6A 36
Leafy Ri. DY3: Lwr G 3H 75
Lea Gdns. WV3: Wolv 3F 43
Lea Grn. Av. DY4: Tip 2E 77
Lea Grn. Dr. B47: Wyt 5C 162
Lea Grn. La. B47: Wyt 3C 162
Lea Hall Rd. B33: Yard 6E 105
Lea Hall Station (Rail) 1F 121
Leahill Cft. B37: F'bri 1B 122
Lea Hill Rd. B20: Hand 5E 83
Leaholme Gdns. DY9: Pedm 3F 125
Leahouse Gdns. B68: O'bry 6G 97
Lea Ho. Rd. B30: Stir 6C 132
Leahouse Rd. B68: O'bry 6G 97
Leahurst Cres. B17: Harb 1G 131
Lea La. WS6: Gt Wyr 2G 7
Lea Mnr. Dr. WV4: Penn 2C 58
Leam Cres. B92: Sol 4F 137
Leamington Rd. B12: Bal H 6A 118
LEAMORE 4H 31
Leamore Cl. WS2: Wals 2G 31
Leamore Ent. Pk. WS2: Wals 3G 31
(Fryer's Rd.)
WS2: Wals 2G 31
(Willenhall La., not continuous)
Leamore Ind. Est. WS2: Wals 3H 31
Leamore La. WS2: Wals 2G 31
WS3: Blox 2G 31
Leamount Dr. B44: K'sdng 3C 68
Leander Cl. WS6: Gt Wyr 4F 7
Leander Gdns. B14: K Hth 2H 147
Leander Rd. DY9: W'cte 1B 126
Leandor Dr. B74: S'tly 4A 52
Lea Rd. B11: S'hll 1D 134
WV3: Wolv 4E 43 (6A 170)
Lear Rd. WV5: Wom 5H 57
Leason La. WV10: Bush 1C 28
Leasow, The WS9: A'rdge 4A 34
Leasow Dr. B15: Edg 2H 131
Leasowe Dr. WV6: Pert 5D 24
Leasowe Rd. B45: Rubery 1F 157
DY4: Tip 3G 77
Leasowes Country Pk., The 1D 128
Leasowes Ct. B63: Hale 3A 128
Leasowes Dr. WV4: Penn 5B 42
Leasowes La. B62: Hale 6D 112
Leasowes Rd. B14: K Hth 4H 133
Leasowes Sports Cen. 5E 113
Leatherhead Cl. B6: Aston 3H 101
Leather Mus., The 6C 32
Lea Va. Rd. DY8: Stourb 3D 124
Leavesden Gro. B26: Sheld 6E 121
Lea Vw. WS9: A'rdge 4A 34
WV12: W'hall 4A 30
Lea Wlk. B45: Rubery 1F 157
Lea Yield Cl. B30: Stir 6C 132
Lechlade Rd. B43: Gt Barr 5A 66
Leckie Rd. WS2: Wals 5C 32
Ledbury Cl. B16: Birm 1C 116
WS9: A'rdge 6E 23
Ledbury Ct. *B29: W Cas* *6G 131*
(off Ruthall Cl.)
WV12: W'hall 5B 30
Ledbury Dr. WV1: Wolv 2D 44
Ledbury Ho. B33: Kitts G 1A 122
Ledbury Way B76: Walm 5E 71
Ledsam Gro. B32: Harb 5D 114
Ledsam St. B16: Birm 1C 116
Ledwell B90: Dic H 3G 163
LEE BANK 3E 117
Lee Bank Middleway B15: Birm 3E 117
Leebank Rd. B63: Hale 3G 127
Leech St. DY4: Tip 2C 78
Lee Ct. WS9: Wals W 4B 22
Lee Cres. B15: Edg 3E 117
Lee Gdns. B67: Smeth 4C 98
Lee Rd. B47: H'wd 2A 162
B64: Crad H 3H 111
Leeson Wlk. B17: Harb 1H 131
Lees Rd. WV14: Bils 2H 61
Lees St. B18: Hock 4B 100
Lees Ter. WV14: Bils 2H 61
Lee St. B70: W Brom 5G 63
Legge La. B1: Birm 6D 100 (2A 4)
WV14: Cose 3F 61
Legge St. B4: Birm 5H 101
B70: W Brom 4B 80
WV2: E'shll 5A 44
Legion Rd. B45: Rubery 2E 157
Legs La. WV10: Bush 3A 16
Leicester Cl. B67: Smeth 2C 114
Leicester Pl. B71: W Brom 6A 64
Leicester Sq. WV6: Wolv 6E 27
Leicester St. WS1: Wals 1C 48
WV6: Wolv 5F 27
Leigham Dr. B17: Harb 4E 115
Leigh Cl. WS4: Wals 5E 33
Leigh Ct. B23: Erd 5C 84
WS4: Wals 6E 33
Leigh Rd. B8: Salt 3E 103
B75: S Cold 6F 55
WS4: Wals 6E 33
Leighs Cl. WS4: S'fld 6G 21
Leighs Rd. WS4: S'fld 6F 21
LEIGHSWOOD 1C 34
Leighswood Av. WS9: A'rdge 2C 34
Leighswood Ct. WS9: A'rdge 3D 34
Leighswood Gro. WS9: A'rdge 2C 34
Leighswood Ind. Est. WS9: A'rdge 6B 22
(Brickyard Rd.)
WS9: A'rdge 2C 34
(Phoenix Dr.)
Leighswood Rd. WS9: A'rdge 2C 34
Leighton Cl. B43: Gt Barr 2E 67
DY1: Dud 5A 76
Leighton Rd. B13: Mose 3H 133
WV4: Penn 5D 42
WV14: Bils 1A 62
Leith Gro. B38: K Nor 1A 160
Lelant Gro. B17: Harb 6E 115

Lellow St. B71: W Brom 5H **63**
Lemar Ind. Est. B30: Stir 4D **132**
Le More B74: Four O 1G **53**
Lemox Rd. B70: W Brom 5G **63**
Lench Cl. B62: B'hth 2C **112**
Lenches, The *B69: O'bry* *4E 97*
(off Shelsley Av.)
Lench's Cl. B13: Mose 3H **133**
Lenchs Grn. B5: Bal H 4G **117**
Lench St. B4: Birm 5G **101** (1F **5**)
Lenchs Trust B32: Quin 5B **114**
Lench's Trust Ho's. B12: Birm 4H **117**
(Conybere St.)
B12: Birm 3A **118**
(Ravenhurst St.)
B16: Birm *2C 116*
(off Ladywood Middleway)
Len Davis Rd. WV12: W'hall 2B **30**
Lennard Gdns. B66: Smeth 3H **99**
Lennox Gdns. WV3: Wolv 3E **43**
Lennox Gro. B73: Bold 6G **69**
Lenton Cft. B26: Yard 1C **136**
Lenwade Rd. B68: O'bry 3B **114**
Leofric Ct. B15: Edg 3E **117**
Leominster Ct. *B45: Rubery* *1F 157*
(off Deelands Rd.)
Leominster Ho. B33: Kitts G 1A **122**
Leominster Rd. B11: S'hll 2E **135**
Leominster Wlk. B45: Rubery 1F **157**
Leona Ind. Est. B62: B'hth 2D **112**
Leonard Av. B19: Loz 1F **101**
Leonard Gro. B19: Loz 1E **101**
Leonard Rd. B19: Loz 1E **101**
DY8: Woll 6A **108**
Leopold Av. B20: Hand 2A **82**
Leopold St. B12: Birm 3H **117**
Lepid Gro. B29: S Oak 3H **131**
Lerryn Cl. DY6: K'wfrd 4D **92**
Lerwick Cl. DY6: K'wfrd 4D **92**
Lesley Dr. DY6: K'wfrd 5C **92**
Leslie Bentley Ho. B1: Birm 3A **4**
Leslie Dr. DY4: Tip 4A **62**
Leslie Ri. B69: Tiv 1C **96**
Leslie Rd. B16: Edg 1B **116**
B20: Hand 5F **83**
B74: Lit A 1B **52**
WV10: Wolv 4B **28**
Lesscroft Cl. WV9: Pend 4E **15**
Lester Gro. WS9: A'rdge 1G **51**
Lester St. WV14: Bils 6H **45**
Levante Gdns. B33: Stech 1B **120**
Leve La. WV13: W'hall 1B **46**
Level St. DY5: Brie H 6H **93**
Leven Cft. B76: Walm 6E **71**
Leven Dr. WV12: W'hall 6B **18**
Levenwick Way DY6: K'wfrd 4E **93**
Leverretts, The B21: Hand 5G **81**
Lever St. WV2: Wolv 3H **43** (6C **170**)
Leverton Ri. WV10: Oxl 3G **27**
Leveson Av. WS6: C Hay 3E **7**
Leveson Cl. DY2: Dud 1G **95**
Leveson Ct. WV13: W'hall 1A **46**
Leveson Cres. CV7: Bal C 6H **169**
Leveson Dr. DY4: Tip 1G **77**
Leveson Rd. WV11: Wed 1H **29**
Leveson St. WV13: W'hall 1A **46**
Leveson Wlk. DY2: Dud 1G **95**
Levington Cl. WV6: Pert 5F **25**
Levis's Trad. Est. B33: Stech 5B **104**
Lewis Av. WV1: Wolv 6D **28**
Lewis Cl. WV12: W'hall 4D **30**
Lewis Gro. WV11: Wed 3F **29**
Lewisham Ind. Est. B66: Smeth 2E **99**
Lewisham Rd. B66: Smeth 2E **99**
WV10: Oxl 5F **15**
Lewisham St. B71: W Brom 3B **80**
Lewis Rd. B30: Stir 6E **133**
B68: O'bry 4H **113**
DY9: Lye 6H **109**
Lewis St. DY4: Tip 2D **78**
WS2: Wals 5B **32**
WV14: Bils 5G **45**
Lewthorn Ri. WV4: Penn 1H **59**
Lexington Grn. DY5: Brie H 4G **109**
Leybourne Cres. WV9: Pend 5D **14**
Leybourne Gro. B25: Yard 5H **119**
Leybrook Rd. B45: Redn 1H **157**
Leyburn Cl. WS2: Wals 5D **30**
Leycester Cl. B31: Longb 2E **159**
Leycroft Av. B33: Kitts G 5H **105**
Leydon Cft. B38: K Nor 5D **146**
LEY HILL **2G 53**
Ley Hill Farm Rd.
B31: N'fld 2C **144**
Ley Hill Rd. B75: Four O 2A **54**
Leylan Cft. B13: Mose 6C **134**
Leyland Av. WV3: Wolv 2D **42**
Leyland Cft. WS3: Pels 3D **20**
Leyland Dr. DY2: Dud 1F **95**
Leyman Cl. B14: Yard W 3C **148**
Ley Ri. DY3: Sed 4G **59**
Leys, The B31: N'fld 2F **145**
WS10: Darl 5C **46**
Leys Cl. DY9: Pedm 3G **125**
Leys Cres. DY5: Brie H 6F **93**
Leysdown Gro. B27: A Grn 5A **136**
Leysdown Rd. B27: A Grn 5A **136**
Leys Rd. DY5: Brie H 6E **93**
Leys Wood Cft. B26: Sheld 5E **121**
Leyton Cl. DY5: Brie H 3G **109**
Leyton Gro. B44: K'sdng 4A **68**
Leyton Rd. B21: Hand 1B **100**
Libbards Ga. B91: Sol 1G **165**
Libbards Way B91: Sol 1F **165**
Liberty Ct. WS6: C Hay 2D **6**
Liberty Pl. B16: Birm 1D **116**
Library, Theatre and Solihull Arts Complex
. . . . 4G **151**
Library Way B45: Rubery 2F **157**
Lich Av. WV11: Wed 2G **29**
Lichen Gdns. B38: K Nor 2H **159**
Lichfield Ct. B90: Shir 5D **148**
WS4: Wals *5E 33*
(off Lichfield Rd.)
Lichfield Pas. WV1: Wolv 1H **43** (2C **170**)
Lichfield Rd. B6: Aston 3A **102**
B46: Col, Wat O 3F **89**
B74: Four O 4F **37**
B76: Curd, Wis 2F **89**
WS3: Blox 5H **19**
WS3: Pels 2E **21**
WS4: Rus, S'fld, Wals 5E **33**
WS8: Bwnhls 5B **10**
WS9: Wals W, Bwnhls 4B **22**
WV11: Wed 4F **29**
WV12: W'hall 2A **30**
Lichfield St. DY4: Tip 5H **61**
WS1: Wals 1D **48**
WV1: Wolv 1G **43** (3B **170**)
WV14: Bils 5F **45**
Lich Gates WV1: Wolv 1G **43** (2B **170**)
Lichwood Rd. WV11: Wed 2H **29**
LICKEY **6G 157**
Lickey Coppice B45: Coft H 5A **158**
Lickey Hills Country Pk. 5G **157**
Lickey Hills Vis. Cen. 6H **157**
Lickey Rd. B45: Redn 4A **158**
DY8: Amb 5F **109**
Liddiard Ct. DY8: Woll 5C **108**
Liddon Gro. B27: A Grn 5A **136**
Liddon Rd. B27: A Grn 5A **136**
LIFFORD **2D 146**
Lifford Cl. B14: K Hth 2D **146**
Lifford La. B30: K Nor 2C **146**
Lifton Cft. DY6: K'wfrd 4D **92**
Lightfields Wlk. B65: Row R 4A **96**
Lighthorne Av. B16: Birm 1C **116**
Lighthorne Rd. B91: Sol 1G **151**
Lighthouse, The 1H **43** (2C **170**)
Lightning Way B31: Longb 2F **159**
Lightwood Cl. B93: Know 1D **166**
Lightwood Rd. DY1: Dud 4C **76**
Lightwoods Hill B67: Smeth 3C **114**
Lightwoods Rd. B67: Smeth 1E **115**
DY9: Pedm 4G **125**
Lilac Av. B12: Bal H 6A **118**
B44: Gt Barr 6G **67**
B74: S'tly 3G **51**
DY4: Tip 6G **61**
WS5: Wals 1E **65**
Lilac Dr. WV5: Wom 1F **73**
Lilac Gro. WS2: Wals 6E **31**
WS10: W'bry 3G **63**
Lilac La. WS6: Gt Wyr 5F **7**
Lilac Rd. DY1: Dud 3D **76**
WV1: Wolv 3D **44**
WV12: W'hall 2E **31**
Lilac Way B62: B'hth 3F **113**
Lilian Gro. WV14: Bils 4G **61**
Lilleshall Cres. WV2: Wolv 4H **43**
Lilleshall Rd. B26: Sheld 4F **121**
Lilley La. B31: Longb 1F **159**
Lillington Cl. B75: S Cold 1E **71**
Lillington Gro. B34: S End 4H **105**
Lillington Rd. B90: Shir 1H **163**
Lillycroft La. B38: Head H 2C **160**
Lily Rd. B26: Yard 5B **120**
Lily St. B71: W Brom 2A **80**
Limberlost Cl. B20: Hand 4C **82**
Limbrick Cl. B90: Shir 5F **149**
Limbury Gro. B92: Sol 5B **138**
Lime Av. B29: S Oak 3B **132**
WS2: Wals 6E **31**
Lime Cl. B47: H'wd 4A **162**
B70: W Brom 3G **79**
DY4: Tip 2G **77**
WS2: Wals 6E **31**
WS6: Gt Wyr 1F **7**
Lime Ct. B11: S'hll 1C **134**
Lime Gro. B10: Small H 3D **118**
B12: Bal H 6H **117**
B19: Loz 1E **101**
B26: Yard 5B **120**
B37: Chel W 2D **122**
B66: Smeth 6F **99**
(Edith Rd.)
B66: Smeth 5F **99**
(Windmill La.)
B73: W Grn 6H **69**
WS4: Rus 3G **33**
WV14: Bils 4E **45**
Limehurst Av. WV3: Wolv 3A **42**
Limehurst Rd. WS4: Rus 4G **33**
Lime Kiln Cl. B38: K Nor 2H **159**
Limekiln La. B14: K Hth 3A **148**
Lime Kiln Wlk. DY1: Dud 5F **77**
Lime La. WS3: Lit W 3D **8**
Limepit La. DY1: Dud 4C **76**
Lime Pitts Nature Reserve 4G **33**
Limerick Cl. DY3: Gorn 5F **75**
Lime Rd. DY3: Sed 4B **60**
WS10: W'bry 1F **63**
Limes, The B11: S'brk 5C **118**
B16: Birm 6B **100**
B24: Erd 4F **85**
DY3: Himl 4H **73**
WS1: Wals 1E **49**
WS4: Rus 2H **33**
Limes Av. B65: Row R 1C **112**
DY5: Brie H 4G **93**
Limescroft Cl. WS4: Rus 2F **33**
Limes Rd. DY1: Dud 4D **76**
WV6: Tett 5A **26**
Lime St. WS1: Wals 2D **48**
WV3: Wolv 3E **43**
WV14: Cose 5C **60**
Limes Vw. DY3: Sed 6H **59**
Lime Ter. B6: Aston 6H **83**
Lime Tree Av. WV6: Tett 6G **25**
Lime Tree Gdns. WV8: Bilb 4H **13**
Lime Tree Gro. B31: N'fld 5F **145**
Lime Tree Rd. B8: Salt 3F **103**
B27: A Grn 6A **120**
WS5: Wals 1E **65**
WV8: Bilb 4H **13**
Limetree Rd. B74: S'tly 2F **51**
Lime Wlk. B38: K Nor 1A **160**
Linacre Ho. B37: F'bri 1B **122**
Linchmere Rd. B21: Hand 5G **81**
Lincoln Av. WV13: W'hall 6D **30**
Lincoln Cl. B27: A Grn 2C **136**
Lincoln Ct. *B29: W Cas* *6G 131*
(off Tugford Rd.)
Lincoln Grn. WV10: Bush 5H **15**
Lincoln Gro. B37: Mars G 2C **122**
Lincoln Rd. B27: A Grn 3B **136**
B67: Smeth 1C **114**
B71: W Brom 4B **64**
DY2: Neth 6F **95**
WS1: Wals 1E **49**
Lincoln Rd. Nth. B27: A Grn 2C **136**

Lincoln Rd. Wharf B92: Olton 3C **136**
Lincoln St. B12: Bal H 6G **117**
WV10: Wolv 6A **28**
Lincoln Twr. *B16: Birm* *2C 116*
(off Morville St.)
Lindale Av. B36: Hodg H 3A **104**
Lindale Cres. DY5: Brie H 5F **109**
Lindale Dr. WV5: Wom 1F **73**
Linden Av. B43: Gt Barr 5H **65**
B62: B'hth 4E **113**
B69: Tiv 1D **96**
Linden Cl. WS2: Wals 1D **46**
Linden Dr. DY8: Stourb 2E **125**
Linden Glade B63: Hale 1A **128**
Linden La. WV12: W'hall 2E **31**
Linden Lea WV3: Wolv 2B **42**
Linden Rd. B30: B'vlle 5A **132**
B66: Smeth 1E **115**
DY1: Dud 4D **76**
Linden Road Instruction Pool 6B **132**
Lindens, The B32: Harb 4C **114**
WV6: Wolv 6C **26**
Lindens Dr. B74: S'tly 6H **51**
Linden Ter. B12: Bal H 6B **118**
Lindenwood B73: S Cold 5H **53**
Lindford Way B38: K Nor 5D **146**
Lindley Av. DY4: Tip 4H **77**
Lindon Cl. WS8: Bwnhls 1C **22**
Lindon Dr. WS8: Bwnhls 6B **10**
Lindon Rd. WS8: Bwnhls 2B **22**
Lindon Vw. WS8: Bwnhls 2C **22**
Lindrick Cl. WS3: Blox 4F **19**
Lindridge Dr. B76: Min 1G **87**
Lindridge Rd. B23: Erd 3B **84**
B75: S Cold 3D **54**
B90: Shir 6F **149**
Lindrosa Rd. B74: S'tly 6H **35**
Lindsay Rd. B42: Gt Barr 4D **66**
Lindsey Av. B31: N'fld 3G **145**
Lindsey Pl. DY5: Brie H 6G **93**
Lindsey Rd. B71: W Brom 6A **64**
Lindsworth App. B30: K Nor 4E **147**
Lindsworth Ct. B30: K Nor 4E **147**
Lindsworth Rd. B30: K Nor 4D **146**
Linfield Gdns. DY3: Sed 4G **59**
Linford Gro. B25: Yard 2B **120**
Linforth Dr. B74: S'tly 4A **52**
Lingard Cl. B7: Nech 4B **102**
Lingard Ho. B76: Walm 5D **70**
Lingard Rd. B75: S Cold 6D **54**
Lingfield Av. B44: Gt Barr 4G **67**
WV10: F'hses 2H **15**
Lingfield Cl. WS6: Gt Wyr 3F **7**
Lingfield Ct. B43: Gt Barr 6H **65**
Lingfield Dr. WS6: Gt Wyr 3F **7**
Lingfield Gdns. B34: S End 3F **105**
Lingfield Grange B74: S'tly 2A **52**
Lingfield Gro. WV6: Pert 5F **25**
Lingfield Rd. WS11: Nort C 1E **9**
Lingfield Way DY6: K'wfrd 4E **93**
Lingham Cl. B92: Sol 6H **137**
Ling Ho. WV10: Wolv 6B **28**
Lingmoor Gro. WS9: A'rdge 2C **34**
Linhope Dr. DY6: K'wfrd 4E **93**
Link, The B27: A Grn 4G **135**
Link One Ind. Pk. DY4: Tip 1E **79**
Link Rd. B16: Edg 6A **100**
WS9: Wals W 4D **22**
WV5: Wom 6G **57**
Links Av. WV6: Tett 2B **26**
Links Cres. B68: O'bry 3H **113**
Links Dr. B45: Rubery 4G **157**
B91: Sol 1F **151**
DY8: Stourb 3C **124**
Links Rd. B14: K Hth 6A **148**
B68: O'bry 3H **113**
WV4: Penn 2E **59**
Links Side Way WS9: A'rdge 1E **35**
Links Vw. B62: Hale 1D **128**
B74: S'tly 2B **52**
Linkswood Cl. B13: Mose 4B **134**
Linkwood Ind. Est. DY8: Woll 5C **108**
Linley Cl. WS9: A'rdge 4A **34**
Linley Dr. WV10: Bush 6A **16**
Linley Gro. B14: K Hth 1E **147**
DY3: Gorn 5F **75**
Linley Lodge Ind. Est. WS9: A'rdge 2A **34**
Linley Rd. WS4: Rus 2H **33**
Linley Wood Rd. WS9: A'rdge 4A **34**
Linnet Cl. B30: B'vlle 5A **132**
B62: Hale 5B **112**
(Lodgefield Rd.)
B62: Hale 4G **127**
(Manor Way)
Linnet Gro. B23: Erd 1B **84**
WV12: W'hall 1B **30**
Linpole Wlk. B14: K Hth 5E **147**
Linsey Rd. B92: Sol 3G **137**
Linslade Cl. WV4: Penn 1H **59**
Linthouse La. WV11: Wed 1F **29**
Linton Av. B91: Sol 6E **151**
Linton Cl. B63: Crad 6F **111**
Linton Cft. WV14: Bils 6F **45**
Linton Rd. B11: Tys 1G **135**
B43: Gt Barr 1E **67**
B64: Old H 6H **95**
WV4: Penn 6C **42**
Linton Wlk. B23: Erd 4B **84**
Linwood Ct. B23: Erd 4E **85**
Linwood Rd. B21: Hand 1A **100**
B91: Sol 2B **150**
DY1: Dud 2D **76**
Lionel St. B3: Birm 6E **101** (3B **4**)
Lion Ind. Pk. WS9: A'rdge 1C **34**
Lion Pas. DY8: Stourb 6D **108**
Lion Rd. B64: Old H 2A **112**
Lion's Den WS7: Hamm 3G **11**
Lion St. DY8: Stourb 6D **108**
Liskeard Rd. WS5: Wals 4H **49**
Lisko Cl. DY5: Brie H 3E **109**
Lismore Cl. B45: Fran 6E **143**
Lismore Dr. B17: Harb 2E **131**
Lissimore Dr. DY4: Tip 5A **78**
Lissimore Ho. *B70: W Brom* *1C 98*
(off Maria St.)
Lisson Gro. B44: Gt Barr 1H **67**
Listelow Cl. B36: Cas B 1F **105**
Lister Cl. DY4: Tip 3A **78**
WS2: Wals 4H **31**
Lister Rd. DY2: Dud 2E **95**
WS2: Wals 4H **31**
Lister St. B7: Birm 5H **101** (1G **5**)
WV13: W'hall 2B **46**
Listowel Rd. B14: K Hth 1F **147**
Lisures Dr. B76: Walm 1B **70**
Lit. Albert St. WS2: Wals 1C **48**
Lit. Ann St. B5: Birm 1H **117** (5H **5**)
LITTLE ASTON 4C **36**
Little Aston Golf Course 5C **36**
Lit. Aston Hall Dr. B74: Lit A 4A **36**
Lit. Aston La. B74: Lit A 3C **36**
Lit. Aston Pk. Rd. B74: Lit A 6A **36**
Lit. Aston Rd. WS9: A'rdge 3D **34**
Lit. Barr St. B9: Birm 1A **118**
Little Birches WV3: Wolv 3D **42**
LITTLE BLOXWICH 4B **20**
Lit. Brick Kiln St.
WV3: Wolv 2G **43** (5A **170**)
LITTLE BROMWICH 1F **119**
Lit. Bromwich Rd. B9: Bord G 2H **119**
Lit. Caldmore WS1: Wals 3C **48**
Lit. Checkhill La. DY7: Stourt 5D **90**
Lit. Clothier St. WV13: W'hall 6A **30**
Lit. Clover Cl. B7: Nech 3C **102**
Little Comn. WS3: Pels 3E **21**
Lit. Cornbow B63: Hale 2B **128**
Littlecote Cft. B14: K Hth 4A **148**
Littlecote Dr. B23: Erd 6F **69**
Lit. Cottage St. DY5: Brie H 1H **109**
Little Cft. B43: Gt Barr 4G **65**
Lit. Cross St. WS10: Darl 4C **46**
Lit. Edward St. B9: Birm 1A **118**
Lit. Fields Way B69: O'bry 2F **97**
Lit. Francis Gro. B7: Birm 4B **102**
Lit. Gorway WS1: Wals 4D **48**
Lit. Green La. B9: Small H 2C **118**
Lit. Green Lanes B73: W Grn 6H **69**
Lit. Hardwick Rd. WS9: A'rdge 1E **51**
LITTLE HAY 1H **37**
Lit. Hay La. WS14: Lit H, W'frd 2H **37**
Lit. Heath Cft. B34: S End 2F **105**
Little Hill WS10: W'bry 2F **63**
Lit. Hill Gro. B38: K Nor 6C **146**
Lit. Hill Ho. B24: Erd 1B **86**
Lit. Hill Way B32: Bart G 3B **130**
Lit. Johnsons La. WS9: A'rdge 3D **50**
Lit. John St. DY5: Brie H 5H **93**
Little La. B71: W Brom 2B **80**
WV12: W'hall 2D **30**
Lit. Lawns Cl. WS8: Wals W 3C **22**
LITTLE LONDON 6A **30**
Little London WS1: Wals 4C **48**
Lit. London Ho. WS1: Wals 4D **48**
Littlemead Av. B31: N'fld 6G **145**
Lit. Meadow Cft. B31: N'fld 3D **144**
Lit. Meadow Wlk. B33: Stech 6C **104**
Littlemead Rd. B90: Maj G 1E **163**
Lit. Moor Hill B67: Smeth 4D **98**
Lit. Newport St. *WS1: Wals* *2C 48*
(off Newport St.)
Lit. Oaks Rd. B6: Aston 1G **101**
Littleover Av. B28: Hall G 1F **149**
Little Pk. B32: Quin 1H **129**
Lit. Park St. WV1: Wolv 1H **43** (3D **170**)
Lit. Pitts Cl. B24: Erd 2B **86**
Lit. Potter St. DY5: Brie H 1H **109**
Lit. Pountney St.
WV2: Wolv 3G **43** (6B **170**)
Lit. Shadwell St. B4: Birm 5G **101** (1E **5**)
Littleshaw Cft. B47: Wyt 5C **162**
Littleshaw La. B47: Wyt 5C **162**
Little's La. WV1: Wolv 1H **43** (1C **170**)
(not continuous)
Lit. Station St. WS2: Wals 1C **48**
Little St. DY2: Dud 6F **77**
LITTLE SUTTON 1A **54**
Lit. Sutton La. B75: S Cold 4A **54**
Lit. Sutton Rd. B75: R'ley 1A **54**
Littleton Cl. B76: Walm 3E **71**
Littleton Cft. B91: Sol 1G **165**
Littleton Rd. WV12: W'hall 2C **30**
Littleton St. E. WS1: Wals 1D **48**
Littleton St. W. WS2: Wals 1C **48**
LITTLEWOOD 1E **7**
Littlewood Cl. B91: Sol 1F **165**
Littlewood La. WS6: C Hay 1E **7**
Littlewood Rd. WS6: C Hay 1E **7**
Lit. Wood St. WV13: W'hall 1A **46**
Littleworth Av. DY1: Dud 1D **76**
LITTLEWORTH END 3G **55**
Littleworth Gro. B76: Walm 1D **70**
LITTLE WYRLEY 5C **8**
Liveridge Cl. B93: Know 3B **166**
Liverpool Cft. B37: Mars G 3B **122**
Liverpool St. B9: Birm 1A **118**
Livery St. B3: Birm 5F **101** (1C **4**)
(not continuous)
Livingstone Av. WV6: Pert 4E **25**
Livingstone Rd. B14: K Hth 1G **147**
B20: Hand 6E **83**
B70: W Brom 6H **79**
WS3: Blox 5C **20**
WV14: Bils 6D **44**
Living Well Heath Club 3D **68** (5A **4**)
Lizafield Ct. B66: Smeth 2C **98**
Lloyd Dr. WV4: Penn 3A **58**
Lloyd Hill WV4: Penn 2A **58**
Lloyd Ho. *B19: Hock* *3E 101*
(off Newtown Dr.)
Lloyd Rd. B20: Hand 3C **82**
WV6: Tett 4B **26**
Lloyd Sq. B15: Edg 3B **116**
Lloyds Rd. B62: B'hth 3C **112**
Lloyd St. B10: Small H 3D **118**
B71: W Brom 3C **80**
DY2: Dud 1F **95**
WS10: W'bry 2E **63**
WV6: Wolv 5D **26**
Locarno Rd. DY4: Tip 2H **77**
Lochalsh Gro. WV12: W'hall 6B **18**
Lochranza Cft. B43: Gt Barr 3A **66**
Lock Dr. B33: Stech 6B **104**
Locke Pl. B7: Birm 6A **102**
Locket Cl. WS2: Wals 5F **31**
Lockfield Cl. DY8: Word 2D **108**
Lockhart Dr. B75: R'ley 2A **54**
Locking Cft. B35: Cas V 4F **87**
Lockington Cft. B62: Quin 5F **113**
Lock Keepers Cl. WS11: Nort C 1D **8**
Lockley Cl. WV10: Wolv 5B **28**
Lock Mus. 2A **46**

Lock Side DY4: Tip 2G **77**
Lockside WS9: A'rdge 2B **34**
WV5: Wom 6E **57**
Lockside Cl. DY5: Brie H 2H **109**
Locksmith Cl. WV13: W'hall 1B **46**
Lock St. WV1: Wolv 6H **27** (1D **170**)
(not continuous)
Locks Vw. DY8: Word 2C **108**
Lockton Rd. B30: Stir 5E **133**
Lockwood Rd. B31: N'fld 3D **144**
LODE HEATH 2H **151**
Lode La. B91: Sol 3F **151**
B92: Olton, Sol 4F **137**
Lode Mill Ct. B92: Olton 5F **137**
Lodge Cl. B62: Hale 2E **129**
WS5: Wals 5H **49**
Lodge Cres. DY2: Neth 5C **94**
Lodge Cft. B31: N'fld 1C **144**
B93: Know 3D **166**
Lodge Dr. B26: Yard 3D **120**
Lodge Farm Cl. B76: Walm 2D **70**
Lodgefield Rd. B62: Hale 5B **112**
Lodge Forge Rd. B64: Crad H 4E **111**
Lodge Forge Trad. Est. B64: Crad H 4E **111**
Lodge Gro. WS9: A'rdge 4C **34**
LODGE HILL 3F **131**
Lodge Hill Crematorium B29: S Oak 4F **131**
Lodge Hill Rd. B29: S Oak 4H **131**
Lodge La. DY6: K'wfrd 3G **91**
WS11: Cann 1C **6**
Lodge Pool Cl. B44: Gt Barr 1G **83**
Lodge Rd. B6: Aston 1G **101**
B18: Win G, Hock 3A **100**
(not continuous)
B67: Smeth 2C **98**
B70: W Brom 4H **79**
B93: Know 3D **166**
WS4: S'fld 6F **21**
WS5: Wals 6H **49**
(not continuous)
WS10: Darl 6D **46**
WV10: Oxl 1F **27**
WV14: Bils 1H **61**
Lodge St. B69: O'bry 2G **97**
WV12: W'hall 4C **30**
Lodge Ter. B17: Harb 6G **115**
Lodge Vw. WS6: C Hay 2C **6**
Loeless Rd. B33: Kitts G 6E **105**
Lofthouse Cres. B31: N'fld 4D **144**
Lofthouse Gro. B31: N'fld 4D **144**
Lofthouse Rd. B20: Hand 4A **82**
Loftus Cl. B29: W Cas 5D **130**
Logan Cl. WV10: Oxl 3G **27**
Lomaine Dr. B30: K Nor 3A **146**
Lomas Dr. B31: N'fld 4C **144**
Lomas St. WV1: Wolv 5G **27**
Lombard Av. DY2: Neth 6F **95**
Lombard St. B12: Birm 3H **117**
B70: W Brom 4A **80**
Lombard St. W. B70: W Brom 4A **80**
Lombardy Cft. B62: Quin 5G **113**
Lombardy Gdns. WV12: W'hall 2E **31**
Lomond Cl. B34: S End 3A **106**
Lomond Rd. DY3: Sed 4G **59**
LONDONDERRY 5B **98**
Londonderry Gro. B67: Smeth 4D **98**
Londonderry Ho. B4: Birm 3F **5**
Londonderry La. B67: Smeth 5B **98**
Londonderry Rd. B68: O'bry 5B **98**
LONDON FIELDS 5B **76**
London Hgts. DY1: Dud 5C **76**
London Rd. B20: Hand 5G **83**
B75: Bass P 6F **39**
B75: Can 4E **39**
B78: Midd 1G **55**
WS14: W'frd 1D **38**
London St. B66: Smeth 4G **99**
London St. Ind. Est. B66: Smeth 4H **99**
Lones Rd. B71: W Brom 1F **99**
Long Acre B7: Nech 3B **102**
WV8: Cod 5F **13**
Longacre WV13: W'hall 3A **46**
Long Acre Ind. Est. B7: Nech 2B **102**
(not continuous)
Longacre Ind. Est. B7: Nech 1C **102**
Longacres B74: Lit A 5C **36**
Long Acre St. WS2: Wals 6B **32**
Longbank Rd. B69: Tiv 1C **96**
Longboat La. DY8: Word 3C **108**
Longboat Quay DY2: Neth 5F **95**
Longbow Rd. B29: W Cas 6D **130**
LONGBRIDGE 1D **158**
Longbridge La. B31: Longb 1C **158**
Longbridge Station (Rail) 1C **158**
Longbrook La. CV7: Bal C 3E **169**
CV8: Fen E 3E **169**
Long Cl. Wlk. B35: Cas V 4F **87**
Longcroft, The B63: Hale 2G **127**
WS4: Rus 2G **33**
Longcroft Av. WS10: W'bry 2G **63**
Longcroft Cl. B35: Cas V 5D **86**
Longdales Rd. B38: K Nor 2H **159**
Longdon Av. WV4: Penn 6H **43**
Longdon Cft. B93: Know 1C **166**
Longdon Dr. B74: Four O 5E **37**
Longdon Rd. B93: Know 3C **166**
Longfellow Rd. B30: K Nor 3H **145**
DY3: Lwr G 2E **75**
Longfield Cl. B28: Hall G 1F **149**
Longfield Dr. B74: Lit A 5D **36**
Longfield Ho. WV10: Wolv 6B **28**
Longfield Rd. B31: N'fld 5C **130**
DY9: Lye 6H **109**
Longford Cl. B32: Bart G 6G **129**
B93: Dorr 6D **166**
WV5: Wom 2D **72**
Longford Gro. B44: K'sdng 2A **68**
Longford Rd. B44: K'sdng 2A **68**
WV10: Wolv 5B **28**
Long Furrow WV8: Pend 6C **14**
Longham Cft. B32: Harb 1D **130**
Longhurst Cft. B31: Longb 2F **159**
Long Hyde Rd. B67: Smeth 2D **114**
Long Innage B63: Crad 5D **110**
Long Knowle La. WV11: Wed 1D **28**
Longlake Av. WV6: Tett 6G **25**
Longlands, The WV5: Wom 1G **73**
Longlands Cl. *B38: K Nor 1G 159*
(off Nearhill Rd.)
Longlands Rd. B62: Hale 2E **129**
Long La. B62: B'hth 2D **112**
B65: B'hth 2D **112**
WS6: Ess, Gt Wyr 2D **18**
WS11: Nort C 1D **8**
Long La. Trad. Est. B62: B'hth 3D **112**
Long Leasow B29: W Cas 6E **131**
Longleat B43: Gt Barr 3H **65**
Longleat Dr. B90: Ches G 4C **164**
DY1: Dud 5A **76**
Longleat Rd. WS9: A'rdge 6C **22**
Long Ley WV10: Wolv 6B **28**
Longley Av. B76: Min 2H **87**
Longley Cres. B26: Yard 1C **136**
Long Leys Ct. B46: Wat O 4D **88**
Longleys Cft. B46: Wat O 5D **88**
Longley Wlk. B37: Chel W 1E **123**
Long Mdw. B65: Row R 6C **96**
Longmeadow Cl. B75: S Cold 6D **54**
Longmeadow Cres. B34: S End 3A **106**
Long Mdw. Dr. DY3: Sed 3F **59**
Longmeadow Gro. B31: Longb 3E **159**
Longmeadow Rd. WS5: Wals 3A **50**
Long Mill Av. WV11: Wed 2D **28**
Long Mill Nth. WV11: Wed 2D **28**
Long Mill Sth. WV11: Wed 2D **28**
Longmoor Cl. WV11: Wed 4H **29**
Longmoor Rd. B63: Hale 2G **127**
B73: S'tly 2B **68**
Longmore Av. WS2: Wals 2F **47**
Longmore Cl. B73: S'tly 6A **52**
Longmore Rd. B90: Shir 5A **150**
Longmore St. B12: Bal H 4G **117**
WS10: W'bry 2F **63**
Long Mynd B63: Hale 4F **127**
Long Mynd Cl. WV12: W'hall 6B **18**
Long Mynd Rd. B31: N'fld 1C **144**
Long Nuke Rd. B31: N'fld 6C **130**
Long Saw Dr. B31: Longb 6B **144**
Longshaw Gro. B34: S End 3H **105**
Longstone Cl. B90: M'path 3F **165**
Longstone Rd. B42: Gt Barr 6E **67**
Long St. B11: S'brk 5A **118**
WS2: Wals 2B **48**
WV1: Wolv 1H **43** (2C **170**)
Long Wood B30: B'vlle 2A **146**
Longwood La. WS4: Wals 1A **50**
WS5: Wals 1A **50**
Longwood Pathway B34: S End 4G **105**
Longwood Ri. WV12: W'hall 4D **30**
Longwood Rd. B45: Redn 2G **157**
WS9: A'rdge 6D **34**
Lonicera Cl. WS5: Wals 2F **65**
Lonsdale Cl. B33: Stech 1B **120**
WV12: W'hall 4B **30**
Lonsdale Ct. B17: Harb 5G **115**
Lonsdale Rd. B17: Harb 5F **115**
B66: Smeth 2B **98**
WS5: Wals 5G **49**
WV3: Wolv 4F **43**
WV14: Bils 5H **45**
Lords B17: Harb 5F **115**
Lords Dr. WS2: Wals 6C **32**
Lordsmore Cl. WV14: Cose 4G **61**
Lord St. B7: Birm 5H **101**
WS1: Wals 4B **48**
(not continuous)
WV3: Wolv 1F **43**
(not continuous)
WV14: Bils 2G **61**
Lord St. W. WV14: Bils 2G **61**
Lordswood Rd. B17: Harb 3E **115**
Lordswood Sq. B17: Harb 4F **115**
Lorimer Way B43: Gt Barr 6F **51**
Lorne St. DY4: Tip 5H **61**
Lorrainer Av. DY5: Brie H 3E **109**
Lothians Rd. WS3: Pels 2E **21**
WV6: Tett 3C **26**
Lottie Rd. B29: S Oak 4A **132**
Lotus Ct. B16: Edg 2A **116**
Lotus Cft. B67: Smeth 5D **98**
Lotus Dr. B64: Old H 1H **111**
Lotus Wlk. B36: Cas B 6B **88**
Lotus Way B65: Row R 5A **96**
Loughton Gro. B63: Hale 1H **127**
Louisa Pl. B18: Hock 4C **100**
Louisa St. B1: Birm 6E **101** (3A **4**)
Louis Ct. B67: Smeth 4D **98**
Louise Ct. B27: A Grn 2A **136**
B91: Sol 6C **150**
Louise Cft. B14: K Hth 5G **147**
Louise Lorne Rd. B13: Mose 1H **133**
Louise Rd. B21: Hand 2B **100**
Louise St. DY3: Gorn 4F **75**
Lount Wlk. B19: Hock 4G **101**
Lovatt Cl. DY4: Tip 4C **62**
Lovatt St. WV1: Wolv 1F **43**
Loveday Ho. B70: W Brom 4B **80**
Loveday St. B4: Birm 5G **101** (1E **5**)
(not continuous)
Lovelace Av. B91: Sol 1H **165**
Love La. B7: Birm 5H **101**
B47: H'wd 2G **161**
B69: Tiv 6A **78**
DY8: Stourb 2E **125**
DY9: Lye 6A **110**
WS1: Wals 4C **48**
WS6: Gt Wyr 2G **7**
WV6: Tett 3B **26**
Lovell Cl. B29: W Cas 1F **145**
Loveridge Cl. WV8: Cod 4F **13**
Lovers Wlk. B6: Aston 1B **102**
WS10: W'bry 2F **63**
Lovett Av. B69: O'bry 4D **96**
Low Av. B43: Gt Barr 3B **66**
Lowbridge Cl. WV12: W'hall 4C **30**
Lowbrook La. B90: Tid G 5D **162**
Lowcroft Gdns. WV10: Bush 1A **28**
Lowden Cft. B26: Yard 1C **136**
Lowe Av. WS10: Darl 4B **46**
Lowe Dr. B73: New O 2D **68**
DY6: K'wfrd 5C **92**
Lwr. Beeches Rd. B31: Longb 5A **144**
LOWER BRADLEY 2A **62**
Lwr. Chapel St. B69: Tiv 5C **78**
Lwr. Church La. DY4: Tip 2B **78**
Lwr. City Rd. B69: Tiv 6C **78**
Lowercroft Way B74: Four O 4E **37**
Lwr. Dartmouth St. B9: Birm 1B **118**
Lwr. Derry St. DY5: Brie H 1H **109**
Lwr. Essex St. B5: Birm 2G **117**
Lwr. Forster St. WS1: Wals 1D **48**

LOWER GORNAL 4H 75
Lower Grn. DY4: Tip 2G 77
  WS10: Darl 3D 46
  WV6: Tett 4C 26
Lwr. Ground Cl. B6: Aston 6H 83
  (off Emscote Rd.)
Lwr. Hall La. WS1: Wals 2C 48
Lwr. Hall St. WV13: W'hall 2B 46
  (off Walsall St.)
Lwr. High St. B64: Crad H 3E 111
  DY8: Stourb 5D 108
  WS10: W'bry 3F 63
Lwr. Higley Cl. B32: Quin 1B 130
Lwr. Lichfield St. WV13: W'hall 1A 46
Lwr. Loveday St. B19: Birm 5F 101 (1D 4)
Lwr. Mall & Up. Mall
  B5: Birm 1G 117 (5F 5)
Lower Moor B30: B'ville 5A 132
Lower Nth. St. WS4: Wals 6D 32
Lower Pde., The B72: S Cold. 6A 54
LOWER PENN. 6G 41
Lwr. Prestwood Rd. WV11: Wed 2E 29
Lwr. Queen St. B72: S Cold 1A 70
Lwr. Reddicroft B73: S Cold. 6A 54
Lwr. Rushall St. WS1: Wals 1D 48
Lwr. Severn St. B1: Birm 1F 117 (5D 4)
Lowerstack Cft. B37: F'bri 6B 106
LOWER STONNALL. 3H 23
Lower St. WV6: Tett 4C 26
Lwr. Temple St. B2: Birm 1F 117 (4D 4)
Lwr. Tower St. B19: Birm. 4G 101
Lwr. Trinity St. B9: Birm 2A 118
  B70: W Brom 6B 80
  (off Glover St.)
Lwr. Valley Rd. DY5: Brie H. 1E 109
Lwr. Vauxhall WV1: Wolv. 1E 43
Lwr. Villiers St. WV2: Wolv. 4G 43
Lwr. White Rd. B32: Quin 6B 114
Lowesmoor Rd. B26: Sheld 4G 121
Lowe St. WV6: Wolv. 5E 27
Loweswater Dr. DY3: Lwr G 4H 75
Loweswater Ho. B38: K Nor 6C 146
Lowfield Cl. B62: Quin. 2G 129
LOW HILL 2A 28
Low Hill Cres. WV10: Bush 1A 28
Lowhill La. B45: Redn 3A 158
Lowland Cl. B64: Old H 2H 111
Lowlands Av. B74: S'tly 3F 51
  WV6: Tett. 3C 26
Lowlands Ct. WV6: Tett 3C 26
Lowndes Rd. DY8: Woll 5C 108
Lowry Cl. B67: Smeth 3D 98
  WV6: Pert 5F 25
  WV13: W'hall 1G 45
Low St. WS6: C Hay. 2D 6
Low Thatch B38: K Nor 2A 160
Lowther Ct. DY5: Brie H. 1H 109
Low Town B69: O'bry. 2G 97
Low Wood Rd. B23: Erd. 2D 84
LOXDALE. 1H 61
Loxdale Ind. Est. WV14: Bils. 1G 61
Loxdale Sidings WV14: Bils. 1H 61
Loxdale St. WS10: W'bry 3F 63
  WV14: Bils. 1H 61
Loxley Av. B14: Yard W 4C 148
  B90: Shir 6F 149
Loxley Cl. B31: N'fld 5C 130
Loxley Rd. B67: Smeth 2D 114
  B75: R'ley. 5B 38
Loxley Sq. B92: Olton 5B 136
Loxton Cl. B74: Lit A 4D 36
Loxton Ct. B7: Birm 4B 102
Loynells Rd. B45: Redn. 2H 157
Loyns Cl. B37: F'bri 6B 106
LOZELLS 2D 100
Lozells Rd. B19: Loz 2D 100
Lozells St. B19: Loz 2E 101
Lozells Wood Cl. B19: Loz. 2D 100
Luanne Cl. B64: Old H 2A 112
Lucas Cir. B19: Nech 4E 101
Lucas Way B90: Shir 2A 164
Luce Cl. B35: Cas V 3F 87
Lucerne Ct. B23: Erd 1D 84
Luce Rd. WV10: Bush 3A 28
Lucknow Rd. WV12: W'hall 5B 30
Lucton Ho. B30: B'ville 2A 146
Luddington Rd. B92: Sol 5A 138

Ludford Cl. B75: S Cold 4C 54
Ludford Rd. B32: Bart G. 4G 129
Ludgate Cl. B46: Wat O 4C 88
  B69: Tiv 1B 96
Ludgate Ct. WS5: Wals 4H 49
Ludgate Hill B3: Birm 6F 101 (2C 4)
Ludgate Ho. B13: Mose. 1H 133
Ludgate Loft Apartments B3: Birm 2C 4
Ludgate St. DY1: Dud 6D 76
Ludlow Cl. B37: Chel W 1E 123
  WV12: W'hall 3B 30
Ludlow Ct. B11: S'brk 5B 118
Ludlow Ho. B13: Mose. 1A 148
  WS3: Blox 3A 32
  (off Providence La.)
Ludlow La. WS2: Wals 5G 31
Ludlow Rd. B8: Salt 6F 103
Ludlow Way DY1: Dud 5A 76
Ludmer Way B20: Hand 5E 83
Ludstone Av. WV4: Penn 6B 42
Ludstone Rd. B29: W Cas 4D 130
Ludworth Av. B37: Mars G 2D 122
Lugtrout La. B91: Cath B, Sol 1A 152
Lukes, The DY2: Neth. 2E 111
Lulworth Cl. B63: Crad 5E 111
Lulworth Rd. B28: Hall G. 5G 135
Lulworth Wlk. WV4: Penn 5A 42
Lumley Gro. B37: Chel W 1F 123
Lumley Rd. WS1: Wals 2E 49
Lundy Vw. B36: Cas B 4D 106
LUNT, THE 4A 46
Lunt Gro. B32: Quin 6B 114
Lunt Pl. WV14: Bils 5A 46
Lunt Rd. WV14: Bils. 5H 45
Lupin Gro. B9: Bord G 6F 103
  WS5: Wals 1F 65
Lupin Rd. DY2: Dud. 6H 77
Lusbridge Cl. B63: Crad. 1D 126
LUTLEY. 2E 127
Lutley Av. B63: Hale 1F 127
Lutley Cl. WV3: Wolv. 4C 42
Lutley Dr. DY9: Pedm 2G 125
Lutley Gro. B32: Bart G 4H 129
Lutley La. B63: Hale, Lutley. 2D 126
  (not continuous)
Lutley Mill Rd. B63: Hale. 1G 127
Luton Rd. B29: S Oak. 2B 132
Luttrell Rd. B74: Four O 3F 53
Lyall Gdns. B45: Fran. 6E 143
Lyall Gro. B27: A Grn. 3G 135
Lychgate Av. DY9: Pedm 4G 125
Lydate Rd. B62: Quin 1F 129
Lydbrook Covert B38: K Nor. 1A 160
Lydbury Gro. B33: Kitts G. 5E 105
Lyd Cl. WV11: Wed 4D 28
Lydd Cft. B35: Cas V 3F 87
Lyddington Dr. B62: Hale 4B 112
Lyde Grn. B63: Crad. 4D 110
Lydford Gro. B24: Erd 5G 85
Lydford Rd. WS3: Blox. 5H 19
Lydgate Rd. DY6: K'wfrd 3D 92
Lydget Gro. B23: Erd 6D 68
Lydham Cl. B44: K'sdng. 1A 84
  WV14: Bils. 1D 60
Lydia Cft. B74: Four O 3E 37
Lydiat Av. B31: Longb 6B 144
LYDIATE ASH 6C 156
Lydiate Ash Rd. B61: L Ash 6B 156
  (not continuous)
Lydiates Cl. DY3: Sed. 6F 59
Lydney Cl. WV12: W'hall 6D 30
Lydney Gro. B31: N'fld. 4D 144
LYE 6A 110
Lye Av. B32: Bart G 3G 129
Lye Bus. Cen. DY9: Lye 5B 110
Lye By-Pass DY9: Lye 5A 110
Lye Cl. La. B32: Bart G. 3F 129
  B62: Hale 3F 129
Lyecroft Av. B37: Chel W 1F 123
Lye Cross Rd. B69: Tiv. 2B 96
Lye Station (Rail) 5A 110
Lye Valley Ind. Est. DY9: Lye 5B 110
Lygon Cl. B62: Hale 5B 112
Lygon Gro. B32: Quin. 1C 130
Lymedene Rd. B42: P Barr 2D 82
Lyme Grn. Rd. B33: Stech 5D 104
Lymer Rd. WV10: Oxl 6G 15

Lymington Rd. WV13: W'hall. 1D 46
Lymsey Cft. DY8: Word 6A 92
Lynbrook Cl. B47: H'wd 2A 162
  DY2: Neth 3F 95
Lyncourt Gro. B32: Quin 5H 113
Lyncroft Rd. B11: Tys 3F 135
Lyndale Dr. WV11: Wed 3G 29
Lyndale Rd. DY2: Dud 3G 95
  DY3: Sed 3F 59
Lyndhurst Dr. DY8: Word 2D 108
Lyndhurst Rd. B24: Erd 5F 85
  B71: W Brom 6C 64
  WV3: Wolv 4E 43
LYNDON 2B 80
Lyndon B71: W Brom 2B 80
Lyndon Cl. B20: Hand. 5E 83
  B36: Cas B 1G 105
  B63: Hale 1G 127
  DY3: Sed 4A 60
Lyndon Ct. B26: Sheld 1G 137
Lyndon Cft. B37: Mars G 4D 122
  B92: Olton 3E 137
LYNDON GREEN 4E 121
Lyndon Gro. B71: W Brom 3B 80
  DY6: W Hth 1H 91
Lyndon Ho. B31: N'fld. 4F 145
Lyndon Rd. B33: Stech. 6C 104
  B45: Rubery 2E 157
  B73: S Cold 6H 53
  B92: Olton 3D 136
Lyndworth Rd. B30: Stir 6E 133
Lyneham Gdns. B76: Walm 1E 87
Lyneham Way B35: Cas V 4D 86
Lynfield Cl. B38: K Nor 2B 160
Lyng La. B70: W Brom. 4A 80
  (not continuous)
Lynmouth Cl. WS9: A'rdge 4C 34
LYNN 2H 23
Lynn Gro. B29: S Oak. 2G 131
Lynn La. WS14: Lynn, Shens. 2H 23
Lynton Av. B66: Smeth 3E 99
  B71: W Brom 6A 64
  WV6: Tett 2C 26
Lynton Ho. B23: Erd 1B 84
Lynton Rd. B6: Aston 2A 102
Lynval Rd. DY5: Quar B 4B 110
Lynwood Av. DY6: W Hth. 2H 91
Lynwood Cl. WV12: W'hall 1E 31
Lynwood Wlk. B17: Harb 1H 131
Lynwood Way B45: Lick 6G 157
Lyon Ct. B72: S Cold 6A 54
  (off Midland Dr.)
Lyons Gro. B11: S'hll 2C 134
Lysander Rd. B45: Fran 5G 143
Lysander Way B35: Cas V 5F 87
Lysways St. WS1: Wals 3D 48
Lytham Cl. B76: Walm 1F 87
  DY8: Stourb 3E 125
Lytham Cft. B15: Birm 3F 117
Lytham Gro. WS3: Blox 3G 19
Lytham Rd. WV6: Pert 5D 24
Lythwood Dr. DY5: Brie H 3G 109
Lyttelton Rd. B16: Edg. 2H 115
  B33: Stech 1B 120
  DY8: Stourb 6B 108
Lyttleton Av. B62: B'hth 4E 113
Lyttleton Cl. DY2: Neth. 5E 95
Lyttleton Ho. B63: Hale 3A 128
Lyttleton St. B70: W Brom 5A 80
Lytton Av. WV4: Penn. 1B 58
Lytton Gro. B27: A Grn 4H 135
Lytton La. B32: Bart G 2D 130

M

Maas Rd. B31: N'fld 4E 145
Macarthur Rd. B64: Crad H 3E 111
Macaulay Ho. B70: W Brom 6B 80
McBean Rd. WV6: Wolv. 5D 26
Macdonald Cl. B69: Tiv 5D 78
McDougall Rd. WS10: W'bry. 2A 64
Mace St. B64: Old H 2G 111
McGregor Cl. B6: Aston 6H 83
Machin Rd. B23: Erd 3F 85
Mackadown La. B33: Kitts G, Sheld . 1H 121
Mackay Rd. WS3: Blox. 5B 20

McKean Rd. B69: O'bry 6G 79
McKen Ct. B70: W Brom 6A 80
Mackenzie Cl. B31: N'fld 5C 130
Mackenzie Rd. B11: S'hll 3C 134
Mackmillan Rd. B65: Row R 1B 112
McLean Rd. WV10: Oxl 5G 15
Macmillan Cl. B69: Tiv 5C 78
Macrome Rd. WV6: Tett 1C 26
Madams Hill Rd. B90: Shir 2B 164
Maddocks Hill B72: W Grn 3A 70
Madehurst Rd. B23: Erd 1E 85
Madeira Av. WV8: Cod 5G 13
Madeleine Ho. B33: Stech 6C 104
Madeley Rd. B11: S'brk 6C 118
　DY6: K'wfrd 5D 92
Madin Rd. DY4: Tip 3G 77
Madison Av. B36: Hodg H 3B 104
　DY5: Brie H 6B 94
　WS2: Wals 1H 47
Madley Cl. B45: Rubery 1E 157
Madresfield Dr. B63: Hale 3B 128
Maer Cl. B65: Row R 5C 96
Mafeking Rd. B66: Smeth 2E 99
Magdala St. B18: Win G 4A 100
Magdalen Cl. DY1: Dud 5C 76
Magdalen Cl. B16: Edg 2A 116
　　　　　　　　　　　(off Vernon Ct.)
Magdalene Rd. WS1: Wals 4E 49
Magna Cl. WS6: C Hay 2E 7
Magness Cres. WV12: W'hall 4C 30
Magnet Wlk. B23: Erd 4C 84
Magnolia Cl. B29: W Cas 6E 131
Magnolia Dr. WS5: Wals 1D 64
Magnolia Gro. WV8: Bilb 4G 13
　WV12: W'hall 5B 30
Magnolia Way DY8: Word 3D 108
Magnum Cl. B74: S'tly 4H 51
Magpie Cl. DY2: Neth 6G 95
Magpie La. CV7: Bal C 2E 169
Magreal Ind. Est. B16: Birm 6B 100
Maidendale Rd. DY6: K'wfrd 2H 91
Maidensbridge Dr. DY6: W Hth 1A 92
Maidensbridge Gdns. DY6: W Hth . . . 6H 73
Maidensbridge Rd. DY6: W Hth 6H 73
Maidstone Dr. DY8: Word 6C 92
Maidstone Rd. B20: Hand 6G 83
Maidwell Dr. B90: Shir 1C 164
Mailbox, The B1: Birm 1F 117 (6C 4)
Mailbox Sq. B1: Birm 1F 117 (5C 4)
Main Rd. B26: Birm A 2B 138
　CV7: Mer 4H 141
Mainstream 47 Ind. Pk. B7: Birm . . . 4C 102
Mainstream Way B7: Birm 5C 102
Main St. B11: S'brk 4A 118
　WS9: Ston 4F 23
Main Ter. B11: S'brk 4A 118
Mainwaring Dr. B75: R'ley 1C 54
Maitland Ho. B36: Cas B 6H 87
Maitland Rd. B8: Salt 5F 103
　DY1: Dud 6A 76
Majestic Way B65: Row R 5C 96
Major Ct. B13: Mose 3B 134
MAJOR'S GREEN 1D 162
Majuba Rd. B16: Edg 5G 99
Malcolm Av. B24: Erd 2A 86
Malcolm Ct. B26: Sheld 6E 121
　WV1: Wolv 6E 27
Malcolm Gro. B45: Redn 2G 157
Malcolm Rd. B90: Shir 6H 149
Malcolmson Cl. B15: Edg 3B 116
Malfield Dr. B27: A Grn 2C 136
Mali Jenkins Ho. WS1: Wals 2F 49
Malins Rd. B17: Harb 6H 115
　WV4: E'shll 6A 44
Malkit Cl. WS2: Wals 5F 31
Mallaby Cl. B90: Shir 1G 163
Mallard Cl. B27: A Grn 2A 136
　DY5: Brie H 4G 109
　WS3: Pels 1E 21
Mallard Dr. B23: Erd 4B 84
　B69: O'bry 5F 97
Mallards Reach B92: Olton 5C 136
Mallender Dr. B93: Know 3B 166
Mallen Dr. B69: Tiv 6B 78
Mallin Gdns. DY1: Dud 1A 94
Mallin St. B66: Smeth 2B 98
Mallory Cres. WS3: Blox 5B 20

Mallory Ri. B13: Mose 4C 134
Mallory Rd. WV6: Pert 6E 25
Mallow Cl. WS5: Wals 2E 65
Mallow Rd. WV6: Wolv 4F 27
Mallow Ri. B23: Erd 6B 68
Malmesbury Pk. B15: Edg 4A 116
Malmesbury Rd. B10: Small H 5E 119
Malpas Dr. B32: Bart G 5A 130
Malpass Gdns. WV8: Cod 3E 13
Malpass Rd. DY5: Quar B 4B 110
Malpas Wlk. WV10: Wolv 4C 28
Malt Cl. B17: Harb 5H 115
Malthouse B66: Smeth 2C 98
Malthouse Cft. B6: Aston 1G 101
Malthouse Dr. DY1: Dud 5C 76
Malthouse Gdns. B19: Loz 2F 101
Malthouse Gro. B25: Yard 2C 120
Malt Ho. La. WV13: W'hall 1A 46
Malthouse La. B8: Salt 3E 103
　B42: Gt Barr 5F 67
　B61: C'wich 4B 156
　　　　　　　　　(not continuous)
　WV6: Tett 3C 26
Malthouse Rd. DY4: Tip 2G 77
Malt Ho. Row B37: Mars G 3C 122
Maltings, The B1: Birm . . . 2E 117 (6B 4)
　WS9: A'rdge 3E 35
　WV1: Wolv 6H 27 (1C 170)
　WV5: Wom. 1G 73
Malt Mill La. B62: B'hth 3C 112
Malton Av. B69: O'bry 3D 96
Malton Gro. B13: Mose 6B 134
Malvern Av. DY9: Lye 6G 109
Malvern Cl. B15: Edg 3G 115
　B71: W Brom 2B 80
　WV12: W'hall 5B 30
Malvern Ct. B27: A Grn 1A 136
　WV10: Bush. 1H 27
Malvern Cres. DY2: Dud 3B 94
Malvern Dr. B76: Walm 5E 71
　WS9: A'rdge 6E 23
　WV1: Wolv. 2D 44
Malvern Ho. B63: Hale. 2A 128
　　　　　　　　(off Pickersleigh Cl.)
Malvern Pk. Rd. B91: Sol 4H 151
Malvern Rd. B21: Hand 6G 81
　B27: A Grn 1A 136
　B45: Lick 6G 157
　B68: O'bry 3H 113
　CV7: Bal C 6H 169
Malvern St. B12: Bal H. 6A 118
Malvern Vw. Rd. DY3: Low'r G 3H 75
Mamble Rd. DY8: Stourb. 6C 108
Mammouth Dr. WV10: Wolv 4H 27
Manby Cl. WV6: Wolv. 5F 27
Manby Rd. B35: Cas V 3E 87
Manby St. DY4: Tip 5H 61
Mancetter Rd. B90: Shir 4A 150
Manchester St. B6: Birm 4G 101
　B69: O'bry 2H 97
Mancroft Cl. DY6: K'wfrd 2H 91
Mancroft Gdns. WV6: Tett 4A 26
Mancroft Rd. WV6: Tett 4A 26
Mandale Rd. WV10: Wolv 3B 28
Mander Cen. WV1: Wolv . . . 1G 43 (3B 170)
Manderley Cl. DY3: Sed 3G 59
Manders Ind. Est. WV1: Wolv 6B 28
Manderston Cl. DY1: Dud 4A 76
Mander Sq. WV1: Wolv 2G 43 (4B 170)
Mander St. WV3: Wolv 3F 43 (6A 170)
Manderville Ho. B31: Longb 1D 158
Mandeville Gdns. WS1: Wals 3D 48
MANEY 1A 70
Maney Cnr. B72: S Cold. 1H 69
Maney Hill Rd. B72: W Grn 2H 69
Manfield Rd. WV13: W'hall 6E 29
Manifoldia Grange B70: W Brom . . . 5H 79
Manilla Rd. B29: S Oak 4D 132
Manitoba Cft. B38: K Nor. 1B 160
Manley Cl. B70: W Brom. 4H 79
Manlove St. WV3: Wolv 3E 43
Manningford Cl. B14: K Hth. 5H 147
Manningford Rd. B14: K Hth 5G 147
Mnr. Abbey Rd. B62: Hale 2E 129

Manor Av. WS6: Gt Wyr. 1G 7
Manor Cl. WV4: Penn 1D 58
　WV8: Bilb. 3H 13
　WV13: W'hall 6A 30
Manor Ct. B27: A Grn 3B 136
　B30: K Nor 5C 146
　B62: Quin. 4B 113
　　　　　　　　　(off Binswood Rd.)
　B93: Dorr 6G 167
　DY2: Neth 5E 95
　WS2: Wals 1A 48
Manor Dr. B73: S Cold 1H 69
　DY3: Gorn. 4F 75
　DY3: Swind 5E 73
Manor Farm Dr. WV12: W'hall. 4D 30
Manor Farm Rd. B11: Tys 1E 135
Manor Fold WV8: Oaken 5D 12
Manorford Av. B71: W Brom 4E 65
Manor Gdns. B33: Stech 1B 120
　WS10: W'bry 1F 63
　WV5: Wom. 6H 57
Manor Hill B73: S Cold 1H 69
Manor Ho. B31: N'fld 6F 131
Manor Ho., The B44: Gt Barr. 3G 67
　　　　　　　　　(off Amblecote Av.)
Manor Ho. Cl. B29: W Cas. 4D 130
Manor Ho. Dr. B31: N'fld 6F 131
Manor Ho. La. B26: Yard. 5D 120
　B46: Wat O. 4D 88
Manor Ho. Pk. WV8: Bilb. 3H 13
Manor Ho. Rd. WS10: W'bry 2F 63
Manorial Rd. B75: R'ley 6C 38
Manor Ind. Est. WS2: Wals 2A 48
Manor La. B61: C'wich, L Ash 4C 156
　B62: Hale 2E 129
　DY8: Stourb 2B 124
Manor Pk. DY6: K'wfrd. 3B 92
Manor Pk. Cl. B13: Mose. 3A 134
Manor Pk. Gro. B31: Longb 6A 144
Manor Pk. Rd. B36: Cas B 2H 105
Manor Rd. B6: Aston 6H 83
　B16: Edg 2H 115
　B33: Stech 6C 104
　B47: Wyt 6A 162
　B67: Smeth 4B 98
　B73: S Cold 6H 53
　B74: S'tly 3A 52
　B91: Sol 2F 151
　B93: Dorr 6A 166
　DY4: Tip 3H 77
　DY8: Word 1C 108
　WS2: Wals 1A 48
　WS10: W'bry 3B 64
　WV4: E'shll 6C 44
　WV4: Penn 1D 58
　WV10: Oxl 2G 27
Manor Rd. Nth. B16: Edg 2H 115
Manor Rd. Pct. WS2: Wals 1A 48
Manor Sq. B91: Sol 4G 151
Manor St. WV6: Tett 4A 26
Manor Wlk. B91: Sol 4G 151
Manor Way B62: Hale 4G 127
　B73: S Cold 1H 69
Mansard Cl. WV3: Wolv. 3D 42
　WV11: Bush. 1D 28
Mansard Ct. B46: Col. 2H 107
Mansell Cl. B63: Crad 4D 110
Mansell Rd. DY4: Tip 5A 62
Mansel Rd. B10: Small H 4E 119
Mansfield Ho. B37: Chel W 6E 107
Mansfield Rd. B6: Aston 1F 101
　B25: Yard 6A 120
Mansion Cl. DY1: Dud 4C 76
Mansion Ct. WV5: Wom 2D 72
　　　　　　　　(off Heath Ho. Dr.)
Mansion Cres. B67: Smeth 5C 98
Mansion Dr. DY4: Tip 2C 78
　WS7: Hamm 1F 11
Manson Dr. B64: Old H 2A 112
Manston Dr. WV6: Pert. 4E 25
Manston Rd. B26: Sheld. 4F 121
Manton Cft. B93: Dorr 6A 166
Manton Ho. B19: Loz 2G 101
Manway Cl. B20: Hand 2B 82
Manwoods Cl. B20: Hand 5D 82
Maple Av. WS10: W'bry 1A 64
Maple Bank B15: Edg. 4C 116

Maplebeck Ct. B91: Sol 2G **151**
Maple Bus. Pk. B7: Nech 3B **102**
Maple Cen., The WS10: Mox 2B **62**
Maple Cl. B21: Hand 6A **82**
DY8: Stourb 3B **124**
WV14: Cose 6C **60**
Maple Ct. *B24: Erd* *4F* ***85***
(off Coppice Cl.)
B66: Smeth 1B **98**
Maple Cft. B13: Mose 1H **147**
Mapledene B13: Mose 3B **134**
Mapledene Rd. B26: Sheld 5H **121**
Maple Dr. B44: K'sdng 5B **68**
DY3: Gorn 5F **75**
WS4: S'fld 1F **33**
WS5: Wals 1F **65**
WS10: Mox 1B **62**
Maple Grn. DY1: Dud 2C **76**
Maple Gro. B19: Loz 1E **101**
B37: K'hrst 3B **106**
DY6: K'wfrd 3C **92**
WV3: Wolv 1A **42**
WV14: Bils 1H **61**
Maple Leaf Dr. B37: Mars G 3D **122**
Maple Leaf Ind. Est. WS2: Wals 6G **31**
Maple Leaf Rd. WS10: W'bry 4C **62**
Maple Ri. B68: O'bry 1A **114**
Maple Rd. B30: B'vlle 5A **132**
B45: Rubery 3F **157**
B62: B'hth 3D **112**
B72: S Cold 2A **70**
DY1: Dud 4E **77**
WS3: Pels 5D **20**
WV3: Wolv 4C **42**
Maple Row DY5: Brie H 1H **109**
Maple St. WS3: Blox 5B **20**
Mapleton Gro. B28: Hall G 6H **135**
Mapleton Rd. B28: Hall G 6H **135**
Maple Tree La. B63: Crad 5E **111**
Maple Wlk. *B37: Chel W* *1D* ***122***
(off Chelmsley Wood Shop. Cen.)
Maple Way B31: Longb 6D **144**
Maplewood B76: Walm 5E **71**
Mapperley Gdns. B13: Mose 2E **133**
Mappleborough Rd. B90: Shir 6E **149**
Marans Cft. B38: K Nor 2H **159**
Marbury Cl. B38: K Nor 5H **145**
Marbury M. DY5: Brie H 2H **109**
Marchant Rd. WV3: Wolv 1D **42**
WV14: Bils 4E **45**
March Cl. WS6: C Hay 4D **6**
MARCH END 4G **29**
March End Rd. WV11: Wed 4F **29**
(not continuous)
Marchmont Rd. B9: Bord G 1G **119**
Marchmount Rd. B72: W Grn 5A **70**
March Way WS9: A'rdge 6E **23**
Marcliff Cres. B90: Shir 5C **148**
Marcos Dr. B36: Cas B 6B **88**
Marcot Rd. B92: Olton 6D **120**
Marden Cl. WV13: W'hall 2H **45**
Marden Gro. B31: Longb 2E **159**
Marden Wlk. B23: Erd 4B **84**
Mardon Rd. B26: Sheld 6F **121**
Maree Gro. WV12: W'hall 6B **18**
Marfield Cl. B76: Walm 1E **87**
Margam Cres. WS3: Blox 5F **19**
Margam Ter. WS3: Blox 5F **19**
Margam Way WS3: Blox 5F **19**
Margaret Av. B63: Hale 1H **127**
Margaret Cl. DY5: Quar B 3A **110**
Margaret Dr. DY8: Stourb 1F **125**
Margaret Gdns. B67: Smeth 4C **98**
Margaret Gro. B17: Harb 4G **115**
Margaret Ho. B17: Harb 6F **115**
Margaret Rd. B17: Harb 6G **115**
B73: New O 4D **68**
WS2: Wals 6E **31**
WS10: Darl 1C **62**
Margarets Ho. B76: Walm 2D **70**
Margaret St. B3: Birm 6F **101** (3C **4**)
B70: W Brom 5H **79**
Margaret Va. DY4: Tip 4C **62**
Margaret Vine Ct. B62: B'hth 2F **113**
Marholm Cl. WV9: Pend 5D **14**
Marian Cft. B26: Sheld 6H **121**
Maria St. B70: W Brom 1C **98**
Marie Dr. B27: A Grn 5H **135**
Marigold Cres. DY1: Dud 3C **76**
Marine Cres. DY8: Word 2C **108**
Marine Dr. B44: K'sdng 1G **83**
Marine Gdns. DY8: Word 2C **108**
Mariner Av. B16: Edg 2A **116**
Marion Cl. DY5: Quar B 1B **110**
Marion Rd. B67: Smeth 3B **98**
Marion Way B28: Hall G 6E **135**
Marita Cl. DY2: Neth 6G **95**
Marjoram Cl. B38: K Nor 1B **160**
Marjorie Av. B30: K Nor 4D **146**
Mark Av. WS10: W'bry 2E **63**
Markby Rd. B18: Win G 3A **100**
Mark Ct. WS1: Wals 6E **33**
Market La. WV4: Lwr P 5F **41**
Market Pl. B65: B'hth 2C **112**
B69: O'bry *1G* ***97***
(off Market St.)
DY2: Dud 6E **77**
DY2: Neth 4E **95**
DY4: Tip 2D **78**
WS3: Blox 6H **19**
WS10: W'bry 3F **63**
WV13: W'hall 2A **46**
Market Sq. B64: Crad H 3E **111**
Market St. B69: O'bry 1G **97**
DY6: K'wfrd 3B **92**
DY8: Stourb 6E **109**
WV1: Wolv 1H **43** (3C **170**)
Market Way DY9: Hag 6G **125**
WV14: Bils 6F **45**
Markfield Rd. B26: Sheld 3F **121**
Markford Wlk. B19: Hock 3F **101**
Markham Cres. B92: Sol 4B **138**
Markham Cft. WV9: Pend 5E **15**
Markham Dr. DY6: K'wfrd 5C **92**
Markham Rd. B73: New O 2C **68**
Mark Ho. B13: Mose 3A **134**
Marklew Cl. WS8: Bwnhls 2C **22**
Marklin Av. WV10: Oxl 6H **15**
Mark Rd. WS10: W'bry 2E **63**
Marksbury Cl. WV6: Wolv 4E **27**
Marlbank Rd. DY8: Word 2E **109**
Marlborough Cl. B74: Four O 3E **37**
Marlborough Ct. *B74: Four O* *1F* ***53***
(off Vesey Cl.)
Marlborough Dr. DY8: Stourb 2E **125**
Marlborough Gdns. DY8: Word 1A **108**
WV6: Wolv 5C **26**
Marlborough Gro. B25: Yard 2B **120**
Marlborough Rd. B10: Small H 2E **119**
B36: Cas B 1G **105**
B66: Smeth 6E **99**
DY3: Sed 6B **60**
Marlborough St. WS3: Blox 6H **19**
Marlbrook Cl. B92: Sol 1G **137**
Marlbrook Dr. WV4: Penn 5F **43**
Marlbrook La. B60: Marl 6D **156**
Marlburn Way WV5: Wom 1E **73**
Marlcliff Gro. B13: Mose 1A **148**
Marldon Rd. B14: K Hth 1G **147**
Marlene Cft. B37: Chel W 2E **123**
Marley Rd. DY6: K'wfrd 5E **93**
Marling Cft. B92: Sol 6A **138**
Marlow Cl. DY2: Neth 6G **95**
Marlowe Dr. WV12: W'hall 2A **30**
Marlow Rd. B23: Erd 2D **84**
Marlow St. B65: B'hth 2B **112**
WS2: Wals 5C **32**
Marlpit La. B75: R'ley 1B **54**
Marlpit Ri. B75: R'ley 6C **38**
Marlpool Dr. WS3: Pels 6E **21**
Marl Rd. DY2: Neth 5D **94**
Marl Top B38: K Nor 5B **146**
Marmion Dr. B43: Gt Barr 3B **66**
Marmion Gro. DY1: Dud 1C **94**
Marmion Way B70: W Brom 1F **79**
Marnel Dr. WV3: Wolv 3B **42**
Marquis Dr. B62: Hale 4A **112**
Marriott Rd. B66: Smeth 2B **98**
DY2: Neth 5E **95**
Marroway St. B16: Birm 6B **100**
Marrowfat La. B21: Hand 2B **100**
Mars Cl. WV14: Cose 4C **60**
Marsden Cl. B92: Olton 4C **136**
Marsh, The WS10: W'bry 2E **63**
Marshall Cl. WS9: A'rdge 5D **34**
Marshall Gro. B44: Gt Barr 6H **67**
Marshall Ho. *WS2: Wals* *3A* ***48***
(off St Quentin St.)
Marshall Lake Rd. B90: Shir 1B **164**
Marshall Rd. B68: O'bry 2A **114**
WV13: W'hall 2E **45**
Marshalls Ind. Est. WV2: Wolv 4G **43**
Marshall St. B1: Birm 2F **117** (6C **4**)
B67: Smeth 2B **98**
Marsham Ct. Rd. B91: Sol 6D **136**
Marsham Rd. B14: K Hth 4H **147**
Marshbrook Cl. B24: Erd 3C **86**
Marsh Cl. B23: Erd 2F **85**
Marsh Cres. DY8: Word 6A **92**
Marsh End B38: K Nor 1C **160**
Marshfield B90: Dic H 4H **163**
Marshfield Gdns. B24: Erd 5E **85**
Marsh Gro. DY3: Swind 5E **73**
Marsh Hill B23: Erd 3B **84**
Marsh Ho. Farm La. B92: H Ard 4D **154**
Marshland Way WS2: Wals 2E **47**
Marsh La. B23: Erd 2D **84**
B46: Wat O 4D **88**
B71: W Brom 6A **64**
B76: Curd 2E **89**
B91: Sol 3A **152**
B92: H Ard 1A **154**
(not continuous)
WS2: Wals 1B **48**
WV10: F'hses 4F **15**
Marsh La. Pde. WV10: Oxl 5G **15**
Marshmont Way B23: Erd 5D **68**
Marsh St. WS2: Wals 1B **48**
Marshwood Cft. B62: Quin 2G **129**
Marsland Cl. B17: Edg 2G **115**
Marsland Rd. B92: Olton 6C **136**
Marston Av. WS10: Darl 5C **46**
Marston Cl. DY8: Stourb 1B **124**
Marston Cft. B37: Mars G 4B **122**
Marston Dr. B37: K'hrst 4C **106**
MARSTON GREEN 3B **122**
Marston Green Station (Rail) 4B **122**
Marston Gro. B43: Gt Barr 5G **65**
Marston Rd. B29: W Cas 5D **130**
B73: Bold 6G **69**
DY1: Dud 1H **93**
WV2: Wolv 4F **43**
Marston Rd. Ind. Est.
WV2: Wolv 4G **43**
Marston St. WV13: W'hall 1C **46**
Martham Dr. WV6: Tett 1H **41**
Martin Cl. B25: Yard 5B **120**
WV14: Cose 6F **61**
Martindale Wlk. DY5: Brie H 5F **109**
Martin Dr. WV12: W'hall 4C **30**
Martineau Pl. B2: Birm 1G **117** (4E **5**)
Martineau Twr. *B19: Birm* *4F* ***101***
(off Uxbridge St.)
Martineau Way *B2: Birm* *4E* ***5***
(off Union St.)
Martingale Cl. WS5: Wals 1D **64**
Martin Hill St. DY2: Dud 1E **95**
Martin Ri. B37: Mars G 3B **122**
Martin Rd. DY4: Tip 2A **78**
WS5: Wals 3G **49**
WV14: Bils 2H **61**
Martin St. WV4: E'shll 6B **44**
Martlesham Sq. B35: Cas V 3E **87**
Martley Cft. B32: Quin 1C **130**
B91: Sol 1F **165**
Martley Dr. DY9: Lye 1G **125**
Martley Rd. B69: O'bry 3D **96**
WS4: S'fld 6G **21**
Marwood Cft. B74: S'tly 1A **52**
Mary Ann St. B3: Birm 5F **101** (1C **4**)
WV1: Wolv 2A **44**
Maryland Av. B34: Hodg H 4C **104**
Maryland Dr. B31: N'fld 2F **145**
Maryland Rd. DY5: Quar B 4B **110**
Marylebone Cl. DY8: Amb 4E **109**
Mary Macarthur Dr.
B64: Crad H 2E **111**
Mary Rd. B21: Hand 2A **100**
B33: Stech 6B **104**
B69: Tiv 1C **96**
B70: W Brom 6B **80**

Mary St.—Meetinghouse La.

Mary St. B3: Birm 5E **101** (1B **4**)
B12: Bal H 6G **117**
WS2: Wals 6B **32**
Maryvale Ct. WS1: Wals 2C **48**
Mary Va. Rd. B30: B'vlle 1A **146**
Marywell Cl. B32: Bart G 6H **129**
Masefield Av. DY1: Dud 6E **61**
Masefield Cl. WV14: Bils 3H **61**
Masefield M. WV10: Bush 6C **16**
Masefield Ri. B62: Hale 2D **128**
Masefield Rd. DY3: Lwr G 3E **75**
WS3: Blox 2C **32**
WV10: Bush 6C **16**
Masefield Sq. B31: N'fld 3G **145**
Masham Cl. B33: Stech 1C **120**
Mashie Gdns. B38: K Nor 6H **145**
Maslen Pl. B63: Hale 2B **128**
Maslin Dr. WV14: Cose 4C **60**
Mason Ct. B27: A Grn 3C **136**
Mason Cres. WV4: Penn 6C **42**
Mason Hall B15: Edg 5C **116**
Mason Ho. B90: Shir 6E **149**
Masonleys Rd. B31: N'fld 4B **144**
Mason Rd. B24: Erd 3G **85**
WS2: Wals 4H **31**
Mason's Cl. B63: Crad 5E **111**
Masons Cotts. B24: Erd 2H **85**
Mason St. B70: W Brom 3H **79**
WV2: Wolv 4G **43**
WV14: Cose 6D **60**
Mason's Way B92: Olton 3C **136**
Massbrook Gro. WV10: Wolv 3B **28**
Massbrook Rd. WV10: Wolv 3B **28**
Masshouse La. B38: K Nor 6B **146**
Masters La. B62: B'hth 2E **113**
Matchlock Cl. B74: S'tly 4G **51**
Matfen Av. B73: S Cold 3F **69**
Math Mdw. B32: Harb 6D **114**
Matlock Cl. DY2: Neth 6F **95**
WS3: Blox 4A **20**
Matlock Rd. B11: Tys 2F **135**
WS3: Blox 4A **20**
Matlock Vs. *B12: Bal H* *6B* ***118***
(off Chesterton Rd.)
Matthews Cl. B65: B'hth 2B **112**
Mattox Rd. WV11: Wed 3F **29**
Matty Rd. B68: O'bry 5H **97**
Maud Rd. B46: Wat O 4F **89**
B70: W Brom 6A **80**
Maughan St. DY1: Dud 6C **76**
DY5: Quar B 3B **110**
Maurice Gro. WV10: Wolv 3C **28**
Maurice Rd. B14: K Hth 2G **147**
B67: Smeth 1C **114**
Mavis Gdns. B68: O'bry 3H **113**
Mavis Rd. B31: N'fld 6C **144**
Maw St. WS1: Wals 5D **48**
Maxholm Rd. B74: S'tly 3G **51**
Max Rd. B32: Quin 6B **114**
Maxstoke Cl. B32: Bart G 6G **129**
B73: New O 3E **69**
CV7: Mer 4H **141**
WS3: Blox 4G **19**
Maxstoke Cft. B90: Shir 1A **164**
Maxstoke La. CV7: Mer 3H **141**
(not continuous)
Maxstoke Rd. B73: New O 3E **69**
Maxstoke St. B9: Birm 1B **118**
Maxted Rd. B23: Erd 5C **68**
Maxwell Av. B20: Hand 6D **82**
Maxwell Rd. WV2: Wolv 3H **43** (6D **170**)
Mayall Dr. B75: R'ley 5A **38**
May Av. B12: Bal H 6A **118**
Maybank B9: Bord G 6F **103**
Maybank Pl. B44: P Barr 1G **83**
Maybank Rd. DY2: Neth 6E **95**
Mayberry Cl. B14: K Hth 5B **148**
Maybridge Dr. B91: Sol 1F **165**
Maybrook Ho. B63: Hale 1A **128**
Maybrook Ind. Est. WS8: Bwnhls 2B **22**
(not continuous)
Maybrook Rd. B76: Min 2E **87**
WS8: Bwnhls 3B **22**
Maybury Cl. WV8: Cod 3E **13**
Maybush Gdns. WV10: Oxl 6G **15**
Maydene Cft. B12: Bal H 5H **117**
MAYERS GREEN 3C **80**
Mayfair *B37: K'hrst* *4B* ***106***
(off Haselour Rd.)
DY9: W'cte 3H **125**
Mayfair Cl. B44: K'sdng 6B **68**
DY1: Dud 5C **76**
Mayfair Dr. DY6: K'wfrd 2A **92**
Mayfair Gdns. DY4: Tip 3A **78**
WV3: Wolv 1B **42**
Mayfair Pde. B44: K'sdng 6B **68**
May Farm Cl. B47: H'wd 3A **162**
Mayfield Av. B29: S Oak 3D **132**
Mayfield Cl. B91: Sol 6G **151**
Mayfield Ct. B13: Mose 3A **134**
Mayfield Cres. B65: Row R 6A **96**
Mayfield Rd. B11: Tys 1G **135**
B13: Mose 3A **134**
B19: Hand 1E **101**
B27: A Grn 2G **135**
B30: Stir 1C **146**
B62: B'hth 2F **113**
B63: Hale 3F **127**
B73: W Grn 3G **69**
B74: S'tly 3H **51**
DY1: Dud 2D **76**
WV1: Wolv 2D **44**
Mayfields Dr. WS8: Bwnhls 3F **9**
Mayflower Cl. B19: Loz 3F **101**
Mayflower Dr. DY5: P'ntt 2E **93**
Mayford Gro. B13: Mose 1B **148**
Maygrove Rd. DY6: K'wfrd 2A **92**
Mayhurst Cl. B47: H'wd 2C **162**
DY4: Tip 5A **62**
Mayhurst Rd. B47: H'wd 2B **162**
Mayland Dr. B74: S'tly 6H **51**
Mayland Rd. B16: Edg 1G **115**
May La. B14: K Hth 2H **147**
B47: H'wd 2A **162**
Maynard Av. DY8: Stourb 2B **124**
Mayou Ct. WS3: Pels 3E **21**
Maypole Cl. B64: Crad H 3D **110**
Maypole Ct. WV5: Wom 1G **73**
Maypole Dr. DY8: Stourb 6C **108**
Maypole Flds. B63: Crad 4C **110**
Maypole Gro. B14: K Hth 5B **148**
Maypole Hill B63: Crad 3C **110**
Maypole La. B14: K Hth 5H **147**
Maypole Rd. B68: O'bry 2H **113**
Maypole St. WV5: Wom 6H **57**
May St. WS3: Blox 3A **32**
Mayswood Dr. WV6: Tett 2F **41**
Mayswood Gro. B32: Quin 1B **130**
Mayswood Rd. B92: Sol 3G **137**
Maythorn Av. B76: Walm 1E **87**
Maythorn Gdns. WV6: Tett 6A **26**
WV8: Bilb 3G **13**
Maythorn Gro. B91: Sol 1F **165**
Maytree Cl. B37: F'bri 1C **122**
May Tree Gro. B20: Hand 4B **82**
May Trees B47: H'wd 3H **161**
Maywell Dr. B92: Sol 5B **138**
Maywood Cl. DY6: K'wfrd 3A **92**
Meaburn Cl. B29: W Cas 6E **131**
Mead, The DY3: Sed 5F **59**
Mead Cl. WS9: A'rdge 3D **34**
Mead Cres. B9: Bord G 6H **103**
Meadfoot Av. B14: K Hth 4H **147**
Meadfoot Dr. DY6: K'wfrd 2H **91**
Meadlands, The WV5: Wom 1E **73**
Meadow Av. B71: W Brom 4D **64**
Meadowbank Grange WS6: Gt Wyr 1E **7**
Meadowbrook Gdns. WV8: Bilb 3H **13**
Mdw. Brook Rd. B31: N'fld 2D **144**
Meadowbrook Rd. B63: Hale 2F **127**
Meadow Cl. B17: Harb 3F **115**
B74: S'tly 1H **51**
B76: Walm 4D **70**
B90: Shir 1B **164**
WS4: S'fld 1G **33**
WV12: W'hall 1C **30**
Meadow Ct. B17: Edg 2F **115**
B20: Hand 4A **82**
Meadow Cft. B47: Wyt 6A **162**
WV6: Pert 6D **24**
Meadow Dr. B92: H Ard 1B **154**
Meadowfield Rd. B45: Rubery 2G **157**
Meadowfields Cl. DY8: Word 1C **108**
Mdw. Grange Dr. WV12: W'hall 2C **30**
Meadow Gro. B92: Olton 4B **136**
WS6: Gt Wyr 3G **7**
Meadow Hill Dr. DY8: Word 1C **108**
Meadow Hill Rd. B38: K Nor 5A **146**
Meadowlands Dr. WS4: S'fld 1H **33**
Meadow La. WV5: Wom 5G **57**
WV10: Cov H 1G **15**
WV12: W'hall 4A **30**
WV14: Cose 3D **60**
(not continuous)
Meadow Pk. Rd. DY8: Woll 3B **108**
Mdw. Pleck La. B90: Dic H 3G **163**
Meadow Ri. B30: B'vlle 6H **131**
CV7: Bal C 5H **169**
Meadow Rd. B17: Harb 2F **115**
B32: Quin 5G **113**
B47: Wyt 6A **162**
B62: B'hth 3C **112**
B67: Smeth 5E **99**
B68: O'bry 1H **113**
DY1: Dud 3C **76**
WS9: A'rdge 5C **34**
WV3: Wolv 3A **42**
Meadows, The DY9: Pedm 5F **125**
WS9: A'rdge 4A **34**
Meadowside Cl. B43: Gt Barr 4A **66**
Meadowside Rd. B74: Four O 5F **37**
Meadow St. B64: Old H 3H **111**
WS1: Wals 3B **48**
Meadowsweet Av. B38: K Nor 1B **160**
Meadowsweet Way DY6: K'wfrd 3E **93**
Meadow Va. WV8: Bilb 5H **13**
Meadow Vw. B13: Mose 5C **134**
DY3: Sed 4G **59**
WV6: Tett 5C **26**
Meadow Vw. Mobile Home Pk.
WV10: Cov H 1G **15**
Meadow Vw. Ter. WV6: Tett 5C **26**
(not continuous)
Meadow Vw. Wharf WV6: Tett 5C **26**
Meadow Wlk. B14: K Hth 6G **147**
B64: Crad H 3F **111**
Meadow Way DY8: Word 1A **108**
WV8: Cod 5E **13**
Mead Ri. B15: Edg 5B **116**
Meadthorpe Rd. B44: Gt Barr 5F **67**
Meadvale Rd. B45: Redn 3H **157**
Meadway B33: Yard 1D **120**
Meadway, The WV6: Tett 4G **25**
Meadwood Ind. Est.
WV14: Bils 6G **45**
Mears Cl. B23: Erd 5D **68**
Mears Coppice DY5: Quar B 5A **110**
DY9: Lye 5A **110**
Mears Dr. B33: Stech 5B **104**
Mease Cft. B9: Birm 1B **118**
Measham Gro. B26: Yard 6C **120**
Measham Way WV11: Wed 2G **29**
Meaton Gro. B32: Bart G 5H **129**
Mecca Bingo
Acocks Green 1H **135**
Bilston 1E **61**
Brierley Hill 1H **109**
Great Barr 2H **67**
Oldbury 2F **97**
Wednesbury 3E **63**
Wolverhampton 2G **43** (4A **170**)
Medcroft Av. B20: Hand 3A **82**
Medina Cl. WV10: Bush 3B **16**
Medina Rd. B11: Tys 1E **135**
Medina Way DY6: K'wfrd 3A **92**
Medley Gdns. DY4: Tip 3D **78**
Medley Rd. B11: S'brk 6D **118**
Medlicott Rd. B11: S'brk 5C **118**
Medway Cl. DY5: P'ntt 3E **93**
Medway Ct. B73: S Cold 6H **53**
Medway Cft. B36: Cas B 2B **106**
Medway Gro. B38: K Nor 1A **160**
Medway Rd. WS8: Bwnhls 3G **9**
Medway Twr. B7: Nech 4B **102**
Medway Wlk. WS8: Bwnhls 3G **9**
Medwin Gro. B23: Erd 6D **68**
Meerash La. WS7: Hamm 2D **10**
Meer End B38: K Nor 2H **159**
Meerhill Av. B90: M'path 3E **165**
Meeting Ho. La. CV7: Bal C 5H **169**
Meetinghouse La. B31: N'fld 3E **145**

Meeting La. DY5: Brie H. 2F **109**
(not continuous)
Meeting La. Ind. Est. DY5: Brie H 2F **109**
Meeting St. DY2: Neth 4E **95**
DY4: Tip 1D **78**
WS10: W'bry 2E **63**
Megabowl
Birmingham 2G **117** (6F **5**)
Brierley Hill 1H **109**
Nechells *1D 102*
(in Star City)
Melbourne Av. B19: Hock 3E **101**
B66: Smeth 2F **99**
Melbourne Cl. B70: W Brom 6G **63**
DY6: K'wfrd 5C **92**
Melbourne Gdns. WS5: Wals 5F **49**
Melbourne Rd. B63: Hale 6B **112**
B66: Smeth 2E **99**
Melbourne St. WV2: Wolv 2H **43** (5C **170**)
Melbury Cl. WV3: Wolv 2E **43**
Melbury Gro. B14: K Hth 2G **147**
Melchett Rd. B30: K Nor 4B **146**
Melcote Gro. B44: Gt Barr 5G **67**
Meldon Dr. WV14: Bils 3A **62**
Melford Cl. DY3: Sed 3G **59**
Melford Hall Rd. B91: Sol 6D **136**
Melfort Gro. B14: K Hth 4A **148**
Melksham Sq. B35: Cas V 4E **87**
Mellis Gro. B23: Erd 2A **84**
Mellish Ct. *WS4: Wals* *6E 33*
(off Mellish Rd.)
Mellish Dr. WS4: Wals 6F **33**
Mellish Rd. WS4: Wals 6E **33**
Mellor Dr. B74: Four O 6E **37**
Mellors Cl. B17: Harb 2F **131**
Mellowdew Rd. DY8: Word 6A **92**
Mell Sq. B91: Sol 3G **151**
Melplash Av. B91: Sol 3E **151**
Melrose Av. *B11: S'hll* *5C 118*
(off Walford Rd.)
B12: Bal H 5A **118**
B71: W Brom 5B **64**
B73: S Cold 3E **69**
DY8: Stourb 3D **124**
Melrose Cl. B38: K Nor 6B **146**
Melrose Cotts. WS14: Muck C. 4H **11**
Melrose Dr. WV6: Pert 5D **24**
Melrose Gro. B19: Loz 2D **100**
Melrose Pl. B66: Smeth 1B **98**
Melrose Rd. B20: Hand 6G **83**
Melstock Cl. DY4: Tip 2F **77**
Melstock Rd. B14: K Hth 6F **133**
Melton Av. B92: Olton 1E **137**
Melton Dr. B15: Edg 4E **117**
Melton Gro. B33: Kitts G 6A **106**
Melton Rd. B14: K Hth 5H **133**
Melverley Gro. B44: K'sdng 5H **67**
Melverton Av. WV10: Bush 1H **27**
Melville Hall B16: Edg 2G **115**
Melville Rd. B16: Edg 2G **115**
Melvina Rd. B7: Birm 5B **102**
Membury Rd. B8: Salt 3D **102**
Memorial Cl. WV13: W'hall 1A **46**
Memory La. WS10: Darl 3D **46**
WV11: Wed 4D **28**
Menai Cl. WV12: W'hall 3C **30**
Menai Wlk. B37: F'bri 5D **106**
Mendip Av. B8: Salt 4E **103**
Mendip Cl. B63: Hale 4F **127**
DY3: Lwr G 4H **75**
WV2: E'shll 5B **44**
Mendip Rd. B8: Salt 5E **103**
B63: Hale 4F **127**
DY8: Amb 5F **109**
Menin Cres. B13: Mose 6B **134**
Menin Pas. B13: Mose 5B **134**
Menin Rd. B13: Mose 5B **134**
DY4: Tip 2F **77**
Mentone Ct. B20: Hand 4A **82**
Meon Gro. B33: Sheld 3F **121**
WV6: Pert 5F **25**
Meon Ri. DY9: Pedm 2G **125**
Meon Way WV11: Wed 2H **29**
Meranti Cl. WV12: W'hall 1C **30**
Mercer Av. B46: Wat O 4C **88**
Mercer Gro. WV11: Wed 2G **29**
Merchants Way WS9: A'rdge 2C **34**
Mercia Dr. B14: K Hth 1F **147**
WV6: Pert 4E **25**
Mercote Hall La. CV7: Mer 2G **155**
Mere Av. B35: Cas V 4E **87**
Mere Cl. WV12: W'hall 4A **30**
Merecote Rd. B92: Olton 6B **136**
Mere Cft. WS11: Nort C 1D **8**
Meredith Rd. DY3: Lwr G 2E **75**
WV11: Wed 1E **29**
Merediths Pool Cl. B18: Hock 3B **100**
Meredith St. B64: Crad H 2F **111**
MERE GREEN **6A 38**
Mere Grn. Cl. B75: Four O 1A **54**
Mere Grn. Rd. B75: Four O 1H **53**
Mere Oak Rd. WV6: Pert 4E **25**
Mere Pool Rd. B75: R'ley 1B **54**
Mere Rd. B23: Erd 4C **84**
DY8: Stourb 2C **124**
Mereside Way B92: Olton 5C **136**
Meres Rd. B63: Crad 6E **111**
Merevale Rd. B92: Sol 3F **137**
Mere Vw. WS4: S'fld 1G **33**
MERIDEN **4H 141**
Meriden Av. DY8: Woll 5B **108**
Meriden Cl. B25: Yard 4H **119**
DY8: Woll 5B **108**
Meriden Dr. B37: K'hrst 3C **106**
Meriden Ri. B92: Sol 2H **137**
Meriden Rd. B92: H Ard 6B **140**
CV7: Mer 6B **140**
WV10: Oxl 1E **27**
Meriden St. B5: Birm 1H **117** (6G **5**)
Merino Av. B31: Longb 1E **159**
Merlin Cl. B35: Cas V 4E **87**
DY1: Dud 1B **94**
Merlin Gro. B26: Sheld 6F **121**
Merrick Cl. B63: Hale 3F **127**
Merrick Rd. WV11: Wed 3A **30**
MERRIDALE **2D 42**
Merridale Av. WV3: Wolv 2D **42**
Merridale Ct. WV3: Wolv 2D **42**
Merridale Cres. WV3: Wolv 1E **43**
Merridale Gdns. WV3: Wolv 2E **43**
Merridale Gro. WV3: Wolv 2C **42**
(not continuous)
Merridale La. WV3: Wolv 1E **43**
Merridale Rd. WV3: Wolv 2D **42**
Merridale St. WV3: Wolv 2F **43** (5A **170**)
Merridale St. W. WV3: Wolv 3E **43**
Merrill Cl. WS6: C Hay 3E **7**
Merrill's Hall La. WV11: Wed 5G **29**
Merrington Cl. B91: Sol 1G **165**
Merrions Cl. B43: Gt Barr 1A **66**
Merrishaw Rd. B31: Longb 1E **159**
Merritts Brook Cl. B29: W Cas 2E **145**
Merritt's Brook La. B31: N'fld 3C **144**
Merritt's Hill B31: N'fld 1B **144**
Merrivale Rd. B62: B'hth 3F **113**
B66: Smeth 1E **115**
Merryfield Cl. B92: Sol 6H **137**
Merryfield Gro. B17: Harb 1G **131**
Merryfield Rd. DY1: Dud 1H **93**
MERRY HILL
Brierley Hill **6A 94**
Wolverhampton **4B 42**
Merry Hill DY5: Brie H, Quar B 2B **110**
Merry Hill Cen. DY5: Brie H 6B **94**
Merry Hill Ct. B66: Smeth 3H **99**
Merryhill Dr. B18: Hock 3B **100**
Merryhills Ent. Pk. WV10: Wolv 4B **28**
Mersey Gro. B38: K Nor 1A **160**
Mersey Pl. WS3: Blox 6C **20**
Mersey Rd. WS3: Blox 6C **20**
Merstal Dr. B92: Sol 6B **138**
Merstone Cl. WV14: Bils 5E **45**
Merstowe Cl. B27: A Grn 2H **135**
Merton Cl. B68: O'bry 1H **113**
Merton Ho. B37: F'bri 1B **122**
Merton Rd. B13: Mose 2B **134**
Mervyn Pl. WV14: Bils 2H **61**
Mervyn Rd. B21: Hand 6A **82**
WV14: Bils 2H **61**
Meryhurst Rd. WS10: W'bry 6G **47**
Messenger La. B70: W Brom 4B **80**
Messenger Rd. B66: Smeth 3F **99**
MESTY CROFT **2H 63**
Metchley Abbey B17: Harb 6H **115**
Metchley Ct. B17: Harb 1H **131**
Metchley Cft. B90: M'path 3D **164**
Metchley Dr. B17: Harb 6G **115**
Metchley Gro. *B18: Win G* *5A 100*
(off Heath Grn. Rd.)
Metchley Ho. B17: Harb 6H **115**
Metchley La. B17: Harb 1H **131**
Metchley Pk. Rd. B15: Edg 1H **131**
Metfield Cft. B17: Harb 1H **131**
DY6: K'wfrd 3D **92**
Metric Wlk. B67: Smeth 4E **99**
Metropolitan Ho. *B16: Birm* *2C 116*
(off Hagley Rd.)
Metropolitan Lofts *DY1: Dud* *6E 77*
(off Parson's St.)
Metro Triangle B7: Nech 2D **102**
Metro Way B66: Smeth 2G **99**
Mews, The B27: A Grn 2H **135**
B44: K'sdng 6B **68**
B65: Row R 1B **112**
Meynell Ho. B20: Hand 4B **82**
Meyrick Rd. B70: W Brom 1G **79**
Meyrick Wlk. B16: Edg 2B **116**
Miall Pk. Rd. B91: Sol 2C **150**
Miall Rd. B28: Hall G 5G **135**
Michael Blanning Gdns. B93: Dorr 6A **166**
Michael Blanning Ho. *B13: Mose* *3B 134*
(off Wake Grn. Pk.)
Michael Blanning Pl. CV7: Bal C 2H **169**
Michael Ct. B5: Edg 5F **117**
Michael Dr. B15: Edg 4E **117**
Michael Rd. B67: Smeth 3C **98**
WS10: Darl 4B **46**
Michelle Cl. B13: Mose 2A **148**
Micklehill Dr. B90: Shir 1H **163**
Mickle Mdw. B46: Wat O 4D **88**
Mickleover Rd. B8: W End 4A **104**
Mickleton Av. B33: Sheld 3G **121**
Mickleton Rd. B92: Olton 5B **136**
Mickley Av. WV10: Wolv 4A **28**
Midacre WV13: W'hall 2A **46**
Middle Acre Rd. B32: Bart G 3C **130**
Middle Av. WV13: W'hall 3G **45**
Middle Bickenhill La. B92: Bick 1A **140**
Middle Cres. WS3: Wals 2E **33**
Middle Cross WV1: Wolv 2H **43** (4D **170**)
Middle Dr. B45: Coft H 5B **158**
Middlefield WV8: Pend 5C **14**
Middlefield Av. B62: B'hth 3F **113**
B93: Know 5D **166**
Middlefield Cl. B62: B'hth 2F **113**
Middlefield Gdns. *B62: B'hth* *3F 113*
(off Hurst Grn. Rd.)
Middlefield Ho. *B14: K Hth* *4H 147*
(off Britford Cl.)
Middle Fld. Rd. B31: N'fld 5G **145**
Middlefield Rd. B69: Tiv 1A **96**
Middle Gdns. WV13: W'hall 1B **46**
MIDDLE HILL JUNC. **1A 6**
Middlehill Ri. B32: Bart G 3B **130**
Middle La. B38: Head H 3E **161**
B47: Wyt 5G **161**
WV8: Oaken 5C **12**
WV9: Coven 3D **14**
Middle Leaford B34: Stech 4E **105**
Middle Leasowe B32: Quin 1A **130**
Middle Mdw. DY4: Tip 2B **78**
Middle Mdw. Av. B32: Quin 6A **114**
Middlemist Gro. B43: Gt Barr 1B **82**
Middlemore Bus. Pk. WS9: A'rdge 4H **33**
Middlemore Ind. Est. B21: Hand 1F **99**
Middlemore La. WS9: A'rdge 3B **34**
Middlemore La. W. WS9: A'rdge 3H **33**
Middlemore Rd. B21: Hand 2F **99**
B31: N'fld 5F **145**
B66: Hand, Smeth 2F **99**
B71: W Brom 2F **99**
Middle Pk. Cl. B29: W Cas 5F **131**
Middle Pk. Dr. B31: N'fld 1F **145**
Middle Pk. Rd. B29: W Cas 5F **131**
Middlepark Rd. DY1: Dud 1A **94**
Middle Rd. B61: Wild 5A **156**
Middleton Cl. WS5: Wals 6D **48**
(not continuous)
Middleton Gdns. B30: K Nor 3H **145**
Middleton Grange B31: N'fld 3G **145**
Middleton Hall Rd. B30: K Nor 3H **145**

Middleton Rd. B14: K Hth 6G **133**
B74: S'tly 2A **52**
B90: Shir 5G **149**
WS8: Bwnhls 4C **10**
Middleton Trad. Est. WV13: W'hall 1G **45**
Middletree Rd. B63: Crad 4E **111**
Middle Vauxhall WV1: Wolv 1E **43**
Middleway B15: Birm. 3D **116**
Middleway Av. DY8: Word 6A **92**
Middleway Grn. WV14: Bils 3E **45**
Middleway Ind. Est. *B12: Birm 4H 117*
(off Moseley Rd.)
Middleway Rd. WV14: Bils. 3E **45**
Middleway Vw. B18: Hock 6C **100**
Midgley Dr. B74: Four O 1G **53**
Midhill Dr. B65: Row R 3C **96**
Midhurst Gro. WV6: Tett 4A **26**
Midhurst Rd. B30: K Nor 4D **146**
Midland Cl. B21: Hand. 2C **100**
Midland Ct. *B3: Birm 5E 101*
(off Cox St.)
Midland Cft. B33: Kitts G. 1H **121**
Midland Dr. B72: S Cold 6A **54**
Midland Karting 5B **32**
Midland Rd. B30: K Nor. 2B **146**
B74: S Cold 4G **53**
WS1: Wals 2B **48**
WS10: Darl. 3C **46**
Midland Sailing Club. 6A **100**
Midlands Art Cen. 1F **133**
Midland St. B8: Birm 6C **102**
Midpoint Blvd. B76: Min 2G **87**
Midpoint Pk. B76: Min. 3G **87**
Midvale Dr. B14: K Hth. 5F **147**
Milburn Rd. B44: K'sdng 2A **68**
Milcote Dr. B73: New O 2C **68**
WV13: W'hall 2F **45**
Milcote Rd. B29: W Cas. 5E **131**
B67: Smeth 1D **114**
B91: Sol 3F **151**
Milcote Way DY6: K'wfrd. 2H **91**
Mildenhall Rd. B42: Gt Barr 4C **66**
Mildred Rd. B64: Old H 1G **111**
Mildred Way B65: Row R. 3C **96**
Milebrook Gro. B32: Bart G 5H **129**
Mile Flat DY6: K'wfrd. 3E **91**
Mile Oak Ct. B66: Smeth 3F **99**
Milesbush Av. B36: Cas B 6H **87**
Miles Gro. DY2: Dud 2H **95**
Miles Mdw. Cl. WV12: W'hall 1C **30**
Milestone Ct. WV6: Tett. 6G **25**
Milestone La. B21: Hand. 1H **99**
Milestone Way WV12: W'hall. 1B **30**
Milford Av. B12: Bal H 5A **118**
WV12: W'hall 4A **30**
Milford Cl. DY8: Word 6C **92**
Milford Copse B17: Harb 6F **115**
Milford Cft. B19: Birm 4F **101**
B65: Row R 3H **95**
Milford Gro. B90: M'path 2G **165**
Milford Pl. B14: K Hth 5G **133**
Milford Rd. B17: Harb 6F **115**
WV2: Wolv. 4G **43**
Milholme Grn. B92: Sol. 5H **137**
MILKING BANK. 5A **76**
Milking Bank DY1: Dud 5H **75**
Milk St. B5: Birm 2H **117** (6H **5**)
Millard Ind. Est. B70: W Brom 6G **79**
Millard Rd. WV14: Cose 4D **60**
Mill Bank DY3: Sed 5H **59**
Millbank Gro. B23: Erd 1B **84**
(not continuous)
Millbank St. WV11: Wed 6H **17**
Mill Brook Dr. B31: Longb 1C **158**
Millbrook Rd. B14: K Hth. 1E **147**
Millbrook Way DY5: Brie H. 3F **109**
Mill Burn Way B9: Birm 1B **118**
Mill Cl. B47: H'wd 2A **162**
Mill Cft. WV14: Bils 5G **45**
Millcroft Cl. B32: Bart G. 3C **130**
Millcroft Rd. B74: S'tly. 3A **52**
Milldale Cres. WV10: F'hses 3H **15**
Milldale Rd. WV10: F'hses 3H **15**
Mill Dr. B66: Smeth 4F **99**
Millenium Gdns. B64: Old H 1H **111**
Millennium Apartments B3: Birm 2C **4**
Millennium Cl. WS3: Pels 4E **21**
Millennium Pk. B70: W Brom 2G **79**
Millennium Point 6H **101** (3H **5**)
Millennium Way WV8: Bilb 3H **13**
Miller Ct. B33: Stech 6C **104**
Miller Cres. WV14: Cose 4C **60**
Millers Cl. WS2: Wals 2F **47**
Millers Ct. *B66: Smeth. 4F 99*
(off Corbett St.)
B90: Shir 5F **149**
Millersdale Dr. B71: W Brom 3D **64**
Millers Grn. Dr. DY6: W Hth 1G **91**
Miller St. B6: Aston 4G **101**
Millers Va. WV5: Wom 2D **72**
Millers Wlk. WS3: Pels 4C **20**
Mill Farm Rd. B17: Harb 2G **131**
Millfield B31: N'fld 3E **145**
Millfield Av. WS3: Blox 5B **20**
WS4: S'fld 6F **21**
Millfield Ct. *DY1: Dud 5C 76*
(off Pelham Dr.)
Millfield Rd. B20: Hand 2A **82**
WS8: Bwnhls 6C **10**
Millfields B33: Kitts G 6H **105**
(not continuous)
Millfields Cl. B71: W Brom 4H **63**
Millfields Rd. B71: W Brom 4H **63**
WV4: E'shll. 6C **44**
WV14: Bils 6C **44**
Millfields Way WV5: Wom. 1E **73**
Millfield Vw. B63: Hale 1G **127**
Millford Cl. B28: Hall G 2G **149**
Mill Gdns. B14: Yard W. 2D **148**
B67: Smeth 6D **98**
MILL GREEN **2A 36**
Mill Grn. WV10: F'hses 3H **15**
Mill Gro. WV8: Bilb 4A **14**
Millhaven Av. B30: Stir 1D **146**
Mill Hill B67: Smeth 6D **98**
Mill Ho. B8: W End 5B **104**
Mill Ho. La. B75: Can 1D **38**
Millhouse Rd. B25: Yard 3H **119**
Millicent Pl. B12: Bal H 5A **118**
Millichip Rd. WV13: W'hall 2G **45**
Millington Rd. B36: Hodg H. 1C **104**
DY4: Tip. 4H **61**
WV10: Bush. 3A **28**
Millison Gro. B90: M'path 2E **165**
Mill La. B5: Birm 2H **117** (6G **5**)
B31: N'fld. 6D **144**
B32: Bart G 3B **130**
B61: Wild 6A **156**
B63: Hale 1C **128**
B69: O'bry 5G **97**
B91: Sol. 4G **151**
B93: Dorr 5A **166**
DY3: Swind 4D **72**
DY7: Env, Stourt. 6A **90**
WS3: Wals 5D **32**
WS4: Wals 5D **32**
WS7: Hamm. 2F **11**
WS9: A'rdge. 2H **35**
WS9: Ston 3H **23**
WV5: Wom. 6H **57**
WV6: Tett. 6G **25**
WV8: Cod 1E **13**
WV11: Wed 2C **28**
WV12: W'hall 4C **30**
Mill La. Arc. *B91: Sol 4G 151*
(off Touchwood Shop. Cen.)
Millmead Lodge B13: Mose. 5D **134**
Mill Mdw. DY8: Amb 5E **109**
Millmead Rd. B32: Bart G 3C **130**
Mill Pl. WS3: Wals. 5C **32**
Millpool, The WV5: Seis 3A **56**
Mill Pool Cl. WV5: Wom 2D **72**
Millpool Gdns. B14: K Hth. 4H **147**
Millpool Hill B14: K Hth. 3H **147**
Millpool Way B66: Smeth 5E **99**
Mill Race La. DY8: Amb 5E **109**
Mill Rd. B64: Crad H 4G **111**
WS4: S'fld 6F **21**
WS8: Bwnhls 6C **10**
Mills Av. B76: Walm. 1C **70**
Mills Cl. WV11: Wed 1D **28**
Mills Cres. WV2: Wolv. 3A **44**
Millside B28: Hall G 4E **149**
WV5: Wom. 2E **73**
Mills Rd. WV2: Wolv 3A **44**
Millstone Cl. B76: Walm 4D **70**
Mill Stream Cl. WV8: Bilb 3H **13**
Mill St. B6: Birm 4H **101**
B63: Crad 4E **111**
B70: W Brom 3A **80**
B72: S Cold 6A **54**
DY4: Tip. 2D **78**
DY5: Brie H 1H **109**
DY8: Word 1C **108**
WS2: Wals 6C **32**
WS10: Darl. 5C **46**
WV13: W'hall 1C **46**
WV14: Bils 6E **45**
Millsum Ho. *WS1: Wals. 2D 48*
(off Paddock La.)
Mills Wlk. DY4: Tip 6H **61**
Millthorpe Cl. B8: W End 4F **103**
Mill Vw. B33: Kitts G 5G **105**
Mill Wlk., The B31: N'fld. 6D **144**
Millwalk Dr. WV9: Pend. 4E **15**
Millward St. B9: Small H 2C **118**
B70: W Brom 4G **79**
Millwright Cl. DY4: Tip 2B **78**
Milner Rd. B29: S Oak. 4C **132**
Milner Way B13: Mose 5D **134**
Milnes Walker Ct. B44: Gt Barr. 4G **67**
Milsom Gro. B34: S End 3H **105**
Milstead Rd. B26: Yard 2E **121**
Milston Cl. B14: K Hth. 6G **147**
Milton Av. B12: Bal H. 5A **118**
Milton Cl. B93: Ben H 5B **166**
DY8: Amb. 4E **109**
WS1: Wals 5B **48**
WV12: W'hall 2E **31**
Milton Ct. B66: Smeth 2E **115**
WV6: Pert. 5E **25**
Milton Cres. B25: Yard. 4B **120**
DY3: Lwr G. 2E **75**
Milton Dr. DY9: Hag. 6H **125**
Milton Gro. B29: S Oak 2B **132**
Milton Pl. WS1: Wals. 5B **48**
Milton Rd. B67: Smeth. 4B **98**
B93: Ben H. 5B **166**
WV10: Wolv 4C **28**
WV14: Cose 5F **61**
Milton St. B71: W Brom. 2H **79**
DY5: P'ntt 3H **93**
WS1: Wals 3B **48**
Milverton Cl. B63: Hale 5A **112**
B76: Walm 6D **70**
Milverton Ct. *B62: Quin 4G 113*
(off Binswood Rd.)
Milverton Rd. B23: Erd. 3E **85**
B93: Know 4E **167**
Mimosa Cl. B29: W Cas 5F **131**
Mimosa Wlk. DY6: K'wfrd 1C **92**
Mincing La. B65: Row R 6D **96**
Mindelsohn Way B15: Edg. 1H **131**
Minden Gro. B29: S Oak. 4F **131**
Minehead Rd. DY1: Dud 1H **93**
WV10: Oxl 5F **15**
Miner St. WS2: Wals 6A **32**
Minerva Cl. WV12: W'hall 5E **31**
Minewood Cl. WS3: Blox 4F **19**
Minith Rd. WV14: Cose 5F **61**
Miniva Dr. B76: Walm 4E **71**
Minivet Dr. B12: Bal H 5G **117**
Minley Av. B17: Harb. 4D **114**
Minories B4: Birm. 6G **101** (3E **5**)
Minories, The DY2: Dud. 6E **77**
Minstead Rd. B24: Erd. 6D **84**
Minster, The WV3: Wolv 4D **42**
Minster Cl. B65: Row R 6E **97**
B93: Know. 1D **166**
Minster Ct. B13: Mose 1A **134**
B29: W Cas 6G 131
(off Abdon Av.)
Minster Dr. B10: Small H. 4D **118**
Minsterley Cl. WV3: Wolv 3C **42**
Mintern Rd. B25: Yard. 3A **120**
Minto Ho. B12: Bal H 6G **117**
Minton Cl. WV1: Wolv 2C **44**
Minton Rd. B32: Quin 1D **130**
MINWORTH 2H **87**
Minworth Ind. Est. B76: Min 1E **87**
Minworth Ind. Pk. B76: Min. 1G **87**

Minworth Rd.—Morley Rd.

Minworth Rd. B46: Wat O 4C 88
Miranda Cl. B45: Fran 4G 143
Mirfield Cl. WV9: Pend 4E 15
Mirfield Rd. B33: Kitts G 1F 121
B91: Sol 1E 151
Mission Cl. B64: Old H. 2A 112
Mission Dr. DY4: Tip 4A 78
Mistletoe Dr. WS5: Wals 2F 65
Mitcham Ct. *B29: W Cas 6G 131*
(off Abdon Av.)
Mitcham Gro. B44: K'sdng 4B 68
Mitcheldean Covert B14: K Hth 5F 147
Mitchell Av. WV14: Cose 4D 60
Mitchells Art & Craft Cen. 1C 54
Mitchel Rd. DY6: K'wfrd 5D 92
Mitford Dr. B92: Sol 6H 137
Mitre Cl. WV11: Ess 4A 18
WV12: W'hall 2D 30
Mitre Ct. B74: S Cold 5A 54
Mitre Fold WV1: Wolv 1G 43 (2A 170)
Mitre Rd. DY9: Lye 6A 110
WS6: C Hay 3C 6
Mitten Av. B45: Fran 6F 143
Mitton Rd. B20: Hand 5A 82
Moatbrook Av. WV8: Cod 3E 13
Moatbrook La. WV8: Cod 2C 12
Moat Coppice B32: Bart G 4H 129
Moat Cft. B37: F'bri 1C 122
B76: Walm 6F 71
Moat Dr. B62: B'hth 2E 113
Moat Farm Dr. B32: Bart G 4G 129
Moat Farm Way WS3: Pels 2E 21
Moatfield Ter. WS10: W'bry 2G 63
Moat Grn. Av. WV11: Wed 2G 29
Moat Ho. B31: Longb 1D 158
Moat Ho. La. E. WV11: Wed 2F 29
Moat Ho. La. W. WV11: Wed 2F 29
Moat Ho. Rd. B8: W End 5G 103
Moat La. B5: Birm 1G 117 (6F 5)
B26: Yard 4C 120
B91: Sol 1G 151
WS6: Gt Wyr 3G 7
Moat Mdws. B32: Quin 1C 130
Moatmead Wlk. B36: Hodg H 1C 104
Moat Rd. B68: O'bry 1H 113
DY4: Tip 6A 62
WS2: Wals 1H 47
Moatside Cl. WS3: Pels 2E 21
Moat St. WV13: W'hall 1A 46
Moatway, The B38: K Nor 2A 160
Mobberley Rd. WV14: Cose 4C 60
Mob La. WS4: S'fld 5G 21
Mockleywood Rd. B93: Know 2D 166
Modbury Av. B32: Bart G 4B 130
Moden Cl. DY3: Up Gor 2H 75
Moden Hill DY3: Sed 1G 75
Mogul La. B63: Crad 4C 110
Moilliett Ct. B66: Smeth 3G 99
Moilliett St. B18: Win G. 5H 99
Moira Cres. B14: Yard W 3C 148
Moises Hall Rd. WV5: Wom 6H 57
Moland St. B4: Birm 5G 101
Mole St. B11: S'brk 5B 118
Molineux 6G 27 (1A 170)
Molineux All. WV1: Wolv 6G 27 (1A 170)
(not continuous)
Molineux Fold WV1: Wolv 6G 27 (1B 170)
Molineux St. WV1: Wolv 6G 27 (1B 170)
Mollington Cres. B90: Shir 4A 150
Molyneux Rd. DY2: Neth 1G 111
Monaco Ho. B5: Birm 3F 117
Monarch Dr. DY4: Tip 1C 78
Monarch Ind. Est. B11: Tys 5G 119
Monarchs Ga. B91: Sol 2A 152
Monarch Way DY2: Neth 5E 95
Mona Rd. B23: Erd 2F 85
Monastery Dr. B91: Sol 1B 150
Monckton Rd. B68: O'bry 4G 113
Moncrieffe Cl. DY2: Dud 1G 95
Moncrieffe St. WS1: Wals 2E 49
Money La. B61: C'wich 4A 156
Monica Rd. B10: Small H 4F 119
Monins Av. DY4: Tip 4A 78
Monk Cl. DY4: Tip 4B 78
Monk Rd. B8: W End 4H 103
Monks Cl. WV5: Wom 1E 73
Monkseaton Rd. B72: W Grn 3H 69
Monksfield Av. B43: Gt Barr 4H 65
Monkshood M. B23: Erd 6B 68
Monkshood Retreat B38: K Nor 1B 160
Monks Kirby Rd. B76: Walm 2D 70
MONKSPATH 3E 165
Monkspath B76: Walm 5D 70
Monkspath Bus. Pk. B90: Shir 1D 164
Monkspath Cl. B90: Shir 2B 164
Monkspath Hall Rd. B90: M'path 3D 164
B91: Sol 1F 165
Monkspath Leisure Pk. 3C 164
Monksway B38: K Nor 6D 146
Monkswell Cl. B10: Small H 4D 118
DY5: Brie H 2H 109
Monkswood Rd. B31: N'fld 5G 145
Monkton Rd. B29: W Cas 2E 131
Monmar Ct. WV12: W'hall 4B 30
Monmer Cl. WV13: W'hall 6B 30
Monmer Cl. Ind. Est. WV13: W'hall 6C 30
Monmer La. WV12: W'hall 5B 30
WV13: W'hall 5B 30
Monmore Bus. Pk. WV2: Wolv 4B 44
MONMORE GREEN 3A 44
Monmore Green Stadium 3C 44
Monmore Pk. Ind. Est. WV2: E'shll 4B 44
Monmore Rd. WV1: Wolv 3C 44
Monmouth Dr. B71: W Brom 6H 63
B73: New O, S Cold 2C 68
Monmouth Ho. B33: Kitts G 1A 122
Monmouth Rd. B32: Bart G 5B 130
B67: Smeth 3C 114
WS2: Wals 6E 31
Monsal Av. WV10: Wolv 5A 28
Monsaldale Cl. WS8: Clay 1H 21
Monsal Rd. B42: Gt Barr 6E 67
Mons Rd. DY2: Dud 6G 77
Montague Rd. B16: Edg 2A 116
B21: Hand 1B 100
B24: Erd 6G 85
B66: Smeth 6F 99
Montague St. B6: Aston 1B 102
B9: Birm 1A 118
Montana Av. B42: P Barr 2C 82
Monteagle Dr. DY6: K'wfrd 6B 74
Montford Gro. DY3: Sed 6H 59
Montfort Rd. B46: Col 4H 107
WS2: Wals 5H 47
Montfort Wlk. B32: Bart G 3G 129
Montgomery Cres. DY5: Quar B 4B 110
Montgomery Cft. B11: S'brk 4C 118
Montgomery Rd. WS2: Wals 1E 47
Montgomery St. B11: S'brk 4B 118
Montgomery St. Bus. Cen.
B11: S'brk 4C 118
Montgomery Wlk. B71: W Brom 3B 80
Montgomery Way B8: Salt 5G 103
Montpelier Rd. B24: Erd 6G 85
Montpellier Gdns. DY1: Dud 5A 76
Montpellier St. B12: Birm 5A 118
Montreal Ho. B5: Bal H. 4F 117
Montrose Dr. B35: Cas V 4E 87
DY1: Dud 1C 94
Montsford Cl. B93: Know 3B 166
Monument Av. DY9: W'cte 1A 126
Monument La. B45: Lick 5F 157
DY3: Sed 4A 60
DY9: Hag 6H 125
Monument Rd. B16: Edg 2B 116
(not continuous)
Monway Ind. Est. WS10: W'bry 2E 63
Monway Ter. WS10: W'bry 2E 63
Monwood Gro. B91: Sol 5D 150
Monyhull Hall Rd. B30: K Nor 5D 146
Moodyscroft Rd. B33: Kitts G 6G 105
Moons La. WS6: C Hay 3D 6
Moor, The B76: Walm 5E 71
Moor Cen., The DY5: Brie H 6H 93
Moorcroft WV14: Bils 2A 62
Moorcroft Dr. WS10: W'bry 3C 62
Moorcroft Pl. B7: Birm 5A 102
Moorcroft Rd. B13: Mose 2G 133
Moordown Av. B92: Olton 3E 137
Moore Cl. B74: Four O 3F 37
WV6: Pert 5F 25
Moore Cres. B68: O'bry 6A 98
Moorend Av. B37: Chel W, Mars G 3B 122
Moor End La. B24: Erd 3G 85
Moore Rd. WV12: W'hall 1D 30
Moore's Row B5: Birm 2H 117 (6H 5)
Moore St. WV1: Wolv 2B 44
Moorfield Av. B93: Know 3A 166
Moorfield Dr. B63: Hale 5H 111
B73: Bold 5F 69
Moorfield Rd. B34: S End 3E 105
WV2: Wolv 4G 43
Moorfoot Av. B63: Hale 4E 127
MOOR GREEN 3F 133
Moor Grn. La. B13: Mose 4E 133
Moor Hall Dr. B75: R'ley 3A 54
Moorhills Cft. B90: Shir 1H 163
Moor Ho. *B14: K Hth 5E 147*
(off Druids La.)
Moorings, The B18: Win G. 4B 100
B69: O'bry 1E 97
DY5: Brie H 5C 94
WV9: Pend 5D 14
Moorland Av. WV10: Oxl 3G 27
Moorland Rd. B16: Edg 2H 115
WS3: Blox 1G 31
Moorlands, The B74: Four O 3F 53
Moorlands Cl. B75: S Cold 5D 54
Moorlands Ct. B65: Row R 5D 96
Moorlands Dr. B90: Shir 4A 150
Moorlands Rd. B71: W Brom 4A 64
Moor La. B6: Witt 1H 83
B65: Row R 1A 112
Moor La. Ind. Est. B6: Witt 3A 84
Moor Leasow B31: N'fld 5G 145
Moor Mdw. Rd. B75: S Cold 4B 54
Moor Pk. WS3: Blox 4H 19
WV6: Pert 4D 24
Moorpark Rd. B31: Longb 6E 145
Moor Pool Av. B17: Harb 5G 115
Moorpool Ter. B17: Harb 5G 115
Moors, The B36: Hodg H 1D 104
Moors Cft. B32: Bart G 4H 129
Moorside Gdns. WS2: Wals 6H 31
Moorside Rd. B14: Yard W 3C 148
Moor's La. B31: N'fld 5C 130
Moors Mill La. DY4: Tip 6D 62
Moorsom St. B6: Aston 4G 101
MOOR STREET 3G 129
Moor St. B5: Birm 5F 5
B70: W Brom 5A 80
DY5: Brie H 6E 93
WS10: W'bry 3H 63
Moor St. Ind. Est. DY5: Brie H. 1G 109
Moor St. Queensway
B4: Birm 1G 117 (4F 5)
Moor St. Sth. WV2: Wolv 4G 43
Moor Street Station (Rail) . . . 1G 117 (4F 5)
Moorville Wlk. B11: S'brk 4A 118
Morar Cl. B35: Cas V 3G 87
Moray Cl. B62: B'hth 3E 113
Morcom Rd. B11: Tys 6E 119
Mordaunt Dr. B75: R'ley 1C 54
Morden Rd. B33: Stech 6B 104
Morefields Cl. WS9: A'rdge 2C 34
Moreland Cft. B76: Walm 1F 87
Morelands, The B31: N'fld 6F 145
Morestead Av. B26: Sheld 6G 121
Moreton Av. B43: Gt Barr 2E 67
WV4: E'shll 1A 60
Moreton Cl. B25: Yard 4H 119
B32: Harb 6D 114
(not continuous)
DY4: Tip 3B 62
Moreton Rd. B90: Shir 5A 150
WV10: Bush 6H 15
Moreton St. B1: Birm 5D 100
Morford Rd. WS9: A'rdge 2C 34
Morgan Cl. B64: Old H. 3G 111
B69: O'bry 1D 96
WV12: W'hall 5B 30
Morgan Ct. B24: Erd 1A 86
Morgan Dr. WV14: Cose 5D 60
Morgan Gro. B36: Cas B 6B 88
Morgans Bus. Pk. WS11: Nort C 1D 8
Morgrove Av. B93: Know 3B 166
Morjon Dr. B43: Gt Barr 3B 66
Morland Rd. B31: N'fld 6D 144
B43: Gt Barr 1E 67
Morley Gro. WV6: Wolv 5G 27
Morley Rd. B8: W End 3H 103

Morlich Ri.—Napton Gro.

Morlich Ri. DY5: Brie H . . . 3F **109**
Morning Pines DY8: Stourb . . . 1C **124**
Morningside B73: S Cold . . . 5H **53**
Mornington Ct. B46: Col . . . 2H **107**
Mornington Rd. B66: Smeth . . . 2F **99**
Morris Av. WS2: Wals . . . 1E **47**
Morris Cl. B27: A Grn . . . 1B **136**
Morris Cft. B36: Cas B . . . 6A **88**
Morris Fld. Cft. B28: Hall G . . . 3E **149**
Morrison Av. WV10: Bush . . . 1H **27**
Morrison Rd. DY4: Tip . . . 3C **78**
Morris Rd. B8: W End . . . 3H **103**
Morris St. B70: W Brom . . . 6A **80**
Mortimers Cl. B14: K Hth . . . 6B **148**
Morton Rd. DY5: Quar B . . . 4H **109**
Morvale Gdns. DY9: Lye . . . 6A **110**
Morvale St. DY9: Lye . . . 6A **110**
Morven Rd. B73: S Cold . . . 3F **69**
Morville Cl. B93: Dorr . . . 6H **165**
Morville Cft. WV14: Bils . . . 1D **60**
Morville Rd. DY2: Neth . . . 5F **95**
Morville St. B16: Birm . . . 2C **116**
(not continuous)
Mosborough Cres. B19: Birm . . . 4E **101**
Mosedale Dr. WV11: Wed . . . 4H **29**
MOSELEY
B13 . . . **2H 133**
WV10 . . . **3C 16**
WV13 . . . **1E 45**
Moseley Bog Nature Reserve . . . 4C 134
Moseley Ct. B13: Mose . . . 3B **134**
WV11: Ess . . . 4H **17**
WV13: W'hall . . . 2F **45**
Moseley Dr. B37: Mars G . . . 3B **122**
Moseley Ga. B13: Mose . . . 2H **133**
Moseley Old Hall WV10: F'stne . . . 2C **16**
Moseley Old Hall La.
WV10: F'stne . . . 2C **16**
Moseley Pk. Sports Cen. . . . 3G 45
Moseley Rd. B12: Bal H, Birm . . . 6H **117**
(not continuous)
WV10: Bush . . . 2B **16**
WV13: W'hall . . . 2F **45**
Moseley Road Swimming Pool . . . 6H 117
Moseley RUFC . . . 2B 132
Moseley St. B5: Birm . . . 2H **117**
B12: Birm . . . 2H **117**
DY4: Tip . . . 6C **62**
WV10: Wolv . . . 5G **27**
Moss Cl. WS4: Wals . . . 6E **33**
WS9: A'rdge . . . 4C **34**
Mossdale Way DY3: Sed . . . 6A **60**
Moss Dr. B72: W Grn . . . 2A **70**
Mossfield Rd. B14: K Hth . . . 6G **133**
Moss Gdns. WV14: Cose . . . 2D **60**
Moss Gro. B14: K Hth . . . 1F **147**
DY6: K'wfrd . . . 2B **92**
Moss Ho. Cl. B15: Birm . . . 2D **116**
Mossley Cl. WS3: Blox . . . 6F **19**
Mossley La. WS3: Blox . . . 5F **19**
Mossvale Cl. B64: Old H . . . 2H **111**
Mossvale Gro. B8: Salt . . . 4F **103**
Moss Way B74: S'tly . . . 4H **51**
Mostyn Cres. B71: W Brom . . . 6H **63**
Mostyn Rd. B16: Edg . . . 1B **116**
B21: Hand . . . 1B **100**
Mostyn St. WV1: Wolv . . . 5F **27**
Mother Teresa Ho. *B70: W Brom . . . 4H 79*
(off Baker St.)
Motorway Trad. Est. B6: Birm . . . 4H **101**
Mott Cl. DY4: Tip . . . 5C **62**
Mottram Cl. B70: W Brom . . . 5G **79**
Mottrams Cl. B72: W Grn . . . 3A **70**
Mott St. B19: Birm . . . 5F **101** (1C **4**)
Mott St. Ind. Est. B19: Birm . . . 5F **101**
Motts Way B46: Col . . . 4H **107**
Mounds, The B38: K Nor . . . 1A **160**
Moundsley Gro. B14: K Hth . . . 4A **148**
Moundsley Ho. B14: K Hth . . . 5G **147**
Mount, The B23: Erd . . . 6D **84**
B64: Old H . . . 2A **112**
B76: Curd . . . 1E **89**
Mountain Ash Dr. DY9: Pedm . . . 3G **125**
Mountain Ash Rd. WS8: Clay . . . 2A **22**
Mount Av. DY5: Brie H . . . 5G **93**
Mountbatten Cl. B70: W Brom . . . 5D **80**
Mountbatten Rd. WS2: Wals . . . 1F **47**
Mount Cl. B13: Mose . . . 1H **133**
DY3: Gorn . . . 5G **75**
WS6: C Hay . . . 3E **7**
WV5: Wom . . . 6G **57**
Mount Ct. WV6: Tett . . . 1H **41**
Mount Dr. WV5: Wom . . . 6G **57**
Mountfield Cl. B14: K Hth . . . 5A **148**
Mountford Cl. B65: Row R . . . 6C **96**
Mountford Cres. WS9: A'rdge . . . 1E **35**
Mountford Dr. B75: Four O . . . 3H **53**
Mountford Ho. *B70: W Brom . . . 6C 80*
(off Glover St.)
Mountford La. WV14: Bils . . . 4F **45**
Mountford Rd. B90: Shir . . . 6D **148**
Mountford St. B11: S'hll . . . 6D **118**
Mount Gdns. WV8: Cod . . . 3F **13**
Mountjoy Cres. B92: Sol . . . 2G **137**
Mount La. DY3: Gorn . . . 5G **75**
Mt. Pleasant B10: Small H . . . 2B **118**
B14: K Hth . . . 4H **133**
DY5: Quar B . . . 2A **110**
DY6: K'wfrd . . . 4H **91**
WS6: C Hay . . . 3D **6**
WV14: Bils . . . 5G **45**
Mt. Pleasant Av. B21: Hand . . . 6A **82**
WV5: Wom . . . 6F **57**
Mt. Pleasant Ct. B10: Small H . . . 2B **118**
Mt. Pleasant St. B70: W Brom . . . 5A **80**
WV14: Cose . . . 5D **60**
Mountrath St. WS1: Wals . . . 2C **48**
Mount Rd. B21: Hand . . . 1H **99**
B65: Row R . . . 6E **97**
B69: Tiv . . . 1C **96**
DY8: Stourb . . . 6F **109**
DY8: Word . . . 1B **108**
WS3: Pels . . . 3E **21**
WV4: E'shll . . . 3B **60**
WV4: Penn . . . 6E **43**
WV5: Wom . . . 6G **57**
WV6: Tett . . . 1G **41**
WV13: W'hall . . . 3G **45**
Mounts Rd. WS10: W'bry . . . 3F **63**
Mount St. B7: Nech . . . 3C **102**
B63: Hale . . . 3A **128**
DY4: Tip . . . 1C **78**
DY8: Stourb . . . 6E **109**
WS1: Wals . . . 3C **48**
Mount St. Bus. Cen. B7: Nech . . . 3C **102**
Mount St. Ind. Est. B7: Nech . . . 2D **102**
Mounts Way B7: Nech . . . 2C **102**
Mount Vw. B75: S Cold . . . 1C **70**
Mountwood Covert WV6: Tett . . . 6H **25**
Mousehall Farm Rd. DY5: Quar B . . . 3H **109**
Mouse Hill WS3: Pels . . . 4D **20**
MOUSESWEET . . . **6G 95**
Mousesweet Brook Nature Reserve . . . 2D 110
Mousesweet Cl. DY2: Neth . . . 5G **95**
Mousesweet La. DY2: Neth . . . 6G **95**
Mousesweet Wlk. B64: Crad H . . . 3D **110**
Mowbray Cl. B45: Fran . . . 5G **143**
Mowbray St. B5: Birm . . . 3G **117**
Mowe Cft. B37: Mars G . . . 4C **122**
Moxhull Cl. WV12: W'hall . . . 6C **18**
Moxhull Dr. B76: Walm . . . 5C **70**
Moxhull Gdns. WV12: W'hall . . . 6C **18**
Moxhull Rd. B37: K'hrst . . . 4C **106**
MOXLEY . . . **1B 62**
Moxley Ct. WS10: Mox . . . 1A **62**
Moxley Ind. Cen. WS10: Mox . . . 1C **62**
Moxley Rd. WS10: Darl . . . 1B **62**
Moyle Dr. B63: Crad . . . 4D **110**
Moyses Cft. B66: Smeth . . . 1E **99**
Muchall Rd. WV4: Penn . . . 6E **43**
MUCKLEY CORNER . . . **4H 11**
Mucklow Hill B62: Hale . . . 1C **128**
Mucklow Hill Trad. Est. B62: Hale . . . 6C **112**
Muirfield Cl. WS3: Blox . . . 4G **19**
Muirfield Cres. B69: Tiv . . . 2A **96**
Muirfield Gdns. B38: K Nor . . . 6H **145**
Muirhead Ho. B5: Edg . . . 5E **117**
Muirville Cl. DY8: Word . . . 6B **92**
Mulberry Dr. B13: Mose . . . 4B **134**
Mulberry Grn. DY1: Dud . . . 2B **76**
Mulberry Pl. WS3: Blox . . . 6F **19**
Mulberry Rd. B30: B'vlle . . . 2G **145**
WS3: Blox . . . 6F **19**
Mulberry Wlk. B74: S'tly . . . 3G **51**
Mull Cl. B45: Fran . . . 6E **143**
Mull Cft. B36: Cas B . . . 2C **106**
Mullens Gro. Rd. B37: K'hrst . . . 4C **106**
Mullett Rd. WV11: Wed . . . 2D **28**
Mullett St. DY5: P'ntt . . . 4F **93**
Mulliners Cl. B37: Chel W . . . 1E **123**
Mullion Cft. B38: K Nor . . . 6A **146**
Mulroy Rd. B74: S Cold . . . 5H **53**
Mulwych Rd. B33: Kitts G . . . 6A **106**
Munslow Gro. B31: Longb . . . 1D **158**
Muntz Ho. B16: Edg . . . 2C **116**
Muntz St. B10: Small H . . . 3D **118**
Murcroft Rd. DY9: W'cte . . . 4H **125**
Murdoch Dr. DY6: K'wfrd . . . 2A **92**
Murdoch Rd. WV14: Bils . . . 5A **46**
Murdock Ct. *WV12: W'hall . . . 2D 30*
(off Huntington Rd.)
Murdock Gro. B21: Hand . . . 2A **100**
Murdock Pl. *B66: Smeth . . . 5F 99*
(off Corbett St.)
Murdock Rd. B21: Hand . . . 1A **100**
B66: Smeth . . . 3H **99**
Murdock Way WS2: Wals . . . 3F **31**
(not continuous)
Murray Ct. B73: S Cold . . . 2G **69**
Murrell Cl. B5: Bal H . . . 4F **117**
Musborough Cl. B36: Cas B . . . 6G **87**
Muscott Gro. B17: Harb . . . 6F **115**
Muscovy Rd. B23: Erd . . . 4C **84**
Mus. of the Jewellery Quarter . . . 4E 101
(off Vyse St.)
Musgrave Cl. B76: Walm . . . 2C **70**
Musgrave Rd. B18: Hock . . . 3B **100**
MUSHROOM GREEN . . . **1D 110**
Mushroom Grn. DY2: Neth . . . 2D **110**
Mushroom Hall Rd. B68: O'bry . . . 4H **97**
Musk La. DY3: Lwr G . . . 4F **75**
Musk La. W. DY3: Lwr G . . . 4F **75**
Muswell Cl. B91: Sol . . . 2H **151**
Muxloe Cl. WS3: Blox . . . 4G **19**
Myatt Av. WS9: A'rdge . . . 4B **34**
WV2: E'shll . . . 5A **44**
Myatt Cl. WV2: E'shll . . . 5A **44**
Myatt Way WS9: A'rdge . . . 4B **34**
Myddleton St. B18: Hock . . . 5C **100**
Myles Ct. DY5: Brie H . . . 5H **93**
Mynors Cres. B47: H'wd . . . 4A **162**
Myring Dr. B75: S Cold . . . 5D **54**
Myrtle Av. B12: Bal H . . . 6A **118**
B14: K Hth . . . 5H **147**
Myrtle Cl. WV12: W'hall . . . 2E **31**
Myrtle Gro. B19: Hand . . . 1E **101**
WV3: Wolv . . . 5C **42**
Myrtle Pl. B29: S Oak . . . 3D **132**
Myrtle Rd. DY1: Dud . . . 4D **76**
Myrtle St. WV2: E'shll . . . 5B **44**
Myrtle Ter. DY4: Tip . . . 3B **62**
Myton Dr. B90: Shir . . . 5D **148**
Mytton Cl. DY2: Dud . . . 6G **77**
Mytton Gro. DY4: Tip . . . 2G **77**
Mytton Rd. B30: B'vlle . . . 2G **145**
B46: Wat O . . . 4C **88**
Myvod Rd. WS10: W'bry . . . 6G **47**

N

Naden Rd. B19: Hock . . . 3D **100**
Nadin Rd. B73: W Grn . . . 5G **69**
Nafford Gro. B14: K Hth . . . 5H **147**
Nagersfield Rd. DY5: Brie H . . . 6E **93**
Nailers Cl. B32: Bart G . . . 3F **129**
Nailers Row WV5: Wom . . . 2F **73**
Nailors Fold WV14: Cose . . . 3F **61**
Nailstone Cres. B27: A Grn . . . 5A **136**
Nairn Cl. B28: Hall G . . . 2F **149**
Nairn Rd. WS3: Blox . . . 3G **19**
Nally Dr. WV14: Cose . . . 3C **60**
Nanaimo Way DY6: K'wfrd . . . 5E **93**
Nansen Rd. B8: Salt . . . 4E **103**
B11: S'hll . . . 2C **134**
Nantmel Gro. B32: Bart G . . . 5A **130**
Naomi Way WS9: Wals W . . . 3D **22**
Napier Dr. DY4: Tip . . . 1C **78**
Napier Rd. WS2: Wals . . . 4G **31**
WV2: Wolv . . . 4H **43**
Napton Gro. B29: W Cas . . . 3D **130**

Narraway Gro. DY4: Tip 5D **62**
Narrowboat Way DY2: Dud 4C **94**
DY5: Brie H 5C **94**
Narrow La. B62: B'hth 3E **113**
WS2: Wals 4H **47**
WS8: Bwnhls 5B **10**
Naseby Dr. B63: Hale 3F **127**
Naseby Rd. B8: Salt 4F **103**
B91: Sol 1F **151**
WV6: Pert 6F **25**
Nash Av. WV6: Pert 6E **25**
Nash Cl. B65: B'hth 2C **112**
Nash Cft. B37: Mars G 3D **122**
Nash Sq. B42: P Barr 3F **83**
Nash Wlk. *B66: Smeth* *4G 99*
(off Poplar St.)
Nately Gro. B29: S Oak 3G **131**
Nathan Cl. B75: S Cold 3H **53**
National Exhibition Cen. 6F **123**
National Indoor Arena 1D **116** (4A **4**)
National Motorcycle Mus. 3A **140**
National Sea Life Cen. 1D **116** (4A **4**)
Naunton Cl. B29: W Cas 6E **131**
Naunton Rd. WS2: Wals 6G **31**
Navenby Cl. B90: Shir 4C **148**
Navigation Dr. DY5: Brie H 5C **94**
Navigation La. WS10: W'bry 3D **64**
Navigation Rdbt. DY4: Tip 1E **79**
Navigation St. B2: Birm 1F **117** (5C **4**)
WS2: Wals 1B **48**
WV1: Wolv 2A **44**
Navigation Way B18: Win G 4B **100**
B70: W Brom 5F **79**
Nayland Cft. B28: Hall G 2G **149**
Naylors Gro. DY3: Up Gor 3A **76**
NEACHELL 1F **45**
Neachells La. WV11: Wed 4F **29**
WV13: W'hall 1F **45**
Neachells La. Ind. Est. WV11: Wed 5F **29**
Neachless Av. WV5: Wom 2G **73**
Neachley Gro. B33: Stech 5D **104**
Neale Ho. B70: W Brom 6B **80**
WV2: Wolv *4G 43*
(off Blakenhall Gdns.)
Neale St. WS2: Wals 1A **48**
Nearhill Rd. B38: K Nor 1G **159**
Near Lands Cl. B32: Quin 1H **129**
Nearmoor Rd. B34: S End 3H **105**
Near Oak Ho. B32: Bart G 5B **130**
Neasden Gro. B44: K'sdng 5B **68**
Neath Rd. WS3: Blox 5F **19**
Neath Way DY3: Sed 1C **76**
WS3: Blox 5F **19**
Nebsworth Cl. B90: Shir 2B **150**
NECHELLS 2D **102**
Nechells Community Sports Cen. 4A **102**
NECHELLS GREEN 4B **102**
Nechells Pk. Rd. B7: Nech 3B **102**
Nechell's Parkway B7: Birm 5A **102**
Nechells Pl. B7: Nech 3B **102**
NEC House B40: Nat E C 6F **123**
Needham St. B7: Nech 2C **102**
Needhill Cl. B93: Know 3B **166**
NEEDLERS END 2H **169**
Needlers End La. CV7: Bal C 3F **169**
Needlers End Rd. CV7: Bal C 2F **169**
Needless All. B2: Birm 1F **117** (4D **4**)
Needwood Cl. WV2: Wolv 5F **43**
Needwood Dr. WV4: E'shll 1B **60**
Needwood Gro. B71: W Brom 4C **64**
Needwood Ho. B27: A Grn 2B **136**
Nelson Av. WV14: Bils 4E **45**
Nelson Ct. B13: Mose 1H **133**
Nelson Ho. DY4: Tip 6A **62**
Nelson Rd. B6: Aston 6H **83**
DY1: Dud 6D **76**
Nelson St. B1: Birm 6D **100**
B69: O'bry 3H **97**
B71: W Brom 2A **80**
WV2: Wolv 3G **43** (6B **170**)
WV13: W'hall 6B **30**
Nene Cl. DY8: Stourb 1E **125**
Nene Way B36: Cas B 1B **106**
Neptune Ind. Est. WV13: W'hall 3B **46**
Neptune St. DY4: Tip 2G **77**
Nesbit Gro. B9: Bord G 6H **103**
Nesfield Cl. B38: K Nor 6G **145**
Nesfield Gro. B92: H Ard 6B **140**
Nesscliffe Gro. B23: Erd 6D **68**
Nest Comn. WS3: Pels 2D **20**
(not continuous)
Neston Gro. B33: Stech 1A **120**
Netheravon Cl. B14: K Hth 5F **147**
Netherby Rd. DY3: Sed 5G **59**
Nethercote Gdns. B90: Shir 4E **149**
Netherdale Cl. B72: W Grn 6A **70**
Netherdale Rd. B14: K Hth 6A **148**
NETHEREND 4C **110**
Netherend Cl. B63: Crad 4C **110**
Netherend La. B63: Crad 4D **110**
Netherend Sq. B63: Crad 4C **110**
Netherfield Gdns. B27: A Grn 2H **135**
Nethergate DY3: Up Gor 2B **76**
Netherstone Gro. B74: Four O 4F **37**
Netherton Bus. Pk. DY2: Neth 5F **95**
(not continuous)
Netherton Gro. B33: Kitts G 6H **105**
Netherton Hill DY2: Neth 4E **95**
Netherton Lodge DY2: Neth 4E **95**
Netherwood Cl. B91: Sol 1C **150**
Nethy Dr. WV6: Tett 4H **25**
Netley Gro. B11: Tys 2F **135**
Netley Ho. B32: Harb 6D **114**
Netley Rd. WS3: Blox 5E **19**
Netley Way WS3: Blox 5E **19**
Network Pk. B8: Salt 5C **102**
Nevada Way B37: Chel W 2E **123**
Neve Av. WV10: Bush 6B **16**
Neve's Opening WV1: Wolv 1B **44**
Neville Av. WV4: Penn 6H **43**
Neville Rd. B23: Erd 4C **84**
B36: Cas B 6A **88**
B90: Shir 6F **149**
Neville Wlk. B35: Cas V 5E **87**
Nevin Gro. B42: P Barr 2E **83**
Nevis Ct. WV3: Wolv 1C **42**
Nevis Gro. WV12: W'hall 6B **18**
Nevison Gro. B43: Gt Barr 1D **66**
Newark Cft. B26: Sheld 5F **121**
Newark Rd. DY2: Neth 1F **111**
WV12: W'hall 2C **30**
New Art Gallery Walsall, The 1C **48**
New Bank Gro. B9: Bord G 6G **103**
New Bartholomew St.
B5: Birm 1H **117** (4G **5**)
New Birmingham Rd. B69: Tiv 5H **77**
DY2: Dud 5H **77**
Newbold Cl. B93: Ben H 4B **166**
Newbold Ct. B63: Hale 2B **128**
NEWBOLDS 3C **28**
Newbolds Rd. WV10: Wolv 3C **28**
Newbolt Rd. WV14: Bils 5G **45**
Newbolt St. WS5: Wals 6C **48**
New Bond St. B9: Birm 2B **118**
DY2: Dud 1F **95**
Newborough Gro. B28: Hall G 3F **149**
Newborough Rd. B28: Hall G 3F **149**
B90: Shir 3F **149**
NEWBRIDGE 6C **26**
Newbridge Av. WV6: Wolv 6C **26**
Newbridge Cres. WV6: Wolv 5C **26**
Newbridge Dr. WV6: Wolv 5C **26**
Newbridge Gdns. WV6: Wolv 5C **26**
Newbridge M. WV6: Wolv 5D **26**
Newbridge Rd. B9: Bord G 3H **119**
DY6: W Hth 1A **92**
Newbridge St. WV6: Wolv 5D **26**
Newburn Cft. B32: Quin 6H **113**
Newbury Cl. B62: Hale 2D **128**
WS6: Gt Wyr 2F **7**
Newbury Ho. B69: O'bry 4D **96**
Newbury La. B69: O'bry 3C **96**
Newbury Rd. B19: Hock 2G **101**
DY8: Word 1A **108**
WS11: Nort C 1E **9**
WV10: F'hses 5G **15**
Newbury Wlk. B65: Row R 3C **96**
Newby Gro. B37: F'bri 4D **106**
New Canal St. B5: Birm 1H **117** (5G **5**)
New Cannon Pas. B2: Birm 1G **117** (4E **5**)
Newcastle Cft. B35: Cas V 4G **87**
Newchurch Gdns. B24: Erd 5E **85**
New Church Rd. B73: Bold 5G **69**
New Cole Hall La. B34: Stech 4F **105**
New Coll. Cl. WS1: Wals 4E **49**
Newcombe Rd. B21: Hand 5H **81**
Newcome Cl. B24: Erd 3B **86**
Newcomen Ct. WS4: Rus 2F **33**
Newcomen Dr. DY4: Tip 4H **77**
Newcott Cl. WV9: Pend 5D **14**
New Ct. *DY5: Brie H* *1H 109*
(off Promenade, The)
New Coventry Rd. B26: Sheld 6D **120**
New Cft. B19: Loz 2G **101**
Newcroft Gro. B26: Yard 4C **120**
NEW CROSS 4C **28**
New Cross Av. WV10: Wolv 5D **28**
WV11: Wed 5D **28**
New Cross Ind. Est. WV1: Wolv 6C **28**
New Cross St. DY4: Tip 2G **77**
WS10: Darl 6D **46**
Newdigate Rd. B75: S Cold 6E **55**
New Dudley Rd. DY6: W Hth 1A **92**
Newells Dr. DY4: Tip 6D **62**
Newells Rd. B26: Yard 3E **121**
New England B62: B'hth 4E **113**
New England Cl. B69: O'bry 6E **79**
Newent Cl. WV12: W'hall 6D **30**
New Ent. Cen. WV1: Wolv 3C **44**
New Enterprise Workshops
B18: Hock 4C **100**
Newent Rd. B31: N'fld 3G **145**
Newey Bus. Pk. DY4: Tip 1F **77**
Newey Cl. B45: Redn 3G **157**
Newey Rd. B28: Hall G 1F **149**
WV11: Wed 1A **30**
Newey St. DY1: Dud 5C **76**
New Farm Rd. DY9: Lye 1G **125**
Newfield Cl. B91: Sol 1H **151**
WS2: Wals 3A **32**
Newfield Cres. B63: Hale 6A **112**
Newfield Dr. DY6: K'wfrd 5C **92**
Newfield La. B63: Hale 6A **112**
Newfield Rd. B69: O'bry 1F **97**
New Forest Rd. WS3: Wals 4C **32**
New Gas St. B70: W Brom 2G **79**
Newhall Ct. B3: Birm 6E **101** (2A **4**)
New Hall Dr. B76: Walm 1B **70**
(not continuous)
Newhall Farm Cl. B76: Walm 1B **70**
Newhall Hill B1: Birm 6E **101** (2A **4**)
Newhall Ho. *WS1: Wals* *3C 48*
(off Newhall St.)
New Hall Pl. WS10: W'bry 2G **63**
Newhall Pl. B3: Birm 2A **4**
Newhall Rd. B65: Row R 6C **96**
New Hall St. WV13: W'hall 1A **46**
Newhall St. B3: Birm 6E **101** (2B **4**)
B70: W Brom 5A **80**
DY4: Tip 5G **61**
WS1: Wals 3C **48**
Newhall Wlk. B72: S Cold 1A **70**
Newhampton Ho.
WV1: Wolv 6F **27** (1A **170**)
New Hampton Lofts B18: Birm 4E **101**
New Hampton Rd. E.
WV1: Wolv 6F **27** (1A **170**)
New Hampton Rd. W. WV6: Wolv 5D **26**
Newhaven Cl. B7: Birm 4A **102**
Newhay Cft. B19: Loz 2E **101**
New Heath Cl. WV11: Wed 4D **28**
New Henry St. B68: O'bry 5G **97**
New High Dr. DY4: Tip 2B **78**
Newhope Cl. B15: Birm 3F **117**
New Hope Rd. B66: Smeth 5G **99**
New Horse Rd. WS6: C Hay 2E **7**
Newhouse Cres. CV7: Bal C 3H **169**
Newhouse Farm Cl. B76: Walm 2D **70**
New Ho. Farm Dr. B31: N'fld 1F **145**
Newick Av. B74: Lit A 6B **36**
Newick Gro. B14: K Hth 3E **147**
Newick St. DY2: Neth 5E **95**
Newington Rd. B37: Mars G 3D **122**
New Inn Rd. B19: Loz 6F **83**
New Inns Cl. B21: Hand 1H **99**
New Inns La. B45: Fran 6E **143**
NEW INVENTION 2D **30**
New John St. B6: Birm 4G **101**
B62: B'hth 2C **112**
New John St. W. B19: Hock 3E **101**
New King St. DY2: Dud 6E **77**

Newland Cl.—Northampton St.

Newland Cl. WS4: S'fld 5G **21**
Newland Ct. B23: Erd 4B **84**
Newland Gdns. B64: Crad H 4G **111**
Newland Gro. DY2: Dud 2B **94**
Newland Rd. B9: Small H 2F **119**
Newlands, The B34: S End 2G **105**
Newlands Cl. WV13: W'hall 2A **46**
Newlands Dr. B62: B'hth 4E **113**
Newlands Grn. B66: Smeth 5E **99**
Newlands La. B37: Mars G 5C **122**
Newlands Rd. B30: Stir 6D **132**
B93: Ben H 5B **166**
Newlands Wlk. *B68: O'bry 5H 97*
(off Jackson St.)
New Landywood La. WV11: Ess 1E **19**
New Leasow B76: Walm 6E **71**
Newlyn Rd. B31: N'fld 4D **144**
B64: Crad H 3F **111**
Newman Av. WV4: E'shll 1B **60**
Newman Coll. Cl. B32: Bart G 5A **130**
Newman Ct. B21: Hand 6A **82**
Newman Pl. WV14: Bils 4H **45**
Newman Rd. B24: Erd 3F **85**
DY4: Tip 4C **62**
WV10: Bush 6C **16**
Newmans Cl. B66: Smeth 5G **99**
Newman Way B45: Redn 2G **157**
Newmarket Cl. WV6: Wolv 4E **27**
Newmarket Rd. WS11: Nort C 1E **9**
New Mkt. St. B3: Birm 6F **101** (3C **4**)
Newmarket Way B36: Hodg H 1H **103**
Newmarsh Rd. B76: Walm 1E **87**
New Mdw. Cl. B31: N'fld 5F **145**
New Meeting St. B4: Birm 1G **117** (4F **5**)
B69: O'bry 1G **97**
New Mills St. WS1: Wals 4B **48**
New Mill St. DY2: Dud 6E **77**
Newmore Gdns. WS5: Wals 6G **49**
New Moseley Rd. B12: Birm 3A **118**
Newnham Gro. B23: Erd 1E **85**
Newnham Ho. B36: Cas B 4D **106**
Newnham Ri. B90: Shir 4B **150**
Newnham Rd. B16: Edg 1G **115**
NEW OSCOTT 4C **68**
New Pool Rd. B64: Crad H 3D **110**
Newport Rd. B12: Bal H 1A **134**
B36: Hodg H 1D **104**
Newport St. WS1: Wals 2C **48**
WV10: Wolv 5A **28**
Newquay Cl. WS5: Wals 4A **50**
Newquay Rd. WS5: Wals 4H **49**
New Railway St. WV13: W'hall 1B **46**
New Rd. B18: Win G 3A **100**
B45: Rubery 2F **157**
B46: Wat O 4D **88**
B47: H'wd 1H **161**
B63: Hale 1B **128**
B91: Sol 4G **151**
DY2: Dud, Neth 3E **95**
DY3: Swind 4A **72**
DY4: Tip 1D **78**
DY8: Stourb 6E **109**
WS8: Bwnhls 6B **10**
WS9: A'rdge 4C **34**
WS10: Darl 5D **46**
WV6: Wolv 5C **26**
WV10: Bush 1D **28**
WV13: W'hall 2A **46**
New Rowley Rd. DY2: Dud 2G **95**
New Royal Briery Experience, The 4F **77**
New Shipton Cl. B76: Walm 4D **70**
New Spring St. B18: Hock 5C **100**
New Spring St. Nth. B18: Hock 4C **100**
Newstead Rd. B44: K'sdng 2A **68**
New St. B2: Birm 1F **117** (4D **4**)
B23: Erd 2F **85**
B36: Cas B 1F **105**
B45: Fran 5F **143**
B66: Smeth 3E **99**
B70: W Brom 6G **63**
(Norbury Rd.)
B70: W Brom 4B **80**
(St Michael St.)
DY1: Dud 6E **77**
DY3: Gorn 4G **75**
DY4: Tip 2H **77**
DY5: Quar B 3C **110**
New St. DY6: K'wfrd 5B **92**
DY6: W Hth 1A **92**
DY8: Stourb 6D **108**
DY8: Word 1B **108**
WS1: Wals 2D **48**
WS3: Blox 6H **19**
WS4: Rus 2F **33**
WS4: S'fld 6H **21**
WS6: Gt Wyr 3G **7**
WS10: Darl 5D **46**
WS10: W'bry 4F **63**
WV2: E'shll 5C **44**
WV3: Wolv 4B **42**
WV4: E'shll 6A **44**
WV11: Ess 4A **18**
WV13: W'hall 2G **45**
New St. Nth. B71: W Brom 4B **80**
New Street Station (Rail) 1F **117** (5D **4**)
New Summer St. B19: Birm 5F **101**
New Swan La. B70: W Brom 2G **79**
New Swinford Hall DY9: Lye 1G **125**
NEWTON 5G **65**
Newton Av. B74: S Cold 4H **53**
Newton Chambers *B2: Birm 4D 4*
(off Cannon St.)
Newton Cl. B43: Gt Barr 4G **65**
Newton Ct. WV9: Pend 4D **14**
Newton Gdns. B43: Gt Barr 5G **65**
Newton Gro. B29: S Oak 3B **132**
Newton Ho. WV13: W'hall 2B **46**
Newton Ind. Est. B9: Bord G 1D **118**
Newton Mnr. Cl. B43: Gt Barr 5H **65**
Newton Pl. B18: Hock 2B **100**
WS2: Wals 3H **31**
Newton Rd. B11: S'hll 6B **118**
B43: Gt Barr 5G **65**
B71: W Brom 1C **80**
B93: Know 2D **166**
WS2: Wals 4H **31**
Newton Sq. B43: Gt Barr 4A **66**
Newton St. B4: Birm 6G **101** (2F **5**)
B71: W Brom 6C **64**
NEW TOWN
Brownhills 4D **10**
West Bromwich 3E **79**
NEWTOWN
Birmingham 3F **101**
Great Wyrley 2G **19**
Netherton 1E **111**
New Town DY5: Brie H 5G **93**
(not continuous)
Newtown DY2: Neth 2E **111**
Newtown Dr. B19: Hock 3E **101**
Newtown La. B62: Roms 6C **142**
B64: Crad H 2F **111**
Newtown Middleway B6: Birm 4G **101**
NEW TOWN ROW 3G **101**
New Town Row B6: Aston 3G **101**
Newtown Shop. Cen. B19: Hock 3G **101**
Newtown St. B64: Crad H 1F **111**
New Village DY2: Neth 2E **111**
New Villas WV11: Wed 4C **28**
New Wood Cl. DY7: Stourt 3A **108**
New Wood Dr. B31: Longb 6B **144**
New Wood Gro. WS9: Wals W 4C **22**
Next Generation Health Club 5H **93**
Ney Ct. DY4: Tip 5H **77**
Niall Cl. B15: Edg 3A **116**
Nicholas Rd. B74: S'tly 3G **51**
Nicholds Cl. WV14: Cose 4D **60**
Nicholls Fold WV11: Wed 4F **29**
Nicholls Rd. DY4: Tip 4G **61**
Nicholls St. B70: W Brom 5C **80**
Nichols Cl. B92: Sol 6B **138**
Nigel Av. B31: N'fld 2E **145**
Nigel Ct. B16: Edg 2A **116**
Nigel Rd. B8: Salt 3E **103**
DY1: Dud 5C **76**
Nightingale Av. B36: Cas B 1C **106**
Nightingale Cl. B23: Erd 6C **68**
Nightingale Ct. B91: Sol 3G **151**
Nightingale Cres. DY5: Brie H 4H **109**
WV12: W'hall 1B **30**
Nightingale Dr. DY4: Tip 2C **78**
Nightingale Pl. WV14: Bils 5F **45**
Nightingale Wlk. B15: Edg 4E **117**
Nightjar Gro. B23: Erd 1C **84**
Nighwood Dr. B74: S'tly 4H **51**
Nijon Cl. B21: Hand 6G **81**
Nimmings Cl. B31: Longb 3D **158**
Nimmings Rd. B62: B'hth 3D **112**
Nineacres Dr. B37: F'bri 1C **122**
Nine Elms La. WV10: Wolv 4A **28**
Nine Leasowes B66: Smeth 2C **98**
Nine Locks Ridge DY5: Brie H 1H **109**
Nine Pails Wlk. B70: W Brom 6B **80**
Ninestiles Community Leisure Cen. 4H **135**
Nineveh Av. B21: Hand 2B **100**
Nineveh Rd. B21: Hand 2A **100**
Ninfield Rd. B27: A Grn 2G **135**
Nith Pl. DY1: Dud 5D **76**
Noakes Ct. WS10: Darl 4F **47**
Nocke Rd. WV11: Wed 6H **17**
Nock St. DY4: Tip 6C **62**
Noddy Pk. WS9: A'rdge 2D **34**
Noddy Pk. Rd. WS9: A'rdge 2D **34**
Noel Av. B12: Bal H 5A **118**
Noel Rd. B16: Edg 2B **116**
Nolton Cl. B43: Gt Barr 5H **65**
Nook, The DY5: P'ntt 4F **93**
WS6: C Hay 4C **6**
Nooklands Cft. B33: Yard 1E **121**
Noose Cres. WV13: W'hall 1G **45**
Noose La. WV13: W'hall 1G **45**
Nora Rd. B11: S'hll 2C **134**
Norbiton Rd. B44: K'sdng 5A **68**
Norbreck Cl. B43: Gt Barr 4H **65**
Norbury Av. WS3: Pels 4D **20**
Norbury Cres. WV4: E'shll 1B **60**
Norbury Dr. DY5: Brie H 2H **109**
Norbury Gro. B92: Olton 2E **137**
Norbury Rd. B44: Gt Barr 2H **67**
B70: W Brom 6G **63**
WV10: Wolv 3B **28**
WV14: Bils 5H **45**
Norcombe Gro. B90: M'path 4E **165**
Nordley Rd. WV11: Wed 4E **29**
Nordley Wlk. WV11: Wed 3E **29**
Norfolk Av. B71: W Brom 6B **64**
Norfolk Cl. B30: Stir 1D **146**
Norfolk Ct. B16: Edg 2H **115**
B29: W Cas 6F **131**
Norfolk Cres. WS9: A'rdge 1D **34**
Norfolk Dr. WS10: W'bry 1B **64**
Norfolk Gdns. B75: S Cold 3H **53**
Norfolk Gro. WS6: Gt Wyr 4F **7**
Norfolk Ho. B23: Erd 2F **85**
B30: K Nor 4C **146**
Norfolk New Rd. WS2: Wals 5G **31**
Norfolk Pl. WS2: Wals 4B **32**
Norfolk Rd. B15: Edg 4H **115**
B23: Erd 2F **85**
B45: Fran 5F **143**
B68: O'bry 4H **113**
B75: S Cold 4H **53**
DY2: Dud 2C **94**
DY8: Woll 3B **108**
WV3: Wolv 3E **43**
Norfolk Twr. B18: Hock 4D **100**
Norgrave Rd. B92: Sol 3G **137**
Norlan Dr. B14: K Hth 4H **147**
Norland Rd. B27: A Grn 4A **136**
Norley Gro. B13: Mose 6C **134**
Norley Trad. Est. B33: Sheld 2G **121**
Norman Av. B32: Harb 4C **114**
Normandy Rd. B20: Hand 6F **83**
Norman Green Athletics Cen. 4E **151**
Norman Rd. B31: N'fld 4F **145**
B67: Smeth 2B **114**
WS5: Wals 3G **49**
Normansell Twr. B6: Aston 1B **102**
Norman St. B18: Win G 4A **100**
DY2: Dud 1F **95**
Norman Ter. B65: Row R 5C **96**
Normanton Av. B26: Sheld 6H **121**
Normanton Twr. B23: Erd 1G **85**
Normid Ct. *B31: N'fld 3G 145*
(off Bunbury Rd.)
Norrington Gro. B31: N'fld 4A **144**
Norrington Rd. B31: N'fld 4A **144**
Norris Dr. B33: Stech 6D **104**
Norris Rd. B6: Aston 6H **83**
Norris Way B75: S Cold 6B **54**
Northampton St. B18: Birm 5E **101**

244 A-Z Birmingham

Northam Wlk. WV6: Wolv. 5F 27
Northanger Rd. B27: A Grn 3H 135
North Av. B40: Nat E C 6G 123
　WV11: Wed 3E 29
Northbrook Ct. B90: Shir 2A 150
Northbrook Rd. B90: Shir. 2A 150
Northbrook St. B16: Birm. 5B 100
Northcote Rd. B33: Stech. 5B 104
Northcote St. WS2: Wals 5B 32
Northcott Rd. DY2: Neth. 5F 95
　WV14: Bils. 1G 61
North Cres. WV10: F'stne. 1D 16
North Dale WV6: Tett 5H 25
Northdown Rd. B91: Sol 6D 150
North Dr. B5: Edg 6E 117
　B20: Hand 1D 100
　B75: S Cold 5A 54
NORTHFIELD 4E 145
Northfield Gro. WV3: Wolv 4A 42
Northfield Pool & Fitness Cen. . . . 4E 145
Northfield Rd. B17: Harb 2E 131
　B30: K Nor 3A 146
　DY2: Neth. 4F 95
Northfield Station (Rail) 5E 145
Northfields Way WS8: Clay 1H 21
North Ga. B17: Harb. 4G 115
Northgate B64: Crad H 3F 111
　WS9: A'rdge 5C 22
Northgate Way WS9: A'rdge. 1C 34
North Grn. WV4: Penn 5B 42
North Holme B9: Bord G 1C 118
Northicote Recreation & Community Cen.
　. . . . . 4A 16
Northland Rd. B90: Shir. 6C 150
Northlands Rd. B13: Mose. 4A 134
Northleach Av. B14: K Hth 5F 147
Northleigh Rd. B8: W End 3G 103
Northmead B33: Yard 1E 121
Northolt B35: Cas V 4E 87
Northolt Gro. B42: Gt Barr 4B 66
North One M. DY3: Sed 4G 59
North Oval DY3: Up Gor 2A 76
Northover Cl. WV9: Pend 5E 15
North Pk. Rd. B23: Erd. 3B 84
North Pathway B17: Harb 4F 115
North Rd. B17: Harb. 5H 115
　B20: Hand 5G 83
　B29: S Oak 2B 132
　DY4: Tip 5B 62
　WV1: Wolv 5G 27
North Roundhay B33: Kitts G 5E 105
Northside Bus. Cen. B18: Win G . . . 4A 100
Northside Dr. B74: S'tly 3H 51
North Solihull Sports Cen. 6C 106
Nth. Springfield DY3: Sed 4A 60
North St. B67: Smeth 4D 98
　DY2: Dud 6F 77
　DY5: Brie H 1G 109
　WS2: Wals 5C 32
　WS10: W'bry 1F 63
　WV1: Wolv 1G 43 (2B 170)
　　　　　　　　　　　　　(not continuous)
North St. Ind. Est. DY5: Brie H 1G 109
Northumberland St. B7: Birm 6A 102
North Vw. Dr. DY5: Brie H 4H 93
North Wlk. B31: N'fld. 6G 145
Nth. Warwick St. B9: Small H 2D 118
Northway B40: Nat E C 5H 123
　DY3: Sed 2G 59
　　　　　　　　　　　　　(Alderdale Av.)
　DY3: Sed 4F 59
　　　　　　　　　　　(Sunningdale Rd.)
Nth. Western Arc. B2: Birm . . . 6G 101 (3E 5)
Nth. Western Rd. B66: Smeth 3D 98
Nth. Western Ter. B18: Hock 2B 100
Northwick Cres. B91: Sol 6F 151
Northwood Ct. DY5: Brie H 1H 109
Northwood Pk. Cl. WV10: Bush. . . . 4H 15
Northwood Pk. Rd.
　WV10: Bush. 4A 16
Northwood St. B3: Birm 5E 101 (2B 4)
Northwood Way DY5: Brie H. 3F 109
North Yd. B9: Birm. 6H 5
Northycote Farm Country Pk. 4C 16
Northycote La. WV10: Bush. 3B 16
NORTON 3C 124
NORTON CANES 1E 9

Norton Cl. B31: N'fld 4E 145
　B66: Smeth 4G 99
　WV4: Penn 2A 58
Norton Cres. B9: Bord G 6H 103
　DY2: Neth. 6G 95
　WV14: Cose 4F 61
Norton Dr. B47: Wyt. 5C 162
Norton E. Rd. WS11: Nort C. 1E 9
Norton Ga. B38: K Nor 6A 146
Norton Grange WS11: Nort C. 1D 8
Norton Grange Cres. WS11: Nort C . . 1D 8
NORTON GREEN 2D 8
Norton Grn. La. B93: Know 6E 167
　WS11: Nort C 1C 8
Norton Hall La. WS11: Nort C 1B 8
Norton La. B47: Tid G, Wyt 5C 162
　B94: Earls 6E 163
　WS6: Gt Wyr 1G 7
　WS11: Cann, Nort C. 1B 8
Norton Rd. B46: Col 6H 89
　DY8: Stourb 4B 124
　WS3: Pels. 1E 21
Norton St. B18: Hock 4C 100
Norton Ter. B30: Stir 1D 146
　　　　　　　　　　　(off Warren Rd.)
Norton Twr. B1: Birm 4A 4
Norton Vw. B14: K Hth 6F 133
Norton Wlk. B23: Erd 4C 84
Nortune Cl. B38: K Nor 5H 145
Norwich Cft. B37: Mars G 2B 122
Norwich Dr. B17: Harb. 3D 114
Norwich Rd. DY2: Neth 1F 111
　WS2: Wals 2H 47
Norwood Av. B64: Crad H 4G 111
Norwood Gro. B19: Hock 2D 100
Norwood Rd. B9: Bord G 1E 119
　DY5: Brie H 5G 93
Nottingham Dr. WV12: W'hall 2C 30
Nottingham New Rd.
　WS2: Wals 4G 31
Nottingham Way DY5: Quar B 1B 110
Nova Ct. B43: Gt Barr 4D 66
Nova Scotia St. B4: Birm . . . 6H 101 (3G 5)
Nowell St. WS10: Darl 6E 47
Nuffield Ho. B36: Cas B 1C 106
Nugent Cl. B6: Aston 2G 101
Nugent Gro. B90: Ches G 6B 164
Number 9 The Gallery. 5A 4
Nursery Av. B12: Bal H 6H 117
　WS9: A'rdge 4D 34
Nursery Cl. B30: K Nor 2B 146
Nursery Dr. B30: K Nor 2B 146
　WV5: Wom 3F 73
Nursery Gdns. B90: Maj G 1E 163
　DY8: Word 2D 108
　WV8: Cod 3F 13
Nursery La. B74: Four O 1G 53
Nursery Rd. B15: Edg 5H 115
　B19: Loz. 3D 100
　WS3: Blox 1H 31
Nursery St. WV1: Wolv. 6G 27 (1B 170)
Nursery Vw. Cl. WS9: A'rdge. 1G 51
Nursery Wlk. WV6: Tett 5B 26
NURTON 6A 24
Nurton Bank WV6: Nur. 6A 24
Nutbush Dr. B31: N'fld 1B 144
Nutfield Wlk. B32: Harb 6D 114
Nutgrove Cl. B14: K Hth 6H 133
Nuthatch Dr. DY5: Brie H 4G 109
Nuthurst B75: S Cold 1F 71
Nuthurst Dr. WS11: Cann 1F 7
Nuthurst Gro. B14: K Hth 5H 147
　B93: Ben H 5C 166
Nuthurst Rd. B31: Longb 3D 158
Nutley Dr. DY4: Tip 5D 62
Nutmeg Gro. WS1: Wals 1E 49
Nuttall Gro. B21: Hand. 2G 99

O

Oak Av. B12: Bal H 6A 118
　B70: W Brom 4H 79
　WS2: Wals 6E 31
　WS6: Gt Wyr 4G 7
Oak Bank B18: Hock 3C 100
Oak Barn Rd. B62: B'hth 3E 113

Oak Cl. B17: Harb. 5E 115
　DY4: Tip 4A 62
Oak Ct. B45: Redn 2A 158
　B63: Hale 3H 127
Oak Cl. B66: Smeth 1A 98
　DY8: Stourb 1E 125
　WS5: Wals 1E 65
Oak Cres. B69: Tiv 6B 78
　WS3: Blox 3B 32
Oak Cft. B37: F'bri 6B 106
Oakcroft Rd. B13: Mose. 6B 134
Oakdale Cl. B68: O'bry 1G 113
　DY5: P'ntt. 2F 93
Oakdale Rd. B36: Hodg H 1C 104
　B68: O'bry 1G 113
Oakdale Trad. Est.
　DY6: K'wfrd 6B 74
Oakdene Cl. WS6: C Hay 3D 6
Oak Dr. B23: Erd. 6C 68
　WV5: Seis 3A 56
OAKEN 5D 12
Oaken Covert WV8: Cod. 5E 13
Oaken Dr. B91: Sol. 2D 150
　WV8: Cod, Oaken. 5D 12
　WV12: W'hall 2E 31
Oaken Grange WS6: Gt Wyr 4F 7
Oaken Gro. WV8: Cod 5E 13
Oakenhayes Cres. B76: Min 2G 87
　WS8: Bwnhls 4B 10
Oakenhayes Dr.
　WS8: Bwnhls 4B 10
Oaken La. WV8: Oaken 4C 12
Oaken Lanes WV8: Cod 4E 13
Oaken Pk. WV8: Cod 5G 13
Oakenshaw Rd. B90: Shir 6B 150
Oakeswell St. WS10: W'bry 2G 63
Oakeywell St. DY2: Dud. 6F 77
OAKFARM 6C 74
Oak Farm Cl. B76: Walm 6E 71
Oak Farm Rd. B30: B'vlle 2H 145
Oakfield Av. B11: S'brk 5C 118
　B12: Bal H 5A 118
　B21: Hand 2H 99
　DY1: Dud 6D 60
　DY6: K'wfrd 4C 92
Oakfield Cl. B66: Smeth 3G 99
　DY8: Word 2D 108
Oakfield Ct. DY5: Brie H 1H 109
　　　　　　　　　　　(off Promenade, The)
Oakfield Dr. B45: Coft H. 5B 158
　WS3: Pels. 2F 21
Oakfield Rd. B12: Bal H. 6G 117
　B24: Erd 4F 85
　B29: S Oak 2C 132
　B66: Smeth 3G 99
　DY8: Word 2E 109
　DY9: W'cte 3B 126
　W8: Bilb. 5H 13
Oakfields Way B91: Cath B 2D 152
Oak Grn. DY1: Dud. 2C 76
　WV6: Tett 6H 25
Oak Grn. Way B68: O'bry. 5G 97
Oak Gro. B31: Longb 6C 144
　WV11: Wed 2D 28
Oakhall Dr. B93: Dorr. 5B 166
OAKHAM 2B 96
Oakham Av. DY2: Dud 2G 95
Oakham Ct. DY2: Dud 1G 95
Oakham Cres. DY2: Dud 2G 95
Oakham Dr. DY2: Dud 1H 95
Oakham Rd. B17: Harb. 4F 115
　B69: Tiv 1G 95
　DY2: Dud 1G 95
Oakham Way B92: Olton 4E 137
Oak Hill WV3: Wolv 3A 42
Oakhill Cl. B17: Harb 3F 115
Oakhill Cres. B27: A Grn 5H 135
Oak Hill Dr. B15: Edg 4A 116
Oakhill Dr. DY5: Brie H 4F 109
Oak Ho. WS6: Gt Wyr 4G 7
Oak House Mus. 5H 79
Oakhurst Rd. B27: A Grn 4H 135
　B72: W Grn 5H 69
Oak Ind. Pk. DY6: K'wfrd 6C 74
Oakington Ho. B35: Cas V 4E 87
Oakland Cl. B91: Sol 3A 152
Oakland Dr. DY3: Gorn. 5F 75

Oakland Rd.—Old Masters Cl.

Oakland Rd. B13: Mose 2A **134**
B21: Hand 1A **100**
(not continuous)
WS3: Blox 2C **32**
Oaklands B31: N'fld 3D **144**
B62: Quin 1G **129**
B76: Curd 1D **88**
Oaklands, The
B37: Mars G 4C **122**
WV3: Wolv 3F **43**
Oaklands Av. B17: Harb 6F **115**
Oaklands Cft. B76: Walm 6F **71**
Oaklands Dr. B20: Hand 5B **82**
B74: S'tly 2H **51**
Oaklands Grn. WV14: Bils 3F **45**
Oaklands Rd. B74: Four O 3H **53**
WV3: Wolv 3F **43**
Oaklands Sports & Social Cen. 1H **99**
Oaklands Way B31: Longb 6H **143**
WS3: Pels 4F **21**
Oak La. B70: W Brom 4H **79**
B92: Bars 6B **154**
DY6: K'wfrd 6C **74**
Oaklea Dr. B64: Old H 1H **111**
Oakleaf Cl. B32: Bart G 3B **130**
Oak Leaf Dr. B13: Mose 2A **134**
Oak Leasow B32: Quin 1H **129**
Oakleigh B31: N'fld 5G **145**
Oakleigh Dr. DY3: Sed 6G **59**
WV8: Bilb 4G **13**
Oakleigh Rd. DY8: Stourb 3E **125**
Oakleighs DY8: Word 2A **108**
Oakleigh Wlk. DY6: K'wfrd 1C **92**
Oakley Av. DY4: Tip 1A **78**
WS9: A'rdge 4C **34**
Oakley Cl. WV4: Penn 6B **42**
Oakley Ct. B15: Edg 6A **116**
Oakley Gro. WV4: Penn 6B **42**
Oakley Rd. B10: Small H 4C **118**
(not continuous)
B30: Stir 2D **146**
WV4: Penn 6B **42**
Oak Leys WV3: Wolv 2A **42**
Oakley Wood Dr. B91: Sol 3A **152**
Oakmeadow Av. B24: Erd 4B **86**
Oakmeadow Cl. B26: Yard 6B **120**
B33: Kitts G 1H **121**
Oakmeadow Way B24: Erd 4B **86**
Oakmount Cl. WS3: Pels 4D **20**
Oak Mt. Rd. B74: S'tly 4A **52**
Oak Pk. Ct. *B74: Four O* *6E 37*
(off Walsall Rd.)
Oak Pk. Leisure Cen. 3B **22**
Oak Pk. Rd. DY8: Word 2D **108**
Oakridge Cl. WV12: W'hall 5C **30**
Oakridge Dr. WS6: C Hay 3F **7**
WV12: W'hall 5C **30**
Oakridge Rd. B31: N'fld 5H **145**
Oak Ri. B46: Col 4H **107**
Oak Rd. B68: O'bry 4H **113**
B70: W Brom 5H **79**
DY1: Dud 4E **77**
DY4: Tip 6G **61**
WS3: Pels 2D **20**
WS4: S'fld 6G **21**
WS9: Wals W 4C **22**
WV13: W'hall 1G **45**
Oaks, The B17: Harb 3F **115**
B34: S End 2F **105**
B38: K Nor 2B **160**
B67: Smeth 4D **98**
B72: W Grn 6H **69**
B76: Walm 2E **71**
WS3: Blox 6G **19**
WV3: Wolv 1E **43**
Oaks Cres. WV3: Wolv 2E **43**
Oaks Dr. WV3: Wolv 1E **43**
WV5: Wom 2G **73**
Oakslade Dr. B92: Sol 5A **138**
Oak St. B64: Crad H 2F **111**
DY2: Neth 5G **95**
DY5: Quar B 2B **110**
DY6: K'wfrd 4A **92**
WV3: Wolv 2E **43**
WV14: Cose 6D **60**
Oak St. Ind. Est. *B64: Crad H* *2F 111*
(off Oak St.)
Oak St. Trad. Est.
DY5: Quar B 2B **110**
Oakthorpe Dr. B37: K'hrst 4B **106**
Oakthorpe Gdns. B69: Tiv 5A **78**
Oak Tree Cl. B93: Ben H 5A **166**
Oak Tree Ct. B28: Hall G 2G **149**
B70: W Brom 4H **79**
Oaktree Cres. B62: Quin 5F **113**
Oak Tree Dr. B8: Salt 3D **102**
Oak Tree Gdns. B28: Hall G 4E **149**
DY8: Word 2E **109**
Oak Tree La. B29: S Oak 4A **132**
B47: H'wd 3B **162**
Oaktree Ri. WV8: Cod 3E **13**
Oaktree Rd. WS10: W'bry 2H **63**
Oak Trees B47: H'wd 3H **161**
Oak Vw. WS2: Wals 6E **31**
Oak Wlk., The B31: Longb 6E **145**
Oak Way B76: Walm 3D **70**
Oakwood Cl. WS9: Wals W 3A **22**
WV11: Ess 4B **18**
Oakwood Cres. DY2: Dud 3B **94**
Oakwood Cft. B91: Sol 6G **151**
Oakwood Dr. B14: K Hth 3F **147**
B74: S'tly 3G **51**
Oakwood Rd. B11: S'hll 2C **134**
B47: H'wd 3A **162**
B67: Smeth 5D **98**
B73: Bold 3E **69**
WS3: Blox 2C **32**
Oakwood St. B70: W Brom 2H **79**
Oast Ho. B8: W End 5A **104**
Oasthouse Cl. DY6: W Hth 2G **91**
Oaston Rd. B36: Cas B 1H **105**
Oatfield Cl. WS7: Chase 1C **10**
Oatlands Wlk. B14: K Hth 5E **147**
Oatlands Way WV6: Pert 6D **24**
Oat Mill Cl. WS10: Darl 6E **47**
Oban Rd. B92: Olton 4D **136**
Oberon Cl. B45: Fran 5G **143**
Oberon Dr. B90: Shir 6G **149**
Occupation Rd. WS8: Wals W 3C **22**
Occupation St. DY1: Dud 5C **76**
Ocean Dr. WS10: W'bry 4D **62**
Ockam Cft. B31: N'fld 5G **145**
OCKER HILL 5C **62**
Ocker Hill Rd. DY4: Tip 4B **62**
O'Connor Dr. DY4: Tip 4C **62**
Oddingley Ct. B23: Erd 4C **84**
Oddingley Rd. B31: N'fld 5G **145**
Odell Cres. WS3: Blox 2A **32**
Odell Pl. B5: Edg 6E **117**
Odell Rd. WS3: Blox 2H **31**
Odell Way WS3: Blox 2H **31**
Odensil Grn. B92: Sol 3F **137**
Odeon Cinema 1G 117 (5E 5)
Offa's Dr. WV6: Pert 4E **25**
Offenham Covert B38: K Nor 1A **160**
Offini Cl. B70: W Brom 5D **80**
Offmoor Rd. B32: Bart G 5H **129**
Ogbury Cl. B14: K Hth 5E **147**
Oglay Hay Rd. WS7: Chase 3C **10**
Ogley Cres. WS8: Bwnhls 6C **10**
Ogley Dr. B75: S Cold 6D **54**
Ogley Hay Rd. WS8: Bwnhls 3C **10**
Ogley Rd. WS8: Bwnhls 6C **10**
O'Hare Ho. WS4: Wals 6D **32**
O'Keeffe Cl. B11: S'brk 5B **118**
Okehampton Dr. B71: W Brom 1A **80**
Okement Dr. WV11: Wed 4D **28**
Old Abbey Gdns. B17: Harb 1H **131**
Oldacre Cl. B76: Walm 1B **86**
Old Acre Dr. B21: Hand 2A **100**
Oldacre Rd. B68: O'bry 4G **113**
Old Bank Pl. B72: S Cold 6A **54**
Old Bank Top B31: N'fld 5F **145**
Old Barn Rd. B30: B'vlle 1H **145**
DY8: Word 2E **109**
Old Beeches B23: Erd 5C **68**
Old Bell Rd. B23: Erd 1H **85**
Oldberrow Cl. B90: M'path 3E **165**
Old Birchills WS2: Wals 6A **32**
Old Birmingham Rd. B45: Lick 6F **157**
Old Bri. St. B19: Hock 3E **101**
Old Bri. Wlk. B65: Row R 4H **95**
Old Bromford La. B8: W End 2H **103**
Old Brookside B33: Stech 1C **120**
OLDBURY 1G **97**
Oldbury Bus. Cen. B68: O'bry 1G **113**
Oldbury Grn. Retail Pk. B69: O'bry 1F **97**
Oldbury Leisure Cen. 3D **96**
Oldbury Ringway B69: O'bry 1F **97**
Oldbury Rd. B65: Row R 1D **112**
B66: Smeth 2A **98**
B70: W Brom 4E **79**
Oldbury Rd. Ind. Est. B66: Smeth 2B **98**
B70: W Brom 5F **79**
Oldbury St. WS10: W'bry 2H **63**
Old Bush St. DY5: Brie H 6A **94**
Old Camp Hill B11: S'brk 3A **118**
Old Canal Wlk. DY4: Tip 2B **78**
Old Castle Gro. WS8: Bwnhls 3B **10**
Old Chapel, The B3: Birm 6F **101** (2C **4**)
Old Chapel Rd. B67: Smeth 6D **98**
Old Chapel Wlk. B68: O'bry 5G **97**
Old Chu. Av. B17: Harb 6G **115**
Old Chu. Grn. B33: Stech 1C **120**
Old Chu. Rd. B17: Harb 6F **115**
B46: Wat O 4D **88**
Old Ct. Cft. B9: Bord G 2C **118**
Old Cft. La. B34: S End 1F **105**
B36: Cas B 1F **105**
Old Cross B4: Birm 2G **5**
Old Cross St. DY4: Tip 2G **77**
Old Crown Cl. B32: Bart G 4H **129**
Old Damson La. B92: Sol 3B **138**
Old Dickens Heath Rd. B90: Dic H 4G **163**
Old Edwardians Sports Club 1A **150**
Olde Hall La. WS6: Gt Wyr 1F **7**
Olde Hall Rd. WV10: F'stne 1E **17**
Old End La. WV14: Cose 6E **61**
Old Fails Cl. WS6: C Hay 2D **6**
OLD FALLINGS 1B **28**
Old Fallings Cres. WV10: Bush 2A **28**
Old Fallings La. WV10: Bush 6B **16**
Old Farm Dr. WV8: Bilb 3G **13**
Old Farm Gro. B14: Yard W 2D **148**
Old Farm Mdw. WV3: Wolv 3A **42**
Old Farm Rd. B33: Stech 5C **104**
Oldfield Dr. DY8: Stourb 2E **125**
Oldfield Rd. B12: Bal H 5A **118**
WV14: Cose 5C **60**
Oldfields B64: Crad H 3F **111**
Oldfield Trad. Est. B64: Crad H 3F **111**
Old Fire Sta., The B17: Harb 5H **115**
Old Flour Mills B70: W Brom 5A **80**
Old Fordrove B76: Walm 2B **70**
Old Forest Way B34: S End 3F **105**
Old Forge Cl. WS1: Wals 3D **48**
Old Forge Trad. Est. DY9: Lye 5A **110**
Old Grange Rd. B11: S'hll 1C **134**
Old Grn. La. B93: Know 6B **168**
Old Gro. Gdns. DY9: W'cte 2H **125**
Old Hall Cl. DY8: Amb 3E **109**
Old Hall Ind. Est. WS3: Blox 1A **32**
Old Hall La. WS9: A'rdge 6D **50**
Old Hall St. WV1: Wolv 2H **43** (4C **170**)
Old Ham La. DY9: Pedm 3G **125**
Old Hampton La. WV10: Bush 5D **16**
Old Hawne La. B63: Hale 6A **112**
Old Heath Cres. WV1: Wolv 2C **44**
Old Heath Rd. WV1: Wolv 2C **44**
Old High St. DY5: Quar B 2B **110**
OLD HILL 3B **112**
Old Hill WV6: Tett 4B **26**
Old Hill By-Pass B64: Old H 1H **111**
Old Hill Station (Rail) 3A **112**
Old Hobicus La. B68: O'bry 4H **97**
Old Horns Cres. B43: Gt Barr 3E **67**
Oldhouse Farm Cl. B28: Hall G 1F **149**
Old Ho. La. B62: Roms 6B **142**
Oldington Gro. B91: Sol 1F **165**
Old Kingsbury Rd. B76: Min 2G **87**
Oldknow Rd. B10: Small H 5E **119**
Old Landywood La. WV11: Ess 1C **18**
Old La. WS3: Blox 2A **32**
WV6: Tett 1F **41**
Old Langley Hall B75: S Cold 1F **71**
Old Level Way DY2: Neth 5F **95**
Old Lime Gdns. B38: K Nor 1A **160**
Old Lindens Cl. B74: S'tly 4G **51**
Old Lode La. B92: Sol 1F **137**
Old Mnr., The WV6: Tett 4B **26**
Old Masters Cl. WS1: Wals 2E **49**

246 A-Z Birmingham

Old Mdw. Rd.—Overbury Rd.

Old Mdw. Rd. B31: Longb 2G **159**
Old Meeting Rd. WV14: Cose 5E **61**
Old Meeting St. B70: W Brom 2H **79**
(not continuous)
Old Mill Cl. B90: Shir 5D **148**
Old Mill Ct. B46: Col 2H **107**
Old Mill Gdns. B33: Stech 1C **120**
WS4: S'fld 5G **21**
Old Mill Gro. B20: Hand 5E **83**
Old Mill House Cl. WS4: S'fld 6F **21**
Old Mill Rd. B46: Col 2H **107**
Old Moat Dr. B31: N'fld 4F **145**
Old Moat Way B8: W End 3H **103**
OLD MOXLEY **1A 62**
Oldnall Cl. DY9: W'cte 1B **126**
Oldnall Rd. B63: Crad 1B **126**
DY9: W'cte 1B **126**
Old Oak Cl. WS9: A'rdge 1D **34**
Old Oak Rd. B38: K Nor 5C **146**
OLD OSCOTT **4G 67**
Old Oscott Hill B44: Gt Barr 4G **67**
Old Oscott La. B44: Gt Barr 5G **67**
Old Pk. B31: N'fld 2E **145**
Old Pk. Cl. B6: Aston 2G **101**
Old Pk. La. B69: O'bry 4G **97**
Old Pk. Rd. DY1: Dud 3B **76**
WS10: Darl, W'bry 5E **47**
Old Pk. Trad. Est. WS10: W'bry 1E **63**
Old Pk. Wlk. B6: Aston 2G **101**
Old Penns La. B46: Col 2H **107**
Old Pl. WS3: Blox 1A **32**
Old Pleck Rd. WS2: Wals 3H **47**
Old Port Cl. DY4: Tip 5B **78**
Old Portway B38: K Nor 2A **160**
Old Postway B19: Loz 2F **101**
Old Quarry Cl. B45: Rubery 1F **157**
Old Quarry Dr. DY3: Up Gor 2H **75**
Old Rectory Gdns. WS9: A'rdge 3E **35**
Old Repertory Theatre, The 1F 117 (5D 4)
Old School Cl. WV13: W'hall 1A **46**
Old School Dr. B65: Row R 6B **96**
Old Scott Cl. B33: Kitts G 1G **121**
Old Snow Hill B4: Birm 5F **101** (1D **4**)
Old Sq. B4: Birm 6G **101** (3F **5**)
Old Sq. Shop. Pct. WS1: Wals 2C **48**
Old Stables Wlk. B7: Nech 2C **102**
Old Sta. Rd. B33: Stech 5B **104**
B92: H Ard 3H **139**
Old Stone Cl. B45: Fran 6F **143**
Old Stow Heath La. WV1: Wolv 2E **45**
OLD SWINFORD **3E 125**
Old Tokengate B17: Harb 5H **115**
Old Town Cl. B38: K Nor 5B **146**
Old Town La. WS3: Pels 4D **20**
Old Union Mill B16: Birm 1D **116**
Old Vicarage Cl. WS3: Pels 5E **21**
WV5: Wom 6H **57**
Old Walsall Rd. B42: P Barr 1B **82**
Old Warstone La. WV11: Ess 5B **6**
Old Warwick Ct. B92: Olton 4C **136**
Old Warwick Rd. B92: Olton 4C **136**
Oldway Dr. B91: Sol 5A **152**
Old Well Cl. WS4: Rus 2F **33**
Old Wharf Rd. DY8: Amb 5D **108**
Olga Dr. DY4: Tip 4B **62**
Olinthus Av. WV11: Wed 2G **29**
Olive Av. WV4: E'shll 6A **44**
Olive Dr. B62: B'hth 3C **112**
Olive Hill Rd. B62: B'hth 3D **112**
Olive La. B62: B'hth 3C **112**
Olive Mt. B69: O'bry 1D **96**
Olive Pl. B14: K Hth 6H **133**
Oliver Cl. DY2: Dud 1G **95**
Oliver Ct. B65: Row R 1B **112**
Oliver Cres. WV14: Bils 3G **61**
Oliver Rd. B16: Birm 1B **116**
B23: Erd 1F **85**
B66: Smeth 6G **99**
Oliver St. B7: Birm 4A **102**
Ollerton Rd. B26: Yard 4D **120**
Ollison Dr. B74: S'tly 1H **51**
Olliver Cl. B62: Quin 2G **129**
Olorenshaw Rd. B26: Sheld 6H **121**
OLTON **4C 136**
Olton Blvd. E. B27: A Grn 3G **135**
Olton Blvd. W. B11: Tys 2F **135**
Olton Cft. B27: A Grn 2B **136**
Olton Mere B92: Olton 4C **136**
Olton Rd. B90: Shir 3H **149**
Olton Station (Rail) **4C 136**
Olton Wharf B92: Olton 3C **136**
Olympus Dr. DY4: Tip 1D **78**
Ombersley Cl. B69: O'bry 4D **96**
Ombersley Rd. B12: Bal H 5A **118**
B63: Hale 3H **127**
Omersley Way B31: N'fld 5H **145**
One Stop Shop. Cen. B42: P Barr 4F **83**
Onibury Rd. B21: Hand 6H **81**
Onslow Cres. B92: Olton 4E **137**
Onslow Rd. B11: Tys 1G **135**
Ontario Cl. B38: K Nor 1C **160**
Oozells Sq. B1: Birm 1E **117** (5A **4**)
Oozells St. B1: Birm 1E **117** (5A **4**)
Oozells St. Nth. B1: Birm 1D **116** (5A **4**)
Open Fld. Cl. B31: N'fld 5F **145**
Openfield Cft. B46: Wat O 5E **89**
Oracle Bldg. B90: Bly P 6E **165**
Oratory, The 2B 116
Orchard, The B37: Mars G 3B **122**
B68: O'bry 5A **98**
WS3: Blox 5B **20**
WV6: Tett 3C **26**
WV14: Bils 6G **45**
Orchard Av. B91: Sol 2H **151**
Orchard Blythe B46: Col 3H **107**
Orchard Cl. B21: Hand 5B **82**
B46: Col 2H **107**
B63: Crad 5E **111**
B65: Row R 6A **96**
B73: Bold 5G **69**
B76: Curd 1D **88**
WS4: Rus 4G **33**
WS6: C Hay 2E **7**
WV3: Wolv 4H **41**
WV13: W'hall 2B **46**
Orchard Ct. B23: Erd 3B **84**
(Marsh Hill)
B23: Erd 2G **85**
(Sutton Rd.)
B65: Row R 6B **96**
DY6: K'wfrd 3B **92**
Orchard Cres. WV3: Wolv 4H **41**
Orchard Dr. B31: Longb 2D **158**
Orchard Gro. B74: Four O 6F **37**
DY3: Lwr G 4F **75**
WS9: A'rdge 5D **34**
WV4: Penn 1E **59**
Orchard Ho. B24: Erd 2G **85**
Orchard La. WV8: Bilb 4H **13**
Orchard Mdw. Wlk. B35: Cas V 4F **87**
Orchard Ri. B26: Yard 4D **120**
Orchard Rd. B12: Bal H 5H **117**
B24: Erd 2G **85**
DY2: Neth 1E **111**
WS5: Wals 2F **65**
WV11: Wed 2E **29**
WV13: W'hall 2B **46**
Orchards, The B47: H'wd 2A **162**
B74: Four O 3G **53**
B90: Ches G 5B **164**
Orchard St. DY4: Tip 5H **77**
DY5: Brie H 5G **93**
Orchards Way B12: Bal H 5G **117**
Orchard Way B27: A Grn 1H **135**
B43: Gt Barr 4B **66**
B47: H'wd 1A **162**
B64: Old H 2H **111**
Orcheston Wlk. B14: K Hth 6F **147**
Orchid Cl. B66: Smeth 2B **98**
Oregon Cl. DY6: K'wfrd 3D **92**
Oregon Dr. WV12: W'hall 2E **31**
Orford Gro. B21: Hand 1G **99**
Oriel Cl. DY1: Dud 5A **76**
Oriel Dr. WV10: F'hses 4H **15**
Oriel Ho. B37: F'bri 6C **106**
Oriel Vs. *B11: S'hll* *6C 118*
(off Warwick Rd.)
Orion Cl. B8: W End 5H **103**
WS6: Gt Wyr 4F **7**
Orkney Av. B34: Hodg H 3D **104**
Orkney Cft. B36: Cas B 2D **106**
Orlando Cl. WS1: Wals 3C **48**
Orlando Ho. *WS1: Wals* *3D 48*
(off Barleyfield Row)
Orme Cl. DY5: Brie H 3E **109**
Ormes La. WV6: Tett 6A **26**
Ormonde Cl. B63: Crad 4D **110**
Ormond Pl. WV14: Bils 5H **45**
Ormond Rd. B45: Fran 6E **143**
Ormsby Ct. B15: Edg 4A **116**
Ormsby Gro. B27: A Grn 6H **135**
Ormscliffe Rd. B45: Redn 3H **157**
Orphanage Rd. B24: Erd 2G **85**
B72: W Grn 1A **86**
Orpington Rd. B44: Gt Barr 2G **67**
Orpwood Rd. B33: Yard 1E **121**
Orslow Wlk. WV10: Wolv 4C **28**
ORTON **2F 57**
Orton Av. B76: Walm 1D **86**
Orton Cl. B46: Wat O 4C **88**
Orton Gro. WV4: Penn 1B **58**
Orton La. WV4: Lwr P 2F **57**
WV5: Wom 2F **57**
Orton Way B35: Cas V 6E **87**
Orwell Cl. DY8: Stourb 1A **124**
WV11: Wed 4H **29**
Orwell Dr. B38: K Nor 1F **159**
B71: W Brom 1B **80**
Orwell Pas. B5: Birm 1G **117** (5F **5**)
Orwell Rd. WS1: Wals 3F **49**
Osberton Dr. DY1: Dud 5B **76**
Osborn Ct. B73: W Grn 4H **69**
Osborne Dr. WS10: Darl 3D **46**
Osborne Gro. B19: Loz 2E **101**
Osborne Rd. B21: Hand 1B **100**
B23: Erd 2F **85**
B70: W Brom 4A **80**
WV4: Penn 6D **42**
Osborne Rd. Sth. B23: Erd 3F **85**
Osborne Twr. B6: Aston 1A **102**
Osborn Rd. B11: S'brk 5C **118**
Osbourne Cl. B6: Aston 2A **102**
DY5: Quar B 3B **110**
Osbourne Cft. B90: Ches G 4B **164**
Oscott Ct. B23: Erd 5E **69**
Oscott Gdns. B42: P Barr 4G **83**
Oscott Rd. B6: Witt 4G **83**
B42: P Barr 4G **83**
Oscott School La.
B44: Gt Barr 3G **67**
Osier Gro. B23: Erd 1B **84**
Osier Pl. WV1: Wolv 1B **44**
Osier St. WV1: Wolv 1B **44**
Osler St. B16: Birm 1B **116**
Osmaston Rd. B17: Harb 2E **131**
DY8: Stourb 3C **124**
Osmington Gro.
B63: Crad 5F **111**
Osprey Dr. DY1: Dud 6B **76**
Osprey Rd. B23: Erd 1C **84**
B27: A Grn 3B **136**
Ostler Cl. DY6: W Hth 2G **91**
Oswestry Ct. B11: S'brk 5B **118**
Oswin Pl. WS3: Wals 4D **32**
Oswin Rd. WS3: Wals 4D **32**
Other Rd. B45: Coft H 4A **158**
Otley Gro. B9: Bord G 6A **104**
Ottawa Twr. B5: Bal H 4F **117**
Otter Cft. B34: S End 4H **105**
Otterstone Cl. DY3: Sed 3G **59**
Oughton Rd. B12: Birm 4A **118**
Oundle Rd. B44: K'sdng 6H **67**
OUNSDALE **1E 73**
Ounsdale Cres. WV5: Wom 6G **57**
Ounsdale Dr. DY2: Neth 6E **95**
Ounsdale Rd. WV5: Wom 6E **57**
Ounty John La.
DY8: Stourb 5E **125**
Outfields B14: K Hth 1G **147**
Outmore Rd. B33: Sheld 2F **121**
Out Wood Dr. B31: Longb 6B **144**
Oval, The B67: Smeth 6B **98**
DY1: Dud 1A **94**
WS10: W'bry 1F **63**
Oval Rd. B24: Erd 6E **85**
DY4: Tip 6H **61**
Overbrook Cl. DY3: Gorn 5G **75**
Over Brunton Cl. B31: N'fld 5F **145**
Overbury Cl. B31: N'fld 4G **145**
B63: Hale 3B **128**
Overbury Rd. B31: N'fld 3G **145**

Overdale Av.—Park Av.

Overdale Av. B76: Walm 2D **86**
Overdale Cl. WS2: Wals. 6C **30**
Overdale Ct. B13: Mose. 1H **133**
Overdale Dr. WV13: W'hall 6C **30**
Overdale Rd. B32: Quin 1C **130**
Overend Rd. B63: Crad. 4F **111**
B64: Crad H 4F **111**
Overend St. B70: W Brom 4B **80**
Overfield Dr. WV14: Cose 2C **60**
Overfield Rd. B32: Bart G 4C **130**
DY1: Dud 1A **94**
Over Grn. Dr. B37: K'hrst. 3B **106**
Overhill Rd. WS7: Burn 1C **10**
Overlea Av. B27: A Grn 2H **135**
Over Mill Dr. B29: S Oak 3D **132**
Over Moor Cl. B19: Loz 2E **101**
Over Pool Rd. B8: W End. 3G **103**
Overseal Rd. WV11: Wed 1G **29**
Overslade Rd. B91: Sol 6D **150**
Oversley Rd. B76: Walm 1E **87**
Overstrand WV9: Pend. 4D **14**
Overton Cl. B28: Hall G 1G **149**
Overton Dr. B46: Wat O 4E **89**
Overton Gro. B27: A Grn 5A **136**
Overton La. WS7: Hamm 1E **11**
Overton Pl. B7: Birm 6A **102**
B71: W Brom 1B **80**
Overton Rd. B27: A Grn. 5H **135**
Overton Wlk. WV4: Penn 5A **42**
Over Wood Cft. B8: Salt. 6D **102**
Owen Pl. WV14: Bils. 5F **45**
Owen Rd. WV3: Wolv. 2E **43**
WV13: W'hall 2C **46**
WV14: Bils 4F **45**
Owen Rd. Ind. Est.
WV13: W'hall. 2C **46**
Owens Cft. B38: K Nor. 6C **146**
Owen St. DY2: Dud 1G **95**
DY4: Tip. 2G **77**
WS10: Darl 4D **46**
Owens Way B64: Old H 2A **112**
Ownall Rd. B34: S End 3G **105**
Oxbarn Av. WV3: Wolv. 5C **42**
Oxenton Cft. B63: Hale 3F **127**
Oxford Cl. B8: W End. 4H **103**
WS6: Gt Wyr 2F **7**
Oxford Ct. B29: W Cas. 6G **131**
Oxford Dr. B27: A Grn 1B **136**
DY8: Stourb. 1D **124**
Oxford Ho. B31: Longb 1D **158**
Oxford Pas. DY1: Dud 6D **76**
Oxford Rd. B13: Mose 3H **133**
B23: Erd 3F **85**
B27: A Grn. 2A **136**
B66: Smeth 1E **99**
(not continuous)
B70: W Brom. 4H **79**
Oxford St. B5: Birm. 2H **117** (6G **5**)
B30: Stir. 6C **132**
DY1: Dud. 6D **76**
WS2: Wals 4A **48**
WS10: W'bry 2H **63**
WV1: Wolv. 2A **44**
WV14: Bils. 6G **45**
Oxford St. Ind. Est.
WV14: Bils 6H **45**
Oxford Ter. WS10: W'bry 3H **63**
Oxford Way DY4: Tip 3F **77**
Oxhayes Cl. CV7: Bal C 6H **169**
Oxhill Rd. B21: Hand 5G **81**
B90: Shir 5C **148**
Ox Leasow B32: Bart G 3A **130**
OXLEY. 1F **27**
Oxley Av. WV10: Oxl 3G **27**
Oxley Cl. DY2: Neth 1D **110**
WS6: Gt Wyr 4F **7**
Oxley Ct. Cvn. Pk.
WV10: Oxl 1E **27**
Oxley Gro. B29: W Cas. 5E **131**
Oxley La. WV1: Wolv. 6G **27**
Oxley Links Rd.
WV10: Oxl 1F **27**
Oxley Moor Rd. WV9: Pend 1E **27**
WV10: Oxl 1E **27**
Ox Leys Rd. B75: S Cold 1F **71**
B76: Walm, Wis 1F **71**
Oxley St. WV1: Wolv 5G **27**
Oxlip Cl. WS5: Wals. 2E **65**
Oxpiece Dr. B36: Hodg H. 1B **104**
Oxstall Cl. B76: Min. 2H **87**
Ox St. DY3: Up Gor 2H **75**
Oxted Cl. WV11: Wed 4H **29**
Oxted Cft. B23: Erd. 4E **85**
Oxwood La. B32: Fran 3D **142**
B62: Hunn 3D **142**

P

Pace Cres. WV14: Bils 3A **62**
Pacific Av. WS10: W'bry 4D **62**
Packhorse La. B38: Head H 3F **161**
B47: H'wd. 3F **161**
Packington Av. B34: S End 4G **105**
Packington Ct. B74: Four O 5E **37**
Packmores B90: Dic H. 4G **163**
Packwood Cl. B20: Hand 5C **82**
B93: Ben H. 5A **166**
WV13: W'hall. 3H **45**
Packwood Cotts. B93: Dorr 6G **167**
Packwood Ct. B29: W Cas 4D **130**
B91: Sol 2G **151**
Packwood Dr. B43: Gt Barr 4H **65**
PACKWOOD GULLET 6F **167**
Packwood Rd. B26: Sheld 3F **121**
B69: Tiv 6A **78**
Padarn Cl. DY3: Sed 4G **59**
Padbury WV9: Pend 4F **15**
Paddington Rd. B21: Hand 6G **81**
Paddington Wlk. WS2: Wals 5F **31**
Paddock, The B31: N'fld 3G **145**
DY3: Up Gor. 2A **76**
DY9: Pedm 4F **125**
WV4: Penn 5F **43**
WV5: Wom. 1E **73**
WV6: Pert 5D **24**
WV8: Cod 5F **13**
WV14: Cose 4F **61**
Paddock Dr. B26: Sheld 4E **121**
B93: Dorr. 6H **167**
Paddock La. WS1: Wals. 2D **48**
(not continuous)
WS6: Gt Wyr 2G **7**
WS9: A'rdge 4C **34**
Paddocks, The B15: Edg 3D **116**
B76: Walm 1E **71**
Paddocks Dr. B47: H'wd 3H **161**
Paddocks Grn. B18: Hock 4C **100**
Paddock Vw. WV6: Wolv 3F **27**
Paddys Wide Water Ind. Est.
DY5: Brie H 4G **93**
Padgate Cl. B35: Cas V 4F **87**
Padstow Rd. B24: Erd 3B **86**
Paganal Dr. B70: W Brom 6C **80**
Paganel Dr. DY1: Dud 4E **77**
Paganel Rd. B29: W Cas 3E **131**
Pagan Pl. *B9: Birm* *6H* ***5***
(off Gibb St.)
Pageant Ct. B12: Bal H 6G **117**
Pages Cl. B75: S Cold 6A **54**
Pages Ct. B43: Gt Barr. 4A **66**
Pages La. B43: Gt Barr 4A **66**
Paget Cl. WV14: Cose 5D **60**
Paget Ho. DY4: Tip. 4B **78**
Paget M. B76: Walm 3D **70**
Paget Rd. B24: Erd. 3B **86**
WV6: Wolv. 1D **42**
Paget St. WV1: Wolv 6F **27**
Pagham Cl. WV9: Pend 5D **14**
Pagnell Gro. B13: Mose. 1C **148**
Paignton Rd. B16: Edg. 6H **99**
Pailton Gro. B29: W Cas. 4F **131**
Pailton Rd. B90: Shir. 2H **149**
Painswick Cl. WS5: Wals 2F **65**
Painswick Rd. B28: Hall G 6E **135**
Paintcup Row DY2: Neth 1E **111**
Painters Cnr. *B66: Smeth* *4G* ***99***
(off Grove La.)
Painters Cft. WV14: Cose 4G **61**
Pakefield Rd. B30: K Nor. 4E **147**
Pakenham Cl. B76: Walm 5D **70**
Pakenham Dr. B76: Walm 5D **70**
Pakenham Ho. B76: Walm. 5D **70**
Pakenham Rd. B15: Edg 4E **117**
Pakenham Village *B15: Edg.* *4E* ***117***
(off Gilldown Pl.)
Pakfield Wlk. B6: Aston. 1H **101**
Palace Cl. B65: Row R 5D **96**
Palace Dr. B66: Smeth. 1B **98**
Palace Rd. B9: Small H 1E **119**
Palefield Rd. B90: M'path 3D **164**
Pale La. B17: Harb. 3D **114**
Pale St. DY3: Up Gor 2A **76**
Palethorpe Rd. DY4: Tip 5A **62**
PALFREY 4A **48**
Palfrey Rd. DY8: Stourb. 6B **108**
Pallasades Shop. Cen., The
B2: Birm 1F **117** (5D **4**)
Palmcourt Av. B28: Hall G 6E **135**
Palm Cft. DY5: Brie H 3G **109**
Palmer Cl. WV11: Wed 6H **17**
Palmers Cl. WV8: Bilb 6A **14**
B90: Shir 2H **149**
PALMER'S CROSS 1B **26**
Palmers Gro.
B36: Hodg H 1C **104**
Palmerston Dr. B69: Tiv. 5D **78**
Palmerston Rd. B11: S'brk 5B **118**
Palmer St. B9: Birm. 1A **118**
Palmer's Way WV8: Bilb 6A **14**
Palm Ho. B20: Hand. 4B **82**
Palmvale Cft. B26: Sheld 5E **121**
Palomino Pl. B16: Birm 1B **116**
Pamela Rd. B31: N'fld 5E **145**
Pan Cft. B36: Hodg H. 2A **104**
Panjab Gdns. B67: Smeth 3D **98**
Pannel Cft. B19: Hock 3F **101**
Panther Cft. B34: S End. 4H **105**
Paper Mill End
B44: Gt Barr 1F **83**
Paper Mill End Ind. Est.
B44: Gt Barr 1F **83**
Papyrus Way B36: Hodg H. 6D **86**
Parade B1: Birm 6E **101** (3A **4**)
B72: S Cold 1H **69**
(Holland St.)
B72: S Cold 6A **54**
(Newhall Wlk.)
Parade, The B37: K'hrst. 3C **106**
B64: Crad H 3G **111**
DY1: Dud 5D **76**
DY6: W Hth 2H **91**
WS8: Bwnhls 4A **10**
Parade Vw. WS8: Bwnhls 5A **10**
PARADISE 1F **95**
Paradise DY2: Dud 1F **95**
Paradise Cir. Queensway
B1: Birm 1E **117** (3B **4**)
Paradise Ct. B28: Hall G 1D **148**
Paradise Gro. WS3: Pels. 4D **20**
Paradise La. B28: Hall G 1E **149**
WS3: Pels 4D **20**
Paradise Pl. B3: Birm 1E **117** (4C **4**)
Paradise St. B1: Birm 1F **117** (4C **4**)
Pardington Cl. B92: Sol 5A **138**
Pargeter Ct. WS2: Wals 1A **48**
Pargeter Rd. B67: Smeth. 1D **114**
Pargeter St. DY8: Stourb 1D **124**
WS2: Wals 1A **48**
Par Grn. B38: K Nor. 6H **145**
Parish Gdns. DY9: Pedm 4F **125**
Park & Ride
Bescot Cres. 6B **48**
Corser St. 2B **44**
Elmdon La. 4B **122**
Monkspath 4F **151**
Plascom 2C **44**
Priestfield 4C **44**
Science Park 3G **27**
Park App. B23: Erd. 5C **84**
Park Av. B12: Bal H 6H **117**
B18: Hock 2C **100**
B30: K Nor 2C **146**
B46: Col. 3H **107**
B65: Row R 6C **96**
B67: Smeth 5D **98**
B68: O'bry 6H **97**
B91: Sol. 4H **151**
DY4: Tip. 2G **77**
WV1: Wolv. 6F **27** (1A **170**)
WV4: Penn. 6G **43**

Park Av. WV5: Wom 2F **73**
  WV13: W'hall 1H **45**
Park Bldgs. DY3: Lwr G 3G **75**
  (off Park Rd.)
Park Cir. B6: Aston 2H **101**
  (not continuous)
Park Cl. B24: Erd 2B **86**
  B69: Tiv 2C **96**
  B92: Sol 3H **137**
  DY1: Dud 6D **60**
  WS6: C Hay 2E **7**
  WS8: Bwnhls 5B **10**
Park Ct. B65: Row R 6C **96**
  B73: Bold 4F **69**
Park Cres. B71: W Brom 3B **80**
  WV1: Wolv 1F **43**
Park Cft. B47: H'wd 4A **162**
PARK DALE 6E **27**
Park Dale WS5: Wals 5G **49**
Parkdale DY3: Sed 5H **59**
Parkdale Av. WS10: W'bry 1G **63**
Parkdale Ct. B24: Erd 5F **85**
Park Dale Ct. WV1: Wolv 6E **27**
Parkdale Dr. B31: Longb 2E **159**
Park Dale E. WV1: Wolv 6E **27**
Parkdale Rd. B26: Sheld 6G **121**
Park Dale W. WV1: Wolv 6E **27**
Park Dr. B74: Four O 1G **53**
  B74: Lit A 5C **36**
  WV4: Penn 6G **43**
Park Edge B17: Harb 4G **115**
Park End B32: Bart G 4B **130**
Parker Ho. B14: K Hth 4H **147**
Park Paul Ind. Est. WV2: Wolv 4G **43**
Parker Rd. WV11: Wed 6H **17**
Parker St. B16: Edg 2B **116**
  WS3: Blox 6G **19**
Parkes Av. WV8: Cod 5H **13**
Parkes' Hall Rd. DY1: Dud 1C **76**
Parkes Ho. B69: O'bry 2G **97**
Parkes La. DY3: Sed 6C **60**
  DY4: Tip 5H **61**
Parkes St. B67: Smeth 5D **98**
  DY5: Brie H 6H **93**
  WV13: W'hall 2B **46**
Parkeston Cres. B44: K'sdng 4C **68**
Park Farm Rd. B43: Gt Barr 1D **66**
PARKFIELD 6B **44**
Parkfield B32: Bart G 3F **129**
Parkfield Chalet Land (Cvn. Pk.)
  WV2: Wolv 5H **43**
Parkfield Cl. B15: Edg 4E **117**
  B62: Quin 6G **113**
Parkfield Colliery WV4: E'shll 6B **44**
Parkfield Ct. B46: Col 2H **107**
  (Park Rd.)
  B46: Col 3H **107**
  (Sumner Rd.)
Parkfield Cres. WV2: E'shll 5A **44**
Parkfield Dr. B36: Cas B 6G **87**
Parkfield Gro. WV2: E'shll 5A **44**
Parkfield Ho. B23: Erd 6E **85**
Parkfield Pl. DY8: Stourb 6F **109**
Parkfield Rd. B8: Salt 6E **103**
  B46: Col 2H **107**
  B68: O'bry 6G **97**
  DY2: Dud 3F **95**
  DY8: Stourb 6E **109**
  WV4: E'shll 5H **43**
Park Gdns. DY9: W'cte 2B **126**
Park Gro. B10: Small H 3D **118**
  B46: Wat O 4E **89**
Park Hall Cl. WS5: Wals 5G **49**
Park Hall Cres. B36: Cas B 1F **105**
Parkhall Cft. B34: S End 2G **105**
Park Hall Rd. WS5: Wals 4G **49**
  WV4: Penn 1H **59**
Parkhead Cres. DY2: Dud 1D **94**
Parkhead Rd. DY2: Dud 1D **94**
Park Hill B13: Mose 1G **133**
  B65: B'hth 2B **112**
  WS10: W'bry 1H **63**
Park Hill Dr. B20: Hand 3B **82**
Park Hill Rd. B17: Harb 5G **115**
  B67: Smeth 4D **98**
Parkhill Rd. B76: Walm 1D **86**
Parkhill St. DY2: Dud 1G **95**

Park Ho. B66: Smeth 4G **99**
  WV11: Ess 4A **18**
Parkhouse Av. WV11: Wed 3D **28**
Parkhouse Dr. B23: Erd 2A **84**
Parkhouse Gdns.
  DY3: Lwr G 3G **75**
Parklands B45: Redn 1G **157**
  B91: Sol 4E **151**
Parklands, The B23: Erd 1D **84**
  DY9: Pedm 2G **125**
  WV3: Wolv 2B **42**
Parklands Ct. B45: Redn 1G **157**
  WS3: Blox 6H **19**
Parklands Dr. B74: Four O 3F **53**
Parklands Gdns.
  WS1: Wals 3E **49**
Parklands Rd. WS10: Darl 6E **47**
  WV1: Wolv 2C **44**
  WV14: Cose 3F **61**
Park La. B6: Aston 2G **101**
  B20: Hand 2F **81**
  B21: Hand 2F **81**
  B35: Cas V 3F **87**
  B63: Crad 5C **110**
  B69: O'bry 3G **97**
  B76: Min 3G **87**
  CV7: Bal C 5G **155**
  DY6: K'wfrd 2C **92**
  WS6: Gt Wyr 2F **7**
  WS10: Darl 4F **47**
  WV10: Bush, Wolv 3A **28**
Park La. E. DY4: Tip 3A **78**
Park La. Est., The B69: O'bry 2G **97**
Park La. Ind. Est. B71: W Brom 6F **81**
Park La. Trad. Est.
  WV10: Wolv 4A **28**
Park La. W. DY4: Tip 2G **77**
Park Lime Dr. WS4: Wals 5F **33**
Park Mall WS1: Wals 1C **48**
Park Mdw. Av. WV14: Bils 3E **45**
Park M. B29: S Oak 4F **131**
Park Pl. B7: Nech 2C **102**
Park Retreat B66: Smeth 5F **99**
Park Ridge B74: S Cold 4G **53**
Park Ridge Dr. B63: Crad 5D **110**
Park Ri. WV3: Wolv 1C **42**
Park Rd. B6: Aston 2A **102**
  B11: S'hll 2C **134**
  B13: Mose 1H **133**
  B18: Hock 3B **100**
  B23: Erd 5C **84**
  B46: Col 3H **107**
  B63: Crad 6C **110**
  B67: Smeth 1D **114**
  B69: Tiv 1C **96**
  B73: S Cold 6H **53**
  B91: Sol 4G **151**
  DY1: Dud 1D **76**
  DY2: Neth 3E **95**
  DY3: Lwr G 3G **75**
  DY5: Quar B 3B **110**
  DY8: Woll 6B **108**
  WS3: Blox 6H **19**
  (not continuous)
  WS4: Rus 4G **33**
  WS5: Wals 6H **49**
  WV13: W'hall 6H **29**
  WV14: Bils 6E **45**
Park Rd. E. WV1: Wolv 6F **27**
Park Rd. Nth. B6: Aston 2A **102**
Park Rd. Sth. B18: Hock 4D **100**
Park Rd. W. DY8: Woll 6A **108**
  WV1: Wolv 6E **27**
Parkrose Ind. Est. B66: Smeth 1F **99**
Parks Cres. WV11: Ess 4A **18**
Parkside B23: Bart G 3A **130**
  B37: Mars G 4F **123**
Parkside Av. WV13: W'hall 1G **45**
Parkside Cl. WS10: W'bry 2H **63**
Parkside Ind. Est. WV1: Wolv 2B **44**
Parkside Rd. B20: Hand 2A **82**
  B63: Crad 6F **111**
Parkside Way B31: Longb 6A **144**
  B74: S'tly 2A **52**
Park Sq. B37: Mars G 3F **123**
Parkstone Cl. WS4: S'fld 1G **33**

Park St. B5: Birm 1G **117** (5F **5**)
  B6: Aston 2A **102**
  (not continuous)
  B64: Crad H 1G **111**
  B65: B'hth 2D **112**
  B69: O'bry 3F **97**
  B70: W Brom 4B **80**
  DY1: Dud 3B **94**
  DY4: Tip 2A **78**
  DY6: K'wfrd 3B **92**
  DY8: Amb 3D **108**
  DY8: Stourb 6E **109**
  DY9: Lye 6B **110**
  WS1: Wals 1C **48**
  WS6: C Hay 2E **7**
  WS10: Darl 6C **46**
  WS10: W'bry 2F **63**
Park St. Arc. WS1: Wals 1C **48**
  (off Park St.)
Park St. Sth. WV2: Wolv 5G **43**
  WS10: Darl 5B **46**
Park Trad. Est. B18: Hock 3C **100**
Pk. Tree Wlk. B24: Erd 3B **86**
Park Vw. B10: Small H 4D **118**
  B18: Win G 5A **100**
  B73: S Cold 5G **53**
  B91: Sol 5F **151**
  WS10: W'bry 5C **46**
Park View Community Leisure Cen. 4F **103**
Parkview Cl. DY6: W Hth 1H **91**
Parkview Cres. WS2: Wals 5G **31**
Parkview Dr. B8: W End 3G **103**
  WS8: Bwnhls 3B **10**
Park Vw. Rd. B31: N'fld 4C **144**
  B74: Four O 6D **36**
  DY9: W'cte 1B **126**
  WV14: Bils 3E **45**
Park Vw. Trad. Est. B30: K Nor 4B **146**
PARK VILLAGE 4B **28**
Park Village Youth Media Activity Cen.
. . . . 4B **28**
Parkville Av. B17: Harb 1F **131**
Park Wlk. DY5: Quar B 3B **110**
Park Way B45: Redn 6H **143**
  WV11: Wed 6A **18**
Parkway B8: W End 4G **103**
Parkway, The B74: Tip 4D **62**
  WS4: S'fld 1G **33**
  WV6: Pert 3D **24**
Parkway Ind. Cen. B7: Birm 5A **102** (1H **5**)
Parkway Ind. Est., The WS10: W'bry 4E **63**
Parkway Rd. DY1: Dud 5C **76**
Parkway Rdbt. WS10: W'bry 4E **63**
Parkwood Cl. WS8: Wals W 2C **22**
Parkwood Cft. B43: Gt Barr 4D **66**
Parkwood Dr. B73: New O 3C **68**
Parkyn St. WV2: Wolv 3A **44**
Parliament St. B6: Aston 3G **101**
  B10: Small H 3C **118**
  B70: W Brom 6B **80**
Parry Rd. WV11: Wed 1A **30**
Parsonage Dr. B45: Coft H 5B **158**
  B63: Crad 4C **110**
Parsonage St. B69: O'bry 2H **97**
  B71: W Brom 1B **80**
Parsons Hill B30: K Nor 5C **146**
  B68: O'bry 2H **113**
Parson's St. DY1: Dud 6E **77**
Parsons Way WS2: Wals 3F **31**
Partons Rd. B14: K Hth 1F **147**
Partridge Av. WS10: Darl 5B **46**
Partridge Cl. B37: Chel W 6E **107**
Partridge Ct. B4: Birm 1E **5**
  WS10: W'bry 2F **63**
Partridge Mill WS3: Pels 4C **20**
Partridge Rd. B26: Yard 2E **121**
  DY8: Stourb 1A **124**
Passey Rd. B13: Mose 3D **134**
Passfield Rd. B33: Yard 6E **105**
Pastures, The WV6: Pert 5D **24**
Pastures Wlk. B38: K Nor 2H **159**
Pasture Vw. WS3: Pels 5D **20**
Patent Dr. WS10: W'bry 3C **62**
Patent Shaft Rdbt.
  WS10: W'bry 2D **62**

Paternoster Row B5: Birm. 1G **117** (4F **5**)
WV1: Wolv 1G **43** (2A **170**)
Paterson Ct. B93: Know 3E **167**
Paterson Pl. WS8: Bwnhls 2D **22**
Pathlow Cres. B90: Shir. 6G **149**
Pathway, The B14: K Hth 2D **146**
Patman Gdns. B16: Edg. 2G **115**
Paton Gro. B13: Mose 3H **133**
Patricia Av. B14: Yard W 3C **148**
WV4: Penn. 6G **43**
Patricia Cres. DY1: Dud. 1D **76**
Patricia Dr. DY4: Tip 5A **78**
Patrick Gregory Rd. WV11: Wed 2H **29**
Patrick Rd. B26: Yard. 4C **120**
Patriot Cl. WS1: Wals 5B **48**
Patshull Av. WV10: F'hses 4F **15**
Patshull Cl. B43: Gt Barr 4H **65**
Patshull Gro. WV10: F'hses 4F **15**
Patshull Pl. B19: Loz 2E **101**
Patterdale Rd. B23: Erd. 3D **84**
Patterdale Way DY5: Brie H 3F **109**
Patterton Dr. B76: Walm 5E **71**
Pattingham Rd. WV6: Pert, Tett. 6A **24**
Pattison Gdns. B23: Erd. 5D **84**
Pattison St. WS5: Wals 6C **48**
Paul Byrne Ct. B20: Hand 6D **82**
Paul Pursehouse Rd. WV14: Cose 2F **61**
Pauls Coppice WS8: Bwnhls 2B **22**
Paul St. WS10: W'bry 3G **63**
WV2: Wolv 3G **43** (6A **170**)
WV14: Cose 4C **60**
Paul Va. DY4: Tip. 2B **78**
Pavenham Dr. B5: Edg. 1E **133**
Pavilion B40: Nat E C. 1G **139**
Pavilion Av. B67: Smeth 6B **98**
Pavilion Cl. WS9: A'rdge 2D **34**
Pavilion Dr. B6: Witt 4H **83**
Pavilion Gdns. DY2: Neth. 1E **111**
Pavilion Rd. B6: Witt. 4H **83**
Pavilions, The B4: Birm 1G **117** (4F **5**)
B37: Mars G 3F **123**
Pavior's Rd. WS7: Chase 1A **10**
Paxford Way B31: N'fld 1D **144**
Paxton Av. WV6: Pert 6E **25**
Paxton Rd. DY9: W'cte. 1C **126**
Payne St. B65: B'hth 2C **112**
Payton Cl. B69: O'bry. 6E **79**
Payton Rd. B21: Hand 1H **99**
PDH Ind. Est. WS10: Mox 1C **62**
Peace Cl. WS6: C Hay 2E **7**
Peace Wlk. B37: Chel W 2D **122**
Peach Av. WS10: Darl 5C **46**
Peachley Cl. B63: Hale. 2B **128**
Peach Ley Rd. B29: W Cas 6D **130**
Peach Rd. WV12: W'hall 3A **30**
Peacock Av. WV11: Wed 1A **30**
Peacock Cl. DY4: Tip 3B **78**
Peacock Cft. WS6: Gt Wyr. 3G **7**
Peacock Rd. B13: Mose. 1H **147**
WS10: Darl. 4B **46**
Peacocks Est. B64: Crad H. 2E **111**
Peak Cft. B36: Hodg H 1B **104**
Peak Dr. DY3: Lwr G 4H **75**
Peake Cres. WS8: Bwnhls 2B **22**
Peake Dr. DY4: Tip. 3B **78**
Peake Rd. WS8: Bwnhls 2C **22**
Peak Ho. Rd. B43: Gt Barr. 2A **66**
Peakman Cl. B45: Redn. 3G **157**
Peak Rd. DY8: Amb 5F **109**
Peal St. WS1: Wals 2D **48**
Pearce Cl. DY1: Dud 1A **94**
Pearl Gro. B18: Win G 5A **100**
B27: A Grn. 2H **135**
Pearman Rd. B45: Fran 6D **142**
B66: Smeth 6E **99**
Pearmans Cft. B47: H'wd. 3A **162**
Pearsall Dr. B69: O'bry 1E **97**
Pearson Ct. WV12: W'hall 5D **30**
Pearson St. B64: Old H 2G **111**
B70: W Brom 3H **79**
DY5: Brie H 6H **93**
DY9: Lye. 1B **126**
WV2: Wolv 3G **43** (6B **170**)
Pear Tree Av. DY4: Tip. 2H **77**
Peartree Av. WV13: W'hall. 2B **46**
Pear Tree Cl. B33: Stech 1B **120**
B43: Gt Barr 4F **65**
Peartree Cl. B90: Shir 5D **148**
Pear Tree Ct. B43: Gt Barr. 5G **65**
B65: Row R 6D **96**
Peartree Cres. B90: Shir 4C **148**
Pear Tree Dr. B43: Gt Barr 5F **65**
B65: Row R 6D **96**
Peartree Dr. DY8: Stourb 3E **125**
Peartree Gro. B90: Shir 5C **148**
Peartree Ho. B68: O'bry. 4A **98**
Peartree Ind. Est. DY2: Dud 3C **94**
Pear Tree La. WS8: Bwnhls. 3G **9**
WV11: Wed 6D **16**
Peartree La. B64: Old H. 2G **111**
DY2: Dud 4C **94**
WV14: Cose 5F **61**
Pear Tree Rd. B34: S End 3G **105**
B43: Gt Barr 4F **65**
B67: Smeth 5C **98**
Peascroft La. WV14: Bils. 5G **45**
(not continuous)
Peasefield Cl. B21: Hand. 1G **99**
Pebble Cl. DY8: Stourb 6F **109**
Pebble Mill Rd. B5: Edg. 1E **133**
Pebworth Av. B90: M'path 3F **165**
Pebworth Cl. B29: S Oak 3D **132**
Pebworth Gro. B33: Sheld 3G **121**
DY1: Dud 4C **76**
Peckham Rd. B44: K'sdng 3A **68**
Peckingham St. B63: Hale 2B **128**
Peckover Cl. B65: B'hth 2C **112**
Peddimore La. B76: Walm 1F **87**
(not continuous)
PEDMORE 4G **125**
Pedmore Ct. Rd. DY8: Stourb 4F **125**
Pedmore Gro. B44: Gt Barr 3H **67**
Pedmore Hall La. DY9: Pedm 5G **125**
Pedmore La. DY9: Hag, Pedm. 4G **125**
Pedmore Rd. DY2: Dud 5B **94**
DY5: Brie H 5B **94**
DY9: Lye 6H **109**
Pedmore Rd. Ind. Est.
DY5: Brie H 5B **94**
Pedmore Wlk. B69: O'bry 4D **96**
Peel Cl. B92: H Ard 1B **154**
WS10: Darl 3D **46**
WV13: W'hall 2A **46**
Peel St. B18: Win G 4A **100**
B71: W Brom 2A **80**
DY2: Dud 1G **95**
DY4: Tip. 3A **78**
WV3: Wolv 2G **43** (4A **170**)
WV13: W'hall 2A **46**
Peel Wlk. B17: Harb 4D **114**
Peel Way B69: Tiv 5C **78**
Pegasus Ct. B75: Four O 6G **37**
Pegasus Wlk. B29: S Oak 4H **131**
Pegleg Wlk. B14: K Hth 5E **147**
Pelham Dr. DY1: Dud. 5C **76**
Pelham Rd. B8: W End 5H **103**
Pelham St. WV3: Wolv. 2E **43**
PELSALL 4E **21**
Pelsall La. WS3: Blox 4B **20**
(not continuous)
WS4: Rus. 1E **33**
Pelsall Rd. WS8: Bwnhls. 1G **21**
PELSALL WOOD 3D **20**
Pemberley Rd. B27: A Grn 3G **135**
Pemberton Cl. B66: Smeth. 6F **99**
Pemberton Cres.
WS10: W'bry 1A **64**
Pemberton Rd. B70: W Brom 1G **79**
WV14: Cose 4F **61**
Pemberton St. B18: Birm. 5D **100**
Pembridge Cl. B32: Bart G 6G **129**
DY5: Quar B. 2B **110**
Pembridge Rd. B93: Dorr 6H **165**
Pembroke Av. WV2: E'shll 4C **44**
Pembroke Cl. *B71: W Brom. 4H 63*
(off Pembroke Rd.)
WV12: W'hall 3C **30**
Pembroke Cft. B28: Hall G. 2G **149**
Pembroke Gdns. DY8: Word 2A **108**
Pembroke Ho. B36: Cas B 2C **106**
WS3: Blox 3A 32
(off Comwall Clo.)
Pembroke Rd. B12: Bal H 1A **134**
B71: W Brom 5H **63**
Pembroke Way B8: Salt 4C **102**
B28: Hall G. 2G **149**
B71: W Brom 6H **63**
Pembury Cl. B74: S'tly. 5H **51**
Pembury Cft. B44: K'sdng 4A **68**
Pencombe Dr. WV4: Penn 6H **43**
Pencroft Rd. B34: S End. 2F **105**
Penda Ct. B20: Hand 1C **100**
Penda Gro. WV6: Pert 4F **25**
Pendeen Rd. B14: Yard W 3B **148**
PENDEFORD. 4E **15**
Pendeford Av. WV6: Tett 1C **26**
Pendeford Bus. Pk. WV9: Pend 4D **14**
Pendeford Cl. WV6: Tett. 1C **26**
Pendeford Hall La.
WV9: Coven, Pend. 2H **13**
Pendeford Hall Mobile Home Pk.
WV9: Pend. 3C **14**
Pendeford La. WV9: Pend 3E **15**
Pendeford Mill La. WV8: Bilb 4H **13**
Pendene Ct. WV4: Penn. 6E **43**
Pendennis Cl. B30: B'vlle. 2H **145**
Pendennis Dr. B69: Tiv 1A **96**
Penderell Cl. WV10: F'stne 1C **16**
Penderel St. WS3: Blox 1A **32**
Pendigo Way B40: Nat E C. 1G **139**
(not continuous)
Pendinas Dr. WV8: Bilb 4H **13**
Pendleton Gro. B27: A Grn 5H **135**
Pendragon Rd. B42: P Barr 3E **83**
Pendrel Cl. WS6: Gt Wyr 5F **7**
Pendrell Cl. B37: F'bri 6C **106**
WV8: Cod. 4G **13**
Pendrell Ct. WV8: Cod. 4G **13**
Pendrill Rd. WV10: Bush. 4A **16**
Penfields Rd. DY8: Amb 5E **109**
Penge Gro. B44: Gt Barr 2G **67**
Penhallow Dr. WV4: E'shll 6A **44**
Penkridge Cl. WS2: Wals. 5B **32**
Penkridge Gro. B33: Stech 5D **104**
Penkridge St. WS2: Wals. 6B **32**
Penk Ri. WV6: Tett. 5G **25**
Penleigh Gdns. WV5: Wom 6F **57**
Penley Gro. B8: W End 3H **103**
Penmark Cl. B35: Cas V. 4F **87**
PENN 6C **42**
Pennant Ct. B65: Row R 6B **96**
Pennant Gro. B29: W Cas. 3E **131**
Pennant Rd. B64: Crad H 2F **111**
B65: Row R 6B **96**
Pennard Gro. B32: Quin. 1D **130**
Penn Cl. WS3: Blox 1A **32**
Penn Comn. Rd. WV4: Penn 4C **58**
Penncricket La. B65: Row R 6E **97**
B68: O'bry 6F **97**
Penncroft La. WV4: Penn. 4D **58**
Penn Dale Cl. B24: Erd 1A **86**
PENN FIELDS 5E **43**
Penn Gro. B29: W Cas 3F **131**
Pennhouse Av. WV4: Penn 6D **42**
Penn Ind. Est. B64: Crad H. 2F **111**
Pennine Dr. DY3: Lwr G. 4H **75**
Pennine Way B8: Salt. 4C **102**
DY8: Amb. 5E **109**
WV12: W'hall. 4D **30**
Pennington Cl. B70: W Brom. 5G **79**
Pennis Ct. B76: Walm 6D **70**
Penn Rd. B65: Row R. 6E **97**
DY3: Sed 4D **58**
WV2: Wolv. 4F **43** (6A **170**)
WV3: Wolv 4F **43**
WV4: Penn. 2B **58**
Penn Rd. Island WV2: Wolv . . . 2G **43** (5A **170**)
Penn Rd. Retail Pk. WV2: Wolv 3G **43**
Penns Lake Rd. B76: Walm 5C **70**
Penns La. B72: W Grn 6A **70**
B76: Walm 6A **70**
Penn St. B4: Birm 6A **102** (2H **5**)
B64: Old H 3H **111**
WV3: Wolv 3F **43**
Penns Wood Cl. DY3: Sed 3G **59**
Penns Wood Dr. B76: Walm. 6D **70**
Pennwood Ct. WV4: Penn 5B **42**
Pennwood La. WV4: Penn 2D **58**
Pennyacre Rd. B14: K Hth 5F **147**
Penny Ct. WS6: Gt Wyr 5F **7**
Pennycress Grn. WS11: Nort C 1D **8**

Pennycroft Ho. B33: Stech 6C **104**
Pennyfield Cft. B33: Stech 6C **104**
Pennyhill La. B71: W Brom 6C **64**
Penny Royal Cl. DY3: Lwr G 5H **75**
Pennyroyal Cl. WS5: Wals 2F **65**
Penrice Dr. B69: Tiv 6H **77**
Penrith Cl. DY5: Brie H 3F **109**
Penrith Cft. B32: Bart G 5B **130**
Penrith Gro. B37: Chel W 1E **123**
Penryn Cl. WS5: Wals 4H **49**
Penryn Rd. WS5: Wals 4H **49**
Pensby Cl. B13: Mose 5D **134**
Pensford Rd. B31: N'fld 4G **145**
Pensham Cft. B90: M'path 3E **165**
Penshaw Cl. WV9: Pend 4E **15**
Penshaw Gro. B13: Mose 4D **134**
Penshurst Av. B20: Hand 6F **83**
PENSNETT 3G **93**
Pensnett Rd. DY1: Dud 2A **94**
DY5: Brie H 4G **93**
Pensnett Trad. Est. DY6: P'ntt 1D **92**
Penstock Dr. B69: O'bry 5G **97**
Penstone La. WV4: Lwr P 1E **57**
Pentland Cft. B12: Birm 4H **117**
Pentland Gdns. WV3: Wolv 1C **42**
Pentos Dr. B11: S'hll 1D **134**
Pentridge Cl. B76: Walm 2D **86**
Penwood Gdns. WV14: Cose 5E **61**
Penzer St. DY6: K'wfrd 2B **92**
Peolsford Rd. WS3: Pels 3E **21**
Peony Wlk. B23: Erd 4B **84**
Peplins Way B30: K Nor 4D **146**
Peplow Rd. B33: Stech 5E **105**
Pepperbox Dr. DY4: Tip 2A **78**
Peppercorn Pl.
B70: W Brom 3A **80**
Pepper Hill DY8: Stourb 1E **125**
Pepper Wood Dr. B31: Longb 6A **144**
Pepys Ct. B43: Gt Barr 6A **66**
Perch Av. B37: F'bri 6C **106**
Perch Cl. WV10: Wolv 5D **28**
Perch Rd. WS2: Wals 5G **31**
Percival Rd. B16: Edg 2G **115**
Percy Bus. Pk. B69: O'bry 2F **97**
Percy Rd. B11: S'hll 2D **134**
Peregrine Cl. DY1: Dud 6B **76**
Pereira Rd. B17: Harb 4G **115**
Perimeter Rd. B40: Nat E C 1F **139**
(not continuous)
Perivale Gro. WV14: Cose 5F **61**
Perivale Way DY8: Amb 3E **109**
Periwinkle Cl. WS8: Clay 1H **21**
Perkins Cl. DY1: Dud 1E **77**
Perks Rd. WV11: Wed 6A **18**
Perott Dr. B75: R'ley 1B **54**
Perrins Gro. B8: W End 3G **103**
Perrin's La. DY9: W'cte 1B **126**
Perrins Ri. DY9: W'cte 1B **126**
Perrott Gdns. DY5: Brie H 2E **109**
Perrott's Folly B16: Edg 2B **116**
Perrott St. B18: Win G 3H **99**
PERRY 1G **83**
Perry Av. B42: P Barr 3E **83**
WV10: Bush 1B **28**
PERRY BARR 2C **82**
Perry Barr Stadium (Greyhound) 4F **83**
Perry Barr Station (Rail) 5F **83**
PERRY BEECHES 6D **66**
Perry Beeches Swimming Pool 6D **66**
Perry Cl. DY2: Dud 1F **95**
PERRY COMMON 5D **68**
Perry Comn. Rd. B23: Erd 6B **68**
Perry Ct. B68: O'bry 4H **113**
Perryford Dr. B91: Sol 1G **165**
Perry Hall Dr. WV12: W'hall 4B **30**
Perry Hall Rd. WV11: Wed 3H **29**
Perry Hill Cres. B68: O'bry 4H **113**
Perry Hill Ho. B68: O'bry 3A **114**
Perry Hill La. B68: O'bry 4H **113**
Perry Hill Rd. B68: O'bry 4H **113**
Perry Pk. Cres. B42: P Barr 1E **83**
Perry Pk. Rd. B64: Old H 2B **112**
B65: B'hth 2B **112**
Perry St. B66: Smeth 2D **98**
DY4: Tip 3A **78**
WS10: Darl 3D **46**
(not continuous)
Perry St. WS10: W'bry 3F **63**
WV14: Bils 2G **61**
Perry Trad. Est. WV14: Bils 2G **61**
Perry Villa Dr. B42: P Barr 2F **83**
Perry Wlk. B23: Erd 1B **84**
Perry Well Dr. B6: Witt 3H **83**
Perry Well Rd. B6: Witt 2H **83**
Perry Wood Rd. B42: Gt Barr 5C **66**
Persehouse St. WS1: Wals 1D **48**
Pershore Av. B29: S Oak 3D **132**
Pershore Cl. WS3: Blox 5F **19**
Pershore Rd. B29: S Oak 6C **132**
B30: K Nor 3C **146**
B63: Hale 3A **128**
WS3: Blox 5F **19**
Pershore Rd. Sth. B30: K Nor 3B **146**
Pershore St. B5: Birm 2G **117** (6E **5**)
Pershore Way WS3: Blox 5F **19**
Pertemps Bees RUFC 3D **150**
Perth Rd. WV12: W'hall 3B **30**
PERTON 5E **25**
Perton Brook Va. WV6: Tett 1F **41**
Perton Gro. B29: W Cas 4E **131**
WV6: Tett 1F **41**
Perton Rd. WV6: Tett 1E **41**
Petchells Cl. DY5: P'ntt 4F **93**
Peter Av. WV14: Bils 3H **61**
Peterbrook B90: Shir 6C **148**
Peterbrook Ri. B90: Shir 6D **148**
Peterbrook Rd. B90: Maj G 2D **162**
B90: Shir 5C **148**
Peterdale Dr. WV4: Penn 2D **58**
Peters Av. B31: N'fld 5D **144**
Petersbourne Ct. B28: Hall G 5E **135**
Petersfield Ct. B28: Hall G 5F **135**
Petersfield Dr. B65: Row R 6E **97**
Petersfield Rd. B28: Hall G 6E **135**
Petersham Pl. B15: Edg 5A **116**
Petersham Rd. B44: K'sdng 4C **68**
Peter's Hill Rd. DY5: Brie H 4G **109**
Petershouse Dr. B74: Four O 4F **37**
Peters St. B70: W Brom 6G **63**
Petford St. B64: Old H 2G **111**
Pettitt Cl. B14: K Hth 5G **147**
Pettyfield Cl. B26: Sheld 5F **121**
Pettyfields Cl. B93: Know 4B **166**
Petworth Cl. WV13: W'hall 3H **45**
Petworth Gro. B26: Yard 5C **120**
Pevensey Cl. B69: Tiv 1H **95**
Peverell Dr. B28: Hall G 6F **135**
Peveril Gro. B76: Walm 1C **70**
Peverill Rd. WV4: E'shll 2A **60**
WV6: Pert 5F **25**
Peveril Way B43: Gt Barr 3B **66**
Pheasant Cft. B36: Cas B 1C **106**
Pheasant Rd. B67: Smeth 1B **114**
Pheasant St. DY5: Brie H 6G **93**
PHEASEY 1F **67**
Philip Ct. B76: Walm 2D **70**
Philip Rd. B63: Hale 2H **127**
DY4: Tip 2D **78**
Philip Sidney Rd. B11: S'hll 2C **134**
Philip St. WV14: Cose 4F **61**
Philip Victor Rd. B20: Hand 6B **82**
Phillimore Rd. B8: Salt 4D **102**
Phillip Rd. WS2: Wals 5A **48**
Phillips Av. WV11: Wed 6H **17**
Phillips St. B6: Aston 3G **101**
Phillips St. Ind. Est. B6: Aston 3H **101**
Phipson Rd. B11: S'hll 1B **134**
Phoenix, The B90: Bly P 6D **164**
Phoenix Ct. B35: Cas V 4D **86**
Phoenix Dr. WS9: A'rdge 2C **34**
Phoenix Grn. B15: Edg 4A **116**
Phoenix Ind. Est. WV14: Bils 1H **61**
Phoenix Intl. Ind. Est. B70: W Brom 2F **79**
Phoenix Pk. B7: Nech 3A **102**
B65: Row R 1E **113**
Phoenix Pas. *DY2: Dud 6F 77*
(off Hall St.)
Phoenix Ri. B23: Erd 6B **68**
WS10: Darl 1D **62**
WV2: Wolv 5G 43
(off Blakenhall Gdns.)
Phoenix Rd. DY4: Tip 1H **77**
WV11: Wed 6F **29**
Phoenix Rd. Ind. Est. WV11: Wed 6F **29**
Phoenix St. B70: W Brom 3F **79**
WV2: Wolv 5H **43**
Phoenix Works Ind. Est. WS10: Darl 4E **47**
Piccadilly Arc. B2: Birm 4D **4**
Piccadilly Cl. B37: Chel W 2E **123**
Pickenham Rd. B14: K Hth 6A **148**
Pickering Cft. B32: Bart G 4A **130**
Pickering Rd. WV11: Wed 4F **29**
Pickersleigh Cl. B63: Hale 2A **128**
Pickford St. B5: Birm 1H **117** (5H **5**)
Pickrell Rd. WV14: Cose 4D **60**
Pickwick Cl. B13: Mose 3B **134**
Pickwick Gro. B13: Mose 3C **134**
Pickwick Pl. WV14: Bils 1G **61**
Picton Cft. B37: Chel W 1F **123**
Picton Gro. B13: Mose 2B **148**
Picturedrome Way WS10: Darl 5D **46**
Piddock Rd. B66: Smeth 4E **99**
Pierce Av. B92: Olton 2C **136**
Piercy St. B70: W Brom 4G **79**
Piers Rd. B21: Hand 2C **100**
(not continuous)
Pier St. WS8: Bwnhls 6B **10**
Piggotts Cft. B37: F'bri 6B **106**
Pike Cl. B20: Hand 6B **82**
Pike Dr. B37: Chel W 6E **107**
Pikehelve St. B70: W Brom 6E **63**
Pikehorne Cft. B36: Cas B 5H **87**
Pike Rd. WS2: Wals 5G **31**
Pikes, The B45: Rubery 1F **157**
Pikewater Rd. B9: Bord G 1E **119**
Pilkington Av. B72: W Grn 2H **69**
Pilson Cl. B36: Hodg H 1D **104**
Pimbury Rd. WV12: W'hall 2D **30**
Pimlico Ct. DY3: Lwr G 4H **75**
Pimpernel Dr. WS5: Wals 2E **65**
Pinbury Cft. B37: Mars G 2D **122**
Pineapple Cl. B14: K Hth 1E **147**
Pineapple Gro. B30: Stir 5E **133**
Pineapple Rd. B30: Stir 6E **133**
Pine Av. B66: Smeth 2C **98**
WS10: W'bry 6F **47**
Pine Cl. B91: Sol 5D **150**
DY6: K'wfrd 4B **92**
WS6: Gt Wyr 1F **7**
WV3: Wolv 2E **43**
Pine Grn. DY1: Dud 1C **76**
Pine Gro. B14: K Hth 2A **148**
Pine Ho. B36: Hodg H 1D **104**
Pinehurst Dr. B38: K Nor 4B **146**
Pine Leigh B74: Four O 2H **53**
Pineneedle Cft. WV12: W'hall 5E **31**
Pine Rd. B69: Tiv 1A **96**
DY1: Dud 2E **77**
Pines, The B45: Redn 6G **143**
B90: Ches G 4B **164**
WS1: Wals 3D **48**
WV3: Wolv 2B **42**
Pine Sq. B37: Chel W 1D **122**
Pine St. WS3: Blox 5B **20**
Pinetree Dr. B74: S'tly 2F **51**
Pineview B31: N'fld 5D **144**
Pine Wlk. B31: N'fld 4F **145**
DY9: W'cte 2H **125**
WV8: Cod 5F **13**
Pinewall Av. B38: K Nor 6C **146**
Pineways B74: Four O 6C **36**
DY8: Word 1A **108**
Pineways, The B69: O'bry 4C **96**
Pineways Dr. WV6: Wolv 5C **26**
Pinewood Cl. B44: Gt Barr 6G **67**
B45: Rubery 1D **156**
WS5: Wals 6E **49**
WS8: Bwnhls 3A **10**
WV3: Wolv 3G **41**
WV5: Wom 1G **73**
WV12: W'hall 3D **30**
Pinewood Dr. B32: Bart G 4G **129**
Pinewood Gro. B91: Sol 5D **150**
Pinewoods B31: N'fld 5D **130**
B32: Bart G 3G **129**
B62: Quin 4G **113**
Pinewood Wlk. DY6: K'wfrd 1C **92**
Pinfold, The WS3: Blox 1A **32**
Pinfold Ct. WS10: Darl 6C **46**
Pinfold Cres. WV4: Penn 5B **42**
Pinfold Gdns. WV11: Wed 4F **29**

Pinfold Gro.—Porter's Fld.

Pinfold Gro. WV4: Penn 5B **42**
Pinfold Ind. Est. WS3: Blox 1A **32**
Pinfold La. WS9: A'rdge 6C **50**
WS11: Nort C 1C **8**
WV4: Penn 5B **42**
Pinfold Rd. B91: Sol 2A **152**
Pinfold St. B2: Birm 1F **117** (4C **4**)
B69: O'bry 1G **97**
WS10: Darl 6C **46**
(not continuous)
WV14: Bils 6F **45**
Pinfold St. Extension WS10: Darl 6C **46**
Pinford La. WS6: C Hay 3C **6**
Pingle Cl. B71: W Brom 4D **64**
Pingle La. WS7: Hamm 1F **11**
Pinkney Pl. B68: O'bry 6A **98**
Pink Pas. B66: Smeth 5F **99**
Pinley Gro. B43: Gt Barr 2E **67**
Pinley Way B91: Sol 1E **165**
Pinner Ct. B17: Harb 5G **115**
Pinner Gro. B32: Quin 1C **130**
Pinson Gdns.
WV13: W'hall 1H **45**
Pinson Rd. WV13: W'hall 1H **45**
Pintail Dr. B23: Erd 5C **84**
Pinto Cl. B16: Birm 1B **116**
Pinza Cft. B36: Hodg H 1B **104**
Pioli Pl. WS2: Wals 4B **32**
Pioneer Way B35: Cas V 5F **87**
Piper Cl. WV6: Pert 5F **25**
Piper Pl. DY8: Amb 3D **108**
Piper Rd. WV3: Wolv 3A **42**
Pipers Grn. B28: Hall G 2F **149**
Piper's Row WV1: Wolv 1H **43** (3D **170**)
Pipes Mdw. WV14: Bils 6G **45**
Pippin Av. B63: Crad 4D **110**
Pirbright Cl. WV14: Bils 2G **61**
Pirrey Cl. WV14: Cose 4G **61**
Pitcairn Cl. B30: Stir 1D **146**
Pitcairn Dr. B62: Hale 6B **112**
Pitcairn Rd. B67: Smeth 2B **114**
Pitclose Rd. B31: N'fld 6F **145**
Pitfield Rd. B33: Kitts G 2A **122**
Pitfield Row DY1: Dud 6D **76**
Pitfields Cl. B68: O'bry 3G **113**
Pitfields Rd. B68: O'bry 3G **113**
Pitfield St. DY1: Dud 6E **77**
Pithall Rd. B34: S End 4H **105**
Pit Leasow Cl. B30: Stir 5D **132**
Pitman Rd. B32: Quin 6A **114**
Pitmaston Ct. B13: Mose 2F **133**
Pitmaston Rd. B28: Hall G 1G **149**
Pitmeadow Ho. *B14: K Hth* *5G 147*
(off Pound Rd.)
Pitsford St. B18: Hock 4C **100**
Pitt La. B92: Bick 3F **139**
Pitts Farm Rd. B24: Erd 2A **86**
Pitt St. B4: Birm 6A **102**
WV3: Wolv 2G **43** (4A **170**)
Pixall Dr. B15: Edg 4D **116**
Pixhall Wlk. B35: Cas V 4F **87**
(not continuous)
Plainview Cl. WS9: A'rdge 1G **51**
Plaistow Av. B36: Hodg H 2A **104**
Plane Gro. B37: Chel W 2D **122**
Planetary Ind. Est.
WV13: W'hall 6E **29**
Planetary Rd.
WV13: W'hall 5D **28**
Plane Tree Rd. B74: S'tly 3F **51**
WS5: Wals 1F **65**
Planet Rd. DY5: Brie H 5H **93**
Plank La. B46: Wat O 5C **88**
Planks La. WV5: Wom 1F **73**
Plantation, The DY5: P'ntt 2F **93**
Plantation Dr. B75: S Cold 5D **54**
Plantation La. DY3: Himl 3H **73**
Plantation Rd. WS5: Wals 1E **65**
Plant Ct. *DY5: Brie H* *1H 109*
(off Hill St.)
Plantsbrook Community Nature Reserve
. . . . 3B 70
Plants Brook Nature Reserve 2E 87
Plants Brook Rd. B76: Walm 1D **86**
Plants Cl. B73: New O 4D **68**
WS6: Gt Wyr 5G **7**
Plants Gro. B24: Erd 2B **86**
Plants Hollow DY5: Brie H 2A **110**
Plant St. B64: Old H 2F **111**
DY8: Word 1C **108**
Plant Way WS3: Pels 3D **20**
Plascom Rd. WV1: Wolv 2C **44**
Platts Cres. DY8: Amb 3C **108**
Platts Dr. DY8: Amb 3C **108**
Platts Rd. DY8: Amb 3C **108**
Platt St. WS10: Darl 6D **46**
Playdon Gro. B14: K Hth 4A **148**
Pleasant Cl. DY6: K'wfrd 5A **92**
Pleasant St. B70: W Brom 5A **80**
(Farm St.)
B70: W Brom 5G **63**
(Lee St.)
Pleasant Vw. DY3: Gorn 5H **75**
PLECK 3H **47**
Pleck Bus. Pk. WS2: Wals 2A **48**
Pleck Ho. *B14: K Hth* *6E 147*
(off Winterbourne Cft.)
Pleck Ind. Est. WS2: Wals 3A **48**
Pleck Rd. WS2: Wals 3A **48**
Pleck Wlk. B38: K Nor 6C **146**
Plestowes Cl. B90: Shir 2H **149**
Plimsoll Gro. B32: Quin 6A **114**
Plough & Harrow Rd.
B16: Edg 2B **116**
Plough Av. B32: Bart G 3A **130**
Ploughmans Pl. B75: R'ley 5B **38**
Ploughmans Wlk. DY6: W Hth 2G **91**
WV8: Pend 6C **14**
Plover Cl. WV10: F'stne 1D **16**
Plover Ct. B33: Stech 6C **104**
Ploverdale Cres. DY6: K'wfrd 2E **93**
Plowden Rd. B33: Stech 5D **104**
Plume St. B6: Aston 1C **102**
Plummers Ho. B6: Aston 2G **101**
Plumstead Rd. B44: K'sdng 5A **68**
Plym Cl. WV11: Wed 4E **29**
Plymouth Cl. B31: Longb 2E **159**
Plymouth Rd. B30: Stir 6D **132**
Plympton M. B71: W Brom 1A **80**
Pocklington Pl. B31: N'fld 1G **145**
Poets Cnr. B10: Small H 4D **118**
Point 3 B3: Birm 6E **101** (2B **4**)
Pointon Cl. WV14: Cose 3C **60**
Polars, The DY5: P'ntt 2F **93**
Polden Cl. B63: Hale 4E **127**
Polesworth Gro. B34: S End 3F **105**
Pollard Rd. B27: A Grn 4A **136**
Pollards, The B23: Erd 5E **69**
Polly Brooks Yd. DY9: Lye 6A **110**
Polo Flds. DY9: Pedm 4F **125**
Pomeroy Rd. B32: Bart G 4A **130**
B43: Gt Barr 1F **67**
Pommel Cl. WS5: Wals 1D **64**
Pond La. WV2: Wolv 3H **43**
Pool Cotts. WS7: Chase 1A **10**
Poole Cres. B17: Harb 2G **131**
WS8: Bwnhls 3G **9**
WV14: Cose 3F **61**
Poole Ho. Rd. B43: Gt Barr 2A **66**
Pool End Cl. B93: Know 3B **166**
Pooles La. WV12: W'hall 1E **31**
Poole St. DY8: Stourb 1C **124**
Pool Farm Rd. B27: A Grn 4H **135**
Pool Fld. Av. B31: N'fld 6C **130**
Poolfield Dr. B91: Sol 4D **150**
POOL GREEN 4B **34**
Pool Grn. WS9: A'rdge 4C **34**
Pool Grn. Ter. WS9: A'rdge 4C **34**
Pool Hall Cres. WV3: Wolv 3F **41**
Pool Hall Rd. WV3: Wolv 3F **41**
Pool Hayes La.
WV12: W'hall 4A **30**
Pool Ho. Rd. WV5: Wom 2D **72**
Pool La. B69: O'bry 5F **97**
Pool Mdw. WS6: C Hay 4D **6**
Poolmeadow B76: Walm 5E **71**
Pool Mdw. Cl. B13: Mose 4C **134**
B91: Sol 6B **152**
Pool Rd. B63: Hale 2B **128**
B66: Smeth 4F **99**
WS7: Chase 1A **10**
(not continuous)
WS8: Bwnhls 3A **10**
WV11: Wed 3A **30**
Pool St. DY1: Dud 1C **76**
WS1: Wals 2D **48**
WV2: Wolv 3G **43** (6A **170**)
(not continuous)
Pooltail Wlk. B31: Longb 6B **144**
Pool Vw. WS4: Rus 2H **33**
WS6: Gt Wyr 1G **7**
Pool Way B33: Yard 2E **121**
Pope Rd. WV10: Bush 1C **28**
Popes La. B69: O'bry 3H **97**
B30: K Nor 3H **145**
B38: K Nor 3H **145**
WV6: Tett 3G **25**
Pope St. B1: Birm 6D **100**
B66: Smeth 2F **99**
Poplar Arc. *B91: Sol* *3G 151*
(off Gardeners Wlk.)
Poplar Av. B11: S'brk 5B **118**
B12: Bal H 1A **134**
B14: K Hth 5H **133**
B17: Edg 2E **115**
B19: Loz 1E **101**
B23: Erd 3F **85**
B37: Chel W 3E **123**
B69: O'bry 5G **97**
B69: Tiv 1B **96**
B70: W Brom 5C **80**
B75: S Cold 4D **54**
DY4: Tip 2F **77**
WS2: Wals 6D **30**
WS5: Wals 1E **65**
WS8: Bwnhls 5C **10**
WV11: Wed 2D **28**
Poplar Cl. B69: Tiv 6C **78**
WS2: Wals 5E **31**
WV5: Wom 1H **73**
Poplar Cres. DY1: Dud 4D **76**
DY8: Stourb 2C **124**
Poplar Dr. B6: Witt 2H **83**
B8: Salt 3D **102**
Poplar Grn. DY1: Dud 1C **76**
Poplar Gro. B19: Loz 1E **101**
B66: Smeth 6F **99**
B70: W Brom 6C **80**
Poplar La. B62: Roms 3A **142**
Poplar Ri. B42: Gt Barr 6D **66**
B69: Tiv 1C **96**
B74: Lit A 4D **36**
Poplar Rd. B11: S'hll 6B **118**
B14: K Hth 5G **133**
B66: Smeth 2E **115**
B69: O'bry 1G **97**
B91: Sol 3G **151**
B93: Dorr 5B **166**
DY6: K'wfrd 4C **92**
DY8: Stourb 2C **124**
WS6: Gt Wyr 4F **7**
WS8: Bwnhls 5C **10**
WS10: W'bry 5G **47**
WV3: Wolv 5E **43**
WV14: Bils 4H **45**
Poplars, The B11: S'brk 5C **118**
B16: Birm 5B **100**
DY8: Word 1D **108**
Poplars Dr. B36: Cas B 1F **105**
WV8: Cod 5F **13**
Poplars Ind. Est., The B6: Witt 2H **83**
Poplar St. B66: Smeth 4G **99**
WV2: Wolv 5H **43**
Poplar Trees *B47: H'wd* *3A 162*
(off May Farm Cl.)
Poplar Way Shop. Cen. B91: Sol 3G **151**
Poplarwoods B32: Bart G 3H **129**
Poppy Dr. WS5: Wals 2D **64**
Poppy Gro. B8: Salt 5F **103**
Poppy La. B24: Erd 2A **86**
Poppymead B23: Erd 5B **68**
Porchester Cl. WS9: Wals W 4C **22**
Porchester Dr. B19: Hock 3F **101**
Porchester St. B19: Hock 3F **101**
Porlock Cres. B31: N'fld 4B **144**
Porlock Rd. DY8: Amb 5E **109**
Portal Rd. WS2: Wals 1F **47**
Portchester Dr. WV11: Wed 4F **29**
Porter Cl. B72: W Grn 6H **69**
Porters Cft. B17: Harb 3E **115**
Porter's Fld. DY2: Dud 6F **77**

Portersfield Ind. Est. B64: Crad H 4F 111
Portersfield Rd. B64: Crad H 3E 111
Portershill Dr. B90: Shir. 6A 150
Porter St. DY2: Dud 6F 77
Porter St. Sth. DY2: Dud 6F 77
Porters Way B9: Bord G 1E 119
Portfield Dr. DY4: Tip 4A 78
Portfield Gro. B23: Erd 1G 85
Porth Kerry Gro. DY3: Sed 6F 59
Port Hope Rd. B11: S'brk. 4A 118
Porthouse Gro. B44: Cose 2D 60
Portia Av. B90: Shir 5H 149
Portland Av. WS3: A'rdge. 4D 34
Portland Ct. WS9: A'rdge. 4D 34
Portland Cres. DY9: Pedm 4F 125
Portland Dr. B69: Tiv 5D 78
   DY9: Pedm 4F 125
Portland Pl. WV14: Cose 6D 60
Portland Rd. B16: Edg 1G 115
   B17: Edg. 6F 99
   WS9: A'rdge. 3D 34
Portland St. B6: Aston 2A 102
   WS2: Wals 6C 32
Port La. WV9: Coven 1H 13
Portman Rd. B13: Mose. 6H 133
PORTOBELLO 3G 45
Portobello Cl. WV13: W'hall. 2F 45
Portobello Rd. B70: W Brom 5G 63
Portrush Av. B38: K Nor 6G 145
Portrush Rd. WV6: Pert 5D 24
Portsdown Rd. WV10: Bush 2B 28
Portsdown Rd. B63: Hale 4E 127
Portsea St. WS3: Blox 3A 32
Port St. WS1: Wals. 4B 48
Portswood Cl. WV9: Pend 6D 14
PORTWAY 4C 96
Portway, The DY6: K'wfrd 4C 92
Portway Cl. B91: Sol 6C 150
   DY6: K'wfrd 4C 92
Portway Hill B65: Row R 3B 96
Portway Rd. B65: Row R 5B 96
   B69: O'bry 2E 97
   WS10: W'bry 2E 63
   WV14: Bils 4G 45
Portway Rd. Ind. Est.
   B69: O'bry 2E 97
Portway Wlk. B65: Row R 3C 96
Posey Cl. B21: Hand 4H 81
Post Office Rd. WV5: Seis 2A 56
Poston Cft. B14: K Hth 3F 147
Potland Ter. B18: Hock 4C 100
                                   (off Crabtree Rd.)
Potter Cl. B23: Erd 5D 68
Potter Ct. DY5: Brie H 1H 109
                                 (off Promenade, The)
Potters Brook DY4: Tip 2B 78
Potters La. WS10: W'bry 3E 63
   B6: Aston 3G 101
Potterton Way B66: Smeth 1D 98
Pottery Rd. B66: Smeth 2E 99
   B68: O'bry 2A 114
Pouk Hill Cl. WS2: Wals 6G 31
Pouk La. WS14: Hilt. 5G 11
Poultney St. B70: W Brom 6F 63
Poulton Cl. B13: Mose 3A 134
Pound Cl. B68: O'bry 6F 97
Pound Grn. B8: Salt 3F 103
Pound La. B32: Fran 4F 143
   B46: Col 5H 107
Poundley Cl. B36: Cas B 1G 105
Pound Rd. B14: K Hth 6G 147
   B68: O'bry 6F 97
                                    (not continuous)
   WS10: W'bry 2G 63
Pountney St. WV2: Wolv. . . 3G 43 (6A 170)
Powell Av. B32: Quin 5G 113
Powell Pl. DY4: Tip 2C 78
   WV14: Bils 2G 61
Powells Ho. B73: New O 3C 68
Powell St. B1: Birm 6D 100
   B63: Hale 2B 128
   WV10: Wolv 5B 28
Powerleague Soccer Cen. 6C 84
Power Way DY4: Tip 5D 62
Powick Pl. B19: Loz 2E 101
Powick Rd. B23: Erd 6D 84
Powis Av. DY4: Tip 1A 78

Powke La. B64: Old H 6H 95
   B65: Row R 1A 112
Powke La. Ind. Est. B65: Row R 1A 112
Powlers Cl. DY9: W'cte 3A 126
Powlett St. WV2: Wolv 2H 43 (5D 170)
Poxon Rd. WS9: Wals W 3C 22
Poynings, The WV6: Tett 4A 26
Precinct, The WV12: W'hall 4B 30
Premier Bus. Pk. WS2: Wals 2B 48
Premier Cl. B30: K Nor 4E 147
Premier Pk. B73: New O 3D 68
Premier Partnership Ind. Est.
   DY6: K'wfrd 6F 93
Premier St. B7: Nech. 1D 102
Premier Trad. Est. B7: Birm 4H 101
Prescot Rd. DY9: Lye 1G 125
Prescott St. B18: Hock. 5D 100
Prestbury Rd. B6: Aston 1G 101
Presthope Rd. B29: W Cas 6F 131
Preston Av. B76: Walm 2C 70
Preston Ho. WS1: Wals 2D 48
                                   (off Paddock La.)
Preston Rd. B18: Win G 3A 100
   B26: Yard 5B 120
Prestons Row WV14: Cose. 2C 60
Prestwick Cl. B75: S Cold 3A 54
Prestwick Rd. B35: Cas V 3F 87
   DY6: K'wfrd 3A 92
Prestwood Av. WV11: Wed 2F 29
Prestwood Rd. B29: W Cas 5F 131
   WV11: Wed 4C 28
Prestwood Rd. W WV11: Wed 3C 28
Pretoria Rd. B9: Bord G 6E 103
Priam Gro. WS3: Pels. 1F 21
Price Cres. WV14: Bils 4F 45
Price Rd. WS10: W'bry 2A 64
Prices Rd. DY3: Gorn. 4G 75
Price St. B4: Birm 5G 101 (1E 5)
   B66: Smeth. 4F 99
   B70: W Brom 4A 80
   DY2: Dud 1G 95
   WV14: Bils 6H 45
PRIESTFIELD 5D 44
Priestfield WV2: E'shll 4C 44
Priestfield Cl. B44: Gt Barr 3E 67
Priestfield St. WV14: Bils 5D 44
Priestland Rd. B34: S End 2F 105
Priestley Cl. B20: Hand 6C 82
   B63: Crad 5D 110
Priestley Rd. B11: S'brk. 4A 118
   WS2: Wals 4G 31
Priestly Wharf B7: Birm 5H 101 (1H 5)
Priest St. B64: Old H 2H 111
Primley Av. B36: Hodg H 2B 104
   WS2: Wals 2H 47
Primley Cl. WS2: Wals 1H 47
Primrose Av. B11: S'hll 5C 118
   DY4: Tip 5C 62
   WV10: F'hses, Bush. 4H 15
Primrose Bank B68: O'bry 5H 97
Primrose Cl. B64: Crad H 3D 110
   WS3: Pels. 2E 21
Primrose Cres. DY1: Dud 3E 77
Primrose Cft. B23: Erd 6C 68
   B28: Hall G 2F 149
Primrose Gdns. B38: K Nor 1B 160
   WV8: Cod. 4G 13
PRIMROSE HILL 5F 95
Primrose Hill B38: K Nor 6B 146
                                    (not continuous)
   B67: Smeth 5B 98
   DY8: Word 2C 108
Primrose Hill Trad. Est. DY2: Neth . . . 5F 95
Primrose La. B28: Hall G 2F 149
   B90: Dic H 4G 163
   WV10: Bush 3A 16
                                       (Cromwell Rd.)
   WV10: Bush 1B 28
                                    (Old Fallings La.)
Primrose Pk. DY5: P'ntt 2G 93
Primrose Rd. DY2: Neth. 5E 95
Primroses, The WS5: Wals 1F 65
Primrose Woods B32: Bart G 3H 129
Primsland Cl. B90: M'path. 2G 165
Prince Albert St. B9: Small H 2D 118
                                    (not continuous)
Prince Andrew Cres. B45: Fran 5E 143

Prince Charles Cl. B45: Fran 5E 143
Prince Charles Rd. WV14: Bils 2H 61
Prince Edward Dr. B45: Fran 5E 143
Prince George Rd. WS10: W'bry 6G 47
Prince of Wales La.
   B14: K Hth, Yard W 5C 148
Prince of Wales Way B66: Smeth 4G 99
Princep Cl. B43: Gt Barr 1F 67
Prince Philip Cl. B45: Fran. 5E 143
Prince Rd. B30: K Nor 4B 146
Princes Av. WS1: Wals. 3E 49
Princes Dr. WV8: Cod 4G 13
PRINCES END 5H 61
Princes End Ind. Est. DY4: Tip 4G 61
Princes Gdns. WV8: Cod 4F 13
Princes Ga. B91: Sol 3F 151
Princes Rd. B69: Tiv 5A 78
   DY8: Stourb 3B 124
Princess Alice Dr.
   B73: New O 3D 68
Princess All. WV1: Wolv. 1H 43 (3C 170)
Princess Anne Dr. B45: Fran 5E 143
Princess Anne Rd. WS2: Wals 6F 31
   WV14: Bils 2H 61
Princess Ct. WV10: Wolv. 3C 28
Princess Cres. B63: Hale 5G 111
Princess Diana Way B45: Fran. 5E 143
Princess Gro. B71: W Brom 5B 64
Princess Pde. B70: W Brom 4B 80
Princess Sq. WV1: Wolv 1H 43 (2C 170)
Princess Rd. B5: Bal H. 5G 117
   B68: O'bry 1B 114
Princess Sq. WV14: Bils 2H 61
Princess St. WV1: Wolv 1H 43 (3C 170)
Princess Way WS10: Darl 3C 46
Prince St. B64: Crad H 3F 111
   DY2: Neth. 3E 95
   WS2: Wals 3A 48
   WS9: Wals W 5B 22
Prince's Way B91: Sol 3F 151
Princethorpe Cl. B34: S End 2H 105
   B90: Shir 5G 149
Princethorpe Rd. B29: W Cas 4E 131
Princeton Gdns. WV9: Pend 5D 14
Prince William Cl. B23: Erd 5D 84
Principal Ct. B67: Smeth 4E 99
Princip St. B4: Birm 5G 101 (1E 5)
Printing Ho. St. B4: Birm 6G 101 (2E 5)
Priors Cl. CV7: Bal C 3H 169
Priors Mill DY3: Up Gor. 2A 76
Priors Way B23: Erd. 5C 68
Priory, The. 4E 77
Priory, The DY3: Sed 5H 59
Priory Av. B29: S Oak. 3D 132
Priory Chambers DY1: Dud 6E 77
                                     (off Priory St.)
Priory Cl. B46: Col 4H 107
   B66: Smeth 5G 99
   B70: W Brom 5D 80
   DY1: Dud 5D 76
   DY8: Stourb 2F 125
Priory Ct. B90: M'path 2F 165
   DY1: Dud 6E 77
   DY8: Stourb 2F 125
   WS9: Wals W 3C 22
   WV1: Wolv 6G 27 (1A 170)
Priory Dr. B68: O'bry 4A 98
Priory Fld. Cl. WV14: Cose 4B 60
Priory Fields Nature Reserve 5D 148
Priory Gdns. B28: Hall G 3D 148
Priory Ga. Way B9: Bord G 1E 119
Priory Ho. B63: Hale 6H 111
Priory Ho. Ind. Est. B18: Hock 4C 100
Priory La. DY3: Sed 6H 59
Priory New Way Ind. Est. B6: Aston . . 4G 101
Priory Queensway, The
   B4: Birm 6G 101 (3E 5)
Priory Rd. B5: Edg 5D 116
   B6: Aston 1B 102
   B14: K Hth 6E 133
   B15: Edg 5D 116
   B28: Hall G. 3D 148
   B62: Hale 1E 129
   DY1: Dud 2E 77
   DY8: Stourb 2F 125
Priory Sq. Shop. Cen. B4: Birm 3F 5
Priory St. DY1: Dud 6E 77

Priory Wlk. B4: Birm . . . 6G **101** (3F **5**)
B72: W Grn . . . 6A **70**
Priory Woods Nature Reserve . . . 3E **81**
Pritchard Av. WV11: Wed . . . 3G **29**
Pritchard Cl. B66: Smeth . . . 4F **99**
Pritchard St. DY5: Brie H . . . 6F **93**
WS10: W'bry . . . 2G **63**
Pritchatts Rd. B15: Edg . . . 6A **116**
Pritchett Av. WV4: E'shll . . . 2B **60**
Pritchett Rd. B31: Longb . . . 2F **159**
Pritchett St. B6: Birm . . . 4G **101**
Pritchett Twr. B10: Small H . . . 2C **118**
Private Way B45: Coft H . . . 5A **158**
Privet Cl. B44: Gt Barr . . . 2G **67**
Probert Rd. WV10: Oxl . . . 1E **27**
Proctor St. B7: Birm . . . 4A **102**
Proffitt Cl. WS2: Wals . . . 5C **32**
WS8: Bwnhls . . . 2C **22**
Proffitt St. WS2: Wals . . . 5C **32**
Prole St. WV10: Wolv . . . 5A **28**
Promenade, The DY5: Brie H . . . 1H **109**
Prospect Gdns. DY8: Stourb . . . 1E **125**
Prospect Hill DY8: Stourb . . . 1E **125**
Prospect La. B91: Sol . . . 2B **150**
Prospect Pl. B12: Bal H . . . 6H **117**
Prospect Rd. B13: Mose . . . 4H **133**
B62: Hale . . . 6C **112**
DY3: Gorn . . . 5F **75**
Prospect Row DY2: Dud . . . 2F **95**
DY8: Stourb . . . 2E **125**
Prospect St. DY4: Tip . . . 4C **62**
WV14: Bils . . . 5G **45**
Prospect Trad. Est. B1: Birm . . . 3A **4**
Prosper Mdw. DY6: K'wfrd . . . 2C **92**
Prospero Cl. B45: Fran . . . 5G **143**
Prosser St. WV10: Wolv . . . 4A **28**
WV14: Bils . . . 6F **45**
Prossers Wlk. B46: Col . . . 2H **107**
Prouds La. WV14: Bils . . . 3F **45**
Provence Cl. WV10: Wolv . . . 5B **28**
Providence Cl. WS3: Blox . . . 2A **32**
(not continuous)
Providence Dr. DY9: Lye . . . 5A **110**
Providence Ind. Est. DY9: Lye . . . 5A **110**
Providence La. WS3: Blox . . . 3A **32**
Providence Row WV14: Cose . . . 5D **60**
Providence St. B64: Crad H . . . 2F **111**
DY4: Tip . . . 2C **78**
DY9: Lye . . . 5A **110**
Pruden Av. WV4: E'shll . . . 2B **60**
Pryor Rd. B68: O'bry . . . 6A **98**
Pudsey Dr. B75: Four O . . . 6A **38**
Pugh Cres. WS2: Wals . . . 1E **47**
Pugh Rd. B6: Aston . . . 2A **102**
WV14: Bils . . . 2G **61**
WV14: Cose . . . 3B **60**
Pugin Cl. WV6: Pert . . . 6D **24**
Pugin Gdns. B23: Erd . . . 5D **68**
Pumphouse Way B69: O'bry . . . 5F **97**
Pump St. WV2: E'shll . . . 4C **44**
Puppy Grn. DY4: Tip . . . 2A **78**
Purbeck Cl. B63: Hale . . . 4F **127**
Purbeck Cft. B32: Harb . . . 6D **114**
Purbrook Rd. WV1: Wolv . . . 3B **44**
Purcel Rd. WV10: Bush . . . 1H **27**
Purdy Rd. WV14: Bils . . . 3G **61**
Purefoy Rd. B13: Mose . . . 2C **148**
Purley Gro. B23: Erd . . . 2A **84**
Purnells Way B93: Know . . . 4C **166**
Purslet Rd. WV1: Wolv . . . 2C **44**
Purslow Gro. B31: N'fld . . . 5E **145**
Putney Av. B20: Hand . . . 6E **83**
Putney La. B62: Roms . . . 5A **142**
Putney Rd. B20: Hand . . . 6D **82**
Putney Wlk. B37: F'bri . . . 6D **106**
Pype Hayes Cl. B24: Erd . . . 3B **86**
Pype Hayes Rd. B24: Erd . . . 3B **86**
Pype Marshbrook Rd. B24: Erd . . . 3B **86**
Pytchley Ho. B20: Hand . . . 4B **82**
Pytman Dr. B76: Walm . . . 6E **71**

Q

Quadrangle, The B30: B'vlle . . . 1B **146**
B90: Shir . . . 1C **164**
Quadrant, The DY3: Sed . . . 4H **59**
Quadrille Lawns WV9: Pend . . . 5D **14**
Quail Grn. WV6: Tett . . . 1F **41**
Qualcast Rd. WV1: Wolv . . . 1B **44**
Quantock Cl. B45: Fran . . . 5H **143**
B63: Hale . . . 3F **127**
WS8: Wals W . . . 3C **22**
Quantock Rd. DY8: Amb . . . 5F **109**
Quantry La. DY9: Belb . . . 1A **156**
Quarrington Gro. B14: K Hth . . . 4A **148**
QUARRY BANK . . . **2C 110**
Quarry Brow DY3: Up Gor . . . 2A **76**
Quarry Cl. WS6: C Hay . . . 2E **7**
Quarry Hill B63: Hale . . . 3H **127**
Quarry Ho. B45: Rubery . . . 1F **157**
Quarry Ho. Cl. B45: Fran . . . 6F **143**
Quarry La. B31: N'fld . . . 4D **144**
B63: Hale . . . 3H **127**
Quarry Pk. Rd. DY8: Stourb . . . 5E **125**
Quarry Ri. B69: Tiv . . . 1B **96**
Quarry Rd. B29: W Cas . . . 4D **130**
DY2: Neth . . . 1D **110**
Quarry Wlk. B45: Redn . . . 2G **157**
Quasar Cen. WS1: Wals . . . 1C **48**
Quatford Gdns. WV10: Wolv . . . 4A **28**
Quayle Gro. DY8: Word . . . 6B **92**
Quayside B18: Win G . . . 4C **100**
Quayside Cl. B69: O'bry . . . 1E **97**
Quayside Dr. WS2: Wals . . . 3A **48**
Qube . . . 3A **4**
Queen Eleanors Dr. B93: Know . . . 1D **166**
Queen Elizabeth Av. WS2: Wals . . . 6F **31**
Queen Elizabeth Ct. B19: Hock . . . 3D **100**
Queen Elizabeth Rd. B45: Fran . . . 5E **143**
Queen Mary St. WS1: Wals . . . 5B **48**
Queen Mother Ct. B30: B'vlle . . . 5H **131**
Queen Mother Gdns. B17: Harb . . . 5E **115**
Queen's Arc. WV1: Wolv . . . 1G **43** (3B **170**)
Queens Av. B14: K Hth . . . 5G **133**
B90: Shir . . . 6H **149**
B18: Hock . . . 3B **100**
B69: Tiv . . . 6B **78**
Queensbridge Rd. B13: Mose . . . 3F **133**
Queens Cl. B24: Erd . . . 5F **85**
B67: Smeth . . . 4E **99**
Queens Ct. B1: Birm . . . 2E **117** (6B **4**)
B3: Birm . . . 5F **101** (1C **4**)
B91: Sol . . . 3H **151**
WV10: Wolv . . . 3C **28**
Queens Ct. Trad. Est. B70: W Brom . . . 4F **79**
Queens Cres. DY8: Amb . . . 4E **109**
WV14: Cose . . . 4C **60**
Queen's Cross DY1: Dud . . . 1D **94**
Queens Dr. B65: Row R . . . 5D **96**
B5: Birm . . . 1F **117** (5D **4**)
B30: K Nor . . . 3C **146**
WS7: Chase . . . 1B **10**
Queens Dr., The B62: Hale . . . 6C **112**
Queens Gdns. B23: Erd . . . 6B **68**
DY2: Neth . . . 5E **95**
WS10: W'bry . . . 2E **63**
WV8: Cod . . . 4F **13**
WV14: Bils . . . 4F **45**
Queen's Head Rd. B21: Hand . . . 2A **100**
Queens Hospital Cl.
B15: Birm . . . 2E **117**
Queens Lea WV12: W'hall . . . 4C **30**
Queens Pde. WS3: Blox . . . 6H **19**
Queen's Pk. Rd. B32: Harb . . . 5D **114**
Queen Sq. WV1: Wolv . . . 1G **43** (3B **170**)
Queen's Ride B5: Edg . . . 1E **133**
Queens Rd. B23: Erd . . . 4C **84**
B67: Smeth . . . 5B **98**
DY8: Stourb . . . 5D **108**
WS5: Wals . . . 5F **49**
B6: Aston . . . 1A **102**
B26: Yard . . . 2D **120**
DY3: Sed . . . 5A **60**
DY4: Tip . . . 2H **77**
WS4: Rus . . . 2G **33**
Queens Sq. B70: W Brom . . . 4B **80**
Queen St. B12: Bal H . . . 6B **118**
B63: Hale . . . 1A **128**
B64: Crad H . . . 2F **111**
B69: O'bry . . . 1G **97**
B70: W Brom . . . 4B **80**
B72: S Cold . . . 1A **70**
DY4: Tip . . . 5H **61**
Queen St. DY5: P'ntt . . . 3G **93**
(not continuous)
DY5: Quar B . . . 3C **110**
(not continuous)
DY6: K'wfrd . . . 2B **92**
DY8: Stourb . . . 6D **108**
DY8: Word . . . 6B **92**
WS2: Wals . . . 2B **48**
WS6: C Hay . . . 2D **6**
WS7: Chase . . . 1B **10**
WS9: Wals W . . . 5A **22**
WS10: Darl . . . 3D **46**
WS10: W'bry . . . 2E **63**
WV1: Wolv . . . 1H **43** (3C **170**)
(not continuous)
WV14: Bils . . . 6G **45**
(Bridge St.)
WV14: Bils . . . 1B **62**
(Tudor Rd.)
Queen St. Ind. Est. WS7: Chase . . . 1B **10**
Queen St. Pas. DY5: Quar B . . . 3C **110**
Queensway B1: Birm . . . 1E **117**
B6: Witt . . . 4H **83**
B63: Hale . . . 2A **128**
B68: O'bry . . . 2H **113**
B74: S'tly . . . 3A **52**
DY9: W'cte . . . 3A **126**
Queensway Cl. B68: O'bry . . . 2H **113**
Queensway Mall *B63: Hale* . . . *2B* ***128***
(off Hagley Mall)
Queensway Trad. Est. B5: Birm . . . 3G **5**
Queenswood Rd. B13: Mose . . . 1A **134**
B75: Four O . . . 2H **53**
Quenby Dr. DY1: Dud . . . 4C **76**
Quendale WV5: Wom . . . 1E **73**
Quentin Dr. DY1: Dud . . . 1B **94**
Queslade Cl. B43: Gt Barr . . . 4C **66**
QUESLETT . . . **3F 67**
Queslett Pk. Golf Cen. . . . *5E 67*
(off Booth's La.)
Queslett Rd. B43: Gt Barr . . . 4B **66**
(not continuous)
Queslett Rd. E. B74: S'tly . . . 6G **51**
Quicksand La. WS9: A'rdge . . . 5B **34**
Quillets Rd. DY8: Word . . . 6A **92**
Quilter Cl. WS2: Wals . . . 6F **31**
WV14: Cose . . . 5C **60**
Quilter Rd. B24: Erd . . . 5H **85**
Quincey Dr. B24: Erd . . . 4A **86**
Quincy Ri. DY5: Brie H . . . 4G **109**
QUINTON . . . **5A 114**
Quinton Av. WS6: Gt Wyr . . . 2F **7**
Quinton Bus. Pk. B32: Quin . . . 6G **113**
Quinton Cl. B92: Sol . . . 2H **137**
Quintondale B90: Shir . . . 1A **164**
Quinton Expressway B32: Quin . . . 1H **129**
Quinton La. B32: Quin . . . 5A **114**
Quinton Pl. WS11: Nort C . . . 1E **9**
Quinton Rd. B17: Harb . . . 2E **131**
Quinton Rd. W. B32: Quin . . . 6H **113**
Qulsnam Ct. B13: Mose . . . 3B **134**
Quorn Cres. DY8: Word . . . 6A **92**
Quorn Gro. B24: Erd . . . 5H **85**
Quorn Ho. B20: Hand . . . 4B **82**

R

Rabone La. B66: Smeth . . . 3F **99**
Raby Cl. B69: Tiv . . . 1H **95**
Raby St. WV2: Wolv . . . 3H **43** (6D **170**)
Racecourse La. DY8: Stourb . . . 3C **124**
Racecourse Rd. WV6: Wolv . . . 4E **27**
Racecourse Rd. Ind. Est. WV6: Wolv . . . 4E **27**
Racemeadow Cres. DY2: Neth . . . 2E **111**
Raceway, The . . . 6D **80**
Rachael Gdns. WS10: W'bry . . . 1H **63**
Rachel Cl. DY4: Tip . . . 4C **62**
Rachel Gdns. B29: S Oak . . . 3H **131**
Radbourn Dr. B74: S Cold . . . 4A **54**
Radbourne Dr. B63: Crad . . . 4C **110**
Radbourne Rd. B90: Shir . . . 4B **150**
Radcliffe Dr. B62: Quin . . . 5E **113**
Radcliffe Twr. B12: Birm . . . 3H **117**
Raddens Rd. B62: Hale . . . 2F **129**
Raddington Dr. B92: Olton . . . 5B **136**
Raddlebarn Farm Dr. B29: S Oak . . . 4B **132**

Raddlebarn Rd. B29: S Oak 4A 132
Radford Cl. WS5: Wals 2E 65
Radford Dr. WS4: S'fld 5G 21
Radford La. WV3: Wolv 5F 41
 WV4: Lwr P 5F 41
Radford Ri. B91: Sol 2A 152
Radford Rd. B29: W Cas 1E 145
Radley Ct. B26: Sheld 4G 121
Radley Gro. B29: W Cas 3E 131
Radley Rd. DY9: W'cte 1B 126
 WS4: Rus 2G 33
Radleys, The B33: Kitts G, Sheld 4G 121
Radley's Wlk. B33: Sheld 4G 121
Radlow Cres. B37: Mars G 3D 122
Radnell Ho. B69: O'bry 3D 96
Radnor Cl. B45: Fran 5H 143
Radnor Ct. WS9: Wals W 3B 22
Radnor Cft. WS5: Wals 2G 65
Radnor Grn. B71: W Brom 6A 64
Radnor Rd. B20: Hand 1D 100
 B68: O'bry 4H 113
 DY3: Sed 5G 59
Radnor St. B18: Hock 3C 100
Radstock Av. B36: Hodg H 2A 104
Radstock Rd. WV12: W'hall 6C 18
Radway Rd. B90: Shir 2C 164
Raeburn Rd. B43: Gt Barr 1E 67
Raford Rd. B23: Erd 1D 84
Ragees Rd. DY6: K'wfrd 5D 92
Raglan Av. B66: Smeth 5G 99
 WV6: Pert 6F 25
Raglan Cl. DY3: Sed 6A 60
 WS9: A'rdge 6H 35
Raglan Rd. B5: Edg 1G 99
 B21: Hand 1G 99
 B66: Smeth 1G 99
Raglan St. DY5: Brie H 5G 93
 WV3: Wolv 1F 43 (3A 170)
Raglan Way B37: Chel W 1F 123
Ragley Cl. B93: Know 2D 166
 WS3: Blox 6G 19
Ragley Dr. B26: Sheld 5G 121
 B43: Gt Barr 3H 65
 WV13: W'hall 3H 45
Ragley Wlk. B65: Row R 6C 96
Ragnall Av. B33: Sheld 4H 121
Rail Bri. Est. B70: W Brom 6G 79
Railswood Dr. WS3: Pels 4E 21
Railway Dr. WV1: Wolv 1H 43 (2D 170)
 WV14: Bils 6G 45
Railway La. WV13: W'hall 2A 46
Railway Rd. B20: Hand 5H 83
 B73: S Cold 6H 53
Railwayside Cl. B66: Smeth 2C 98
                            (off Forest Cl.)
Railway St. B70: W Brom 3H 79
 DY4: Tip 2C 78
 WV1: Wolv 1H 43 (2D 170)
 WV13: W'hall 2A 46
 WV14: Bils 6G 45
Railway Ter. B7: Nech 3B 102
 B42: Gt Barr 1B 82
 WS10: W'bry 3F 63
Railway Vw. B10: Small H 4C 118
Railway Wlk. WS11: Nort C 1E 9
Railwharf Sidings DY2: Neth 5F 95
Rainbow St. WV2: Wolv 3G 43
 WV14: Cose 2F 61
Rainford Way B38: K Nor 1G 159
                          (off Nearhill Rd.)
Rainham Cl. DY4: Tip 2F 77
Rainsbrook Dr. B90: M'path 3D 164
Rake Way B15: Birm 2D 116 (6A 4)
Raleigh Cl. B21: Hand 6F 81
Raleigh Cft. B43: Gt Barr 2A 66
Raleigh Ind. Est. B21: Hand 6F 81
Raleigh Rd. B9: Bord G 6D 102
 WV14: Bils 2H 61
Raleigh St. B71: W Brom 3A 80
 WS2: Wals 1A 48
Ralph Barlow Gdns. B44: K'sdng 5B 68
Ralph Gdns. B44: K'sdng 5B 68
Ralph Rd. B8: Salt 5D 102
 B90: Shir 3H 149
Ralphs Mdw. B32: Bart G 3B 130
Ralston Cl. WS3: Blox 3G 19
Ramblers Way B75: R'ley 6C 38

Ramillies Cres. WS6: Gt Wyr 4F 7
Ramp Rd. B26: Birm A 6E 123
Ramsay Rd. B68: O'bry 2A 114
Ramsden Cl. B29: W Cas 6F 131
Ramsey Cl. B45: Fran 6E 143
 B71: W Brom 5D 64
Ramsey Ho. WS2: Wals 4A 48
Ramsey Rd. B7: Nech 2C 102
 DY4: Tip 6G 61
 WS2: Wals 4G 31
Randall Cl. DY6: K'wfrd 5D 92
Randall Lines Ho. WV1: Wolv 6G 27
Randle Dr. B75: R'ley 6A 38
Randle Rd. DY9: Lye 1G 125
Randwick Gro. B44: Gt Barr 4F 67
Ranelagh Ho. WV2: Wolv 4H 43
                       (off Blakenhall Gdns.)
Ranelagh Rd. WV2: Wolv 5G 43
Rangeview Cl. B74: S'tly 5H 51
Rangeways Rd. DY6: K'wfrd 5D 92
Rangoon Rd. B92: Sol 1A 138
Ranleigh Av. DY6: K'wfrd 5D 92
Rannoch Cl. DY5: Brie H 3F 109
Ranscombe Dr. DY3: Gorn 5H 75
Ransom Rd. B23: Erd 3C 84
Ranworth Ri. WV4: Penn 1H 59
Ratcliffe Cl. DY3: Sed 6B 60
Ratcliffe Rd. B91: Sol 6G 137
 WV11: Wed 3A 30
Ratcliffe Wlk. B69: O'bry 2G 97
Ratcliff Way DY4: Tip 1D 78
Rathbone Cl. B5: Bal H 4G 117
 WV14: Bils 6F 45
Rathbone Rd. B67: Smeth 1D 114
Rathlin Cl. WV9: Pend 4E 15
Rathlin Cft. B36: Cas B 3D 106
Rathmore Cl. DY8: Stourb 3B 124
Rathwell Cl. WV9: Pend 5E 15
Rattle Cft. B33: Stech 6C 104
Ravenall Cl. B34: S End 2F 105
Raven Cl. WS6: C Hay 3D 6
Raven Ct. DY5: Brie H 1H 109
                       (off Lit. Potter St.)
Raven Cres. WV11: Wed 1H 29
Ravenfield Cl. B8: W End 4F 103
Ravenhayes La. B32: Fran 6G 129
Raven Hays Rd. B31: Longb 5A 144
Ravenhill Dr. WV8: Cod 4G 13
Ravenhurst Dr. B43: Gt Barr 2A 66
Ravenhurst M. B23: Erd 4E 85
Ravenhurst Rd. B17: Harb 4G 115
Raven Rd. WS5: Wals 5F 49
Ravensbourne Gro. WV13: W'hall 1C 46
Ravens Ct. WS8: Bwnhls 6B 10
Ravenscroft B13: Woll 5A 108
Ravenscroft Rd. B92: Olton 5E 137
 WV12: W'hall 4B 30
Ravensdale Cl. WS5: Wals 4F 49
Ravensdale Gdns. WS5: Wals 5F 49
Ravensdale Rd. B10: Small H 4F 119
Ravenshaw B91: Sol 5D 152
Ravenshaw La. B91: Sol 3D 152
                          (not continuous)
Ravenshaw Rd. B16: Edg 1G 115
Ravenshaw Way B91: Sol 5C 152
Ravenshill Rd. B14: Yard W 3C 148
Ravensholme WV6: Tett 1F 41
Ravenside Retail Pk. B24: Erd 4C 86
Ravensitch Wlk. DY5: Brie H 2A 110
Ravenswood B15: Edg 3A 116
Ravenswood Cl. B74: Four O 3H 53
Ravenswood Dr. B91: Sol 6D 150
Ravenswood Dr. Sth. B91: Sol 6C 150
Ravenswood Hill B46: Col 2H 107
Raven Wlk. B15: Edg 4E 117
Rawdon Gro. B44: K'sdng 5B 68
Rawlings Rd. B67: Smeth 1D 114
Rawlins Cft. B35: Cas V 4G 87
Rawlins St. B16: Birm 2C 116
Raybon Cft. B45: Redn 3G 157
Rayboulds Bri. Rd. WS2: Wals 5A 32
Raybould's Fold DY2: Neth 4E 95
Rayford Dr. B71: W Brom 3D 64
Ray Hall La. B43: Gt Barr 4E 65
Rayleigh Ho. B27: A Grn 2B 136
Rayleigh Rd. WV3: Wolv 3E 43
Raymond Av. B42: Gt Barr 1D 82

Raymond Cl. WS2: Wals 4B 32
Raymond Gdns. WV11: Wed 4G 29
Raymond Rd. B8: Salt 5E 103
Raymont Gro. B43: Gt Barr 1D 66
Rayners Cft. B26: Yard 2D 120
Raynor Rd. WV10: Wolv 3B 28
RBSA Gallery 6E 101 (2B 4)
Rea Av. B45: Rubery 1E 157
Reabrook Rd. B31: Longb 1D 158
Rea Bus. Pk. B7: Birm 5C 102
Rea Cl. B31: Longb 2E 159
Readers Wlk. B43: Gt Barr 4B 66
Rea Fordway B45: Fran 6F 143
Reansway Sq. WV6: Wolv 5E 27
Reapers Cl. WV12: W'hall 4D 30
Reapers Wlk. WV8: Pend 6D 14
Rea Rd. B31: N'fld 6D 144
Reaside Cres. B14: K Hth 2D 146
Reaside Cft. B12: Bal H 5G 117
Reaside Dr. B45: Redn 1H 157
Rea St. B5: Birm 2H 117 (6G 5)
Rea St. Sth. B5: Birm 3G 117
Rea Ter. B5: Birm 1H 117 (5H 5)
Rea Twr. B19: Birm 4E 101
                    (off Mosborough Cres.)
Rea Valley Dr. B31: N'fld 5F 145
Reaview Dr. B29: S Oak 3D 132
Reaymer Cl. WS2: Wals 3H 31
Reay Nadin Dr. B73: S'tly 1B 68
Rebecca Dr. B29: S Oak 3A 132
Rebecca Gdns. WV4: Penn 1D 58
Recreation St. DY2: Neth 4F 95
Rectory Av. WS10: Darl 5D 46
Rectory Cl. DY8: Stourb 2F 125
Rectory Flds. DY8: Word 1C 108
Rectory Gdns. B36: Cas B 1E 105
 B68: O'bry 4H 97
 B91: Sol 4G 151
 DY8: Stourb 2F 125
Rectory Gro. B18: Win G 3A 100
Rectory La. B36: Cas B 1E 105
Rectory Pk. Av. B75: S Cold 1C 70
Rectory Pk. Cl. B75: S Cold 1C 70
Rectory Pk. Cl. B75: S Cold 5D 54
Rectory Pk. Rd. B26: Sheld 6F 121
Rectory Rd. B31: N'fld 4F 145
 B75: S Cold 6A 54
 B91: Sol 4G 151
 DY8: Stourb 2F 125
Rectory St. DY8: Word 6B 92
Redacre Rd. B73: Bold 3F 69
Redacres WV6: Tett 3C 26
Redbank Av. B23: Erd 4C 84
Redbourn Rd. WS3: Blox 3G 19
Red Brick Cl. B64: Crad H 4F 111
Redbrook Covert B38: K Nor 1A 160
Red Brook Rd. WS2: Wals 4G 31
Redbrooks Cl. B91: Sol 6E 151
Redburn Dr. B14: K Hth 5F 147
Redcar Cft. B36: Hodg H 1A 104
Redcar Rd. WV10: F'hses 3H 15
Redcliffe Dr. WV5: Wom 1H 73
Redcott's Cl. WV10: Bush 1C 28
Redcroft Dr. B24: Erd 2A 86
Redcroft Rd. DY2: Dud 3G 95
Red Cross Wlk. WV1: Wolv 6G 27
Reddal Hill Rd. B64: Old H 2G 111
REDDICAP HEATH 1C 70
Reddicap Heath Rd. B75: S Cold 1C 70
Reddicap Hill B75: S Cold 1C 70
Reddicap Trad. Est. B75: S Cold 6B 54
Reddicroft B73: S Cold 6A 54
Reddings, The B47: H'wd 4A 162
Reddings La. B11: Tys 3E 135
Reddings Rd. B13: Mose 3F 133
Redditch Ho. B33: Kitts G 1A 122
Redditch Rd. B31: Longb 3G 159
 B48: Hopw 6G 159
Redfern Cl. B92: Olton 4F 137
Redfern Pk. Way B11: Tys 6G 119
Redfern Rd. B11: Tys 6F 119
Redfly La. DY5: P'ntt 3G 93
Redford Cl. B13: Mose 3B 134
Redgate Cl. B38: K Nor 5H 145
Redhall Rd. B32: Harb 4C 114
 DY3: Gorn 5G 75

Red Hill—Richmond Rd.

Red Hill DY8: Stourb 1F **125**
Redhill DY2: Dud 1F **95**
Redhill Av. WV5: Wom 1G **73**
Red Hill Cl. DY8: Stourb 1F **125**
Redhill Ct. DY8: Stourb 2F **125**
Red Hill Gro. B38: K Nor 2B **160**
Redhill La. B45: Rubery 4C **156**
B61: C'wich 4C **156**
Redhill Pl. B62: Hunn 6A **128**
Redhill Rd. B25: Yard 5G **119**
B31: Longb 1F **159**
B38: K Nor, Head H 1F **159**
Red Hill St. WV1: Wolv 6G **27**
Redholme Ct. DY8: Stourb 1E **125**
Red Ho. Av. WS10: W'bry 2H **63**
Redhouse Cl. B93: Ben H 4A **166**
Redhouse Cone & Mus. 2C **108**
Redhouse Ind. Est. WS9: A'rdge 3H **33**
Redhouse La. WS9: A'rdge 4A **34**
Red Ho. Pk. Rd. B43: Gt Barr 3A **66**
Redhouse Rd. B33: Stech 6C **104**
WV6: Tett 4G **25**
Redhouse St. WS1: Wals 4C **48**
Redhurst Dr. WV10: F'hses 4F **15**
Redlake Dr. DY9: Pedm 4F **125**
Redlake Rd. DY9: Pedm 4F **125**
Redlands Cl. B91: Sol 2H **151**
Redlands Rd. B91: Sol 2G **151**
Redlands Way B74: S'tly 2A **52**
Red La. DY3: Sed 5F **59**
WV11: Ess 6C **18**
Red Leasowes Rd. B63: Hale 2H **127**
Redliff Av. B36: Cas B 6H **87**
Red Lion Av. WS11: Nort C 1E **9**
Red Lion Cl. B69: Tiv 1A **96**
Red Lion Cres. WS11: Nort C 1E **9**
Red Lion La. WS11: Nort C 1E **9**
Red Lion St. WS2: Wals 6C **32**
WV1: Wolv 1G **43** (2A **170**)
Redmead Cl. B30: K Nor 3G **145**
Redmoor Gdns. WV4: Penn 6E **43**
Redmoor Way B76: Min 1H **87**
REDNAL 3H **157**
Rednal Hill La. B45: Rubery 3F **157**
Rednall Dr. B75: R'ley 6A **38**
Rednal Mill Dr. B45: Redn 2B **158**
Rednal Rd. B38: K Nor 1G **159**
Redoak Ho. WV10: Wolv 6B **28**
Redpine Crest WV12: W'hall 5D **30**
Red River Rd. WS2: Wals 4G **31**
Red Rock Dr. WV8: Cod 5F **13**
Red Rooster Ind. Est. WS9: A'rdge 3A **34**
Redruth Cl. DY6: K'wfrd 1B **92**
WS5: Wals 4H **49**
Redruth Rd. WS5: Wals 4H **49**
Redstone Dr. WV11: Wed 4H **29**
Redstone Farm Rd. B28: Hall G 1H **149**
Redstone Way DY3: Lwr G 3H **75**
Redthorn Gro. B33: Stech 6B **104**
Redvers Rd. B9: Small H 2E **119**
Redway Ct. B75: S Cold 1C **70**
Redwing Cl. WS7: Hamm 1F **11**
Redwing Gro. B23: Erd 6B **68**
Red Wing Wlk. B36: Cas B 1C **106**
Redwood Av. DY1: Dud 2B **76**
Redwood Bus. Pk. B66: Smeth 2A **98**
Redwood Cl. B30: K Nor 3A **146**
B74: S'tly 1H **51**
Redwood Cft. B14: K Hth 6G **133**
Redwood Dr. B69: Tiv 5B **78**
Redwood Gdns. B27: A Grn 6H **119**
Redwood Ho. B37: K'hrst 4C **106**
Redwood Rd. B30: K Nor 3A **146**
WS5: Wals 1F **65**
WV14: Cose 3F **61**
Redwood Way WV12: W'hall 1B **30**
Redworth Ho. *B45: Rubery 1F 157*
(off Deelands Rd.)
Reedham Gdns. WV4: Penn 6B **42**
Reedly Rd. WV12: W'hall 6C **18**
Reedmace Cl. B38: K Nor 1B **160**
Reedswood Cl. WS2: Wals 6A **32**
Reedswood Gdns. WS2: Wals 6A **32**
Reedswood La. WS2: Wals 6A **32**
Reedswood Retail Pk. WS2: Wals 5H **31**
Reedswood Way WS2: Wals 5G **31**
Rees Dr. WV5: Wom 6H **57**
Reeves Gdns. WV8: Cod 3G **13**
Reeves Rd. B14: K Hth 1E **147**
Reeves St. WS3: Blox 1H **31**
Reflex Ind. Pk. WV13: W'hall 6H **29**
Reform St. B70: W Brom 4B **80**
Regal Cft. B36: Hodg H 1H **103**
Regal Dr. WS2: Wals 3A **48**
Regan Av. B90: Shir 6G **149**
Regan Ct. B75: S Cold 6G **55**
Regan Cres. B23: Erd 1E **85**
Regan Dr. B69: O'bry 1D **96**
Regency Cl. B9: Small H 2D **118**
Regency Ct. WV1: Wolv 6G **27** (1A **170**)
Regency Dr. B38: K Nor 5B **146**
Regency Gdns. B14: Yard W 4C **148**
Regency Wlk. B74: Four O 4D **36**
Regent Av. B69: Tiv 6A **78**
Regent Cl. B5: Edg 5F **117**
B63: Hale 1A **128**
B69: Tiv 1A **96**
DY6: K'wfrd 3B **92**
Regent Ct. *B62: Quin 4G 113*
(off Binswood Rd.)
B66: Smeth 4E **99**
Regent Dr. B69: Tiv 6A **78**
Regent Ho. *WS2: Wals 6B 32*
(off Green La.)
WV1: Wolv 6F **27** (2A **170**)
Regent Pde. B1: Birm 5E **101** (1A **4**)
Regent Pk. Rd. B10: Small H 3C **118**
Regent Pl. B1: Birm 5E **101** (1A **4**)
B69: Tiv 5B **78**
Regent Rd. B17: Harb 5H **115**
B21: Hand 1H **99**
B69: Tiv 1A **96**
WV4: Penn 6C **42**
Regent Row B18: Birm 5E **101** (1A **4**)
Regents, The B15: Edg 3H **115**
Regent St. B1: Birm 5E **101** (1A **4**)
B30: Stir 6C **132**
B64: Old H 1H **111**
B66: Smeth 3E **99**
DY1: Dud 1E **77**
DY4: Tip 5G **61**
WV13: W'hall 6A **30**
WV14: Bils 5F **45**
Regents Way B75: S Cold 5D **54**
Regent Wlk. B8: W End 2H **103**
Regina Av. B44: Gt Barr 5F **67**
Regina Cl. B45: Fran 5E **143**
Regina Cres. WV6: Tett 5H **25**
Regina Dr. B42: P Barr 4E **83**
WS4: Wals 5F **33**
Reginald Rd. B8: Salt 5D **102**
B67: Smeth 1D **114**
Regis Beeches WV6: Tett 4A **26**
Regis Gdns. B65: Row R 1C **112**
Regis Heath Rd. B65: Row R 1D **112**
Regis Rd. B65: Row R 2C **112**
WV6: Tett 4H **25**
Regus Bldg. B90: Bly P 6D **164**
Reid Av. WV12: W'hall 3D **30**
Reid Rd. B68: O'bry 2A **114**
Reigate Av. B8: W End 5H **103**
Reliance Trad. Est. WV14: Bils 6D **44**
Relko Dr. B36: Hodg H 2A **104**
Remembrance Rd.
WS10: W'bry 2A **64**
Remington Pl. WS2: Wals 4A **32**
Remington Rd. WS2: Wals 3H **31**
Renaissance Ct. B12: Birm 2A **118**
Renfrew Cl. DY8: Word 6A **92**
Renfrew Sq. B35: Cas V 3F **87**
Rennie Gro. B32: Quin 6B **114**
Rennison Dr. WV5: Wom 1G **73**
Renown Cl. DY5: P'ntt 1F **93**
Renton Gro. WV10: Oxl 6E **15**
Renton Rd. WV10: Oxl 6E **15**
Repington Way B75: S Cold 5F **55**
Repton Av. WV6: Pert 6E **25**
Repton Gro. B9: Bord G 6H **103**
Repton Ho. B23: Erd 1F **85**
Repton Rd. B9: Bord G 6H **103**
Reservoir Cl. WS2: Wals 3H **47**
Reservoir Pas. WS10: W'bry 2F **63**
Reservoir Pl. WS2: Wals 3H **47**
Reservoir Retreat B16: Edg 2B **116**
Reservoir Rd. B16: Edg 1B **116**
B23: Erd 3D **84**
B29: S Oak 2F **131**
B45: Coft H 6A **158**
B65: Row R 6C **96**
B68: O'bry 5A **98**
B92: Olton 5D **136**
Reservoir St. WS2: Wals 3H **47**
Retallack Cl. B66: Smeth 1F **99**
Retford Dr. B76: Walm 1C **70**
Retford Gro. B25: Yard 5A **120**
Retreat, The B64: Crad H 4G **111**
Retreat Gdns. DY3: Sed 6A **60**
Retreat St. WV3: Wolv 3F **43** (6A **170**)
Revesby Wlk. B7: Birm 5A **102**
Revival St. WS3: Blox 6H **19**
Reynards Cl. DY3: Sed 6C **60**
Reynolds Cl. DY3: Swind 5E **73**
Reynolds Ct. B68: O'bry 4H **113**
Reynolds Gro. WV6: Pert 4F **25**
Reynolds Ho. *B19: Loz 2G 101*
(off Newbury Rd.)
Reynolds Rd. B21: Hand 2A **100**
Reynoldstown Rd. B36: Hodg H 1A **104**
Reynolds Wlk. WV11: Wed 1B **30**
Rhayader Rd. B31: N'fld 2C **144**
Rhodes Cl. DY3: Lwr G 3E **75**
Rhone Cl. B11: S'hll 2C **134**
Rhoose Cft. B35: Cas V 4F **87**
Rhys Thomas Cl. WV12: W'hall 5D **30**
Rian Ct. B64: Crad H 3F **111**
Ribbesford Av. WV10: Oxl 1F **27**
Ribbesford Cl. B63: Crad 6F **111**
Ribbesford Cres. WV14: Cose 4F **61**
Ribble Ct. B73: S Cold 6H **53**
Ribblesdale Rd. B30: Stir 6C **132**
Ribble Wlk. B36: Cas B 1B **106**
Richard Lighton Ho. B1: Birm 3A **4**
Richard Pl. WS5: Wals 3G **49**
Richard Rd. WS5: Wals 3G **49**
Richards Cl. B31: Longb 3D **158**
B65: Row R 5E **97**
Richards Ho. B69: O'bry 5D **96**
WS2: Wals 6B 32
(off Burrowes St.)
Richardson Dr. DY8: Amb 3C **108**
Richards Rd. DY4: Tip 4H **61**
Richards St. WS10: Darl 3D **46**
Richard St. B6: Aston 4H **101**
B7: Birm 4H **101**
B70: W Brom 4H **79**
Richard St. Sth. B70: W Brom 5A **80**
Richard St. W. B70: W Brom 5H **79**
Richard Williams Rd. WS10: W'bry 3H **63**
Richborough Dr. DY1: Dud 4A **76**
Riches St. WV6: Wolv 6D **26**
Richford Gro. B33: Kitts G 1H **121**
Richmere Ct. WV6: Tett 6H **25**
Richmond Ashton Dr. DY4: Tip 2A **78**
Richmond Av. B12: Bal H 6H **117**
WV3: Wolv 2D **42**
Richmond Cl. B20: Hand 4C **82**
B47: H'wd 2B **162**
Richmond Ct. *B15: Edg 3D 116*
(off Enfield Rd.)
B29: W Cas 6G **131**
B63: Hale 2G **127**
B68: O'bry 4A **98**
B72: W Grn 6H **69**
DY9: Pedm 4F 125
(off Redlake Rd.)
Richmond Cft. B42: Gt Barr 1B **82**
Richmond Dr. WV3: Wolv 2C **42**
WV6: Pert 5F **25**
Richmond Gdns. DY8: Amb 4D **108**
WV5: Wom 2G **73**
Richmond Gro. DY8: Woll 3C **108**
Richmond Hill B68: O'bry 4A **98**
Richmond Hill Gdns. B15: Edg 4A **116**
Richmond Hill Rd. B15: Edg 5A **116**
Richmond Ho. B37: Chel W 2E **123**
Richmond Pk. DY6: W Hth 1A **92**
Richmond Pl. B14: K Hth 5H **133**
Richmond Rd. B18: Hock 3D **100**
B33: Stech 1B **120**
B45: Rubery 2E **157**
B66: Smeth 1E **115**

Richmond Rd. B73: S Cold 5H 53
   B92: Olton 4C 136
   DY2: Dud 1E 95
   DY3: Sed 6A 60
   WV3: Wolv 1C 42
Richmond St. B63: Hale 1A 128
   B70: W Brom 1F 79
   WS1: Wals 2D 48
Richmond St. Sth.
   B70: W Brom 2E 79
Richmond Way B37: Chel W 6E 107
Rickard Cl. B93: Know 4A 166
Rickman Dr. B15: Birm 3F 117
Rickyard Cl. B25: Yard 2B 120
   B29: W Cas 1E 145
Rickyard Piece B32: Quin 1C 130
Riddfield Rd. B36: Hodg H 1C 104
Ridding La. WS10: W'bry 3F 63
Riddings, The B33: Stech 5C 104
   B76: Walm 5F 71
   DY9: W'cte 3H 125
   WV10: Bush 2C 28
Riddings Cres. WS3: Pels 3D 20
Riddings Hill CV7: Bal C 5H 169
RIDGACRE 5B 114
Ridgacre Ent. Pk. B71: W Brom 1H 79
Ridgacre La. B32: Quin 5H 113
Ridgacre Rd. B32: Quin 5H 113
   (not continuous)
   B71: W Brom 1H 79
Ridgacre Rd. W. B32: Quin 5G 113
Ridge Cl. B13: Mose 1C 148
   WS2: Wals 6D 30
Ridgefield Rd. B62: B'hth 3C 112
Ridge Gro. DY9: Lye 6G 109
Ridge Hill DY8: Word 6D 92
Ridge La. WV11: Wed 2F 29
Ridgemount Dr. B38: K Nor 2H 159
Ridge Rd. DY6: K'wfrd 4H 91
Ridge St. DY8: Woll 5A 108
Ridgewater Cl. B45: Redn 3H 157
Ridge Way B32: Quin 1G 129
Ridgeway B71: Edg 1F 115
   WS9: A'rdge 5D 34
Ridgeway, The B23: Erd 1A 84
   DY3: Sed 1H 75
   WS7: Burn 1C 10
Ridgeway Av. B62: Quin 5G 113
Ridgeway Ct. WS2: Wals 2F 47
Ridgeway Dr. WV4: Penn 2D 58
Ridgeway Rd. DY4: Tip 5A 62
   DY8: Word 1D 108
Ridgewood B34: S End 3F 105
Ridgewood Av. DY8: Woll 4A 108
Ridgewood Cl. WS1: Wals 3D 48
Ridgewood Dr. B75: Four O 2H 53
Ridgewood Gdns. B44: Gt Barr 6G 67
Ridgmont Cft. B32: Quin 6C 114
Riding Cl. B71: W Brom 5D 64
Riding Way WV12: W'hall 3D 30
Ridley St. B1: Birm 2E 117 (6B 4)
Ridpool Rd. B33: Kitts G 6F 105
Rifle St. WV14: Cose 5C 60
Rigby St. WS10: W'bry 4F 63
Riland Av. B75: S Cold 6B 54
Riland Ct. B72: W Grn 6A 70
Riland Gro. B75: S Cold 6A 54
Riland Ind. Est. B75: S Cold 6B 54
Riland Rd. B75: S Cold 6B 54
Riley Cres. WV3: Wolv 5D 42
Riley Dr. B36: Cas B 6C 88
Riley Rd. B14: Yard W 4D 148
Riley St. WV13: W'hall 1B 46
Rilstone Rd. B32: Harb 6D 114
Rindleford Av. WV4: Penn 5A 42
Ring, The B25: Yard 3A 120
Ringhills Rd. WV8: Bilb 5H 13
Ringinglow Rd.
   B44: Gt Barr 3E 67
Ringmere Av. B36: Cas B 1F 105
Ring Rd. Nth. B15: Edg 1B 132
Ring Rd. St Andrews
   WV1: Wolv. 1F 43 (3A 170)
Ring Rd. St Davids
   WV1: Wolv 1H 43 (3D 170)
Ring Rd. St Georges
   WV2: Wolv 2H 43 (5C 170)

Ring Rd. St Johns
   WV2: Wolv 2G 43 (5A 170)
Ring Rd. St Marks
   WV3: Wolv 2F 43 (4A 170)
Ring Rd. St Patricks
   WV1: Wolv 6H 27 (1C 170)
Ring Rd. St Peters
   WV1: Wolv 1G 43 (2A 170)
Ring Rd. Sth. B15: Edg 1B 132
Ringswood Rd. B92: Olton. 1C 136
Ringway Bus. Pk. B7: Birm 4A 102
Ringwood Av. WS9: A'rdge 4D 34
Ringwood Dr. B45: Fran. 6G 143
Ringwood Rd. WV10: Bush 6H 15
Ripley Cl. B69: Tiv 1H 95
Ripley Gro. B23: Erd 2B 84
Ripon Dr. B71: W Brom 4B 64
Ripon Rd. B14: Yard W 3C 148
   WS2: Wals 1H 47
   WV10: Oxl 2G 27
Rippingille Rd. B43: Gt Barr 1E 67
Ripple Rd. B30: Stir 6D 132
Risborough Ho. B31: Longb 1D 158
Rischale Way WS4: Rus 1H 33
Rise, The B37: Mars G 4C 122
   B42: Gt Barr 5C 66
   B48: Hopw 5F 159
   DY6: K'wfrd 4C 92
Rise Av. B45: Redn 2G 157
Riseley Cres. B5: Bal H 5F 117
Rising Brook WV6: Tett 5H 25
Rissington Av. B29: S Oak 5C 132
Ritchie Cl. B13: Mose 4A 134
Rivendell Cl. B28: Hall G 4E 135
Rivendell Gdns. WV6: Tett. 4H 25
Riverbank Rd. WV13: W'hall 1D 46
River Brook Dr. B30: Stir 5D 132
River Lee Rd. B11: Tys 6E 119
Rivermead Pk. B34: S End. 4E 105
Riversdale Rd. B14: Yard W 4D 148
Riverside Cl. B38: K Nor 4H 145
   B46: Col 2H 107
   (off Prossers Wlk.)
Riverside Cres. B28: Hall G 3D 148
Riverside Dr. B29: S Oak 2E 133
   B33: Stech 5B 104
   B91: Sol 5A 152
Riverside Gdns. WV8: Bilb 3H 13
Riversleigh Dr. DY8: Word 3C 108
River St. B5: Birm. 1A 118 (5H 5)
Riverway WS10: W'bry 3H 63
Rivington Cl. DY8: Stourb 1C 124
Rivington Cres. B44: K'sdng 4C 68
Roach Cl. B37: Chel W 6E 107
   DY5: Brie H 4H 93
Roach Cres. WV11: Wed 1H 29
Roach Pool Cft. B16: Edg 1G 115
Robert Av. B23: Erd 1E 85
Robert Ct. B13: Mose. 3B 134
Robert Rd. B20: Hand 6D 82
   DY4: Tip. 1H 77
Roberts Cl. WS9: Wals W 5B 22
   WS10: Mox 1B 62
Roberts Ct. B24: Erd 1A 86
Roberts Grn. Rd. DY3: Up Gor 3A 76
Roberts La. DY9: Pedm 5F 125
Robertson Knoll B36: Hodg H 2D 104
Robertsons Gdns. B7: Nech 2C 102
Roberts Rd. B27: A Grn 2A 136
   WS3: Wals 4D 32
   WS10: W'bry 2C 64
Robert St. DY3: Lwr G 3H 75
Robert Wynd WV14: Cose 4B 60
Robeson Cl. DY4: Tip 2F 77
Robin Cl. B36: Cas B 1C 106
   DY6: K'wfrd 3E 93
Robin Gro. WV11: Wed 2E 29
Robin Hood Crematorium
   B90: Shir 2H 149
Robin Hood Cres. B28: Hall G 6E 135
Robin Hood Cft. B28: Hall G 1F 149
Robin Hood Island B28: Hall G 2G 149
   (off Stratford Rd.)
Robin Hood La. B28: Hall G 6D 134
Robin Hood Rd. DY5: Quar B. 1B 110
Robin Rd. B23: Erd. 3E 85
Robins Bus. Pk. DY4: W Brom 6E 63

Robins Cl. DY8: Stourb 2E 125
   WS6: C Hay 4D 6
Robins Ct. B14: K Hth 4H 133
Robinsfield Dr. B31: Longb 2E 159
Robinsons Way B76: Min. 2H 87
Robin Wlk. WS2: Wals 6F 31
Robottom Cl. WS2: Wals 3H 31
Robson Cl. B70: W Brom 1F 79
Rocester Av. WV11: Wed. 2G 29
Rochdale Wlk. B10: Small H 4C 118
Roche Rd. WS3: Blox 6F 19
Rochester Cft. WS2: Wals 5G 31
Rochester Rd. B31: N'fld 3E 145
Roche Way WS3: Blox 6F 19
Rochford Cl. B45: Rubery 2E 157
   B63: Hale 3H 127
   B76: Walm 5E 71
   WS2: Wals 4A 48
Rochford Ct. B90: M'path 3E 165
Rochford Gro. WV4: Penn 6B 42
Rock, The WV6: Tett. 4B 26
Rock Av. B45: Redn 2A 158
Rockface, The 6H 101 (2H 5)
Rockford Rd. B42: Gt Barr 6C 66
Rock Gro. B92: Olton 2C 136
Rockingham Cl. B93: Dorr. 6H 165
   DY3: Gorn. 4F 75
   WS3: Blox 6H 19
Rockingham Dr. WV6: Pert 6E 25
Rockingham Gdns. B74: S Cold. 5H 53
Rockingham Hall Gdns.
   DY9: Hag 6H 125
Rockingham Rd. B25: Yard 3B 120
Rockland Dr. B33: Stech 5C 104
Rockland Gdns. WV13: W'hall 3H 45
Rocklands Dr. B75: S Cold 3H 53
Rockley Gro. B45: Redn. 2H 157
Rockley Rd. B65: Row R 3A 96
Rockmead Av. B44: Gt Barr 3H 67
Rockmoor Cl. B37: K'hrst. 6A 106
Rock Rd. B92: Olton. 2C 136
   WV14: Cose 5B 60
Rocks Hill DY5: Brie H. 2H 109
Rock St. DY3: Up Gor. 2A 76
Rockville Rd. B8: Salt 5G 103
Rocky La. B6: Aston. 3A 102
   B7: Nech 3A 102
   B42: Gt Barr 1C 82
Rodborough Rd. B26: Sheld 5F 121
   B93: Dorr 6F 167
Rodbourne Rd. B17: Harb 2G 131
Roddis Cl. B23: Erd 5D 68
Roderick Dr. WV11: Wed 2F 29
Roderick Rd. B11: S'brk. 6C 118
Rodlington Av. B44: Gt Barr. 4H 67
Rodman Cl. B15: Edg. 3H 115
Rodney Cl. B16: Birm. 1C 116
   B92: Olton 4F 137
Rodney Rd. B92: Olton 4F 137
Rodway Cl. B19: Loz 2G 101
   DY5: Quar B 4H 109
   WV4: E'shll. 2H 59
Rodwell Gro. B44: K'sdng 5A 68
Roebuck Cl. B34: S End 4A 106
Roebuck Glade WV12: W'hall. 5E 31
Roebuck La. B66: Smeth 2C 98
   B70: W Brom 6C 80
Roebuck Pl. WS3: Blox 3C 32
Roebuck Rd. WS3: Blox. 3C 32
Roebuck St. B70: W Brom 6D 80
Roedean Cl. B44: K'sdng 6B 68
Roford Ct. DY3: Up Gor 1A 76
Rogerfield Rd. B23: Erd. 1G 85
Rogers Cl. WV11: Wed 6A 18
Rogers Rd. B8: W End. 4H 103
Rokeby Cl. B76: Walm 1C 70
Rokeby Rd. B43: Gt Barr 3B 66
Rokeby Wlk. B34: Hodg H 3D 104
Rokewood Cl. DY6: K'wfrd. 6B 74
Roland Gdns. B19: Loz. 1E 101
Roland Gro. B19: Loz 1E 101
Rolan Dr. B90: Maj G 1E 163
Roland Rd. B19: Loz 1E 101
Roland Vernon Way
   DY4: Tip 6C 62
Rolfe St. B66: Smeth 3E 99

Rollason Rd. B24: Erd 4G **85**
DY2: Dud 1F **95**
Rollesby Dr. WV13: W'hall 3H **45**
Rollingmill Bus. Pk.
WS2: Wals 2A **48**
Rolling Mill Cl. B5: Bal H 4G **117**
Rollingmill St. WS2: Wals 2A **48**
Rollswood Dr. B91: Sol 3D **150**
Roman Cl. WS8: Bwnhls 3A **10**
Roman Ct. B38: K Nor 1C **160**
Roman La. B74: Lit A 5B **36**
Roman Pk. B46: Col 6H **89**
B74: Lit A 5B **36**
Roman Pl. B74: Lit A 1B **52**
Roman Rd. B74: Lit A 4C **36**
DY7: Stourb 3A **124**
DY8: Stourb 1A **124**
(not continuous)
Roman Vw. WS11: Cann 1F **7**
Roman Way B15: Edg 2H **131**
B46: Col 5G **89**
B65: Row R 5C **96**
Romany Rd. B45: Fran 6D **142**
Romany Way DY8: Stourb 2A **124**
Roma Rd. B11: Tys 6E **119**
Romford Cl. B26: Sheld 5F **121**
Romilly Av. B20: Hand 5D **82**
Romilly Cl. B76: Walm 1E **71**
DY8: Woll 5C **108**
Romney Cl. B28: Hall G 6F **135**
Romney Ho. Ind. Est. *WS10: Darl* *4B* ***46***
(off Wolverhampton St.)
Romney Way B43: Gt Barr 1F **67**
Romsey Gro. WV10: F'hses 4G **15**
Romsey Rd. WV10: F'hses 4G **15**
Romsey Way WS3: Blox 4F **19**
ROMSLEY **3A 142**
Romsley Cl. B45: Rubery 1E **157**
B63: Hale 3B **128**
WS4: S'fld 5G **21**
ROMSLEY HILL **5A 142**
Romsley Rd. B32: Bart G 5H **129**
B68: O'bry 1H **113**
DY9: Lye 6G **109**
Romulus Cl. B20: Hand 4D **82**
Ronald Gro. B36: Cas B 6H **87**
Ronald Pl. B9: Bord G 1E **119**
Ronald Rd. B9: Bord G 1D **118**
Ron Davis Cl. B66: Smeth 4F **99**
ROOD END **3A 98**
Rood End Rd. B68: O'bry 3A **98**
B69: O'bry 2A **98**
Rooker Av. WV2: E'shll 4A **44**
Rooker Cres. WV2: E'shll 5B **44**
Rookery, The B62: Quin 3G **129**
Rookery Av. DY5: Brie H 1E **109**
WV4: E'shll 2C **60**
Rookery La. WS9: A'rdge 3D **34**
WV3: Wolv 5E **43**
Rookery Pde. WS9: A'rdge 3D **34**
Rookery Pk. DY5: P'ntt 4F **93**
Rookery Ri. WV5: Wom 1H **73**
Rookery Rd. B21: Hand 1A **100**
B29: S Oak 3B **132**
WV4: E'shll 2C **60**
WV5: Wom 1H **73**
Rookery St. WV11: Wed 4E **29**
Rookwood Dr. WV6: Tett 1F **41**
Rookwood Rd. B27: A Grn 1H **135**
Rooth St. WS10: W'bry 1H **63**
Roper Wlk. DY3: Sed 1B **76**
Roper Way DY3: Sed 1B **76**
Rope Wlk. WS1: Wals 2E **49**
Rosafield Av. B62: Quin 5F **113**
Rosalind Av. DY1: Dud 6D **60**
Rosalind Gro. WV11: Wed 4A **30**
Rosamond St. WS1: Wals 4B **48**
Rosary Rd. B23: Erd 4D **84**
Rosary Vs. B11: S'hll 6B **118**
Rose Av. B68: O'bry 4B **114**
DY6: K'wfrd 4D **92**
Rose Bank B74: Lit A 4D **36**
Rose Bank Dr. WS3: Wals 5C **32**
Rosebay Av. B38: K Nor 1B **160**
Rosebay Gro. WV5: Wom 1E **73**
Rosebery Rd. B66: Smeth 5G **99**
Rosebery St. B18: Hock 5C **100**
Rosebriars B90: Maj G 2E **163**
Rose Cl. B66: Smeth 4G **99**
Rose Cott. Dr. *DY8: Word* *6B* ***92***
(off Barnett La.)
Rose Cotts. B29: S Oak 3B **132**
B30: Stir 1C **146**
Rose Ct. CV7: Bal C 1H **169**
Rosecroft Rd. B26: Sheld 5G **121**
Rosedale Av. B23: Erd 4E **85**
B66: Smeth 4G **99**
Rosedale Gro. B25: Yard 3A **120**
Rosedale Pl. WV13: W'hall 3A **46**
Rosedale Rd. B25: Yard 3A **120**
Rosedale Wlk. DY6: K'wfrd 1C **92**
Rosedene Dr. B20: Hand 5B **82**
Rose Dr. WS8: Clay 1A **22**
Rosefield Ct. B67: Smeth 5E **99**
Rosefield Cft. B6: Aston 2H **101**
Rosefield Rd. B67: Smeth 5E **99**
Rosefields B31: N'fld 2F **145**
Rose Gdns., The B63: Hale 3G **127**
Rosehall Cl. B91: Sol 6D **150**
Rose Hill B45: Coft H, Lick 6G **157**
DY5: Quar B 2C **110**
WV13: W'hall 3A **46**
Rose Hill Cl. B36: Cas B 1F **105**
Rosehill Ct. *DY1: Dud* *6E* ***77***
(off Wolverhampton St.)
Rose Hill Gdns. WV13: W'hall 2A **46**
Rose Hill Rd. B21: Hand 2C **100**
Rosehip Cl. WS5: Wals 2E **65**
Roseland Av. DY2: Dud 6H **77**
Roseland Way B15: Birm 2D **116**
Rose La. B69: Tiv 5C **78**
Roseleigh Rd. B45: Redn 3H **157**
Rosemary Av. WS6: C Hay 2D **6**
WV4: Penn 5G **43**
WV14: Bils 5H **45**
Rosemary Cl. WS8: Clay 1H **21**
Rosemary Ct. WV11: Wed 2H **29**
Rosemary Cres. DY1: Dud 1B **76**
WV4: Penn 6G **43**
Rosemary Cres. W. WV4: Penn 6F **43**
Rosemary Dr. B74: Lit A 6C **36**
Rosemary Hill Rd. B74: Four O 6C **36**
Rosemary La. DY8: Stourb 2B **124**
Rosemary Nook B74: Lit A 4D **36**
Rosemary Rd. B33: Stech 1D **120**
B63: Hale 3F **127**
DY4: Tip 1A **78**
WS6: C Hay 1D **6**
(not continuous)
Rosemoor Dr. DY5: Brie H 4F **109**
Rosemount B32: Quin 1C **130**
Rose Pl. B18: Birm 5E **101** (1A **4**)
Rose Rd. B17: Harb 5H **115**
B46: Col 1H **107**
Rose St. WV14: Bils 3H **61**
ROSEVILLE **6D 60**
Roseville Ct. *WV14: Cose* *5E* ***61***
(off Castle St.)
Roseville Gdns. WV8: Cod 3G **13**
Roseville Pct. *WV14: Cose* *5E* ***61***
(off Castle St.)
Rosewood Cl. B74: Lit A 4D **36**
Rosewood Dr. B23: Erd 5D **84**
WV12: W'hall 1B **30**
Rosewood Gdns. WV11: Ess 4B **18**
Rosewood Pk. WS6: C Hay 3D **6**
Rosewood Rd. DY1: Dud 2D **76**
Roshven Rd. B12: Bal H 1A **134**
Roslin Gro. B19: Hock 3E **101**
Roslyn Cl. B66: Smeth 3E **99**
Ross B65: Row R 1B **112**
Ross Cl. WV3: Wolv 1C **42**
Ross Dr. DY6: K'wfrd 2A **92**
Rosse Ct. B92: Sol 5B **138**
Rossendale Cl. B63: Crad 5F **111**
Ross Hgts. B65: Row R 6B **96**
Rosslyn Rd. B76: Walm 1D **86**
Ross Rd. WS3: Wals 3D **32**
Rostrevor Rd. B10: Small H 2F **119**
Rotary Ho. DY1: Dud 6B **76**
Rotherby Gro. B37: Mars G 4D **122**
Rotherfield Rd. B26: Sheld 3F **121**
Rothesay Cft. B32: Bart G 6H **129**
Rothesay Dr. DY8: Word 6A **92**
Rothesay Way WV12: W'hall 3B **30**
Rothley Wlk. B38: K Nor 1G **159**
Rothwell Dr. B91: Shir 2B **150**
Rotton Pk. Rd. B16: Edg 5H **99**
(not continuous)
Rotton Pk. St. B16: Birm 6B **100**
ROTTON ROW **5E 167**
Rough Coppice Wlk. B35: Cas V 5E **87**
ROUGH HAY **4C 46**
Rough Hay Pl. WS10: Darl 4C **46**
Rough Hay Rd. WS10: Darl 4C **46**
Rough Hill Dr. B65: Row R 3H **95**
Rough Hills Cl. WV2: E'shll 5B **44**
Rough Hills Rd. WV2: E'shll 5B **44**
Roughlea Av. B36: Hodg H 2D **104**
ROUGHLEY **6A 38**
Roughley Dr. B75: R'ley 1A **54**
Roughley Farm Rd. B75: R'ley 6C **38**
Rough Rd. B44: K'sdng 2A **68**
Rough Wood Country Pk. **3E 31**
Rouncil Cl. B92: Sol 6H **137**
Roundabout, The B31: Longb 6B **144**
Round Cft. WV13: W'hall 1A **46**
Round Hill DY3: Sed 3H **59**
Round Hill Av. DY9: Pedm 4G **125**
Roundhill Cl. B76: Walm 2C **70**
Roundhill Ho. DY6: K'wfrd 6B **74**
Roundhills Rd. B62: B'hth 3F **113**
Roundhill Ter. B62: B'hth 2E **113**
Roundhill Way WS8: Bwnhls 3B **10**
Roundhouse Rd. DY3: Up Gor 3A **76**
Roundlea Cl. WV12: W'hall 1B **30**
Roundlea Rd. B31: N'fld 5C **130**
Round Moor Wlk. B35: Cas V 4E **87**
ROUND OAK **5H 93**
Round Rd. B24: Erd 5H **85**
Roundsaw Cft. B45: Rubery 1F **157**
ROUND'S GREEN **2E 97**
Round's Grn. Rd. B69: O'bry 2E **97**
Rounds Hill Rd. WV14: Cose 5F **61**
Rounds Rd. WV14: Cose 2F **61**
Round St. DY2: Neth 3E **95**
Roundway Down WV6: Pert 6E **25**
Rounton Cl. B74: Four O 5D **36**
Rousay Cl. B45: Fran 6F **143**
Rousdon Gro. B43: Gt Barr 5H **65**
Rover Dr. B27: A Grn 1B **136**
B36: Cas B 6B **88**
Rovex Bus. Pk. B11: Tys 6F **119**
Rowallan Rd. B75: R'ley 2B **54**
Rowan Cl. B47: H'wd 4B **162**
B76: Walm 3D **70**
Rowan Ct. B30: K Nor 5C **146**
B66: Smeth 1B **98**
Rowan Cres. WV3: Wolv 4C **42**
WV14: Cose 4D **60**
Rowan Dr. B28: Hall G 2G **149**
WV11: Ess 4B **18**
Rowan Grange B74: Lit A 4C **36**
Rowan Ri. DY6: K'wfrd 3C **92**
Rowan Rd. B72: S Cold 3A **70**
DY3: Sed 4B **60**
WS5: Wals 1D **64**
Rowantrees B45: Redn 4H **157**
Rowan Way B31: Longb 6D **144**
B37: Chel W 2E **123**
Roway La. B69: O'bry 6E **79**
Rowbrook Cl. B90: Maj G 1E **163**
Rowchester Ct. B4: Birm 2E **5**
Rowcroft Covert B14: K Hth 4E **147**
Rowdale Rd. B42: Gt Barr 6E **67**
Rowden Dr. B23: Erd 1G **85**
B91: Sol 5C **150**
Rowena Gdns. DY3: Sed 3G **59**
Rowheath Ho. B30: B'vlle 1A **146**
Rowheath Rd. B30: K Nor 3B **146**
Rowington Av. B65: Row R 6D **96**
Rowington Rd. B34: S End 3A **106**
Rowland Gdns. WS2: Wals 6A **32**
Rowland Hill Dr. DY4: Tip 2C **78**
Rowlands Av. WS2: Wals 6E **31**
WV1: Wolv 1D **44**
Rowlands Cl. WS2: Wals 5E **31**
Rowlands Cres. B91: Sol 5F **137**
Rowlands Rd. B26: Yard 4C **120**
Rowland St. WS2: Wals 6A **32**
Rowley Gro. B33: Kitts G 6H **105**

Rowley Hall Av. B65: Row R 5C 96
Rowley Hill Vw. B64: Crad H 3H 111
Rowley Pl. WS4: Rus 2F 33
ROWLEY REGIS 6C 96
Rowley Regis Crematorium
  B65: Row R 1A 112
Rowley Regis Station (Rail) 1E 113
Rowley St. WS1: Wals 1D 48
Rowley Vw. B70: W Brom 4H 79
  WS10: Darl 1C 62
  WV14: Bils 2A 62
Rowley Village B65: Row R 6C 96
Rowney Cft. B28: Hall G 2E 149
Rowood Dr. B91: Sol 6G 137
  B92: Sol 6H 137
Rowthorn Cl. B74: S'tly 4A 52
Rowthorn Dr. B90: M'path 3E 165
Rowton Av. WV6: Pert 6E 25
Rowton Dr. B74: S'tly 6H 51
Roxburgh Gro. B43: Gt Barr 1E 67
Roxburgh Rd. B73: S Cold 2G 69
Roxby Gdns. WV6: Wolv 4E 27
Royal Arch Apartments
  B1: Birm 2E 117 (6B 4)
Royal Cl. B65: Row R 4C 96
  DY5: Brie H 3G 109
Royal Ct. B72: W Grn. 3H 69
Royal Doulton Crystal 4D 108
Royal Gro. B23: Erd 6B 68
Royal Oak Rd. B62: Quin 1F 129
  B65: Row R 4H 95
Royal Rd. B72: S Cold 6A 54
Royal Scot Gro. WS1: Wals 6C 48
Royal Star Cl. B33: Kitts G 1G 121
Royal Stop, The (MM). 2A 44
Royal Way DY4: Tip 5A 78
Roydon Rd. B27: A Grn 5A 136
Roylesden Cres. B73: New O 3C 68
Royston Chase B74: Lit A 6B 36
Royston Ct. B13: Mose. 3B 134
                    (off Wake Grn. Pk.)
Royston Cft. B12: Bal H 5H 117
Royston Way DY3: Sed 5G 59
RSPB Sandwell Valley Nature Reserve
                                      . . . . 1G 81
Rubens Cl. DY3: Up Gor 2H 75
RUBERY 2F 157
Rubery By-Pass B45: Rubery 2E 157
Rubery Cl. WS10: Darl 4C 46
Rubery Farm Gro. B45: Rubery 1F 157
Rubery Fld. Cl. B45: Redn. 6G 143
Rubery La. B45: Fran 6F 143
Rubery La. Sth. B45: Rubery 1F 157
Rubery St. WS10: Darl 3D 46
Ruckley Av. B19: Loz 2E 101
Ruckley Rd. B29: W Cas 5E 131
Rudd Gdns. WV10: Wolv 5D 28
Ruddington Way B19: Hock. 4G 101
Rudge Av. WV1: Wolv 6D 28
Rudge Cl. WV12: W'hall. 5C 30
Rudge Cft. B33: Kitts G 5E 105
Rudge St. WV14: Cose. 3G 61
Rudge Wlk. B18: Hock. 6C 100
Rudgewick Cft. B6: Aston 3H 101
Rudyard Cl. WV10: Bush 3A 16
Rudyard Gro. B33: Kitts G 6E 105
Rudyngfield Dr. B33: Stech 6D 104
Rufford Cl. B23: Erd 5D 68
Rufford Rd. DY9: Lye 1G 125
Rufford St. DY9: Lye 5H 109
Rufford Way WS9: A'rdge 2A 34
Rugby Rd. DY8: Woll 4B 108
Rugby St. WV1: Wolv 6F 27
Rugeley Av. WV12: W'hall 1D 30
Rugeley Cl DY4: Tip 2G 77
Ruislip Cl. B35: Cas V 3E 87
RUITON 3H 75
Ruiton St. DY3: Lwr G 3H 75
Rumbow B63: Hale 2A 128
RUMBUSH 6E 163
Rumbush La. B90: Dic H 6E 163
                         (Dickens Heath Rd.)
  B90: Dic H, Tid G 6E 163
                               (Norton La.)
  B94: Earls. 6E 163
Runcorn Cl. B37: F'bri 5E 107
Runcorn Rd. B12: Bal H. 6H 117

Runnymede Dr. CV7: Bal C 6H 169
Runnymede Rd. B11: S'hll. 2E 135
Rupert St. B7: Birm 5A 102
  WV3: Wolv 1E 43
RUSHALL. 2F 33
Rushall Cl. DY8: Word. 3C 108
  WS4: Wals 5F 33
Rushall Cl. B43: Gt Barr. 6A 66
                                   (off West Rd.)
Rushall Mnr. Cl. WS4: Wals. 5F 33
Rushall Mnr. Rd. WS4: Wals 5F 33
Rushall Rd. WV10: Bush 5A 16
Rushbrook Cl. B92: Olton. 3C 136
  WS8: Clay 1A 22
Rushbrooke Cl. B13: Mose 1H 133
Rushbrooke Dr. B73: New O 2C 68
Rushbrook Gro. B14: K Hth 4E 147
Rushbury Cl. B90: Shir 3B 150
  WV14: Bils 6D 44
Rushden Cft. B44: K'sdng 4H 67
Rushes Mill WS3: Pels. 4C 20
Rushey La. B11: Tys 6G 119
Rushford Av. WV5: Wom 1G 73
Rushford Cl. B90: M'path. 2E 165
Rush Grn. B32: Bart G 3C 130
Rushlake Grn. B34: S End 4F 105
Rushleigh Rd. B90: Maj G 1E 163
Rushmead Gro. B45: Redn 2G 157
Rushmere Rd. DY4: Tip 5A 62
Rushmoor Cl. B74: S Cold. 5H 53
Rushmore Ho. B45: Rubery 1F 157
Rushton Cl. CV7: Bal C 5H 169
Rushwater Cl. WV5: Wom 1E 73
Rushwick Cft. B34: S End 3H 105
Rushwick Gro. B90: M'path 3E 165
Rushwood Cl. WS4: Wals. 6E 33
Rushy Piece B32: Bart G 2B 130
Ruskin Av. B65: Row R 1D 112
  DY3: Lwr G. 2E 75
  WV4: E'shll 3B 60
Ruskin Cl. B6: Aston 2H 101
Ruskin Ct. B66: Smeth. 2B 98
  B68: O'bry 3H 113
Ruskin Gro. B27: A Grn 3H 135
Ruskin Hall Gro. B6: Aston 2H 101
Ruskin St. B71: W Brom 2A 80
Russell Bank Rd. B74: Four O 5E 37
Russell Cl. B69: Tiv 5D 78
  DY4: Tip 4C 62
  WV11: Wed 6H 17
Russell Ct. B74: Four O 6D 36
  WV3: Wolv 2F 43
Russell Ho. WS10: W'bry. 3F 63
  WV8: Cod 3E 13
Russell Rd. B13: Mose. 2F 133
  B28: Hall G 3E 135
  WV14: Bils 4H 45
Russells, The B13: Mose 2F 133
RUSSELL'S HALL 6B 76
Russells Hall Rd. DY1: Dud. 6A 76
Russell St. DY1: Dud. 6D 76
  WS10: W'bry 3F 63
  WV3: Wolv 2F 43
  WV13: W'hall 1B 46
Russett Cl. WS5: Wals 3A 50
Russett Way DY5: P'ntt 2F 93
Russet Wlk. WV8: Pend 6C 14
Russet Way B31: N'fld 1C 144
Ruston St. B16: Birm 2D 116
Ruthall Cl. B29: W Cas 6G 131
Ruth Cl. DY4: Tip 3C 62
Rutherford Rd. B23: Erd. 6E 69
  WS2: Wals 3G 31
Rutland Av. WV4: Penn 1B 58
Rutland Cl. B29: W Cas 6G 131
Rutland Cres. WS9: A'rdge 6D 22
  WV14: Bils 4F 45
Rutland Dr. B26: Yard 4C 120
Rutland Pas. DY1: Dud 6E 77
Rutland Pl. DY8: Woll 3B 108
Rutland Rd. B66: Smeth. 2E 115
  B71: W Brom 6A 64
  WS10: W'bry 1A 64
Rutland St. WS3: Wals. 4C 32
Rutland Ter. B18: Hock 4C 100
                                (off Crabtree Rd.)

Rutley Gro. B32: Quin 1D 130
Rutters Mdw. B32: Quin. 1H 129
Rutter St. WS1: Wals 4B 48
Ryan Av. WV11: Wed 1A 30
Ryan Pl. DY2: Neth. 3E 95
                                 (not continuous)
Rycroft Gro. B33: Kitts G 1G 121
Rydal Cl. B74: S'tly 1H 51
  WV11: Wed 2E 29
Rydal Dr. WV6: Pert 5F 25
Rydal Ho. B69: O'bry. 4D 96
Rydal Way B28: Hall G 6F 135
Rydding La. B71: W Brom. 5H 63
Rydding Sq. B71: W Brom. 5H 63
Ryde Gro. B27: A Grn 4G 135
Ryde Pk. Rd. B45: Redn 3A 158
Ryde Ho. B70: W Brom. 4E 79
Ryders Grn. Rd. B70: W Brom 3E 79
Ryders Hayes La. WS3: Pels 3E 21
Ryder St. B4: Birm 6G 101 (2F 5)
  B70: W Brom 2F 79
  DY8: Word 1B 108
Ryebank Cl. B30: B'vlle 2G 145
Ryeclose Cft. B37: Chel W 6F 107
RYECROFT 5B 32
Rye Cft. B27: A Grn 6A 120
  B47: H'wd 4A 162
  WV9: W'cte 2A 126
Ryecroft Av. WV4: Penn 6F 43
Ryecroft Cl. DY3: Sed 5G 59
Ryecroft Pk. WS2: Wals 6C 32
Ryecroft Pl. WS3: Wals 3D 32
Ryecroft St. WS2: Wals 6C 32
Ryefield WV8: Pend 5C 14
Ryefield Cl. B91: Sol 2C 150
Ryefield Way DY6: K'wfrd 3A 92
Rye Grass Wlk. B35: Cas V 4F 87
Rye Gro. B11: Tys. 1F 135
Ryemarket DY8: Stourb 6E 109
Ryhope Wlk. WV9: Pend 4E 15
                                 (not continuous)
Ryknild Cl. B74: Four O 3F 37
Ryland Cl. B63: Hale 3G 127
  DY4: Tip 2B 78
Ryland Ho. B19: Birm. 4F 101
                              (off Gt. Hampton Row)
Ryland Rd. B11: S'hll. 1D 134
  B15: Edg. 4E 117
  B24: Erd 6F 85
Rylands Dr. WV4: Penn 1D 58
Ryland St. B16: Birm 2D 116
Ryle St. WS3: Blox. 5B 20
Rymond Rd. B34: Hodg H 3C 104
Ryton Cl. B73: S Cold 6H 53
  WV10: Wolv 4C 28
Ryton End La. B92: Bars 6C 154
Ryton Gro. B34: S End 2H 105

S

Sabell Rd. B67: Smeth 3D 98
Sabrina Rd. WV6: Tett 2E 41
Saddlers Cen. WS1: Wals 2C 48
Saddlers Cl. B63: Crad 6D 110
Saddlers Cl. WS2: Wals. 4H 47
Saddlers Ct. Ind. Est. WS2: Wals . . . 2G 31
Saddlers M. B91: Sol. 6G 151
Saddleworth Rd. WS3: Blox 3G 19
Sadler Cres. B11: S'hll. 1D 134
                                    (off Lea Rd.)
Sadler Ho. B19: Hock. 3E 101
                                 (off Guest Gro.)
Sadler Rd. B75: S Cold 4D 54
  WS8: Bwnhls 6C 10
Sadlers Mill WS8: Bwnhls 6C 10
Sadlers Wlk. B16: Edg. 2C 116
Saffron Gdns. WV4: Penn. 1E 59
Saffron Ho. B38: K Nor 1A 160
Sage Cft. B31: N'fld 2D 144
St Agatha's Rd. B8: W End 4H 103
St Agnes Cl. B13: Mose 3B 134
St Agnes Rd. B13: Mose 3B 134
St Aidans Wlk. B10: Small H 3C 118
St Albans Cl. B67: Smeth. 3C 98
  WV11: Wed 1A 30
St Albans Ho. B32: Harb 6D 114

St Albans Rd. B67: Smeth 3C 98
  B13: Mose 2A 134
St Alphege Cl. B91: Sol 4G 151
St Andrew's Av. WS3: Pels. 2E 21
St Andrews Cl. WV6: Wolv. 5E 27
  B32: Bart G. 2E 131
  DY3: Lwr G. 4E 75
  DY8: Stourb 3D 124
St Andrews Dr. B69: Tiv 2B 96
  WV6: Pert 4D 24
St Andrews Ind. Est.
  B9: Bord G 1C 118
St Andrews Rd. B9: Birm 1B 118
  B75: S Cold 4A 54
St Andrews Stadium 2C 118
St Andrews Cl. DY2: Neth 4E 95
  B9: Birm .1B 118
St Annes Cl. WS7: Chase. 1A 10
  B20: Hand 3B 82
St Annes Ct. WV13: W'hall. 2B 46
  B13: Mose 1G 133
  B44: K'sdng 6A 68
  B64: Crad H 2E 111
St Annes Gro. B93: Know. 3C 166
St Annes Ind. Est.
  WV13: W'hall 6B 30
St Annes Rd. B64: Crad H 2E 111
  WV10: Oxl 5G 15
  WV13: W'hall 6B 30
St Anne's Way B44: K'sdng 1A 84
St Ann's Ter. WV13: W'hall 6B 30
St Anthony's Dr. WS3: Pels 2F 21
St Athan Cft. B35: Cas V 4F 87
St Audries Ct. B91: Sol 5D 150
St Augustine's Rd. B16: Edg 2H 115
St Augustus Cl. B70: W Brom 5D 80
St Austell Rd. WS5: Wals 4A 50
St Bartholomew's Ter. WS10: W'bry . . .2F 63
St Benedict's Cl. B70: W Brom 5D 80
St Benedicts Rd. B10: Small H. 4F 119
  WV5: Wom. 1G 73
St Bernards Rd. B92: Olton 2B 150
  B72: W Grn 3A 70
St Blaise Av. B46: Wat O 5D 88
St Blaise Rd. B75: R'ley. 6B 38
St Brades Cl. B69: Tiv 2C 96
St Brides Cl. DY3: Sed. 5G 59
  WV5: Wom 1F 73
Saintbury Dr. B91: Sol 2G 165
St Caroline Cl. B70: W Brom 5D 80
St Catharines Cl. WS1: Wals 4E 49
St Catherines Cl. DY2: Neth 6A 78
  B75: S Cold 4D 54
St Catherine's Ct. B91: Sol. 3F 151
St Catherine's Cres. WV4: Penn 1D 58
St Chads WV14: Cose 6D 60
St Chads Cir. Queensway
  B4: Birm 5F 101 (1D 4)
St Chad's Cl. DY3: Lwr G 4F 75
St Chads Ind. Est. B19: Birm 4F 101
St Chad's Queensway
  B4: Birm 5G 101 (2D 4)
St Chads RC Cathedral. 5G 101 (1D 4)
St Chads Rd. B45: Rubery 2F 157
  B75: S Cold 6C 54
  WV10: Bush 1B 28
  WV14: Bils. 4H 45
St Christopher Cl. B70: W Brom 5D 80
St Christophers B20: Hand. 3B 82
St Clements Av. WS3: Blox 2B 32
St Clements Cl. B63: Hale 2A 128
St Clements La. B71: W Brom. 3B 80
St Clements Rd. B7: Nech 3C 102
St Columbas Dr. B45: Redn 2A 158
St Cuthbert's Cl. B70: W Brom 5D 80
St David's Cl. B70: W Brom. 5D 80
  WS3: Pels 2F 21
St Davids Cl. B69: O'bry 2G 97
St Davids Dr. B32: Quin 6H 113
St Davids Gro. B20: Hand 3B 82
St Davids Pl. WS3: Blox 5B 20
St Denis Rd. B29: W Cas 1E 145
St Dennis Ho. B16: Edg 2H 115
                               (off Melville Rd.)
St Dominic's Rd. B24: Erd 6E 85
                               (not continuous)
St Edburgh's Rd. B25: Yard 2C 120

St Edmund's Cl. B70: W Brom 5D 80
  WV6: Wolv. 6D 26
St Edwards Rd. B29: S Oak 3B 132
St Eleanors Cl. B70: W Brom 5D 80
St Francis Av. B91: Sol 1C 150
St Francis' Cl. WS3: Pels 2F 21
St Francis Factory Est.
  B70: W Brom 5B 80
St George Dr. B66: Smeth 2E 99
ST GEORGES 2H 43 (4C 170)
St Georges Av. B23: Erd 2G 85
St Georges Cl. B75: S Cold 5D 54
  WS10: Darl 4D 46
  B15: Edg .4C 116
St Georges Ct. WS10: Darl 4D 46
                              (off St George's St.)
  B30: B'ville 6A 132
  B74: Four O 4E 37
  WS1: Wals 1F 48
                              (off Persehouse St.)
St George's Pde.
  WV2: Wolv 2H 43 (4C 170)
St Georges Pl. B70: W Brom 4A 80
  WS1: Wals 1D 48
St Georges Rd. DY2: Dud. 3F 95
  DY8: Stourb 3B 124
  B90: Shir .1B 164
St George's St. B19: Birm 5F 101
  WS10: Darl 4D 46
St Gerards Cl. B91: Sol. 5C 150
St Gerards Rd. B91: Sol. 5C 150
St Giles Av. B65: Row R 5B 96
St Giles Cl. B65: Row R 5C 96
St Giles Ct. B65: Row R. 6D 96
  WV13: W'hall 2B 46
St Giles Cres. WV1: Wolv 1C 44
St Giles Rd. B33: Kitts G 1H 121
  WV1: Wolv 1C 44
  WV13: W'hall 2B 46
St Giles Row DY8: Stourb 5E 109
                              (off Lwr. High St.)
St Giles St. DY2: Neth 4E 95
St Helens Av. DY4: Tip. 2C 78
St Helens Pas. B1: Birm 5E 101 (1A 4)
St Helens Rd. B91: Sol. 1E 151
St Heliers Rd. B31: N'fld 3C 144
St Ives Rd. WS5: Wals. 4H 49
St James Av. B65: Row R 5B 96
St James Cl. B70: W Brom 5D 80
  WS3: Pels. 2F 21
St James Gdns. WS8: Bwnhls 1A 22
St James Pl. B7: Birm 6A 102
  B15: Edg .3D 116
  B90: Shir .5H 149
St James Rd. B69: O'bry. 1D 96
  B75: Four O 1A 54
  B21: Hand 1H 99
St James's Rd. DY1: Dud 5D 76
St James's Ter. DY1: Dud 5C 76
St James St. WS10: W'bry. 3E 63
  WV1: Wolv 2A 44
  DY3: Lwr G 4H 75
St James Wlk. WS8: Bwnhls 6B 10
                              (off Short St.)
St John Bosco Cl. B71: W Brom 6H 63
St John Cl. B75: R'ley 5B 38
St John's Arc. WV1: Wolv. 1G 43 (3B 170)
St Johns Av. B65: Row R 5B 96
St Johns Cl. B70: W Brom 5D 80
  B93: Know. 3D 166
  DY3: Swind 5D 72
  WS9: Wals W 4B 22
St Johns Ct. B31: N'fld 6F 145
  B17: Harb 5F 115
  DY5: Brie H 1H 109
                              (off Hill St.)
  WS3: Blox 6H 19
  WS10: W'bry 3F 63
St Johns Gro. B37: K'hrst. 6B 106
St John's Ho. B70: W Brom 5A 80
St Johns Retail Pk.
  WV1: Wolv 2G 43 (6B 170)
St Johns Rd. B11: S'hll 6C 118
  B17: Harb. 5H 115
  B63: Hale .1G 127
  B68: O'bry 4A 98
  DY2: Dud. 1G 95

St Johns Rd. DY8: Stourb 5E 109
  WS2: Wals 3H 47
  WS3: Pels. 2F 21
  DY4: Tip. .6H 61
  WS8: Bwnhls 2C 22
  WS10: Darl. 6C 46
  WV11: Ess 4A 18
St John's Sq. WV2: Wolv 2G 43 (5B 170)
St John's St. DY2: Neth 4E 95
  WV1: Wolv. 3B 170
St Johns Wlk. B42: P Barr 3F 83
St John's Way B93: Know 3E 167
St Johns Wood B45: Redn. 4H 157
St Joseph's Av. B31: N'fld 2F 145
St Josephs Cl. WS3: Pels. 3E 21
St Joseph's Ct. WV4: Penn 5A 42
St Joseph's Rd. B8: W End 4A 104
St Joseph St. DY2: Dud 6F 77
St Judes Cl. B14: K Hth 5H 147
  B75: S Cold 5D 54
St Jude's Cl. WV6: Wolv 6D 26
St Judes Pas. B5: Birm 2F 117 (6D 4)
St Jude's Rd. WV6: Wolv. 6D 26
St Jude's Rd. W. WV6: Wolv 6D 26
St Katherines Rd. B68: O'bry 1H 113
St Kenelms Av. B63: Hale 4G 127
St Kenelm's Cl. B70: W Brom 5D 80
St Kenelm's Rd. B62: Roms 3A 142
St Kilda's Rd. B8: Salt 5E 103
St Laurence M. B31: N'fld 4E 145
St Laurence Rd. B31: N'fld. 2F 145
St Lawrence Cl. B93: Know 4D 166
St Lawrence Ho. B16: Edg. 2H 115
                              (off Melville Rd.)
St Lawrence Way WS10: Darl 4D 46
St Leonard's Cl. B37: Mars G 4C 122
St Loye's Cl. B62: B'hth. 3D 112
St Lukes Cl. B65: Row R 5B 96
St Luke's Rd. B5: Birm 3F 117
                              (not continuous)
  WS10: W'bry 2G 63
St Lukes St. B64: Crad H 2F 111
St Luke's Ter. DY1: Dud 1C 94
St Margaret's B74: Four O 6C 36
St Margarets Av. B8: W End 3H 103
St Margaret's Ct. B92: Olton 4C 136
St Margarets Dr. B63: Hale 3H 127
St Margarets Rd. B8: W End 3G 103
  B43: Gt Barr 3B 66
  B92: Olton 4C 136
  WS3: Pels. 3E 21
St Marks Cl. WS6: Gt Wyr 1F 7
St Marks Cres. B1: Birm 6C 100
St Mark's Factory Cen. DY9: Lye. 6H 109
St Marks Rd. DY2: Dud 5H 77
  DY4: Tip. .5H 61
  WS3: Pels. 3E 21
  WV3: Wolv 2E 43
                              (not continuous)
  B67: Smeth 6B 98
  DY9: Lye .6H 109
  WS8: Bwnhls 2C 22
St Marks St. WV3: Wolv 2F 43 (4A 170)
  B1: Birm. .6D 100
St Martins Cl. B70: W Brom 5D 80
  WV2: E'shll. 5A 44
St Martins Dr. DY4: Tip 2A 78
St Martins Ind. Est. B69: O'bry 3H 97
                              (Engine St.)
  B69: O'bry 2H 97
                              (Parsonage St.)
St Martin's Queensway
  B2: Birm 1G 117 (5E 5)
St Martin's Rd. B75: S Cold. 6D 54
St Martin's St. B15: Birm. 2D 116
St Martin's Ter. WV14: Bils 1G 61
St Marys Cl. B24: Erd 3B 86
  B27: A Grn 2H 135
  DY3: Sed .5B 60
St Marys Ct. WV13: W'hall. 1A 46
                              (off Wolverhampton St.)
  DY5: Brie H 1H 109
St Mary's Hall WV2: Wolv 2H 43 (5C 170)
St Mary's La. DY8: Stourb 2F 125
St Mary's Mobile Home Pk.
  B47: Wyt .6G 161
St Mary's Rd. B17: Harb 6G 115

St Mary's Rd. B67: Smeth 2D **114**
WS10: W'bry 2F **63**
St Marys Row B4: Birm. 6G **101** (2E **5**)
B13: Mose 2H **133**
St Mary's St. WV1: Wolv 1H **43** (2C **170**)
St Mary's Vw. B23: Erd 5D **68**
St Marys Way WS9: A'rdge 4C **34**
St Matthews Cl. WS3: Pels. 2F **21**
WS1: Wals 2D **48**
St Matthews Rd. B66: Smeth. 4G **99**
B68: O'bry 1G **113**
(not continuous)
St Matthews St. WV1: Wolv. 2B **44**
St Mawes Rd. WV6: Pert 6F **25**
St Mawgan Cl. B35: Cas V. 3G **87**
St Michaels Cl. WS3: Pels 5E **21**
St Michaels Ct. B70: W Brom 4A **80**
WV6: Tett 4C **26**
St Michaels Cres. B69: O'bry. 5F **97**
St Michael's Gro. DY2: Dud. 6A **78**
St Michael's Hill B18: Hock. 2C **100**
St Michael's M. B69: Tiv 5A **78**
St Michael's Rd. B18: Hock. 2C **100**
B73: Bold 5F **69**
DY3: Lwr G 2D **74**
St Michael St. B70: W Brom 4A **80**
WS1: Wals 3C **48**
St Michaels Way DY4: Tip 4A **78**
St Nicholas Cl. WS3: Pels 3E **21**
St Nicholas Gdns. B38: K Nor 5B **146**
St Nicholas Wlk. B76: Curd 1D **88**
St Oswald's Ct. B10: Small H. 3E **119**
St Oswald's Rd. B10: Small H 3E **119**
St Patricks Cl. B14: K Hth 2G **147**
St Paul's Av. B12: Bal H 6A **118**
St Paul's Cl. WS1: Wals. 1C **48**
St Pauls Ct. B46: Wat O. 4D **88**
B65: B'hth 2D **112**
St Paul's Cres. B46: Col. 2H **107**
B70: W Brom 6E **63**
WS3: Pels. 3F **21**
St Pauls Dr. B62: B'hth 2D **112**
DY4: Tip. 3B **78**
St Paul's Rd. B12: Bal H 5H **117**
B66: Smeth 2B **98**
DY2: Neth. 4F **95**
WS10: W'bry 6H **47**
St Paul's Sq. B3: Birm. 6E **101** (2B **4**)
St Pauls Stop (MM) **5F 101** (**1C 4**)
St Paul's St. WS1: Wals. 1C **48**
St Pauls Ter. B3: Birm 5E **101** (1B **4**)
St Peters Cl. B72: W Grn 2H **69**
DY4: Tip. 3D **78**
WS9: Ston 3G **23**
B28: Hall G. 1D **148**
B46: Wat O. 5D **88**
WV1: Wolv 1G **43** (2B **170**)
St Peters Ct. WS3: Blox. 6H **19**
St Peter's Dr. WS3: Pels. 3E **21**
St Peters La. B92: Bick. 4F **139**
St Peters Rd. B17: Harb 6F **115**
B20: Hand 6E **83**
DY2: Dud, Neth. 3F **95**
DY9: Pedm. 4G **125**
St Peter's Sq. WV1: Wolv. 1G **43** (2B **170**)
St Peters Ter. WS2: Wals. 5C **32**
St Philips Av. WV3: Wolv. 4D **42**
St Philips Cathedral. 6F 101 (3D 4)
St Philips Gro. WV3: Wolv. 4D **42**
St Philips Pl. B3: Birm 6G **101** (3E **5**)
St Phillips Ct. B46: Col 2H **107**
St Quentin St. WS2: Wals 3A **48**
St Saviours Cl. WV2: E'shll 5B **44**
St Saviour's Rd. B8: Salt 5D **102**
St Silas' Sq. B19: Loz 2D **100**
St Simons Cl. B75: S Cold 5D **54**
St Stephens Av. WV13: W'hall 1H **45**
St Stephen's Cen. B21: Hand. 3A **100**
St Stephen's Ct. WV13: W'hall. 2H **45**
St Stephens Gdns. WV13: W'hall. 1A **46**
St Stephens Rd. B29: S Oak 5D **132**
B71: W Brom 6F **81**
St Stephen's St. B6: Aston. 3G **101**
St Thomas Cl. B75: S Cold 6D **54**
WS3: Wals 3C **32**
WS9: A'rdge. 6D **22**
St Thomas' Rd. B23: Erd 4D **84**
St Thomas St. DY2: Neth 4E **95**
DY8: Stourb 6D **108**
St Valentines Cl. B70: W Brom 5D **80**
St Vincent Cres. B70: W Brom. 1F **79**
St Vincent St. B16: Birm 1D **116**
St Vincent St. W. B16: Birm. 1C **116**
Saladin Av. B69: O'bry 4E **97**
Salcombe Av. B26: Sheld. 6G **121**
Salcombe Dr. DY5: Brie H 4G **109**
Salcombe Gro. WV14: Cose 4F **61**
Salcombe Rd. B66: Smeth 4F **99**
Saldavian Ct. WS2: Wals. 5H **47**
Salem St. DY4: Tip 2D **78**
Salford Circ. B6: Aston 6D **84**
Salford St. B6: Aston 1C **102**
Salford Trad. Est. B6: Aston 1C **102**
Salisbury Cl. B13: Mose 1G **133**
DY1: Dud 4B **76**
Salisbury Ct. B91: Sol 3G **151**
Salisbury Dr. B46: Wat O 4E **89**
Salisbury Gro. B72: W Grn 6A **70**
Salisbury Rd. B8: Salt 4E **103**
B13: Mose 1G **133**
B19: Loz 1F **101**
B66: Smeth. 5F **99**
B70: W Brom 6C **80**
Salisbury St. WS10: Darl 4E **47**
Salisbury Twr. B18: Hock. 6C **100**
Sallow Gro. WS8: Bwnhls 4B **10**
Sally Ward Dr. WS9: Wals W. 3C **22**
Salop Cl. B71: W Brom 1H **79**
Salop Dr. B68: O'bry 1A **114**
Salop Rd. B68: O'bry 6A **98**
Salop St. B12: Birm. 3H **117**
B69: O'bry 6E **79**
DY1: Dud 5D **76**
WV3: Wolv 2G **43** (4A **170**)
WV14: Bils 1G **61**
Salstar Cl. B6: Aston 3G **101**
Saltash Gro. B25: Yard. 2A **120**
Saltbrook Rd. B63: Crad 4C **110**
DY9: Lye. 4B **110**
Saltbrook Trad. Est. B63: Crad 4C **110**
Salter Rd. DY4: Tip 6H **61**
Salter's La. B71: W Brom 3C **80**
Salter's Rd. WS9: Wals W 3C **22**
SALTER STREET **6A 164**
Salter St. B94: Earls, H'ley H 6A **164**
Salters Va. B70: W Brom. 6C **80**
SALTLEY **5D 102**
Saltley Bus. Pk. B8: Salt 3D **102**
Saltley Cotts. B24: Erd 1F **103**
Saltley Ind. Cen. B8: Salt. 6C **102**
Saltley Leisure Cen. 6G 103
Saltley Rd. B7: Birm 4B **102**
Saltley Trad. Est. B8: Salt 3D **102**
Saltley Viaduct B7: Birm 4C **102**
B8: Salt 4C **102**
Saltney Cl. B24: Erd. 2B **86**
Saltwells La. DY2: Neth. 1C **110**
DY5: Brie H, Quar B 1B **110**
Saltwells Nature Reserve 6C 94
Saltwells Rd. DY2: Neth 1D **110**
Salwarpe Gro. B29: W Cas 3D **130**
Sambourn Cl. B91: Sol. 1A **152**
Sambourne Dr. B34: S End 2H **105**
Sambrook Rd. WV10: Wolv 3C **28**
Sampson Cl. B21: Hand. 6G **81**
B69: Tiv 2C **96**
Sampson Rd. B11: S'brk 4B **118**
Sampson Rd. Nth. B11: S'brk 3B **118**
Sampson St. WS10: W'bry 2H **63**
Sams La. B70: W Brom 5A **80**
Samuels Rd. B32: Quin 6G **113**
Samuel St. WS3: Blox 6H **19**
Sanda Cft. B36: Cas B 3D **106**
Sandalls Cl. B31: Longb 6B **144**
Sandal Ri. B91: Sol 4A **152**
Sandals Ri. B62: Hale 2D **128**
Sandalwood Cl. WV12: W'hall 1B **30**
Sandbank WS3: Blox 6G **19**
Sandbarn Cl. B90: M'path 3D **164**
Sandbeds Rd. WV12: W'hall 5C **30**
Sandbourne Rd. B8: W End 5G **103**
Sanderling Ri. DY6: K'wfrd 3E **93**
Sanders Cl. DY2: Dud 2G **95**
Sanders St. DY4: Tip 2B **78**
Sandfield B66: Smeth 2C **98**
Sandfield Bri. DY5: P'ntt 6F **75**
Sandfield Cl. B90: Shir 1G **163**
Sandfield Farm Home Pk.
WS8: Bwnhls 4D **10**
Sandfield Gro. DY3: Gorn. 5F **75**
Sandfield Rd. B71: W Brom. 4C **64**
DY8: Word 1D **108**
Sandfields Av. B10: Small H 3B **118**
Sandfields Rd. B68: O'bry 1A **114**
Sandford Av. B65: Row R. 6C **96**
Sandford Ri. WV6: Tett 3C **26**
Sandford Rd. B13: Mose 1A **134**
DY1: Dud 6A **76**
Sandford Wlk. B12: Bal H 6H **117**
Sandgate Rd. B28: Hall G. 3F **149**
DY4: Tip 5A **62**
Sandhill Farm Cl. B19: Loz 2F **101**
Sandhills Cres. B91: Sol 1F **165**
Sandhill St. WS3: Blox 6G **19**
Sandhurst Av. B36: Hodg H 3B **104**
DY9: W'cte. 3H **125**
Sandhurst Dr. WV4: Penn. 1E **59**
Sandhurst Gro. DY8: Word 6C **92**
Sandhurst Ho. B38: K Nor 6C **146**
Sandhurst Rd. B13: Mose 3G **133**
B74: Four O 4F **37**
DY6: K'wfrd 5E **93**
Sandland Cl. WV14: Bils 5H **45**
Sandland Rd. WV12: W'hall. 1D **30**
Sandmartin Cl. DY2: Neth 1E **111**
Sandmeadow Pl. DY6: K'wfrd 4A **92**
Sandmere Gro. B14: Yard W 4D **148**
Sandmere Ri. WV10: Bush 6A **16**
Sandmere Rd. B14: Yard W. 4D **148**
Sandon Gro. B24: Erd 3H **85**
Sandon Rd. B17: Edg 2E **115**
B66: Smeth 1E **115**
DY9: W'cte 1B **126**
WV10: F'hses 5F **15**
Sandown Av. WS6: C Hay. 2E **7**
Sandown Ct. B29: W Cas. 6G **131**
Sandown Dr. WV6: Pert 5F **25**
Sandown Rd. B36: Hodg H 1B **104**
Sandown Twr. B31: N'fld 6E **145**
Sandpiper Cl. DY9: W'cte 6B **110**
Sandpiper Gdns. B38: K Nor 2B **160**
Sandpiper Way B23: Erd 1C **84**
Sandpit Cl. WS10: W'bry. 3C **64**
Sand Pits B1: Birm 6D **100** (3A **4**)
Sandpits, The B30: B'vlle. 5A **132**
Sandpits Cl. B76: Curd 1D **88**
Sandpits Ind. Est. B1: Birm 6D **100**
Sandra Cl. WS9: A'rdge. 4D **34**
Sandringham Av. WV12: W'hall. 2B **30**
Sandringham Ct. B43: Gt Barr 4B **66**
Sandringham Dr. B65: Row R 5C **96**
WS9: A'rdge. 6D **22**
Sandringham Pl. DY8: Word 2B **108**
Sandringham Rd. B42: P Barr 1D **82**
B62: Hale 4B **112**
DY8: Word 2A **108**
WV4: Penn 1E **59**
WV5: Wom 1F **73**
Sandringham Way DY5: Brie H 3G **109**
Sandstone Av. B45: Rubery 1G **157**
Sandstone Cl. DY3: Lwr G. 3H **75**
Sand St. B70: W Brom 3E **79**
Sandway Gdns. B8: Salt. 3D **102**
Sandway Gro. B13: Mose. 6C **134**
SANDWELL **1E 99**
Sandwell & Dudley Station (Rail). . . . **6G 79**
Sandwell Av. WS10: Darl. 6B **46**
Sandwell Bus. Development Cen.
B66: Smeth 2A **98**
Sandwell Bus. Pk. B66: Smeth 1A **98**
Sandwell Cen. B70: W Brom 4B **80**
Sandwell Ct. B21: Hand. 1H **99**
Sandwell Ind. Est. B66: Smeth 1A **98**
Sandwell Pk. Farm 4D 80
Sandwell Pl. B66: Smeth 1E **99**
WV12: W'hall. 2D **30**
Sandwell Rd. B21: Hand 6H **81**
B70: W Brom 3A **80**
WV10: Oxl 6F **15**
Sandwell Rd. Nth. B71: W Brom 3B **80**
Sandwell Rd. Pas. B70: W Brom. 3A **80**

Sandwell St.—Selly Av.

Sandwell St. WS1: Wals 3D **48**
Sandwell Valley Country Pk.
Forge La. 1E 81
Salter's La. 3D 80
Tanhouse Av. 1G 81
Sandwell Wlk. WS1: Wals 3D **48**
Sandwood Dr. B44: Gt Barr 5H **67**
Sandy Acre Way DY8: Stourb 6F **109**
Sandy Cres. WV11: Wed 1A **30**
Sandy Cft. B13: Mose 6C **134**
Sandycroft B72: W Grn 2A **70**
Sandyfields Rd.
DY3: Lwr G, Sed 2D **74**
Sandy Gro. WS8: Bwnhls 4B **10**
Sandy Hill Ri. B90: Shir 3G **149**
Sandy Hill Rd. B90: Shir 3G **149**
Sandy Hollow WV6: Tett 1A **42**
Sandy La. B6: Aston 2B **102**
B42: Gt Barr 5E **67**
B61: L Ash, Wild 4A **156**
DY8: Stourb 1B **124**
WS10: W'bry 2D **64**
WV6: Tett 3C **26**
WV8: Cod 3F **13**
WV10: Bush 6A **16**
Sandy Mt. WV5: Wom 6H **57**
Sandymount Rd. WS1: Wals 3D **48**
Sandy Rd. DY8: Stourb 4B **124**
Sandys Gro. DY4: Tip 2G **77**
Sandy Way B15: Birm 2D **116** (6A **4**)
Sangwin Rd. WV14: Cose 6E **61**
Sansome Ri. B90: Shir 5F **149**
Sansome Rd. B90: Shir 5F **149**
Sanstone Cl. WS3: Blox 4A **20**
Sanstone Rd. WS3: Blox 4H **19**
Santolina Dr. WS5: Wals 2E **65**
Sant Rd. B31: Longb 2F **159**
Sapcote Bus. Pk. B10: Small H 5E **119**
Sapcote Trad. Cen. B64: Old H 6H **95**
Saplings, The B76: Walm 5E **71**
Sapphire Ct. B3: Birm 5E **101** (1B **4**)
B92: Olton 4D **136**
Sapphire Hgts. B1: Birm 6D **100**
Sapphire Ho. E. B91: Sol 3E **151**
Sapphire Ho. W. B91: Sol 3E **151**
Sapphire Twr. *B6: Aston* *3H **101***
(off Park La.)
Saracen Dr. B75: S Cold 5D **54**
CV7: Bal C 3E **169**
Sara Cl. B74: Four O 6G **37**
Sarah Cl. WV14: Bils 4G **61**
Sarah Ct. B73: New O 4D **68**
Sarah Gdns. WS5: Wals 1D **64**
Sarah St. B9: Birm 1B **118**
Saredon Cl. WS3: Pels 6E **21**
Saredon Rd. WS6: C Hay 1B **6**
WV10: Share 1A **6**
(not continuous)
Sarehole Mill Mus. 5D 134
Sarehole Rd. B28: Hall G 6D **134**
Sargent Cl. B43: Gt Barr 1F **67**
Sargent Ho. B16: Birm 1D **116**
Sargent's Hill WS5: Wals 5G **49**
Sargent Turner Trad. Est.
DY9: Lye 5B **110**
Sark Dr. B36: Cas B 3D **106**
Satellite Ind. Pk.
WV13: W'hall 5F **29**
Saturday Bri. B1: Birm 6B **4**
Saunton Rd. WS3: Blox 4G **19**
Saunton Way B29: S Oak 4G **131**
Saveker Dr. B76: Walm 1C **70**
Savernake Cl. B45: Fran 5G **143**
Saville Cl. B45: Redn 2H **157**
Savoy Cl. B32: Harb 6D **114**
Saw Mill Cl. WS4: Wals 6C **32**
Saxelby Cl. B14: K Hth 5G **147**
(not continuous)
Saxelby Ho. B14: K Hth 5G **147**
Saxon Cl. WS6: Gt Wyr 3G **7**
Saxon Ct. WV6: Tett 4A **26**
Saxondale Av. B26: Sheld 5D **120**
Saxon Dr. B65: Row R 5C **96**
Saxonfields WV6: Tett 4A **26**
Saxons Way B14: K Hth 5A **148**
Saxon Way B37: K'hrst 6B **106**
Saxon Wood Cl. B31: N'fld 3E **145**
Saxon Wood Rd.
B90: Ches G 4B **164**
Saxton Dr. B74: Four O 3F **37**
Scafell Dr. B23: Erd 2D **84**
WV14: Bils 4H **45**
Scafell Rd. DY8: Amb 5F **109**
Scampton Cl. WV6: Pert 4E **25**
Scarborough Cl. WS2: Wals 3H **47**
Scarborough Rd. WS2: Wals 3H **47**
Scarecrow La. B75: R'ley 5C **38**
Scarsdale Rd. B42: Gt Barr 5F **67**
Schofield Av. B71: W Brom 5H **63**
Schofield Rd. B37: K'hrst 4C **106**
Scholars Ga. B33: Kitts G 1F **121**
Scholars Wlk. WS4: Rus 2F **33**
Scholefield Twr. *B19: Birm* *4F **101***
(off Uxbridge St.)
Schoolacre Ri. B74: S'tly 2G **51**
Schoolacre Rd. B34: S End 3F **105**
School Av. WS3: Blox 1A **32**
WS8: Bwnhls 5B **10**
School Cl. B35: Cas V 4F **87**
B37: K'hrst 3C **106**
B69: Tiv 2C **96**
WV3: Wolv 4H **41**
WV5: Try 5C **56**
WV8: Cod 3G **13**
School Dr. B47: Wyt 6A **162**
B73: S Cold 1H **69**
DY8: Amb 3D **108**
WV14: Bils 3A **62**
School Dr., The DY2: Dud 2F **95**
Schoolgate Cl. B8: W End 3G **103**
WS4: S'fld 6H **21**
School Grn. WV14: Bils 3E **45**
Schoolhouse Cl. B38: K Nor 5D **146**
School La. B33: Yard 2D **120**
B34: S End 3F **105**
B63: Hale 3H **127**
B91: Sol 2H **151**
DY5: Brie H 5F **93**
DY9: Hag 6H **125**
WS3: Lit W 3C **8**
WS3: Pels 3D **20**
WV3: Wolv 2G **43** (4A **170**)
WV10: Bush 5H **15**
School Pas. DY5: Quar B 2C **110**
School Rd. B13: Mose 4H **133**
B14: Yard W 3B **148**
B28: Hall G 5F **135**
B45: Rubery 3E **157**
B90: Shir 5H **149**
DY3: Himl 4H **73**
DY5: Quar B 1C **110**
WS10: W'bry 3B **64**
WV5: Try 5C **56**
WV5: Wom 6H **57**
WV6: Tett 5G **25**
WV11: Wed 3D **28**
School St. B64: Crad H 2F **111**
DY1: Dud 6D **76**
(not continuous)
DY3: Sed 5A **60**
DY5: P'ntt 2H **93**
DY8: Stourb 5D **108**
WS4: S'fld 6H **21**
WS10: Darl 5C **46**
(Alma St.)
WS10: Darl 6E **47**
(Nowell St., not continuous)
WV3: Wolv 2G **43** (4A **170**)
WV13: W'hall 1H **45**
WV14: Cose 5E **61**
School St. W. WV14: Cose 5E **61**
School Ter. B29: S Oak 3B **132**
School Wlk. WV14: Bils 3E **45**
Scorers Cl. B90: Shir 1H **149**
Scotchings, The B36: Hodg H 1C **104**
Scotland La. B32: Bart G 5H **129**
Scotland Pas. B70: W Brom 4B **80**
SCOTLANDS 1C 28
Scotland St. B1: Birm 6E **101** (3A **4**)
Scott Arms Shop. Cen. B42: Gt Barr 4B **66**
Scott Av. WS10: W'bry 3H **63**
WV4: Penn 1C **58**
Scott Cl. B71: W Brom 2B **80**
Scott Gro. B92: Olton 2C **136**
Scott Ho. B43: Gt Barr 6B **66**
Scott Rd. B43: Gt Barr 3B **66**
B92: Olton 2C **136**
WS5: Wals 5H **49**
SCOTT'S GREEN **1C 94**
Scotts Grn. Cl. DY1: Dud 1B **94**
Scotts Grn. Island DY1: Dud 2B **94**
Scott's Rd. DY8: Stourb 5D **108**
Scott St. DY4: Tip 2C **78**
Scotwell Cl. B65: Row R 6B **96**
Scout Cl. B33: Kitts G 1G **121**
Scribbans Cl. B66: Smeth 5F **99**
Scriber's La. B28: Hall G 3D **148**
Scribers Mdw. B28: Hall G 3E **149**
Scrimshaw Ho. *WS2: Wals* *4A **48***
(off Pleck Rd.)
Seacroft Av. B25: Yard 2C **120**
Seafield Cl. DY6: K'wfrd 5C **92**
Seaforth Gro. WV12: W'hall 6B **18**
Seagar St. B71: W Brom 3C **80**
Seagers La. DY5: Brie H 1H **109**
Seagull Bay Dr. WV14: Cose 4F **61**
Seal Cl. B76: Walm 1C **70**
Seals Grn. B38: K Nor 2H **159**
Seamless Dr. WV11: Wed 5F **29**
Sear Hills Cl. CV7: Bal C 3H **169**
Sear Retail Pk. B90: Shir 6B **150**
Seaton Cl. WV11: Wed 4H **29**
Seaton Gro. B13: Mose 4F **133**
Seaton Pl. DY8: Word 1A **108**
Seaton Rd. B66: Smeth 4F **99**
Second Av. B6: Witt 4H **83**
B9: Bord G 2E **119**
B29: S Oak 2D **132**
DY6: P'ntt 2D **92**
WS8: Bwnhls 4C **10**
WV10: Bush 2A **28**
Second Exhibition Av. B40: Nat E C . . . 1F **139**
Security Ho. WV1: Wolv 2G **43** (4B **170**)
Sedge Av. B38: K Nor 4B **146**
Sedgeberrow Covert B38: K Nor 1A **160**
Sedgeberrow Rd. B63: Hale 3A **128**
Sedgebourne Way B31: Longb 6A **144**
Sedgefield Cl. DY1: Dud 4A **76**
Sedgefield Gro. WV6: Pert 5F **25**
Sedgefield Way WS11: Nort C 1E **9**
Sedgeford Cl. DY5: Brie H 3H **109**
Sedgehill Av. B17: Harb 1F **131**
Sedgemere Gro. CV7: Bal C 6H **169**
WS4: S'fld 1G **33**
Sedgemere Rd. B26: Yard 2D **120**
SEDGLEY 5H 59
Sedgley Gro. B20: Hand 3A **82**
Sedgley Hall Av. DY3: Sed 5G **59**
Sedgley Hall Est. DY3: Sed 4G **59**
Sedgley Rd. DY1: Dud 1D **76**
WV4: Penn 2C **58**
Sedgley Rd. E. DY4: Tip 3A **78**
Sedgley Rd. W. DY4: Tip 1F **77**
Seedhouse Ct. B64: Old H 3A **112**
Seeds La. WS8: Bwnhls 5B **10**
Seeleys Rd. B11: Tys 6D **118**
Sefton Dr. B65: Row R 3H **95**
Sefton Gro. DY4: Tip 3C **62**
Sefton Rd. B16: Edg 1B **116**
Segbourne Rd. B45: Rubery 1E **157**
Segundo Cl. WS5: Wals 1D **64**
Segundo Rd. WS5: Wals 1D **64**
SEISDON 3A 56
Seisdon Hollaway WV5: Seis 2A **56**
Seisdon Rd. WV5: Seis, Try 3A **56**
Selborne Cl. WS1: Wals 2E **49**
Selborne Gro. B13: Mose 2C **148**
Selborne Rd. B20: Hand 5C **82**
DY2: Dud 2F **95**
Selborne St. WS1: Wals 2E **49**
Selbourne Cres. WV1: Wolv 2D **44**
Selby Cl. B26: Yard 2D **120**
Selby Gro. B13: Mose 2B **148**
Selby Ho. B69: O'bry 3D **96**
Selby Way WS3: Blox 5E **19**
Selcombe Way B38: K Nor 2B **160**
Selco Way B76: Min 2E **87**
Selcroft Av. B32: Harb 6D **114**
Selecta Av. B44: Gt Barr 3F **67**
Selkirk Cl. B71: W Brom 1A **80**
Selly Av. B29: S Oak 3C **132**

Selly Cl. B29: S Oak 3D **132**
Selly Hall Cft. B30: B'vlle 1C **146**
Selly Hill Rd. B29: S Oak 3B **132**
SELLY OAK 4A **132**
Selly Oak Ind. Est. B29: S Oak 4A **132**
Selly Oak Rd. B30: B'vlle 6A **132**
Selly Oak Station (Rail) 3A **132**
SELLY PARK 3D **132**
Selly Pk. Rd. B29: S Oak 2C **132**
Selly Wharf B29: S Oak 3A **132**
Selly Wick Dr. B29: S Oak 3D **132**
Selly Wick Rd. B29: S Oak 3C **132**
Sellywood Rd. B30: B'vlle 6H **131**
Selma Gro. B14: Yard W 2D **148**
Selman's Hill WS3: Blox 4A **20**
Selman's Pde. WS3: Blox 5A **20**
Selsdon Cl. B47: Wyt 4C **162**
Selsdon Rd. WS3: Blox 4F **19**
Selsey Av. B17: Edg 6F **99**
Selsey Rd. B17: Edg 6F **99**
Selston Rd. B6: Aston 2G **101**
Selvey Av. B43: Gt Barr 2D **66**
Selworthy Rd. B36: Cas B 2B **106**
Selwyn Cl. WV2: Wolv 4G **43**
Selwyn Ho. B37: Chel W 6F **107**
Selwyn Rd. B16: Edg 6H **99**
WV14: Bils 5H **45**
Selwyn Wlk. B74: Lit A 5C **36**
Senior Cl. WV11: Ess 4A **18**
Senneley's Pk. Rd.
B31: N'fld 5C **130**
Sennen Cl. WV13: W'hall 2H **45**
Sensall Rd. DY9: W'cte 2B **126**
Sentry Way B75: S Cold 5D **54**
Serpentine Rd. B6: Aston 6A **84**
B17: Harb 5G **115**
B29: S Oak 2C **132**
Servite Ct. B14: K Hth 5A **148**
Servite Ho. B44: Gt Barr 3H **67**
B92: Olton 6B **136**
Seth Somers Track 3C **128**
Settle Av. B34: Hodg H 3E **105**
Settle Cft. B37: F'bri 2B **122**
Setton Dr. DY3: Sed 6A **60**
Seven Acres WS9: A'rdge 4D **34**
Seven Acres Rd. B31: N'fld 6G **145**
B62: Quin 6G **113**
Sevendwellings Vw.
DY5: Brie H 2G **109**
Seven Star Rd. B91: Sol 2E **151**
Seven Stars Rd. B69: O'bry 2G **97**
Severn Cl. B36: Cas B 2B **106**
DY4: Tip 2H **77**
WV12: W'hall 2A **30**
Severn Ct. B23: Erd 4B **84**
B73: S Cold 6H **53**
Severn Dr. DY5: P'ntt 2F **93**
WV6: Pert 5E **25**
Severne Gro. B27: A Grn 4A **136**
Severne Rd. B27: A Grn 5A **136**
Severn Gro. B11: S'brk 5C **118**
B19: Loz 2E **101**
(not continuous)
Severn Rd. B63: Crad 6D **110**
DY8: Stourb 2D **124**
WS3: Blox 6C **20**
WS8: Bwnhls 3G **9**
Severn St. B1: Birm 2F **117** (6C **4**)
Severn St. Pl. B1: Birm 6C **4**
Severn Twr. B7: Nech 4B **102**
Severn Way B47: Wyt 6G **161**
Sevington Cl. B91: Sol 1G **165**
Seymour Cl. B29: S Oak 3C **132**
WS6: C Hay 4D **6**
Seymour Gdns. B74: Four O 6E **37**
Seymour Rd. B69: O'bry 2A **98**
DY4: Tip 4C **62**
DY9: W'cte 6B **110**
Shackleton Dr. WV6: Pert 4E **25**
Shackleton Hall B15: Edg 5C **116**
Shackleton Rd. WS3: Blox 5B **20**
Shadowbrook La.
B92: H Ard 5F **139**
Shadwell Dr. DY3: Lwr G 4H **75**
Shadwell St. B4: Birm 5F **101** (1D **4**)
Shady La. B44: Gt Barr 3F **67**
Shadymoor Dr. DY5: Brie H 3G **109**
Shaftesbury Av. B63: Crad 4D **110**
DY9: Pedm 2G **125**
Shaftesbury Rd. WS10: W'bry 3H **63**
Shaftesbury Sq. B71: W Brom 2A **80**
Shaftesbury St. B70: W Brom 3A **80**
B71: W Brom 3A **80**
Shaftmoor Ind. Est.
B28: Hall G 3F **135**
Shaftmoor La. B27: A Grn 3G **135**
B28: Hall G 3E **135**
Shaftsbury Cl. WV14: Bils 4H **45**
Shaftsbury Rd. B26: Sheld 6G **121**
Shahjalal Rd. B8: Salt 4D **102**
Shakespeare Cl. WV14: Cose 3F **61**
Shakespeare Cres. WS3: Blox 1C **32**
(not continuous)
Shakespeare Dr. B90: Shir 6G **149**
Shakespeare Ho. B31: Longb 1E **159**
Shakespeare Pl. WS3: Blox 2C **32**
Shakespeare Rd. B23: Erd 4B **84**
B67: Smeth 5C **98**
B90: Shir 6B **150**
DY3: Lwr G 3E **75**
DY4: Tip 5A **62**
Shakespeare St. B11: S'hll 6C **118**
WV1: Wolv 2A **44**
Shaldon Wlk. B66: Smeth 4F **99**
Shales, The WV5: Wom 2E **73**
Shale St. WV14: Bils 6E **45**
Shalford Rd. B92: Olton 1C **136**
Shallcross La. DY3: Lwr G 4H **75**
Shalnecote Gro. B14: K Hth 2E **147**
Shambles, The WS10: W'bry 3F **63**
Shandon Cl. B32: Bart G 2D **130**
Shanklyn Cl. WS6: Gt Wyr 2F **7**
Shannon Dr. WS8: Bwnhls 3G **9**
Shannon Rd. B38: K Nor 2H **159**
Shannon Wlk. WS8: Bwnhls 3G **9**
Shanti Niketan WV2: Wolv 4H **43**
Shapinsay Dr. B45: Fran 6F **143**
SHARD END 2G **105**
Shard End Cres. B34: S End 3G **105**
Shardlow Rd. WV11: Wed 1G **29**
Shardway, The B34: S End 4G **105**
(not continuous)
Sharesacre St. WV13: W'hall 6B **30**
Sharington Cl. DY2: Dud 1G **95**
Sharman Rd. WV10: Bush 3A **28**
SHARMANS CROSS 3C **150**
Sharmans Cross Rd. B91: Sol 3C **150**
Sharon Cl. WV4: E'shll 6A **44**
Sharps Cl. B45: Redn 2G **157**
Sharrat Fld. B75: R'ley 1B **54**
Sharrocks St. WV2: Wolv 2A **44**
SHAVER'S END 4D **76**
Shawberry Av. B35: Cas V 4E **87**
Shawberry Rd. B37: K'hrst 4B **106**
SHAWBROOK 5H **161**
Shawbrook Gro. B14: K Hth 4A **148**
Shawbury Gro. B12: Birm 3H **117**
WV6: Pert 4E **25**
Shawbury Rd. WV10: Wolv 4B **28**
Shaw Dr. B33: Yard 1C **120**
Shawfield B47: H'wd 4A **162**
Shaw Hall La. WV10: Cov H 1F **15**
Shawhellier Av. DY5: Brie H 1A **110**
Shaw Hill Gro. B8: W End 5G **103**
Shaw Hill Rd. B8: W End 5G **103**
Shawhurst Cft. B47: H'wd 2A **162**
Shawhurst Gdns. B47: H'wd 2B **162**
Shawhurst La. B47: H'wd 4A **162**
Shaw La. WV6: Tett 6H **25**
Shawley Cft. B27: A Grn 1C **136**
Shaw Pk. Bus. Village WV10: Bush . . . 3H **27**
Shaw Rd. DY2: Dud 2D **94**
(not continuous)
DY4: Tip 3C **78**
WV2: Wolv 5G **43**
WV10: Bush 3G **27**
(not continuous)
WV14: Cose 4D **60**
Shawsdale Rd. B36: Hodg H 2D **104**
Shaws La. WS6: Gt Wyr 3G **7**
Shaw's Pas. B5: Birm 1H **117** (5G **5**)
Shaw St. B70: W Brom 5E **63**
WS2: Wals 1B **48**
Sheaf La. B26: Sheld 6F **121**
Sheapecote Ho. B71: W Brom 3D **64**
Shearers Pl. B75: R'ley 6C **38**
Shearwater Cl. B45: Rubery 3F **157**
Shearwater Dr. DY5: Brie H 4G **109**
Shearwater Wlk. B23: Erd 6B **68**
Sheaves Cl. WV14: Cose 2D **60**
Shedden St. DY2: Dud 1F **95**
Sheddington Rd. B23: Erd 6D **68**
Sheen Rd. B44: Gt Barr 1G **67**
Sheepclose Dr. B37: F'bri 6C **106**
Sheepcote St. B16: Birm 1D **116** (6A **4**)
Sheepfold Cl. B65: Row R 5A **96**
Sheepmoor Cl. B17: Harb 3D **114**
Sheepwash La. DY4: Tip 2D **78**
Sheepwash Nature Reserve 3D **78**
Sheffield Rd. B73: Bold 6G **69**
Sheffield St. DY5: Quar B 2C **110**
Shefford Rd. B6: Aston 4H **101**
Sheila Av. WV11: Wed 2G **29**
Shelah Rd. B63: Hale 5H **111**
Shelbourne Cl. B69: Tiv 5D **78**
SHELDON 6H **121**
Sheldon Av. WS10: W'bry 1G **63**
Sheldon Cl. WV14: Bils 2F **61**
Sheldon Country Pk. 5G **121**
Sheldon Dr. B31: Longb 5B **144**
Sheldonfield Rd. B26: Sheld 6H **121**
Sheldon Gro. B26: Sheld 6F **121**
Sheldon Hall Av. B33: Kitts G 6H **105**
(not continuous)
Sheldon Health Leisure Cen. 3G **121**
Sheldon Heath Rd. B26: Yard, Sheld . . . 2E **121**
Sheldon Rd. B71: W Brom 5C **64**
WV10: Oxl 6E **15**
Sheldon Wlk. B33: Sheld 2G **121**
SHELFIELD 6G **21**
Shelfield Rd. B14: K Hth 4E **147**
Shelley Av. DY4: Tip 5A **62**
Shelley Cl. DY3: Lwr G 2E **75**
DY8: Amb 3E **109**
Shelley Dr. B23: Erd 4B **84**
B74: Four O 3F **37**
Shelley Rd. WV10: F'hses 5H **15**
WV12: W'hall 2E **31**
Shelley Twr. B31: N'fld 4G **145**
Shelly Cl. B37: F'bri 1B **122**
Shelly Cres. B90: M'path 2F **165**
Shelly Cft. B33: Kitts G 6E **105**
Shelly Ho. B68: O'bry 5H **97**
Shelly La. B90: M'path 3F **165**
Shelly Manor Mus. 5B **132**
Shelly Shop. Cen. B90: M'path 2F **165**
Shelsley Av. B69: O'bry 4D **96**
Shelsley Dr. B13: Mose 4B **134**
Shelsley Way B91: Sol 6F **151**
Shelton Cl. WS10: W'bry 6A **48**
Shelton La. B63: Crad 6G **111**
Shelwick Gro. B93: Dorr 5A **166**
Shenley Av. DY1: Dud 1D **76**
Shenley Court Leisure Cen. 6C **130**
SHENLEY FIELDS 1C **144**
Shenley Flds. Dr. B31: N'fld 5C **130**
Shenley Flds. Rd. B29: W Cas 6D **130**
Shenley Gdns. B29: W Cas 6E **131**
Shenley Grn. B29: W Cas 1E **145**
Shenley Hill B31: N'fld 1C **144**
Shenley La. B29: W Cas 4D **130**
Shenley Lane Community & Sports Cen.
. . . . 1E **145**
Shenstone Av. B62: Hale 6E **113**
DY8: Stourb 2B **124**
Shenstone Cl. B74: Four O 3E **37**
Shenstone Ct. B90: Shir 5D **148**
WV3: Wolv 5E **43**
Shenstone Dr. CV7: Bal C 3G **169**
WS9: A'rdge 1C **34**
Shenstone Flats B62: Quin 6F **113**
Shenstone Rd. B14: K Hth 6A **148**
B16: Edg 6G **99**
B43: Gt Barr 5A **66**
Shenstone Trad. Est. B63: Hale 1C **128**
Shenstone Valley Rd. B62: Quin 5E **113**
Shenstone Wlk. B62: Hale 6D **112**
SHENSTONE WOODEND 1G **37**
Shenton Wlk. B37: K'hrst 4C **106**
Shepheard Rd. B26: Sheld 6H **121**
Shepherd Dr. WV12: W'hall 4C **30**

Shepherds Brook Rd. DY9: Lye 6H 109
Shepherds Fold B65: Row R 1B 112
Shepherds Gdns. B15: Birm 2D 116
Shepherds Grn. Rd. B24: Erd 5F 85
Shepherds La. CV7: Mer 2G 141
Shepherds Pool Rd. B75: R'ley 1C 54
Shepherds Standing
    B34: S End 3F 105
Shepherds Wlk. WV8: Pend. 5D 14
Shepherds Way B23: Erd 5C 68
Shepley Rd. B45: Redn 3H 157
Sheppey Dr. B36: Cas B. 4D 106
SHEPWELL GREEN 1C 46
Shepwell Grn. WV13: W'hall 2C 46
Sherard Cft. B36: Cas B 3D 106
Sheraton Cl. WS9: A'rdge 3D 34
Sheraton Grange DY8: Stourb 3D 124
Sherborne Cl. B46: Col 5H 107
    WS3: Blox 2A 32
Sherborne Gdns. WV8: Cod. 4G 13
Sherborne Gro. B1: Birm 6C 100
Sherborne Lofts B16: Birm 1D 116
Sherborne M. WV10: Bush. 6H 15
Sherborne St. B16: Birm 1D 116
Sherborne Wharf B16: Birm. 1D 116
Sherbourne Ct. B27: A Grn 1A 136
Sherbourne Dr. B27: A Grn 1A 136
Sherbourne Rd. B12: Bal H 5H 117
                                        (Arter St.)
    B12: Bal H 4G 117
                                    (Longmore St.)
    B27: A Grn 1A 136
    B64: Old H 3A 112
    DY8: Stourb 1F 125
Sherdmore Cft. B90: M'path. 3E 165
Sheridan Cl. WS2: Wals 4H 47
Sheridan Gdns. DY3: Lwr G. 2D 74
Sheridan St. B71: W Brom. 3B 80
    WS2: Wals 4H 47
Sheridan Wlk. B35: Cas V 4E 87
Sheriff Dr. DY5: Quar B 1B 110
Sherifoot La. B75: Four O 5H 37
Sheringham B15: Edg 3A 116
Sheringham Rd. B30: K Nor 4D 146
Sherington Dr. WV4: Penn. 6H 43
Sherlock Cl. WV12: W'hall. 4D 30
Sherlock St. B5: Birm 4G 117
Sherrans Dell WV4: E'shll 2A 60
Sherratt Cl. B76: Walm 5D 70
Sherringham Dr. WV11: Ess 6C 18
Sherron Gdns. B12: Bal H 6H 117
Sherston Covert B30: K Nor 5E 147
Shervale Cl. WV4: Penn. 5E 43
Sherwin Av. WV4: Cose 3C 60
Sherwood Av. DY4: Tip 3H 77
Sherwood Cl. B28: Hall G 2F 149
    B92: Olton 6D 136
Sherwood Dr. DY5: Quar B. 2B 110
Sherwood M. B28: Hall G 1E 149
Sherwood Rd. B28: Hall G 6E 135
    B67: Smeth 2E 115
    DY8: Woll 4C 108
Sherwood St. WV1: Wolv. 6G 27
Sherwood Wlk. B45: Fran 4H 143
    WS9: A'rdge 2A 34
Shetland Cl. B16: Birm 1B 116
    WV6: Wolv 4F 27
Shetland Dr. B66: Smeth 2B 98
Shetland Wlk. B36: Cas B 3D 106
Shidas La. B69: O'bry 2E 97
Shifnal Rd. WV7: Alb 6A 12
Shifnal Wlk. B31: Longb 1D 158
Shifrall Way B75: S Cold 4D 54
Shillcock Gro.
    B19: Birm. 4G 101
Shilton Cl. B90: M'path 3D 164
Shilton Gro. B29: W Cas 5D 130
Shinwell Cres. B69: Tiv 5C 78
Shipbourne Cl. B32: Harb 6D 114
Shipley Flds. B24: Erd. 4G 85
Shipley Gro. B29: W Cas 5E 131
Shipston Rd. B31: N'fld 6F 145
Shipton Cl. DY1: Dud 4A 76
Shipton Rd. B72: S Cold 2A 70
Shipway Rd. B25: Yard 4G 119
Shirebrook Cl. B6: Aston 1G 101
Shire Brook Cl. B19: Loz 1F 101

Shire Cl. B16: Birm 1B 116
    B68: O'bry 1H 113
Shireland Brook Gdns.
    B18: Win G 5H 99
Shireland Cl. B20: Hand 4A 82
Shireland Rd. B66: Smeth 5F 99
Shire Lea WS8: Bwnhls 1D 22
SHIRE OAK 2B 22
Shire Oak Pk. (Nature Reserve) 3D 22
Shire Ridge WS9: Wals W 3C 22
Shirestone Rd. B33: Kitts G. 1H 121
Shireview Gdns. WS3: Pels 3E 21
Shireview Rd. WS3: Pels 3E 21
Shirland Rd. B37: Mars G 2C 122
SHIRLEY 4H 149
Shirleydale B90: Shir. 6A 150
Shirley Dr. B72: S Cold 1A 70
SHIRLEY HEATH 1H 163
Shirley Pk. Rd. B90: Shir. 5H 149
Shirley Rd. B27: A Grn 4H 135
    B28: Hall G 1G 149
    B30: K Nor 2C 146
    B68: O'bry 3A 98
    DY2: Dud 1G 95
Shirley Station (Rail) 6F 149
SHIRLEY STREET 5H 149
Shirley Trad. Est. B90: Shir. 1D 164
Shirrall Dr. B78: Dray B 5G 39
Shirrall Gro. B37: K'hrst 4B 106
Sholing Cl. WV8: Pend 6D 14
Shooters Cl. B5: Bal H 5F 117
Shooters Hill B72: S Cold 3B 70
Shop La. WV6: Tres 4B 40
    WV8: Oaken 6C 12
Shopton Rd. B34: S End. 2E 105
Shoreham Cl. WV13: W'hall 2F 45
Short Acre St. WS2: Wals 6B 32
SHORT CROSS 1H 127
Shorters Av. B14: K Hth 3B 148
Shortfield Cl. CV7: Bal C 2H 169
SHORT HEATH
    Erdington 1D 84
    Willenhall 4D 30
Short Heath Ct. B23: Erd 2F 85
Short Heath Rd. B23: Erd 1D 84
Shortland Cl. B93: Know 2C 166
Shortlands Cl. B30: K Nor 5C 146
Shortlands La. WS3: Pels 3D 20
Short La. WS6: C Hay. 2E 7
Short Rd. B67: Smeth 6B 98
    WV10: Bush 6A 16
Short St. B63: Hale 1H 127
    B65: B'hth, Row R 1C 112
                                    (not continuous)
    B90: Dic H 4G 163
    DY1: Dud 5C 76
    DY4: Tip 5G 61
    DY8: Stourb 6D 108
    WS2: Wals 2B 48
    WS8: Bwnhls 5B 10
    WS10: Darl 4F 47
    WS10: W'bry 2E 63
    WV1: Wolv 1H 43 (2C 170)
    WV12: W'hall 4C 30
    WV14: Bils 5F 45
Shorwell Pl. DY5: Brie H 3G 109
Shottery Cl. B76: Walm 4D 70
Shottery Gro. B76: Walm 4D 70
Shottery Rd. B90: Shir 6H 149
Shotteswell Rd. B90: Shir 2H 163
Showcase Cinema
    Dudley 5G 77
    Tyburn 5B 86
    Walsall 2G 47
Showell Cir. WV10: Bush. 2A 28
SHOWELL GREEN 1B 134
Showell Grn. La. B11: S'hll 2B 134
Showell Ho. B69: O'bry 2G 97
Showell La. WV4: Lwr P 2G 57
Showell Rd. WV10: Bush. 3H 27
Showell Rd. Ind. Est. WV10: Wolv 3H 27
Showells Gdns. B7: Nech. 2C 102
Shrawley Cl. B45: Rubery 2F 157
    B63: Hale 3A 128
Shrawley Rd. B31: N'fld. 5G 145
Shrewley Cres. B33: Kitts G. 2A 122
Shrewsbury Cl. WS3: Blox 6F 19

Shrewton Av. B14: K Hth 6F 147
Shrubbery, The B16: Birm 6B 100
    DY1: Dud 5D 76
    DY4: Tip. 1C 78
Shrubbery Av. DY4: Tip 2F 77
Shrubbery Cl. B76: Walm. 1B 86
Shrublands Av. B68: O'bry. 4H 113
Shrub La. B24: Erd. 3H 85
Shugborough Cl. WS3: Blox 6H 19
Shugborough Dr. DY1: Dud 5A 76
Shustoke La. WS5: Wals 1F 65
Shustoke Rd. B34: S End. 3G 105
    B91: Sol. 2H 151
SHUT END 6E 75
Shutlock La. B13: Mose 4F 133
Shyltons Cft. B16: Birm 1C 116
Sibdon Gro. B31: Longb. 1E 159
Sidaway Cl. B65: Row R 3C 96
Sidaway St. B64: Old H 2G 111
Sidbury Gro. B93: Dorr 6A 166
Sidcup Cl. WV14: Cose 2D 60
Sidcup Rd. B44: K'sdng 4A 68
Siddeley Wlk. B36: Cas B 6B 88
Siddons Factory Est. B70: W Brom 5F 63
Siddons Rd. WV14: Cose 3F 61
Siddons Way B70: W Brom 6G 63
Sidenhill Cl. B90: Shir. 1H 163
Sidford Gdns. B24: Erd 4A 86
Sidford Gro. B23: Erd. 6E 69
Sidings, The B20: Hand 1E 101
    B70: W Brom 5A 80
Sidlaw Cl. B63: Hale. 3F 127
    WV10: Oxl 3G 27
Sidney St. WV2: Wolv. 3G 43 (6A 170)
Sidwick Cres. WV2: E'shll 5D 44
Sigmund Cl. WV1: Wolv 6D 28
Signal Gro. WS3: Blox 6G 19
Signal Hayes Rd. B76: Walm 3D 70
                                    (not continuous)
Silesbourne Cl. B36: Cas B 1G 105
Silhill Hall Rd. B91: Sol. 1E 151
Silva Av. DY6: K'wfrd. 5D 92
Silver Birch Cl. B8: Salt. 3D 102
Silver Birch Coppice B74: Four O 4D 36
Silverbirch Cl. B24: Erd. 1H 85
Silver Birch Dr. B47: H'wd 3B 162
Silver Birch Rd. B24: Erd. 1H 85
    B37: K'hrst 3B 106
    B74: S'tly 2H 51
    WS11: Nort C 1F 9
    WV2: Wolv 4H 43
Silverbirch Rd. B91: Sol 4A 152
Silver Ct. WS8: Bwnhls 6B 10
Silver Ct. Gdns. WS8: Bwnhls 6B 10
Silvercroft Av. B20: Hand. 4G 81
Silverdale Dr. WV10: Wolv 5A 28
Silverdale Gdns. DY8: Word 6A 92
Silverdale Rd. B24: Erd 2B 86
SILVER END 2F 109
Silver End Bus. Est. DY5: Brie H. 2G 109
Silver End Ind. Est. DY5: Brie H. 2F 109
Silverfield Cl. B14: K Hth 5G 133
Silver Innage B63: Crad 4E 111
Silverlands Av. B68: O'bry. 6H 97
Silverlands Cl. B28: Hall G 4F 135
Silvermead Ct. B47: Wyt 4H 161
Silvermead Rd. B73: W Grn 4G 69
Silvermere Rd. B26: Sheld 5H 121
Silvers Cl. WS3: Pels 2D 20
Silverstone Cl. WS2: Wals 6E 31
Silverstone Dr. B74: S'tly 5H 51
SILVER STREET 4G 161
Silver St. B14: K Hth 5G 133
    B38: Head H 4F 161
    B47: Wyt 4G 161
    DY5: Brie H 2G 109
    WS8: Bwnhls 6A 10
Silverthorne Av. DY4: Tip 2F 77
Silverthorne La. B64: Crad H. 2D 110
Silverton Cres. B13: Mose. 4D 134
Silverton Hgts. B67: Smeth 3D 98
Silverton Rd. B67: Smeth 3C 98
Silverton Way WV11: Wed. 4H 29
Silvertrees Rd. DY4: Tip 2G 77
Silvester Ct. B70: W Brom. 4B 80
Silvester Rd. WV14: Bils 5G 45
Silvester Way DY5: Brie H 3F 109

Silvington Cl. B29: W Cas 6G **131**
Simcox Gdns. B32: Bart G 3B **130**
Simcox Rd. WS10: W'bry 6F **47**
Simeon Bissell Cl. DY4: Tip 2A **78**
Simeon's Wlk. DY5: Quar B 4B **110**
Simmonds Cl. WS3: Blox 4B **20**
Simmonds Pl. WS3: Blox 4B **20**
WS10: Darl 4E **47**
Simmonds Rd. WS3: Blox 4B **20**
Simmonds Way WS8: Bwnhls 2C **22**
Simmons Dr. B32: Quin 6A **114**
Simmons Leasow
B32: Bart G 3B **130**
Simmons Rd. WV11: Wed 6B **18**
Simms La. B47: H'wd 4A **162**
(not continuous)
DY2: Neth 4E **95**
Simon Cl. B71: W Brom 4C **64**
Simon Rd. B47: H'wd 2A **162**
Simpkins Cl. WS9: Wals W 4C **22**
Simpson Gro. WV10: Bush 3A **28**
Simpson Rd. B72: W Grn 4A **70**
WS2: Wals 4H **31**
WV10: Bush 3A **28**
Simpson St. B69: O'bry 2G **97**
Sinclair Ct. B13: Mose 1G **133**
Singer Cft. B36: Cas B 6B **88**
Singh Cl. B21: Hand 6A **82**
Sion Cl. DY5: Brie H 6H **93**
Sir Alfred's Way B76: Walm 2C **70**
Sir Harrys Rd. B15: Edg 5D **116**
Sir Hilton's Rd. B31: Longb 2F **159**
Sir Johns Rd. B29: S Oak 2E **133**
Sir Richards Dr. B17: Harb 4D **114**
Sisefield Rd. B38: K Nor 6C **146**
Siskin Cl. WS7: Hamm 1F **11**
Siskin Dr. B12: Bal H 5G **117**
Siskin Rd. DY9: W'cte 2H **125**
Sister Dora Bldgs. *WS1: Wals 2C 48*
(off Bridge, The)
Sister Dora Gdns. WS1: Wals 2C **48**
Siviters Cl. B65: Row R 6C **96**
Siviters La. B65: Row R 6B **96**
Siviter St. B63: Hale 1B **128**
Six Acres B32: Quin 1A **130**
Sixes Sports Cen. 6C 74
Six Foot Rd. DY2: Neth 4E **95**
Six Towers Rd. WS2: Wals 5A **32**
Six Ways B23: Erd 3F **85**
Skelcher Rd. B90: Shir 3G **149**
Skemp Cl. WV14: Bils 2F **61**
Sketchley Cl. B66: Smeth 4E **99**
Skidmore Av. WV3: Wolv 3D **42**
Skidmore Dr. B70: W Brom 4G **79**
Skidmore Rd. WV14: Cose 3F **61**
Skinner La. B5: Birm 2G **117**
Skinner St. WV1: Wolv 1G **43** (3A **170**)
Skip La. WS5: Wals 6H **49**
Skipton Grn. WV6: Wolv 4E **27**
Skipton Rd. B16: Edg 2C **116**
Skomer Cl. B45: Fran 6E **143**
Skye Cl. B36: Cas B 3D **106**
Skye Wlk. B64: Old H 2G **111**
Sky Lark Cl. DY5: P'ntt 6G **75**
Skylark Cl. B23: Erd 6C **68**
Skywalk B40: Nat E C 1F **139**
Slack La. B20: Hand 5A **82**
Slacky La. WS3: Blox 6C **20**
Slade Cl. B71: W Brom 3D **64**
Sladefield Rd. B8: W End 4G **103**
Slade Gdns. WV8: Cod 3G **13**
Slade Gro. B93: Know 3B **166**
Slade Hill WV6: Wolv 6D **26**
Slade La. B28: Hall G 4E **149**
B75: R'ley 6E **39**
Slade Lanker B34: Stech 4E **105**
Sladepool Farm Rd. B14: K Hth 4H **147**
Slade Rd. B23: Erd 3D **84**
B63: Crad 5E **111**
B75: R'ley, Can 6C **38**
WV10: F'hses 4G **15**
Slaithwaite Rd. B71: W Brom 3C **80**
Slaney Ct. WS2: Wals 4A **48**
Slaney Rd. WS2: Wals 5H **47**
Slatch Ho. Rd. B67: Smeth 1C **114**
Slate La. WV8: Cod 2D **12**
Slateley Cres. B90: M'path 3E **165**
Slater Cl. B64: Old H 2H **111**
Slate Row WS3: Pels 4E **21**
Slater Rd. B93: Ben H 5A **166**
Slater's La. WS2: Wals 4H **47**
Slater's Pl. WS2: Wals 4H **47**
Slater St. DY4: Tip 3A **78**
(Crompton Rd.)
DY4: Tip 2D **78**
(Sheepwash La.)
WS10: Darl 4D **46**
WV13: W'hall 6C **30**
WV14: Bils 1G **61**
Sleaford Gro. B28: Hall G 6G **135**
Sleaford Rd. B28: Hall G 6H **135**
Sledmore Rd. DY2: Dud 2F **95**
Slieve, The B20: Hand 4C **82**
Slim Av. WV14: Bils 2G **61**
Slimbridge Cl. B90: M'path 3E **165**
Slim Rd. WS2: Wals 1E **47**
Slims Ga. B63: Hale 1A **128**
Sling, The DY2: Neth 3E **95**
Slingfield Rd. B31: N'fld 5G **145**
Slitting Mill Cl. B21: Hand 1G **99**
Sloane Ho. B1: Birm 2A **4**
Sloane St. B1: Birm 6E **101** (3A **4**)
Slough La. B38: Head H 1G **161**
B47: H'wd 1G **161**
Smallbrook La. WV5: Wom 6H **57**
Smallbrook Queensway
B5: Birm 2F **117** (6D **4**)
Small Cl. B67: Smeth 4B **98**
Smalldale Rd. B42: Gt Barr 6F **67**
SMALL HEATH **3D 118**
Small Heath Bri. B10: Small H 3B **118**
B11: S'brk 4B **118**
Small Heath Bus. Pk. B10: Small H 4F **119**
Small Heath Highway B10: Small H . . . 3B **118**
Small Heath Leisure Cen. 3D 118
Small Heath Station (Rail) **4D 118**
Small Heath Trad. Est.
B11: Small H 5D **118**
Smallshire Cl. WV11: Wed 4H **29**
Smallshire Way DY8: Word 3B **108**
Small St. B71: W Brom 1H **79**
WS1: Wals 3C **48**
Smallwood Cl. B24: Erd 4B **86**
B76: Walm 2C **70**
Smallwood Rd. WV8: Pend 5C **14**
Smarts Av. WS14: Shen W 2G **37**
Smeaton Gdns. B18: Win G 5A **100**
Smeed Gro. B24: Erd 4H **85**
SMESTOW 3C **72**
Smestow Ga. DY3: Swind 2B **72**
Smestow La. DY3: Swind 3C **72**
Smestow St. WV10: Wolv 5H **27**
Smestow Valley Local Nature Reserve
. . . . 3D 26
Smestow Wildlife Cen. 3D 72
SMETHWICK 4E **99**
Smethwick Galton Bridge Station (Rail)
. . . . **2C 98**
Smethwick New Ent. Cen.
B66: Smeth 3E **99**
Smethwick Rolfe Street Station (Rail)
. . . . **3E 99**
Smethwick Swimming Cen. 1D 114
Smirrells Rd. B28: Hall G 2E **149**
Smith Av. WS10: Darl 1D **62**
Smith Cl. B67: Smeth 6B **98**
WV14: Cose 4C **60**
Smithfield Rd. WS3: Blox 6B **20**
Smithfields DY8: Stourb 6E **109**
Smithfield St. B5: Birm 2G **117** (6G **5**)
Smith Ho. WS3: Blox 4A **20**
Smithmoor Cres. B71: W Brom 5D **64**
Smith Pl. DY4: Tip 3B **78**
Smith Rd. WS2: Wals 5A **48**
WS10: W'bry 4E **63**
Smiths Cl. B32: Bart G 3H **129**
Smiths La. B93: Know 3A **166**
Smith St. B19: Birm 4E **101**
DY2: Dud 2F **95**
WV14: Bils 6F **45**
Smiths Way B46: Wat O 4C **88**
SMITH'S WOOD 2C **106**
Smithy, The B26: Sheld 5G **121**
Smithy Dr. WS3: Pels 3E **21**
Smithy La. DY5: P'ntt 6F **75**
Smout Cres. WV14: Cose 3B **60**
Snapdragon Dr. WS5: Wals 2D **64**
Snape Rd. WV11: Wed 6A **18**
Snapes Lodge WV12: W'hall 3C **30**
Sneyd Hall Cl. WS3: Blox 1G **31**
Sneyd Hall Rd. WS3: Blox 6G **19**
Sneyd La. WS3: Blox 6F **19**
WV11: Ess 5B **18**
Snowberry Dr. DY5: P'ntt 6G **75**
Snowberry Gdns. B27: A Grn 6A **120**
Snowdon Gro. B63: Hale 4F **127**
Snowdon Ri. DY3: Sed 1H **75**
Snowdon Rd. DY8: Amb 5F **109**
Snowdon Way WV10: Oxl 3F **27**
WV12: W'hall 6B **18**
Snowdrop Cl. WS8: Clay 1H **21**
Snowford Cl. B90: Shir 6F **149**
Snow Hill WV2: Wolv 2H **43** (4C **170**)
Snow Hill Junc.
WV2: Wolv 2H **43** (5C **170**)
Snow Hill Queensway
B4: Birm 6G **101** (2D **4**)
Snow Hill Station (Rail & MM)
. . . . **6F 101 (2D 4)**
Snowshill Dr. B90: Ches G 4B **164**
Snowshill Gdns. DY1: Dud 3B **76**
Soberton Cl. WV11: Wed 2H **29**
SOHO 2G **99**
Soho Av. B18: Hock 2C **100**
Soho Benson Road Stop (MM) **3B 100**
Soho Cl. B66: Smeth 4G **99**
Soho Hill B19: Hock 2C **100**
Soho Ho. B66: Smeth 4G **99**
Soho Pool Way B18: Hock 3C **100**
Soho Rd. B21: Hand 1A **100**
Soho St. B66: Smeth 3G **99**
Soho Way B66: Smeth 3F **99**
Solari Cl. DY4: Tip 5C **62**
Solent Cl. WV9: Pend 5D **14**
Solent Ct. B73: S Cold 6H **53**
SOLIHULL **4G 151**
Solihull By-Pass B91: Sol 2G **151**
Solihull Ice Rink 2F 137
Solihull La. B28: Hall G 1G **149**
SOLIHULL LODGE 5C **148**
Solihull Parkway B37: Mars G 4F **123**
Solihull Retail Pk. B90: Shir 6B **150**
Solihull Rd. B11: S'hll 2D **134**
B90: Shir 4A **150**
B92: H Ard 1E **153**
Solihull Station (Rail) **3E 151**
Soliway Cl. WS10: W'bry 1A **64**
Solly Gro. DY4: Tip 6D **62**
Solva Cl. WV1: Wolv 2D **44**
Somerby Dr. B91: Sol 1E **165**
Somercotes Rd. B42: Gt Barr 5F **67**
Somerdale Rd. B31: N'fld 3G **145**
Somerfield Cl. WS4: S'fld 6G **21**
Somerfield Rd. WS3: Blox 1H **31**
Somerford Cl. WS6: Gt Wyr 4E **7**
Somerford Gdns. WV10: Bush 5A **16**
Somerford Pl. WV13: W'hall 2H **45**
Somerford Rd. B29: W Cas 5D **130**
Somerford Way WV14: Cose 5D **60**
Somerland Rd. B26: Yard 2E **121**
Somerset Cres. WS10: W'bry 1B **64**
Somerset Dr. B31: Longb 2D **158**
DY8: Woll 4B **108**
Somerset Rd. B15: Edg 5A **116**
B20: Hand 5B **82**
B23: Erd 1F **85**
B71: W Brom 1B **80**
WS4: Wals 5E **33**
WV13: W'hall 1D **46**
Somers Rd. B62: Hale 6C **112**
CV7: Mer 4F **141**
WS2: Wals 4G **47**
Somers Wood Cvn. & Camping Pk.
CV7: Mer 4F **141**
Somerton Dr. B23: Erd 1G **85**
B37: Mars G 4C **122**
Somerville Ct. B73: S Cold 3G **69**
Somerville Dr. B73: S Cold 1G **69**
Somerville Ho. B37: Chel W 6F **107**
Somerville Rd. B10: Small H 3D **118**
B73: S Cold 1G **69**

Somery Rd. B29: W Cas. 3E 131
   DY1: Dud 4E 77
Sommerfield Rd. B32: Bart G 3A 130
Sonning Dr. WV9: Pend. 5D 14
Sopwith Cft. B35: Cas V 5E 87
Sorrel Cl. B69: Tiv 5B 78
Sorrel Dr. WS5: Wals 2E 65
Sorrel Gro. B24: Erd. 4B 86
Sorrel Ho. B24: Erd 4B 86
Sorrell Dr. B27: A Grn 3H 135
Sorrel Wlk. DY5: Brie H 5F 109
Sorrento Ct. B13: Mose 2A 134
Sot's Hole Nature Reserve 2C 80
Souters Ho. B32: Bart G 5B 130
Southacre Av. B5: Birm 3G 117
       (not continuous)
Southall Cres. WV14: Cose 4E 61
Southall Rd. WV11: Wed 1A 30
Southalls La. DY1: Dud. 6D 76
Southam Cl. B28: Hall G. 5E 135
Southam Dr. B73: W Grn 4H 69
Southam Ho. B13: Mose 6A 134
Southampton St.
   WV1: Wolv 6H 27 (1D 170)
Southam Rd. B28: Hall G 5E 135
South Av. DY8: Stourb 1D 124
   WV11: Wed 4E 29
Southbank Rd. B64: Old H. 2G 111
Southbank Vw. DY6: K'wfrd 5C 92
Southbourne Av. B34: Hodg H 3B 104
   WS2: Wals 2H 47
Southbourne Cl. B29: S Oak 3C 132
Southbourne Rd. WV10: F'hses. 4G 15
Sth. Car Pk. Rd. B40: Nat E C 2G 139
Southcote Gro. B38: K Nor 6H 145
Southcott Av. DY5: Brie H 3H 109
South Cres. WV10: F'stne 1D 16
South Dene B67: Smeth. 4D 98
Southdown Av. B18: Hock 3C 100
South Dr. B5: Edg 1E 133
   B46: Col 2F 107
   B75: S Cold 5A 54
Southern Cl. DY6: K'wfrd 6D 92
Southerndown Rd. DY3: Sed 6F 59
Southern Rd. B8: W End 4A 104
Southern Way WS10: Mox 2C 62
   WS10: W'bry 2C 62
Southey Cl. B91: Sol. 1F 165
   WV12: W'hall 1E 31
Southfield Av. B16: Edg 6H 99
   B36: Cas B 1E 105
Southfield Cl. WS9: A'rdge 3C 34
Southfield Dr. B28: Hall G 2G 149
Southfield Gro. WV3: Wolv 4A 42
Southfield Rd. B16: Edg 6H 99
   WV11: Wed 4H 29
Southfields Cl. B46: Col. 5H 107
Southfields Rd. B91: Sol 6D 150
Southfield Way WS6: Gt Wyr 3F 7
Southgate B64: Crad H. 3F 111
   WV1: Wolv 1F 43
Southgate Rd. B44: Gt Barr 3G 67
South Grn. WV4: Penn 6B 42
South Gro. B6: Aston 1F 101
   B19: Hand 1D 100
   B23: Erd 2F 85
South Holme B9: Bord G 1C 118
Southlands Rd. B13: Mose 4A 134
Southminster Dr. B14: K Hth 1G 147
South Oval DY3: Up Gor. 2A 76
South Pde. B72: S Cold 6A 54
South Pk. M. DY5: Brie H 1G 109
South Range B11: Bal H 5B 118
South Rd. B11: S'brk 4B 118
   B14: K Hth 5G 133
   B18: Hock 2C 100
   B23: Erd 3F 85
   B31: N'fld. 5D 144
   B67: Smeth 4D 98
   DY4: Tip 5B 62
   DY8: Stourb 1B 124
South Rd. Av. B18: Hock 3C 100
South Roundhay B33: Kitts G 6E 105
Southside Bus. Cen. B12: Bal H 6A 118
      (off Ladypool Rd.)
Sth. Staffordshire Bus. Pk.
   WS11: Cann. 1C 6

South Staffordshire Golf Course 3B 26
South St. B17: Harb 6H 115
   DY5: Brie H 1G 109
   WS1: Wals 3B 48
   WV10: Oxl 3G 27
   WV13: W'hall 2H 45
South St. Gdns. WS1: Wals 3B 48
South Vw. B43: Gt Barr 6A 66
South Vw. Cl. WV8: Bilb 5H 13
   WV10: F'stne 1D 16
Southview Ridge DY5: Brie H 4H 109
South Vw. Rd. DY3: Sed 5G 59
Southville Bungalows B14: K Hth 3B 148
South Wlk. B31: N'fld. 6G 145
South Way B40: Nat E C 2H 139
Southway Ct. DY6: K'wfrd 5D 92
Southwick Pl. WV14: Bils 4F 45
Southwick Rd. B62: B'hth 3D 112
Southwold Av. B30: K Nor 4E 147
Southwood Av. B34: S End 2F 105
Southwood Cl. DY6: K'wfrd 4C 92
Southwood Covert B14: K Hth 5F 147
SOUTH YARDLEY 5B 120
Sovereign Cl. B1: Birm 6E 101 (2A 4)
Sovereign Dr. DY1: Dud 5A 76
Sovereign Hgts. B31: Longb 6A 144
Sovereign Rd. B30: K Nor 3B 146
Sovereign Wlk. WS1: Wals 1E 49
Sovereign Way B13: Mose. 1H 133
Sowerby March B24: Erd 3B 86
Sowers Cl. WV12: W'hall 4D 30
Sowers Ct. B75: R'ley 5B 38
Sowers Gdns. WV12: W'hall 4D 30
Spa Gro. B30: Stir 5E 133
SPARKBROOK. 4B 118
SPARKHILL 1C 134
Sparkhill Pool & Fitness Cen. 1C 134
Spark St. B11: S'brk. 4A 118
Sparrey Dr. B30: Stir 5C 132
Sparrow Cl. WS10: W'bry 6H 47
Spartan Ind. Cen. B70: W Brom 1E 79
Speakers Cl. B69: Tiv. 2B 96
Speed Rd. DY4: Tip 1G 77
Speedwell Cl. B25: Yard 5G 119
   WS9: A'rdge 4B 34
   WV11: Wed 4G 29
Speedwell Dr. CV7: Bal C 3G 169
Speedwell Gdns. DY5: Brie H. 5F 109
Speedwell Ho. B38: K Nor 6C 146
Speedwell Rd. B5: Bal H 5F 117
   B25: Yard. 5G 119
Speedwell Trad. Est. B11: Tys. 5G 119
Spelter Works WS3: Blox. 2G 31
Spencer Av. WV14: Cose 5E 61
Spencer Cl. B24: Erd 3B 86
   B69: Tiv 1B 96
   B71: W Brom 5D 64
   DY3: Lwr G. 3E 75
Spencer St. B18: Birm 4E 101 (1A 4)
      (not continuous)
Spenser Av. WV6: Pert 5F 25
Spernall Gro. B29: W Cas 4E 131
Spey Cl. B5: Edg. 5F 117
Spiceland Rd. B31: N'fld 1D 144
Spiers Cl. B93: Know 3C 166
Spies Cl. B62: Quin 5F 113
Spies La. B62: Quin 6F 113
Spills Mdw. DY3: Up Gor. 2A 76
Spilsbury Cft. B91: Sol 1E 165
Spindle La. B90: Dic H 3G 163
      (not continuous)
Spinners End Dr. B64: Crad H 2F 111
Spinners End Ind. Est. B64: Crad H . . . 3F 111
Spinney, The B15: Edg. 6A 116
   B20: Hand 3A 82
   B38: K Nor 6B 146
   B47: Wyt 5B 162
   B74: Lit A 4B 36
   B91: Sol. 1G 165
   DY3: Gorn 5G 75
   WV3: Wolv 2B 42
Spinney Cl. B31: N'fld 4E 145
   DY8: Word 6A 92
   WS3: Pels. 5E 21
Spinney Dr. B90: Ches G 5B 164
Spinney Wlk. B76: Walm 6D 70
Spiral Cl. B62: B'hth. 3E 113

Spiral Ct. B24: Erd 5E 85
   B76: Walm. 2D 70
   DY3: Lwr G 4H 75
      (off Yorkdale Cl.)
   DY8: Stourb 1E 125
   WV11: Wed. 2F 29
Spiral Grn. B24: Erd. 3A 86
Spitfire Pk. B24: Erd 5B 86
Spitfire Rd. B24: Erd 5A 86
Spitfire Way B35: Cas V 5E 87
Spondon Gro. B34: S End 4G 105
Spondon Rd. WV11: Wed 1G 29
Spon La. B70: W Brom 6B 80
Spon La. Ind. Est. B66: Smeth 1B 98
Spon La. Sth. B66: Smeth 1B 98
   B70: Smeth, W Brom 1B 98
Spon La. Trad. Est. B70: W Brom 5B 80
Spoon Dr. B38: K Nor 5H 145
Spooner Cft. B5: Birm 3G 117
Spooners Cl. B92: Sol 6B 138
Spot La. WS8: Clay 1B 22
Spouthouse La. B43: Gt Barr 6A 66
Spout La. WS1: Wals 4C 48
      (not continuous)
Spreadbury Cl. B17: Harb 3D 114
Sprig Cft. B36: Hodg H. 1A 104
Spring Av. B65: Row R. 1C 112
Spring Avon Cft. B17: Harb 5F 115
SPRING BANK 6B 30
Springbank B9: Bord G. 6F 103
Spring Bank Ho. WV13: W'hall 6A 30
Springbank Rd. B15: Edg 4E 117
Springbrook Cl. B36: Cas B 6H 87
Spring Cl. B91: Sol 4D 150
   WS4: S'fld 5G 21
Spring Coppice Dr. B93: Dorr 6C 166
Spring Ct. B66: Smeth 4G 99
   B70: W Brom 5B 80
   WS1: Wals 4E 49
Spring Cres. B64: Crad H. 4H 111
Springcroft Rd. B11: Tys 3F 135
Spring Dr. WS6: Gt Wyr. 3G 7
Spring Dr. Ind. Est.
   WV4: E'shll 1C 60
SPRINGFIELD
   Moseley. 4D 134
   Rowley Regis 3H 95
   Wolverhampton 6A 28
Springfield B23: Erd. 4D 84
Springfield Av. B12: Bal H 5A 118
   B68: O'bry 5A 98
   DY3: Sed 4A 60
   DY9: W'cte 1A 126
Springfield Cl. B65: Row R 4A 96
Springfield Ct. B28: Hall G 5F 135
   B75: S Cold 6G 55
Springfield Cres. B70: W Brom 6C 80
   B76: Walm 1E 71
   B92: Sol. 2G 137
   DY2: Dud 1H 95
Springfield Dr. B14: K Hth 4G 133
   B62: B'hth 4D 112
Springfield Grn. DY3: Sed 4A 60
Springfield Ind. Est. B69: O'bry 2H 97
Springfield La. B65: Row R 4H 95
   WV10: F'hses. 3H 15
Springfield Rd. B13: Mose 4D 134
   B14: K Hth 5H 133
   B36: Cas B 1H 105
   B62: B'hth 4D 112
   B68: O'bry 5A 98
   B76: Walm 3D 70
   DY5: Brie H 1F 109
   WV10: Wolv 5A 28
   WV14: Bils. 4G 45
Springfields B46: Col. 4H 107
   WS4: Rus 2F 33
Springfield Ter. B65: Row R 4H 95
Spring Gdns. B21: Hand. 2A 100
   B66: Smeth. 6F 99
   DY2: Dud 1F 95
   DY3: Gorn 5G 75
Spring Gro. B19: Hock. 3D 100
Spring Gro. Gdns. B18: Hock. 3B 100
Spring Head WS10: W'bry 3F 63
SPRING HILL 1A 58

SPRINGHILL
  Essington. 2D **18**
  Lynn 6G **11**
Spring Hill B1: Birm. 6D **100**
  B18: Hock 5C **100**
  B24: Erd 4F **85**
Springhill Av. WV4: Penn. 2A **58**
Springhill Cl. WS4: S'fld 6H **21**
  WV12: W'hall 2D **30**
Springhill Gro. WV4: Penn. 1A **58**
Spring Hill Ind. Est.
  B18: Hock 6C **100**
Springhill La. WV4: Lwr P 6F **41**
  WV4: Penn. 2A **58**
Springhill Pk. WV4: Penn 2H **57**
Springhill Rd. WS1: Wals 2D **48**
  WS8: Bwnhls 6C **10**
  WV11: Wed 1G **29**
Spring Hill Ter. WV4: Penn 5E **43**
Spring Ho. B37: K'hrst 4D **106**
Spring La. B24: Erd 4G **85**
  WS4: S'fld 5G **21**
  WV12: W'hall 5B **30**
Spring Mdw. B63: Hale 3H **127**
  B64: Old H 2H **111**
  DY4: Tip 1C **78**
  WS6: C Hay 4D **6**
Springmeadow Gro. B19: Hock . . . 3F **101**
Springmeadow Rd. DY2: Neth 1E **111**
Spring Mdws. Cl. WV8: Bilb 3H **13**
Spring Parklands DY1: Dud 1C **94**
Spring Rd. B11: Tys 2F **135**
  B15: Edg. 4F **117**
  B66: Smeth 1B **98**
  DY2: Neth 3F **95**
  WS4: S'fld 6H **21**
  WV4: E'shll 6C **44**
Spring Rd. Ind. Est. WV4: E'shll . . . 1C **60**
Spring Road Station (Rail). 3G **135**
Springs, The B64: Old H 2A **112**
Springslade B32: Harb. 6D **114**
Springslade Dr. B24: Erd 4B **86**
SPRINGS MIRE. 1A **94**
Spring St. B15: Birm. 3F **117**
  B63: Crad 5E **111**
  DY4: Tip 2A **78**
  (Alexandra Rd.)
  DY4: Tip 5C **62**
  (Oaker Hill Rd.)
  DY9: Lye 1A **126**
Springthorpe Grn. B24: Erd 3A **86**
Springthorpe Rd. B24: Erd 4B **86**
  (Pype Hayes Rd.)
  B24: Erd 3B **86**
  (Woodcote Rd.)
SPRING VALE. 1D **60**
Springvale Av. WS5: Wals 4G **49**
  WV14: Bils 1D **60**
Springvale Bus. Cen. WV14: Bils . . 1D **60**
Spring Va. Cl. WV14: Cose 4C **60**
Spring Va. Ind. Pk. WV14: Bils 6E **45**
Spring Va. Rd. B65: Row R 4A **96**
Springvale St. WV13: W'hall 6B **30**
Springvale Way WV14: Bils 1E **61**
Spring Vs. B63: Hale 2A **128**
Spring Wlk. B63: Hale 4F **127**
  B69: O'bry 4G **97**
  WS2: Wals 6H **31**
Sproat Av. WS10: Darl 6C **46**
Spruce Gro. B24: Erd 5H **85**
Spruce Rd. WS5: Wals 2F **65**
Spruce Way WV3: Wolv 2B **42**
Spur Tree Av. WV3: Wolv 2G **41**
Squadron Cl. B35: Cas V 3G **87**
Square, The B15: Birm 2D **116**
  B17: Harb. 6G **115**
  (off High St.)
  B17: Harb 5F **115**
  (Carless Av.)
  B91: Sol 4G **151**
  DY2: Dud 3B **94**
  DY4: Tip 6D **62**
  WS9: A'rdge 3D **34**
  WV2: Wolv 3H **43** (6D **170**)
  WV8: Cod 3F **13**
  WV12: W'hall 1D **30**

Square Cl. B32: Bart G 2A **130**
Squires Ct. DY5: Brie H 3G **109**
Squires Cft. B76: Walm 4E **71**
Squires Ga. Wlk. B35: Cas V 4E **87**
Squires Wlk. WS10: W'bry. 2F **63**
Squirrel Hollow B76: Walm 3E **71**
Squirrels Hollow B68: O'bry 4B **114**
Squirrel Wlk. B74: Lit A 4C **36**
  WV4: Penn 1E **59**
Stable Ct. DY3: Sed 1A **76**
Stable Cft. B71: W Brom 6D **64**
Stableford Cl. B32: Bart G 2D **130**
Stables, The B29: S Oak 3C **132**
Stablewood Gro. WS1: Wals 4E **49**
Stacey Cl. B64: Old H 2G **111**
Stacey Dr. B13: Mose. 2A **148**
Stacey Grange Gdns.
  B45: Redn 3G **157**
Stackhouse Cl. WS9: Wals W 3C **22**
Stackhouse Dr. WS3: Pels 3E **21**
Staddlestones, The WV6: Pert. . . . 5D **24**
Stadium Cl. WV13: W'hall 6B **30**
Stadium Dr. DY2: Neth 2E **111**
Stafford Cl. WS3: Blox. 5H **19**
Stafford Ct. *B43: Gt Barr* 6A **66**
  (off West Rd.)
  B71: W Brom 1H **79**
Stafford Ho. B33: Kitts G 1A **122**
Stafford La. WV8: Cod. 6D **12**
Stafford Rd. B21: Hand 1B **100**
  WS3: Blox 1G **19**
  WS6: Gt Wyr 1G **19**
  WS10: Darl. 5C **46**
  WV10: Cov H 1H **15**
  WV10: F'hses, Oxl, Wolv 1G **27**
Staffordshire Pool Cl. *B6: Aston* . . . *RH 83*
  (off Emscote Rd.)
Stafford St. DY1: Dud 6D **76**
  WS2: Wals 6C **32**
  WS10: W'bry 3E **63**
  WV1: Wolv 5G **27** (1C **170**)
  WV13: W'hall 1A **46**
  (not continuous)
  WV14: Bils 6F **45**
Stafford St. Junc.
  WV1: Wolv 6G **27** (1B **170**)
Stafford Twr. B4: Birm 6H **101** (2F **5**)
Stafford Way B43: Gt Barr 6A **66**
Stag Cres. WS3: Blox. 3C **32**
Stag Hill Rd. WS3: Blox. 2C **32**
Stag Ind. Est. WV14: Bils. 1H **61**
Stag Wlk. B76: Walm 6B **70**
Stainsby Av. B19: Birm. 4E **101**
Stainsby Cft. B90: M'path. 4F **165**
Stallings La. DY6: K'wfrd 1B **92**
Stambermill Cl. DY9: Lye 6H **109**
Stambermill Ho. DY9: Lye 6A **110**
Stambermill Ind. Est.
  DY9: Lye 5G **109**
Stamford Cft. B91: Sol 5F **151**
Stamford Gro. B20: Hand 6E **83**
Stamford Rd. B20: Hand 6E **83**
  DY5: Brie H 4G **109**
  DY8: Amb 6F **109**
Stamford St. DY8: Amb 4D **108**
Stamford Way WS9: A'rdge 5D **22**
Stanbrook Rd. B90: M'path. 3E **165**
Stanbury Av. WS10: Darl 5B **46**
Stanbury Rd. B14: K Hth 3B **148**
Stancroft Gro. B26: Yard 3E **121**
Standard Way B24: Erd 1F **103**
Standbridge Way
  DY4: Tip 2A **78**
Standhills Rd. DY6: K'wfrd 3C **92**
Standlake Av. B36: Hodg H 2B **104**
Standleys Twr. B23: Erd 1G **85**
Stanfield Rd. B32: Quin 4B **114**
  B43: Gt Barr 6F **51**
Stanford Av. B42: Gt Barr 6C **66**
Stanford Dr. B65: Row R 5B **96**
Stanford Gro. B63: Hale 4E **127**
Stanford Rd. WV2: Wolv 4G **43**
Stanford Way *B69: O'bry* *5E 97*
  (off Kempsey Cl.)
Stanhoe Cl. DY5: Brie H 3H **109**
Stanhope Rd. B67: Smeth 6D **98**

Stanhope St. B12: Birm. 4H **117**
  DY2: Neth 5G **95**
  WV3: Wolv. 2F **43** (4A **170**)
Stanhope Way B43: Gt Barr 1F **67**
Stanhurst Way B71: W Brom 3E **65**
Stanier Cl. WS4: Rus 2F **33**
Stanier Gro. B20: Hand 5D **82**
Staniforth St. B4: Birm 5G **101** (1F **5**)
Stanley Av. B32: Harb 4C **114**
  B75: S Cold 1D **70**
  B90: Shir 3H **149**
Stanley Cl. B28: Hall G 2G **149**
  WV11: Wed 1H **29**
Stanley Ct. *B13: Mose* *3B 134*
  (off Wake Grn. Pk.)
  WV6: Pert. 5E **25**
Stanley Dr. DY3: Swind 5E **73**
Stanley Gro. B11: S'brk 5B **118**
Stanley Pl. B13: Mose. 2H **133**
  WS4: Rus 3F **33**
  WV14: Bils 6D **44**
Stanley Rd. B7: Nech 2C **102**
  B14: K Hth 6F **133**
  B68: O'bry 3A **114**
  B71: W Brom 6C **64**
  DY8: Stourb 2D **124**
  WS4: Rus 3F **33**
  WS10: Darl 6D **46**
  WV10: Bush. 6H **15**
Stanley St. WS3: Blox 1A **32**
Stanmore Gro. B62: Quin. 2G **129**
Stanmore Rd. B16: Edg 2G **115**
Stansbury Ho. *WS2: Wals* *3A 48*
  (off St Quentin St.)
Stanton Av. DY1: Dud. 1B **76**
Stanton Gro. B26: Yard 3D **120**
  B90: Shir 3G **149**
  DY4: Tip 2A **78**
Stanton Ho. B71: W Brom 4D **64**
Stanton Rd. B43: Gt Barr 6H **65**
  B90: Shir 3G **149**
  WV1: Wolv. 1B **44**
Stanville Rd. B26: Sheld 5G **121**
Stanway Gdns. B71: W Brom 1B **80**
Stanway Gro. B44: Gt Barr 2H **67**
Stanway Rd. B71: W Brom 1B **80**
  B90: Shir 4H **149**
Stanwell Gro. B23: Erd 1E **85**
Stanwick Av. B33: Kitts G 6A **106**
Stapenhall Rd. B90: M'path. 3E **165**
Stapleford Cft. B14: K Hth 5E **147**
Stapleford Gro. DY8: Word 6C **92**
Staplehall Rd. B31: N'fld 5F **145**
Staplehurst Rd. B28: Hall G 5F **135**
Staple Lodge Rd. B31: N'fld 6F **145**
Stapleton Cl. B76: Walm 1F **87**
Stapleton Dr. B37: F'bri 6D **106**
Stapleton Rd. WS9: A'rdge 4B **34**
Stapylton Av. B17: Harb 6F **115**
Stapylton Ct. *B17: Harb* *6F 115*
  (off Old Church Rd.)
Starbank Rd. B10: Small H 3G **119**
Starbold Ct. B93: Know 3D **166**
Starbold Cres. B93: Know 4C **166**
Star City 1D **102**
Star Cl. DY4: Tip 2C **78**
  WS2: Wals 5F **31**
Starcrest Ind. Est. DY5: Brie H 2A **110**
Starcross Rd. B27: A Grn. 3A **136**
Star Hill B15: Edg 3D **116**
Starkey Cft. B37: Chel W 1E **123**
Starkie Dr. B68: O'bry 5A **98**
Starley Way B37: Mars G 5E **123**
Star St. DY9: Lye 6B **110**
  WV3: Wolv. 3C **42**
Start Point Trad. Est.
  B11: S'hll 1D **134**
Statham Dr. B16: Edg 1G **115**
Station App. B73: S Cold 5H **53**
  B74: Four O 3F **37**
  B91: Sol 3E **151**
  B93: Dorr. 6G **167**
Station Av. B16: Edg 2G **115**
Station Bldgs. *B46: Wat O* *4D 88*
  (off Minworth Rd.)
Station Cl. WS3: Blox 1H **31**
  WV8: Cod 4F **13**

Station Dr. B28: Hall G 4F 135
 B46: Wat O. 4D 88
 B74: Four O 3H 53
 B92: Olton 4C 136
 DY4: Tip 3B 78
 DY5: Brie H 1A 110
  (Brierley Hill)
 DY5: Brie H. 2F 109
  (Silver End)
Station Link Rd. B26: Birm A 1F 139
 B40: Nat E C 1F 139
Station Pl. WS3: Blox 1H 31
Station Rd. B6: Aston 6H 83
 B14: K Hth 5F 133
 B17: Harb. 5G 115
 B21: Hand 1G 99
 B23: Erd 2F 85
 B27: A Grn 2A 136
 B30: K Nor 2A 146
 B31: N'fld 5E 145
 B33: Stech 5B 104
 B37: Mars G 3B 122
 B38: K Nor 2A 146
 B46: Col 1H 107
 B47: Wyt 6A 162
 B64: Old H 2H 111
 B65: Row R 1D 112
 B69: O'bry 4G 97
 B73: Bold, W Grn. 4G 69
 B91: Sol 3F 151
 B92: H Ard 6B 140
 B93: Dorr. 6C 166
 CV7: Bal C 3G 169
 DY5: Brie H 5G 93
 DY9: Lye. 5A 110
 WS3: Pels. 4E 21
 WS4: Rus. 3E 33
 WS6: Gt Wyr 1F 7
 WS7: Hamm 2G 11
 WS9: A'rdge 4C 34
 WV5: Wom. 5G 57
 WV8: Cod. 4E 13
 WV14: Bils 6G 45
Station Rd. Ind. Est. B65: Row R 1D 112
Station St. B5: Birm 2F 117 (6D 4)
 B64: Crad H 3E 111
 B73: S Cold 6H 53
 DY4: Tip 2B 78
 WS2: Wals 2B 48
 WS3: Blox 1H 31
 WS6: C Hay 2E 7
 WS10: Darl. 5E 47
Station Ter. WV14: Cose 4E 61
Station Way B37: Mars G 2F 139
 B40: Nat E C 1F 139
Staulton Grn. B69: O'bry 5E 97
Staveley Rd. B14: K Hth. 1F 147
 WV1: Wolv. 5G 27
Stead Cl. DY4: Tip 4B 62
 WS2: Wals 4A 32
Steadman Cft. DY4: Tip 5D 62
STECHFORD 1C 120
Stechford Cascades. 6C 104
Stechford La. B8: W End 4A 104
Stechford Retail Pk. B33: Stech 5C 104
Stechford Rd. B34: Hodg H 4B 104
Stechford (Rail). 6B 104
Stechford Trad. Est. B33: Stech. 6C 104
Steel Bright Rd. B66: Smeth 3G 99
Steel Dr. WV10: Bush 1H 27
Steel Gro. B25: Yard 4A 120
Steelhouse La. B4: Birm. 6G 101 (2E 5)
 WV2: Wolv 2A 44
Steelmans Rd. WS10: Darl. 4F 47
Steelpark Rd. B62: Hale. 4B 112
Steelpark Way WV11: Wed 5F 29
Steel Rd. B31: N'fld 5D 144
Steel Rdbt. WV1: Wolv 3E 63
Steene Gro. B31: N'fld 4B 144
Steeples, The DY8: Stourb. 2F 125
Steepwood Cft. B30: K Nor 3H 145
Stella Cft. B37: Chel W. 1E 123
Stella Gro. B43: Gt Barr 5F 65
Stella Rd. DY4: Tip 1H 77
Stenbury Cl. WV10: Bush 3B 16
Stencills Rd. WS4: Wals 6F 33
Stencills Rd. WS4: Wals 5F 33

Stennels Cres. B62: Hale 1E 129
Stephens Cl. WV11: Wed. 1H 29
Stephens Ind. Est. B11: Tys. 1F 135
Stephenson Av. WS2: Wals 3G 31
Stephenson Dr. B37: Chel W 6D 106
 WV6: Pert. 3E 25
Stephenson Pl. B2: Birm. 1G 117 (4E 5)
Stephenson Sq. WS2: Wals. 4H 31
Stephenson St. B2: Birm. 1F 117 (4D 4)
 WV3: Wolv 2F 43
Stephenson Twr. B5: Birm 5D 4
Stephens Rd. B76: Walm 1E 71
Stepping Stone Cl.
 WS2: Wals 5F 31
Stepping Stones DY8: Stourb. 6F 109
Steppingstone St. DY1: Dud 6D 76
Sterling Pk. DY5: Brie H. 5B 94
Sterndale Rd. B42: Gt Barr 1E 83
Steven Dr. WV14: Bils 4G 61
Stevens Av. B32: Bart G. 3B 130
Stevens Ga. WV2: Wolv 3G 43 (6B 170)
Stevens Rd. DY9: W'cte. 3H 125
Steward St. B18: Hock. 6C 100
Stewart Rd. B6: K'wfrd 5B 92
 WS9: Wals W 4C 22
Stewarts Rd. B62: B'hth. 4D 112
Stewart St. WV2: Wolv 3G 43 (6B 170)
Stewkins DY8: Word 3C 108
Steyning Rd. B26: Yard 6C 120
Stickley La. DY3: Lwr G. 3G 75
Stilehouse Cres. B65: Row R 1C 112
Stilthouse Gro. B45: Redn. 2G 157
STIRCHLEY 1D 146
Stirchley Indoor Bowling Cen. 6C 132
Stirchley Trad. Est. B30: Stir 6D 132
Stirling Ct. B16: Edg 2B 116
Stirling Cres. WV12: W'hall 3B 30
Stirling Rd. B16: Edg 2A 116
 B73: New O 3D 68
 B90: Shir 1C 164
 DY2: Dud 3G 95
 WV14: Bils 2H 61
Stirrup Cl. WS5: Wals 1D 64
Stockbridge Cl. WV6: Tett 1F 41
Stockdale Pl. B15: Edg 3H 115
Stock Exchange Bldg.
 B3: Birm. .3C 4
STOCKFIELD. 6A 120
Stockfield Rd. B25: Yard 6A 120
 B27: A Grn 1H 135
Stockhill Dr. B45: Rubery. 3F 157
Stocking St. DY9: Lye 6B 110
Stockland Ct. B74: S'tly 3A 52
STOCKLAND GREEN 3C 84
Stockland Green Community Leisure Cen.
 . . . . .3C 84
Stockland Rd. B23: Erd 3D 84
Stockley Cres. B90: Shir 4B 150
Stockmans Cl. B38: K Nor 1A 160
Stocks Wood B30: B'vlle. 5B 132
Stockton Cl. B76: Min 2G 87
 B93: Know. 5D 166
 WS2: Wals 5B 32
Stockton Ct. WV14: Cose. 5D 60
Stockton Gro. B33: Kitts G. 2H 121
Stockwell Av. DY5: Quar B. 3H 109
STOCKWELL END 4B 26
Stockwell End WV6: Tett 3B 26
Stockwell Ri. B92: Sol. 6H 137
Stockwell Rd. B21: Hand 5A 82
 WV6: Tett. 4B 26
Stokes Av. DY4: Tip 5A 62
 WV13: W'hall 3H 45
Stokesay Av. WV6: Pert 6F 25
Stokesay Cl. B69: Tiv. 1A 96
Stokesay Gro. B31: Longb 1D 158
Stokesay Ho. B23: Erd 1F 85
Stokesay Ri. DY1: Dud. 4A 76
Stokes St. WS3: Blox 1H 31
Stoke Way B15: Birm 2E 117 (6A 4)
Stom Rd. WV14: Bils 6D 44
Stoneacre Cl. WV3: Wolv 2G 41
Stone Av. B75: S Cold 6E 55
Stonebow Av. B91: Sol 1F 165
STONEBRIDGE 3C 140
Stonebridge Cres.
 B37: K'hrst 4B 106

Stonebridge Rd. B46: Col 2H 107
  (not continuous)
Stonebrook Way B29: W Cas. 3D 130
Stonebury B15: Edg 3H 115
Stonechat Dr. B23: Erd. 5C 84
Stone Cl. B38: K Nor 5B 146
Stonecroft Av. B45: Redn. 2G 157
Stonecrop Cl. B38: K Nor. 1B 160
 WS8: Clay 1H 21
Stonecross B46: Wat O 4D 88
Stonedown Cl. WV14: Cose 2C 60
Stonefield Dr. DY5: P'ntt 2F 93
Stonefield Rd. WV14: Bils 6F 45
Stonefield Wlk. WV14: Bils 6F 45
  (off Stonefield Rd.)
Stoneford Rd. B90: Shir. 3G 149
Stonehaven Gro. B28: Hall G. 5H 135
Stonehenge Cft. B14: K Hth 6F 147
Stone Hill Cft. B90: M'path 3D 164
Stonehouse Av. WV13: W'hall 5H 29
Stonehouse Cres.
 WS10: W'bry 3H 63
Stonehouse Dr. B74: Lit A 5C 36
Stonehouse Gro. B32: Bart G 3B 130
Stonehouse Hill B29: W Cas 2E 131
Stonehouse La. B32: Bart G. 3B 130
Stonehouse Rd. B73: S Cold 2F 69
Stonehurst Rd. B43: Gt Barr. 1E 67
Stone Lea WS9: A'rdge 4D 34
Stonelea Cl. B71: W Brom. 5C 64
Stoneleigh Cl. B74: Four O. 3F 53
Stoneleigh Gdns. WV8: Cod. 3F 13
Stoneleigh Ho. B32: Harb 6C 114
Stoneleigh Rd. B20: Hand 6G 83
 B91: Sol 2B 150
Stoneleigh Way DY3: Up Gor 1H 75
Stonepine Pl. DY3: Up Gor 1A 76
Stone Rd. B15: Edg 4F 117
Stonerwood Av. B28: Hall G 5E 135
Stones Grn. B23: Erd 1F 85
Stone St. B69: O'bry. 2G 97
 DY1: Dud 6E 77
 WV14: Bils 6G 45
Stoneton Cres. CV7: Bal C 3G 169
Stoneton Gro. B29: W Cas 5E 131
Stone Yd. B12: Birm 2H 117 (6H 5)
 B64: Crad H 3E 111
Stoneybrook Leys WV5: Wom 2E 73
Stoney Cl. B92: Sol 6A 138
Stoneycroft Twr. B36: Hodg H 1C 104
Stoneyford Gro.
 B14: Yard W. 3B 148
Stoneyhurst Rd. B24: Erd. 6F 85
Stoney La. B12: Bal H 6B 118
 B25: Yard 3B 120
 B32: Quin. 5H 113
 B71: W Brom 3B 80
 DY2: Neth 6E 95
 WS3: Blox 4H 19
  (not continuous)
 WV4: Penn 6F 43
Stoneymoor Dr. B36: Cas B 6G 87
Stoneythorpe Cl. B91: Sol 6F 151
Stonnal Gro. B23: Erd 1G 85
STONNALL. 3G 23
Stonnall Ga. WS9: A'rdge 1E 35
Stonnall Rd. WS9: A'rdge. 1E 35
Stonor Pk. Rd. B91: Sol. 2D 150
Stonor Rd. B28: Hall G 2G 149
Stony La. B67: Smeth 4D 98
Stony St. B67: Smeth 3D 98
Stornoway Rd. B35: Cas V 3F 87
Storrs Cl. B9: Small H 2D 118
Storrs Pl. B10: Small H 2D 118
Storrs Way, The B32: Bart G 6H 129
Stotfold Rd. B14: K Hth 5H 147
STOURBRIDGE 6E 109
Stourbridge Crematorium
 DY8: Stourb 1B 124
Stourbridge Ind. Est. DY8: Amb. 5E 109
Stourbridge Junction Station (Rail)
 . . . . .2F 125
Stourbridge Lawn Tennis & Squash Club
 . . . . .4A 124
Stourbridge Rd. B63: Hale. 6G 111
 DY1: Dud 4A 94
 DY3: Himl. 3A 74

Stourbridge Rd. DY5: Brie H 4A **94**
   DY9: Hag 6G **125**
   DY9: Lye 6G **109**
   WV4: Penn 5A **58**
   WV5: Wom. 2H **73**
Stourbridge Town Station (Rail) . . . 6E **109**
Stour Cl. B63: Hale. 5G **111**
Stourdale Rd. B64: Crad H. 4E **111**
Stourdell Rd. B63: Crad 5G **111**
Stour Hill DY5: Quar B 4C **110**
Stourmore Cl.
   WV12: W'hall 3D **30**
Stour St. B18: Hock 6C **100**
   B70: W Brom 4E **79**
Stourton Cl. B76: Walm 1D **70**
   B93: Know 2D **166**
Stourton Dr. WV4: Penn 6A **42**
Stourton Rd. B32: Quin 6H **113**
Stour Va. Rd. DY9: Lye 5B **110**
Stour Valley Cl. DY5: Quar B 4H **109**
Stourville Ind. Est. DY9: Lye 5B **110**
Stow Dr. DY5: Brie H 5F **109**
Stowell Rd. B44: K'sdng 6H **67**
Stowe St. WS3: Blox 2A **32**
Stow Gro. B36: Hodg H 2C **104**
STOW HEATH 4D **44**
Stowheath La. WV1: Wolv 4D **44**
Stow Heath Pl. WV1: Wolv 4D **44**
STOW LAWN 3E **45**
Stowmans Cl. WV14: Cose 2D **60**
Straight Rd. WV12: W'hall 3D **30**
STRAITS, THE 3E **75**
Straits, The DY3: Lwr G 2D **74**
Straits Est. DY3: Lwr G 3E **75**
Straits Grn. DY3: Lwr G 3F **75**
Straits Rd. DY3: Lwr G 4F **75**
Stratford Cl. B72: S Cold 2H **69**
   B90: Shir 1B **164**
Stratford Dr. WS9: A'rdge 1E **35**
Stratford Pl. B12: Birm. 3A **118**
Stratford Rd. B11: S'brk 4A **118**
   (not continuous)
   B28: Hall G. 2G **149**
   B90: M'path, Shir 3C **164**
   B94: H'ley H, Lapw 6F **165**
Stratford St. Nth. B11: S'brk 3A **118**
   (not continuous)
Stratford St. Sth. B11: S'hll 6C **118**
Stratford Wlk. B36: Hodg H 2A **104**
Strathdene Gdns. B29: S Oak 4G **131**
Strathdene Rd. B29: S Oak 3G **131**
Strathern Dr. WV14: Cose 4C **60**
Strathfield Wlk. WV4: Penn 5A **42**
Strathmore Cres.
   WV5: Wom. 4G **57**
Strathmore Rd. DY4: Tip 5A **62**
Stratton St. WV10: Wolv 5A **28**
Strawberry Cl. B69: Tiv 2C **96**
Strawberry Flds. CV7: Mer 4H **141**
Strawberry La.
   WS6: Gt Wyr 5E **7**
   WV13: W'hall 6E **29**
Strawberry La. Ind. Est.
   WV13: W'hall 1E **45**
Strawmoor La.
   WV8: Oaken, Cod 5B **12**
Stray, The DY5: P'ntt 3G **93**
Stream Mdw. WS4: S'fld 6G **21**
Stream Pk. DY6: K'wfrd 5C **92**
Stream Rd. DY6: K'wfrd 4B **92**
   (Greenfields Rd.)
   DY6: K'wfrd 5C **92**
   (Lesley Dr.)
   DY8: Word 4B **92**
Streamside Way B92: Sol 1H **137**
   WS4: S'fld 1H **33**
Streatham Gro. B44: K'sdng 3A **68**
Streather Rd. B75: R'ley 2A **54**
STREETLY 2H **51**
Streetly Crematorium
   WS9: A'rdge 1F **51**
Streetly Cres. B74: Four O 6D **36**
Streetly Dr. B74: Four O 6D **36**
Streetly La. B74: Four O 1C **52**
Streetly Rd. B23: Erd. 2D **84**
Streetly Wood B74: S'tly 1A **52**

Streetsbrook Rd. B90: Shir 1H **149**
   B91: Sol 2C **150**
Streets Cnr. Gdns.
   WS9: Wals W 3C **22**
Streets La. WS6: Gt Wyr 5E **7**
Strensham Cl. B13: Mose 1G **133**
Strensham Hill B13: Mose 1G **133**
Strensham Rd. B12: Bal H 1G **133**
Stretton Cl. B24: Erd 5E **85**
Stretton Gdns. WV8: Cod 3F **13**
Stretton Gro. B8: W End. 3A **104**
   B11: S'brk *5C* **118**
   (off Sydenham Rd.)
   B19: Loz 2E **101**
Stretton Pl. DY2: Neth 5C **94**
   WV14: Cose 4C **60**
Stretton Rd. B90: Shir 1H **163**
   WV12: W'hall 1C **30**
Stringer Cl. B75: Four O 5G **37**
Stringes Cl. WV13: W'hall 6C **30**
Stringes La. WV13: W'hall 1B **46**
Strode Rd. WV2: Wolv 5G **43**
Stronsay Cl. B45: Fran 6F **143**
Stroud Av. WV12: W'hall 5C **30**
Stroud Cl. WV12: W'hall. 5C **30**
Stroud Rd. B90: Shir. 5F **149**
Strutt Cl. B15: Edg 3H **115**
Stuart Cres. DY2: Dud 6G **77**
Stuart Ho. B46: Col 2H **107**
Stuart Rd. B62: Quin. 6F **113**
   B65: Row R 5C **96**
Stuarts Dr. B33: Stech 2B **120**
Stuarts Grn. DY9: Pedm 5F **125**
Stuarts Rd. B33: Stech. 1B **120**
Stuart St. B7: Nech. 2C **102**
   WS3: Blox 1H **31**
Stuarts Way B32: Bart G 6G **129**
STUBBERS GREEN 1A **34**
Stubbers Grn. Rd.
   WS9: A'rdge 6H **21**
Stubbington Cl.
   WV13: W'hall 2F **45**
Stubbs Rd. WV3: Wolv 4E **43**
Stubby La. WV11: Wed 3H **29**
Stubley Dr. WV10: Wolv. 3A **28**
Studland Rd. B28: Hall G 5G **135**
Stud La. B33: Stech. 6D **104**
Studley Cft. B92: Sol 1H **137**
Studley Dr. DY5: Brie H 3G **109**
Studley Ga. DY8: Stourb 1B **124**
Studley Rd. WV3: Wolv 3A **42**
Studley St. B12: Bal H 5B **118**
Studley Twr. *B12: Birm* 4H **117**
   (off Canford Cl.)
Sturman Dr. B65: B'hth 2B **112**
Suckling Grn. La. WV8: Cod 5F **13**
Sudbury Cl. WV11: Wed 1G **29**
Sudbury Gro. B44: K'sdng 3B **68**
Sudeley Cl. B36: Cas B 6F **87**
Sudeley Gdns. DY1: Dud. 5H **75**
Suffield Gro. B23: Erd 2B **84**
Suffolk Cl. B68: O'bry 5H **97**
   WV11: Wed 2E **29**
Suffolk Dr. DY5: Brie H 4G **109**
Suffolk Gro. WS9: A'rdge 1D **34**
Suffolk Ho. B23: Erd 2F **85**
Suffolk Pl. B1: Birm. 2F **117** (6D **4**)
   WS2: Wals 4B **32**
Suffolk Rd. DY2: Dud 2C **94**
Suffolk St. Queensway
   B1: Birm 1F **117** (5C **4**)
Suffrage St. B66: Smeth. 4F **99**
Sugar Loaf La. DY7: I'ley. 5A **124**
Sulgrave Cl. DY1: Dud. 4B **76**
Sumburgh Cft. B35: Cas V 4E **87**
Summercourt Dr.
   DY6: K'wfrd 3A **92**
Summercourt Ho. B29: S Oak 4F **131**
Summercourt Sq.
   DY6: K'wfrd 4A **92**
Summer Dr. DY3: Lwr G 4G **75**
Summerfield Av. B70: W Brom 3A **80**
   (not continuous)
   DY6: W Hth 2A **92**
Summerfield Cen. B18: Win G 5A **100**
Summerfield Ct. B15: Edg. 3G **115**

Summerfield Cres.
   B16: Edg 6A **100**
Summerfield Dr. B29: W Cas 6E **131**
Summerfield Gro. B18: Win G 5A **100**
Summerfield Ind. Est.
   B18: Win G 5C **100**
Summerfield Rd. B16: Edg 6A **100**
   B92: Olton 3E **137**
   DY2: Dud 2F **95**
Summerfields Av. B62: B'hth 3F **113**
Summergate DY3: Lwr G 4G **75**
SUMMER HILL 5A **62**
SUMMERHILL 5G **11**
Summer Hill B63: Hale. 2B **128**
   DY6: K'wfrd 3A **92**
Summer Hill Ind. Pk. *B1: Birm* 6D **100**
   (off Anderton St.)
Summer Hill Rd. B1: Birm. 6D **100**
   WV14: Cose 4F **61**
Summerhill Rd. DY4: Tip. 6H **61**
Summer Hill St. B1: Birm 6D **100**
Summer Hill Ter. B1: Birm . . . 6D **100** (3A **4**)
Summerhouse Rd.
   WV14: Cose 4C **60**
Summer La. B19: Birm 5F **101** (1D **4**)
   B76: Min 1H **87**
   DY3: Lwr G 4G **75**
   WS4: S'fld 5G **21**
Summerlee Rd. B24: Erd. 5H **85**
Summer Rd. B15: Edg 4E **117**
   (not continuous)
   B23: Erd 2F **85**
   B27: A Grn 3G **135**
   B65: Row R 6D **96**
   DY1: Dud 3C **76**
Summer Row B3: Birm 6E **101** (3A **4**)
   WV2: Wolv 2G **43** (4B **170**)
Summer St. B71: W Brom 3B **80**
   DY6: K'wfrd 3B **92**
   DY8: Stourb 6D **108**
   DY9: Lye. 6A **110**
   WV13: W'hall 1H **45**
Summerton Rd. B69: O'bry 6D **78**
Summerville Ter. B17: Harb 6G **115**
Summit, The DY9: W'cte 1H **125**
Summit Cres. B66: Smeth. 1C **98**
Summit Gdns. B63: Hale 2H **127**
Summit Pl. DY3: Gorn 5F **75**
Sumner Rd. B46: Col 3H **107**
Sunbeam Cl. B36: Cas B 6B **88**
Sunbeam Dr. WS6: Gt Wyr 2F **7**
Sunbeam St. WV2: Wolv 4G **43**
Sunbeam Way B33: Kitts G 1G **121**
Sunbury Cl. WV14: Cose 4G **61**
Sunbury Cotts. B31: N'fld 3E **145**
Sunbury Rd. B31: Longb 2C **158**
   B63: Hale 1H **127**
Suncroft B32: Quin 6A **114**
Sundbury Ri. B31: N'fld 2F **145**
Sunderland Dr. DY8: Amb 3E **109**
Sunderton Rd. B14: K Hth 2G **147**
Sundew Cft. B36: Hodg H 1B **104**
Sundial La. B43: Gt Barr 4B **66**
Sundour Cres. WV11: Wed 6D **16**
Sundridge Rd. B44: Gt Barr. 1G **67**
Sundridge Wlk. WV4: Penn 5A **42**
Sunleigh Gro. B27: A Grn 1C **136**
Sunningdale B62: Hale 1E **129**
Sunningdale Av. WV6: Pert 4D **24**
Sunningdale Cl. B20: Hand 3A **82**
   B73: W Grn 3G **69**
   DY8: Stourb 3D **124**
Sunningdale Dr. B69: Tiv 2A **96**
Sunningdale Rd. B11: Tys. 2G **135**
   DY3: Sed 5F **59**
Sunningdale Way WS3: Blox. 4G **19**
Sunny Av. B12: Bal H 6A **118**
Sunnybank Av. B44: K'sdng 6B **68**
Sunnybank Cl. WS9: A'rdge 1G **51**
Sunny Bank Ct. B68: O'bry 4A **114**
Sunny Bank Rd. B68: O'bry 4A **114**
Sunnybank Rd.
   B73: Bold, W Grn. 5G **69**
   DY3: Up Gor. 2B **76**
Sunnydale Wlk. B71: W Brom 3A **80**
Sunnydene B8: W End 4G **103**
Sunny Hill Cl. WV5: Wom 1H **73**

Sunnymead Rd. B26: Sheld . . . 5D **120**
Sunnymead Way B74: S'tly . . . 4H **51**
Sunnymede Rd.
DY6: K'wfrd . . . 5E **93**
Sunnyside B69: Tiv. . . . 2B **96**
WS9: Wals W. . . . 5C **22**
Sunnyside Av. B23: Erd . . . 4E **85**
Sunnyside Cl. CV7: Bal C. . . . 5H **169**
Sunnyside La. CV7: Bal C . . . 5H **169**
Sunnyside Ter. CV7: Bal C . . . 5H **169**
Sunridge Av. B19: Hock . . . 3F **101**
WV5: Wom. . . . 6G **57**
Sunrise Wlk. B68: O'bry . . . 6A **98**
Sunset Cl. WS6: Gt Wyr . . . 2F **7**
Sunset Pl. WV4: E'shll . . . 2B **60**
Sun St. DY5: Quar B. . . . 2B **110**
WS1: Wals . . . 4B **48**
(not continuous)
WV1: Wolv . . . 1A **44**
WV10: Wolv . . . 1A **44**
Surfeit Hill Rd. B64: Crad H. . . . 3F **111**
Surrey Cres. B71: W Brom . . . 5G **63**
Surrey Dr. DY6: K'wfrd. . . . 5D **92**
WV3: Wolv . . . 2C **42**
Surrey Rd. B44: Gt Barr. . . . 1G **67**
DY2: Dud . . . 2C **94**
Surrey Wlk. WS9: A'rdge . . . 6C **22**
Sussex Av. B71: W Brom . . . 1A **80**
WS9: A'rdge. . . . 1C **34**
WS10: W'bry . . . 1B **64**
Sussex Ct. B29: W Cas . . . 6G **131**
Sussex Dr. WV3: Wolv . . . 2C **42**
Sutherland Av. B90: Shir . . . 4A **150**
WV2: Wolv . . . 3B **44**
Sutherland Cl. B43: Gt Barr . . . 1F **67**
Sutherland Dr. B13: Mose . . . 1H **133**
WV5: Wom. . . . 5G **57**
Sutherland Gro. WV6: Pert. . . . 5F **25**
Sutherland Ho. WV1: Wolv . . . 1E **43**
Sutherland Pl. WV2: Wolv . . . 2H **43** (5D **170**)
Sutherland Rd. B64: Old H . . . 3G **111**
WS6: C Hay . . . 2E **7**
WV4: Penn . . . 6F **43**
Sutherland St. B6: Aston . . . 1B **102**
Sutton App. B8: W End . . . 5G **103**
Sutton Arts Theatre. . . . 1A **70**
Sutton Coalfield Crematorium
B75: S Cold . . . 1E **55**
SUTTON COLDFIELD . . . 6A **54**
Sutton Coldfield By-Pass
B75: Bass P, S Cold . . . 1F **55**
B76: Min, Wis . . . 1G **87**
Sutton Coldfield Station (Rail) . . . 6H **53**
Sutton Coldfield Tennis & Squash Club
. . . 3H **69**
Sutton Ct. B43: Gt Barr. . . . 6A **66**
B75: S Cold . . . 4A **54**
(not continuous)
WV4: E'shll. . . . 3A **60**
Sutton Cres. B70: W Brom. . . . 4G **79**
Sutton Lodge B91: Sol . . . 4E **151**
Sutton New Rd. B23: Erd . . . 3F **85**
Sutton Oak Cnr. B73: S'tly . . . 6A **52**
Sutton Oak Rd. B73: S'tly. . . . 1A **68**
Sutton Pk. . . . 4E **53**
Sutton Pk. Ct. B72: W Grn. . . . 3H **69**
Sutton Pk. Vis. Cen. . . . 6G **53**
Sutton Rd. B23: Erd . . . 2G **85**
B24: Erd. . . . 1H **85**
WS1: Wals . . . 3D **48**
WS5: Wals . . . 3F **49**
WS10: Mox . . . 6A **46**
Suttons Dr. B43: Gt Barr. . . . 1B **66**
Sutton Sq. B76: Min. . . . 1A **88**
Sutton St. B1: Birm. . . . 2F **117**
B6: Aston . . . 3H **101**
DY8: Word . . . 2C **108**
Suttton Rd. WS9: A'rdge . . . 2A **50**
Swains Gro. B44: Gt Barr. . . . 1H **67**
Swale Gro. B38: K Nor. . . . 6B **146**
WV13: W'hall . . . 1D **46**
Swale Rd. B76: Walm . . . 4E **71**
Swallow Av. B36: Cas B . . . 1C **106**
Swallow Cl. B12: Bal H . . . 6B **118**
DY2: Neth . . . 1F **111**
WS10: W'bry . . . 1H **63**
Swallow Ct. WV10: Bush . . . 2H **27**
Swallowdale WS9: Wals W . . . 3D **22**
WV6: Tett . . . 1F **41**
Swallowfall Av. DY8: Stourb . . . 1A **124**
Swallowfields Rd. DY3: Sed . . . 3G **59**
Swallows Cl. WS3: Pels. . . . 2E **21**
Swallows Mdw. B90: Shir . . . 1B **164**
(not continuous)
Swallows Ri. Bus. Pk. DY5: Brie H . . . 6A **94**
Swallow St. B2: Birm . . . 1F **117** (5C **4**)
B70: W Brom. . . . 3G **79**
Swanage Rd. B10: Small H . . . 3D **118**
Swan Av. B66: Smeth. . . . 2C **98**
Swan Bank WV4: Penn. . . . 1D **58**
Swan Cl. WS6: C Hay. . . . 3D **6**
Swan Copse B25: Yard. . . . 6A **120**
Swancote Dr. WV4: Penn . . . 5A **42**
Swancote Rd. B33: Stech . . . 4D **104**
DY1: Dud . . . 6D **76**
Swancote St. DY1: Dud . . . 1C **94**
Swan Courtyard B26: Yard. . . . 5B **120**
Swan Cres. B69: O'bry . . . 5F **97**
Swancroft Rd. DY4: Tip . . . 5H **61**
Swan Dr. WS8: Bwnhls . . . 6A **10**
Swanfield Rd. DY8: Word . . . 2D **108**
Swan Gdns. B23: Erd . . . 3F **85**
Swanhurst Community Leisure Cen. . . . 6A **134**
Swan Island B25: Yard. . . . 5B **120**
Swan La. B70: W Brom . . . 2G **79**
DY8: Word. . . . 1D **108**
Swan La. Ind. Est. B70: W Brom. . . . 2G **79**
Swanley Cl. B62: Quin. . . . 2G **129**
Swanmore Cl. WV3: Wolv . . . 3C **42**
Swann Rd. WV14: Cose . . . 3C **60**
Swann Wlk. DY4: Tip . . . 5A **62**
Swan Pool Gro. WS4: S'fld . . . 6H **21**
Swan Rdbt. B70: W Brom. . . . 2F **79**
Swansbrook Gdns. B38: K Nor. . . . 5E **147**
Swan Shop. Cen., The B25: Yard . . . 5B **120**
Swanshurst La. B13: Mose . . . 5C **134**
Swan St. DY2: Neth . . . 3E **95**
DY5: P'ntt . . . 2G **93**
DY8: Stourb. . . . 6C **108**
WV1: Wolv. . . . 1B **44**
Swanswell Rd. B92: Olton. . . . 5B **136**
Swanswood Gro. B37: Chel W . . . 6E **107**
SWAN VILLAGE
Bilston. . . . 6D **60**
West Bromwich . . . 2G **79**
Swan Village B70: W Brom. . . . 2G **79**
Swan Village Ind. Est. B70: W Brom . . . 2G **79**
Swarthmore Rd. B29: W Cas . . . 6E **131**
Sweetbriar La. WV12: W'hall. . . . 4D **30**
Sweetbriar Rd. WV2: E'shll . . . 4C **44**
Sweetbrier Dr. DY8: Word . . . 2C **108**
Sweetman Pl. WV6: Wolv . . . 6E **27**
Sweetman St. WV6: Wolv . . . 5D **26**
(not continuous)
Sweetmoor Cl. B36: Cas B. . . . 1G **105**
Swift Cl. B36: Cas B. . . . 1C **106**
Swinbrook Gro. B44: Gt Barr. . . . 4G **67**
Swinbrook Way B90: Shir . . . 3B **150**
Swincross Rd. DY8: Stourb . . . 1F **125**
Swindell Rd. DY9: Pedm . . . 4G **125**
SWINDON . . . 5E **73**
Swindon Rd. B17: Edg . . . 6F **99**
DY6: K'wfrd . . . 1F **91**
Swinford Gro. B93: Dorr . . . 6A **166**
Swinford Leys WV5: Wom . . . 2D **72**
Swinford Rd. B29: W Cas. . . . 2E **131**
DY8: Stourb . . . 3E **125**
WV10: Wolv. . . . 4A **28**
Swin Forge Way DY3: Swind . . . 5E **73**
Swiss Dr. DY8: Word . . . 1D **108**
Swynnerton Dr. WV11: Ess . . . 3H **17**
Sycamore Av. B12: Bal H. . . . 6A **118**
Sycamore Cl. B24: Erd . . . 4F **85**
B76: Walm . . . 3D **70**
DY8: Stourb . . . 3B **124**
WS4: S'fld . . . 1F **33**
Sycamore Ct. B23: Erd. . . . 6C **68**
B30: K Nor . . . 3A **146**
Sycamore Cres. B24: Erd . . . 4F **85**
B37: Mars G. . . . 3C **122**
DY4: Tip. . . . 6H **61**
Sycamore Dr. B47: H'wd . . . 4A **162**
WV3: Wolv. . . . 2B **42**
Sycamore Grn. DY1: Dud. . . . 2B **76**
Sycamore Ho. B13: Mose . . . 2A **134**
B31: N'fld . . . 4F ***145***
(off Rectory Rd.)
Sycamore Ind. Est. B21: Hand. . . . 2H **99**
Sycamore Paddock DY8: Word . . . 2E **109**
Sycamore Pl. B67: Smeth . . . 5D **98**
WV14: Bils . . . 2A **62**
Sycamore Rd. B6: Aston . . . 1A **102**
B21: Hand . . . 2H **99**
B23: Erd . . . 6F **69**
B30: B'vlle . . . 6B **132**
B43: Gt Barr. . . . 2A **66**
B66: Smeth. . . . 6F **99**
B69: O'bry . . . 5G **97**
DY6: K'wfrd . . . 3C **92**
WS4: S'fld . . . 1F **33**
WS5: Wals. . . . 6D **48**
WS10: W'bry . . . 3G **63**
Sycamores, The WV10: Bush . . . 1B **28**
Sycamore Ter. B14: K Hth . . . 1E **147**
Sycamore Way B27: A Grn. . . . 1A **136**
Sydenham Rd. B11: S'brk . . . 5C **118**
B66: Smeth . . . 2E **99**
WV1: Wolv. . . . 1D **44**
Sydney Cl. B70: W Brom. . . . 6G **63**
Sydney Ho. B34: S End . . . 3A **106**
Sydney Rd. B9: Bord G . . . 1C **118**
B64: Crad H . . . 2E **111**
B67: Smeth . . . 1C **114**
Sylvan Av. B31: N'fld . . . 4D **144**
Sylvan Grn. B62: Hale . . . 6D **112**
Sylvan Gro. B90: Shir . . . 2H **149**
Sylvia Av. B31: Longb . . . 1F **159**
Symphony Ct. *B16: Birm . . . 1D* ***116***
(off Delius Ho.)
Sych La. WV5: Wom. . . . 2G **73**

T

Tack Farm Rd. DY8: Word. . . . 2B **108**
Tackford Cl. B36: Cas B. . . . 6G **87**
Tackley Cl. B90: Shir . . . 1H **163**
Tadmore Cl. WV14: Bils . . . 6E **45**
Tadworth Cl. WV1: Wolv . . . 1C **44**
Tait Cft. B92: Sol . . . 5B **138**
Talaton Cl. WV9: Pend . . . 5E **15**
Talbot Av. B74: Lit A. . . . 6B **36**
Talbot Cl. B23: Erd. . . . 5D **68**
WS2: Wals . . . 3A **32**
Talbot Pas. *DY8: Stourb. . . . 6E* ***109***
(off Talbot St.)
Talbot Pl. WV14: Bils . . . 5E **45**
Talbot Rd. B66: Smeth . . . 6E **99**
DY2: Neth . . . 5D **94**
WV2: Wolv. . . . 5G **43**
Talbots La. DY5: Brie H . . . 2A **110**
Talbot St. B18: Hock . . . 3B **100**
B63: Crad . . . 5E **111**
DY5: Brie H . . . 6H **93**
(Adelaide St.)
DY5: Brie H . . . 6H **93**
(Albion St.)
DY8: Stourb . . . 6E **109**
DY9: Lye. . . . 6B **110**
Talbot Way B10: Small H . . . 4F **119**
Talfourd St. B9: Small H . . . 2D **118**
Talgarth Covert B38: K Nor . . . 2A **160**
Talke Rd. WS5: Wals . . . 6D **48**
Talladale B32: Bart G. . . . 6H **129**
Tallington Rd. B33: Sheld . . . 4G **121**
Tall Trees Cl. B74: Four O . . . 5D **36**
WV12: W'hall . . . 3D **30**
Tall Trees Dr. DY9: Pedm. . . . 3H **125**
Talton Cl. B90: M'path . . . 4E **165**
Tamar Cl. WS8: Bwnhls. . . . 3G **9**
Tamar Dr. B36: Cas B. . . . 1B **106**
B76: Walm . . . 6F **71**
DY3: Sed . . . 1B **76**
Tamar Gro. WV6: Pert . . . 5E **25**
WV13: W'hall . . . 1C **46**
Tamarisk Cl. B29: W Cas . . . 5F **131**
Tamar Ri. DY8: Amb . . . 3E **109**
Tame Av. WS10: W'bry . . . 1H **63**
Tame Bri. WS5: Wals. . . . 1D **64**
Tame Bri. Factory Est. WS5: Wals . . . 3F **65**
Tamebridge Ind. Est. B42: P Barr . . . 3G **83**

Tame Bridge Parkway Station (Rail)
. . . . 3D 64
Tame Cl. WS1: Wals 5C 48
Tame Cres. B71: W Brom 1A 80
Tame Dr. WS3: Pels 6E 21
Tame Ri. B68: O'bry 3H 113
Tame Rd. B6: Witt 5A 84
  B68: O'bry 3G 113
  DY4: Tip 2C 78
Tame Rd. Ind. Est. B6: Witt 6A 84
Tamerton Rd. B32: Bart G 4B 130
Tameside Dr. B6: Witt 3H 83
  B35: Cas V 6D 86
Tame St. B70: W Brom 5F 63
  WS1: Wals 5C 48
  WV14: Bils 6H 45
Tame St. E. WS1: Wals 5D 48
Tamworth Cl. WS8: Bwnhls 3B 10
Tamworth Rd. B75: Bass P 1F 55
  B75: S Cold 4A 54
Tanacetum Dr. WS5: Wals 2F 65
Tandy Ct. B14: K Hth 4H 147
Tandy Dr. B14: K Hth 4H 147
Tanfield Cl. WV6: Tett 6H 25
Tanfield Rd. B33: Stech 6D 104
  DY2: Dud 2D 94
Tanford Rd. B92: Sol 2G 137
Tanglewood Cl. B32: Quin 6H 113
  B34: S End 4G 105
Tanglewood Gro. DY3: Sed 3G 59
Tangmere Cl. WV6: Pert. 4E 25
Tangmere Dr. B35: Cas V 5D 86
Tangmere Sq. B35: Cas V 4D 86
Tanhouse Av. B43: Gt Barr 6G 65
Tanhouse Farm Rd. B92: Sol 3G 137
Tanhouse La. B63: Crad 5D 110
Tanners Cl. B75: S Cold 4D 54
Tanners La. WS1: Wals 3C 48
Tannery Cl. WS2: Wals 6B 32
Tansey B74: Four O. 4F 37
Tansey Ct. DY5: P'ntt 2F 93
TANSEY GREEN 2F 93
Tansey Grn. Rd. DY5: P'ntt 6E 75
Tansley Cl. B93: Dorr. 5B 166
Tansley Gro. B44: K'sdng 4H 67
Tansley Hill Av. DY2: Dud 1H 95
Tansley Hill Rd. DY2: Dud 1G 95
Tansley Rd. B44: K'sdng 5H 67
Tansley Vw. WV2: Wolv 4H 43
Tantallon Dr. B32: Bart G 4B 130
Tantany La. B71: W Brom 3A 80
Tantarra St. WS1: Wals 2D 48
                                (not continuous)
Tanwood Cl. B91: Sol 1F 165
Tanworth Gro. B12: Bal H 5H 117
Tanworth La. B90: Shir 2H 163
Tanyards B27: A Grn 2A 136
Tapestries Av. B70: W Brom 3G 79
Tapton Cl. WS3: Blox 4A 20
Tarmac Rd. WV4: E'shll 6D 44
Tarragon Gdns. B31: Longb 5A 144
Tarrant Gro. B32: Harb. 6D 114
Tarrington Covert
  B38: K Nor 1A 160
Tarry Hollow Rd. DY5: P'ntt 1F 93
Tarry Rd. B8: Salt 5E 103
Tarvin M. DY5: Brie H 2H 109
Taryn Dr. WS10: Darl 4D 46
Tasker St. B70: W Brom 3E 79
  WS1: Wals 3B 48
Tasman Gro. WV6: Pert 4E 25
TAT BANK 3H 97
Tat Bank Rd. B68: O'bry 3H 97
  B69: O'bry 2G 97
Taunton Av. WV10: F'hses 3H 15
Taunton Cl. B31: Longb 4A 144
Taunton Rd. B12: Bal H 1A 134
Taverners Cl. WV12: W'hall 6C 18
Taverners Grn. B20: Hand 4B 82
Tavistock Rd. B27: A Grn 6A 136
Taw Cl. B36: Cas B. 1B 106
Tay Cft. B37: F'bri 5E 107
Tay Gro. B38: K Nor 1B 160
  B62: B'hth 3E 113
Taylor Av. WS3: Blox 1B 32
Taylor Ho. WS2: Wals 4A 48
                                (off Oxford St.)

Taylor Rd. B13: Mose 2H 147
  DY2: Neth 1G 111
  WV4: E'shll 6B 44
Taylors La. B69: O'bry 2E 97
  B71: W Brom 3B 80
  B67: Smeth 4D 98
Taylors Orchard B23: Erd 3B 84
Taylor St. WV11: Wed 4F 29
Taylor Way B69: Tiv 1B 96
Taynton Covert B30: K Nor 4E 147
Tay Rd. B45: Fran 6H 143
Taysfield Rd. B31: N'fld 1C 144
Taywood Dr. B10: Small H 4C 118
Tealby Gro. B29: S Oak 4C 132
Teal Dr. B23: Erd 4B 84
Teal Gro. WS10: Mox. 2B 62
Teall Ct. B27: A Grn 2A 136
Teall Rd. B8: Salt 4E 103
Tean Cl. B11: Tys 2G 135
Teasdale Way DY9: W'cte 1H 125
Teasel Rd. WV11: Wed 4G 29
Teazel Av. B30: B'ville 1H 145
Tebworth Cl. WV9: Pend 5D 14
Tedbury Cres. B23: Erd 1E 85
Tedder Rd. WS2: Wals 1F 47
Teddesley Gro. B33: Kitts G 5G 105
Teddesley St. WS4: Wals 6D 32
Teddington Cl. B73: S Cold 3G 69
Teddington Gro. B42: P Barr 4F 83
Tedstone Rd. B32: Quin 6C 114
Teesdale Av. B34: Hodg H 3D 104
Teesdale Cl. WV1: Wolv 1C 44
Tees Gro. B38: K Nor 1B 160
Teignmouth Rd.
  B29: S Oak 3B 132
Telford Av. WS6: Gt Wyr. 2F 7
Telford Cl. B67: Smeth 2B 114
  B71: W Brom 5G 63
  WS2: Wals 4G 31
Telford Gdns. WV3: Wolv 4B 42
Telford Rd. WS2: Wals 4G 31
Telford Way B66: Smeth 2D 98
Teme Gro. WV13: W'hall 1D 46
Teme Rd. B63: Crad 6D 110
  DY8: Stourb 2D 124
Tempest St. WV2: Wolv 2H 43 (4C 170)
Templars, The B69: O'bry 4E 97
Templars Wlk. WV13: W'hall 6A 30
Temple Av. B28: Hall G 1G 149
  CV7: Bal C 3F 169
TEMPLE BALSALL 5C 168
Temple Bar WV13: W'hall 1A 46
Temple Ct. B46: Col 6H 89
Templefield Gdns. B9: Bord G 2C 118
Templefield Sq. B15: Edg 4D 116
Templefield St. B9: Bord G 2C 118
Temple La. B93: Know. 6A 168
Temple Mdws. Rd.
  B71: W Brom 2C 80
Templemore Dr. B43: Gt Barr 6A 66
Temple Pas. B2: Birm 1F 117 (4D 4)
Temple Rd. B93: Dorr 6C 166
  WV13: W'hall 6A 30
Temple Row B2: Birm 1F 117 (4D 4)
Temple Row W. B2: Birm 1F 117 (3D 4)
Temple Sq. WV13: W'hall 6B 30
Temple St. B2: Birm 1F 117 (4D 4)
  B70: W Brom 3A 80
  DY3: Lwr G 4H 75
  WV2: Wolv 2G 43 (4B 170)
  WV14: Bils 6G 45
Templeton Cl. B93: Dorr 6C 166
Templeton Rd. B44: Gt Barr 3G 67
Temple Way B46: Col 6G 89
  B69: Tiv 5C 78
Tenacre La. DY3: Up Gor 1A 76
TEN ACRES 5D 132
Ten Acres End B30: Stir 5D 132
Ten Acres Works B30: Stir 5D 132
Ten Ashes La. B45: Coft H 5A 158
Tenbury Cl. WS2: Wals 6D 30
  WS9: A'rdge 1E 35
Tenbury Gdns. WV4: Penn 6B 42
Tenbury Gdns. WV4: Penn 1B 58
Tenbury Ho. B63: Hale 2A 128
                                (off Highfield La.)
Tenbury Rd. B14: K Hth 1F 147

Tenby Ct. B29: W Cas 6G 131
                                (off Tugford Rd.)
Tenby Rd. B13: Mose. 4D 134
Tenby St. B1: Birm 5D 100 (1A 4)
Tenby St. Nth. B1: Birm 5D 100 (1A 4)
Tenby Twr. B31: N'fld 6E 145
Tenlands Rd. B63: Hale 2H 127
Tennal Dr. B32: Harb 5D 114
Tennal Gro. B32: Harb 5D 114
Tennal La. B32: Harb 6C 114
Tennal Rd. B32: Harb 5C 114
Tennant St. B15: Birm 2D 116 (6A 4)
Tennis Ct. B30: K Nor 3H 145
Tennis Ct., The B15: Edg 6C 116
Tennis Ct. Flats B15: Edg 6C 116
Tennscore Av. WS6: C Hay 2E 7
Tennyson Av. B74: Four O 3F 37
Tennyson Ho. B31: Longb 1E 159
  B68: O'bry 5A 98
Tennyson Rd. B10: Small H 4E 119
  DY3: Lwr G 2E 75
  WS3: Blox 1C 32
  WV10: Bush 6C 16
  WV12: W'hall 1E 31
Tennyson St. DY5: P'ntt 3H 93
Tenter Ct. B63: Hale 1B 128
Tenter Dr. B63: Hale 1B 128
Tenterfields B63: Hale 1B 128
Tern Cl. WV4: E'shll 2H 59
Tern Gro. B38: K Nor 6A 146
Terrace, The B64: Crad H 3G 111
  WV3: Wolv 2A 42
Terrace Rd. B15: Edg 2B 132
  B19: Hock 2C 100
Terrace St. B65: Row R 2B 112
  DY5: Brie H 4A 94
  WS10: W'bry 2G 63
Terry Dr. B76: Walm. 4D 70
Terrys La. B24: Erd 4A 86
Terry St. DY2: Dud 6F 77
Tessall La. B31: Longb 6H 143
                                (not continuous)
Tetbury Gro. B31: N'fld. 4B 144
Tetley Av. WS4: Wals 5F 33
Tetley Rd. B11: S'hll 2E 135
Tetnall St. DY2: Dud 1F 95
TETTENHALL 5A 26
Tettenhall Rd. WV6: Wolv 5C 26
TETTENHALL WOOD 1G 41
Teviot Gdns. DY5: P'ntt 3E 93
  WV8: Bilb 2G 13
Teviot Gro. B38: K Nor 1B 160
Teviot Twr. B19: Birm 4E 101
                                (off Mosborough Cres.)
Tewkesbury Dr. DY2: Neth 6F 95
Tewkesbury Rd. B20: Hand 6G 83
  WS3: Blox 5E 19
Tew Pk. Rd. B21: Hand 2A 100
Thackeray Rd. B30: B'ville 2H 145
Thames Cl. DY5: P'ntt 2F 93
Thames Ct. B47: Wyt. 6G 161
                                (off Chapel La.)
  B73: S Cold 6H 53
Thames Gdns. WV14: Cose 4C 60
Thames Rd. WS3: Blox 1B 32
Thames Twr. B7: Nech 4B 102
Thanet Cl. DY6: K'wfrd. 3A 92
Thanet Gro. B42: P Barr 3E 83
Thatchers, The B62: B'hth 3E 113
Thatchway Gdns. B38: K Nor 2A 160
Thaxted Rd. B33: Kitts G 1A 106
Theatre App. B5: Birm 2G 117 (6E 5)
Thelbridge Rd. B31: Longb 3C 158
Thelma Rd. DY4: Tip 2G 77
Thelma St. WS1: Wals 4B 48
Thelsford Way B92: Sol 5H 137
Theodore Cl. B17: Harb 1H 131
  B69: O'bry 6E 79
Theresa Rd. B11: S'brk 4B 118
The Swallows Ind. Est.
  B90: Shir 1B 164
Thetford Cl. DY4: Tip 2F 77
Thetford Gdns. WV11: Wed 3F 29
Thetford Rd. B42: Gt Barr 6D 66
Thetford Way WS5: Wals 2G 65
Thickett Cl. WS2: Wals 3H 47
Thicknall Dr. DY9: Pedm 3F 125

Thimble Dr. B76: Walm 4D **70**
THIMBLE END 4D **70**
Thimble End Rd. B76: Walm 2D **70**
Thimble La. B93: Know 3E **167**
Thimble Mill La. B6: Aston 2B **102**
B7: Nech 2B **102**
Thimblemill Rd. B67: Smeth 5B **98**
Thinktank 6H 101 (3H 5)
Third Av. B6: Witt 4H **83**
B9: Bord G 1F **119**
B29: S Oak 2E **133**
DY6: P'ntt 1D **92**
WS8: Bwnhls 4C **10**
WV10: Bush 2A **28**
Third Exhibition Av.
B40: Nat E C 1F **139**
Third Rd. B61: Wild 5A **156**
Thirlmere Cl. WV6: Tett 1B **26**
Thirlmere Dr. B13: Mose 5C **134**
WV11: Ess 5A **18**
Thirlmere Gro. WV6: Pert 5F **25**
Thirlmere Ho. B15: Edg 2H **131**
Thirlmere Rd. WV6: Tett 1B **26**
Thirlmere Wlk. DY5: Brie H 4F **109**
Thirsk Cft. B36: Hodg H 1A **104**
Thirston Cl. WV11: Wed 4A **30**
Thistle Cl. DY3: Sed 1B **76**
Thistle Cft. WV11: Wed 4F **29**
Thistle Down Cl. B74: S'tly 1A **52**
Thistledown Rd. B34: S End 2G **105**
Thistledown Wlk. DY3: Sed 4G **59**
Thistle Grn. B38: K Nor 2A **160**
Thistle Grn. Cl. B65: Row R 4H **95**
Thistlegreen Rd. DY2: Neth 5G **95**
Thistle Ho. B36: Hodg H 1B **104**
Thistle La. B32: Bart G 5H **129**
Thomas Benson Pl. B12: Birm 4H **117**
Thomas Cres. B66: Smeth 4G **99**
Thomas Guy Rd. B70: W Brom 6E **63**
Thomas Ho. WS3: Blox 4B **20**
Thomas Mason Cl.
WV11: Wed 2F **29**
Thomas St. B6: Aston 3H **101**
B66: Smeth 4F **99**
B70: W Brom 5B **80**
WS2: Wals 1B **48**
WV2: Wolv 3G **43** (6B **170**)
Thomas Wlk. B35: Cas V 4F **87**
Thompson Av. WV2: Wolv 4H **43**
Thompson Cl. DY2: Neth 1D **110**
WV13: W'hall 6A **30**
Thompson Dr. B24: Erd 1F **103**
Thompson Gdns. B67: Smeth 5D **98**
Thompson Ho. DY4: Tip 5C **62**
Thompson Rd. B67: Smeth 5D **98**
B68: O'bry 5H **97**
Thompson St. WV13: W'hall 6A **30**
WV14: Bils 6F **45**
Thomson Av. B38: K Nor 6G **145**
Thoresby Cft. DY1: Dud 4B **76**
Thornberry Dr. DY1: Dud 1H **93**
Thornberry Wlk. B7: Nech 3C **102**
Thornbridge Av. B42: Gt Barr 6E **67**
Thornbridge Gro. WS9: Wals W 4B **22**
Thorn Brook Ct. *WS4: Wals* *6D **32***
(off Butts Rd.)
Thornbury Ct. WV6: Pert 6G **25**
Thornbury Rd. B20: Hand 5F **83**
Thornby Av. B91: Sol 2F **151**
Thornby Rd. B23: Erd 5C **68**
Thorncliffe Rd. B44: Gt Barr 3G **67**
Thorn Cl. WS10: W'bry 1F **63**
Thorncroft Way WS5: Wals 1F **65**
Thorne Av. WV10: Bush 2A **28**
Thorne Pl. B65: Row R 1C **112**
Thorne Rd. WV13: W'hall 6A **30**
THORNES 4G **23**
Thornes Cft. WS9: Ston 3G **23**
Thorne St. WV2: E'shll 4C **44**
Thorneycroft La. WV10: Wolv 4C **28**
Thorneycroft Pl. WV14: Bils 2B **62**
Thorneycroft Rd. WV14: Bils 2A **62**
Thorneyfield Rd. B90: Shir 4A **150**
Thorney Rd. B74: S'tly 2H **51**
Thornfield Cft. DY3: Sed 6A **60**
Thornfield Rd. B27: A Grn 3A **136**
Thorngrove Av. B91: Sol 1G **165**
Thornham Way B14: K Hth 6F **147**
Thornhill Gro. B21: Hand 1B **100**
Thornhill Pk. B74: S'tly 3A **52**
Thornhill Rd. B11: S'hll 2D **134**
B21: Hand 2B **100**
B63: Hale 2G **127**
B74: S'tly 5A **52**
B91: Sol 6G **137**
DY1: Dud 3E **77**
DY5: Quar B 2A **110**
Thornhurst Av. B32: Quin 4C **114**
Thornleigh DY3: Up Gor 2H **75**
Thornleigh Trad. Est.
DY2: Dud 2C **94**
Thornley Cl. B13: Mose 4A **134**
WV11: Wed 6H **17**
Thornley Cft. WS6: C Hay 4D **6**
Thornley Gro. B76: Min 1G **87**
Thornley Rd. WV11: Wed 6H **17**
Thornley St. WV1: Wolv 1H **43** (2C **170**)
Thorn Rd. B30: B'vlle 6A **132**
Thorns Av. DY5: Quar B 2A **110**
Thornsett Gro. B90: Shir 1H **149**
Thorns Leisure Cen. 3A 110
Thorns Rd. DY5: Quar B 4A **110**
Thornthwaite Cl. B45: Fran 5H **143**
Thornton Cl. B69: Tiv 5C **78**
Thornton Dr. DY5: Brie H 2A **110**
Thornton Ho. *B19: Hock* *4G **101***
(off Ruddington Way)
Thornton Rd. B8: W End 4H **103**
B90: M'path 3D **164**
WV1: Wolv 2D **44**
Thornwood Cl. B68: O'bry 4A **98**
Thornyfield Cl. B90: Shir 4A **150**
Thorpe Cl. B75: S Cold 3A **54**
Thorpe Ct. B91: Sol 1D **150**
Thorpe Rd. WS1: Wals 4C **48**
Thorp St. B5: Birm 2F **117** (6D **4**)
Three Acres La. B90: Dic H 3F **163**
Three Cnr. Cl. B90: Maj G 1E **163**
Three Leasows DY4: Tip 2C **78**
THREE MAYPOLES 3H **163**
Three Oaks Rd. B47: Wyt 5C **162**
Three Shires Oak Rd.
B67: Smeth 1D **114**
Three Tuns La. WV10: Oxl 5G **15**
Three Tuns Pde. WV10: Oxl 5G **15**
Threshers Dr. WV12: W'hall 3D **30**
Threshers Way WV12: W'hall 3D **30**
Throne Cl. B65: Row R 4C **96**
Throne Cres. B65: Row R 4D **96**
Throne Rd. B65: Row R 4C **96**
Throstles Cl. B43: Gt Barr 6A **66**
Thrushel Wlk. WV11: Wed 4E **29**
Thrush Rd. B68: O'bry 1F **113**
Thruxton Cl. B14: K Hth 4H **147**
Thurcroft Cl. B8: W End 5F **103**
Thuree Rd. B67: Smeth 1C **114**
Thurleigh Cl. DY9: Pedm 3G **125**
Thurlestone Rd. B31: Longb 2C **158**
Thurloe Cres. B45: Fran 6E **143**
Thurlston Av. B92: Olton 1D **136**
Thurlstone Dr. WV4: Penn 1D **58**
Thurlstone Rd. WS3: Blox 4H **19**
Thursfield Rd. B71: W Brom 5C **64**
DY4: Tip 1A **78**
Thurston Av. B69: O'bry 3F **97**
Thynne St. B70: W Brom 5C **80**
Tibbats Cl. B32: Bart G 2A **130**
Tibberton Cl. B63: Hale 2C **128**
B91: Sol 1E **165**
WV3: Wolv 4B **42**
Tibbets La. B17: Harb 1E **131**
Tibbington Rd. DY4: Tip 6G **61**
Tibbington Ter. DY4: Tip 6G **61**
Tibbits Ho. *WS2: Wals* *6B **32***
(off Burrowes St.)
Tibblestone B90: Dic H 4G **163**
Tiberius Cl. B46: Col 6H **89**
Tibland Rd. B27: A Grn 4A **136**
TIDBURY GREEN 5E **163**
Tiddington Cl. B36: Cas B 6F **87**
Tideswell Rd. B42: Gt Barr 1E **83**
Tidmarsh Cl. CV7: Bal C 3G **169**
Tidworth Cft. B14: K Hth 4A **148**
Tierney Dr. DY4: Tip 1C **78**
Tiffany La. WV9: Pend 5D **14**
Tiffield Rd. B25: Yard 6A **120**
Tigley Av. B32: Bart G 4B **130**
Tilbury Cl. WV3: Wolv 3G **41**
Tilbury Gro. B13: Mose 4F **133**
Tildasley St. B70: W Brom 2H **79**
Tildesley Dr. WV12: W'hall 4B **30**
TILE CROSS 1G **121**
Tile Cross Rd. B33: Kitts G 2H **121**
Tile Cross Trad. Est.
B33: Kitts G 2H **121**
Tiled Ho. La. DY5: P'ntt 4F **93**
Tile Gro. B37: K'hrst 4C **106**
TILEHOUSE GREEN 2B **166**
Tilehouse Grn. La.
B93: Know 2B **166**
Tilehouse La. B90: Tid G 5E **163**
Tilesford Cl. B90: M'path 4E **165**
Tiller Gro. B75: R'ley 5B **38**
Tilley St. WS10: Darl 5E **47**
Tillyard Cft. B29: S Oak 4G **131**
Tilshead Cl. B14: K Hth 4G **147**
Tilsley Gro. B23: Erd 2B **84**
Tilston Dr. DY5: Brie H 2H **109**
Tilton Rd. B9: Bord G 2C **118**
(not continuous)
Timbercombe Way B21: Hand 1H **99**
Timberdine Cl. B63: Crad 5F **111**
Timberlake Cl. B90: M'path 3F **165**
Timberley Cft. B34: S End 2H **105**
Timberley La. B34: S End 3G **105**
(not continuous)
Timber Mill Ct. B17: Harb 5F **115**
Timbers Way B11: S'brk 5A **118**
B24: Erd 3D **86**
Timbertree Cres. B64: Crad H 4G **111**
Timbertree Rd. B64: Crad H 4G **111**
Times Sq. Av. DY5: Brie H 1A **110**
Timmins Cl. B91: Sol 2A **152**
Timmis Cl. WV14: Cose 2D **60**
Timmis Rd. DY9: Lye 5G **109**
Timothy Rd. B69: Tiv 2C **96**
Tinacre Hill WV6: Tett 1E **41**
Tinchbourne St. DY1: Dud 6E **77**
Tindal St. B12: Bal H 6H **117**
Tinker's Farm Gro. B31: N'fld 4C **144**
Tinker's Farm Rd. B31: N'fld 4C **144**
Tinmeadow Cres. B45: Redn 2A **158**
Tinsley St. DY4: Tip 2E **79**
Tintagel Cl. WV6: Pert 6F **25**
Tintagel Dr. DY1: Dud 5A **76**
Tintagel Way WS9: A'rdge 3A **34**
Tintern Cl. B74: S'tly 4A **52**
Tintern Ct. WV6: Pert 5E **25**
Tintern Cres. WS3: Blox 4F **19**
Tintern Ho. B32: Harb 6D **114**
Tintern Rd. B20: Hand 6G **83**
Tintern Vs. *B12: Bal H* *6B **118***
(off Chesterton Rd.)
Tintern Way WS3: Blox 5F **19**
Tipperary Cl. B36: Hodg H 1C **104**
Tipperary Wlk. B69: O'bry 2F **97**
Tipper Trad. Est. DY9: Lye 6C **110**
Tippity Grn. B65: Row R 5B **96**
Tipps Stone Cl. DY4: Tip 3G **77**
TIPTON 2F **77**
Tipton Ind. Est. WV14: Cose 6F **61**
Tipton Leisure Cen. 4A 62
Tipton Rd. B69: Tiv 4B **78**
DY1: Dud 3G **77**
DY3: Sed 6A **60**
Tipton Station (Rail) 1H **77**
Tipton St. DY3: Sed 6A **60**
Tipton Swimming Cen. 2H 77
Tipton Trad. Est. WV14: Cose 6F **61**
Tirley Rd. B33: Stech 4E **105**
Titania Cl. B45: Fran 4H **143**
Titchfield Cl. WV10: Bush 3A **16**
Titford Cl. B69: O'bry 5F **97**
Titford La. B65: Row R 5E **97**
Titford Rd. B69: O'bry 5F **97**
(not continuous)
Tithe Cft. WV10: Wolv 6B **28**
Tithe Rd. WV11: Wed 3F **29**
Titterstone Rd. B31: Longb 1E **159**
Tiverton Cl. DY6: K'wfrd 6D **92**
Tiverton Dr. B71: W Brom 1A **80**

Tiverton Gro. B67: Smeth 3D **98**
(off Dibble Rd.)
Tiverton Rd. B29: S Oak. 3B **132**
B66: Smeth. 4F **99**
Tiverton Road Pool & Fitness Cen. . . 3B **132**
TIVIDALE 6A **78**
Tividale Rd. B69: Tiv 5H **77**
DY4: Tip 5H **77**
Tividale St. DY4: Tip 4A **78**
Tivoli, The B25: Yard 5B **120**
(off Church Rd.)
Tixall Rd. B28: Hall G. 2E **149**
Toadnest La. WV6: Pert 6A **24**
Toberland WS2: Wals. 2H **31**
Tobruk Wlk. DY5: Brie H 6H **93**
WV13: W'hall 2G **45**
Toll End Rd. DY4: Tip. 6C **62**
Tollgate Cl. B31: Longb 1D **158**
Tollgate Dr. B20: Hand. 2C **100**
Tollgate Pct. B67: Smeth 3D **98**
Toll Ho. Rd. B45: Redn 2A **158**
Tollhouse Way B66: Smeth 2D **98**
WV5: Wom 6E **57**
Tolworth Gdns. WV2: Wolv 4A **44**
Tolworth Hall Rd. B24: Erd 4H **85**
Tomey Rd. B11: S'brk 6D **118**
Tomlan Rd. B31: Longb. 2G **159**
Tomlinson Rd. B36: Cas B 6H **87**
Tompstone Rd. B71: W Brom 5D **64**
Tonadine Cl. WV11: Wed. 6A **18**
Tonbridge Rd. B24: Erd 6G **85**
Tong Cl. WV1: Wolv 5G **27**
Tong St. WS1: Wals 2E **49**
Topcroft Rd. B23: Erd 6F **69**
Topfield Ho. B14: K Hth 6G **147**
Top Fld. Wlk. B14: K Hth 5F **147**
Topland Gro. B31: Longb. 5A **144**
Top Rd. B61: Wild 4A **156**
Topsham Cft. B14: K Hth 2F **147**
Topsham Rd. B67: Smeth 3C **98**
Torfield WV8: Pend 5C **14**
Tor Lodge Dr. WV6: Tett. 1H **41**
Toronto Gdns. B32: Harb 5C **114**
Torre Av. B31: N'fld 5C **144**
Torrey Gro. B8: W End 5A **104**
Torridge Dr. WV11: Wed. 4E **29**
Torridon Cft. B13: Mose 2F **133**
Torridon Rd. WV12: W'hall. 6B **18**
Tor Va. Rd. WV6: Tett 1G **41**
Tor Way WS3: Pels. 4D **20**
Totnes Gro. B29: S Oak 3B **132**
Totnes Rd. B67: Smeth 3D **98**
Tottenham Cres. B44: K'sdng. 3B **68**
Touchwood Hall Cl. B91: Sol 3G **151**
Touchwood Shop. Cen.
B91: Sol. 4G **151**
Tourist Info. Cen.
Birmingham 1G 117 (4E **5**)
Birmingham International 1F **139**
Broad St. 1E 117 (4A **4**)
Dudley 6F **77**
Solihull 4G **151**
Wolverhampton 1G 43 (3B **170**)
Worcester St. 1G 117 (5E **5**)
Towcester Cft. B36: Hodg H 1B **104**
Tower Cft. B37: F'bri 5D **106**
TOWER HILL 1D **82**
Tower Hill Rd. B42: Gt Barr 1C **82**
Tower Ri. B69: Tiv 2C **96**
Tower Rd. B6: Aston 2H **101**
(not continuous)
B69: Tiv 2B **96**
B75: Four O 6H **37**
Tower St. B19: Birm 4F **101**
(not continuous)
DY1: Dud 6E **77**
DY3: Sed 4H **59**
WS1: Wals 1C **48**
WV1: Wolv 1H 43 (3C **170**)
Tower Vw. Rd. WS6: Gt Wyr 5F **7**
Tower Works Ind. Est.
WV3: Wolv 2E **43**
Town End Sq. WS1: Wals. 1C **48**
(off Park St.)
Townend St. WS2: Wals 1C **48**
Town Fold WS3: Pels 3E **21**
Town Ga. Retail Pk. DY1: Dud 5H **77**

Town Hall Stop (MM) 4A **80**
Townley Gdns. B6: Aston. 6G **83**
Townsend Av. DY3: Sed 5H **59**
Townsend Dr. B76: Walm. 6D **70**
Townsend Pl. DY6: K'wfrd 3B **92**
Townsend Way B1: Birm . . 6D 100 (3A **4**)
Townshend Gro. B37: K'hrst 5B **106**
Townson Rd. WV11: Wed. 1A **30**
Townwell Fold WV1: Wolv . . 1G 43 (3A **170**)
Town Wharf Bus. Pk. WS2: Wals . . 2B **48**
Town Yd. WV13: W'hall 2A **46**
Towpath Cl. B9: Birm 1B **118**
Towyn Rd. B13: Mose 3D **134**
Toy's La. B63: Crad 6E **111**
Tozer St. DY4: Tip 6H **61**
Traceys Mdw. B45: Redn 2G **157**
Tractor Spares Ind. Est.
WV13: W'hall 1F **45**
Trafalgar Cl. B69: Tiv. 6B **78**
Trafalgar Gro. B25: Yard 5G **119**
Trafalgar Rd. B13: Mose. 2H **133**
B21: Hand 1A **100**
B24: Erd 4F **85**
B66: Smeth. 5F **99**
B69: Tiv 6B **78**
Trafalgar Ter. B66: Smeth. 5F **99**
Trajan Hill B46: Col 6H **89**
Tram Way B66: Smeth 2A **98**
Tramway Cl. WS10: Darl 4E **47**
WV14: Bils 4H **45**
Tranter Rd. B8: W End 4G **103**
Tranwell Cl. WV9: Pend. 5D **14**
Traquain Dr. DY1: Dud 4C **76**
Travellers Way B37: Chel W 6F **107**
Treaford La. B8: W End 5H **103**
Treddles La. B70: W Brom. 4B **80**
Tredington Cl. B29: W Cas 6E **131**
Tree Acre Gro. B63: Crad 1E **127**
Treeford Cl. B91: Sol. 6D **150**
Trees Rd. WS1: Wals 5D **48**
Treeton Ct. B33: Yard 1E **121**
Tree Tops WV5: Wom 5E **57**
Treetops Dr. WV12: W'hall 4E **31**
Trefoil Cl. B29: W Cas 6E **131**
(not continuous)
Tregarron Rd. B63: Crad 6E **111**
Tregea Ri. B43: Gt Barr 6G **65**
Trehern Cl. B93: Know. 4C **166**
Trehernes Dr. DY9: Pedm 4F **125**
Trehurst Av. B42: Gt Barr 5E **67**
Trejon Rd. B64: Crad H 3G **111**
Tremaine Gdns. WV10: Wolv. 5H **27**
Trenchard Cl. B75: S Cold 6D **54**
Trent Cl. DY8: Stourb 1E **125**
WV6: Pert. 5E **25**
Trent Ct. B73: S Cold 6H **53**
Trent Cres. B47: Wyt 6G **161**
Trent Dr. B36: Cas B 1B **106**
Trentham Av. WV12: W'hall 4A **30**
Trentham Gro. B26: Sheld 6C **120**
Trentham Ri. WV2: E'shll 4B **44**
Trent Pl. WS3: Blox 1B **32**
Trent Rd. WS3: Pels 6E **21**
Trent St. B5: Birm 1H 117 (5H **5**)
Trent Twr. B7: Birm. 5A **102**
Trenville Av. B11: S'hll. 6B **118**
B12: Bal H 6B **118**
Tresco Cl. B45: Fran 6E **143**
TRESCOTT 4B **40**
Trescott Rd. B31: N'fld 4B **144**
Tresham Rd. B44: Gt Barr 4G **67**
DY6: K'wfrd 1B **92**
Trevanie Av. B32: Quin. 5A **114**
Trevelyan Ho. B37: Chel W 2E **123**
Trevor Av. WS6: Gt Wyr 2G **7**
Trevorne Cl. B12: Bal H 5H **117**
Trevor Rd. WS3: Pels. 3D **20**
Trevor St. WS3: Nech 3C **102**
Trevor St. W. B7: Nech. 3C **102**
Trevose Cl. WS3: Blox 4F **19**
Trevose Retreat B12: Bal H 6H **117**
Trewman Cl. B76: Walm 5D **70**
Treyamon Rd. WS5: Wals 4H **49**
Treynham Cl. WV1: Wolv 2E **45**
TRIANGLE 1D **10**
Triangle, The B18: Hock 3A **100**
Trickley Dr. B75: S Cold 5D **54**

Tricorn Ho. B16: Edg 2C **116**
Trident Blvd. B35: Cas V. 5F **87**
Trident Cen. DY1: Dud 6E **77**
Trident Cl. B23: Erd 6G **69**
B76: Walm 6D **70**
Trident Cl. B20: Hand. 4C **82**
B37: Mars G. 3G **123**
Trident Dr. B68: O'bry 4H **97**
WS10: W'bry 2D **62**
Trident Ho. B15: Birm 2E 117 (6A **4**)
Trident Retail Pk. B9: Birm 1A **118**
Trident Rd. B26: Birm A 1E **139**
Trigen Ho. B90: Bly P. 6D **164**
Trigo Cft. B36: Hodg H 1C **104**
Trimpley Cl. B93: Dorr 6A **166**
Trimpley Gdns. WV4: Penn 2C **58**
Trimpley Rd. B32: Bart G. 5H **129**
Trinder Rd. B67: Smeth 1B **114**
Trindle Cl. DY2: Dud. 6F **77**
Trindle Rd. DY2: Dud 6F **77**
Tring Cl. WV6: Wolv. 5D **26**
Trinity Cen. B64: Old H 1G **111**
Trinity Cl. B92: Olton 4F **137**
DY8: Word 1B **108**
Trinity Ct. B6: Aston 6F **83**
B64: Old H 2G **111**
WV3: Wolv 1E **43**
WV13: W'hall 2G **45**
(not continuous)
Trinity Gro. WS10: W'bry 2G **63**
Trinity Hill B72: S Cold. 6A **54**
Trinity Pk. B37: Mars G 2F **139**
Trinity Pl. B72: S Cold 6A **54**
Trinity Rd. B6: Aston 6F **83**
B75: Four O 2H **53**
DY1: Dud 6E **77**
DY8: Amb 3E **109**
WV12: W'hall 3D **30**
WV14: Bils 6H **45**
(not continuous)
Trinity Rd. Nth. B70: W Brom 6B **80**
(not continuous)
Trinity Rd. Sth.
B70: W Brom 6B **80**
Trinity St. B64: Old H 2G **111**
B67: Smeth 3E **99**
B69: O'bry 4G **97**
B70: W Brom 5B **80**
DY5: Brie H 6H **93**
Trinity Ter. B11: S'brk. 3A **118**
Trinity Way B70: W Brom. 6B **80**
Trinity Way Stop (MM) 6B **80**
Trippleton Av. B32: Bart G 5H **129**
Tristram Av. B31: N'fld 6F **145**
Triton Cl. WS6: Gt Wyr 4F **7**
Trittiford Rd. B13: Mose. 1B **148**
Triumph Wlk. B36: Cas B 6C **88**
Tromans Cl. B64: Crad H 4G **111**
Tromans Ind. Est. DY2: Neth 6F **95**
Troon Cl. B75: S Cold. 3B **54**
WS3: Blox 4G **19**
Troon Ct. WV6: Pert. 4D **24**
Troon Pl. DY8: Word 6A **92**
Trotter's La. B71: W Brom. 6G **63**
Trouse La. WS10: W'bry 2E **63**
Troutbeck Dr. DY5: Brie H. 3F **109**
Troy Gro. B14: K Hth. 3F **147**
Truck Stop Bus. Pk. B11: Tys. . . . 6H **119**
Truda St. WS1: Wals 4B **48**
TRUEMAN'S HEATH 2C **162**
Trueman's Heath La.
B47: H'wd 2B **162**
B90: Maj G. 2B **162**
Truro Cl. B65: Row R 5E **97**
Truro Rd. WS5: Wals 4H **49**
Truro Twr. B16: Birm 1C **116**
Truro Wlk. B37: Chel W 1C **122**
Trustin Cres. B92: Sol 5A **138**
Tryon Pl. WV14: Bils 5G **45**
TRYSULL 4C **56**
Trysull Av. B26: Sheld 1G **137**
Trysull Gdns. WV3: Wolv 4B **42**
Trysull Holloway WV5: Try 1C **56**
Trysull Rd. WV3: Wolv 4B **42**
WV5: Wom 5E **57**
Trysull Way DY2: Neth 6E **95**
Tudbury Rd. B31: N'fld 3B **144**
Tudman Cl. B76: Walm. 6E **71**

Tudor Cl. B13: Mose 1H 147
  B14: K Hth 6A 148
  B73: New O 3D 68
  CV7: Bal C 3G 169
  WS6: C Hay 2E 7
Tudor Ct. B1: Birm 3A 4
  B72: S Cold 6A 54
  B74: Four O 1G 53
  DY4: Tip 3A 78
  WV11: Ess 4H 17
Tudor Cres. WV2: Wolv 5F 43
Tudor Cft. B37: F'bri 2B 122
Tudor Gdns. B23: Erd 4E 85
  DY8: Stourb 6C 108
Tudor Grange Pk. 4E 151
Tudor Grange Sports Cen. 4F 151
TUDOR HILL 5H 53
Tudor Hill B73: S Cold 5G 53
Tudor Ind. Est. B11: Tys 6H 119
Tudor Pk. Ct. B74: Four O 6F 37
Tudor Pl. DY3: Up Gor 1A 76
Tudor Rd. B13: Mose 3H 133
  B65: Row R 4C 96
  B68: O'bry 5A 98
  B73: S Cold 6H 53
  DY3: Up Gor 1A 76
  WV10: Wolv 5C 28
  WV14: Bils 1B 62
Tudors Cl. B10: Small H 3C 118
Tudor St. B18: Win G 5H 99
  DY4: Tip 3A 78
Tudor Ter. B17: Harb 5G 115
  DY2: Dud 6G 77
Tudor Va. DY3: Up Gor 1A 76
Tudor Way B72: W Grn 3H 69
  WS6: C Hay 4D 6
Tufnell Gro. B8: W End 2G 103
Tugford Rd. B29: W Cas 6G 131
Tulips Gdns. B29: W Cas 6D 130
Tulip Wlk. B37: Chel W 3E 123
Tulsi Cen. B19: Birm 5E 101
Tulyar Cl. B36: Hodg H 1A 104
Tunnel La. B30: K Nor, K Hth 3D 146
Tunnel Rd. B70: W Brom 5G 63
Tunnel St. WV14: Cose. 5E 61
Tunstall Rd. DY6: K'wfrd 4E 93
Turchill Dr. B76: Walm 5E 71
Turf Cl. WS11: Nort C 1E 9
Turfpits La. B23: Erd 1D 84
Turf Pitts La. B75: Can. 6D 38
                (not continuous)
Turks Head Way
  B70: W Brom 5A 80
Turley St. DY1: Dud 1C 76
Turls Hill Rd. DY3: Sed 5A 60
  WV14: Cose 5C 60
Turls St. DY3: Sed 5A 60
Turnberry Cl. WV6: Pert. 4D 24
Turnberry Rd. B42: Gt Barr 5D 66
  WS3: Blox. 4F 19
Turner Av. WV14: Cose 3B 60
Turner Dr. DY5: Quar B 4H 109
Turner Gro. WV6: Pert 5G 25
Turners Cft. B71: W Brom 5E 65
TURNER'S HILL 3B 96
Turner's Hill B65: Row R 3B 96
Turners Hill Rd. DY3: Lwr G 3G 75
Turner's La. DY5: Brie H 3G 109
Turner St. B11: S'brk 5A 118
  B70: W Brom 3G 79
  DY1: Dud 1D 94
  DY3: Lwr G 4H 75
  DY4: Tip 6H 61
Turney Rd. DY8: Stourb 5D 108
Turnham Gro. WV6: Pert 6E 25
Turnhouse Rd. B35: Cas V 3F 87
Turnley Rd. B34: S End 3G 105
Turnpike Cl. B11: S'brk 5A 118
  CV7: Bal C 2H 169
Turnpike Dr. B46: Wat O 4E 89
Turnstone Dr. WV10: F'stne 1D 16
Turton Cl. WS3: Blox 3G 19
Turton Rd. B70: W Brom 5H 79
  DY4: Tip 4H 61
Turtons Cft. WV14: Cose 2D 60

TURVES GREEN 6E 145
Turves Grn. B31: Longb, N'fld 2D 158
Turves Green Leisure & Adult Education Cen.
                     . . . . 6E 145
Turville Rd. B20: Hand 6E 83
Tustin Gro. B27: A Grn 5A 136
Tutbury Av. WV6: Pert. 6F 25
Tuxford Cl. WV10: Wolv 5A 28
Twatling Rd. B45: B Grn, Lick 6G 157
Tweeds Well B32: Bart G 6H 129
Tweed Twr. B20: Hand 5F 83
Twickenham Ct. DY8: Woll. 4A 108
Twickenham Rd. B44: K'sdng 4B 68
Two Gates B63: Crad 6D 110
Two Gates La. B63: Crad 6E 111
Two Locks DY5: Brie H. 5C 94
Two Woods La. DY5: Brie H 2A 110
Twycross Gro. B36: Hodg H 2B 104
Twydale Av. B69: Tiv 5C 78
Twyford Cl. WS9: A'rdge 4D 34
Twyford Gro. WV11: Wed. 2H 29
Twyford Rd. B8: W End 4A 104
Twyning Rd. B16: Edg 5H 99
  B30: Stir. 6D 132
Tyber Dr. B20: Hand 4D 82
Tyberry Cl. B90: Shir 6G 149
TYBURN 4E 87
Tyburn Gro. B24: Erd 4B 86
Tyburn Rd. B24: Erd. 6D 84
  WV1: Wolv 2E 45
Tyburn Sq. B24: Erd 4B 86
Tyburn Trad. Est. B35: Cas V 5B 86
Tyebeams B34: S End 4G 105
Tye Gdns. DY9: Pedm. 4F 125
Tyler Cl. B24: Erd 4F 85
Tyler Gdns. WV13: W'hall 2B 46
Tyler Gro. B43: Gt Barr. 4C 66
Tyler Rd. WV13: W'hall 3A 46
Tylers Grn. B38: K Nor. 5D 146
Tylers Gro. B90: M'path. 3D 164
Tylney Cl. B5: Bal H 4F 117
Tyndale Cres. B43: Gt Barr. 2E 67
Tyndall Wlk. B32: Bart G 3G 129
Tyne Cl. B37: F'bri 5D 106
  WS8: Bwnhls 3G 9
Tyne Ct. B73: S Cold 6H 53
Tynedale Cres. WV4: E'shll 2A 60
Tynedale Rd. B11: Tys 2F 135
Tyne Gro. B25: Yard 3B 120
Tyne Pl. DY5: Quar B 1B 110
Tyning Cl. WV9: Pend. 5E 15
Tyninghame Av. WV6: Tett 3B 26
Tynings La. WS9: A'rdge 4C 34
Tyrley Cl. WV6: Tett 1H 41
Tyrol Cl. DY8: Woll. 6B 108
TYSELEY 6G 119
Tyseley Hill Rd. B11: Tys. 1G 135
Tyseley Ind. Est. B11: Tys 6E 119
Tyseley La. B11: Tys 1G 135
Tyseley Station (Rail) 6F 119
Tysoe Dr. B76: Walm 1D 70
Tysoe Rd. B44: K'sdng. 6H 67
Tythebarn Dr. DY6: W Hth 2G 91
Tythe Barn La. B90: Dic H 3E 163
                (not continuous)
Tyzack Cl. DY5: Brie H 1G 109

U

UCI Cinema
  Brierley Hill 1A 110
  Shirley 2C 164
Udall Rd. WV14: Cose 2F 61
Uffculme Rd. B30: Stir 5F 133
Uffmoor Est. B63: Hale. 3G 127
Uffmoor La. B62: Roms, Hale. 6F 127
  B63: Hale 4G 127
Uffmoor Wood Nature Reserve 6G 127
Ufton Cl. B90: Shir. 4C 150
Ufton Cres. B90: Shir. 4B 150
UGC Cinema
  Birmingham 2G 117 (6E 5)
  Bishopsgate St. 2D 116
  Rednal. 1G 157
Ullenhall Rd. B76: Walm 4C 70
  B93: Know 3C 166

Ullenwood B21: Hand 2H 99
Ulleries Rd. B92: Olton 3D 136
Ullrick Grn. B24: Erd 5F 85
Ullswater Cl. B32: Bart G. 3D 130
Ullswater Gdns. DY6: K'wfrd 3B 92
Ullswater Ho. B69: O'bry. 4D 96
Ullswater Ri. DY5: Brie H 4H 93
Ullswater Rd. WV12: W'hall. 6B 18
Ulster Dr. DY6: K'wfrd 5C 92
Ulverley Ct. B92: Olton 5D 136
Ulverley Cres. B92: Olton 5D 136
ULVERLEY GREEN 5D 136
Ulverley Grn. Rd. B92: Olton 4C 136
Ulwine Dr. B31: N'fld. 3D 144
Umberslade Rd. B29: S Oak 4B 132
Uncle Ben's Cl. B69: O'bry. 5F 97
Underhill La. WV10: Bush 4B 16
Underhill Rd. B8: Salt. 6F 103
  DY4: Tip 1C 78
Underhill St. B69: O'bry 4G 97
Underhill Wlk. B69: O'bry 4G 97
Underley Cl. DY6: W Hth. 2H 91
Underpass, The B40: Nat E C 1F 139
Underwood Cl. B15: Edg 1H 131
  B23: Erd. 3C 84
Underwood Rd. B20: Hand 2A 82
Unett Ct. B66: Smeth 4G 99
Unett St. B19: Hock 4E 101
                  (not continuous)
  B66: Smeth 5G 99
Unett Wlk. B19: Birm 4E 101
Union Cen. WS10: W'bry 3F 63
Union Dr. B73: Bold 3F 69
Union La. WV5: Try 4D 56
Union Mill St. WV1: Wolv 1A 44
Union Pas. B2: Birm 1G 117 (4E 5)
Union Pl. B29: S Oak 3D 132
Union Rd. B6: Aston. 1B 102
  B69: O'bry 6E 79
  B70: W Brom 5F 79
  B90: Shir 5A 150
  B91: Sol 3G 151
Union Row B21: Hand 1B 100
Union St. B2: Birm 1G 117 (4E 5)
  B65: B'hth 2C 112
  B70: W Brom 1B 98
  DY2: Dud 6E 77
  DY4: Tip 5H 61
                   (Attwell Rd.)
  DY4: Tip 2H 77
                   (Unity Wlk.)
  DY8: Stourb 6E 109
  DY9: Lye. 6A 110
  WS1: Wals 1D 48
  WS10: W'bry 3F 63
  WV1: Wolv 1H 43 (3D 170)
  WV13: W'hall 1A 46
  WV14: Bils 6E 45
Unisant Trad. Est.
  B64: Old H 1H 111
Unitt Dr. B64: Old H 3G 111
Unity Cl. WS10: Darl 1C 62
Unity Pl. B29: S Oak. 3B 132
  B69: O'bry 1G 97
Unity Wlk. DY4: Tip 2G 77
University of Aston
  Chemical Engineering Building
                  . . . . 6H 101
  Gem Sports Hall 6H 101
University of Birmingham
  Edgbaston Pk. Rd. 6B 116
  Selly Oak Campus 5H 131
  University Rd. E. 1B 132
University of Central England
  Bournville Campus 6A 132
  Department of Art. 6F 101 (3C 4)
  Gosta Green Campus . . . 5H 101 (1G 5)
  Hamstead Campus 4A 82
  Perry Barr Campus 4F 83
  School of Jewellery 5E 101 (1A 4)
  Sycamore Rd. 6B 132
  Westbourne Campus 3C 116
University of Wolverhampton
  Molineux Rd. 6G 27 (1B 170)
  St Peter's Sq. 1G 43 (2B 170)
  Walsall Campus 4E 49
University Rd. E. B15: Edg 1B 132

University Rd. W. B15: Edg 1A **132**
University Station (Rail) **1A 132**
Unketts Rd. B67: Smeth. 6C **98**
Unwin Cres. DY8: Stourb 6C **108**
Upavon Cl. B35: Cas V 3E **87**
Upland Rd. B29: S Oak 3C **132**
Uplands B63: Hale 3F **127**
Uplands, The B67: Smeth 4D **98**
Uplands Av. B65: Row R 6D **96**
WV3: Wolv 3B **42**
WV13: W'hall 2F **45**
Uplands Cl. DY2: Dud 2H **95**
Uplands Dr. DY3: Sed 5H **59**
WV3: Wolv 3C **42**
WV5: Wom. 1G **73**
Uplands Gro. WV13: W'hall 2E **45**
Uplands Rd. B21: Hand 5H **81**
DY2: Dud 2G **95**
WV13: W'hall 2E **45**
Up. Ashley St. B62: B'hth 2C **112**
Up. Balsall Heath Rd.
B12: Bal H 5H **117**
Up. Brook St. WS2: Wals 2B **48**
Up. Castle St. WS10: Darl 3D **46**
Up. Chapel St. B69: Tiv 5B **78**
Up. Church La. DY4: Tip 5H **61**
Up. Clifton Rd. B73: S Cold 6H **53**
Upper Cl. B32: Bart G. 2B **130**
Up. Conybere St. B12: Birm 4H **117**
Up. Dean St. B5: Birm 2G **117** (6E **5**)
Up. Ettingshall Rd.
WV14: Cose 5C **60**
Up. Forster St. WS4: Wals 6D **32**
UPPER GORNAL **2A 76**
Up. Gough St. B1: Birm. 2F **117** (6C **4**)
Upper Grn. WV6: Tett. 4B **26**
Up. Grosvenor Rd. B20: Hand 5D **82**
Up. Hall La. WS1: Wals 2C **48**
Up. Highgate St. B12: Birm. 4H **117**
Up. High St. B64: Crad H 2F **111**
WS10: W'bry 2F **63**
Up. Holland Rd. B72: S Cold 1A **70**
UPPER LANDYWOOD **5E 7**
Up. Landywood La. WS6: C Hay 4D **6**
Up. Lichfield St. WV13: W'hall 1A **46**
Up. Mall E. B5: Birm 1G **117** (5F **5**)
Up. Mall W. B5: Birm 1G **117** (5E **5**)
Up. Marshall St. B1: Birm. 2F **117** (6C **4**)
Up. Meadow Rd. B32: Quin 6A **114**
Up. Navigation St. WS2: Wals 1B **48**
Up. Portland St. B6: Aston. 2A **102**
Up. Rushall St. WS1: Wals 2D **48**
Up. Russell St. WS10: W'bry 3F **63**
Up. St Mary's Rd. B67: Smeth 2D **114**
Up. Short St. WS2: Wals 2B **48**
Up. Sneyd Rd. WV11: Ess 5B **18**
Up. Stone Cl. B76: Walm 1C **70**
Upper St. WV6: Tett 4B **26**
Up. Sutton St. B6: Aston 2H **101**
Up. Thomas St. B6: Aston 2H **101**
(not continuous)
Up. Trinity St. B9: Birm 2A **118**
Up. Vauxhall WV1: Wolv 1E **43**
Up. Villiers St. WV2: Wolv 5G **43**
Up. William St. B1: Birm 2E **117** (6A **4**)
Up. Zoar St. WV3: Wolv 3F **43**
Upton Ct. *B23: Erd 4B 84*
(off Alwynn WLk.)
Upton Gdns. WV14: Bils 6E **45**
Upton Gro. B33: Stech 2A **120**
Upton Rd. B33: Stech. 1A **120**
Upton St. DY2: Neth 4E **95**
Upwey Av. B91: Sol 3E **151**
USAM Trad. Est.
WV10: F'hses. 5H **15**
Usk Way B36: Cas B. 1B **106**
Uttoxeter Cl. WV6: Wolv. 3F **27**
Uxbridge Cl. DY3: Lwr G 4H **75**
Uxbridge Ct. WS7: Chase. 1A **10**
Uxbridge St. B19: Birm. 4F **101**

V

Valbourne Rd. B14: K Hth 3E **147**
Vale, The B11: S'hll 3C **134**
B15: Edg 5C **116**
Vale Av. DY3: Up Gor. 1H **75**
WS9: A'rdge 6F **35**
Vale Cl. B32: Bart G. 2D **130**
Vale Head Dr. WV6: Tett 1G **41**
Valencia Cft. B35: Cas V 3F **87**
Valentine Cl. B74: S'tly 5H **51**
Valentine Ct. B14: K Hth 4H **133**
Valentine Rd. B14: K Hth. 4G **133**
B68: O'bry 1A **114**
Valepits Rd. B33: Sheld. 2G **121**
Valerian B74: Four O 5F **37**
Valerie Gro. B43: Gt Barr. 5G **65**
Vale Rd. DY2: Neth 5G **95**
Vale Row DY3: Up Gor. 2H **75**
Vales Cl. B76: Walm 6C **70**
Vale St. B71: W Brom 1C **80**
DY3: Up Gor 2H **75**
DY8: Amb. 3E **109**
WV2: E'shll. 5C **44**
Vale Vw. WS9: A'rdge 5D **34**
Valiant Ho. B35: Cas V. 2F **87**
Valiant Way B92: Sol 5G **137**
Vallan Cft. B36: Hodg H. 2D **104**
Valley Farm Rd. B45: Rubery. 3F **157**
Valley Grn. WS6: C Hay 3E **7**
Valley Rd. B43: Gt Barr 6G **65**
B62: B'hth. 3F **113**
B64: Crad H 4G **111**
B67: Smeth 6D **98**
B74: S'tly 4H **51**
B92: Sol. 2G **137**
DY3: Up Gor. 1A **76**
DY9: Lye. 6B **110**
Valley Rd. WS3: Blox. 1A **32**
WV10: Wolv 4B **28**
Valleyside WS3: Pels. 5D **20**
Valley Vw. WS8: Bwnhls 6C **10**
Vanborough Wlk. DY1: Dud. 5C **76**
Vanbrugh Ct. WV6: Pert 6E **25**
Van Diemans Rd. WV5: Wom 2E **73**
Vanguard Cl. B36: Hodg H. 1C **104**
Vanguard Rd. B26: Birm A. 1E **139**
Vann Cl. B10: Small H 3C **118**
(not continuous)
Vantage Point *B70: W Brom 5A 80*
(off Blacksmith Way)
Varden Cft. B5: Bal H 4F **117**
Vardon Way B38: K Nor. 6H **145**
Varley Rd. B24: Erd 3B **86**
Varley Va. B24: Erd 3B **86**
Varlins Way B38: K Nor. 2H **159**
Varney Av. B70: W Brom 5B **80**
Vaughan Cl. B74: Four O 3F **37**
Vaughan Gdns. WV8: Cod 3F **13**
Vaughan Rd. WV13: W'hall 2F **45**
Vaughan Trad. Est. DY4: Tip 3B **78**
Vaughton Dr. B75: S Cold 5C **54**
Vaughton St. B12: Birm. 3H **117**
Vaughton St. Sth. B5: Birm 3G **117**
B12: Birm. 3G **117**
VAUXHALL **4B 102**
Vauxhall Av. WV1: Wolv. 1E **43**
Vauxhall Bus. Pk. B7: Birm 4C **102**
Vauxhall Cres. B36: Cas B 6B **88**
Vauxhall Gdns. DY2: Dud 2G **95**
Vauxhall Gro. B7: Birm 6B **102**
Vauxhall Ho. *WV1: Wolv 1E 43*
(off Upper Vauxhall)
Vauxhall Pl. B7: Birm. 6A **102**
Vauxhall Rd. B7: Birm 6A **102**
DY8: Stourb 6E **109**
Vauxhall St. DY1: Dud. 1D **94**
Vauxhall Ter. B7: Birm. 5B **102**
Vauxhall Trad. Est. B7: Birm 5B **102**
Vector Ind. Pk. B71: W Brom. 1A **80**
Velsheda Rd. B90: Shir 5G **149**
Venetia Rd. B9: Bord G 1C **118**
Venice Ct. B13: Mose. 3B **134**
Venning Gro. B43: Gt Barr. 6H **65**
Ventnor Av. B19: Hock 2E **101**
B36: Hodg H 2B **104**
Ventnor Cl. B68: O'bry. 4A **114**
Ventnor Rd. B92: Sol 2G **137**
Venture Ct. WV10: F'hses 2H **15**
Venture Way B7: Birm 5H **101** (1H **5**)
Vera Rd. B26: Yard. 4C **120**
Verbena Gdns. B7: Birm 4A **102**
Verbena Rd. B31: N'fld 1D **144**
Vercourt B74: Lit A. 6B **36**
Verdun Cres. DY2: Dud 5H **77**
Vere St. B5: Birm 3F **117**
Verity Wlk. DY8: Word. 2C **108**
Verney Av. B33: Sheld 4H **121**
Vernier Av. DY6: K'wfrd 4E **93**
Vernon Av. B20: Hand 3B **82**
DY4: Tip. 3G **77**
WS8: Bwnhls 5C **10**
Vernon Cl. B62: B'hth. 3C **112**
B74: Four O 4E **37**
WV11: Ess 3H **17**
WV13: W'hall. 2G **45**
Vernon Ct. B16: Edg. 2A **116**
B68: O'bry 4H **113**
Vernon Rd. B16: Edg 2H **115**
B62: B'hth 3C **112**
B68: O'bry 3A **98**
WV14: Bils 5H **45**
Vernon St. B70: W Brom 4E **79**
WV14: Cose 3G **61**
Vernon Trad. Est. B62: B'hth 3C **112**
Vernon Way WS3: Blox 6D **18**
Veronica Av. WV4: E'shll 6A **44**
Veronica Cl. B29: W Cas 1D **144**
Veronica Rd. DY6: K'wfrd 3E **93**
Verstone Cft. B31: N'fld 5E **145**
Verstone Rd. B90: Shir 3A **150**
Verwood Cl. WV13: W'hall 2F **45**
Vesey Cl. B46: Wat O. 5D **88**
B74: Four O 1F **53**
Vesey Rd. B73: W Grn. 4H **69**
Vesey St. B4: Birm 5G **101** (1E **5**)
Vestry Cl. B64: Old H. 2H **111**
Vestry Ct. DY8: Woll. 5C **108**
Viaduct Dr. WV6: Wolv 3F **27**
Viaduct St. B7: Birm. 6A **102**
Vibart Rd. B26: Yard 3D **120**
Vicarage Cl. B30: Stir. 6E **133**
B42: Gt Barr 6F **67**
DY4: Tip. 2G **77**
DY5: Brie H 3G **109**
WS8: Bwnhls 5C **10**
(not continuous)
Vicarage Gdns. B65: B'hth. 2C **112**
B76: Walm 6D **70**
Vicarage La. B46: Wat O 5D **88**
DY5: P'ntt 1H **93**
Vicarage Pl. WS1: Wals. 2C **48**
Vicarage Prospect DY1: Dud. 6D **76**
Vicarage Rd. B6: Aston 2A **102**
(not continuous)
B14: K Hth 1E **147**
B15: Edg 3B **116**
B17: Harb 6F **115**
B18: Hock 2C **100**
B33: Yard. 2C **120**
B62: B'hth. 2C **112**
B67: Smeth 4D **98**
B68: O'bry. 5H **97**
B71: W Brom 1B **80**
B94: Earls. 6A **164**
DY3: Up Gor. 2B **76**
DY5: Brie H 4G **109**
DY8: Amb. 4E **109**
DY8: Woll. 4A **108**
DY9: Lye. 6B **110**
WS3: Pels. 5E **21**
WS8: Bwnhls 6B **10**
WS10: W'bry 2F **63**
WV2: Wolv. 3H **43**
WV4: Penn 2B **58**
WV11: Wed 3D **28**
WV14: Cose 6E **61**
Vicarage Rd. Sth. DY9: Lye. 6A **110**
Vicarage Rd. W. DY1: Dud 1D **76**
Vicarage St. B68: O'bry. 4H **97**
Vicarage Ter. WS2: Wals 3A **48**
Vicarage Wlk. WS1: Wals 2C **48**
Vicar St. DY2: Dud. 6E **77**
DY3: Sed 5H **59**
WS10: W'bry. 2G **63**
Vicars Wlk. DY9: W'cte 3A **126**
Viceroy Cl. B5: Edg 5E **117**
DY6: K'wfrd 4E **93**
Victor Cl. WV2: E'shll. 5D **44**

Victoria Arc. WV1: Wolv 1G **43** (3B **170**)
Victoria Av. B10: Small H. 3D **118**
 B21: Hand 1B **100**
 B62: Quin 5F **113**
 B66: Smeth 4E **99**
 WS3: Blox 6H **19**
Victoria Bldgs. B16: Birm 6A **100**
 (off Barford Rd.)
Victoria Ct. B13: Mose. 1H **133**
 B62: Quin 4G **113**
 (off Binswood Rd.)
 B66: Smeth. 3F **99**
 DY5: Brie H 6H **93**
 WS11: Nort C 1F **9**
Victoria Fold WV1: Wolv . . 2G **43** (4A **170**)
Victoria Gdns. B64: Old H 1H **111**
Victoria Gro. B18: Win G 5A **100**
 WV5: Wom. 5G **57**
Victoria Ho. B16: Birm. 1D **116**
 (off Bellcroft)
 WS3: Blox 1B **32**
 WS10: Darl. 5C **46**
 (off Factory St.)
Victoria M. B69: O'bry 6F **97**
 WS4: Wals 6E **33**
Victoria New Works WS10: Darl . . 3D **46**
Victoria Pk. Rd. B66: Smeth 4F **99**
Victoria Pas. DY8: Stourb 6E **109**
 WV1: Wolv 1G **43** (3B **170**)
Victoria Rd. B6: Aston 2G **101**
 (not continuous)
 B17: Harb 6F **115**
 B21: Hand 2A **100**
 B23: Erd 4D **84**
 B27: A Grn 3A **136**
 (not continuous)
 B30: Stir 6C **132**
 B33: Stech 6B **104**
 B62: B'hth 2D **112**
 B64: Old H 1H **111**
 B68: O'bry 3A **98**
 B72: S Cold 6A **54**
 DY3: Sed 5A **60**
 DY4: Tip 2H **77**
 DY5: Quar B 2C **110**
 WS3: Pels. 4E **21**
 WS10: Darl 5D **46**
 WV3: Wolv 4C **42**
 WV6: Tett 4C **26**
 WV10: Wolv 4B **28**
 WV11: Wed 3D **28**
Victoria Sq. B2: Birm. 1F **117** (4C **4**)
 WV1: Wolv 1H **43** (3C **170**)
Victoria St. B9: Small H 2D **118**
 B63: Hale 1A **128**
 B70: W Brom 2F **79**
 (Phoenix St.)
 B70: W Brom 4A **80**
 (Price St.)
 DY5: Brie H 6H **93**
 DY5: P'ntt 2G **93**
 DY6: W Hth 6H **73**
 DY8: Stourb 6E **109**
 WS10: W'bry 3E **63**
 WV1: Wolv 2G **43** (4B **170**)
 WV13: W'hall 6A **30**
Victoria Ter. WS4: Wals 6E **33**
Victor Rd. B18: Win G 3A **100**
 B92: Sol 2H **137**
Victor St. WS1: Wals 4C **48**
 WS3: Pels. 6E **21**
Victor Twr. B7: Nech. 3B **102**
Victory Av. B65: Row R 1B **112**
 WS10: Darl. 1C **62**
Victory Ho. B13: Mose 1H **133**
Victory La. WS2: Wals 5G **31**
Victory Ri. B71: W Brom 2A **80**
View Dr. DY2: Dud 1G **95**
Viewfield Cres. DY3: Sed 6H **59**
Viewlands Dr. WV6: Tett 1G **41**
View Point B69: Tiv 1B **96**
VIGO 4B **22**
Vigo Cl. WS9: Wals W 5B **22**
Vigo Pl. WS9: A'rdge 1B **34**
Vigo Rd. WS9: Wals W 5B **22**
Vigo Ter. WS9: Wals W 5B **22**
Viking Ri. B65: Row R 5C **96**

VILLAGE, THE 2C **92**
Village, The DY6: K'wfrd 3G **92**
Village M., The WV6: Tett 4A **26**
Village Rd. B6: Aston. 6A **84**
Village Sq. B31: Longb 5A **144**
Village Wlk. WS10: W'bry 2H **63**
Village Way B76: Walm 5D **70**
 WV14: Bils 6E **45**
Villa Park 6H **83**
Villa Rd. B19: Hock 2C **100**
Villa St. B19: Loz 2D **100**
 (not continuous)
 DY8: Amb. 3E **109**
Villa Wlk. B19: Hock 3E **101**
Villette Gro. B14: Yard W 3C **148**
Villiers Av. WV14: Bils 4F **45**
Villiers Ho. WV2: Wolv 4G **43**
 (off Blakenhall Gdns.)
Villiers Pl. WV14: Bils 4F **45**
Villiers Sq. WV14: Bils 4F **45**
Villiers St. WS1: Wals 4C **48**
 WV13: W'hall 1A **46**
Villiers Trad. Est. WV2: Wolv. . . . 4F **43**
Vimy Rd. B13: Mose 6B **134**
 WS10: W'bry 1G **63**
Vimy Ter. WS10: W'bry 1G **63**
Vincent Cl. B12: Bal H 5H **117**
Vincent Dr. B15: Edg 2H **131**
Vincent Pde. B12: Bal H. 5H **117**
Vincent Rd. B75: S Cold. 4C **54**
Vincent St. B12: Bal H 6H **117**
 (not continuous)
 WS1: Wals 4D **48**
Vince St. B66: Smeth 6E **99**
Vinculum Way WV13: W'hall 3B **46**
Vine Av. B12: Bal H 6A **118**
Vine Cres. B71: W Brom 1B **80**
Vine Gdns. B64: Old H 1H **111**
Vine La. B63: Hale 2B **128**
Vineries, The B27: A Grn 1B **136**
Vine St. B6: Aston 2B **102**
 DY5: Brie H 4A **94**
 DY8: Word 2C **108**
Vine Ter. B17: Harb 6G **115**
Vineyard Cl. B18: Hock 2B **100**
Vineyard Rd. B31: N'fld 2D **144**
Vinnall Gro. B32: Bart G 5H **129**
Vintage Cl. B34: Stech 4E **105**
Violet Cft. DY4: Tip 4C **62**
Virgin Active 6D **164**
Virginia Dr. WV4: Penn 1D **58**
Viscount Cl. B35: Cas V 5E **87**
Viscount Dr. B35: Cas V 5F **87**
Viscount Ho. B26: Birm A. 1E **139**
Vista, The DY3: Sed 4H **59**
Vista Grn. B38: K Nor. 6C **146**
 (not continuous)
Vittoria St. B1: Birm 5E **101** (1A **4**)
 B66: Smeth 3H **99**
Vivian Cl. B17: Harb 6G **115**
Vivian Rd. B17: Harb 6G **115**
Vixen Cl. B76: Walm 6B **70**
Vue Cinema 1D **102**
 (in Star City)
Vulcan Ind. Est. WS2: Wals 3A **32**
Vulcan Rd. B91: Sol 1G **151**
 WV14: Bils 6H **45**
Vulcan Rd. Ind. Est. B91: Sol 1G **151**
Vyrnwy Gro. B38: K Nor 1A **160**
Vyse St. B6: Aston 1B **102**
 B18: Birm 4E **101** (1A **4**)

W

Wadbarn B90: Dic H. 4G **163**
Waddell Cl. WV14: Cose 3B **60**
Waddens Brook La. WV11: Wed . . 4G **29**
Waddington Av. B43: Gt Barr . . . 4A **66**
Wades Cl. DY4: Tip 2G **77**
Wadesmill Lawns WV10: Bush . . 3A **16**
Wadham Cl. B65: Row R 3C **96**
Wadham Ho. B37: Chel W 6E **107**
Wadhurst Rd. B17: Edg 1F **115**
Wadley's Rd. B91: Sol 1D **150**
Waen Cl. DY4: Tip 5B **62**
Waggoners La. B78: Hints 2H **39**

Waggon St. B64: Old H 1H **111**
Waggon Wlk. B38: K Nor. 1G **159**
 (not continuous)
Wagoners Cl. B8: Salt 3F **103**
Wagon La. B92: Olton 1D **136**
Wagstaff Cl. WV14: Cose 5F **61**
Waine Ho. WS8: Bwnhls 1C **22**
Wainwright Cl. DY6: W Hth 2G **91**
Wainwright St. B6: Aston. 2A **102**
Waite Rd. WV13: W'hall 3G **45**
Wakefield Cl. B73: Bold. 3G **69**
Wakefield Ct. B13: Mose 3B **134**
 B29: W Cas 6G **131**
 (off Abdon Av.)
Wakefield Gro. B46: Wat O 4D **88**
Wakeford Rd. B31: N'fld 6G **145**
WAKE GREEN 3A **134**
Wake Grn. Pk. B13: Mose 3B **134**
Wake Grn. Rd. B13: Mose. 2H **133**
 DY4: Tip 4A **62**
Wakelam Gdns. B43: Gt Barr. . . . 4H **65**
Wakelams Fold DY3: Gorn 4G **75**
Wakeley Hill WV4: Penn 1D **58**
Wakelin Rd. B90: Shir 2H **163**
Wakeman Ct. WV11: Ess 4H **17**
Wakeman Dr. B69: Tiv 1B **96**
Wakeman Gro. B33: Sheld. 4H **121**
Wakes Cl. WV13: W'hall 2B **46**
Wakes Rd. WS10: W'bry 3G **63**
Walcot Cl. B75: Four O 6H **37**
Walcot Dr. B43: Gt Barr 1B **82**
Walcot Gdns. WV14: Bils 1D **60**
Walcot Grn. B93: Dorr 6H **167**
Waldale Cl. WV11: Ess 6C **18**
Walden Gdns. WV4: Penn 5C **42**
Walden Rd. B11: Tys 2G **135**
Waldeve Gro. B92: Sol 5B **138**
Waldley Gro. B24: Erd 4A **86**
Waldon Wlk. B36: Cas B 1B **106**
Waldron Av. DY5: Brie H 1F **109**
Waldron Cl. WS10: W'bry 5F **47**
Waldrons Moor B14: K Hth 2E **147**
Walford Av. WV3: Wolv 3D **42**
Walford Dr. B92: Sol 2H **137**
Walford Grn. B32: Bart G. 6H **129**
Walford Rd. B11: S'brk 5B **118**
Walford St. B69: Tiv 5A **78**
Walhouse Cl. WS1: Wals. 1D **48**
Walhouse Rd. WS1: Wals 1D **48**
 (not continuous)
Walk, The DY3: Sed. 4H **59**
Walker Av. B69: Tiv 2C **96**
 DY5: Quar B 4H **109**
 DY9: W'cte. 2H **125**
 WV10: Bush 1A **28**
Walker Dr. B24: Nech. 1E **103**
Walker Grange DY4: Tip 6H **61**
Walker Pl. WS3: Blox. 1C **32**
Walker Rd. WS3: Blox 1B **32**
Walkers Fold WV12: W'hall 3D **30**
WALKER'S HEATH 5C **146**
Walkers Heath Rd. B38: K Nor . . . 6D **146**
Walker St. DY2: Neth 5E **95**
 DY4: Tip 6B **62**
Walk La. WV5: Wom 6G **57**
Walkmill La. WS11: Cann 1D **6**
Wallace Cl. B69: O'bry 3D **96**
 WS11: Nort C 1D **8**
Wallace Ct. WS6: C Hay 4D **6**
Wallace Ho. B69: O'bry 4D **96**
Wallace Ri. B64: Crad H 4G **111**
Wallace Rd. B29: S Oak 3D **132**
 B69: O'bry 3D **96**
 WS8: Bwnhls 5A **10**
 WV14: Bils 2A **62**
Wall Av. B46: Col 4H **107**
Wallbank Rd. B8: W End 3G **103**
WALLBROOK 5F **61**
Wallbrook St. WV14: Cose 5F **61**
Wall Cft. WS9: A'rdge 2D **34**
Wall Dr. B74: Four O 5F **37**
Wall End Cl. WS2: Wals 2G **31**
Wallface B71: W Brom 6G **63**
WALL HEATH 1H **91**
Wallheath Cres. WS9: Ston. 2G **23**
Wall Heath La. WS9: Ston. 2H **23**
Walling Cft. WV14: Cose 2D **60**

Wallington Cl. WS3: Blox 5H 19
WALLINGTON HEATH 5G 19
Wallington Heath WS3: Blox 5H 19
Wallis Ct. B13: Mose 3B 134
Wallows Ind. Est., The
   DY5: Brie H 4H 93
Wallows La. WS1: Wals 5A 48
   WS2: Wals 5A 48
Wallows Pl. DY5: Brie H 4G 93
Wallows Rd. DY5: Brie H 5G 93
Wallows Wood DY3: Lwr G 3E 75
Wall Av. WV1: Wolv 1D 44
Wall Well B63: Hale 2H 127
Wall Well La. B63: Hale 2H 127
Walmead Cft. B17: Harb 4D 114
Walmer Gro. B23: Erd 2B 84
Walmer Mdw. WS9: A'rdge 2D 34
Walmers, The WS9: A'rdge 2D 34
Walmers Wlk., The B31: Longb 6B 144
Walmer Way B37: Chel W 6E 107
Walmesley Way B31: N'fld 4C 144
WALMLEY 5D 70
WALMLEY ASH 2D 86
Walmley Ash La. B76: Walm, Min 1F 87
Walmley Ash Rd. B76: Walm, Min 6D 70
Walmley Cl. B63: Crad 4D 110
   B76: Walm 5D 70
Walmley Rd. B76: Walm 1C 70
Walnut Av. WV8: Bilb 4G 13
Walnut Cl. B37: Chel W 2D 122
   DY9: Pedm 4F 125
Walnut Dr. B66: Smeth 4F 99
   WV3: Wolv 2B 42
Walnut Ho. B20: Hand 4B 82
Walnut La. WS10: W'bry 3G 63
Walnut Rd. WS5: Wals 1E 65
Walnut Way B31: Longb 1D 158
Walpole St. WV6: Wolv 6E 27
Walpole Wlk. B70: W Brom 6B 80
WALSAL END 4A 154
Walsal End La. B92: H Ard 4H 153
WALSALL 2D 48
Walsall Bus. Pk. WS9: A'rdge 6A 34
Walsall Enterprise Pk. WS2: Wals 3A 48
Walsall FC 5B 48
Walsall Gala Baths 1D 48
Walsall Library & Mus. 1D 48
                              (off Tower La.)
Walsall Local History Cen. 5C 32
Walsall New Firms Cen., The
   WS1: Wals 3B 48
Walsall Rd. B42: Gt Barr, P Barr 4B 66
   B71: W Brom 6B 64
   B74: Four O 5D 36
   B74: Lit A 3C 36
   WS3: Pels 5E 21
   WS4: S'fld 6H 21
   WS5: Wals 1D 64
   WS6: Gt Wyr 1F 7
   WS9: A'rdge 6A 34
   WS9: Wals W 5H 21
   WS10: Darl 5D 46
   WS10: W'bry 3C 64
   WS11: Nort C. 2D 8
   WS14: Hilt, Lynn, Muck C, Wall 6F 11
   WV13: W'hall 1B 46
Walsall Station (Rail) 2C 48
Walsall St. B70: W Brom 4B 80
   WS10: Darl 4D 46
   WS10: W'bry 2F 63
   WV1: Wolv 2A 44
   WV13: W'hall 2B 46
   WV14: Bils 5H 45
WALSALL WOOD 3C 22
Walsall Wood Rd. WS9: A'rdge 5C 22
Walsgrave Cl. B92: Sol 1H 151
Walsgrave Dr. B92: Sol 6H 137
Walsham Cft. B34: S End 4G 105
Walsh Dr. B76: Walm 1D 70
Walsh Gro. B23: Erd 5D 68
Walsingham St. WS1: Wals 2E 49
Walstead Cl. WS5: Wals 6G 49
Walstead Rd. WS5: Wals 6D 48
Walstead Rd. W. WS5: Wals 6C 48
Walt Dene Cl. B43: Gt Barr 3A 66
Walter Burden Ho. B66: Smeth 6G 99
Walter Cobb Dr. B73: W Grn 4G 69

Walter Rd. B67: Smeth 3C 98
   WV14: Bils 2G 61
Walters Cl. B31: Longb 3D 158
Walters Rd. B68: O'bry 4G 113
Walters Row DY1: Dud 6C 76
Walter St. B7: Nech 3B 102
   B70: W Brom 5C 80
   WS3: Pels 6E 21
Waltham Gro. B44: K'sdng 3B 68
Waltham Ho. B38: K Nor 6C 146
   B70: W Brom 4B 80
Walthamstow Ct. DY5: Brie H 2H 109
Walton Av. B65: B'hth 3B 112
Walton Cl. B63: Hale 3H 127
   B65: Row R 5A 96
Walton Ct. B63: Hale 2H 127
Walton Cres. WV4: E'shll 6A 44
Walton Cft. B91: Sol 6F 151
Walton Dr. DY9: Lye. 6G 109
Walton Gdns. WV8: Cod 3F 13
Walton Gro. B30: K Nor 5D 146
Walton Heath WS3: Blox 4F 19
Walton Ho. B16: Birm 1D 116
Walton Rd. B68: O'bry 1H 113
   DY8: Amb 5E 109
   WS9: A'rdge 6C 22
   WS10: W'bry 3A 64
   WV4: E'shll 6A 44
Walton St. DY4: Tip 2H 77
Wanderers Av. WV2: Wolv 5G 43
Wanderer Wlk. B36: Hodg H 6C 86
Wandle Gro. B11: Tys 2G 135
Wandsworth Rd. B44: Gt Barr 2G 67
Wansbeck Gro. B38: K Nor 1A 160
Wansbeck Wlk. DY3: Sed 1B 76
Wanstead Gro. B44: K'sdng 4A 68
Wantage Rd. B46: Col 6G 89
Ward Cl. B8: W End 4G 103
Warden Av. B73: Bold. 5F 69
WARD END 3G 103
Ward End Cl. B8: Salt 3F 103
Ward End Hall Gro. B8: W End 3G 103
Ward End Ho. B8: W End 3G 103
Ward End Pk. Rd. B8: Salt 4F 103
Wardend Rd. B8: W End 3G 103
Warden Rd. B73: Bold 5F 69
Ward Gro. WV4: E'shll 2A 60
Wardle Cl. B75: Four O 5G 37
Wardles La. WS6: Gt Wyr 3F 7
Wardlow Cl. WV4: Penn 5F 43
Wardlow Rd. B7: Birm 4B 102
                           (not continuous)
Wardour Dr. B37: Chel W 1E 123
Wardour Gro. B44: K'sdng 5C 68
Ward Rd. WV4: Penn 6H 43
   WV8: Cod 4F 13
Ward St. B19: Birm 5G 101
   WS1: Wals 1D 48
   WV1: Wolv 1A 44
                           (not continuous)
   WV2: E'shll. 4D 44
   WV13: W'hall 6B 30
   WV14: Cose 5D 60
Wareham Cl. WS3: Wals 4D 32
Wareham Ho. B28: Hall G 4E 149
Wareham Rd. B45: Fran 5H 143
Wareing Dr. B23: Erd 5D 68
Warewell Cl. WS1: Wals 1D 48
Warewell St. WS1: Wals 2D 48
Waring Cl. DY4: Tip 5G 61
Waring Rd. DY4: Tip 5A 62
Warings, The WV5: Wom 3F 73
War La. B17: Harb 6F 115
Warley Cft. B68: O'bry 3C 114
Warley Hall Rd. B68: O'bry 3B 114
Warley Rd. B68: O'bry 4A 98
WARLEY WOODS 2C 114
Warmington Dr. B73: S Cold 1H 69
Warmington Rd. B26: Sheld 6G 121
   B47: H'wd 3A 162
Warmley Cl. B91: Sol 2H 151
   WV6: Wolv 4F 27
Warner Dr. DY5: Brie H 2H 109
Warner Pl. WS3: Wals 3D 32
Warner Rd. WS3: Wals 3D 32
   WS10: W'bry 3A 64
   WV8: Cod 4F 13

Warner St. B12: Birm 3A 118
Warners Wlk. B10: Small H 3C 118
Warnford Wlk. WV4: Penn 5A 42
Warple Rd. B32: Quin 6A 114
Warren Av. B13: Mose 3H 133
   WV10: Wolv 4B 28
Warren Cl. DY4: Tip 6H 61
Warren Dr. B65: Row R 4H 95
   B93: Dorr 6C 166
   DY3: Sed 4G 59
Warren Farm Rd. B44: K'sdng 5H 67
Warren Gdns. DY6: K'wfrd 3A 92
Warren Gro. B8: Salt 3E 103
Warren Hill Rd. B44: K'sdng 1H 83
Warren Ho. Ct. B76: Walm 4D 70
Warren Ho. Wlk. B76: Walm 4D 70
Warren La. B45: Lick 6H 157
Warren Pl. WS8: Bwnhls 6C 10
Warren Rd. B8: Salt 3E 103
   B30: Stir 6C 132
   B44: K'sdng 1A 84
Warrens Cft. WS5: Wals 6H 49
Warrens End B38: K Nor 1B 160
Warrens Hall Nature Reserve. 3H 95
Warrens Hall Rd. DY2: Dud 2F 95
Warrington Cl. B76: Walm 4E 71
Warrington Dr. B23: Erd 5D 68
Warsash Cl. WV1: Wolv. 3D 44
WARSTOCK 4B 148
Warstock La. B14: K Hth 2A 148
Warstock Rd. B14: K Hth 4A 148
Warston Av. B32: Bart G 3B 130
WARSTONE 6B 6
Warstone Ct. B18: Birm 5E 101 (1A 4)
Warstone Dr. B71: W Brom 3C 80
Warstone La. B18: Birm 5D 100 (1A 4)
Warstone M. B18: Birm 1A 4
Warstone Pde. E. B18: Birm 5D 100
Warstone Rd. WV10: Share 3A 6
   WV11: Ess 3A 6
Warstones Cres. WV4: Penn 6B 42
Warstones Dr. WV4: Penn 5A 42
Warstones Gdns. WV4: Penn 5A 42
Warstones Ho. WV4: Penn. 5B 42
Warstones Rd. WV4: Penn. 2A 58
Warstone Ter. B21: Hand 1A 100
Warstone Twr. B36: Hodg H 1A 104
Wartell Bank DY6: K'wfrd 2B 92
Wartell Bank Ind. Est. DY6: K'wfrd 2C 92
Warwards La. B29: S Oak 4C 132
Warwell La. B26: Yard 5B 120
Warwick Av. WS10: W'bry 1A 64
   WV6: Pert 6F 25
   WV13: W'hall 1D 46
Warwick Cl. B68: O'bry 1H 113
   B70: W Brom 6E 63
   DY3: Lwr G 4H 75
Warwick Ct. B13: Mose 3A 134
   B29: W Cas. 6F 131
   B37: Chel W 1F 123
   B91: Sol 2F 151
Warwick Crest B15: Edg 4D 116
Warwick Cft. B36: Hodg H 1A 104
Warwick Dr. WV8: Cod. 3E 13
Warwick Gdns. B69: Tiv. 5C 78
Warwick Grange B91: Sol 6D 136
Warwick Gro. B92: Olton 4C 136
Warwick Pk. Ct. B92: Olton 5D 136
Warwick Pas. B2: Birm 1G 117 (4E 5)
Warwick Rd. B6: Witt. 5G 83
                           (not continuous)
   B11: S'hll 6C 118
                           (not continuous)
   B27: A Grn 1D 134
   B68: O'bry 4B 114
   B73: New O 3C 68
   B91: Sol 2E 151
   B93: Chad E, Know. 4E 167
   DY2: Neth 6G 95
   DY8: Word 2B 108
Warwick Rd. Trad. Est. B11: S'hll 1D 134
Warwickshire County Cricket Club
   Edgbaston 6F 117
Warwick St. B12: Birm. 2A 118
   WS4: Wals 6D 32
   WV1: Wolv 2A 44
   WV14: Bils 6G 45

Warwick Wlk. WS9: A'rdge 6C **22**
Wasdale Dr. DY6: K'wfrd 3C **92**
Wasdale Rd. B31: N'fld 3D **144**
WS8: Clay 1H **21**
Waseley Hills Country Pk. 6C 142
Waseley Hills Country Pk. Vis. Cen. 6C 142
Waseley Rd. B45: Rubery 1E **157**
Washbrook La. WS11: Nort C 1A **8**
Washbrook Rd. B8: W End 3G **103**
Washford Gro. B25: Yard 3H **119**
Washington Cen. DY2: Neth. 6F **95**
Washington Ct. B1: Birm 6B **4**
WV3: Wolv 2B **42**
Washington Dr. B20: Hand 4D **82**
Washington St. B1: Birm. 2E **117** (6B **4**)
DY2: Neth 6F **95**
Washington St. Ind. Est. DY2: Neth. 6F **95**
Washington Wharf B1: Birm 2E **117** (6B **4**)
Wash La. B25: Yard 4A **120**
WASHWOOD HEATH 3E 103
Washwood Heath Rd. B8: Salt. 4D **102**
Wasperton Cl. B36: Cas B 1F **105**
Wassell Ct. B63: Hale 3G **127**
Wassell Gro. Bus. Cen. DY9: Hag 3C **126**
Wassell Gro. La. DY9: Hag 5B **126**
Wassell Rd. B63: Hale. 3G **127**
DY9: W'cte. 3B **126**
WV14: Bils 4F **45**
Wast Hill Gro. B38: K Nor 2B **160**
Wast Hills La. B38: Hopw 5H **159**
B48: Hopw. 5H **159**
Wastwater Ct. WV6: Pert 5F **25**
Watchbury Cl. B36: Cas B 6G **87**
Watchman Av. DY5: Quar B 4B **110**
Waterbridge La. WV5: Wom 6E **57**
Water Dale WV3: Wolv 1C **42**
Waterdale B90: Ches G 4B **164**
WV5: Wom 2E **73**
Waterfall Cl. B66: Smeth 2C **98**
Waterfall La. B64: Old H 2A **112**
B65: B'hth 2B **112**
Waterfall La. Trad. Est. B64: Old H. . . . 2A **112**
Waterfall Rd. DY5: Brie H 4G **109**
Waterfield Cl. DY4: Tip 2E **77**
Waterfield Ho. WV5: Wom 6H **57**
Waterfield Way B26: Sheld 4G **121**
Waterford Ct. B23: Erd. 3B **84**
Waterford Pl. B33: Kitts G 6H **105**
Waterford Rd. DY6: K'wfrd 2B **92**
Waterfront, The DY5: Brie H 5A **94**
Waterfront Bus. Pk. DY5: Brie H 6H **93**
Waterfront E. DY5: Brie H 5A **94**
Waterfront Way DY5: Brie H 5A **94**
WS2: Wals 1B **48**
Waterfront W. DY5: Brie H. 5A **94**
Waterglade La. WV13: W'hall 2A **46**
Waterhaynes Cl. B45: Rubery 3G **157**
Waterhead Cl. WV10: Bush 5C **16**
Waterhead Dr. WV10: Bush 5C **16**
Water La. B71: W Brom. 6D **64**
Waterlinks Blvd. B6: Aston 2A **102**
Waterlinks Ho. *B7: Birm* *4H* ***101***
(off Richard St.)
Waterloo Av. B37: F'bri 5D **106**
Waterloo Ind. Est. B37: F'bri. 4D **106**
Waterloo Pas. B2: Birm 1F **117**
Waterloo Rd. B14: K Hth 5G **133**
B25: Yard 5H **119**
B66: Smeth 6E **99**
WV1: Wolv 1G **43** (2A **170**)
Waterloo Rd. Junc.
WV1: Wolv 1G **43** (2A **170**)
Waterloo St. B2: Birm 1F **117** (4C **4**)
DY1: Dud 1D **94**
DY4: Tip. 2G **77**
Waterloo St. E. DY4: Tip 2H **77**
Waterloo Ter. WV1: Wolv 6F **27**
Watermarque B16: Birm 1D **116**
Watermead Grange WS8: Bwnhls 6A **10**
Watermeadow Dr. WS4: S'fld 6H **21**
Watermere WS4: S'fld. 1H **33**
Water Mill Cl. B29: S Oak 2H **131**
Watermill Cl. WV10: F'hses. 4H **15**
Water Mill Cres. B76: Walm 4D **70**
WATER ORTON. 4D 88
Water Orton La. B76: Min 2H **87**
Water Orton Rd. B36: Cas B 1G **105**
Water Orton Station (Rail). **4C 88**
Water Rd. DY3: Gorn. 5G **75**
Waters Dr. B74: Four O 6D **36**
Waters Edge, The B1: Birm. 1E **117** (5A **4**)
Waterside B15: Birm 2E **117**
B43: Gt Barr. 6A **66**
Waterside Cl. B9: Birm 1C **118**
B24: Erd 2E **87**
Waterside Ct. *B16: Birm* *1D* ***116***
(off Vincent St.)
Waterside Dr. B18: Win G 4B **100**
Waterside Est. DY2: Neth. 6E **95**
Waterside Ind. Est. B65: Row R 5H **95**
WV2: E'shll. 5C **44**
Waterside Orchard Cvn. Pk.
B48: Hopw 6F **159**
Waterside Pk. DY4: Tip 6D **62**
Waterside Vw. B18: Hock 4C **100**
DY5: Brie H. 3F **109**
Waterside Way WS8: Bwnhls 3G **9**
WV9: Pend 4E **15**
Waterson Cft. B37: Chel W. 6F **107**
Water St. B3: Birm 6F **101** (2C **4**)
B70: W Brom 5B **80**
DY6: K'wfrd 2B **92**
WV10: Wolv. 6H **27**
Waters Vw. WS3: Pels 2F **21**
Waterward Cl. B17: Harb. 6G **115**
Waterway Ct. B14: Yard W. 4C **148**
Waterways Dr. B69: O'bry 6E **79**
Waterways Gdns. DY8: Word 2C **108**
Waterworks Cotts. B71: W Brom. 6C **64**
Water Works Dr. B31: N'fld 2B **144**
Waterworks Rd. B16: Edg 2B **116**
Waterworks St. B6: Aston 1B **102**
Watery La. B32: Quin. 2G **129**
B48: A'chu, Hopw. 6A **160**
B67: Smeth 4E **99**
B93: Know 5G **167**
B94: Earls. 5A **164**
DY4: Tip 2H **77**
(not continuous)
DY8: Word 1C **108**
WS1: Wals 4B **48**
(not continuous)
WV8: Cod. 3G **13**
WV13: W'hall 6F **29**
Watery La. Ind. Est. WV13: W'hall 6G **29**
Watery La. Middleway B9: Birm 1B **118**
WATFORD GAP 3F 37
Watford Gap Rd. WS14: Lit H 2G **37**
Watford Rd. B30: K Nor 2B **146**
Wathan Av. WV14: Cose 3B **60**
Watkins Gdns. B31: N'fld 4F **145**
Watkins Rd. WV12: W'hall. 4C **30**
Watland Grn. B34: Stech 4E **105**
Watling St. WS8: Bwnhls. 4H **9**
WS11: Cann, Four C, Nort C. 1F **7**
(not continuous)
WS14: Lich, Muck C, Shens, Wall, W'frd
. . . . 3E **11**
Watling St. Bus. Pk. WS3: Lit W 3E **9**
Watney Gro. B44: K'sdng. 5C **68**
Watson Cl. B72: W Grn 3A **70**
Watson Rd. B8: W End 4F **103**
WS10: Mox 6A **46**
WV10: F'hses 5F **15**
WV14: Cose 3C **60**
Watson Rd. E. B7: Nech 2D **102**
Watsons Cl. DY2: Dud 1G **95**
Watson's Grn. Flds. DY2: Dud. 1H **95**
Watson's Grn. Rd. DY2: Dud. 6G **77**
Watson Way CV7: Bal C 5H **169**
Wattisham Sq. B35: Cas V. 3E **87**
Wattis Rd. B67: Smeth. 1E **115**
Wattle Grn. B70: W Brom. 4F **79**
Wattle Rd. B70: W Brom 4F **79**
Watton Cl. WV14: Cose 4C **60**
Watton Grn. B35: Cas V 5E **87**
(not continuous)
Watton La. B46: Wat O. 5E **89**
Watton St. B70: W Brom 5B **80**
Watt Rd. B23: Erd. 3E **85**
DY4: Tip. 5B **62**
Watts Cl. DY4: Tip 2E **77**
Watt's Rd. B10: Small H 3D **118**
Watt St. B21: Hand 2H **99**
B66: Smeth. 3F **99**
Wattville Av. B21: Hand. 1G **99**
Wattville Rd. B66: Hand, Smeth. 2F **99**
Watwood Rd. B28: Hall G. 4F **149**
B90: Hall G, Shir. 4F **149**
Waugh Cl. B37: Chel W 1D **122**
Waugh Dr. B63: Hale 5F **127**
Wavell Rd. B8: Salt 4E **103**
DY5: Quar B 4B **110**
WS2: Wals 1E **47**
Waveney Av. WV6: Pert 5E **25**
Waveney Cft. B36: Cas B. 1B **106**
Wavenham Cl. B74: Four O 4E **37**
Waverhill Rd. B21: Hand. 2B **100**
Waverley Av. B43: Gt Barr 1D **66**
Waverley Cres. B62: Roms 3A **142**
WV2: Penn 5F **43**
WV4: E'shll. 2B **60**
Waverley Gdns. WV5: Wom 6H **57**
Waverley Gro. B91: Sol 4D **150**
Waverley Rd. B10: Small H 4D **118**
WS3: Blox. 5F **19**
WS10: Darl 5D **46**
Waverley St. DY2: Dud 1C **94**
Waxland Rd. B63: Hale 3B **128**
Wayfield Cl. B90: Shir 4A **150**
Wayfield Rd. B90: Shir 4A **150**
Wayford Dr. B72: W Grn 6B **70**
Wayford Glade WV13: W'hall. 3H **45**
Wayford Gro. B8: W End 5H **103**
Waynecroft Rd. B43: Gt Barr 3A **66**
Wayside B37: Mars G. 3B **122**
WV8: Pend 5C **14**
Wayside Acres WV8: Cod. 5F **13**
Wayside Dr. B74: Lit A. 6C **36**
B75: R'ley. 6C **38**
Wayside Gdns.
WV12: W'hall 5E **31**
Wayside Wlk. WS2: Wals 6G **31**
Wealden Hatch WV10: Bush 3A **16**
Wealdstone Dr. DY3: Lwr G. 5H **75**
Weaman St. B4: Birm 6G **101** (2E **5**)
Weates Yd. B27: A Grn 1A **136**
Weatheroak Rd. B11: S'hll. 6C **118**
Weather Oaks B17: Harb 6F **115**
Weatheroaks B62: Quin 4G **113**
WS9: Wals W. 3D **22**
Weaver Av. B26: Sheld. 5F **121**
B76: Walm 4E **71**
Weaver Cl. DY5: P'ntt 3E **93**
Weaver Ct. B75: R'ley 6C **38**
Weaver Gro. WV13: W'hall 1D **46**
Weavers Ri. DY2: Neth. 6F **95**
Webb Av. WV6: Pert. 4E **25**
Webbcroft Rd. B33: Stech 5C **104**
Webb La. B28: Hall G. 1E **149**
Webb Rd. DY4: Tip. 6C **62**
Webb St. WV13: W'hall 1H **45**
WV14: Cose 3E **61**
Webley Ri. WV10: Bush. 3B **16**
Webnor Ind. Est. WV2: E'shll. 5C **44**
Webster Cl. B11: S'brk. 5B **118**
B72: W Grn 6H **69**
Webster Rd. WS2: Wals. 4B **32**
WV13: W'hall 6A **30**
Webster Way B76: Walm 4E **71**
Weddell Wynd WV14: Bils. 4G **61**
Wedgbury Way DY5: Brie H 2F **109**
Wedge Ct. *WS1: Wals* *2D* ***48***
(off Union St.)
Wedge St. WS1: Wals 1D **48**
Wedgewood Av. B70: W Brom 6F **63**
Wedgewood Cl. WV5: Wom. 6F **57**
Wedgewood Ct. *WS4: S'fld* *6G* ***21***
(off Green La.)
Wedgewood Ho. B37: F'bri 5D **106**
Wedgewood Pl. B70: W Brom 6F **63**
Wedgewood Rd. B32: Quin 6A **114**
Wedgwood Cl. WV1: Wolv. 2C **44**
Wedgwood Dr. B20: Hand 5D **82**
Wedmore Rd. B73: Bold. 4F **69**
WEDNESBURY 3F 63
Wednesbury Great Western Street Stop (MM) 3E 63
Wednesbury Leisure Cen. 2E 63
Wednesbury Mus. & Art Gallery 3F 63

Wednesbury New Ent. Cen.
WS10: Mox 2C **62**
Wednesbury Oak Rd. DY4: Tip 4A **62**
Wednesbury Parkway Stop (MM) . . . 3D **62**
Wednesbury Rd. WS2: Wals 4A **48**
Wednesbury Trad. Est.
WS10: W'bry 1E **63**
WEDNESFIELD 4F **29**
Wednesfield High Sports Cen. 4G **29**
Wednesfield Rd.
WV10: Wolv 6H **27** (1D **170**)
WV13: W'hall 6A **30**
Wednesfield Way
WV10: Wolv 5C **28**
WV11: Wed 5D **28**
Wednesfield Way Ind. Est.
WV11: Wed 5F **29**
Weeford Dell B75: R'ley 6C **38**
Weeford Dr. B20: Hand 3B **82**
Weeford Rd. B75: R'ley 1C **54**
Weirbrook Cl. B29: W Cas 6F **131**
Weland Cl. B46: Wat O 5D **88**
Welbeck Av. WV10: Bush 2H **27**
Welbeck Cl. B62: Quin 6E **113**
Welbeck Dr. WS4: Rus 2H **33**
Welbeck Gro. B23: Erd 2B **84**
Welbury Gdns. WV6: Wolv 4D **26**
Welby Ga. CV7: Bal C 4H **169**
Welby Rd. B28: Hall G 4F **135**
Welch Cl. DY4: Tip 6B **62**
Welches Cl. B31: N'fld 2F **145**
Welcombe Dr. B76: Walm 6D **70**
Welcombe Gro. B91: Sol 4D **150**
Welford Av. B26: Yard 3D **120**
Welford Gro. B74: Four O 6F **37**
Welford Rd. B20: Hand 1C **100**
B73: New O 4E **69**
B90: Shir 3A **150**
Welham Cft. B90: M'path 3E **165**
Welland Dr. DY8: Amb 3E **109**
Welland Gro. B24: Erd 4A **86**
WV13: W'hall 1C **46**
Welland Rd. B63: Hale 3A **128**
Welland Way B76: Walm 6E **71**
Well Cl. B36: Hodg H 1C **104**
Wellcroft Rd. B34: S End 2E **105**
Wellcroft St. WS10: W'bry 2F **63**
Wellesbourne Cl. WV3: Wolv 3H **41**
Wellesbourne Dr. WV14: Cose 6D **60**
Wellesbourne Rd. B20: Hand 6D **82**
Wellesbourne Twr. B5: Birm 3G **117**
Wellesley Dr. DY4: Tip 2H **77**
Wellesley Gdns. B13: Mose 4D **134**
Wellesley Rd. B68: O'bry 3H **97**
Wellfield Gdns. DY2: Dud 3G **95**
Wellfield Rd. B28: Hall G 1H **149**
WS9: A'rdge 1D **34**
Wellhead La. B42: P Barr 5G **83**
Wellhead Way B6: Witt 5G **83**
Wellington Av. WV3: Wolv 4D **42**
Wellington Cl. DY6: K'wfrd 5C **92**
Wellington Ct. B20: Hand 5E **83**
B32: Harb 6D **114**
B64: Old H 1H **111**
(off Vine Gdns.)
Wellington Cres. B20: Hand 5D **82**
Wellington Gro. B91: Sol 1D **150**
Wellington Ho. B32: Quin 1D **130**
Wellington Ind. Est.
WV14: Cose 6E **61**
Wellington Pas. B2: Birm 4D **4**
Wellington Pl. WV13: W'hall 6H **29**
Wellington Rd. B15: Edg 5D **116**
B20: Hand 5D **82**
B67: Smeth 6E **99**
DY1: Dud 1D **94**
DY4: Tip 3A **78**
WS5: Wals 5G **49**
WV14: Bils 4D **44**
Wellington St. B18: Win G 3H **99**
B64: Old H 1H **111**
B66: Smeth 3H **99**
B69: O'bry 3H **97**
B71: W Brom 3A **80**
WS2: Wals 4H **47**
Wellington St. Sth.
B70: W Brom 3A **80**

Wellington Ter. B19: Loz 2D **100**
WV13: W'hall 6H **29**
Wellington Twr. B31: N'fld 6E **145**
Wellington Way B35: Cas V 5F **87**
Well La. B5: Birm 1H **117** (5F **5**)
WS3: Blox 2C **32**
WS6: Gt Wyr 4G **7**
WV11: Wed 5E **29**
Wellman Cft. B29: S Oak 4H **131**
Wellman's Rd. WV13: W'hall 2C **46**
Well Mdw. B45: Redn 3G **157**
Wellmeadow Gro. B92: H Ard 6A **140**
Wellmead Wlk. B45: Rubery 1F **157**
Well Pl. WS3: Blox 1C **32**
Wells Av. WS10: Darl 5B **46**
Wells Cl. DY4: Tip 4A **62**
WV6: Pert 5D **24**
Wells Ct. B71: W Brom 5B **64**
DY2: Neth 4E **95**
(off Meeting St.)
Wellsford Av. B92: Olton 1E **137**
WELLS GREEN 6F **121**
Wells Grn. Rd. B92: Olton 1D **136**
Wells Grn. Shop. Cen.
B26: Sheld 1F **137**
Wells Rd. B65: Row R 5E **97**
B92: Sol 1G **137**
DY5: Brie H 6F **93**
WV4: Penn 6D **42**
WV14: Bils 2G **61**
Wells Twr. B16: Birm 1C **116**
Well St. B19: Birm 4E **101**
WS10: Darl 5E **47**
Wells Wlk. B37: Mars G. 2C **122**
Welney Gdns. WV9: Pend 4E **15**
Welsby Av. B43: Gt Barr 6A **66**
Welsh Ho. Farm Rd.
B32: Quin, Harb 1D **130**
Welshmans Hill B73: New O 3B **68**
Welton Cl. B76: Walm 3E **71**
Welwyndale Rd. B72: W Grn 1A **86**
Wembley Gro. B25: Yard 3A **120**
Wem Gdns. WV11: Wed 3F **29**
Wendell Crest WV10: Bush 3B **16**
Wendover Ho. B31: Longb 1D **158**
Wendover Rd. B23: Erd 6C **68**
B65: Row R 4A **96**
WV4: E'shll. 3B **60**
Wendron Gro. B14: K Hth 3F **147**
Wenlock Av. WV3: Wolv 3C **42**
Wenlock Cl. B63: Hale 3F **127**
DY3: Sed 6G **59**
Wenlock Gdns. WS3: Wals 4C **32**
Wenlock Rd. B20: Hand 6H **83**
DY8: Amb 5F **109**
Wenman St. B12: Bal H 5H **117**
Wensley Cft. B90: Shir 1H **149**
Wensleydale Rd. B42: P Barr 1C **82**
Wensley Rd. B26: Sheld 5D **120**
Wentbridge Rd. WV1: Wolv 2E **45**
Wentworth Av. B36: Cas B 1F **105**
Wentworth Ct. B24: Erd 5F **85**
B74: Four O 2H **53**
Wentworth Dr. B69: Tiv 2A **96**
Wentworth Ga. B17: Harb. 5F **115**
Wentworth Gro. WV6: Pert 4D **24**
Wentworth Pk. Av. B17: Harb 5F **115**
Wentworth Ri. B62: Hale 1D **128**
Wentworth Rd. B17: Harb 5E **115**
B74: Four O 4G **53**
B92: Olton 2D **136**
DY8: Woll 4B **108**
WS3: Blox. 3F **19**
WV10: Bush 5A **16**
Wentworth Way B32: Bart G 2D **130**
Wenyon Cl. DY4: Tip 3B **78**
Weoley Av. B29: S Oak 3G **131**
WEOLEY CASTLE 4D **130**
Weoley Castle 3E **131**
Weoley Castle Rd. B29: W Cas 4D **130**
Weoley Hill B29: S Oak 5G **131**
Weoley Pk. Rd. B29: S Oak 4F **131**
WERGS 3F **25**
Wergs Dr. WV6: Tett. 2G **25**
Wergs Hall Rd. WV6: Tett 1F **25**
WV8: Cod 6F **13**
Wergs Rd. WV6: Tett 3F **25**

Werneth Gro. WS3: Blox 3G **19**
Wesley Av. B63: Crad 3D **110**
WS6: C Hay 2D **6**
WV8: Bilb 5H **13**
Wesley Cl. B64: Old H 2H **111**
WV5: Wom 2F **73**
Wesley Ct. B16: Edg 6H **99**
B64: Old H 3H **111**
WV13: W'hall 2G **45**
Wesley Gro. WS10: W'bry 2E **63**
Wesley Ho. WS2: Wals 4A **48**
(off Oxford St.)
Wesley Pl. DY4: Tip 6C **62**
Wesley Rd. B23: Erd 2F **85**
DY5: P'ntt 4F **93**
WV8: Bilb 5H **13**
WV12: W'hall 3C **30**
Wesley's Fold WS10: Darl 5D **46**
Wesley St. B69: O'bry 1G **97**
B70: W Brom 4H **79**
WV2: E'shll 5C **44**
WV14: Bils 3G **61**
Wessex Cl. WS8: Bwnhls. 6B **10**
Wessex Rd. WV2: E'shll 5B **44**
Wesson Gdns. B63: Hale 2A **128**
Wesson Rd. WS10: Darl. 3C **46**
Westacre WV13: W'hall 2H **45**
Westacre Cres. WV3: Wolv 3H **41**
W. Acre Dr. DY5: Quar B 3B **110**
Westacre Gdns. B33: Stech 6D **104**
West Av. B20: Hand 3B **82**
B36: Cas B 1H **105**
B69: Tiv 2B **96**
WV11: Wed 3E **29**
West Blvd. B32: Quin, Bart G 5C **114**
Westbourne Av. B34: Hodg H 3C **104**
WS6: C Hay 1E **7**
Westbourne Ct. WS4: Wals 6E **33**
(off Lichfield Rd.)
Westbourne Cres. B15: Edg 3C **116**
Westbourne Gdns. B15: Edg 4C **116**
Westbourne Gro. B21: Hand 2B **100**
Westbourne Rd. B15: Edg 4B **116**
B21: Hand 6H **81**
B62: B'hth 4E **113**
B70: W Brom 5H **79**
B92: Olton 5D **136**
WS4: Wals 5D **32**
WS10: Darl 4F **47**
WV4: Penn 6E **43**
Westbourne St. WS4: Wals 6D **32**
WEST BROMWICH 4B **80**
West Bromwich Albion FC 6F **81**
West Bromwich Central Stop (MM) . . . 5A **80**
West Bromwich Crematorium
B71: W Brom 6E **65**
W. Bromwich Parkway B70: W Brom . . . 4H **79**
(Dartmouth St.)
B70: W Brom 6C **80**
(Springfield Cres.)
W. Bromwich Ringway B70: W Brom . . . 4B **80**
(New St.)
B70: W Brom 4A **80**
(St Michael St.)
W. Bromwich Rd. WS1: Wals 5C **48**
(not continuous)
W. Bromwich St. B69: O'bry. 6F **79**
WS1: Wals 3C **48**
Westbrook Av. WS9: A'rdge 4A **34**
Westbrook Way WV5: Wom 2F **73**
Westbury Av. WS10: W'bry 5F **47**
Westbury Ct. DY5: Brie H. 1H **109**
(off Lit. Potter St.)
Westbury Rd. B17: Edg 6F **99**
WS10: W'bry 5F **47**
Westbury St. WV1: Wolv . . . 1H **43** (2C **170**)
Westcliffe Pl. B31: N'fld 3D **144**
Westcombe Gro. B32: Bart G 4G **129**
W. Coppice Rd.
WS8: Bwnhls 5G **9**
Westcote Av. B31: Longb. 5A **144**
Westcote Cl. B92: Olton 3E **137**
Westcott Cl. DY6: K'wfrd 6D **92**
Westcott Rd. B26: Yard 3E **121**
WESTCROFT 5D **16**
Westcroft Av. WV10: Bush 6C **16**
Westcroft Gro. B38: K Nor 4G **145**

Westcroft Rd. DY3: Sed 3F 59
WV6: Tett 3F 25
Westcroft Way B14: K Hth 6B 148
DY1: Dud 1D 94
W. Cross Shop. Cen. B66: Smeth 2B 98
W. Dean Cl. B62: Hale 1C 128
West Dr. B5: Birm 6E 117
B20: Hand 1D 100
West End Av. B66: Smeth 2B 98
Westerdale Cl. DY3: Sed 6C 60
Westerham Cl. B93: Know 3B 166
Westeria Cl. B36: Cas B 1G 105
Westering Parkway WV10: Bush 3A 16
Westerings B20: Hand 5E 83
Western Av. B19: Loz 2E 101
B62: Hale 1E 129
DY3: Sed 5F 59
DY5: Brie H 1F 109
WS2: Wals 6D 30
Western Bus. Pk. B62: Hale 4B 112
Western Cl. WS2: Wals 6D 30
Western Ct. B9: Birm 2A 118
(off Bromley St.)
Western Rd. B18: Win G 5B 100
B24: Erd 4G 85
B64: Crad H 3G 111
B69: O'bry 4H 97
B73: W Grn 4G 69
DY8: Stourb 1D 124
Western Way WS10: Mox, W'bry 1C 62
Westfield Av. B14: K Hth 6B 148
Westfield Cl. B93: Dorr 6F 167
Westfield Dr. WS9: A'rdge 3C 34
WV5: Wom 6F 57
Westfield Grange B14: K Hth. 4G 133
Westfield Gro. WV3: Wolv 3A 42
Westfield Hall B16: Edg. 2G 115
Westfield Ho. B36: Cas B. 2C 106
Westfield Mnr. B75: Four O 5G 37
Westfield Rd. B14: K Hth 5F 133
B15: Edg 3G 115
B27: A Grn 2H 135
B62: B'hth 2E 113
B67: Smeth 5D 98
DY2: Dud 2F 95
DY3: Sed 4H 59
DY5: Quar B 3B 110
WV13: W'hall 3G 45
WV14: Bils 4D 44
Westford Gro. B28: Hall G 4E 149
West Ga. B1: Birm 6D 100
B16: Edg 6A 100
B69: O'bry 5E 97
Westgate B15: Edg 1A 132
WS9: A'rdge 2H 33
Westgate Cl. DY3: Sed. 6A 60
Westgate Trad. Est. WS9: A'rdge. 3A 34
West Grn. WV4: Penn 6A 42
West Grn. Cl. B15: Edg 3D 116
West Gro. Av. B90: M'path 3D 164
Westhall Ga. WS3: Blox 5H 19
Westham Ho. B37: F'bri 5D 106
Westhaven Dr. B31: N'fld 6C 130
Westhaven Rd. B72: S Cold 5A 54
Westhay Rd. B28: Hall G 6H 135
WEST HEATH 6F 145
W. Heath Rd. B18: Win G 5H 99
B31: N'fld 5F 145
Westhill WV3: Wolv 1A 42
Westhill Cl. B92: Olton 5C 136
West Hill Ct. B14: K Hth. 3E 147
Westhill Rd. B38: K Nor 4B 146
West Holme B9: Birm. 1C 118
Westholme Cft. B30: B'vlle 6A 132
Westhorpe Gro. B19: Birm 4E 101
Westhouse Gro. B14: K Hth 3F 147
Westland Av. WV3: Wolv 1D 42
West Land Cl. B23: Erd 2F 85
Westland Gdns. DY8: Amb 4D 108
WV3: Wolv 1E 43
Westland Rd. WV3: Wolv 1D 42
Westlands Est. DY8: Word. 2C 108
Westlands Rd. B13: Mose 4A 134
B76: Walm 1D 86
Westland Wlk. B35: Cas V 5D 86
Westleigh Rd. WV5: Wom 2F 73
Westley Brook Cl. B26: Sheld 6F 121
Westley Cl. B28: Hall G 1H 149

Westley Rd. B27: A Grn. 2H 135
Westley St. B9: Birm 1A 118
DY1: Dud 1D 94
Westmead Cres. B24: Erd 3A 86
W. Mead Dr. B14: K Hth 1G 147
Westmead Dr. B68: O'bry 5H 97
W. Mill Cft. B38: K Nor 2A 160
Westminster B37: K'hrst 4B 106
Westminster Av. WV4: Penn 6F 43
Westminster Cl. DY1: Dud 5C 76
Westminster Dr. B14: K Hth 1G 147
Westminster Ind. Est.
DY2: Neth 1F 111
Westminster Rd. B20: Hand. 5E 83
B29: S Oak 4C 132
B71: W Brom 4B 64
DY8: Word 1A 108
WS4: Rus 2F 33
Westmore Way WS10: W'bry. 6B 48
Westmorland Ct. B71: W Brom 6B 64
Westmorland Rd. B71: W Brom 6B 64
Weston Av. B11: S'brk 5C 118
Weston Cl. B93: Dorr. 6H 167
WS1: Wals 5C 48
Weston Ct. B9: Birm. 2A 118
(off Allcock St.)
WV1: Wolv 5G 27
Weston Cres. WS9: A'rdge 4D 34
Weston Dr. DY4: Tip. 3C 62
WS6: Gt Wyr 5E 7
WV14: Bils 1D 60
Weston Ho. B19: Hock. 3G 101
Weston Ind. Est. B11: Tys 1E 135
Weston La. B11: Tys 1E 135
Weston Rd. B19: Hock. 2D 100
B67: Smeth 1D 114
Weston St. WS1: Wals 5C 48
Weston Ter. B19: Loz 1F 101
(off New Inn Rd.)
Westover Rd. B20: Hand 3A 82
West Pk. Av. B31: N'fld 5C 144
West Pk. Cl. WS9: A'rdge 4A 34
West Pk. Ct. WV1: Wolv. 1E 43
West Pk. Rd. B67: Smeth 2B 98
West Pathway B17: Harb 5G 115
West Point B15: Edg 3G 115
Westport Cres. WV11: Wed 4H 29
Westray Cl. B45: Fran 6E 143
Westridge DY3: Sed. 5G 59
Westridge Rd. B13: Mose 6C 134
West Ri. B75: S Cold 5A 54
West Rd. B6: Witt 5G 83
B43: Gt Barr 6A 66
B63: Crad 5D 110
DY4: Tip 5B 62
West Rd. Sth. B63: Crad 5D 110
Westside Dr. B32: Bart G 4B 130
WEST SMETHWICK 2B 98
West St. B65: B'hth 2C 112
DY3: Gorn 4H 75
DY5: Quar B 3B 110
DY8: Stourb 6D 108
WS3: Blox 2A 32
WV10: Wolv 4G 27
West Vw. B8: W End 5A 104
West Vw. Ct. B75: S Cold 5C 54
West Vw. Dr. DY6: K'wfrd 4C 92
West Vw. Rd. B75: S Cold 5C 54
Westville Rd. WS2: Wals 6G 31
Westward Cl. B44: K'sdng 5H 67
West Way B31: Longb 2F 159
WS4: S'fld 5F 21
Westwick Cl. WS9: Ston 3G 23
Westwood Av. B11: Tys 1D 134
DY8: Stourb 2A 124
Westwood Bus. Pk. B6: Witt 6B 84
Westwood Ct. B73: S'tly 1B 68
Westwood Dr. B45: Redn 6H 143
Westwood Gro. B91: Sol 5D 150
Westwood Rd. B6: Witt 6A 84
B73: S'tly 1A 68
Westwood Vw. B24: Erd. 4A 86
Wetherby Cl. B36: Hodg H 1B 104
WV10: F'hses. 3H 15

Wetherby Rd. B27: A Grn. 3A 136
WS3: Blox 3G 19
Wetherfield Rd. B11: Tys. 2G 135
Wexford Cl. DY1: Dud 5B 76
Wexler Lofts B1: Birm 2A 4
Weybourne Rd. B44: Gt Barr 3G 67
Weycroft Rd. B23: K'sdng 6B 68
Weyhill Cl. WV9: Pend 5D 14
Weymoor Rd. B17: Harb 2E 131
Weymouth Dr. B74: Four O. 5F 37
Wharf, The B1: Birm 1E 117 (5B 4)
Wharf App. WS9: A'rdge 2B 34
Wharfdale Rd. B11: Tys 6G 119
Wharfedale Cl. DY6: W Hth. 2H 91
Wharfedale St. WS10: W'bry 3F 63
Wharf La. B91: Sol. 1H 151
WS8: Bwnhls 2C 10
Wharf Rd. B11: Tys 6H 119
B30: K Nor 5C 146
Wharf Rd. Ind. Est.
B11: Tys. 6H 119
Wharfside B69: O'bry 2F 97
Wharfside Leisure Complex 2D 146
Wharfside St. B1: Birm 2F 117 (6C 4)
Wharf St. B6: Aston 2A 102
B18: Hock 3C 100
WV1: Wolv 2A 44
Whar Hall Rd. B92: Sol 5A 138
Wharton Av. B92: Sol 6A 138
Wharton Rd. B66: Smeth 2G 99
Wharton St. B7: Nech 1D 102
Wharwell La. WS6: Gt Wyr 4G 7
Whatcote Grn. B92: Sol 5H 137
Whatecroft, The B17: Harb. 5F 115
Whateley Av. WS3: Wals 3D 32
Whateley Cres. B36: Cas B 1H 105
Whateley Grn. B36: Cas B. 1G 105
B74: Four O 3G 53
Whateley Hall Cl. B93: Know. 2E 167
Whateley Hall Rd. B93: Know. 2D 166
Whateley Lodge Dr. B36: Cas B 1G 105
Whateley Pl. WS3: Wals 3D 32
Whateley Rd. B21: Hand 1A 100
WS3: Wals 3D 32
Wheatcroft Cl. B62: B'hth. 3F 113
B75: R'ley. 6C 38
Wheatcroft Dr. B37: Chel W 2E 123
Wheatcroft Gro. DY2: Dud 6H 77
Wheatcroft Rd. B33: Yard 1D 120
Wheaten Cl. B37: Chel W 6F 107
Wheatfield Cl. B36: Cas B 2C 106
Wheatfield Vw. B31: N'fld 1B 144
Wheat Hill WS5: Wals 3A 50
Wheathill Cl. WV4: Penn 2C 58
Wheatland Gro. WS9: A'rdge. 5D 34
Wheatlands, The WV6: Pert 6D 24
Wheatlands Cft. B33: Kitts G 6A 106
Wheatley Cl. B68: O'bry 3B 114
B75: Four O 6A 38
B92: Sol 5A 138
Wheatley Grange B46: Col. 3H 107
Wheatley Gro. WS6: Gt Wyr 3G 7
Wheatley Rd. B68: O'bry 3A 114
Wheatley St. B70: W Brom 4G 79
WV2: E'shll. 5A 44
Wheatmoor Ri. B75: S Cold 5C 54
Wheatmoor Rd. B75: S Cold 4D 54
Wheaton Cl. WV10: Oxl 2G 27
Wheaton Va. B20: Hand. 4A 82
Wheatridge Cl. DY6: W Hth. 1G 91
Wheats Av. B17: Harb. 2F 131
Wheatsheaf Cl. B75: R'ley. 5C 38
Wheatsheaf Rd. B16: Edg 1H 115
B69: Tiv 1A 96
WV8: Pend 6C 14
Wheatstone Cl. DY3: Sed. 1A 76
Wheatstone Gro. B33: Stech 4D 104
Wheel Av. WV8: Cod 4F 13
Wheel Ct., The WV8: Cod 4F 13
Wheeler Cl. WV8: Cod 3E 13
Wheeler Ho. B69: O'bry. 2G 97
Wheeler Rd. WV11: Wed 1E 29
Wheeler's Fold WV1: Wolv. . . 1H 43 (3C 170)
Wheeler's Hill DY8: Stourb 5D 108
(off Lwr. High St.)
Wheeler's La. B13: Mose 1G 147
Wheeler St. DY8: Stourb 6D 108

Wheeler St. Shop. Cen. B19: Hock 3F 101
Wheeley Moor Rd. B37: K'hrst 4C 106
Wheeley Rd. B92: Sol 6H 137
Wheeley's La. B15: Birm 3E 117
Wheeley's Rd. B15: Edg 4D 116
Wheelfield WV8: Cod 4F 13
Wheelock Cl. B74: S'tly 4H 51
Wheelwright Ct. B24: Erd 5E 85
Wheelwright Rd. B24: Erd 5E 85
Wheldrake Av. B34: S End 4G 105
Whernside Dr. WV6: Wolv 4E 27
Wherretts Well La. B91: Sol 2A 152
Whetstone Cl. B15: Edg 6B 116
Whetstone Grn. WV10: Bush 6H 15
Whetstone Gro. WV10: Bush 1H 27
Whetstone La. WS9: A'rdge 5D 34
Whetstone Rd. WV10: Bush 1H 27
Whetty Bri. Rd. B45: Rubery 3E 157
Whetty La. B45: Rubery 2E 157
Whichbury Ct. B65: Row R 5D 96
Whichford Cl. B76: Walm 1B 86
Whichford Gro. B9: Bord G 1H 119
While Rd. B72: S Cold 1H 69
Whilmot Cl. WV10: F'stne 1D 16
Whinberry Ri. DY5: P'ntt 6G 75
Whisley Brook La. B28: Hall G 3F 135
Whistler Gro. WV10: Bush 1C 28
Whiston Av. WV11: Wed 2A 30
Whiston Gro. B29: W Cas 5F 131
Whiston Ho. WS1: Wals 2D 48
Whitacre La. WS14: Lynn 6G 11
Whitacre Rd. B9: Bord G 6E 103
  B93: Know 2D 166
Whitbourne Cl. B12: Bal H 6B 118
Whitburn Av. B42: P Barr 2C 82
Whitburn Cl. WV9: Pend 5E 15
Whitby Cl. WS3: Blox 4F 19
Whitby Rd. B12: Bal H 1A 134
Whitchurch La. B90: Dic H 3G 163
Whitcot Gro. B31: Longb 1D 158
Whitebeam Cl. DY3: Lwr G 3G 75
  WS8: Clay 1A 22
Whitebeam Cft. B38: K Nor 6A 146
Whitebeam Rd. B37: Chel W 3E 123
White City Rd. DY5: Quar B 2C 110
White Cl. DY9: Pedm 3G 125
Whitecrest B43: Gt Barr 3B 66
Whitecroft Rd. B26: Sheld 6G 121
White Falcon Ct. B91: Sol 5D 150
White Farm Rd. B74: Four O 4E 37
Whitefield Av. B17: Harb 5E 115
Whitefield Cl. WV8: Bilb 5H 13
Whitefields Cres. B91: Sol 5F 151
Whitefields Ga. B91: Sol 6E 151
Whitefields Rd. B91: Sol 6E 151
  (not continuous)
Whitefriars Dr. B63: Hale 1A 128
Whitegates Rd. WV14: Cose 2F 61
Whitehall Dr. B63: Hale 1B 128
  DY1: Dud 5C 76
Whitehall Ind. Pk. DY4: Tip 2E 79
Whitehall Rd. B9: Small H 1D 118
  B21: Hand 2C 100
  B63: Hale 1B 128
  B64: Crad H 3E 111
  B70: W Brom 2E 79
  DY4: Tip 2D 78
  DY6: K'wfrd 3A 92
  DY8: Stourb 3F 125
  WS1: Wals 4C 48
  WV4: Penn 1F 59
White Hart, The WS1: Wals 3C 48
  (off Caldmore Grn.)
Whitehead Dr. B76: Min 1H 87
Whitehead Gro. CV7: Bal C 2H 169
Whitehead Rd. B6: Aston 2G 101
Whiteheath Ct. B69: O'bry 5E 97
  (off Birchfield La.)
White Hill B31: N'fld 2F 145
Whitehill La. B29: W Cas 2E 145
White Hollies WS3: Pels 3D 20
White Horse Rd. WS8: Bwnhls 3A 10
Whitehouse Av. WS10: Darl 4B 46
  WS10: W'bry 2F 63
  WV3: Wolv 3B 42
  WV11: Wed 2H 29
White Ho. Cl. B91: Sol 4D 150

WHITEHOUSE COMMON 4D 54
Whitehouse Comn. Rd. B75: S Cold . . 3C 54
Whitehouse Ct. B75: S Cold 6D 54
Whitehouse Cres. B75: S Cold 3C 54
  WV11: Wed 6H 17
Whitehouse Dr. B66: Smeth 2E 99
WHITEHOUSE GATE 5E 97
White Ho. Grn. B91: Sol 4D 150
Whitehouse La. DY3: Swind 6A 72
  DY7: Env 6A 72
  WV8: Cod, Cod W 1B 12
White Ho. Pl. B45: Rubery 3F 157
White Ho's. La. WV10: F'stne 1C 16
  (not continuous)
Whitehouse St. B6: Aston 3H 101
  DY4: Tip 5A 78
  WS2: Wals 6B 32
  WV14: Cose 5E 61
White Ho. Way B91: Sol. 4E 151
Whitehouse Way WS9: A'rdge 5B 34
Whitemoor Dr. B90: M'path 2E 165
White Oak Dr. DY6: K'wfrd. 3A 92
  WV3: Wolv 3A 42
Whitepoplars Cl. DY5: Brie H 5G 93
White Rd. B11: S'brk 4C 118
  B32: Quin 5B 114
  B67: Smeth 3C 98
White Row WV5: Try 4C 56
Whites Dr. DY3: Sed 5A 60
Whiteslade Cl. B93: Know 2C 166
Whitesmiths Cl. DY3: Sed 5H 59
Whitesmiths Cft. B14: K Hth 5G 133
Whites Rd. B71: W Brom 1A 80
WHITE STITCH 1H 141
Whitestitch La. CV7: Mer. 2H 141
Whitestone Rd. B63: Hale 5A 112
White St. B12: Bal H 6A 118
  WS1: Wals 3C 48
Whites Wood WV5: Wom 2G 73
Whitethorn Cres. B74: S'tly 2F 51
Whitethorn Rd. DY8: Word 2E 109
Whitewood Glade
  WV12: W'hall 5E 31
Whitford Dr. B90: M'path 2F 165
Whitgreave Av. WV10: Bush 1A 28
  WV10: F'stne 1D 16
Whitgreave Ct. WV10: F'stne. 1D 16
Whitgreave St. B70: W Brom. 4E 79
Whitland Cl. B45: Redn 3H 157
Whitland Dr. B14: K Hth 4H 147
Whitley Cl. WV6: Tett. 1H 41
Whitley Cl. B20: Hand 4A 82
Whitley Ct. Rd. B32: Quin 5A 114
Whitley Dr. B74: S'tly 3A 52
Whitley St. WS10: W'bry 2E 63
Whitlock Gro. B14: K Hth. 4A 148
WHITLOCKS END 4E 163
Whitlock's End Station (Rail) 2E 163
Whitminster Av. B24: Erd 4H 85
Whitminster Cl. WV12: W'hall. 5C 30
Whitmore Hill WV1: Wolv. . . . 1G 43 (2A 170)
Whitmore Ho. WV6: Wolv 5E 27
WHITMORE REANS 5E 27
Whitmore Rd. B10: Small H 3C 118
  DY8: Stourb 6B 108
Whitmore St. B18: Hock 4D 100
  WS1: Wals 4B 48
  WV1: Wolv 1H 43 (2C 170)
Whitnash Cl. CV7: Bal C 3G 169
Whitney Av. DY8: Woll 5B 108
Whittaker St. WV2: E'shll 5A 44
Whittall St. B4: Birm 6G 101 (2E 5)
Whittimere St. WS1: Wals. 1D 48
Whittingham Gro. WV11: Wed 3H 29
Whittingham Rd. B63: Hale 6A 112
Whittington Cl. B14: K Hth 2G 147
  B71: W Brom 5D 64
Whittington Gro. B33: Yard 1D 120
Whittington Hall La. DY7: Kinv 1A 124
Whittington Oval B33: Yard 1E 121
Whittington Rd. DY8: Stourb 2B 124
Whittle Cft. B35: Cas V 4D 86
Whittleford Gro. B36: Cas B 6G 87
Whitton St. WS10: Darl 5E 47
Whitwell Cl. B90: M'path 4E 165
Whitworth Cl. WS10: Darl 4E 47
Whitworth Dr. B71: W Brom 4C 64

Whitworth Ind. Pk. B9: Bord G 1C 118
Whyle St. B63: Hale 1B 128
Whyley St. B70: W Brom 3G 79
Whyley Wlk. B69: O'bry 4G 97
Whynot St. B63: Crad 6D 110
Wibert Cl. B29: S Oak 4C 132
Wichnor Rd. B92: Olton 6D 120
Wicketts Twr. B5: Edg 6E 117
Wickham Gdns. WV11: Wed 3D 28
Wickham Sq. B70: W Brom 5H 79
Wicklow Cl. B63: Hale 4F 127
Wideacre Dr. B44: Gt Barr 6G 67
Wide Acres B45: Fran 6F 143
Widney Av. B29: S Oak 3G 131
  WS9: A'rdge 6D 22
Widney Cl. B93: Ben H. 4B 166
Widney La. B91: Sol 6C 150
Widney Mnr. Rd. B91: Sol. 5G 151
Widney Manor Station (Rail) 1G 165
Widney Rd. B93: Ben H, Know 4A 166
Wiggin Cotts. B17: Harb 6G 115
Wiggin Ho. WS3: Blox 4A 20
Wiggins Cft. B76: Walm. 2D 70
Wiggins Hill Rd. B76: Min, Wis. 1B 88
Wigginsmill Rd. WS10: W'bry 4D 62
Wiggin St. B16: Birm 6B 100
Wight Cft. B36: Cas B 3D 106
Wightman Cl. WS10: W'bry 6C 46
Wightwick Bank WV6: Tett 2G 41
Wightwick Cl. WS3: Blox 6H 19
Wightwick Ct. WV6: Tett 1G 41
Wightwick Gro. WV6: Tett 1G 41
Wightwick Hall Rd. WV6: Tett 2E 41
Wightwick Leys WV6: Tett 1F 41
Wightwick Manor 2F 41
Wigland Way B38: K Nor 6C 146
Wigmore Gro. B44: K'sdng 5B 68
Wigmore La. B71: W Brom 5E 65
  (not continuous)
Wigorn La. DY9: Pedm. 5F 125
Wigorn Rd. B67: Smeth 2D 114
Wilberforce Way B92: Sol 6B 138
Wilbraham Rd. WS2: Wals 2A 48
Wilcote Gro. B27: A Grn 5A 136
Wildacres DY8: Woll 5A 108
Wilday Cl. DY4: Tip 2A 78
Wilde Cl. B14: K Hth 3F 147
Wilden Cl. B31: N'fld 4A 144
Wilderness La. B43: Gt Barr 3H 65
Wildfell Rd. B27: A Grn 3B 136
WILDMOOR 5A 156
Wildmoor La. B61: Cats, Wild 6A 156
Wildmoor Rd. B90: Shir. 2H 149
Wildside Activity Cen. 4D 26
Wildtree Av. WV10: Bush. 5C 16
Wiley Av. WS10: Darl. 5C 46
Wiley Av. Sth. WS10: Darl 6C 46
Wilford Gro. B76: Walm 1F 87
  B91: Sol 5F 151
Wilford Rd. B71: W Brom 1B 80
Wilkes Av. WS2: Wals 1F 47
Wilkes Cl. WS3: Pels 4C 20
Wilkes Cft. DY3: Sed 6H 59
Wilkes Rd. WV8: Cod 3F 13
Wilkes St. B71: W Brom 6C 64
  WV13: W'hall 2A 46
Wilkin, The WS8: Bwnhls 3G 9
Wilkin Rd. WS8: Bwnhls 3G 9
Wilkins Ho. WS3: Blox 6G 19
  (off Sandbank)
Wilkinson Av. WV14: Bils 2G 61
Wilkinson Cl. B73: W Grn 3H 69
Wilkinson Cft. B8: W End. 3A 104
Wilkinson Rd. WS10: Mox. 6A 46
Wilkins Rd. WV14: Bils 4F 45
Wilks Grn. B21: Hand 4H 81
Willard Rd. B25: Yard 5A 120
Willaston Rd. B33: Sheld. 4H 121
Willclare Rd. B26: Sheld 5E 121
Willcock Rd. WV2: Wolv 4A 44
WILLENHALL 1B 46
Willenhall Ind. Est. WV13: W'hall. 6C 30
Willenhall La. WS2: Wals 2F 31
  WS3: Blox. 2F 31
Willenhall La. Ind. Est.
  WS3: Blox 1G 31
Willenhall Leisure Cen. 2B 46
Willenhall Library & Mus. 2B 46

Willenhall Rd. WS10: Darl 2D **46**
WV1: Wolv 2C **44**
WV13: W'hall 2C **44**
WV14: Bils 5H **45**
Willenhall St. WS10: Darl 3C **46**
Willenhall Trad. Est. WV13: W'hall 2A **46**
Willerby Fold WV10: Bush 3B **16**
Willersey Rd. B13: Mose 5D **134**
Willes Ct. *B62: Quin* *4G 113*
(off Binswood Rd.)
Willes Rd. B18: Win G 3A **100**
Willett Av. WS7: Chase 1A **10**
Willett Rd. B71: W Brom 5C **64**
Willetts Dr. B63: Crad 1D **126**
Willetts Rd. B31: N'fld 6E **145**
Willetts Way B64: Old H 1H **111**
Willey Gro. B24: Erd 5H **85**
William Bentley Ct. WV11: Wed 4E **29**
William Booth La. B4: Birm 5F **101** (1D **4**)
William Cook Rd. B8: W End 4H **103**
William Ct. B13: Mose 1H **133**
B16: Edg 2A **116**
William Edward St. B12: Birm 3H **117**
William Grn. Rd. WS10: W'bry 2A **64**
William Harper Rd. WV13: W'hall 2B **46**
William Kerr Rd. DY4: Tip 2C **78**
William Rd. B31: N'fld 6D **144**
B67: Smeth 6B **98**
William's Cl. WV12: W'hall 4C **30**
Williamson St. WV3: Wolv 3F **43** (6A **170**)
William St. B15: Birm 2E **117** (6A **4**)
B70: W Brom 2E **79**
DY5: Brie H 6G **93**
WS4: Wals 6D **32**
William St. Nth. B19: Birm 5F **101**
William St. W. B66: Smeth 2F **99**
William Wiggin Av. WS3: Blox 5H **19**
Willingsworth Rd.
WS10: W'bry 4C **62**
Willingworth Cl. WV14: Cose 2C **60**
Willis Pearson Av. WV14: Bils 3H **61**
Willmore Gro. B38: K Nor 1B **160**
Willmore Rd. B20: Hand 5F **83**
Willmott Cl. B75: R'ley 6B **38**
Willmott Rd. B75: R'ley 6B **38**
Willoughby Dr. B91: Sol 6F **151**
Willoughby Gro. B29: W Cas 4E **131**
Willow Av. B17: Edg 1E **115**
WS10: W'bry 1F **63**
WV11: Wed 1C **28**
Willow Bank WV3: Wolv 2A **42**
Willowbank Rd. B93: Know 3B **166**
Willow Cl. B21: Hand 1H **99**
B64: Old H 2G **111**
Willow Coppice B32: Bart G 4A **130**
Willow Ct. B13: Mose 2A **134**
B66: Smeth 1B **98**
Willowdale Grange WV6: Tett 4C **26**
Willow Dr. B21: Hand 6G **81**
B69: Tiv 2C **96**
B90: Ches G 5B **164**
WV8: Bilb 4H **13**
Willow End DY9: W'cte 2H **125**
Willow Gdns. B16: Birm 5B **100**
Willow Gro. WV11: Ess 4B **18**
Willow Hgts. B64: Crad H 3A **112**
Willowherb Cl. WS5: Wals 2E **65**
Willowherb Way B90: Dic H 4G **163**
Willow Ho. *B7: Birm* *5A 102*
(off Vauxhall Rd.)
Willow M. B29: S Oak 4F **131**
Willow Pk. Dr. DY8: Stourb 3E **125**
Willow Ri. DY5: Brie H 2G **109**
Willow Rd. B30: B'vlle 5B **132**
B43: Gt Barr 4B **66**
B91: Sol 5C **150**
DY1: Dud 3C **76**
WV3: Wolv 3B **42**
Willows, The B27: A Grn 3H **135**
B47: H'wd 3A **162**
B74: Four O 1F **53**
B76: Walm 3D **70**
DY2: Neth 4G **95**
WV5: Wom 2F **73**
Willowsbrook Rd. B62: B'hth 3F **113**
Willows Cres. B12: Bal H 6F **117**
Willowside WS4: S'fld 1G **33**
Willows Rd. B12: Bal H 6G **117**
WS1: Wals 2E **49**
WS4: S'fld 1G **33**
Willow Wlk. B76: Walm 6D **70**
Willow Way B37: Chel W 1D **122**
Wills Av. B71: W Brom 5H **63**
Willsbridge Covert B14: K Hth 5F **147**
Wills Ho. B70: W Brom 5A **80**
Willson Cft. B28: Hall G 4D **148**
Wills St. B19: Loz 2D **100**
Wills Way B66: Smeth 5G **99**
Wilmcote Cl. B12: Bal H 5G **117**
Wilmcote Dr. B75: Four O 6H **37**
Wilmcote Rd. B91: Sol 1D **150**
Wilmcote Twr. B12: Birm 4H **117**
Wilmington Rd. B32: Quin 5H **113**
Wilmore La. B47: Wyt 5H **161**
Wilmot Av. B46: Col 3H **107**
Wilmot Cl. CV7: Bal C 1H **169**
Wilmot Dr. B23: Erd 1G **85**
DY4: Tip 1G **77**
Wilmot Gdns. DY1: Dud 5C **76**
Wilnecote Gro. B42: P Barr 3F **83**
Wilner's Vw. WS3: Pels 2D **20**
Wilsford Cl. B14: K Hth 6F **147**
WS4: S'fld 1G **33**
Wilson Dr. B75: S Cold 6E **55**
(not continuous)
Wilson Rd. B19: Loz 1F **101**
B66: Smeth 6F **99**
B68: O'bry 3B **114**
DY5: Brie H 5G **93**
WV14: Cose 6E **61**
Wilsons Rd. B93: Know 3E **167**
Wilson St. DY4: Tip 2A **78**
WV1: Wolv 6H **27**
Wilton Cl. DY3: Sed 6A **60**
Wilton Rd. B11: S'hll 6B **118**
B20: Hand 6D **82**
B23: Erd 2G **85**
CV7: Bal C 3H **169**
Wilton St. B19: Loz 1F **101**
Wiltshire Cl. WS2: Wals 5B **32**
Wiltshire Ct. *B29: W Cas* *6G 131*
(off Tugford Rd.)
Wiltshire Dr. B63: Crad 4D **110**
Wiltshire Way B71: W Brom 6A **64**
Wimbledon Dr. DY8: Stourb 3F **125**
Wimborne Rd. WV10: Wolv 3C **28**
Wimbourne Rd. B16: Edg 6H **99**
B76: Walm 1E **71**
Wimhurst Mdw. WV10: Bush 3B **16**
Wimperis Way B43: Gt Barr 1E **67**
Wimpole Gro. B44: K'sdng 6B **68**
Wincanton Cft. B36: Hodg H 1A **104**
Winceby Rd. WV6: Pert 6F **25**
Winchcombe Cl. B92: Olton 3F **137**
DY1: Dud 4A **76**
Winchcombe Rd. B92: Olton 3F **137**
Winchester Cl. B65: Row R 5E **97**
DY9: Hag 6E **125**
Winchester Ct. *B74: Four O* *1F 53*
(off Vesey Cl.)
Winchester Dr. B37: Chel W 1C **122**
DY8: Stourb 2E **125**
Winchester Gdns. B31: N'fld 4E **145**
Winchester Gro. B21: Hand 1G **99**
Winchester M. WS9: A'rdge 5D **34**
Winchester Ri. DY1: Dud 5C **76**
Winchester Rd. B20: Hand 6F **83**
B71: W Brom 5H **63**
WV10: F'hses 4G **15**
Winchfield Dr. B17: Harb 3D **114**
Wincote Dr. WV6: Tett 5A **26**
Wincrest Way B34: S End 4G **105**
Windermere Dr. B74: S'tly 6H **35**
DY6: K'wfrd 3B **92**
Windermere Ho. *B15: Edg* *2H 131*
(off Vincent Rd.)
B69: O'bry 4D **96**
Windermere Rd. B13: Mose 4B **134**
B21: Hand 5A **82**
WV6: Tett 1B **26**
Windfall Ct. B24: Erd 3B **86**
Winding Mill Nth. DY5: Quar B 4A **110**
Winding Mill Sth. DY5: Quar B 4A **110**
Windlass Cft. B31: N'fld 2D **144**
Windleaves Rd. B36: Cas B 1A **106**
Windley Cl. B19: Birm 4E **101**
Windley Ho. B73: New O 3C **68**
Windmill Av. B45: Rubery 1E **157**
B46: Col 2H **107**
Windmill Bank WV5: Wom 6G **57**
Windmill Cl. B31: N'fld 2G **145**
Windmill Cres. B66: Smeth 4G **99**
WV3: Wolv 2G **41**
Windmill End DY2: Neth 4G **95**
Windmill Gro. DY6: W Hth 1H **91**
Windmill Hill B31: N'fld 2F **145**
B63: Crad 5E **111**
Windmill La. B66: Smeth 5F **99**
WV3: Wolv 2G **41**
Windmill Pct. B66: Smeth 4F **99**
Windmill Rd. B90: Shir 5E **149**
Windmill St. B1: Birm 2F **117** (6D **4**)
DY1: Dud 5C **76**
DY3: Up Gor 2H **75**
WS1: Wals 3C **48**
WS10: W'bry 2G **63**
Windmill Ter. WS10: W'bry 2G **63**
Windmill Vw. DY1: Dud 6D **60**
Windridge Cres. B92: Sol 5B **138**
Windrow, The WV6: Pert 5D **24**
Windrush Cl. B92: Olton 3E **137**
Windrush Gro. B29: S Oak 5C **132**
Windrush Rd. B47: H'wd 2B **162**
Windsor Arc. B4: Birm 6G **101** (3E **5**)
Windsor Av. B68: O'bry 6G **97**
WV4: Penn 5C **42**
Windsor Cl. B31: Longb 3E **159**
B45: Fran 5G **143**
B63: Hale 2H **127**
B65: Row R 5C **96**
DY3: Gorn 6F **75**
Windsor Ct. B38: K Nor 6B **146**
Windsor Cres. DY2: Dud 3F **95**
Windsor Dr. B24: Erd 2A **86**
B92: Sol 2F **137**
Windsor Gdns. WV3: Wolv 4G **41**
WV8: Cod 4F **13**
Windsor Ga. WV12: W'hall 5C **30**
Windsor Gro. DY8: Word 2C **108**
WS4: S'fld 5G **21**
Windsor Ho. B23: Erd 1F **85**
Windsor Ind. Est. B7: Birm 4A **102**
Windsor Lodge B92: Olton 5B **136**
Windsor Pl. B7: Birm 6A **102**
B23: Erd 4E **85**
Windsor Rd. B30: Stir 2D **146**
B36: Cas B 2B **106**
B63: Hale 1H **127**
B65: Row R 5C **96**
B68: O'bry 6G **97**
B71: W Brom 5H **63**
B73: New O 4D **68**
DY4: Tip 5A **62**
DY8: Stourb 2B **124**
WS6: C Hay 1E **7**
WV4: E'shll 6B **44**
WV5: Wom 1F **73**
Windsor St. B7: Birm 4H **101**
WS1: Wals 4C **48**
WV14: Bils 5E **45**
Windsor St. Sth. B7: Birm 5A **102**
Windsor Ter. B16: Edg 2B **116**
Windsor Vw. B32: Bart G 6H **129**
Windsor Wlk. WS10: Darl 3D **46**
Windsor Way WS4: Rus 2H **33**
Winds Point DY9: Hag 6E **125**
Windward Way B36: Cas B 1B **106**
Windward Way Ind. Est. B36: Cas B . . . 1B **106**
Windy Mnr. Rd. B93: Know 5G **151**
Windyridge Rd. B76: Walm 1D **86**
Winford Av. DY6: K'wfrd 5C **92**
Wingate Cl. B30: K Nor 3B **146**
Wingate Ct. B74: Four O 5E **37**
Wingate Rd. WS2: Wals 1E **47**
Wing Cl. WS2: Wals 5F **31**
Wingfield Cl. B37: F'bri 6B **106**
Wingfield Ho. B37: K'hrst 4B **106**
Wingfield Rd. B42: Gt Barr 6E **67**
B46: Col 4H **107**
Wingfoot Av. WV10: Bush 1A **28**
Wingfoot Way B24: Erd 6A **86**

Wing Yip Cen. B7: Nech. 3B **102**
Winifride Ct. B17: Harb 6F **115**
Winkle St. B70: W Brom 3H **79**
Winleigh Rd. B20: Hand 5B **82**
Winnall Cl. WV14: Cose 3F **61**
Winn Ho. *WS2: Wals 6B 32*
(off Burrowes St.)
Winnie Rd. B29: S Oak 4A **132**
Winnington Rd. B8: W End 2G **103**
Winnipeg Rd. B38: K Nor. 1C **160**
Winrush Cl. DY3: Gorn 4H **75**
Winscar Cft. DY3: Lwr G 4A **76**
Winsford Cl. B63: Hale 5A **112**
B76: Walm 2C **70**
CV7: Bal C 3G **169**
Winsham Gro. B21: Hand 1A **100**
Winslow Av. B8: W End 5H **103**
Winslow Dr. WV6: Wolv. 5D **26**
Winslow Ho. B29: S Oak 4F **131**
WINSON GREEN **4A 100**
Winson Green/ Outer Circle Stop (MM)
2A 100
Winson Grn. Rd. B18: Win G 4A **100**
Winson St. B18: Win G 5H **99**
Winspear Cl. CV7: Mer 4H **141**
Winstanley Rd. B33: Stech 1B **120**
Winster Av. B93: Dorr 5A **166**
Winster Gro. B44: Gt Barr 3F **67**
Winster Gro. Ind. Est. B44: Gt Barr 3F **67**
Winster Rd. B43: Gt Barr 5H **65**
WV1: Wolv 2D **44**
Winston Churchill Ct. WV14: Bils 3E **45**
Winston Dr. B20: Hand 6D **82**
B62: Roms 3A **142**
Winston Rd. DY3: Swind 5E **73**
Winterbourne Cft. B14: K Hth 6E **147**
Winterbourne Rd. B91: Sol 3D **150**
Winterdene CV7: Bal C. 2H **169**
Winterley Gdns. DY3: Sed 1A **76**
Winterley La. WS4: Rus 2G **33**
Winterton Rd. B44: K'sdng. 2A **68**
Winthorpe Dr. B91: Sol 1G **165**
Wintney Cl. B17: Harb 4E **115**
Winton Gro. B76: Walm 1E **87**
Winwood Rd. B65: Row R 6E **97**
Winwoods Gro. B32: Bart G. 5G **129**
Wiremill Cl. B44: Gt Barr. 1G **83**
Wirral Rd. B31: N'fld 1D **144**
Wiseacre Cft. B90: Shir 5E **149**
Wiseman Gro. B23: Erd. 4D **68**
Wisemore WS1: Wals 1C **48**
(not continuous)
Wishaw Cl. B90: Shir. 5E **149**
Wishaw Gro. B37: K'hrst 4B **106**
Wishaw La. B76: Curd. 1D **88**
B76: Min, Wis 1H **87**
Wisley Way B32: Harb. 6D **114**
Wistaria Cl. B31: N'fld 1E **145**
Wisteria Dr. WS5: Wals 1D **64**
WS8: Bwnhls 3G **9**
Wisteria Gro. B44: Gt Barr. 3G **67**
Wistmans Cl. DY1: Dud 5A **76**
Wistwood Hayes WV10: Bush 3B **16**
Witham Cl. B76: Walm. 4E **71**
Witham Cft. B91: Sol 6G **151**
Withdean Cl. B11: S'brk 6D **118**
Witherford Cl. B29: S Oak 5G **131**
Witherford Cft. B91: Sol. 5B **150**
Witherford Way B29: S Oak. 5G **131**
Withern Way DY3: Gorn. 4G **75**
Withers Rd. WV8: Bilb 4H **13**
Withers Way B71: W Brom 3B **80**
Withington Covert B14: K Hth 5F **147**
Withington Gro. B93: Ben H, Dorr 5A **166**
Withybrook Rd. B90: Shir 1H **163**
Withy Gro. B37: K'hrst 4B **106**
Withy Hill Rd. B75: S Cold 4D **54**
Withymere La. WV5: Wom 5A **58**
Withymoor Rd. DY2: Neth 5G **95**
DY8: Amb 4E **109**
WITHYMOOR VILLAGE **2H 109**
Withy Rd. WV14: Bils 2E **61**
Withy Rd. Ind. Est. WV14: Bils 2E **61**
Withywood Cl. WV12: W'hall 6C **18**
Witley Av. B63: Hale 1G **127**
B91: Sol 5G **151**
Witley Cres. B69: O'bry 4E **97**
Witley Farm Cl. B91: Sol 5G **151**
Witley Rd. B31: N'fld 5H **145**
Witney Dr. B37: F'bri 1B **122**
Witney Gro. WV10: F'hses 4F **15**
Wittersham Ct. *WV13: W'hall 1B 46*
(off Birmingham St.)
WITTON **4H 83**
Witton Bank B62: Quin 4F **113**
Witton La. B6: Aston 6H **83**
B71: W Brom 5G **63**
Witton Lodge Rd. B23: Erd 6B **68**
Witton Rd. B6: Aston 1G **101**
WV4: Penn 5E **43**
Witton Station (Rail) **6H 83**
Witton St. DY8: Stourb. 1C **124**
Wixford Cft. B34: S End 2E **105**
Wixford Gro. B90: Shir. 5B **150**
Wobaston Rd. WV9: Pend 4B **14**
WV10: F'hses 3E **15**
Woburn Av. WV12: W'hall 3B **30**
Woburn Cres. B43: Gt Barr 4H **65**
Woburn Dr. B62: Hale. 4B **112**
DY5: Brie H. 4F **109**
Woburn Gro. B27: A Grn 4A **136**
Woburn Ho. *B15: Edg. 4E 117*
(off Woodview Dr.)
Wodehouse Cl. WV5: Wom 2E **73**
Wodehouse La. DY3: Sed 5A **58**
WV5: Wom. 5A **58**
Woden Av. WV11: Wed. 3E **29**
Woden Cl. WV5: Wom 6F **57**
Woden Cres. WV11: Wed 3E **29**
Woden Pas. WS10: W'bry 3F **63**
Woden Rd. WV10: Wolv. 5A **28**
Woden Rd. E. WS10: W'bry. 1H **63**
Woden Rd. Nth. WS10: W'bry 6E **47**
Woden Rd. Sth. WS10: W'bry 4F **63**
Woden Rd. W. WS10: Darl 1D **62**
WS10: W'bry 1D **62**
Wodensfield Twr. WV11: Wed 4E **29**
Woden Way WV11: Wed. 3E **29**
Wolcot Gro. B6: Witt 2H **83**
Wold Wlk. B13: Mose 1B **148**
Wolfsbane Dr. WS5: Wals 2E **65**
Wolfson Dr. B15: Edg. 1H **131**
WOLLASTON **5B 108**
Wollaston Ct. DY8: Woll 5A **108**
WS1: Wals 1D 48
(off Lwr. Rushall St.)
Wollaston Cres. WV11: Wed 3F **29**
Wollaston Rd. DY7: Stourt. 4A **108**
DY8: Amb. 4C **108**
Wollerton Gro. B75: S Cold 5D **54**
WOLLESCOTE **6B 110**
Wollescote Bus. Pk. DY9: Lye 6B **110**
Wollescote Dr. B91: Sol 6F **151**
Wollescote Rd. DY9: W'cte 2G **125**
(not continuous)
Wolmer Rd. WV11: Wed 5H **17**
Wolseley Av. B27: A Grn 1B **136**
Wolseley Bank WV10: Bush. 2B **28**
Wolseley Cl. B36: Cas B 6C **88**
WV10: Bush 2B **28**
Wolseley Dr. B8: W End 2G **103**
Wolseley Ga. WV10: Bush. 2B **28**
Wolseley Rd. B70: W Brom 6E **63**
WV14: Bils 4D **44**
Wolseley St. B9: Birm 1B **118**
(not continuous)
Wolston Cl. B90: Shir 2H **149**
WOLVERHAMPTON **1A 44 (4D 170)**
Wolverhampton Art Gallery & Mus. *2C 170*
(off Lichfield St.)
Wolverhampton Race Course 3E **27**
Wolverhampton Rd. B68: O'bry 6G **97**
B69: O'bry 2D **96**
DY3: Sed 4H **59**
DY6: W Hth 6A **74**
WS2: Wals 1G **47**
(not continuous)
WS3: Blox 6H **19**
WS3: Pels 4C **20**
WS6: C Hay 4B **6**
WS11: Cann 1B **6**
WV6: Nur 6A **24**
WV8: Cod 3F **13**
(not continuous)
Wolverhampton Rd. WV10: Share 3A **6**
(Saredon Rd., not continuous)
WV10: Share 4B **6**
(Warstone Rd.)
WV10: Wolv 6B **28**
WV11: Ess 4H **17**
Wolverhampton Rd. E. WV4: Penn 6H **43**
Wolverhampton Rd. Sth. B32: Quin 4C **114**
Wolverhampton Rd. W. WS2: Wals 1C **46**
WV13: W'hall 1C **46**
Wolverhampton Science Pk.
WV10: Wolv. 3G **27**
Wolverhampton Sports Arena 4E **27**
Wolverhampton Station (Rail)
1H 43 (2D 170)
Wolverhampton St. DY1: Dud 5D **76**
WS2: Wals 1B **48**
WS10: Darl. 4B **46**
WV13: W'hall 2H **45**
WV14: Bils 5E **45**
Wolverhampton Wanderers FC
6G **27** (1A **170**)
Wolverley Av. DY8: Woll 5A **108**
WV4: Penn. 6B **42**
Wolverley Cres. B69: O'bry 4D **96**
Wolverley Rd. B32: Bart G. 5H **129**
B63: Hale 3H **127**
B92: Sol 3H **137**
Wolverson Cl. WV12: W'hall 5C **30**
Wolverson Rd. WS9: Wals W 3C **22**
Wolverton Rd. B37: Mars G. 4D **122**
B45: Redn 3A **158**
DY2: Dud 6G **77**
WOMBOURNE **2F 73**
Wombourne Cl. DY3: Sed 5G **59**
Wombourne Ent. Pk. WV5: Wom 2D **72**
Wombourne Leisure Cen. 6F **57**
Wombourne Pk. WV5: Wom. 2F **73**
Wombourne Rd. DY3: Swind 5E **73**
Wombrook Bus. Cen.
WV5: Wom. 1E **73**
Wombrook Dale WV5: Wom 1D **72**
Woodacre Rd. B24: Erd 3A **86**
Woodall Rd. B6: Aston 6H **83**
Woodall St. B64: Crad H 2E **111**
WS3: Blox 6A **20**
(not continuous)
Woodard Rd. DY4: Tip 6C **62**
Wood Av. DY3: Lwr G 3G **75**
WV11: Wed. 3F **29**
Wood Bank B26: Yard. 4C **120**
Wood Bank Rd. WV3: Wolv 3G **41**
Woodbank Rd. DY3: Sed 6G **59**
Woodberry Dr. B76: Walm 3E **71**
Woodberry Wlk. B27: A Grn. 2B **136**
Woodbine Av. B10: Small H. 3D **118**
Woodbine Cft. B26: Sheld 5E **121**
Woodbine Wlk. B37: Chel W 1F **123**
Woodbourne B15: Edg 3H **115**
(not continuous)
Woodbourne Rd. B15: Edg 3G **115**
B17: Harb 3F **115**
B67: Smeth 1C **114**
Woodbridge Cl. WS3: Blox 4G **19**
WS4: S'fld 6H **21**
Woodbridge Rd. B13: Mose. 2H **133**
Woodbrooke Gro. B31: N'fld 1G **145**
Woodbrooke Rd. B30: B'vlle 6H **131**
Woodbrook Ho. B37: Chel W 1D **122**
Woodburn Rd. B66: Smeth 2H **99**
Woodbury Cl. B62: B'hth 3F **113**
DY5: Brie H 1A **110**
Woodbury Gro. B91: Sol. 6F **151**
Woodbury Rd. B62: B'hth. 3F **113**
B62: Quin 4F **113**
Woodchester Rd. B93: Dorr 6F **167**
Woodchurch Grange B73: Bold 5F **69**
Wood Cl. B46: Col 2H **107**
Woodclose Rd. B37: F'bri 6B **106**
Woodcock Cl. B31: Longb 6A **144**
WOODCOCK HILL **6C 130**
Woodcock La. B27: A Grn 2B **136**
(not continuous)
B31: N'fld. 6C **130**
Woodcock La. Nth. B27: A Grn 1B **136**
Woodcock Sports Cen. *5H 101*
(off Woodcock St.)

Woodcock St. B7: Birm. 5H **101** (1G **5**)
Woodcombe Cl. DY5: Brie H 4F **109**
Wood Comn. Grange
  WS3: Pels 3D **20**
Woodcote Dr. B8: Salt 4F **103**
  B93: Dorr 6H **167**
Woodcote Pl. B19: Loz. 2E **101**
Woodcote Rd. B24: Erd 2B **86**
  WV6: Tett 5A **26**
Woodcote Way B18: Hock 4C **100**
  B74: S'tly 5H **51**
Wood Ct. B20: Hand 5C **82**
Woodcroft Av. B20: Hand 4A **82**
  DY4: Tip 2E **77**
Woodcroft Cl. B64: Old H. 3H **111**
WOODCROSS 3B **60**
Woodcross La. WV14: Cose. 3C **60**
Woodcross St. WV14: Cose 3B **60**
WOOD END 2E **29**
Woodend B20: Hand. 1A **82**
Wood End La. B24: Erd 4F **85**
Woodend Pl. WV6: Tett 5H **25**
Wood End Rd. B24: Erd 4F **85**
  WS5: Wals 3H **49**
  WV11: Wed. 2F **29**
Woodend Way WS9: A'rdge 6D **22**
Woodfall Av. B30: K Nor 2B **146**
Woodfield Av. B64: Crad H 3F **111**
  B69: O'bry 5G **97**
  DY5: P'ntt. 2F **93**
  DY9: W'cte. 3B **126**
  WV4: Penn. 5D **42**
Woodfield Cl. B74: Four O. 3H **53**
  WS5: Wals 6A **50**
Woodfield Cres. B12: Bal H 5A **118**
Woodfield Hgts. WV6: Tett. 5B **26**
Woodfield Rd. B12: Bal H 5A **118**
  B13: K Hth 5H **133**
  B91: Sol 1F **151**
  DY3: Lwr G 3G **75**
Woodfield Social & Sports Club 5E **43**
Woodfold Cft. WS9: A'rdge 2D **34**
Woodford Av. B36: Cas B 1F **105**
Woodford Cl. WV9: Pend 5D **14**
Woodford Grn. Rd. B28: Hall G 5G **135**
Woodford La. WV5: Try, Wom 5C **56**
Woodford Way WV5: Wom 1D **72**
Woodfort Rd. B43: Gt Barr 6A **66**
WOODGATE 5H **129**
Woodgate Bus. Pk. B32: Bart G. 3H **129**
Woodgate Dr. B32: Bart G. 4G **129**
Woodgate Gdns. B32: Bart G 3G **129**
Woodgate La. B32: Bart G. 3G **129**
Woodgate Valley Country Pk. 3H **129**
Woodgate Valley Country Pk. Vis. Cen.
  . . . . 3H **129**
Woodgate Valley Urban Farm
  B32: Bart G 3G **129**
Woodglade Cft. B38: K Nor 5A **146**
WOOD GREEN 6H **47**
Wood Grn. WS6: C Hay 1E **7**
Woodgreen Cft. B68: O'bry 4A **114**
Wood Grn. Rd. B18: Win G 5H **99**
  WS10: W'bry 1G **63**
Woodgreen Rd. B68: O'bry 4A **114**
Woodhall Cl. DY4: Tip 5A **62**
Woodhall Cft. B92: Olton 2D **136**
Woodhall Ho. WS3: Blox 1A **32**
                 (off Woodhall St.)
Woodhall Rd. WV4: Penn 1C **58**
Woodham Cl. B45: Fran 6E **143**
Woodhaven WS4: S'fld 6H **21**
WOOD HAYES 6E **17**
Wood Hayes Cft. WV10: Bush 5E **17**
Wood Hayes Rd. WV10: Bush 5D **16**
  WV11: Wed 6E **17**
Woodhill Cl. WV5: Wom 1F **73**
Wood Hill Dr. WV5: Wom 2F **73**
Wood Ho. WS1: Wals. 4D **48**
Woodhouse Cl. DY5: Quar B 2C **110**
Woodhouse Fold WV11: Wed. 4F **29**
Woodhouse Rd. B32: Quin. 5C **114**
  WV6: Tett 5H **25**
Woodhouse Rd. Nth. WV6: Tett. 5H **25**
Woodhouse Way B64: Crad H 2E **111**
Woodhurst Rd. B13: Mose. 1A **134**

Wooding Cres. DY4: Tip. 4B **62**
Woodington Rd. B75: S Cold 6E **55**
Woodland Av. DY1: Dud. 4E **77**
  DY5: Quar B 2C **110**
  WV6: Tett 6H **25**
Woodland Cl. DY9: Pedm 4H **125**
  WV12: W'hall 3D **30**
Woodland Cl. WS14: Shen W 2G **37**
Woodland Cres. WV3: Wolv. 4B **42**
Woodland Dr. B66: Smeth 2C **98**
  WS6: C Hay 1E **7**
Woodland Ri. B43: Gt Barr 2A **66**
  DY3: Gorn. 4F **75**
Woodland Ri. B64: Crad H. 3H **111**
Woodland Rd. B21: Hand 1G **99**
  B31: N'fld 4F **145**
  B62: B'hth 3D **112**
  WV3: Wolv 4B **42**
Wood Lands, The B75: S Cold 5E **55**
Woodlands, The B64: Crad H. 4A **112**
  DY8: Stourb 3E **125**
  WV8: Cod. 5G **13**
Woodlands Av. B46: Wat O 5D **88**
  WS5: Wals 6A **50**
Woodlands Cen., The WV12: W'hall . . . 2E **31**
Woodlands Cotts. WV4: Penn 1C **58**
Woodlands Crematorium B46: Col. . . . 4E **107**
Woodlands Cres. WS3: Pels 2D **20**
Woodlands Farm Rd. B24: Erd 3D **86**
Woodlands La. B90: Shir. 1H **163**
Woodlands Paddock WV4: Penn 1C **58**
Woodlands Pk. Rd. B30: B'vlle 1G **145**
Woodlands Rd. B8: Salt 5F **103**
  B11: S'hll 2B **134**
  B45: Rubery 2D **156**
  WV5: Wom. 2G **73**
Woodlands St. B66: Smeth 4G **99**
Woodlands Wlk. WV4: Penn 6C **42**
Woodlands Way B37: Chel W 6F **107**
Wood La. B17: Harb. 5E **115**
  B20: Hand 5C **82**
  B24: Erd. 6G **85**
  B32: Bart G 4G **129**
              (not continuous)
  B37: Mars G. 3C **122**
  B70: W Brom 4G **79**
  B74: S'tly 2G **51**
  B92: Bars 5G **153**
  WS3: Pels 2D **20**
  WS9: A'rdge 6H **23**
  WS14: Foot 6H **23**
  WV10: F'hses 6H **15**
  WV12: W'hall 2E **31**
Wood La. Cl. WV12: W'hall 2E **31**
Woodlawn B91: Sol 3A **152**
Woodlawn Gro. DY6: K'wfrd 4B **92**
Woodlea Dr. B24: Erd. 5F **85**
  B91: Sol 2C **150**
Wood Leasow B32: Bart G 3B **130**
Wood Leaves B47: H'wd 1H **161**
Woodleigh Av. B17: Harb. 1H **131**
Woodleigh Cl. B63: Hale 5A **112**
Woodleigh Ct. B38: K Nor 6B **146**
Woodleigh Rd. B72: W Grn 4A **70**
Woodleys, The B14: K Hth. 3B **148**
Woodloes Rd. B90: Shir 1H **163**
Woodman Cl. B63: Hale 2C **128**
  WS10: W'bry 1H **63**
Woodman Gro. B75: R'ley 6C **38**
Woodman La. WS6: C Hay 1E **7**
Woodman Rd. B14: K Hth 6A **148**
  B63: Hale 2C **128**
Woodman Wlk. B23: Erd 2A **84**
Woodmeadow Rd. B30: K Nor. 4D **146**
Woodnorton Dr. B13: Mose. 3G **133**
Woodnorton Rd. B65: Row R 1F **113**
Woodpecker Gro. B36: Cas B. 2C **106**
Woodperry Av. B91: Sol. 6G **151**
Woodridge B6: Aston. 6G **83**
Woodridge Av. B32: Quin. 1H **129**
Woodridge Rd. B63: Hale. 6A **112**
Wood Rd. DY3: Lwr G 4G **75**
  WV5: Wom. 5H **57**
  WV6: Tett 6H **25**
  WV8: Cod. 2D **12**
Woodrough Dr. B13: Mose. 3H **133**

Woodrow Cres. B93: Know 4C **166**
Woodrow La. B61: Cats 6B **156**
Woodruff Way WS5: Wals 1D **64**
Woodrush Dr. B47: H'wd 4A **162**
WOODS, THE 1A **64**
Woods, The B14: K Hth 4H **133**
WOODS BANK 5D **46**
Woods Bank Est., The WS10: Darl . . . 1D **62**
Woods Bank Ter. WS10: Darl 6C **46**
Woods Cres. DY5: Quar B 2C **110**
WOODSETTON 1B **76**
Woodsetton Cl. DY1: Dud 1D **76**
Woodshires Rd. B92: Olton 6C **136**
WOODSIDE 3B **94**
Wood Side WV11: Wed 1A **30**
Woodside B37: K'hrst. 4A **106**
  B74: Four O 1E **53**
Woodside Cl. WS5: Wals. 5H **49**
Woodside Cres. B93: Know. 5D **166**
Woodside Dr. B74: Lit A. 4C **36**
Woodside Gro. WV8: Bilb 4H **13**
Woodside Ho. B34: S End 4A **106**
Woodside Ind. Est. DY5: Brie H. 4B **94**
Woodside Rd. B29: S Oak 4C **132**
              (not continuous)
  DY2: Dud 3B **94**
  WS5: Wals 5H **49**
Woodside Way B32: Bart G 5G **129**
  B91: Sol 2C **150**
  WS9: A'rdge 4D **34**
  WV12: W'hall 2E **31**
Woods La. B64: Crad H 3E **111**
  DY5: Brie H 4H **109**
Woodsome Gro. B23: Erd 6C **68**
Woodsorrel Rd. DY1: Dud 3B **76**
Woodstile B75: R'ley 6B **38**
Woodstile Way B34: S End. 3F **105**
Woodstock Cl. DY1: Dud 1C **94**
  DY8: Word 2A **108**
  WS5: Wals 2E **65**
Woodstock Cres. B93: Dorr 6B **166**
Woodstock Dr. B74: Four O 5D **36**
  DY8: Word 2A **108**
Woodstock Ho. B13: Mose. 6A **134**
  B21: Hand 1B **100**
  WV1: Wolv. 2D **44**
Woodston Gro. B91: Sol 1G **165**
Wood St. B16: Birm 1C **116**
  DY2: Dud 3B **94**
  DY4: Tip 1G **77**
  DY8: Woll 4B **108**
  DY9: Lye. 6B **110**
  WS10: Darl 5F **47**
  WV4: E'shll. 2C **60**
  WV10: Wolv 4B **28**
  WV13: W'hall. 1A **46**
  WV14: Bils 6F **45**
Woodthorne WV6: Tett. 3H **25**
Woodthorne Cl. DY3: Gorn 5H **75**
Woodthorne Rd. WV6: Tett 3G **25**
Woodthorne Rd. Sth.
  WV6: Tett 5G **25**
Woodthorpe Wlk. DY6: K'wfrd. 1C **92**
Woodthorpe Dr. DY9: W'cte 2H **125**
Woodthorpe Gdns. B14: K Hth. 2G **147**
Woodthorpe Rd. B14: K Hth 2F **147**
Woodvale Dr. B28: Hall G 3E **149**
Woodvale Rd. B28: Hall G 3E **149**
  B32: Bart G 4G **129**
Woodview Dr. B15: Edg 4E **117**
Woodville Ct. B23: Erd. 5E **85**
             (off Gravelly Hill)
Woodville Gdns. DY3: Sed. 4B **60**
Woodville Rd. B14: K Hth 5H **133**
  B17: Harb. 5E **115**
Woodward Pl. DY9: Lye 1G **125**
Woodwards Cl. WS2: Wals 3H **47**
Woodwards Pl. WS2: Wals 3H **47**
Woodwards Rd. WS2: Wals 3H **47**
Woodward St. B71: W Brom 3C **80**
Woodway B24: Erd. 2H **85**
Woodwells Rd. B8: W End. 4G **103**
Woody Bank WS6: C Hay 3E **7**
Woolacombe Lodge Rd. B29: S Oak . . 3G **131**
Woolmore Rd. B23: Erd 3B **84**
Woolpack All. WV1: Wolv. 1G **43** (3B **170**)

Woolpack Cl. B65: Row R 5A **96**
Woolpack St.
    WV1: Wolv 1G **43** (3B **170**)
Wooton Gro. B44: K'sdng. 5C **68**
Wootton Av. WV11: Wed. 2F **29**
Wootton Cl. DY5: Brie H. 3F **109**
WOOTTON GREEN 6G **155**
Wootton Grn. La. CV7: Bal C 6G **155**
Wootton La. CV7: Bal C 6E **155**
Wootton Rd. B31: Longb 2E **159**
    WV3: Wolv 4B **42**
Woottons Sq. WV14: Bils. 3G **61**
Worcester Arc. B2: Birm 5E **5**
(off New St.)
Worcester Bar 1E 117 (5A 4)
Worcester Cl. B75: R'ley 6B **38**
Worcester Ct. WV3: Wolv. 5E **43**
Worcester Grn. B71: W Brom 6A **64**
Worcester Gro. WV6: Pert 5D **24**
Worcester Ho. B36: Cas B 1C **106**
    B63: Hale 2A **128**
(off Hill St.)
Worcester La. B75: R'ley 6B **38**
    DY8: Stourb 4F **125**
    DY9: Hag, Pedm 4F **125**
Worcester Ri. B29: S Oak 4D **132**
Worcester Rd. B6: Witt 5H **83**
    B68: O'bry 3G **113**
    DY2: Neth 6G **95**
    DY9: Hag 6F **125**
    WV13: W'hall 1D **46**
Worcester St. B2: Birm 5E **5**
    DY8: Stourb 1D **124**
    WV2: Wolv 2G **43** (5A **170**)
Worcester Wlk. B2: Birm . . . 1G **117** (5E **5**)
    B37: Mars G. 3B **122**
Word Hill B17: Harb. 4D **114**
WORDSLEY 1B **108**
Wordsley Ct. DY8: Word 6B **92**
Wordsley Grn. DY8: Word 1B **108**
(not continuous)
Wordsley Grn. Shop. Cen.
    DY8: Word 1B **108**
Wordsworth Av. WV4: E'shll 1A **60**
    WV6: Pert. 5E **25**
Wordsworth Cl. DY4: Tip 5A **62**
Wordsworth Ho. B31: Longb 1E **159**
    B68: O'bry 5A **98**
Wordsworth Rd. B10: Small H 4D **118**
    DY3: Lwr G 2F **75**
    WS3: Blox 1C **32**
    WV10: Bush 1C **28**
    WV12: W'hall 2E **31**
Wordsworth St. B71: W Brom 2A **80**
Worfield Cl. WS4: Wals 5E **33**
Worfield Gdns. WV3: Wolv 5D **42**
Works Rd. B26: Birm A 2B **138**
WORLDS END 6D **136**
Worlds End Av. B32: Quin 5B **114**
Worlds End La. B32: Quin 5B **114**
Worlds End Rd. B20: Hand 4C **82**
Worleys Wharf Av. WS10: W'bry 3C **64**
Worsey Dr. DY4: Tip. 1D **78**
Worthen Gro. B31: Longb 1E **159**
Worthings, The B30: Stir 1D **146**
Worthy Down WV11: Wed 4H **29**
Worthy Down Wlk. B35: Cas V 4F **87**
Wortley Av. WV10: Wolv 3A **28**
Worton Rd. DY9: W'cte 3A **126**
Woverhampton Cricket Ground 3A **26**
Wragby Cl. WV9: Pend 4F **15**
Wrekin Cl. B63: Hale 4E **127**
Wrekin Dr. DY9: W'cte 1H **125**
    WV3: Wolv 3C **42**
    WV6: Tett 4G **25**
Wrekin Gro. WV12: W'hall 6B **18**
Wrekin La. WV6: Tett 4G **25**
Wrekin Rd. B44: K'sdng. 1H **83**
    B73: Bold 4G **69**
Wrekin Vw. WS8: Bwnhls 2C **22**
    WV1: Wolv 1G **43** (2A **170**)
Wrekin Vw. Rd. DY3: Sed 5G **59**
Wren Av. WV6: Pert 6D **24**
Wrens Av. DY4: Tip 2E **77**
    DY6: K'wfrd 5E **93**
Wrens Hill Rd. DY1: Dud. 2C **76**
WREN'S NEST 3C **76**

Wren's Nest Geological Nature Reserve
. . . . 2D **76**
Wren's Nest La. B90: Dic H. 4G **163**
Wrens Nest Pl. DY1: Dud. 2C **76**
Wrens Nest Rd. DY1: Dud. 2C **76**
Wrens Pk. Av. B76: Walm 6C **70**
Wren St. DY1: Dud. 1D **76**
    DY2: Neth 4D **94**
Wrentham St. B5: Birm 3F **117**
Wretham Ct. B19: Hock. 2D **100**
Wretham Rd. B19: Hock 3D **100**
Wrexham Av. WS2: Wals 2F **47**
Wright Av. WV11: Wed 2F **29**
Wrighton Cl. WV12: W'hall 1C **30**
Wrighton Dr. DY5: P'ntt 6G **75**
Wright Rd. B8: Salt. 4E **103**
Wright's La. B64: Old H. 1H **111**
Wright St. B10: Small H. 3D **118**
    B63: Hale 1B **128**
    WV10: Wolv 5H **27**
    WV14: Bils. 1G **61**
Wrottesley Pk. Rd. WV6: Pert 1D **40**
Wrottesley Rd. B43: Gt Barr 4H **65**
    WV6: Tett 4H **25**
Wrottesley Rd. W. WV6: Tett 3F **25**
Wrottesley St. B5: Birm 2G **117** (6E **5**)
Wroxall Cl. DY5: Brie H. 3F **109**
Wroxall Gro. B13: Mose. 1A **148**
Wroxall Rd. B91: Sol 1C **150**
Wroxham Glen WV13: W'hall. 4H **45**
Wroxton Rd. B26: Yard. 3C **120**
Wulfruna Ct. WV3: Wolv. 2F **43**
Wulfruna Gdns. WV3: Wolv 2D **42**
Wulfruna St. WV1: Wolv. . . . 1G **43** (2B **170**)
Wulfrun Cen. WV1: Wolv . . . 2G **43** (4B **170**)
Wulfrun Sq. WV1: Wolv 2H **43** (4C **170**)
Wulfrun Trad. Est. WV10: Wolv 4G **27**
Wulfrun Way WV1: Wolv . . . 2G **43** (4B **170**)
Wyatt Cl. B5: Edg. 6E **117**
Wyatt Rd. B75: S Cold 5F **55**
Wychall Dr. WV10: Bush 3A **16**
Wychall La. B31: K Nor. 5H **145**
Wychall Pk. Gro. B38: K Nor 5H **145**
Wychall Rd. B31: N'fld 4F **145**
Wychbold Cl. WV12: W'hall 6D **18**
Wychbold Ct. DY9: Pedm. 5G **125**
Wychbold Cres. B33: Kitts G 6G **105**
Wychbold Way WV12: W'hall 6D **18**
Wychbury B76: Walm. 4E **71**
Wychbury Ct. B63: Hale 2A **128**
    DY1: Dud 1D **94**
Wychbury Dr. DY9: Hag. 6G **125**
Wychbury Rd. B32: Bart G. 5G **129**
    DY5: Quar B. 3A **110**
    DY9: W'cte. 4H **125**
    WV3: Wolv 4A **42**
Wyche Av. B14: K Hth. 3F **147**
Wychelm Farm Rd. B14: K Hth 6A **148**
Wych Elm Rd. WS8: Clay. 2A **22**
Wycherley Way B64: Old H 3G **111**
Wychnor Gro. B71: W Brom. 3C **64**
Wychwood Av. WV3: Know 1D **166**
Wychwood Cres. B26: Sheld 5D **120**
Wyckham Cl. B17: Harb 1E **131**
Wyckham Rd. B36: Cas B 1A **106**
Wycome Rd. B28: Hall G 1F **149**
Wye Cliff Rd. B20: Hand 1D **100**
Wye Cl. B76: Walm 6E **71**
    WV6: Pert. 5F **25**
Wyegate Cl. B36: Cas B 1B **106**
Wyemanton Cl. B43: Gt Barr 4G **65**
Wye Rd. WS3: Blox 6C **20**
Wykeham Gro. WV6: Pert 6D **24**
Wyken Cl. B93: Dorr. 6F **167**
Wyld Cl. B71: W Brom. 5G **63**
Wylde Cres. B65: Row R 5C **96**
WYLDE GREEN 4A **70**
Wylde Grn. Rd. B72: W Grn. 4A **70**
    B76: Walm 4A **70**
Wylde Green Station (Rail) 4H **69**
Wymering Av. WV11: Wed 2H **29**
Wynall La. DY9: W'cte 1B **126**
Wynall La. Sth. DY9: W'cte 2C **126**
Wynbrook Gro. B90: M'path 3F **165**
Wynchcombe Av. WV4: Penn 1B **58**
Wynd, The DY3: Sed 4H **59**
Wyndcliff Rd. B9: Small H 2D **118**

Wyndham Gdns. B30: K Nor 3H **145**
Wyndham Rd. B16: Edg. 2B **116**
Wyndhurst Rd. B33: Stech 5C **104**
Wyndley Cl. B74: Four O 3F **37**
Wyndley Dr. B73: S Cold 1H **69**
Wyndley Gro. B72: W Grn 3A **70**
Wyndley La. B73: S Cold. 1G **69**
Wyndley Leisure Cen. 6G **53**
Wyndley Mnr. B74: Four O. 3G **37**
Wyndley Swimming Baths 1G **69**
Wyndmill Cres. B71: W Brom 4D **64**
Wynds Covert B14: K Hth 5F **147**
Wynds Point B31: N'fld. 2F **145**
Wynfield Gdns. B14: K Hth 2H **147**
Wynford Rd. B27: A Grn. 6A **120**
Wynford Rd. Ind. Est. B27: A Grn 6A **120**
Wynne Cres. WV4: Penn 2A **58**
Wynn Griffith Dr. DY4: Tip 4A **78**
Wynn Rd. WV4: Penn. 5D **42**
Wynn St. B15: Birm 3F **117**
Wynstead Covert B14: K Hth 5E **147**
Wyntor La. B71: W Brom. 5H **63**
Wyre Cl. B45: Fran. 6H **143**
    WS9: Wals W 3B **22**
Wyre Rd. DY8: Woll 5C **108**
Wyrley Cl. WS8: Bwnhls 2B **10**
    WV12: W'hall. 2D **30**
Wyrley Ho. B23: Erd 1D **84**
    DY4: Tip 4B **78**
Wyrley La. WS3: Lit W. 4C **8**
Wyrley Rd. B6: Witt. 4A **84**
    B75: R'ley. 2B **54**
    WV11: Wed 3A **30**
Wyrley St. WV10: Wolv 1B **44**
Wyrley Way B23: Erd 1A **84**
WYTHALL 6A **162**
Wythall Grn. Way B47: Wyt. 5G **161**
Wythall Rd. B63: Hale 3A **128**
Wythall Station (Rail) 5C **162**
Wythwood Cl. DY9: Pedm 4H **125**
Wythwood Gro. B47: H'wd 3C **162**
    DY4: Tip 5A **62**
Wythwood Rd. B47: H'wd 3B **162**
Wyton Av. B68: O'bry 1A **114**
Wyvern Cl. B68: O'bry 5H **97**
    B74: S Cold 4H **53**
    WV12: W'hall 2A **30**
Wyvern Gro. B29: S Oak 3G **131**
Wyvern Rd. B74: S Cold 4H **53**
Wyvis Cl. WV3: Wolv 1C **42**

Y

Yale Dr. WV11: Wed 4G **29**
YARDLEY 3B **120**
Yardley Cl. B68: O'bry 2H **113**
Yardley Crematorium B25: Yard 6B **120**
Yardley Flds. Rd. B33: Stech 1B **120**
Yardley Grn. Rd. B9: Bord G 2F **119**
    B33: Stech 2A **120**
Yardley Rd. B27: A Grn 1A **136**
Yardley St. DY9: Lye 5G **109**
    WS10: Darl. 4C **46**
YARDLEY WOOD 4C **148**
Yardley Wood Rd. B13: Mose 2B **134**
    B14: Yard W 2B **148**
Yardley Wood Station (Rail) 2D **148**
Yare Gro. WV13: W'hall 1D **46**
Yarnborough Hill DY8: Stourb 3E **125**
Yarnbury Cl. B14: K Hth. 6G **147**
Yarn Cl. B47: H'wd. 4A **162**
Yarner Cl. DY1: Dud. 5A **76**
Yarnfield Rd. B11: Tys. 2G **135**
Yarningale Rd. B14: K Hth 3E **147**
Yarningdale B90: Shir 6A **150**
Yarn La. B90: Dic H 3G **163**
Yarrow Cl. WS3: Pels 2E **21**
    WV11: Wed 4H **29**
Yarrow Dr. B38: K Nor 1B **160**
Yarwell Cl. WV10: Wolv. 5H **27**
Yateley Av. B42: Gt Barr. 6C **66**
Yateley Cres. B42: Gt Barr 6C **66**
Yateley Rd. B15: Edg 4A **116**
Yatesbury Av. B35: Cas V. 4D **86**
Yates Cft. B74: Four O 3F **37**
Yates La. B65: Row R. 1F **113**

Yeadon Gdns. WV3: Wolv 3B 42
Yeames Cl. B43: Gt Barr 1E 67
Yelverton Cl. WS3: Blox. 3H 19
Yelverton Dr. B15: Edg. 3A 116
Yeman Rd. B68: O'bry 6B 98
Yems Cft. WS4: Rus. 3E 33
Yemscroft WS6: Gt Wyr 5G 7
Yemscroft Flats WS4: Rus 3E 33
Yenton Ct. B24: Erd 1H 85
Yenton Gro. B24: Erd 1A 86
Yeomanry Cl. B75: S Cold 5E 55
Yeomans Garage B75: S Cold 5D 54
                                    (off Yeomans Way)
Yeomans Way B75: S Cold 5D 54
Yeovil Ct. DY5: Brie H 1H 109
                                        (off Hill St.)
Yerbury Gro. B23: Erd 3B 84
Yew Cft. Av. B17: Harb 5E 115
Yewdale B17: Harb. 1G 131
Yewhurst Rd. B91: Sol 3C 150
Yew Pl. B66: Smeth 6F 99
Yew St. WV3: Wolv. 2E 43
YEW TREE 1F 65
Yew Tree Av. B26: Yard 4C 120
Yew Tree Gdns. WS5: Wals 1F 65
        WV8: Cod. 3G 13
Yew Tree Hills DY2: Neth. 5E 95
Yew Tree La. B25: Yard 4C 120
        B32: Fran 4D 142
        B91: Sol 2A 152
        WS10: W'bry 3G 63
        WV6: Tett. 3G 25

Yewtree La. B65: Row R 1B 112
        WV14: Cose 4F 61
Yew Tree Pl. B62: Roms 2A 142
        WS3: Blox 4B 20
Yew Tree Retail Pk. B25: Yard. 3B 120
Yew Tree Ri. B76: Walm 2D 70
Yew Tree Rd. B6: Aston 6A 84
        B13: Mose 3F 133
        B15: Edg. 3E 117
        B36: Cas B 1A 106
        B67: Smeth 5C 98
        B73: Bold 6G 69
        B74: S'tly 3F 51
        DY2: Neth. 5E 95
        WS4: S'fld 6F 21
        WS5: Wals 6E 49
Yewtree Rd. B63: Hale. 2H 127
Yew Tree Vs. B73: Bold 6G 69
Yew Wlk. B37: Chel W 1D 122
Yockleton Rd. B33: Kitts G. 6G 105
York Av. WS2: Wals 1H 47
        WV3: Wolv. 2C 42
        WV13: W'hall. 1D 46
Yorkbrook Dr. B26: Sheld 6F 121
York Cl. B30: B'vlle. 2C 146
        DY4: Tip 3F 77
York Cres. B70: W Brom 1G 79
        DY8: Woll. 4B 108
        WS10: Darl 5D 46
        WV3: Wolv. 2C 42
Yorkdale Cl. DY3: Lwr G 4H 75
York Dr. B36: Hodg H. 1H 103

Yorke Av. DY5: Brie H. 2E 109
York Gdns. WV3: Wolv 2C 42
Yorklea Cft. B37: F'bri 1B 122
Yorkminster Dr.
        B37: Chel W 1E 123
York Rd. B14: K Hth. 5G 133
        B16: Edg 2A 116
        B21: Hand 1B 100
        B23: Erd 3F 85
        B28: Hall G. 3E 135
        B65: Row R 6E 97
        DY2: Neth 6G 95
        WS4: Rus. 2H 33
        WV3: Wolv. 3H 41
York St. B17: Harb 5H 115
        WV1: Wolv 2A 44
Yorks Wood Dr. B37: K'hrst 3B 106
York Ter. B18: Birm 4E 101
Young St. B70: W Brom 4G 79
Yoxall Gro. B33: Kitts G 6E 105
Yoxall Rd. B90: Shir. 5B 150

Z

Zion Cl. WS6: C Hay 2D 6
Zions Cl. B64: Old H 2H 111
Zion St. DY4: Tip 5H 61
Zoar St. DY3: Gorn. 4G 75
Zouche Cl. DY8: Amb. 3C 108

HOSPITALS and HOSPICES
covered by this atlas
with their map square reference

N.B. Where Hospitals and Hospices are not named on the map, the reference given is for the road in which they are situated.

ACORNS CHILDREN'S HOSPICE 5A **132**
103 Oak Tree Lane
BIRMINGHAM
B29 6HZ
Tel: 0121 2484850

ACORNS CHILDREN'S HOSPICE (WALSALL)
.... 6D **48**
Walstead Road
WALSALL
WS5 4NL
Tel: 01922 422500

BIRMINGHAM CHILDREN'S HOSPITAL
(DIANA PRINCESS OF WALES HOSPITAL)
.... 6G **101** (2F **5**)
Steelhouse Lane
BIRMINGHAM
B4 6NH
Tel: 0121 3339999

BIRMINGHAM DENTAL HOSPITAL
.... 6G **101** (2E **5**)
St Chad's Queensway
BIRMINGHAM
B4 6NN
Tel: 0121 2368611

BIRMINGHAM HEARTLANDS HOSPITAL
.... 1H **119**
Bordesley Green East
BIRMINGHAM
B9 5ST
Tel: 0121 4242000

BIRMINGHAM NUFFIELD HOSPITAL, THE
.... 6B **116**
22 Somerset Road
BIRMINGHAM
B15 2QQ
Tel: 0121 4562000

BIRMINGHAM WOMENS HOSPITAL
.... 1H **131**
Metchley Park Road
BIRMINGHAM
B15 2TG
Tel: 0121 4721377

BLOXWICH HOSPITAL 1H **31**
Reeves Sreet
WALSALL
WS3 2JJ
Tel: 01922 858600

BRADBURY HOSPICE 1H **113**
494 Wolverhampton Road
OLDBURY
B68 8DG
Tel: 0121 5442712

BUSHEY FIELDS HOSPITAL 2A **94**
Bushey Fields Rd.
DUDLEY
DY1 2LZ
Tel: 01384 457373

CITY HOSPITAL (BIRMINGHAM) 5B **100**
Dudley Road
BIRMINGHAM
B18 7QH
Tel: 0121 5543801

COMPTON HOSPICE 1A **42**
Compton Road West
WOLVERHAMPTON
WV3 9DH
Tel: 01902 774500

CORBETT HOSPITAL 4E **109**
Vicarage Rd.
STOURBRIDGE
DY8 4JB
Tel: 01384 456111

DOROTHY PATTISON HOSPITAL 2H **47**
Alumwell Close
WALSALL
WS2 9XH
Tel: 01922 858000

EDWARD STREET HOSPITAL 4A **80**
Edward Street
WEST BROMWICH
B70 8NL
Tel: 0121 5537676

GOOD HOPE HOSPITAL 5B **54**
Rectory Road
SUTTON COLDFIELD
B75 7RR
Tel: 0121 3782211

GOSCOTE HOSPITAL 1D **32**
Goscote Lane
WALSALL
WS3 1SJ
Tel: 01922 710710

GUEST HOSPITAL 4G **77**
Tipton Rd.
DUDLEY
DY1 4SE
Tel: 01384 456111

HAMMERWICH HOSPITAL 1D **10**
Hospital Rd.
BURNTWOOD
WS7 0EH
Tel: 01543 675754

HEATH LANE HOSPITAL 6B **64**
Heath Lane
WEST BROMWICH
B71 2BG
Tel: 0121 5531831

HIGHCROFT HOSPITAL 4D **84**
Fentham Road
BIRMINGHAM
B23 6AL
Tel: 0121 6235500

JOHN TAYLOR HOSPICE 2A **86**
76 Grange Road
BIRMINGHAM
B24 0DF
Tel: 0121 2552400

LITTLE ASTON BUPA HOSPITAL 4B **36**
Little Aston Hall Dri.
SUTTON COLDFIELD
B74 3UP
Tel: 0121 3532444

LITTLE BLOXWICH DAY HOSPICE 4B **20**
Stoney Lane
WALSALL
WS3 3DW
Tel: 01922 858735

MANOR HOSPITAL (WALSALL) 2A **48**
Moat Road
WALSALL
WS2 9PS
Tel: 01922 721172

MARY STEVENS HOSPICE 3F **125**
221 Hagley Rd.
STOURBRIDGE
DY8 2JR
Tel: 01384 443010

MOSELEY HALL HOSPITAL 2G **133**
Alcester Road
BIRMINGHAM
B13 8JL
Tel: 0121 4424321

MOSSLEY DAY UNIT 6G **19**
Sneyd Lane
WALSALL
WS3 2LW
Tel: 01922 858680

NEW CROSS HOSPITAL (WOLVERHAMPTON)
.... 4D **28**
Wolverhampton Road
WOLVERHAMPTON
WV10 0QP
Tel: 01902 307999

NORTHCROFT HOSPITAL 3D **84**
Reservoir Road
BIRMINGHAM
B23 6DW
Tel: 0121 3782211

PARKWAY BUPA HOSPITAL 2A **152**
1 Damson Parkway
SOLIHULL
B91 2PP
Tel: 0121 7041451

PENN HOSPITAL 1C **58**
Penn Road
WOLVERHAMPTON
WV4 5HN
Tel: 01902 444141

PRIORY HOSPITAL, THE 6D **116**
Priory Road
BIRMINGHAM
B5 7UG
Tel: 0121 4402323

QUEEN ELIZABETH HOSPITAL 1A **132**
Edgbaston
BIRMINGHAM
B15 2TH
Tel: 0121 6271627

QUEEN ELIZABETH PSYCHIATRIC HOSPITAL
.... 1A **132**
Mindelsohn Way
BIRMINGHAM
B15 2QZ
Tel: 0121 678000

RIDGE HILL HOSPITAL 6C **92**
Brierly Hill Rd.
STOURBRIDGE
DY8 5ST
Tel: 01384 456111

ROWLEY REGIS COMMUNITY HOSPITAL
.... 1B **112**
Moor Lane
ROWLEY REGIS
B65 8DA
Tel: 0121 6073465

ROYAL ORTHOPAEDIC HOSPITAL 2F **145**
Bristol Road South
BIRMINGHAM
B31 2AP
Tel: 0121 685 4000

RUSSELLS HALL HOSPITAL 2H **93**
Pensnett Rd.
DUDLEY
DY1 2HQ
Tel: 01384 456111

ST DAVID'S HOUSE (DAY HOSPITAL) ... 6G **57**
Planks La.
WOLVERHAMPTON
WV5 8DU
Tel: 01902 326001

ST MARY'S HOSPICE 4C **132**
176 Raddlebarn Road
BIRMINGHAM
B29 7DA
Tel: 0121 4721191

SANDWELL DISTRICT GENERAL HOSPITAL
.... 2B **80**
Lyndon
WEST BROMWICH
B71 4HJ
Tel: 0121 5531831

SELLY OAK HOSPITAL 4B **132**
Raddlebarn Road
BIRMINGHAM
B29 6JD
Tel: 0121 6271627

SOLIHULL HOSPITAL 3G **151**
Lode Lane
SOLIHULL
B91 2JL
Tel: 0121 4242000

SUTTON COLDFIELD COTTAGE HOSPITAL
.... 1H **69**
Birmingham Road
SUTTON COLDFIELD
B72 1QH
Tel: 0121 255 4000

WARREN PEARL MARIE CURIE HOSPICE
.... 3H **151**
911-913 Warwick Road
SOLIHULL
B91 3ER
Tel: 0121 2547800

WEST HEATH HOSPITAL 1G **159**
Rednal Road
BIRMINGHAM
B38 8HR
Tel: 0121 6271627

WEST MIDLANDS HOSPITAL 6F **111**
Colman Hill
HALESOWEN
B63 2AH
Tel: 01384 560123

WEST PARK REHABILITATION HOSPITAL
.... 1E **43**
Park Road West
WOLVERHAMPTON
WV1 4PW
Tel: 01902 444000

WOLVERHAMPTON EYE INFIRMARY ... 1E **43**
Compton Road
WOLVERHAMPTON
WV3 9QR
Tel: 01902 307999

WOLVERHAMPTON NUFFIELD HOSPITAL
.... 5A **26**
Wood Road
WOLVERHAMPTON
WV6 8LE
Tel: 01902 754177

WOODBOURNE PRIORY HOSPITAL ... 3G **115**
23 Woodbourne Road
BIRMINGHAM
B17 8BY
Tel: 0121 4344343

WORDSLEY HOSPITAL 5C **92**
Stream Rd.
STOURBRIDGE
DY8 5QX
Tel: 01384 456111

Printed and bound in the United Kingdom by Polestar Wheatons Ltd., Exeter.